culture

What makes *CULTURE* special?

What's Inside

Engaging pedagogy designed to be eye-catching and visually appealing can be found throughout the text.

As You READ

As You Read introduces the reading with important questions discussed in the chapter.

STUDY TIP

Study Tips call attention to important concepts and suggest effective strategies for learning and studying.

Pop Quiz

Pop Quiz helps students to master key chapter material.

CULTURE THINK

CULTURE Think questions throughout each chapter prompt students to think more deeply about a topic discussed in the text.

POPCULTURE

Pop CULTURE teaches anthropological concepts through popular culture familiar to students.

CULTURE Clips connects students to anthropological videos through a smartphone or any mobile phone with a camera.

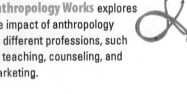

Anthropology Works

Anthropology Works explores the impact of anthropology on different professions, such as teaching, counseling, and marketing.

Get Involved sections push students to actively participate in anthropological issues that are relevant to them.

get involved

Did You Know provides short, engaging nuggets of information relevant to the chapter.

Did You Know

For REVIEW

For Review summarizes the key points of each chapter in an easy-to-read format.

Name: Lisa Gezon

Education: My B.A. in Anthropology is from Albion College in Albion, MI. I got my Ph.D. from the University of Michigan (Conrad Kottak was my advisor).

Occupation: Professor, mother

Hobbies: I like to do yoga with friends, and I sing in a women's chorus. I like to swim, bicycle, take walks, and pet my cats.

Favorite places to travel: As an anthropologist, I enjoy traveling anywhere, but I especially like Madagascar, France, and Costa Rica.

Family: I am the mother of two boys (12 and 13 years old) and aunt to four nephews.

Last books read: The Gift by Hafiz; Little Bee by Chris Cleave; Far From the Madding Crowd by Thomas Hardy

Favorite films: The Color of Paradise, Mississippi Masala, 8 Mile

Latest accomplishment: One month of fieldwork in Madagascar in June, 2010

Favorite quote: "A little learning is a dang'rous thing; Drink deep, or taste not the Pierian spring." —Alexander Pope, 1711, from "An Essay on Criticism"

Name: Conrad Kottak

Education: Columbia College and Columbia University

Occupation: Professor, Anthropologist

Hobbies: Swimming, movies, theater, television

Favorite places to travel: Brazil, New York, San Francisco, London, Paris

Family: Married with two adult children and three grandchildren

Last books read: Person or Persons Unknown by Bruce Alexander

Favorite films: Star Wars (the original one) and Casablanca

Latest accomplishment: Finishing the fourth edition of On Being Different: Diversity and Multiculturalism in the North American Mainstream

Favorite quote: "Never doubt that a small group of concerned citizens can change the world. Indeed, it's the only thing that ever has." —Margaret Mead

culture

Lisa Gezon
University of West Georgia

Conrad Phillip Kottak
University of Michigan

With Additional Materials from

ANNUAL EDITIONS
Anthropology 11/12
Thirty-Fourth Edition

Elvio Angeloni
Pasadena City College

Mc
Graw
Hill
Education

Culture
With Additional Material

This book is a McGraw-Hill Learning Solutions textbook and contains select material from the following sources:
Culture by Lisa Gezon and Conrad Phillip Kottak. Copyright © 2012 by The McGraw-Hill Companies, Inc.
Annual Editions: Antropology 11/12, Thirty-Fourth Edition by Elvio Angeloni. Copyright © 2011, 2010, 2009, 2008 by The McGraw-Hill Companies, Inc.
Both are reprinted with permission of the publisher. Many custom published texts are modified versions or adaptations of our best-selling textbooks. Some adaptations are printed in black and white to keep prices at a minimum, while others are in color.

7 8 9 0   KNG KNG   17 16 15 14

ISBN-13: 978-0-07-752175-2
ISBN-10: 0-07-752175-7

Learning Solutions Specialist: Jennifer Harrington
Production Editor: Lynn Nagel
Printer/Binder: King Printing

Table of Contents

1

What Is Anthropology? 1

>> The Cross-Cultural Perspective   2

>> Human Adaptability   3
   Adaptation, Variation, and Change   4

>> General Anthropology   5

>> Human Biological Diversity
   and the Race Concept   6
   Explanatory Approaches to Human Diversity   9

>> The Subdisciplines of Anthropology   12

Cultural Anthropology   12
Archaeological Anthropology   12
Biological, or Physical, Anthropology   14
Linguistic Anthropology   15

>> Anthropology and Other
   Academic Fields   16

>> Applied Anthropology   16

Culture 20

>> What Is Culture 22

Culture Is Learned 23

Culture Is Symbolic 23

Culture Is Shared 24

Culture and Nature 24

Culture Is All-Encompassing 25

Culture Is Integrated 25

Culture Can Be Adaptive and Maladaptive 26

>> Culture's Evolutionary Basis 26

What We Share with Other Primates 27

How We Differ from Other Primates 28

>> Universality, Generality, and Particularity 29

Universals and Generalities 29

Particularity: Patterns of Culture 30

>> Culture and the Individual: Agency and Practice 31

>> Levels of Culture 31

>> Ethnocentrism, Cultural Relativism, and Human Rights 32

>> Mechanisms of Cultural Change 34

>> Globalization 36

Ethics and Methods   40

>> **Ethics and Anthropology**   42

>> **Research Methods**   44

>> **Ethnography: Anthropology's Distinctive Strategy**   44

>> **Ethnographic Techniques**   45

Observation and Participant Observation   45

Conversation, Interviewing, and Interview Schedules   46

The Genealogical Method   47

Key Cultural Consultants   48

Life Histories   48

Local Beliefs and Perceptions, and the Ethnographer's   48

>> **The Evolution of Ethnography**   49

Problem-Oriented Ethnography   51

Longitudinal Research   51

Team Research   51

Culture, Space, and Scale   52

>> **Survey Research**   53

Applying Anthropology   58

>> **What is Applied Anthropology?**   60

>> **The Role of the Applied Anthropologist**   61

Early Applications   61

Academic and Applied Anthropology   61

Applied Anthropology Today   62

>> **Development Anthropology**   63

Equity   63

>> **Strategies for Innovation**   64

Overinnovation   64

Underdifferentiation   65

Indigenous Models   66

>> **Anthropology and Education**   66

>> **Urban Anthropology**   67

Urban versus Rural   68

>> **Medical Anthropology**   70

>> **Anthropology and Business**   73

>> **Careers and Anthropology**   74

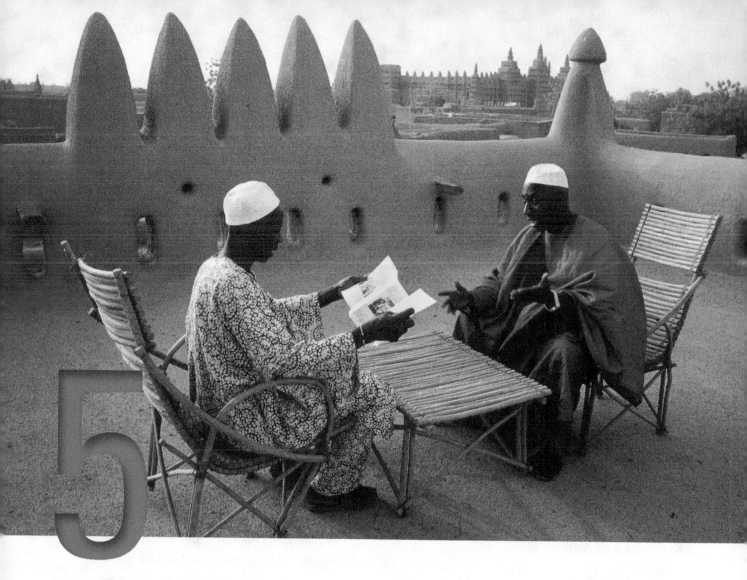

Language and Communication 78

>> **Language** 80

>> **Nonhuman Primate Communication** 80
Call Systems 80
Sign Language 81
The Origin of Language 83

>> **Nonverbal Communication** 84

>> **The Structure of Language** 85
Speech Sounds 85

>> **Language, Thought, and Culture** 86
The Sapir-Whorf Hypothesis 87

Focal Vocabulary 88

>> **Sociolinguistics** 89
Linguistic Diversity within Nations 90
Gender Speech Contrasts 90
Stratification and Symbolic Domination 91
Black English Vernacular (BEV) 92

>> **Historical Linguistics** 93
Language Loss 94

6

Making a Living   98

>> **Adaptive Strategies**   100

   Foraging   100

      Correlates of Foraging   *102*

>> **Adaptive Strategies Based on
Food Production**   103

   Horticulture   103

   Agriculture   104

      Domesticated Animals   *104*

      Irrigation   *104*

      Terracing   *104*

      Costs and Benefits of Agriculture   *105*

   Agricultural Intensification:
People and the Environment   105

   Pastoralism   106

>> **Economic Systems**   107

   Division of Labor   107

Means of Production   108

   Land as a Means of Production   *108*

   Labor, Tools, and Specialization   *109*

Alienation in Industrial Economies   109

   A Case of Industrial Alienation   *109*

>> **Economizing and Maximization**   110

   Alternative Ends   111

>> **Distribution, Exchange**   112

   The Market Principle   112

   Redistribution   112

   Reciprocity   112

   Coexistence of Exchange Principles   114

   Potlatching   114

Political Systems 118

>> **What Is "The Political"?** 120

>> **Types and Trends in Political Organization** 121

>> **Band Organization** 122
The San 122
The Inuit 123

>> **Tribal Societies** 124
The Village Head 124
The "Big Man" 125
Pantribal Sodalities and Age Grades 127
Nomadic Politics 129

>> **Chiefdoms** 130
Political and Economic Systems in Chiefdoms 131
Social Status in Chiefdoms 132
Status Systems in Chiefdoms and States 132
The Emergence of Stratification 132
Open- and Closed-Class Systems 133

>> **States** 134
Population Control 134
Judiciary Systems 135
Enforcement Systems 136
Fiscal Systems 136

8

Families, Kinship, and Marriage   140

>> **Families**   142
  Nuclear and Extended Families   143
  Industrialism and Family Organization   144
  Changes in North American Kinship   145
  The Family among Foragers   148

>> **Descent**   149
  Characteristics of Descent Groups   149
  Lineages, Clans, and Residence Rules   150

>> **Marriage**   151
  Incest and Exogamy   152
    Although Tabooed, Incest Does Happen   153
  Endogamy   153
    Caste   153

>> **Marital Rights and Same-Sex Marriage**   154

>> **Marriage across Cultures**   156
  Bridewealth and Dowry   156
  Durable Alliances   157
    Sororate   157
    Levirate   157

>> **Divorce**   157

>> **Plural Marriages**   159
  Polygny   159
  Polyandry   160

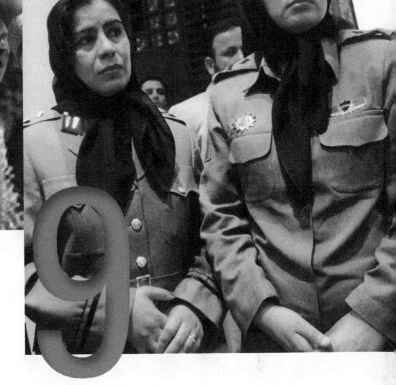

9

Gender   162

>> **Nature and Nurture**   164

>> **Recurrent Gender Patterns**   165

>> **Gender among Foragers**   169

>> **Gender among Horticulturalists**   170
  Reduced Gender Stratification—
  Matrilineal–Matrilocal Societies   171
  Matriarchy   172
  Increased Gender Stratification—
  Patrilineal–Patrilocal Societies   172

>> **Gender among Agriculturists**   173

>> **Patriarchy and Violence**   174

>> **Gender and Industrialism**   175
  The Feminization of Poverty   177

>> **What Determines Gender Variation?**   178

>> **Sexual Orientation**   178

Religion 184

>> **Defining Religion** 186

>> **Expressions of Religion** 187

Spiritual Beings 187

Powers and Forces 187

Magic 188

Uncertainty, Anxiety, Solace 188

Rituals 189

Rites of Passage 190

Totemism 192

>> **Religion and Social Control** 192

>> **Kinds of Religion** 194

>> **World Religions** 196

>> **Religion and Change** 197

Revitalization Movements 197

Cargo Cults 198

>> **Secular Rituals** 199

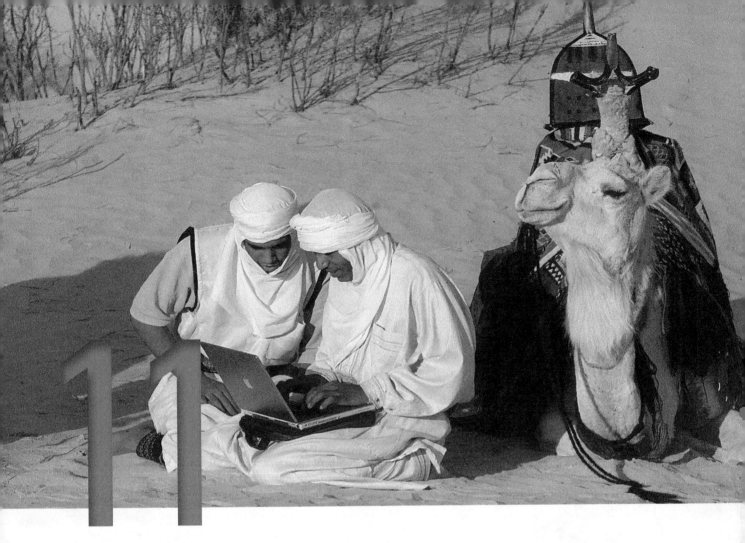

The World System and Colonialism 202

>> **The World System** 204

The Emergence of the World System 205

>> **Industrialization** 206

Causes of the Industrial Revolution 206

>> **Socioeconomic Effects of Industrialization** 207

Industrial Stratification 208

>> **Colonialism** 210

British Colonialism 211

French Colonialism 212

Colonialism and Identity 213

Postcolonial Studies 214

>> **The Role of Development in the World System** 215

Neoliberalism 215

>> **The Second World** 216

Communism 216

Postsocialist Transitions 217

>> **The World System Today** 217

Industrial Degradation 219

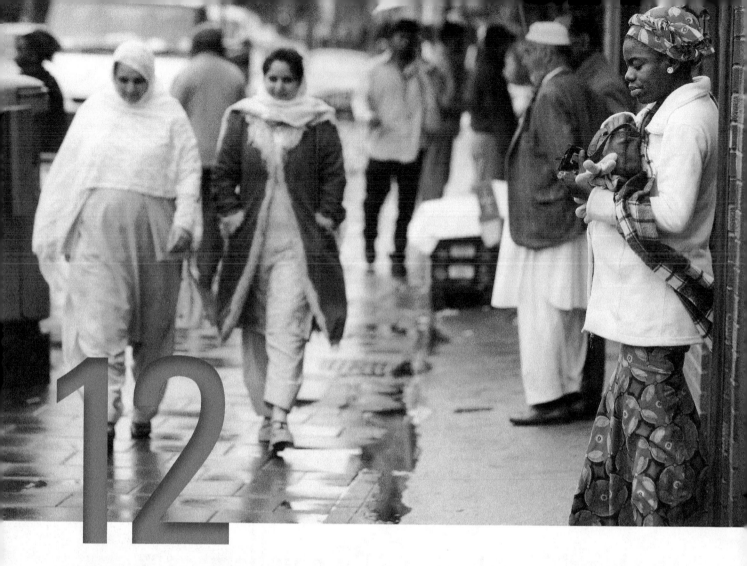

12

Ethnicity and Race 224

>> **Ethnic Groups and Ethnicity** 226

Status Shifting 227

>> **Race and Ethnicity** 228

>> **The Social Construction of Race** 229

Hypodescent: Race in the United States 229

Race in the U.S. Census 230

"Not Us": Race in Japan 231

Phenotype and Fluidity: Race in Brazil 233

>> **Ethnic Groups, Nations, and Nationalities** 234

Nationalities and Imagined Communities 234

>> **Ethnic Tolerance and Accommodation** 235

Assimilation 235

The Plural Society 236

Multiculturalism and Ethnic Identity 236

>> **Roots of Ethnic Conflict** 238

Prejudice and Discrimination 238

Chips in the Mosaic 239

Aftermaths of Oppression 239

Anthropology's Role in a Globalizing World   245

>> **Global Climate Change** 246

>> **Environmental Anthropology** 249
  Global Assaults on Local Autonomy 251
  Deforestation 252

>> **Interethnic Contact** 253
  Religious Change 253
  Cultural Imperialism 254

>> **Making and Remaking Culture** 256

  Indigenizing Popular Culture 256
  A Global System of Images 256
  A Global Culture of Consumption 257

>> **People in Motion** 258

>> **Indigenous Peoples** 259
  Identity in Indigenous Politics 261

>> **The Continuance of Diversity** 261

Preface   iv

Correlation Guide   x

Topic Guide   xi

Internet References   xiv

World Map   xvi

UNIT 1
Anthropological Perspectives

Unit Overview xviii

1. **A Dispute in Donggo: Fieldwork and Ethnography,** John Monaghan and
   Peter Just, *Social and Cultural Anthropology: A Very Short Introduction,* Oxford
   University Press, 2000

   In this account of **dispute resolution in an Indonesian community,** the authors illustrate the
   unique features of **anthropological fieldwork. Participant observation,** involving prolonged
   exposure to the daily lives of people, allows for contextual understanding of events and
   motivations that go beyond superficial appearances.   2

2. **Doing Fieldwork among the Yąnomamö,** Napoleon A. Chagnon, from
   Yąnomamö: The Fierce People, Holt, Rinehart, and Winston, 1992

   Although an anthropologist's first field experience may involve **culture shock,** Napoleon
   Chagnon reports that the long process of **participant observation** may transform personal
   hardship and frustration into confident understanding of exotic cultural patterns.   10

3. **Eating Christmas in the Kalahari,** Richard Borshay Lee, *Natural History,*
   December 1969

   Anthropologist Richard Borshay Lee gives an account of the misunderstanding and confusion
   that often accompany **cross-cultural experience.** In this case, he violated a basic principle of
   the !Kung Bushmen's social relations—**food sharing.**   22

4. **Tricking and Tripping: Fieldwork on Prostitution in the Era of AIDS,** Claire E.
   Sterk, *Tricking and Tripping: Prostitution in the Era of AIDS,* Social Change Press,
   2000

   As unique as Claire E. Sterk's report on **prostitution** may be, she discusses issues common
   to anthropologists wherever they conduct **fieldwork:** How does one build trusting relationships
   with informants and what are the **ethical obligations** of an anthropologist toward them?   26

5. **Can White Men Jump?: Ethnicity, Genes, Culture and Success,** David Shenk
   from *The Genius in All of Us,* Doubleday, 2010

   Clusters of **ethnic and geographical athletic success** prompt **suspicions of hidden genetic
   advantages.** The real advantages are much more cultural, more nuanced, and less hidden.   32

UNIT 2
Culture and Communication

Unit Overview 36

6. **Whose Speech Is Better?,** Donna Jo Napoli, *Language Matters: A Guide to
   Everyday Questions About Language,* Oxford University Press, 2003

   Although we cannot explicitly state the **rules of our language,** we do choose to follow
   different rules in different contexts. Depending on the situation, we manipulate every aspect of
   language, from simple differences in **pronunciation** and **vocabulary** to the more complicated
   changes in **phrasing** and **sentence structure.**   38

The concepts in bold italics are developed in the article. For further expansion, please refer to the Topic Guide.

7. **Do You Speak American?,** Robert MacNeil, *USA Today Magazine,* January 2005

It is a common assumption that the mass media is making all Americans speak in a similar manner. **Linguists** point out, however, that while some national trends in language are apparent, **regional speech differences** are not only thriving, but in some places they are becoming even more distinctive.

44

8. **Fighting for Our Lives,** Deborah Tannen, *The Argument Culture,* Random House, 1998

In America today, a **pervasive warlike tone seems to prevail in public dialogue.** The prevailing belief is that there are only two sides to an issue and opposition leads to truth. Often, however, an issue is more like a crystal, with many sides, and the truth is in the complex middle, not in the **oversimplified extremes.**

49

9. **Shakespeare in the Bush,** Laura Bohannan, *Natural History,* August/September 1966

It is often claimed that great literature has **cross-cultural** significance. In this article, Laura Bohannan describes the difficulties she encountered and the lessons she learned as she attempted to relate the story of **Hamlet** to the Tiv of West Africa in their own **language.**

60

UNIT 3
The Organization of Society and Culture

Unit Overview

64

10. **Macho Origin Myths,** Franz de Waal, from *The Age of Empathy,* Harmony Books, 2009

Without any understanding of the vast knowledge accumulated by such sciences as **anthropology,** too many economists and politicians have modeled their views on **human nature** based upon the **narrow perspective of Western society.** One only needs to know our past to understand that **humans are not naturally warlike, competitive, and individualistic.**

66

11. **How Cooking Frees Men,** Richard Wrangham, from *Catching Fire,* Basic Books, 2009

The classic explanation for why there is a **universal sexual division of labor in foraging societies** has to do with **men hunting and women gathering.** Even more important, says Wrangham, is the advent of **cooked food.** This dietary change has fostered **anatomical and physiological changes** as well.

70

12. **When Cousins Do More than Kiss,** Anthony Layng, *USA Today,* September 2009

Given the variability of **incest taboos** cross-culturally, it is very unlikely that humans have some sort of **instinct against inbreeding** or that **genetic closeness** is the major concern. The more likely explanation is that requiring young people to find their mates outside their group **fostered cooperation and exchange of food** between hunting and gathering bands.

75

13. **Meet the Alloparents,** Sarah Blaffer Hrdy, *Natural History,* April 2009

A growing body of evidence from traditional societies is making it clear that **multiple caregivers of children**—not just the mother alone—**provide greater assurance that offspring will survive and prosper.**

77

14. **The Inuit Paradox,** Patricia Gadsby, *Discover,* October 2004

The **traditional diet** of the Far North, with its **high-protein, high-fat** content, shows that there are no essential foods—only **essential nutrients.**

81

15. **Ties That Bind,** Peter M. Whiteley, *Natural History,* November 2004

The **Hopi** people offer **gifts** in a much broader range of circumstances than people in **Western cultures** do, tying individuals and groups to each other and to the realm of the spirits.

85

16. **Sick of Poverty,** Robert Sapolsky, *Scientific American,* December 2005

While it has long been known that people with **low socioeconomic status** have **higher disease risks and shorter life spans,** new studies indicate that material deprivation may only be part of the explanation. Perhaps an even more important aspect has to do with the **psychosocial stresses** that go with their place in society.

88

The concepts in bold italics are developed in the article. For further expansion, please refer to the Topic Guide.

UNIT 4
Other Families, Other Ways

Unit Overview   92

17. **When Brothers Share a Wife: Among Tibetans, the Good Life Relegates Many Women to Spinsterhood,** Melvyn C. Goldstein, *Natural History,* March 1987

While the custom of **fraternal polyandry** relegated many Tibetan women to spinsterhood, this unusual **marriage** form promoted personal security and economic well-being for its participants.   94

18. **Death without Weeping,** Nancy Scheper-Hughes, *Natural History,* October 1989

In the Shantytowns of Brazil, the seeming indifference of mothers who allow some of their **children** to die is a **survival strategy,** geared to circumstances in which only some may live.   98

19. **Arranging a Marriage in India,** Serena Nanda, *Stumbling Toward Truth: Anthropologists at Work,* Waveland Press, 2000

Arranging a marriage in India is far too serious a business for the young and inexperienced. Instead, the parents make the decision on the basis of the families' **social position,** reputation, and ability to get along.   103

20. **Who Needs Love! In Japan, Many Couples Don't,** Nicholas D. Kristof, *New York Times,* February 11, 1996

Paradoxically, **Japanese families** seem to survive, not because husbands and wives love each other more than American couples do, but rather because they perhaps love each other less. And as **love marriages** increase, with the compatibility factor becoming more important in the decision to marry, the **divorce rate** is rising.   108

UNIT 5
Gender and Status

Unit Overview   112

21. **The Berdache Tradition,** Walter L. Williams, *The Meaning of Difference,* Beacon Press, 2000

Not all societies agree with the **Western cultural view** that all humans are either women or men. In fact, many Native American cultures recognize an **alternative role** called the "berdache," a morphological male who has a non-masculine character. This is just one way for a society to recognize and assimilate some **atypical individuals** without imposing a change on them or stigmatizing them as deviants.   114

22. **Where Fat Is a Mark of Beauty,** Ann M. Simmons, *Los Angeles Times,* September 30, 1998

In a **rite of passage,** some Nigerian girls spend months gaining weight and learning customs in a "fattening room." A woman's rotundity is seen as a sign of **good health, prosperity, and feminine beauty.**   120

23. **. . . but What If It's a Girl?,** Carla Power, *New Statesman,* April 25, 2006

In some parts of Asia, a combination of the traditional **preference for male heirs,** increased **consumerism,** and **population control** efforts has resulted in an **imbalance in the sex ratios,** an increase in **violence toward females,** and a potentially "**hypermacho society**" of "**sex-starved males.**"   122

24. **Missing Girls,** Michelle Goldberg, from *The Means of Reproduction,* Penguin, 2009

Motivated by economic need and runaway consumerism and fueled by **modern technology,** such as **ultrasound, sex selection in favor of sons** has become **a tool for limiting population** in much of Asia. The resulting **imbalance in the sex ratio threatens to impede women's rights, destabilize entire regions, and prevent men from marrying at all.**   125

The concepts in bold italics are developed in the article. For further expansion, please refer to the Topic Guide.

25. **Rising Number of Dowry Deaths in India,** Amanda Hitchcock, International Committee of the Fourth International, July 4, 2001

Traditionally, a dowry in India allowed a woman to become a member of her husband's family with her own wealth. However, with the development of a cash economy, increased consumerism, and a status-striving society, heightened demands for dowry and the inability of many brides' families to meet such demands have led to thousands of deaths each year. **137**

UNIT 6
Religion, Belief, and Ritual

Unit Overview **140**

26. **Shamanisms: Past and Present,** David Kozak, *Religion and Culture,* Pearson Prentice Hall, 2008

This article explains how few generalizations about **shamanism** do justice to the **varying social contexts** and individual **cultural histories** of the shamans, and discusses the past **perceptual biases** on the part of ethnographic observers. **142**

27. **The Adaptive Value of Religious Ritual,** Richard Sosis, *American Scientist,* March/April 2004

Rituals promote **group cohesion** by requiring members to engage in behavior that is too costly to fake. Groups that do so are more likely to attain their **collective goals** than the groups whose members are less committed. **152**

28. **Understanding Islam,** Kenneth Jost, *CQ Researcher,* November 3, 2005

As the world's second largest religion after Christianity, **Islam** teaches **piety, virtue, and tolerance.** Yet, with the emphasis of some Islamists on a **strong relationship between religion and state,** and with an increasing number of Islamic militants calling for **violence against the West,** communication and mutual understanding are becoming more important than ever. **158**

29. **The Secrets of Haiti's Living Dead,** Gino Del Guercio, *Harvard Magazine,* January/February 1986

In seeking scientific documentation of the existence of zombies, anthropologist Wade Davis found himself looking beyond the stereotypes and mysteries of **voodoo,** and directly into a cohesive system of **social control** in rural Haiti. **163**

30. **Body Ritual among the Nacirema,** Horace Miner, *American Anthropologist,* June 1956

The **rituals,** beliefs, and **taboos,** of the Nacirema provide us with a test case of the objectivity of ethnographic description and show us the extremes to which human behavior can go. **167**

31. **Baseball Magic,** George Gmelch, Original Work, 2008

Professional baseball players, like Trobriand Islanders, often resort to **magic,** in **situations of chance and uncertainty.** As irrational as it may seem, magic creates confidence, competence, and control in the practitioner. **170**

UNIT 7
Sociocultural Change

Unit Overview **176**

32. **Why Can't People Feed Themselves?,** Frances Moore Lappé and Joseph Collins, *Food First: Beyond the Myth of Scarcity,* Random House, 1977

When **colonial governments** force the conversion of **subsistence farms to cash crop plantations,** peasants are driven into marginal lands or into a large pool of cheap labor. In either case, the authors maintain their stand that the farmers are no longer able to feed themselves. **178**

The concepts in bold italics are developed in the article. For further expansion, please refer to the Topic Guide.

33. **The Tractor Invasion,** Laura Graham, *Cultural Survival Quarterly,* Summer 2009

The **Brazilian Cerrado** is one of the world's most **biologically diverse** tropical Savanna regions. Its **indigenous people** are struggling to survive the onslaught of **agribusiness, deforestation, environmental pollution, and exotic diseases.** What legal rights they have to the land are being trampled and their cries for help are largely ignored.   **183**

34. **Yanomamo,** Leslie E. Sponsel, *Encyclopedia of Anthropology,* (H. James Birx, ed.), Sage Publications, 2006

As one of the few indigenous cultures remaining in the Amazon rain forest, the **Yanomami** have become increasingly **endangered from outside contact.** In calling for more **social responsibility and relevance in anthropological research,** the author questions whether it is any longer "justifiable" to collect scientific data merely to feed **careerism** and the vague promise of "contributing to human knowledge."   **188**

35. **The Arrow of Disease,** Jared Diamond, *Discover,* October 1992

The most deadly weapon **colonial Europeans** carried to other continents was their germs. The most intriguing question to be answered here is, why did the flow of **disease** not move in the opposite direction?   **192**

36. **The Americanization of Mental Illness,** Ethan Watters, **New Scientist,** January 20, 2010

According to some anthropologists and cross-cultural psychiatrists, **mental illness has varied in time and place** much more than previously thought. **American-led globalization, however, is undermining local conceptions of self and modes of healing** and, says Watters, is **"homogenizing the way the world goes mad."**   **199**

37. **The Price of Progress,** John Bodley, *Victims of Progress,* Mayfield Publishing, 1998

As **traditional cultures** are sacrificed in the process of **modernization,** tribal peoples not only lose the security, autonomy, and quality of life they once had, but they also become **powerless, second-class citizens** who are discriminated against and exploited by the dominant society.   **205**

38. **Seeing Conservation through the Global Lens,** Jim Igoe, *Conservation and Globalization,* Wadsworth, 2004

Before **economic globalization** took hold, most **traditional peoples** lived in ways that **ensured the continued availability of resources** for future generations. Because most Western models of conservation are based on the total exclusion of indigenous peoples, it is not surprising that they **speak of conservation with disdain.**   **213**

39. **Der Indianer,** Noemi Lopinto, *Alberta Views,* July/August 2008

Apparently sensing something missing in their own lives, **tens of thousands of Germans claim a spiritual link to Native American myths and ceremonies.** They even spend weekends trying to live as Indians did two centuries ago. While their hearts might be in the right place, their tendency to improvise on the most sacred rituals and **their sense of ownership over aboriginal culture ultimately demeans the very people they claim to admire.**   **224**

40. **What Native Peoples Deserve,** Roger Sandall, *Commentary,* May 2005

What should be done about **endangered enclave societies** in the midst of a modern nation such as Brazil? The main priority, says Roger Sandall, must be to ensure that no one should have to play the role of **historical curiosity** and that those who want to **participate in the modern world** should be able to do so, whether on the reservation or off it.   **228**

41. **Being Indigenous in the 21st Century,** Wilma Mankiller, *Cultural Survival Quarterly,* Spring 2009

With a **shared sense of history** and a growing set of tools, the **world's indigenous peoples** are moving into **a future of their own making** without losing sight of who they are and where they come from.   **233**

Test-Your-Knowledge Form   **236**
Article Rating Form   **237**

The concepts in bold italics are developed in the article. For further expansion, please refer to the Topic Guide.

WHAT IS ANTHROPOLOGY?

WHAT'S TO COME

The Cross-Cultural Perspective

Human Adaptability

General Anthropology

Human Biological Diversity and the Race Concept

The Subdisciplines of Anthropology

Anthropology and Other Academic Fields

Applied Anthropology

UNDERSTANDING OURSELVES

When you were young, your parents might have told you that drinking milk and eating vegetables would help you grow up "big and strong." They probably didn't as readily recognize the role that *culture* plays in shaping bodies, personalities, and personal health. If nutrition matters in growth, so, too, do cultural guidelines. Our bodies are affected by the kinds of work we do, the homes we live in, the ways we play and relax, the gender roles of males and females, our religion, and the ways we relate to our family, friends, and neighbors. Culture is an environmental force that affects our development as much as do nutrition, heat, cold, and altitude.

Think about the phrases and sentences you would use to describe yourself in a personal ad or on a networking site—your likes and dislikes, hobbies and habits. How many of these descriptors would be the same if you had been born in a different place or time? We usually think about "who we are" as a collection of set characteristics and tendencies, but this idea is as culturally determined as any of the traits we might put on an "about me" list. In other cultures, people might describe themselves by referencing their relationship to one or more gods, their success as a hunter, or their roles as family members.

Among scholarly disciplines, anthropology stands out as the field that provides the cross-cultural test. How much would we know about human behavior, thought, and feeling if we studied only our own kind? What if our entire understanding of human behavior were based on analysis of questionnaires filled out by college students in Oregon? One culture, age group, or gender can't tell us everything we need to know about what it means to be human. Often culture is "invisible," and thus unexamined, until it is placed in comparison to another culture. For example, to appreciate how watching television affects us as human beings, we need to study not just North America today but some other place—and perhaps also some other time (such as Brazil in the 1980s; see Kottak 1990b). The cross-cultural test is fundamental to the anthropological approach, which orients this textbook.

- What is anthropology, and how does it differ from other fields that study human beings?
- How useful is the race concept in understanding human diversity?
- What are the four subfields of anthropology?

>> The Cross-Cultural Perspective

"That's just human nature." "People are pretty much the same all over the world." Such opinions, which we hear in conversations, in the mass media, and in a dozen scenes in daily life, promote the erroneous idea that people in other countries have the same desires, feelings, values, and aspirations that we do. Such statements proclaim that because people are essentially the same, they are eager to receive the ideas, beliefs, values, institutions, practices, and products of an expansive North American culture. Often this assumption turns out to be wrong.

ethnography Fieldwork in a particular culture.

Anthropology offers a broader view—a distinctive comparative, cross-cultural perspective. Most people think that anthropologists study nonindustrial societies, and they do—but that's not all they do. Although Lisa Gezon has done some research on sustainable agriculture and water use in the state of Georgia, USA, she has spent most of her research time in Madagascar, a large island off the southeast coast of Africa. With Conrad Kottak as her graduate school adviser, she first studied how people in a local chiefdom responded to forest conservation. In her next study, she traced the drug *khat* as it went from farmers' fields, into the hands of traders, and finally into the mouths of urban consumers. Conrad Kottak's research also has taken him to remote villages in Brazil and Madagascar. In Brazil he sailed with fishers in simple sailboats on Atlantic waters. Among Madagascar's Betsileo people he worked in rice fields and took part in ceremonies in which he entered tombs to rewrap the corpses of decaying ancestors.

Anthropology, which originated as the study of nonindustrial peoples, is a comparative science that now extends to all societies, ancient and modern, simple and complex. Most of the other social sciences tend to focus on a single society, usually an industrial nation such as the United States or Canada. Anthropology offers a unique cross-cultural perspective, constantly comparing the customs of one society with those of others.

To become a cultural anthropologist, one normally does **ethnography** (the first-

In Mozambique's Gaza province, the Dutch ethnographer Janine van Vugt (red hair) sits on a mat near reed houses, talking to local women.

STUDY TIP

Two key assumptions of anthropology:

- Understanding human nature requires comparative, cross-cultural studies;

- People are best understood holistically, incorporating the whole of the human condition, including biological and cultural influences.

hand, personal study of local settings). Ethnographic fieldwork usually entails spending a year or more in another society, living with the local people and learning about their way of life. No matter how much the ethnographer discovers about the society, he or she remains an alien there. That experience of alienation has a profound impact. Having learned to respect other customs and beliefs, anthropologists can never forget that there is a wider world. There are normal ways of thinking and acting other than our own.

>> Human Adaptability

Anthropologists study human beings wherever and whenever they find them—in a Turkish café, a Mesopotamian tomb, or a North American shopping mall. Anthropology is the exploration of human diversity in time and space. Anthropology studies the whole of the human condition: past, present, and future; biology, society, language, and culture. Of particular interest is the diversity that comes through human adaptability.

Humans are among the world's most adaptable animals. In the Andes of South America, people wake up in villages

A culture produces a degree of consistency among members of the same society. Cultural celebrations, such as this Kurdish wedding, are patterned in particular ways based on cultural traditions.

16,000 feet above sea level and then trek 1,500 feet higher to work in tin mines. Tribes in the Australian desert worship animals and discuss philosophy. People survive malaria in the tropics. Men have walked on the moon. The model of the starship *Enterprise* in Washington's Smithsonian Institution symbolizes the desire to "seek out new life and civilizations, to boldly go where no one has gone before." Wishes to know the unknown, control the uncontrollable, and create order out of chaos find expression among all peoples. Creativity, adaptability, and flexibility are basic human attributes, and human diversity is the subject matter of anthropology.

Students often are surprised by the breadth of **anthropology,** which is the study of the human species and its immediate ancestors. Anthropology is a uniquely comparative and **holistic** science. *Holism* refers to the study of the whole of the human condition: past, present, and future; biology, society, language, and culture.

People share *society*—organized life in groups—with other animals, including baboons, wolves, and even ants. Culture, however, is more distinctly human. **Cultures** are traditions and customs, transmitted through learning, that form and guide the beliefs and behavior of the people exposed to them. Children learn such a tradition by growing up in a particular society, through a process called enculturation. Cultural traditions include customs and opinions, developed over the generations, about proper and improper behavior. These traditions answer such questions as: How should we do things? How do we make sense of the world? How do we tell right from wrong? What is right, and what is wrong? A culture produces a degree of consistency in behavior and thought among the people who live in a particular society.

> **anthropology** The study of the human species and its immediate ancestors.
>
> **holistic** Pertaining to the whole of the human condition, past, present, and future; biology, society, language, and culture.
>
> **culture** Traditions and customs that govern behavior and beliefs; distinctly human; transmitted through learning.

The most critical element of cultural traditions is their transmission through learning rather than through biological inheritance. Culture is not itself biological, but it rests on certain features of human biology. For more than a million years, humans have had at least some of the biological capacities on which culture depends. These abilities are to learn, to think symbolically, to use language, and to employ tools and other products in organizing their lives and adapting to their environments.

Anthropology confronts and ponders major questions of human existence as it explores human biological and cultural diversity in time and space. By examining ancient bones and tools, we unravel the mysteries of human origins. When did our ancestors separate from those remote great-aunts and great-uncles whose descendants are the apes? Where and when did *Homo sapiens* originate? How has our species changed? What are we now, and where are we going? How have changes in culture and society influenced biological change? Our genus, *Homo,* has been changing for more than one million years. Humans continue to adapt and change both biologically and culturally.

adaptation The process by which organisms cope with environmental stresses.

food production Plant cultivation and animal domestication.

general anthropology The field of anthropology as a whole, consisting of cultural, archaeological, biological, and linguistic anthropology.

ADAPTATION, VARIATION, AND CHANGE

Adaptation refers to the processes by which organisms cope with environmental forces and stresses, such as those posed by climate and *topography,* or terrains, also called landforms. How do organisms change to fit their environments, such as dry climates or high mountain altitudes? Like other animals, humans use biological means of adaptation. But humans are unique in also having cultural means of adaptation. Table 1.1 summarizes the cultural and biological means that humans use to adapt to high altitudes.

Mountainous terrains pose particular challenges, those associated with high altitude and oxygen deprivation. Consider four ways (one cultural and three biological) in which humans may cope with low oxygen pressure at high altitudes. Illustrating cultural (technological) adaptation would be a pressurized airplane cabin equipped with oxygen masks. There are three ways of adapting biologically to high altitudes: genetic adaptation, long-term physiological adaptation, and short-term physiological adaptation. First, native populations of high-altitude areas, such as the Andes of Peru and the Himalayas of Tibet and Nepal, seem to have acquired certain genetic advantages for life at very high altitudes. The Andean tendency to develop a voluminous chest and lungs probably has a genetic

CULTURETHINK

How have people adapted to changing economic conditions? Different jobs are available now than were available two generations ago. Talk with people (for example, your grandparents) who sought jobs at an earlier time in history. What kinds of jobs did they see as available? What kind of training did they require? How have things changed for you?

Forms of Cultural and Biological Adaptation (to High Altitude)

Form of Adaptation	Type of Adaptation	Example
Technology	Cultural	Pressurized airplane cabin with oxygen masks
Genetic adaptation (occurs over generations)	Biological	Larger "barrel chests" of native highlanders
Short-term physiological adaptation (occurs spontaneously when the individual organism enters a new environment)	Biological	Increased heart rate, hyperventilation
Long-term adaptation (occurs during growth and development of the individual organism)	Biological	More efficient respiratory system, to extract oxygen from "thin air"

basis. Second, regardless of their genes, people who grow up at a high altitude become physiologically more efficient there than genetically similar people who have grown up at sea level would be. This illustrates long-term physiological adaptation during the body's growth and development. Third, humans also have the capacity for short-term or immediate physiological adaptation. Thus, when lowlanders arrive in the highlands, they immediately increase their breathing and heart rates. Hyperventilation increases the oxygen in their lungs and arteries. As the pulse also increases, blood reaches their tissues more rapidly. All these varied adaptive responses—cultural and biological—achieve a single goal: maintaining an adequate supply of oxygen to the body.

The Sherpas of Nepal, one of whom is shown here (on the right) with a female trekker, have adapted culturally and biologically to their high altitude environment.

As human history has unfolded, the social and cultural means of adaptation have become increasingly important. In this process, humans have devised diverse ways of coping with the range of environments they have occupied in time and space. The rate of cultural adaptation and change has accelerated, particularly during the past ten thousand years. For millions of years, hunting and gathering of nature's bounty—*foraging*—was the sole basis of human subsistence. It took only a few thousand years, however, for **food production** (the cultivation of plants and domestication of animals), which originated some ten to twelve thousand years ago, to replace foraging in most areas. The first civilizations rose between 6000 and 5000 B.P. ("before the present"—years ago, in this case, five to six thousand years ago). These were large, powerful, and complex societies, such as ancient Egypt, that conquered and governed large geographic areas.

Much more recently, the spread of industrial production has profoundly affected human life. Throughout human history, major innovations have spread at the expense of earlier ones. Each economic revolution has had social and cultural repercussions. Today's global economy and communications link all contemporary people, directly or indirectly, in the modern world system. People must cope with forces generated by progressively larger systems—region, nation, and world. The study of such contemporary adaptations generates new challenges for anthropology: "The cultures of world peoples need to be constantly rediscovered as these people reinvent them in changing historical circumstances" (Marcus and Fischer 1986, p. 24).

>> General Anthropology

The academic discipline of anthropology, also known as **general anthropology,** or "four-field" anthropology, includes four main subdisciplines or subfields. They are sociocultural, archaeological, biological, and linguistic anthropology. (From here on, the shorter term *cultural anthropology* will be used as a synonym for "sociocultural anthropology.") Of the subfields, cultural anthropology has the largest membership. Most departments of anthropology teach courses in all four subfields.

There are historical reasons for the inclusion of four subfields in a single discipline. The origin of anthropol-

CULTURETHINK

What unites the four subdisciplines of anthropology into a single discipline? How might anthropology's diversity—as a discipline that includes biological as well as cultural perspectives, for example—be a strength? How might it be a weakness?

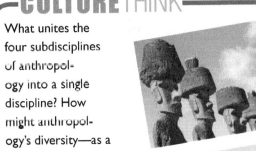

ogy as a scientific field, and of American anthropology in particular, can be traced to the nineteenth century. Early American anthropologists were concerned especially with the history and cultures of the native peoples of North America. Interest in the origins and diversity of Native Americans brought together studies of customs, social life, language, and physical traits. Anthropologists still ponder such questions as: Where did Native Americans come from? How many waves of migration brought them to the New World? What are the linguistic, cultural, and biological links among Native Americans and between them and Asia? (Note that a unified four-field anthropology did not develop in Europe, where the subfields tend to exist separately.)

racial classification The attempt to assign humans to discrete categories (purportedly) based on common ancestry.

There also are logical reasons for the unity of American anthropology. Each subfield considers variation in time and space (that is, in different geographic areas). Cultural and archaeological anthropologists study (among many other topics) changes in social life and customs. Archaeologists use studies of living societies to imagine what life might have been like in the past. Biological anthropologists examine evolutionary changes in physical form, for example, anatomical changes that might have been associated with the origin of tool use or language. Linguistic anthropologists may reconstruct the basics of ancient languages by studying modern ones.

Ely S. Parker, or Ha-sa-no-an-da, was a Seneca Indian who made significant contributions to early anthropology.
....

The subfields influence each other as anthropologists talk to each other, read books and journals, and meet in professional organizations. Anthropologists share certain key assumptions. Perhaps the most fundamental is the idea that sound conclusions about "human nature" cannot be derived from studying a single population, nation, society, or cultural tradition. A comparative, cross-cultural approach is essential.

General anthropology explores the basics of human biology, society, and culture and considers their interrelations. The four-field approach has been particularly effective in examining the relation between biology (e.g., "race"—see below) and culture. About seventy years ago, the famed anthropologist Ruth Benedict realized, "In World history, those who have helped to build the same

culture are not necessarily of one race, and those of the same race have not all participated in one culture" (Benedict 1940, Ch. 2). This statement is even truer in today's globalizing world. How do contemporary anthropologists deal with issues of human biological diversity and race?

>> Human Biological Diversity and the Race Concept

The photos in this book offer only a glimpse of the range of human biological variation. Additional illustration comes from your own experience. Look around you in your classroom or library, or at the mall or multiplex. Inevitably you'll see people whose ancestors lived in many lands. The first (Native) Americans had to cross a land bridge that once linked Siberia to North America. For later immigrants, perhaps including your own parents or grandparents, the voyage may have been across the sea or overland from nations to the south. They came for many reasons. Some came voluntarily, while others were brought here in chains. The scale of migration in today's world is so vast that millions of people routinely cross national borders or live far from the homelands of their grandparents. Now meeting every day are diverse human beings whose biological features reflect adaptation to a wide range of environments other than the ones they now inhabit. Physical contrasts are evident to anyone. Anthropology's job is to explain them.

Historically, scientists have approached the study of human biological diversity in two main ways: (1) racial classification (now largely abandoned) versus (2) the current explanatory approach, which focuses on understanding specific differences. First we'll consider problems with **racial classification**—the attempt to assign humans to discrete categories (purportedly) based on common ancestry. Then we'll offer some explanations for specific aspects of human biological diversity (in this case, light versus dark skin color). *Biological differences are real, important, and apparent to us all.* Modern scientists find it most productive to seek explanations for this diversity, rather than trying to pigeonhole people into categories called races.

What is race anyway? In theory, a biological race would be a geographically isolated subdivision of a species. (A *species* is a population whose members can interbreed to produce offspring that can live and reproduce.) Such a *subspecies* would be capable of interbreeding with other subspecies of the same species, but it would not actually do so because of its geographic isolation. Some biologists also use "race" to refer to "breeds," as of

Photos, from left to right: an Aymaran woman from Bolivia; a Samburu woman from Kenya; a woman from Guangzhou province, People's Republic of China; a young Norwegian woman with blonde hair and blue eyes.

dogs or roses. Thus, a pit bull and a Chihuahua would be different races of dogs. Such domesticated "races" have been bred by humans for generations. Humanity (*Homo sapiens*) lacks such races because human populations have not been isolated enough from one another to develop into such discrete groups. Nor have humans experienced controlled breeding like that which has created the various kinds of dogs and roses.

A race is supposed to reflect shared *genetic* material (inherited from a common ancestor), but early scholars instead used *phenotypical* traits (usually skin color) for human racial classification. **Phenotype** refers to an organism's evident traits, its "manifest biology"—anatomy and physiology. Humans display hundreds of evident (detectable) physical traits. They range from skin color, hair form, eye color, and facial features (which are visible) to blood groups and enzyme production (which become evident through testing).

Racial classifications based on phenotype raise the problem of deciding which traits are most important. Should races be defined by height, weight, body shape, facial features, teeth, skull form, or skin color? Like their fellow citizens, early European and American scientists gave priority to skin color. Many school books and encyclopedias still proclaim the existence of three great races: the white, the black, and the yellow. This overly simplistic classification was compatible with the political use of race during the colonial period of the late nineteenth and early twentieth centuries. Such a tripartite scheme kept white Europeans neatly separate from their African, Asian, and Native American subjects. Then colonial empires began to break up, and after World War II, scientists began to question established racial categories.

Politics aside, one obvious problem with such racial labels is that they don't accurately describe skin color. "White" people are more pink, beige, or tan than white. "Black" people are various shades of brown, and "yellow" people are tan or beige. These terms also have been dignified by more scientific-*sounding* synonyms— Caucasoid, Negroid, and Mongoloid—which actually have no more of a scientific basis than do white, black, and yellow.

> **phenotype** An organism's evident traits, its "manifest biology"—anatomy and physiology.

It's true also that many human populations don't fit neatly into any one of the three "great races." For example, where does one put the Polynesians? Polynesia is a triangle of South Pacific islands formed by Hawaii to the north, Easter Island to the east, and New Zealand to the southwest. Does the bronze skin color of Polynesians place them with the Caucasoids or the Mongoloids? Some scientists, recognizing this problem, enlarged the original tripartite scheme to include the Polynesian race. Native Americans present an additional problem. Are they red or yellow? Again, some scientists add a fifth race—the red, or Amerindian—to the major racial groups.

Many people in southern India have dark skins, but scientists have been reluctant to classify them with black Africans because of their Caucasoid facial features and hair form. Some, therefore, have created a separate race for these people. What about the Australian aborigines, hunters and gatherers native to the most isolated continent? By skin color, one might place some Native Australians in the same race as tropical Africans. However, similarities to Europeans in hair color (light or reddish) and facial features have led some scientists to classify them as Cauca-

CULTURETHINK

Try to identify the people shown in these photos using traditional racial categories: Race typically is assigned based on a combination of ancestry and appearance. Without knowing their ancestry, can you identify their "race"?

Answers: (left to right): Polynesian, southern Indian, Native Australian, San

soids. But there is no evidence that Australians are closer genetically or historically to either of these groups than they are to Asians. Recognizing this problem, scientists often regard Native Australians as a separate race.

Finally, consider the San ("Bushmen") of the Kalahari Desert in southern Africa. Scientists have perceived their skin color as varying from brown to yellow. Those who regard San skin as yellow have placed them in the same category as Asians. In theory, people of the same race share more recent common ancestry with each other than they do with any others; but there is no evidence for recent common ancestry between San and Asians. More reasonably, the San are classified as members of the Capoid (from the Cape of Good Hope) race, which is seen as being different from other groups inhabiting tropical Africa.

biocultural Referring to the inclusion and combination (to solve a common problem) of both biological and cultural approaches—one of anthropology's hallmarks.

Similar problems arise when any single trait is used as a basis for racial classification. An attempt to use facial features, height, weight, or any other phenotypical trait is fraught with difficulties. For example, consider the Nilotes, natives of the upper Nile region of Uganda and Sudan. Nilotes tend to be tall and to have long, narrow noses. Certain Scandinavians also are tall, with similar noses. Given the distance between their homelands, to classify them as members of the same race makes little sense. There is no reason to assume that Nilotes and Scandinavians are more closely related to each other than either is to shorter (and nearer) populations with different kinds of noses.

Would it be better to base racial classifications on a combination of physical traits? This would avoid some of the problems just discussed, but others would arise. First, skin color, stature, skull form, and facial features (nose form, eye shape, lip thickness) don't go together as a unit. For example, people with dark skin may be tall or short and have hair ranging from straight to very curly. Dark-haired populations may have light or dark skin, along with various skull forms, facial features, and body sizes and shapes. The number of combinations is very large, and the amount that heredity (versus environment) contributes to such phenotypical traits is often unclear.

There is a final objection to racial classification based on phenotype. The phenotypical characteristics on which races are based supposedly reflect genetic material that is shared and that has stayed the same for long periods. But phenotypical similarities and differences don't necessarily have a genetic basis. Because of changes in the environment that affect individuals during growth and development, the range of phenotypes characteristic of a population may change without any genetic change. There are several examples. In the early twentieth century, the anthropologist Franz Boas (1940/1966) described changes in skull form among the children of Europeans who had migrated to the United States. The reason for this wasn't a change in genes, since the European immigrants tended to marry among themselves. Some of their children had been born in Europe and merely raised in the United States. Something in the new environment, probably in the diet, was producing this change. We know now that changes in average height and weight produced by dietary differences in a few generations are common and have nothing to do with race or genetics.

Anthropology's comparative, biocultural perspective recognizes that environmental factors, including customary diet and other cultural forces, constantly mold human biology. (**Biocultural** refers to the inclusion and combination of both biological and cultural perspectives and approaches to comment on or solve a particular issue or problem.) Culture is a key environmental force in determining how human bodies grow and develop. Cultural traditions promote certain activities and abilities, discourage others, and set standards of physical well-being and attractiveness.

CULTURETHINK

The fact that race lacks a biological basis does not make it irrelevant. How is race an issue for many people today?

STUDY TIP

What's wrong with classifying people by race?

- Human groups haven't been isolated from each other long enough to form genetically separate groups.

- Many individuals, and even whole human populations, don't fit neatly into common racial categories.

- Not all phenotypic differences have a genetic basis.

Bodies—ideal and actual—vary from culture to culture and within one culture over time. Ideal bodies change from generation to generation and, with the influence of the mass media, even from decade to decade. Old movies make it easy for us to study bodies and clothing over time. Such movie stars of the past as Humphrey Bogart and Barbara Stanwyck wore stylish hats and smoked cigarettes. Contemporary American men and women wear baseball caps and lift weights. When asked how he recognized Americans in the street, one European mentioned lifting (of weights, and its effects on the body) and tennis shoes (an item of dress considered inelegant in Europe, but a mainstay of hard-core American touring).

"The purpose of anthropology is to make the world safe for human differences."

Ruth Benedict

EXPLANATORY APPROACHES TO HUMAN DIVERSITY

Traditional racial classification assumed that biological characteristics were determined by heredity and were stable (immutable) over long periods. We know now that a biological similarity doesn't necessarily indicate recent common ancestry. Dark skin color, for example, can be shared by tropical Africans and Native Australians for reasons other than common ancestry. It is not possible to *define human races* biologically. Still, scientists have made much progress in *explaining* variation in skin color, along with many other expressions of human biological diversity. We shift now from classification to *explanation,* in which natural selection plays a key role.

First recognized by Charles Darwin and Alfred Russel Wallace, **natural selection** is the process by which the forms most fit to survive and reproduce in a given environment—such as the tropics—do so in greater numbers than others in the same population do. Over the years, the less fit organisms die out and the favored types survive by producing more offspring. The role of natural selection

in producing variation in skin color illustrates the explanatory approach to human biological diversity. Comparable explanations have been provided for many other aspects of human biological variation.

Melanin, the primary determinant of human skin color, is a chemical substance manufactured in the epidermis, or outer skin layer. The melanin cells of darker-skinned people produce more and larger granules of melanin than do those of lighter-skinned people. By screening out ultraviolet (uv) radiation from the sun, melanin offers protection against a variety of maladies, including sunburn and skin cancer.

Before the sixteenth century, most of the world's very dark skinned populations lived in the **tropics,** a belt extending about 23 degrees north and south of the equator, between the Tropic of Cancer and the Tropic of Capricorn. The association between dark skin color and a tropical habitat existed throughout the Old World, where humans and their ancestors have lived for millions of years. The darkest populations of Africa evolved not in shady equatorial forests but in sunny open grassland, or savanna, country.

Outside the tropics, skin color tends to be lighter. Moving north in Africa, for example, there is a gradual transition from dark brown to medium brown. Average skin color continues to lighten as one moves through the Middle East, into southern Europe, through central Europe, and to the north. South of the tropics skin color also is lighter. In the Americas, by contrast, tropical populations don't have very dark skin. This is because the settlement of the New World, by light-skinned Asian ancestors of Native Americans, was relatively recent, probably dating back no more than eighteen thousand years.

How, aside from migrations, can we explain the geographic distribution of human skin color? Natural selection provides an answer. In the tropics, intense UV radiation poses a series of threats that make light skin color an adaptive disadvantage. First, UV radiation can cause severe sunburn, which aside from discomfort can lead to vulnerabilities in the body. By damaging sweat glands, sunburn reduces the body's ability to perspire and thus to regulate its own temperature (thermoregulation). Sunburn also can increase susceptibility to disease. Yet another disadvantage of having light skin color in the tropics is that exposure to UV radiation can cause skin cancer (Blum 1961). Melanin, nature's own sunscreen, confers a selective advantage (i.e., a

> **natural selection** Originally formulated by Charles Darwin and Alfred Russel Wallace; the process by which nature selects the forms most fit to survive and reproduce in a given environment, such as the tropics.
>
> **tropics** Geographic belt extending about 23 degrees north and south of the equator, between the Tropic of Cancer (north) and the Tropic of Capricorn (south).

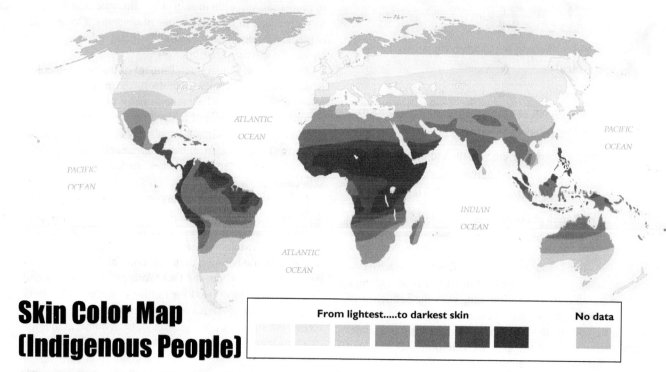

Skin Color Map (Indigenous People)

| From lightest.....to darkest skin | No data |

Before the sixteenth century, most of the world's very dark skinned populations lived in the tropics, a belt extending about 23 degrees north and south of the equator. Outside the tropics, skin color tends to be lighter.

Source: G. Chaplin, "Geographic Distribution of Environmental Factors Influencing Human Skin Coloration," *American Journal of Physical Anthropology* 125:292–302, 2004; map updated in 2007.

better chance to survive and reproduce) on darker-skinned people living in the tropics because it helps protect them from sunburn and skin cancer.

Another selective factor in the geographic distribution of human skin color relates to the manufacture (synthesis) of vitamin D in the body. Years ago, W. F. Loomis (1967) focused on the role of UV radiation in stimulating the manufacture of vitamin D by the human body. The unclothed human body can produce its own vitamin D when exposed to sufficient sunlight. However, in a cloudy environment that also is so cold that people have to dress themselves much of the year (such as northern Europe, where very light skin color evolved), clothing interferes with the body's manufacture of vitamin D. The ensuing shortage of vitamin D diminishes the absorption of calcium in the intestines. A nutritional disease known as rickets, which softens and deforms the bones, may develop. In women, deformation of the pelvic bones from rickets can interfere with childbirth. In cold northern areas, light skin color maximizes the absorption of UV radiation and the synthesis of vitamin D by the

few parts of the body that are exposed to direct sunlight. There has been selection against dark skin color in northern areas because melanin screens out UV radiation.

This natural selection continues today: East Asians who have migrated recently from India and Pakistan to northern areas of the United Kingdom have a higher incidence of rickets and osteoporosis (also related to vitamin D and calcium deficiency) than the general British population. A related illustration involves Eskimos (Inuit) and other indigenous inhabitants of northern Alaska and northern Canada. According to Nina Jablonski (quoted in Iqbal 2002), "Looking at Alaska, one would think that the native people should be pale as ghosts." One reason they aren't is that they haven't inhabited this region very long in terms of geological time. Even more important, their traditional diet, which is rich in seafood, including fish oils, supplies sufficient vitamin D so as to make a reduction in pigmentation unnecessary. However, and again illustrating natural selection at work today, "when these people don't eat their aboriginal diets of fish and marine mammals, they suffer tremendously high rates of vitamin D-deficiency diseases such as rickets in children and osteoporosis in adults" (Jablonski quoted in Iqbal 2002). Far from being immutable, skin color can become an evolutionary liability very quickly.

According to Jablonski and George Chaplin (2000), another key factor explaining the geographic distribution of skin color involves the effects of UV radiation on folate, an essential nutrient that the human body manufactures from folic acid. Folate is needed for cell division and the production of new DNA. Pregnant women require large

Did You Know ?

Before the 1930s, when milk first was fortified with vitamin D, rickets was a major health concern in the United States. The National Institutes of Health directly linked vitamin D deficiency with low sun exposure. You could say that fortifying milk is a cultural adaptation to the environmental stress of low sun exposure.

	UV Index			
No Protection Required		Protection Required		Extra Protection
1 2		3 4 5	6 7	8 9	10 11

The Sun's Rays

This color-coded map of the world shows the mean annual UV radiation level in 2003, with purple designating the lowest radiation levels, and red designating the highest. How does this data fit with the skin color map on page 10?

amounts of folate to support rapid cell division in the embryo, and there is a direct connection between folate and individual reproductive success. Folate deficiency causes neural tube defects (NTDs) in human embryos. NTDs are marked by the incomplete closure of the neural tube, so the spine and spinal cord fail to develop completely. One NTD, anencephaly (with the brain an exposed mass), results in stillbirth or death soon after delivery. With spina bifida, another NTD, survival rates are higher, but babies have severe disabilities, including paralysis. NTDs are the second-most-common human birth defect after cardiac abnormalities. Today, women of reproductive age are advised to take folate supplements to prevent serious birth defects such as spina bifida.

Natural sunlight and UV radiation destroy folate in the human body. Because melanin, as we have seen, protects against UV hazards, such as sunburn and its consequences, dark skin coloration is adaptive in the tropics. Now we see that melanin also is adaptive because it conserves folate in

Rickets, based on a significant vitamin D deficiency, can lead to softening of the bones, which may result in bow legs as illustrated by the child shown in this nineteenth century photo.

the human body and thus protects against NTDs, which are much more common in light-skinned than in darker-skinned populations (Jablonski and Chaplin 2000). Studies confirm that Africans and African Americans have a low incidence of severe folate deficiency, even among individuals with marginal nutritional status. Folate also plays a role in another process that is central to reproduction, spermatogenesis—the production of sperm. In mice and rats, folate deficiency can cause male sterility; it may well play a similar role in humans.

Today, of course, cultural alternatives to biological adaptation permit light-skinned people to survive in the tropics and darker-skinned people to live in the far north. People can clothe themselves and seek shelter from the sun; they can use artificial sunscreens if they lack the natural protection that melanin provides. Dark-skinned people living in the north can, indeed must, get vitamin D from their diet or take supplements. Today, pregnant women are routinely advised to take folic acid or folate supplements as a hedge against NTDs. Even so, light skin color still is correlated with a higher incidence of spina bifida. Jablonski and Chaplin (2000) explain variation in human skin color as resulting from a balancing act between the evolutionary needs to (1) protect against all UV hazards (favoring dark skin in the tropics) and (2) have an adequate supply of vitamin D (favoring lighter skin outside the tropics).

cultural anthropology The study of human society and culture; describes, analyzes, interprets, and explains social and cultural similarities and differences.

ethnology The theoretical, comparative study of society and culture; compares cultures in time and space.

This discussion of skin color shows that common ancestry, the presumed basis of race, is not the only reason for biological similarities. Natural selection, still at work today, makes a major contribution to variations in human skin color, as well as to many other human biological differences and similarities.

>> The Subdisciplines of Anthropology

CULTURAL ANTHROPOLOGY

The study of human society and culture, known as **cultural anthropology,** is the subfield that describes, analyzes, interprets, and explains social and cultural similarities and differences. To study and interpret cultural diversity, cultural anthropologists engage in two kinds of activity: ethnography (based on fieldwork) and ethnology (based on cross-cultural comparison). Ethnography provides an account of a particular community, society, or culture. During ethnographic fieldwork, the ethnographer gathers data that he or she organizes, describes, analyzes, and interprets to build and present that account, which may be in the form of a book, article, or film. Traditionally, ethnographers have lived in small communities and studied local behavior, beliefs, customs, social life, economic activities, politics, and religion (see Wolcott 2008).

The anthropological perspective derived from ethnographic field work often differs radically from that of economics or political science. Those fields focus on national and official organizations and policies and often on elites. The groups that anthropologists traditionally have studied usually have been relatively poor and powerless. Ethnographers often observe discriminatory practices directed toward such people, who experience food shortages, dietary deficien-

President Barack Obama and his mother, Ann Dunham, who was a cultural and applied anthropologist, in an undated photo from the 1960s.
....

cies, and other aspects of poverty. Political scientists tend to study programs that national planners develop, while anthropologists discover how these programs work on the local level.

Cultures are not isolated. As noted by Franz Boas (1940/1966) many years ago, contact between neighboring tribes always has existed and has extended over enormous areas. Human populations construct their cultures in interaction with one another, and not in isolation (Wolf 1982, p. ix). Villagers increasingly participate in regional, national, and world events. Exposure to external forces comes through the mass media, migration, and modern transportation. City and nation increasingly invade local communities with the arrival of tourists, development agents, government and religious officials, and political candidates. Such linkages are prominent components of regional, national, and international systems of politics, economics, and information. These larger systems increasingly affect the people and places anthropology traditionally has studied. The study of such linkages and systems is part of the subject matter of modern anthropology.

Ethnology examines, interprets, analyzes, and compares the results of ethnography—the data gathered in different societies. It uses such data to compare and contrast and to make generalizations about society and culture. Looking beyond the particular to the more general, ethnologists attempt to identify and explain cultural differences and similarities, to test hypotheses, and to build theory to enhance our understanding of how social and cultural systems work. Ethnology gets its data for comparison not just from ethnography but also from the other subfields, particularly from archaeological anthropology, which reconstructs social systems of the past. (Table 1.2 summarizes the main contrasts between ethnography and ethnology.)

ARCHAEOLOGICAL ANTHROPOLOGY

The subfield **archaeological anthropology** (more simply, "archaeology") reconstructs, describes, and interprets human behavior and cultural patterns through material remains. At sites where people live or have lived, archaeologists find *artifacts*—material items that humans have made, used, or modified, such as tools, weapons, campsites, buildings, and garbage. Plant and animal remains and ancient garbage tell stories about consumption and activities. Wild and domesticated grains have different characteristics, which allow archaeologists to distinguish between gathering and cultivation. Examination of animal bones reveals the ages of slaughtered animals and provides other infor-

Field notes

Ethnography and Ethnology— Two Dimensions of Cultural Anthropology

Ethnography	Ethnology
Requires field work to collect data	Uses data collected by a series of researchers
Often descriptive	Usually synthetic
Group/community specific	Comparative/cross-cultural

mation useful in determining whether species were wild or domesticated.

Analyzing such data, archaeologists answer several questions about ancient economies. Did the group get its meat from hunting, or did it domesticate and breed animals, killing only those of a certain age and sex? Did plant food come from wild plants or from sowing, tending, and harvesting crops? Did the residents make, trade for, or buy particular items? Were raw materials available locally? If not, where did they come from? From such information, archaeologists reconstruct patterns of production, trade, and consumption.

Archaeologists have spent much time studying potsherds, fragments of earthenware. Potsherds are more durable than many other artifacts, such as textiles and wood. The quantity of pottery fragments allows estimates of population size and density. The discovery that potters used materials that were not available locally suggests systems of trade. Similarities in manufacture and decoration at different sites may be proof of cultural connections. Groups with similar pots may be historically related. Perhaps they shared common cultural ancestors, traded with each other, or belonged to the same political system.

Many archaeologists examine paleoecology. *Ecology* is the study of interrelations among living things in an environment. The organisms and environment together constitute an *ecosystem,* a patterned arrangement of energy flows and exchanges. Human ecology studies ecosystems that include people, focusing on the ways in which human use "of nature influences and is influenced by social organization and cultural values" (Bennett 1969, pp. 10–11). *Paleoecology* looks at the ecosystems of the past.

In addition to reconstructing ecological patterns, archaeologists may infer cultural transformations, for example, by observing changes in the size and type of sites

and the distance between them. A city develops in a region where only towns, villages, and hamlets existed a few centuries earlier. The number of settlement levels (city, town, village, hamlet) in a society is a measure of social complexity. Buildings offer clues about political and religious features. Temples and pyramids suggest that an ancient society had an authority structure capable of marshaling the labor needed to build such monuments. The presence or absence of certain structures, like the pyramids of ancient Egypt and Mexico, reveals differences in function between settlements. For example, some towns were places where people came to

> **archaeological anthropology**
> The branch of anthropology, commonly known as archaeology, that reconstructs, describes, and interprets human behavior and cultural patterns through material remains; best known for the study of prehistory.

PUPCULTURE

Consider any one of the four *Indiana Jones* movies directed by Steven Spielberg. Archaeologists often complain that these movies distort public perceptions of their field by portraying archaeologists as greedy, adventurous, amoral, unscientific looters. How, if at all, has Indiana Jones influenced your views about archaeology? More generally, do media portrayals of archaeologists make you think more favorably or less favorably about the field of archaeology?

An archaeological team works at Harappa, one site from an ancient Indus River civilization dating back some 4,800 years.

attend ceremonies. Others were burial sites; still others were farming communities.

Archaeologists also reconstruct behavior patterns and lifestyles of the past by excavating. This involves digging through a succession of levels at a particular site. In a given area, through time, settlements may change in form and purpose, as may the connections between settlements. Excavation can document changes in economic, social, and political activities.

Although archaeologists are best known for studying prehistory—that is, the period before the invention of writing—they also study the cultures of historical and even living peoples (see Sabloff 2008). Studying sunken ships off the Florida coast, archaeologists have been able to verify the living conditions on the vessels that brought ancestral African Americans to the New World as enslaved people. In a research project begun in 1973 in Tucson, Arizona, archaeologist William Rathje has learned about contemporary life by studying modern garbage. The value of "garbology," as Rathje calls it, is that it provides "evidence of what people did, not what they think they did, what they think they should have done, or what the interviewer thinks they should have done" (Harrison, Rathje, and Hughes 1994, p. 108). What people report may contrast strongly with their real behavior as revealed by garbology. For example, the garbologists discovered that the three Tucson neighborhoods that reported the lowest beer consumption actually had the highest number of discarded beer cans per household (Podolefsky and Brown 1992, p. 100)! Rathje's garbology also exposed misconceptions about how much of different kinds of trash are in landfills: While most people thought that fast-food containers and disposable diapers were major waste problems, in fact they were relatively insignificant compared with paper, including environmentally friendly, recyclable paper (Rathje and Murphy 2001).

BIOLOGICAL, OR PHYSICAL, ANTHROPOLOGY

The subject matter of **biological,** or **physical, anthropology** is human biological diversity in time and space. The focus on biological variation unites five special interests within biological anthropology:

- Human evolution as revealed by the fossil record (paleoanthropology)
- Human genetics
- Human growth and development
- Human biological plasticity (the body's ability to change as it copes with stresses, such as heat, cold, and altitude)
- The biology, evolution, behavior, and social life of monkeys, apes, and other nonhuman primates

These interests link physical anthropology to other fields: biology, zoology, geology, anatomy, physiology, medicine, and public health. *Osteology*—the study of bones—helps paleoanthropologists, who examine skulls, teeth, and bones, to identify human ancestors and to chart changes in anatomy over time. A *paleontologist* is a scientist who studies fossils. A *paleoanthropologist* is one sort of paleontologist, one who studies the fossil record of human evolution. Paleoanthropologists often collaborate with archaeologists, who study artifacts, in reconstructing biological and cultural aspects of human evolution. Fossils and tools often are found together. Different types of tools provide information about the habits, customs, and lifestyles of the ancestral humans who used them.

More than a century ago, Charles Darwin noticed that the variety that exists within any population permits some individuals (those with the favored characteristics) to do better than others at surviving and reproducing. Genetics, which developed later, enlightens us about the causes and transmission of this variety. However, it isn't just genes that cause variety. During any individual's lifetime, the environment works along with heredity to determine biological features. For example, people with a genetic tendency to be tall will be shorter if they are poorly nourished during childhood. Thus, biological anthropology also investigates the influence of environment on the body as it grows and matures. Among the environmental factors that influence the body as it develops are nutrition, altitude, temperature, and disease, as well as cultural factors, such as the standards of attractiveness we considered previously.

biological (physical) anthropology The branch of anthropology that studies human biological diversity in time and space—for instance, hominid evolution, human genetics, human biological adaptation; also includes primatology (behavior and evolution of monkeys and apes).

primates Members of the zoological order that includes humans, apes, monkeys, and prosimians, such as lemurs.

Biological anthropology (along with zoology) also includes primatology. The **primates** include our closest relatives—apes and monkeys. Primatologists study their biology, evolution, behavior, and social life, often in the primates' natural environments. Primatology assists paleoanthropology, because primate behavior may shed light on early human behavior and human nature.

LINGUISTIC ANTHROPOLOGY

We don't know (and probably never will) when our ancestors acquired the ability to speak, although biological anthropologists have looked to the anatomy of the face and the skull to speculate about the origin of language. And primatologists have described the communication systems of mon-

Primatologists study the evolution, biology, behavior, and social life of monkeys and apes, such as these young orangutans.

keys and apes. We do know that well-developed, grammatically complex languages have existed for thousands of years. Linguistic anthropology offers further illustration of anthropology's interest in comparison, variation, and change. **Linguistic anthropology** studies language in its social and cultural context, across space and over time. Some linguistic anthropologists make inferences about universal features of language, linked perhaps to uniformities in the human brain. Others reconstruct ancient languages by comparing their contemporary descendants and in so doing make discoveries about history. Still others study linguistic differences to discover varied perceptions and patterns of thought in different cultures.

Historical linguistics considers variation in time, such as the changes in sounds, grammar, and vocabulary between Middle English (spoken from approximately 1050 to 1550 C.E.) and modern English. **Sociolinguistics** investigates relationships between social and linguistic variation. No language is a homogeneous system in which everyone speaks just like everyone else. How do different speakers use a given language? How do linguistic features correlate with social factors, including class and gender differences (Tannen 1990)? One reason for variation is geography, as in regional dialects and accents. Linguistic variation also is expressed in the bilingualism of ethnic groups. Linguistic and cultural anthropologists collaborate in studying links between language and many other aspects of culture, such as how people reckon kinship and how they perceive and classify colors.

>> Anthropology and Other Academic Fields

As mentioned previously, one of the main differences between anthropology and the other fields that study people is holism, anthropology's unique blend of biological, social, cultural, linguistic, historical, and contemporary perspectives. Paradoxically, while distinguishing anthropology, this breadth is what also links it to many other disciplines. Techniques used to date fossils and artifacts have come to anthropology from physics, chemistry, and geology. Because plant and animal remains often are found with human bones and artifacts, anthropologists collaborate with botanists, zoologists, and paleontologists.

As a discipline that is both scientific and humanistic, anthropology has links with many other academic fields.

Anthropology is a **science**—a "systematic field of study or body of knowledge that aims, through experiment, observation, and deduction, to produce reliable explanations of phenomena, with references to the material and physical world" (*Webster's New World Encyclopedia* 1993, p. 937). The following chapters present anthropology as a humanistic science devoted to discovering, describing, understanding, and explaining similarities and differences in time and space among humans and our ancestors. Clyde Kluckhohn (1944) described anthropology as "the science of human similarities and differences" (p. 9). His statement of the need for such a field still stands: "Anthropology provides a scientific basis for dealing with the crucial dilemma of the world today: how can peoples of different appearance, mutually unintelligible languages, and dissimilar ways of life get along peaceably together?" (p. 9). Anthropology has compiled an impressive body of knowledge that this textbook attempts to encapsulate.

Besides its links to the natural sciences (e.g., geology, zoology), and social sciences (e.g., sociology, psychology), anthropology also has strong links to the humanities. The humanities include English, comparative literature, classics, folklore, philosophy, and the arts. These fields study languages, texts, philosophies, arts, music, performances, and other forms of creative expression. Ethnomusicology, which studies forms of musical expression on a worldwide basis, is especially closely related to anthropology. Also linked is folklore, the systematic study of tales, myths, and legends from a variety of cultures. One might well argue that anthropology is among the most humanistic of all academic fields because of its fundamental respect for human diversity. *Humanism* refers to respect for human diversity and welfare. Anthropologists listen to, record, and represent voices from a multitude of nations and cultures. Anthropology values local knowledge, diverse worldviews, and alternative philosophies. Cultural anthropology and linguistic anthropology in particular bring a comparative and nonelitist perspective to forms of creative expression, including language, art, narratives, music, and dance, viewed in their social and cultural context.

CULTURETHINK

How is anthropology among the most humanistic of all academic disciplines? How does each of the subdisciplines contribute to its humanism? *Humanism* refers to respect for human diversity and welfare.

>> Applied Anthropology

Anthropology is not a science of the exotic carried on by quaint scholars in ivory towers. Rather, anthropology has a lot to tell the public. Anthropology's foremost professional organization, the American Anthropological Association (AAA), has formally acknowledged a public service role by recognizing that anthropology has two dimensions:

Anthropology Works

People in many different careers can use anthropological insights. For example, a psychologist, nurse, teacher, politician, or even a business executive would benefit from being sensitive to cultural differences.

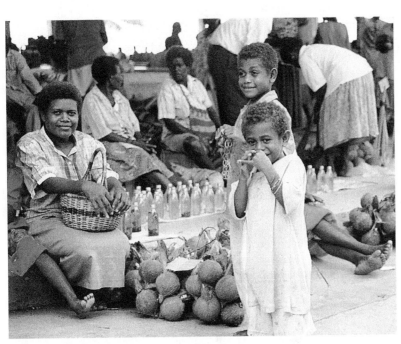

Bronislaw Malinowski is famous for his field work among the matrilineal Trobriand Islanders of the South Pacific. Does this Trobriand market scene suggest anything about the status of Trobriand women?

(1) academic or general anthropology and (2) practicing, or **applied anthropology.** The latter refers to the application of anthropological data, perspectives, theory, and methods to identify, assess, and solve contemporary social problems. As Erve Chambers (1987, p. 309) states it, applied anthropology is the "field of inquiry concerned with the relationships between anthropological knowledge and the uses of that knowledge in the world beyond anthropology." More and more anthropologists from the four subfields now work in such "applied" areas as public health, family planning, business, economic development, and cultural resource management.

Applied anthropology encompasses any use of the knowledge and/or techniques of the four subfields to identify, assess, and solve practical problems. Because of anthropology's breadth, it has many applications. For example, applied medical anthropologists consider both the sociocultural and the biological contexts and implications of disease and illness. Perceptions of good and bad health, along with actual health threats and problems, differ among societies. Various ethnic groups recognize different illnesses, symptoms, and causes and have developed different health care systems and treatment strategies.

Applied archaeology, usually called *public archaeology,* includes such activities as cultural resource management, contract archaeology, public educational programs, and historic preservation. An important role for public archaeology has been created by legislation requiring evaluation of sites threatened by dams, highways, and other construction activities. To decide what needs saving, and to preserve significant information about the past when sites cannot be saved, is the work of **cultural resource management (CRM).** CRM involves not only preserving sites but also allowing their destruction if they are not significant. The "management" part of the term refers to the evaluation and decision-making process. Cultural resource managers work for federal, state, and county agencies and other clients. Applied cultural anthropologists sometimes work with the public archaeologists, assessing the human problems generated by the proposed change and determining how they can be reduced.

applied anthropology The application of anthropological data, perspectives, theory, and methods to identify, assess, and solve contemporary social problems.

cultural resource management (CRM) The branch of applied archaeology aimed at preserving sites threatened by dams, highways, and other projects.

Learn more about the breadth and unity of the four subfields of anthropology at americananthropologicalassociation .org, the website of American anthropologists' foremost professional society. Under "About AAA," click on "What Is Anthropology?" While you're there, also explore "What Do Anthropologists Do?"

get involved!

For REVIEW

I. **What is anthropology, and how does it differ from other fields that study human beings?**

- Anthropology is the holistic, biocultural, and comparative study of humanity. Unlike other fields that study humans, anthropology explores the whole of the human condition: the origins of, and changes in, our biological and cultural adaptations, and the world's vast diversity of societies, languages, customs, and beliefs. Anthropology seeks to explain both the differences and the similarities among peoples everywhere, past, present, and future.

II. **How useful is the race concept in understanding human diversity?**

- Race is a problematic concept because humans do not fit neatly into any racial classifications. Contemporary anthropology's biocultural perspective offers a much more fruitful approach to human biological diversity than pigeonholing humans into racial categories. Anthropologists today focus on specific biological differences, such as skin color, and use the concept of natural selection to explain them.

III. **What are the four subfields of anthropology?**

- The four subfields are cultural, archaeological, biological, and linguistic anthropology. Cultural anthropology explores human society and culture, describing and explaining cultural similarities and differences. Archaeology reconstructs, describes, and interprets cultural patterns, often of prehistoric populations, through material remains. Biological anthropology studies human biological diversity in time and space. Linguistic anthropology studies language in its social and cultural context across time and space. These subfields have a strong academic dimension, but anthropologists from each subfield are increasingly applying their knowledge to identify, assess, and solve contemporary social problems.

CULTURE CLIPS

TO ACCESS THESE VIDEOS ON YOUR COMPUTER, VISIT

www.mhhe.com/gezonqr

I-1

I-2

I-3

Pop Quiz

1. Which of the following statements most completely characterizes anthropology as a unique field of study?

   a. It studies only ancient and nonindustrial societies.

   b. It includes biology.

   c. It deals with crucial world dilemmas.

   d. It is comparative and holistic.

2. What is the most critical element of cultural traditions?

   a. Their stability owing to the unchanging characteristics of human biology.

   b. Their tendency to change radically every generation.

    c. Their transmission through learning rather than through biological inheritance.

    d. Their tendency to remain unchanged despite changing historical circumstances.

3. How has human reliance on cultural means of adaptation changed?

    a. Humans are just beginning to depend on them.

    b. Human have become increasingly dependent on them.

    c. Humans have become entirely reliant on biological means.

    d. Humans no longer use cultural means.

4. Anthropology's focus on both culture and biology:

    a. Is not a characteristic of anthropology in America.

    b. Means that biological anthropologists do not collaborate with other biological scientists.

    c. Allows anthropology to address how culture influences biological traits and vice versa.

    d. Is insignificant, since biology is studied by biological anthropologists while culture is studied by cultural anthropologists.

5. Which of the following expresses scientists' preference for explaining biological differences among humans rather than pigeonholing humans into racial classifications?

    a. Skin color presents a useful basis for assigning humans to racial classifications.

    b. All human populations fit neatly into one or other of the so-called great races.

    c. Scientists who have used four to five or so physical traits to classify races find that these traits always go together as a unit in a population.

    d. Natural selection, such as that against the concentration of melanin in skin in northern regions, contributes to differences in human skin color.

6. Four-field anthropology:

    a. Was shaped largely by early American anthropologists' interests in Native Americans.

    b. Lacks unity, since only archaeology and biological anthropology consider variation in time and space.

    c. Lacks unity because the four subfields do not share key assumptions.

    d. Is weak in examining the relation between biology and culture.

7. Which of the following accurately distinguishes ethnography from ethnology?

    a. Ethnology focuses on the study of particular cultures, while ethnography looks at cultures comparatively.

    b. Traditionally, ethnography was done in large societies with wealth and power, while ethnology focused on small societies with little wealth.

    c. Ethnography studies cultures that are isolated from one another, while ethnology studies nations influenced by globalization.

    d. Ethnologists look beyond the particular cultural data that ethnographers describe and interpret to compare and contrast and make generalizations about society and culture.

8. Archaeological anthropology is *not* likely to use which of the following approaches in reconstructing human cultural patterns:

    a. Examination of paleoecology.

    b. Excavation.

    c. Recovery and interpretation of human material remains.

    d. Observation of nonhuman primates in their natural settings.

9. Anthropology is a humanistic science most particularly because:

    a. The techniques it uses come from a variety of sciences, including those that study humans' relations with other animals.

    b. It discovers, describes, and attempts to explain similarities and differences among humans, with concern for the full diversity of worldviews and voices.

    c. It is a systematic study that respects experiment, observation, and deduction as applied to both contemporary human life and human evolution.

    d. Over the years it has compiled an impressive body of knowledge about human life.

10. All of the following are true about applied anthropology *except* that:

    a. It uses the knowledge, perspectives, or methods of the four subfields to identify, assess, and solve practical human problems.

    b. It is a growing aspect of anthropology, with increasingly more anthropologists developing applied components of their work.

    c. It is less relevant for archaeology, since archaeology concerns the material culture of societies that no longer exist.

    d. It has many applications because of anthropology's breadth.

1. (d), 2. (c), 3. (c), 4. (c), 5. (d), 6. (a), 7. (d), 8. (d), 9. (b), 10. (c)

2

CULTURE

WHAT'S TO COME

What Is Culture?

Culture's Evolutionary Basis

Universality, Generality, and Particularity

Culture and the Individual: Agency and Practice

Levels of Culture

Ethnocentrism, Cultural Relativism,
    and Human Rights

Mechanisms of Cultural Change

Globalization

UNDERSTANDING OURSELVES

How special are you? To what extent are you "your own person," and to what extent are you a product of your particular culture? Americans may not fully appreciate the power of culture because of the value their culture places on "the *individual*." Yet individualism itself is a distinctive *shared* value, a feature of American culture, transmitted constantly in our daily lives. From the late Mr. (Fred) Rogers of daytime TV to parents, grandparents, and teachers, our enculturative agents insist we are all "someone special." That we are individuals first and members of groups second is the opposite of this chapter's lesson about culture. Certainly we have distinctive features because we are individuals, but we have other distinct attributes because we belong to cultural groups.

For example, a comparison of the United States with Brazil, Italy, or virtually any Latin nation reveals striking contrasts between a national culture (American) that discourages physical affection and national cultures in which the opposite is true. Brazilians approach, touch, and kiss one another much more frequently than North Americans do. In personal encounters, the Brazilian characteristically moves closer, while the North American is apt to retreat. Such movements are products of years of exposure to particular cultural traditions. Middle-class Brazilians teach their kids—both boys and girls—to kiss every adult relative they see. Given the size of Brazilian extended families, this can mean hundreds of people. Women continue kissing all those people throughout their lives, while men typically continue to kiss female relatives and friends, as well as their fathers and uncles.

Do you kiss your father? Your uncle? Your grandfather? How about your mother, aunt, or grandmother? The answer to these questions may differ between men and women, and for male and female relatives. Culture can help us to make sense of these differences.

As You
READ

- What is culture, and why do we study it?
- What is the relation between culture and the individual?
- How does culture change?

>> What Is Culture?

Humans share *society,* organized life in groups, with other animals—social animals, such as monkeys, wolves, and ants. Other animals, especially the great apes, have rudimentary cultural abilities, but only humans have fully elaborated cultures—distinctive traditions and customs transmitted over the generations through learning and through language.

The concept of culture has long been basic to anthropology. Well over a century ago, in his book *Primitive Culture,* the British anthropologist Edward Tylor proposed that cultures—systems of human behavior and thought—obey natural laws and therefore can be studied scientifically. Tylor's definition of culture still offers an overview of the subject matter of anthropology and is widely quoted.

"Culture . . . is that complex whole which includes knowledge, belief, arts, morals, law, custom, and any other

People learn and share beliefs and behavior as members of cultural groups, for example, in this Muslim primary school in Marrakesh, Morocco.

capabilities and habits acquired by man as a member of society" (Tylor 1871/1958, p. 1). The crucial phrase here is "acquired . . . as a member of society." Tylor's definition focuses on attributes that people acquire not through biological inheritance but by growing up in a particular society in which they are exposed to a specific cultural tradition. **Enculturation** is the process by which a child *learns* his or her culture.

CULTURE IS LEARNED

The ease with which children absorb any cultural tradition rests on the uniquely elaborated human capacity to learn. Other animals may learn from experience, so that, for example, they avoid fire after discovering that it hurts. Social animals also learn from other members of their group. Wolves, for instance, learn hunting strategies from other pack members. Such social learning is particularly important among monkeys and apes, our closest biological relatives. But our own *cultural learning* depends on the uniquely developed human capacity to use **symbols,** signs that have no necessary or natural connection to the things they stand for or signify.

On the basis of cultural learning, people create, remember, and deal with ideas. They grasp and apply specific systems of symbolic meaning. Anthropologist Clifford Geertz defined culture as ideas based on cultural learning and symbols. Cultures have been characterized as sets of "control mechanisms—plans, recipes, rules, instructions, what computer engineers call programs for the governing of behavior" (Geertz 1973, p. 44). These programs are absorbed by people through enculturation in particular traditions. People gradually internalize a previously established system of meanings and symbols, which helps guide their behavior and perceptions throughout their lives.

Every person begins immediately, through a process of conscious and unconscious learning and interaction with others, to internalize, or incorporate, a cultural tradition through the process of enculturation. Sometimes culture is taught directly, as when parents tell their children to say "thank you" when someone gives them something or does them a favor.

Culture also is transmitted through observation. Children pay attention to the things that go on around them. They modify their behavior not just because other people tell them to do so but as a result of their own observations and growing awareness of what their culture considers right and wrong. Culture also is absorbed unconsciously. North Americans acquire their culture's notions about how far apart people should stand when they talk, not by being told directly to maintain a certain distance, but through a gradual process of observation, experience, and conscious and unconscious behavior modification. No one tells Latins to stand closer together than North Americans do; they learn to do so as part of their cultural tradition.

> **enculturation** The social process by which culture is learned and transmitted across the generations.
>
> **symbol** A verbal or nonverbal sign that arbitrarily and by convention stands for something else, with which it has no necessary or natural connection.

CULTURE IS SYMBOLIC

Symbolic thought is unique and crucial to humans and to cultural learning. A symbol is something verbal or nonverbal, within a particular language or culture, that comes to stand for something else. Anthropologist Leslie White defined culture as

> dependent upon symbolling. . . . Culture consists of tools, implements, utensils, clothing, ornaments, customs, institutions, beliefs, rituals, games, works of art, language, etc. (White 1959, p. 3)

For White, culture originated when our ancestors acquired the ability to use symbols, that is, to originate and bestow meaning on a thing or event and, correspondingly, to grasp and appreciate such meanings (White 1959, p. 3).

There need be no obvious, natural, or necessary connection between the symbol and what it symbolizes. The familiar pet that barks is no more naturally a *dog* than it is a *chien, Hund,* or *mbwa,* the words for "dog" in French, German, and Swahili, respectively. Language is one of the distinctive possessions of *Homo sapiens.* No other animal has developed anything approaching the complexity of language, with its multitude of symbols.

Symbols often are linguistic. There also are myriad nonverbal symbols, such as flags, which stand for various countries, and the arches that symbolize a particular fast-food chain. Holy water is a potent symbol in Roman Catholicism. As is true of all symbols, the association be-

STUDY **TIP**

Culture is transmitted in three ways: direct teaching, observation, and unconscious absorption.

tween a symbol (water) and what is symbolized (holiness) is arbitrary and conventional. Water probably is not intrinsically holier than milk, blood, or other natural liquids. Nor is holy water chemically different from ordinary water. Holy water is a symbol within Roman Catholicism, which is part of an international cultural system. A natural thing has been associated arbitrarily with a particular meaning for Catholics, who share common beliefs and experiences that are based on learning and transmitted across the generations.

For hundreds of thousands of years, humans have shared the abilities on which culture rests—the abilities to learn, to think symbolically, to manipulate language, and to use tools and other cultural products in organizing their lives and coping with their environments. Every contemporary human population has the ability to use symbols and thus to create and maintain culture. Our nearest relatives—chimpanzees and gorillas—have rudimentary cultural abilities. However, no other animal has elaborated cultural abilities to the extent that *Homo* has.

CULTURE IS SHARED

Culture is an attribute not of individuals per se but of individuals as members of *groups*. Culture is transmitted in society. Don't we learn our culture by observing, listening, talking, and interacting with many other people? Shared beliefs, values, memories, and expectations link people who grow up in the same culture. Enculturation unifies people by providing us with common experiences.

Today's parents were yesterday's children. If they grew up in North America, they absorbed certain values and beliefs transmitted over the generations. People become agents in the enculturation of their children, just as their parents were for them. Although a culture constantly changes, certain fundamental beliefs, values, worldviews, and child-rearing practices endure. Consider a simple American example of enduring shared enculturation. As children, when we didn't finish a meal, our parents may have reminded us to think of starving children in some

foreign country, just as our grandparents might have done a generation earlier. The specific country changes (China, India, Bangladesh, Ethiopia, Somalia, Rwanda—what was it in your home?). Still, American culture goes on transmitting the idea that by eating all our brussels sprouts or broccoli, we can justify our own good fortune, compared to a hungry child in an impoverished or war-ravaged country.

CULTURE AND NATURE

Culture takes the natural biological urges we share with other animals and teaches us how to express them in particular ways. People have to eat, but culture teaches us what, when, and how. In many cultures people have their main meal at noon, but most North Americans prefer a large dinner. English people eat fish for breakfast, but North Americans prefer hotcakes and cold cereals. Brazilians put hot milk into strong coffee, whereas many North Americans pour cold milk into a weaker brew. Midwesterners dine at five or six, Spaniards at ten.

Cultural habits, perceptions, and inventions mold "human nature" into many forms. People have to eliminate wastes from their bodies. But some cultures teach people to defecate standing, while others tell them to do it sitting down. Peasant women in the Andean highlands squat in the streets and urinate, getting all the privacy they need from their massive skirts. All these habits are parts of cultural traditions that have converted natural acts into cultural customs.

Our culture—and cultural changes—affect how we perceive nature, human nature, and "the natural." Through science, invention, and discovery, cultural advances have overcome many "natural" limitations. We prevent and cure diseases such as polio and smallpox, which felled our ancestors. We use Viagra to enhance or restore sexual potency. Through cloning, scientists have challenged the way we think about biological identity and the meaning of life itself. Culture, of course, does not always protect us from natural threats. Hurricanes, floods, earthquakes, and other natural forces regularly overthrow our wishes to modify

English people eat fish for breakfast, but North Americans prefer hot cakes and cold cereal.

Culture is all encompassing. Lady Gaga is part of American culture as well as American popular culture.

the environment through building, development, and expansion. Can you think of other ways in which nature strikes back at culture?

CULTURE IS ALL-ENCOMPASSING

For anthropologists, culture includes much more than refinement, good taste, sophistication, education, and appreciation of the fine arts. Not only college graduates but all people are "cultured." The most interesting and significant cultural forces are those that affect people every day of their lives, particularly those that influence children during enculturation.

Culture, as defined anthropologically, encompasses features that are sometimes regarded as trivial or unworthy of serious study, such as those of "popular" culture. To understand contemporary North American culture, we must consider television, fast-food restaurants, sports, and games. As a cultural manifestation, a rock star may be as interesting as a symphony conductor (or vice versa); a comic book may be as significant as a book-award winner.

CULTURE IS INTEGRATED

Cultures are not haphazard collections of customs and beliefs. Cultures are integrated, patterned systems. If one part of the system (the overall economy, for instance) changes, other parts change as well. For example, during the 1950s most American women planned domestic careers as homemakers and mothers. Most of today's college women, by contrast, expect to get paying jobs when they graduate.

What are some of the social repercussions of this particular economic change? Attitudes and behavior regarding marriage, family, and children have changed. Late marriage, "living together," and divorce have become more common. The average age at first marriage for American women rose from twenty years old in 1955 to twenty-six in 2007. The comparable figures for men were twenty-three and twenty-eight (U.S. Census Bureau 2007). The number of currently divorced Americans quadrupled from four million in 1970 to about twenty-three million in 2007 (U.S. Census Bureau 2008). Work competes with marriage and family responsibilities and reduces the time available to invest in child care.

STUDY TIP

Name the seven characteristics of culture described in this chapter (hint: start with "learned").

Anthropology Works

Anthropology teaches people working for disaster relief agencies to be aware of how proposed solutions (change of residence, for example) will affect all aspects of people's lives. How might life be different for people who have to move to a new neighborhood or city, away from their friends, schools, workplace, and family? What if they move from multifamily compounds to single-family residences?

and cultural means of adaptation has increased during human evolution and plays a crucial role.

Sometimes, adaptive behavior that offers short-term benefits to particular subgroups or individuals may harm the environment and threaten the group's long-term survival. Economic growth may benefit some people while it depletes resources needed for society at large or for future generations. Thus, cultural traits, patterns, and inventions can also be *maladaptive,* threatening the group's continued existence (survival and reproduction). Air conditioners help us deal with heat, as fires and furnaces protect us against the cold. Automobiles permit us to make a living by getting us from home to workplace. But the by-products of such "beneficial" technology often create new problems.

>> Culture's Evolutionary Basis

The human capacity for culture has an evolutionary basis that extends back at least two and a half million years to early toolmakers. Evidence for these toolmakers exists in the archeological record. Based on observation of tool use and manufacture by apes, however, scientists believe the evolutionary basis for culture may extend even further back.

Similarities between humans and apes, our closest relatives, are evident in anatomy, brain structure, genetics, and biochemistry. Most closely related to us are the African great apes: chimpanzees and gorillas. *Hominidae* is the zoological family that includes fossil and living humans, as well as chimps and gorillas. We refer to members of this family as **hominids.** We use the term **hominins** for the group that leads to humans but not to chimps and gorillas and that encompasses all the human species that have ever existed.

Many human traits reflect the fact that our primate ancestors lived in the trees. These traits include grasping ability and manual dexterity (especially opposable thumbs), depth and color vision, learning ability based on a large brain, substantial parental investment in a limited number of offspring, and tendencies toward sociality and cooperation. Like other primates, humans have flexible, five-fingered hands and *opposable thumbs:* Each thumb can touch all the other fingers on the same hand. Like monkeys and apes, humans also have excellent depth and color vision. Our eyes are placed forward in the skull and look directly ahead, so that their fields of vision overlap. Depth perception, impossible without overlapping visual fields, proved adaptive—for judging distance, for example—in the trees. Having color and depth vision also facilitates the identification of various food sources, as well as mutual grooming—picking out burrs, insects, and other small ob-

core values Key, basic, or central values that integrate a culture and help distinguish it from others.

hominids Members of the zoological family that includes fossil and living humans, chimps, and gorillas.

hominins Members of the evolutionary line leading to and including modern humans, as distinct from chimps and gorillas.

Cultures are integrated not simply by their dominant economic activities and related social patterns but also by sets of values, ideas, symbols, and judgments. Cultures train their individual members to share certain personality traits. A set of characteristic **core values** (key, basic, central values) integrates each culture and helps distinguish it from others. For instance, the work ethic and individualism are core values that have integrated American culture for generations. Different sets of dominant values influence the patterns of other cultures.

CULTURE CAN BE ADAPTIVE AND MALADAPTIVE

Humans have both biological and cultural ways of coping with environmental stresses. Besides our biological means of adaptation, we also use "cultural adaptive kits," which contain customary activities and tools that aid us. Although humans continue to adapt biologically, reliance on social

CULTURETHINK

Many cultural patterns such as overconsumption and pollution appear to be maladaptive in the long run. Do you agree? Can you think of others?

jects from hair. Such grooming is one way of forming and maintaining social bonds.

The combination of manual dexterity and depth perception allows monkeys, apes, and humans to pick up small objects, hold them in front of their eyes, and appraise them. Our ability to thread a needle reflects an intricate interplay of hands and eyes that took millions of years of primate evolution to achieve. Such dexterity, including the opposable thumb, confers a tremendous advantage in manipulating objects and is essential to a major human adaptive capacity: toolmaking.

In primates, and especially in humans, the ratio of brain size to body size exceeds that of most mammals. Even more important, the brain's outer layer—concerned with memory, association, and integration—is relatively larger. Monkeys, apes, and humans store an array of images in their memories, which permits them to learn more. Such a capacity for learning is another tremendous adaptive advantage. Like most other primates, humans usually give birth to a single offspring. Receiving more parental attention, that one infant has enhanced learning opportunities. The need for longer and more attentive care of offspring places a selective value on support by a social group. Humans have developed considerably the primate tendency to be social animals, living and interacting regularly with other members of their species.

WHAT WE SHARE WITH OTHER PRIMATES

There is a substantial gap between primate *society* (organized life in groups) and fully developed human *culture,* which is based on symbolic thought. Nevertheless, studies of nonhuman primates reveal many similarities with humans, such as the ability to learn from experience and change behavior as a result. Apes and monkeys, like humans, learn throughout their lives. For example, in one group of Japanese macaques (land-dwelling monkeys), a three-year-old female started washing sweet potatoes before she ate them. First her mother, then her age peers, and finally the entire troop began washing sweet potatoes as well. The ability to benefit from experience confers a tremendous adaptive advantage, permitting the avoidance of fatal mistakes. Faced with environmental change, humans and other primates don't have to wait for a genetic or physiologi-cal response. They can modify learned behavior and social patterns instead.

Although humans employ tools much more than any other animal does, tool use also turns up among several nonhuman species, including birds, beavers, sea otters, and especially apes (see Mayell 2003). Humans are also not the only animals that make tools with a specific purpose in mind. Chimpanzees living in the Tai forest of Ivory Coast make and use stone tools to break open hard, golf-ball-sized nuts (Mercader, Panger, and Boesch 2002). At specific sites, the chimps gather nuts, place them on stumps or flat rocks, which are used as anvils, and pound the nuts with heavy stones. The chimps must select hammer stones suited to smashing the nuts and carry them to where the nut trees grow. Nut cracking is a learned skill, with mothers showing their young how to do it.

In 1960, Jane Goodall (1996) began observing wild chimps—including their tool use and hunting behavior—at Gombe Stream National Park in Tanzania, East Africa. The most studied form of ape toolmaking involves "termiting," in which chimps make tools to probe termite hills. They choose twigs, which they modify by removing leaves and peeling off bark to expose the sticky surface beneath. They carry the twigs to termite hills, dig holes with their fingers, and insert the twigs. Finally, they pull out the twigs and dine on termites that were attracted to the sticky surface. Given what is known about ape tool use and manufacture, it is almost certain that early hominins shared this ability, although the first evidence for hominin stone toolmaking dates back only two and a half million years. In addition, *bipedalism* (moving around upright on two legs) would have permitted the carrying and use of tools and weapons against predators and competitors in an open grassland habitat.

Tool use by chimps. These chimps in Liberia are using stone tools to crack palm nuts, as described in the text.

The apes have other abilities essential to culture. Wild chimps and orangs aim and throw objects. Gorillas build nests, and they throw branches, grass, vines, and other objects. Hominins have elaborated the capacity to aim and throw, without which we never would have developed projectile technology and weaponry—or baseball.

Like toolmaking, hunting once was cited as a distinctive human activity not shared with the apes. Again, however, primate research shows that other primates, especially chimpanzees, are habitual hunters. For example, in Uganda's Kibale National Park, chimps form large hunting parties, including an average of twenty-six individuals (almost always adult and adolescent males). Most hunts (78 percent) result in at least one prey item being caught—a much higher success rate than that among lions (26 percent), hyenas (34 percent), or cheetahs (30 percent). Chimps' favored prey in Kibale Park is the red colobus monkey (Mitani and Watts 1999).

Archaeological evidence suggests that humans hunted by at least two and a half million years ago, based on stone meat-cutting tools found at Olduvai Gorge in Tanzania. Given our current understanding of hunting and toolmaking by chimps, we can infer that hominids may have been hunting much earlier than the first archaeological evidence attests. However, because chimps typically devour the monkeys they kill, leaving few remains, we may never find archaeological evidence for the first hominin hunt, especially if it was done without stone tools.

HOW WE DIFFER FROM OTHER PRIMATES

Although chimps often share meat from a hunt, apes and monkeys (except for nursing infants) tend to feed themselves individually. Cooperation and sharing are much more developed among humans. Until fairly recently (twelve thousand to ten thousand years ago), all humans were hunter-gatherers living in small social groups called bands. In some world areas, the hunter-gatherer way of life

Cultural Features of Chimpanzees (Rudimentary) and Humans (Fully Developed)

	Chimpanzees	Humans
Cultural Learning	Rudimentary	Fully developed
Tool Use	Occasional	Habitual
Tool Manufacture	Occasional: hammer stones, termiting	Habitual and sophisticated
Aimed Throwing	Occasional objects, not tools	Projectile technology
Hunting	Significant, but no tools	Basic hominin subsistence strategy, with tools
Food Sharing	Meat sharing after hunt	Basic to human life
Cooperation	Occasional in hunting	Basic to human life
Mating and Marriage	Female estrus cycle, limited pair bonds	Year-round mating, marriage, and exogamy
Kin Ties	Limited by dispersal at adolescence	Maintained through sons and daughters

persisted into recent times, permitting study by ethnographers. In such societies, men and women bring resources back to the camp and share them. Everyone shares the meat from a large animal. Nourished and protected by younger band members, elders live past reproductive age and are respected for their knowledge and experience. Humans are among the most cooperative of the primates—in the food quest and other social activities. In addition, the amount of information stored in a human band is far greater than that in any other primate group.

Another difference between humans and other primates involves mating. Among baboons and chimps, most mating occurs when females enter estrus, during which they ovulate. In estrus, the vaginal area swells and reddens, and receptive females form temporary bonds with, and mate with, males. Human females, by contrast, lack a visible estrus cycle, and their ovulation is concealed. Not knowing when ovulation is occurring, humans maximize their reproductive success by mating throughout the year. Human pair bonds for mating are more exclusive and more durable than are those of chimps. Related to our more constant sexuality, all human societies have some form of marriage. Marriage gives mating a reliable basis and grants to each spouse special, though not always exclusive, sexual rights in the other.

Marriage creates another major contrast between humans and nonhuman primates: exogamy and kinship systems. Most cultures have rules of *exogamy* requiring marriage outside one's kin or local group. Coupled with the recognition of kinship, exogamy confers adaptive advantages because it creates ties between the spouses' different kin groups. Their children have relatives, and therefore allies, in two kin groups rather than just one. The key point here is that ties of affection and mutual support between members of different local groups tend to be absent among primates other than *Homo*. Other primates tend to disperse at adolescence. Among chimps and gorillas, females tend to migrate, seeking mates in other groups. Humans also choose mates from outside the natal group, and usually at least one spouse moves. However, *humans maintain lifelong ties with sons and daughters.* The systems of kinship and marriage that preserve these links provide a major contrast between humans and other primates. Table 2.1 lists differences in the cultural abilities of humans and chimpanzees, our nearest relatives.

>> Universality, Generality, and Particularity

Anthropologists agree that cultural learning is uniquely elaborated among humans and that all humans have culture. Anthropologists also accept a doctrine termed in the nineteenth century "the psychic unity of man." This means that although *individuals* differ in their emotional and intellectual tendencies and capacities, all human *populations* have equivalent capacities for culture. Regardless of their

genes or their physical appearance, people can learn *any* cultural tradition.

To understand this point, consider that contemporary Americans and Canadians are the genetically mixed descendants of people from all over the world. Our ancestors were biologically varied, lived in different countries and continents, and participated in hundreds of cultural traditions. However, early colonists, later immigrants, and their descendants all have become active participants in American and Canadian life. All now share a common national culture.

To recognize biopsychological equality is not to deny differences among populations. In studying human diversity in time and space, anthropologists distinguish among the universal, the generalized, and the particular. Certain biological, psychological, social, and cultural features are **universal,** found in every culture. Others are merely **generalities,** common to several but not all human groups. Still other traits are **particularities,** unique to certain cultural traditions.

universal Something that exists in every culture.

generality Culture pattern or trait that exists in some but not all societies.

particularity Distinctive or unique culture trait, pattern, or integration.

UNIVERSALS AND GENERALITIES

Biologically based universals include a long period of infant dependency, year-round (rather than seasonal) sexuality, and a complex brain that enables us to use symbols, languages, and tools. Among the social universals is life in groups and in some kind of family (see Brown 1991). Generalities occur in certain times and places but not in all cultures. They may be widespread, but they are not universal. One cultural generality that is present in many but not all societies is the *nuclear family,* a kinship group consisting of parents and children. Although many middle-class Americans ethnocentrically view the nuclear family as a proper and "natural" group, it is not universal. It was absent, for example, among the Nayars, located on India's Malabar Coast. Traditionally, the Nayars lived in female-headed households, and husbands and wives did not live together. In many other societies, the nuclear family is submerged in larger kin groups, such as extended families, lineages, and clans.

Societies can share the same beliefs and customs because of borrowing or through (cultural) inheritance from

CULTURE THINK

Anthropologists tend to emphasize cultural diversity, but humans share many characteristics. Think about a person or a group of people who are very different from you. What do you have in common—for example, in terms of biology, meaningful social attachments, or values?

a common cultural ancestor. Speaking English is a generality shared by North Americans and Australians because both countries had English settlers. Another reason for generalities is domination, as in colonial rule, when a more powerful culture imposes customs and procedures on another one. In many countries, use of the English language reflects colonial history. More recently, English has spread through *diffusion* (cultural borrowing) to many other countries, as it has become the world's foremost language for business and travel.

PARTICULARITY: PATTERNS OF CULTURE

A cultural particularity is a trait or feature of culture that is not generalized or widespread; rather it is confined to a single place, culture, or society. Yet because of cultural borrowing, which has accelerated through modern transportation and communication systems, traits that once were limited in their distribution have become more widespread. Traits that are useful, that have the capacity to please large audiences, and that don't clash with the cultural values of potential adopters are more likely to be borrowed than others are. Still, certain cultural particularities persist. One example is a particular food dish (e.g., pork barbeque with a mustard-based sauce available only in South Carolina,

or the pastie—beef stew baked in pie dough characteristic of Michigan's upper peninsula). McDonald's food outlets, on the other hand, once confined to San Bernardino, California, have spread across the globe through diffusion. But there are other reasons why cultural particularities are increasingly rare. Many cultural traits are shared as cultural universals and as a result of independent invention. When facing similar problems, people in different places have come up with similar solutions. Again and again, similar cultural causes have produced similar cultural results.

At the level of the individual cultural trait or element (e.g., bow and arrow, hot dog, MTV), particularities may be getting rarer. But at a higher level, particularity is more obvious. Different cultures emphasize different things. Cultures are integrated and patterned differently and display tremendous variation and diversity. When cultural traits are borrowed, they are modified to fit the culture that adopts them. They are reintegrated—patterned anew—to fit their new setting. MTV in Germany or Brazil isn't at all the same thing as MTV in the United States. As stated in the earlier section "Culture Is Integrated," patterned beliefs, customs, and practices lend distinctiveness to particular cultural traditions.

Consider universal life-cycle events, such as birth, puberty, marriage, parenthood, and death, that many cultures observe and celebrate. The occasions (e.g., marriage, death) may be the same and universal, but the patterns of ceremonial observance may be dramatically different. Cultures vary in just which events merit special celebration. Americans, for example, regard expensive weddings as more socially appropriate than lavish funerals. The Betsileo of Madagascar take the opposite view. The marriage ceremony is a minor event that brings together just the couple and a few close relatives. A funeral is a measure of the deceased person's social position and lifetime achievement, and it may attract a thousand people. Why use money on a house, the Betsileo say, when one can use it on the tomb where one will spend eternity in the company of dead relatives? How unlike contemporary Americans' dreams of home ownership and preference for quick and inexpensive funerals. Cremation, an increasingly common option in the United States, would horrify the Betsileo, for whom ancestral bones and relics are important ritual objects.

Cultures use rituals to mark such universal life-cycle events as birth, puberty, marriage, parenthood, and death. But particular cultures differ as to which events merit special celebration and in the emotions expressed during their rituals. Compare the wedding party (left) in Bali, Indonesia, with the funeral (right) among the Tanala of eastern Madagascar. How would you describe the emotions suggested by the photos?

Cultures vary tremendously in their beliefs, practices, integration, and patterning. By focusing on and trying to explain alternative customs, anthropology forces us to reappraise our familiar ways of thinking. In a world full of cultural diversity, contemporary American culture is just one cultural variant, more powerful perhaps, but no more natural, than the others.

>> Culture and the Individual: Agency and Practice

Generations of anthropologists have theorized about the relationship between the "system," on one hand, and the "person" or "individual" on the other. The system can refer to various concepts, including culture, society, social relations, or social structure. Individual human beings always make up, or constitute, the system. But, living within that system, humans also are constrained (to some extent, at least) by its rules and by the actions of other individuals. Cultural rules provide guidance about what to do and how to do it, but people don't always do what the rules say should be done. People use their culture actively and creatively, rather than blindly following its dictates. Humans aren't passive beings doomed to follow their cultural traditions like programmed robots. Cultures are dynamic and constantly changing. People learn, interpret, and manipulate the same rule in different ways—or they emphasize different rules that better suit their interests. Culture is *contested:* Different groups in society struggle with one another over whose ideas, values, goals, and beliefs will prevail. Even common symbols may have radically different meanings to different individuals and groups in the same culture. Golden arches may cause one person to salivate while another plots a vegetarian protest. The same flag may be waved to support or oppose a given war.

Even when they agree about what should be done, people don't always do as their culture directs or as other people expect. Many rules are violated, some very often (for example, automobile speed limits). Some anthropologists find it useful to distinguish between ideal and real culture. The *ideal culture* consists of what people say they should do and what they say they do. *Real culture* refers to their actual behavior as observed by the anthropologist.

Culture is both public and individual, both in the world and in people's minds. Anthropologists are interested not only in public and collective behavior but also in how individuals think, feel, and act. The individual and culture are linked because human social life is a process in which individuals internalize the meanings of public (i.e., cultural) messages. Then, alone and in groups, people influence culture by converting their private (and often divergent) understandings into public expressions (D'Andrade 1984).

Conventionally, culture has been seen as social glue transmitted across the generations, binding people through their common past, rather than as something being continually

created and reworked in the present. The tendency to view culture as an entity rather than as a process is changing. Contemporary anthropologists now emphasize how day-to-day action, practice, or resistance can make and remake culture (Gupta and Ferguson 1997b). *Agency* refers to the actions that individuals take, both alone and in groups, in forming and transforming cultural identities.

The approach to culture known as *practice theory* (Ortner 1984) recognizes that individuals within a society or culture have diverse motives and intentions and different degrees of power and influence. Such contrasts may be associated with gender, age, ethnicity, class, and other social variables. Practice theory focuses on how such varied individuals—through their ordinary and extraordinary actions and practices—manage to influence, create, and transform the world they live in. Practice theory appropriately recognizes a reciprocal relation between culture (the system—see above) and the individual. The system shapes how individuals experience and respond to external events, but individuals also play an active role in how society functions and changes. Practice theory recognizes both constraints on individuals and the flexibility and changeability of cultures and social systems.

national culture Cultural experiences, beliefs, learned behavior patterns, and values shared by citizens of the same nation.

international culture Cultural traditions that extend beyond national boundaries.

>> Levels of Culture

We distinguish between different levels of culture: national, international, and subcultural. In today's world these distinctions are increasingly important. **National culture** embodies those beliefs, learned behavior patterns, values, and institutions shared by citizens of the same nation. **International culture** extends beyond and across national boundaries. Because culture is transmitted through learning rather than genetically, cultural

Levels of Culture, with Examples from Sports and Food

Levels of Culture	Sports Examples	Food Examples
International	Soccer, basketball	Pizza
National	Monster truck rallies	Apple pie
Subculture	Bocce	Big Joe Pork Barbecue (South Carolina)

traits can spread through borrowing or diffusion from one group to another.

Because of diffusion, migration, colonialism, and globalization, many cultural traits and patterns have acquired international scope. The contemporary United States, Canada, Great Britain, and Australia share cultural traits they have inherited from their common linguistic and cultural ancestors in Great Britain. Roman Catholics in many different countries share beliefs, symbols, experiences, and values transmitted by their church. The World Cup has become an international cultural event, as people in many countries know the rules of, play, and follow soccer.

subcultures Different cultural symbol-based traditions associated with subgroups in the same complex society.

ethnocentrism The tendency to view one's own culture as best and to judge the behavior and beliefs of culturally different people by one's own standards.

Cultures also can be smaller than nations (see Jenks 2005). Although people who live in the same country share a national cultural tradition, all cultures also contain diversity. Individuals, families, communities, regions, classes, and other groups within a culture have different learning experiences as well as shared ones. **Subcultures** are different symbol-based patterns and traditions associated with particular groups in the same complex society. In large or diverse nations such as the United States or Canada, a variety of subcultures originate in region, ethnicity, language, class, and religion. The religious backgrounds of Jews, Baptists, and Roman Catholics create subcultural differences between them. While sharing a common national culture, U.S. northerners and southerners also differ in their beliefs, values, and customary behavior as a result of national and regional history. French-speaking Canadians sometimes pointedly contrast with English-speaking people in the same country. Italian Americans have ethnic traditions different from those of Irish, Polish, and African Americans. Table 2.2 lists sports and food examples illustrating levels of culture.

Nowadays, many anthropologists are reluctant to use the term *subculture*. They feel that the prefix *sub-* is offensive because it means "below." Subcultures thus may be perceived as "less than" or somehow inferior to a dominant, elite, or national culture. In this discussion of levels of culture, we intend no such implication. Our point is simply that nations may contain many different culturally defined groups. As mentioned earlier, culture is contested. Various groups may strive to promote the correctness and value of their own practices, values, and beliefs in comparison with those of other groups or the nation as a whole.

>> Ethnocentrism, Cultural Relativism, and Human Rights

The tendency to view one's own culture as superior and to apply one's own cultural values in judging the behavior and beliefs of people raised in other cultures is known as **ethnocentrism.** We hear ethnocentric statements all the time. Ethnocentrism contributes to social solidarity, a sense of value and community, among people who share a cultural tradition. People everywhere think that the familiar explanations, opinions, and customs are true, right, proper, and moral. They regard different behavior as strange, immoral, or savage. Often other societies are not considered fully human. Their members may be castigated as cannibals, thieves, or people who do not bury their dead.

CULTURETHINK

Cite one or more examples of ethnocentrism you have encountered.

Among several tribes in the Trans-Fly region of Papua New Guinea, homosexuality was valued over heterosexuality (see Chapter 9). Men who grew up in the Etoro tribe (Kelly 1976) favored oral sex between men, while their neighbors the Marind-anim encouraged men to engage in anal sex. (In both groups heterosexual coitus was stigmatized and allowed only for reproduction.) Etoro men considered Marind-anim

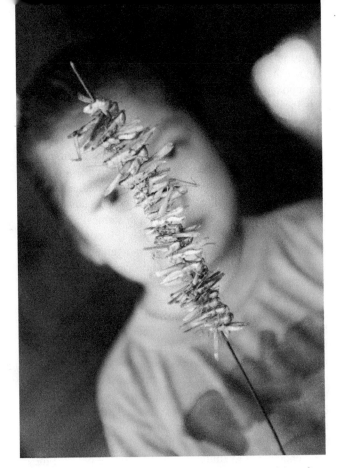

Would you say you have an ethnocentric position on eating grasshoppers?

anal sex to be disgusting, while seeing nothing abnormal about their own oral homosexual practices.

Opposing ethnocentrism is **cultural relativism,** the viewpoint that behavior in one culture should not be judged by the standards of another culture. This position also presents problems. At its most extreme, cultural relativism argues that there is no superior, international, or universal morality, that the moral and ethical rules of all cultures deserve equal respect. In the extreme relativist view, Nazi Germany would be evaluated as nonjudgmentally as Athenian Greece.

In today's world, human rights advocates challenge many tenets of cultural relativism. For example, several societies in Africa and the Middle East have traditions of female genital modification (FGM). *Clitoridectomy* is the removal of a girl's clitoris. Infibulation involves sewing the lips (labia) of the vagina, to constrict the vaginal opening. Both procedures reduce female sexual pleasure, and, it is believed in some cultures, the likelihood of adultery. Human rights advocates, especially women's rights groups, oppose such prac-

tices. The idea is that the tradition infringes on a basic human right—control over one's body and one's sexuality. Some African countries have banned or otherwise discouraged the procedures, as have Western nations that receive immigrants from such cultures. Similar issues arise with circumcision and other male genital operations. Is it right for a baby boy to be circumcised without his permission, as has been done routinely in the United States? Is it proper to require adolescent boys to undergo collective circumcision to fulfill cultural tradition, as has been done in parts of Africa and Australia?

Some argue that the problems with relativism can be solved by distinguishing between methodological and moral relativism. In anthropology, cultural relativism is not a moral position, but a methodological one: To understand another culture fully, you must try to see how the people in that culture see things. What motivates them—what are they thinking—when they do those things? Such an approach does not preclude making moral judgments or taking action. When faced with Nazi atrocities, a methodological relativist would have a moral obligation to stop doing anthropology and take action to intervene. In the FGM example, one can understand the *motivations* for the practice by looking at the situation from the point of view of those who engage in it. Having done this, one then faces the moral question of whether to intervene to stop it. We should recognize as well that different people and groups living in the same society—for example, women and men, old and

> **cultural relativism** The position that the values and standards of cultures differ and deserve respect. Anthropology is characterized by methodological rather than moral relativism: In order to understand another culture fully, anthropologists try to understand its members' beliefs and motivations. Methodological relativism does not preclude making moral judgments or taking action.

Human rights activists in Lafayette Park across from the White House urge action on behalf of the people of Sudan's Darfur region, where a protracted civil war has killed at least 200,000 people and displaced two million others.

END THE KILLING IN DARFUR

young, the more and less powerful—can have widely different views about what is proper, necessary, and moral (see Hunt 2007).

The idea of **human rights** invokes a realm of justice and morality beyond and superior to the laws and customs of particular countries, cultures, and religions (see R. Wilson 1996). Human rights include the right to speak freely, to hold religious beliefs without persecution, and not to be murdered, injured, or enslaved or imprisoned without charge. Such rights are seen as *inalienable* (nations cannot abridge or terminate them) and international (larger than and superior to individual nations and cultures). Four United Nations documents describe nearly all the human rights that have been internationally recognized. Those documents are the U.N. Charter; the Universal Declaration of Human Rights; the Covenant on Economic, Social and Cultural Rights; and the Covenant on Civil and Political Rights.

Alongside the human rights movement has arisen an awareness of the need to preserve cultural rights. Unlike human rights, **cultural rights** are vested not in individuals but in groups, such as religious and ethnic minorities and indigenous societies. Cultural rights include a group's ability to preserve its culture, to raise its children in the ways of its forebears, to continue its language, and not to be deprived of its economic base by the nation in which it is located (Greaves 1995). The related notion of indigenous **intellectual property rights (IPR)** has arisen in an attempt to conserve each society's cultural base—its core beliefs, knowledge, and practices (see Merry 2006). Much traditional cultural knowledge has commercial value. Examples include ethnomedicine (traditional medical knowledge and techniques), cosmetics, cultivated plants, foods, folklore, arts, crafts, songs, dances, costumes, and rituals (see Nazarea 2006). According to the IPR concept, a particular group may determine how indigenous knowledge and its products may be used and distributed and the level of compensation required.

The notion of cultural rights is related to the idea of cultural relativism, and the problem discussed previously arises again. What does one do about cultural rights that interfere with human rights? We believe that anthropology's main job is to present accurate accounts and explanations of cultural phenomena. The anthropologist doesn't have to approve infanticide, cannibalism, or torture to record their existence and determine their causes and the motivations behind them. However, each anthropologist has a choice about where he or she will do fieldwork. Some anthropologists choose not to study a particular culture because they discover in advance or early in fieldwork that behavior they consider morally repugnant is practiced there. Anthropologists respect human diversity. Most ethnographers try to be objective, accurate, and sensitive in their accounts of other cultures. However, objectivity, sensitivity, and a cross-cultural perspective don't mean that anthropologists have to ignore international standards of justice and morality. What do you think?

human rights Doctrine that invokes a realm of justice and morality beyond and superior to particular countries, cultures, and religions. Human rights, usually seen as vested in individuals, include the right to speak freely, to hold religious beliefs without persecution, and not to be enslaved.

cultural rights Doctrine that certain rights are vested not in individuals but in identifiable groups, such as religious and ethnic minorities and indigenous societies.

intellectual property rights (IPR) Each society's cultural base—its core beliefs and principles. IPR is claimed as a group right—a cultural right, allowing indigenous groups to control who may know and use their collective knowledge and its applications.

CULTURETHINK

Where should we draw the line between acceptance based on cultural relativism and objection based on a violation of human rights? Some examples are easy: The Holocaust was clearly unacceptable. What about some current controversial issues: Is arranged marriage always wrong? Female (or male) circumcision? Drug dealing? Think of other controversial issues that require cultural understanding in order to accurately assess whether they involve unacceptable human rights violations.

>> Mechanisms of Cultural Change

Why and how do cultures change? We gave some examples earlier of **diffusion,** or borrowing of traits between cultures. Such exchange of information and products has gone on throughout human history because cultures have never been truly isolated. Contact between neighboring groups has always existed and has extended over vast areas (Boas 1940/1966). Diffusion is *direct* when two cultures trade with, intermarry among, or wage war on one another. Diffusion is *forced* when one culture subjugates another and imposes its customs on the dominated group. Diffusion is *indirect* when items or traits move from group A to group C via group B without any firsthand contact between A and C. In this case, group B might consist of traders or merchants who take products from a variety of places to new markets. Or group B might be geographically situated between A and C, so that what it gets from A eventually winds up in C, and vice versa. In today's world,

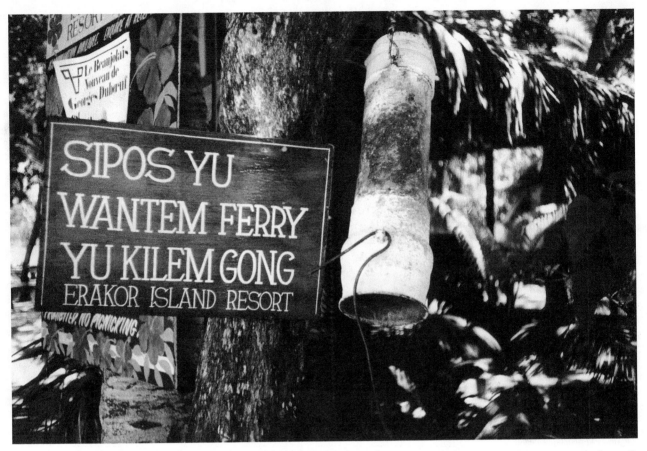

Illustrating acculturation is this sign in pidgin English at a landing on Efate Island, Vanuatu, South Pacific. It reads, "If you want the ferry to come, strike the gong."

much international diffusion is indirect—culture spread by the mass media and advanced information technology.

Acculturation, a second mechanism of cultural change, is the exchange of cultural features that results when groups have continuous firsthand contact. The cultures of either or both groups may be changed by this contact (Redfield, Linton, and Herskovits 1936). With acculturation, parts of the cultures change, but each group remains distinct. One example of acculturation is a *pidgin,* a mixed language that develops to ease communication between members of different cultures in contact. This usually happens in situations of trade or colonialism. Pidgin English, for example, is a simplified form of English. It blends English grammar with the grammar of a native language. Pidgin English was first used for commerce in Chinese ports.

Similar pidgins developed later in Papua New Guinea and West Africa. In situations of continuous contact, cultures have also exchanged and blended foods, recipes, music, dances, clothing, tools, and technologies.

Independent invention—the process by which humans innovate, creatively finding solutions to problems—is a third mechanism of cultural change. Faced with comparable problems and challenges, people in different societies have innovated and changed in similar ways, which is one reason cultural generalities exist.

diffusion Borrowing between cultures either directly or through intermediaries.

acculturation The exchange of cultural features that results when groups come into continuous firsthand contact; the original cultural patterns of either or both groups may be altered, but the groups remain distinct.

independent invention Development of the same culture trait or pattern in separate cultures as a result of comparable needs and circumstances.

In our interlinked, twenty-first century world, even men in remote villages may have access to computers and the Internet. Shown here, two men with a laptop in the village of Bhaktapur, Nepal.

One example is the independent invention of agriculture in the Middle East and Mexico. Over the course of human history, major innovations have spread at the expense of earlier ones. Often a major invention, such as agriculture, triggers a series of subsequent interrelated changes. These economic revolutions have social and cultural repercussions. Thus in both Mexico and the Middle East, agriculture led to many social, political, and legal changes, including notions of property and distinctions in wealth, class, and power (see Naylor 1996).

>> Globalization

The term **globalization** encompasses a series of processes, including diffusion, migration, and acculturation, working to promote change in a world in which nations and people are increasingly interlinked and mutually dependent. Promoting such linkages are economic and political forces, as well as modern systems of transportation and communication. The forces of globalization include international

globalization A set of processes, including diffusion, migration, and acculturation, that promote change in today's interlinked world.

STUDY **TIP**

Globalization is a complex set of processes. It helps to think of it as having three main characteristics:

- Increasing global political and economic interdependence;

- Increased mobility of people (migration and travel);

- Fast and efficient communications technologies that link people across the globe.

commerce and finance, travel and tourism, transnational migration, the media, and various high-tech information flows (see Appadurai 2001; Friedman and Friedman 2008; Scholte 2000). During the Cold War, which ended with the fall of the Soviet Union, the basis of international alliance was political, ideological, and military. More recent international pacts have shifted toward trade and economic issues. New economic unions (which have met considerable resistance in their member nations) have been created through the North American Free Trade Agreement (NAFTA), the World Trade Organization (WTO), and the European Union (EU).

Communication systems and the media play a significant role in today's process of globalization. Long-distance communication is easier, faster, and cheaper than ever, and extends to remote areas. The mass media help propel a globally spreading culture of consumption. Within nations and across their borders, the media spread information about products, services, rights, institutions, lifestyles, and the perceived costs and benefits of globalization. Emigrants transmit information and resources transnationally, as they maintain their ties with home (phoning, faxing, emailing, making visits, sending money). In a sense, such people live *multilocally*—in different places and cultures at once. They learn to play various social roles and to change behavior and identity depending on the situation (see Cresswell 2006).

The effects of globalization are broad and not always welcome. Local people must cope increasingly with forces generated by progressively larger systems—region, nation, and world. An army of outsiders now intrudes on people everywhere. Tourism has become the world's number one industry (see Holden 2005). Economic development agents and the media promote the idea that work should be for cash rather than mainly for subsistence. Indigenous peoples and traditional societies have devised various strategies to deal with threats to their autonomy, identity, and livelihood (Maybury-Lewis

2002). New forms of political mobilization and cultural expression, including the rights movements discussed previously, are emerging from the interplay of local, regional, national, and international cultural forces (see Ong and Collier 2005).

get involved!

Interview a friend, a classmate, or a relative who is a member of an immigrant group. If no one you know meets this description, perhaps a friend can recommend someone who does. Ask about particular beliefs, traditions, values, or symbols. Which of these views or traditions might other Americans see as strange or improper? Can you determine what the person you interview finds odd in America's national culture? Note any ethnocentric statements you hear from this person and any ethnocentrism you experience yourself during the interview.

66 I learned much more about acting from philosophy courses, psychology courses, history and anthropology than I ever learned in acting class. 99

Tim Robbins

For REVIEW

CULTURECLIPS

TO ACCESS THESE VIDEOS ON
YOUR COMPUTER, VISIT
www.mhhe.com/gezonqr

2-1

2-2

2-3

I.   What is culture, and why do we study it?

- Culture, which is distinctly human, refers to customary behavior and beliefs that are passed on through learning and symbols. We study culture to understand the human condition: our origins in our primate ancestors' evolving capacity for culture, our shared human capacity for culture, culture's unique and universal forms, how we think and act as members of groups, and how we organize and change our lives and our relations with others. The study of culture also teaches us about our unique relation to nature, the significance of understanding ourselves as biocultural creatures, and our interactions, both adaptive and maladaptive, with our environments.

II. What is the relation between culture and the individual?

- Cultural rules constrain individuals but do not dictate their behavior. People use culture actively and creatively. They interpret and manipulate the rules in different ways, emphasize rules that best suit their needs, and contest the rules. People play an active role in how society functions and changes. Having internalized the meanings of cultural messages, individuals then influence their culture by converting their private (often divergent) understandings into public expressions.

III. How does culture change?

- Culture changes through three chief mechanisms: diffusion, acculturation, and independent invention. Diffusion is the spread of cultural traits as groups borrow from one another. Acculturation involves the exchange of cultural features that results when groups have continuous first-hand contact. Independent invention is the development of the same cultural trait in separate cultures as a result of comparable circumstances. In addition, globalization—a series of processes that includes diffusion, acculturation, and migration—promotes change in our contemporary world, where nations and peoples are increasingly linked and interdependent.

Pop Quiz

1. Which of the following is *not* one of the ways in which individuals acquire culture?
   a. Genetic transmission
   b. Conscious and unconscious learning
   c. Observation
   d. Direct instruction

2. Which of the following statements about culture is false?
   a. Despite increased reliance on cultural means of adaptation, humans still adapt biologically.
   b. Cultural traditions are transmitted through learning.
   c. Cultural patterns might offer short-term benefits to a particular group but nevertheless threaten that group's long-term survival.
   d. If certain cultural patterns offer short-term benefits, they usually are adaptive in the long run as well.

3. The chapter's discussion of the similarities and differences between humans and apes:
   a. States that all hominids have evolved the same capacities for culture.
   b. Emphasizes culture's evolutionary basis, stressing the interaction between biology and culture.
   c. States that genetics has been more important than culture in determining our particular evolutionary path.
   d. Illustrates how human females' lack of a visible estrus cycle determined our unique capacity for culture.

4. The "psychic unity" of humans, a doctrine that most anthropologists accept, means that:
   a. Psychology is the exclusive domain of the academic discipline of psychology.
   b. Genetically mixed descendants of people from around the world will not be capable of acquiring the common national culture of the country they now live in.
   c. Although individuals differ in their emotional and intellectual tendencies, all human populations have equivalent capacities for culture.
   d. Psychological attributes are determined by our genes.

5. Anthropologists have found that certain biological, psychological, social, and cultural features are universal, found in every society. All the following are examples of universal features *except*:
   a. A long period of infant dependency.
   b. Seasonal (rather than year-round) sexuality.
   c. Life in groups and in some kind of family.
   d. Capacity to use symbols, languages, and tools.

6. Which of the following statements about culture is false?
   a. All human groups possess some form of culture.
   b. Culture is the major reason for human adaptability.
   c. Human groups differ in their capacities for culture.
   d. The capacity for culture has its basis in human evolution.

7. Anthropologists have noted that culture is often contested. This means that:
   a. Different groups in a society struggle over whose ideas, values, goals, and beliefs will prevail.
   b. Certain symbols may have different meanings to specific individuals and groups, even though most common symbols are agreed upon by everyone in a culture.
   c. Humans are passive beings who must follow their cultural traditions.
   d. "Real" culture (the actual behavior of individuals in a society) is of primary importance to anthropological study, while "ideal" culture has no significance.

8. In anthropology, cultural relativism:
   a. Is primarily a methodological position rather than a moral one.
   b. Is equally a moral and a methodological stance toward other cultures.
   c. Is synonymous with moral relativism.
   d. Is a political position that argues for the defense of human rights, regardless of culture.

9. Agriculture developed in at least seven different regions of the world. Therefore, agriculture is an example of which mechanism of cultural change?
   a. Acculturation
   b. Enculturation
   c. Independent invention
   d. Diffusion

10. The series of processes that are making nations and people increasingly interlinked and mutually dependent is known as:
    a. Acculturation
    b. Independent invention
    c. Diffusion
    d. Globalization

1. (a), 2. (d), 3. (b), 4. (c), 5. (b), 6. (c), 7. (a), 8. (a), 9. (c), 10. (d)

Chapter 2 / Culture • 39

3

ETHICS
AND METHODS

WHAT'S TO COME

Ethics and Anthropology

Research Methods

Ethnography: Anthropology's Distinctive Strategy

Ethnographic Techniques

The Evolution of Ethnography

Survey Research

UNDERSTANDING OURSELVES

"Been on any digs lately?" Ask your instructor if she or he has been asked this question. Then ask how often he or she actually has been on a dig. Remember that anthropology has four subfields, only two of which (archaeology and biological anthropology) require much digging—in the ground at least. To be sure, cultural anthropologists "dig out" information about varied lifestyles. Traditionally cultural anthropologists have done a variant on the *Star Trek* mission of seeking out, if not new, at least different "life" and "civilizations."

Despite globalization, the cultural diversity under anthropological scrutiny right now may be as great as ever, because anthropologists now study modern nations. Today's cultural anthropologists are as likely to be studying artists in Miami or bankers in Beirut as Trobriand sailors in the South Pacific. Still, we can't forget that anthropology did originate in non-Western, nonindustrial societies. Its research techniques were developed to deal with small populations. Even when working in modern nations, anthropologists still consider ethnography with small groups to be an excellent way of learning about how people live their lives and make decisions.

Before this course, did you know the names of any anthropologists? If so, which ones? For the general public, biological anthropologists tend to be better known than cultural anthropologists because of what they study. You're more likely to have seen film of Jane Goodall with chimps or a paleoanthropologist holding a skull than an ethnographer at work. One particularly wise and charismatic cultural anthropologist and an important public figure through her death in 1978 was Margaret Mead. Famed for her work on teen sexuality in Samoa and gender roles in New Guinea, Mead may well be the most famous anthropologist who ever lived. She appeared regularly on NBC's *Tonight Show*. In all her ventures—including teaching, museum work, TV, anthropological films, popular books, and magazines—Mead helped Americans appreciate the relevance of anthropology to understanding their daily lives. Her work is featured here and elsewhere in this book.

As You READ

- What ethical concerns and issues must anthropologists consider?
- Where and how do cultural anthropologists do fieldwork?
- What are some ways of studying complex societies in modern nations?

>> Ethics and Anthropology

As the main organization representing the breadth of anthropology (all four subfields, academic, and applied dimensions), the American Anthropological Association (AAA) believes that generating and using knowledge of the peoples of the world, past and present, is a worthy goal. The mission of the AAA is to advance anthropological research and encourage the spread of anthropological knowledge through publications, teaching, public education, and application. Part of that mission is to help educate AAA members about ethical obligations and challenges (http://www.aaanet.org).

Anthropologists increasingly are mindful of the fact that science exists in society, and in the context of law and ethics. Anthropologists can't study things simply because they happen to be interesting or of value to science. As anthropologists conduct research and engage in other professional activities, ethical issues inevitably arise. Anthropologists typically have worked abroad, outside their own society. In the context of international contacts and cultural diversity, different value systems will meet, and often compete. To guide its members in making decisions involving ethics and values, the AAA offers a Code of Ethics.

The most recent revision of the code, adopted in 2009, recognizes that anthropologists have obligations to their scholarly field, to the wider society and culture, and to the human species, other species, and the environment. This code's aim is to offer guidelines and to promote discussion and education, rather than to investigate allegations of misconduct. The AAA code addresses several contexts in which anthropologists work. Its main points may be summarized as follows:

> Anthropologists should be open and honest about . . . their research projects with all parties affected by the research. These parties should be informed about the nature, procedures, purpose(s), potential impacts, and source(s) of support for the research. Researchers should not compromise anthropological ethics in order to conduct research. They should . . . pay attention to proper relations between themselves as guests and the host nations and communities where they work. The AAA does not advise anthropologists to avoid taking stands on issues. Indeed, . . . seeking to shape actions and policies may be as ethically justifiable as inaction.

The full Code of Ethics is available at the AAA website (http://www.aaanet.org/issues/policy-advocacy/Code-of-Ethics.cfm).

Most ethnographers (field-workers in cultural anthropology) work outside their nations of origin. In the host country (the nation where the research takes place), the ethnographer seeks permissions, cooperation, and knowledge from government officials, scholars, and many others, most importantly the people of the community being studied. Cultural sensitivity is paramount when the research subjects are living people into whose lives the anthropologist intrudes. Anthropologists need to establish and maintain appropriate, collaborative, and nonexploit-

CULTURETHINK

Ethical decisions rarely are easy or obvious. They require thoughtful consideration of whom and what may be harmed—physically, socially, psychologically, or otherwise. What difficult ethical decisions have you had to make? Looking back, do you think you made the right decision?

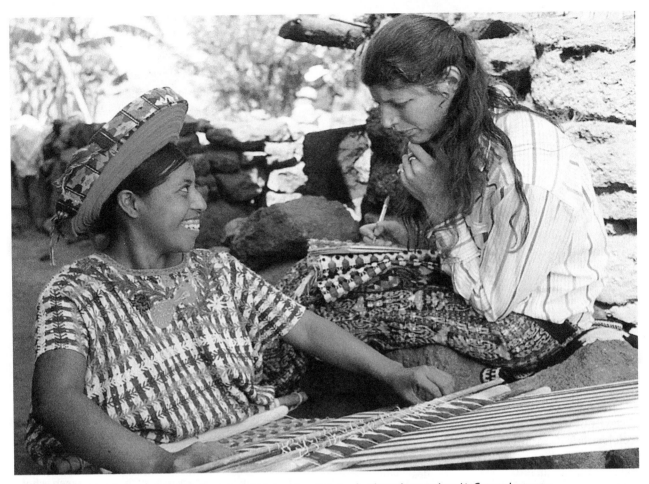

Anthropologists such as Christie Kiefer typically form personal relationships with their cultural consultants, such as this Guatemalan weaver.

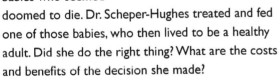
ative relationships with colleagues and communities in the host country.

To work in a host country and community, researchers must inform officials and colleagues there about the purpose and funding, and the anticipated results and impacts, of the research. Researchers have to gain the informed consent of all affected parties—from the authorities who control access to the field site to the members of the community to be studied. Before the research begins, people should be informed about the purpose, nature, and procedures of the research and its potential costs and benefits to them. **Informed consent** (agreement to take part in the research, after having been so informed) should be obtained from anyone who provides information or who might be affected by the research.

> **informed consent** An agreement sought by ethnographers from community members to take part in research.

According to the AAA code, anthropologists have a debt to the people they work with in the field, and they should reciprocate in appropriate ways. For example, it

At the age of twenty-four, famed anthropologist Margaret Mead arrived, via steamship, on the island of Samoa, where she spent the next nine months studying the lives of adolescents. Back in the United States, she became America's best-known anthropologist, presenting her findings to the general public through her writing and lectures until her death in 1978.

is highly appropriate for North American anthropologists working in another country to (1) include host country colleagues in their research plans and funding requests, (2) establish collaborative relationships with those colleagues and their institutions, and (3) include host country colleagues in publication of the research results. Of course, in cultural anthropology, as in all the subfields, anthropologists' primary ethical obligation is to the people being studied. Their welfare and interests come first.

>> Research Methods

Cultural anthropology and sociology share an interest in social relations, organization, and behavior. Important differences between these disciplines arose, however, from the kinds of societies each traditionally studied. Initially, sociologists focused on the industrial West; anthropologists, on nonindustrial societies. Different methods of data collection and analysis emerged to deal with those different kinds of societies. To study large-scale, complex nations, sociologists came to rely on questionnaires and

World-famous anthropologist Margaret Mead in the field in Bali, Indonesia, in 1957.

other means of gathering masses of quantifiable data. For many years, sampling and statistical techniques have been basic to sociology, whereas statistical training has been less common in anthropology (although this is changing somewhat as anthropologists work increasingly in modern nations).

Traditional ethnographers studied small, nonliterate (without writing) populations and relied on ethnographic methods appropriate to that context. "Ethnography is a research process in which the anthropologist closely observes, records, and engages in the daily life of another culture—an experience labeled as the fieldwork method—and then writes accounts of this culture, emphasizing descriptive detail" (Marcus and Fischer 1986, p. 18). One key method described in this quote is **participant observation**—taking part in the events one is observing, describing, and analyzing.

Anthropology started to separate from sociology around 1900. Early students of society, such as the French scholar Émile Durkheim, were among the founders of both sociology and anthropology. Comparing the organization of simple and complex societies, Durkheim studied the religions of Native Australians (Durkheim 1912/2001), as well as mass phenomena (such as suicide rates) in modern nations (Durkheim 1897/1951). Eventually, anthropology would specialize in the former, sociology, in the latter.

>>Ethnography: Anthropology's Distinctive Strategy

Anthropology developed into a separate field as early scholars worked on Indian (Native American) reservations and traveled to distant lands to study small groups of foragers (hunters and gatherers) and cultivators. Traditionally, the process of becoming a cultural anthropologist has required a field experience in another society. Early ethnographers lived in small-scale, relatively isolated societies, with simple technologies and economies.

Ethnography thus emerged as a research strategy in societies with greater cultural uniformity and less social differentiation than are found in large, modern, industrial nations. Traditionally, ethnographers have tried to understand the whole of a particular culture (or, more realistically, as much as they can, given limitations of time and perception). To pursue this goal, ethnographers adopt a free-ranging strategy for gathering information. In a given society or community, the ethnographer moves from setting to setting, place to place, and subject to subject to discover the totality and interconnectedness of social life. By expanding our knowledge of the range of human diversity, ethnography provides a foundation for generalizations about human behavior and social life. Ethnographers draw on varied techniques to piece together a picture of otherwise alien lifestyles. Anthropologists usually employ several (but rarely all) of the techniques discussed here (see also Bernard 2006; Wolcott 2008).

Researchers discuss their work on fishing in Ambuea village, Kaledupa Island, Sulawesi, Indonesia.

>> Ethnographic Techniques

The characteristic *field techniques* of the ethnographer include the following:

- Direct, firsthand observation of behavior, including *participant observation.*

- Conversation with varying degrees of formality, from the daily chitchat, which helps maintain rapport and provides knowledge about what is going on, to prolonged *interviews,* which can be unstructured or structured.

- The *genealogical method.*

- Detailed work with *key consultants,* or *informants,* about particular areas of community life.

- In-depth interviewing, often leading to the collection of *life histories* of particular people (narrators).

- Discovery of local (native) beliefs and perceptions, which may be compared with the ethnographer's own observations and conclusions.

- Problem-oriented research of many sorts.

- Longitudinal research—the continuous long-term study of an area or site.

- Team research—coordinated research by multiple ethnographers.

OBSERVATION AND PARTICIPANT OBSERVATION

Ethnographers must pay attention to hundreds of details of daily life, seasonal events, and unusual happenings. They should record what they see as they see it. Things never will seem quite as strange as they do during the first few weeks in the field. The ethnographer eventually gets used to, and accepts as normal, cultural patterns that initially were alien. Staying a bit more than a year in the field allows the ethnographer to repeat the season of his or her arrival, when certain events and processes may have been missed because of initial unfamiliarity and culture shock.

> **participant observation**
> A characteristic ethnographic technique; taking part in the events one is observing, describing, and analyzing.

Many ethnographers record their impressions in a personal *diary,* which is kept separate from more formal *field notes.* Later, this record of early impressions will help point out some of the most basic aspects of cultural diversity. Such aspects include distinctive smells, noises people make, how they cover their mouths when they eat, and how they gaze at others. These patterns, which are so basic as to seem almost trivial, are part of what Bronislaw Malinowski called "the imponderabilia of native life and of typical behavior" (Malinowski 1922/1961, p. 20). These features of culture are so fundamental that natives take them for granted. They are too basic even to talk about, but the unaccustomed eye of the fledgling ethnographer picks them up. Thereafter, becoming familiar, they fade to the edge of consciousness. Initial impressions are valuable and should be recorded. First and foremost, ethnographers should try to be accurate observers, recorders, and reporters of what they see in the field.

As ethnographers, we strive to establish *rapport,* a good, friendly working relationship based on personal contact, with our hosts. One of ethnography's most characteristic procedures is participant observation, which means that we take part in community life as we study it. As human beings living among others, we cannot be totally impartial and detached observers. We take part in many events and processes we are observing and trying to comprehend. By participating, we learn why local people

find such events meaningful, as we see how they are organized and conducted.

In Arembepe, Brazil, Conrad Kottak learned about fishing by sailing on the Atlantic with local fishers. He gave Jeep rides to malnourished babies, to pregnant mothers, and once to a teenage girl possessed by a spirit. All of those people needed to consult specialists outside the village. He danced at Arembepe's festive occasions, drank libations commemorating new births, and became a godfather to a village girl. Most anthropologists have similar field experiences. The common humanity of the student and the studied, the ethnographer and the research community, makes participant observation inevitable.

CONVERSATION, INTERVIEWING, AND INTERVIEW SCHEDULES

Participating in local life means that ethnographers constantly talk to people and ask questions. As our knowledge of the native language and culture increases, we understand more. There are several stages in learning a field language. First is the naming phase—asking name after name of the objects around us. Later we are able to pose more complex questions and understand the replies. We begin to understand simple conversations between two villagers. If our language expertise proceeds far enough, we eventually become able to comprehend rapid-fire public discussions and group conversations.

Seated blonde woman (on the right) meets with villagers during field work in Kenya.

One data-gathering technique Kottak has used in both Arembepe and Madagascar involves an ethnographic survey that includes an interview schedule. In 1964, Kottak and his fellow field-workers attempted to complete an interview schedule in each of Arembepe's 160 households. They entered almost every household (fewer than 5 percent refused to participate) to ask a set of questions on a printed form. Their results provided them with a census and basic information about the village. They wrote down the name, age, and gender of each household member. They gathered data on family type, religion, present and previous jobs, income, expenditures, diet, possessions, and many other items on their eight-page form.

Although they were doing a survey, their approach differed from the survey research design routinely used by sociologists and other social scientists working in large, industrial nations. That survey research, discussed below, involves sampling (choosing a small, manageable study group from a larger population). Kottak and his colleagues did not select a partial sample from the total population. Instead, they tried to interview in all households in the community (that is, to have a total sample). They used an interview schedule rather than a questionnaire. With the **interview schedule,** the ethnographer talks face-to-face with people, asks the questions, and writes down the answers. *Questionnaire* procedures tend to be more indirect and impersonal; often the respondent fills in the form.

Kottak's goal of getting a total sample allowed him to meet almost everyone in the village and helped establish rapport. Decades later, Arembepeiros still talk warmly about how these ethnographers were interested enough in them to visit their homes and ask them questions. This stood in sharp contrast to the other outsiders the villagers had known, who considered them too poor and backward to be taken seriously.

Like other survey research, however, Kottak's interview schedule did gather comparable quantifiable information. It gave his group of researchers a basis for assessing patterns and exceptions in village life. Their schedules included a core set of questions that were posed to everyone. Interesting side issues often came up during the interview, which they would pursue then or later.

Kottak and his colleagues followed such leads into many dimensions of village life. One woman, for instance—a midwife—became the key cultural consultant

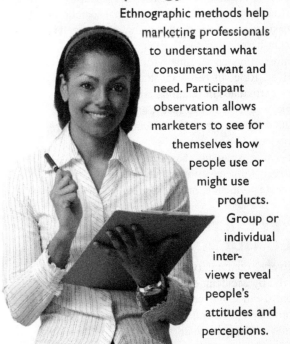
they sought out later when they wanted detailed information about local childbirth. Another woman had done an internship in an Afro-Brazilian cult (*candomblé*) in the city. She still went there regularly to study, dance, and get possessed. She became their candomblé expert.

Thus, their interview schedule provided a structure that *directed but did not confine* them as researchers. It enabled their ethnography to be both quantitative and qualitative. The quantitative part consisted of the basic information gathered and later analyzed statistically. The qualitative dimension came from follow-up questions, open-ended discussions, pauses for gossip, and work with key consultants.

interview schedule
Ethnographic tool for structuring a formal interview. A prepared form guides interviews with households or individuals being compared systematically. This contrasts with a questionnaire because the researcher has personal contact and records people's answers.

genealogical method
Procedures by which ethnographers discover and record connections of kinship, descent, and marriage, using diagrams and symbols.

STUDY TIP

An interview schedule uses both qualitative and quantitative methods. It is similar to a *survey* in that it obtains data from many individuals that can be analyzed statistically. It is similar to *ethnographic research* in that the researcher sits with the respondent, asks questions, and writes down the answers.

THE GENEALOGICAL METHOD

As ordinary people, many of us learn about our own ancestry and relatives by tracing our genealogies. Various computer programs now allow us to trace our "family tree" and degrees of relationship. The **genealogical method** is a well-established ethnographic technique. Early ethnographers developed notation and symbols to deal with kinship, descent, and marriage. Genealogy is a prominent building block in the social organization of nonindustrial societies, where people live and work each day with their close kin. Anthropologists need to collect genealogical data to understand current social relations and to reconstruct history. In many nonindustrial societies, kin links are basic to social life. Anthropologists even call such cultures "kin-based societies." Everyone is related, and spends most of his or her time with relatives. Rules of behavior attached to particular kin relations are basic to everyday life (see Carsten 2004). Marriage also is crucial in organizing nonindustrial societies because strategic marriages between villages, tribes, and clans create political alliances.

KEY CULTURAL CONSULTANTS

Every community has people who by accident, experience, talent, or training can provide the most complete or useful information about particular aspects of life. These people are **key cultural consultants,** also called *key informants.* In Ivato, the Betsileo village in Madagascar where Kottak spent most of his time, a man named Rakoto was particularly knowledgeable about village history. When asked to work on a genealogy of the fifty to sixty people buried in the village tomb, however, he called in his cousin Tuesdaysfather, who knew more about that subject. Tuesdaysfather had survived an epidemic of influenza that ravaged Madagascar, along with much of the world, around 1919. Immune to the disease himself, Tuesdaysfather had the grim job of burying his kin as they died. He kept track of everyone buried in the tomb. Tuesdaysfather helped Kottak with the tomb genealogy. Rakoto joined him in providing personal details about the deceased villagers.

LIFE HISTORIES

In nonindustrial societies as in our own society, individual personalities, interests, and abilities vary. Some villagers prove to be more interested in the ethnographer's work and are more helpful, interesting, and pleasant than others are. Anthropologists develop likes and dislikes in the field as

we do at home. Often, when we find someone unusually interesting, we collect his or her **life history.** This recollection of a lifetime of experiences provides a more intimate and personal cultural portrait than would be possible otherwise. Life histories, which may be recorded or videotaped for later review and analysis, reveal how specific people perceive, react to, and contribute to changes that affect their lives. Such accounts can illustrate diversity, which exists within any community, since the focus is on how different people interpret and deal with some of the same problems. Many ethnographers include the collection of life histories as an important part of their research strategy.

LOCAL BELIEFS AND PERCEPTIONS, AND THE ETHNOGRAPHER'S

One goal of ethnography is to discover local (native) views, beliefs, and perceptions, which may be compared with the ethnographer's own observations and conclusions. In the field, ethnographers typically combine two research strategies, the *emic* (native-oriented) and the *etic* (scientist-oriented). These terms, derived from linguistics, have been applied to ethnography by various anthropologists. Marvin Harris (1968/2001) popularized the following meanings of the terms: An **emic** approach investigates how local people think. How do they perceive and categorize the world? What are their rules for behavior? What has meaning for them? How do they imagine and explain things? Operating emically, the ethnographer seeks the "native viewpoint," relying on local people to explain things and to say whether something is significant or not. The term **cultural consultant,** or *informant,* refers to individuals the ethnographer gets to know in the field, the people who teach him or her about their culture, who provide the emic perspective.

The **etic** (scientist-oriented) approach shifts the focus from local observations, categories, explanations, and interpretations to those of the anthropologist. The etic approach recognizes that members of a culture often are too involved in what they are doing to interpret their cultures impartially. Operating etically, the ethnographer emphasizes what he or she (the observer) notices and considers important. As a trained scientist, the ethnographer should try to bring an objective and comprehensive view-

key cultural consultant An expert on a particular aspect of local life who helps the ethnographer understand that aspect.

life history Of a cultural consultant; provides a personal cultural portrait of existence or change in a culture.

emic The research strategy that focuses on native explanations and criteria of significance.

etic The research strategy that emphasizes the observer's rather than the natives' explanations, categories, and criteria of significance.

point to the study of other cultures. Of course, like any other scientist, the ethnographer is also a human being with cultural blinders that prevent complete objectivity. As in other sciences, proper training can reduce, but not totally eliminate, the observer's bias. But anthropologists do have special training to compare behavior between different societies.

What are some examples of emic versus etic perspectives? Consider our holidays. For North Americans, Thanksgiving Day has special significance. In our view (emically), it is a unique cultural celebration that commemorates particular historical themes. But a wider, etic perspective sees Thanksgiving as just one more example of the postharvest festivals held in many societies. Another example: Local people (including many Americans) may believe that chills and drafts cause colds, which scientists know are caused by germs. In cultures that lack the germ theory of disease, illnesses are emically explained by various causes, ranging from spirits to ancestors to witches. *Illness* refers to a culture's (emic) perception and explanation of bad health, whereas *disease* refers to the scientific—etic—explanation of poor health, involving known pathogens.

Ethnographers typically combine emic and etic strategies in their fieldwork. The statements, perceptions, categories, and opinions of local people help ethnographers understand how cultures work. Local beliefs are also interesting and valuable in themselves. However, people often fail to admit, or even recognize, certain causes and consequences of their behavior. This is as true of North Americans as it is of people in other societies.

POPCULTURE

Set on another globe, *Avatar,* the most popular film ever made to date, is about what it means to be human and not human, while still cultured in the anthropological sense. *Avatar* also raises ethical questions involving humanoid rights and proper loyalties for humans—to nature, indigenous "peoples," science, and commerce. *Avatar* portrays the struggle that local cultures face in resisting and surviving the powerful forces and threats they face from outside.

The movie also features a quasi-anthropologist, Dr. Grace Augustine, played by Sigourney Weaver. As you watch *Avatar,* pay attention to how Grace's attitudes, beliefs, and opinions differ from those of other members of the cast. What are her main similarities and differences to the anthropologists discussed in this chapter?

>> The Evolution of Ethnography

The Polish anthropologist Bronislaw Malinowski (1884–1942), who spent most of his professional life in England, is generally considered the founder of ethnography. Like most anthropologists of his time, Malinowski did *salvage ethnography,* in the belief that the ethnographer's job is to study and record cultural diversity threatened by Westernization. Early ethnographic accounts (ethnographies), such as Malinowski's classic *Argonauts of the Western Pacific* (1922/1961), were similar to earlier traveler and explorer accounts in describing the writer's discovery of unknown people and places. However, the *scientific* aims of ethnographies set them apart from books by explorers and amateurs.

> **cultural consultant** Someone the ethnographer gets to know in the field, who teaches him or her about their society and culture (also called *informant*).

The style that dominated "classic" ethnographies was *ethnographic realism.* The writer's goal was to present an accurate, objective, scientific account of a different way of life, written by someone who knew it firsthand. This knowledge came from an "ethnographic adventure" involving immersion in an alien language and culture. Ethnographers derived their authority—both as scientists and as voices of "the native" or "the other"—from this personal research experience.

CULTURETHINK

Why do people practice religion? Think of a specific religious practice. What would be an emic answer to this question? In other words, how would the people themselves answer?

Bronislaw Malinowski (1884–1942), who was born in Poland but spent most of his professional life in England, did fieldwork in the Trobriand Islands from 1914 to 1918. Malinowski is generally considered to be the father of ethnography. Does this photo suggest anything about his relationship with Trobriand villagers?

Malinowski's ethnographies were guided by the assumption that aspects of culture are linked and intertwined. Beginning by describing a Trobriand sailing expedition, the ethnographer then follows the links between that entry point and other areas of the culture, such as magic, religion, myths, kinship, and trade. Compared with Malinowski, today's ethnographies tend to be less inclusive and holistic, focusing on particular topics, such as kinship or religion.

According to Malinowski, a primary task of the ethnographer is "to grasp the native's point of view, his relation to life, to realize *his* vision of *his* world" (1922/1961, p. 25—Malinowski's italics). This is a good statement of the need for the emic perspective, as discussed earlier. Since the 1970s, *interpretive anthropology* has considered the task of describing and interpreting that which is meaningful to natives. Interpretivists such as Clifford Geertz (1973) view cultures as meaningful texts that natives constantly "read" and ethnographers must decipher. According to Geertz, anthropologists may choose anything in a culture that interests them, fill in details, and elaborate to inform their readers about meanings in that culture. Meanings are carried by public symbolic forms, including words, rituals, and customs.

A current trend in ethnographic writing is to question traditional goals, methods, and styles, including ethnographic realism and salvage ethnography (Clifford 1982,

STUDY TIP

Malinowski's ethnography is characterized by salvage ethnography, ethnographic realism, use of the ethnographic present, and holism.

1988; Marcus and Cushman 1982). Marcus and Fischer argue that experimentation in ethnographic writing is necessary because all peoples and cultures have already been "discovered" and must now be "rediscovered . . . in changing historical circumstances" (1986, p. 24).

In general, experimental anthropologists see ethnographies as works of art as well as works of science. Ethnographic texts may be viewed as literary creations in which the ethnographer, as mediator, communicates information from the "natives" to readers. Some experimental ethnographies are "dialogic," presenting ethnography as a dialogue between the anthropologist and one or more native informants (e.g., Behar 1993; Dwyer 1982). These works draw attention to ways in which ethnographers, and by extension their readers, communicate with other cultures. Some ethnographies of this type have been criticized for spending too much time talking about the anthropologist and too little time describing the local people and their culture.

The dialogic ethnography is one genre within a larger experimental category—*reflexive ethnography*. Here the ethnographer puts his or her personal feelings and reactions to the field situation right in the text. Experimental writing strategies are prominent in reflexive accounts. The ethnographer may adopt some of the conventions of the novel, including first-person narration, conversations, dialogues, and humor. Experimental ethnographies, using new ways of showing what it means to be a Samoan or a Brazilian, may convey to the reader a richer and more complex understanding of human experience.

CULTURETHINK

Those doing reflexive anthropology have recognized that not even anthropologists can be completely objective. That's why they call for authors to reflect on their own biases and perspectives. Consider yourself: What kinds of biases and perspectives do you think would be found in your own writing?

Linked to salvage ethnography was the idea of the *ethnographic present*—the period before Westernization, when the "true" native culture flourished. This notion often gives classic ethnographies an unrealistic timeless quality. Providing the only jarring note in this idealized picture are occasional comments by the author about traders or missionaries, suggesting that in actuality the natives were already part of the world system.

Anthropologists now recognize that the ethnographic present is a rather unrealistic construct. Cultures have been in contact—and have been changing—throughout history. Most native cultures had at least one major foreign encounter before any anthropologist ever came their way. Most of them already had been incorporated in some fashion into nation-states or colonial systems.

Contemporary ethnographies usually recognize that cultures constantly change and that an ethnographic account applies to a particular moment. A current trend in ethnography is to focus on the ways in which cultural ideas serve political and economic interests. A related trend is the anthropology of globalization, which describes how various particular "natives" participate in broader historical, political, and economic processes (Shostak 1981).

PROBLEM-ORIENTED ETHNOGRAPHY

We see, then, a tendency to move away from holistic accounts toward more problem-focused and experimental ethnographies. Although anthropologists are interested in the whole context of human behavior, it is impossible to study everything. Most ethnographers now enter the field with a specific problem to investigate, and they collect data relevant to that problem (see Chiseri-Strater and Sunstein 2001; Kutsche 1998). Local people's answers to questions are not the only data source. Anthropologists also gather information on factors such as population density, environmental quality, climate, physical geography, diet, and land use. Sometimes this involves direct measurement—of rainfall, temperature, fields, yields, dietary quantities, or time allocation (Bailey 1990; Johnson 1978). Often it means that we consult government records or archives.

The information of interest to ethnographers is not limited to what local people can and do tell us. In an increasingly interconnected and complicated world, local people lack knowledge about many factors that affect their lives. Our local consultants may be as mystified as we are by the exercise of power from regional, national, and international centers.

LONGITUDINAL RESEARCH

Geography limits anthropologists less now than in the past, when it could take months to reach a field site, and return visits were rare. New systems of transportation allow anthropologists to widen the area of their research and to return repeatedly. Ethnographic reports now routinely include data from two or more field stays. **Longitudinal research** is the long-term study of a community, region, society, culture, or other unit, usually based on repeated visits.

One example of such research is the longitudinal study of Gwembe District, Zambia. This study, planned in 1956 as a longitudinal project by Elizabeth Colson and Thayer Scudder, continues with Colson, Scudder, and their associates of various nationalities. Thus, as is often the case with longitudinal research, the Gwembe study also illustrates team research—coordinated research by multiple ethnographers (Colson and Scudder 1975; Scudder and Colson 1980). In this study, four villages in different areas have been followed for five decades. Periodic village censuses provide basic data on population, economy, kinship, and religious behavior. Censused people who have moved are traced and interviewed to see how their lives compare with those of people who have stayed in the villages.

A series of different research questions have emerged, while basic data on communities and individuals continue to be collected. The first focus of study was the impact of a large hydroelectric dam, which subjected the Gwembe people to forced resettlement. The dam also spurred road building and other activities that brought the people of Gwembe more closely in touch with the rest of Zambia. In subsequent research Scudder and Colson (1980) examined how education provided access to new opportunities as it also widened a social gap between people with different educational levels. A third study then examined a change in brewing and drinking patterns, including a rise in alcoholism, in relation to changing markets, transportation, and exposure to town values (Colson and Scudder 1988).

> **longitudinal research** Long-term study of a community, society, culture, or other unit, usually based on repeated visits.

TEAM RESEARCH

As mentioned, longitudinal research often is team research. Kottak's field site of Arembepe, Brazil, for example, first entered the world of anthropology as a field-team village in the 1960s. It was one of four sites for the now defunct Columbia-Cornell-Harvard-Illinois Summer Field Studies Program in Anthropology. For at least three years, that program sent a total of about twenty undergraduates annually,

Conrad Kottak with his Brazilian nephew, Gui Roxo, in the field in Arembepe, Bahia, Brazil.

STUDY TIP

Approaches that enhance traditional ethnography include study of government and archival documents, longitudinal research, multisited research, and team research.

have studied various topics in Arembepe. In 1990 Doug Jones, a Michigan student doing biocultural research, used Arembepe as a field site to investigate standards of physical attractiveness. In 1996–1997, Janet Dunn studied family planning and changing female reproductive strategies. Chris O'Leary, who first visited Arembepe in summer 1997, investigated a striking aspect of religious change there—the arrival of Protestantism; his dissertation research then examined changing food habits and nutrition in relation to globalization (O'Leary 2002). Arembepe is thus a site where various field-workers have worked as members of a longitudinal team. The more recent researchers have built on prior contacts and findings to increase knowledge about how local people meet and manage new circumstances.

CULTURE, SPACE, AND SCALE

The previous sections on longitudinal and team research illustrate an important shift in cultural anthropology. Traditional ethnographic research focused on a single community or "culture," treated as more or less isolated and unique in time and space. The shift has been toward recognition of ongoing and inescapable flows of people, technology, images, and information. The study of such flows and linkages is now part of the anthropological analysis. In reflecting today's world—in which people, images, and information move about as never before—fieldwork must be more flexible and on a larger scale. Ethnography increasingly is multitimed and multisited. Malinowski could focus on Trobriand culture and spend most of his field time in a particular community. Nowadays we cannot afford to ignore, as Malinowski did, the "outsiders" who increasingly impinge on the places we study (e.g., migrants, refugees, terrorists, warriors, tourists, developers). Integral to our analyses now are the external organizations and forces (e.g., governments, businesses, nongovernmental organizations) now laying claim to land, people, and resources throughout the world. Also important is increased recognition of power differentials and how they affect cultures, and of the importance of diversity within cultures and societies.

the author included, to do brief summer research abroad. They were stationed in rural communities in four countries: Brazil, Ecuador, Mexico, and Peru. Since Kottak's wife, Isabel Wagley Kottak, and he began studying it in 1962, Arembepe has become a longitudinal field site. Three generations of researchers have monitored various aspects of change and development. The community has changed from a village into a town and illustrates the process of globalization at the local level. Its economy, religion, and social life have been transformed (Kottak 2006).

Conrad Kottak has been studying Arembepe since 1962. His most recent field trip there was in March 2010. It used to be rare for anthropologists to return to the field, but they do it all the time now because of improved means of transoportation.

Brazilian and American researchers worked with Kottak on team research projects during the 1980s (on television's impact) and the 1990s (on ecological awareness and environmental risk perception). Graduate students from the University of Michigan have drawn on baseline information from the 1960s as they

Lisa Gezon in Diego Suarez, Madagascar, sitting with her friend (right) who is selling khat, a leafy plant that people chew for a stimulant effect. On the left are Lisa Gezon's Malagasy daughter and sister.

In two volumes of essays edited by Akhil Gupta and James Ferguson (1997a, 1997b), several anthropologists describe problems in trying to locate cultures in bounded spaces. John Durham Peters (1997), for example, notes that, particularly because of the mass media, contemporary people simultaneously experience the local and the global. He describes them as culturally "bifocal"—both "nearsighted" (seeing local events) and "farsighted" (seeing images from far away). Given their bifocality, their interpretations of the local always are influenced by information from outside. Thus, their attitude about a clear blue sky at home is tinged by their knowledge, through weather reports, that a hurricane may be approaching.

The mass media, which anthropologists increasingly study, are oddities in terms of culture and space. Whose image and opinions are these?

What culture or community do they represent? They certainly aren't local. Media images and messages flow electronically. TV brings them right to you. The Internet lets you discover new cultural possibilities at the click of a mouse. The Internet takes us to virtual places, but in truth the electronic mass media are placeless phenomena, which are transnational in scope and play a role in forming and maintaining cultural identities.

Anthropologists increasingly study people in motion. Examples include people living on or near national borders, nomads, seasonal migrants, homeless and displaced people, immigrants, and refugees. Anthropological research today may take us traveling along with the people we study, as they move from village to city, cross the border, or travel internationally on business. As we'll see in the chapter "Global Issues Today," ethnographers increasingly follow the people and images they study. As fieldwork changes, with less and less of a spatially set field, what can we take from traditional ethnography? Gupta and Ferguson correctly cite the "characteristically anthropological emphasis on daily routine and lived experience" (1997a, p. 5). The treatment of communities as discrete entities may be a thing of the past. However, "anthropology's traditional attention to the close observation of particular lives in particular places" has an enduring importance (Gupta and Ferguson 1997b, p. 25). The method of close observation helps distinguish cultural anthropology from sociology and survey research, to which we now turn.

>> Survey Research

As anthropologists work increasingly in large-scale societies, they have developed innovative ways of blending ethnography and survey research (Fricke 1994). Before examining such combinations of field methods, let's consider survey research and the main differences between survey research and ethnography. Working mainly in large, populous nations, sociologists, political scientists, and economists have developed and refined the **survey research** design, which involves sampling, impersonal data collection, and statistical analysis. Survey research usually draws a **sample** (a manageable study group) from a much larger population. By studying a properly selected and representative sample, social scientists can make accurate inferences about the larger population.

In smaller-scale societies and communities, ethnographers get to know most of the people. Given the greater size and complexity of nations, survey research cannot help being more impersonal. Survey researchers call the people they study *respondents.* These are people who respond to questions during a survey. Sometimes survey researchers personally interview them. Sometimes, after an initial meeting, they ask respondents to fill out a questionnaire. In other cases researchers mail or email printed questionnaires to randomly selected sample members or have paid assistants interview or telephone them. In a **random sample,** all members of the population have an equal statistical chance of being chosen for inclusion. A random sample is selected by randomizing procedures, such as tables of random numbers, which are found in many statistics textbooks.

> **survey research** Characteristic research procedure among social scientists other than anthropologists, which studies society through sampling, statistical analysis, and impersonal data collection.
>
> **sample** A smaller study group chosen to represent a larger population.
>
> **random sample** A sample in which all members of the population have an equal statistical chance of being included.

What kind of social science research is illustrated by exit polling?

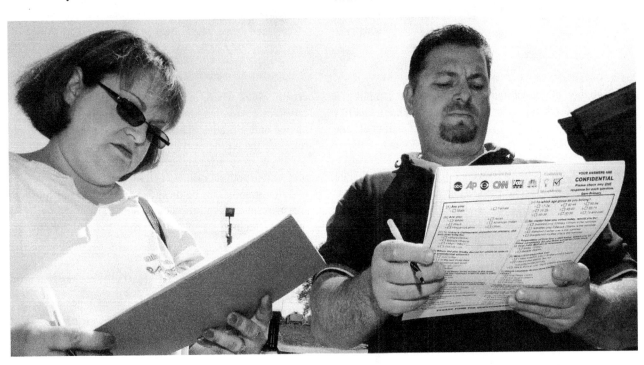

Ethnography and Survey Research Contrasted

Ethnography (Traditional)	Survey Research
Studies whole, functioning communities	Studies a small sample of a larger population
Usually is based on firsthand field work, during which information is collected after rapport, based on personal contact, is established between researcher and hosts	Often is conducted with little or no personal contact between study subjects and researchers, as interviews are frequently conducted by assistants over the phone or in printed form
Traditionally is interested in all aspects of local life (holistic)	Usually focuses on small number of variables (e.g., factors that influence voting) rather than on the totality of people's lives
Traditionally has been conducted in nonindustrial, small-scale societies, where people often do not read and write	Normally is carried out in modern nations, where most people are literate, permitting respondents to fill in their own questionnaires
Makes little use of statistics, because the communities being studied tend to be small, with little diversity besides that based on age, gender, and individual personality variation	Depends heavily on statistical analyses to make inferences regarding a large and diverse population, based on data collected from a small subset of that population

Probably the most familiar example of sampling is the polling used to predict political races. The media hire agencies to estimate outcomes and do exit polls to find out what kinds of people voted for which candidates. During sampling, researchers gather information about age, gender, religion, occupation, income, and political party preference. These characteristics (**variables**—attributes that vary among members of a sample or population) are known to influence political decisions.

Many more variables affect social identities, experiences, and activities in a modern nation than in the small communities where ethnography grew up. In contemporary North America hundreds of factors influence our behavior and attitudes. These social predictors include our religion; the region of the country we grew up in; whether we come from a town, suburb, or city; and our parents' professions, ethnic origins, and income levels.

Ethnography can be used to supplement and fine-tune survey research. Anthropologists can transfer the personal, firsthand techniques of ethnography to virtually any set-

variables Attributes (e.g., sex, age, height, weight) that differ from one person or case to the next.

complex societies Nations; large and populous, with social stratification and central governments.

CULTURETHINK

What are the advantages and disadvantages of doing survey research? What about participant observation and other ethnographic techniques?

ting that includes human beings. A combination of survey research and ethnography can provide new perspectives on life in **complex societies** (large and populous societies with social stratification and central governments). Preliminary ethnography also can help develop culturally appropriate questions for inclusion in surveys.

In any complex society, many predictor variables (*social indicators*) influence behavior and opinions. Because we must be able to detect, measure, and compare the influence of social indicators, many contemporary anthropological studies have a statistical foundation. Even in rural fieldwork, more anthropologists now draw samples, gather quantitative data, and use statistics to interpret them (see Bernard

1998, 2006). Quantifiable information may permit a more precise assessment of similarities and differences among communities. Statistical analysis can support and round out an ethnographic account of local social life.

In the best studies, the hallmark of ethnography remains: Anthropologists enter the community and get to know the people. They participate in local activities, networks, and associations in the city, town, or countryside. They observe and experience social conditions and problems. They watch the effects of national and international policies and programs on local life. The ethnographic method and the emphasis on personal relationships in social research are valuable gifts that cultural anthropology brings to the study of any society.

"The way to do fieldwork is never to come up for air until it is all over."

Margaret Mead

Join a club or use your classroom to practice participant observation. Your goal as an ethnographer is to take part in the group as you study it. Do you have good enough rapport with group members to take part in their activities? What "imponderabilia" do you observe in the life of the group? Record these. What differences might you see in group members' behavior if they did not know you were an ethnographer observing them rather than being honestly informed, as anthropological ethics demand?

get involved!

For REVIEW

I. **What ethical concerns and issues must anthropologists consider?**

- Anthropologists need to establish collaborative relationships with colleagues and communities in the host country. Cultural sensitivity is paramount. The AAA Code of Ethics advises researchers to be honest about their research, its purposes, funding, methods, and potential results and impacts. Researchers must obtain the informed consent of all affected parties—from the authorities who control access to the field to the members of the community studied. Ethnographers need not avoid taking stands on community issues; shaping policy may be ethically justifiable.

II. **Where and how do cultural anthropologists do fieldwork?**

- Early anthropologists worked in small, relatively isolated, societies with a certain cultural uniformity. Ethnographers sought to create a holistic account, revealing a culture's totality and interconnectedness. Ethnographers have developed a variety of techniques. A key method is participant observation, taking part in community life as it is studied. Ethnographers also gather data from conversations and interviews, and by tracing genealogies, working with key cultural consultants, and collecting life histories. Ethnography seeks also to discover the native viewpoint.

- In today's interlinked world, anthropologists increasingly study people on the move. Ethnographers now tend to enter the field with a particular problem to investigate. Enabled by modern systems of transportation, ethnographers often return for multiple stays to monitor change. Such longitudinal research may entail coordinated team research.

III. **What are some ways of studying complex societies in modern nations?**

- Working in populous, large-scale societies, anthropologists have learned to blend ethnography with survey research. Survey research involves sampling, collecting impersonal data, and statistical analysis. Social scientists make inferences about the larger population by surveying a sample of "respondents." Such quantifiable information allows a more precise assessment of similarities and differences among communities and rounds out the ethnographic account. By providing data acquired by personal, firsthand techniques, ethnography supplements and fine-tunes survey research.

Pop Quiz

1. Which of the following is *not* a part of the AAA Code of Ethics?
   a. The recognition that anthropologists are obligated to their scholarly field, to the wider society and culture, and to the human species.
   b. The recommendation that anthropologists avoid taking stands on issues that arise in their dealings with another culture.
   c. The requirement that all parties involved in doing anthropological research be informed about the nature, procedures, purpose, and potential impacts of the research.
   d. The recommendation that the people anthropologists work with in the field be acknowledged and reciprocated in appropriate ways.

2. Which of the following statements about ethnography is false?
   a. Early ethnographers tried to understand the culture they studied as a whole (that is, sought to make a holistic account).
   b. Ethnographers see little value in collecting quantitative data.
   c. Bronislaw Malinowski, considered the founder of ethnography, sought to grasp the natives' points of view and visions of their world.
   d. Ethnographers today recognize that the culture they study is described only in a moment of time.

3. The friendly working relationship that ethnographers strive to establish with their hosts is known as:
   a. The imponderabilia of native life
   b. Rapport
   c. An interview schedule
   d. Ethnographic realism

4. Which of the following techniques did ethnographers develop as a specific response to the importance of kinship, descent, and marriage in the social organization of nonindustrial societies?
   a. The life history
   b. Participant observation
   c. The interview schedule
   d. The genealogical method

5. All the following are true about ethnography *except:*
   a. It was traditionally used to study whole communities.
   b. It is based on firsthand fieldwork.
   c. It is more personal than survey research.
   d. It privileges ethnographers' observations and conclusions over the local people's views and beliefs.

6. Trends in doing ethnography include the following *except:*
   a. A move away from holistic accounts toward investigations of specific problems.
   b. The inclusion of field-gathered data from two or more stays in the field (longitudinal research).
   c. Doing more work for colonial governments.
   d. Giving increased attention to contacts from outside the communities being studied.

7. Which of the following is not a key difference between an ethnographic survey approach and the survey procedures commonly used by sociologists? An ethnographic survey:
   a. Typically studies a partial sample.
   b. Uses an interview schedule.
   c. Includes face-to-face interviews with subjects.
   d. Encourages researchers to establish rapport.

8. In a modern world in which people, images, and information move around as never before, ethnography:
   a. Is becoming increasingly challenging for those wishing to focus on a spatially set culture.
   b. Is becoming a less useful and less valuable tool for understanding culture.
   c. Has become more traditional.
   d. Now requires that researchers stay in the same site for more than three years.

9. Which of the following statements is *not* true of the survey approach?
   a. It was developed by social scientists working in large populous nations.
   b. It entails less face-to-face interaction than ethnography.
   c. Quantifiable information obtained from the survey approach is useful for assessing similarities and differences between communities.
   d. Surveying's statistical approach does *not* benefit from being combined with ethnography.

10. Which of the following most completely characterizes the ethnographic approach?
    a. It relies on firsthand contact with the community being studied, including participation in its cultural life and observation of its social conditions.
    b. It takes into consideration people in motion and may require the anthropologist to follow the people being studied.
    c. It involves team research projects.
    d. Sources of data for ethnography include local people's answers to the anthropologist's questions, measurement of environmental conditions, and consultation of government records.

1. (b), 2. (b), 3. (b), 4. (d), 5. (d), 6. (c), 7. (a), 8. (a), 9. (d), 10. (a)

4

APPLYING
ANTHROPOLOGY

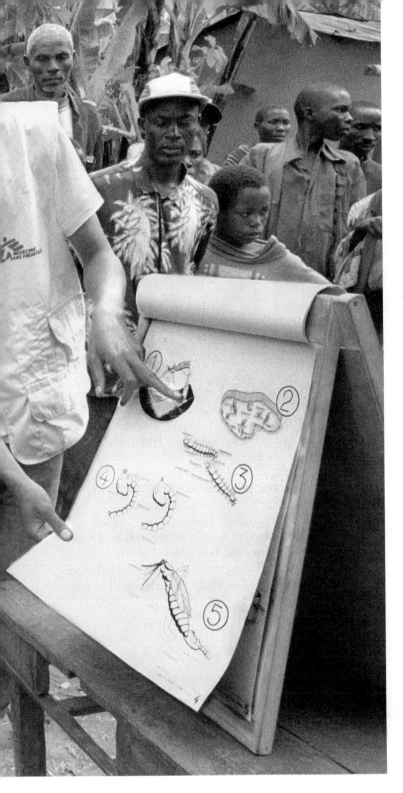

WHAT'S TO COME

What Is Applied Anthropology?

The Role of the Applied Anthropologist

Development Anthropology

Strategies for Innovation

Anthropology and Education

Urban Anthropology

Medical Anthropology

Anthropology and Business

Careers and Anthropology

UNDERSTANDING OURSELVES

Is change always good? The idea that innovation is inherently desirable is axiomatic in American culture, especially in advertising. "New and improved" is a slogan we hear all the time—a lot more often than "old reliable." Which do you think is best—change or the status quo? That "new" isn't always "improved" is a painful lesson learned by the Coca-Cola Company (TCCC) in 1985 when it changed the formula of its premier soft drink and introduced "New Coke." After hordes of customers protested, TCCC brought back old, familiar, reliable Coke under the name "Coca-Cola Classic," which thrives today. New Coke, now history, offers a classic case of how not to treat consumers. TCCC tried a *top-down change* (a change initiated at the top of a hierarchy rather than inspired by the people most affected by the change). Customers didn't ask TCCC to change its product; executives made that decision.

The field of market research, which employs a good number of anthropologists, is based on the need to appreciate what actual and potential customers do, think, and want. Smart planners study and listen to people to try to determine *locally based demand*. What changes do the people—and which people—want? How can conflicting wishes and needs be accommodated? Applied anthropologists help answer these questions, which are crucial in understanding whether change is needed and how it will work.

Innovation succeeds best when it is culturally appropriate. This axiom of applied anthropology is a useful guide for international programs aimed at social and economic change as well as for businesses. Each time an organization expands to a new nation, it must devise a culturally appropriate strategy for fitting into the new setting. In their international expansion, companies and organizations have learned that more money, and more progress, can be made by fitting in with, rather than trying to Americanize, local habits.

As You
READ

- How can change be bad?
- How can anthropology be applied to education, medicine, and business?
- How does the study of anthropology fit into a career path?

>> What Is Applied Anthropology?

Anthropology has two dimensions: applied anthropology and theoretical/academic anthropology. Applied, or *practical,* anthropology is the use of anthropological data, perspectives, theory, and methods to identify, assess, and solve contemporary problems involving human behavior and social and cultural forces, conditions, and contexts (see Ervin 2005). For example, medical anthropologists have worked as cultural interpreters in public health programs to facilitate their fit into local culture. Many applied anthropol-ogists have worked for or with international development agencies, such as the World Bank and the U.S. Agency for International Development (USAID). In North America, garbologists help the Environmental Protection Agency, the paper industry, and packaging and trade associations. Archaeology is applied as well in cultural resource management and historic preservation. Biological anthropologists work in public health, nutrition, genetic counseling, substance abuse, epidemiology, aging, and mental illness. Forensic anthropologists work with the police, medical examiners, the courts, and international organizations to identify victims of crimes, accidents, wars, and terrorism. Linguistic anthropologists study physician–patient inter-

TABLE 4.1

The Four Subfields and Two Dimensions of Anthropology	
Anthropology's Subfields (Academic Anthropology)	**Examples of Application (Applied Anthropology)**
Cultural anthropology	Development anthropology
Archaeological anthropology	Cultural resource management (CRM)
Biological or physical anthropology	Forensic anthropology
Linguistic anthropology	Study of linguistic diversity in classrooms

STUDY TIP

Two major differences between
anthropologists and many other experts are
(1) anthropologists' emphasis on talking
with local people, using ethnographic
techniques, and (2) anthropologists'
holistic approach.

actions and show how dialect differences influence classroom learning. The goal of most applied anthropologists is to find humane and effective ways of helping local people.

One of the most valuable tools in applying anthropology is the ethnographic method. Ethnographers study societies firsthand, living with and learning from ordinary people. Ethnographers are participant observers, taking part in the events they study in order to understand local thought and behavior. Applied anthropologists use ethnographic techniques in both foreign and domestic settings. Other "expert" participants in social-change programs may be content to converse with officials, read reports, and copy statistics. The applied anthropologist's likely early request, however, is some variant of "take me to the local people." We know that people must play an active role in the changes that affect them and that "the people" have information "the experts" lack.

Anthropological theory, the body of findings and generalizations of the four subfields, also guides applied anthropology. Anthropology's holistic perspective—its interest in biology, society, culture, and language—permits the evaluation of many issues that affect people. Theory aids practice, and application fuels theory. As we compare social-change policy and programs, our understanding of cause and effect increases. We add new generalizations about culture change to those discovered in traditional and ancient cultures.

>> The Role of the Applied Anthropologist

EARLY APPLICATIONS

Application was a central concern of early anthropology in Great Britain (in the context of colonialism) and the United States (in the context of Native American policy). Before turning to the new, we should consider some dangers of the old. For the British empire, specifically its African colonies, Malinowski (1929) proposed that "practical anthropology" (his term for colonial applied anthropology) should focus on **Westernization**—the diffusion of European culture into tribal societies. Malinowski questioned

neither the legitimacy of colonialism nor the anthropologist's role in making it work. He saw nothing wrong with aiding colonial regimes by studying land tenure and land use in order to recommend how much of their land local people should be allowed to keep and how much Europeans should get. Malinowski's views exemplify a historical association between early anthropology, particularly in Europe, and colonialism (Maquet 1964).

CULTURETHINK

Malinowski and other early anthropologists have been criticized for supporting the colonial missions of the Western nations that hired them to do ethnographic research. Ethically, whose needs and goals do you think anthropologists should be representing? What would have been the risks and benefits of advocating for local people's rights in Malinowski's day?

During World War II, American anthropologists studied Japanese and German "culture at a distance" in an attempt to predict the behavior of the enemies of the United States. After that war, applied anthropologists worked on Pacific islands to promote local-level cooperation with American policies in various trust territories.

ACADEMIC AND APPLIED ANTHROPOLOGY

Applied anthropology did not disappear during the 1950s and 1960s, but academic anthropology did most of the growing after World War II. The baby boom, which began in 1946 and peaked in 1957, fueled expansion of the American educational

> **Westernization** The diffusion of European cultures into tribal societies.

system and thus of academic jobs. New junior, community, and four-year colleges opened, and anthropology became a standard part of the college curriculum. During the 1950s and 1960s, most American anthropologists were college professors, although some still worked in agencies and museums.

This era of academic anthropology continued through the early 1970s. Especially during the Vietnam War, undergraduates flocked to anthropology classes to learn about other cultures. Students were especially interested in Southeast Asia, whose indigenous societies were being disrupted by war. Many anthropologists protested the superpowers' apparent disregard for non-Western lives, values, customs, and social systems.

During the 1970s, and increasingly thereafter, although most anthropologists still worked in academia, others found jobs with international organizations, government, business, hospitals, and schools. This shift toward appli-

During the Vietnam War, many anthropologists protested the superpowers' disregard for the values, customs, social systems, and lives of indigenous peoples. Several anthropologists attended this all-night Columbia University teach-in about the war in 1965.

cal arena. However, applied anthropologists also solve problems for clients who are neither poor nor powerless. Applied anthropologists working for businesses try to solve the problem of expanding profits for their employer or client. In market research, ethical issues may arise as anthropologists attempt to help companies operate more efficiently and profitably. Ethical ambiguities are present as well in cultural resource management (CRM), in deciding how to preserve significant remains and information when sites are threatened by development or public works. A CRM firm typically is hired by someone seeking to build a road or a factory. In such cases, the client may have a strong interest in an outcome in which no sites are found that need protecting.

Contemporary applied anthropologists still face ethical questions: To whom does the researcher owe loyalty? What problems are involved in holding firm to the truth? What happens when applied anthropologists don't make the policies they are told to implement? How does one criticize programs in which one has participated (see Escobar 1991, 1994)? Anthropology's professional organizations have addressed such questions by establishing codes of ethics and ethics committees. See http://www.aaanet.org for the Code of Ethics of the AAA. As Tice (1997) notes, attention to ethical issues is paramount in the teaching of applied anthropology today.

By instilling an appreciation for human diversity, the entire field of anthropology combats *ethnocentrism*— the tendency to view one's own culture as superior and to use one's own cultural values in judging the behavior

cation, though only partial, has benefited the profession. It has forced anthropologists to consider the wider social value and implications of their research.

APPLIED ANTHROPOLOGY TODAY

Today, most applied anthropologists see their work as radically removed from the colonial perspective. Modern applied anthropology usually is seen as a helping profession, devoted to assisting local people, as anthropologists speak up for the disenfranchised in the international politi-

Supervised by archaeologists from India, with funding from the United Nations, these workers are cleaning and restoring the front façade of Cambodia's historical Angkor Wat temple. To decide what needs saving, and to preserve significant information about the past even when sites cannot be saved, is the work of cultural resource management (CRM).

and beliefs of people raised in other societies. Anthropology's broadening, educational role affects the knowledge, values, and attitudes of people exposed to its teachings. This chapter focuses specifically on this question: What specific contributions can anthropology make in identifying and solving problems stirred up by contemporary currents of economic, social, and cultural change, including globalization?

Because anthropologists are experts on human problems and social change and because they study, understand, and respect cultural values, they are highly qualified to suggest, plan, and implement policy affecting people. Proper roles for applied anthropologists include (1) identifying needs for change that local people perceive, (2) working with those people to design culturally appropriate and socially sensitive change, and (3) protecting local people from harmful policies and projects that may threaten them.

Anthropology's systemic perspective recognizes that changes don't occur in a vacuum. A program or project always has multiple effects, some of which are unforeseen. In an American example of unintended consequences, a program aimed at enhancing teachers' appreciation of cultural differences led to ethnic stereotyping (Kleinfield 1975). Specifically, Native American students did not welcome teachers' frequent comments about their Indian heritage. The students felt set apart from their classmates and saw this attention to their ethnicity as patronizing and demeaning. Internationally, dozens of economic development projects intended to increase productivity through irrigation have worsened public health by creating waterways where diseases thrive.

>> Development Anthropology

The branch of applied anthropology that focuses on social issues in, and the cultural dimension of, economic development is called **development anthropology.** Develop-

CULTURETHINK

What's the difference between equity and equality? (*Equality* means that each person or group would be treated the same and receive the same benefits.) What are the challenges in striving for equality as a development goal?

ment anthropologists do not just carry out development policies planned by others; they also plan and guide policy. (For more detailed discussions of issues in development anthropology, see Edelman and Haugerud 2004; Escobar 1995; Ferguson 1995; Nolan 2002; and Robertson 1995.)

Ethical dilemmas often confront development anthropologists (Escobar 1991, 1995). Our respect for cultural diversity often is offended because efforts to extend industry and technology may entail profound cultural changes. Foreign aid usually doesn't go where the need and suffering are greatest. It is spent on political, economic, and strategic priorities as international donors, political leaders and powerful interest groups perceive them. Planners' interests don't always coincide with the best interests of the local people. Although the aim of most development projects is to enhance the quality of life, living standards often decline in the target area (Bodley 1988).

EQUITY

A commonly stated goal of recent development policy is to promote equity. **Increased equity** means reduced poverty and a more even distribution of wealth. If projects are to increase equity, however, they must have the support of reform-minded governments. Wealthy and powerful people typically resist projects that threaten their vested interests.

Some types of development projects, particularly irrigation schemes, are more likely than others to widen wealth disparities, that is, to have a negative equity impact. An initial uneven distribution of resources (particularly land) often becomes the basis for greater skewing after the project. The social impact of new technology tends to be more severe, contributing negatively to quality of life and to equity, when inputs are channeled to or through the rich.

Many fisheries projects also have had negative equity results (see Durrenberger and King 2000). In Bahia, Brazil (Kottak 2006), sailboat owners (but not nonowners) received loans to buy motors for their boats. To repay the loans, the owners increased the percentage of the catch they took from the men who fished in their boats. Over the years, they used their rising profits to buy larger and more

development anthropology The branch of applied anthropology that focuses on social issues in, and the cultural dimension of, economic development.

equity, increased A reduction in absolute poverty and a fairer (more even) distribution of wealth.

A mix of boats harbored at Dai-Lanh fishing village in Vietnam. A boat owner receives a loan to buy a motor. To repay the loan, he increases the share of the catch he takes from his crew. Later, he uses his rising profits to buy a more expensive boat and takes even more from his crew. Can a more equitable solution be found?

expensive boats. The result was stratification—the creation of a group of wealthy people within a formerly egalitarian community. These events hampered individual initiative and interfered with further development of the fishing industry. With new boats so expensive, ambitious young men who once would have sought careers in fishing no longer had any way to obtain their own boats. They sought wage labor on land instead. To avoid such results, credit-granting agencies must seek out enterprising young fishers rather than giving loans only to owners and established businesspeople.

overinnovation Characteristic of development projects that require major changes in people's daily lives, especially ones that interfere with customary subsistence pursuits.

>> Strategies for Innovation

Development anthropologists, who are concerned with social issues in, and the cultural dimension of, economic development, must work closely with local people to assess and help them realize their own wishes and needs for change. Development anthropologists can help identify, plan, and implement beneficial projects by consulting with local people and responding to their expressed needs (Cernea 1991).

In a comparative study of sixty-eight rural development projects from around the world, Conrad Kottak found the *culturally compatible* economic development projects to be twice as successful financially as the incompatible ones (Kottak 1990b, 1991). This finding shows that using anthropological expertise in planning to ensure cultural compatibility is cost effective. To maximize social and economic benefits, projects must (1) be culturally compatible, (2) respond to locally perceived needs, (3) involve men and women in planning and carrying out the changes that affect them, (4) harness traditional organizations, and (5) be flexible.

OVERINNOVATION

In Kottak's comparative study, the compatible and successful projects avoided the fallacy of **overinnovation** (too much change). We would expect people to resist development projects that require major changes in their daily lives. People usually want to change just enough to keep what they have. Motives for modifying behavior come from the traditional culture and the small concerns of ordinary life. Peasants' values are not such abstract ones as "learning a better way," "progressing," "increasing technical know-how," "improving efficiency," or "adopting modern techniques." (Those phrases exemplify intervention philosophy.)

Instead, people's objectives are down-to-earth and specific ones. They want to improve yields in a rice field, amass resources for a ceremony, get a child through school, or have enough cash to pay the tax bill. The goals and values of subsistence producers differ from those of people who produce for cash, just as they differ from the intervention philosophy of development planners. Different value systems must be considered during planning.

In Kottak's comparative study, the projects that failed were usually incompatible both economically and culturally. For example, one South Asian project promoted the cultivation of onions and peppers, expecting this practice to fit into a preexisting labor-intensive system of rice growing. Cultivation of these cash crops wasn't traditional in the area. It conflicted with existing crop priorities and other interests of farmers. Also, the labor peaks for pepper and onion production coincided with those for rice, to which the farmers gave priority.

Throughout the world, project problems have arisen from inadequate attention to, and consequent lack of fit with, local culture. Another naive and incompatible project was an overinnovative scheme in Ethiopia. Its major fallacy was to try to convert nomadic herders into sedentary cultivators. It ignored traditional land rights. Outsiders—commercial farmers—were to get much of the herders' territory. The pastoralists were expected to settle down and start farming. This project helped wealthy outsiders instead of the local people. The planners naively expected free-ranging herders to give up a generations-old way of life to work three times harder growing rice and picking cotton for bosses.

STUDY **TIP**

Be able to identify the five criteria for successful projects that maximize social and economic benefits.

UNDERDIFFERENTIATION

The fallacy of **underdifferentiation** is the tendency to view the "less developed countries" as more alike than they are. Development agencies have often ignored cultural diversity (e.g., between Brazil and Burundi) and adopted a uniform approach to deal with very different sets of people. Neglecting cultural diversity, many projects also have tried to impose incompatible property notions and social units. Most often, the faulty social design assumes either (1) individualistic productive units that are privately owned by an individual or couple and worked by a nuclear family or (2) cooperatives that are at least par-tially based on models from the former Eastern bloc and Socialist countries.

One example of faulty Euro-American models (the individual and the nuclear family) was a West African project designed for an area where the extended family was the basic social unit. The project succeeded despite its faulty social design because the participants used their traditional extended family networks to attract additional settlers. Eventually, twice as many people as planned benefited as extended family members flocked to the project area. Here, settlers modified the project design that had been imposed on them by following the principles of their traditional society.

The second dubious foreign social model that is common in development strategy is the cooperative. In the comparative study of rural development projects, new cooperatives fared badly. Cooperatives succeeded only when they harnessed preexisting local-level communal institutions. This is a corollary of a more general rule: Participants' groups are most effective when they are based on traditional social organization or on a socioeconomic similarity among members.

Neither foreign social model—the nuclear family farm nor the cooperative—has an unblemished record in development. An alternative is needed: greater use of indigenous social models in economic development. These are traditional social units, such as the clans, lineages, and other extended kin groups

> **underdifferentiation** Planning fallacy of viewing less-developed countries as an undifferentiated group; ignoring cultural diversity and adopting a uniform approach (often ethnocentric) for very different types of project beneficiaries.

To maximize benefits, development projects should respond to locally perceived needs. Shown here (foreground) is the president of a Nicaraguan cooperative that makes and markets hammocks. This cooperative has been assisted by a nongovernmental organization (NGO) whose goals include increasing the benefits that women derive from economic development.

of Africa, Oceania, and many other nations, with their communally held estates and resources. The most humane and productive strategy for change is to base the social design for innovation on traditional social forms in each target area.

INDIGENOUS MODELS

Many governments are not genuinely, or realistically, committed to improving the lives of their citizens. Interference by major powers also has kept governments from enacting needed reforms. In some nations, however, the government acts more as an agent of the people. Madagascar provides an example. The people of Madagascar, the Malagasy, had been organized into descent groups before the origin of the state. The Merina, creators of the major precolonial state of Madagascar, wove descent groups into its structure, making members of important groups advisers to the king and thus giving them authority in government. The Merina state made provisions for the people it ruled. It collected taxes and organized labor for public works projects. In return, it redistributed resources to peasants in need. It also granted them some protection against war and slave raids and allowed them to cultivate their rice fields in peace. The government maintained the water works for rice cultivation. It opened to ambitious peasant boys the chance of becoming, through hard work and study, state bureaucrats.

> **anthropology and education** Anthropological research in classrooms, homes, and neighborhoods, viewing students as total cultural creatures whose enculturation and attitudes toward education belong to a larger context that includes family, peers, and society.

Throughout the history of the Merina state—and continuing in modern Madagascar—there have been strong relationships between the individual, the descent group, and the state. Local Malagasy communities, where residence is based on descent, are more cohesive and homogeneous than are communities in Latin America or North America. Madagascar gained political independence from France in 1960. Although it still was economically dependent on France when Conrad Kottak first did research there in 1966–1967, the new government had an economic development policy aimed at increasing the ability of the Malagasy to feed themselves. Government policy emphasized increased production of rice, a subsistence crop, rather than cash crops. Furthermore, local communities, with their traditional cooperative patterns and solidarity based on kinship and descent, were treated as partners in, not obstacles to, the development process.

In a sense, the descent group is preadapted to equitable national development. In Madagascar, members of local descent groups have customarily pooled their resources to educate their ambitious members. Once educated, these men and women gain economically secure positions in the nation. They then share the advantages of their new positions with their kin. For example, they give room and board to rural cousins attending school and help them find jobs.

Malagasy administrations appear generally to have shared a commitment to democratic economic development. Perhaps this is because government officials are of the peasantry or have strong personal ties to it. By contrast, in Latin American countries, the elites and the lower class have different origins and no strong connections through kinship, descent, or marriage.

Furthermore, societies with descent-group organization contradict an assumption that many social scientists and economists seem to make. It is not inevitable that as nations become more tied to the world capitalist economy, indigenous forms of social organization will break down into nuclear family organization, impersonality, and alienation. Descent groups, with their traditional communalism and corporate solidarity, have important roles to play in economic development.

Realistic development promotes change but not over-innovation. Many changes are possible if the aim is to preserve local systems while making them work better. Successful economic development projects respect, or at least don't attack, local cultural patterns. Effective development draws on indigenous cultural practices and social structures.

>> Anthropology and Education

Attention to culture also is fundamental to **anthropology and education,** involving research that extends from classrooms into homes, neighborhoods, and communities (see Spindler 2000, 2005). In classrooms, anthropologists have observed interactions among teachers, students, parents, and visitors. Jules Henry's classic account of the American elementary school classroom (1955) shows how students learn to conform to and compete with their peers. Anthropologists view children as total cultural creatures whose enculturation and

Afghan girls attend a lesson at the secondary school in Sarkani village, Kunar Province, eastern Afghanistan. What do you see here that differs from classrooms in your country?

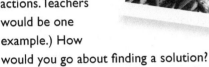

The anthropologists also found that certain practices were preventing Hispanics from being adequately educated. For example, the teachers' union and the board of education had agreed to teach "English as a foreign language." However, they had provided no bilingual teachers to work with Spanish-speaking students. The school was assigning all students (including non-Hispanics) with low reading scores and behavior problems to the English-as-a-foreign-language classroom. This educational disaster brought together in the classroom a teacher who spoke no Spanish, children who barely spoke English, and a group of English-speaking students with reading and behavior problems. The Spanish speakers were falling behind not just in reading but in all subjects. They could at least have kept up in the other subjects if a Spanish speaker had been teaching them science, social studies, and math until they were ready for English-language instruction in those areas.

attitudes toward education belong to a context that includes family and peers.

Sociolinguists and cultural anthropologists work side by side in education research. For example, in a study of Puerto Rican seventh-graders in the urban Midwest (Hill-Burnett 1978), anthropologists uncovered some misconceptions held by teachers. The teachers mistakenly had assumed that Puerto Rican parents valued education less than did non-Hispanics, but in-depth interviews revealed that the Puerto Rican parents valued it more.

>> Urban Anthropology

Alan and Josephine Smart (2003) note that cities have long been influenced by global forces, including world capitalism and colonialism. The roles of cities in the world system have changed recently, however, as a result of the time-space compression made possible by modern transportation and communication systems. That is, everything appears closer today because contact and movement are so much easier.

One-sixth of Earth's population lives in urban slums. Roçinha (shown here) is a populous shantytown within the city of Rio de Janeiro, Brazil. How might anthropologists study slums?

Watch a few episodes of the Fox TV series *Bones*—based on characters created by Kathy Reichs, a physical and forensic anthropologist. *Bones* is one of the very few TV programs featuring a professional anthropologist, the character Temperance Brennan, aka "Bones" to her FBI agent partner, Seely Booth. As you watch the program, pay attention to the following questions: How do Dr. Brennan's attitudes, beliefs, and opinions differ from those of other members of the cast? How do her statements compare and contrast with anthropological perspectives as presented in this textbook? Ask your professor what she or he thinks about some of the statements you write down and quote from Dr. Brennan.

In the context of contemporary globalization, the mass media can become as important as local factors in guiding daily routines, dreams, and aspirations. People live in particular places, but their imaginations and attachments don't have to be locally confined (Appadurai 1996). People migrate to cities partly for economic reasons, but also to be where the action is. Rural Brazilians routinely cite *movimento*, urban movement and excitement, as something to be valued. International migrants tend to settle in the largest cities, where the most is happening. For example, in Canada, which has the second highest percentage of foreign-born population after Australia, 71.2 percent of immigrants settled in Toronto, Vancouver, or Montreal. Nearly half of Toronto's citizens were born outside Canada (Smart and Smart 2003).

urban anthropology The anthropological study of life in and around world cities, including the study of urban social problems, differences between urban and other environments, and adaptation to city life.

The proportion of the world's population living in cities has been increasing ever since the Industrial Revolution. About 3 percent of people were city dwellers in 1800, compared with 13 percent in 1900, over 40 percent in 1980, and about 50 percent today (see Smart and Smart 2003). The More Developed Countries (MDCs) were 76 percent urbanized in 1999, compared with 39 percent for the Less Developed Countries (LDCs). However, the urbanization growth rate is much faster in the LDCs (Smart and Smart 2003). The world had 16 cities with more than a million people in 1900, but there were 314 such cities in 2005. By 2025, 60 percent of the global population will be urban (Butler 2005; Stevens 1992).

About one billion people, one-sixth of Earth's population, live in urban slums, mostly without water, sanitation, public services, and legal security (Vidal 2003). If current trends continue, urban population increase and the concentration of people in slums will be accompanied by rising rates of crime, along with water, air, and noise pollution. These problems will be most severe in the LDCs.

As industrialization and urbanization spread globally, anthropologists increasingly study these processes and the social problems they create. **Urban anthropology,** which has theoretical (basic research) and applied dimensions, is the cross-cultural and ethnographic study of global urbanization and life in cities (see Aoyagi, Nas, and Traphagan 1998; Gmelch and Zenner 2002; Smart and Smart 2003; Stevenson 2003). The United States and Canada have become popular arenas for urban anthropological research on topics such as immigration, ethnicity, poverty, class, and urban violence (Mullings 1987; Vigil 2003).

URBAN VERSUS RURAL

Recognizing that a city is a social context that is very different from a tribal or peasant village, an early student of urbanization, the anthropologist Robert Redfield, focused on contrasts between rural and urban life. He contrasted rural communities, whose social relations are on a face-to-face basis, with cities, where impersonality characterizes many aspects of life. Redfield (1941) proposed that urbanization be studied along a rural–urban continuum. He described differences in values and social relations in four sites that spanned such a continuum. In Mexico's Yucatán peninsula, Redfield compared an isolated Maya-speaking Indian community, a rural peasant village, a small provincial city, and a large capital. Several studies in Africa (Little 1971) and Asia were influenced by Redfield's view that cities are centers through which cultural innovations spread to rural and tribal areas.

In any nation, urban and rural represent different social systems. However, cultural diffusion or borrowing occurs as people, products, images, and messages move from one to the other. Migrants bring rural practices and beliefs to cities and take urban patterns back home. The experiences and social forms of the rural area affect adaptation to city life. City folk also develop new institutions to meet specific urban needs (Mitchell 1966).

An applied anthropology approach to urban planning would start by identifying key social groups in the urban context. After identifying those groups, the anthropologist might elicit their wishes for change, convey those needs to funding agencies, and work with agencies and local people to realize those goals. In Africa relevant groups might include ethnic associations, occupational groups, social clubs, religious groups, and burial societies. Through membership in such groups, urban Africans maintain wide networks of personal contacts and support (Banton 1957; Little 1965). These groups also have links with, and provide cash support and urban lodging for, their rural relatives. Sometimes such groups think of themselves as a gigantic kin group, a clan that includes urban and rural members. Members may call one another "brother" and "sister." As in an extended family, rich members help their poor relatives. A member's improper behavior can lead to expulsion—an unhappy fate for a migrant in a large ethnically heterogeneous city.

One role for the urban applied anthropologist is to help relevant social groups deal with urban institutions, such as legal and social services, with which recent migrants may be unfamiliar. In certain North American cities, as in Africa, kin-based ethnic associations are relevant urban groups. One example comes from Los Angeles, which has the largest Samoan immigrant community (over twelve thousand people) in the United States. Samoans in Los Angeles draw on their traditional system of *matai* (*matai* means "chief"; the matai system now refers to respect for elders) to deal with modern urban problems. One example: In 1992, a white police officer shot and killed two unarmed Samoan brothers. When a judge dismissed charges against the officer, local leaders used the matai system to calm angry youths (who have formed gangs, like other ethnic groups in the Los Angeles area). Clan leaders and elders organized a well-attended community meeting, in which they urged young members to be patient. The Samoans then used the American judicial system. They brought a civil case against the officer in question and pressed the U.S. Justice Department to initiate a civil rights case in the matter (Mydans 1992b). Not all conflicts involving gangs and law enforcement end so peacefully.

James Vigil (2003) examines gang violence in the context of large-scale immigrant adaptation to American cities. He notes that before the 1970s most gangs were located in white ethnic enclaves in eastern and midwestern cities. Back then, gang incidents typically were brawls involving fists, sticks, and knives. Today, gangs more often are composed of non-white ethnic groups, and handguns have replaced the less lethal weapons of the past. Gangs still consist mostly of male adolescents who have grown up together, usually in a low-income neighborhood, where it's estimated that about 10 percent of young men join gangs. Female gang members are much rarer—from 4 to 15 percent of gang members. With gangs organized hierarchically by age, older members push younger ones (usually fourteen- to eighteen-year-olds) to carry out violent acts against rivals (Vigil 2003).

The populations that include most of today's gang members settled originally in poorer urban areas. On the East Coast these usually were run-down neighborhoods where a criminal lifestyle already was present. Around Los Angeles, urban migrants created squatterlike settlements in previously empty spaces. Immigrants tend to reside in neighborhoods apart from middle-class people, thus limiting their opportunities for integration. Confined in this manner, and facing residential overcrowding, poor people often experience frustration, which can lead to aggressive acts (Vigil 2003). At the same time, industries and jobs have moved from inner cities to distant suburbs and foreign nations. Urban minority youth have limited access to entry-level jobs; often they receive harsh treatment from authorities, especially law enforcement. Frustration and competition over resources can spark aggressive incidents, fueling urban violence. For survival, many residents of abandoned neighborhoods have turned to informal and illegal economic arrangements, of which drug trafficking in particular has heightened gang violence (Vigil 2003). How might an applied anthropologist approach the problem of urban violence? Which groups would need to be involved in the study?

> "I must admit that I personally measure success in terms of the contributions an individual makes to her or his fellow human beings."
>
> Margaret Mead

CULTURETHINK

How might an applied anthropologist approach the problem of urban violence? Which groups would need to be involved in the study?

>> Medical Anthropology

The branch of anthropology known as **medical anthropology** is both academic/theoretical and applied/practical and includes anthropologists from all four subfields (see Anderson 1996; Briggs 2005; Brown 1998; Dressler et al. 2005; Joralemon 2006; Singer and Baer 2007; Trevathan, Smith, and McKenna 2007). Medical anthropologists examine such questions as which diseases and health conditions affect particular populations (and why) and how illness is socially constructed, diagnosed, managed, and treated in various societies.

medical anthropology
Unites biological and cultural anthropologists in the study of disease, health problems, health care systems, and theories about illness in different cultures and ethnic groups.

disease An etic, or scientifically identified, health threat caused by a bacterium, virus, fungus, parasite, or other pathogen.

illness An emic condition of poor health felt by the individual.

Disease refers to a scientifically identified health threat caused genetically or by a bacterium, virus, fungus, parasite, or other pathogen. **Illness** is a condition of poor health perceived or felt by an individual (Inhorn and Brown 1990). Perceptions of good and bad health, along with health threats and problems, are culturally constructed. Various ethnic groups and cultures recognize different illnesses, symptoms, and causes and have developed different health care systems and treatment strategies.

The incidence and severity of *disease* vary as well (see Baer, Singer, and Susser 2003; Barnes 2005). Group differences are evident in the United States. Keppel, Pearch, and Wagener (2002) examined data between 1990 and 1998 using ten health status indicators in relation to racial and ethnic categories from the U.S. census: non-Hispanic white, non-Hispanic black, Hispanic, American Indian or Alaska Native, and Asian or Pacific Islander. Black Americans' rates for six measures (total mortality, heart disease, lung cancer, breast cancer, stroke, and homicide) exceeded those of other groups by a factor ranging from 2.5 to almost 10. Other ethnic groups had higher rates for suicide (white Americans) and motor vehicle accidents (American Indians and Alaskan Natives). Overall, Asians had the longest life spans (see Dressler et al. 2005).

Hurtado and colleagues (2005) note the prevalence of poor health and unusually high rates of early mortality among indigenous populations in South America. Life expectancy at birth is at least twenty years shorter among indigenous groups compared with other South Americans. In 2000, the life expectancy of indigenous peoples in Brazil and Venezuela was lower than that in Sierra Leone, which had the lowest reported national life expectancy in the world (Hurtado et al. 2005).

How can applied anthropologists help ameliorate the large health disparity between indigenous peoples and other populations? Hurtado and colleagues (2005) suggest three steps: (1) Identify the most pressing health problems that indigenous communities face; (2) gather information on solutions to those problems; and (3) implement solutions in partnership with the agencies and organizations in charge of public health programs for indigenous populations.

In many areas, the world system and colonialism worsened the health of indigenous peoples by spreading diseases, warfare, servitude, and other stressors. Traditionally and in ancient times, hunter-gatherers, because of their small numbers, mobility, and relative isolation from other groups, lacked most of the epidemic infectious diseases that affect agrarian and urban societies (Cohen and Armelagos 1984; Inhorn and Brown 1990). Epidemic diseases such as cholera, typhoid, and bubonic plague thrive in dense populations, and thus among farmers and city dwellers. The spread of malaria has been linked to population growth and deforestation associated with food production.

Certain diseases, and physical conditions such as obesity, have spread with economic development and globalization (Ulijaszek and Lofink 2006). *Schistosomiasis,* or bilharzia (blood and liver flukes), is probably the fastest-spreading and most dangerous parasitic infection now known. It is propagated by snails that live in ponds, lakes, and waterways, usually those created by irrigation projects. A study done in a Nile Delta village in Egypt (Farooq 1966) illustrated the role of culture (religion) in the spread of schistosomiasis. The disease was more common among Muslims than among Christians because of an Islamic practice called *wudu*—ritual ablution (bathing) before prayer. The applied anthropology approach to reducing such diseases is to see if local people perceive a connection between the vector (e.g., snails in the water) and the disease. If not, such information may be provided by enlisting active local groups, schools, and the media.

The highest global rates of HIV infection and AIDS-related deaths are in Africa, especially southern Africa. As it kills productive adults, AIDS leaves behind children and seniors who have difficulty replacing the

STUDY TIP

Three ways of identifying, classifying, and explaining illness, called disease theories, are (1) personalistic, (2) naturalistic, and (3) emotionalistic.

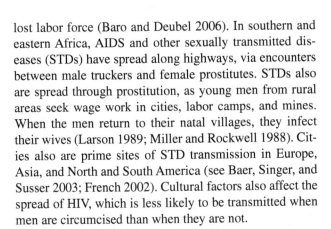

believe their health suffers when they eat or drink hot or cold substances together or under inappropriate conditions. For example, one shouldn't drink something cold after a hot bath or eat a pineapple (a "cold" fruit) when one is menstruating (a "hot" condition).

Emotionalistic disease theories assume that emotional experiences cause illness. For example, Latin Americans may develop *susto,* an illness caused by anxiety or fright (Bolton 1981; Finkler 1985). Its symptoms (lethargy, vagueness, distraction) are similar to those of "soul loss," a diagnosis of similar symptoms made by people in Madagascar. Modern psychoanalysis also focuses on the role of the emotions in physical and psychological well-being.

All societies have **health care systems** consisting of beliefs, customs, specialists, and techniques aimed at ensuring health and at preventing, diagnosing, and curing illness. A society's illness-causation theory influences treatment. When illness has a personalistic cause, magicoreligious specialists may be good curers. They draw on varied techniques (occult and practical) that are part of their special expertise. A shaman may cure soul loss by enticing the spirit back into the body. Shamans may ease difficult childbirths by asking spirits to travel up the birth canal to guide the baby out (Lévi-Strauss 1967). A shaman may cure a cough by counteracting a curse or removing a substance introduced by a sorcerer.

If there is a "world's oldest profession" besides hunter and gatherer, it is **curer,** often a shaman. The curer's role has some universal features (Foster and Anderson 1978). Thus curers emerge through a culturally defined process of

health care systems Beliefs, customs, and specialists concerned with ensuring health and preventing and curing illness; a cultural universal.

curer Specialized role acquired through a culturally appropriate process of selection, training, certification, and acquisition of a professional image; the curer is consulted by patients, who believe in his or her special powers, and receives some form of special consideration; a cultural universal.

lost labor force (Baro and Deubel 2006). In southern and eastern Africa, AIDS and other sexually transmitted diseases (STDs) have spread along highways, via encounters between male truckers and female prostitutes. STDs also are spread through prostitution, as young men from rural areas seek wage work in cities, labor camps, and mines. When the men return to their natal villages, they infect their wives (Larson 1989; Miller and Rockwell 1988). Cities also are prime sites of STD transmission in Europe, Asia, and North and South America (see Baer, Singer, and Susser 2003; French 2002). Cultural factors also affect the spread of HIV, which is less likely to be transmitted when men are circumcised than when they are not.

The kinds of and incidence of disease vary among societies, and cultures interpret and treat illness differently. Standards for sick and healthy bodies are cultural constructions that vary in time and space (Martin 1992). Still, all societies have what George Foster and Barbara Anderson call "disease-theory systems" to identify, classify, and explain illness. According to Foster and Anderson (1978), there are three basic theories about the causes of illness: personalistic, naturalistic, and emotionalistic. *Personalistic disease theories* blame illness on agents, such as sorcerers, witches, ghosts, or ancestral spirits. *Naturalistic disease theories* explain illness in impersonal terms. One example is Western medicine, or *biomedicine,* which aims to link illness to scientifically demonstrated agents that bear no personal malice toward their victims. Thus Western medicine attributes illness to organisms (e.g., bacteria, viruses, fungi, or parasites), accidents, toxic materials, or genes.

Other naturalistic ethnomedical systems blame poor health on unbalanced body fluids. Many Latin societies classify food, drink, and environmental conditions as "hot" or "cold." People

A traditional healer at work in Malaysia. Shown here, mugwort, a small, spongy herb, is burned to facilitate healing. The healer lights one end of a moxa stick, roughly the shape and size of a cigar, and attaches it, or holds it close, to the area being treated for several minutes until the area turns red. The purpose of moxibustion is to strengthen the blood, stimulate spiritual energy, and maintain general health.

STUDY TIP

Strengths of Western use of biomedicine are (1) effective drugs, (2) preventive health care, and (3) safe surgical procedures. Weaknesses are (1) overprescription of drugs, (2) opposition between mind and body, (3) unnecessary surgery, and (4) distant physician–patient relationships.

selection (parental prodding, inheritance, visions, dream instructions) and training (apprentice shamanship, medical school). Eventually, the curer is certified by older practitioners and acquires a professional image. Patients believe in the skills of the curer, whom they consult and compensate.

We should not lose sight, ethnocentrically, of the difference between **scientific medicine** and Western medicine per se. Despite advances in technology, genomics, molecular biology, pathology, surgery, diagnostics, and applications, many Western medical procedures have little justification in logic or fact. Overprescription of drugs, unnecessary surgery, and the impersonality and inequality of the physician–patient relationship are questionable features of Western medical systems (see Briggs 2005 for linguistic aspects of this inequality). Also, overuse of antibiotics, not just for people but also in animal feed, seems to be triggering an explosion of resistant microorganisms, which may pose a long-term global public health hazard.

> **scientific medicine** As distinguished from Western medicine, a health care system based on scientific knowledge and procedures, encompassing such fields as pathology, microbiology, biochemistry, surgery, diagnostic technology, and applications.

Still, biomedicine surpasses tribal treatment in many ways. Although medicines such as quinine, coca, opium, ephedrine, and rauwolfia were discovered in nonindustrial societies, thousands of effective drugs are available today to treat myriad diseases. Preventive health care improved during the twentieth century. Today's surgical procedures are much safer and more effective than those of traditional societies.

But industrialization and globalization have spawned their own health problems. Modern stressors include poor nutrition, dangerous machinery, impersonal work, isolation, poverty, homelessness, substance abuse, and noise, air, and water pollution (see McElroy and Townsend 2003). Health problems in industrial nations are caused as much by economic, social, political, and cultural factors as by pathogens. In modern North America, for example, poverty contributes to many illnesses, including arthritis, heart conditions, back problems, and hearing and vision impairment (see Bailey 2000). Poverty also is a factor in the differential spread of infectious diseases.

In the United States and other developed countries today, good health has become something of an ethical imperative (Foucault 1990). Individuals are expected to regulate their behavior and shape themselves in keeping with new medical knowledge. Those who do so acquire the status of sanitary citizens—people with modern understanding of the body, health, and illness, who practice hygiene and depend on doctors and nurses when they are sick. People who act differently (e.g., smokers, overeaters, those who avoid doctors) are stigmatized as unsanitary and blamed for their own health problems (Briggs 2005; Foucault 1990).

Even getting an epidemic disease such as cholera or living in an infected neighborhood may be interpreted today as a moral failure. It's assumed that people who are properly informed and act rationally can avoid such "preventable" diseases. Individuals are expected to follow scientifically based imperatives (e.g., "boil water," "don't smoke"). People (e.g., gay men, Haitians, smokers, veterans) can become objects of avoidance and discrimination simply by belonging to a group seen as having a greater risk of getting a particular disease (Briggs 2005).

Medical anthropologists have served as cultural interpreters in public health programs, which must pay attention to local theories about the nature, causes, and treatment of illness. Health interventions cannot simply be forced on communities. They must fit into local cultures and be accepted by local people. When Western medicine is introduced, people usually retain many of their old methods while also accepting new ones (see Green 1987/1992). Native curers may go on treating certain conditions (spirit possession), whereas doctors may deal with others. If both modern and traditional specialists are consulted and the patient is cured, the native curer may get as much or more credit than the physician.

A more personal treatment of illness that emulates the non-Western curer-patient-community relationship could probably benefit Western systems. Western medicine tends to draw a rigid line between biological and psychological causation. Non-Western theories usually lack this sharp distinction, recognizing that poor health has intertwined physical, emotional, and social causes. The mind-body opposition is part of Western folk taxonomy, not of science (see also Brown 1998; Helman 2001; Joralemon 2006; Strathern and Stewart 1999).

Medical anthropologists increasingly are examining the impact of new scientific and medical techniques on ideas about life, death, and *personhood* (what is and is not a person). For decades, disagreements about personhood—about when life begins and ends—have been part of political and religious discussions of contraception, abortion, assisted suicide, and euthanasia (mercy killing). More recent additions to such discussions include stem cell research, frozen embryos, assisted reproduction, genetic screening, cloning, and life-prolonging medical treatments. Ideas about what it means to be human and to be alive or dead are being reformulated.

In the United States, the controversy surrounding the death of Terri Schiavo in 2005 brought such questions into public debate. Kaufman and Morgan (2005) emphasize the contrast between what they call low-tech and high-tech births and deaths in today's world. A desperately poor young mother dies of AIDS in Africa while half a world away an American child of privilege is born as the result of a $50,000 in-vitro fertilization procedure. Medical anthropologists increasingly are concerned with new and contrasting conditions that allow humans to enter, live, and depart life, and with how the boundaries of life and death are being questioned and negotiated in the twenty-first century.

CULTURE THINK

Consider one of the controversial health issues listed on pp. 72–73. What do you think, for example, of life-prolonging medical treatments and assisted suicide for terminal patients?

>> Anthropology and Business

Carol Taylor (1987) discusses the value of an "anthropologist-in-residence" in a large, complex organization, such as a hospital or a business. When information and decisions usually move through a rigid hierarchy, a free-ranging ethnographer can be a perceptive oddball. If allowed to observe and converse freely with all types and levels of personnel, the anthropologist may acquire a unique perspective on organizational conditions and problems. Also, high-tech companies, such as Xerox, IBM, and Apple, have employed anthropologists in various roles. Closely observing how people actually use computer products, anthropologists work with engineers to design products that are more user-friendly.

For many years anthropologists have used ethnography to study business settings (Arensberg 1987; Jordan 2003). For example, ethnographic research in an auto factory may view workers, managers, and executives as different social categories participating in a common social system. Each group has characteristic attitudes, values, and behavior patterns. These are transmitted through *microenculturation*, the process by which people learn particular roles in a limited social system. The free-ranging nature of ethnography takes the anthropologist back and forth from worker to executive. Each is an individual with a personal viewpoint and a cultural creature whose perspective is, to some extent, shared with other members of a group. Applied anthropologists have acted as "cultural brokers," translating managers' goals or workers' concerns to the other group (see Ferraro 2006).

For business, key features of anthropology include (1) ethnography and observation as ways of gathering data, (2) cross-cultural expertise, and (3) focus on cultural diversity. A primary business application of anthropology has to do with knowledge of how consumers use products.

By studying social interactions in factories such as this one, applied anthropologists have acted as "cultural brokers," translating managers' goals or workers' concerns to the other.

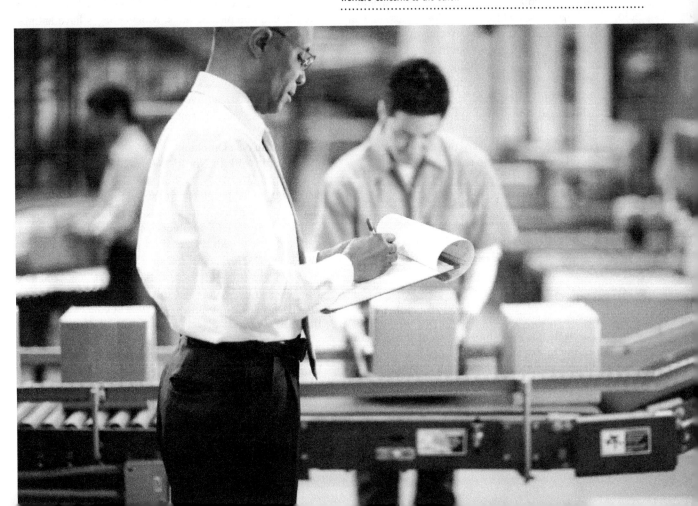

Businesses hire anthropologists because of the usefulness of observation in natural settings and the focus on cultural diversity. Thus, Hallmark Cards has hired anthropologists to observe parties, holidays, and celebrations of ethnic groups to improve its ability to design cards for targeted audiences. Anthropologists go into people's homes to see how they actually use products (see Sunderland and Denny 2007).

>> Careers and Anthropology

Many college students find anthropology interesting and consider majoring in it. However, their parents or friends may discourage them by asking, "What kind of job are you going to get with an anthropology major?" The first step in answering this question is to consider the more general question, "What do you do with any college major?" The answer is, "Not much, without a good bit of effort, thought, and planning." A survey of graduates of the University of Michigan's literary college showed that few had jobs that were clearly linked to their majors. Medicine, law, and many other professions require advanced degrees. Although many colleges offer bachelor's degrees in engineering, business, accounting, and social work, master's degrees often are needed to get the best jobs in those fields. Anthropologists, too, need an advanced degree, almost always a PhD, to find gainful employment in academic, museum, or applied anthropology.

A broad college education, and even a major in anthropology, can be an excellent foundation for success in many fields. A recent survey of women executives showed that most had not majored in business but in the social sciences or humanities. Only after graduating did they study business, obtaining a master's degree in business administration. These executives felt that the breadth of their college educations had contributed to their business careers. Anthropology majors go on to medical, law, and business schools and find success in many professions that often have little explicit connection to anthropology.

─CULTURE THINK─

What job(s) are you interested in having someday? How would anthropology be useful to you?

Anthropology's breadth provides knowledge and an outlook on the world that are useful in many kinds of work. For example, an anthropology major combined with a master's degree in business is excellent preparation for work in international business. Breadth is anthropology's hallmark. Anthropologists study people biologically, culturally, socially, and linguistically, across time

Anthropology Works

Employees of governmental social service agencies, such as family and children's services or departments of corrections, use anthropological sensitivities to understand cultural diversity and find solutions to problems. In one case, state employees assumed a young mother was neglecting her newborn and were about to put the child into foster care. An anthropologically trained caseworker realized that where the woman came from in Central America, mothers spent one month lying in while their extended family cared for the infant.

and space, in developed and underdeveloped nations, in simple and complex settings. Most colleges have anthropology courses that compare cultures and others that focus on particular world areas, such as Latin America, Asia, and Native North America. The knowledge of foreign areas acquired in such courses can be useful in many jobs. Anthropology's comparative outlook, its longstanding Third World focus, and its appreciation of diverse lifestyles combine to provide an excellent foundation for overseas employment (see Omohundro 2001).

Even for work in North America, the focus on culture is valuable. Every day we hear about cultural differences and about social problems whose solutions require a multicultural viewpoint—an ability to recognize and reconcile ethnic differences. Government, schools, and private firms constantly deal with people from different social classes, ethnic groups, and tribal backgrounds. Physicians, attorneys, social workers, police officers, judges, teachers, and students can all do a better job if they understand social differences in a part of the world such as ours that is one of the most ethnically diverse in history.

Planning and carrying out programs that affect the many social groups within a modern nation requires knowledge about the traditions and beliefs of those groups. Attention to social background and cultural categories helps ensure the welfare of affected ethnic groups, communities, and neighborhoods. Experience in planned social change—whether community organization in North America or economic development overseas—shows that a proper social study should be done before a project or policy is implemented. When local people want the change and it fits their lifestyle and traditions, it will be more successful, beneficial, and cost effective. There will be not only a more humane but also a more economical solution to a real social problem.

People with anthropology backgrounds are doing well in many fields. Even if one's job has little or nothing to do with anthropology in a formal or obvious sense, a background in anthropology provides a useful orientation when we work with our fellow human beings. For most of us, this means every day of our lives.

Talk with three fellow students of various cultural backgrounds (different ethnicity, religion, or region). Explain that you are investigating how different groups perceive and respond to illness and its treatment. Ask each student the following questions about their last illness:

- What symptoms did you note?
- What causes did you suspect?
- Does your group have any specific beliefs about the illness, its causes, and its treatment?
- Did you consult a physician or other health care practitioner? If so, what was the diagnosis and the recommended treatment? Did you find the diagnosis acceptable and the treatment, if you tried it, effective? (If you did not consult a practitioner, explain how you attempted to manage your illness.)
- Describe your level of comfort with the setting in which you received diagnosis and treatment.

From these cases, what conclusions can you draw about how cultural background influences our experience of illness, disease, and treatment?

For REVIEW

CULTURECLIPS

TO ACCESS THESE VIDEOS ON
YOUR COMPUTER, VISIT
www.mhhe.com/gezonqr

4-1

4-2

4-3

I. How can change be bad?

- Applied anthropology recognizes that designs for social or economic change may have unforeseen negative consequences. When foreign aid goes to the developmental priorities as seen by powerful interests rather than to where the need is greatest, the living standards of the needy may actually decline. Channeling inputs through the rich may severely widen economic disparities. Development projects that begin with an uneven distribution of resources often create greater skewing after the project. Projects not implemented by culturally compatible means, failing to use indigenous social models, are less likely to benefit the targeted area.

II. How can anthropology be applied to education, medicine, and business?

- Anthropology and education researchers study the various settings relevant to education. Researchers may identify problematic school practices, misconceptions held by teachers, and problems in interaction among teachers, students, and parents. Researchers then make policy recommendations. Medical anthropologists consider different societies' divergent health care systems and the cultural construction of health and illness. Medical anthropologists serve as cultural interpreters in public health programs and help ensure that interventions fit into local cultures. In businesses and other organizations, ethnographers develop a unique perspective on organizational conditions. They help resolve issues of cultural diversity, study how consumers use products, and translate managers' goals and workers' concerns to the other group.

III. How does the study of anthropology fit into a career path?

- Anthropology's comparative perspective, four-field breadth, and multicultural outlook provide a basis for working in international business and in careers in government, schools, medicine, private firms, or with interest groups that require the ability to recognize and reconcile ethnic differences and understand social problems. Anthropologists with advanced degrees can find employment in academic, museum, or applied anthropology. A background in anthropology can aid and enrich our work with people regardless of the type of employment.

Pop Quiz

1. The use of anthropological data, perspectives, theory, and methods to identify, assess, and solve contemporary problems is known most generally as:
   a. Scientific anthropology
   b. Urban anthropology
   c. Applied anthropology
   d. Development anthropology

2. According to the text, what is the most valuable and distinctive tool of the applied anthropologist?
   a. Knowledge of genetics.
   b. Familiarity with environmental problems.
   c. Statistical expertise.
   d. The ethnographic method.

3. An applied anthropologist today would most likely do which of the following?
   a. Supply information to help colonial regimes.
   b. Offer assistance to local people who lack a voice in the international political arena.
   c. Use survey research to solve economic problems for clients able to pay them.
   d. Supervise the controlled flooding of archaeological sites for underwater archaeology.

4. What situation or event does this chapter use to illustrate some dangers of the old applied anthropology?
   a. The drafting of the American Anthropological Association's ethics guidelines.
   b. Robert Redfield's work contrasting urban and rural communities.
   c. Malinowski's focus on Westernization and his aid of colonial expansion.
   d. The increase in undergraduate anthropology enrollments during the Vietnam War.

5. Which of the following would *not* be a goal of an applied anthropological approach to urban programs?
   a. Work with the target community to ensure that a proposed change is implemented effectively.
   b. Create a universal policy to be applied to all urban communities.
   c. Identify key social groups in the urban context.
   d. Elicit needs and desires from the target community and translate them to funding agencies.

6. In 1992 a white Los Angeles policeman shot and killed two unarmed Samoan brothers. Local Samoan leaders used the traditional *matai* ("chief") system to calm angry youths. This example illustrates:
   a. How an immigrant community can draw on its cultural traditions to adapt to urban life.

   b. That judicial anthropology has little application in urban settings.
   c. The tension between adjustment to a new environment and cultural traditions.
   d. That traditional "clan mentality" often results in excessive violence in urban settings.

7. Most generally, medical anthropology studies:
   a. How indigenous peoples maintain their traditional treatments in societies that offer technologically advanced health care.
   b. The application of traditional health knowledge to the Western medical system.
   c. The academic study and application of Western medicine to solve health problems around the world.
   d. How illness and its diagnosis and treatment are socially constructed and managed in different societies.

8. Which term refers most generally to beliefs, customs, specialists, and techniques aimed at ensuring health and diagnosing and curing illness?
   a. Disease theory
   b. Medical anthropology
   c. Health care system
   d. Shamanism

9. Why would a business or other complex organization hire an anthropologist?
   a. To gain access to the unique, ethnographic perspective on organizational problems.
   b. To learn about the Code of Ethics of the American Anthropological Association.
   c. To ensure that workers' concerns remain those of the workers, and are not translated to managers.
   d. Because anthropologists are cheaper than sociologists and tend to be more presentable.

10. Which of the following points about anthropology and careers is false?
    a. Anthropology offers broad knowledge about human life that is useful in many kinds of work.
    b. The knowledge of foreign cultures acquired in anthropology courses can serve as preparation for work in international business.
    c. Anthropology's focus on culture and its diversity is valuable to any career in which solutions require a multicultural viewpoint.
    d. To gain employment in academic, applied, or museum anthropology, students of anthropology rarely need an advanced degree.

1. (c), 2. (d), 3. (b), 4. (c), 5. (b), 6. (a), 7. (d), 8. (c), 9. (a), 10. (d)

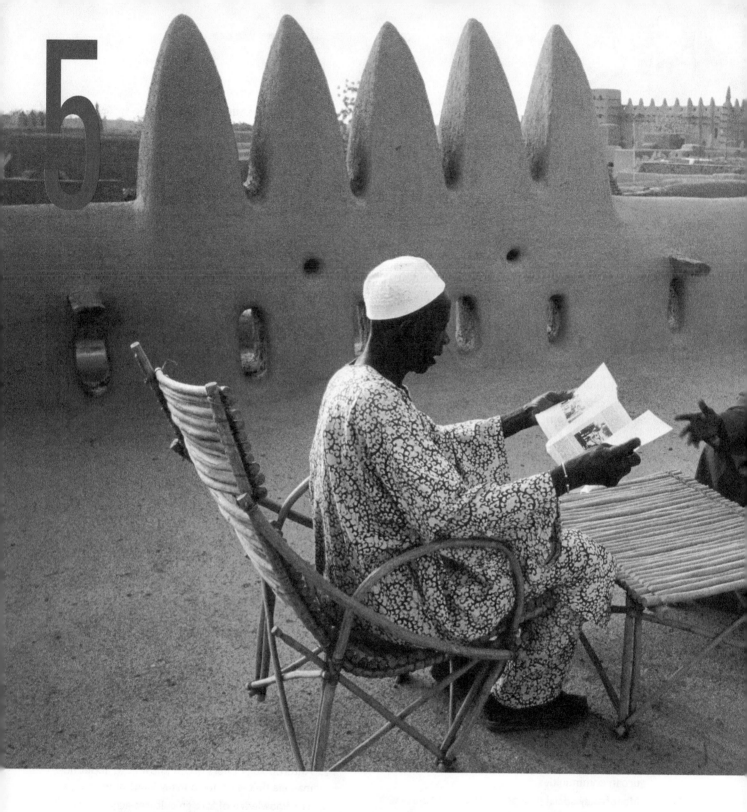

5

LANGUAGE AND COMMUNICATION

WHAT'S TO COME

Language

Nonhuman Primate Communication

Nonverbal Communication

The Structure of Language

Language, Thought, and Culture

Sociolinguistics

Historical Linguistics

UNDERSTANDING OURSELVES

Can you identify anything distinctive or unusual about the way you talk? If you're from Canada, Virginia, or Savannah, you may say "oot" instead of "out." A southerner may request a "soft drink" rather than the New Yorker's "soda." How might a "Valley Girl" or "surfer dude" talk? Usually when we pay attention to the way we talk, it's because someone else comments on our speech. It may be only when you move from one state or region to another that you realize how much of a regional accent you have.

Unlike grammarians, linguistic anthropologists are interested in what people do say, rather than what they should say. Speech differences are associated with, and tell us a lot about, social variation, such as region, education, ethnic background, and gender. Men and women talk differently. We're sure you can think of examples based on your own experience, although you probably never realized that women tend to peripheralize their vowels (think of the sounds in "weasel" and "whee"), whereas men tend to centralize them (think of "rough" and "ugh"). Men are more likely to speak "ungrammatically" than women are.

Men and women also show differences in their sports and color terminologies. Men typically know more terms related to sports, make more distinctions among them (e.g., *runs* versus *points*), and try to use the terms more precisely than women do. Correspondingly, influenced more by the fashion and cosmetics industries, women use more color terms and attempt to use them more precisely than men do. For example, women are much more likely than men to distinguish between various shades of purple, such as mauve, lilac, lavender, and wisteria. Rare is the man who on the spur of the moment can imagine the difference between fuchsia and magenta or grape and aubergine.

- What makes language different from other forms of communication?
- How do anthropologists and linguists study language in general, and specific languages in particular?
- How does language change over short and long periods?

>> Language

Linguistic anthropology illustrates anthropology's characteristic interests in diversity, comparison, and change—but here the focus is on language. Language, spoken (*speech*) and written (*writing,* which has existed for about six thousand years), is our primary means of communication. Like culture in general, of which language is a part, language is transmitted through learning. Language is based on arbitrary, learned associations between words and the things they stand for. Unlike the communication systems of other animals, language allows us to discuss the past and future, share our experiences with others, and benefit from their experiences.

call systems Systems of communication among nonhuman primates, composed of a limited number of sounds that vary in intensity and duration; tied to environmental stimuli.

Anthropologists study language in its social and cultural context (see Bonvillain 2008; Salzmann 2007). Some linguistic anthropologists reconstruct ancient languages by comparing their contemporary descendants and, in doing so, make discoveries about history. Others study linguistic differences to discover the varied worldviews and patterns of thought in a multitude of cultures. Sociolinguists examine dialects and styles in a single language to show how speech reflects social differences, as in the above discussion of regional speech contrasts. Linguistic anthropologists also explore the role of language in colonization and globalization (Geis 1987; Thomas 1999).

歡迎
Welcome
Bienvenue
Bienvenido
Willkommen
Benvenuto
Boas-Vindas
환영
ようこそ

>> Nonhuman Primate Communication

CALL SYSTEMS

Only humans speak. No other animal has anything approaching the complexity of language. The natural communication systems of other primates (monkeys and apes) are **call systems.** These vocal systems consist of a limited number of sounds—*calls*—that are produced only when particular environmental stimuli are encountered. Such calls may be varied in intensity and duration, but they are much less flexible than language because they are automatic and can't be combined. When primates encounter food and danger simultaneously, they can make only one call. They can't combine the calls for food and danger into a single utterance, indicating that both are present. At some point in human evolution, however, our ancestors began to combine calls and to understand the combinations. The number of calls also expanded, eventually becoming too great to be transmitted even partly through the genes. Communication came to rely almost totally on learning.

STUDY TIP

Call systems, used in animal communication, have three features:

- They have a limited number of sounds;

- They are used only when certain stimuli are present;

- They cannot be combined to produce more complex messages.

Although wild primates use call systems, the vocal tract of apes is not suitable for speech. Until the 1960s, attempts to teach spoken language to apes suggested that they lack linguistic abilities. In the 1950s, a couple raised a chimpanzee, Viki, as a member of their family and systematically tried to teach her to speak. Viki learned only four words: "mama," "papa," "up," and "cup."

Apes, such as these Congo chimpanzees, use call systems to communicate in the wild. Their vocal systems consist of a limited number of sounds—calls—that are produced only when they encounter particular environmental stimuli.

Hearing-impaired dancers in China's Disabled People's Performing Art Troupe communicate through sign language while undergoing physical conditioning.

SIGN LANGUAGE

More recent experiments have shown that apes can learn to use language, if not speak it (Fouts 1997; Miles 1983). Several apes have learned to converse with people through means other than speech. One such communication system is American Sign Language (ASL), which is widely used by hearing-impaired people in the United States, Canada, and several other nations. British Sign Language (BSL), used in the United Kingdom, differs significantly from ASL, and the two are not mutually intelligible. Sign languages employ a limited number of basic gesture units that are analogous to sounds in spoken language. These units combine to form words and larger units of meaning.

The first chimpanzee to learn ASL was Washoe, a female, who died in 2007 at the age of forty-two. Captured in West Africa, R. Allen Gardner and Beatrice Gardner, scientists at the University of Nevada in Reno, acquired Washoe in 1966, when she was a year old. Four years later, she moved to Norman, Oklahoma, to a converted farm that had become the Institute for Primate Studies. Washoe revolutionized the discussion of the language-learning abilities of apes (Carey 2007). At first she lived in a trailer and heard no spoken language. The researchers always used ASL to communicate with each other in her presence. The chimp gradually acquired a vocabulary of more than one hundred signs representing English words (Gardner, Gardner, and

Did You Know?

Kanzi is a bonobo, a great ape similar to a chimpanzee but genetically and behaviorally closer to humans. He learned to communicate using symbols, or lexigrams, when he was very young. His primary mentor, Sue Savage-Rumbaugh, reported that eight-year-old Kanzi could communicate with grammatical complexity similar to that of a two-year-old child.

her son Sequoia, who died in infancy (Fouts, Fouts, and Van Cantfort 1989).

Because of their size and strength as adults, gorillas are less likely subjects than chimps for such experiments. Lean adult male gorillas in the wild weigh 400 pounds (180 kilograms), and full-grown females can easily reach 250 pounds (110 kilograms). Because of this, psychologist Penny Patterson's work with gorillas at Stanford University seems more daring than the chimp experiments. Patterson raised her now full-grown female gorilla, Koko, in a trailer next to a Stanford museum. Koko's vocabulary surpasses that of any chimp. She regularly employs four hundred ASL signs and has used about seven hundred at least once.

Koko and the chimps also show that apes share still another linguistic ability with humans: **productivity.** Speakers routinely use the rules of their language to produce entirely new expressions that are comprehensible to other native speakers. A human speaker could, for example, create "baboonlet" to refer to a baboon infant. This is done through analogy with English words in which the suffix -*let* designates the young of a species. Anyone who speaks English immediately understands the meaning of the new word. Koko, Washoe, Lucy, and others have shown that apes also are able to use language productively. Lucy used gestures she already knew to create "drinkfruit" for watermelon. Washoe, seeing a swan for the first time, coined "waterbird." Koko, who knew the gestures for "finger" and "bracelet," formed "finger bracelet" when she was given a ring.

Chimps and gorillas have a rudimentary capacity for language. They may never have invented a meaningful gesture system in the wild. Given such a system, however, they show many humanlike abilities in learning and using it. Of course, language use by apes is a product of human intervention and teaching. The experiments mentioned here do not suggest that apes can invent language (nor are human children ever faced with that task). However, young apes have managed to learn the basics of gestural language. They can employ it productively and creatively, although not with the sophistication of human ASL users.

Apes also have demonstrated linguistic **displacement.** Absent in call systems, this is a key ingredient in language. Normally, each call is tied to an environmental stimulus, such as food. Calls are uttered only when that stimulus is present. Displacement means

Van Cantfort 1989). At the age of two, Washoe began to combine as many as five signs into rudimentary sentences, such as "You, me, go out, hurry."

The second chimp to learn ASL was Lucy, Washoe's junior by one year. Lucy died, or was murdered by poachers, in 1986, after having been introduced to "the wild" in Africa in 1979 (Carter 1988). From her second day of life until her move to Africa, Lucy lived with a family in Norman, Oklahoma. Roger Fouts, a researcher from the nearby Institute for Primate Studies, came two days a week to test and improve Lucy's knowledge of ASL. During the rest of the week, Lucy used ASL to converse with her foster parents. After acquiring language, Washoe and Lucy exhibited several human traits: swearing, joking, telling lies, and trying to teach language to others (Fouts 1997).

cultural transmission A basic feature of language; transmission through learning.

productivity The ability to use the rules of one's language to create new expressions comprehensible to other speakers; a basic feature of language.

When irritated, Washoe called her monkey neighbors at the institute "dirty monkeys." Lucy insulted her "dirty cat." On arrival at Lucy's place, Fouts once found a pile of excrement on the floor. When he asked the chimp what it was, she replied, "dirty, dirty," her expression for feces. Asked whose "dirty, dirty" it was, Lucy named Fouts's coworker, Sue. When Fouts refused to believe her about Sue, the chimp blamed the excrement on Fouts himself.

Cultural transmission of a communication system through learning is a fundamental attribute of language. Washoe, Lucy, and other chimps have tried to teach ASL to other animals, including their own offspring. Washoe taught gestures to other institute chimps, including

"He says he wants a lawyer."

Human Language

Human Language	Primate Call Systems
Has the capacity to speak of things and events that are not present (displacement).	Are stimuli-dependent; the food call will be made in the presence of food; it cannot be faked.
Has the capacity to generate new expressions by combining other expressions (productivity).	Consist of a limited number of calls that cannot be combined to produce new calls.
Is group specific in that all humans have the capacity for language, but each linguistic community has its own language, which is culturally transmitted.	Tend to be species specific, with little variation among communities of the same species for each call.

Primate Call Systems

that humans can talk about things that are not present. We don't have to see the objects before we say the words. Human conversations are not limited by place. We can discuss the past and future, share our experiences with others, and benefit from theirs.

Patterson has described several examples of Koko's capacity for displacement (Patterson 1978). The gorilla once expressed sorrow about having bitten Penny three days earlier. Koko has used the sign "later" to postpone doing things she doesn't want to do. Table 5.1 summarizes the contrasts between language, whether sign or spoken, and call systems.

Certain scholars doubt the linguistic abilities of chimps and gorillas (Sebeok and Umiker-Sebeok 1980; Terrace 1979). They contend that Koko and the chimps are comparable to trained circus animals and don't really have linguistic ability. In defense of Patterson and the other researchers (Hill 1978; Van Cantfort and Rimpau 1982), only one of their critics has worked with an ape. This was Herbert Terrace, whose experience teaching a chimp sign language lacked the continuity and personal involvement that have contributed so much to Patterson's success with Koko.

No one denies the huge difference between human language and gorilla signs. There is a major gap between the ability to write a book or say a prayer and the few hundred gestures employed by a well-trained chimp. Apes aren't people, but they aren't just animals either. Let Koko express it: When asked by a reporter whether she was a person or an animal, Koko chose neither. Instead, she signed "fine animal gorilla" (Patterson 1978). For the latest on Koko, see http://koko.org.

Hieroglyphics from an Egyptian tomb illustrate this early form of writing. Language has been around a lot longer than writing. How much longer, do you think?

THE ORIGIN OF LANGUAGE

Although the capacity to remember and combine linguistic symbols may be latent in the apes (Miles 1983), human evolution was needed for this seed to flower into language. A mutated gene known as FOXP2 helps explain why humans speak and chimps don't (Paulson 2005). The key role of FOXP2 in speech came to light in a study of a British family, identified only as KE, half of whose members had an inherited, severe deficit in speech (Trivedi 2001). The same variant form of FOXP2 that is found in chimpanzees causes this disorder. Those who have the nonspeech version of the gene cannot make the fine tongue and lip movements necessary for clear speech, and their speech is unintelligible—even to other members of the KE family (Trivedi 2001). Chimps have the same (genetic) sequence as the KE family members with the speech deficit. Comparing chimp and human genomes, it appears that the speech-friendly form of FOXP2 took hold in humans around 150,000 years ago. This mutation conferred selec-

> **displacement** A linguistic capacity that allows humans to talk about things and events that are not present.

tive advantages (linguistic and cultural abilities) that allowed those who had it to spread at the expense of those who did not (Paulson 2005).

Language offered a tremendous adaptive advantage to *Homo sapiens.* Language permits the information stored by a human society to exceed by far that of any nonhuman group. Language is a uniquely effective vehicle for learning. Because we can speak of things we have never experienced, we can anticipate responses before we encounter the stimuli. Adaptation can occur more rapidly in *Homo* than in the other primates because our adaptive means are more flexible.

CULTURE THINK

How does language provide an adaptive advantage? In other words, how do you think it has helped humans survive?

>> Nonverbal Communication

Language is our principal means of communicating, but it isn't the only one we use. We *communicate* when we transmit information about ourselves to others and receive such information from them. Our expressions, stances, gestures, and movements, even if unconscious, convey information and are part of our

kinesics The study of communication through body movements, stances, gestures, and facial expressions.

communication styles. Deborah Tannen (1990) discusses differences in the communication styles of American men and women, and her comments go beyond language. She notes that American girls and women tend to look directly at each other when they talk, whereas American boys and men do not. Males are more likely to look straight ahead rather than turn and make eye contact with someone, especially another man, seated beside them. Also, in conversational groups, American men tend to relax and sprawl out. American women may adopt a similar relaxed posture in all-female groups, but when they are with men, they tend to draw in their limbs and adopt a tighter stance.

Kinesics is the study of communication through body movements, stances, gestures, and expressions. Linguists pay attention not only to what is said but to how it is said, and to features besides language itself that convey meaning. A speaker's enthusiasm is conveyed not only through words, but also through facial expressions, gestures, and other signs of animation. We use gestures, such as a jab of the hand, for emphasis. We vary our intonation and the pitch or loudness of our voices. We communicate through strategic pauses, and even by being silent. An effective communication strategy may be to alter pitch, voice level, and grammatical forms, such as declaratives ("I am . . ."), imperatives ("Go forth . . ."), and questions ("Are you . . . ?"). Culture teaches us that certain manners and styles should accompany certain kinds of speech. Our demeanor, verbal and nonverbal, when our favorite team is winning would be out of place at a funeral or when a somber subject is being discussed.

Culture always plays a role in shaping the "natural." Cross-culturally, nodding does not always mean affirmative, nor does head shaking from side to side always mean negative. Brazilians wag a finger to mean no. Americans say "uh huh" to affirm, whereas in Madagascar a similar

Men and women have different communication styles, as illustrated in these two photos. Men, for example, are less likely to engage in face-to-face conversation than women are. What differences do you notice in the gender-based communication styles shown here?

CULTURETHINK

The late anthropologist Edward T. Hall coined the term *proxemics* to refer to the study of spatial relations between people. Cross-culturally there are different norms regarding personal space. Once you know the norms, you can learn a lot by observing the distance between people. How big is your personal space "bubble"? Does it get larger or smaller when you are with strangers, friends, intimate others?

taining all its morphemes and their meanings. **Syntax** refers to the arrangement and order of words in phrases and sentences. For example, do nouns usually come before or after verbs? Do adjectives normally precede or follow the nouns they modify?

SPEECH SOUNDS

From the movies and TV, and from meeting foreigners, we know something about foreign accents and mispronunciations. We know that someone with a marked French accent doesn't pronounce *r* like an American does. But at least someone from France can distinguish between "craw" and "claw," which someone from Japan may not be able to do. The difference between *r* and *l* makes a difference in English

> **descriptive linguistics** The scientific study of a spoken language, including its phonology, morphology, lexicon, and syntax.
>
> **phonology** The study of sounds used in speech.
>
> **morphology** The study of form; used in linguistics (the study of morphemes and word construction) and for form in general—for example, biomorphology relates to physical form.
>
> **lexicon** Vocabulary; a dictionary containing all the morphemes in a language and their meaning.
>
> **syntax** The arrangement and order of words in phrases and sentences.
>
> **phoneme** Significant sound contrast in a language that serves to distinguish meaning, as in minimal pairs.

sound is made to deny. Americans point with their fingers; the people of Madagascar point with their lips.

Body movements communicate social differences. In Japan, bowing is a regular part of social interaction, but different bows are used depending on the social status of the people who are interacting. In Madagascar and Polynesia, people of lower status should not hold their heads above those of people of higher status. When one approaches someone older or of higher status, one bends one's knees and lowers one's head as a sign of respect. In Madagascar, one always does this, for politeness, when passing between two people. Although our gestures, facial expressions, and body stances have roots in our primate heritage, and can be seen in the monkeys and the apes, they have not escaped cultural shaping. Language, which is so highly dependent on the use of symbols, is the domain of communication in which culture plays the strongest role.

CULTURETHINK

Sometimes the meaning of headlines is unclear due to confusion about parts of speech and word order. This is technically referred to as *syntactic* (from syntax) *ambiguity*. What, specifically, makes these headlines confusing—and humorous? Squad Helps Dog Bite Victim; Drunk Gets Nine Months in Violin Case; Iraqi Head Seeks Arms.

>> The Structure of Language

The scientific study of a spoken language, called **descriptive linguistics,** involves several interrelated areas of analysis: phonology, morphology, lexicon, and syntax. **Phonology,** the study of speech sounds, considers which sounds are present and significant in a given language. **Morphology** studies the way sounds combine to form *morphemes*—words and their meaningful parts. Thus, the word *cats* would be analyzed as containing two morphemes—*cat,* the name for a kind of animal, and *-s,* a morpheme indicating plurality. A language's **lexicon** is a dictionary con-

and in French, but it doesn't in Japanese. In linguistics we say that the difference between *r* and *l* is *phonemic* in English and French but not in Japanese. In English and French, *r* and *l* are phonemes but not in Japanese. A **phoneme** is a sound contrast that makes a difference, that differentiates meaning.

We find the phonemes in a given language by comparing *minimal pairs*—words that resemble each other in all but one sound. The words have different meanings, but they differ in just one sound. The contrasting sounds are therefore phonemes in that language. An example in English is the minimal pair *pit/bit*. These two words are distinguished by a single sound contrast between /p/ and /b/ (we enclose phonemes in slashes). Thus /p/ and /b/ are phonemes in English. Another example

Source: From Aspects of Language, 3rd ed. by Bolinger, Fig. 2.1. Copyright © 1981 Heinle/Arts & Sciences, a part of Cengage Learning, Inc. Reprinted by permission.

Vowel Phonemes in Standard American English

Tongue high

i   u

ɪ   ʊ

Mid   e   ə   o

ɛ   ɔ

Tongue low   æ   a

	Tongue front	Central	Tongue back

High front (spread)	[i]	as in *beat*
Lower high front (spread)	[ɪ]	as in *bit*
Mid front (spread)	[e]	as in *bait*
Lower mid front (spread)	[ɛ]	as in *bet*
Low front	[æ]	as in *bat*
Central	[ə]	as in *butt*
Low back	[a]	as in *pot*
Lower mid back (rounded)	[ɔ]	as in *bought*
Mid back (rounded)	[o]	as in *boat*
Lower high back (rounded)	[ʊ]	as in *put*
High back (rounded)	[u]	as in *boot*

Vocal phonemes are shown according to height of tongue and tongue position at front, center, or back of mouth. Phonetic symbols are identified by English words that include them; note that most are minimal pairs.

is the different vowel sound of *bit* and *beat* (see "Vowel Phonemes in Standard American English," above). This contrast serves to distinguish these two words and the two vowel phonemes written /ɪ/ and /i/ in English.

Standard (American) English (SE), the "region-free" dialect of TV network newscasters, has about thirty-five phonemes—at least eleven vowels and twenty-four consonants. The number of phonemes varies from language to language—from fifteen to sixty, averaging between thirty and forty. The number of phonemes also varies between dialects of a given language. In North American English, for example, vowel phonemes vary noticeably from dialect to dialect. Try pronouncing the words in the figure above, paying attention to (or asking someone else) whether you (or your partner) can distinguish each of the vowel sounds. Most North Americans don't pronounce them all.

Phonetics is the study of speech sounds in general, what people actually say in various languages. **Phonemics** studies only the *significant* sound contrasts (phonemes) of a given language. In English, like /r/ and /l/ (remember *craw* and *claw*), /b/ and /v/ also are phonemes, occurring in minimal pairs like *bat* and *vat*. In Spanish, however, the contrast between [b] and [v] doesn't distinguish meaning, and they therefore are not phonemes (we enclose sounds that are not phonemic in brackets). Spanish speakers

phonetics The study of speech sounds in general; what people actually say in various languages.

phonemics The study of significant sound contrasts (phonemes) of a particular language.

normally use the [b] sound to pronounce words spelled with either *b* or *v*.

In any language, a given phoneme extends over a phonetic range. In English the phoneme /p/ ignores the phonetic contrast between the [pʰ] in *pin* and the [p] in *spin*. Most English speakers don't even notice that there is a phonetic difference. The [pʰ] is aspirated, so that a puff of air follows the [p]. The [p] in *spin* is not. (To see the difference, light a match, hold it in front of your mouth, and watch the flame as you pronounce the two words.) The contrast between [pʰ] and [p] is phonemic in some languages, such as Hindi (spoken in India). That is, there are words whose meaning is distinguished only by the contrast between an aspirated and an unaspirated [p].

Native speakers vary in their pronunciation of certain phonemes, such as the /e/ phoneme in the midwestern United States. This variation is important in the evolution of language. Without shifts in pronunciation, there could be no linguistic change. The section on sociolinguistics later in the chapter considers phonetic variation and its relationship to social divisions and the evolution of language.

CULTURE THINK

Say the following words casually, with an informal but acceptable pronunciation: top, stop, little, kitten, Atlanta. Are the *t*'s all pronounced the same? How many variants can you count? (Note: One of them is aspirated.) The sound we think of as *t* can be pronounced in several ways.

>> Language, Thought, and Culture

The well-known linguist Noam Chomsky (1957) has argued that the human brain contains a limited set of rules for organizing language, so that all languages have a common structural basis. (Chomsky calls this set of rules *universal grammar.*) The fact that people can learn foreign languages and that words and ideas translate from one language to another supports Chomsky's position that all humans have similar linguistic abilities and thought processes. Another line of support comes from creole languages. Such languages develop from pidgins—languages that form in situations of acculturation, when different societies come into contact and must devise a system of communication. Pidgins based on English and native languages developed through trade and colonialism in many world areas, including China, Papua New Guinea, and West Af-

Imagine life without Twitter, Facebook, and texting—means of communication that allow people to stay in almost constant contact with others. Facebook, created in 2004, allows people to send public posts and private messages, share photos, organize events, and remember birthdays. Twitter, launched in 2006, was developed as a way of sending text messages to multiple people. People now use it to keep track of their friends and celebrity favorites (e.g., Ashton Kutcher, Sarah Palin). People emit "tweets" to update people who "follow" them. According to Mashable: The Social Media Guide (mashable.com), Twitter helps people get to know new sides of other people. How does cybercommunication change the quality and quantity of friendships and family ties? How does it affect our awareness of world, national, and local events? Try going a day or even a week without any form of communication that is not absolutely necessary.

rica. Eventually, after generations of being spoken, pidgins may develop into *creole languages*. These are more mature languages, with developed grammatical rules and native speakers (people who learn the language as their primary one during enculturation).

Creoles are spoken in several Caribbean societies. Gullah, which is spoken by African Americans on coastal islands in South Carolina and Georgia, is a creole language. Supporting the idea that creoles are based on universal grammar is the fact that such languages all share certain features. Syntactically, all use particles (e.g., will, was) to form future and past tenses and multiple negation to deny or negate (e.g., he don't got none). Also, all form questions by changing inflection rather than by changing word order. For example, "You're going home for the holidays?" (with a rising tone at the end) rather than "Are you going home for the holidays?"

THE SAPIR-WHORF HYPOTHESIS

Other linguists and anthropologists take a different approach to the relation between language and thought. Rather than seeking universal linguistic structures and processes, they believe that different languages produce different ways of thinking. This position sometimes is known as the **Sapir-Whorf hypothesis,** after Edward Sapir (1931) and his student Benjamin Lee Whorf (1956), its prominent early advocates. Sapir and Whorf argued that the grammatical categories of particular languages lead their speakers to think about things in different ways. For example, English divides time into past, present,

> **Sapir-Whorf hypothesis**
> Theory that different languages produce different ways of thinking.

and future. Hopi, a language of the Pueblo region of the Native American Southwest, does not. Rather, Hopi distinguishes between events that exist or have existed (what we use present and past to discuss) and those that don't or don't yet (our future events, along with imaginary and hypothetical events). Whorf argued that this difference leads Hopi speakers to think about time and reality in different ways than English speakers do.

A similar example comes from Portuguese, which employs a future subjunctive verb form, introducing a degree of uncertainty into discussions of the future. In English we routinely use the future tense to talk about something we think will happen. We don't feel the need to qualify "The sun'll come out tomorrow," by adding "if it doesn't go supernova." We don't hesitate to proclaim, "I'll see you next year," even when we can't be absolutely sure we will. The Portuguese future subjunctive qualifies the future

Shown here (in 1995) is Leigh Jenkins, who was or is director of cultural preservation for the Hopi council. The Hopi language would not distinguish between was and is in the previous sentence. For the Hopi, present and past are real and are expressed grammatically in the same way, while the future remains hypothetical and has a different grammatical expression.

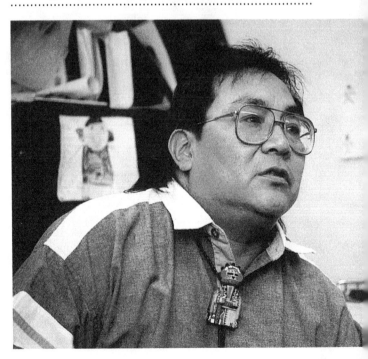

event, recognizing that the future can't be certain. Our way of expressing the future as certain is so ingrained that we don't even think about it, just as the Hopi don't see the need to distinguish between present and past, both of which are real, while the future remains hypothetical. It seems, however, that language does not tightly restrict thought, because cultural changes can produce changes in thought and in language, as we'll see in the next section (see also Gumperz and Levinson 1996).

FOCAL VOCABULARY

As mentioned earlier, a lexicon (or vocabulary) is a language's dictionary, its set of names for things, events, and ideas. Lexicon influences perception. Thus, Eskimos (or Inuit) have several distinct words for differ-

focal vocabulary A set of words and distinctions that are particularly important to certain groups (those with particular foci of experience or activity), such as types of snow to Eskimos or skiers.

ent types of snow that in English are all called *snow*. Most English speakers never notice the differences between these types of snow and might have trouble seeing them even if someone pointed them out. Eskimos recognize and think about differences in snow that English speakers don't see because our language gives us just one word.

Illustrating focal vocabulary, Eskimos, or Inuit, have several distinct words for different types of snow that in English are all called "snow."

CULTURETHINK

Much of what we communicate is nonverbal and refers to our emotional states and intentions. This leads to frequent miscommunication in texting and online messaging. People use emoticons (☺, ☹, :~/ [confused], :~0 ['hah!' no way!]) and abbreviations (lol—laugh out loud; lmao—laugh my a** off; wtf—what the f**; omg—oh my god) to fill in what would otherwise be communicated by tone of voice, laughter, and facial expression. Have you ever had any miscommunications when texting or emailing? What strategies do you use to communicate more clearly?

Similarly, the Nuer of Sudan have an elaborate vocabulary to describe cattle. Eskimos have several words for snow, and Nuer have dozens for cattle because of their particular histories, economies, and environments (Brown 1958; Eastman 1975). When the need arises, English speakers can also elaborate their snow and cattle vocabularies. For example, skiers name varieties of snow with words that are missing from the lexicons of Florida retirees. Similarly, the cattle vocabulary of a Texas rancher is much more ample than that of a salesperson in a New York City department store. Such specialized sets of terms and distinctions that are particularly important to certain groups (those with particular *foci* of experience or activity) are known as **focal vocabulary.**

Vocabulary is the area of language that changes most readily. New words and distinctions, when needed, appear and spread. For example, who would have "texted" or sent a "tweet" a generation ago? Names for items get simpler as they become common and important. A television has become a *TV,* an automobile a *car,* a digital video disc a *DVD,* and cell phone applications *apps.*

Language, culture, and thought are interrelated. Opposing the Sapir-Whorf hypothesis, however, it might be more accurate to say that changes in culture produce changes in language and thought than to say the reverse. Consider differences between female and male Americans

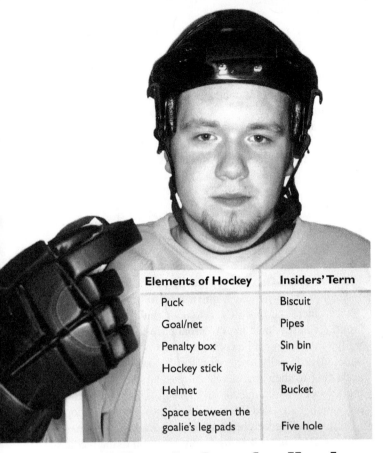

Elements of Hockey	Insiders' Term
Puck	Biscuit
Goal/net	Pipes
Penalty box	Sin bin
Hockey stick	Twig
Helmet	Bucket
Space between the goalie's leg pads	Five hole

Focal Vocabulary for Hockey

regarding the color terms they use (Lakoff 2004). Distinctions implied by such terms as *salmon, rust, peach, beige, teal, mauve, cranberry,* and *dusky orange* aren't in the vocabularies of most American men. Many of them weren't even in American women's lexicons fifty years ago. These changes reflect changes in American economy, society, and culture. Color terms and distinctions have increased with the growth of the fashion and cosmetic industries. A similar contrast (and growth) in Americans' lexicons shows up in football, basketball, and hockey vocabularies. Sports fans, more often males than females, use more terms concerning, and make more elaborate distinctions between, the games they watch, such as hockey. Thus, cultural contrasts and changes affect lexical distinctions (for instance, *peach* versus *salmon*) within semantic domains (for instance, color terminology). **Semantics** refers to a language's meaning system.

The ways in which people divide the world—the lexical contrasts they perceive as meaningful or significant—reflect their experiences (see Bicker, Sillitoe, and Pottier 2004). Anthropologists have discovered that certain sets of vocabulary items evolve in a determined order. For example, after studying more than a hundred languages, Berlin and Kay (1969/1992) discovered ten basic color terms: *white, black,*

red, yellow, blue, green, brown, pink, orange, and *purple* (they evolved in more or less that order). The number of terms varied with cultural complexity. Representing one extreme were Papua New Guinea cultivators and Australian hunters and gatherers, who used only two basic terms, which translate as *black* and *white* or *dark* and *light.* At the other end of the continuum were European and Asian languages with all the color terms. Color terminology was most developed in areas with a history of using dyes and artificial coloring.

>> Sociolinguistics

No language is a uniform system in which everyone talks just like everyone else. The field of **sociolinguistics** investigates relationships between social and linguistic variation (Romaine 2000; Trudgill 2000). How do different speakers use a given language? How do linguistic features correlate with social diversity and stratification, including class, ethnic, and gender differences (Tannen 1990, 1993)? How is language used to express, reinforce, or resist power (Geis 1987; Lakoff 2000)?

Sociolinguists focus on features that vary systematically with social position and situation. To study variation, sociolinguists observe, define, and measure variable use of language in real-world situations. To show that linguistic features correlate with social, economic, and political differences, social attributes of speakers must be measured and related to speech (Fasold 1990; Labov 1972a).

> **semantics** A language's meaning system.
>
> **sociolinguistics** Study of relationships between social and linguistic variation; study of language in its social context.

How might social variation show up in texting?

Anthropology Works

Understanding language variation can help educators identify the difference between genuine speech disabilities and dialect differences. Anthropological training shows that different ways of pronouncing words are not necessarily due to individual deficiencies.

Variation within a language at a given time is historical change in progress. The same forces that, working gradually, have produced large-scale linguistic change over the centuries are still at work today. Linguistic change doesn't occur in a vacuum but in society. When new ways of speaking are associated with social factors, they are imitated, and they spread. In this way, a language changes.

LINGUISTIC DIVERSITY WITHIN NATIONS

As an illustration of the linguistic variation encountered in all nations, consider the contemporary United States. Ethnic diversity is revealed by the fact that millions of Americans learn first languages other than English. Spanish is the most common. Most of those people eventually become bilinguals, adding English as a second language. In many multilingual (including colonized) nations, people use two languages on different occasions—one in the home, for example, and the other on the job or in public.

style shifts Variations in speech in different contexts.

diglossia The existence of "high" (formal) and "low" (familial) dialects of a single language, such as German.

Whether bilingual or not, we all vary our speech in different contexts; we engage in **style shifts.** In certain parts of Europe, people regularly switch dialects. This phenomenon, known as **diglossia,** applies to "high" and "low" variants of the same language, for example, in German and Flemish (spoken in Belgium). People employ the high variant at universities and in writing, professions, and the mass media. They use the low variant for ordinary conversation with family members and friends.

Just as social situations influence our speech, so do geographical, cultural, and socioeconomic differences. Many dialects coexist in the United States with Standard (American) English (SE). SE itself is a dialect that differs, say, from "BBC English," which is the preferred dialect in Great Britain. Different dialects are equally effective as systems of communication, which is language's main job. Our tendency to think of particular dialects as cruder or more sophisticated than others is a social rather than a linguistic judgment. We rank certain speech patterns as better or worse because we recognize that they are used by groups that we also rank. People who say *dese, dem,* and *dere* instead of *these, them,* and *there* communicate perfectly well with anyone who recognizes that the *d* sound systematically replaces the *th* sound in their speech. However, this form of speech has become an indicator of low social rank. We call it, like the use of *ain't,* "uneducated speech." The use of *dem, dese,* and *dere* is one of many phonological differences that Americans recognize and look down on.

GENDER SPEECH CONTRASTS

Comparing men and women, there are differences in phonology, grammar, and vocabulary, and in the body stances and movements that accompany speech (Eckert and McConnell-Ginet 2003; Lakoff 2004; Tannen 1990). In phonology, American women tend to pronounce their vowels more peripherally ("rant," "rint" when saying "rent"), whereas men tend to pronounce theirs more centrally ("runt"). In public contexts, Japanese women tend to adopt an artificially high voice, for the sake of politeness, according to their traditional culture. Women tend to be more careful about uneducated speech. This trend shows up in both the United States and England. Men may adopt working-class speech because they associate it with masculinity. Perhaps women pay more attention to the media, in which standard dialects are employed.

According to Robin Lakoff (2004), the use of certain types of words and expressions has been associated with women's traditional lesser power in American society (see also Coates 1986; Romaine 1999; Tannen 1990, 1993). For example, "Oh dear," "Oh fudge," and "Goodness!" are less forceful than "Hell" and "Damn." Watch the lips of a disgruntled male athlete in a televised competition, such as a football game. What's the likelihood he's saying "Phooey on you"? Women also are more likely to use such adjec-

CULTURE THINK

The text identifies several factors that make the speech of men and women different, including pronunciation, types of words and expressions, and overall linguistic styles. Pay attention to the conversations around you: Do you notice these differences? Do you agree with Tannen that men tend to value hierarchy, while women focus on building relationships?

tives as *adorable, charming, sweet, cute, lovely,* and *divine* than men are.

Differences in the linguistic strategies and behavior of men and women are examined in several books by the well-known sociolinguist Deborah Tannen (1990, 1993). Tannen uses the terms "rapport" and "report" to contrast women's and men's overall linguistic styles. Women, says Tannen, typically use language and the body movements that accompany it to build rapport—social connections with others. Men, on the other hand, tend to make reports, reciting information that serves to establish a place for themselves in a hierarchy, as they also attempt to determine the relative ranks of their conversation mates.

STRATIFICATION AND SYMBOLIC DOMINATION

We use and evaluate speech in the context of *extralinguistic* forces—social, political, and economic. Mainstream Americans evaluate the speech of low-status groups negatively, calling it "uneducated." This is not because these ways of speaking are bad in themselves but because they have come to symbolize low status. Consider variation in the pronunciation of *r.* In some parts of the United States, *r* is regularly pronounced, and in other (*r*less) areas, it is not. Originally, American *r*less speech was modeled on the fashionable speech of England. Because of its prestige, *r*lessness was adopted in many areas and continues as the norm around Boston and in the South.

New Yorkers sought prestige by dropping their *r*'s in the nineteenth century, after having pronounced them in the eighteenth. Contemporary New Yorkers are going back to the eighteenth-century pattern of pronouncing *r*'s. What matters, and what governs linguistic change, is not the reverberation of a strong midwestern *r* but social evaluation, whether *r*'s happen to be "in" or "out."

Studies of *r* pronunciation in New York City have clarified the mechanisms of phonological change. William Labov (1972b) focused on whether *r* was pronounced after vowels in such words as *car, floor, card,* and *fourth.* To get data on how this linguistic variation correlated with social class, he used a series of rapid encounters with employees in three New York City department stores, each of whose prices and locations attracted a different socioeconomic group. Saks Fifth Avenue (68 encounters) catered to the upper middle class, Macy's (125) attracted middle-class shoppers, and S. Klein's (71) had predominantly lower-middle-class and working-class customers. The class origins of store personnel reflected those of their customers.

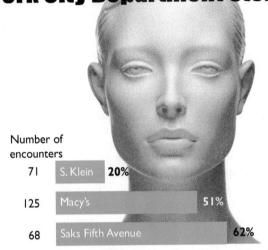

Pronunciation of *r* in New York City Department Stores

Number of encounters	Store	Percentage r pronunciation
71	S. Klein	20%
125	Macy's	51%
68	Saks Fifth Avenue	62%

Having already determined that a certain department was on the fourth floor, Labov approached ground-floor salespeople and asked where that department was. After the salesperson had answered, "Fourth floor," Labov repeated his "Where?" in order to get a second response. The second reply was more formal and emphatic, the salesperson presumably thinking that Labov hadn't heard or understood the first answer. For each salesperson, therefore, Labov had two samples of /r/ pronunciation in two words.

Labov calculated the percentages of workers who pronounced /r/ at least once during the interview. These were 62 percent at Saks, 51 percent at Macy's, but only 20 percent at S. Klein's. He also found that on upper floors, where he asked, "What floor is this?" (and where more expensive items were sold), personnel pronounced *r* more often than ground-floor salespeople did.

In Labov's study, *r* pronunciation was clearly associated with prestige. Certainly the job interviewers who had hired the salespeople never counted *r*'s before offering employment. However, they did use speech evaluations to make judgments about how effective certain people would be in selling particular kinds of merchandise. In other words, they practiced sociolinguistic discrimination, using linguistic features in deciding who got certain jobs.

Our speech habits help determine our access to employment and other material resources. Because of this, "proper language" itself becomes a strategic resource—and a path to wealth, prestige, and power (Gal 1989; Thomas and Wareing 2004). Illustrating this, many ethnographers have described the importance of verbal skill and oratory in politics (Beeman 1986; Bloch 1975; Brenneis 1988; Geis 1987; Lakoff 2000). Ronald Reagan, known as a "great communicator," dominated American society in the 1980s as a two-term president. Another twice-elected president, Bill Clinton, despite his southern accent, was known for his verbal skills in certain contexts (e.g., televised debates

STUDY TIP

Sociolinguistics investigates language variation within a population. Language differences correlate with such factors as dialect, gender, class, and ethnicity.

How should schools treat children who speak different languages and dialects? Should they require them to use the standard, prestigious speech pattern?

and town-hall meetings). Communications flaws may have helped doom the presidencies of Gerald Ford, Jimmy Carter, and George Bush the elder. Does his use of language affect your perception of Barack Obama?

The French anthropologist Pierre Bourdieu views linguistic practices as *symbolic capital* that properly trained people may convert into economic and social capital. The value of a dialect—its standing in a "linguistic market"—depends on the extent to which it provides access to desired positions in the labor market. In turn, this reflects its legitimation by formal institutions—educational institutions, state, church, and prestige media. Even people who don't use the prestige dialect accept its authority and correctness, its "symbolic domination" (Bourdieu 1982, 1984). Thus, linguistic forms, which lack power in themselves, take on the power of the groups they symbolize. The education system, however (defending its own worth), denies linguistic relativity. It misrepresents prestige speech as being inherently better. The linguistic insecurity often felt by lower-class and minority speakers is a result of this symbolic domination.

Black English Vernacular (BEV) A rule-governed dialect of American English (sometimes called ebonics) with roots in southern English. African American youth and many adults speak BEV in their casual, intimate speech.

BLACK ENGLISH VERNACULAR (BEV)

The sociolinguist William Labov and several associates, both white and black, have conducted detailed studies of what they call **Black English Vernacular (BEV).** (*Vernacular* means ordinary, casual speech.) BEV is the "relatively uniform dialect spoken by the majority of black youth in most parts of the United States today, especially in the inner-city areas of New York, Boston, Detroit, Philadelphia, Washington,

Although never a native speaker of BEV, President Barack Obama, speaking here in 2009 to the National Academy of Sciences, exemplifies an upwardly mobile person with an unusually effective mastery of SE.

Cleveland, . . . and other urban centers. It is also spoken in most rural areas and used in the casual, intimate speech of many adults" (Labov 1972a, p. xiii). This does not imply that all, or even most, African Americans speak BEV.

BEV is a complex linguistic system with its own rules, which linguists have described. Consider some of the phonological and grammatical differences between BEV and SE. One phonological difference is that BEV speakers are less likely to pronounce *r* than SE speakers are. Actually, many SE speakers don't pronounce *r*'s that come right before a consonant (card) or at the end of a word (car). But SE speakers usually do pronounce an *r* that comes right before a vowel, either at the end of a word (four o'clock) or within a word (Carol). BEV speakers, by contrast, are much more likely to omit such intervocalic (between vowels) *r*'s. The result is that speakers of the two dialects have different *homonyms* (words that sound the same but have different meanings). BEV speakers who don't pronounce intervocalic *r*'s have the following homonyms: Carol/Cal; Paris/pass.

Observing different phonological rules, BEV speakers pronounce certain words differently than SE speakers do. Particularly in the elementary school context, the homonyms of BEV-speaking students typically differ from those of their SE-speaking teachers. To evaluate reading accuracy, teachers should determine whether students are recognizing the different meanings of such BEV homonyms as *passed, past,* and *pass.* Teachers need to make sure students understand what they are reading, which is probably more important than whether they are pronouncing words correctly according to the SE norm.

Phonological rules may lead BEV speakers to omit *-ed* as a past-tense marker and *-s* as a marker of plurality. However, other speech contexts demonstrate that BEV speakers do understand the difference between past and present verbs, and between singular and plural nouns. Confirming this are irregular verbs (e.g., *tell, told*) and irregular plurals (e.g., *child, children*), in which BEV works the same as SE.

SE is not superior to BEV as a linguistic system, but it does happen to be the prestige dialect—the one used in the mass media, in writing, and in most public and professional contexts. SE is the dialect that has the most "symbolic capital." In areas of Germany where there is diglossia, speakers of Plattdeusch (Low German) learn the High German dialect to communicate appropriately in the national context. Similarly, upwardly mobile BEV-speaking students learn SE.

Rap and hip-hop weave BEV into musical expression. Here we see Common performing with Pharrell Williams, Shay Haley and Chad Hugo of N.E.R.D during the 2008 BET Hip Hop Awards.

>> Historical Linguistics

Sociolinguists study contemporary variation in speech, which is language change in progress. **Historical linguistics** deals with longer-term change. Historical linguists can reconstruct many features of past languages by studying contemporary **daughter languages.** These are languages that descend from the same parent language and that have been changing separately for hundreds or even thousands of years. We call the original language from which they diverge the **protolanguage.** Romance languages such as French and Spanish, for example, are daughter languages of Latin, their common protolanguage. German, English, Dutch, and the Scandinavian languages are daughter languages of proto-Germanic. The Romance languages and the Germanic languages all belong to the Indo-European language family. Their common protolanguage is called Proto-Indo-European (PIE). Historical linguists classify languages according to their degree of relationship (see "PIE Family Tree" on page 94).

Language changes over time. It evolves—varies, spreads, divides into **language subgroups** (those within a taxonomy of related languages that are most closely related). Dialects of a single parent language become distinct daughter languages, especially if they are isolated from one another. Some of them split, and new "granddaughter" languages develop. If people remain in the ancestral homeland, their speech patterns also change. The evolving speech in the ancestral homeland should be considered a daughter language like the others.

A close relationship between languages doesn't necessarily mean that their speakers are closely related biologically or culturally, because people can adopt new languages. In the equatorial forests of Africa, "pygmy" hunters have discarded their ancestral languages and now speak those of the cultivators who have migrated to the area. Immigrants to the United States spoke many different languages on arrival, but their descendants now speak fluent English.

historical linguistics Subdivision of linguistics that studies languages over time.

daughter languages Languages developing out of the same parent language; for example, French and Spanish are daughter languages of Latin.

protolanguage Language ancestral to several daughter languages.

language subgroups Languages within a taxonomy of related languages that are most closely related.

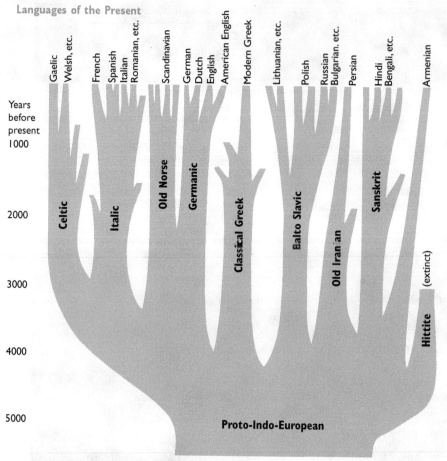

Years
before
present
1000

2000

3000

4000

5000

Proto-Indo-European

PIE Family Tree

Main languages and subgroups of the Indo-European language stock, showing approximate time to their divergence.

Knowledge of linguistic relationships often is valuable to anthropologists interested in history, particularly events during the past five thousand years. Cultural features may (or may not) correlate with the distribution of language families. Groups that speak related languages may (or may not) be more culturally similar to each other than they are to groups whose speech derives from different linguistic ancestors. Of course, cultural similarities aren't limited to speakers of related languages. Even groups whose members speak unrelated languages have contact through trade, intermarriage, and warfare. Ideas and inventions diffuse widely among human groups. Many items of vocabulary in contemporary English, particularly food items, such as "beef" and "pork," come from French. Even without written documentation of France's influence after the Norman Conquest of England in 1066, linguistic evidence in contemporary English

Papua New Guinea, an island with just over six million people, once had at least 841 spoken languages. Many of those languages are endangered, and some have no living speakers.

would reveal a long period of important firsthand contact with France. Similarly, linguistic evidence may confirm cultural contact and borrowing when written history is lacking. By considering which words have been borrowed, we also can make inferences about the nature of the contact.

LANGUAGE LOSS

One aspect of linguistic history is language loss. When languages disappear, cultural diversity is reduced as well. According to linguist K. David Harrison, "When we lose a language, we lose centuries of thinking about time, seasons, sea creatures, reindeer, edible flowers, mathematics, landscapes, myths, music, the unknown and the everyday" (quoted in Maugh 2007). Harrison's recent book, *When Languages Die* (2007), notes that an indigenous language goes extinct every two weeks, as its last speakers die. The world's linguistic diversity has been cut in half (measured by number of distinct languages) in the past five hundred years, and half of the remaining languages are predicted to disappear during this century. Colonial languages (e.g., English, Spanish, Portuguese, French, Dutch, Russian) have expanded at the expense of indigenous ones. Of approximately seven thousand remaining languages, about 20 percent are endangered, compared with 18 percent of mammals, 8 percent of plants, and 5 percent of birds (Maugh 2007).

Harrison, who teaches at Swarthmore College in Pennsylvania, is director of research for the Living Tongues Institute for Endangered Languages (http://www.livingtongues.org), which works to maintain, preserve, and revitalize endangered languages through multimedia documentation projects. Researchers from the institute use digital audio and video equipment to record the last speakers of the most endangered languages. *National Geographic*'s Enduring Voices Project (http://www.nationalgeographic.com/mission/enduringvoices/) strives to preserve endangered languages by identifying the geographic areas with unique, poorly understood, or threatened languages and by documenting those languages and cultures.

The website shows various language hot spots where the endangerment rate ranges from low to severe. In the United States, the rate is high in an area encompassing Oklahoma, Texas, and New Mexico, where 40 Native American languages are at risk. The top hot spot is northern Australia, where 153 Aboriginal languages are endangered (Maugh 2007). Other hot spots are in central South America, the

Internet Top 10 Languages

Millions of users

Language	Millions of users
English	464
Chinese	321
Spanish	131
Japanese	94
French	74
Portuguese	73
German	65
Arabic	41
Russian	38
Korean	37
Rest of world languages	258

Pacific Northwest of North America, and eastern Siberia. In all these areas, indigenous tongues have yielded, either voluntarily or through coercion, to a colonial language.

Despite language loss, linguistic diversity is alive and well in many countries, including India. Despite that nation's colonial history, only about a tenth of the Indian population speaks English. Even many of those English speakers prefer to read, and to seek Internet content, in their own regional languages. Local entrepreneurs and international companies such as Google, Yahoo, and Microsoft are rushing to meet the demand for Web content in local languages. This example illustrates one of the main lessons of applied anthropology, that external inputs fit in best when they are tailored properly to local settings.

get **involved!**

Sociolinguists have studied the ways that speech patterns differ between American men and American women. Save emails from your male and female friends and family members to see if there are comparable differences in electronic communication styles. Are there different ratios of what sociolinguist Deborah Tannen calls "rapport" (building social connections) and "report" (reciting information)? How about differences in kinds of words used, size and completeness of sentences, and typography? Does the use of emoticons vary, both in type (joking or serious, reassuring or negative) and in number? Keep a table of your findings: women's style on one side, men's on the other.

For REVIEW

I. **What makes language different from other forms of communication?**

- The communication systems used by other animals lack the complexity and adaptive advantages characteristic of language. Wild primates use calls—sounds limited in number and produced only when particular environmental stimuli are encountered. Calls are automatic and cannot be combined. Language, by contrast, is based on arbitrary, learned associations between words and the things they represent. The fundamental attributes of language are (1) cultural transmission through learning; (2) productivity—the ability to produce new expressions by combining other expressions; and (3) displacement—the ability to talk about things not present.

II. **How do anthropologists and linguists study language in general and specific languages in particular?**

- Anthropologists and linguists study a specific spoken language by describing its significant sounds and how they combine to form words and their meaningful parts. These scientists also compile a lexicon of the language's morphemes and their meanings, and they study syntax, the order and arrangement of words in phrases and sentences. Phonetics is the study of speech sounds in general. Some linguists seek universal linguistic structures and processes. Still others examine how different linguistic structures produce varied ways of thinking.

III. **How does language change over short and long periods?**

- Sociolinguists study relationships between social and linguistic variation in a society, including linguistic diversity within nations, gender speech contrasts, and the stratification of language. Such contemporary variation within a language is language change in progress. When new ways of speaking are associated with social factors, these ways spread, and language changes. Dealing with long-term change, historical linguists reconstruct features of past languages by studying contemporary daughter languages, descendants of the same parent language that have been changing separately for hundreds or even thousands of years. Language evolves, spreads, and divides into subgroups. Another area of language change is language loss. The past five hundred years have seen the world's linguistic diversity reduced by half. Colonial languages have expanded at the expense of indigenous languages.

Pop Quiz

1. Studies of communication among nonhuman primates reveal that:
   a. Like humans, though to a lesser degree, apes possess the linguistic ability of productivity.
   b. Nonhuman primates can create flexible call systems, so that, for example, a call for food may be combined with a call indicating that danger is also present.
   c. Nonhuman primate call systems vary greatly among communities of the same species.
   d. Primates other than humans can speak.

2. Washoe and Lucy's effort to teach sign language to other chimpanzees is an example of:
   a. A call system
   b. Displacement
   c. Productivity
   d. Cultural transmission

3. Recent research on the origin of language suggests that:
   a. The capacity to remember and combine linguistic symbols is latent in all mammals.
   b. A mutation in humans that occurred around 150,000 years ago may have conferred selective advantages (linguistic and cultural abilities) to those who had it.
   c. Fine tongue and lip movements that are necessary for clear speech are passed on through enculturation.
   d. The earliest forms of language slowed human adaptation because they were less effective for information storage and learning than were call systems.

4. The study of communication through body movements, stances, gestures, and facial expressions is called:
   a. Semantics
   b. Kinesics
   c. Protolanguage
   d. Diglossia

5. The area of analysis of a spoken language that refers to all of a language's morphemes and their meanings is:
   a. Syntax
   b. Semantics
   c. Phonology
   d. Lexicon

6. The Sapir-Whorf hypothesis states that:
   a. The Hopi do not divide time into past, present, and future; the Hopi have no concept of time.
   b. Different languages produce different ways of thinking.
   c. Changes in culture produce changes in language and thought.
   d. All languages share the same grammatical categories.

7. Studies of the differences in the use of color terms between female and male Americans suggest that:
   a. Changes in culture produce changes in language and thought.
   b. Changes in the American economy, society, and culture have no impact on the use of color terms.
   c. Women and men are equally susceptible to the marketing tactics of the cosmetic industry.
   d. Different languages produce different ways of thinking.

8. Which of the following statements about sociolinguistics is false:
   a. It investigates the relationships between social and linguistic variation.
   b. It has found that speakers retain their speech patterns even as the social context changes.
   c. It has found that men and women's speech varies in all these ways: phonology, grammar, vocabulary, body stances, and movements accompanying speech.
   d. It considers the different social standings of a society's dialects, which include a prestige language that provides greater access to desirable jobs and is legitimized by the society's formal institutions.

9. Which of the following statements about Black English Vernacular (BEV) is true?
   a. BEV is a simple linguistic system with its own rules.
   b. All African Americans speak BEV.
   c. As a linguistic system, Standard English is superior to BEV.
   d. Upwardly mobile BEV-speaking students typically consider Standard English to be society's prestige dialect and learn it.

10. Historical linguistics studies all of the following except:
    a. Features of past languages reconstructed from the study of contemporary, or daughter, languages.
    b. The nature of contact between groups by way of linguistic evidence.
    c. Short-term language change.
    d. The loss of indigenous languages as colonial languages have expanded.

1. (a), 2. (d), 3. (b), 4. (b), 5. (d), 6. (b), 7. (a), 8. (b), 9. (d), 10. (c)

6

MAKING A LIVING

WHAT'S TO COME

Adaptive Strategies

Adaptive Strategies Based on Food Production

Economic Systems

Economizing and Maximization

Distribution, Exchange

UNDERSTANDING OURSELVES

In the non-Western societies where ethnography originated, the need to balance work (making a living) and family wasn't as stark as it is for us. In traditional societies, one's workmates usually were also one's kin. There was no need for a "take your child to work" day because most women did that every day. People didn't work with strangers. Home and office, society and economy, were intertwined.

The fact that subsistence and sociality are both basic human needs creates conflicts in modern society. People have to make choices about allocating their time and energy between work and family. Think about the choices your parents have made in terms of economic versus social goals. Have their decisions maximized their incomes, their lifestyles, their individual happiness, family benefits, or what? What about you? What factors motivated you when you chose to apply to and attend college? Did you want to stay close to home, to attend college with friends, or to maintain a romantic attachment (all social reasons)? Did you seek the lowest tuition and college costs—or get a generous scholarship (economic decisions)? Did you choose prestige, or perhaps the likelihood that one day you would earn more money because of the reputation of your alma mater (maximizing prestige and future wealth)? Economists tend to assume that the profit motive rules in contemporary society. However, different individuals, like different cultures, may choose to pursue goals other than monetary gain.

Studies show that most American women now expect to join the paid labor force, just as men do. But the family remains attractive. Most young women and some men also plan to stay home with small children and return to work once their children enter school. How about you? If you have definite career plans, how do you imagine your work will fit in with your future family life—if you have one planned? What do your parents want most for you—a successful career or a happy family life, with children? Probably both. Will it be easy to fulfill such expectations?

As You READ

- What are the major adaptive strategies found in nonindustrial societies?
- What is an economy, and what is economizing behavior?
- What principles regulate the exchange of goods and services in various societies?

>> Adaptive Strategies

In today's globalizing world, communities and societies are being incorporated, at an accelerating rate, into larger systems. The origin (around ten thousand years ago) and spread of food production (plant cultivation and animal domestication) led to the formation of larger and more powerful social and political systems. Food production led to major changes in human life. The pace of cultural transformation increased enormously. This chapter provides a framework for understanding a variety of human adaptive strategies and economic systems.

The anthropologist Yehudi Cohen (1974) used the term *adaptive strategy* to describe a society's system of economic production. Cohen argued that the most important reason for similarities between two (or more) unrelated societies is their possession of a similar adaptive strategy. In other words, similar economic causes have similar sociocultural effects. For example, there are clear similarities among societies that have a foraging (hunting and gathering) strategy. Cohen developed a typology of societies based on correlations between their economies and their social features. His typology includes these five adaptive strategies: foraging, horticulture, agriculture, pastoralism, and industrialism. Industrialism is discussed in the chapter, "The World System and Colonialism." This chapter focuses on the first four adaptive strategies.

Drag net fishing at China Beach (aka My Khe Beach) Danang, Vietnam. Fishing is a form of foraging.

FORAGING

Until ten thousand years ago all humans were foragers. However, environmental differences created substantial contrasts among the world's foragers. Some, like the people who lived in Europe during the ice ages, were big-game hunters. Today, hunters in the Arctic still focus on large animals and herd animals; they have much less vegetation and variety in their diets than do tropical foragers. Moving from colder to hotter areas, the number of species increases. The tropics contain tremendous biodiversity, and tropical foragers typically hunt and gather a wide range of plant and animal species. The same may be true in temperate areas. For example, on the North Pacific Coast of North America, foragers could draw on varied sea, river, and land species, such as salmon and other fish, sea mammals, berries, and mountain goats. Despite differences caused by such environmental variation, all foraging economies have shared one essential feature: People rely on nature to make their living.

Animal domestication (initially of sheep and goats) and plant cultivation (of wheat and barley) began ten to twelve

STUDY TIP

Foraging has several characteristics:

- People rely on nature to make a living, with little management of natural resources;

  - It requires less work than farming;

  - Foraging traditionally correlates with the band social unit and with a mobile lifestyle;

- Modern foragers live on marginal lands (lands not good for agricultural production) and do not survive solely by foraging.

thousand years ago in the Middle East. Cultivation based on different crops, such as corn (maize), manioc (cassava), and potatoes, arose independently in the Americas. In both hemispheres most foragers eventually turned to food production. Today most foragers have at least some dependence on food production or on food producers (Kent 1992).

The foraging way of life survived into modern times in certain forests, deserts, islands, and very cold areas—places where food production was not practicable with simple technology (see Lee and Daly 1999). In many areas, foragers were exposed to the "idea" of food production but never adopted it because their own economies provided a perfectly adequate and nutritious diet—with a lot less work. In some places, people reverted to foraging after trying food production and abandoning it. In most areas where hunter-gatherers did survive, foraging should be described as "recent" rather than "contemporary." *All modern foragers live in nation-states and depend to some extent on government assistance.* They are in contact with food-producing neighbors as well as with missionaries and other outsiders. We should not view contemporary foragers as isolated or pristine survivors of the Stone Age. Modern foragers are influenced by national and international policies and political and economic events in the world system.

Although foraging is disappearing rapidly as a way of life, we can trace the outlines of Africa's two broad belts of recent foraging. One is the Kalahari Desert of southern Africa. This is the home of the San ("Bushmen"), who include the Ju/'hoansi (see Kent 1996; Lee 2003). The other main African foraging area is the equatorial forest of central and eastern Africa, home of the Mbuti, Efe, and other "pygmies" (Bailey et al. 1989; Turnbull 1965).

People still do, or until recently did, subsistence foraging in certain remote forests in Madagascar, Southeast Asia, Malaysia, the Philippines, and on certain islands off the Indian coast. Some of the best-known recent foragers are the aborigines of Australia. Those Native Australians lived on their island continent for more than sixty thousand years without developing food production.

The Western Hemisphere also had recent foragers. The Eskimos, or Inuit, of Alaska and Canada are well-known hunters. These (and other) northern foragers now use modern technology, including rifles and snowmobiles, in their subsistence activities (Pelto 1973). The native populations of California, Oregon, Washington, and British Columbia all were foragers, as were those of inland subarctic Canada and the Great Lakes. For many Native Americans, fishing, hunting, and gathering remain important subsistence (and sometimes commercial) activities.

Coastal foragers also lived near the southern tip of South America, in Patagonia. On the grassy plains of Argentina, southern Brazil, Uruguay, and Paraguay, there were other hunter-gatherers. The contemporary Aché of Paraguay usually are called hunter-gatherers, although they now get just a third of their livelihood from foraging. The Aché also grow crops, have domesticated animals, and live in or near mission posts, where they receive food from missionaries (Hawkes, O'Connell, and Hill 1982; Hill et al. 1987).

Throughout the world, foraging survived in environments that posed major obstacles to food production. (Some foragers took refuge in such areas after the rise of food production, the state, colonialism, or the modern world system.) The difficulties of cultivating at the North Pole are obvious. In southern Africa, the Dobe Ju/'hoansi San area studied by Richard Lee and others is surrounded by a waterless belt 43 to 124 miles (70 to 200 kilometers) in breadth (Solway and Lee 1990).

Environmental obstacles to food production aren't the only reason foragers survived. As shown in "Worldwide Distribution of Recent Hunter-Gatherers," their niches had one thing in common—their marginality. Their environments were not of immediate interest to farmers, herders, or colonialists. The foraging way of life persisted in a few areas that could be cultivated, even after contact with farmers. Those tenacious foragers, like the indigenous peoples of what is now California and the Pacific Northwest, did not adopt food production, because they were supporting themselves adequately by hunting and gathering. As the modern world system spreads, the number of foragers continues to decline.

Most of the estimated one hundred thousand San who survive today live in poverty on society's fringes. Each year more and more foragers come under the control of nation-states and are influenced by forces of globalization. As described by Motseta (2006), between 1997 and 2002, the government of Botswana in southern Africa relocated about three thousand Basarwa San Bushmen outside their ancestral territory, which was converted into a reserve for wildlife protection. The Basarwa received some compensation for their land, along with access to schools, medical facilities, and job training in resettlement centers. Critics claim this resettlement turned a society of free hunter-gatherers into communities dependent on food aid and government handouts (Motseta 2006).

In 2006 Botswana's High Court ruled that the Basarwa had been wrongly evicted from the "Central Kalahari Game Reserve." In the context of global political action for cultural rights, this verdict was hailed as a victory for

Historically Known Foragers (Hunter-gatherers)

1. Eskimos or Inuit
2. Subarctic Indians
3. Northwest Coast Indians
4. Plateau Indians
5. California Indians
6. Great Basin Indians
7. Plains Indians
8. Amazon Basin Hunter-gatherers
9. Gran Chaco Indians
10. Tehuelche
11. Fuegians
12. "Pygmies"
13. Okiek
14. Hadza
15. San

16. Native Australians
17. Maori
18. Toala
19. Agta
20. Punan
21. Kubu
22. Semang
23. Andaman Islanders
24. Mlabri
25. Vedda
26. Kadar
27. Chenchu
28. Birhor
29. Ainu
30. Chukchi

Worldwide Distribution of Recent Hunter-Gatherers

Souce: Adaptation from map by Ray Sim, in Göran Burenhult, ed. *Encyclopedia of Humankind: People of the Stone Age,* p. 193. © 1933. Reprinted by permission of Weldon Owen Pty. Ltd.

correlation An association between two or more variables such that when one changes (varies), the other(s) also change(s) (covaries); for example, temperature and sweating.

band Basic unit of social organization among foragers. A band includes fewer than 100 people; it often splits up seasonally.

indigenous peoples around the world (Motseta 2006). In December 2006, Botswana's attorney general recognized the court order to allow the Basarwa to return to their ancestral lands, while imposing conditions likely to prevent most of them from doing so. Only the 189 people who filed the lawsuit would have automatic right of return with their children, compared with some 2,000 Basarwa wishing to return. The others would have to apply for special permits. Returning Basarwa would be allowed to build only temporary structures and to use enough water for subsistence needs. Water would be a major obstacle because the government shut the main well in 2002, and water is scarce in the Kalahari. Furthermore, anyone wishing to hunt would have to apply for a permit. So goes the foraging way of life in the world today.

CULTURETHINK

The case of the Botswana Basarwa San is typical of global indigenous rights issues. Why do you think the government of Botswana removed the San from their ancestral territory? What were the costs and potential benefits for the San people of moving out? After they won the lawsuit in 2006, was moving back to the territory an attractive option for the San? Why or why not?

Correlates of Foraging Typologies, such as Cohen's adaptive strategies, are useful because they suggest **correlations**—association or covariation between two or more variables. (Correlated variables are factors that are linked and interrelated, such as food intake and body weight, such that when one increases or decreases, the other changes too.) Ethnographic studies in hundreds of societies have revealed many correlations between the economy and social life. Associated (correlated) with each adaptive strategy is a bundle of particular sociocultural features. Correlations, however, rarely are perfect. Some foragers lack cultural features usually associated with foraging, and some of those features are found in groups with other adaptive strategies.

What, then, are some correlates of foraging? People who subsisted by hunting and gathering often, but not always (see the section "Potlatching" at the end of the chapter), lived in band-organized societies. Their basic social unit, the **band,** was a small group of fewer than a hundred people, all related by kinship or marriage. Among some foragers, band size stayed about the same year-round. In others, the band split up for part of the year. Families left to gather resources that were better exploited by just a few people. Later, they regrouped for cooperative work and ceremonies.

One typical characteristic of the foraging life was mobility. In many San groups, as among the Mbuti of Congo, people shifted band membership several times in a lifetime. One might be born, for example, in a band in which one's mother had kin. Later, one's family might move to a band in which the father had relatives. Because bands were exogamous (people married outside their own band) one's parents came from two different bands, and one's grandparents might have come from four. People could join any band to which they had kin or marital links. A couple could live in, or shift between, the husband's and the wife's band.

All human societies have some kind of division of labor based on gender. (See the chapter "Gender" for more on this.) Among foragers, men typically hunt and fish while women gather and collect, but the specific nature of the work varies among cultures. Sometimes women's work contributes most to the diet. Sometimes male hunting and fishing predominate. Among foragers in tropical and semitropical areas, gathering tends to contribute more to the diet than hunting and fishing do.

All foragers make social distinctions based on age. Old people often receive great respect as guardians of myths, legends, stories, and traditions. Younger people value the elders' special knowledge of ritual and practical matters. Most foraging societies are *egalitarian*. This means that contrasts in prestige are minor and are based on age and gender.

When considering issues of "human nature," we should remember that the egalitarian band was a basic form of human social life for most of our history. Food production has existed less than 1 percent of the time *Homo* has spent on Earth. However, it has produced huge social differences. We now consider the main economic features of food-producing strategies.

>> Adaptive Strategies Based on Food Production

In Cohen's typology, the three adaptive strategies based on food production in nonindustrial societies are horticulture, agriculture, and pastoralism. Just as they do in the United States and Canada, people in nonindustrial societies carry out a variety of economic activities. Each adaptive strategy refers to the main economic activity. Pastoralists (herders), for example, consume milk, butter, blood, and meat from their animals as mainstays of their diet. However, they also add grain to their diet by doing some cultivating or by trading with neighbors.

HORTICULTURE

Two types of cultivation found in nonindustrial societies are horticulture and agriculture. Both differ from the farming systems of industrial nations such as the United States and Canada, which use large land areas, machinery, and petrochemicals. According to Cohen, **horticulture** is cul-

Horticulture systems typically use simple technology. Here, after the land has been cleared using slash-and-burn techniques, a woman uses a digging stick to plant mountain rice in Madagascar.

CULTURE THINK

In slash-and-burn horticulture, the land is cleared by cutting down (slashing) and burning trees and bush, using simple technology. What are the likely environmental effects of this kind of cultivation with low population numbers? What if the population increases?

tivation that makes intensive use of *none* of the factors of production: land, labor, capital, and machinery. Horticulturalists use simple tools such as hoes and digging sticks to grow their crops. Their fields lie fallow for varying lengths of time. Horticulture often involves *slash-and-burn* techniques. Here, horticulturalists clear land by cutting down (slashing) and burning forest or bush or by setting fire to the grass covering the plot. The vegetation is broken down, pests are killed, and the ashes remain to fertilize the soil. Crops then are sown, tended, and harvested. Use of the plot is not continuous. Often it is cultivated only for a year or two.

When horticulturalists abandon a plot because of soil exhaustion or a thick weed cover, they clear another piece of land, and the original plot reverts to forest. After several

horticulture Nonindustrial system of plant cultivation in which plots lie fallow for varying lengths of time.

Agriculture requires more labor than horticulture does and uses land intensively and continuously. Labor demands associated with agriculture reflect its use of domesticated animals, irrigation, and terracing. Shown here, rice farmers in Saramsa, Sikkim, India, work in flooded terraces.

years of fallowing, the cultivator returns to farm the original plot again. Because the relationship between people and land is not permanent, horticulture also is called *shifting cultivation*. Shifting cultivation does not mean that whole villages must move when plots are abandoned. Among the Kuikuru of the South American tropical forest, one village of 150 people remained in the same place for ninety years (Carneiro 1956). Kuikuru houses were large and well made. Because the work involved in building them was substantial, the Kuikuru preferred to walk farther to their fields than to construct a new village. They shifted their plots rather than their settlements. On the other hand, horticulturalists in the montaña (Andean foothills) of Peru lived in small villages of about thirty people (Carneiro 1961/1968). Their houses were small and simple. After a few years in one place, these people built new villages near virgin land. Because their houses were so simple, they preferred rebuilding to walking even a half mile to their fields.

agriculture Nonindustrial system of plant cultivation characterized by continuous and intensive use of land and labor.

AGRICULTURE

The intensive and continuous use of land in **agriculture** requires more labor than horticulture does. The greater labor demands associated with agriculture reflect its use of domesticated animals, irrigation, or terracing.

Domesticated Animals Many agriculturists use animals as means of production—for transport, as cultivating machines, and for their manure. Asian farmers typically incorporate cattle and/or water buffalo into their agricultural economies. Those rice farmers may use cattle to trample pre-tilled flooded fields, thus mixing soil and water, before

transplanting. Many agriculturists attach animals to plows and harrows for field preparation before planting or transplanting. Also, agriculturists typically collect manure from their animals, using it to fertilize their plots, thus increasing yields. Animals are attached to carts for transport and also to implements of cultivation.

Irrigation While horticulturalists must await the rainy season, agriculturists can schedule their planting in advance because they control water. Like other irrigation experts in the Philippines, the Ifugao water their fields with canals from rivers, streams, springs, and ponds. Irrigation makes it possible to cultivate a plot year after year. Irrigation enriches the soil because the irrigated field is a unique ecosystem with several species of plants and animals, many of them minute organisms, whose wastes fertilize the land.

An irrigated field is a capital investment that usually increases in value. It takes time for a field to start yielding; it reaches full productivity only after several years of cultivation. The Ifugao, like other irrigators, have farmed the same fields for generations. In some agricultural areas, including the Middle East, however, salts carried in the irrigation water can make fields unusable after fifty or sixty years.

Terracing The Ifugao also have mastered the agricultural technique of terracing. Their homeland has small valleys separated by steep hillsides. Because the population is dense, people need to farm the hills. If they simply planted on the steep hillsides, fertile soil and crops would be washed away during the rainy season. To prevent this, the Ifugao cut into the hillside and build stage after stage of terraced fields rising above the valley floor. Springs located above the terraces supply their irrigation water. The labor necessary to build and maintain a system of terraces is great. Terrace walls crumble each year and must be partially rebuilt. The canals that bring water down through the terraces also demand attention.

Costs and Benefits of Agriculture

Agriculture requires human labor to build and maintain irrigation systems, terraces, and other works. People must feed, water, and care for their animals. But agricultural land can yield one or two crops annually for years, or even generations. An agricultural field does not necessarily produce a higher single-year yield than does a horticultural plot. The first crop grown by horticulturalists on long-idle land may be larger than that from an agricultural plot of the same size. Furthermore, because agriculturists work harder than horticulturalists do, agriculture's yield relative to the labor invested also is lower. Agriculture's main advantage is that the long-term yield per area is far greater and more dependable. Because a single field sustains its owners year after year, there is no need to maintain a reserve of uncultivated land as horticulturalists do. This is why agricultural societies tend to be more densely populated than horticultural ones.

AGRICULTURAL INTENSIFICATION: PEOPLE AND THE ENVIRONMENT

The range of environments available for food production has widened as people have increased their control over nature. For example, in arid areas of California, where Native Americans once foraged, modern irrigation technology now sustains rich agricultural estates. Agriculturists live in many areas that are too arid for nonirrigators or too hilly for non-terracers. Increasing labor intensity and permanent land use have major demographic, social, political, and environmental consequences.

Thus, because of their permanent fields, agriculturists are sedentary. People live in larger and more permanent communities located closer to other settlements. Growth in population size and density increases contact between individuals and groups. There is more need to regulate interpersonal relations, including conflicts of interest. Economies that support more people usually require more coordination in the use of land, labor, and other resources (see the next chapter).

Intensive agriculture has significant environmental effects. Irrigation ditches and paddies (fields with irrigated rice) become repositories for organic wastes, chemicals (such as salts), and disease microorganisms. Intensive agriculture typically spreads at the expense of trees and forests, which are cut down to be replaced by fields. Accompanying such deforestation is loss of environmental diversity (see Srivastava, Smith, and Forno 1999). Agricultural economies grow increasingly specialized. They focus on one or a few caloric staples, such as rice, and on the animals that aid the agricultural economy. Because tropical horticulturalists typically cultivate dozens of plant species simultaneously, a horticultural plot mirrors the botanical diversity found in a tropical forest. Agricultural plots, by contrast, reduce ecological diversity by cutting down trees and concentrating on a few staple foods. Such crop specialization is true of agriculturists both in the tropics (e.g., Indonesian paddy farmers) and outside the tropics (e.g., Middle Eastern irrigation farmers).

Agriculturists attempt to reduce risk in production by favoring stability in the form of a reliable annual harvest and long-term production. Tropical foragers and horticulturalists, by contrast, attempt to reduce risk by relying on multiple species and benefiting from ecological diversity. The agricultural strategy is to put all one's eggs in one big and very dependable basket. The strategy of tropical foragers and horticulturalists is to have several smaller baskets, a few of which may fail without endangering subsistence.

The agricultural strategy makes sense when there are lots of children to raise and adults to be fed. Foraging and horticulture, of course, are associated with smaller, sparser, and more mobile populations.

Agricultural economies also pose a series of regulatory problems. How is water to be managed? How are disputes about access to and distribution of water to be resolved? With more people living closer together on more valuable land, agriculturists are more likely to come into conflict than are foragers and horticulturalists. The social and political implications of food production and intensification are examined more fully in the next chapter.

pastoralists People who use a food-producing strategy of adaptation based on caring for herds of domesticated animals.

nomadism, pastoral Movement throughout the year by the whole pastoral group (men, women, and children) with their animals. More generally, such constant movement in pursuit of strategic resources.

transhumance One of two variants of pastoralism in which part of the population moves seasonally with the herds while the other part remains in home villages.

PASTORALISM

Herders, or **pastoralists,** are people whose activities focus on such domesticated animals as cattle, sheep, goats, camels, yak, and reindeer. They live in North and sub-Saharan Africa, the Middle East, Europe, and Asia. East African pastoralists, like many others, live in symbiosis with their herds. (*Symbiosis* is an obligatory interaction between groups—here, humans and animals—that is beneficial to each.) Herders attempt to protect their animals and to ensure their reproduction in return for food and other products, such as leather. Herds provide dairy products and meat.

People use livestock in various ways. Natives of North America's Great Plains, for example, didn't eat, but only rode, their horses. (Europeans reintroduced horses to the Western Hemisphere; the native American horse had become extinct thousands of years earlier.) For Plains Indians, horses served as "tools of the trade," means of production used to *hunt* buffalo, a main target of their economies. So the Plains Indians were not true pastoralists but hunters who used horses—as many agriculturists use animals—as means of production.

Pastoralists, by contrast, typically use their herds for food. They consume their meat, blood, and milk, from which they make yogurt, butter, and cheese. Although some pastoralists rely on their herds more completely than others do, it is impossible to base subsistence solely on animals. Most pastoralists therefore supplement their diet by hunting, gathering, fishing, cultivating, or trading.

In the sixteenth century, the Samis (also known as Lapps or Laplanders) of Norway, Sweden, and Finland domesticated the reindeer, which their ancestors used to hunt. Like other herders, they follow their animals as they make an annual trek, in this case from coast to interior. Today's Samis use modern technology, such as snowmobiles and four-wheel-drive vehicles, to accompany their herds on their annual nomadic trek. Although their environment is harsher, the Samis, like other herders, live in nation-states and must deal with outsiders, including government officials, as they follow their herds and make their living through animal husbandry, trade, and sales (Hoge 2001).

Unlike foraging and cultivation, which existed throughout the world before the Industrial Revolution, pastoralism was confined almost totally to the Old World. Before European conquest, the only pastoralists in the Americas lived in the Andean region of South America. They used their llamas and alpacas for food and wool and in agriculture and transport. Much more recently, Navajo of the southwestern United States developed a pastoral economy based on sheep, which were brought to North America by Europeans. The populous Navajo became the major pastoral population in the Western Hemisphere.

Two patterns of movement occur with pastoralism: *nomadism* and *transhumance*. Both are based on the fact that herds must move to use pasture available in particular places in different seasons. In pastoral **nomadism,** the entire group—women, men, and children—moves with the animals throughout the year. The Middle East and North Africa provide numerous examples of pastoral nomads. In Iran, for example, the Basseri and the Qashqai ethnic groups traditionally followed a nomadic route more than 300 miles (480 kilometers) long (see Salzman 2004).

CULTURE THINK

Many agree that pastoral nomadism could only have emerged after the rise of agriculture. Why would this be true?

With **transhumance,** part of the group moves with the herds, but most people stay in the home village. There are examples from Europe and Africa. In Europe's Alps only the shepherds and goatherds—not the whole village—accompany the flocks to highland meadows in summer. Among the Turkana of Uganda, men and boys accompany the herds to distant pastures, while much of the village stays put and does some horticultural farming. During their annual trek, pastoral nomads trade for crops and other products with more sedentary people. Transhumants don't have to trade for crops. Because only part of the population accompanies the herds, transhumants can maintain year-round villages and grow their own crops. Table 6.1 summarizes Cohen's adaptive strategies discussed in this chapter.

Did You Know?

One underlying cause of the conflict in Darfur, Sudan, is rivalry between agriculturalists and pastoralist groups due to drought-related land and water scarcity. The involvement of the Sudanese military exacerbated tensions and escalated violence between local populations.

Yehudi Cohen's Adaptive Strategies (Economic Typology) Summarized

Adaptive Strategy	Also Known As	Key Features/Varieties
Foraging	Hunting-gathering	Mobility, use of nature's resources
Horticulture	Slash-and-burn, shifting cultivation, swiddening, dry farming	Fallow period
Agriculture	Intensive farming	Continuous use of land, intensive use of labor
Pastoralism	Herding	Nomadism and transhumance
Industrialism	Industrial production	Factory production, capitalism, socialist production

STUDY TIP

The four adaptive strategies discussed in this chapter are

- Foraging
- Horticulture
- Agriculture
- Pastoralism

>> Economic Systems

An **economy** is a system of production, distribution, and consumption of resources; *economics* is the study of such systems. Economists focus on modern nations and capitalist systems. Anthropologists have broadened understanding of economic principles by gathering data on nonindustrial economies. Economic anthropology studies economics from a comparative perspective (see Gudeman 1999; Plattner 1989; Sahlins 2004; Wilk 1996).

A **mode of production** is a way of organizing production—"a set of social relations through which labor is deployed to wrest energy from nature by means of tools, skills, organization, and knowledge" (Wolf 1982, p. 75). In the capitalist mode of production, money buys labor power, and a social gap between the people (bosses and workers) is involved in the production process. By contrast, in nonindustrial societies, labor usually is not bought but is given

as a social obligation. In such a *kin-based* mode of production, mutual aid in production is one among many expressions of a larger web of social relations.

Societies representing each of the adaptive strategies just discussed (e.g., foraging) tend to have similar modes of production. Differences in the mode of production within a given strategy may reflect differences in environments, target resources, or cultural traditions (Kelly 1995). Thus a foraging mode of production may be based on individual hunters or teams, depending on whether the game is a solitary or a herd animal. Gathering usually is more individualistic than hunting, although teams of collectors may assemble when abundant resources ripen and must be harvested quickly. Fishing may be done alone (as in ice or spear fishing) or in crews (as with open-sea fishing and hunting of sea mammals).

> **economy** A population's system of production, distribution, and consumption of resources.
>
> **mode of production** Way of organizing production—a set of social relations through which labor is deployed to wrest energy from nature by means of tools, skills, and knowledge.

DIVISION OF LABOR

Although some kind of division of economic labor related to age and gender is a cultural universal, the specific tasks assigned to each sex and to people of different ages vary (see the chapter "Gender"). Many horticultural societies assign a major productive role to women, but some make men's work primary. Similarly, among pastoralists, men generally tend large animals, but in some societies women

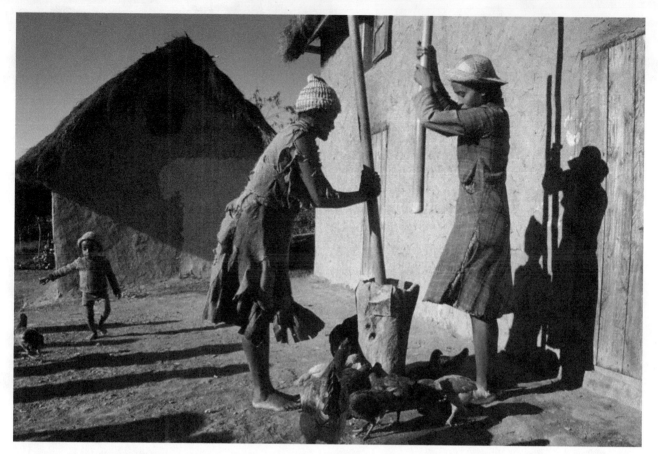

Women hull rice in a Betsileo village. In the village of Ivato, farmers who traditionally grew only rice in their fields now use the same land for commercial crops, such as carrots, after the annual rice harvest.

do the milking. Jobs accomplished through teamwork in some cultivating societies are done in other societies by smaller groups or by individuals working over a longer period.

The Betsileo of Madagascar have two stages of teamwork in rice cultivation: transplanting and harvesting. Both feature a traditional division of labor by age and gender that is well known and repeated across the generations. The first job in transplanting is the trampling of a flooded, previously tilled field by young men driving cattle in order to mix earth and water. They bring cattle to the fields just before transplanting. The young men yell at and beat the cattle, striving to drive them into a frenzy so they will trample the fields properly. Trampling breaks up clumps of earth and mixes irrigation water with soil to form a smooth mud. Once the tramplers leave the field, older men arrive. With their spades they break up the clumps the cattle missed. Meanwhile, the owner and other adults uproot rice seedlings and bring them to the field. Women plant the seedlings.

At harvest time, four or five months later, young men cut the rice off the stalks. Young women carry it to the clearing above the field. Older women arrange and stack it. The oldest men and women then stand on the stack,

> **means (or factors) of production** Land, labor, technology, and capital—major productive resources.

stomping and compacting it. Three days later, young men thresh the rice, beating the stalks against a rock to remove the grain. Older men then beat the stalks with sticks to make sure all the grains have fallen off.

MEANS OF PRODUCTION

In nonindustrial societies the relationship between the worker and the means of production is more intimate than it is in industrial nations. **Means, or factors, of production** include land (territory), labor, and technology.

Land as a Means of Production Among foragers, ties between people and land were less permanent than among food producers. Although many bands had territories, the boundaries usually were not marked, and there

STUDY TIP

Mode of production refers to the way of organizing production: capitalist or kin-based. *Means of production* refers to the materials or factors with which production is carried out: land, labor, and technology.

was no way they could be enforced. The hunter's stake in an animal was more important than where the animal finally died. A person acquired the rights to use a band's territory by being born in the band or by joining it through a tie of kinship or marriage. In Botswana in southern Africa, Ju/'hoansi San women habitually used specific tracts of berry-bearing trees. When a woman changed bands, she immediately acquired a new gathering area.

Among food producers, rights to the means of production also come through kinship and marriage. Descent groups (groups whose members claim common ancestry) are common among nonindustrial food producers. Those who descend from the founder share the group's territory and resources. If the adaptive strategy is horticulture, the estate includes gardens and fallow land for shifting cultivation. As members of a descent group, pastoralists have access to animals to start their own herds, to grazing land, to garden land, and to other means of production.

Labor, Tools, and Specialization Like land, labor is a means of production. In nonindustrial societies, access to both land and labor comes through social links such as kinship, marriage, and descent. Mutual aid in production is merely one aspect of ongoing social relations that are expressed on many other occasions.

Nonindustrial societies contrast with industrial nations regarding another means of production—technology. Manufacturing often is linked to age and gender. Women may weave and men may make pottery, or vice versa. Most people of a particular age and gender share the technical knowledge associated with that age and gender. If married women customarily make baskets, most married women know how to make baskets. Neither technology nor technical knowledge is very specialized.

Some tribal societies, however, do promote specialization. Among the Yanomami of Venezuela and Brazil, for instance, certain villages manufacture clay pots and others make hammocks. They don't specialize, as one might suppose, because certain raw materials happen to be available near particular villages. Clay suitable for pots is widely available. Everyone knows how to make pots, but not everybody does so. Craft specialization reflects the social and political environment rather than the natural environment. Such specialization promotes trade, which is the first step in creating an alliance with enemy villages (Chagnon 1997).

ALIENATION IN INDUSTRIAL ECONOMIES

There are significant contrasts between industrial and nonindustrial economies. When factory workers produce for their employer's profit, they may be *alienated* from the items they make: They don't feel strong pride in or personal identification with their products. They see their product as belonging to someone other than the man or woman whose labor actually produced it. In nonindustrial societies, by contrast, people usually see their work through from start to finish and feel a sense of accomplishment.

In nonindustrial societies the economic relation between coworkers is just one aspect of a more general social relation. They aren't just coworkers but kin or in-laws. In industrial nations, people usually don't work with relatives and neighbors. If coworkers are friends, the personal relationship often develops out of their common employment rather than being based on a previous association.

Thus, industrial workers have impersonal relations with their products, coworkers, and employers. People sell their labor for cash, and work stands apart from family life. In nonindustrial societies, the relations of production, distribution, and consumption are *social relations with economic aspects*. Economy is not a separate entity but is *embedded* in the society.

A Case of Industrial Alienation For decades, the government of Malaysia has promoted export-oriented industry, allowing transnational companies to install manufacturing operations in rural Malaysia. In search of cheaper labor, corporations headquartered in Japan, Western Europe, and the United States have moved labor-intensive factories to developing countries. Malaysia has hundreds of Japanese and American subsidiaries, which produce garments, foodstuffs, and electronics components. Thousands of young Malaysian women from peasant families now assemble microchips and microcomponents for transistors and capacitors. Aihwa Ong (1987) studied electronics assembly workers in an area where 85 percent of the workers were young unmarried females from nearby villages.

Ong found that, unlike village women, female factory workers had to cope with a rigid work routine and constant supervision by men. The discipline that factories value was being taught in local schools, where uniforms helped prepare girls for the factory dress code. Village women wear loose, flowing tunics, sarongs, and sandals, but factory workers had to don tight overalls and heavy rubber gloves, in which they felt constrained. Assembling electronics components requires precise, concentrated labor. Labor in these factories illustrates the separation of intellectual and manual activity—the alienation that Karl Marx considered the defining feature of industrial work. One woman said about her bosses, "They exhaust us very much, as if they

How might factory work, as shown here in this Chinese garment factory, create alienation?

do not think that we too are human beings" (Ong 1987, p. 202). Nor does factory work bring women a substantial financial reward, given low wages, job uncertainty, and family claims on wages. Although young women typically work just a few years, production quotas, three daily shifts, overtime, and surveillance take their toll in mental and physical exhaustion.

One response to factory relations of production has been spirit possession (factory women are possessed by spirits). Ong interprets this phenomenon as the women's unconscious protest against labor discipline and male control of the industrial setting. Sometimes possession takes the form of mass hysteria. Spirits have simultaneously invaded as many as 120 factory workers. *Weretigers* (the Malay equivalent of the werewolf) arrive to avenge the construction of a factory on aboriginal burial grounds. Disturbed earth and grave spirits swarm on the shop floor. First the women see the spirits; then their bodies are invaded. The weretigers send the women into sobbing, laughing, and shrieking fits. To deal with possession, factories employ local medicine men, who sacrifice chickens and goats to fend off the spirits. This solution works only some of the time; possession still goes on. Ong argues that spirit possession expresses anguish at, and resistance to, capitalist relations of production. By engaging in this form of rebellion, however, factory women avoid a direct confrontation with the source of their distress. Ong concludes that spirit possession, while expressing repressed resentment, doesn't do much to modify factory conditions. (Other tactics, such as union-

ization, would do more.) Spirit possession may even help maintain the current system by operating as a safety valve for accumulated tensions.

>> Economizing and Maximization

Economic anthropologists have been concerned with two main questions:

- How are production, distribution, and consumption organized in different societies? This question focuses on *systems* of human behavior and their organization.

- What motivates people in different societies to produce, distribute or exchange, and consume? Here the focus is not on systems of behavior but on the *individuals* who participate in those systems.

Anthropologists view economic systems and motivations in a cross-cultural perspective. Motivation is a concern of psychologists, but it also has been a concern of economists and anthropologists. American economists assume that producers and distributors make decisions rationally, using the *profit motive,* as do consumers when they shop around for the best value. Although anthropologists know that the profit motive is not universal, the assumption that individuals try to maximize profits is basic to capitalism and to Western economic theory. In fact, the subject matter of economics often is defined as *economizing,* or the rational allocation of scarce means (or resources) to alternative ends (or uses).

What does that mean? Classical economic theory assumes that our wants are infinite, while our means are limited. People must make choices about how to use their scarce resources—their time, labor, money, and capital. Western economists assume that when confronted with choices and decisions, people tend to make the one that maximizes profit. This is assumed to be the most rational choice.

The idea that individuals choose to maximize profits was a basic assumption of the classical economists of the nineteenth century and one held by many contemporary economists. Certain economists now recognize that individuals may be motivated by many other goals. Depending on the society and the situation, people may try to maximize profit, wealth, prestige, pleasure, comfort, or social harmony. Individuals may want to realize their personal or family ambitions or those of another group to which they belong (see Sahlins 2004).

ALTERNATIVE ENDS

To what uses do people put their scarce resources? Throughout the world, people devote some of their time and energy to building up a *subsistence fund* (Wolf 1966). In other words, they have to work to eat, to replace the calories they use in daily activity. People also must invest in a *replacement fund*. They must maintain their technology and other items essential to production. If a hoe or plow breaks, they must repair or replace it. They also must obtain and replace items that are essential not to production but to everyday life, such as clothing and shelter.

People everywhere also have to invest in a *social fund*. They must help their friends, relatives, in-laws, and neighbors. It is useful to distinguish between a social fund and a *ceremonial fund*. The latter term refers to expenditures on ceremonies or rituals. To prepare a festival honoring one's ancestors, for example, requires time and the outlay of wealth.

Citizens of nonindustrial states also must allocate scarce resources to a *rent fund*. We think of rent as payment for the use of property. Rent fund, however, has a wider meaning. It refers to resources that people must render to an individual or agency that is superior politically or economically. Tenant farmers and sharecroppers, for example, either pay rent or give some of their produce to their landlords, as peasants did under feudalism.

Peasants are small-scale agriculturists who live in nonindustrial states and have rent fund obligations (see Kearney 1996). They produce to feed themselves, to sell their produce, and to pay rent. All peasants have two things in common:

- They live in state-organized societies;
- They produce food without the elaborate technology—chemical fertilizers, tractors, airplanes to spray crops, and so on—of modern farming or agribusiness.

Besides paying rent to landlords, peasants must satisfy government obligations, paying taxes in the form of money, produce, or labor. The rent fund is not simply an *additional* obligation for peasants. Often it becomes their foremost and unavoidable duty. Sometimes their own diets suffer as a result. The demands of social superiors may divert resources from subsistence, replacement, social, and ceremonial funds.

> **peasant** Small-scale agriculturist living in a state, with rent fund obligations.

CULTURE THINK

Think of examples of how you and your family set money aside for various purposes in subsistence, replacement, social, ceremonial, and rent funds.

Motivations vary from society to society, and people often lack freedom of choice in allocating their resources. Because of obligations to pay rent, peasants may allocate their scarce means toward ends that are not their own but those of government officials. Thus, even in societies in which there is a profit motive, people often are prevented from rationally maximizing self-interest by factors beyond their control.

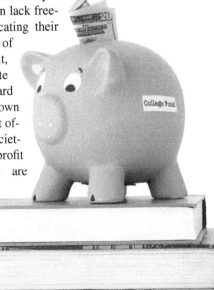

>> Distribution, Exchange

The economist Karl Polanyi (1968) stimulated the comparative study of exchange, and several anthropologists followed his lead. Polanyi defined three principles that guide exchanges: the market principle, redistribution, and reciprocity. These principles all can be present in the same society, but in that case they govern different kinds of transactions. In any society, one of them usually dominates. The principle of exchange that dominates in a given society is the one that allocates the means of production.

THE MARKET PRINCIPLE

In today's world capitalist economy, the **market principle** dominates. It governs the distribution of the means of production—land, labor, natural resources, technology, and capital. With market exchange, items are bought and sold, using money, with an eye to maximizing profit, and value is determined by the *law of supply and demand* (things cost more the scarcer they are and the more people want them). Bargaining is characteristic of market-principle exchanges. The buyer and seller strive to maximize—to get their "money's worth." Bargaining doesn't require that the buyer and seller meet. Consumers bargain whenever they shop around or use advertisements or the Internet in their decision making (see Madra 2004).

market principle Profit-oriented principle of exchange that dominates in states, particularly industrial states. Goods and services are bought and sold, and values are determined by supply and demand.

redistribution Major exchange mode of chiefdoms, many archaic states, and some states with managed economies.

reciprocity One of the three principles of exchange. Governs exchange between social equals; major exchange mode in band and tribal societies.

REDISTRIBUTION

The movement of goods, services, or their equivalent from the local level to a center is known as **redistribution.** The center may be a capital, a regional collection point, or a storehouse near a chief's residence. Products often move through a hierarchy of officials for storage at the center. Along the way, officials and their dependents may consume some of the products, but the exchange principle here is *re*distribution. The flow of goods eventually reverses direction—out from the center, down through the hierarchy, and back to the common people.

One example of a redistributive system comes from the Cherokee (the original owners of the Tennessee Valley), productive farmers who subsisted on maize, beans, and squash, supplemented by hunting and fishing. The Cherokee had chiefs, and each of their main villages had a central plaza, where meetings of the chief's council took place and where redistributive feasts were held. According to Cherokee custom, each family farm had an area where the family could set aside part of their annual harvest for the chief. This supply of corn was used to feed the needy, as well as travelers and warriors journeying through friendly territory. This store of food was available to all who needed it, with the understanding that it "belonged" to the chief and was available through his generosity. The chief also hosted the redistributive feasts held in the main settlements (Harris 1978).

RECIPROCITY

The exchange between social equals, who normally are related by kinship, marriage, or another close personal tie, is known as **reciprocity.** Because it occurs between social equals, it is dominant in the more egalitarian societies—among foragers, cultivators, and pastoralists. There are three degrees of reciprocity: *generalized, balanced,* and *negative* (Sahlins 1968, 2004; Service 1966). These may be imagined as areas of a continuum defined by these questions:

- How closely related are the parties to the exchange?
- How quickly and unselfishly are gifts reciprocated?

Generalized reciprocity, the purest form of reciprocity, is characteristic of exchanges between closely related people. In *balanced reciprocity,* social distance increases, as does the need to reciprocate. In *negative reciprocity,* social distance is greatest and reciprocation is most calculated. This range, from generalized to negative, is called the **reciprocity continuum.**

With generalized reciprocity, someone gives to another person and expects nothing immediate in return. Such exchanges are not primarily economic transactions but expressions of personal relationships. Most parents don't

STUDY TIP

Three principles of exchange are

- The market principle
- Redistribution
- Reciprocity

Think of how you engage in generalized and balanced reciprocity. To whom and under what circumstances do you give gifts? Send holiday cards or formal electronic greetings? Who do you invite over for dinner or a party? Who pays when you are on a date? Are each of these examples of balanced or generalized reciprocity for you (refer to the definitions in the book)?

keep accounts of every penny they spend on their children. They merely hope their children will respect their culture's customs involving obligations to parents.

Among foragers, generalized reciprocity usually has governed exchanges. People routinely have shared with other band members (Bird-David 1992; Kent 1992). So strong is the ethic of sharing that most foragers have lacked an expression for "thank you." To offer thanks would be impolite because it would imply that a particular act of sharing, which is the keystone of egalitarian society, was unusual. Among the Semai, foragers of central Malaysia (Dentan 1979), to express gratitude would suggest surprise at the hunter's success (Harris 1974).

Balanced reciprocity applies to exchanges between people who are more distantly related than are members of the same band or household. In a horticultural society, for example, a man presents a gift to someone in another village. The recipient may be a cousin, a trading partner, or a brother's fictive kinsman. The giver expects something in return. This may not come immediately, but the social relationship will be strained if there is no reciprocation.

Exchanges in nonindustrial societies also may illustrate negative reciprocity, mainly in dealing with people on the fringes of or outside their social systems. To people who live in a world of close personal relations, exchanges with outsiders are full of ambiguity and distrust. Exchange is one way of establishing friendly relations, but when trade begins, the relationship is still tentative. Often the initial exchange is close to being purely economic; people want to get something back immediately. Just as in market economies, but without using money, they try to get the best possible immediate return for their investment.

Generalized reciprocity and balanced reciprocity are based on trust and a social tie. Negative reciprocity involves the attempt to get something for as little as possible, even if it means being cagey or deceitful or cheating. Among the most extreme and "negative" examples of negative reciprocity was nineteenth-century horse thievery by North American Plains Indians. Men would sneak into camps and villages of neighboring tribes to steal horses. A similar pattern of livestock (cattle) raiding continues today in East Africa, among tribes such as the Kuria (Fleisher 2000). In these cases, the party that starts the raiding can expect reciprocity—a raid on their own village—or worse. The Kuria hunt down cattle thieves and kill them. It's still reciprocity, governed by "Do unto others as they have done unto you."

One way of reducing the tension in situations of potential negative reciprocity is to engage in "silent trade." One example was the silent trade of the Mbuti pygmy foragers of the African equatorial forest and their neighboring horticultural villagers. There was no personal contact during their exchanges. A Mbuti hunter left game, honey, or another forest product at a customary site. Villagers collected it and left crops in exchange. Often the parties bargained silently. If one felt the return was insufficient, he or she simply left it at the trading site. If the other party wanted to continue trade, it was increased.

> **reciprocity continuum**
> Regarding exchanges, a range running from generalized reciprocity (closely related/deferred return) through balanced reciprocity, to negative reciprocity (strangers/immediate return).

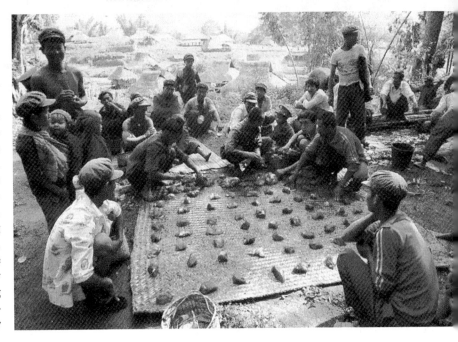

Sharing the fruits of production, a keystone of many nonindustrial societies, also has been a goal of socialist nations, such as China. These workers in Yunnan province strive for an equal distribution of meat.

COEXISTENCE OF EXCHANGE PRINCIPLES

In today's North America, the market principle governs most exchanges, from the sale of the means of production to the sale of consumer goods. We also have redistribution. Some of our tax money goes to support the government, but some of it also comes back to us in the form of social services, education, health care, and road building. We also have reciprocal exchanges. Generalized reciprocity characterizes the relationship between parents and children.

> **potlatch** Competitive feast among Indians on the North Pacific Coast of North America.

However, even here the dominant market mentality surfaces in comments about the high cost of raising children and in the stereotypical statement of the disappointed parent: "We gave you everything money could buy."

Exchanges of gifts, cards, and invitations exemplify reciprocity, usually balanced. Everyone has heard remarks like "They invited us to their daughter's wedding, so when ours gets married, we'll have to invite them" and "They've been here for dinner three times and haven't invited us yet. I don't think we should ask them back until they do." Such precise balancing of reciprocity would be out of place in a foraging band, where resources are communal (common to all) and daily sharing based on generalized reciprocity is an essential ingredient of social life and survival.

Location of Potlatching Groups

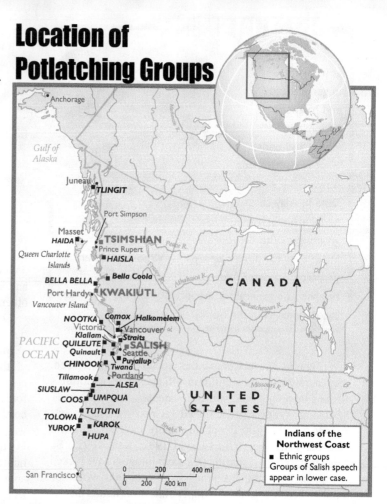

Indians of the Northwest Coast
■ Ethnic groups
Groups of Salish speech appear in lower case.

0   200   400 mi
0   200   400 km

Many hip-hop lyrics center around how much money the artist has in comparison to others, how much more money the artist has now than before his or her music career took off, and how this money often leads to problems. Locate and read the lyrics to these songs: "Beamer, Benz, or Bentley," "Mo Money Mo Problems," and "It's All about the Benjamins." What do they say about the music industry and the artist? Do you believe that these musicians have as much money as they say they have, or is their bragging a technique to place themselves above others, a lesson in bravado? Might these lyrics entice you into beginning a seemingly lucrative music career? Why or why not? What does this say about our culture?

POTLATCHING

One of the most famous cultural practices studied by ethnographers is the **potlatch.** This is a festive event within a regional exchange system among tribes of the North Pacific Coast of North America, including the Salish and Kwakiutl of Washington and British Columbia. Some tribes still practice the potlatch, sometimes as a memorial to the dead (Kan 1986, 1989). At each such event, assisted by members of their communities, potlatch sponsors traditionally gave away food, blankets, pieces of copper, or other items. In return for this, they got prestige. To give a potlatch enhanced one's reputation. Prestige increased with the lavishness of the potlatch—the value of the goods given away in it.

The potlatching tribes were foragers, but atypical ones for relatively recent times. They were sedentary and had chiefs. They had access to a wide variety of land and sea resources. Among their most important foods were salmon, herring, candlefish, berries, mountain goats, seals, and porpoises (Piddocke 1969).

According to classical economic theory, the profit motive is universal, with the goal of maximizing material benefits. How then does one explain the potlatch, in which substantial wealth is given away? In his influential book *Theory of the Leisure Class* (1899/1992), economist and social commentator Thorstein Veblen cited potlatching as an example of conspicuous con-

This historic photo shows Tlingit clan members attending a potlatch at Sitka, Alaska, in 1904. Such ancestral headdresses have been repatriated recently from museums back to Tlingit clans. Have you ever partaken in anything like a potlatch?

sumption, claiming that potlatching was based on an economically irrational drive for prestige. This interpretation stressed the lavishness and supposed wastefulness, especially of the Kwakiutl displays, to support the contention that in some societies people strive to maximize prestige at the expense of their material well-being. This interpretation has been challenged.

Ecological anthropology, also known as *cultural ecology,* is a theoretical school that attempts to interpret cultural practices, such as the potlatch, in terms of their long-term role in helping humans adapt to their environments. Wayne Suttles (1960) and Andrew Vayda (1961/1968) saw potlatching not in terms of its immediate wastefulness, but in terms of its long-term role as a cultural adaptive mechanism. This view also helps us understand similar patterns of lavish feasting throughout the world. Here is the ecological interpretation: *Customs such as the potlatch are cultural adaptations to alternating periods of local abundance and shortage.*

How does this work? Although the natural environment of the North Pacific Coast is favorable, resources do fluctuate from year to year and place to place. Salmon and herring aren't equally abundant every year in a given locality. One village can have a good year while another is experiencing a bad one. Later their fortunes reverse. In this context, the potlatch cycle had adaptive value, and the potlatch was not a competitive display that brought no material benefit.

A village enjoying an especially good year had a surplus of subsistence items, which it could trade for more durable wealth items, such as blankets, canoes, or pieces of copper. Wealth, in turn, by being distributed, could be converted into prestige. Members of several villages were invited to any potlatch and took home the resources that were given away. In this way, potlatching linked villages together in a regional economy—an exchange system that distributed food and wealth from wealthy to needy communities. In return, the potlatch sponsors and their villages got prestige. The decision to potlatch was determined by the health of the local economy. If there had been subsistence surpluses, and thus a buildup of wealth over several good years, a village could afford a potlatch to convert its surplus food and wealth into prestige.

The long-term adaptive value of intercommunity feasting becomes clear when a formerly prosperous village had a run of bad luck. Its people started accepting invitations to potlatches in villages that were doing better. The tables were turned as the temporarily rich became temporarily poor and vice versa.

The newly needy accepted food and wealth items. They were willing to receive rather than bestow gifts and thus to relinquish some of their stored-up prestige. They hoped their luck would eventually improve so that resources could be recouped and prestige regained.

The potlatch linked local groups along the North Pacific Coast into a regional alliance and exchange network. Potlatching and intervillage exchange had adaptive functions, regardless of the motivations of the individual participants. The anthropologists who stressed rivalry for prestige were not wrong. They were merely emphasizing *motivations* at the expense of an analysis of economic and ecological *systems.*

The use of feasts to enhance individual and community reputations and to redistribute wealth is not peculiar to populations of the North Pacific Coast. Competitive feasting is widely characteristic of nonindustrial food producers. But among most surviving foragers, who live in marginal areas, resources are too meager to support feasting on such a level. In such societies, sharing rather than competition prevails.

How do aspects of modern economic life compare to tribal North Pacific Coast potlatching? Talk with friends from wealthy families or go into an affluent neighborhood and observe its inhabitants' lifestyles and consumption behavior. What roles might huge mansions, lavish parties, and private jets, for example, have other than flaunting wealth? Can you think of ways in which they might help connect people (within or between families, social clubs, or large political or economic networks)? Stoke the larger economy? Help distribute wealth to the needy? Do any of the practices you see suggest that Americans may favor competition and social prestige at the expense of society's overall social and environmental well-being?

get INVOLVED!

For REVIEW

CULTURECLIPS

TO ACCESS THESE VIDEOS ON
YOUR COMPUTER, VISIT
www.mhhe.com/gezonqr

6-1

6-2

6-3

I. **What are the major adaptive strategies found in non-industrial societies?**

  • Foraging, or hunting and gathering, was the only human adaptive strategy until the advent of food production. Modern foragers depend in part on food production or food producers. Horticulture is cultivation that does not make intensive use of land, labor, capital, or machinery. After cultivating a plot for one or two years, horticulturalists abandon it, seek other land to cultivate, then return to the original plot after a fallow period. Agriculture is cultivation characterized by continuous, intensive use of land and labor. Agriculturalists may use irrigation, terracing, or domesticated animals for production. Pastoralism is the herding of domesticated animals used for food and other products. In pastoral nomadism, the entire group moves with the animals to pasturage throughout the year, often trading for crops with sedentary people. With transhumance, part of the group moves with the herds; the other part stays in the village and grows crops.

II. **What is an economy, and what is economizing behavior?**

  • An economy is a system of production, distribution, and consumption of resources. Western economists assume that when confronted with choices, people tend to make the one that maximizes profit. These theorists focus on economizing, the rational allocation of scarce resources to alternative uses. However, in nonindustrial societies, indeed even in our own society, people often maximize alternative values, such as pleasure or social harmony. Even in societies where there is a profit motive, factors beyond their control may prevent people from rationally maximizing self-interest.

III. **What principles regulate the exchange of goods and services in various societies?**

  • The market principle dominates in the world capitalist economy. It involves buying and selling items, using money, with the goal of maximizing profit; the law of supply and demand determines value. The redistribution principle operates when goods or services move from the local level to a center. The flow of goods eventually moves out of the center and back to the people. In reciprocity, exchange occurs between social equals related by kinship, marriage, or other close ties. With generalized reciprocity, someone gives to another person and expects nothing immediate in return. As social distance increases, reciprocity becomes balanced and, finally, negative. The potlatch was a North Pacific Coast tribal feast in which sponsors gave away goods in return for prestige. The exchange served to distribute wealth from wealthy to needy communities.

Pop Quiz

1. The concept of an adaptive strategy:
   a. Establishes random causal connections rather than associations or correlations between economic and cultural variables.
   b. Was designed to analyze the economic activities associated with food production in nonindustrial societies engaged in the cultivation of food.
   c. Is used to describe any society's system of economic production.
   d. Has become incorporated into anthropologists' approach to categorizing societies, replacing the use of cultural patterns.

2. Which of the following statements about foraging is false?
   a. All modern foragers have contacts with nonforaging societies.
   b. Some foragers have incorporated modern technology, such as rifles and snowmobiles, into their subsistence activities.
   c. All modern foragers live in nation-states and are influenced by national and international policies and by events in the world system.
   d. Foraging societies have all changed in similar ways because they have faced similar circumstances that encourage their adoption of food production.

3. Which of the following is associated with horticulture?
   a. Intensive use of land and human labor.
   b. Use of irrigation and terracing.
   c. Use of draft animals.
   d. Periodic cycles of cultivation and fallowing.

4. Which of the following statements about horticulture is true?
   a. It typically supports life in dense populations, including cities.
   b. It may lead to soil exhaustion or thick weed cover after many years of having cultivated a plot.
   c. It makes use of simple tools for growing crops.
   d. It requires more labor than does agriculture.

5. The key factor that distinguishes agriculturists from horticulturalists is that agriculturalists:
   a. Can produce one or two crops annually but only for a very few years.
   b. Clear a tract of land they wish to use by cutting down trees and setting fire to the forest or bush.
   c. Use land intensively and continuously.
   d. Generally have much more leisure time at their disposal than do horticulturalists.

6. Which of the following is not a consequence of agriculture?

a. Agriculture promotes nomadism to allow farmers to take full advantage of their land.
   b. Agriculture often spreads at the expense of trees and forests, which are cut down to make room for fields, thus reducing ecological diversity.
   c. By favoring dependability and size of the long-term yield, agricultural societies tend to be more densely populated than horticultural societies.
   d. Agriculture poses regulatory problems, such as resolving disputes about access to water and coordinating the use of land, labor, and other resources.

7. Which of the following is found in all adaptive strategies?
   a. The use of domesticated animals as a means of production.
   b. Transhumance.
   c. Some kind of division of labor based on gender.
   d. Intensive use of land.

8. Most generally, economic alienation in industrial societies comes about as a result of:
   a. Separation of workers from the products they make.
   b. Loss of land.
   c. Negative reciprocity.
   d. Discontent due to low pay.

9. Which of these statements about generalized reciprocity is true?
   a. It involves the immediate return of the object exchanged.
   b. It usually develops after the evolution of redistribution but before the market principle.
   c. It is the characteristic form of exchange in egalitarian societies.
   d. It disappears with the origin of the state.

10. All of the following are true about potlatching except:
   a. It is a festive event among North Pacific Coast tribes that involves potlatch sponsors, assisted by their communities, giving away valuable goods.
   b. The prestige of the potlatch sponsor increases with the lavishness of the potlatch and the value of the goods given away.
   c. Potlatching links villages in a regional exchange system that distributes food and wealth from wealthy to needy communities.
   d. The giving away of substantial wealth in the potlatch indicates that it is a classic case of economically wasteful behavior.

1. (c), 2. (d), 3. (d), 4. (c), 5. (c), 6. (a), 7. (c), 8. (a), 9. (c), 10. (d)

7

POLITICAL SYSTEMS

WHAT'S TO COME

What Is "The Political"?

Types and Trends in Political Organization

Band Organization

Tribal Societies

Chiefdoms

States

UNDERSTANDING OURSELVES

A "big man on campus" is a collegian who is very well known and/or popular. Useful in becoming a BMOC (see http://www.ehow.com/how_2112834_be-big-man-campus.html) are lots of friends, a cool car, a hip wardrobe, a nice smile, a sports connection, and a sense of humor. "Big man" has a related meaning in anthropology. Many indigenous cultures had a political figure that anthropologists call the "big man." Such a leader achieved his status through hard work, amassing wealth in the form of pigs and other native riches. The personality characteristics that enabled the big man to attract loyal supporters (aka lots of friends), included wealth, generosity, eloquence, physical fitness, bravery, and supernatural powers.

Do any of these factors contribute to political success today? Although contemporary politicians may use their own wealth to finance their campaigns, they also solicit labor and money (rather than pigs) from supporters. And, like big men, successful American politicians try to be generous with their supporters. Payback may take the form of largesse (e.g., earmarks) to a particular area. Tribal big men amass wealth and then give away pigs. Successful American politicians dish out "pork."

As with the big man, eloquence and communication skills contribute to political success (e.g., Barack Obama, Bill Clinton, and Ronald Reagan), although lack of such skills isn't necessarily fatal (e.g., either President Bush). What about physical fitness? Hair, height, health (and even a nice smile) are certainly political advantages. Bravery, as demonstrated through military service, can help political careers, but it certainly isn't required. Nor does it guarantee success. Just ask John McCain or John Kerry. Supernatural powers? Candidates who proclaim themselves atheists are as rare as self-identified witches.

Contemporary politics isn't just about personality, however, as it is in big man systems. We live in a state-organized, stratified society with inherited wealth, power, and privilege, all of which have political implications. As is typical of states, inheritance and kin connections play a role in political success. Just think of Kennedys, Bushes, Gores, and Clintons.

As You READ

- What kinds of political systems have existed worldwide, and what are their social and economic correlates?

- What is social status, and how does it relate to political systems?

- How does the state differ from other forms of political organization?

>> What Is "The Political"?

Anthropologists and political scientists share an interest in political systems and organization, but the anthropological approach is global and comparative and includes nonstates as well as the states and nation-states usually studied by

Through public action, citizens can influence government policy. Shown here is a 2008 student rally in Rome. They are protesting educational reforms proposed by the government.

political scientists. Anthropological studies have revealed substantial variation in power, authority, and legal systems in different societies. (*Power* is the ability to exercise one's will over others; *authority* is the socially approved use of power.) (See Gledhill 2000; Kurtz 2001; Lewellen 2003; Nugent and Vincent 2004; Wolf with Silverman 2001.)

Morton Fried offered this definition of political organization:

> Political organization comprises those portions of social organization that specifically relate to the individuals or groups that manage the affairs of public policy or seek to

control the appointment or activities of those individuals or groups. (Fried 1967, pp. 20–21)

This definition certainly fits contemporary North America. Under "individuals or groups that manage the affairs of public policy" come federal, state (provincial), and local (municipal) governments. Those who seek to influence public policy include such interest groups as political parties, unions, corporations, consumers, activists, action committees, religious groups, and nongovernmental organizations (NGOs).

Fried's definition is much less applicable to nonstates, where it often was difficult to detect any "public policy." For this reason, we prefer to speak of *socio*political organization in discussing the regulation or management of relations among groups and their representatives. Political regulation includes such processes as decision making, social control, and conflict resolution. The study of political regulation draws our attention to those who make decisions and resolve conflicts—whether or not there are formal leaders.

Ethnographic and archaeological studies in hundreds of places have revealed many correlations between economy and social and political organization.

>> Types and Trends in Political Organization

Decades ago, the anthropologist Elman Service (1962) listed four types, or levels, of political organization: band, tribe, chiefdom, and state. Today, none of the first three types can be studied as a self-contained form of political organization, since all exist within the context of nation-states and are subject to state control (see Ferguson 2002). There is archaeological evidence for early bands, tribes, and chiefdoms that existed before the first states appeared. But because anthropology came into being long after the origin of the state, anthropologists never have been able to observe "in the flesh" a band, tribe, or chiefdom outside the influence of some state. There still may be local political leaders (e.g., village heads) and regional figures (e.g., chiefs) of the sort discussed in this chapter,

but all now exist and function within the context of state organization.

We saw earlier that a *band* refers to a small *kin-based* group (all its members are related by kinship or marriage) found among foragers. **Tribes** had economies based on non-intensive food production (horticulture and pastoralism). Living in villages and organized into kin groups based on common descent (clans and lineages—see the next chapter), tribes lacked a formal government and had no reliable means of enforcing political decisions. **Chiefdom** refers to a form of sociopolitical organization intermediate between the tribe and the state. In chiefdoms, social relations were based mainly on kinship, marriage, descent, age, generation, and gender—just as they were in bands and tribes. Although chiefdoms were kin-based, they featured differential access to resources (some people had more wealth, prestige, and power than others did) and a permanent political structure. The **state** is a form of sociopolitical organization based on a formal government structure and socioeconomic stratification.

The four labels in Service's typology are much too simple to account for the full range of political diversity and complexity known to archaeology and ethnography. We'll see, for instance, that tribes have varied widely in their political systems and institutions. Nevertheless, Service's typology does highlight some significant contrasts in political organization, especially those between states and nonstates. For example, in bands and tribes—unlike states, which have clearly visible governments—political organization did not stand out as separate and distinct from the total social order. In bands and tribes, it was difficult to characterize an act or event as political rather than merely social.

Service's labels "band," "tribe," "chiefdom," and "state" are categories or types within a **sociopolitical typology.** These types are correlated with the adaptive strategies (economic typology) discussed in the chapter "Making a

tribe Form of sociopolitical organization usually based on horticulture or pastoralism. Socioeconomic stratification and centralized rule are absent in tribes, and there is no means of enforcing political decisions.

chiefdom Form of sociopolitical organization intermediate between the tribe and the state; kin-based with differential access to resources and a permanent political structure.

state (nation-state) Complex sociopolitical system that administers a territory and populace with substantial contrasts in occupation, wealth, prestige, and power. An independent, centrally organized political unit, a government.

sociopolitical typology Classification scheme based on the scale and complexity of social organization and the effectiveness of political regulation; includes band, tribe, chiefdom, and state.

STUDY TIP

Service's four levels of political organization include

- Bands (foraging; small, kin-based)

- Tribes (based on nonintensive food production)

- Chiefdoms (intermediate between tribe and state)

- State (formal government with stratification)

Living." Thus, foragers (an economic type) tended to have band organization (a sociopolitical type). Similarly, many horticulturalists and pastoralists lived in tribes. Although most chiefdoms had farming economies, herding was important in some Middle Eastern chiefdoms. Nonindustrial states usually had an agricultural base.

With food production came larger, denser populations and more complex economies than was the case among foragers. These features posed new regulatory problems, which gave rise to more complex relations and linkages. Many sociopolitical trends reflect the increased regulatory demands associated with food production. Archaeologists have studied these trends through time, and cultural anthropologists have observed them among more contemporary groups.

This chapter examines a series of societies with different political systems. We address a common set of questions for each one: What kinds of social groups does the society have? How do the groups link with larger ones? How do the groups represent themselves to each other? How are their internal and external relations regulated? To answer these questions, we begin with bands and tribes and then consider chiefdoms and states.

>> Band Organization

Modern hunter-gatherers represent today's remnants of foraging band societies. The strong ties they maintain with sociopolitical groups outside the band make them markedly different from Stone Age hunter-gatherers. Modern foragers live in nation-states and an interlinked world. The pygmies of Congo, for example, have for generations shared a social world and economic exchanges with their neighbors who are cultivators. All foragers now trade with food producers. In addition, most contemporary hunter-gatherers rely on governments and on missionaries for at least part of what they consume.

THE SAN

The Basarwa San are an example of foraging bands whose lives have been impacted significantly by outside groups. In the previous chapter, "Making a Living," we saw how the Basarwa San are affected by policies of the government of Botswana, which relocated them after converting their ancestral lands into a

wildlife reserve (Motseta 2006). The government of Botswana is not the first to implement policies and systems that affect the Basarwa San. San speakers ("Bushmen") of southern Africa have been influenced by Bantu speakers (farmers and herders) for two thousand years and by Europeans for centuries. Edwin Wilmsen (1989) argues that many San descend from herders who were pushed into the desert by poverty or oppression. He sees the San today as a rural underclass in a larger political and economic system dominated by Europeans and Bantu food producers. As a result of this system, many San now tend cattle for wealthier Bantu rather than foraging independently. They also have domesticated animals, indicating their movement away from their foraging lifestyle.

Susan Kent (1992, 1996) notes a tendency to stereotype foragers, to treat them all as alike. They used to be stereotyped as isolated, primitive survivors of the Stone Age. A new stereotype sees them as culturally deprived people forced by states, colonialism, or world events into marginal environments. Although this view often is exaggerated, it probably is more accurate than the former one.

Kent (1996) stresses variation among foragers, focusing on diversity in time and space among the San. The nature of San life has changed considerably since the 1950s and 1960s, when a series of anthropologists from Harvard University, including Richard Lee, embarked on a systematic study of life in the Kalahari. Lee and others have documented many of the changes in various publications (Lee 1979, 1984, 2003; Silberbauer 1981; Tanaka 1980). Such longitudinal research monitors variation in time, while fieldwork in many San areas has revealed variation in space. One of the most important contrasts was found to be that between settled (sedentary) and nomadic groups (Kent and Vierich 1989). Although sedentary lifestyles have increased substantially in recent years, some San groups (along rivers) have been sedentary for generations. Others, including the Dobe Ju/'hoansi San studied by Lee (1984, 2003) and the Kutse San that Kent studied, have retained more of the hunter-gatherer lifestyle.

Among tropical foragers, women make an important economic contribution through gathering, as is true among the San shown here in Namibia. What evidence do you see in this photo that contemporary foragers participate in the modern world system?

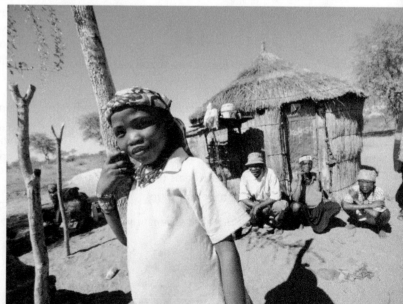

To the extent that foraging has been the basis of subsistence for bands, however, contemporary and recent hunter-gatherers like the San can illustrate links between a foraging economy and other aspects of band society and culture. For example, San groups that still are mobile, or that were so until recently, emphasize social, political, and gender equality, which are traditional band characteristics. A social system based on kinship, reciprocity, and sharing is appropriate for an economy with few people and limited resources. The nomadic pursuit of wild plants and animals tends to discourage permanent settlement, wealth accumulation, and status distinctions. In this context, families and bands have been adaptive social units. People have to share meat when they get it; otherwise it rots.

CULTURE THINK

What were some characteristics of traditional bands—ones that had foraging as the basis of the economy? What has changed for foraging bands in contemporary times?

In the past, foraging bands—small, nomadic or seminomadic social units—formed seasonally when component nuclear families got together. The particular families in a band varied from year to year. Marriage and kinship created ties between members of different bands. Trade and visiting also linked them. Band leaders were leaders in name only. In such an egalitarian society, they were first among equals. Sometimes they gave advice or made decisions, but they had no way to enforce their decisions. Given the spread of states and the modern world system, it is increasingly difficult for ethnographers to find and observe such patterns of band organization.

THE INUIT

The aboriginal Inuit (Hoebel 1954, 1954/1968), another group of foragers, provide a good example of methods of settling disputes—**conflict resolution**—in stateless societies. All societies have ways of settling disputes (of variable effectiveness) along with cultural rules or norms about proper and improper behavior. *Norms* are cultural standards or guidelines that enable individuals to distinguish between appropriate and inappropriate behavior in a given society (N. Kottak 2002). Rules and norms are cultural universals, but only state societies, those with established governments, have formal laws that are formulated, proclaimed, and enforced.

Foragers lacked formal **law** in the sense of a legal code with trial and enforcement, but they did have methods of social control and dispute settlement. The absence of law did not mean total anarchy. As described by E. A. Hoebel (1954) in a classic ethnographic study of conflict resolution, a sparse population of some twenty thousand Inuit spanned 6,000 miles (9,500 kilometers) of the Arctic region (see "Location of the Inuit"). The most significant social groups were the nuclear family and the band. Personal re-

conflict resolution The means by which disputes are socially regulated and settled; found in all societies, but the resolution methods tend to be more formal and effective in states than in nonstates.

law A legal code, including trial and enforcement; characteristic of state-organized societies.

Location of the Inuit

lationships linked the families and bands. Some bands had headmen. There were also shamans (part-time religious specialists). However, these positions conferred little power on those who occupied them.

Hunting and fishing by men were the primary Inuit subsistence activities. The diverse and abundant plant foods available in warmer areas, where female labor in gathering is important, were absent in the Arctic. Traveling on land and sea in a bitter environment, Inuit men faced more dangers than women did. The traditional male role took its toll in lives, so that adult women outnumbered men. This permitted some men to have two or three wives. The ability to support more than one wife conferred a certain amount of prestige, but it also encouraged envy. (*Prestige* is esteem, respect, or approval for culturally valued acts or qualities.) If a man seemed to be taking additional wives just to enhance his reputation, a rival was likely to steal one of them. Most disputes were between men and originated over women, caused by wife stealing or adultery.

A jilted husband had several options. He could try to kill the wife stealer. If he succeeded, however, one of his rival's kinsmen surely would try to kill him in retaliation. One dispute could escalate into several deaths as relatives avenged a succession of murders. No government existed to intervene and stop such a *blood feud* (a murderous feud between families). On the other hand, one also could challenge a rival to a song battle. In a public setting, contestants made up insulting songs about each other. At the end of the match, the audience proclaimed the winner. If a man whose wife had been stolen won, there was no guarantee she would return. Often she stayed with her abductor.

Thefts are common in societies with marked property differentials, like our own, but thefts are uncommon among foragers. Each Inuit had access to the resources needed to sustain life. Every man could hunt, fish, and make the tools necessary for subsistence. Every woman could obtain the materials needed to make clothing, prepare food, and do domestic work. Inuit men could even hunt and fish in the territories of other local groups. There was no notion of private ownership of territory or animals.

>> Tribal Societies

As is true of foraging bands, there are no totally autonomous tribes in today's world. Still, there are societies, for example, in Papua New Guinea and in South America's tropical forests, in which tribal principles continue to operate. Tribes typically have a horticultural or pastoral economy and are organized by village life or membership in *descent groups* (kin groups whose members trace descent from a common ancestor). Tribes lack socioeconomic stratification (i.e., a class structure) and a formal government of their own. A few tribes still conduct small-scale warfare, in the form of intervillage raiding. Tribes have more effective regulatory mechanisms than foragers do, but tribal societies have no sure means of enforcing political decisions. The main regulatory officials are village heads, big men, descent-group leaders, village councils, and leaders of pantribal associations (discussed later in the chapter). All these figures and groups have limited authority.

Like foragers, horticulturalists tend to be egalitarian, although some have marked *gender stratification:* an unequal distribution of resources, power, prestige, and personal freedom between men and women (see the chapter "Gender"). Horticultural villages usually are small, with low population density and open access to strategic resources. Age, gender, and personal traits determine how much respect people receive and how much support they get from others. Egalitarianism diminishes, however, as village size and population density increase. Horticultural villages usually have headmen—rarely, if ever, headwomen.

THE VILLAGE HEAD

The Yanomami (Chagnon 1997) are Native Americans who live in southern Venezuela and the adjacent part of Brazil. Their tribal society has about 26,000 people living in 200 to 250 widely scattered villages, each with a population between 40 and 250. The Yanomami are horticulturalists who also hunt and gather. Their staple crops are bananas and plantains (a bananalike crop). There are more significant social groups among the Yanomami than exist in a foraging society. The Yanomami have families, villages, and descent groups. Their descent groups, which span more than one village, are patrilineal (ancestry is traced back through males only) and exogamous (people must marry outside their own descent group). However, local branches of two different descent groups may live in the same village and intermarry.

As has been true in many village-based tribal societies, traditionally among the Yanomami the only leadership position has been that of **village head** (always a man). His authority, like that of a foraging band's leader, is severely limited. If a headman wants something done, he must lead by example and persuasion. The headman lacks the right to issue orders. He can only persuade, harangue, and try to influence public opinion. For example, if he wants people to clean up the central plaza in preparation for a feast, he must start sweeping it himself, hoping his covillagers will take the hint and relieve him.

When conflict erupts within the village, the headman may be called on as a mediator who listens to both sides. He will give an opinion and advice. If a disputant is unsatisfied, the headman has no power to back his decisions and no way to impose punishments. Like the band leader, he is first among equals.

A Yanomami village headman also must lead in generosity. Because he must be more generous than any other villager, he cultivates more land. His garden provides much of the food consumed when his village holds a feast for another village. The headman represents the village in its dealings with outsiders, including agents of the governments of Venezuela and Brazil.

The way a person acts as headman depends on his personal traits and the number of supporters he can muster. One village headman, Kaobawa, intervened in a dispute between a husband and a wife and kept him from killing her (Chagnon 1983/1992). He also guaranteed safety to a delegation from a village with which a covillager of his wanted to start a war. Kaobawa was a particularly effective headman. He had demonstrated his fierceness in battle, but he also knew how to use diplomacy to avoid offending other villagers. No one in the village had a better personality for the headmanship. Nor (because Kaobawa had many brothers) did anyone have more sup-

porters. Among the Yanomami, when a group is dissatisfied with a village headman, its members can leave and found a new village; this is done from time to time.

Yanomami society, with its many villages and descent groups, is more complex than a band-organized society. The Yanomami also face more regulatory problems. A headman sometimes can prevent a specific violent act, but intervillage raiding has been a feature of some areas of Yanomami territory, particularly those studied by Chagnon (1997).

We also must stress that the Yanomami are not isolated from outside events, including missionization. They live in two nation-states, Venezuela and Brazil, and external warfare waged by Brazilian ranchers and miners increasingly has threatened them (Chagnon 1997; *Cultural Survival Quarterly* 1989; Ferguson 1995). During a Brazilian gold rush between 1987 and 1991, one Yanomami died each day, on average, from external attacks. By 1991, there were some forty thousand Brazilian miners in the Brazilian Yanomami homeland. Some Indians were killed outright. The miners introduced new diseases, and the swollen population ensured that old diseases became epidemic. In 1991, a commission of the American Anthropological Association reported on the plight of the Yanomami (*Anthropology Newsletter,* September 1991). Brazilian Yanomami were dying at a rate of 10 percent annually, and their fertility rate had dropped to zero. Since then, both the Brazilian and Venezuelan governments have intervened to protect the Yanomami. One Brazilian president declared a huge Yanomami territory off-limits to outsiders. Unfortunately, local politicians, miners, and ranchers have increasingly evaded the ban. The future of the Yanomami remains uncertain.

> **village head** Leadership position in a village (as among the Yanomami, where the head is always a man); has limited authority; leads by example and persuasion.
>
> **big man** Figure often found among tribal horticulturalists and pastoralists. The big man occupies no office but creates his reputation through entrepreneurship and generosity to others. Neither his wealth nor his position passes to his heirs.

THE "BIG MAN"

Many societies of the South Pacific, particularly in the Melanesian Islands and Papua New Guinea, had a kind of political leader that we call the big man. The **big man** (almost always a male) was an elaborate version of the village head, but with one significant difference. The village head's leadership is within one village; the big man had supporters in several villages. The big man therefore was a regulator of *regional* political organization.

The Kapauku Papuans live in Irian Jaya, Indonesia (which is on the island of New Guinea). Anthropologist Leopold Pospisil (1963) studied the Kapauku (then

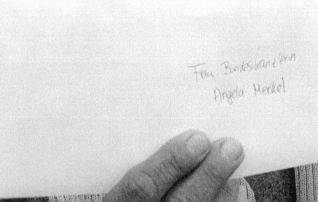

A Yanomami leader today—no longer just a village head. Kopenawa Yanomami, claiming to represent his people, holds a letter for German Chancellor Angela Merkel.

The big man persuades people to organize feasts, which distribute pork and wealth. Shown here is such a regional event, drawing on several villages, in Papua New Guinea. Big men owe their status to their individual personalities rather than to inherited wealth or position. Does our society have equivalents of big men?

forty-five thousand people), who grow crops (with the sweet potato as their staple) and raise pigs. Their economy is too complex to be described as simple horticulture. Kapauku cultivation has used varied techniques for specific kinds of land. Labor-intensive cultivation in valleys involves mutual aid in turning the soil before planting. The digging of long drainage ditches, which a big man often helped organize, is even more complex. Kapauku plant cultivation supports a larger and denser population than does the simpler horticulture of the Yanomami. Kapauku society could not survive in its current form without collective cultivation and political regulation of the more complex economic tasks.

The key political figure among the Kapauku was the big man, known as a *tonowi*. A tonowi achieved his status through hard work, amassing wealth in the form of pigs and other native riches.

The term *status* often is used as a synonym for prestige. In that context, "She's got a lot of status" means she's got a lot of prestige; people look up to her. Among social scientists, that's not the primary meaning of status. Social scientists use *status* more neutrally—for any social position, no matter what the prestige. In this sense, **status** encompasses the various positions that people occupy in society, such as spouse, parent, trading partner, teacher, student, salesperson, big man, and many others. People always occupy multiple statuses (e.g., son, brother, father, big man). Among the statuses we occupy, particular ones dominate in particular settings, such as son or daughter at home and student in the classroom (see "Social Statuses").

Some statuses are **ascribed:** People have little or no choice about occupying them. Age is an ascribed status; we can't choose not to age. One's status as a member of the nobility, or as a male or a female, usually is ascribed; people are born members of a certain social category and remain so all their lives. **Achieved statuses,** by contrast, aren't automatic; they come through

High School Popularity

What makes high school girls popular?

According to college women:		According to college men:
1	Grades/intelligence	2
2	Participation in sports	3
3	General sociability	4
4	Physical attractiveness	1
	Popularity with boys	5
5	Clothes	

What makes high school boys popular?

According to college women:		According to college men:
1	Participation in sports	1
2	Grades/intelligence	2
	Popularity with girls	3
3	General sociability	4
4	Physical attractiveness	
5	School clubs/government	
	Car	5

How does this big man on campus compare with the Melanesian big man?

Note: Students at the following universities were asked in which ways adolescents in their high schools had gained prestige with their peers: Cornell University, Louisiana State University, Southeastern Louisiana University, State University of New York at Albany, State University of New York at Stony Brook, the University of Georgia, and the University of New Hampshire.

Source: Suitor et al. 2001:445.

Social Statuses

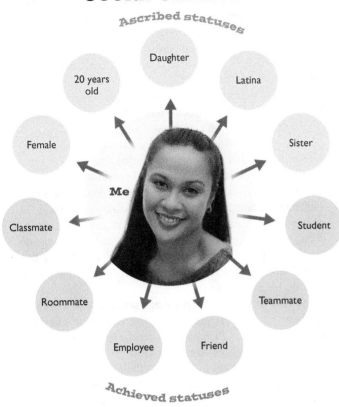

Ascribed statuses

- Daughter
- Latina
- 20 years old
- Sister
- Female
- Me
- Student
- Classmate
- Roommate
- Teammate
- Employee
- Friend

Achieved statuses

porters. He sponsored ceremonial pig feasts in which pigs were slaughtered and their meat distributed to guests.

Unlike the Yanomami village head, a big man's wealth exceeded that of his fellows. His supporters, recognizing his past favors and anticipating future rewards, recognized him as a leader and accepted his decisions as binding. The big man was an important regulator of regional events in Kapauku life. He helped determine the dates for feasts and markets. He persuaded people to sponsor feasts, which distributed pork and wealth. He initiated economic projects requiring the cooperation of a regional community.

The Kapauku big man again exemplifies a generalization about leadership in tribal societies: If someone achieves wealth and widespread respect and support, he or she must be generous. The big man worked hard not to hoard wealth but to give away the fruits of his labor, to convert wealth into prestige and gratitude. A stingy big man would lose his support, his reputation plummeting. Selfish and greedy big men sometimes were murdered by their fellows (Zimmer-Tamakoshi 1997).

> **status** Any position that determines where someone fits in society; may be ascribed or achieved.
>
> **ascribed status** Social status that people have little or no choice about occupying (e.g., race or gender).
>
> **achieved status** Social status that comes through talents, actions, efforts, activities, and accomplishments (e.g., big man or convicted felon).

choices, actions, efforts, talents, or accomplishments, and may be positive or negative. Examples of achieved statuses include big man, healer, senator, convicted felon, terrorist, salesperson, union member, father, and college student.

The achieved status of big men rested on certain characteristics that distinguished the big man from his fellows: wealth, generosity, eloquence, physical fitness, bravery, and supernatural powers. Men became big men because they had certain personalities. They amassed resources during their own lifetime; they did not inherit their wealth or position. A determined man could become a big man, creating wealth through hard work and good judgment. Wealth resulted from successful pig breeding and trading. As a man's pig herd and prestige grew, he attracted sup-

PANTRIBAL SODALITIES AND AGE GRADES

Big men could forge regional political organization, albeit temporarily, by mobilizing people from several villages. Other social and political mechanisms in tribal societies—such as a belief in common ancestry, kinship, or descent—could be used to link local groups within a region. The same descent group might span several villages, and its dispersed members might follow a descent group leader.

To what extent has the political success of the Kennedys family been achieved, or ascribed?

Superhero films celebrate differences in power between those heroes and ordinary people. Power differentials also are key interests in political anthropology. Some superheroes (e.g., the X-Men) are born with their special powers. Others (e.g., Iron Man and Batman) use technology to become superhuman. Still others (e.g., Spiderman and the Fantastic Four) get their powers accidentally. In each case, is superherodom an ascribed status or an achieved status? How about Superman?

POPCULTURE

Principles other than kinship also can link local groups. In a modern nation, a labor union, national sorority or fraternity, political party, or religious denomination may provide such a nonkin-based link. In tribes, nonkin groups called *associations,* or *sodalities,* may serve the same linking function. Often, sodalities are based on common age or gender, with all-male sodalities more common than all-female ones.

Pantribal sodalities (those that extend across the whole tribe, spanning several villages) sometimes arose in areas where two or more different cultures came into regular contact. Such sodalities were especially likely to develop in the presence of warfare between tribes. Drawing their membership from different villages of the same tribe, pantribal sodalities could mobilize men in many local groups for attack or retaliation against another tribe.

CULTURE THINK

Do you or your family belong to any kind of sodality, or nonkin group?

In the cross-cultural study of nonkin groups, we must distinguish between those that are confined to a single village and those that span several local groups. Only the latter, the pantribal groups, are important in general military mobilization and regional political organization. Localized men's houses and clubs, limited to particular villages, are found in many horticultural societies in tropical South America, Melanesia, and Papua New Guinea. These groups may organize village activities and even intervillage raiding. However, their leaders are similar to village heads, and their political scope is mainly local. The following discussion concerns pantribal groups.

pantribal sodality A nonkin-based group that exists throughout a tribe, spanning several villages.

age set Group uniting all men or women (usually men) born during a certain time span; this group controls property and often has political and military functions.

The best examples of pantribal sodalities come from the Central Plains of North America and from tropical Africa. During the eighteenth and nineteenth centuries, Native American societies of the Great Plains of the United States and Canada experienced a rapid growth of pantribal sodalities. This development reflected an economic change that followed the spread of horses, which had been reintroduced to the Americas by the Spanish, to the states between the Rocky Mountains and the Mississippi River. Many Plains Indian societies changed their adaptive strategies because of the horse. At first they had been foragers who hunted bison (buffalo) on foot. Later they adopted a mixed economy based on hunting, gathering, and horticulture. Finally they changed to a much more specialized economy based on horseback hunting of bison (eventually with rifles).

As the Plains tribes were undergoing these changes, other Indians also adopted horseback hunting and moved into the Plains. Attempting to occupy the same area, groups came into conflict. A pattern of warfare developed in which the members of one tribe raided another, usually for horses. The new economy demanded that people follow the movement of the bison herds. During the winter, when the bison dispersed, a tribe fragmented into small bands and families. In the summer, as huge herds assembled on the Plains, members of the tribe reunited. They camped together for social, political, and religious activities, but mainly for communal bison hunting.

Only two activities in the new adaptive strategy demanded strong leadership: organizing and carrying out raids on enemy camps (to capture horses) and managing the summer bison hunt. All the Plains societies developed pantribal sodalities, and leadership roles within them, to police the summer hunt. Leaders coordinated hunting efforts, making sure that people did not cause a stampede with an early shot or an ill-advised action. Leaders imposed severe penalties, including seizure of a culprit's wealth, for disobedience.

Some Plains sodalities were **age sets** of increasing rank. Each set included all the men—from that tribe's component bands—born during a certain time span. Each set had its distinctive dances, songs, possessions, and privileges. Members of each set had to pool their wealth to buy admission to the next higher level as they moved up the age hierarchy. Most Plains societies had pantribal warrior associations whose rituals celebrated militarism. As noted previously, the leaders of these associations organized bison hunting and raiding. They also arbitrated disputes during the summer, when many people came together.

Many tribes that adopted this Plains strategy of adaptation had once been foragers for whom hunting and gathering had been individual or small-group affairs. They never had come together previously as a single social unit. Age and gender were available as social principles that could quickly and efficiently forge unrelated people into pantribal groups.

Raiding of one tribe by another, this time for cattle rather than horses, also was common in eastern and southeastern Africa, where pantribal sodalities, including age sets, also developed. Among the pastoral Masai of Kenya, men born during the same four-year period were circumcised together and belonged to the same named group, an age set, throughout their lives. The sets moved through age grades, the most important of which was the warrior grade. Members of a set felt a strong allegiance to one another.

CULTURE THINK

The text describes three forms of tribal leadership: village heads, big men, and pantribal sodalities. What characteristics do they have in common? How are they different? Think, for example, about the amount of authority each has and the size of the group governed.

Here we see the Masai warrior (ilmurran) age grade dancing with a group of girls of a lower age grade (intoyie). Do we have any equivalents of age sets or grades in our own society?

Masai women lacked comparable set organization, but they also passed through culturally recognized age grades: the initiate, the married woman, and the postmenopausal woman.

To understand the difference between an age set and an age grade, think of a college class, the Class of 2014, for example, and its progress through the university. The age set would be the group of people constituting the Class of 2014, while the first ("freshman"), sophomore, junior, and senior years would represent the age grades.

Not all societies with age grades also have age sets. When there are no sets, men can enter or leave a particular grade individually or collectively, often by going through a predetermined ritual. The grades most commonly recognized in Africa are these:

- Recently initiated youths
- Warriors
- One or more grades of mature men who play important roles in pantribal government
- Elders, who may have special ritual responsibilities

In certain parts of West and Central Africa, the pantribal sodalities are *secret societies,* made up exclusively of men or women. Like our college fraternities and sororities, these associations have secret initiation ceremonies. Among the Mende of Sierra Leone, men's and women's secret societies were very influential. The men's group, the Poro, trained boys in social conduct, ethics, and religion and supervised political and economic activities.

Leadership roles in the Poro often overshadowed village headship and played an important part in social control, dispute management, and tribal political regulation. Age, gender, and ritual can link members of different local groups into a single social collectivity in a tribe and thus create a sense of ethnic identity, of belonging to the same cultural tradition.

NOMADIC POLITICS

Although many pastoralists, such as the Masai, live in tribes, a range of demographic and sociopolitical diversity occurs with pastoralism. A comparison of pastoralists shows that as regulatory problems increase, political hierarchies are more complex. Political organization is less personal, more formal, and less kinship-oriented. The pastoral strategy of adaptation does not dictate any particular political organization. Unlike the Masai and other tribal herders, some pastoralists have chiefs and live in nation-states.

The scope of political authority among pastoralists expands considerably as regulatory problems increase in densely populated regions. Consider two Iranian pastoral nomadic tribes—the Basseri and the Qashqai (Salzman 1974). Starting each year from a plateau near the coast, these groups took their animals to grazing land 17,000 feet (5,400 meters) above sea level. The Basseri and the Qashqai shared this route with one another and with several other ethnic groups (see "Location of the Basseri and Qashqai" on page 130).

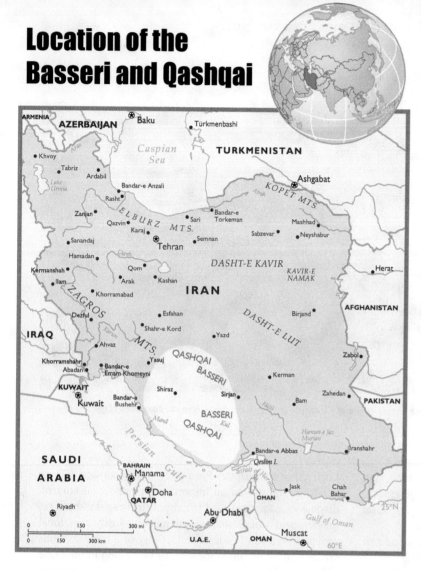

Location of the Basseri and Qashqai

In Qashqai society, allegiance shifted from the person to the office. The Qashqai had multiple levels of authority and more powerful chiefs, or khans. Managing four hundred thousand people required a complex hierarchy. Heading it was the il-khan, helped by a deputy, under whom were the heads of constituent tribes, under each of whom were descent-group heads.

A case illustrates just how developed the Qashqai authority structure was. A hailstorm prevented some nomads from joining the annual migration at the appointed time. Although everyone recognized that they were not responsible for their delay, the il-khan assigned them less favorable grazing land, for that year only, in place of their usual pasture. The tardy herders and other Qashqai considered the judgment fair and didn't question it. Thus, Qashqai authorities regulated the annual migration. They also adjudicated disputes between people, tribes, and descent groups.

These Iranian cases illustrate the fact that pastoralism often is just one among many specialized economic activities within complex nation-states and regional systems. As part of a larger whole, pastoral tribes are constantly pitted against other ethnic groups. In these nations, the state becomes a final authority, a higher-level regulator that attempts to limit conflict between ethnic groups. State organization arose not just to manage agricultural economies but also to regulate the activities of ethnic groups within expanding social and economic systems (see Das and Poole 2004).

>> Chiefdoms

Having looked at bands and tribes, we turn to more complex forms of sociopolitical organization—chiefdoms and states. The first states emerged in the Old World about fifty-five hundred years ago. The first chiefdoms developed perhaps a thousand years earlier, but few survive today. In many parts of the world, the chiefdom was a transitional form of organization that emerged during the evolution of tribes into states. State formation began in Mesopotamia (currently Iran and Iraq). It next occurred in Egypt, the Indus Valley of Pakistan and India, and northern China. A few thousand years later states arose in two parts of the Western Hemisphere—Mesoamerica (Mexico, Guatemala, Belize) and the central Andes (Peru and Bolivia). Early states are known as *archaic states,* or nonindustrial states, in contrast to modern industrial nation-states. Robert Carneiro defines the state as "an autonomous political unit encompassing many communities within its territory, having a centralized government with the power to collect

Use of the same pasture land at different times was carefully scheduled. Ethnic-group movements were tightly coordinated. Expressing this schedule is *il-rah,* a concept common to all Iranian nomads. A group's il-rah is its customary path in time and space. It is the schedule, different for each group, of when specific areas can be used in the annual trek.

Each tribe had its own leader, known as the *khan* or *il-khan.* The Basseri khan, because he dealt with a smaller population, faced fewer problems in coordinating its movements than did the leaders of the Qashqai. Correspondingly, his rights, privileges, duties, and authority were weaker. Nevertheless, his authority exceeded that of any political figure discussed so far. The khan's authority still came from his personal traits rather than from his office. That is, the Basseri followed a particular khan not because of a political position he happened to fill but because of their personal allegiance and loyalty to him as a man. The khan relied on the support of the heads of the descent groups into which Basseri society was divided.

office Permanent political position.

taxes, draft men for work or war, and decree and enforce laws" (Carneiro 1970, p. 733).

The chiefdom and the state, like many categories used by social scientists, are *ideal types*. That is, they are labels that make social contrasts seem sharper than they really are. In reality there is a continuum from tribe to chiefdom to state. Some societies had many attributes of chiefdoms but retained tribal features. Some advanced chiefdoms had many attributes of archaic states and thus are difficult to assign to either category. Recognizing this "continuous change" (Johnson and Earle 2000), some anthropologists speak of "complex chiefdoms" (Earle 1987, 1997), which are almost states.

CULTURETHINK

Consider the pros and cons of ideal types. Is such a typology a valuable way of presenting information, or is it misleading? Do the categories of band, tribe, chiefdom, and state help you understand cross-cultural politics?

POLITICAL AND ECONOMIC SYSTEMS IN CHIEFDOMS

Areas with chiefdoms included the circum-Caribbean (e.g., Caribbean islands, Panama, Colombia), lowland Amazonia, what is now the southeastern United States, and Polynesia. Between the emergence and spread of food production and the expansion of the Roman empire, much of Europe was organized at the chiefdom level. Europe reverted to this level for centuries after the fall of Rome in the fifth century c.e. Chiefdoms created the megalithic cultures of Europe, such as the one that built Stonehenge. Bear in mind that chiefdoms and states can fall (disintegrate) as well as rise.

Chiefdoms created the megalithic cultures of Europe, such as the one that built Stonehenge more than five thousand years ago. Between the emergence and spread of food production and the expansion of the Roman empire, much of Europe was organized at the chiefdom level, to which it reverted after the fall of Rome.

Much of our ethnographic knowledge about chiefdoms comes from Polynesia, where they were common at the time of European exploration. In chiefdoms, social relations are based mainly on kinship, marriage, descent, age, generation, and gender—just as they are in bands and tribes. This is a fundamental difference between chiefdoms and states. States bring nonrelatives together and oblige them all to pledge allegiance to a government.

Unlike bands and tribes, however, chiefdoms are characterized by *permanent political regulation* of the territory they administer. They have a clear-cut and enduring regional political system. Chiefdoms may include thousands of people living in many villages or hamlets. Regulation is carried out by the chief and his or her assistants, who occupy political offices. An **office** is a permanent position, which must be refilled when it is vacated by death or retirement. Because offices are refilled systematically, the structure of a chiefdom endures across the generations, ensuring permanent political regulation.

In the Polynesian chiefdoms, the chiefs were full-time political specialists in charge of regulating the economy— production, distribution, and consumption. Polynesian chiefs relied on religion to buttress their authority. They regulated production by commanding or prohibiting (using religious taboos) the cultivation of certain lands and crops. Chiefs also regulated distribution and consumption. At certain seasons—often on a ritual occasion such as a first-fruit ceremony—people would offer part of their harvest to the chief through his or her representatives. Products moved up the hierarchy, eventually reaching the chief. Conversely, illustrating obligatory sharing with kin, chiefs sponsored feasts at which they gave back much of what they had received.

Such a flow of resources to and then from a central office is known as *chiefly redistribution*. Redistribution offers economic advantages. If the different areas specialized in particular crops, goods, or services, chiefly redistribution made those products available to the entire society. Chiefly redistribution also played a role in risk management. It stimulated production beyond the immediate subsistence level and provided a central storehouse for goods that might become scarce at times of famine (Earle 1987, 1997).

STUDY TIP

Neither band nor tribal leaders have permanent positions or can enforce decisions, unlike chiefs and state leaders, who hold offices and have clear-cut authority.

SOCIAL STATUS IN CHIEFDOMS

Social status in chiefdoms was based on seniority of descent. Because rank, power, prestige, and resources came through kinship and descent, Polynesian chiefs kept extremely long genealogies. Some chiefs (without writing) managed to trace their ancestry back fifty generations. All the people in the chiefdom were thought to be related to each other. Presumably, all were descended from a group of founding ancestors.

The status of chief was ascribed, based on seniority of descent. The chief would be the oldest child (usually son) of the oldest child of the oldest child, and so on. Degrees of seniority were calculated so intricately on some islands that there were as many ranks as people. For example, the third son would rank below the second, who in turn would rank below the first. The children of an eldest brother, however, would all rank above the children of the next brother, whose children would in turn outrank those of younger brothers. However, even the lowest-ranking person in a chiefdom was still the chief's relative. In such a kin-based context, everyone, even a chief, had to share with his or her relatives.

Because everyone had a slightly different status, it was difficult to draw a line between elites and common people. Other chiefdoms calculated seniority differently and had shorter genealogies than did those in Polynesia. Still, the concern

differential access Unequal access to resources; basic attribute of chiefdoms and states. Superordinates have favored access to such resources, while the access of subordinates is limited by superordinates.

This photo, taken in 1981 in Neiafu, Savaii, Western Samoa, shows an orator chief, or tulafale. His speaking staff and the fly whisk over his shoulder symbolize his status as a tulafale. Traditional Samoa provides one example of a Polynesian chiefdom. How do chiefs differ from ordinary people?

for seniority and the lack of sharp gaps between elites and commoners are features of all chiefdoms.

STATUS SYSTEMS IN CHIEFDOMS AND STATES

The status systems of chiefdoms and states are similar in that both are based on **differential access** to resources. This means that some men and women had privileged access to power, prestige, and wealth. They controlled strategic resources such as land and water. Earle characterizes chiefs as "an incipient aristocracy with advantages in wealth and lifestyle" (1987, p. 290). Nevertheless, differential access in chiefdoms was tied very much to kinship. The people with privileged access were generally chiefs and their nearest relatives and assistants.

Compared with chiefdoms, archaic states drew a much firmer line between elites and masses, distinguishing at least between nobles and commoners. Kinship ties did not extend from the nobles to the commoners because of *stratum endogamy*—marriage within one's own group. Commoners married commoners; elites married elites.

Such a division of society into socioeconomic strata contrasts strongly with bands and tribes, whose status systems are based on prestige, rather than on differential access to resources. The prestige differentials that do exist in bands reflect special qualities and abilities. Successful hunters get respect from their fellows if they are generous. So does a skilled curer, dancer, storyteller—or anyone else with a talent or skill that others appreciate.

In tribes, some prestige goes to descent-group leaders, to village heads, and especially to the big man. All these figures must be generous, however. If they accumulate more resources—such as property or food—than others in the village, they must share them with the others. Since strategic resources are available to everyone, social classes based on the possession of unequal amounts of resources can never exist.

In many tribes, particularly those with patrilineal descent (descent traced through males only), men have much greater prestige and power than women do. The gender contrast in rights may diminish in chiefdoms, where prestige and access to resources are based on seniority of descent, so that some women are senior to some men. Unlike big men, chiefs are exempt from ordinary work and have rights and privileges that are unavailable to the masses. Like big men, however, they still return much of the wealth they take in.

THE EMERGENCE OF STRATIFICATION

The status system in chiefdoms, although based on differential access, differed from the status system in states because the privileged few were always relatives and assistants of the chief. However, this type of status sys-

Max Weber's Three Dimensions of Stratification

Wealth = Economic status   Power = Political status   Prestige = Social status

tem didn't last very long. Chiefs would start acting like kings and try to erode the kinship basis of the chiefdom. In Madagascar they would do this by demoting their more distant relatives to commoner status and banning marriage between nobles and commoners (Kottak 1980). Such moves, if accepted by the society, created separate social strata—*unrelated* groups that differ in their access to wealth, prestige, and power. (A *stratum* is one of two or more groups that contrast in social status and access to strategic resources. Each stratum includes people of both sexes and all ages.) The creation of separate social strata is called **stratification,** and its emergence signified the transition from chiefdom to state. *The presence of stratification* is one of the key distinguishing features of a state.

The influential sociologist Max Weber (1922/1968) defined three related dimensions of social stratification: (1) Economic status, or **wealth,** encompasses all a person's material assets, including income, land, and other types of property; (2) **power,** the ability to exercise one's will over others—to do what one wants—is the basis of political status; (3) **prestige**—the basis of social status—refers to esteem, respect, or approval for acts, deeds, or qualities considered exemplary. Prestige involves worth, respect, and "cultural capital" (Bourdieu 1984), which often bring economic benefits as well.

In archaic states—for the first time in human evolution—there were contrasts in wealth, power, and prestige between entire groups (social strata) of men and women. Each stratum included people of both sexes and all ages. The **superordinate** (the higher, or elite) stratum had privileged access to wealth, power, and other valued resources. Access to resources by members of the **subordinate** (lower, or underprivileged) stratum was limited by the privileged group.

OPEN- AND CLOSED-CLASS SYSTEMS

Inequalities, which are built into the structure of state-organized societies, tend to persist across the genera-

tions. The extent to which they do or don't is a measure of the openness of the stratification system—the ease of social mobility it permits. **Vertical mobility** is an upward or downward change in a person's social status. A truly **open-class system** would facilitate mobility. Individual achievement and personal merit would determine social rank. Hierarchical social statuses would be achieved on the basis of people's efforts. Ascribed statuses (family background, ethnicity, gender, religion) would be less important.

Stratification has taken many forms, including caste, slavery, and class systems. **Caste systems** are closed, hereditary systems of stratification that often are dictated by religion. Hierarchical social status is ascribed at birth, so that people are locked into their parents' social position. Caste lines are clearly defined, and legal and religious sanctions are applied against those who seek to cross them.

In **slavery,** the most inhumane, coercive, and degrading form of legal stratification, people who are conquered or stolen from their homelands become

stratification Characteristic of a system with socioeconomic strata.

wealth All a person's material assets, including income, land, and other types of property; the basis of economic status.

power The ability to exercise one's will over others—to do what one wants; the basis of political status.

prestige Esteem, respect, or approval for acts, deeds, or qualities considered exemplary.

superordinate The higher, or privileged, group in a stratified system.

subordinate The lower, or underprivileged, group in a stratified system.

vertical mobility Upward or downward change in a person's social status.

open-class system Stratification system that facilitates social mobility, with individual achievement and personal merit determining social rank.

caste system Closed, hereditary system of stratification, often dictated by religion; hierarchical social status is ascribed at birth, so that people are locked into their parents' social position.

slavery The most extreme, coercive, abusive, and inhumane form of legalized inequality; people are treated as property.

Dalit ("untouchable") women work with cow dung on the outskirts of the northern Indian city of Lucknow.

someone's property. In the Atlantic slave trade, millions of human beings were treated as commodities. The plantation systems of the Caribbean, the southeastern United States, and Brazil were based on forced slave labor. Lacking control over the means of production as well as their own destinies, slaves were forced to live and work at their master's whim. Defined as lesser—or less than—human beings, slaves lacked legal rights. They could be sold and resold; their families were split apart. Unlike the poorest nonslaves, enslaved people had nothing to sell—not even their own labor (Mintz 1985).

Modern class structures, featuring forms of stratification more open than slavery, caste systems, or the status systems of ancient states, have developed in recent times. Still, socioeconomic stratification continues as a defining feature of all states, archaic or industrial. The elites control a significant part of the means of production—for example, land, herds, water, capital, farms, or factories. Those born at the bottom of the hierarchy have reduced chances of so-

CULTURETHINK—

Is there an open-class system in your country? To what extent is there vertical mobility? What factors make it difficult for people to move up or down from their family's status?

cial mobility. Because of elite ownership rights, ordinary people lack free access to resources. Only in states do the elites get to keep their differential wealth. Unlike big men and chiefs, they don't have to give it back to the people whose labor has built and increased it.

>> States

Table 7.1 summarizes the information presented so far on bands, tribes, chiefdoms, and states. States, remember, are autonomous political units with social classes and a formal government, based on law. States tend to be large and populous, as compared to bands, tribes, and chiefdoms. Certain statuses, systems, and subsystems with specialized functions are found in all states (see Sharma and Gupta 2006). They include the following:

- *Population control:* fixing of boundaries, establishment of citizenship categories, and the taking of a census.
- *Judiciary:* laws, legal procedure, and judges.
- *Enforcement:* permanent military and police forces.
- *Fiscal:* taxation.

In archaic states, these subsystems were integrated by a ruling system or government composed of civil, military, and religious officials (Fried 1960).

POPULATION CONTROL

To know whom they govern, states typically conduct censuses. States demarcate boundaries that separate them from other societies. Customs agents, immigration officers, navies, and coast guards patrol frontiers. Even nonindustrial states have boundary-maintenance forces. In Buganda, an archaic state on the shores of Lake Victoria in Uganda, the king rewarded military officers with estates in outlying provinces. They became his guardians against foreign intrusion.

States also control population through administrative subdivision: provinces, districts, "states," counties, subcounties, and parishes. Lower-level officials manage the populations and territories of the subdivisions.

In nonstates, people work and relax with their relatives, in-laws, and agemates—people with whom they have a personal relationship. Such a personal social life existed throughout most of human history, but food production spelled its eventual decline. After millions of years of human evolution, it took only a few thousand years for the population increase and regulatory problems spawned by food production to lead from tribe to chiefdom to state. With state organization, kinship's pervasive role diminished. Descent groups may continue as kin groups within archaic states, but their importance in political organization declines.

Economic Basis of and Political Regulation in Bands, Tribes, Chiefdoms, and States

Sociopolitical Type	Economic Type	Examples	Type of Regulation
Band	Foraging	Inuit, San	Local
Tribe	Horticulture, pastoralism	Yanomami, Kapauku, Masai	Local, temporary regional
Chiefdom	Productive horticulture, pastoral nomadism, agriculture	Qashqai, Polynesia, Cherokee	Permanent regional
State	Agriculture, industrialism	Ancient Mesopotamia, contemporary U.S., Canada	Permanent regional

States foster geographic mobility and resettlement, severing long-standing ties among people, land, and kin (Smith 2003). Population displacements have increased in the modern world and with globalization. War, famine, and job seeking across national boundaries churn up migratory currents. People in states come to identify themselves by new statuses, both ascribed and achieved—including ethnicity, residence, occupation, party, religion, and team or club affiliation—rather than only as members of a descent group or extended family.

CULTURETHINK

Compare and contrast leadership characteristics among bands, tribes, chiefdoms, and states. Are they permanent or temporary positions? Do they have the authority to enforce decisions? How much territory or how many people do they govern? Try drawing a chart or some other visual representation of this information.

States also manage their populations by granting different rights and obligations to citizens and noncitizens. Status distinctions among citizens are also common. Many archaic states granted different rights to nobles, commoners, and slaves. Unequal rights within state-organized societies persist in today's world. In recent American history, before the Emancipation Proclamation, there were different laws for enslaved and free people. In European colonies, separate courts judged cases involving only natives and cases involving Europeans. In contemporary America, a military code of justice and court system continue to coexist alongside the civil judiciary.

JUDICIARY SYSTEMS

States have *laws* based on precedent and legislative proclamations. Without writing, laws may be preserved in oral tradition, with justices, elders, and other specialists responsible for remembering them. Oral traditions as repositories of legal wisdom have continued in some nations with writing, such as Great Britain. Laws regulate relations between individuals and groups.

Crimes are violations of the legal code, with specified types of punishment. However, a given act, such as killing someone, may be legally defined in different ways (e.g., as manslaughter, justifiable homicide, or first-degree murder). Furthermore, even in contemporary North America, where justice is supposed to be "blind" to social distinctions, the poor are prosecuted more often and more severely than are the rich.

To handle disputes and crimes, all states have courts and judges. Precolonial African states had subcounty, county, and district courts, plus a high court formed by the king or queen and his or her advisers. Most states allow appeals to higher courts, although people are encouraged to solve problems locally.

A striking contrast between states and nonstates is intervention in family affairs. In states, aspects of parenting and marriage enter the domain of public law. Governments step in to halt blood feuds and regulate previously private disputes. States attempt to curb *internal* conflict, but they aren't always successful. About 85 percent of the world's armed conflicts since 1945 have begun within states—in efforts to overthrow a ruling regime or as disputes over tribal, religious, and ethnic minority issues (see Chatterjee 2004). Only 15 percent have been fights across national borders (Barnaby 1984). Rebellion, resistance, repression, terrorism, and warfare continue (see Nordstrom 2004; Tishkov 2004). Indeed, recent states have perpetrated some of history's bloodiest deeds.

> "Treat all men alike. Give them the same law. Give them an even chance to live and grow."
>
> Chief Joseph

All states have law enforcement officials, such as this U.S. Marshal.

ENFORCEMENT SYSTEMS

All states have agents to enforce judicial decisions. Confinement requires jailers. If there is a death penalty, it requires executioners. Agents of the state have the power to collect fines and confiscate property.

As a relatively new form of sociopolitical organization, states have competed successfully with nonstates throughout the world. A government suppresses internal disorder (with police) and guards the nation against external threats (with the military). Military organization helps states subdue neighboring nonstates, but this is not the only reason for the spread of state organization. Although states impose hardships, they also offer advantages. They provide protection from outsiders and preserve internal order. By promoting internal peace, states enhance production. Their economies support massive, dense populations, which supply armies and colonists to promote expansion. A major concern of government is to defend hierarchy, property, and the power of the law.

FISCAL SYSTEMS

A financial, or **fiscal,** system is needed in states to support rulers, nobles, officials, judges, military personnel, and thousands of other specialists. As in the chiefdom, the state intervenes in production, distribution, and consumption. The state may decree that a certain area will produce certain things or forbid certain activities in particular places. Although, like chiefdoms, states also have redistribution (through taxation), generosity and sharing are played down. Less of what comes in flows back to the people.

In nonstates, people customarily share with relatives, but residents of states face added obligations to bureaucrats and officials. Citizens must turn over a substantial portion of what they produce to the state. Of the resources that the state collects, it reallocates part for the general good and uses another part (often larger) for the elite.

The state does not bring more freedom or leisure to the common people, who usually work harder than do people in nonstates. They may be called on to build monumental public works. Some of these projects, such as dams and irrigation systems, may be economically necessary. People also build temples, palaces, and tombs for the elites.

Markets and trade usually are under at least some state control, with officials overseeing distribution and exchange, standardizing weights and measures, and collecting taxes on goods passing into or through the state. Taxes support government and the ruling class, which is clearly separated from the common people in regard to activities, privileges, rights, and obligations. Taxes also support the many specialists—administrators, tax collectors, judges, lawmakers, generals, scholars, and priests. As the state matures, the segment of the population freed from direct concern with subsistence grows.

The elites of archaic states reveled in the consumption of *sumptuary goods*—jewelry, exotic food and drink, and stylish clothing reserved for, or affordable only by, the rich. Peasants' diets suffered as they struggled to meet government demands. Commoners perished in territorial wars that had little relevance to their own needs. Are any of these observations true of contemporary states?

fiscal Pertaining to finances and taxation.

Can you find parallels to the Melanesian "big man" on your campus? Talk with dorm residents or members of Greek houses or other social circles to see which students tend to take charge and acquire prestige. Or think back to high school. Who were the big men and women in your graduating class? How did their achievements compare with those described for big men in the text? Typically such individuals are self-made, gaining respect through efforts and personal qualities. But ask what effect family privilege, race, or ethnicity might have on their status. Consider too what values or actions might serve to level that status, bringing it in line with campus norms. Think of a campus big man or woman you know. Would you want to level or support his or her status? Why?

get **involved!**

For
REVIEW

I. What kinds of political systems have existed world-wide, and what are their social and economic correlates?

- Bands are small groups of foragers related by kinship or marriage. Foraging encourages equality, reciprocity, and sharing as well as mobility. Band leaders are first among equals; they lack sure ways to enforce decisions and have only local influence. Tribes, which have horticultural or pastoral economies, are organized around village life and descent groups. The village headman and the "big man," a regional leader, have limited authority. Chiefdoms have horticultural, pastoral nomadic, or agricultural economies. While kin-based, they feature differential access to resources and permanent political regulation of a territory. Chiefs, whose status is based on seniority of descent, receive products that come upward through the hierarchy, then redistribute them to the people. The state is an independent, centrally organized political unit with marked socioeconomic stratification. The economy is typically agricultural or industrial. Political regulation is permanent and regional.

II. What is social status, and how does it relate to political systems?

- *Status* refers to social position. Ascribed status is automatic; achieved status comes through choice, personality, talent, or accomplishment. In bands, successful hunters or talented curers earn respect but do not inherit positions nor enjoy differential access to resources. In tribes, descent group leaders, village heads, and, especially, the big man must be generous. The big man amasses resources through effort; his achieved status gives him authority to regulate events and persuade people. In chiefdoms, chiefs and their assistants occupy political offices, which are permanent positions. States emerged when chiefs started to erode the kinship basis of the chiefdom and create separate strata—unrelated groups differing in economic, political, and social status. New kinds of statuses arise in states, such as ethnic, party, and occupational.

III. How does the state differ from other forms of political organization?

- Marked social stratification distinguishes states from other forms of political organization. Whereas chiefdoms allowed differential access to resources, it was closely tied to kinship seniority; in states, each social stratum comprises unrelated groups. Inequalities are built into states and tend to persist across generations. Also distinctive of states is formal government. Government fixes boundaries, establishes citizenship, and conducts censuses; decrees and enforces laws; handles disputes through courts; guards the nation and promotes expansion with a military; and collects taxes. States tend to be large and populous and to foster geographic mobility, severing long-standing ties among people, land, and kin.

Pop Quiz

1. The text argues that the term *sociopolitical* is preferable to Morton Fried's *political organization* because:
   a. Both anthropologists and political scientists prefer *sociopolitical*.
   b. Fried spoke of the management of "public policy" in his definition of *political organization,* making this term less applicable to nonstates.
   c. Nonstate societies show more correlations between social and political organization than do state societies.
   d. The term *political* refers only to contemporary Western states.

2. Band societies:
   a. Lack develop political systems that encourage equality.
   b. Are isolated survivors of the Stone Age.
   c. Have cultural rules that help members to distinguish between proper and improper behavior.
   d. Lack means for conflict resolution since bands do not have established governments or formal laws.

3. All the following statements about the San of southern African are true *except:*
   a. The San live within nation-states and are affected by world events.
   b. San society and economy vary in time and space, with settled ways of life on the increase among many San while others have retained more of their hunter-gatherer lifestyle.
   c. One researcher sees the San today as a rural underclass in a larger political and economic system.
   d. No San today retain their foraging lifestyle.

4. Which of the following factors is responsible for the recent changes in Yanomami tribal society?
   a. Big men have amassed so much wealth that the Yanomami have begun to regard them as chiefs.
   b. The Brazilian and Venezuelan governments have relocated Yanomami to other territories to protect them from big business enterprises.
   c. Intervillage trade and cooperation have led to the expansion of Yanomami tribal society.
   d. Gold miners and cattle ranchers have encroached on Yanomami territory and attacked its people; the miners have introduced new diseases.

5. Why are pantribal sodalities and age grades described in a chapter on political systems?
   a. They are organizing principles used to mobilize and link local groups to form alliances.
   b. They are among the statuses and systems with specialized functions that are found in all states.
   c. They are organizing principles that stress the importance of kinship ties.
   d. The leadership roles within them are important factors in the evolution of states.

6. The comparison between the Basseri and the Qashqai, two Iranian nomadic tribes, illustrates that:
   a. Among tribal sociopolitical organizations, pastoralists are the least likely to interact with other populations in the same space and time.
   b. As regulatory problems increase, political hierarchies become more complex.
   c. As regulatory problems decrease, political hierarchies become more complex.
   d. State organization arises to manage agricultural economies.

7. In foraging and tribal societies, what is the basis for the degree of respect or status attached to an individual?
   a. Prestige inherited from parents.
   b. Personal attributes, such as wisdom, leadership skills, and generosity.
   c. The amount of possessions one owns and the ability to convert them into cash.
   d. The amount of territory a person owns.

8. In what kind of society does differential access to strategic resources based on social stratification occur?
   a. Chiefdoms
   b. Bands
   c. States
   d. Tribes

9. All the following are interrelated dimensions of social stratification as defined by the sociologist Max Weber *except:*
   a. Power over others.
   b. Prestige, the basis of social status.
   c. The permanence of social position.
   d. Wealth, or economic status.

10. Which of the following would not constitute a status or specialized function that is found in all states?
    a. Control of populations.
    b. Agents to enforce judicial decisions, police the society, and guard the nation against external threats.
    c. Elimination of different rights granted to different social classes.
    d. Taxation.

1. (b), 2. (c), 3. (d), 4. (d), 5. (a), 6. (b), 7. (b), 8. (c), 9. (c), 10. (c)

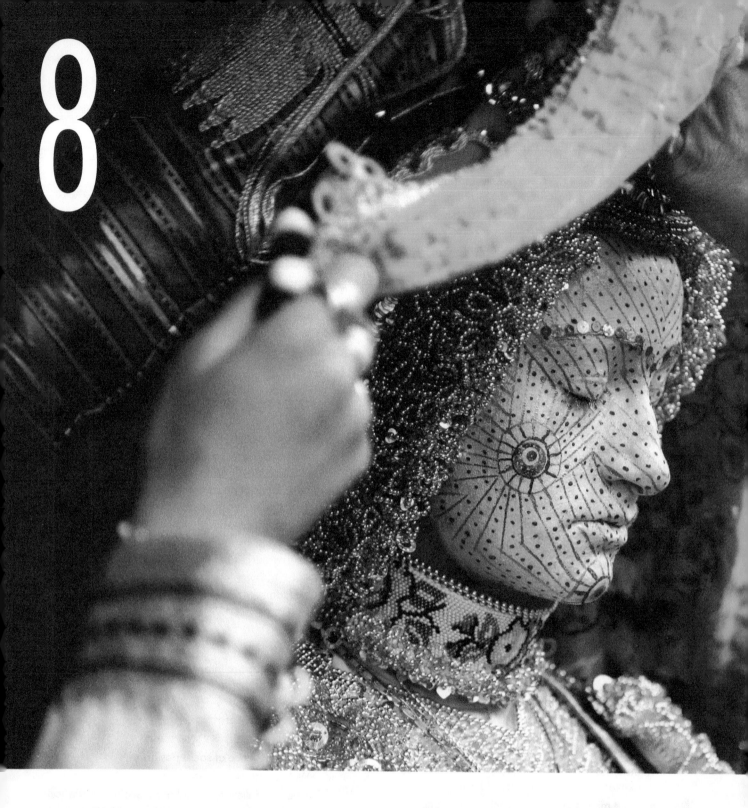

8

FAMILIES, KINSHIP, AND MARRIAGE

WHAT'S TO COME

Families

Descent

Marriage

Marital Rights and Same-Sex Marriage

Marriage across Cultures

Divorce

Plural Marriages

UNDERSTANDING OURSELVES

Although it remains something of an ideal in our culture, the nuclear family (mom, dad, and kids) now accounts for fewer than one-fourth of all American households. What kind of family raised you? According to the radio talk show psychologist (and undergraduate anthropology major) Dr. Joy Browne, the dual job of parents or caretakers is to give their kids "roots and wings." Roots, she says, are the easier part. In other words, it's easier to raise children than to let them go. Has that been true of those who raised you? We've heard comments about today's "helicopter parents" hovering over even their college-aged kids, using cell phones, email, and texting to follow their progeny more closely than in previous generations.

It can be difficult to make the transition between the family that raised us (our family of orientation) and the family we create when (or if) we form a long-term romantic partnership and have children (our family of procreation). Contemporary Americans usually get a head start by "leaving home" long before we marry. We go off to college or find a job that enables us to support ourselves so that we can live independently, or with roommates. In nonindustrial societies a woman often must leave her home village and her own kin and move in with her husband and his relatives. Many such women complain about feeling isolated in their husband's village, where they may be mistreated by their husband or in-laws.

Even in contemporary North America, conflicts with in-laws aren't at all uncommon. Just read "Dear Abby" or listen to Dr. Joy Browne (cited above) for a week. Even more of a challenge is learning to live with our spouse or domestic partner. Cohabitation always raises issues of accommodation and adjustment. Initially the couple is just that, unless there are children from a previous marriage. If there are, adjustment issues will involve stepparenthood and likely a prior spouse or partner. Once a couple has its own child, family loyalty shifts, but not completely, from the family of orientation to the family that includes spouse and child(ren). The cycle of "marriage and the family" begins anew.

As You READ

- What forms of kinship exist cross-culturally, and what are their social correlates?

- How do families and descent groups differ?

- How is marriage defined and regulated, and what rights does it convey?

>> Families

The societies anthropologists traditionally have studied have stimulated a strong interest in families, along with larger systems of kinship and marriage. The wide web of kinship—as vital in daily life in nonindustrial societies as work outside the home is in our own—has become an essential part of anthropology because of its importance to the people we study. We are ready to take a closer look at the systems of kinship and marriage that have organized human life for much of our history.

Ethnographers quickly recognize social divisions, or groups, within any society they study. They learn about significant groups by observing their activities and membership. Often people live in the same village or neighborhood or work, socialize, or celebrate together because they are related in some way. A significant kin group might consist of descendants of the same grandfather. These people live in neighboring houses, farm adjoining fields, and help each other in daily tasks. Groups based on other kin links get together less often in that society.

This polygynous family (a man with multiple wives) in Mali, West Africa, displays their normal weekly diet on the roof of their mud-brick home. Ethnographers have studied many family types besides the nuclear family—the traditional American ideal.

How strong is your extended family support system, compared with that of your best friend, roommate, or romantic partner? Write down the names of everyone in your extended family and how they are related to you.

The nuclear family (parents and children) is one kind of kin group that is widespread in human societies. Other kin groups include extended families (families consisting of three or more generations) and descent groups—lineages and clans.

Much of kinship is *culturally constructed,* that is, based on learning and variable from culture to culture (McKinnon 2005; Schneider 1967). Different societies have different kinds of families, households, kin groups, marriage customs, and living arrangements. Consider the term *family,* which is basic, *familiar* (so much so it even shares its root with *familiar*), and difficult to define in a way that applies to all cultures. A **family** is a group of people (e.g., parents, children, siblings, grandparents, grandchildren, uncles, aunts, nephews, nieces, cousins, spouses, siblings-in-law, parents-in-law, children-in-law) who are considered to be related in some way, such as by "blood" (common ancestry or descent) or marriage. Some families, such as the nuclear family, are residentially based; its members live together. Others are not; they live apart but come together for family reunions of various sorts from time to time.

Consider a striking contrast between the United States and Brazil, the two most populous countries of the Western Hemisphere, in the meaning and role of family. American adults usually define their family as consisting of their spouse and children. When middle-class Brazilians talk about their family (*família*), they mean their parents, siblings, aunts, uncles, grandparents, and cousins. Later they add their children, but rarely the husband or wife, who has his or her own family. The children are shared by the two families. Because middle-class Americans typically lack an extended family support system, marriage assumes more importance. The husband–wife relationship is supposed to take precedence over either spouse's relationship with his or her own parents. This places a significant strain on North American marriages.

Living in a less mobile society, Brazilians stay in closer face-to-face contact with their relatives, includ-ing members of the extended family, than North Americans do. Residents of Rio de Janeiro and São Paulo, two of South America's largest cities, are reluctant to leave those urban centers to live away from family and friends. Brazilians find it hard to imagine, and unpleasant to live in, social worlds without relatives. Contrast this with a characteristic American theme: learning to live with strangers.

NUCLEAR AND EXTENDED FAMILIES

A nuclear family is *impermanent;* it lasts only as long as the parents and children remain together. Most people belong to at least two nuclear families at different times in their lives. They are born into a family consisting of their parents and siblings. When they reach adulthood, they may marry and establish a nuclear family that includes the spouse and eventually children. Since most societies permit divorce, some people establish more than one family through marriage.

Anthropologists distinguish between the **family of orientation** (the family in which one is born and grows up) and the **family of procreation** (formed when one marries and has children). From the individual's point of view, the critical relationships are with parents and siblings in the family of orientation and with spouse and children in the family of procreation. In Brazil, as we just saw, the family of orientation predominates, whereas in the United States it is the family of procreation.

In most societies, relations with nuclear family members (parents, siblings, and children) take precedence over

family A group of people (e.g., parents, children, siblings, grandparents, grandchildren, uncles, aunts, nephews, nieces, cousins, spouses, siblings-in-law, parents-in-law, children-in-law) who are considered to be related in some way, such as by "blood" (common ancestry or descent) or marriage.

family of orientation Nuclear family in which one is born and grows up.

family of procreation Nuclear family established when one marries and has children.

relations with other kin. Nuclear family organization is very widespread but not universal, and its significance in society differs greatly from one place to another. In a few societies, such as the classic Nayar case described a little later in the chapter, nuclear families are rare or nonexistent. In others, the nuclear family plays no special role in social life. Other social units—most notably descent groups and extended families—can assume many of the functions otherwise associated with the nuclear family.

neolocality Postmarital residence pattern in which a couple establishes a new place of residence rather than living with or near either set of parents.

extended family household Expanded household including three or more generations.

Consider an example from the former Yugoslavia. Traditionally, among the Muslims of western Bosnia, nuclear families lacked autonomy (Lockwood 1975). Several such families lived in an extended family household called a *zadruga*. The zadruga was headed by a male household head and his wife, the senior woman. It included married sons and their wives and children, and unmarried sons and daughters. Each nuclear family had a sleeping room, decorated and partly furnished from the bride's trousseau. Zadruga members shared possessions, however—even clothing and trousseau items. Such a residential unit is known as a *patrilocal* extended family because each couple resides in the husband's father's household after marriage.

The zadruga took precedence over its component units. There were three successive meal settings—for men, women, and children, respectively. Traditionally, all children over the age of twelve slept together in boys' or girls' rooms. When a woman wished to visit another village, she sought the permission of the male zadruga head. Although men usually felt closer to their own children than to those of their brothers, they were obliged to treat them equally. Children were disciplined by any adult in the household. When a nuclear family broke up, children under age seven went with the mother. Older children could choose between their parents. Children were considered part of the household where they were born even if their mother left. One widow who remarried had to leave her five children, all over the age of seven, in their father's zadruga, now headed by his brother.

Another example of an alternative to the nuclear family is provided by the Nayar (or Nair), a large and powerful caste on the Malabar Coast of southern India (Gough 1959; Shivaram 1996). Their traditional kinship system was matrilineal (descent traced only through females). Nayar lived in matrilineal extended family compounds called *tarawads*—a residential complex with several buildings, its own temple, granary, water well, orchards, gardens, and land holdings. Headed by a senior woman, assisted by her brother, the tarawad housed her siblings, sisters' children, and other *matrikin*—matrilineal relatives.

Traditional Nayar marriage seems to have been hardly more than a formality: a kind of coming-of-age ritual. A young woman would go through a marriage ceremony with a man, after which they might spend a few days together at her tarawad. Then the man would return to his own tarawad, where he lived with his sisters, aunts, and other matrikin. Nayar men belonged to a warrior class, who left home regularly for military expeditions, returning permanently to their tarawad on retirement. Nayar women could have multiple sexual partners. Children became members of the mother's tarawad; they were not considered to be relatives of their biological father. Indeed, many Nayar children didn't even know who their biological father (genitor) was. Child care was the responsibility of the tarawad. Nayar society therefore reproduced itself biologically without the nuclear family.

INDUSTRIALISM AND FAMILY ORGANIZATION

For many Americans and Canadians, the nuclear family is the only well-defined kin group. Family isolation arises from geographic mobility, which is associated with industrialism, so that a nuclear family focus is characteristic of many modern nations. Born into a family of orientation, North Americans leave home for college or work, and the break with parents is under way. Selling our labor on the market, we often move to places where jobs are available. Eventually most North Americans marry and start a family of procreation.

Many married couples live hundreds of miles from their parents. Their jobs have determined where they live. Such a postmarital residence pattern is **neolocality:** Married couples are expected to establish a new place of residence—a "home of their own." Among middle-class North Americans, neolocal residence is both a cultural preference

Unable to survive economically as nuclear family units, relatives may band together in an expanded family household and pool their resources. This photo, taken in 2002 in Munich, Germany, shows German Roma, or Gypsies. Together with her children and grandchildren, this grandmother resides in an expanded family household.

In their 2009 book *Media and Middle-Class Moms: Images and Realities of Work and Family,* Lara Descartes and Conrad Kottak point out that, contrary to popular belief, it is the 1980s—not the 1950s—that best qualifies as the golden decade of the TV family. Not only did such family-oriented programs as *The Cosby Show* and *Family Ties* dominate Nielsen's top ten, there also was a revival of interest in earlier family shows. The now iconic series *Leave It to Beaver,* for example, never made it into even the Nielsen top thirty shows during its original broadcast years, 1957–1963. In the mid-1980s, *Beaver* reappeared in syndication, in a reunion telemovie, and in a sequel series. Idealized media representations of traditional nuclear families increased in tandem with the subversion of that structure by socioeconomic fact, as the divorce rate rose and more and more women joined the workforce. To be sure, 1980s shows featured working women like Claire Huxtable and Elyze Keaton. And they, too, were idealized in their ability to blend professional success with exemplary motherhood. Watch a few episodes, and evaluate Claire or Elyze as role models compared with the reality of your own family life.

and a statistical norm. Most middle-class Americans eventually establish households and nuclear families of their own.

There are significant differences between middle-class and poorer North Americans. For example, in the lower class, the incidence of expanded family households (those that include nonnuclear relatives) is greater than it is in the

middle class. When an *expanded family household* includes three or more generations, it is an **extended family household,** such as the zadruga. Another type of expanded family is the *collateral household,* which includes siblings and their spouses and children.

The higher proportion of expanded family households among poorer Americans has been explained as an adaptation to poverty (Stack 1975). Unable to survive economically as nuclear family units, relatives band together in an expanded household and pool their resources. Adaptation to poverty causes kinship values and attitudes to diverge from middle-class norms. Thus, when North Americans raised in poverty achieve financial success, they often feel obligated to provide financial help to a wide circle of less fortunate relatives (see Willie 2003).

CHANGES IN NORTH AMERICAN KINSHIP

Although the nuclear family remains a cultural ideal for many Americans, the "Changes in Organization" chart on page 146 shows that nuclear families accounted for 23 percent of American households in 2007 (see "Households by Type" also on page 146). Other domestic arrangements now outnumber the "traditional" American household more than four to one. There are several reasons for this changing household composition. Women increasingly are joining men in the cash workforce. This often removes them from their family of orientation while making it economically feasible to

CULTURETHINK

The average age of first marriage in 2009 was almost twenty-six for women and twenty-eight for men. Consider the people you know: How much (if at all) do they vary from this national norm?

Changes in Family and Household Organization in the United States, 1970 vs. 2007

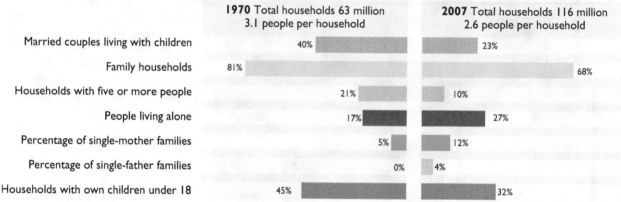

1970 Total households 63 million
3.1 people per household

2007 Total households 116 million
2.6 people per household

	1970	2007
Married couples living with children	40%	23%
Family households	81%	68%
Households with five or more people	21%	10%
People living alone	17%	27%
Percentage of single-mother families	5%	12%
Percentage of single-father families	0%	4%
Households with own children under 18	45%	32%

Sources: From U.S. Census data in J. M. Fields, "America's Families and Living Arrangements: 2003," *Current Population Reports*, P20–553, November 2004, http://ww.census .gov/prod/2004pubs/p20-553.pdf, p. 4; J. M. Fields and L. M. Casper, "America's Families and Living Arrangements: Population Characteristics 2000," *Current Population Reports*, P20–537, June 2001, http://www.census.gov/prod/2001pubs/p20-537.pdf; U.S. Census Bureau, *Statistical Abstract of the United States 2009*, Tables 58, 60, 63, http://www.census.gov/compendia/statab/2009edition.html.

Households by Type: Selected Years, 1970–2007

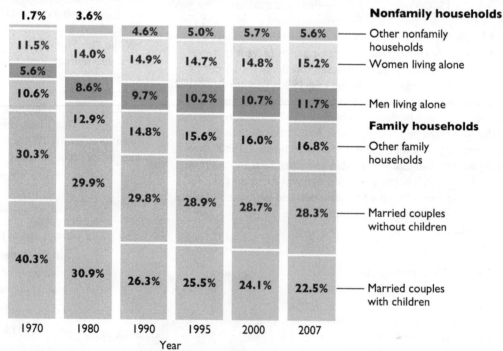

Nonfamily households

Year	1970	1980	1990	1995	2000	2007	
Other nonfamily households	1.7%	3.6%	4.6%	5.0%	5.7%	5.6%	Nonfamily households
Women living alone	11.5%	14.0%	14.9%	14.7%	14.8%	15.2%	
Men living alone	5.6% / 10.6%	8.6%	9.7%	10.2%	10.7%	11.7%	
Other family households		12.9%	14.8%	15.6%	16.0%	16.8%	Family households
Married couples without children	30.3%	29.9%	29.8%	28.9%	28.7%	28.3%	
Married couples with children	40.3%	30.9%	26.3%	25.5%	24.1%	22.5%	

Sources: J. M. Fields, "America's Families and Living Arrangements: 2003," *Current Population Reports*, P20–553. November 2004, http://www.census.gov/prod2004pubs/p20-553.pdf, p. 4; *Statistical Abstract of the United States* 2009, Table 58, p. 52, and Table 60, p. 53, http://www.census.gov/compendia/statab/2009edition.html.

Ratio of Divorces to Marriages per 1,000 U.S. Population, Selected Years, 1950–2006

Ratio of divorces to marriages per 1,000 U.S. population

Year

Source: Statistical Abstract of the United States 2009, Table 77, p. 63, http://www.census.gov/compendia/statab/2009edition.html.

delay marriage. Furthermore, job demands compete with romantic attachments. The median age at first marriage for American women rose from twenty-one years in 1970 to twenty-six in 2009. For men the comparable ages were twenty-three and twenty-eight (U.S. Census Bureau 2010).

The U.S. divorce rate also has risen, making divorced Americans much more common today than they were in 1970. U.S. Census Bureau figures show that between 1970 and 2007 the number of divorced Americans quintupled—some 23 million in 2007 versus 4.3 million in 1970. (Note, however, that each divorce creates two divorced people.) The figure above shows the ratio of divorces to marriages in the United States for selected years between 1950 and 2006. The major jump in the American divorce rate took place between 1960 and 1980. During that period the ratio of divorces to marriage doubled. Since 1980 the ratio has stayed the same, slightly below 50 percent. That is, each year there are about half as many new divorces as there are new marriages.

The rate of growth in single-parent families also has outstripped population growth, quintupling from fewer than 4 million in 1970 to 19 million in 2007. (The overall American population in 2007 was 1.5 times its size in 1970.) The percentage (22.6 percent) of children living in fatherless (mother-headed, no resident dad) households in 2007 was more than twice the 1970 rate, while the percentage (3.2 percent) in motherless (father-headed, no resident mom) homes increased fourfold. About 57 percent of American women and 60 percent of American men were currently married in 2006, versus 60 and 65 percent, respectively, in 1970 (Fields 2004; Fields and Casper 2001; *Statistical Abstract of the United States* 2009). Recent census data also reveal that more American women are now living without a husband than with one. In 2005, 51 percent of women said they were living without a spouse, compared with 35 percent in 1950 and 49 percent in 2000 (Roberts et al. 2007).

In contemporary North America, single-parent families have increased at a rapid rate. In 1960, 88 percent of American children lived with both parents, compared with 68 percent today. This divorced mom, Valerie Jones, enjoys a candlelight dinner with her kids. What do you see as the main differences between nuclear families and single-parent families?

To be sure, contemporary Americans maintain social lives through work, friendship, sports, clubs, religion, and organized social activities. But the growing isolation from kin that these figures suggest may well be unprecedented in human history.

Rise of Single-Parent Families in the United States, 1970–2004

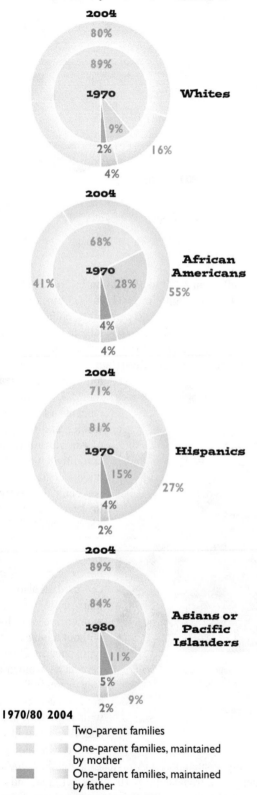

2004

80%

89%

1970　**Whites**

9%

2%　16%

4%

2004

68%

1970　**African Americans**

41%　28%　55%

4%

4%

2004

71%

81%

1970　**Hispanics**

15%

27%

4%

2%

2004

89%

84%

1980　**Asians or Pacific Islanders**

11%

5%

2%　9%

1970/80　2004

　Two-parent families

　One-parent families, maintained by mother

　One-parent families, maintained by father

Note: "Children" refers to children under 18. Early data for Asian Americans are for 1980. Hispanics can be of any race. Not included are unrelated people living together with no children present. All data exclude the 4 percent of children in nonparental households.

Source: Bureau of the Census 1994:63; Kreider 2008.

The "Households and Family Size" chart documents similar changes in family and household size in the United States and Canada between 1980 and 2007. Those figures confirm a general trend toward smaller families and living units in North America. This trend is also detectable in Western Europe and other industrial nations.

Immigrants often are shocked by what they perceive as weak kinship bonds and lack of proper respect for family in contemporary North America. In fact, most of the people whom middle-class North Americans see every day are either nonrelatives or members of the nuclear family. On the other hand, Stack's (1975) study of welfare-dependent families in a ghetto area of a midwestern city shows that regular sharing with nonnuclear relatives is an important strategy that the urban poor use to adapt to poverty.

THE FAMILY AMONG FORAGERS

Foraging societies are far removed from industrial nations in terms of social complexity, but they feature geographic mobility, which is associated with nomadic or seminomadic hunting and gathering. Here again, the nuclear family often is the most significant kin group, although in no foraging society is it the only group based on kinship. The two basic social units of traditional foraging societies are the nuclear family and the band.

Unlike middle-class couples in industrial nations, foragers don't usually reside neolocally. Instead, they join a band in which either the husband or the wife has relatives. However, couples and families may move from one band to another several times. Although nuclear families are ultimately as impermanent among foragers as they are in any other society, they usually are more stable than bands are.

Many foraging societies lacked year-round band organization. The Native American Shoshone of Utah and Nevada provide an example. The resources available to the Shoshone were so meager that for most of the year families traveled alone through the countryside hunting and gathering. In certain seasons families assembled to hunt cooperatively as a band, but after just a few months together they dispersed.

In neither industrial nor foraging economies are people permanently tied to the land. The mobility and the emphasis on small, economically self-sufficient family units promote the nuclear family as a basic kin group in both types of societies.

CULTURETHINK

Think of the nuclear family as an economic adaptation. What features do foragers and people living in industrial nations have in common that make the nuclear family practical? How is this different from nonindustrial food-producing societies?

Household and Family Size in the United States and Canada, 1980 vs. 2007

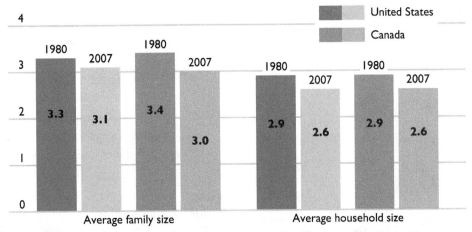

Legend: United States | Canada

Average family size:
- 1980: 3.3
- 2007: 3.1
- 1980: 3.4
- 2007: 3.0

Average household size:
- 1980: 2.9
- 2007: 2.6
- 1980: 2.9
- 2007: 2.6

Sources: J. M. Fields, "America's Families and Living Arrangements: 2003," *Current Population Reports*, P20–553. November 2004, http://www.census.gov/prod2004pubs/p20-553.pdf, pp. 3–4; U.S. Census Bureau, *Statistical Abstract of the United States,* 2009, Table 58, p. 52; Statistics Canada, 2006 Census, http://www12.statcan.ca/english/census06/data/topics/, http://www40.statcan.ca/101/cst01/famil532.

>> Descent

We've seen that the nuclear family is important in industrial nations and among foragers. The analogous group among nonindustrial food producers is the descent group. A **descent group** is a *permanent* social unit whose members claim common ancestry. Descent group members believe they all descend from those common ancestors. The group endures even though its membership changes, as members are born and die, move in and move out. Often, descent-group membership is determined at birth and is lifelong. In this case, it is an ascribed status.

CHARACTERISTICS OF DESCENT GROUPS

Descent groups frequently are exogamous (members seek their mates from other descent groups). Two common rules serve to admit certain people as descent-group members while excluding others. With a rule of **patrilineal descent,** people automatically have lifetime membership in their father's group. The children of the group's men join the group, but the children of the group's women are excluded. With **matrilineal descent,** people join the mother's group automatically at birth and stay members throughout life. Matrilineal descent groups therefore include only the children of the group's women.

Matrilineal and patrilineal descent are types of **unilineal descent.** This means the descent rule uses one line only, either the male or the female line. Patrilineal descent is much more common than matrilineal descent. In a sample of 564 societies (Murdock 1957), about three times as many were found to be patrilineal (247 to 84).

> **descent group** A permanent social unit whose members claim common ancestry; fundamental to tribal society.
>
> **patrilineal descent** Unilineal descent rule in which people join the father's group automatically at birth and stay members throughout life.
>
> **matrilineal descent** Unilineal descent rule in which people join the mother's group automatically at birth and stay members throughout life.
>
> **unilineal descent** Matrilineal or patrilineal descent.

A Patrilineage Five Generations Deep

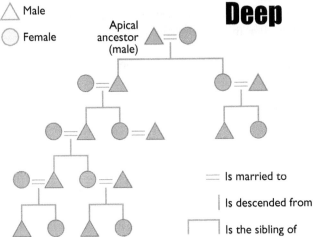

△ Male
○ Female

Apical ancestor (male)

═ Is married to
| Is descended from
⎣ Is the sibling of

Lineages are based on demonstrated descent from an apical ancestor. With patrilineal descent, children of the group's men (blue) are included as descent-group members. Children of the group's women are excluded; they belong to their father's patrilineage.

A Matrilineage Five Generations Deep

Apical ancestor (female)

△ Male

○ Female

Matrilineages are based on demonstrated descent from a female ancestor. Only the children of the group's women (blue) belong to the matrilineage. The children of the group's men are excluded; they belong to their mother's matrilineage.

STUDY TIP

Two important ways of organizing kin are the nuclear family and the descent group. The *nuclear family* is impermanent, includes only parents and children, and is common in foraging and industrial societies. The *descent group*, which is common among nonindustrial food producers (horticulturalists, agriculturalists, and pastoralists), is permanent and includes multiple generations.

Descent groups may be **lineages** or **clans.** Common to both is the belief that members descend from the same *apical ancestor*, the person who stands at the apex, or top, of the common genealogy. For example, Adam and Eve are the apical ancestors of the biblical Jews, and, according to the Bible, of all humanity. Since Eve is said to have come from Adam's rib, Adam stands as the original apical ancestor for the patrilineal genealogy laid out in the Bible.

How do lineages and clans differ? A lineage uses *demonstrated descent.* Members recite the names of their forebears from the apical ancestor through the present. (This doesn't mean their recitations are accurate, only that lineage members think they are.) In the Bible the litany of men who "begat" other men is a demonstration of genealogical descent for a large patrilineage that ultimately includes Jews and Arabs (who share Abraham as their last common apical ancestor).

Unlike lineages, clans use *stipulated descent.* Clan members merely say they descend from the apical ancestor, without trying to trace the actual genealogical links. The Betsileo of Madagascar have both clans and lineages. Descent may be demonstrated for the most recent eight to ten generations, then stipulated for the more remote past—sometimes with mermaids and vaguely defined foreign royalty mentioned among the founders (Kottak 1980). Like the Betsileo, many societies have both lineages and

lineage Unilineal descent group based on demonstrated descent.

clan Unilineal descent group based on stipulated descent.

patrilocality Customary residence with the husband's relatives after marriage, so that children grow up in their father's community.

matrilocality Customary residence with the wife's relatives after marriage, so that children grow up in their mother's community.

clans. In such a case, clans have more members and cover a larger geographical area than lineages do. Sometimes a clan's apical ancestor is not a human at all but an animal or plant (called a *totem*).

The economic types that usually have descent group organization are horticulture, pastoralism, and agriculture. Such societies tend to have several descent groups. Any one of them may be confined to a single village, but usually they span more than one village. Two or more local branches of different descent groups may live in the same village. Descent groups in the same village or different villages may establish alliances through frequent intermarriage.

LINEAGES, CLANS, AND RESIDENCE RULES

As we've seen, descent groups, unlike families, are permanent and enduring units, with new members added in every generation. Members have access to the lineage estate, where some of them must live, in order to benefit from and manage that estate across the generations. An easy way to keep members at home is to have a rule about who belongs to the descent group and where they should live after they get married. Patrilineal and matrilineal descent, and the postmarital residence rules that usually accompany them, ensure that about half the people born in each generation will spend their lives on the ancestral estate.

Patrilocality is the rule that when a couple marries, it moves to the husband's community, so that their children will grow up in their father's village. Patrilocality is associated with patrilineal descent. This makes sense. If the group's male members are expected to exercise their rights in the ancestral estate, it's a good idea to raise them on that estate and to keep them there after they marry. This can be done by having wives move to the husband's village, rather than vice versa.

A less common postmarital residence rule, often associated with matrilineal descent, is **matrilocality:** Married couples live in the wife's community, and their children grow up in their mother's village. This rule keeps related

Most societies have a prevailing opinion about where couples should live after they marry; this is called a postmarital residence rule. A common rule is patrilocality: The couple lives with the husband's relatives, so that the children grow up in their father's community. The image at left shows a twelve-year-old Muslim bride (veiled in pink) in the West African country of Guinea Bissau. On the last day of her three-day wedding ceremony, she will collect laundry from her husband's family, wash it with her friends, and be taken to his village on a bicycle. In the image below, in Lendak, Slovakia, women transport part of the bride's dowry to the groom's house.

women together. Together, patrilocality and matrilocality are known as *unilocal* rules of postmarital residence.

>> Marriage

"Love and marriage," "marriage and the family": These familiar phrases show how we link the romantic love of two individuals to marriage, and how we link marriage to reproduction and family creation. But marriage is an institution with significant roles and functions in addition to reproduction. What is marriage, anyway?

No definition of marriage is broad enough to apply easily to all societies and situations. A commonly quoted definition comes from *Notes and Queries on Anthropology:*

> Marriage is a union between a man and a woman such that the children born to the woman are recognized as legitimate offspring of both partners. (Royal Anthropological Institute 1951, p. 111)

This definition isn't valid universally for several reasons. In many societies, marriages unite more than two spouses. Here we speak of *plural marriages,* as when a man weds two (or more) women, or a woman weds a group of brothers—an arrangement called *fraternal polyandry* that is characteristic of certain Himalayan cultures. In the Brazilian community of Arembepe, people can choose among various forms of marital union. Most people live in long-term "common-law" domestic partnerships that are not legally sanctioned. Some have civil marriages, which are licensed and legalized by a justice of the peace. Still others go through religious ceremonies, so they are united in "holy matrimony," although not legally. And some have both civil and religious ties. The different forms of union permit someone to have multiple spouses (e.g., one common-law, one civil, one religious) without ever getting divorced.

Some societies recognize various kinds of same-sex marriages. In Sudan, a Nuer woman could marry a woman if her father had only daughters but no male heirs, who are necessary if his patrilineage is to survive. He might ask his daughter to stand as a son in order to take a bride. This daughter would become the socially recognized husband of another woman (the wife). This was a symbolic and social relationship rather than a sexual one. The "wife" had sex with a man or men (whom her female "husband" had to approve) until she got pregnant. The children born to the wife were accepted as the offspring of both the female husband and the wife. Although the female husband was not the actual *genitor* (the biological father) of the children, she was their *pater,* or socially recognized father. What's important in this Nuer case is *social* rather than *biological paternity.* We see again how kinship is socially constructed. The bride's children were considered the legitimate offspring of her female husband, who was biologically a woman but socially a man, and the descent line continued.

A study of online dating found that, online, men tend to lie about their height and women about their weight. Those farther from the norm lied more. Both men and women tend to use deliberately deceptive photographs but are honest about their relationship information.

Did You Know?

Incest refers to sexual relations with a relative. All cultures have taboos against it. Although the taboo is a cultural universal, cultures define their kin, and thus incest, differently. When unilineal descent is very strongly developed, the parent who belongs to a different descent group than your own isn't considered a relative. Thus, with strict patrilineality, the mother is not a relative but a kind of in-law who has married a member of your own group—your father. With strict matrilineality, the father isn't a relative because he belongs to a different descent group.

The Lakher of Southeast Asia are strictly patrilineal (Leach 1961). Using the male ego (the reference point, the person in question) in the figure below, let's suppose that ego's father and mother get divorced. Each remarries and has a daughter by a second marriage. A Lakher always belongs to his or her father's group, all the members of which (one's *agnates,* or patrikin) are considered too closely related to marry because they are members of the same patrilineal descent group. Therefore, ego can't marry his father's daughter by the second marriage, just as in contemporary North America it's illegal for half-siblings to marry.

In contrast to our society, where all half-siblings are tabooed in marriage, the Lakher would permit ego to marry his mother's daughter by a different father. She is not ego's relative because she belongs to her own father's descent group rather than ego's. The Lakher illustrate very well that definitions of relatives, and therefore of incest, vary from culture to culture.

INCEST AND EXOGAMY

In nonindustrial societies, a person's social world includes two main categories—friends and strangers. Strangers are potential or actual enemies. Marriage is one of the primary ways of converting strangers into friends, of creating and maintaining personal and political alliances, relationships of affinity. **Exogamy,** the practice of seeking a mate outside one's own group, has

exogamy Mating or marriage outside one's kin group; a cultural universal.

incest Sexual relations with a close relative.

adaptive value because it links people into a wider social network that nurtures, helps, and protects them in times of need.

On February 15, 1946, in Tokyo, American sailor Charles D. Seabolt and his Japanese girlfriend Kaneko are photographed in a park. International marriages are a form of exogamy.

Patrilineal Descent-Group Identity and Incest among the Lakher

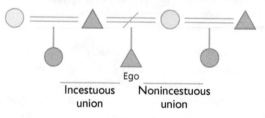

Ego

Incestuous union   Nonincestuous union

⬤, ▲ : Ego's patrilineage

⬤, ▲ : Ego's mother's second husband's patrilineage

⬤ : Ego's mother's patrilineage

⬤ : Ego's father's second wife's patrilineage

⚯ : Separation or divorce.

FD: by second marriage is a comember of ego's descent group and is included within the incest taboo.

MD: by second marriage is not a comember of ego's descent group and is not tabooed.

Although Tabooed, Incest Does Happen There is no simple or universally accepted explanation for the fact that all cultures ban incest. Do primate studies offer any clues? Research with primates shows that adolescent males (among monkeys) or females (among apes) often move away from the group in which they were born (Rodseth et al. 1991). This emigration reduces the frequency of incestuous unions, but it doesn't eliminate them. DNA testing of wild chimps has confirmed incestuous unions between adult sons and their mothers, who reside in the same group. Human behavior with respect to mating with close relatives may express a generalized primate tendency, in which we see both urges and avoidance.

A cross-cultural study of eighty-seven societies (Meigs and Barlow 2002) revealed that incest occurred in several of them. For example, among the Yanomami, Chagnon reported that "incest, far from being feared, is widely practiced" (1967, p. 66). Meyer Fortes observed about the Ashanti: "In the old days it [incest] was punished by death. Nowadays the culprits are heavily fined" (Fortes 1950, p. 257). Among twenty-four Ojibwa individuals from whom he obtained information about incest, A. Irving Hallowell found eight cases of parent–child incest and ten cases of brother–sister incest (Hallowell 1955, pp. 294–295).

In ancient Egypt, sibling marriage apparently was allowed not just for royalty but for commoners as well, in at least some districts. Based on official census records from Roman Egypt (first to third centuries C.E.) preserved on papyrus, 24 percent of all documented marriages in the Arsinoites district were between brothers and sisters. In the second century C.E., the rates were 37 percent for the city of Arsinoe and 19 percent for the surrounding villages. These figures are much higher than any other documented levels of inbreeding among humans (Scheidel 1997).

> "An ounce of blood is worth more than a pound of friendship."
>
> Spanish proverb

CULTURE THINK

We tend to think of incest as wrong because of the potential for genetic defects due to inbreeding. Many states, however, consider it incestuous to have sexual relations with categories of relatives who are not biologically related, such as stepparents and siblings by adoption. Why are these considered wrong?

According to Anna Meigs and Kathleen Barlow (2002), for Western societies with nuclear family organization, father–daughter incest is most common with stepfathers, but it also happens with biological fathers, especially those who were absent or did little caretaking of their daughters in childhood (Williams and Finkelhor 1995). In a carefully designed study, Linda M. Williams and David Finkelhor (1995) found father–daughter incest to be least likely when there was substantial paternal parenting of daughters who were four to five years old. This experience enhanced the father's parenting skills and his feelings of nurturance, protectiveness, and identification with his daughter, thus reducing the risk of incest.

It has been argued (Hobhouse 1915; Lowie 1920/1961) that the incest taboo is universal because incest horror is instinctive: Humans have a genetically programmed disgust toward incest. Because of this feeling, early humans banned it. However, cultural universality doesn't necessarily entail an instinctual basis. Fire making, for example, is a cultural universal, but it certainly isn't an ability transmitted by the genes. Furthermore, if people really did have an instinctive horror of mating with blood relatives, a formal incest taboo would be unnecessary. No one would do it. As we have just seen, and as social workers, judges, psychiatrists, and psychologists know, incest is more common than we might suppose.

ENDOGAMY

The practice of exogamy pushes social organization outward, establishing and preserving alliances among groups. In contrast, rules of **endogamy** dictate mating or marriage within a group to which one belongs. Endogamic rules are less common but are still familiar to anthropologists. Indeed, most cultures *are* endogamous units, although they usually do not need a formal rule requiring people to marry someone from their own society. In our own society, classes and ethnic groups are quasi-endogamous groups. Members of an ethnic or religious group often want their children to marry within that group, although many of them do not do so. The outmarriage rate varies among such groups, with some more committed to endogamy than others.

> **endogamy** Marriage between people of the same social group.

Caste An extreme example of endogamy is India's caste system, which was formally abolished in 1949, although its structure and effects linger. Castes are stratified groups in which membership is ascribed at birth and is lifelong. Indian castes are grouped into five major categories, or *varna*. Each is ranked relative to the other four, and these categories extend throughout India. Each varna includes a large number of castes (*jati*), each of which includes people within a region who may intermarry. All the jati in a single varna in a given region are ranked, just as the varna themselves are ranked.

Occupational specialization often sets off one caste from another. A community may include castes of agricultural workers, merchants, artisans, priests, and sweepers. The untouchable varna, found throughout India, includes castes whose ancestry, ritual status, and occupations are considered so impure that higher-caste people hold even casual contact with untouchables to be defiling.

The belief that intercaste sexual unions lead to ritual impurity for the higher-caste partner has been important in maintaining endogamy. A man who has sex with a lower-caste woman can restore his purity with a bath and a prayer. A woman who has intercourse with a man of a lower caste has no such recourse. Her defilement cannot be undone. Because the women have the babies, these differences protect the purity of the caste line, ensuring the pure ancestry of high-caste children. Although Indian castes are endogamous groups, many of them are internally subdivided into exogamous lineages. Traditionally this meant that Indians had to marry a member of another descent group from the same caste. This shows that rules of exogamy and endogamy can coexist in the same society.

Couple getting married in San Francisco after a state supreme court ruling to allow same-sex marriage and before Proposition 8, a state constitutional amendment, banned the practice, and before Proposition 8 was voided by an Appeals Court judge in 2010.

>> Marital Rights and Same-Sex Marriage

The British anthropologist Edmund Leach (1955) observed that, depending on the society, several kinds of rights are allocated by marriage. According to Leach, marriage can, but doesn't always, accomplish the following:

- Establish the legal father of a woman's children and the legal mother of a man's.
- Give either or both spouses a monopoly in the sexuality of the other.
- Give either or both spouses rights to the labor of the other.
- Give either or both spouses rights over the other's property.
- Establish a joint fund of property—a partnership—for the benefit of the children.
- Establish a socially significant "relationship of affinity" between spouses and their relatives.

The discussion of same-sex marriage that follows will serve to illustrate the six rights just listed by seeing what happens in their absence (see also Stone 2004). What if same-sex marriages, which by and large remain illegal in the United States, were legal? Could a same-sex marriage establish legal parentage of children born to one or both partners after the partnership is formed? In the case of a different-sex marriage, children born to the wife after the marriage takes place usually are defined legally as her husband's regardless of whether he is the genitor.

Nowadays, DNA testing makes it possible to establish paternity, just as modern reproductive technology makes it possible for a lesbian couple to have one or both partners artificially inseminated (see Levine 2008). When same-sex marriage is legal, the social construction of kinship easily can make both partners parents. If a Nuer woman married to a woman can be the pater of a child she did not father, why can't two lesbians be the *maters* (socially recognized mothers) of a child one of them did not father? And if a married different-sex couple can adopt a child and have it be theirs through the social and legal construction of kinship, the same logic could be applied to a gay male or lesbian couple.

Continuing with Leach's list of the rights transmitted by marriage, same-sex marriage certainly could give each spouse rights to the sexuality of the other. Same-sex marriages, as forms of monogamous commitment, have been endorsed by representatives of many religions, including Unitarians, Quakers (the Society of Friends), and reform Jewish synagogues (Eskridge 1996). In June 2003 a court ruling established same-sex marriages as legal in the province of Ontario, Canada. On June 28, 2005, Canada's House of Commons voted to guarantee full marriage rights to same-sex couples throughout that nation. In the United States six states—Massachusetts, Connecticut, Iowa, Vermont, Maine, and New Hampshire—allowed same-sex marriage as of 2009 (see "Same-Sex Marriage Laws"). California rejoined that list in 2010. Civil unions for same-sex couples are legal in New Jersey. In reaction to same-sex marriage, voters in at least eighteen U.S. states have approved measures in their state constitutions defining marriage as an exclusively heterosexual union. On November 4, 2008, Californians voted 52 percent to 48 percent for Proposition 8, overturning the right to same-sex marriage, which the courts had approved earlier that year. An appeals court judge ruled Proposition 8 unconstitutional in 2010 and allowed same-sex marriages in California to resume.

Legal same-sex marriages can easily give each spouse rights to the other spouse's labor and its products. Some societies allow marriage between members of the same biological sex. Several Native American groups had figures known as *berdaches*. These were biological men who assumed many of the manner-

isms, behavior patterns, and tasks of women. Sometimes berdaches married men, who shared the products of their labor from hunting and traditional male roles, as the berdache fulfilled the traditional wifely role. Also, in some Native American cultures, a marriage of a "manly-hearted woman" to another woman brought the traditional male–female division of labor to their household. The manly woman hunted and did other male tasks, while the wife played the traditional female role.

There's no logical reason why same-sex marriage cannot give spouses rights over the other's property. But in the United States, the same inheritance rights that apply to male–female couples usually do not apply to same-sex couples. For instance, even in the absence of a will, property can pass to a widow or a widower without going through probate. The wife or husband pays no inheritance tax. This benefit is not available to gay men and lesbians. When a same-sex partner is in a nursing home, prison, or hospital, the other partner may not have the same visiting rights as would a husband, wife, or biological relative (Weston 1991).

What about Leach's fifth right—to establish a joint fund of property—to benefit the children? Here again, gay and lesbian couples are at a disadvantage. If there are children, property is separately, rather than jointly, transmitted. Some organizations do make staff benefits, such as health and dental insurance, available to same-sex domestic partners.

Finally, there is the matter of establishing a socially significant "relationship of affinity" between spouses and their relatives. In many societies, one of the main roles of marriage is to establish an alliance between groups, in addition to the individual bond. *Affinals* are relatives through

> "Of all the peoples whom I have studied, from city dwellers to cliff dwellers, I always find that at least 50 percent would prefer to have at least one jungle between themselves and their mothers-in-law."
>
> Margaret Mead

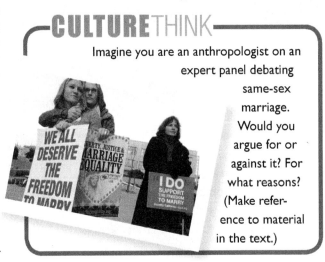

CULTURETHINK

Imagine you are an anthropologist on an expert panel debating same-sex marriage. Would you argue for or against it? For what reasons? (Make reference to material in the text.)

marriage, such as a brother-in-law or mother-in-law. For same-sex couples in contemporary North America, affinal relations are problematic. In an unofficial union, terms like "daughter-in-law" and "mother-in-law" may sound strange. Many parents are suspicious of their children's sexuality and lifestyle choices and may not recognize a relationship of affinity with a child's partner of the same sex.

This discussion of same-sex marriage is intended to illustrate the different kinds of rights that typically accompany marriage, by seeing what may happen when there is a permanent pair bond without legal sanction. In just six of the United States are such unions fully legal. As we have seen, same-sex unions have been recognized in different historical and cultural settings. In certain African cultures, including the Igbo of Nigeria and the Lovedu of South Africa, women could marry other women. In situations in which women, such as prominent market women in West Africa, are able to amass property and other forms of wealth, they may take a wife. Such marriage allows the prominent woman to strengthen her social status and the economic importance of her household (Amadiume 1987).

bridewealth A customary gift before, at, or after marriage from the husband and his kin to the wife and her kin.

progeny price A gift from the husband and his kin to the wife and her kin before, at, or after marriage; legitimizes children born to the woman as members of the husband's descent group.

dowry A marital exchange in which the wife's group provides substantial gifts to the husband's family.

>> Marriage across Cultures

Outside industrial societies, marriage often is more a relationship between groups than one between individuals. We think of marriage as an individual matter. Although the bride and groom usually seek their parents' approval, the final choice (to live together, to marry, to divorce) lies with the couple. The idea of romantic love symbolizes this individual relationship.

Anthropology Works

Counselors or clinical psychologists would find it helpful to know about cross-cultural patterns of marriage and divorce to better understand the pressures their clients face.

In nonindustrial societies, although there can be romantic love (Goleman 1992), marriage is a group concern. People don't just take a spouse; they assume obligations to a group of in-laws. When residence is patrilocal, for example, a woman must leave the community where she was born. She faces the prospect of spending the rest of her life in her husband's village, with his relatives. She may even have to transfer her major allegiance from her own group to her husband's.

BRIDEWEALTH AND DOWRY

In societies with descent groups, people enter marriage not alone but with the help of the descent group. Descent-group members often contribute to the **bridewealth,** a customary gift before, at, or after the marriage from the husband and his kin to the wife and her kin. Another word for bridewealth is *brideprice,* but this term is inaccurate because people with the custom don't usually think of marriage as a commercial relationship between a man and an object to be bought and sold.

Bridewealth compensates the bride's group for the loss of her companionship and labor. More important, it makes the children born to the woman full members of her husband's descent group. For this reason, the institution also is called **progeny price.** Rather than the woman herself, it is her children who are permanently transferred to the husband's group. Whatever we call it, such a transfer of wealth at marriage is common in patrilineal groups. In matrilineal societies, children are members of the mother's group, and there is no reason to pay a progeny price.

Dowry is a marital exchange in which the wife's group provides substantial gifts to the husband's family. Dowry, best known from India but also practiced in Europe, correlates with low female status. Women are perceived as burdens. When husbands and their families take a wife, they expect to be compensated for the added responsibility.

Bridewealth exists in many more cultures than dowry does, but the nature and quantity of transferred items differ. In many African societies, cattle constitute bridewealth, but the number of cattle given varies from society to society. As the value of bridewealth increases, marriages become more stable. Bridewealth is insurance against divorce.

Imagine a patrilineal society in which a marriage requires the transfer of about twenty-five cattle from the groom's descent group to the bride's. Michael, a member of descent group A, marries Sarah from group B. His relatives help him assemble the bridewealth. He gets the most help from his close agnates—his older brother, father, father's brother, and closest patrilineal cousins.

The distribution of the cattle once they reach Sarah's group mirrors the manner in which they were assembled. Sarah's father, or her oldest brother if the father is dead, receives her bridewealth. He keeps most of the cattle to use as bridewealth for his sons' marriages. However, a share also goes to everyone who will be expected to help when Sarah's brothers marry.

When Sarah's brother David gets married, many of the cattle go to a third group—C, which is David's wife's group. Thereafter, they may serve as bridewealth to still other groups. Men constantly use their sisters' bridewealth cattle to acquire their own wives. In a decade, the cattle given when Michael married Sarah will have been exchanged widely.

In such societies marriage entails an agreement between descent groups. If Sarah and Michael try to make their marriage succeed but fail to do so, both groups may conclude that the marriage can't last. Here it becomes especially obvious that marriages are relationships between groups as well as between individuals. If Sarah has a younger sister or niece (her older brother's daughter, for example), the concerned parties may agree to Sarah's replacement by a kinswoman.

However, incompatibility isn't the main problem that threatens marriage in societies with bridewealth. Infertility is a more important concern. If Sarah has no children, she and her group have not fulfilled their part of the marriage agreement. If the relationship is to endure, Sarah's group must furnish another woman, perhaps her younger sister, who can have children. If this happens, Sarah may choose to stay in her husband's village. Perhaps she will someday have a child. If she does stay on, her husband will have established a plural marriage.

Most nonindustrial food-producing societies, unlike most industrial nations, allow **plural marriages,** or *polygamy.* There are two varieties; one is common and the other is very rare. The more common variant is **polygyny,** in which a man has more than one wife. The rare variant is **polyandry,** in which a woman has more than one husband. If the infertile wife remains married to her husband after he has taken a substitute wife provided by her descent group, this is polygyny.

DURABLE ALLIANCES

It is possible to exemplify the group-alliance nature of marriage by examining still another common practice—continuation of marital alliances when one spouse dies.

Sororate What happens if Sarah dies young? Michael's group will ask Sarah's group for a substitute, often her sister. This custom is known as the **sororate**. If Sarah has no sister, or if all her sisters already are married, another woman from her group may be available. Michael marries her, there is no need to return the bridewealth, and the alliance continues.

The sororate exists in both matrilineal and patrilineal societies. In a matrilineal society with matrilocal postmarital residence, a widower may remain with his wife's group by marrying her sister or another female member of her matrilineage.

Levirate What happens if the husband dies? In many

> **plural marriage** Marriage of a man to two or more women (polygyny) or marriage of a woman to two or more men (polyandry) at the same time.
>
> **sororate** Custom by which a widower marries the sister of the deceased wife.
>
> **levirate** Custom by which a widow marries the brother of her deceased husband.

CULTURETHINK

Consider how each of the following illustrates the importance of marriage as an alliance between groups: arranged marriage, bridewealth, sororate and levirate.

Examples of the sororate and levirate

Sororate

Levirate

● : Sarah's descent group

▲ : Michael's descent group

societies, the widow may marry his brother. This custom is known as the **levirate.** Like the sororate, it is a continuation marriage that maintains the alliance between descent groups, in this case by replacing the husband with another member of his group. The implications of the levirate vary with age. One study found that in African societies the levirate, although widely permitted, rarely involves cohabitation of the widow and her new husband. Furthermore, widows don't automatically marry the husband's brother just because they are allowed to. Often they prefer to make other arrangements (Potash 1986).

>> Divorce

In some societies marriages may seem to go on forever, but in our own they are fairly brittle. Ease of divorce varies across cultures. What factors work for and against divorce? As we've seen, marriages that are political alliances between groups are more difficult to dissolve than are marriages that are more individual affairs, of concern mainly to the married couple and their children. Substantial bridewealth may decrease the divorce rate for individuals; replacement marriages (levirate and sororate)

One sociologist has found what he calls a "divorce divide": People with college degrees are less likely to get a divorce than those without degrees. The divorce rate among college graduates actually decreased between the 1970s and the 1990s.

also work to preserve group alliances. Divorce tends to be more common in matrilineal than in patrilineal societies. When residence is matrilocal (in the wife's home village), the wife may simply send off a man with whom she's incompatible.

Among the Hopi of the American Southwest, houses were owned by matrilineal clans, with matrilocal postmarital residence. The household head was the senior woman of that household, which also included her daughters and their husbands and children. A son-in-law had no important role there; he returned to his own mother's home for his clan's social and religious activities. In this matrilineal society, women were socially and economically secure, and the divorce rate was high. Consider the Hopi of Oraibi (Orayvi) pueblo, northeastern Arizona (Levy 1992; Titiev 1992). In a study of the marital histories of 423 Oraibi women, Mischa Titiev found 35 percent to have been divorced at least once. Jerome Levy found that 31 percent of 147 adult women had been divorced and remarried at least once. For comparison, of all ever-married women in the United States, only 4 percent had been divorced in 1960, 10.7 percent in 1980, and 11.5 percent in 2004. Titiev characterizes Hopi marriages as unstable. Part of this brittleness was due to conflicting loyal-

ties to matrikin versus spouse. Most Hopi divorces appear to have been matters of personal choice. Levy generalizes that, cross-culturally, high divorce rates are correlated with a secure female economic position. In Hopi society women were secure in their home and land ownership and in the custody of their children. In addition, there were no formal barriers to divorce.

Divorce is harder in a patrilineal society, especially when substantial bridewealth would have to be reassembled and repaid if the marriage failed. A woman residing patrilocally (in her husband's household and community) might be reluctant to leave him. Unlike the Hopi, where the kids stay with the mother, in patrilineal, patrilocal societies the children of divorce would be expected to remain with their father, as members of his patrilineage. From the women's perspective this is a strong impediment to divorce.

Among foragers, different factors favor or oppose divorce. What factors work against durable marriages? Since foragers tend to lack descent groups, the political alliance functions of marriage are less important to them than they are to food producers. Foragers also tend to have minimal material possessions. The process of dissolving a joint fund of property is less complicated when spouses do not hold substantial resources in common. What factors work in opposition to divorce among foragers? In societies in which

STUDY TIP

Divorce is less common (1) when marriage involves political alliances; (2) where there is brideprice; (3) in patrilineal societies; (4) when women have a low economic position.

the family is an important year-round unit with a gender-based division of labor, ties between spouses tend to be durable. Also, sparse populations mean few alternative spouses if a marriage doesn't work out.

In contemporary Western societies, we have the idea that romantic love is necessary for a good marriage (see Ingraham 2008). When romance fails, so may the marriage (see "Trends in Marriage and Divorce in the United States"). Or it may not fail, if the other rights associated with marriage, as discussed previously in this chapter, are compelling. Economic ties and obligations to children, along with other factors, such as concern about public opinion, or simple inertia, may keep marriages intact after sex, romance, or companionship fade.

Trends in Marriage and Divorce in the United States, 1920–2008

>> Plural Marriages

In contemporary North America, where divorce is fairly easy and common, **polygamy** (marriage to more than one spouse at the same time) is against the law. Marriage in industrial nations joins individuals, and relationships between individuals can be severed more easily than can those between groups. North Americans are allowed to practice *serial monogamy:* Individuals may have more than one spouse but never, legally, more than one at the same time. As stated earlier, the two forms of polygamy are polygyny and polyandry. Polyandry is practiced in only a few societies, notably among certain groups in Tibet, Nepal, and India. Polygyny is much more common.

POLYGYNY

We must distinguish between the social approval of plural marriage and its actual frequency in a particular society. Many cultures approve of a man's having more than one wife. But even when polygyny is encouraged, most people are monogamous, and polygyny characterizes only a fraction of the marriages. Why?

One reason is equal sex ratios. In the United States, about 105 males are born for every 100 females. In adulthood the ratio of men to women equalizes, and eventually it reverses. The average North American woman outlives the average man. In many nonindustrial societies as well, the male-biased sex ratio among children reverses in adulthood.

The custom of men marrying later than women also promotes polygyny. Among Nigeria's Kanuri people (Cohen 1967), men got married between the ages of eighteen and thirty; women, between twelve and fourteen. The age difference between spouses meant there were more widows than widowers. Most of the widows remarried, some in polygynous unions. Among the Kanuri and in other polygynous societies, such as the Tiwi of northern Australia, widows made up a large number of the women involved in plural marriages (Hart, Pilling, and Goodale 1988).

In certain societies, the first wife requests a second wife to help with household chores. The second wife's status is lower than that of the first; they are senior and junior wives. The senior wife sometimes chooses the junior one from among her close kinswomen. Among the Betsileo of Madagascar, the different wives always lived in different villages. A man's first and senior wife, called "Big Wife," lived in the village where he cultivated his best rice field and spent most of his time. High-status men with several rice fields and multiple wives had households near each field. They spent most of their

Shown here in Mali is an Islamic marabout (religious teacher) with his two wives and children. Would you expect most marriages to be polygynous in a society that allows polygyny?

time with the senior wife but visited the others throughout the year.

Plural wives can play important political roles in nonindustrial states. The king of the Merina, a populous society in the highlands of Madagascar, had palaces for each of his twelve wives in different provinces. He stayed with them when he traveled through the kingdom. They were his local agents, overseeing and reporting on provincial matters. The king of Buganda, the major precolonial state of Uganda, took hundreds of wives, representing all the clans in his nation. Everyone in the kingdom became the king's in-law, and all the clans had a chance to provide the next ruler. This was a way of giving the common people a stake in the government.

These examples show there is no single explanation for polygyny. Its context and function vary from society to society and even within the same society. Some men are

> **polygamy** Marriage with three or more spouses, at the same time.

Explore your family's history like an anthropologist. Search on one of the free genealogy websites, such as familysearch.org or the family history or public archives sites of a particular state or country. On either (or both) your mother's or your father's side, look for changes across generations: Who got married to whom (from which towns, of which nationalities) and at what ages? Where did the couple reside relative to their parents? Were there divorces? Obtaining this information online may be difficult, but look at any kinship data you do uncover with an eye for investigating social change. If you can't trace your own family history online, choose some well-known person and investigate his or her family history.

get involved!

polygynous because they have inherited a widow from a brother. Others have plural wives because they seek prestige or want to increase household productivity. Men and women with political and economic ambitions cultivate marital alliances that serve their aims. In many societies, including the Betsileo of Madagascar and the Igbo of Nigeria, women arrange the marriages.

POLYANDRY

Most of the world's polyandrous peoples live in South Asia—Tibet, Nepal, India, and Sri Lanka. Polyandry is rare and practiced under very specific conditions. In some of these areas, polyandry seems to be a cultural adaptation to mobility associated with customary male travel for trade, commerce, and military operations. Polyandry ensures there will be at least one man at home to accomplish male activities within a gender-based division of labor. Fraternal polyandry is also an effective strategy when resources are scarce. Brothers with limited resources (in land) pool their resources in expanded (polyandrous) households. They take just one wife. Polyandry restricts the number of wives and heirs. Less competition among heirs means that land can be transmitted with minimal fragmentation.

For REVIEW

CULTURE CLIPS

TO ACCESS THESE VIDEOS ON YOUR COMPUTER, VISIT

www.mhhe.com/gezonqr

8-1

8-2

8-3

I. **What forms of kinship exist cross-culturally, and what are their social correlates?**

- The nuclear family consists of a married couple and their children. It assumes importance in societies with geographic mobility, which promotes small, economically self-sufficient family units. In industrial societies, a couple typically starts its own nuclear family in a new home. The forager family usually joins a band in which either the husband or the wife has relatives. Extended families include three or more generations. Extended family households occur more frequently where kinspeople need to pool resources. The descent group is a basic kin group among nonindustrial food producers. This perpetual kin group manages an estate across generations.

II. **How do families and descent groups differ?**

- The descent group is a larger system of kinship and marriage than the family. It is important in nonindustrial food-producing societies. The descent group endures even though its membership changes. Descent group members are admitted into their group based on whether they belong to the father's (patrilineal) or the mother's (matrilineal) side. Descent groups take the form of a lineage or a clan. Members of lineages trace genealogical links, while clan members merely say they descend from the same ancestor. The rule of descent and postmarital residence ensure that at least some members spend their lives on the descent group's estate.

III. **How is marriage defined and regulated, and what rights does it convey?**

- Worldwide, marriage has various forms, roles, and functions. In many societies, marriage unites more than two spouses: A man may wed two or more women; a woman may wed a group of brothers. Some societies also recognize same-sex marriage. Generally, marriage establishes the legal parents of children, gives spouses the rights to the sexuality, labor, and property of the other, and establishes a socially significant "relationship of affinity." In societies with descent groups, the transfer of wealth from the groom and his kin to the bride and her kin creates and maintains group alliances. Marital alliances can continue when a man marries the sister of his deceased wife or a woman marries the brother of her deceased husband.

Pop Quiz

1. Which of the following explains the reasons for the primacy of the nuclear family in modern North America?
   a. The nuclear family is prefered by North Americans of all ethnicities and social classes.
   b. Geographic mobility separates North Americans from their extended families.
   c. Households tend to be smaller among the urban poor.
   d. The North American family life has evolved parallel with families worldwide, where the nuclear family has become the most developed form of domestic arrangement.

2. Which of the following is *not* true about the nuclear family?
   a. It is universally present in human societies.
   b. Functions associated with nuclear families may be assumed by other social units.
   c. Nuclear families have no special adaptive advantage in conditions associated with poverty.
   d. The geographic mobility of foraging societies encourages the development of the nuclear family.

3. A lineage is distinguished from a clan by this particular characteristic:
   a. The lineage uses stipulated descent.
   b. The lineage believes all its members descend from the same apical ancestor.
   c. Lineage members can name their forebears from the apical ancestor through the present.
   d. Lineages establish alliances with other descent groups.

4. The following is generally true about incest:
   a. All cultures define incest in more or less the same way.
   b. Human behavior with respect to mating with close relatives may express a generalized primate tendency, including both urges and avoidance.
   c. The horror of incest is instinctive.
   d. Incestuous behavior is extremely rare.

5. The rule of endogamy in India's caste system is an extreme example of that practice. All of the following are true of endogamy in India *except*:
   a. The untouchable *varna* is considered so impure by higher-caste people that even casual contact with untouchables is believed to be defiling.
   b. Although the caste system was formally abolished in 1949, its endogamous practices continue to affect Indian society.
   c. Castes are never subdivided into exogamous lineages.

   d. A woman cannot undo the attribution of defilement she suffers by having sexual intercourse with a man of a lower caste.

6. In societies where same-sex marriage is legal, Edmund Leach's rules about the allocation of rights by marriage apply in all of the following ways, *except*:
   a. Both marital partners can be made parents.
   b. Spouses each have rights to the sexuality of the other.
   c. Native American societies that allowed legal same-sex marriages gave each spouse rights to the other spouse's labor and its products.
   d. In contemporary North American society, parents typically recognize affinity, or relation through marriage, with a child's partner of the same sex.

7. The practice by which the husband's group makes a substantial gift to the wife and her kin is called:
   a. Dowry
   b. Bridewealth
   c. Polygyny
   d. Levirate

8. Which of the following statements about divorce is false?
   a. Divorce is less common in matrilineal societies than in patrilineal societies.
   b. Marriage is harder to dissolve when it creates political alliances.
   c. Divorce is rarer in societies in which the husband and his kin group provide substantial bridewealth.
   d. The Western idea of romantic love is not necessarily a strong cement between spouses.

9. Polygamy includes all of these cases *except*:
   a. A man who has three unrelated wives.
   b. A woman who has three husbands, all of whom are brothers.
   c. A man who marries, then divorces, then marries again, then divorces again.
   d. A man who has three related wives.

10. Which of the following statements about marriage is true?
    a. Marriage must involve at least one biological male and at least one biological female.
    b. Marriage involves a woman and the genitor of her children.
    c. Outside industrial societies, marriage is often more a relationship between groups than one between individuals.
    d. Rings must be exchanged.

1. (b), 2. (a), 3. (c), 4. (c), 5. (b), 6. (c), 7. (b), 8. (a), 9. (c), 10. (c)

9

GENDER

WHAT'S TO COME

Nature and Nurture

Recurrent Gender Patterns

Gender among Foragers

Gender among Horticulturalists

Gender among Agriculturists

Patriarchy and Violence

Gender and Industrialism

What Determines Gender Variation?

Sexual Orientation

UNDERSTANDING OURSELVES

Did you have chores when you were growing up? Was there any gender bias in what you were asked to do compared with your siblings? If you were raised by two parents, did any tension arise over their division of labor? Based on cross-cultural data from societies worldwide, a table in this chapter lists activities that are generally male, generally female, or swing (either male or female). Before you look at that table, see if you can assign the following to one gender or the other (M or F):

hunting large animals ___

gathering wild vegetable foods ___

tending crops ___

fishing ___

cooking ___

fetching water ___

making baskets ___

making drinks ___

Now consult Table 9.1 on page 166 and see how you did. Reflect on your results.

Ideas about gender have changed along with the employment patterns of men and women. Still, the lingering American expectation that proper female behavior should be polite, restrained, and/or meek poses a challenge for women, because American culture also values decisiveness. A man's assertiveness may be admired, but a woman's similar behavior may be labeled "aggressive"—or worse.

Both men and women are constrained by their cultural training. For example, American culture stigmatizes male crying. Becoming a man typically means stifling this natural expression of joy and sadness. American men also are trained to make decisions and stick to them. Our stereotypes associate changing one's mind more with women than with men. What a strange idea—that people shouldn't change their positions if they find a better way. Males, females, and humanity may be equally victimized by aspects of cultural training.

- How are biology and culture expressed in human sex/gender systems?

- How do gender, gender roles, and gender stratification correlate with other social, economic, and political variables?

- What is sexual orientation, and how do sexual practices vary cross-culturally?

>> Nature and Nurture

Because anthropologists study biology, society, and culture, they are in a unique position to comment on nature (biological predispositions) and nurture (environment) as determinants of human behavior. Human attitudes, values, and behavior are limited not only by our genetic predispositions—which often are difficult to identify—but also by our experiences during enculturation. Our attributes as adults are determined both by our genes and by our environment during growth and development.

Questions about nature and nurture emerge in the discussion of human sex/gender roles and sexuality. Men and women differ genetically. Women have two X chromosomes, and men have an X and a Y. The father determines a baby's sex because only he has the Y chromosome to transmit. The mother always provides an X chromosome.

The chromosomal difference is expressed in hormonal and physiological contrasts. Humans are sexually dimorphic, more so than some primates, such as gibbons (small tree-living Asiatic apes) and less so than others, such as gorillas and orangutans. **Sexual dimorphism** refers to differences in male and female biology besides the contrasts in breasts and genitals. Women and men differ not just in primary (genitalia and reproductive organs) and secondary (breasts, voice, hair distribution) sexual characteristics, but in average weight, height, strength, and longevity. Women tend to live longer than men and have excellent endurance capabilities. In a given population, men tend to be taller

sexual dimorphism Marked differences, such as in height and weight, in male and female biology besides the contrasts in breasts and genitals.

gender roles The tasks and activities that a culture assigns to each sex.

gender stereotypes Oversimplified but strongly held ideas about the characteristics of males and females.

and to weigh more than women do. Of course, there is a considerable overlap between the sexes in terms of height, weight, and physical strength, and there has been a pronounced reduction in sexual dimorphism during human biological evolution.

Just how far, however, do such genetically and physiologically determined differences go? What effects do they have on the way men and women act and are treated in different societies? Anthropologists have discovered both similarities and differences in the roles of men and women in different cultures. The predominant anthropological position on sex–gender roles and biology may be stated as follows:

> The biological nature of men and women [should be seen] not as a narrow enclosure limiting the human organism, but rather as a broad base upon which a variety of structures can be built. (Friedl 1975, p. 6)

Although in most societies men tend to be somewhat more aggressive than women are, many behavioral and attitudinal differences between the sexes emerge from culture rather than biology. Sex differences are biological, but gender encompasses all the traits that a culture assigns to and inculcates in males and females. *Gender*, in other words, refers to the cultural construction of whether one is female, male, or something else.

STUDY **TIP**

Sex refers to biological differences, and *gender* to cultural constructions of sex differences. There may be more than two recognized genders in a given society.

Given the "rich and various constructions of gender within the realm of cultural diversity," Susan Bourque and Kay Warren (1987) note that the same images of masculinity and femininity do not always apply. Anthropologists have gathered systematic ethnographic data about similarities and differences involving gender in many cultural settings (Bonvillain 2008; Brettell and Sargent 2005; Gilmore 2001; Kimmel 2007; Mascia-Lees and Black 2000; Nanda 2000; Ward and Edelstein 2008). Anthropologists can detect recurrent themes and patterns involving gender differences. They also can observe that gender roles vary with environment, economy, adaptive strategy, and type of political system. Before we examine the cross-cultural data, some definitions are in order.

Gender roles are the tasks and activities a culture assigns to the sexes. Related to gender roles are **gender stereotypes,** which are oversimplified but strongly held ideas about the characteristics of males and females. **Gender stratification** describes an unequal distribution of rewards (socially valued resources, power, prestige, human rights, and personal freedom) between men and women, reflecting their different positions in a social hierarchy. According to Ann Stoler (1977), the economic determinants of gender status include freedom or autonomy (in disposing of one's labor and

POPCULTURE

In an episode of *The Simpsons* titled "Lisa vs. Malibu Stacy," eight-year-old Lisa is outraged when her talking doll (Stacy) says things like, "Let's buy makeup so boys will like us." The doll's statement, and Lisa's reaction to it, expose American cultural values reflecting consumerism, gender roles, and gender stereotypes. Watch a few episodes of *The Simpsons, South Park,* or *Family Guy.* What can we learn about gender roles and stereotypes (and about culture and society more generally) by analyzing such popular culture products?

CULTURETHINK

Advertisements communicate gender stereotypes. Focusing on different kinds of products (e.g., cars, cleaning products, clothing, beer), analyze three to five TV ads for the messages they send about what it means to be a man or a woman.

its fruits) and social power (control over the lives, labor, and produce of others).

In stateless societies, gender stratification often is more obvious in regard to prestige than it is in regard to wealth. In her study of the Ilongots of northern Luzon in the Philippines, Michelle Rosaldo (1980a) described gender differences related to the positive cultural value placed on adventure, travel, and knowledge of the external world. More often than women, Ilongot men, as headhunters, visited distant places. They acquired knowledge of the external world, amassed experiences there, and returned to express

their knowledge, adventures, and feelings in public oratory. They received acclaim as a result. Ilongot women had inferior prestige because they lacked external experiences on which to base knowledge and dramatic expression. On the basis of Rosaldo's study and findings in other stateless societies, Ong (1989) argues that we must distinguish between prestige systems and actual power in a given society. High male prestige may not entail economic or political power held by men over their families.

gender stratification Unequal distribution of rewards (socially valued resources, power, prestige, and personal freedom) between men and women, reflecting their different positions in a social hierarchy.

>> Recurrent Gender Patterns

Ethnologists compare ethnographic data from several cultures (i.e., cross-cultural data) to discover and explain differences and similarities. Data relevant to the cross-cultural study of gender can be drawn from the domains of economics, politics, domestic activity, kinship, and marriage. Table 9.1 shows cross-cultural data from 185 randomly selected societies on the division of labor by gender.

Remembering the discussion of universals, generalities, and particularities in the chapter "Culture," the findings in

Chapter 9 / Gender • 165

Generalities in the Division of Labor by Gender, Based on Data from 185 Societies

Generally Male Activities	Swing (Male or Female) Activities	Generally Female Activities
Hunting of large aquatic animals (e.g., whales, walrus)	Making fire	Gathering fuel (e.g., firewood)
Smelting of ores	Body mutilation	Making drinks
Metalworking	Preparing skins	Gathering wild vegetal foods
Lumbering	Gathering small land animals	Dairy production (e.g., churning)
Hunting large land animals	Planting crops	Spinning
Working wood	Making leather products	Doing the laundry
Hunting fowl	Harvesting	Fetching water
Making musical instruments	Tending crops	Cooking
Trapping	Milking	Preparing vegetal foods (e.g., processing cereal grains)
Building boats	Making baskets	
Working stone	Carrying burdens	
Working bone, horn, and shell	Making mats	
Mining and quarrying	Caring for small animals	
Setting bones	Preserving meat and fish	
Butchering*	Loom weaving	
Collecting wild honey	Gathering small aquatic animals	
Clearing land	Clothing manufacture	
Fishing	Making pottery	
Tending large herd animals		
Building houses		
Preparing the soil		
Making nets		
Making rope		

*All the activities above "butchering" are almost always done by men; those from "butchering" through "making rope" usually are done by men.

Table 9.1 about the division of labor by gender illustrate generalities rather than universals. That is, among the societies known to ethnography, there is a very strong tendency for men to build boats, but there are exceptions. One was the Hidatsa, a Native American group in which the women made the boats used to cross the Missouri River. (Traditionally, the Hidatsa were village farmers and bison hunters on the North American Plains; they now live in North Dakota.) Another exception: Pawnee women worked wood; this is the only Native American group that assigned this activity to women. (The Pawnee, also traditionally Plains farmers and bison hunters, originally lived in what is now central Nebraska and central Kansas; they now live on a reservation in north central Oklahoma.)

Exceptions to cross-cultural generalizations may involve societies or individuals. A society like the Hidatsa can contradict the cross-cultural generalization that men build boats by assigning that task to women. Or, in a society where the cultural expectation is that only men build boats, a particular woman or women can contradict that expectation by doing the male activity. Table 9.1 shows that in a sample of 185 societies, certain activities ("swing activities") are assigned to either or both men and women. Among the most important of such activities are planting, tending, and harvesting crops. We'll see below that some societies customarily assign more farming chores to women, whereas others call on men to be the main farm laborers. Among the tasks almost always assigned to men (Table 9.1), some (e.g., hunting large animals on land and sea) seem clearly related to the greater average size and strength of males. Others, such as working wood and making musical instruments, seem more culturally arbitrary. And women, of course, are not exempt from arduous and time-consuming physical labor, such as gathering firewood and fetching water. In Arembepe, Bahia, Brazil, women routinely transported water in five-gallon tins, balanced on their heads, from wells and lagoons located long distances from their homes.

Time and Effort Expended on Subsistence Activities by Men and Women*

More by men	16%
Roughly equal	61%
More by women	23%

* Percentage of 88 randomly selected societies for which information was available on this variable.

Who Does the Domestic Work?*

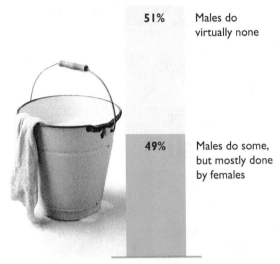

| 51% | Males do virtually none |
| 49% | Males do some, but mostly done by females |

* Percentage of 92 randomly selected societies for which information was available on this variable.

Both women and men have to fit their activities into twenty-four-hour days. Based on cross-cultural data, the figure at left shows that the time and effort spent in subsistence activities by men and women tend to be about equal. If anything, men do slightly less subsistence work than women do. Think about how female domestic activities could have been specified in greater detail in Table 9.1. The original coding of the data in Table 9.1 probably illustrates a male bias, because extradomestic activities received much more prominence than domestic activities did. For example, is collecting wild honey (listed in Table 9.1) more necessary or time-consuming than cleaning a baby's bottom (absent from Table 9.1)? Also, notice that Table 9.1 does not mention trade and market activity, in which either or both men and women are active.

Cross-culturally the subsistence contributions of men and women are roughly equal. But in domestic activities and child care, female labor predominates. "Who Does the Domestic Work?" shows that in about half the societies studied, men did virtually no domestic work. Even in societies where men did some domestic chores, the bulk of such work was done by women. Adding together their subsistence activities and their domestic work, women tend to work more hours than men do. Has this changed in the contemporary world?

What about child care? Women tend to be the main caregivers in most societies, but men often play a role. Cross-cultural data is used to answer the question, "Who—men or women—has final authority over the care, handling, and discipline of children younger than four years?" in a figure on page 168. Women have primary authority over infants in two-thirds of the societies. Given the critical role of breast-feeding in ensuring infant survival, it makes

Who Has the Final Authority over the Care, Handling, and Discipline of Infant Children (under Four Years Old)?*

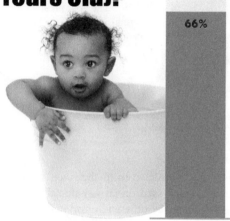

18%	Males have more say
16%	Roughly equal
66%	Females have more say

Percentage of 67 randomly selected societies for which information was available on this variable.

Does the Society Allow Multiple Spouses?*

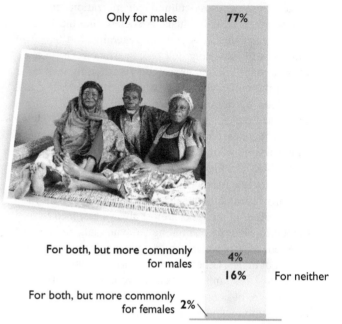

Only for males **77%**

For both, but more commonly for males **4%**

For both, but more commonly for females **2%**

16% For neither

Percentage of 92 randomly selected societies for which information was available on this variable.

sense, for infants especially, for the mother to be the primary caregiver.

There are differences in male and female reproductive strategies. Women work to ensure their progeny will survive by establishing a close bond with each baby. It's also advantageous for a woman to have a reliable mate to ease the child-rearing process and ensure the survival of her children. (Again, there are exceptions, such as the matrilineal Nayar discussed in the previous chapter.) Women can have only so many babies during their reproductive years, which begin after menarche (the advent of first menstruation) and end with menopause (cessation of menstruation). Men, in contrast, have a longer reproductive period, which can last into the elder years. If they choose to do so, men can enhance their reproductive success by impregnating several women over a longer time. Although men do not always have multiple mates, they have a greater tendency to do so than women do, as the next three figures show. Among the societies known to

domestic–public dichotomy Contrast between women's role in the home and men's role in public life, with a corresponding social devaluation of women's work and worth.

ethnography, polygyny is much more common than polyandry, as shown above.

Men mate, within and outside marriage, more than women do. The "Double Standard" figure on the next page shows cross-cultural data on premarital sex, and the

CULTURETHINK

Increasing numbers of men are staying at home to be full-time parents. What do you see as the benefits and challenges of stay-at-home fatherhood? What did you think of the stay-at-home fathers you may have known when you grew up?

bottom one summarizes the data on extramarital sex. In both cases men are less restricted than women are, although the restrictions are equal in about half the societies studied.

Double standards that restrict women more than men illustrate gender stratification. Several studies have shown that economic roles affect gender stratification. In one cross-cultural study, Sanday (1974) found that gender stratification decreased when men and women made roughly equal contributions to subsistence. She found that gender stratification was greatest when the women contrib-

Is There a Double Standard with Respect to Premarital Sex?*

44% Females are more restricted

56% Equal restrictions on males and females

* Percentage of 73 randomly selected societies for which information was available on this variable.

Is There a Double Standard with Respect to Extramarital Sex?*

43% Females are more restricted

55% Equal restrictions on males and females

3% Males punished more severely for transgressions

* Percentage of 75 randomly selected societies for which information was available on this variable.

uted either much more or much less than the men did.

>> Gender among Foragers

In foraging societies gender stratification was most marked when men contributed much *more* to the diet than women did. This was true among the Inuit and other northern hunters and fishers. Among tropical and semitropical foragers, by contrast, gathering usually supplies more food than hunting and fishing do. Gathering generally is women's work. Men usually hunt and fish, but women also do some fishing and may hunt small animals. When gathering is prominent, gender status tends to be more equal than it is when hunting and fishing are the main subsistence activities.

Gender status also is more equal when the domestic and public spheres aren't sharply separated. (*Domestic* means within or pertaining to the home.) Strong differentiation between the home and the outside world is called the **domestic–public dichotomy** or the *private–public contrast.* The outside world can include politics, trade, warfare, or work. Often when domestic and public spheres are clearly separated, public activities have greater prestige than domestic ones do. This can promote gender stratification, because men are more likely to be active in the public domain than women are. Cross-culturally, women's activities tend to be closer to home than men's are. Thus, another reason hunter-gatherers have less gender stratification than food producers do is that the domestic–public dichotomy is less developed among foragers.

CULTURETHINK

Consider the domestic–public dichotomy in your society. Are domestic (home) and public (the outside world) spheres clearly separated, or do they overlap? Think, for example, about where religious, political, economic, and educational activities tend to take place.

In many societies women routinely do hard physical labor, as illustrated by these women working together to move logs at a sawmill in Langziang, China. Anthropologists have described both commonalities and differences in gender roles and activities among the world's societies.

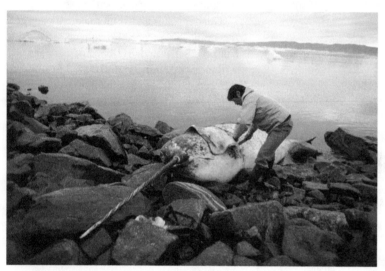

Among foragers, gender stratification tends to increase when men contribute much more to the diet than women do—as has been true among the Inuit and other northern hunters and fishers. Shown here, Mikile, an Inuit hunter, opens up a narwhal he hunted and killed near Qeqertat in northwestern Greenland.

STUDY TIP

Gender status tends to be more equal (in other words, there is less gender stratification) when (1) men and women have similar freedom over their labor and control over the products and labor of others; (2) women and men make roughly equal economic contributions; (3) the domestic and public spheres are not sharply separated; (4) men and women have access to equal prestige.

Certain roles tend to be more sex-linked than others. Men are the usual hunters and warriors. Given such weapons as spears, knives, and bows, men make better fighters because they are bigger and stronger on average than are women in the same population (Divale and Harris 1976). The male hunter–fighter role also reflects a tendency toward greater male mobility. In foraging societies, women are either pregnant or lactating during much of their childbearing years. Late in pregnancy and after childbirth, carrying a baby limits a woman's movements. Among the Agta of the Philippines, however, women not only gather, but they also hunt with dogs while carrying their babies with them (Griffin and Estioko-Griffin 1985). Still, considering cross-cultural data, women rarely are the primary hunters (Friedl 1975). Warfare, which also requires mobility, is not found in most foraging societies, nor is interregional trade well developed. Warfare and trade are two public arenas that contribute to status inequality of males and females among food producers.

The Ju/'hoansi San illustrate the extent to which the activities and spheres of influence of men and women may overlap among foragers (Draper 1975). Traditional Ju/'hoansi gender roles were interdependent. During gathering, women discovered information about game animals, which they passed on to the men. Men and women spent about the same amount of time away from the camp, but neither worked more than three days a week. The Ju/'hoansi saw nothing wrong in doing the work of the other gender. Men often gathered food and collected water. A general sharing ethos dictated that men distribute meat and that women share the fruits of gathering.

It is among foragers that the public and private spheres are least separate, hierarchy is least marked, aggression and competition are most discouraged, and the rights, activities, and spheres of influence of men and women overlap the most. Our ancestors lived entirely by foraging until ten thousand years ago. Despite the popular stereotype of the club-wielding caveman dragging his mate by the hair, relative gender equality is a much more likely ancestral pattern.

>> Gender among Horticulturalists

Gender roles and stratification among cultivators vary widely, depending on specific features of the economy and social structure. Demonstrating this, Martin and Voorhies (1975) studied a sample of 515 horticultural societies, representing all parts of the world. They looked at several factors, including descent and postmarital residence, the percentage of the diet derived from cultivation, and the relative productivity of men and women.

Women turned out to be the main producers in horticultural societies. In 50 percent of those societies, women did most of the cultivating. In 33 percent, contributions to cultivation by men and women were equal (see the figure below). In only 17 percent did men do most of the work. Women tended to do a bit more cultivating in matrilineal compared with patrilineal societies. They dominated horticulture in 64 percent of the matrilineal societies versus 50 percent of the patrilineal ones.

REDUCED GENDER STRATIFICATION—MATRILINEAL–MATRILOCAL SOCIETIES

Cross-cultural variation in gender status is related to rules of descent and postmarital residence (Friedl 1975; Martin and Voorhies 1975). Among horticulturalists with matrilineal descent and *matrilocality* (residence after marriage with the wife's relatives), female status tends to be high. Matriliny and matrilocality disperse related males, rather than consolidating them. By contrast, patriliny and *patrilocality* (residence after marriage with the husband's kin) keep male relatives together—an advantage given warfare. Matrilineal–matrilocal systems tend to occur in societies where population pressure on strategic resources is minimal and warfare is infrequent.

Women tend to have high status in matrilineal, matrilocal societies for several reasons. Descent-group membership, succession to political positions, allocation of land, and overall social identity all come through female links. Among the matrilineal Malays of Negeri Sembilan, Malaysia (Peletz 1988), matriliny gave women sole inheritance of ancestral rice fields. Matrilocality created solidary clusters of female kin. These Malay women had considerable influence beyond the household (Swift 1963). In such matrilineal contexts, women are the basis of the entire social structure. Although public authority nominally may be assigned to the men, much of the power and decision making actually may belong to the senior women.

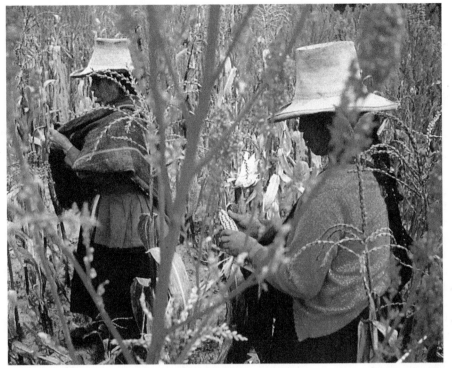

Women are the main producers in horticultural societies. Women like these South American corn farmers do most of the cultivating in such societies. What kinds of roles do women play in contemporary North American farming?

Male and Female Contributions to Production in Cultivating Societies

Horticulture

50%

17%

33%

(percentage of 104 societies)

Agriculture

81%

15%

3%

(percentage of 93 societies)

▢ Women are primary cultivators

▢ Men are primary cultivators

▢ Equal contributions to cultivation

MATRIARCHY

Cross-culturally, anthropologists have described tremendous variation in the roles of men and women, and the power differentials between them. If a patriarchy is a political system ruled by men, what would a matriarchy be? Would a **matriarchy** be a political system ruled by women, or a political system in which women play a much more prominent role than men do in social and political organization? Anthropologist Peggy Sanday (2002) has concluded that matriarchies exist, but not as mirror images of patriarchies. The superior power that men typically have in a patriarchy isn't matched by women's equally disproportionate power in a matriarchy. Many societies, including the Minangkabau of West Sumatra, Indonesia, whom Sanday has studied for decades, lack the substantial power differentials that typify patriarchal systems. Minangkabau women play a central role in social, economic, and ceremonial life and as key symbols. The primacy of matriliny

matriarchy A political system in which women play a much more prominent role than men do in social and political organization.

A Minangkabau bride and groom in West Sumatra, Indonesia, where anthropologist Peggy Reeves Sanday has conducted several years of ethnographic fieldwork.

Anthropology Works

People working on international development projects need to be aware of the role women play in family households and economy. Assuming that men are in charge of household budgets or agricultural decision making, for example, would be a mistake in many places.

and matriarchy is evident at the village level, as well as regionally, where seniority of matrilineal descent serves as a way to rank villages.

The four million Minangkabau constitute one of Indonesia's largest ethnic groups. Located in the highlands of West Sumatra, their culture is based on the coexistence of matrilineal custom and a nature-based philosophy called *adat,* complemented by Islam, a more recent (sixteenth-century) arrival. The Minangkabau view men and women as cooperative partners for the common good rather than competitors ruled by self-interest. People gain prestige when they promote social harmony rather than by vying for power.

Sanday considers the Minangkabau a matriarchy because women are the center, origin, and foundation of the social order. Senior women are associated with the central pillar of the traditional house, the oldest one in the village. The oldest village in a cluster is called the "mother village." In ceremonies, women are addressed by the term used for their mythical Queen Mother. Women control land inheritance, and couples reside matrilocally. In the wedding ceremony, the wife collects her husband from his household and, with her female kin, escorts him to hers. If there is a divorce, the husband simply takes his things and leaves. Yet despite the special position of women, the Minangkabau matriarchy is not the equivalent of female rule, given the Minangkabau belief that all decision making should be by consensus.

INCREASED GENDER STRATIFICATION—PATRILINEAL–PATRILOCAL SOCIETIES

Martin and Voorhies (1975) link the decline of matriliny and the spread of the **patrilineal–patrilocal complex** (consisting of patrilineality, patrilocality, warfare, and male supremacy) to pressure on resources. Faced with scarce resources, patrilineal–patrilocal cultivators such as the Yanomami often wage warfare against other villages. This favors patrilocality and patriliny, customs that keep related men together in the same village, where they make strong allies in battle. Such societies tend to have a sharp domestic–public dichotomy, and men tend to dominate the prestige hierarchy. Men may use their public roles in warfare and trade and their greater prestige to

Matrilineal and *matrilocal* societies occur
where little pressure on resources and
low population densities exist. Pressure
on resources leads to warfare and
intensified production, which favors
patrilocality and *patrilineality*.

symbolize and reinforce the devaluation or oppression of women.

The patrilineal–patrilocal complex characterizes many societies in highland Papua New Guinea. Women work hard growing and processing subsistence crops, raising and tending pigs (the main domesticated animal and a favorite food), and doing domestic cooking, but they are isolated from the public domain, which men control. Men grow and distribute prestige crops, prepare food for feasts, and arrange marriages. The men even get to trade the pigs and control their use in ritual.

In densely populated areas of the Papua New Guinea highlands, male–female avoidance is associated with strong pressure on resources (Lindenbaum 1972). Men fear all female contacts, including sex. They think that sexual contact with women will weaken them. Indeed, men see

In some parts of Papua New Guinea, the patrilineal–patrilocal complex has extreme social repercussions. Regarding females as dangerous and polluting, men may segregate themselves in men's houses (such as this one, located near the Sepik River), where they hide their precious ritual objects from women. Are there places like this in your society?

everything female as dangerous and polluting. They segregate themselves in men's houses and hide their precious ritual objects from women. They delay marriage, and some never marry.

By contrast, the sparsely populated areas of Papua New Guinea, such as recently settled areas, lack taboos on male–female contacts. The image of woman as polluter fades, heterosexual intercourse is valued, men and women live together, and reproductive rates are high.

patrilineal–patrilocal complex An interrelated constellation of patrilineality, patrilocality, warfare, and male supremacy.

extradomestic Outside the home; within or pertaining to the public domain.

>> Gender among Agriculturists

When the economy is based on agriculture, women typically lose their role as primary cultivators. Certain agricultural techniques, particularly plowing, have been assigned to men because of their greater average size and strength (Martin and Voorhies 1975). Except when irrigation is used, plowing eliminates the need for constant weeding, an activity usually done by women.

Cross-cultural data illustrate these contrasts in productive roles between agricultural and horticultural economies. Women were the main workers in 50 percent of the horticultural societies surveyed but in only 15 percent of the agricultural groups. As shown in the figure on page 171, male subsistence labor dominated 81 percent of the agricultural societies but only 17 percent of the horticultural ones (Martin and Voorhies 1975).

With the advent of agriculture, women were cut off from production for the first time. Belief systems started contrasting men's valuable extradomestic labor with women's domestic role, now viewed as inferior. (**Extradomestic** means outside the home; within or pertaining to the public domain.) Changes in kinship and postmarital residence patterns also hurt women. Descent groups and polygyny declined with agriculture, and the nuclear family became more common. Living with her husband and children, a woman was isolated from her kinswomen and cowives. Female sexuality is carefully supervised in agricultural economies; men have easier access to divorce and extramarital sex, reflecting a "double standard."

Still, female status in agricultural societies is not inevitably bleak. Gender stratification is associated with plow agriculture rather than with intensive cultivation per se. Studies of peasant gender roles and stratification in France and Spain (Harding 1975; Reiter 1975), which have plow agriculture, show that people think of the house as the female sphere and the fields as the male domain. Such a dichotomy is not inevitable, though, as Conrad Kottak's own research among Betsileo agriculturists in Madagascar shows.

Betsileo women play a prominent role in agriculture, contributing a third of the hours invested in rice production. They have their customary tasks in the division of labor, but their work is more seasonal than men's is. No one has much to do during the ceremonial season, between mid-June and mid-September. Men work in the rice fields almost daily the rest of the year. Women's cooperative work occurs during transplanting (mid-September through November) and harvesting (mid-March through early May). Along with other members of the household, women do daily weeding in December and January. After the harvest, all family members work together winnowing the rice and then transporting it to the granary.

patriarchy Political system ruled by men in which women have inferior social and political status, including fewer basic human rights.

If we consider the strenuous daily task of husking rice by pounding (a part of food preparation rather than production per se), women actually contribute slightly more than 50 percent of the labor devoted to producing and preparing rice before cooking.

Not just women's prominent economic role but also their traditional social organization enhances female status among the Betsileo. Although postmarital residence is mainly patrilocal, descent rules permit married women to keep membership in and a strong allegiance to their own descent groups. Kinship is broadly and bilaterally (on both sides—as in contemporary North America) calculated. The Betsileo exemplify Aihwa Ong's (1989) generalization that bilateral (and matrilineal) kinship systems, combined with subsistence economies in which the sexes have complementary roles in food production and distribution, are characterized by reduced gender stratification. Such societies are common among South Asian peasants (Ong 1989).

Traditionally, Betsileo men participate more in politics, but the women also hold political office. Women sell their produce and products in markets, invest in cattle, sponsor ceremonies, and are mentioned during offerings to ancestors. Arranging marriages, an important extradomestic activity, is more women's concern than men's. Sometimes Betsileo women seek their own kinswomen as wives for their sons, reinforcing their own prominence in village life and continuing kin-based female solidarity in the village.

The Betsileo illustrate the idea that intensive cultivation does not necessarily entail sharp gender stratification. We can see that gender roles and stratification reflect not just the type of adaptive strategy but also specific cultural attributes. Betsileo women continue to play a significant role in their society's major economic activity, rice production.

>> Patriarchy and Violence

A political system ruled by men in which women have inferior social and political status, including fewer basic human rights, is known as **patriarchy.** Barbara Miller (1997), in a study of systematic neglect of females, describes women in rural northern India as "the endangered sex." Societies that feature a full-fledged patrilineal–patrilocal complex, replete with warfare and intervillage raiding, also typify

India has been described as a patriarchal culture, in which women routinely are harassed when they move from private (domestic) to public space. The women shown here enjoy their ride, unmolested, on the "Ladies Special" train from Palwal to Delhi.

patriarchy. Such practices as dowry murders, female infanticide, and clitoridectomy exemplify patriarchy, which extends from tribal societies such as the Yanomami to state societies such as India and Pakistan.

Although more prevalent in certain social settings than in others, family violence and domestic abuse of women are worldwide problems. Domestic violence certainly occurs in nuclear family settings, such as Canada and the United States. Cities, with their impersonality and isolation from extended kin networks, are breeding grounds for domestic violence.

We've seen that gender stratification typically is reduced in matrilineal, matrifocal, and bilateral societies in which women have prominent roles in the economy and social life. When a woman lives in her own village, she has kin nearby to look after and protect her interests. Even in patrilocal polygynous settings, women often count on the support of their cowives and sons in disputes with potentially abusive husbands. Such settings, which tend to provide a safe haven for women, are retracting rather than expanding in today's world, however. Isolated families and patrilineal social forms have spread at the expense of matrilineality. Many nations have declared polygyny illegal. More and more women, and men, find themselves cut off from extended kin and families of orientation.

With the spread of the women's rights movement and the human rights movement, attention to domestic violence and abuse of women has increased. Laws have been passed and mediating institutions established. Brazil's female-run police stations for battered women provide an example, as do shelters for victims of domestic abuse in the United States and Canada. But patriarchal institutions do persist in what should be a more enlightened world.

Domestic violence isn't limited to tribal societies. It also occurs in nuclear family settings including the United States, Canada, and the United Kingdom. Shown here, women rally in London, England, on International Women's Day, March 8, 2008.

>> Gender and Industrialism

The domestic–public dichotomy, which is developed most fully among patrilineal–patrilocal food producers and plow agriculturists, also has affected gender stratification in industrial societies, including the United States and Canada. Gender roles have been changing rapidly in North America. The "traditional" idea that "a woman's place is in the home" actually emerged in the United States as industrialism spread after 1900. Earlier, pioneer women in the Midwest and West had been recognized as fully productive workers in farming and home industry. Under industrialism, attitudes about gendered work came to vary with class and region. In early industrial Europe, men, women, and children had flocked to factories as wage laborers. Enslaved Americans of both sexes had done grueling work in cotton fields. With abolition, southern African American women continued working as field hands and domestics. Poor white women labored in the South's early cotton mills. In the 1890s more than one million American women held menial and repetitious unskilled factory positions (Margolis 1984; Martin and Voorhies 1975).

After 1900, European immigration produced a male labor force willing to work for wages lower than those of American-born men. Those immigrant men moved into factory jobs that previously had gone to women. As machine tools and mass production further reduced the need for female labor, the notion that women were biologically unfit for factory work began to gain ground (Martin and Voorhies 1975).

Maxine Margolis (1984, 2000) has shown how gendered work, attitudes, and beliefs have varied in response to American economic needs. For example, wartime shortages of men have promoted the idea that work outside the home is women's patriotic duty. During the world wars the notion that women are unfit for hard

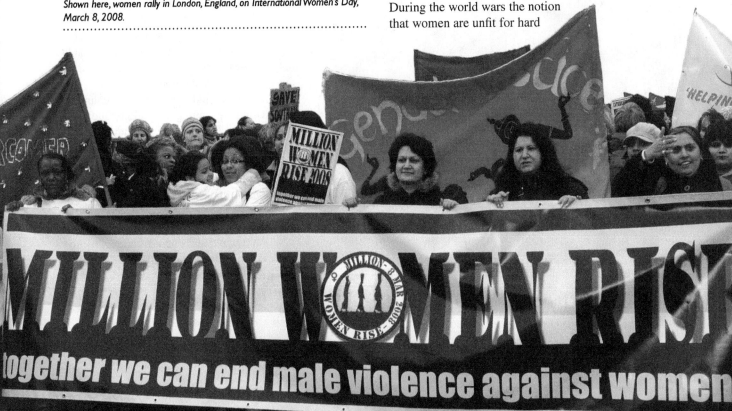

physical labor faded. Inflation and the culture of consumption also have spurred female employment. When prices or demand rise, multiple paychecks help maintain family living standards.

The steady increase in female paid employment since World War II also reflects the baby boom and industrial expansion. American culture traditionally has defined clerical work, teaching, and nursing as female occupations. With rapid population growth and business expansion after World War II, the demand for women to fill such jobs grew steadily. Employers also found they could increase their profits by paying women lower wages than they would have to pay returning male war veterans.

Margolis (1984, 2000) contends that changes in the economy lead to changes in attitudes toward and about

CULTURETHINK

What circumstances shape public attitudes toward women working outside the home, according to the text? Ask around: Is it acceptable, or desirable, for women to work for wages? What reasoning do people use to explain their answers?

women. Economic changes paved the way for the contemporary women's movement, which also was spurred by the publication of Betty Friedan's book *The Feminine Mystique* in 1963 and the founding of the National Organization of Women (NOW), in 1966. The movement in turn promoted expanded work opportunities for women, including the goal of equal pay for equal work. Between 1970 and 2007, the female percentage of the American workforce rose from 38 percent to 46 percent. In other words, almost half of all Americans who work outside the home are women. Over 71 million women now have paid jobs, compared with 82 million men. Women fill more than half (56 percent) of all professional jobs (*Statistical Abstract of the United States 2009*, p. 384). And it's not mainly single women working, as once was the case. The ever-increasing cash employment of American wives and mothers, including those with children under six years old, is shown in the top figure on the next page.

Note in the top figure that the cash employment of American married men has been falling while that of American married women has been rising. There has been a dramatic change in behavior and attitudes since 1960, when 89 percent of all married men worked, compared with just 32 percent of married women. The comparable figures in 2007 were 77 percent and 62 percent. Ideas about the gender roles of males and females have changed. Compare your grandparents and your parents. Chances are you have a working mother, but your grandmother was more likely a stay-at-home mom. Your grandfather is more likely than your father to have worked in manufacturing and to have belonged to a union. Your father is more likely than your grandfather to have shared child care and domestic responsibilities. Age at marriage has been delayed for both men and women. College educations and professional degrees have increased.

During the world wars the notion that women were biologically unfit for hard physical labor faded. Shown here is World War II's famous Rosie the Riveter. Is there a comparable poster woman today? What does her image say about modern gender roles?

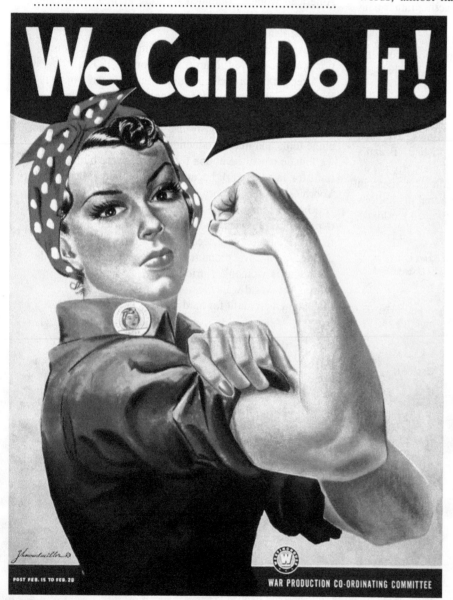

Cash Employment of American Mothers, Wives, and Husbands, 1960–2007*

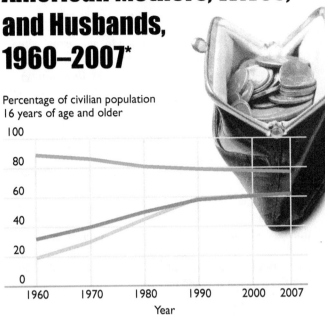

Percentage of civilian population
16 years of age and older

— Percentage of all married men (wife present)
— Percentage of all married women (husband present)
— Percentage of all married women (husband present, with children under six)

erty line, more than double the number in 1959. Married couples are much more secure economically than single mothers are. The median one-earner family maintained by a single woman had an annual income of $28,829 in 2006, less than half the median income ($69,404) of a married-couple household (*Statistical Abstract of the United States, 2009*, p. 446).

The feminization of poverty isn't just a North American trend. The percentage of female-headed households has been increasing worldwide. In Western Europe, for example, female-headed households rose from 24 percent in 1980 to 31 percent in 1990. The figure ranges from below 20 percent in certain South Asian and Southeast Asian countries to almost 50 percent in certain African countries and the Caribbean (Buvinic 1995).

CULTURETHINK

Although many women are now earning more than men, the feminization of poverty shows that others are earning increasingly less. What are the problems with making general statements about "women" without considering differences among them? What differences besides income would you need to consider?

Trends in U.S. Women's Participation in the Paid Labor Force, 1890–2008

Single women

Married women

2008

What other changes do you associate with the increase in female employment outside the home?

THE FEMINIZATION OF POVERTY

Alongside the economic gains of many American women stands an opposite extreme: the feminization of poverty, or the increasing representation of women (and their children) among America's poorest people. Women head over half of U.S. households with incomes below the pov-

Why must so many women be solo household heads? Where are the men going, and why are they leaving? Among the causes are male migration, civil strife (men off fighting), divorce, abandonment, widowhood, unwed adolescent parenthood, and, more generally, the idea that children are women's responsibility. Globally, households headed by women tend to be poorer than those headed by men. In one study, the percentage of single-parent families considered poor was 18 percent in Britain, 20 percent in Italy, 25 percent in Switzerland, 40 percent in Ireland, 52 percent in Canada, and 63 percent in the United States.

It is widely believed that one way to improve the situation of poor women is to encourage them to organize. New women's groups can in some cases revive or replace traditional forms of social organization that have been disrupted. Membership in a group can help women mobilize resources, enhance production, and reduce the risks and costs associated with credit. By organizing, women also develop self-confidence and decrease dependence on others. Through such organization, poor women throughout the world are working to determine their own needs and priorities and to change things so as to improve their social and economic situation (Buvinic 1995).

>> What Determines Gender Variation?

We see that gender roles and stratification have varied widely across cultures and through history. Among many foragers and matrilineal cultivators, there is little gender stratification. Competition for resources leads to warfare and the intensification of production, which favor patriliny and patrilocality. To the extent that women lose their productive roles in agricultural societies, the domestic–public dichotomy is accentuated and gender stratification is sharpened. With industrialism, attitudes about gender vary in the context of female extradomestic employment. Gender is flexible and varies with cultural, social, political, and economic factors. The variability of gender in time and space suggests that it will continue to change. The biology of the sexes is not a narrow enclosure limiting humans but a broad base upon which a variety of structures can be built (Friedl 1975).

>> Sexual Orientation

A person's habitual sexual attraction to, and sexual activities with, persons of the opposite sex (*heterosexuality*), the same sex (*homosexuality*), or both sexes (*bisexuality*) is termed their **sexual orientation.** *Asexuality*—indifference toward, or lack of attraction to either sex—also is a sexual orientation. All four of these forms are found in contemporary North America and throughout the world. But each type of desire and experience holds different meanings for individuals and groups. For example, an asexual disposition may be acceptable in some places but perceived as a character flaw in others. Male–male sexual activity may be a private affair in Mexico, rather than public, socially sanctioned, and encouraged as among the Etoro (see below) of Papua New Guinea (see also Blackwood and Wieringa 1999; Boellstorff 2007; Kimmel and Plante 2004; Kottak and Kozaitis 2008; Nanda 2000).

Neither man nor woman, hijras constitute India's third gender. Many hijras get their income from performing at ceremonies, begging, or prostitution. The beauty contest shown here was organized by an AIDS prevention and relief organization that works with the local hijra community.

Recently in the United States the tendency has been to see sexual orientation as fixed and biologically based. There is not enough information at this time to determine the exact extent to which sexual orientation is based on biology. What we can say is that all human activities and preferences, including erotic expression, are at least partially culturally constructed.

In any society, individuals will differ in the nature, range, and intensity of their sexual interests and urges. No one knows for sure why such individual sexual differences exist. Part of the answer probably is biological, reflecting genes or hormones (Wade 2005). Another part may have to do with experiences during growth and development. But whatever the reasons for individual variation, culture always plays a role in molding individual sexual urges toward a collective norm. And such sexual norms vary from culture to culture.

twenty—left their families and shared quarters with adult fighting men, who paid bridewealth for them and had sex with them. During this apprenticeship, the young men performed the domestic duties of women. Upon reaching warrior status, these young men took their own younger male brides. Later, retiring from the warrior role, Azande men married women. Flexible in their sexual expression, Azande males had no difficulty shifting from sex with older men (as male brides), to sex with younger men (as warriors), to sex with women (as husbands) (see Murray and Roscoe 1998).

> **sexual orientation** A person's habitual sexual attraction to, and activities with persons of the opposite sex (heterosexuality), the same sex (homosexuality), or both sexes (bisexuality); also, the lack of attraction (asexuality).

Consider also the Etoro (Kelly 1976), a group of four hundred people who subsist by hunting and horticulture

"As far as I'm concerned, being any gender is a drag."

Patti Smith

What do we know about variation in sexual norms from society to society, and over time? A classic cross-cultural study (Ford and Beach 1951) found wide variation in attitudes about masturbation, bestiality (sex with animals), and homosexuality. In a single society, such as the United States, attitudes about sex differ over time and with socioeconomic status, region, and rural versus urban residence. However, even in the 1950s, prior to the "age of sexual permissiveness" (the pre-HIV period from the mid-1960s through the 1970s), research showed that almost all American men (92 percent) and more than half of American women (54 percent) admitted to masturbation. In the famous Kinsey report (Kinsey, Pomeroy, and Martin 1948), 37 percent of the men surveyed admitted having had at least one sexual experience leading to orgasm with another male. In a later study of twelve hundred unmarried women, 26 percent reported same-sex sexual activities. (Because Kinsey's research relied on nonrandom samples, it should be considered merely illustrative, rather than a statistically accurate representation, of sexual behavior at the time.)

Sex acts with people of the same sex were absent, rare, or secret in 37 percent of seventy-six societies for which data were available in the Ford and Beach study (1951). In the other societies, various forms of same-sex sexual activity were acceptable. Sometimes sexual relations between people of the same sex involved transvestism on the part of one of the partners (see Kulick 1998). Transvestism did not characterize male–male sex among the Sudanese Azande, who valued the warrior role (Evans-Pritchard 1970). Prospective warriors—young men aged twelve to

in the Trans-Fly region of Papua New Guinea. The Etoro illustrate the power of culture in molding human sexuality. The following account, based on ethnographic fieldwork by Raymond C. Kelly in the late 1960s, applies only to Etoro males and their beliefs. Etoro cultural norms prevented the male anthropologist who studied them from gathering comparable information about female attitudes. Note, also, that the activities described have been discouraged by missionaries. Since there has been no restudy of the Etoro specifically focusing on these activities, the extent to which these practices continue today is unknown. For this reason, we'll use the past tense in describing them.

Etoro opinions about sexuality were linked to their beliefs about the cycle of birth, physical growth, maturity, old age, and death. Etoro men believed that semen was necessary to give life force to a fetus, which was, they believed, implanted in a woman by an ancestral spirit. Sexual intercourse during pregnancy nourished the growing fetus. The Etoro believed that men had a limited lifetime supply of semen. Any sex act leading to ejaculation was seen as draining that supply, and as sapping a man's virility and vitality. The birth of children, nurtured by semen, symbolized a necessary

> **Did You Know?**
> For the first time in U.S. history, the 2010 census counted gay couples as married, even if they were not legally married. In 2000, they could only designate themselves as "unmarried partners" living in the same household.

sacrifice that would lead to the husband's eventual death. Heterosexual intercourse—required only for reproduction—was otherwise discouraged. Women who wanted too much sex were viewed as witches, hazardous to their husbands' health. Etoro culture allowed heterosexual intercourse only about one hundred days a year. The rest of the time it was tabooed. Seasonal birth clustering shows the taboo was respected.

So objectionable was male–female sex that it was removed from community life. It could occur neither in sleeping quarters nor in the fields. Coitus could happen only in the woods, where it was risky because poisonous snakes, the Etoro claimed, were attracted by the sounds and smells of male–female sex.

Although coitus was discouraged, sex acts between men were viewed as essential. Etoro believed that boys could not produce semen on their own. To grow into men and eventually give life force to their children, boys had to acquire semen orally from older men. From the age of ten until adulthood, boys were inseminated by older men. No taboos were attached to this. Such oral insemination could proceed in the sleeping area or garden. Every three years, a group of boys around the age of twenty were formally initiated into manhood. They went to a secluded mountain lodge, where they were visited and inseminated by several older men.

> "Society as a whole benefits immeasurably from a climate in which all persons, regardless of race or gender, may have the opportunity to earn respect, responsibility, advancement and remuneration based on ability."
>
> Sandra Day O'Connor

Male–male sex among the Etoro was governed by a code of propriety. Although sexual relations between older and younger males were considered culturally essential, those between boys of the same age were discouraged. A boy who took semen from other youths was believed to be sapping their life force and stunting their growth. A boy's rapid physical development might suggest he was getting semen from other boys. Like a sex-hungry wife, he might be shunned as a witch.

These sexual practices among the Etoro rested not on hormones or genes but on cultural beliefs and traditions. The Etoro shared a cultural pattern, which Gilbert Herdt (1984) calls "ritualized homosexuality," with some fifty other tribes in Papua New Guinea, especially in that country's Trans-Fly region. These societies illustrate one extreme of a male–female avoidance pattern that is widespread in Papua New Guinea and indeed in many patrilineal–patrilocal societies.

Flexibility in sexual expression seems to be an aspect of our primate heritage. Both masturbation and same-sex sexual activity exist among chimpanzees and other primates. Male bonobos (pygmy chimps) regularly engage in a form of mutual masturbation known as "penis fencing." Females get sexual pleasure from rubbing their genitals against those of other females (de Waal 1997). Our primate sexual potential is molded by culture, the environment, and reproductive necessity. Heterosexual coitus is practiced in all human societies—which, after all, must reproduce themselves—but alternatives also are widespread (Rathus, Nevid, and Fichner-Rathus 2008). Like gender roles and attitudes more generally, the sexual component of human personality and identity—just how we express our "natural" sexual urges—is a matter that culture and environment determine and limit.

CULTURETHINK

People in the United States tend to think of sexual orientation as fixed and unchanging. How does this contrast with sexual practices and identities in other cultures, such as the Azande and the Etoro?

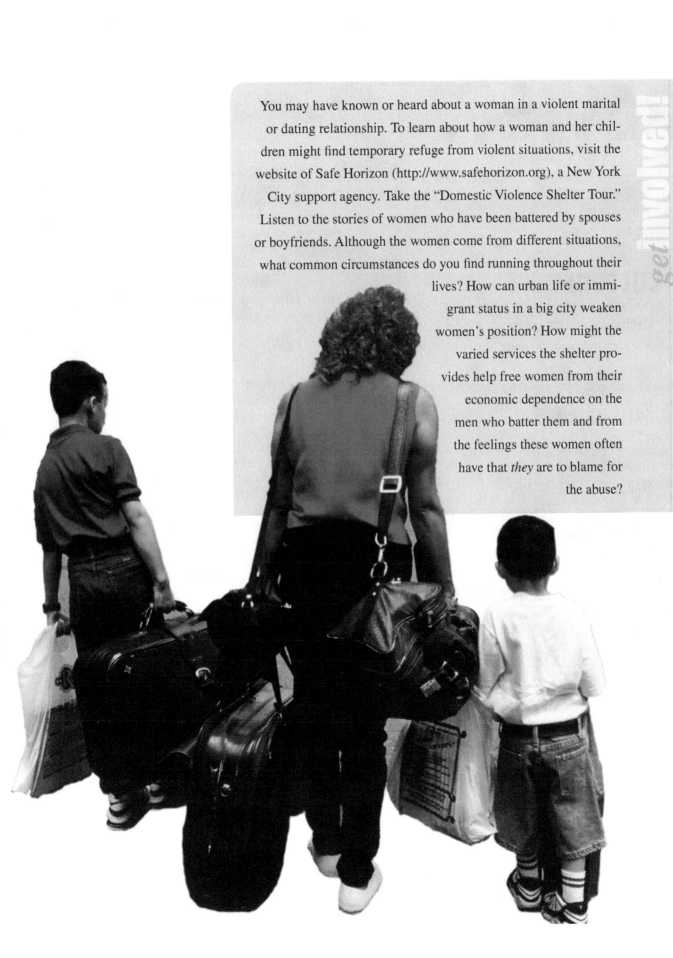

get **involved!**

You may have known or heard about a woman in a violent marital or dating relationship. To learn about how a woman and her children might find temporary refuge from violent situations, visit the website of Safe Horizon (http://www.safehorizon.org), a New York City support agency. Take the "Domestic Violence Shelter Tour." Listen to the stories of women who have been battered by spouses or boyfriends. Although the women come from different situations, what common circumstances do you find running throughout their lives? How can urban life or immigrant status in a big city weaken women's position? How might the varied services the shelter provides help free women from their economic dependence on the men who batter them and from the feelings these women often have that *they* are to blame for the abuse?

For REVIEW

CULTURECLIPS

TO ACCESS THESE VIDEOS ON
YOUR COMPUTER, VISIT

www.mhhe.com/gezonqr

9-1

9-2

9-3

I. **How are biology and culture expressed in human sex/ gender systems?**

   • Although sexual dimorphism decreased during human evolution, males and females still differ physiologically and anatomically.

   Anthropologists have shown that culture is the source of many differences between the sexes and that the roles of men and women both differ and resemble one another in different cultures. "The biological nature of men and women [should be seen] not as a narrow enclosure limiting the human organism, but rather as a broad base upon which a variety of structures can be built." This statement sums up the predominant anthropological position today. Sex differences are biological, but gender encompasses the traits that a culture assigns to males and females. Gender refers to the cultural construction of whether one is female, male, or something else.

II. **How do gender, gender roles, and gender stratification correlate with other social, economic, and political variables?**

   • In foraging societies both the domestic–public dichotomy and gender stratification are limited, and male and female activities tend to overlap. Female status is high among horticulturalists with matrilineal descent and matrilocality. With the advent of plow agriculture, women lost their role as primary cultivators and became more homebound; gender stratification sharpened. Competition for resources favors the patrilineal-patrilocal complex. The superior power that men typically have in a patriarchy isn't matched by women's power in a matriarchy. Industrialization in the United States initially contributed to the notion that women were unfit for factory work, but industrial expansion after World War II increased female paid employment. The rise in poverty of women is a global phenomenon.

III. **What is sexual orientation, and how do sexual practices vary cross-culturally?**

   • Sexual orientation refers to a person's habitual sexual attraction to, and sexual activities with, persons of the opposite sex (heterosexuality), the same sex (homosexuality), or both sexes (bisexuality). Asexuality is indifference toward, or lack of attraction to, either sex. All four forms of orientation occur worldwide but hold different meanings for individuals and groups. Anthropologists generally see sexual orientation as at least partially culturally constructed. In the United States, attitudes about sex have differed over time and with socioeconomic status, region, and rural versus urban residence. Flexibility in sexual expression seems to be an aspect of our primate heritage.

Pop Quiz

1. Consider this quote: "The biological nature of men and women [should be seen] not as a narrow enclosure limiting the human organism, but rather as a broad base upon which a variety of structures can be built." Which of the following best describes this quote's significance?
   a. The quote reflects a cultural generality, rather than a cultural universal.
   b. The quote reflects the predominant anthropological position on sex/gender roles and biology.
   c. This quote summarizes how biological determinists think.
   d. This quote ignores considerable evidence.

2. Hidatsa women made boats, and Pawnee women worked wood. These two cases suggest that:
   a. Biology has nothing to do with gender roles.
   b. Anthropologists are too optimistic about finding a society with gender equality.
   c. There are exceptions to cross-cultural generalizations about the kinds of work men and women usually do in different societies.
   d. A Hidatsa or Pawnee man would never do the female task.

3. Among foragers:
   a. Warfare and trade make men dominant over women.
   b. Female status falls when gathering is more important than hunting.
   c. The lack of a clear domestic–public dichotomy is related to relatively weak gender stratification.
   d. Men and women are completely equal.

4. Which of the following statements about gender status and power in horticultural societies is false?
   a. Where matriliny and matrilocality disperse related males, female status tends to be high.
   b. Matriarchy describes systems in which the women hold superior power to, and rule, the men.
   c. Pressure on resources encourages the spread of the patrilineal–patrilocal complex.
   d. Men may use their public roles to reinforce the devaluation of women.

5. Which of the following is false about gender roles and statuses among agriculturalists?
   a. With agriculture, women tend to lose their role as primary cultivators.
   b. The advent of agriculture in horticultural societies gave women a further advantage in the prestige hierarchy.
   c. With agriculture, polygyny and descent groups declined.
   d. Reduced gender stratification is found in bilateral and matrilineal kinship systems with complementary gender roles in food production.

6. In which kind of society do anthropologists most typically find female genital operations, warfare, female infanticide, and dowry murders?
   a. Patrilineal–patrilocal
   b. Matrilineal–patrilocal
   c. Matrilineal–matrilocal
   d. Patrilineal–matrilocal

7. The idea that "a woman's place is in the home":
   a. Emerged in the United States as industrialism spread after 1900.
   b. Is found in virtually all societies.
   c. Reflects the weakening of a domestic–public dichotomy.
   d. Fuels the contemporary women's movement.

8. In comparing gender roles and status in different societies, we can say that the following is true:
   a. Generally, women's status is relatively high among horticulturalists with matrilineal descent and matrilocal residence.
   b. In a large number of societies women control the strategic resources and carry out the most prestigious activities.
   c. The more women contribute to the domestic sphere, the more power they hold.
   d. The less women contribute to the public sphere, the more power they achieve.

9. "The feminization of poverty" means that:
   a. Poverty has been dressed up to seem more bearable.
   b. Single mothers are more secure economically than are married couples.
   c. Women and their children are increasingly represented among the world's poorest people.
   d. An increasing percentage of female-headed households shows the growing power and independence of women.

10. All the following are key ideas to take away from this chapter's discussion of sexual orientation *except*:
    a. Different types of sexual desires and experiences hold different meanings for individuals and groups.
    b. In any society, individuals will differ in the nature, range, and intensity of sexual interests and urges.
    c. Culture always plays a role in molding individual sexual urges toward a collective norm.
    d. There is conclusive scientific evidence that sexual orientation is genetically determined.

1. (b), 2. (c), 3. (c), 4. (b), 5. (b), 6. (a), 7. (a), 8. (a), 9. (c), 10. (d)

10

RELIGION

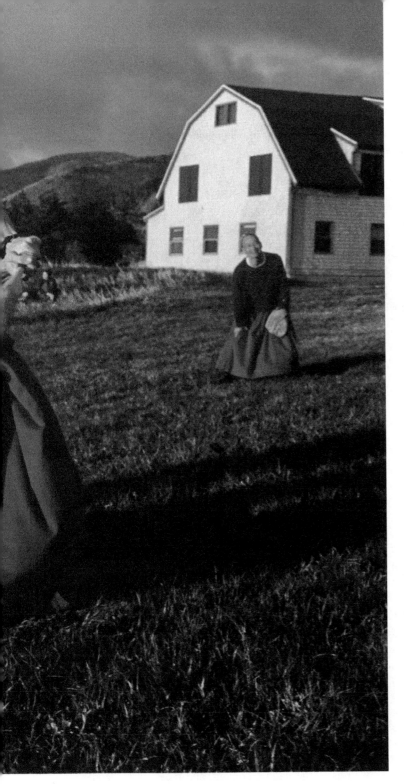

WHAT'S TO COME

Defining Religion

Expressions of Religion

Religion and Social Control

Kinds of Religion

World Religions

Religion and Change

Secular Rituals

UNDERSTANDING OURSELVES

Ever notice how much baseball players spit? Football players, with their customary headgear, don't spit, nor do basketball players, who might slip on the court. No spitting by tennis players, golfers, gymnasts, or swimmers. But watch any baseball game, and you'll see spitting galore. The custom likely originated on the mound and continues today as a carryover from the days when pitchers routinely chewed tobacco, believing that nicotine enhanced their concentration. The spitting custom spread to other players, who unabashedly spew saliva from the outfield to the dugout steps.

For the student of custom, ritual, and magic, baseball is an especially interesting game, to which lessons from anthropology are easily applied. The pioneering anthropologist Bronislaw Malinowski, writing about Pacific islanders, noted their use of all sorts of magic in sailing, a hazardous activity. He proposed that people turn to magic when they face uncertainty and conditions they can't control (e.g., wind and weather). Like sailing magic, baseball magic, in the form of rituals, taboos, and sacred objects, serves to reduce psychological stress, creating an illusion of control when real control is lacking.

All sorts of magical behaviors surround pitching and batting, which are full of uncertainty. There are fewer rituals for fielding, over which players have more control. Especially obvious are the rituals (like the spitting) of pitchers, who may: tug their cap between pitches, spit in a particular direction, magically manipulate the resin bag, talk to the ball, or wash their hands after giving up a run. Batters have their rituals, too. One major leaguer routinely would spit, then ritually touch his gob with his bat to enhance his success at the plate.

To keep hope alive in situations of uncertainty, and for outcomes we can't control, all societies draw on magic and religion as sources of nonmaterial comfort, explanation, and control. What are your rituals?

- What is religion, and what are its various forms, social correlates, and functions?
- What is ritual, and what are its various forms and expressions?
- What role does religion play in maintaining and changing societies?

>> Defining Religion

The anthropologist Anthony F. C. Wallace defined **religion** as "belief and ritual concerned with supernatural beings, powers, and forces" (1966, p. 5). The supernatural is the extraordinary realm outside (but believed to impinge on) the observable world. It is nonempirical and inexplicable in ordinary terms. It must be accepted "on faith."

religion Beliefs and rituals concerned with supernatural beings, powers, and forces.

Supernatural beings—gods and goddesses, ghosts, and souls—are not of the material world. Nor are supernatural forces, some of which may be wielded by beings. Other sacred forces are impersonal; they simply exist. In many societies, however, people believe they can benefit from, become imbued with, or manipulate supernatural forces (see Bowen 2008; Bowie 2006; Crapo 2006; Lambek 2008; Stein and Stein 2008; Warms, Garber, and McGee 2009).

Another definition of religion (Reese 1999) focuses on bodies of people who gather together regularly for worship. These congregants or adherents subscribe to and internalize a common system of meaning. They accept (adhere to or believe in) a set of doctrines involving the relationship between the individual and divinity, the supernatural, or whatever is taken to be the ultimate nature of reality. Anthropologists have stressed the collective, shared, and enacted nature of religion, the emotions it generates, and the meanings it embodies. Emile Durkheim (1912/2001), an early scholar of religion, stressed religious *effervescence,* the bubbling up of collective emotional intensity generated by worship. Victor Turner (1969/1995) updated Durkheim's notion, using the term *communitas,* an intense community spirit, a feeling of great social solidarity, equality, and togetherness. The word *religion* derives from the Latin *religare*—"to tie, to bind," but it is not necessary for all members of a given religion

to meet together as a common body. Subgroups meet regularly at local congregation sites. They may attend occasional meetings with adherents representing a wider region. And they may form an imagined community with people of similar faith throughout the world.

CULTURE THINK

Have you ever felt the intense community spirit of *communitas*? What are some secular settings where people might experience *communitas,* or collective effervescence?

Like ethnicity and language, religion also is associated with social divisions within and between societies and nations. Religion both unites and divides. Participation in common rites may affirm, and thus maintain, the social solidarity of a religion's adherents. However, as we know from daily headlines, religious difference also may be associated with bitter enmity.

In studying religion cross-culturally, anthropologists pay attention to the social nature and roles of religion as well as to the nature, content, and meaning to people of religious doctrines, acts, events, settings, practitioners, and organizations. We also consider such verbal manifestations of religious beliefs as prayers, chants, myths, texts, and statements about ethics and morality (see Cunningham 1999; Klass 2003; Lehmann, Meyers, and Moro 2005; Stein and Stein 2005). Religion, by either definition offered here, exists in all human societies. It is a cultural universal. However, we'll see that distinguishing the supernatural from the natural isn't always easy and that different societies conceptualize divinity, supernatural entities, and ultimate realities very differently.

STUDY TIP

Religion has several characteristics:
(1) It is concerned with the supernatural;
(2) it serves emotional needs; (3) it is a collective system of meaning;
(4) it explains the unexplainable;
(5) it is social in nature, based on religious roles.

>> Expressions of Religion

When did religion begin? No one knows for sure. There are suggestions of religion in Neandertal burials and on European cave walls, where painted stick figures may represent shamans—early religious specialists. Nevertheless, any statement about when, where, why, and how religion arose, or any description of its original nature, can be only speculative. Although inconclusive, many such speculations have revealed important functions and effects of religious behavior. Several theories will be examined now.

SPIRITUAL BEINGS

The founder of the anthropology of religion was the Englishman Sir Edward Burnett Tylor (1871/1958). Religion was born, Tylor thought, as people tried to understand conditions and events they could not explain by reference to daily experience. Tylor believed that our ancestors—and contemporary nonindustrial peoples—were particularly intrigued with death, dreaming, and trance. People see images they may remember when they wake up or come out of the trance state. Tylor concluded that attempts to explain dreams and trances led early humans to believe that two entities inhabit the body, one active during the day and the other—a double or soul—active during sleep and trance states. Although they never meet, they are vital to each other. When the double permanently leaves the body, the person dies. Death is departure of the soul. From the Latin for soul, *anima,* Tylor named this belief animism. The soul was one sort of spiritual entity; people remembered various images from their dreams and trances—other spirits. For Tylor, **animism,** the earliest form of religion, was a belief in spiritual beings.

Tylor proposed that religion evolved through stages, beginning with animism. *Polytheism* (the belief in multiple gods) and then *monotheism* (the belief in a single, all-powerful deity) devel-

This image of Apollo, with a lyre, and Artemis, sacrificing over an alter fire, illustrates ancient Greek polytheism. The red-figured terra-cotta vessel dates from ca. 2500 B.P.

oped later. Because religion originated to explain things people didn't understand, Tylor thought it would decline as science offered better explanations. To an extent, he was right. We now have scientific explanations for many things that religion once explained. Nevertheless, because religion persists, it must do something more than explain the mysterious. It must, and does, have other functions and meanings.

CULTURE THINK

What kinds of questions does religion answer that science cannot? Do you think, like Tylor did, that religion declines as science provides better answers?

POWERS AND FORCES

Besides animism—and sometimes coexisting with it in the same society—is a view of the supernatural as a domain of impersonal power, or *force,* which people can control under certain conditions. (You'd be right to think of *Star Wars.*) Such a conception of the supernatural is particularly prominent in Melanesia, the area of the South Pacific that includes Papua New Guinea and adjacent islands. Melanesians believed in **mana,** a sacred impersonal force existing in the universe. Mana can reside in people, animals, plants, and objects.

animism Belief in souls or doubles.

mana Sacred impersonal force in Melanesian and Polynesian religions.

Melanesian mana was similar to our notion of efficacy or luck. Melanesians attributed success to mana, which people could acquire or manipulate in different ways, such as through magic. Objects with mana could change someone's luck. For example, a charm or amulet belonging to a successful hunter might transmit the hunter's mana to the next person who held or wore it. A woman might put a rock in her garden, see her yields improve dramatically, and attribute the change to the force contained in the rock.

Beliefs in manalike forces are widespread, although the specifics of the religious doctrines vary. Consider the contrast between mana in Melanesia and Polynesia (the islands included in a triangular area marked by Hawaii to the north, Easter Island to the east, and New Zealand to the southwest). In Melanesia, one could acquire mana by chance, or by working hard to get it. In Polynesia, mana wasn't potentially available to everyone but was attached to political offices. Chiefs and nobles had more mana than ordinary people did.

So charged with mana were the highest chiefs that contact with them was dangerous to the commoners. The mana of chiefs flowed out of their bodies wherever they went. It could infect the ground, making it dangerous for others to walk in the chief's footsteps. It could permeate the containers and utensils chiefs used in eating. Contact between chief and commoners was dangerous because mana could have an effect like an electric shock. Because high chiefs had so much mana, their bodies and possessions were **taboo** (set apart as sacred and off-limits to ordinary people). Contact between a high chief and commoners was forbidden. Because ordinary people couldn't bear as much sacred current as royalty could, when commoners were accidentally exposed, purification rites were necessary.

taboo Prohibition backed by supernatural sanctions.

magic Use of supernatural techniques to accomplish specific aims.

One function of religion is to explain. A belief in souls explains what happens in sleep, trance, and death. Melanesian mana explains differential success that people can't understand in ordinary, natural terms. People fail at hunting, war, or gardening not because they are lazy, stupid, or inept but because success comes—or doesn't come—from the supernatural world.

The beliefs in spiritual beings (e.g., animism) and supernatural forces (e.g., mana) fit within the definition of religion given at the beginning of this chapter. Most religions include both spirits and impersonal forces. Likewise the supernatural beliefs of contemporary North Americans include beings (gods, saints, souls, demons) and forces (charms, talismans, crystals, and sacred objects).

MAGIC

Magic refers to supernatural techniques intended to accomplish specific aims. These techniques include spells, formulas, and incantations used with deities or with impersonal forces. Magicians use *imitative magic* to produce a desired effect by imitating it. If magicians wish to injure or kill someone, they may imitate that effect on an image of the victim. Sticking pins in "voodoo dolls" is an example. With *contagious magic,* whatever is done to an object is believed to affect a person who once had contact with it. Sometimes practitioners of contagious magic use body products from prospective victims—their nails or hair, for example. The spell performed on the body product is believed to reach the person eventually and work the desired result (see Stein and Stein 2008).

We find magic in societies with diverse religious beliefs. It can be associated with animism, mana, polytheism, or monotheism. Magic is neither simpler nor more primitive than animism or the belief in mana.

UNCERTAINTY, ANXIETY, SOLACE

Religion and magic don't just explain things. They serve emotional needs as well as cognitive (e.g., explanatory) ones. For example, supernatural beliefs and practices can help reduce anxiety. Religion helps people face death and endure life crises. Magical techniques can dispel doubts that arise when outcomes are beyond human control.

Although all societies have techniques to deal with everyday matters, there are certain aspects of people's lives over which they lack control. When people face uncertainty and danger, according to Malinowski, they turn to magic. As mentioned in "Understanding Ourselves" at the beginning of this chapter, Malinowski found that the Trobriand Islanders used magic when sailing, a hazardous activity. He proposed that because people can't control matters such as wind, weather, and the fish supply, they turn to magic (Malinowski 1931/1978). Gmelch's research on baseball and magic, also discussed in "Understanding Ourselves," confirms Malinowski's conclusion that magic is most prevalent in situations of chance or uncertainty, especially pitching and batting.

Malinowski noted that it was only when confronted by situations they could not control that Trobrianders, out of psychological stress, turned from technology to magic. Despite our improving technical skills, we still can't con-

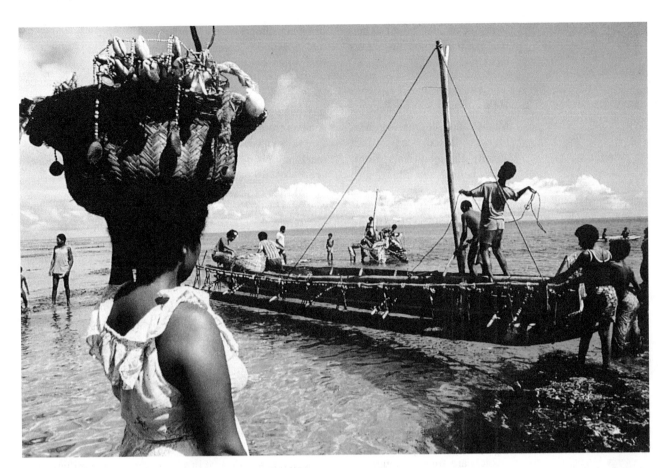

Trobriand Islanders prepare a traditional trading canoe for use in the Kula, a regional exchange system. The woman brings trade goods in a basket, while the men prepare the long boat to set sail. Magic is often associated with uncertainty, such as sailing in unpredictable waters.

CULTURE THINK

Think about superstitions, such as knocking on wood to prevent an unwanted outcome. Think of three additional superstitious behaviors. How many of them are used, like magic, to produce an illusion of control in an uncertain situation?

special (sacred) places and at set times. Rituals include *liturgical orders*—sequences of words and actions invented prior to the current performance of the ritual in which they occur.

These features link rituals to plays, but there are important differences. Plays have audiences rather than participants. Actors merely *portray* something, but ritual performers—who make up congregations—are in *earnest*. Rituals convey information about the participants and their traditions. Repeated year after year, generation after generation, rituals translate enduring messages, values, and sentiments into action.

Rituals are *social* acts. Inevitably, some participants are more committed than others to the beliefs that lie behind the rites. However, just by taking part in a joint public act, the performers signal that they accept a com-

> **ritual** Behavior that is formal, stylized, repetitive, and stereotyped, performed earnestly as a social act; rituals are held at set times and places and have liturgical orders.

trol every outcome, and magic persists in contemporary societies.

RITUALS

Several features distinguish **rituals** from other kinds of behavior (Rappaport 1974, 1999). Rituals are formal—stylized, repetitive, and stereotyped. People perform them in

STUDY TIP

Rituals serve two purposes:

• They convey messages, values, and sentiments;

• They encourage a common social order.

mon social and moral order, one that transcends their status as individuals.

RITES OF PASSAGE

Magic and religion, as Malinowski noted, can reduce anxiety and allay fears. Ironically, beliefs and rituals also can *create* anxiety and a sense of insecurity and danger (Radcliffe-Brown 1962/1965). Anxiety may arise *because* a rite exists. Indeed, participation in a collective ritual may build up stress, whose common reduction, through the completion of the ritual, enhances the solidarity of the participants.

Rites of passage, such as the collective circumcision of teenagers, can be very stressful. The traditional vision quests of Native Americans, particularly the Plains Indians, illustrate **rites of passage** (customs associated with the transition from one place or stage of life to another), which are found throughout the world. Among the Plains Indians, to move from boyhood to manhood, a youth temporarily separated from his community. After a period of isolation in the wilderness, often featuring fasting and

rites of passage Culturally defined activities associated with the transition from one place or stage of life to another.

liminality The critically important marginal or in-between phase of a rite of passage.

drug consumption, the young man would see a vision, which would become his guardian spirit. He would then return to his community as an adult.

The rites of passage of contemporary societies include confirmations, baptisms, bar and bat mitzvahs, and fraternity hazing. Passage rites involve changes in social status, such as from boyhood to manhood and from nonmember to sorority sister. More generally, a rite of passage may mark any change in place, condition, social position, or age.

All rites of passage have three phases: separation, liminality, and incorporation. In the first phase, people withdraw from the group and begin moving from one place or status to another. In the third phase, they reenter society, having completed the rite. The *liminal* phase is the most interesting. It is the period between states, the limbo during which people have left one place or state but haven't yet entered or joined the next (Turner 1967/1974).

Liminality always has certain characteristics. Liminal people occupy ambiguous social positions. They exist apart from ordinary distinctions and expectations, living in a time out of time. They are cut off from normal social contacts. A variety of contrasts may demarcate liminality from regular social life. For example, among the Ndembu of Zambia, a chief underwent a rite of passage before taking office. During the liminal period, his past and future positions in society were ignored, even reversed. He was subjected to a variety of insults, orders, and humiliations.

Passage rites often are collective. Several individuals—boys being circumcised, fraternity or sorority initiates, men at military boot camps, football players in summer training camps, women becoming nuns—pass through the rites together as a group. Table 10.1 summarizes the contrasts, or oppositions, between liminality and normal social life. Most notable is a social aspect of *collective*

Passage rites are often collective. A group—such as these initiates in Togo or these Navy trainees in San Diego—passes through the rites as a unit. Such liminal people experience the same treatment and conditions and must act alike. They share communitas, an intense community spirit, a feeling of great social solidarity or togetherness.

Oppositions Between Liminality and Normal Social Life

Liminality	Normal Social Structure
Transition	State
Homogeneity	Heterogeneity
Communitas	Structure
Equality	Inequality
Anonymity	Names
Absence of property	Property
Absence of status	Status
Absence of rank	Rank
Humility	Pride
Nakedness or uniform dress	Dress distinctions
Sexual continence or excess	Sexuality
Minimization of sex distinctions	Maximization of sex distinctions
Disregard of personal appearance	Care for personal appearance
Unselfishness	Selfishness
Total obedience	Obedience only to superior rank
Sacredness	Secularity
Sacred instruction	Technical Knowledge
Silence	Speech
Simplicity	Complexity
Acceptance of pain and suffering	Avoidance of pain and suffering

Source: From *The Ritual Process* by Victor Turner. Copyright © 1969 by Aldine Publishers. Reprinted by permission of Aldine Transaction, a division of Transaction Publishers.

liminality called **communitas** (Turner 1967/1974), an intense community spirit, a feeling of great social solidarity, equality, and togetherness. People experiencing liminality together form a community of equals. The social distinctions that have existed before or will exist afterward are forgotten temporarily. Liminal people experience the same treatment and conditions and must act alike. Liminality may be marked ritually and symbolically by *reversals* of ordinary behavior. For example, sexual taboos may be intensified, or conversely, sexual excess may be encouraged. Liminal symbols mark entities and circumstances as extraordinary—outside and beyond ordinary social space and routine social events.

Liminality is basic to every passage rite. Furthermore, in certain societies, including our own, liminal symbols may be used to set off one (religious) group from another,

and from society as a whole. Such "permanent liminal groups" (e.g., sects, brotherhoods, and cults) are found most characteristically in nation-states. Such liminal features as humility, poverty, equality, obedience, sexual abstinence, and silence may be required for all sect or cult members. Those who join such a group agree to its rules. As if they were undergoing a passage rite—but in this case a never-ending one—they may rid themselves of their previous possessions and cut themselves off from former social links, including those with family members.

communitas Intense community spirit, a feeling of great social solidarity, equality, and togetherness; characteristic of people experiencing liminality together.

Identity as a group member is expected to transcend individuality. Cult members often wear uniform clothing.

They may try to reduce distinctions based on age and gender by using a common hairstyle (shaved head, short hair, or long hair). With such cults, the individual, so important in American culture, is submerged in the collective. This is one reason Americans are so fearful and suspicious of "cults."

Not all collective rites are rites of passage. Most societies observe occasions on which people come together to worship and, in doing so, affirm and reinforce their solidarity. Rituals such as the totemic ceremonies described below are *rites of intensification:* They demand collective adherence to the rules of ritual behavior and create emotions (the collective spiritual effervescence described by Durkheim 1912/2001) that enhance and intensify social solidarity.

TOTEMISM

The religions of the Native Australians included totemism. *Totems* could be animals, plants, or geographical features. In each tribe, groups of people had particular totems. Members of each totemic group believed themselves to be descendants of their totem. They customarily neither killed nor ate it, but this taboo was lifted once a year, when people assembled for ceremonies dedicated to the totem. These annual rites were believed to be necessary for the totem's survival and reproduction.

Totemism uses nature as a model for society. The totems are usually animals and plants, which are part of nature. People relate to nature through their totemic association with natural species. Because each group has a different totem, social differences mirror natural contrasts. Diversity in the natural order becomes a model for diversity in the social order. However, although totemic plants and animals occupy different niches in nature, on another level they are united because they all are part of nature. The unity of the human social order is enhanced by symbolic association with and imitation of the natural order (Durkheim 1912/2001; Lévi-Strauss 1963; Radcliffe-Brown 1962/1965).

In contemporary nations, too, totems continue to mark groups, such as states and universities (e.g., Badgers, Buckeyes, and Wolverines), professional teams (Lions, Tigers, and Bears), and political parties (donkeys and elephants). Although the modern context is more secular, one can still witness, in intense college football rivalries, some of the effervescence Durkheim noted in Australian totemic religion and other rites of intensification.

Totems are sacred emblems symbolizing common identity. This is true not just among Native Australians, but also among Native American groups of the North Pacific Coast of North America, whose totem poles are well known. Their totemic carvings, which commemorated, and told visual stories about, ancestors, animals, and spirits, were also associated with ceremonies. In totemic rites, people gather together to honor their totem. In so doing, they use ritual to maintain the social oneness that the totem symbolizes.

>> Religion and Social Control

Religion has meaning for people. It helps them cope with adversity and tragedy. It offers hope that things will get better. Lives can be transformed through spiritual healing. Sinners can repent and be saved—or they can go on sinning and be damned. If the faithful truly internalize a system of religious rewards and punishments, their religion becomes a powerful influence on their beliefs, behavior, and what they teach their children.

Many people engage in religious activity because it seems to work. Prayers get answered. Faith healers heal. Sometimes it doesn't take much to convince the faithful that religious actions are effective. Many American Indian people in southwestern Oklahoma use faith healers at high monetary costs, not just because it makes them feel better

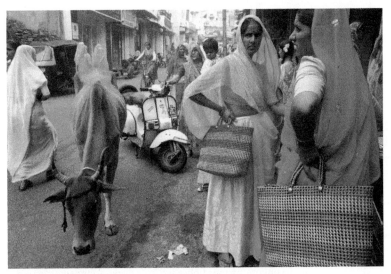

A wandering cow does not perturb these shoppers in Udaipur, Rajasthan. India's zebu cattle are protected by the doctrine of asimsa, a principle of nonviolence that forbids the killing of animals generally. This Hindu doctrine puts the full power of organized religion behind the command not to destroy a valuable resource even in times of extreme need.

Religion can work by getting inside people and mobilizing their emotions—their joy, their wrath, their righteousness. People feel a deep sense of shared joy, meaning, experience, communion, belonging, and commitment to their religion. The power of religion affects action. When religions meet, they can coexist peacefully, or their differences can be a basis for enmity and disharmony, even battle. Religious fervor has inspired Christians on crusades against the infidel and has led Muslims to wage holy wars against non-Islamic peoples. Throughout history, political leaders have used religion to promote and justify their views and policies.

By late September 1996, the Taliban Movement had firmly imposed an extreme form of social control through religious repression on Afghanistan and its people. Led by Muslim clerics, the Taliban aimed to create their version of an Islamic society modeled on the teachings of the Koran (Burns 1997). Various repressive measures were instituted. The Taliban barred women from work and girls from school. Females past puberty were prohibited from talking to men unrelated to them. Women needed an approved reason, such as shopping for food, to leave their homes. Men, who were required to grow bushy beards, also faced an array of bans—against playing cards, listening to music, keeping pigeons, and flying kites.

To enforce their decrees, the Taliban sent armed enforcers throughout the country. These agents took charge

about the uncertain, but because it works (Lassiter 1998). Each year legions of Brazilians visit a church, Nosso Senhor do Bomfim, in the city of Salvador, Bahia. They vow to repay "Our Lord" (Nosso Senhor) if healing happens. Showing that the vows work, and are repaid, are the thousands of *ex votos,* plastic impressions of every conceivable body part, that adorn the church, along with photos of people who have been cured.

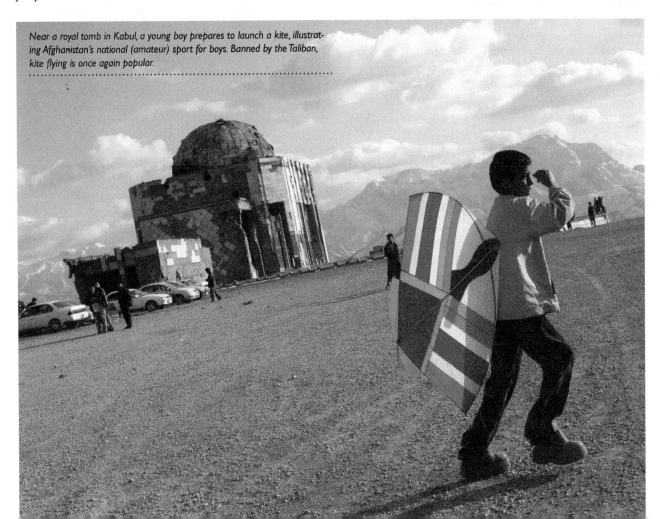

Near a royal tomb in Kabul, a young boy prepares to launch a kite, illustrating Afghanistan's national (amateur) sport for boys. Banned by the Taliban, kite flying is once again popular.

Karl Marx famously referred to religion as "the opiate of the masses." What do you think he meant by that?

Witchcraft accusations often are directed at socially marginal or anomalous individuals. Among the Betsileo of Madagascar, for example, who prefer patrilocal postmarital residence, men living in their wife's or their mother's village violate a cultural norm. Linked to their anomalous social position, just a bit of unusual behavior (e.g., staying up late at night) on their part is sufficient for them to be called witches and avoided as a result. In tribes and peasant communities, people who stand out economically, especially if they seem to be benefiting at the expense of others, often face witchcraft accusations, leading to social ostracism or punishment. In this case witchcraft accusation becomes a **leveling mechanism,** a custom or social action that operates to reduce status differences and thus to bring standouts in line with community norms—another form of social control.

To ensure proper behavior, religions offer rewards (e.g., the fellowship of the religious community) and punishments (e.g., the threat of being cast out or excommunicated). Religions, especially the formal organized ones typically found in state societies, often prescribe a code of ethics and morality to guide behavior. The Judaic Ten Commandments laid down a set of prohibitions against killing, stealing, adultery, and other misdeeds. Crimes are breaches of secular laws,

of "beard checks" and other forms of scrutiny on behalf of a religious police force known as the General Department for the Preservation of Virtue and the Elimination of Vice (Burns 1997). By late fall 2001 the Taliban had been overthrown, with a new interim government established in Kabul, the Afghan capital, on December 22. The collapse of the Taliban followed American bombing of Afghanistan in response to the September 11, 2001, attacks on New York's World Trade Center and Washington's Pentagon. As the Taliban yielded Kabul to victorious northern alliance forces, local men flocked to barbershops to have their beards trimmed or shaved. They were using a key Taliban symbol to celebrate the end of religious repression.

"God has no religion."

Mahatma Gandhi

as sins are breaches of religious strictures. Some rules (e.g., the Ten Commandments) proscribe or prohibit behavior; others prescribe behavior. The Golden Rule, for instance, is a religious guide to do unto others as you would have them do unto you. Moral codes are ways of maintaining order and stability. Codes of morality and ethics are constantly repeated in religious sermons, catechisms, and the like. They become internalized psychologically. They guide behavior and produce regret, guilt, shame, and the need for forgiveness, expiation, and absolution when they are not followed.

Note that in the case of the Taliban, forms of social control were used to support a strict religious orthodoxy. This wasn't repression in religion's name, but repressive religion. In other countries, secular leaders seeking power may use religious rhetoric to get it.

How may leaders mobilize communities and, in so doing, gain support for their own policies? One way is by persuasion; another is by instilling hatred or fear. Consider witchcraft accusations.

leveling mechanisms Customs and social actions that operate to reduce differences in wealth and thus to bring standouts in line with community norms.

shaman A part-time religious practitioner who mediates between ordinary people and supernatural beings and forces.

Witch hunts can be powerful means of social control by creating a climate of danger and insecurity that affects everyone, not just the people who are likely targets. No one wants to seem deviant, to be accused of being a witch. Witch hunts often take aim at people who can be accused and punished with least chance of retaliation. During the great European witch craze of the fifteenth, sixteenth, and seventeenth centuries (Harris 1974), most accusations and convictions were against poor women with little social support.

>> Kinds of Religion

Religion is a cultural universal. But religions exist in particular societies, and cultural differences show up systematically in religious beliefs and practices. For example, the religions of stratified, state societies differ from those of societies with less marked social contrasts and power differentials.

Considering several societies, Wallace (1966) identified four types of religion: shamanic, communal, Olympian, and monotheistic (Table 10.2). The simplest type is shamanic religion. Unlike priests, **shamans** aren't full-time religious officials but part-time religious figures who mediate between people and supernatural beings and forces. All societies have medico-magico-religious specialists. *Shaman* is the general term encompassing curers ("witch doctors"), mediums, spiritualists, astrologers, palm read-

Wallace's Typology of Religions

Type of Religion	Type of Practitioner	Conception of Supernatural	Type of Society
Monotheistic	Priests, ministers, etc.	Supreme being	States
Olympian	Priesthood	Hierarchical pantheon with powerful deities	Chiefdoms and archaic states
Communal	Part-time specialists; occasional community-sponsored events, including collective rites	Several deities with some control over nature	Food-producing tribes
Shamanic	Shaman (part-time practitioner)	Zoomorphic (plants and animals)	Foraging bands

ers, and other diviners. Wallace found shamanic religions to be most characteristic of foraging societies.

Shamans sometimes set themselves off symbolically from ordinary people by assuming a different or ambiguous sex or gender role. (In nation-states, priests, nuns, and vestal virgins do something similar by taking vows of celibacy and chastity.) Among the Chukchee of Siberia (Bogoras 1904), male shamans copied the dress, speech, hair arrangements, and lifestyles of women. These shamans took other men as husbands and sex partners and received respect for their supernatural and curative expertise. Female shamans could join a fourth gender, copying men and taking wives.

Communal religions have, in addition to shamans, community rituals such as harvest ceremonies and collective rites of passage. Although communal religions lack *full-time* religious specialists, they believe in several deities (**polytheism**) who control aspects of nature. Although some hunter-gatherers, including Australian totemites, have communal religions, these religions are more typical of farming societies.

Olympian religions, which arose with state organization and marked social stratification, add full-time religious specialists—professional *priesthoods*. Like the state itself, the priesthood is hierarchically and bureaucratically organized. The term *Olympian* comes from Mount Olympus, home of the classical Greek gods. Olympian religions are polytheistic. They include powerful anthropomorphic

gods with specialized functions, for example, gods of love, war, the sea, and death. Olympian *pantheons* (collections of supernatural beings) were prominent in the religions of many nonindustrial nation-states, including the Aztecs of Mexico, several African and Asian kingdoms, and classical Greece and Rome. Wallace's fourth type—**monotheism**—also has priesthoods and notions of divine power, but it views the supernatural differently. In monotheism, all supernatural phenomena are manifestations of, or are under the control of, a single eternal, omniscient, omnipotent, and omnipresent supreme being.

Robert Bellah (1978) coined the term "world-rejecting religion" to describe most forms of Christianity. The first world-rejecting religions arose in ancient civilizations, along with literacy and a specialized priesthood. These religions are so-named because of their tendency to reject the natural (mundane, ordinary, material, secular) world and to focus instead on a higher (sacred, transcendent)

communal religions In Wallace's typology, these religions have—in addition to shamanic cults—communal cults in which people organize community rituals such as harvest ceremonies and rites of passage.

polytheism Belief in several deities who control aspects of nature.

Olympian religions In Wallace's typology, religions that develop with state organization; have full-time religious specialists—professional priesthoods.

monotheism Worship of an eternal, omniscient, omnipotent, and omnipresent supreme being.

realm of reality. The divine is a domain of exalted morality to which humans can only aspire. Salvation through fusion with the supernatural is the main goal of such religions.

>> World Religions

The number of adherents of the world's major religions today is shown below in "Major World Religions." Based on people's claimed religions, Christianity is the world's largest, with some 2.1 billion adherents. Islam, with some 1.5 billion practitioners, is next, followed by Hinduism, then Chinese traditional religion (also known as Chinese folk religion or Confucianism), and Buddhism. More than a billion people claim no official religion, but only about a fifth of them are self-proclaimed atheists. Worldwide,

Islam is growing at a rate of about 2.9 percent annually, versus 2.3 percent for Christianity, whose overall growth rate is the same as the rate of world population increase (Adherents.com 2002; Ontario Consultants 2001).

Within Christianity, the growth rate varies. There were an estimated 680 million "born-again" Christians (e.g., Pentecostals and Evangelicals) in the world in 2001, with an annual worldwide growth rate of 7 percent, versus just 2.3 percent for Christianity overall. (This would translate into 1.2 billion Pentecostals/Evangelicals by 2010.) The global growth rate of Roman Catholics has been estimated at only 1.3 percent, compared with a Protestant growth rate of 3.3 percent per year (Winter 2001). Much of this explosive growth, especially in Africa, is of a type of Protestantism that would be scarcely recognizable to most Americans, given its incorporation of many animistic elements.

Religions of the World*

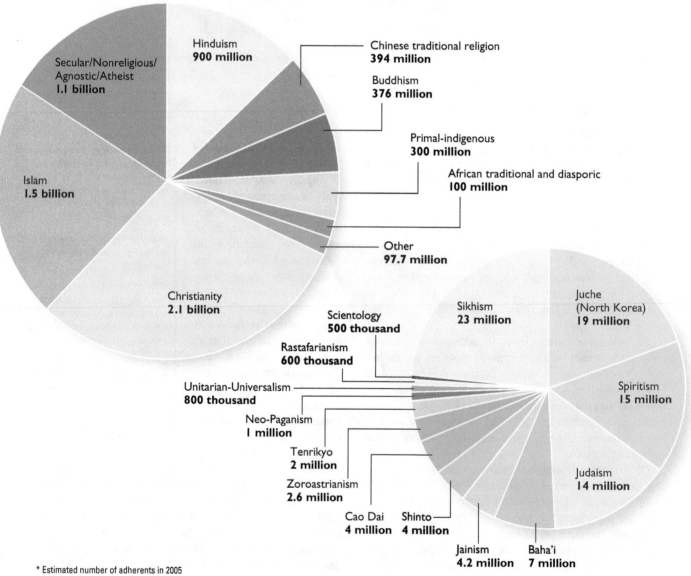

* Estimated number of adherents in 2005

Source: B.A. Robinson, "Religions of the World," Ontario Consultants on Religious Tolerance, www.religioustolerance.org/worldrel.html. Reprinted by permission.

In an analysis of more than a thousand films, Jack Shaheen (2006, 2009) found that only 5 percent of Arab and Muslim characters were presented in a positive light. Arabs repeatedly were caricatured as villains, buffoons, lechers, incompetents, and terrorists. Watch a film or TV show featuring Arab or Islamic characters (e.g., *Babel, Syriana, 24*). How are those characters portrayed? Is religion an important part of the portrayal? Do characters with other ethnic backgrounds (e.g., Latinos, African Americans, non-Hispanic whites) have as many religious markers? How do you account for the differences you note in these portrayals?

>> Religion and Change

Religious fundamentalists seek order based on strict adherence to purportedly traditional standards, beliefs, rules, and customs. Christian and Islamic fundamentalists recognize, decry, and attempt to redress change, yet they also contribute to change (Antoun 2008). In a worldwide process, new religions challenge established churches. In the United States, for example, conservative Christian TV hosts have become influential broadcasters and opinion shapers. In Latin America, evangelical Protestantism is winning millions of converts from Roman Catholicism.

Like political organization, religion helps maintain social order. And like political mobilization, religious energy can be harnessed not just for change but also for revolution. Reacting to conquest or to actual or perceived foreign domination, for instance, religious leaders may seek to al-

Anthropology Works

A politician or a diplomat dealing with foreign affairs would benefit from anthropological perspectives on religious responses to social change. What appear to be struggles over religion often have much deeper roots in unequal access to social and economic goods.

ter or revitalize their society. In an "Islamic Revolution," for example, Iranian ayatollahs marshaled religious fervor to create national solidarity and radical change. We call such movements *nativistic movements* (Linton 1943) or *revitalization movements* (Wallace 1956).

REVITALIZATION MOVEMENTS

Social movements that occur in times of change, in which religious leaders emerge and undertake to alter or revitalize a society, are termed **revitalization movements.** Christianity originated as a revitalization movement. Jesus was one of several prophets who preached new religious doctrines while the Middle East was under Roman rule. It was a time of social unrest, when a foreign power ruled the land. Jesus inspired a new, enduring, and major religion. His contemporaries were not so successful.

The Handsome Lake religion arose around 1800 among the Iroquois of New York State (Wallace 1969). Handsome Lake, the founder of this revitalization movement, was a leader of one of the Iroquois tribes. The Iroquois had suffered because of their support of the British against the American colonials. After the colonial victory and a wave of immigration to their homeland, the Iroquois were dispersed on small reservations. Unable to pursue traditional horticulture and hunting in their homeland, the Iroquois became heavy drinkers and quarreled among themselves.

> **revitalization movements** Movements that occur in times of change, in which religious leaders emerge and undertake to alter or revitalize a society.

Handsome Lake was a heavy drinker who started having visions from heavenly messengers. The spirits warned him that unless the Iroquois changed their ways, they would be destroyed. His visions offered a plan for coping with the new order. Witchcraft, quarreling, and drinking would end. The Iroquois would copy European farming techniques, which, unlike traditional Iroquois horticulture, stressed male rather than female labor. Handsome Lake preached that the Iroquois should also abandon their communal long houses and matrilineal descent groups for more permanent marriages and individual family households. The teachings of Handsome Lake produced a new church and religion, one that still has members in New York and Ontario. This revitalization movement helped the Iroquois adapt to and survive in a modified environment. They eventually gained a reputation among their non-Indian neighbors as sober family farmers.

CARGO CULTS

Like the Handsome Lake religion just discussed, **cargo cults** are revitalization movements. Such movements may emerge when natives have regular contact with industrial societies but lack their wealth, technology, and living standards. Some cargo cults attempt to *explain* European domination and wealth and to achieve similar success magically by mimicking European behavior and manipulating symbols of the desired life style. The cargo cults of Melanesia and Papua New Guinea weave Christian doctrine with aboriginal beliefs. They take their name from their focus on cargo—European goods of the sort natives have seen unloaded from the cargo holds of ships and airplanes.

In one early cult, members believed that the spirits of the dead would arrive in a ship. These ghosts would bring manufactured goods for the natives and would kill all the

cargo cults Postcolonial, acculturative, religious movements common in Melanesia that attempt to explain European domination and wealth and to achieve similar success magically by mimicking European behavior.

whites. More recent cults replaced ships with airplanes (Worsley 1959/1985). Many cults have used elements of European culture as sacred objects. The rationale is that Europeans use these objects, have wealth, and therefore must know the "secret of cargo." By mimicking how Europeans use or treat objects, natives hope also to come upon the secret knowledge needed to gain cargo.

Having seen Europeans' reverent treatment of flags and flagpoles, for example, the members of one cult began to worship flagpoles. They believed the flagpoles were sacred towers that could transmit messages between the living and the dead. Other natives built airstrips to entice planes bearing canned goods, portable radios, clothing, wristwatches, and motorcycles. Near the airstrips they made effigies of towers, airplanes, and radios. They talked into the cans in a magical attempt to establish radio contact with the gods. Can you think of anything in your own society (including the media) that features similar behavior?

Some cargo cult prophets proclaimed that success would come through a reversal of European domination and native subjugation. The day was near, they preached, when natives, aided by God, Jesus, or native ancestors, would turn the tables. Native skins would turn white, and those of Europeans would turn brown; Europeans would die or be killed.

Cargo cults blend aboriginal and Christian beliefs. Melanesian myths told of ancestors shedding their skins and changing into powerful beings and of dead people returning to life. Christian missionaries, who had been in Melanesia since the late nineteenth century, also spoke of resurrection. The cults' preoccupation with cargo is related to traditional Melanesian big man systems. In the chapter "Political Systems," we saw that a Melanesian big man had to be generous. People worked for the big man, helping him amass wealth, but eventually he had to give a feast and give away all that wealth.

Because of their experience with big man systems, Melanesians believed that all wealthy people eventually had to give away their wealth. For decades they had attended Christian missions and worked on plantations. All the while they expected Europeans to return the fruits of their labor as their own big men did. When the Europeans refused to distribute the wealth or even to let natives know the secret of its production and distribution, cargo cults developed.

Like arrogant big men, Europeans would be leveled, by death if necessary. However, natives lacked the physical means of doing what their traditions said they should do. Thwarted by well-armed colonial forces, natives resorted to magical leveling. They called on supernatural beings to intercede, to kill or otherwise deflate the European big men and redistribute their wealth.

Cargo cults are religious responses to the expansion of the world capitalist economy. However, this religious mobilization had political and economic results. Cult participation gave

A cargo cult in Vanuatu, a country in Melanesia. Boys and men march with spears, imitating British colonial soldiers. Does anything in your own society remind you of a cargo cult?

Melanesians a basis for common interests and activities and thus helped pave the way for political parties and economic interest organizations. Previously separated by geography, language, and customs, Melanesians started forming larger groups as members of the same cults and followers of the same prophets. The cargo cults paved the way for political action through which the indigenous peoples eventually regained their autonomy.

>> Secular Rituals

In concluding this discussion of religion, we may recognize some problems with the definition of religion given at the beginning of this chapter. The first problem: If we define religion with reference to supernatural beings, powers, and forces, how do we classify ritual-like behaviors that occur in secular contexts? Some anthropologists believe there are both sacred and secular rituals. Secular rituals include formal, invariant, stereotyped, earnest, repetitive

get **involved!**

Find a group on campus or in town that might be considered a "permanent liminal group." If you can't find one, read about cults and sects and choose one in the United States or another society you may know well. Learn something about the group's practices and beliefs. Using Table 10.1, list liminal features that seem to fit this group. For example, do you see an absence of rank and a sharing of communitas? Note how such features are revealed in behavior patterns. How would the contrasts between liminality and "normal" social life help explain why outsiders might consider this group strange or even threatening?

behavior and rites of passage that take place in nonreligious settings.

A second problem: If the distinction between the supernatural and the natural is not consistently made in a society, how can we tell what is religion and what isn't? The Betsileo of Madagascar, for example, view witches and dead ancestors as real people who play roles in ordinary life. However, their occult powers are not empirically demonstrable.

A third problem: The behavior considered appropriate for religious occasions varies tremendously from culture to culture. One society may consider drunken frenzy the surest sign of faith, whereas another may inculcate quiet reverence. Who is to say which is "more religious"?

For REVIEW

CULTURE CLIPS

TO ACCESS THESE VIDEOS ON YOUR COMPUTER, VISIT

www.mhhe.com/gezonqr

10-1

10-2

10-3

I. **What is religion, and what are its various forms, social correlates, and functions?**

- Wallace defined religion as "belief and behavior concerned with supernatural beings, powers, and forces." Religion also encompasses the feelings, meanings, and congregations associated with such belief and behavior. Wallace defined three types of religion: shamanic, which is common in foraging societies; communal, which is typical of farming societies; and Olympian, which is associated with states. Tylor proposed three stages in the evolution of religion: animism, polytheism, and monotheism. Expressions of religion include mana, a sacred impersonal force, and totemism, which uses nature as a model for society. Magic employs supernatural techniques to accomplish specific aims. Magic and religion help to explain the world and serve emotional needs, such as helping people cope with adversity and reducing anxiety, although rites also can create anxiety. Religion can divide as well as unite.

II. **What is ritual, and what are its various forms and expressions?**

- Rituals consist of behavior that is formal—stylized, repetitive, and stereotyped. People perform rituals in sacred places and at set times. Rituals convey information about the participants and translate enduring messages and values into action. Through ritual people subordinate their particular beliefs to a social collectivity. Rites of passage mark changes in place, condition, age, or social position. These rites have three stages: separation, liminality, and incorporation. In separation, people withdraw from the group; incorporation involves reentering it. Liminality is the limbo in between. In communitas, a liminal characteristic, participants experience social solidarity and equality. Rituals may be secular as well as religious.

III. **What role does religion play in maintaining and changing societies?**

- Religion establishes and maintains social control through moral and ethical beliefs and real and imagined rewards and punishments. Religion also can mobilize communities for collective action; leaders may use religious rhetoric to gain support for their policies. Some orthodox groups may institute repressive measures to control people's behavior and exclude them from certain activities. Leveling actions bring standouts in line with social norms. Religion can promote change through revitalization movements led by religious figures trying to alter a society and help its people adapt to change. Cargo cults blend aboriginal and Christian beliefs to explain European domination and wealth and achieve similar success magically.

Pop Quiz

1. According to Tylor, through what sequence did religion evolve?
   a. Animism, polytheism, monotheism.
   b. Imitative magic, polytheism, monotheism.
   c. Mana, polytheism, monotheism.
   d. Olympianism, animism, monotheism.

2. Which of the following describes the concept of mana in Polynesian and Melanesian cultures?
   a. Things charged with mana were taboo.
   b. In Melanesia, mana was similar to the notion of luck, anyone could get it; in Polynesia, mana was attached to political elites.
   c. Most anthropologists agree that mana was the most primitive religious doctrine in both areas.
   d. In both Polynesia and Melanesia, mana was concerned with supernatural beings rather than with powers or forces.

3. What is an irony this chapter highlights when describing rites of passage?
   a. Participants in rites of passage often are tricked into believing there is a big change in their status.
   b. The main goal of such rites is to worsen the anxieties caused by other aspects of religion.
   c. Beliefs and rituals can both diminish and create anxiety and a sense of danger.
   d. Rites of passage would be more effective if they did not include the third phase of the rite.

4. What is typically observed during the liminal phase of a rite of passage?
   a. Intensification of social hierarchy.
   b. Symbolic reversals of ordinary behavior.
   c. Formation of a ranking system.
   d. No change in the social norms.

5. This chapter describes how Afghanistan's Taliban movement imposed an extreme form of social control through repressive religion. However:
   a. Secular leaders also use religion for social control.
   b. Religion is used this way only by Muslim clerical leaders.
   c. The Taliban movement had no interest in women's lives; it focused only on men.
   d. The Taliban's extreme forms of social control did not influence people's actions.

6. Which of the following statements does not completely apply to Wallace's typology of religions?
   a. Olympian religions arose with state organization and added full-time religious specialists in the form of professional priesthoods.
   b. Communal religions, typical of farming societies, lack full-time religious specialists.

   c. Shamans are full-time religious officials who mediate between people and the supernatural.
   d. In monotheism, supernatural phenomena are manifestations of a single eternal, omnipotent supreme being.

7. Which of the following points is not consistent with the chapter's discussion of world religions?
   a. Christianity is the world's largest major religion.
   b. Islam is growing at a faster rate than Christianity.
   c. There is no variation in the growth rate of different groups of Christians.
   d. More than a billion people claim no religion.

8. Which statement most accurately defines a revitalization movement?
   a. It seeks to maintain order through strict adherence to purportedly traditional standards, customs, and beliefs.
   b. More correctly known as a nativistic movement, a revitalization movement seeks to maintain the old native ways of life.
   c. It is a colonial religious movement that lacked adaptive value for the people involved.
   d. It is a social movement that occurs in times of change in which religious leaders undertake to revitalize a society.

9. Cargo cults, which mix Melanesian and Christian beliefs, are:
   a. Religious responses to the expansion of the world capitalistic economy, often with political and economic consequences.
   b. Cultural acts that mock the widespread but erroneous belief of European cultural supremacy.
   c. Movements that arise when natives begin to acquire and benefit from the wealth, technology, and living standards of industrial societies.
   d. Attempts to explain European domination without actually trying to achieve similar successes.

10. Which one of the following would not represent a problem with Wallace's definition of religion?
   a. The definition excludes ritual-like behaviors that occur in nonreligious settings.
   b. His concept of the supernatural does not fit with the idea of this realm being outside the observable world.
   c. It fails to consider societies in which the distinction between the supernatural and the natural is not consistently made.
   d. It fails to consider behavior that may be considered appropriate for religious occasions in one culture but not in another.

1. (a), 2. (b), 3. (c), 4. (b), 5. (a), 6. (c), 7. (c), 8. (d), 9. (a), 10. (b)

11

THE WORLD SYSTEM AND COLONIALISM

WHAT'S TO COME

The World System

Industrialization

Socioeconomic Effects of Industrialization

Colonialism

The Role of Development in the World System

The Second World

The World System Today

UNDERSTANDING OURSELVES

In today's world system, people are linked as never before, and descendants of villagers who hosted ethnographers a generation ago now live transnational lives. Conrad Kottak (2010) reports on how transnationalism has affected a village in Madagascar, Ivato, that he first studied in 1966 and 1967.

When Kottak was not "in the field" in Ivato, he rented a small house in Ambalavao, a town whose residents included Indian cloth merchants, Chinese grocers, and a few French people, including two young men in the French equivalent of the Peace Corps. (Madagascar had been a French colony.) One of them, Noel, was courting Lenore, a young woman from a prominent local family originally from Ivato.

On Kottak's next trip to Madagascar, in 1981, he discovered that an active exchange program, including study abroad, had been established between Madagascar and the Soviet Union. One result of this program was that Kottak missed one of his best friends from Ivato who was spending three months studying in Moscow.

When Kottak next visited Madagascar, in 1990, he met Emily, the twenty-two-year-old daughter of Noel and Lenore, whose courtship he had witnessed in 1967. Emily was about to travel to the United States to study marketing. When Kottak saw her again a few months later in Gainesville, Florida, she inquired about her father, whom she had never met. She had sent several letters to France, but Noel never responded.

Descendants of Ambalavao now live all over the world. Emily, a child of colonialism, has two aunts in France and another in Germany. Members of her family, which is not especially wealthy, have traveled to Russia, Canada, the United States, France, Germany, and West Africa. How many of your classmates, including perhaps you, yourself, have recent transnational roots? The son of a man from a rural Kenyan village has even been elected president of the United States.

As You READ

- When and why did the world system develop, and what is it like today?

- When and how did European colonialism develop, and how is its legacy expressed in postcolonial studies?

- How do colonialism, development, industrialization, neoliberalism, and Communism exemplify intervention philosophies?

>> The World System

Although fieldwork in small communities has been anthropology's hallmark, isolated groups are impossible to find today. Truly isolated societies probably never have existed. For thousands of years, human groups have been in contact with one another. Local societies always have participated in a larger system, which today has global dimensions—we call it the *modern world system,* by which we mean a world in which nations are economically and politically interdependent.

The world system and the relations among the countries within it are shaped by the capitalist world economy. A huge increase in international trade during and after the fifteenth century led to the **capitalist world economy** (Wallerstein 1982, 2004b), a single world system committed to production for sale or exchange, with the object of maximizing profits, rather than supplying domestic needs. **Capital** refers to wealth or resources invested in business, with the intent of using the means of production to make a profit.

World-system theory can be traced to the French social historian Fernand Braudel. In his three-volume work *Civi-*

capitalist world economy The single world system, which emerged in the sixteenth century, committed to production for sale, with the object of maximizing profits, rather than supplying domestic needs.

capital Wealth or resources invested in business, with the intent of producing a profit.

lization and Capitalism, 15th–18th Century (1981, 1982, 1992), Braudel argued that society consists of interrelated parts assembled into a system. Societies are subsystems of larger systems, with the world system the largest. The key claim of **world-system theory** is that an identifiable social system, based on wealth and power differentials, extends beyond individual countries. That system is formed by a set of economic and political relations that has characterized much of the globe since the sixteenth century, when the Old World established regular contact with the New World (see Bodley 2008).

According to Wallerstein (1982, 2004b), countries within the world system occupy three different positions of economic and political power: core, semiperiphery, and periphery. The geographic center, or **core,** which is the dominant position in the world system, includes the strongest and most powerful nations, such as the United States, Germany, and Japan. In core nations, "the complexity of economic activities and the level of capital accumulation is the greatest" (Thompson 1983, p. 12). With its sophisticated technologies and mechanized production, the core churns out products that flow mainly to other core countries. Some also go to the periphery and semiperiphery. According to Arrighi (1994), the core monopolizes the most profitable activities, especially the control of world finance.

Semiperiphery and periphery countries have less power, wealth, and influence than the core does. The **semiperiphery** is intermediate between the core and the periphery. Contemporary nations of the semiperiphery, including Brazil, India, and China, are industrialized. Like core nations, they export both industrial goods and commodities, but they lack the power and economic dominance of core nations, although their power and influence are growing rapidly. Brazil, a semiperiphery nation, exports automobiles to Nigeria (a periphery nation) and auto engines, or-

STUDY TIP

There are three positions in the world system:

- Core (most powerful nations, largest capital accumulation, sophisticated technologies, control over finance).

- Semiperiphery (intermediate between core and periphery, industrialized, exports to core and periphery nations, source of cheap labor).

- Periphery (least powerful nations, less mechanized industries, exports raw materials and agricultural commodities, source of cheap labor).

ange juice extract, coffee, and shrimp to the United States (a core nation). The **periphery** includes the world's least privileged and powerful countries, including Bangladesh, Guatemala, Haiti, and Madagascar, among many others. Economic activities there are less mechanized than are those in the semiperiphery, although some degree of industrialization has reached even peripheral nations. The periphery produces raw materials, agricultural commodities, and, increasingly, human labor for export to the core and the semiperiphery (Shannon 1996).

In the United States and Western Europe today, immigration—legal and illegal—from the periphery and semiperiphery supplies cheap labor for agriculture in core countries. U.S. states as distant as California, Michigan, and South Carolina make significant use of farm labor from Mexico. The availability of relatively cheap workers from noncore nations such as Mexico (in the United States) and Turkey (in Germany) benefits farmers and business owners in core countries, while also supplying remittances to families in the semiperiphery and periphery. As a result of twenty-first-century telecommunications technology, cheap labor doesn't even need to migrate to the United States. Thousands of families in India are being

supported as American companies outsource jobs—from telephone assistance to software engineering—to nations outside the core.

THE EMERGENCE OF THE WORLD SYSTEM

As Europeans took to ships, developing a transoceanic trade-oriented economy, people throughout the world entered Europe's sphere of influence. In the fifteenth century, Europe established regular contact with Asia, Africa, and eventually the New World (the Caribbean and the Americas). Christopher Columbus's first voyage from Spain to the Bahamas and the Caribbean in 1492 was soon followed by additional voyages. These journeys opened the way for a major exchange of people, resources, products, ideas, and diseases, as the Old and New Worlds were forever linked (Crosby 2003; Diamond 1997; Fagan 1998; Viola and Margolis 1991). Led by Spain and Portugal, Europeans extracted silver and gold, conquered the natives (taking some as slaves), and colonized their lands.

Previously in Europe as throughout the world, rural people had produced mainly for their own needs, growing their own food and making clothing, furniture, and tools from local products. Production beyond immediate needs was undertaken to pay taxes and to purchase trade items such as salt and iron. As late as 1650 the English diet was based on locally grown starches (Mintz 1985). In the two hundred years that followed, however, the English became extraordinary consumers of imported goods. One of the earliest and most popular of those goods was sugar (Mintz 1985).

world-system theory Argument for the historic and contemporary social, political, and economic significance of an identifiable global system, based on wealth and power differentials, that extends beyond individual countries.

core Dominant structural position in the world system; consists of the strongest and most powerful states with advanced systems of production.

semiperiphery Structural position in the world system intermediate between core and periphery; exporters of goods and commodities, but lacking the power of core nations.

periphery Weakest structural position in the world system; less mechanized producers of raw materials, agricultural commodities, and human labor.

Sugarcane originally was domesticated in Papua New Guinea, and sugar was first processed in India. Reaching Europe via the Middle East and the eastern Mediterranean, it was carried to the New World by Columbus (Mintz 1985). The climate of Brazil and the Caribbean proved ideal for growing sugarcane, and Europeans built plantations there to supply the growing demand for sugar. This led to the development in the seventeenth century of a plantation economy based on a single cash crop—a system known as *monocrop* production.

The demand for sugar in a growing international market spurred the development of the transatlantic slave trade and New World plantation economies based on slave labor. By the eighteenth century, an increased English demand for raw cotton led to rapid settlement of

CULTURE THINK

Look at the labels on your clothing: Where was it made? Where do those nations fit into the world system? (See p. 218 for a map.)

MADE IN BANGLADESH

what is now the southeastern United States and the emergence there of another slave-based mono-crop production system. Like sugar, cotton was a key trade item that fueled the growth of the world system.

>> Industrialization

By the eighteenth century the stage had been set for the **Industrial Revolution**—the historical transformation (in Europe, after 1750) of "traditional" into "modern" societies through industrialization of the economy. Industrialization required capital for investment. The established system of transoceanic trade and commerce supplied this capital from the enormous profits it generated. Wealthy people sought investment opportunities and eventually found them in machines and engines to drive machines. Capital and scientific innovation fueled invention. Industrialization increased production in both farming and manufacturing.

European industrialization developed from (and eventually replaced) the *domestic system* of manufacture (or home-handicraft system). In this system, an organizer-entrepreneur supplied the raw materials to workers in their homes and collected the finished products from them. The entrepreneur, whose sphere of operations might span several villages, owned the materials, paid for the work, and arranged the marketing.

CAUSES OF THE INDUSTRIAL REVOLUTION

The Industrial Revolution began with cotton products, iron, and pottery. These were widely used goods whose

From producer to consumer, in the modern world system. The top photo, taken in the Caribbean nation of Dominica, shows the hard labor required to extract sugar using a manual press. In the bottom photo, consumers thousands of miles from the Caribbean take afternoon tea, sweetened with imported sugar. Which of the ingredients in your breakfast today were imported?

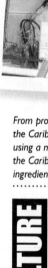

POPCULTURE

McDonald's is a global chain, and the ingredients in its products illustrate the historical world system in miniature. Consider just the Big Mac. Its two all-beef patties come from cattle, an Old World domesticate. Its special sauce is similar to mayonnaise, invented in France. Lettuce comes from Egypt; cheese from cow's milk (Old World), pickles from India, onions from Iran and West Pakistan. It comes on a sesame seed (India) bun (wheat—Middle East). The Egg McMuffin includes eggs, from chickens (Southeast Asia), and Canadian bacon, from pork (western Asia). The breakfast burrito is based on maize, or corn, a New World product—like the chocolate you might have in your milk or shake. Keep a food diary for two days. Then Google "food origins" or consult a site like http://www.foodtimeline .org/ to see how your own diet illustrates the diverse origins of the foods we eat every day.

STUDY **TIP**

Industrialism draws labor to a central location of production (say, a factory), while people work in their homes in the *domestic system* of manufacture.

manufacture could be broken into simple routine motions that machines could perform. When manufacturing moved from homes to factories, where machinery replaced handwork, agrarian societies evolved into industrial ones. As factories produced cheap staple goods, the Industrial Revolution led to a dramatic increase in production. Industrialization fueled urban growth and created a new kind of city, with factories crowded together in places where coal and labor were cheap.

The Industrial Revolution began in England rather than in France. Why? Unlike the English, the French didn't have to transform their domestic manufacturing system by industrializing. Faced with an increased need for products, with a late eighteenth-century population at least twice that of Great Britain, France could simply augment its domestic system of production by drawing in new homes. Thus, the French increased production *without innovating*—they could enlarge the existing system rather than adopt a new

In the home-handicraft, or domestic, system of production, an organizer supplied raw materials to workers in their homes and collected their products. Family life and work were intertwined, as in this English scene. Is there a modern equivalent to the domestic system of production?

The ART of STOCKING-FRAME-WORK-KNITTING.

grav'd for the Universal Magazine 1750 for J. Hinton at the Kings Arms in S.t Pauls Church Yard LONDON.

one. To meet mounting demand for staples—at home and in the colonies—England had to industrialize.

As its industrialization proceeded, Britain's population began to increase dramatically. It doubled during the eighteenth century (especially after 1750) and did so again between 1800 and 1850. This demographic explosion fueled consumption, but British entrepreneurs couldn't meet the increased demand with the traditional production methods. This spurred further experimentation, innovation, and rapid technological change.

English industrialization drew on national advantages in natural resources. Britain was rich in coal and iron ore, and had navigable waterways and easily negotiated coasts. It was a seafaring island-nation located at the crossroads of international trade. These features gave Britain a favored position for importing raw materials and exporting manufactured goods. Another factor in England's industrial growth was the fact that much of its eighteenth-century colonial empire was occupied by English settler families who looked to the mother country as they tried to replicate European civilization in the New World. These colonies bought large quantities of English staples.

> **Industrial Revolution** The historical transformation (in Europe, after 1750) of "traditional" into "modern" societies through industrialization of the economy.

STUDY **TIP**

The Industrial Revolution began in England for several reasons: (1) a dramatic population increase (within England and its colonies) fueled demand for goods; (2) it was rich in raw materials (coal and iron ore) essential to production; (3) expertise in navigation facilitated importing and exporting; (4) the growth of Protestantism among the middle class encouraged a work ethic.

It also has been argued that particular cultural values and religion contributed to industrialization. Many members of the emerging English middle class were Protestant nonconformists. Their beliefs and values encouraged industry, thrift, the dissemination of new knowledge, inventiveness, and willingness to accept change (Weber 1904/1958).

>> Socioeconomic Effects of Industrialization

The socioeconomic effects of industrialization were mixed. English national income tripled between 1700 and 1815 and increased thirty times more by 1939.

Standards of comfort rose, but prosperity was uneven. At first, factory workers' wages were higher than those available in the domestic system. Later, owners started recruiting labor in places where living standards were low and labor (including that of women and children) was cheap.

Social ills worsened with the growth of factory towns and industrial cities, amid conditions like those Charles Dickens described in *Hard Times*. Filth and smoke polluted the nineteenth-century cities. Housing was crowded and unsanitary, with insufficient water and sewage disposal facilities. People experienced rampant disease and rising death rates. This was the world of Ebenezer Scrooge, Bob Cratchit, Tiny Tim—and Karl Marx.

bourgeoisie One of Karl Marx's opposed classes; owners of the means of production (factories, mines, large farms, and other sources of subsistence).

working class (proletariat) Those who must sell their labor to survive; the antithesis of the bourgeoisie in Marx's class analysis.

INDUSTRIAL STRATIFICATION

Social theorists Karl Marx and Max Weber focused on the stratification systems associated with industrialization. From his observations in England and his analysis of nineteenth-century industrial capitalism, Marx (Marx and Engels 1848/1976) saw socioeconomic stratification as a sharp and simple division between two opposed classes: the bourgeoisie (capitalists) and the proletariat (propertyless workers). The bourgeoisie traced its origins to overseas ventures and the world capitalist economy, which had created a wealthy commercial class.

Industrialization shifted production from farms and cottages to mills and factories, where mechanical power was available and where workers could be assembled to operate heavy machinery. The **bourgeoisie** were the owners of the factories, mines, large farms, and other means of production. The **working class,** or **proletariat,** were people who had to sell their labor to survive. With the decline of subsistence production and the rise of urban migration and the possibility of unemployment, the bourgeoisie came to stand between workers and the means of production.

Industrialization hastened the process of *proletarianization*—the separation of workers from the means of production. The bourgeoisie also came to dominate the means of communication, the schools, and other key institutions. *Class consciousness* (recognition of collective interests and personal identification with one's economic group) was a vital part of Marx's view of class. He saw bourgeoisie and proletariat as socioeconomic divisions with radically opposed interests. Marx viewed classes as powerful collective forces that could mobilize human energies to influence the course of history. On the basis of their common experience, workers would develop class consciousness, which could lead to revolutionary change. Although no proletarian revolution was to occur in England, workers did develop organizations to protect their interests and increase their share of industrial profits. During the nineteenth century, trade unions and socialist parties emerged to express a rising anticapitalist spirit. The concerns of the English labor movement were to remove young children from factories and limit the hours during which women and children could work. The profile of stratification in industrial core nations gradually took shape. Capitalists controlled production, but labor was organizing for better wages and working conditions. By 1900 many governments had factory legislation and social-welfare programs. Mass living standards in core nations rose as population grew.

In today's capitalist world system the class division between owners and workers is now worldwide. However, publicly traded companies complicate the division between capitalists and workers in industrial nations. Through pension plans and personal investments, some American workers now have a proprietary interest in the means of production. They are part owners rather than propertyless workers. The key difference is that the wealthy have *control* over these means. The key capitalist now is not the factory owner, who may have been replaced by thousands of stockholders, but the CEO or the chair of the board of directors, neither of whom may actually own the corporation.

Modern stratification systems aren't simple and dichotomous. They include (particularly in core and semiperiphery nations) a middle

Karl Marx observed and analyzed nineteenth-century industrial capitalism. He saw socioeconomic stratification in terms of two opposed classes: bourgeoisie and proletariat.

During the nineteenth and early twentieth centuries, women and children often worked long hours in factories, as in this Macon, Georgia textile mill in 1909.

class of skilled and professional workers. Gerhard Lenski (1966) argues that social equality tends to increase in advanced industrial societies. The masses improve their access to economic benefits and political power. In Lenski's scheme, the shift of political power to the masses reflects the growth of the middle class, which reduces the polarization between owning and working classes. The proliferation of middle-class occupations creates opportunities for social mobility. The stratification system grows more complex (Giddens 1973).

CULTURETHINK

Ask some of the people you know what social class they think they belong to. How about you—what's your class? Why do you think so many Americans identify with the middle class? What are some cultural values associated with being middle class?

In the United States this complex stratification system has gone largely unnoticed by many Americans. Most contemporary Americans, for example, think they belong

to, and claim identity with, the middle class, which they tend to perceive as a vast undifferentiated group. However, there are substantial differences in income and wealth between the richest and the poorest Americans, and the gap is widening. According to U.S. Census data from 1967 to 2000, the top (richest) fifth, or quintile, of American households increased their share of national income by 13.5 percent, while all other quintiles fell. The percentage share of the lowest fifth fell most dramatically—by 17.6 percent. The divergence continues: In 2006 the highest quintile of households received 50.5 percent (versus 49.7 percent in 2000) of all national income, while the lowest fifth received 3.4 percent (versus 3.6 in 2000). Comparable figures in 1967 were 43.8 percent and 4.0 percent. The 2006 ratio was 15:1, versus 14:1 in 2000 and 11:1 in 1967. In other words, the richest fifth of American households, with a mean annual income of $168,170, is now 15 times wealthier than the poorest fifth, with a mean annual income of $11,352 (DeNavas-Walt, Proctor, and Lee; U. S. Census Bureau 2006, http://www.census.gov/hhes/www/income/histinc/h03ar.html). When we consider wealth (investments, property, possessions, etc.) rather than income, the contrast is even more striking: 1 percent of American families hold just over one-third of the nation's wealth (Council on International and Public Affairs 2006). As the chart on page 210 ("Percentage of Wealth Owned, by Percentile") shows, the top 1 percent owns 33.4 percent of all wealth in the United States. By contrast, the bottom 50 percent owns

United States Wealth Owned, 2004

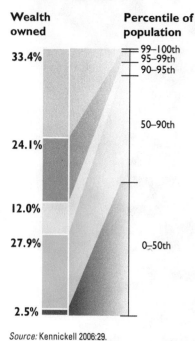

Wealth owned	Percentile of population
33.4%	99–100th / 95–99th / 90–95th
24.1%	50–90th
12.0%	
27.9%	0–50th
2.5%	

Source: Kennickell 2006:29.

contrasts, the modern world system is cross-cut by collective identities based on ethnicity, religion, and nationality (Shannon 1996). Class conflicts tend to occur within nations, and nationalism has prevented global class solidarity, particularly of proletarians.

Although the capitalist class dominates politically in most countries, growing wealth has made it easier for core nations to grant higher wages (Hopkins and Wallerstein 1982). However, the improvement in core workers' living standards wouldn't have occurred without the world system. Without the periphery, core capitalists would have trouble maintaining their profits and also satisfying the demands of core workers. In the periphery, wages and living standards are much lower. The current *world stratification system* features a substantial contrast between both

just 2.5 percent. In fact, the top 1 percent owns more than the bottom 90 percent combined.

Weber faulted Marx for an overly simple and exclusively economic view of stratification. As we saw in the chapter "Political Systems," Weber (1922/1968) defined three dimensions of social stratification: wealth, power, and prestige. Although, as Weber showed, wealth, power, and prestige are separate components of social ranking, they tend to be correlated. Weber also believed that social identities based on ethnicity, religion, race, nationality, and other attributes could take priority over class (social identity based on economic status). In addition to class

Max Weber (1864–1920). Did Weber improve on Marx's view of stratification?

capitalists and workers in the core nations and workers on the periphery (see Kerbo 2006).

>> Colonialism

World-system theory stresses the existence of a global culture and economy. It emphasizes historical contacts, linkages, and power differentials between local people and international forces. The major forces influencing cultural interaction during the past five hundred years have been commercial expansion, industrial capitalism, and the dominance of colonial and core nations (Wallerstein 1982, 2004b; Wolf 1982). As state formation had done previously, industrialization accelerated local participation in larger networks. According to Bodley (2007), perpetual expansion is a distinguishing feature of industrial economic systems. Bands and tribes were small, self-sufficient, subsistence-based systems. Industrial economies, by contrast, are large, highly specialized systems in which market exchanges occur with profit as the primary motive (Bodley 2007).

During the nineteenth century, European business interests initiated a concerted search for markets. This process led to European imperialism in Africa, Asia, and Oceania. **Imperialism** refers to a policy of extending the rule of a country or empire over foreign nations and of taking and holding foreign colonies. Imperialism goes back to early states, including Egypt in the Old World and the Incas in the New. Alexander the Great forged a Greek empire, and Julius Caesar and his successors spread the Roman empire. More recent examples include the British, French, and Soviet empires (Scheinman 1980).

After 1850, European imperial expansion was aided by improved transportation, which facilitated the colonization of vast areas of sparsely settled lands in the interior of North and South America and Australia. The new colonies purchased masses of goods from the industrial centers and shipped back wheat, cotton, wool, mutton, beef, and leather. The first phase of European colonialism had been the exploration and exploitation of the Americas and the Caribbean after Columbus. A new second phase began as European nations competed for colonies between 1875 and 1914, setting the stage for World War I.

Colonialism is the political, social, economic, and cultural domination of a territory and its people by a foreign power for an extended time (see Bremen and Shimizu 1999; Cooper and Stoler 1997). If imperialism is almost as old as the state, colonialism can be traced back to the Phoenicians, who established colo-

STUDY TIP

Three dimensions of social stratification, according to Weber, are power, prestige, and wealth.

On January 1, 1900, a British officer in India receives a pedicure from a servant. What does this photo say to you about colonialism? Who gives pedicures in your society?

nies along the eastern Mediterranean three thousand years ago. The ancient Greeks and Romans were avid colonizers, as well as empire builders.

The first phase of modern colonialism began with the European "Age of Discovery"—of the Americas and of a sea route to the Far East. After 1492, the Spanish, the original conquerors of the Aztecs and Incas, explored and colonized widely in the New World—the Caribbean, Mexico, the southern portions of what was to become the United States, and Central and South America. In South America, Portugal ruled over Brazil. Rebellions and wars aimed at independence ended the first phase of European colonialism by the early nineteenth century. Brazil declared independence from Portugal in 1822. By 1825 most of Spain's colonies were politically independent. Spain

STUDY TIP

The two phases of European colonialism include first, the exploration and exploitation of the New World after Columbus; and second, the competition for colonies, ending with World War I.

held onto Cuba and the Philippines until 1898, but otherwise withdrew from the colonial field. During the first phase of colonialism, Spain and Portugal, along with Britain and France, were major colonizing nations. Britain and France dominated the second phase.

BRITISH COLONIALISM

At its peak about 1914, the British empire covered a fifth of the world's land surface and ruled a fourth of its population (see "Map of British Empire in 1765 and 1914" on page 212). Like several other European nations, Britain had two stages of colonialism. The first began with the Elizabethan voyages of the sixteenth century. During the seventeenth century, Britain acquired most of the eastern coast of North America, Canada's St. Lawrence basin, islands in the Caribbean, slave stations in Africa, and interests in India.

imperialism A policy of extending the rule of a nation or empire over foreign nations and of taking and holding foreign colonies.

colonialism The political, social, economic, and cultural domination of a territory and its people by a foreign power for an extended time.

The British shared the exploration of the New World with the Spanish, Portuguese, French, and Dutch. The British by and large left Mexico, along with Central and South America, to the Spanish and the Portuguese. The end of the Seven Years' War in 1763 forced a French retreat

Map of British Empire in 1765 and 1914

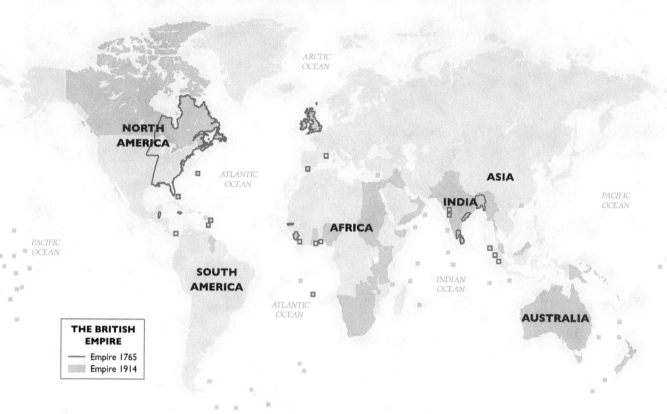

from most of Canada and India, where France previously had competed with Britain (Cody 1998; Farr 1980).

The American Revolution ended the first stage of British colonialism. A second colonial empire, on which the "sun never set," rose from the ashes of the first. Beginning in 1788, but intensifying after 1815, the British settled Australia. Britain had acquired Dutch South Africa by 1815. The establishment of Singapore in 1819 provided a base for a British trade network that extended to much of South Asia and along the coast of China. By this time, the empires of Britain's traditional rivals, particularly Spain, had been severely diminished in scope. Britain's position as imperial power and the world's leading industrial nation was unchallenged (Cody 1998; Farr 1980).

During the Victorian Era (1837–1901), as Britain's acquisition of territory and of further trading concessions continued, Prime Minister Benjamin Disraeli implemented a foreign policy justified by a view of imperialism as shouldering "the white man's burden"—a phrase coined by the

poet Rudyard Kipling. People in the empire were seen as unable to govern themselves, so that British guidance was needed to civilize and Christianize them. This paternalistic and racist doctrine served to legitimize Britain's acquisition and control of parts of central Africa and Asia (Cody 1998).

After World War II, the British empire began to fall apart, with nationalist movements for independence. India became independent in 1947, as did Ireland in 1949. Decolonization in Africa and Asia accelerated during the late 1950s. Today, the ties that remain between Britain and its former colonies are mainly linguistic or cultural rather than political (Cody 1998).

FRENCH COLONIALISM

Two phases also characterized French colonialism. The first began with the explorations of the early 1600s. Before the French revolution in 1789, missionaries, explorers, and traders had carved out niches for France in Canada, the Louisiana territory, several Caribbean islands, and parts of India (Harvey 1980). The Treaty of Paris of 1763 ended the Seven Years' War, the American counterpart of which was the French and Indian War. That treaty awarded Canada to Great Britain, while France retained the prosperous West Indian sugar islands of Guadeloupe and Martinique.

The foundations of the second French empire were established between 1830 and 1870. In Great Britain the

CULTURETHINK

The idea of the "white man's burden" was a world-view that made colonialism seem legitimate. Does anything like the "white man's burden" shape current events in politics?

Map of the French Empire at Its Height around 1914

Source: From the *Academic American Encyclopedia*, Vol 3, p. 309. 1998 Edition. Copyright 1998 by Grolier Incorporated. Reprinted with permission.

sheer drive for profit led expansion, but French colonialism was spurred more by the state, church, and armed forces than by pure business interests. France acquired Algeria and part of what eventually became Indochina (Cambodia, Laos, and Vietnam). By 1914 the French empire covered four million square miles and included some sixty million people (see "Map of the French Empire at Its Height"). By 1893 French rule had been fully established in Indochina. Tunisia and Morocco became French protectorates in 1883 and 1912, respectively (Harvey 1980).

To be sure, the French, like the British, had substantial business interests in their colonies, but they also sought, again like the British, international glory and prestige. The French promulgated a *mission civilisatrice,* their equivalent of Britain's "white man's burden." The goal was to implant French culture, language, and religion, Roman Catholicism, throughout the colonies (Harvey 1980).

The French used two forms of colonial rule: *indirect rule,* governing through native leaders and established political structures, in areas with long histories of state organization, such as Morocco and Tunisia; and *direct rule* by French officials in many areas of Africa, where the French imposed new government structures to control diverse societies, many of them previously stateless. Like the British empire, the French empire began to disintegrate after World War II. France fought long—and ultimately futile—wars to keep its empire intact in Indochina and Algeria (Harvey 1980).

COLONIALISM AND IDENTITY

Many geopolitical labels in the news today had no equivalent meaning before colonialism. Whole countries, along with social groups and divisions within them, were colonial inventions. In West Africa, for example, by geographic logic, several adjacent countries could be one (Togo, Ghana, Ivory Coast, Guinea, Guinea-Bissau, Sierra Leone, Liberia). Instead, they are separated by linguistic, political, and economic contrasts promoted under colonialism.

Hundreds of ethnic groups and "tribes" are colonial constructions (see Ranger 1996). The Sukuma of Tanzania, for instance, were first registered as a single tribe by the colonial administration. Then missionaries standardized a series of dialects into a single Sukuma language into which they translated the Bible and other religious texts. Thereafter, those texts were taught in missionary schools and to European foreigners and other non-Sukuma speakers. Over time this standardized the Sukuma language and ethnicity (Finnstrom 1997).

As in most of East Africa, in Rwanda and Burundi farmers and herders live in the same areas and speak the same language. Historically they have shared the same social world, although their social organization is "extremely hierarchical," almost "castelike" (Malkki 1995, p. 24). There has been a tendency to see the pastoral Tutsis as superior to the agricultural Hutus. Tutsis have been presented as nobles, Hutus as commoners. Yet when distributing identity

Tutsi and Hutu originated as arbitrary colonial categories. They became "ethnic" groups subject to mass killings (genocide) in Rwanda in 1994, as portrayed in the film Hotel Rwanda, shown here.

postcolonial Referring to interactions between European nations and the societies they colonized (mainly after 1800); more generally, it may be used to signify a position against imperialism and Eurocentrism.

cards in Rwanda, the Belgian colonizers simply identified all people with more than ten head of cattle as Tutsi. Owners of fewer cattle were registered as Hutus (Bjuremalm 1997). Years later, these arbitrary colonial registers were used systematically for "ethnic" identification during the mass killings (genocide) that took place in Rwanda in 1994 (as portrayed vividly in the film *Hotel Rwanda*).

POSTCOLONIAL STUDIES

In anthropology, history, and literature, the field of postcolonial studies has gained prominence since the 1970s (see Ashcroft, Griffiths, and Tiffin 1989; Cooper and Stoler 1997). **Postcolonial** refers to the interactions between European nations and the societies they colonized (mainly after 1800). In 1914, European empires, which

CULTURETHINK

Do you think the critique of Eurocentrism is legitimate? Does the perspective of white Europeans (or their descendants) dominate thinking about history and culture? What perspectives do you think a non-Eurocentric point of view would consider?

broke up after World War II, ruled more than 85 percent of the world (Petraglia-Bahri 1996). The term *postcolonial* also has been used to describe the second half of the twentieth century in general, the period succeeding colonialism. Even more generically, *postcolonial* may be used to signify a position against imperialism and Eurocentrism (Petraglia-Bahri 1996).

The former colonies (*postcolonies*) can be divided into settler, nonsettler, and mixed (Petraglia-Bahri 1996). The settler countries, with large numbers of European colonists and sparser native populations, include Australia and Canada. Examples of nonsettler countries include India, Pakistan, Bangladesh, Sri Lanka, Malaysia, Indonesia, Nigeria, Senegal, Madagascar, and Jamaica. All these had substantial native populations and relatively few European settlers. Mixed countries include South Africa, Zimbabwe, Kenya, and Algeria. Such countries had significant European settlement despite having sizable native populations.

Given the varied experiences of such countries, postcolonial has to be a loose term. The United States, for instance, was colonized by Europeans and fought a war for independence from Britain. Is the United States a postcolony? It usually isn't perceived as such, given its current world power position, its treatment of native Americans (sometimes called internal colonization), and its annexation of other parts of the world (Petraglia-Bahri 1996). Research in postcolonial studies is growing, permitting a wide-ranging investigation of power relations in varied contexts. Broad topics in the field include the formation of an empire, the impact of colonization, and the state of the postcolony today (Petraglia-Bahri 1996).

Anthropology Works

A social studies educator can use insights from anthropology to make connections between historical events and contemporary conditions. Economic expansion during and before European colonialism helped shape the current world system, shedding light on why some nations are poorer than others today.

>> The Role of Development in the World System

During the Industrial Revolution, a strong current of thought viewed industrialization as a beneficial process of organic development and progress. Many economists still assume that industrialization increases production and income. They seek to create in Third World ("developing") countries a process like the one that first occurred spontaneously in eighteenth-century Great Britain.

We have seen that Britain used the notion of a white man's burden to justify its imperialist expansion and that France claimed to be engaged in a *mission civilisatrice*—a civilizing mission—in its colonies. Both these ideas illustrate an **intervention philosophy,** an ideological justification for outsiders to guide native peoples in specific directions. Economic development plans also have intervention philosophies. John Bodley (2008) argues that the basic belief behind interventions—whether by colonialists, missionaries, governments, or development planners—has been the same for more than a hundred years. This belief is that industrialization, modernization, Westernization, and individualism are desirable evolutionary advances and that development schemes that promote them will bring long-term benefits to local people. In a more extreme form, intervention philosophy may pit the assumed wisdom of enlightened colonial or other First World planners against the purported conservatism, ignorance, or "obsolescence" of "inferior" or "backward" local people.

NEOLIBERALISM

One currently influential intervention philosophy, neoliberalism, encompasses a set of assumptions that have become widespread during the last thirty years. Neoliberal policies are being implemented in developing nations, including postsocialist societies (e.g., those of the former Soviet Union). **Neoliberalism** is the current form of the classic economic liberalism laid out in Adam Smith's famous capitalist manifesto, *The Wealth of Nations,* published in 1776, soon after the Industrial Revolution. Smith

advocated laissez-faire (hands-off) economics as the basis of capitalism: The government should stay out of its nation's economic affairs. Free trade, Smith thought, was the best way for a nation's economy to develop. There should be no restrictions on manufacturing, no barriers to commerce, and no tariffs. This philosophy is called liberalism because it aimed at liberating, or freeing, the economy from government controls. Economic liberalism encouraged "free" enterprise and competition, with the goal of generating profits. (Note the difference between this meaning of *liberal* and the one that has been popularized on American talk radio, in which people use "liberal"—usually as a derogatory term—as the opposite of "conservative." Ironically, Adam Smith's liberalism is today's capitalist conservatism.)

Economic liberalism prevailed in the United States until President Franklin Roosevelt's New Deal during the 1930s. The Great Depression produced a turn to Keynesian economics, which challenged liberalism. John Maynard Keynes (1927, 1936) insisted that full employment was necessary for capitalism to grow, that governments and central banks should intervene to increase employment, and that government should promote the common good.

> **intervention philosophy** Guiding principle of colonialism, conquest, missionization, or development; an ideological justification for outsiders to guide native peoples in specific directions.
>
> **neoliberalism** Revival of Adam Smith's classic economic liberalism, the idea that governments should not regulate private enterprise and that free market forces should rule; a currently dominant intervention philosophy.

STUDY **TIP**

Three phases in the economics of capitalism have been (1) Adam Smith's liberalism (government stays out of the economy); (2) Keynesian economics (the government stimulates the economy); (3) neoliberalism (government promotes free trade).

Especially since the fall of Communism (1989–1991), there has been a revival of economic liberalism, now known as neoliberalism, which has been spreading globally. Around the world, powerful financial institutions, such as the International Monetary Fund (IMF), the World Bank, and the Inter-American Development Bank, have imposed neoliberal policies (see Edelman and Haugerud 2004). Neoliberalism entails open (tariff- and barrier-free) international trade and investment. Profits are sought through lowering of costs, whether through improving productivity, laying off workers, or seeking workers who accept lower wages. In exchange for loans, the governments of postsocialist and developing nations

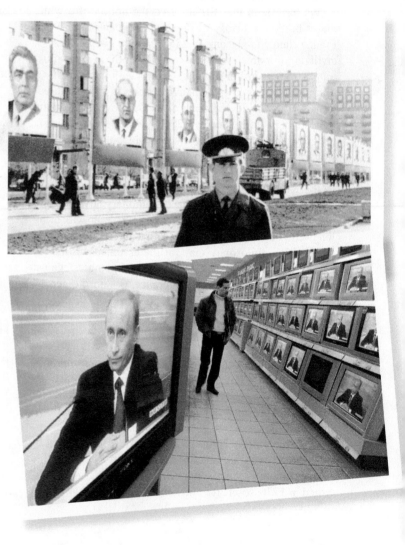

Citizens of former colonies often reject neoliberal reforms. For example, people across the world—from women's groups in India to the Kayapó indigenous people of the Amazon basin—have organized to protest the building of hydroelectric dams.

have been required to accept the neoliberal premise that deregulation leads to economic growth, which will eventually benefit everyone through a process sometimes called "trickle down." Accompanying the belief in free markets and the idea of cutting costs is a tendency to impose austerity measures that cut government expenses. This can entail reduced public spending on education, health care, and other social services (Martinez and Garcia 2000).

>> The Second World

The labels "First World," "Second World," and "Third World" represent a common, although ethnocentric, way of categorizing nations. The *First World* refers to the "democratic West"—traditionally conceived in opposition to a "Second World" ruled by "Communism." The *Second World* refers to the former Soviet Union and the socialist and once-socialist countries of Eastern Europe and Asia. Proceeding with this classification, the "less-developed countries" or "developing nations" make up the *Third World*.

communism Spelled with a lowercase c, describes a social system in which the community owns property and people work for the common good.

Communism Spelled with an uppercase C, describes a political movement and doctrine seeking to overthrow capitalism and to establish a form of communism such as that which prevailed in the Soviet Union (USSR) from 1917 to 1991.

COMMUNISM

The two meanings of communism involve how it is written, whether with a lowercase (small) or an uppercase (large) *c*. Small-*c* **communism** describes a social system in which the community owns property and people work for the common good. Large-*C* **Communism** was a political movement and doctrine seeking to overthrow capitalism and establish a form of communism such as that which prevailed in the Soviet Union (USSR) from 1917 to 1991. The heyday of Communism was a forty-year period from 1949 to 1989, when more Communist regimes existed than at any time before or after. Today only five Communist states remain—China, Cuba, Laos, North Korea, and Vietnam—compared with twenty-three in 1985.

Communism, which originated with Russia's Bolshevik Revolution in 1917, and took its inspiration from Karl Marx and Friedrich Engels, was not uniform

over time or among countries. All Communist systems were *authoritarian* (promoting obedience to authority rather than individual freedom). Many were *totalitarian* (banning rival parties and demanding total submission of the individual to the state). Several features distinguished Communist societies from other authoritarian regimes (e.g., Spain under Franco) and from socialism of a social democratic type. First, the Communist Party monopolized power in every Communist state. Second, relations within the party were highly centralized and strictly disciplined. Third, Communist nations had state ownership, rather than private ownership, of the means of production. Finally, all Communist regimes, with the goal of advancing communism, cultivated a sense of belonging to an international movement (Brown 2001).

Social scientists have tended to refer to such societies as socialist rather than Communist. Today research by anthropologists is thriving in *postsocialist* societies—those that once emphasized bureaucratic redistribution of wealth according to a central plan (Verdery 2001). In the postsocialist period, states that once had planned economies

Before and after Communism. Top: on May Day (May 1, 1975), large photos of Politburo members (Communist Party leaders) adorn buildings in Moscow. Bottom: on January 31, 2006, in a Moscow electronics store, a potential customer considers a display of TV sets, broadcasting the annual press conference of Russian then-president, now prime minister Vladimir Putin.

have been following the neoliberal agenda, by divesting themselves of state-owned resources in favor of privatization. Some of them have moved toward formal liberal democracy, with political parties, elections, and a balance of powers (Grekova 2001).

POSTSOCIALIST TRANSITIONS

Neoliberal economists assumed that dismantling the Soviet Union's planned economy would raise gross domestic product (GDP) and living standards. The goal was to enhance production by substituting a decentralized market system and providing incentives through privatization. In October 1991, Boris Yeltsin, who had been elected president of Russia that June, announced a program of radical market-oriented reform, pursuing a changeover to capitalism. Yeltsin's program of "shock therapy" cut subsidies to farms and industries and ended price controls. Since then, postsocialist Russia has faced many problems. The anticipated gains in productivity did not materialize. After the fall of the Soviet Union, Russia's GDP fell by half. Poverty increased, with a quarter of the population now living below the poverty line. Life expectancy and the birth rate declined. Another problem to emerge in the postsocialist transition is corruption. In response, the World Bank and other international organizations have launched anticorruption programs worldwide. *Corruption* is defined as the abuse of public office for private gain.

The World Bank's approach to corruption assumes a clear and sharp distinction between the state (the public or official domain) and the private sphere, and that the two should be kept separate. The idea that the public sphere can be separated neatly from the private sphere is ethnocentric. According to Janine Wedel (2002), postsocialist states provide rich contexts in which to explore variability in relations between public and private domains. Alexei Yurchak (2002, 2005) describes two spheres that operate in Russia today; these spheres do not mesh neatly with the assumption of a public–private split. He calls them the official–public sphere and the personal–public sphere, referring to domains that coexist and sometimes overlap. State officials may respect the law (official–public), while also working with informal or even criminal groups (personal–public). Officials switch from official–public to personal–public behavior all the time, in order to accomplish specific tasks.

>> The World System Today

The process of industrialization continues today, although nations have shifted their positions within the world system (Table 11.1). By 1900, the United States had become a core nation within the world system and had overtaken Great Britain in iron, coal, and cotton production. In a few decades (1868–1900), Japan had changed from a medieval handicraft economy to an industrial one, joining the semiperiphery by 1900 and moving to the core between 1945 and 1970. "The World System in 2000" map on page 218 shows the modern world system.

Twentieth-century industrialization added hundreds of new industries and millions of new jobs. Production increased, often beyond immediate demand, spurring strategies, such as advertising, to sell everything industry could churn out. Mass production gave rise to a culture of consumption, which valued acquisitiveness and conspicuous consumption (Veblen 1934). Industrialization entailed a shift from reliance on renewable resources to the use of fossil fuels. Fossil fuel energy, stored over millions of years, is being depleted rapidly to support a previously unknown and probably unsustainable level of consumption. (See also Chapter 13.)

Did You Know?

The Chinese economy has grown considerably in the past twenty years. In 2009, the United States' trade deficit with China was $226 billion, up from $68 billion in 1999, and $6 million in 1985. The United States imported $226 billion more in goods, resources, and materials from China than it exported to China. Over 70 percent of Walmart's goods are made in China.

Ascent and Decline of Nations within the World System

Periphery to Semiperiphery	Semiperiphery to Core	Core to Semiperiphery
United States (1800–1860)	United States (1860–1900)	Spain (1620–1700)
Japan (1868–1900)	Japan (1945–1970)	
Taiwan (1949–1980)	Germany (1870–1900)	
S. Korea (1953–1980)		

Source: Copyright © 1996 Thomas R. Shannon. Reprinted by permission of Westview Press, a member of Perseus Book Group.

The World System Today

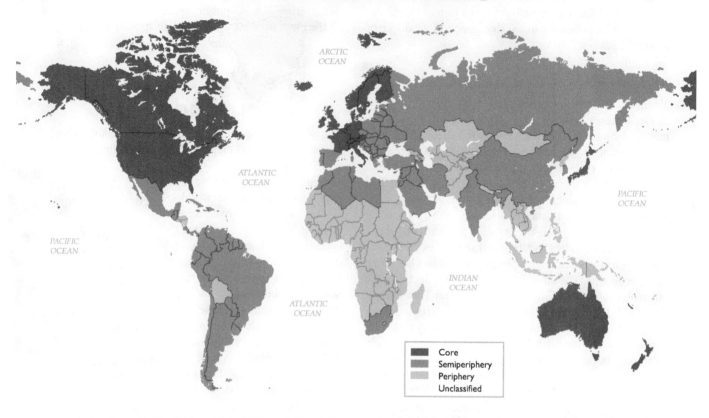

Energy Consumption in Various Contexts

Daily kilocalories per person   **Type of society**

Bands and tribes **4,000–12,000**

Preindustrial states **26,000** (maximum)

Early industrial states **70,000**

Americans in 1970 **230,000**

Americans in 1990 **275,000**

● = 1,000 kCal

Americans are the world's foremost consumers of nonrenewable resources as shown in "Energy Consumption in Various Contexts." In terms of energy consumption, the average American is about thirty-five times more expensive than the average forager or tribesperson. Since 1900, the United States has tripled its per capita energy use. It also has increased its total energy consumption thirtyfold.

"Energy Consumption in Selected Countries" compares energy use, per capita and total, in the United States and selected other countries. The United States represents 21.1 percent of the world's annual energy consumption, com-

CULTURE THINK

The amount of energy an individual consumes is sometimes called her or his "ecological footprint." How big is your footprint? What kinds of things do you use energy for each day? How much of that comes from fossil fuels?

Energy Consumption in Selected Countries, 2006

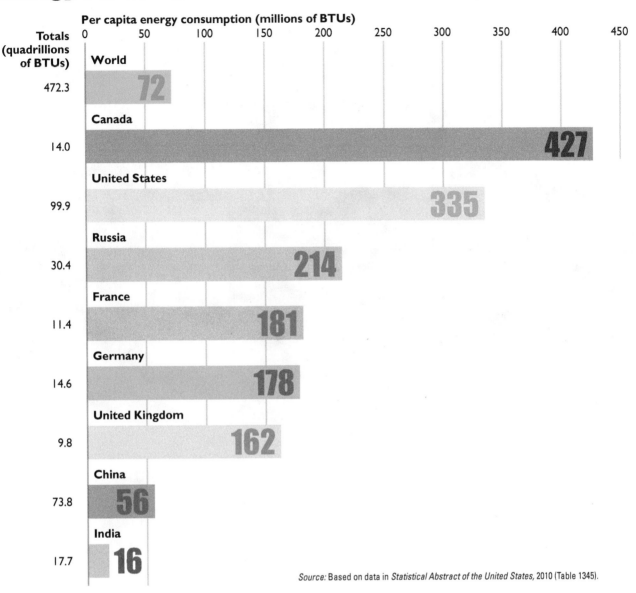

Per capita energy consumption (millions of BTUs)

Totals (quadrillions of BTUs)	Country	Per capita
472.3	World	72
14.0	Canada	427
99.9	United States	335
30.4	Russia	214
11.4	France	181
14.6	Germany	178
9.8	United Kingdom	162
73.8	China	56
17.7	India	16

Source: Based on data in *Statistical Abstract of the United States,* 2010 (Table 1345).

pared with China's 15.6 percent, but the average American consumes six times the energy used by the average Chinese and twenty-one times the energy used by the average inhabitant of India.

INDUSTRIAL DEGRADATION

Industrialization and factory labor now characterize many societies in Latin America, Africa, the Pacific, and Asia. One effect of the spread of industrialization has been the destruction of indigenous economies, ecologies, and populations. Two centuries ago, as industrialization was developing, fifty million people still lived in politically independent bands, tribes, and chiefdoms. Occupying vast areas, those nonstate societies, although not totally isolated, were only marginally affected by nation-states

and the world capitalist economy. In 1800, bands, tribes, and chiefdoms controlled half the globe and 20 percent of its population (Bodley 2008). Industrialization tipped the balance in favor of states (see Hornborg and Crumley 2007).

As industrial states have conquered, annexed, and "developed" nonstates, there has been genocide on a grand scale. *Genocide* refers to a deliberate policy of exterminating a group through warfare or murder. Examples include the Holocaust, Rwanda in 1994, and Bosnia in the early 1990s. Bodley (2008) estimates that an average of 250,000 indigenous people perished annually between 1800 and 1950. Besides warfare, the causes included foreign diseases (to which natives lacked resistance), slavery, land grabbing, and other forms of dispossession and impoverishment.

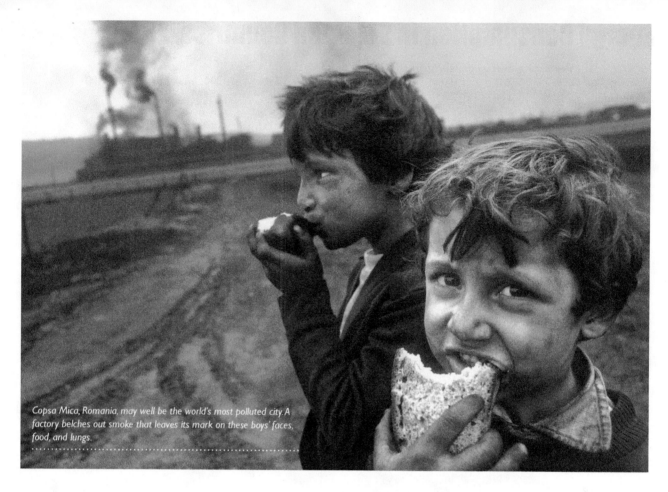

Copsa Mica, Romania, may well be the world's most polluted city. A factory belches out smoke that leaves its mark on these boys' faces, food, and lungs.

"Such is the Old Town of Manchester, and on re-reading my description, I am forced to admit that instead of being exaggerated, it is far from black enough to convey a true impression of the filth, ruin and uninhabitableness, the defiance of all consideration of cleanliness, ventilation, and health which characterise the construction of this single district. . . . Everything which here arouses horror and indignation is of recent origin, belongs to the industrial epoch."

Friedrich Engels, *The Condition of the Working-Class in England*

Many native groups have been incorporated within nation-states, in which they have become ethnic minorities. Some such groups have been able to recoup their population. Many **indigenous peoples** survive and maintain their ethnic identity despite having lost their ancestral cultures to varying degrees (partial ethnocide). And many descendants of tribespeople live on as culturally distinct and self-conscious colonized peoples, many of whom aspire to autonomy. As the original inhabitants of their territories, they are called indigenous peoples (see Maybury-Lewis 2002).

Around the world contemporary nations are repeating—at an accelerated rate—the process of resource depletion that started in Europe and the United States during the Industrial Revolution. Fortunately, today's world has some environmental watchdogs that did not exist during the first centuries of the Industrial Revolution. Given national and international cooperation and sanctions, the modern world may benefit from the lessons of the past (see Hornborg, McNeill, and Martinez-Alier 2007).

indigenous peoples The original inhabitants of particular territories; often descendants of tribespeople who live on as culturally distinct colonized peoples, many of whom aspire to autonomy.

get involved

Learn to read your dinner plate like a map of the world system. The American diet relies heavily on imports of both goods and labor. Supplementing information on the source of a particular food item (packaging often identifies sources) with Internet research, use the food you eat to gain information on global capitalism and global inequality. For example, let's say your cauliflower came from California. Hondurans who migrated across Mexico to work on farms in California may have harvested your cauliflower. Although working for extremely low wages, Honduran migrant workers manage collectively to send huge remittances in U.S. dollars back to Honduras. Who in the United States might benefit from this and how? Who in Honduras might benefit? Given these facts, what would you suspect is Honduras's position of economic power in the world system?

I. When and why did the world system develop, and what is it like today?

- A global system of economic and political relations emerged in the fifteenth century, as Europeans established transoceanic trade with other peoples, who then entered Europe's sphere of influence. Over the next several hundred years, an exchange of people, resources, products, ideas, and diseases linked the Old and the New Worlds. By the eighteenth century, European industrialization, fed by capital from transoceanic trade, hastened the separation of workers from the means of production. Today's capitalistic world economy maintains the contrast between owners and workers, but a partial shift in power to the masses has reduced the polarization. Currently, world stratification features a contrast between both capitalists and workers in the core nations and workers on the periphery. Industrialization is implicated in the destruction of indigenous economies, ecologies, and populations and an accelerated rate of resource depletion.

II. When and how did European colonialism develop, and how is its legacy expressed in postcolonial studies?

- The first phase of European colonialism began with the exploration and exploitation of the Americas after Columbus. In the nineteenth century, the search for new markets led European nations to take and hold foreign colonies. During this new phase of colonialism (1875–1914), Britain and France promoted their commercial interests in their respective colonies and sought to "civilize" native peoples. Colonizers constructed whole countries and divisions within them. *Postcolonial* refers to the lasting effects of European colonization and the study of the period after it. The settler, nonsettler, and mixed countries that were former colonies had different colonial experiences. The United States, although colonized, usually isn't perceived as postcolonial because of its current world power position, its treatment of Native Americans, and its annexation of foreign territories.

III. How do colonialism, development, industrialization, neoliberalism, and Communism exemplify intervention philosophies?

- These ideologies and historical developments have been shaped by justifications for guiding native peoples in specific directions. Colonial powers have engaged in political, social, economic, and cultural domination. Paternalistic views of non-Western peoples' "backwardness" helped colonial powers to legitimize imperialist expansion. Development plans assume that retracing the "First World's" path among "developing" countries will promote long-term benefits for them. Powerful financial institutions impose neoliberal policies, entailing open trade and investment, cost control, and austerity measures that cut government aid for social services. Communism has promoted obedience to authority and often demanded total submission of individuals to the state.

CULTURECLIPS
TO ACCESS THESE VIDEOS ON
YOUR COMPUTER, VISIT
www.mhhe.com/gezonqr

11-1

11-2

11-3

Pop Quiz

1. The modern world system is best understood as:
   a. A system in which ethnic groups are increasingly isolated from nation-states.
   b. A system of social class stratification mirroring Karl Marx's theory of class conflict.
   c. A global system in which nations are economically and politically interdependent.
   d. A system whose major contrast pits capitalists against workers in core nations.

2. Which of the following statements about world-system theory is false?
   a. The three different positions of economic and political power are core, semiperiphery, and periphery.
   b. The theory sees society as consisting of inter-related parts.
   c. The theory claims that a set of economic and political relations has characterized much of the globe since the Old World and New World established regular contact.
   d. The theory applies mainly to economic and political relations among Western nations.

3. European development of a transoceanic trade-oriented economy, led to all of the following *except:*
   a. Peoples of Asia, Africa, and the Americas entered Europe's sphere of influence.
   b. Europeans' consumption of imports spurred the rise of plantation economies in the Americas.
   c. Contact led to a major exchange of people, resources, ideas, and diseases.
   d. Demand for fossil fuels spurred development of slave-based production in the New World.

4. Marx argued that class consciousness results from:
   a. The intersection of ethnic and national identities with social class identity.
   b. Recognizing collective economic interests and identifying with a group sharing those interests.
   c. A growing distinction among religions.
   d. The extension of notions of kinship beyond the boundaries of actual biological relations.

5. Imperialism refers to extending rule of a country or empire over foreign nations and holding foreign colonies, while colonialism refers specifically to:
   a. The political, social, economic, and cultural domination of a territory and its people by a foreign power for an extended time.
   b. Imperial influence that disappears when former colonies gain independence.
   c. European domination of a territory.
   d. Efforts to civilize the world by implanting European languages.

6. Colonial administrators registered the Sukuma of Tanzania as a single tribe. In Rwanda and Burundi, the distribution of colonial identity cards created arbitrary ethnic divisions. These two cases:
   a. Suggest that strong ethnic identities are a key ingredient of development.
   b. Illustrate that ethnic groups and tribes may be colonial constructions.
   c. Show how well-informed administrators were about local cultures.
   d. Show the importance of making clear tribal and ethnic distinctions to reduce conflict.

7. Since the fall of Communism, neoliberalism:
   a. Is no longer seen as a viable economic policy.
   b. Has been associated with open international trade and investment.
   c. Has rejected attempts to lower costs with layoffs.
   d. Has favored increased public spending on education and other social services.

8. Although Communism was not uniform over time or among countries that adopted it:
   a. All Communist systems have been authoritarian.
   b. Few Communist systems have been totalitarian.
   c. All Communist nations mix state ownership with private ownership of means of production.
   d. Few Communist regimes have stressed identification with the international movement.

9. All the following statements about postsocialist societies are supported by research, *except:*
   a. They typically experience gains in productivity and a higher living standard.
   b. Such societies have promoted privatization to enhance production.
   c. The World Bank's approach to corruption assumes that the public (state) domain should be kept separate from the private domain.
   d. Postsocialist states provide rich contexts in which to explore variability in relations between public and private domains.

10. Which of the following statements does *not* characterize the modern world system?
    a. Twentieth-century industrialization added hundreds of new industries and millions of new jobs.
    b. Mass production has given rise to a culture of consumption.
    c. The U.S. lags behind India and China in total energy consumption.
    d. Industrialization has caused the destruction of indigenous economies, ecologies, and populations.

1. (c), 2. (d), 3. (d), 4. (b), 5. (a), 6. (b), 7. (b), 8. (a), 9. (a), 10. (c)

12

ETHNICITY AND RACE

Ethnic Groups and Ethnicity

Race and Ethnicity

The Social Construction of Race

Ethnic Groups, Nations, and Nationalities

Ethnic Tolerance and Accommodation

Roots of Ethnic Conflict

WHAT'S TO COME

UNDERSTANDING OURSELVES

How do you imagine human "diversity"? Maybe you associate that word with "race" or "ethnicity." Perhaps you think of differences—like skin or eye color, hair form, or height—that can be observed by the naked eye. In fact, human biological diversity encompasses much more than observable physical differences. It includes, for example, our variable abilities to digest various foods and our innate resistance or susceptibility to particular diseases.

Meeting every day in contemporary North America are people whose ancestors lived in many lands. The first (Native) Americans had to cross a land bridge that once linked Siberia to North America. For later immigrants, perhaps including your own parents or grandparents, the voyage may have been across the sea, or overland from nations to the south. They came for many reasons; some came voluntarily, while others were brought in chains. The scale of migration in today's world is so vast that millions of people routinely cross national borders or live far from the homelands of their grandparents. The American population includes millions of people whose biological features reflect adaptations to environments other than the ones they now inhabit.

Diversity also includes the various identities that the same person may hold in different situations. Part of human adaptive flexibility is our ability to consciously (and sometimes subconsciously) shift self presentation in response to context. Italians, for example, maintain separate sets of clothing to be worn inside and outside the home. They invest much more in their outside wardrobe—thus supporting a vibrant Italian fashion industry—and what it says about their public persona than in indoor garb, which is for family and intimates to see. Both behavior and identities can change with context. One person can be both black and Hispanic, or a father and a ballplayer. One identity is claimed or perceived in certain settings, another in different ones. Among African Americans a "Hispanic" baseball player might be black; among Hispanics, Hispanic. When asked "who are you?" what first comes to mind? How might that vary according to situation?

- How are race and ethnicity socially constructed?
- How does contemporary racial classification differ in three contemporary nations: the United States, Japan, and Brazil?
- What are the positive and negative aspects of ethnicity?

>> Ethnic Groups and Ethnicity

As with any culture, members of an **ethnic group** *share* certain beliefs, values, habits, customs, and norms because of their common background. They define themselves as different and special because of cultural features. This distinction may arise from language, religion, historical experience, geographic placement, kinship, or "race" (see

Spickard 2004). Markers of an ethnic group may include a collective name, belief in common descent, a sense of solidarity, and an association with a specific territory, which the group may or may not hold (Ryan 1990, pp. xiii, xiv). Table 12.1 lists American ethnic groups, based on 2008 figures.

According to Fredrik Barth (1969), ethnicity can be said to exist when people claim a certain ethnic identity for themselves and are defined by others as having that identity. **Ethnicity** means identification with, and feeling part of, an ethnic group and exclusion from certain other groups because of this affiliation. Ethnic feelings and associated behavior vary in intensity within ethnic groups and countries and over time. A change in the degree of importance attached to an ethnic identity may reflect political changes (Soviet rule ends—ethnic feeling rises) or individual life-cycle changes (young people relinquish, or old people reclaim, an ethnic background).

Cultural differences may be associated with ethnicity, class, region, or religion. Individuals often have more than one group identity. People may be loyal (depending on circumstances) to their neighborhood, school, town, state or province, region, nation, continent, religion, ethnic group, or interest group (Ryan 1990, p. xxii). In a complex society such as the United States or Canada, people constantly negotiate their social identities. All of us "wear dif-

TABLE 12.1

Racial/Ethnic Identification in the United States, 2008 (estimated by U.S. Census Bureau)

Claimed Identity	Number (millions)	Percentage
White (non-Hispanic)	199.5	65.6
Hispanic	46.2	15.2
Black	37.2	12.2
Asian	13.2	4.4
American Indian	2.3	0.8
Pacific Islander	0.4	0.1
Two or more races	5.2	1.7
Total population	304.1	100.0

Source: Statistical Abstract of the United States, 2010, Table 6.

ferent hats," presenting ourselves sometimes as one thing, sometimes as another.

CULTURETHINK

What identities other than ethnicity do people negotiate depending on the situation they are in?

STATUS SHIFTING

Sometimes our identities (aka social statuses) are mutually exclusive. It's hard to be both black and white or male and female. Sometimes, assuming an identity or joining a group requires a conversion experience, acquiring a new and overwhelming primary identity, such as becoming a born-again Christian.

Some statuses aren't mutually exclusive, but contextual. People can be both black and Hispanic or both a mother and a senator. One identity is used in certain settings, another in different ones. We call this the *situational negotiation of social identity* (Leman 2001). Hispanics, for example, may shift ethnic affiliations as they negotiate their identities. "Hispanic" is a category based mainly on language. It includes whites, blacks, and "racially" mixed Spanish speakers and their ethnically conscious descendants. (There also are Native American and even

Asian Hispanics.) "Hispanics," the fastest-growing ethnic group in the United States, lumps together people of diverse geographic origin—Puerto Rico, Mexico, Cuba, El Salvador, Guatemala, the Dominican Republic, and other Spanish-speaking countries of Central and South America and the Caribbean. "Latino" is a broader category, which also can include Brazilians (who speak Portuguese). The national origins of American Hispanics/Latinos (excluding Brazilians) in 2008 are shown in the graph below.

Mexican Americans (Chicanos), Cuban Americans, and Puerto Ricans may mobilize to promote general Hispanic issues (e.g., opposition to English-only laws) but act as three separate interest groups in other contexts. Cuban Americans are richer on average than Chicanos and Puerto Ricans are, and their class interests and voting patterns differ. Cubans often vote Republican, but Puerto Ricans and Chicanos are more likely to favor Democrats. Some Mexican Americans whose families have lived in the United States for generations have little in common with new Hispanic immigrants, such as those from Central America. Many Americans (especially those fluent in English) claim Hispanic ethnicity in some contexts but shift to a general "American" identity in others.

In many societies a racial, ethnic, or caste status is associated with a position in the social–political hierarchy. Certain groups, called **minority groups,** are subordinate. They have inferior power and less secure access to resources than do **majority groups** (which are superordinate, dominant, or controlling). Often ethnic groups are minorities. When an ethnic group is assumed to have a biological basis (distinctively shared "blood" or genes), it is called a **race.** Discrimination against such a group is called **racism** (Cohen 1998; Montagu 1997; Scupin 2003; Shanklin 1995; Wade 2002).

> **ethnic group** Group distinguished by cultural similarities (shared among members of that group) and differences (between that group and others); ethnic group members share beliefs, values, habits, customs, and norms, and a common language, religion, history, geography, kinship, and/or race.
>
> **ethnicity** Identification with, and feeling part of, an ethnic group and exclusion from certain other groups because of this affiliation.
>
> **minority groups** Subordinate groups in a social–political hierarchy, with inferior power and less secure access to resources than majority groups have.
>
> **majority groups** Superordinate, dominant, or controlling groups in a social–political hierarchy.
>
> **race** An ethnic group assumed to have a biological basis.
>
> **racism** Discrimination against an ethnic group assumed to have a biological basis.

American Hispanics/ Latinos, 2008

Puerto Rican
8.8%

Cuban
3.5%

Central and South American
16.5%

Mexican
65.8%

Other Hispanic/Latino origin
5.4%

Source: Statistical Abstract of the United States, 2010, Table 6.

STUDY **TIP**

Identity consists both of how people define themselves and how others define them.

After Barack Obama's election to the presidency in 2008, some claimed this as evidence that we live in a "postracial" world, where race is no longer a barrier to success. Do you agree?

>> Race and Ethnicity

Race, like ethnicity in general, is a cultural category rather than a biological reality. That is, ethnic groups, including "races," derive from contrasts perceived and perpetuated in particular societies, rather than from scientific classifications based on common genes (see Wade 2002).

Human races cannot be defined biologically. Only cultural constructions of race are possible—even though the

"Hispanic" and "Latino" are ethnic categories that cross-cut "racial" contrasts such as between "black" and "white." Note the physical diversity among these multiracial schoolchildren in Havana, Cuba.

average person conceptualizes "race" in biological terms (see Mukhopadhyay, Heuze, and Moses 2007). The belief that human races exist and are important is much more common among the public than it is among scientists. Most Americans, for example, believe that their population includes biologically based races to which various labels have been applied. These labels include "white," "black," "yellow," "red," "Caucasoid," "Negroid," "Mongoloid," "Amerindian," "Euro-American," "African American," "Asian American," and "Native American."

We hear the words *ethnicity* and *race* frequently, but American culture doesn't draw a clear line between them. As illustration, consider two articles in the *New York Times* of May 29, 1992. One, discussing the changing ethnic composition of the United States, explains (correctly) that Hispanics "can be of any race" (Barringer 1992, p. A12). In other words, "Hispanic" is an ethnic category that cross-cuts racial contrasts such as that between "black" and "white." The other article reports that during the Los Angeles riots of spring 1992, "hundreds of Hispanic residents were interrogated about their immigration status on the basis of their *race* alone [emphasis added]" (Mydans 1992a, p. A8). Use of "race" here seems inappropriate because "Hispanic" usually is perceived as referring to a linguistically based (Spanish-speaking) ethnic group, rather than a biologically based race. Since these Los Angeles residents were being interrogated because they were Hispanic, the article is actually reporting on ethnic, not racial, discrimination. Given the lack of a precise distinction between

Despite the increasing diversity of American society, some recently popular TV shows (e.g., *Seinfeld*, *Sex and the City*, *Entourage*, *Curb Your Enthusiasm*) have principal characters who are ethnically homogeneous. Other programs, from *Glee*, which is fictional, to MTV's *The Real World* and CBS's *Survivor*, which are classified as "reality shows," make diversity a key part of their cast of characters. What kinds of diversity are shown on *Glee* and *The Real World*? How might you explain the presence or absence of diversity in these seven shows?

HYPODESCENT: RACE IN THE UNITED STATES

How is race culturally constructed in the United States? In American culture, one acquires his or her racial identity at birth, as an ascribed status, but race isn't based on biology or on simple ancestry. Take the case of the child of a "racially mixed" marriage involving one black and one white parent. We know that 50 percent of the child's genes come from one parent and 50 percent from the other. Still, American culture overlooks heredity and classifies this child as black. This rule is arbitrary. On the basis of genotype (genetic composition), it would be just as logical to classify the child as white.

American rules for assigning racial status can be even more arbitrary. In some states, anyone known to have any black ancestor, no matter how remote, is classified as a member of the black race. This is a rule of **descent** (it assigns social identity on the basis of ancestry), but of a sort that is rare outside the contemporary United

race and ethnicity, the term "ethnic group" is preferable to "race" to describe *any* such social group—for example, African Americans, Asian Americans, Irish Americans, Anglo Americans, or Hispanics.

States. It is called **hypodescent** (Harris and Kottak 1963) because it automatically places the children of a union between members of different groups in the minority group (*hypo* means "lower"). Hypodescent divides American society into groups that have been unequal in their access to wealth, power, and prestige.

The following case from Louisiana is an excellent illustration of the arbitrariness of the hypodescent rule and of the role that governments (federal or, in

> **descent** Rule assigning social identity on the basis of some aspect of one's ancestry.
>
> **hypodescent** A rule that automatically places the children of a union or mating between members of different socioeconomic groups in the less privileged group.

>> The Social Construction of Race

Races are ethnic groups assumed (by members of a particular culture) to have a biological basis, but actually race is socially constructed. The "races" we hear about every day are cultural, or social, rather than biological categories. Many Americans mistakenly assume that whites and blacks, for example, are biologically distinct and that these terms stand for discrete races. But these labels, like racial terms used in other societies, really designate culturally perceived rather than biologically based groups.

this case, state) play in legalizing, inventing, or eradicating race and ethnicity (B. Williams 1989). Susie Guillory Phipps, a light-skinned woman with Caucasian features and straight black hair, discovered as an adult that she was black. When Phipps ordered a copy of her birth certificate, she found her race listed as "colored." Since she had been "brought up white and married white twice," Phipps challenged a 1970 Louisiana law declaring anyone with at least one-thirty-second "Negro blood" to be legally black. Although the state's lawyer admitted that Phipps "looks like a white person," the state of Louisiana insisted that her racial classification was proper (Yetman 1991, pp. 3–4).

CULTURETHINK

Based on your own experiences, think of several ways in which skin color and ethnicity affect judgments and evaluations of people.

Cases like Phipps's are rare because racial identity usually is ascribed at birth and doesn't change. The rule of hypodescent affects blacks, Asians, Native Americans, and Hispanics differently (see Hunter 2005). Native American or Hispanic identity is easier to negotiate than black identity. The ascription rule isn't as definite, and the assumption of a biological basis isn't as strong.

To be considered Native American, one ancestor out of eight (great-grandparents) or out of four (grandparents) may suffice. This depends on whether the assignment is by federal or state law or by an Indian tribal council. The child of a Hispanic may (or may not, depending on context) claim Hispanic identity. Many Americans with an Indian or Latino grandparent consider themselves white and lay no claim to minority group status.

RACE IN THE U.S. CENSUS

The U.S. Census Bureau has gathered data by race since 1790. Initially this was done because the Constitution specified that a slave counted as three-fifths of a white person, and because Indians were not taxed. The racial categories

A biracial American, Halle Berry, with her mother. What is Halle Berry's race?

included in the 1990 census were "White," "Black or Negro," "Indian (American)," "Eskimo," "Aleut or Pacific Islander," and "Other." A separate question was asked about Spanish–Hispanic heritage. Check out the reproduction of the questionnaire on racial categories in the 2010 census.

Attempts by social scientists and interested citizens to add a "multiracial" census category have been opposed by the National Association for the Advancement of Colored People (NAACP) and the National Council of La Raza (a Hispanic advocacy group). Racial classification is a political issue (Goldberg 2002) involving access to resources, including jobs, voting districts, and federal funding of programs aimed at minorities. The hypodescent rule results in all the population growth being attributed to the minority category. Minorities fear their political clout will decline if their numbers go down.

But things are changing. Choice of "some other race" in the U.S. Census more than doubled from 1980 (6.8 million) to 2000 (over 15 million)—suggesting imprecision in and dissatisfaction with the existing categories (Mar 1997). In the 2000 census, 2.4 percent of Americans, or 6.8 million people, chose a first-ever option of identifying themselves as belonging to more than one race. The number of interracial marriages and children is increasing, with implications for the traditional system of American racial classification. "Interracial," "biracial,"

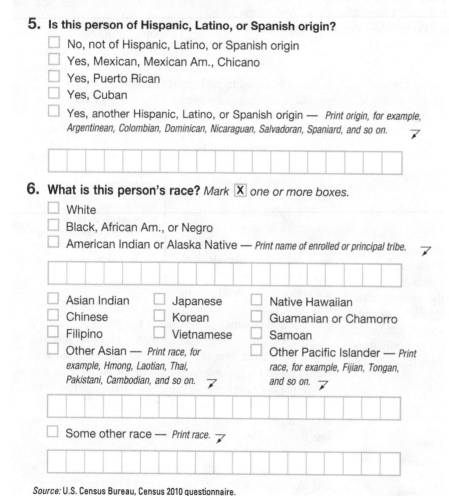

Questions on Race and Hispanic Origin from Census 2010

5. **Is this person of Hispanic, Latino, or Spanish origin?**

☐ No, not of Hispanic, Latino, or Spanish origin
☐ Yes, Mexican, Mexican Am., Chicano
☐ Yes, Puerto Rican
☐ Yes, Cuban
☐ Yes, another Hispanic, Latino, or Spanish origin — *Print origin, for example, Argentinean, Colombian, Dominican, Nicaraguan, Salvadoran, Spaniard, and so on.* ⬂

6. **What is this person's race?** *Mark* ☒ *one or more boxes.*

☐ White
☐ Black, African Am., or Negro
☐ American Indian or Alaska Native — *Print name of enrolled or principal tribe.* ⬂

☐ Asian Indian   ☐ Japanese   ☐ Native Hawaiian
☐ Chinese   ☐ Korean   ☐ Guamanian or Chamorro
☐ Filipino   ☐ Vietnamese   ☐ Samoan
☐ Other Asian — *Print race, for example, Hmong, Laotian, Thai, Pakistani, Cambodian, and so on.* ⬂   ☐ Other Pacific Islander — *Print race, for example, Fijian, Tongan, and so on.* ⬂

☐ Some other race — *Print race.* ⬂

Source: U.S. Census Bureau, Census 2010 questionnaire.

Visible Minority Population of Canada, 2006 Census

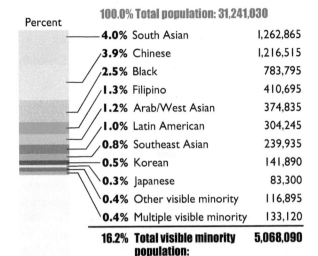

Percent

100.0% Total population: 31,241,030

4.0%	South Asian	1,262,865
3.9%	Chinese	1,216,515
2.5%	Black	783,795
1.3%	Filipino	410,695
1.2%	Arab/West Asian	374,835
1.0%	Latin American	304,245
0.8%	Southeast Asian	239,935
0.5%	Korean	141,890
0.3%	Japanese	83,300
0.4%	Other visible minority	116,895
0.4%	Multiple visible minority	133,120
16.2%	**Total visible minority population:**	**5,068,090**

83.8%
Not visible minority (i.e. majority):
26,172,940

Source: From Statistics Canada, 2006 Census, http://www12
.statcan.ca/english/census06/data/highlights/ethnic.

or "multiracial" children who grow up with both parents undoubtedly identify with particular qualities of either parent. To have so important an identity as race dictated by the arbitrary rule of hypodescent is troubling for many of them. It may be especially discordant when racial identity doesn't parallel gender identity, for instance, a boy with a white father and a black mother, or a girl with a white mother and a black father.

How does the Canadian census compare with the American census in its treatment of race? Rather than race, the Canadian census asks about "visible minorities." That country's Employment Equity Act defines such groups as "persons, other than Aboriginal peoples [aka First Nations in Canada, Native Americans in the United States], who are non-Caucasian in race or non-white in colour" (Statistics Canada 2001a). The "Visible Minority Population" figure shows that "South Asian" and "Chinese" are Canada's largest visible minorities. Note that Canada's total visible minority population of 16.2 percent (up from 11.2 percent in 1996) contrasts with a figure of about 25 percent for the United States in the 2000 census and over 33 percent in 2007. In particular, Canada's black population of 2.5 percent contrasts with the American figure

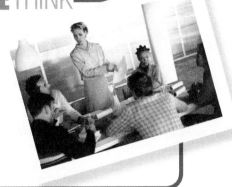
of 12.9 percent (2007) for African Americans, while Canada's Asian population is significantly higher than the U.S. figure of 4.5 percent (2007) on a percentage basis. Only a tiny fraction of the Canadian population (0.4 percent) claimed multiple visible minority affiliation, compared with 2.4 percent claiming "more than one race" in the United States in 2000.

Canada's visible minority population has been increasing steadily. In 1981, 1.1 million visible minorities accounted for 4.7 percent of the total population, versus 16.2 percent today. Visible minorities are growing much faster than is Canada's total population. Between 2001 and 2006, the total population increased 5 percent, while visible minorities rose 27 percent. If recent immigration trends continue, by 2016, visible minorities will account for 20 percent of the Canadian population.

"NOT US": RACE IN JAPAN

American culture ignores considerable diversity in biology, language, and geographic origin as it socially constructs race in the United States. North Americans also overlook diversity by seeing Japan as a nation that is homogeneous in race, ethnicity, language, and culture—an image the Japanese themselves cultivate. Thus in 1986 former Prime Minister Nakasone created an international furor by contrasting his country's supposed homogeneity (responsible, he suggested, for Japan's success at that time in international business) with the ethnically mixed United States.

Japan is hardly the uniform entity Nakasone described. Scholars estimate that 10 percent of Japan's national population are minorities of various sorts. These include aboriginal Ainu, annexed Okinawans, outcast *burakumin,* children of mixed marriages, and immigrant nationalities, especially Koreans, who number more than seven hundred thousand (De Vos, Wetherall, and Stearman 1983; Lie 2001).

To describe racial attitudes in Japan, Jennifer Robertson (1992) uses Kwame Anthony Appiah's (1990) term "intrinsic racism"—the belief that a (perceived) racial difference is a sufficient reason to value one person less than another. In Japan the valued group is majority ("pure") Japanese, who are believed to share "the same blood." Thus, the caption to a printed photo of a Japanese American model reads: "She was born in Japan but raised in Hawaii. Her nationality is American but no foreign blood flows in her veins" (Robertson 1992, p. 5). Something like hypodescent also operates in Japan, but less precisely than in the United States, where mixed offspring automatically become members of the minority group. The children of mixed marriages between majority Japanese and others (including Euro-Americans) may not get the same "racial" label as their minority parent, but they are still stigmatized for their non-Japanese ancestry (De Vos and Wagatsuma 1966).

How is race culturally constructed in Japan? The (majority) Japanese define themselves by opposition to others, whether minority groups in their own nation or outsiders—anyone who is "not us." The "not us" should stay that way; assimilation generally is discouraged. Cultural mechanisms, especially residential segregation and taboos on "interracial" marriage, work to keep minorities "in their place."

In its construction of race, Japanese culture regards certain ethnic groups as having a biological basis, when there is no evidence that they do. The best example is the *burakumin,* a stigmatized group of at least four million outcasts, sometimes compared to India's untouchables. The burakumin are physically and genetically indistinguishable from other Japanese. Many of them "pass" as (and marry) majority Japanese, but a deceptive marriage can end in divorce if burakumin identity is discovered (Aoki and Dardess 1981).

Burakumin are perceived as standing apart from majority Japanese. Through ancestry, descent (and thus, it is

assumed, "blood," or genetics) burakumin are "not us." Majority Japanese try to keep their lineage pure by discouraging mixing. The burakumin are residentially segregated in neighborhoods (rural or urban) called *buraku,* from which the racial label is derived. Compared with majority Japanese, the burakumin are less likely to attend high school and college. When burakumin attend the same schools as majority Japanese, they face discrimination. Majority children and teachers may refuse to eat with them because burakumin are considered unclean.

In applying for university admission or a job and in dealing with the government, Japanese must list their address, which becomes part of a household or family registry. This list makes residence in a buraku, and likely burakumin social status, evident. Schools and companies use this information to discriminate. (The best way to pass is to move so often that the buraku address eventually disappears from the registry.) Majority Japanese also limit "race" mixture by hiring marriage mediators to check out the family histories of prospective spouses. They are especially careful to check for burakumin ancestry (De Vos et al. 1983).

The origin of the burakumin lies in a historical tiered system of stratification (from the Tokugawa period—1603–1868). The top four ranked categories were warrior-administrators (*samurai*), farmers, artisans, and merchants. The ancestors of the burakumin were below this hierarchy, an outcast group who did unclean jobs such as animal slaughter and disposal of the dead. Burakumin still do similar jobs, including work with leather and other animal products. The burakumin are more likely than majority Japanese to do manual labor (including farm work) and to belong to the national lower class. Burakumin and other Japanese minorities also are more likely to have careers in crime, prostitution, entertainment, and sports (De Vos et al. 1983).

Japan's stigmatized burakumin are physically and genetically indistinguishable from other Japanese. In response to burakumin political mobilization, Japan has dismantled the legal structure of discrimination against burakumin. This Sports Day for burakumin children is one kind of mobilization.

Like blacks in the United States, the burakumin are class-stratified. Because certain jobs are reserved for the burakumin, people who are successful in those occupations (e.g., shoe factory owners) can be wealthy. Burakumin also have found jobs as government bureaucrats. Financially successful burakumin can temporarily escape their stigmatized status by travel, including foreign travel.

Discrimination against the burakumin is strikingly like the discrimination that blacks have experienced in the United States. The burakumin often live in villages and neighborhoods with poor housing and sanitation. They have limited access to education, jobs, amenities, and health facilities. In response to burakumin political mobilization, Japan has dismantled the legal structure of discrimination against burakumin and has worked to improve conditions in the buraku. (The website http://blhrri.org/index_e.htm is sponsored by the Buraku Liberation and Human Rights Research Institute and includes the most recent information about the Buraku liberation movement.) Still Japan has yet to institute American-style affirmative action programs for education and jobs. Discrimination against nonmajority Japanese is still the rule in companies. Some employers say that hiring burakumin would give their company an unclean image and thus create a disadvantage in competing with other businesses (De Vos et al. 1983).

PHENOTYPE AND FLUIDITY: RACE IN BRAZIL

There are more flexible, less exclusionary ways of constructing social race than those used in the United States and Japan. Along with the rest of Latin America, Brazil has less

exclusionary categories, which permit individuals to change their racial classification. Brazil shares a history of slavery with the United States, but it lacks the hypodescent rule. Nor does Brazil have racial aversion of the sort found in Japan.

Brazilians use many more racial labels—over five hundred were once reported (Harris 1970)—than Americans or Japanese do. In northeastern Brazil, Conrad Kottak found forty different racial terms in use in Arembepe, a village of only seven hundred and fifty people (Kottak 2006). Through their traditional classification system Brazilians recognize and attempt to describe the physical variation that exists in their population. The system used in the United States, by recognizing only three or four races, blinds Americans to an equivalent range of evident physical contrasts. The system Brazilians use to construct social race has other special features. In the United States one's race is an ascribed status; it is assigned automatically by hypodescent and usually doesn't change. In Brazil racial identity is more flexible, more of an achieved status. Brazilian racial classification pays attention to phenotype. As discussed in the chapter "What Is Anthropology," **phenotype** refers to an organism's evident traits, its "manifest biology"—physiology and anatomy, including skin color, hair form, facial features, and eye color. A Brazilian's phenotype and racial label may change because of environmental factors, such as the tanning rays of the sun or the effects of humidity on the hair.

> **phenotype** An organism's evident traits, its "manifest biology"—anatomy and physiology.

These photos, taken in Brazil by Conrad Kottak in 2003 and 2004, give just a glimpse of the spectrum of phenotypical diversity encountered among contemporary Brazilians.

As physical characteristics change (sunlight alters skin color, humidity affects hair form), so do racial terms. Furthermore, racial differences may be so insignificant in structuring community life that people may forget the terms they have applied to others. Sometimes they even forget the ones they've used for themselves. In Arembepe, Kottak made it a habit to ask the same person on different days to tell him the races of others in the village (and his own). In the United States he is "white" or "Euro-American," but in Arembepe he was given several terms besides *branco* ("white"). He could be *claro* ("light"), *louro* ("blond"), *sarará* ("light-skinned redhead"), *mulato claro* ("light mulatto"), or *mulato* ("mulatto"). The racial term used to describe Kottak or anyone else varied from person to person, week to week, even day to day. His best informant, a man with very dark skin color, changed the term he used for himself all the time—from *escuro* ("dark") to *preto* ("black") to *moreno escuro* ("dark brunet").

The American and Japanese racial systems are creations of particular cultures, rather than scientific—or even accurate—descriptions of human biological differences. Brazilian racial classification also is a cultural construction, but Brazilians have developed a way of describing human biological diversity that is more detailed, fluid, and flexible than the systems used in most cultures. Brazil lacks Japan's racial aversion, and it also lacks a rule of descent like that which ascribes racial status in the United States (Degler 1970; Harris 1964).

For centuries the United States and Brazil have had mixed populations, with ancestors from Native America, Europe, Africa, and Asia. Although races have mixed in both countries, Brazilian and American cultures have constructed the results differently.

nation-state An autonomous political entity, a country, such as the United States or Canada.

The historical reasons for this contrast lie mainly in the different characteristics of the settlers of the two countries. The mainly English early settlers of the United States came as women, men, and families, but Brazil's Portuguese colonizers were mainly men—merchants and adventurers. Many of these Portuguese men married Native American women and recog-

nized their racially mixed children as their heirs. Like their North American counterparts, Brazilian plantation owners had sexual relations with their slaves. But the Brazilian landlords more often freed the children that resulted—for demographic and economic reasons. (Sometimes these were their only children.) Freed offspring of master and slave became plantation overseers and foremen and filled many intermediate positions in the emerging Brazilian economy. They were not classed with the slaves, but were allowed to join a new intermediate category. No hypodescent rule developed in Brazil to ensure that whites and blacks remained separate (see Degler 1970; Harris 1964).

>> Ethnic Groups, Nations, and Nationalities

The term *nation* once was synonymous with *tribe* or *ethnic group*. All three of these terms have been used to refer to a single culture sharing a single language, religion, history, territory, ancestry, and kinship. Thus one could speak interchangeably of the Seneca (American Indian) nation, tribe, or ethnic group. Now *nation* has come to mean *state*—an independent, centrally organized political unit, or a government. *Nation* and *state* have become synonymous. Combined in **nation-state** they refer to an autonomous political entity, a country—like the United States, "one nation, indivisible" (see Farner 2004; Gellner 1997; Hastings 1997).

Because of migration, conquest, and colonialism, most nation-states are not ethnically homogeneous. A 2003 study by Fearon found that about 70 percent of all countries have an ethnic group that forms an absolute majority of the population, and the average population share of such groups is 65 percent. The average size of the *second* largest group, or largest ethnic minority, is 17 percent. Only 18 percent of all countries have a single ethnic group that accounts for 90 percent or more of its population.

NATIONALITIES AND IMAGINED COMMUNITIES

Ethnic groups that once had, or wish to have or regain, autonomous political status (their own country) are called **nationalities.** In the words of Benedict Anderson (1991), they are "imagined communities." Even when they become nation-states, they remain imagined communities because most of their members, though feeling comradeship, will never meet (Anderson 1991, pp. 6–10). They can only imagine they all participate in the same unit.

CULTURETHINK

In what ways is the United States an imagined community? What role does the media play in this community creation?

Anderson traces Western European nationalism, which arose in imperial powers such as England, France, and Spain, back to the eighteenth century. He stresses that language and print played a crucial role in the growth of European national consciousness. The novel and the newspaper were "two forms of imagining" communities (consisting of all the people who read the same sources and thus witnessed the same events) that flowered in the eighteenth century (Anderson 1991, pp. 24–25).

Over time, political upheavals, wars, and migration have divided many imagined national communities that arose in the eighteenth and nineteenth centuries. The German and Korean homelands were artificially divided after wars, according to communist and capitalist ideologies. World War I split the Kurds, who remain an imagined community, forming a majority in no state. Kurds are a minority group in Turkey, Iran, Iraq, and Syria.

In creating multitribal and multiethnic states, colonialism often erected boundaries that corresponded poorly with preexisting cultural divisions. But colonial institutions also helped create new "imagined communities" beyond nations. An example is the idea of *négritude* ("Black identity") developed by African intellectuals in Francophone (French-speaking) West Africa. Négritude can be traced to the association and common experience in colonial times of youths from Guinea, Mali, the Ivory Coast, and Senegal at the William Ponty school in Dakar, Senegal (Anderson 1991, pp. 123–124).

> **nationalities** Ethnic groups that once had, or wish to have or regain, autonomous political status (their own country).
>
> **assimilation** The process of change that a minority group may experience when it moves to a country where another culture dominates; the minority is incorporated into the dominant culture to the point that it no longer exists as a separate cultural unit.

>> Ethnic Tolerance and Accommodation

Ethnic diversity may be associated with positive group interaction and coexistence or with conflict (discussed shortly). There are nation-states, including some less developed countries, in which multiple cultural groups live together in reasonable harmony.

ASSIMILATION

The process of change that a minority ethnic group may experience when its members move to a country where another culture dominates is known as **assimilation.** By assimilating, the minority adopts the patterns and norms of its host culture. It is incorporated into the dominant culture to the point that it no longer exists as a separate cultural unit. Some countries, such as Brazil, are more assimilationist than others. Germans, Italians, Japanese, Middle Easterners, and East Europeans started migrating

The United States is increasingly a multicultural society. It features growing ethnic enclaves such as New York's Chinatown, shown here, often located right next to others, such as Little Italy in the same city.

to Brazil late in the nineteenth century. These immigrants have assimilated to a common Brazilian culture, which has Portuguese, African, and Native American roots. The descendants of these immigrants speak the national language (Portuguese) and participate in the national culture. (During World War II, Brazil, which was on the Allied side, forced assimilation by banning instruction in any language other than Portuguese—especially in German.)

THE PLURAL SOCIETY

Assimilation isn't inevitable, and ethnic harmony can exist without it. Ethnic distinctions can persist despite generations of interethnic contact. Through a study of three ethnic groups in Swat, Pakistan, Fredrik Barth (1958/1968) challenged an old idea that interaction always leads to assimilation. He showed that ethnic groups can be in contact for generations without assimilating and can live in peaceful coexistence.

plural society A society that combines ethnic contrasts, ecological specialization (i.e., use of different environmental resources by each ethnic group), and the economic interdependence of those groups.

multiculturalism The view of cultural diversity in a country as something good and desirable; a multicultural society socializes individuals not only into the dominant (national) culture, but also into an ethnic culture.

Barth (1958/1968, p. 324) defines **plural society** (an idea he extended from Pakistan to the entire Middle East) as a society combining ethnic contrasts, ecological specialization (i.e., use of different environmental resources by each ethnic group), and the economic interdependence of those groups. Consider his description of the Middle East (in the 1950s): "The 'environment' of any one ethnic group is not only defined by natural conditions, but also by the presence and activities of the other ethnic groups on which it depends. Each group exploits only part of the total environment, and leaves large parts of it open for other groups to exploit." The ecological interdependence (or, at least, the lack of competition) between ethnic groups may be based on different activities in the same region or on long-term occupation of different regions in the same nation-state.

In Barth's view, ethnic boundaries are most stable and enduring when the groups occupy different ecological niches. That is, they make their living in different ways and don't compete. Ideally, they should depend on each other's activities and exchange with one another. When different ethnic groups exploit the *same* ecological niche, the militarily more powerful group will normally replace the weaker one. If they exploit more or less the same niche, but the weaker group is better able to use marginal environments, they also may coexist (Barth 1958/1968, p. 331). Given niche specialization, ethnic boundaries and interdependence can be maintained, although the specific cultural features of each group may change. By shifting the analytic focus from individual cultures or ethnic groups to *relationships* between cultures or ethnic groups, Barth (1958/1968, 1969) has made important contributions to ethnic studies.

MULTICULTURALISM AND ETHNIC IDENTITY

The view of cultural diversity in a country as something good and desirable is called **multiculturalism** (see Kottak and Kozaitis 2008). The multicultural model is the opposite of the assimilationist model, in which minorities are expected to abandon their cultural traditions and values, replacing them with those of the majority population. The multicultural view encourages the practice of cultural–ethnic traditions. A multicultural society socializes individuals not only into the dominant (national) culture but also into an ethnic culture. Thus in the United States millions of people speak both English and another language, eat both "American" (apple pie, steak, hamburgers) and "ethnic" foods, and celebrate both national (July 4, Thanksgiving) and ethnic–religious holidays.

In the United States and Canada multiculturalism is of growing importance. This reflects an awareness that the number and size of ethnic groups have grown dramatically in recent years. If this trend continues, the ethnic composition of the United States will change dramatically (see "Ethnic Composition of the United States").

Even now, because of immigration and differential population growth, minorities outnumber whites in many urban areas. For example, of the 8,274,527 people living in New York City in 2007, 25 percent were black, 27 per-

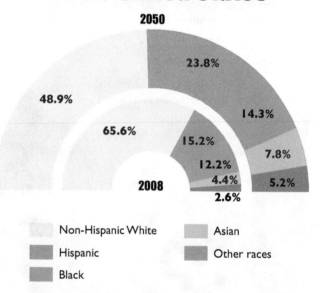

Ethnic Composition of the United States

2050

23.8%

14.3%

48.9%

15.2%

7.8%

65.6%

12.2%

4.4%

5.2%

2008

2.6%

Non-Hispanic White   Asian

Hispanic   Other races

Black

The proportion of the American population that is white and non-Hispanic is declining. The projection for 2050 shown here comes from a U.S. Census Bureau report issued in March 2004. Note especially the dramatic rise in the Hispanic portion of the American population between 2008 and 2050.

Source: Based on data from U.S. Census Bureau, International Data Base, Table 094, http://www.census.gov/ipc/www.idbprint.html; Files 2005 and http://www.census.gov/Press-Release/www/releases/archives/population/010048.html, and Table 12.1 on p. 226.

cent Hispanic, 12 percent Asian, and 36 percent other—including non-Hispanic whites. The comparable figures for Los Angeles (which had 3,770,590 people in 2007) were 10 percent black, 48 percent Hispanic, 11 percent Asian, and 31 percent other, including non-Hispanic whites (U.S. Census Bureau 2008, 2009).

In October 2006, the population of the United States reached 300 million people, just thirty-nine years after reaching 200 million and ninety-one years after reaching the 100 million mark (in 1915). The country's ethnic composition has changed dramatically in the past forty years. The 1970 census, the first to attempt an official count of Hispanics, found they represented no more than 4.7 percent of the American population, compared with 15.2 percent in 2008. The number of African Americans increased from 11.1 percent in 1967 to 12.2 percent in 2008, while (non-Hispanic) whites ("Anglos") declined from 83 percent to 65.6 percent. In 1967 less than 10 million people in the United States (5 percent of the population) had been born elsewhere, compared with more than 36 million immigrants (12 percent) today (Ohlemacher 2006).

In 1973, 78 percent of the students in American public schools were white, and 22 percent were minorities: blacks, Hispanics, Asians, Pacific Islanders, and "others." By 2004, 57 percent of public school students were white, and 43 percent were minorities. If current trends continue, minority students will outnumber (non-Hispanic) white students by 2015. They already do in California, Hawaii, Mississippi, New Mexico, and Texas (Dillon 2006).

Immigration, mainly from southern and eastern Europe, had a similar effect on classroom diversity, at least in the largest American cities, a century ago. A study of American public schools in 1908–1909 found that 42 percent of those urban students were native-born, while 58 percent were immigrants. In a very different (multicultural now versus assimilationist then) context, today's American classrooms have regained the ethnic diversity they demonstrated in the early 1900s, when author Conrad Kottak's German-speaking Austro-Hungarian-born father and grandparents immigrated to the United States.

One response to ethnic diversification and awareness has been for many whites to reclaim ethnic identities (Italian, Albanian, Serbian, Lithuanian, etc.) and to join ethnic associations (clubs, gangs). Some such groups are new. Others have existed for decades, although they lost members during the assimilationist years of the 1920s through the 1950s.

Multiculturalism seeks ways for people to understand and interact that don't depend on sameness but rather on respect for differences. Multiculturalism stresses the interaction of ethnic groups and their contribution to the country. It assumes that each group has something to offer to and learn from the others. Several forces have propelled North America away from the assimilationist model toward multiculturalism. First, multiculturalism reflects the fact of recent large-scale migration, particularly from the "less developed countries" to the "developed" nations of North America and Western Europe. The global scale of

modern migration introduces unparalleled ethnic variety to host nations. Multiculturalism is related to globalization: People use modern means of transportation to migrate to nations whose lifestyles they learn about through the media and from tourists who increasingly visit their own countries (see Inda and Rosaldo 2008).

Migration also is fueled by rapid population growth, coupled with insufficient jobs (both for educated and uneducated people), in the less developed countries. As traditional rural economies decline or mechanize, displaced farmers move to cities, where they and their children often are unable to find jobs. As people in the less developed countries get better educations, they seek more skilled employment. They hope to partake of an international culture of consumption that includes such modern amenities as refrigerators, televisions, and automobiles (Ahmed 2004).

In a world with growing rural–urban and transnational migration, ethnic identities are used increasingly to form self-help organizations focused mainly on enhancing the group's economic competitiveness (Williams 1989). People claim and express ethnic identities for political and economic reasons. Michel Laguerre's (1984, 1998) studies of Haitian immigrants in the United States show that they mobilize to deal with the discriminatory structure (racist in this case, since Haitians tend to be black) of American society. Ethnicity (their common Haitian creole language and cultural background) is a basis for their mobilization. Haitian ethnicity helps distinguish them from African Americans and other ethnic groups.

STUDY **TIP**

The United States has moved toward the multicultural model for two primary reasons:

- Ethnic variety has increased with globalization, as people migrate for opportunities in education and skilled employment;

- Ethnic self-help organizations increasingly keep ethnic groups united and mobilized politically.

In the face of globalization, much of the world, including Europe and North America, is experiencing an ethnic revival. The new assertiveness of long-resident ethnic groups extends to the Basques and Catalans in Spain, the Bretons and Corsicans in France, and the Welsh and Scots in the United Kingdom. The United States and Canada are becoming increasingly multicultural, focusing on their internal diversity (see Laguerre 1999). "Melting pots" no longer, they are better described as ethnic "salads" (each ingredient remains distinct, although in the same bowl, with the same dressing).

⌐CULTURETHINK⌐

Think about a neighborhood or town you know well. Has it experienced an ethnic revival? Does it more resemble a melting pot or a salad bowl?

>> Roots of Ethnic Conflict

Ethnicity, based on perceived cultural similarities and differences in a society or nation, can be expressed in peaceful multiculturalism or in discrimination or violent interethnic confrontation. The roots of ethnic differentiation—and therefore, potentially, of ethnic conflict—can be political, economic, religious, linguistic, cultural, or racial (see Kuper 2006). Why do ethnic differences often lead to conflict and violence? The causes include a sense of injustice because of resource distribution, economic or political competition, and reaction to discrimination, prejudice, and other expressions of devalued identity (see Friedman 2003; Ryan 1990, p. xxvii).

prejudice Devaluing (looking down on) a group because of its assumed behavior, values, capabilities, or attributes.

stereotypes Fixed ideas—often unfavorable—about what members of a group are like.

discrimination Policies and practices that harm a group and its members.

In Iraq, under the dictator Saddam Hussein, one Muslim group (Sunnis) discriminated against others (Shiites and Kurds). Sunnis, although a numeric minority within Iraq's population, enjoyed privileged access to power, prestige, and position. After the 2005 elections, which many Sunnis chose to boycott, Shiites gained political control. A civil war developed out of *sectarian violence* (conflicts among sects of the same religion) as Sunnis (and

their foreign supporters) fueled an insurgency against the new government and its foreign supporters, including the United States. Shiites retaliated against Sunni attacks and a history of Sunni privilege and perceived discrimination against Shiites, as Shiite militias engaged in ethnic (sectarian) cleansing of their own.

PREJUDICE AND DISCRIMINATION

Ethnic conflict often arises in reaction to prejudice (attitudes and judgments) or discrimination (action). **Prejudice** means devaluing (looking down on) a group because of its assumed behavior, values, capabilities, or attributes. People are prejudiced when they hold stereotypes about groups and apply them to individuals. (**Stereotypes** are fixed ideas—often unfavorable—about what the members of a group are like.) Prejudiced people assume that members of the group will act as they are "supposed to act" (according to the stereotype) and interpret a wide range of individual behaviors as evidence of the stereotype. They use this behavior to confirm their stereotype (and low opinion) of the group.

⌐CULTURETHINK⌐

What stereotypes affect people besides those related to ethnicity? Give several examples of how stereotypes can lead to discrimination. What are some ways of fighting against harmful stereotypes—and discrimination?

Discrimination refers to policies and practices that harm a group and its members. Discrimination may be *de facto* (practiced, but not legally sanctioned) or *de jure* (part of the law). An example of de facto discrimination is the harsher treatment that American minorities (compared with other Americans) tend to get from the police and the judicial system. This unequal treatment isn't legal, but it happens anyway. Segregation in the southern United States and *apartheid* in South Africa provide two examples of de jure discrimination, which no longer are in existence. In both systems, by law, blacks and whites had different rights and privileges. Their social interaction ("mixing") was legally curtailed.

Anthropology Works

Law enforcement agents benefit from anthropological understandings of race and ethnicity. Being aware of the human tendency to hold stereotypes and prejudices, agents can work to combat discrimination, both in their own organization and within the community.

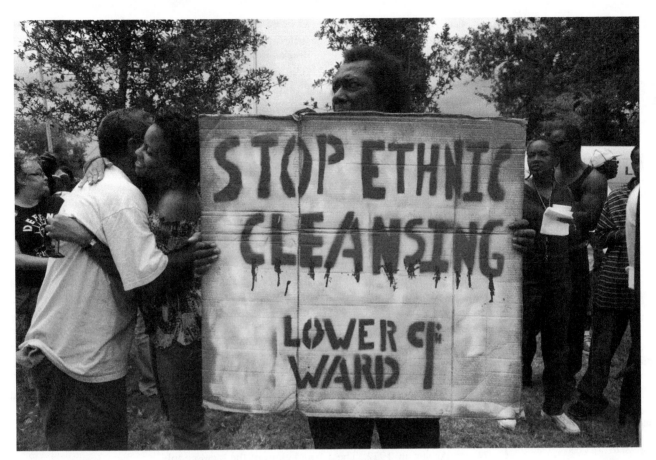

Discrimination *refers to policies and practices that harm a group and its members. This protest sign, hoisted in New Orleans' lower 9th ward, shows that at least some community residents see ethnic and racial bias.*

CHIPS IN THE MOSAIC

Although the multicultural model is increasingly prominent in North America, ethnic competition and conflict also are evident. There is conflict between newer arrivals—for instance, Central Americans and Koreans—and longer-established ethnic groups, such as African Americans. Ethnic antagonism flared in South-Central Los Angeles in spring 1992 in rioting that followed the acquittal of four white police officers who were tried for the videotaped beating of Rodney King (see Abelmann and Lie 1995).

Angry blacks attacked whites, Koreans, and Latinos. This violence expressed frustration by African Americans about their prospects in an increasingly multicultural society. A *New York Times* CBS News poll conducted just after the Los Angeles riots found that blacks had a bleaker outlook than whites about the effects of immigration on their lives. Only 23 percent of the blacks felt they had more opportunities than recent immigrants, compared with twice that many whites (Toner 1992).

Korean stores were hard hit during the 1992 riots, and more than a third of the businesses destroyed were Latino-owned. A third of those who died in the riots were Latinos. These mainly recent migrants lacked deep roots to the neighborhood and, as Spanish speakers, faced language barriers (Newman 1992). Many Koreans also had trouble with English.

Koreans interviewed on ABC's *Nightline* on May 6, 1992, recognized that blacks resented them and considered them unfriendly. One man explained, "It's not part of our culture to smile." African Americans interviewed on the same program did complain about Korean unfriendliness. "They come into our neighborhoods and treat us like dirt." These comments suggest a shortcoming of the multicultural perspective: Ethnic groups (blacks here) expect other ethnic groups in the same nation-state to assimilate to some extent to a shared (national) culture. The African Americans' comments invoked a general American value system that includes friendliness, openness, mutual respect, community participation, and "fair play." Los Angeles blacks wanted their Korean neighbors to act more like generalized Americans—and good neighbors.

> **genocide** Policies aimed at, and/or resulting in, the physical extinction (through mass murder) of a people perceived as a racial group, that is, as sharing defining physical, genetic, or other biological characteristics.

AFTERMATHS OF OPPRESSION

Fueling ethnic conflict are such forms of discrimination as genocide, forced assimilation, ethnocide, and cultural colonialism. The most extreme form of ethnic discrimination is **genocide,** the deliberate elimination of a group (such as Jews in Nazi Germany, Muslims in Bosnia, or Tutsi in Rwanda) through mass murder. A dominant group may try to destroy the cultures of certain ethnic groups (**ethnocide**) or force them to adopt the dominant culture (*forced assimilation*). Many countries have penalized or banned the language and customs of an ethnic group (including its religious observances). One example of forced assimilation is the anti-Basque campaign that the dictator Francisco Franco (who ruled between 1939 and 1975) waged in Spain. Franco banned Basque books, journals, newspapers, signs, sermons, and tombstones and imposed fines for using the Basque language in schools (Ryan 1990). His policies led to the formation of a Basque terrorist group and spurred strong nationalist sentiment in the Basque region.

A policy of *ethnic expulsion* aims at removing culturally different groups from a country. There are many examples, including Bosnia-Herzegovina in the 1990s. Uganda expelled 74,000 Asians in 1972. The neofascist parties of contemporary Western Europe advocate repatriation (expulsion) of immigrant workers (West Indians in England, Algerians in France, and Turks in Germany) (see Friedman 2003; Ryan 1990, p. 9). A policy of expulsion may create **refugees**—people who have been forced (involuntary refugees) or who have chosen (voluntary refugees) to flee a country, to escape persecution or war.

ethnocide Destruction by a dominant group of the culture of an ethnic group.

refugees People who have been forced (involuntary refugees) or who have chosen (voluntary refugees) to flee a country, to escape persecution or war.

cultural colonialism Within a nation or empire, domination by one ethnic group or nationality and its culture/ ideology over others—e.g., the dominance of Russian people, language, and culture in the former Soviet Union.

In many countries, colonial nation-building left ethnic strife in its wake. Thus, over a million Hindus and Muslims were killed in the violence that accompanied the division of the Indian subcontinent into India and Pakistan. Problems between Arabs and Jews in Palestine began during the British mandate period.

Multiculturalism may be growing in the United States and Canada, but the opposite is happening in the former Soviet Union, where ethnic groups (nationalities) want their own nation-states. The flowering of ethnic feeling and conflict as the Soviet empire disintegrated illustrates that years of political repression and ideology provide insufficient common ground for lasting unity. **Cultural colonialism** refers to internal domination—by one group and its culture or ideology over others. One example is the domination over the former Soviet empire by Russian people, language, and culture, and by communist ideology. The dominant culture makes itself the official culture. This is reflected in schools, the media, and public interaction. Under Soviet rule ethnic minorities had very limited self-rule in republics and regions controlled by Moscow. All the republics and their peoples were to be united by the oneness of "socialist internationalism." One common technique in cultural colonialism is to flood ethnic areas with members of the dominant ethnic group. Thus, in the former Soviet Union, ethnic Russian colonists were sent to many areas, to diminish the cohesion and clout of the local people.

The Commonwealth of Independent States (CIS), founded in 1991 and headquartered in Minsk, Belarus, is what remains of the once-powerful Soviet Union (see Yurchak 2005). In Russia and other formerly Soviet na-

Two faces of ethnic difference in the former Soviet empire. A propaganda poster depicts a happy mix of nationalities that make up the population of Kyrgyzstan, Central Asia (left); ethnic Georgians in a refugee camp near Tblisi, Georgia, in August 2008 (right). They fled Georgia's breakaway province, the self-proclaimed new republic of South Ossetia, where Russians were fighting the Georgian army. A cease-fire did not end the tension; Georgia still views South Ossetia as a Russian-occupied territory.

tions, ethnic groups (nationalities) have sought, and continue to seek, to forge separate and viable nation-states based on cultural boundaries. This celebration of ethnic autonomy is part of an ethnic flowering that—as surely as globalization and transnationalism—is a trend of the late twentieth and early twenty-first centuries.

get involved!

Test your stereotypes about ethnicity and "race" in sports. What ethnicity do you assume to be especially common among players in each of the following: hockey, baseball, football, and basketball? Pick a city near you with a professional sports team or a college or university sports program you know well. Find rosters of players, then use photos of the players and their family names to help you ascertain ethnic backgrounds. Watch a game in each sport and see who plays the most. How do your stereotypes accord with the rosters and the players you see in the games? Might players of a particular ethnic background excel in or even dominate certain sports? If so, what roles do you think society's ethnic stereotypes, players' early enculturation, and their family's regional and social class background might play in this dominance?

For
REVIEW

CULTURECLIPS

TO ACCESS THESE VIDEOS ON
YOUR COMPUTER, VISIT

www.mhhe.com/gezonqr

12-1

12-2

12-3

I.   **How are race and ethnicity socially constructed?**

* Both ethnic groups and "races" derive from contrasts perceived and perpetuated in particular societies. Members of an ethnic group define themselves through a common language, religion, historical experience, geographic placement, kinship, and/or "race." Other people regard the group as having the ethnic identity it claims. Ethnic group markers include a collective name, belief in common descent, sense of solidarity, and association with a territory, real or imagined. Race is an ethnic group that is assumed to have a biological basis. Racial labels really designate *culturally* perceived groups. American culture assigns racial status arbitrarily. Children of a union between members of different groups are assigned the status of the minority group.

II. **How does contemporary racial classification differ in three contemporary nations: the United States, Japan, and Brazil?**

* In the United States, race is assumed to have a biological basis and racial status is ascribed. Traditional American racial categories are changing as biracial and multiracial children begin to resist having the hypodescent rule dictate their identity. In Japan, a perceived racial difference is sufficient reason to value one person less than another. Offspring of marriages between "pure" majority Japanese and members of a minority are stigmatized. In Brazil, classification is more flexible and racial identity is more of an achieved status. If a Brazilian's phenotype changes because of environmental factors, racial labels change accordingly.

III. **What are the negative and positive aspects of ethnicity?**

* Ethnic diversity may be associated both with conflict and with positive group interaction and coexistence. The assimilation of an ethnic minority group may be expected or even forced. Although multiculturalism seeks ways for different groups to interact with and learn from one other, it does not necessarily end conflict. Unequal access to resources, economic or political competition, prejudice, and discrimination may lead to conflict and violence. Genocide is the deliberate elimination of a group. Ethnocide, forced expulsion, and cultural colonialism also endanger ethnic groups and fuel conflict. Ethnicity may be the basis for mobilizing group members to self-help and dealing with discrimination. It also may be the basis for seeking to forge separate nation-states.

Pop Quiz

1. What is the term for identifying with, and feeling part of, an ethnic group, and excluded from other ethnic traditions?
   a. Cultural relativism
   b. Ethnicity
   c. Assimilation
   d. Ethnocentrism

2. When a person's identities are not mutually exclusive, but one identity is used in a certain setting while another identity is used in another setting, we say that:
   a. The person is having an identity crisis.
   b. The identities are situationally nonnegotiable.
   c. Affiliation shifts as identity is negotiated.
   d. Shifting identities is unlikely, because people always have one overwhelming primary identity.

3. Which of the following statements would apply to both ethnicity and race?
   a. Both terms describe a minority group.
   b. Both terms are cultural rather than biological categories.
   c. American culture defines these terms in a way that sharply distinguishes one from the other.
   d. The basis of both of these terms is biological.

4. The rule or principle that automatically places the children of a union between members of different socioeconomic groups in the minority group is called:
   a. Hypodescent
   b. Natural descent
   c. Racial mixing
   d. Achieved status

5. What distinguishes racial classification in Brazil from that in the United States?
   a. Race in Brazil is ascribed.
   b. Brazilians have created a profusion of racial labels that often leads to mislabeling a person's race.
   c. Brazilian racial identity is flexible, more of an achieved status.
   d. A Brazilian's phenotype remains fixed.

6. A nationality is considered:
   a. One nation-state.
   b. One ethnic community that is politically united.
   c. A minority within a single state.
   d. An imagined community.

7. Which of the following is *not* true about minority groups that move to a country where another culture dominates?
   a. They usually assimilate by the second or, at latest, the third generation.
   b. Their members may continue to speak their own languages and practice their ways yet still live in ethnic harmony with the dominant culture.
   c. If they maintain their ethnicity and use environmental resources different from those used by other groups, they may live in a state of ecological interdependence with those groups.
   d. The boundaries between ethnic groups are most stable and enduring when the groups occupy different ecological niches.

8. Which of the following statements is *not* true about multiculturalism?
   a. It contrasts with assimilation, the process by which a minority abandons its traditions and adopts the patterns of the majority culture.
   b. Living together in a multicultural society with little interaction among them, ethnic groups have little to teach or offer one another.
   c. The number and size of ethnic groups in the United States have grown dramatically in recent years.
   d. Multiculturalism is related to globalization.

9. Which one of the following is *not* generally one of the roots of ethnic conflict?
   a. Differential access to resources and prospects for the future.
   b. Political conflict.
   c. Reaction to prejudice and discrimination.
   d. People's understanding that many ethnic groups cannot assimilate readily to a shared national culture.

10. What is the term for a dominant group's attempt to destroy the cultures of certain ethnic groups or attempt to force them to adopt the dominant culture?
    a. Colonialism
    b. Genocide
    c. Ethnocide
    d. Ethnic expulsion

1. (b), 2. (c), 3. (b), 4. (a), 5. (c), 6. (d), 7. (a), 8. (b), 9. (d), 10. (c)

13

ANTHROPOLOGY'S ROLE IN A GLOBALIZING WORLD

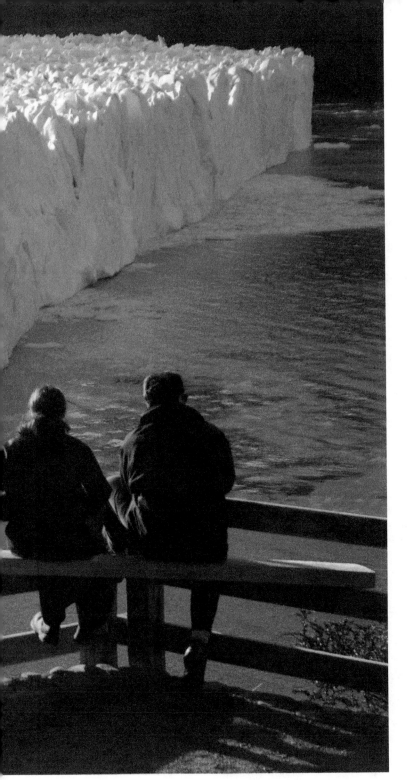

WHAT'S TO COME

Global Climate Change

Environmental Anthropology

Interethnic Contact

Making and Remaking Culture

People in Motion

Indigenous Peoples

The Continuance of Diversity

UNDERSTANDING OURSELVES

Modern technology makes it easier than ever for us to perceive the Earth as both a planet and our world. Images of Earth taken from space have become commonplace. Anthropologists have even used such images to choose communities to study on Earth. Interested in the causes of deforestation in Madagascar, for example, Lisa Gezon, Conrad Kottak, and their colleagues examined a series of satellite images taken in successive years to determine areas where the forest cover had diminished significantly. Then they traveled to Madagascar to study those areas on the ground.

Intensifying global trends include reliance on fossil fuels and increased fossil-fuel emissions, human population increase, and the shift from subsistence to cash economies. These trends promote agricultural intensification, resource depletion (from deforestation to oil spills), and emigration.

Worldwide, young people are abandoning traditional subsistence pursuits. An old popular song asked, "How ya' gonna keep 'em down on the farm after they've seen Paree." Nowadays most people *have* seen Paree—Paris, that is—along with other world capitals, maybe not in person, but in print or on-screen images. Young people today are better educated and wiser in the ways of the world than ever before. They are increasingly exposed to the promises of a better life away from the farm. They seek paying jobs, but work is scarce, spurring migration within and across national boundaries. In turn, transnational migration increases cultural diversity in the United States, Canada, and western European countries.

Small towns throughout America now have Chinese restaurants. Pizza and tacos are as American as apple pie. Your McDonald's outlet sells burritos, lattes, and cappuccino. Every day you encounter not just products, but people whose ancestral countries and cultures have been studied by anthropologists for generations—making cultural anthropology all the more relevant to our daily lives in an increasingly interconnected world.

- What is global climate change, and how can anthropologists study it, along with other environmental threats?

- What is cultural imperialism, and what forces work to favor and oppose it?

- What are indigenous peoples, and how and why has their importance increased in recent years?

>> Global Climate Change

The Earth's surface temperatures have risen about 1.48 degrees Fahrenheit (0.78 degrees Centigrade) since the early twentieth century. About two-thirds of this increase has been since 1978 (see "Global Temperature Change").

Along with rising temperatures, shrinking glaciers and melting polar ice provide additional evidence for global warming. Scientific measurements confirm that global warming is not due to increased solar radiation. The causes are mainly anthropogenic—caused by humans and their activities.

Because our planet's climate is always changing, the key question becomes this: How much global warming is

Global Temperature Change

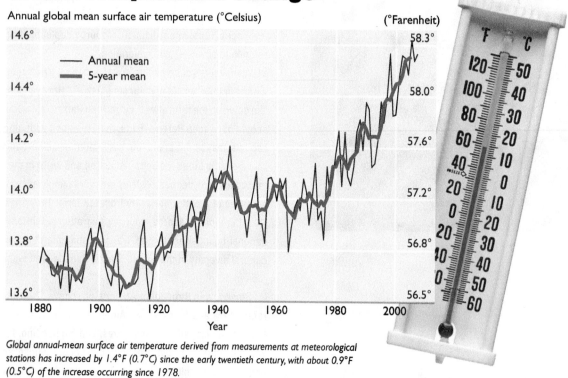

Annual global mean surface air temperature (°Celsius)

- Annual mean
- 5-year mean

(°Farenheit)

Global annual-mean surface air temperature derived from measurements at meteorological stations has increased by 1.4°F (0.7°C) since the early twentieth century, with about 0.9°F (0.5°C) of the increase occurring since 1978.

Source: Goddard Institute for Space Studies, from "Understanding and Responding to Climate Change: Highlights of National Academies Reports," http://dels.nas.edu/basc/Climate-HIGH.pdf.

Is the future depicted in the movie Wall-E a likely one, and how does it relate, if at all, to global climate change?

due to human activities versus natural climate variability? Most scientists agree that human activities play a major role in global climate change. How can the human factor not be significant given population growth and rapidly increasing use of fossil fuels, which produce greenhouse gases in the atmosphere?

The role of one such gas—carbon dioxide (CO_2)—in warming the Earth's surface has been known for over a century. For hundreds of thousands of years, world temperatures have varied depending on the amount of CO_2 in the atmosphere. The burning of fossil fuels (oil, natural gas, and coal) releases substantial amounts of carbon dioxide. The recent rapid rise in both CO_2 and the Earth's surface temperature is one proof that humans are fueling global warming.

The **greenhouse effect** is a natural phenomenon that keeps the Earth's surface warm. Without greenhouse gases—water vapor (H_2O), carbon dioxide (CO_2), methane (CH_4), nitrous oxide (N_2O), halocarbons, and ozone (O_3)—life as we know it wouldn't exist. Like a greenhouse window, such gases allow sunlight to enter and then prevent heat from escaping the atmosphere. All those gases have increased since the Industrial Revolution. Today, the atmospheric concentration of greenhouse gases has reached its highest level in four hundred thousand years. It will continue to rise—as will global temperatures—without actions to slow it down (National Academies 2006).

Scientists prefer the term **climate change** to *global warming*. The former term points out that, beyond rising temperatures, there have been changes in sea levels, precipitation, storms, and ecosystem effects. (Table 13.1 summarizes forces that work to warm and cool the earth.) Along with many ordinary people, some scientists see recent weather events as reflecting climate change. Such events include Pakistan's floods of 2010, Florida's 2007 worst-in-a-century drought, the 2005 hurricane season featuring Katrina, the first-ever hurricane in the South Atlantic in 2004, and the severe European heat wave of 2003. Although linking any one event to climate change is difficult, the conjunction of several events may indicate climate change is playing a role.

The precise effects of climate change on regional weather patterns have yet to be determined. Land areas are expected to warm more than oceans, with the greatest warming in higher latitudes, such as Canada, the northern United States, and northern Europe. Global warming may benefit these areas, offering milder winters and extended growing seasons. However, many more people worldwide probably will be harmed. Already we know that in the Arctic, temperatures have risen almost twice as much as the global average. Arctic landscapes and ecosystems are changing rapidly and perceptibly.

The Intergovernmental Panel on Climate Change (IPCC) is composed of hundreds of scientists from the United States and other countries. In 2001 the IPCC predicted that by 2100 average global surface temperatures will rise 2.5 to 10.4 degrees Fahrenheit (1.4 to 5.8 degrees Centigrade) above 1990 levels. The IPCC also forecast ocean warming trends—the combined effects of melting glaciers, melting ice caps, and seawater expansion. The global average sea level is projected to rise 4 to 35 inches (0.1 to 0.9 meters) between 1990 and 2100.

> **greenhouse effect** Warming from trapped atmospheric gases.
>
> **climate change** Global warming, plus changing sea levels, precipitation, storms, and ecosystem effects.

Coastal communities can anticipate increased flooding and more severe storms and surges. At risk are people, animals, plants, freshwater supplies, and such industries as tourism and farming. Along with many island nations, Bangladesh, one of the world's poorest countries, is projected to lose a significant portion (17.5 percent) of its land, displacing millions of people (National Academies 2006). Given the political will, developed countries might use sci-

TABLE 13.1

What Heats, What Cools, the Earth?

Warming	
Carbon dioxide (CO$_2$)	Has natural and human sources; levels increasing due to burning of fossil fuels.
Methane (CH$_4$)	Has risen due to an increase in human activities, including livestock raising, rice growing, landfill use, and the extraction, handling, and transport of natural gas.
Ozone (O$_3$)	Has natural sources, especially in the stratosphere, where chemicals have depleted the ozone layer; ozone also produced in the troposphere (lower part of the atmosphere) when hydrocarbons and nitrogen oxide pollutants react.
Nitrous oxide (N$_2$O)	Has been rising from agricultural and industrial sources.
Halocarbons	Include chlorofluorocarbons (CFCs), which remain from refrigerants in appliances made before CFC ban.
Aerosols	Some airborne particles and droplets warm the planet; black carbon particles (soot) produced when fossil fuels or vegetation are burned; generally have a warming effect by absorbing solar radiation.
Cooling	
Sea ice	Reflects sunlight back to space.
Tundra	Reflects sunlight back to space.
Aerosols	Some cool the planet; (SO$_4$) aerosols from burning fossil fuels reflect sunlight back to space.
Volcanic eruptions	Emit gaseous SO$_2$ which, once in the atmosphere, forms sulfate aerosol; and ash. Both reflect sunlight back to space.
Warming/Cooling	
Forests	Deforestation creates land areas that reflect more sunlight back to space (cooling); it also removes trees that absorb CO$_2$ (warming).

ence and technology to anticipate and deal with climate impacts and to help less developed countries adapt to climate change.

The U.S. National Academy of Sciences and other national academies have issued several reports on climate change. Citations and highlights of these reports can be found in a brochure titled "Understanding and Responding to Climate Change: Highlights of National Academies Reports" (http://dels.nas.edu/basc/Climate-HIGH .pdf), on which some of this discussion is based (see also Crate and Nuttall 2008).

Meeting energy needs is the single greatest obstacle to slowing climate change. In the United States, about 80 percent of all energy used comes from fossil fuels. Worldwide, energy use continues to grow with economic and popula-

tion expansion. China and India in particular are rapidly increasing their use of energy, mainly from fossil fuels, and consequently their emissions of CO$_2$ (see "Projected Emission of Greenhouse Gases"). These emissions could be reduced by using energy more efficiently or by using renewable sources. One alternative is ethanol, of which the United States is a limited producer. American policy makers give lip service to the value of ethanol, while restricting its inflow from nations, such as Brazil, that produce it most effectively.

Among the alternatives to fossil fuels are nuclear power and such renewable energy technologies as solar, wind, and biomass generators. Replacing coal-fired electric power plants with more efficient natural-gas-fired turbines would reduce carbon emissions. In the United States, these

Many scientists see recent weather catastrophes as reflecting climate change. Such events include the 2005 hurricane season featuring Katrina and fires that devastated Southern California in late October 2007. The map above shows Hurricane Katrina, which sustained winds of 140 m.p.h., in the Gulf of Mexico. The photo (right) shows one of dozens of epic fires that swept Southern California. Shown here, firefighters watch as a San Diego Fire Department helicopter drops water on a fire in Via Conejo, between Lake Hodges and Escondido.

Projected Emission of Greenhouse Gases, 2025

Trillions of tons of carbon equivalent

| 0 | 2 | 4 | 6 | 8 | 10 | 12 | 14 | 16 |

World — 57%

Developed — 35%

Developing — 84%

| 0 | .5 | 1 | 1.5 | 2 | 2.5 | 3 |

U.S. — 39%

China — 118%

EU — 19%

Former Soviet Union — 42%

India — 70%

Africa — 80%

Brazil — 68%

Japan — 26%

Mexico — 124%

■ 2000 emissions

● Projected emissions, 2025

50% Projected increase from 2000 levels

Greenhouse gasses do not include CO_2 from land use change.

In 2000, the United States was the largest emitter of CO_2 from fossil fuels. China is expected to take the lead by 2025.

Source: Baumert 2005.

CULTURETHINK

Ethanol, made from corn, has been criticized as an alternative source of fuel. Some analysts claim that it raises the price of food and that producing ethanol uses more energy than it yields. Others maintain that it has significant environmental benefits. Do an online search. What is the current status of this debate?

technologies currently are too expensive, or, in the case of nuclear power, they raise environmental or other concerns. This could change with the development and increasing use of new technologies and as the cost of fossil fuels rises.

>> Environmental Anthropology

Anthropology always has been concerned with how environmental forces influence humans and how human activities affect the biosphere and the Earth itself. The 1950s–1970s witnessed the emergence of an area of study

Did You Know?

Traditional ecological knowledge often provides solutions to contemporary problems. One development project in southern Peru revived an ancient irrigation and drainage system that had been abandoned a thousand years ago. This permitted food production in low-lying, flood-prone, poorly drained lands.

known as *cultural ecology* or **ecological anthropology.** That field focused on how cultural beliefs and practices helped human populations adapt to their environments, and how people used elements of their culture to maintain their ecosystems.

Early ecological anthropologists showed that many indigenous groups did a reasonable job of managing their resources and preserving their ecosystems. Such groups had traditional ways of categorizing resources, regulating their use, and preserving the environment. An **ethnoecology** is any society's set of environmental practices and perceptions—that is, the society's cultural model of the environment and its relation to people and society. Indigenous ethnoecologies increasingly are being challenged, as migration, media, and commerce spread people, institutions, information, and technology. In the face of national and international incentives to exploit and degrade, ethnoecological systems that once preserved local and regional environments increasingly are ineffective or irrelevant.

ecological anthropology Study of cultural adaptations to environments.

ethnoecology A culture's set of environmental practices and perceptions.

Anthropologists routinely witness threats to the people they study and their environments. Among such threats are commercial logging, industrial pollution, and the imposition of external management systems on local ecosystems (see Johnston 2009). Today's ecological anthropology, aka *environmental anthropology,* attempts not only to understand but also to find solutions to environmental problems. Such problems must be tackled at the national and international levels (e.g., global warming). Even in remote places, ecosystem management now involves multiple levels. For example, author Lisa Gezon found that among the Antankarana of northern Madagascar (Gezon 2006), several levels of authority claim the right to use and regulate natural resources and local ecosystems. Actual or would-be regulators there include local communities, traditional leaders (the regional king or chief), provincial and national governments, and the WWF, the Worldwide Fund for Nature (formerly the World Wildlife Fund), an international nongovernmental organization (NGO). Local people, their landscapes, their ideas, their values, and their traditional management systems face attacks from all sides. Outsiders attempt to remake native landscapes and cultures in their own image. The aim of many agricultural development projects, for example, seems to be to make the world as much like a midwestern American agricultural state as possible. Often there is an attempt to impose mechanized farming and nuclear family ownership, even though these institutions may be inappropriate in areas far removed from the midwestern United States. Development projects usually fail when they try to replace indigenous institutions with culturally alien concepts (Kottak 1990b).

The world's most populous nations, China and India, are rapidly increasing their use of energy, mainly from fossil fuels, and consequently their emissions of CO_2. Pictured here are crowds of cars and busses moving slowly during a serious Beijing traffic jam.

CULTURE THINK

Do you do anything because it is "good for the globe"? What advice would you give to an environmentalist who wanted to convince people in your town or community to buy environmentally friendly goods, even if they cost more money?

GLOBAL ASSAULTS ON LOCAL AUTONOMY

A clash of cultures related to environmental change may occur when development threatens indigenous peoples and their environments. A second clash of cultures related to environmental change may occur when external regulation aimed at conservation confronts indigenous peoples and their ethnoecologies. Like development projects, conservation schemes may ask people to change their ways in order to satisfy planners' goals rather than local goals. In places as different as Madagascar, Brazil, and the Pacific Northwest of the United States, people have been asked, told, or forced to abandon basic economic activities because to do so is good for "nature" or "the globe." "Good for the globe" doesn't play very well in Brazil, whose Amazon is a focus of international environmentalist attention. Brazilians complain that outsiders (e.g., Europeans and North Americans) promote "global needs" and "saving the Amazon" after having destroyed their own forests for economic growth. Well-intentioned conservation plans can be as insensitive as development schemes that promote radical changes without involving local people in planning and carrying out the policies that affect them. When people are asked to give up the basis of their livelihood, they usually resist.

The spread of environmentalism may expose radically different notions about the "rights" and value of plants and animals versus humans. In Madagascar, many intellectuals and officials complain that foreigners seem more concerned about lemurs and other endangered species than about the people of Madagascar (the Malagasy). As a geographer there remarked to Conrad Kottak, "The next time you come to Madagascar, there'll be no more Malagasy. All the people will have starved to death, and a lemur will have to meet you at the airport." Most Malagasy perceive human poverty as a more pressing problem than animal and plant survival.

Still, who can doubt that conservation, including the preservation of biodiversity, is a worthy goal? The challenge for applied ecological anthropology is to devise culturally appropriate strategies for achieving biodiversity conservation in the face of unrelenting population growth and commercial expansion. How does one get people to support conservation measures that may, in the short run at least, diminish their access to resources? Like development plans in general, the most effective conservation strategies pay attention to the needs and wishes of the local people.

STUDY TIP

A clash of cultures over environmental issues occurs (1) when development projects degrade local resources; (2) when external authorities impose conservation measures on local people.

A scene from the "great red island" of Madagascar. On that island, the effects of deforestation, water runoff, and soil erosion are visible to the naked eye.

DEFORESTATION

Forest loss—a global concern—can lead to increased greenhouse gas (CO_2) production, which contributes to global warming. The destruction of tropical forests also is a major factor in the loss of global biodiversity, since many species, often of limited distribution and including many primates, live in forests. Tropical forests contain at least half of Earth's species while covering just 6 percent of the planet's land surface. Yet tropical forests are disappearing at the rate of ten million to twenty million hectares per year (the size of New York State).

Generations of anthropologists have studied how human economic activities (ancient and modern) affect the environment. Anthropologists know that food producers (farmers and herders) typically do more to degrade the environment than foragers do. Population increase and the need to expand farming caused deforestation in many parts of the ancient Middle East and Mesoamerica (see Hornborg and Crumley 2007). Even today, many farmers think of trees as giant weeds to be removed and replaced with productive fields.

Often, deforestation is demographically driven—caused by population pressure. For example, Madagascar's population is growing at a rate of 3 percent annually, doubling every generation. Population pressure leads to migration, including rural–urban migration. Madagascar's capital, Antananarivo, had one hundred thousand people in 1967. The population grew to about two million by 2007.

Urban growth promotes deforestation if city dwellers rely on fuel wood from the countryside, as is true in Madagascar. As forested watersheds disappear, crop productivity declines. Madagascar is known as the "great red island," after the color of its soil. On that island, the effects of soil erosion and water runoff are visible to the naked eye. From the look of its rivers, Madagascar appears to be bleeding to death. Increasing runoff of water no longer trapped by trees causes erosion of low-lying rice fields near swollen rivers as well as siltation in irrigation canals (Kottak 2007).

The global scenarios of deforestation include demographic pressure (from births or immigration) on subsistence economies, commercial logging, road building, cash cropping, fuel wood needs associated with urban expansion, and clearing and burning associated with livestock and grazing. The fact that forest loss has several causes has a policy implication: Different deforestation scenarios require different conservation strategies.

Applied anthropology uses anthropological perspectives to identify and solve contemporary problems that affect humans. Deforestation is one such problem. Here women take part in a reforestation project in coastal Tanzania near Dar es Salaam.

What can be done? On this question applied anthropology weighs in (see Chapter 4), spurring policy makers to think about new conservation strategies. The traditional approach has been to restrict access to forested areas designated as parks, then employ park guards and punish violators. Modern strategies are more likely to consider the needs, wishes, and abilities of the people (often impoverished) living in and near the forest. Since effective conservation depends on the cooperation of the local people, their concerns must be addressed in devising conservation strategies.

Reasons to change behavior must make sense to local people (see Sillitoe 2007). In Madagascar, the economic value of the forest for agriculture (as an antierosion mechanism and reservoir of potential irrigation water) provides a much more powerful incentive against forest degradation than do such global goals as "preserving biodiversity." Most Malagasy have no idea that lemurs and other endemic species exist only in Madagascar. Nor would such knowledge provide much of an incentive for them to conserve the forests if doing so jeopardized their livelihoods.

To curb the global deforestation threat, we need conservation strategies that work. Laws and enforcement may

CULTURETHINK

People concerned with conservation debate which is more effective: putting up fences and hiring guards to keep people out of areas to be preserved, or engaging local people as partners and allowing limited use of endangered resources. What do you think would be the strengths and weaknesses of each approach?

help reduce commercially driven deforestation caused by burning and clear-cutting. But local people also use and abuse forested lands. A challenge for the environmentally oriented applied anthropologist is to find ways to make forest preservation attractive to local people and ensure their cooperation. Applied anthropologists must work to make "good for the globe" good for the people.

>> Interethnic Contact

Since at least the 1920s anthropologists have investigated the changes—on both sides—that arise from contact between industrial and nonindustrial societies. Studies of "social change" and "acculturation" are abundant. British and American ethnographers, respectively, have used these terms to describe the same process. *Acculturation* refers to changes that result when groups come into continuous firsthand contact—changes in the cultural patterns of either or both groups (Redfield, Linton, and Herskovits 1936, p. 149).

Acculturation differs from diffusion, or cultural borrowing, which can occur without firsthand contact. For example, most North Americans who eat hot dogs ("frankfurters") have never been to Frankfurt, Germany, nor have most North American Toyota owners or sushi eaters ever visited Japan. Although *acculturation* can be applied to any case of cultural contact and change, the term most often has described *Westernization*—the influence of Western expansion on indigenous peoples and their cultures. Thus, local people who wear store-bought clothes, learn Indo-European languages, and otherwise adopt Western customs are called acculturated. Acculturation may be voluntary or forced, and there may be considerable resistance to the process.

Different degrees of destruction, domination, resistance, survival, adaptation, and modification of native cultures may follow interethnic contact. In the most destructive encounters, native and subordinate cultures face obliteration. In cases where contact between the indigenous societies and more powerful outsiders leads to destruction—a situation that is particularly characteristic of colonialist and expansionist eras—a "shock phase" often follows the initial encounter (Bodley 2008). Outsiders may attack or exploit the native people. Such exploitation may increase mortality, disrupt subsistence, fragment kin groups, damage social support systems, and inspire new religious movements, such as the cargo cults examined in the chapter "Religion" (Bodley 2008). During the shock

STUDY TIP

Diffusion is a form of cultural borrowing that can occur without firsthand contact, while *acculturation*, which may be voluntary or forced, refers to changes that occur with firsthand contact.

Anthropology Works

People in all fields need to know about the effects of globalization. A school administrator, for example, can design better programming when he or she understands the social, economic, and cultural issues confronting immigrant populations.

phase, there may be civil repression backed by military force. Such factors may lead to the group's cultural collapse (*ethnocide*) or physical extinction (*genocide*).

RELIGIOUS CHANGE

Religious proselytizing can promote ethnocide, as native beliefs and practices are replaced by Western ones. Sometimes a religion and associated customs are replaced by ideology and behavior more compatible with Western culture. One example is the Handsome Lake religion (as described in the chapter on religion), which led the Iroquois to copy European farming techniques, stressing male rather than female labor. The Iroquois also gave up their communal longhouses and matrilineal descent groups for nuclear family households. The teachings of Handsome Lake led to a new church and religion. This revitalization movement helped the Iroquois survive in a drastically modified environment, but much ethnocide was involved.

Handsome Lake was a native who created a new religion, drawing on Western models. More commonly, missionaries and proselytizers representing the major world religions, especially Christianity and Islam, are the proponents of religious change. Protestant and Catholic missionization continues even in remote corners of the world. Evangelical Protestantism, for example, is advancing today in Peru, Brazil, and other parts of Latin America. It challenges an often jaded Catholicism that has too few priests and that is sometimes seen mainly as women's religion.

Sometimes the political ideology of a nation-state is pitted against traditional religion. Officials of the former Soviet empire discouraged Catholicism, Judaism, and Islam. In Central Asia, Soviet dominators destroyed Muslim mosques and discouraged religious practice. On the other hand, governments often use their power to advance a religion, such as Islam in Iran or Sudan.

A military government seized power in Sudan in 1989. It immediately launched a campaign to change that country of more than thirty-five million people, where one-quarter were not Muslims, into an Islamic nation. Sudan adopted a policy of religious, linguistic, and cultural imperialism. The government sought to extend Islam and the Arabic language to the non-Muslim south. This was an area of Christianity and tribal religions that had resisted the central government for a decade (Hedges 1992).

Arab militias have forced black Africans off their land in the Darfur region of western Sudan through a campaign of killing, rape, and pillage. Since the violence began in March 2003, more than two million people have fled to refugee camps in Sudan and Chad. In this photo, children play among thousands of makeshift huts in the El-Geneina camp.

This resistance continues and has spilled over into Sudan's drought-stricken and impoverished western province of Darfur. As of this writing, more than two million Sudanese are living in camps, having fled years of fighting in the region. Sudan's government and pro-government Arab militias have been accused of war crimes against the region's black African population. The Darfur conflict began early in 2003 as non-Islamic rebels waged attacks against government targets, claiming the government was oppressing black Africans in favor of Arabs. Darfur has faced many years of tension over land and grazing rights between nomadic Arabs and black African farmers. One of the two main rebel groups, the Sudan Liberation Army (SLA), includes Nuer and other Nilotic populations.

cultural imperialism The rapid spread or advance of one culture at the expense of others, or its imposition on other cultures, which it modifies, replaces, or destroys—usually because of differential economic or political influence.

CULTURAL IMPERIALISM

Children in the French colonial empire learned French history, language, and culture from standard textbooks also used in France. Tahitians, Malagasy, Vietnamese, and Senegalese learned the French language by reciting from books about "our ancestors the Gauls." This is an example of **cultural imperialism**—the spread or advance of one culture at the expense of others, or its imposition on other cultures, which it modifies, replaces, or destroys, usually because of differential economic or political influence.

To what extent is modern technology, especially the mass media, an agent of cultural imperialism? Some commentators see modern technology as erasing cultural differences, as homogeneous products reach more people worldwide. But others see a role for modern technology in allowing social groups (local cultures) to express themselves and to survive (Marcus and Fischer 1999). Modern radio and TV, for example, constantly bring local happenings (for example, a "chicken festival" in Iowa) to the

Native children throughout the French colonial empire learned the French language by reciting from books about "our ancestors the Gauls." More recently, French citizens have criticized or resisted what they see as American "cultural imperialism"—one prominent symbol of which has been Euro Disneyland. Has there also been resistance to the expansion of Disney enterprises in the United States?

In San Gimignano, Italy, boys and young men don medieval costumes and beat drums in a parade through the streets during one of the town's many pageants. Increasingly, local communities perform "traditional" ceremonies for TV and tourists.

attention of a larger public. The North American media play a role in stimulating local activities of many sorts. Similarly, in Brazil, local practices, celebrations, and performances are changing in the context of outside forces, including the mass media and tourism.

In the town of Arembepe, Brazil (Kottak 2006), TV coverage has stimulated participation in a traditional annual performance, the *Chegança*. This is a fishermen's danceplay that reenacts the Portuguese discovery of Brazil. Arembepeiros have traveled to the state capital to perform the *Chegança* before television cameras, for a TV program featuring traditional performances from many rural communities.

One national Brazilian Sunday-night variety program (*Fantástico*) is especially popular in rural areas because it shows such local events. In several towns along the Amazon River, annual folk ceremonies are now staged more lavishly for TV cameras. In the Amazon town of Parantíns, for example, boatloads of tourists arriving any time of year are shown a videotape of the town's annual Bumba Meu Boi festival. This is a costumed performance mimicking bullfighting, parts of which have been shown on *Fantástico*. This pattern, in which local communities preserve, revive, and intensify the scale of traditional ceremonies to perform for TV and tourists, is expanding.

Brazilian television also has played a "top-down" role, by spreading the popularity of holidays like Carnaval and Christmas (Kottak 1990a). TV has aided the national spread of Carnaval beyond its traditional urban centers. Still, local reactions to the nationwide broadcasting of Car-

naval and its trappings (elaborate parades, costumes, and frenzied dancing) are not simple or uniform responses to external stimuli.

Rather than direct adoption of Carnaval, local Brazilians respond in various ways. Often they don't take up Carnaval itself but modify their local festivities to fit Carnaval images. Others actively spurn Carnaval. One example is Arembepe, where Carnaval has never been important, probably because it occurs around the same time as the main local festival, which is held in February to honor Saint Francis of Assisi. In the past, villagers couldn't afford to celebrate both occasions. Now, not only do the people of Arembepe reject Carnaval; they are also increasingly hostile to their own main festival. Arembepeiros resent the fact that the Saint Francis festival has become "an outsiders' event," because it draws thousands of tourists to Arembepe each February. The villagers think that commercial interests and outsiders have appropriated Saint Francis.

In opposition to these trends, many Arembepeiros now say they like and participate more in the traditional June festivals honoring Saint John, Saint Peter, and Saint Anthony. In the past, these were observed on a much smaller scale than was the festival honoring Saint Francis. Arembepeiros celebrate them now with a new vigor and enthusiasm, as they react to outsiders and their celebrations, real and televised.

CULTURETHINK

To what extent do you think modern technology, especially the mass media, is an agent of cultural imperialism?

>> Making and Remaking Culture

To understand culture change, we must recognize that meaning may be locally manufactured. People assign their own meanings and value to the texts, messages, and products they receive. Those meanings reflect their cultural backgrounds and experiences.

INDIGENIZING POPULAR CULTURE

When forces from world centers enter new societies, they are **indigenized**—modified to fit the local culture. This is true of cultural forces as different as fast food, music, housing styles, science, terrorism, celebrations, and political ideas and institutions (Appadurai 1990). Consider the reception of the movie *Rambo* in Australia as an example of how popular culture may be indigenized. One researcher (Michaels 1986) found that the character Rambo was very popular among aborigines in the deserts of central Australia, who had manufactured their own meanings from the film. Their "reading" was different from the one imagined by the movie's creators and by most North Americans. The

indigenized Modified to fit the local culture.

Illustrating a process of indigenizing offerings of the modern world system, children dress as Colonel Sanders to promote egg tarts (a local dish now offered by an international restaurant chain) at a KFC store in Shanghai, China.

Native Australians saw Rambo as a representative of the Third World who was engaged in a battle with the white officer class. This reading expressed their negative feelings about white paternalism and about existing race relations. The Native Australians also imagined that there were tribal ties and kin links between Rambo and the prisoners he was rescuing. All this made sense, based on their experience. Native Australians are disproportionately represented in Australian jails. Their most likely liberator would be someone with a personal link to them. These readings of *Rambo* were relevant meanings produced *from* the text, not by it (Fiske 1989).

A GLOBAL SYSTEM OF IMAGES

All cultures express imagination—in dreams, fantasies, songs, myths, and stories. Today, however, more people in many more places imagine "a wider set of 'possible' lives than they ever did before. One important source of this change is the mass media [radio, TV, movies, video games, and the Internet], which present a rich, ever-changing store of possible lives" (Appadurai 1991, p. 197). The United States as a media center has been joined by Canada, Japan, Western Europe, Brazil, Mexico, Nigeria, Egypt, India, and Hong Kong.

As print has done for centuries (Anderson 1991), the electronic mass media also can spread, even help create, national and ethnic identities. Like print, television, radio, and the Internet can diffuse the cultures of different countries within their own boundaries, thus enhancing national cul-

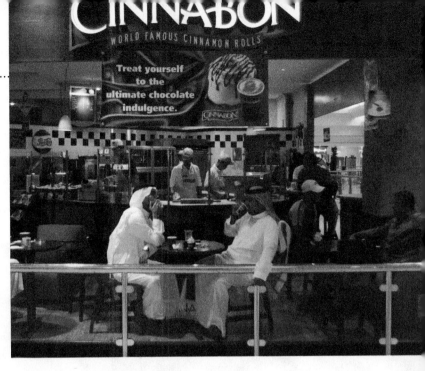

Foods offered in such chains as McDonald's, KFC, and Cinnabon (shown here) are now consumed internationally, though always indigenized somewhat to meet local expectations.

tural identity. For example, millions of Brazilians who were formerly cut off (by geographic isolation or illiteracy) from urban and national events and information now participate in a national—even international—communication system, through TV and the Internet (Kottak 2009). Social networking media such as Facebook permit regular communication among Brazilians in their own country and throughout Brazil's global diaspora.

Cross-cultural studies of television contradict a belief Americans ethnocentrically hold about televiewing in other countries. This misconception is that American programs inevitably triumph over local products. This doesn't happen when there is appealing local competition. In Brazil, for example, the most popular network (TV Globo) relies heavily on native productions, especially *telenovelas*. Globo plays each night to one of the world's largest and most devoted audiences (perhaps eighty million viewers throughout the nation and beyond—via satellite TV). The programs that attract this horde are made by Brazilians, for Brazilians. Thus, it is not North American culture but a new pan-Brazilian national culture that Brazilian TV is propagating. Brazilian productions also compete internationally. They are exported to over a hundred countries, spanning Latin America, Europe, Asia, and Africa.

We may generalize that culturally alien programming won't do very well anywhere when a quality local choice is available. Confirmation comes from many countries. National productions are highly popular in Japan, Mexico, India, Egypt, and Nigeria. In a survey during the mid-1980s, 75 percent of Nigerian viewers preferred local productions. Only 10 percent favored imports, and the remaining 15 percent liked the two options equally. Local productions are successful in Nigeria because "they are filled with everyday moments that audiences can identify with. These shows are locally produced by Nigerians" (Gray 1986). Thirty million people watched one of the most popular series, *The Village Headmaster,* each week. That program brought rural values to the screens of urbanites who had lost touch with their rural roots (Gray 1986).

CULTURETHINK

One way that media help establish a national identity is to create the sense that those who are not citizens of that nation are different. What images of non-Western peoples do television and other media provide? Do you think these images represent those people fairly?

The mass media also can play a role in maintaining ethnic and national identities among people who lead transnational lives. Arabic-speaking Muslims, including migrants, in several countries follow the TV network Al Jazeera, based in Qatar, which helps reinforce ethnic and religious identities. As groups move, they can stay linked to each other and to their homeland through the media. **Diasporas**—people who have spread out from an original, ancestral homeland— have enlarged the markets for media, communication, and travel services targeted at specific ethnic, national, or religious audiences. For a fee, a PBS station in Fairfax, Virginia, offers more than thirty hours a week to immigrant groups in the D.C. area, to make programs in their own languages.

> **diaspora** people who have spread out from an original, ancestral homeland.

A GLOBAL CULTURE OF CONSUMPTION

Besides the electronic media, another key transnational force is finance. Multinational corporations and other business interests look beyond national boundaries for places to invest and draw profits. As Arjun Appadurai (1991, p. 194) puts it, "money, commodities, and persons unendingly chase each other around the world." Residents of many Latin American communities now depend on outside cash, remitted from international labor migration. Also, the U.S. economy is increasingly influenced by foreign investment, especially from Britain, China, Canada, Germany, the Netherlands, and Japan (Rouse 1991). The American economy also has increased its dependence on foreign labor—through both the immigration of laborers and the export of jobs.

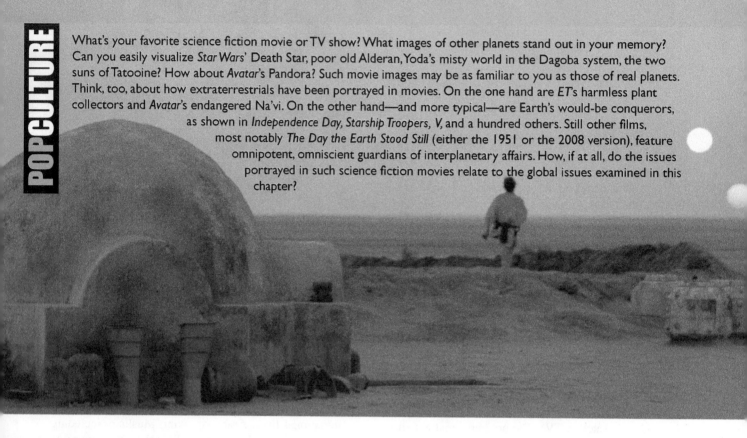

What's your favorite science fiction movie or TV show? What images of other planets stand out in your memory? Can you easily visualize *Star Wars'* Death Star, poor old Alderan, Yoda's misty world in the Dagoba system, the two suns of Tatooine? How about *Avatar's* Pandora? Such movie images may be as familiar to you as those of real planets. Think, too, about how extraterrestrials have been portrayed in movies. On the one hand are *ET*'s harmless plant collectors and *Avatar's* endangered Na'vi. On the other hand—and more typical—are Earth's would-be conquerors, as shown in *Independence Day, Starship Troopers, V,* and a hundred others. Still other films, most notably *The Day the Earth Stood Still* (either the 1951 or the 2008 version), feature omnipotent, omniscient guardians of interplanetary affairs. How, if at all, do the issues portrayed in such science fiction movies relate to the global issues examined in this chapter?

The flow of people, technology, finance, information, images, and ideology drive contemporary global culture (Appadurai 1990, 2001). Business, technology, and the media have increased the craving for commodities and images throughout the world (Gottdiener 2000). This has forced nation-states to open to a global culture of consumption. Almost everyone today participates in this culture. Few people have never seen a T-shirt advertising a Western product. American and English rock stars' recordings blast through the streets of Rio de Janeiro, while taxi drivers from Toronto to Madagascar play Brazilian music tapes. Peasants and tribal people participate in the modern world system not only because they have been hooked on cash, but also because their products and images are appropriated by world capitalism (Root 1996). They are commercialized by others (like the San in the movie *The Gods Must Be Crazy*). Furthermore, indigenous peoples also market their own images and products, through outlets like Cultural Survival (see Mathews 2000).

> **postmodernity** Condition of a world in flux, with people on the move, in which established groups, boundaries, identities, contrasts, and standards are reaching out and breaking down.

elytizers, laborers, businesspeople, development workers, employees of nongovernmental organizations, politicians, terrorists, soldiers, sports figures, or media-borne images, people appear to travel more than ever.

In previous chapters, we saw that foragers and herders are typically seminomadic or nomadic. Today, the scale of human movement has expanded dramatically. So important is transnational migration that many Mexican villagers find "their most important kin and friends are as likely to be living hundreds or thousands of miles away as immediately around them" (Rouse 1991). Most migrants maintain their ties with their native land (phoning, emailing, visiting, sending money, watching "ethnic TV"). In a sense, they live multilocally—in different places at once. Dominicans in New York City, for example, have been characterized as living "between two islands": Manhattan and the Dominican Republic (Grasmuck and Pessar 1991). Many Dominicans—like migrants from other countries—migrate to the United States temporarily, seeking cash to transform their lifestyles when they return to the Caribbean.

>> People in Motion

The linkages in the modern world system have both enlarged and erased old boundaries and distinctions. Arjun Appadurai (1990, p. 1) characterizes today's world as a "translocal" "interactive system" that is "strikingly new." Whether as refugees, migrants, tourists, pilgrims, pros-

CULTURETHINK

With so many people having ties across the globe, anthropologists face new challenges in fieldwork. What methods and techniques do you think ethnographers could use to learn about phenomena that span geographical zones, such as migration?

With so many people "in motion," the unit of anthropological study expands from the local community to the diaspora. As anthropologists, we increasingly follow descendants of the villages we have studied as they move from rural to urban areas and across national boundaries.

Postmodernity describes our time and situation: today's world in flux, these people on the move who have learned to manage multiple identities depending on place and context. In its most general sense, **postmodern** refers to the blurring and breakdown of established canons (rules or standards), categories, distinctions, and boundaries. The word is taken from **postmodernism**—a style and movement in architecture that began in the 1970s and followed modernism. Postmodern architecture rejected the rules, geometric order, and austerity of modernism. Modernist buildings were expected to have a clear and functional design. Postmodern design is "messier" and more playful. It draws on a diversity of styles from different times and places—including popular, ethnic, and non-Western cultures. Postmodernism extends "value" well beyond classic, elite, and Western cultural forms. *Postmodern* is now used to describe comparable developments in music, literature, and visual art. From this origin, *postmodernity* describes a world in which traditional standards, contrasts, groups, boundaries, and identities are opening up, reaching out, and breaking down.

New kinds of political and ethnic units are emerging. In some cases, cultures and ethnic groups have banded together in larger associations. There is a growing pan-Indian identity (Nagel 1996) and an international pantribal movement as well. Thus, in June 1992, the World Conference of Indigenous Peoples met in Rio de Janeiro concurrently with UNCED (the United Nations Conference on the Environment and Development). Along with diplomats, journalists, and environmentalists came 300 representatives of the tribal diversity that survives in the modern world—from Lapland to Mali (Brooke 1992; see also Maybury-Lewis 2002).

>> Indigenous Peoples

The term *indigenous people* entered international law with the creation in 1982 of the United Nations Working Group on Indigenous Populations (WGIP). This group, which meets annually, has members from six continents. The draft of the Declaration of Indigenous Rights, produced by the WGIP in 1989, was accepted by the UN for discussion in 1993. Convention 169, an ILO (International Labor Organization) document that supports cultural diversity and indigenous empowerment, was approved in 1989. Such documents, along with the work of the WGIP, have influenced governments, NGOs, and international agencies to adopt policies aimed at benefiting indigenous peoples. Social movements worldwide now use the term "indigenous people" as a self-identifying label in their quests for social, cultural, and political rights (Brower and Johnston 2007; de la Peña 2005).

In Spanish-speaking Latin America, social scientists and politicians now favor the term *indígena* (indigenous person) over *indio* (Indian). The latter is a colonial term that European conquerors used for Native Americans, whose situation did not necessarily improve after Latin American nations gained independence from Spain and Portugal, mostly by the 1820s. For the white and *mestizo* (mixed) elites of the new nations, *indios* and their lifestyle seemed alien to (European) civilization (de la Peña 2005).

Until the mid- to late 1980s, Latin American public policy emphasized assimilation. Indians were associated with a romanticized past, but marginalized in the present, except for museums, tourism, and folkloric events. Indigenous Bolivians and Peruvians were encouraged to self-identify as *campesinos* (peasants). The last thirty years have

postmodern In its most general sense, describes the blurring and breakdown of established canons (rules, standards), categories, distinctions, and boundaries.

postmodernism A style and movement in architecture that followed modernism. Compared with modernism, it is less geometric, less functional, less austere, more playful, and more willing to include elements from diverse times and cultures; *postmodern* now describes comparable developments in music, literature, and visual art.

Working to promote cultural survival is a growing international pantribal movement. In June 1992, the World Conference of Indigenous Peoples met in Rio de Janeiro. Along with diplomats, journalists, and environmentalists came 300 representatives of the tribal diversity that survives in the modern world.

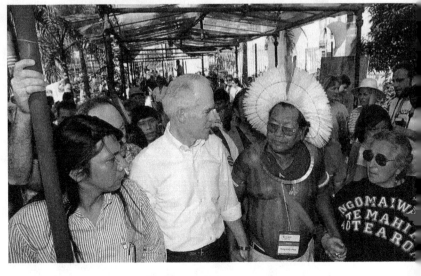

witnessed a dramatic shift from assimilation—*mestizaje*—to cultural difference. In Ecuador, groups seen previously as Quichua-speaking peasants are classified now as indigenous communities with their own territories. Brazil has recognized thirty new indigenous communities in the northeast, a region previously seen as having lost its native population. Guatemala, Nicaragua, Brazil, Colombia, Mexico, Paraguay, Ecuador, Argentina, Bolivia, Peru, and Venezuela now are officially multicultural (Jackson and Warren 2005). Several national constitutions recognize the rights of indigenous peoples to cultural distinctiveness and political representation. In Colombia, indigenous territories have the same benefits as any local government (dc la Pcña 2005).

essentialism The process of viewing an identity as established, real, and frozen, so as to hide the historical processes and politics within which that identity developed.

The indigenous rights movement exists in the context of globalization, including transnational movements focusing on human rights, women's rights, and environmentalism. Transnational organizations have helped indigenous peoples to influence legislation. Since the 1980s there has been a general shift in Latin America from authoritarian to democratic rule. Still, inequality and discrimination

Bolivians claiming an Indian (indigenous) identity rally for indigenous rights and the nationalization of that country's natural gas resources. In December 2005, Bolivians elected as their president Evo Morales, the candidate of the Indigenous Movement toward Socialism party. The party made further gains in 2006 parliamentary elections.

persist, and there has been resistance to indigenous mobilization, including assassinations of leaders and their supporters. Guatemala, Peru, and Colombia have witnessed severe repression. There have been thousands of indigenous deaths, refugees, and internally displaced persons (Jackson and Warren 2005).

Ceuppens and Geschiere (2005) explore a recent upsurge, in multiple world areas, of the notion of *autochthony* (being native to, or formed, in the place where found), with an implicit call for excluding strangers. The terms *autochthony* and *indigenous* both go back to classical Greek history, with similar implications. Autochthony refers to self and soil. Indigenous literally means born inside, with the connotation in classical Greek of being born "inside the house." Both notions stress the need to safeguard ancestral lands (patrimony) from strangers, along with the rights of first-comers to special rights and protection versus later immigrants—legal or illegal (Ceuppens and Geschiere 2005).

During the 1990s, autochthony became an issue in many parts of Africa, inspiring violent efforts to exclude (European and Asian) "strangers." Simultaneously, autochthony became a key notion in debates about immigration and multiculturalism in Europe. European majority groups have claimed the label *autochthon*. This term highlights the prominence that the exclusion of strangers has assumed in day-to-day politics worldwide (Ceuppens and Geschiere 2005). One familiar example is the United States, as represented in the congressional debate in 2006–2007, over illegal immigration.

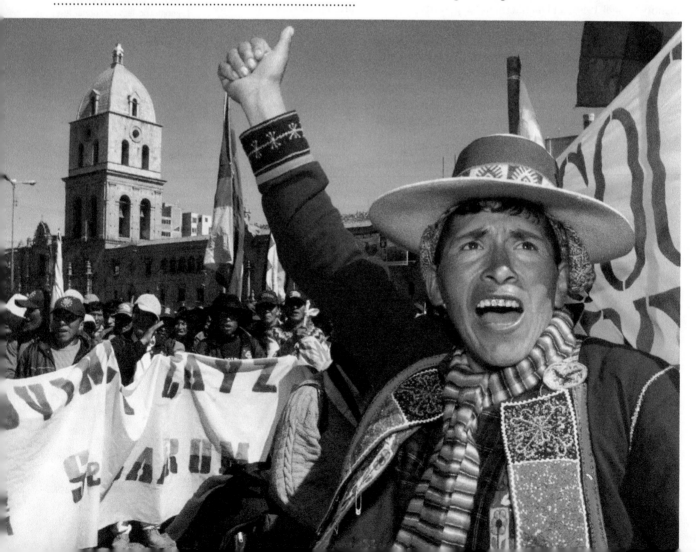

IDENTITY IN INDIGENOUS POLITICS

Essentialism describes the process of viewing an identity as established, real, and frozen, so as to hide the historical processes and politics within which that identity developed. Identities, emphatically, are not fixed. We saw in the chapter "Ethnicity and Race" that identities can be fluid and multiple. People seize on particular, sometimes competing, self-labels and identities. Some Peruvian groups, for instance, self-identify as mestizos but still see themselves as indigenous. Identity is a fluid, dynamic process, and there are multiple ways of being indigenous. Neither speaking an indigenous language nor wearing "native" clothing is required. Identities are asserted at particular times and places by particular individuals and groups and after various kinds of negotiations. Indigenous identity coexists with, and must be managed in the context of, other identity components, including religion, race, and gender. Identities always must be seen as (1) potentially plural, (2) emerging through a specific process, (3) ways of being someone or something in particular times and places (Jackson and Warren 2005).

>> The Continuance of Diversity

Anthropology has a crucial role to play in promoting a more humanistic vision of social change, one that respects the value of human biological and cultural diversity. The existence of anthropology is itself a tribute to the continuing need to understand similarities and differences among human beings throughout the world. Anthropology teaches us that the adaptive responses of humans can be more flexible than those of other species because our main adaptive means are sociocultural. However, the cultural forms, institutions, values, and customs of the past always influence subsequent adaptation, producing continued diversity and giving a certain uniqueness to the actions and reactions of different groups. With our knowledge and our awareness of our professional responsibilities, let us work to keep anthropology, the study of humankind, the most humanistic of all the sciences.

get involved!

Pay attention to the behavior of members of ethnic dance or music groups who perform on your campus or in your town or city. What do they wear when performing that expresses their traditional or indigenous culture? Does any other part of their dress or performance seem to conflict or compete with this traditional element? Observe or inquire about these people's behavior in various places and contexts. For example, do they speak English at certain times but not others? How often do they use their own language when talking among themselves? How would you evaluate whether their traditional ethnic identities are being lost or reinforced? Give a few examples of how their ethnic identity seems to be a matter of time, place, and negotiation.

For REVIEW

I. What is global climate change, and how can anthropologists study it, along with other environmental threats?

- Earlier ecological anthropology studied how culture helps human populations adapt to their environments. Today this field focuses on understanding and finding solutions to environmental threats that must be tackled at the national and international as well as local levels. Global climate change includes rising temperatures and changes in sea levels, precipitation, storms, and ecosystems. Human population growth and the increasing use of fossil fuels contribute to these changes. Global forces challenge indigenous peoples; outside environmental regulation confronts their ethnoecologies. Anthropologists believe that the most effective conservation strategies are those that pay attention to the needs and wishes of local people.

II. What is cultural imperialism, and what forces work to favor and oppose it?

- Cultural imperialism is the spread or advance of one culture at the expense of others, or its imposition on other cultures, which it modifies, replaces, or destroys. Modern mass media are alternately viewed as agents of cultural imperialism and means for allowing local cultures to express themselves. Electronic mass media can reinforce national and ethnic identities. Cultural forces entering new societies from world centers are often modified to fit the local culture. Business, technology, and mass media have increased the craving for commodities and images worldwide. Peasants and tribal peoples participate in the world system in part because world capitalism appropriates their products and images, but indigenous peoples may market their own images and products to the world.

III. What are indigenous peoples, and how and why has their importance increased in recent years?

- Social movements worldwide use the term *indigenous people* as a self-identifying political label that is based on past oppression but now signals a quest for social, cultural, and political rights. International law and the work of the UN's Working Group on Indigenous Populations have influenced governments, nongovernmental organizations, and international agencies to adopt policies aimed at recognizing and benefiting indigenous peoples. The indigenous rights movement exists in the global context of transnational movements that focus on human rights, women's rights, and environmentalism. Various world areas have seen an upsurge in the notion of *autochthony*, with an implicit call from native peoples to exclude strangers. Indigenous identities are fluid, multiple, and sometimes competing, asserted at particular times and places.

Pop Quiz

1. Scientific measurements confirm that global warming isn't caused by increased solar radiation. Rather, the causes are mainly anthropogenic. This means that:

   a. Humans and their activities cause global warming.

   b. The causes are indigenized.

   c. Global warming caused by normal climate fluctuations affects humans.

   d. The causes are social constructions used for political purposes.

2. All the following are true about global climate change *except*:

   a. The atmospheric concentration of greenhouse gases has reached its highest level in four hundred thousand years.

   b. The recent rise in CO_2 and the Earth's surface temperature is one proof that humans are fueling global warming.

   c. Worldwide, energy use has been falling, thanks to increased energy efficiency.

   d. Scientists prefer the term *climate change* to *global warming*.

3. Ecological anthropology:

   a. Is concerned with ethnoecology—how indigenous societies' environmental practices become irrelevant as national policies replace them.

   b. Focuses on the local community, because other levels of authority lack the right to use and regulate local ecosystems.

   c. Attempts to understand and solve environmental problems.

   d. Favors top-down agricultural development projects.

4. Which of the following statements about concern for environmental change and conservation is *false*?

   a. Some indigenous peoples have been forced to abandon basic economic activities because to do so is "good for nature" or for "the globe."

   b. Environmentalism began in Brazil in response to local and international attention given to the destruction of tropical Amazonian forests.

   c. Conservation plans should involve local people in planning and implementing policies that affect them.

   d. Applied anthropologists must make forest preservation attractive to local people to ensure their cooperation.

5. Which of the following is *not* true of changes arising from contact between native cultures and more powerful outsiders?

   a. Such changes typically occur on just one side of the contact.

   b. Westernization is a form of acculturation involving the influence of Western expansion on indigenous peoples and their cultures.

   c. Interethnic contact may cause destruction, domination, resistance, adaptation, and modification of native cultures.

   d. Religious proselytizing can promote ethnocide.

6. The spread or advance of one culture at the expense of others, or its imposition on other cultures, which it modifies, replaces, or destroys, is most accurately called:

   a. Cultural relativism

   b. Westernization

   c. Cultural imperialism

   d. Acculturation

7. When forces from world centers are modified to fit the local culture, this process is called:

   a. Religious proselytizing

   b. Indigenization

   c. Acculturation

   d. Assimilation

8. Which of the following statements about mass media is true?

   a. The United States is unique among media centers in offering varied images of possible lives.

   b. Media images and ideas are too general to help create or spread national and ethnic identities.

   c. American television programs don't necessarily triumph over local competition.

   d. Mass media can only work to maintain ethnic identities when people live inside their nation of origin.

9. What term does Arjun Appadurai use to refer to both the enlargening and the erasing of old boundaries and distinctions in the modern world?

   a. "Translocal" interactive system

   b. Postmodernism

   c. Essentialism

   d. Diaspora

10. In Latin America, which of the following would be an exception to the drive by indigenous peoples for indigenous identity and empowerment?

   a. Favoring of the term *indígena* over *indio* (Indian).

   b. A shift in policy from cultural difference to assimilation.

   c. National constitutions recognizing rights of indigenous peoples to political representation.

   d. Participation in transnational indigenous rights movements.

A

acculturation   The exchange of cultural features that results when groups come into continuous firsthand contact; the original cultural patterns of either or both groups may be altered, but the groups remain distinct.

achieved status   Social status that comes through talents, actions, efforts, activities, and accomplishments (e.g., big man, convicted felon).

adaptation   The process by which organisms cope with environmental stresses.

age set   Group uniting all men or women (usually men) born during a certain time span; this group controls property and often has ritual, political, and military functions.

agriculture   Nonindustrial system of plant cultivation characterized by continuous and intensive use of land and labor.

animism   Belief in souls or doubles.

anthropology   The study of the human species and its immediate ancestors

anthropology and education   Anthropological research in classrooms, homes, and neighborhoods, viewing students as total cultural creatures whose enculturation and attitudes toward education belong to a larger context that includes family, peers, and society.

applied anthropology   The application of anthropological data, perspectives, theory, and methods to identify, assess, and solve contemporary social problems.

archaeological anthropology   The branch of anthropology, commonly known as "archaeology," that reconstructs, describes, and interprets human behavior and cultural patterns through material remains; best known for the study of prehistory.

ascribed status   Social status that people have little or no choice about occupying (e.g., race, gender).

assimilation   The process of change that a minority group may experience when it moves to a country where another culture dominates; the minority is incorporated into the dominant culture to the point that it no longer exists as a separate cultural unit.

B

band   Basic unit of social organization among foragers. A band includes fewer than 100 people; it often splits up seasonally.

big man   Figure often found among tribal horticulturalists and pastoralists. The big man occupies no office but creates his reputation through entrepreneurship and generosity to others. Neither his wealth nor his position passes to his heirs.

biocultural   Referring to the inclusion and combination (to solve a common problem) of both biological and cultural approaches—one of anthropology's hallmarks.

biological anthropology   Also called *physical anthropology,* the branch of anthropology that studies human biological diversity in time and space—for instance, hominid evolution, human genetics, human biological adaptation; also includes primatology (behavior and evolution of monkeys and apes).

Black English Vernacular (BEV)   A rule-governed dialect of American English (sometimes called "ebonics") with roots in southern English. Many African American youth and adults speak BEV in their casual, intimate speech.

bourgeoisie   One of Karl Marx's opposed classes; owners of the means of production (factories, mines, large farms, and other sources of subsistence).

bridewealth   A customary gift before, at, or after marriage from the husband and his kin to the wife and her kin; see also *progeny price.*

C

call systems   Systems of communication among nonhuman primates, composed of a limited number of sounds that vary in intensity and duration; tied to environmental stimuli.

capital   Wealth or resources invested in business, with the intent of producing a profit.

capitalist world economy   The single world system, which emerged in the sixteenth century, committed to production for sale, with the object of maximizing profits rather than supplying domestic needs.

cargo cults   Postcolonial, acculturative, religious movements common in Melanesia that attempt to explain European domination and wealth and to achieve similar success magically by mimicking European behavior.

caste system   Closed, hereditary system of stratification, often dictated by religion; hierarchical social status is ascribed at birth, so that people are locked into their parents' social position.

chiefdom   Form of sociopolitical organization intermediate between the tribe and the state; kin-based with differential access to resources and a permanent political structure.

clan   Unilineal descent group based on stipulated descent.

climate change   Global warming, plus changing sea levels, precipitation, storms, and ecosystem effects.

colonialism   The political, social, economic, and cultural domination of a territory and its people by a foreign power for an extended time.

communal religions   In Wallace's typology, these religions have—in addition to shamanic cults—communal cults in which people organize community rituals such as harvest ceremonies and rites of passage.

communism   Spelled with a lowercase *c,* describes a social system in which the community owns property and people work for the common good.

Communism   Spelled with an uppercase *C,* describes a political movement and doctrine seeking to overthrow capitalism and to establish a form of communism such as that which prevailed in the Soviet Union (USSR) from 1917 to 1991.

communitas Intense community spirit, a feeling of great social solidarity, equality, and togetherness; characteristic of people experiencing liminality together.

complex societies Nations; large and populous, with social stratification and central governments.

conflict resolution The means by which disputes are socially regulated and settled; found in all societies, but the resolution methods tend to be more formal and effective in states than in nonstates.

core Dominant structural position in the world system; consists of the strongest and most powerful states with advanced systems of production.

core values Key, basic, or central values that integrate a culture and help distinguish it from others.

correlation An association between two or more variables such that when one changes (varies), the other(s) also change(s) (covaries); for example, temperature and sweating.

cultural anthropology The study of human society and culture; describes, analyzes, interprets, and explains social and cultural similarities and differences.

cultural colonialism Within a nation or empire, domination by one ethnic group or nationality and its culture/ ideology over others—e.g., the dominance of Russian people, language, and culture in the former Soviet Union.

cultural consultant Someone the ethnographer gets to know in the field, who teaches him or her about their society and culture (also called "informant").

cultural imperialism The rapid spread or advance of one culture at the expense of others, or its imposition on other cultures, which it modifies, replaces, or destroys—usually because of differential economic or political influence.

cultural relativism The position that the values and standards of cultures differ and deserve respect. Anthropology is characterized by methodological rather than moral relativism: In order to understand another culture fully, anthropologists try to understand its members' beliefs and motivations. Methodological relativism does not preclude making moral judgments or taking action.

cultural resource management (CRM) The branch of applied archaeology aimed at preserving sites threatened by dams, highways, and other projects.

cultural rights Doctrine that certain rights are vested not in individuals but in identifiable groups, such as religious and ethnic minorities and indigenous societies.

cultural transmission A basic feature of language; transmission through learning.

culture Traditions and customs that govern behavior and beliefs; distinctly human; transmitted through learning.

curer Specialized role acquired through a culturally appropriate process of selection, training, certification, and acquisition of a professional image; the curer is consulted by patients, who believe in his or her special powers, and receives some form of special consideration; a cultural universal.

D

daughter languages Languages developing out of the same parent language; for example, French and Spanish are daughter languages of Latin.

descent Rule assigning social identity on the basis of some aspect of one's ancestry.

descent group A permanent social unit whose members claim common ancestry; fundamental to tribal society.

descriptive linguistics The scientific study of a spoken language, including its phonology, morphology, lexicon, and syntax.

development anthropology The branch of applied anthropology that focuses on social issues in, and the cultural dimension of, economic development.

diaspora people who have spread out from an original, ancestral homeland.

differential access Unequal access to resources; basic attribute of chiefdoms and states. *Superordinates* have favored access to such resources, while the access of *subordinates* is limited by superordinates.

diffusion Borrowing between cultures either directly or through intermediaries.

diglossia The existence of "high" (formal) and "low" (familial) dialects of a single language, such as German.

discrimination Policies and practices that harm a group and its members.

disease An *etic,* or scientifically identified, health threat caused by a bacterium, virus, fungus, parasite, or other pathogen.

displacement A linguistic capacity that allows humans to talk about things and events that are not present.

domestic–public dichotomy Contrast between women's role in the home and men's role in public life, with a corresponding social devaluation of women's work and worth.

dowry A marital exchange in which the wife's group provides substantial gifts to the husband's family.

E

ecological anthropology Study of cultural adaptations to environments.

economy A population's system of production, distribution, and consumption of resources.

emic The research strategy that focuses on native explanations and criteria of significance.

enculturation The social process by which culture is learned and transmitted across the generations.

endogamy Marriage between people of the same social group.

equity, increased   A reduction in absolute poverty and a fairer (more even) distribution of wealth.

essentialism   The process of viewing an identity as established, real, and frozen, so as to hide the historical processes and politics within which that identity developed.

ethnic group   Group distinguished by cultural similarities (shared among members of that group) and differences (between that group and others); ethnic group members are thought to share beliefs, values, habits, customs, and norms, and a common language, religion, history, geography, kinship, and/or race.

ethnicity   Identification with, and feeling part of, an ethnic group, and exclusion from certain other groups because of this affiliation.

ethnocentrism   The tendency to view one's own culture as best and to judge the behavior and beliefs of culturally different people by one's own standards.

ethnocide   Destruction by a dominant group of the culture of an ethnic group.

ethnoecology   A culture's set of environmental practices and perceptions.

ethnography   Fieldwork in a particular culture.

ethnology   The theoretical, comparative study of society and culture; compares cultures in time and space.

etic   The research strategy that emphasizes the observer's rather than the natives' explanations, categories, and criteria of significance.

exogamy   Mating or marriage outside one's kin group; a cultural universal.

extended family household   Expanded household including three or more generations.

extradomestic   Outside the home; within or pertaining to the public domain.

F

family   A group of people (e.g., parents, children, siblings, grandparents, grandchildren, uncles, aunts, nephews, nieces, cousins, spouses, siblings-in-law, parents-in-law, children-in-law) who are considered to be related in some way, such as by "blood" (common ancestry or descent) or marriage.

family of orientation   Nuclear family in which one is born and grows up.

family of procreation   Nuclear family established when one marries and has children.

fiscal   Pertaining to finances and taxation.

focal vocabulary   A set of words and distinctions that are particularly important to certain groups (those with particular foci of experience or activity), such as types of snow to Eskimos or skiers.

food production   Plant cultivation and animal domestication.

G

gender roles   The tasks and activities that a culture assigns to each sex.

gender stereotypes   Oversimplified but strongly held ideas about the characteristics of males and females.

gender stratification   Unequal distribution of rewards (socially valued resources, power, prestige, and personal freedom) between men and women, reflecting their different positions in a social hierarchy.

genealogical method   Procedures by which ethnographers discover and record connections of kinship, descent, and marriage, using diagrams and symbols.

general anthropology   The field of anthropology as a whole, consisting of cultural, archaeological, biological, and linguistic anthropology.

generality   Culture pattern or trait that exists in some but not all societies.

genocide   Policies aimed at, and/or resulting in, the physical extinction (through mass murder) of a people perceived as a racial group, that is, as sharing defining physical, genetic, or other biological characteristics.

globalization   A set of processes, including *diffusion,* migration, and *acculturation,* that promote change in today's interlinked world.

greenhouse effect   Warming from trapped atmospheric gases.

H

head, village   See *village head.*

health care systems   Beliefs, customs, and specialists concerned with ensuring health and preventing and curing illness; a cultural universal.

historical linguistics   Subdivision of linguistics that studies languages over time.

holistic   Interested in the whole of the human condition past, present, and future; biology, society, language, and culture.

hominids   Members of the zoological family that includes fossil and living humans, chimps, and gorillas.

hominins   Members of the evolutionary line leading to and including modern humans, as distinct from chimps and gorillas.

horticulture   Nonindustrial system of plant cultivation in which plots lie fallow for varying lengths of time.

human rights   Doctrine that invokes a realm of justice and morality beyond and superior to particular countries, cultures, and religions. Human rights, usually seen as vested in individuals, include the right to speak freely, to hold religious beliefs without persecution, and not to be enslaved.

hypodescent   A rule that automatically places the children of a union or mating between members of different socioeconomic groups in the less privileged group.

I

illness   An *emic* condition of poor health felt by the individual.

imperialism   A policy of extending the rule of a nation or empire over foreign nations and of taking and holding foreign colonies.

incest   Sexual relations with a close relative.

independent invention   Development of the same culture trait or pattern in separate cultures as a result of comparable needs and circumstances.

indigenized   Modified to fit the local culture.

indigenous peoples   The original inhabitants of particular territories; often descendants of tribespeople, they live on as culturally distinct colonized peoples, many of whom aspire to autonomy.

Industrial Revolution   The historical transformation (in Europe, after 1750) of "traditional" into "modern" societies through industrialization of the economy.

informed consent   An agreement sought by ethnographers from community members to take part in research.

intellectual property rights (IPR)   Each society's cultural base—its core beliefs and principles. IPR is claimed as a group right—a cultural right, allowing indigenous groups to control who may know and use their collective knowledge and its applications.

international culture   Cultural traditions that extend beyond national boundaries.

intervention philosophy   Guiding principle of colonialism, conquest, missionization, or development; an ideological justification for outsiders to guide native peoples in specific directions.

interview schedule   Ethnographic tool for structuring a formal interview. A prepared form that guides interviews with households or individuals being compared systematically. This contrasts with a questionnaire because the researcher has personal contact and records people's answers.

K

key cultural consultant   An expert on a particular aspect of local life who helps the ethnographer understand that aspect.

kinesics   The study of communication through body movements, stances, gestures, and facial expressions.

L

language subgroups   Languages within a taxonomy of related languages that are most closely related.

law   A legal code, including trial and enforcement; characteristic of state-organized societies.

leveling mechanisms   Customs and social actions that operate to reduce differences in wealth and thus to bring standouts in line with community norms.

levirate   Custom by which a widow marries the brother of her deceased husband.

lexicon   Vocabulary; a dictionary containing all the morphemes in a language and their meaning.

life history   Of a cultural consultant; provides a personal cultural portrait of existence or change in a culture.

liminality   The critically important marginal or in-between phase of a rite of passage.

lineage   Unilineal descent group based on demonstrated descent.

linguistic anthropology   The branch of anthropology that studies linguistic variation in time and space, including interrelations between language and culture; includes historical linguistics and sociolinguistics.

longitudinal research   Long-term study of a community, society, culture, or other unit, usually based on repeated visits.

M

magic   Use of supernatural techniques to accomplish specific aims.

majority groups   Superordinate, dominant, or controlling groups in a social–political hierarchy.

mana   Sacred impersonal force in Melanesian and Polynesian religions.

market principle   Profit-oriented principle of exchange that dominates in states, particularly industrial states. Goods and services are bought and sold, and values are determined by supply and demand.

matriarchy   A political system in which women play a much more prominent role than men do in social and political organization.

matrilineal descent   Unilineal descent rule in which people join the mother's group automatically at birth and stay members throughout life.

matrilocality   Customary residence with the wife's relatives after marriage, so that children grow up in their mother's community.

means (or factors) of production   Land, labor, technology, and capital—major productive resources.

medical anthropology   Unites biological and cultural anthropologists in the study of disease, health problems, health care systems, and theories about illness in different cultures and ethnic groups.

minority groups   Subordinate groups in a social–political hierarchy, with inferior power and less secure access to resources than majority groups have.

mode of production   Way of organizing production—a set of social relations through which labor is deployed to wrest energy from nature by means of tools, skills, and knowledge.

monotheism   Worship of an eternal, omniscient, omnipotent, and omnipresent supreme being.

morphology   The study of form; used in linguistics (the study of morphemes and word construction) and for form in general—for example, biomorphology relates to physical form.

multiculturalism   The view of cultural diversity in a country as something good and desirable; a multicultural society socializes individuals not only into the dominant (national) culture, but also into an ethnic culture.

N

national culture   Cultural experiences, beliefs, learned behavior patterns, and values shared by citizens of the same nation.

nationalities   Ethnic groups that once had, or wish to have or regain, autonomous political status (their own country).

nation-state   An autonomous political entity, a country like the United States or Canada. See also *state*.

natural selection   Originally formulated by Charles Darwin and Alfred Russel Wallace; the process by which nature selects the forms most fit to survive and reproduce in a given environment, such as the tropics.

neoliberalism   Revival of Adam Smith's classic economic liberalism, the idea that governments should not regulate private enterprise and that free market forces should rule; a currently dominant intervention philosophy.

neolocality   Postmarital residence pattern in which a couple establishes a new place of residence rather than living with or near either set of parents.

nomadism, pastoral   Movement throughout the year by the whole pastoral group (men, women, and children) with their animals. More generally, such constant movement in pursuit of strategic resources.

O

office   Permanent political position.

Olympian religions   In Wallace's typology, religions that develop with state organization; have full-time religious specialists—professional priesthoods.

open-class system   Stratification system that facilitates social mobility, with individual achievement and personal merit determining social rank.

overinnovation   Characteristic of development projects that require major changes in people's daily lives, especially ones that interfere with customary subsistence pursuits.

P

pantribal sodality   A nonkin-based group that exists throughout a tribe, spanning several villages.

participant observation   A characteristic ethnographic technique; taking part in the events one is observing, describing, and analyzing.

particularity   Distinctive or unique culture trait, pattern, or integration.

pastoralists   People who use a food-producing strategy of adaptation based on caring for herds of domesticated animals.

patriarchy   Political system ruled by men in which women have inferior social and political status, including fewer basic human rights.

patrilineal descent   Unilineal descent rule in which people join the father's group automatically at birth and stay members throughout life.

patrilineal–patrilocal complex   An interrelated constellation of patrilineality, patrilocality, warfare, and male supremacy.

patrilocality   Customary residence with the husband's relatives after marriage, so that children grow up in their father's community.

peasant   Small-scale agriculturist living in a state, with rent fund obligations.

periphery   Weakest structural position in the world system; less mechanized producers of raw materials, agricultural commodities, and human labor.

phenotype   An organism's evident traits, its "manifest biology"—anatomy and physiology.

phoneme   Significant sound contrast in a language that serves to distinguish meaning, as in minimal pairs.

phonemics   The study of the sound contrasts (phonemes) of a particular language.

phonetics   The study of speech sounds in general; what people actually say in various languages.

phonology   The study of sounds used in speech.

physical anthropology   See *biological anthropology*.

plural marriage   Marriage of a man to two or more women (polygyny) or marriage of a woman to two or more men (polyandry)—at the same time; see also *polygamy*.

plural society   A society that combines ethnic contrasts, ecological specialization (i.e., use of different environmental resources by each ethnic group), and the economic interdependence of those groups.

polyandry   Variety of plural marriage in which a woman has more than one husband.

polygamy   Marriage with three or more spouses, at the same time; see also *plural marriage*.

polygyny   Variety of plural marriage in which a man has more than one wife.

polytheism   Belief in several deities who control aspects of nature.

postcolonial   Referring to interactions between European nations and the societies they colonized (mainly after 1800); more generally, it may be used to signify a position against imperialism and Eurocentrism.

postmodern In its most general sense, describes the blurring and breakdown of established canons (rules, standards), categories, distinctions, and boundaries.

postmodernism A style and movement in architecture that followed modernism. Compared with modernism, it is less geometric, less functional, less austere, more playful, and more willing to include elements from diverse times and cultures; *postmodern* now describes comparable developments in music, literature, and visual art.

postmodernity Condition of a world in flux, with people on the move, in which established groups, boundaries, identities, contrasts, and standards are reaching out and breaking down.

potlatch Competitive feast among Indians on the North Pacific Coast of North America.

power The ability to exercise one's will over others—to do what one wants; the basis of political status.

prejudice Devaluing (looking down on) a group because of its assumed behavior, values, capabilities, or attributes.

prestige Esteem, respect, or approval for acts, deeds, or qualities considered exemplary.

primates Members of the zoological order that includes humans, apes, monkeys, and prosimians (e.g., lemurs).

productivity The ability to use the rules of one's language to create new expressions comprehensible to other speakers; a basic feature of language.

proletariat See *working class*.

progeny price A gift from the husband and his kin to the wife and her kin before, at, or after marriage; legitimizes children born to the woman as members of the husband's descent group.

protolanguage Language ancestral to several daughter languages.

R

race An ethnic group assumed to have a biological basis.

racial classification The attempt to assign humans to discrete categories (purportedly) based on common ancestry.

racism Discrimination against an ethnic group assumed to have a biological basis.

random sample A sample in which all members of the population have an equal statistical chance of being included.

reciprocity One of the three principles of exchange. Governs exchange between social equals; major exchange mode in band and tribal societies.

reciprocity continuum Regarding exchanges, a range running from generalized reciprocity (closely related/deferred return) through balanced reciprocity, to negative reciprocity (strangers/immediate return).

redistribution Flow of goods into the center, then back out; characteristic of chiefdoms, many archaic states, and some states with managed economies.

refugees People who have been forced (involuntary refugees) or who have chosen (voluntary refugees) to flee a country, to escape persecution or war.

religion Beliefs and rituals concerned with supernatural beings, powers, and forces.

revitalization movements Movements that occur in times of change, in which religious leaders emerge and undertake to alter or revitalize a society.

rites of passage Culturally defined activities associated with the transition from one place or stage of life to another.

ritual Behavior that is formal, stylized, repetitive, and stereotyped, performed earnestly as a social act; rituals are held at set times and places and have liturgical orders.

S

sample A smaller study group chosen to represent a larger population.

Sapir-Whorf hypothesis Theory that different languages produce different ways of thinking.

science A systematic field of study or body of knowledge that aims, through experiment, observation, and deduction, to produce reliable explanations of phenomena, with reference to the material and physical world.

scientific medicine A health care system based on scientific knowledge and procedures, encompassing such fields as pathology, microbiology, biochemistry, surgery, diagnostic technology, and applications.

semantics A language's meaning system.

semiperiphery Structural position in the world system intermediate between core and periphery; exporters of goods and commodities, but lacking the power of core nations.

sexual dimorphism Marked differences, such as in height and weight, in male and female biology besides the contrasts in breasts and genitals.

sexual orientation A person's habitual sexual attraction to, and activities with, persons of the opposite sex (heterosexuality), the same sex (homosexuality), or both sexes (bisexuality); also, the lack of sexual attraction (asexuality).

shaman A part-time religious practitioner who mediates between ordinary people and supernatural beings and forces.

slavery The most extreme, coercive, abusive, and inhumane form of legalized inequality; people are treated as property.

sociolinguistics Study of relationships between social and linguistic variation; study of language in its social context.

sociopolitical typology Classification scheme based on the scale and complexity of social organization and the effectiveness of political regulation; includes band, tribe, chiefdom, and state.

sodality See *pantribal sodality*.

sororate Custom by which a widower marries the sister of the deceased wife.

state (nation-state) Complex sociopolitical system that administers a territory and populace with substantial contrasts in occupation, wealth, prestige, and power. An independent, centrally organized political unit, a government.

status Any position that determines where someone fits in society; may be ascribed or achieved.

stereotypes Fixed ideas—often unfavorable—about what members of a group are like.

stratification Characteristic of a system with socioeconomic strata.

style shifts Variations in speech in different contexts.

subcultures Different cultural symbol-based traditions associated with subgroups in the same complex society.

subordinate The lower, or underprivileged, group in a stratified system.

superordinate The higher, or privileged, group in a stratified system.

survey research Characteristic research procedure among social scientists other than anthropologists, which studies society through sampling, statistical analysis, and impersonal data collection.

symbol Something, verbal or nonverbal, that arbitrarily and by convention stands for something else, with which it has no necessary or natural connection.

syntax The arrangement and order of words in phrases and sentences.

T

taboo Prohibition backed by supernatural sanctions.

transhumance One of two variants of pastoralism; part of the population moves seasonally with the herds while the other part remains in home villages.

tribe Form of sociopolitical organization usually based on horticulture or pastoralism. Socioeconomic stratification and centralized rule are absent in tribes, and there is no means of enforcing political decisions.

tropics Geographic belt extending about 23 degrees north and south of the equator, between the Tropic of Cancer (north) and the Tropic of Capricorn (south).

typology, sociopolitical See *sociopolitical typology*.

U

underdifferentiation Planning fallacy of viewing less-developed countries as an undifferentiated group; ignoring cultural diversity and adopting a uniform approach (often ethnocentric) for very different types of project beneficiaries.

unilineal descent Matrilineal or patrilineal descent.

universal Something that exists in every culture.

urban anthropology The anthropological study of life in and around world cities, including the study of urban social problems, differences between urban and other environments, and adaptation to city life.

V

variables Attributes (e.g., sex, age, height, weight) that differ from one person or case to the next.

vertical mobility Upward or downward change in a person's social status.

village head Leadership position in a village (as among the Yanomami, where the head is always a man); has limited authority; leads by example and persuasion.

W

wealth All of a person's material assets, including income, land, and other types of property; the basis of economic status.

Westernization The acculturation influence of European cultures on tribal societies.

working class (proletariat) Those who must sell their labor to survive; the antithesis of the bourgeoisie in Marx's class analysis.

world-system theory Argument for the historic and contemporary social, political, and economic significance of an identifiable global system, based on wealth and power differentials, that extends beyond individual countries.

Abelmann, N., and J. Lie. 1995. *Blue Dreams: Korean Americans and the Los Angeles Riots.* Cambridge, MA: Harvard University Press.

Adams, Beatrice. 2007. McDonald's Strange Menu Around the World. http://thrifter.com/practical-travel/budget-travel/mcdonald%E2%80%99s-strange-menu-around-the-world/.

Adherents.com. 2002. Major Religions of the World Ranked by Number of Adherents. http://www.adherents.com/Religions_By_Adherents.html.

Ahmed, A. S. 1992. *Postmodernism and Islam: Predicament and Promise.* New York: Routledge.

———. 2004. *Postmodernism and Islam: Predicament and Promise.* Rev. ed. New York: Routledge.

Amadiume, I. 1987. *Male Daughters, Female Husbands.* Atlantic Highlands, NJ: Zed.

American Anthropological Association. *Anthropology Newsletter.* Published nine times annually by the American Anthropological Association, Washington, DC.

———. 2010. Anthropologists Challenge New Arizona Immigration Law. http://aaanet.org/issues/press/Arizona-Immigration.cfm.

Anderson, B. 1991. *Imagined Communities: Reflections on the Origin and Spread of Nationalism.* Rev. ed. London: Verso.

Anderson, R. 1996. *Magic, Science, and Health: The Aims and Achievements of Medical Anthropology.* Fort Worth, TX: Harcourt Brace.

Antoun, R. T. 2008. *Understanding Fundamentalism: Christian, Islamic, and Jewish Movements.* 2nd ed. Lanham, MD: AltaMira.

Aoki, M. Y., and M. B. Dardess, eds. 1981. *As the Japanese See It: Past and Present.* Honolulu: University Press of Hawaii.

Aoyagi, K., P. J. M. Nas, and J. Traphagan, eds. 1998. *Toward Sustainable Cities: Readings in the Anthropology of Urban Environments.* Leiden: Leiden Development Studies, Institute of Cultural and Social Studies, University of Leiden.

Appadurai, A. 1990. Disjuncture and Difference in the Global Cultural Economy. *Public Culture* 2(2):1–24.

———. 1991. Global Ethnoscapes: Notes and Queries for a Transnational Anthropology. In *Recapturing Anthropology: Working in the Present,* R. G. Fox, ed., pp. 191–210. Santa Fe, NM: School of American Research Advanced Seminar Series.

———. 1996. *Modernity at Large. Cultural Dimensions of Globalization.* Minneapolis: University of Minnesota Press.

———. 2001. *Globalization.* Durham, NC: Duke University Press.

Appiah, K. A. 1990. Racisms. In *Anatomy of Racism,* David Theo Goldberg, ed., pp. 3–17. Minneapolis: University of Minnesota Press.

Applebome, P. 1996. English Unique to Blacks Is Officially Recognized. *New York Times,* December 20. http://www.nytimes.com.

Arensberg, C. 1987. Theoretical Contributions of Industrial and Development Studies. In *Applied Anthropology in America,* 2nd ed., E. M. Eddy and W. L. Partridge, eds. New York: Columbia University Press.

Arrighi, G. 1994. *The Long Twentieth Century; Money, Power, and the Origins of Our Times.* New York: Verso.

Ashcroft, B., G. Griffiths, and H. Tiffin. 1989. *The Empire Writes Back: Theory and Practice in Post-colonial Literatures.* New York: Routledge.

Baer, H., and M. Singer. 2008. *Global Warming and the Political Ecology of Health.* Walnut Creek, CA: Left Coast Press.

Baer, H. A., M. Singer, and I. Susser. 2003. *Medical Anthropology and the World System.* Westport, CT: Praeger.

Bailey, E. J. 2000. *Medical Anthropology and African American Health.* Westport, CT: Bergin and Garvey.

Bailey, R. C. 1990. *The Behavioral Ecology of Efe Pygmy Men in the Ituri Forest, Zaire.* Ann Arbor: Anthropological Papers, Museum of Anthropology, University of Michigan, no. 86.

Bailey, R. C., G. Head, M. Jenike, B. Owen, R. Rechtman, and E. Zechenter. 1989. Hunting and Gathering in Tropical Rain Forests: Is It Possible? *American Anthropologist* 91:59–82.

Banton, M. 1957. *West African City. A Study in Tribal Life in Freetown.* London: Oxford University Press.

Barber, B. R. 1992. Jihad vs. McWorld. *Atlantic Monthly* 269(3):53–65, March 1992.

———. 1995. *Jihad vs. McWorld.* New York: Times Books.

Barker, C. 1997. *Global Television: An Introduction.* Malden, MA: Blackwell.

———. 2003. *Cultural Studies: Theory and Practice.* Thousand Oaks, CA: Sage.

Barnaby, F., ed. 1984. *Future War: Armed Conflict in the Next Decade.* London: M. Joseph.

Barnes, E. 2005. *Diseases and Human Evolution.* Albuquerque: University of New Mexico Press.

Baro, M., and T. F. Deubel. 2006. Persistent Hunger: Perspectives on Vulnerability, Famine, and Food Security in Sub-Saharan Africa. *Annual Review of Anthropology* 35:521–538.

Barringer, F. 1992. New Census Data Show More Children Living in Poverty. *New York Times,* May 29, pp. A1, A12–A13.

Barth, F. 1968. (orig. 1958). Ecologic Relations of Ethnic Groups in Swat, North Pakistan. In *Man in Adaptation: The Cultural Present,* Yehudi Cohen, ed., pp. 324–331. Chicago: Aldine.

———. 1969. *Ethnic Groups and Boundaries: The Social Organization of Cultural Difference.* London: Allen & Unwin.

Bearak, B. 2010. Shaky Rule in Madagascar Threatens Trees. *New York Times,* May 24. http://www.nytimes.com.

Beeman, W. 1986. *Language, Status, and Power in Iran.* Bloomington: Indiana University Press.

Behar, R. 1993. *Translated Woman: Crossing the Border with Esperanza's Story.* Boston: Beacon Press.

Bell, W. 1981. Neocolonialism. In *Encyclopedia of Sociology,* p. 193. Guilford, CT: DPG Publishing.

Bellah, R. N. 1978. Religious Evolution. In *Reader in Comparative Religion: An Anthropological Approach,* 4th ed., W. A. Lessa and E. Z. Vogt, eds., pp. 36–50. New York: Harper and Row.

Benedict, R. 1940. *Race, Science and Politics.* New York: Modern Age Books.

Berlin, B., and P. Kay. 1992. *Basic Color Terms: Their Universality and Evolution.* 2nd ed. Berkeley: University of California Press.

Bernard, H. R. 2002. *Research Methods in Anthropology: Qualitative and Quantitative Methods.* 3rd ed. Walnut Creek, CA: AltaMira.

———. 2006. *Research Methods in Anthropology: Qualitative and Quantitative Approaches.* 4th ed. Lanham, MD: AltaMira.

Bernard, H. R., ed. 1998. *Handbook of Methods in Cultural Anthropology,* Walnut Creek, CA: AltaMira.

Bicker, A., P. Sillitoe, and J. Pottier. 2004. *Investigating Local Knowledge: New Directions, New Approaches.* Burlington, VT: Ashgate.

Bird-David, N. 1992. Beyond "The Original Affluent Society": A Culturalist Reformulation. *Current Anthropology* 33(1):25–47.

Bjuremalm, H. 1997. Rattvisa kan skippas i Rwanda: Folkmordet 1994 gar attt forklara och analysera pa samma satt som forintelsen av judarna. *Dagens Nyheter* [06–03–1997, p. B3].

Blackwood, E., and S. Wieringa, eds. 1999. *Female Desires: Same-Sex Relations and Transgender Practices across Cultures.* New York: Columbia University Press.

Bloch, M., ed. 1975. *Political Language and Oratory in Traditional Societies.* London: Academic Press.

Boas, F. 1966 (orig. 1940). *Race, Language, and Culture.* New York: Free Press.

Bodley, J. H. 2003. *The Power of Scale: A Global History Approach.* Armonk, NY: M. E. Sharpe.

———. 2007. *Anthropology and Contemporary Human Problems.* 5th ed. Lanham, MD: AltaMira.

———. 2008. *Victims of Progress.* 5th ed. Lanham, MD: AltaMira.

Bodley, J. H., ed. 1988. *Tribal Peoples and Development Issues: A Global Overview.* Mountain View, CA: Mayfield.

Boellstorff, T. 2007. Queer Studies in the House of Anthropology. *Annual Review of Anthropology* 36:375–389.

Bogoras, W. 1904. The Chukchee. In *The Jesup North Pacific Expedition*, F. Boas, ed. New York: Memoir of the American Museum of Natural History.

Bolinger, D., and D. Sears. 1981. *Aspects of Language*. 3rd ed. New York: Harcourt Brace Jovanovich.

Bolton, R. 1981. Susto, Hostility, and Hypoglycemia. *Ethnology* 20(4): 227–258.

Bonvillain, N. 2001. *Women and Men: Cultural Constructions of Gender*. 3rd ed. Upper Saddle River, NJ: Prentice Hall.

———. 2008. *Language, Culture, and Communication: The Meaning of Messages*. 5th ed. Upper Saddle River, NJ: Prentice Hall.

Boserup, E. 1970. *Women's Role in Economic Development*. London: Allen and Unwin.

Bourdieu, P. 1977. *Outline of a Theory of Practice*. R. Nice (trans.). Cambridge: Cambridge University Press.

———. 1982. *Ce Que Parler Veut Dire*. Paris: Fayard.

———. 1984. *Distinction: A Social Critique of the Judgment of Taste*. R. Nice (trans.). Cambridge, MA: Harvard University Press.

Bourque, S. C., and K. B. Warren. 1987. Technology, Gender and Development. *Daedalus* 116(4):173–197.

Bowen, J. R. 2008. *Religion in Practice: An Approach to Anthropology of Religion*. 4th ed. Boston: Pearson/Allyn and Bacon.

Bowie, F. 2006. *The Anthropology of Religion: An Introduction*. Malden, MA: Blackwell.

Braudel, F. 1981. *Civilization and Capitalism, 15th–18th Century*, Vol. I, *The Structure of Everyday Life: The Limits*. S. Reynolds (trans.). New York: Harper and Row.

———. 1982. *Civilization and Capitalism, 15th–18th Century*, Vol. II, *The Wheels of Commerce*. New York: Harper and Row.

———. 1992. *Civilization and Capitalism, 15th–18th Century*, Vol. III, *The Perspective of the World*. Berkeley: University of California Press.

Bremen, J. V., and A. Shimizu, eds. 1999. *Anthropology and Colonialism in Asia and Oceania*. London: Curzon.

Brenneis, D. 1988. Language and Disputing. *Annual Review of Anthropology* 17:221–237.

Brettell, C. B., and C. F. Sargent, eds. 2005. *Gender in Cross-Cultural Perspective*. Upper Saddle River, NJ: Pearson/Prentice Hall.

Briggs, C. L. 2005. Communicability, Racial Discourse, and Disease. *Annual Review of Anthropology* 34:269–291.

Brooke, J. 1992. Rio's New Day in Sun Leaves Laplander Limp. *New York Times*, June 1, p. A7.

Brower, B., and B. R. Johnston 2007. *Disappearing Peoples?: Indigenous Groups and Ethnic Minorities in South and Central Asia*. Walnut Creek, CA: Left Coast Press.

Brown, A. 2001. Communism. *International Encyclopedia of the Social & Behavioral Sciences*, pp. 2323–2326. New York: Elsevier.

Brown, D. 1991. *Human Universals*. New York: McGraw-Hill.

Brown, P. J. 1998. *Understanding and Applying Medical Anthropology*. Mountain View, CA: Mayfield.

Brown, R. W. 1958. *Words and Things*. Glencoe, IL: Free Press.

Burns, J. F. 1992a. Bosnian Strife Cuts Old Bridges of Trust. *New York Times*, May 22, pp. A1, A6.

———. 1992b. A Serb, Fighting Serbs, Defends Sarajevo. *New York Times*, July 12, sec. 4, p. E3.

———. 1997. A Year of Harsh Islamic Rule Weighs Heavily for Afghans. September 24. www.nytimes.com.

Butler, R. 2005. World's Largest Cities: [Ranked by City Population]. http://www.mongabay.com/cities_pop_01.htm.

Buvinic, M. 1995. The Feminization of Poverty? Research and Policy Needs. In *Reducing Poverty through Labour Market Policies*. Geneva: International Institute for Labour Studies.

Carey, B. 2007. Washoe, a Chimp of Many Words Dies at 42. *New York Times*, November 1. http://www.nytimes.com.

Carneiro, R. L. 1956. Slash-and-Burn Agriculture: A Closer Look at Its Implications for Settlement Patterns. In *Men and Cultures*, Selected Papers of the Fifth International Congress of Anthropological and Ethnological Sciences, pp. 229–234. Philadelphia: University of Pennsylvania Press.

———. 1968 (orig. 1961). Slash-and-Burn Cultivation among the Kuikuru and Its Implications for Cultural Development in the Amazon Basin. In *Man in Adaptation: The Cultural Present*, Y. A. Cohen, ed., pp. 131–145. Chicago: Aldine.

———. 1970. A Theory of the Origin of the State. *Science* 69: 733–738.

Carsten, J. 2004. *After Kinship*. New York: Cambridge University Press.

Carter, J. 1988. Freed from Keepers and Cages, Chimps Come of Age on Baboon Island. *Smithsonian*, June, pp. 36–48.

Cernea, M., ed. 1991. *Putting People First: Sociological Variables in Rural Development*. 2nd ed. New York: Oxford University Press (published for the World Bank).

Ceuppens, B., and P. Geschiere. 2005. Autochthony: Local or Global? New Modes in the Struggle over Citizenship and Belonging in Africa and Europe. *Annual Review of Anthropology* 34:385–407.

Chagnon, N. A. 1967. *Yanomamo Warfare: Social Organization and Marriage Alliances*. Ann Arbor, MI: University Microfilms.

———. 1992 (orig. 1983). *Yanomamo: The Fierce People*. 4th ed. New York: Harcourt Brace.

———. 1997. *Yanomamo*. 5th ed. Fort Worth, TX: Harcourt Brace.

Chambers, E. 1987. Applied Anthropology in the Post-Vietnam Era: Anticipations and Ironies. *Annual Review of Anthropology* 16:309–337.

Chatterjee, P. 2004. *The Politics of the Governed: Reflections on Popular Politics in Most of the World*. New York: Columbia University Press.

Chiseri-Strater, E., and B. S. Sunstein. 2001. *Fieldworking: Reading and Writing Research*. 2nd ed. Upper Saddle River, NJ: Prentice Hall.

Chomsky, N. 1957. *Syntactic Structures*. The Hague: Mouton.

Christensen, L. 2003. The Politics of Correction. *Rethinking Schools Online*. Fall. http://www.rethinkingschools.org/archive/18_01/corr181.html.

Clifford, J. 1982. *Person and Myth: Maurice Leenhardt in the Melanesian World*. Berkeley: University of California Press.

———. 1988. *The Predicament of Culture: Twentieth-Century Ethnography, Literature and Art*. Cambridge, MA: Harvard University Press.

Coates, J. 1986. *Women, Men, and Language*. London: Longman.

Cody, D. 1998. British Empire. http://www.stg.brown.edu/projects/hypertext/landow/victorian/history/Empire.html, May 18.

Cohen, M. 1998. *Culture of Intolerance: Chauvinism, Class, and Racism*. New Haven, CT: Yale University Press.

Cohen, M. N., and Armelagos, G., eds. 1984. *Paleopathology at the Origins of Agriculture*. New York: Academic Press.

Cohen, R. 1967. *The Kanuri of Bornu*. New York: Holt, Rinehart & Winston.

Cohen, Y. 1974. Culture as Adaptation. In *Man in Adaptation: The Cultural Present*, 2nd ed., Y. A. Cohen, ed., pp. 45–68. Chicago: Aldine.

Colson, E., and T. Scudder. 1975. New Economic Relationships between the Gwembe Valley and the Line of Rail. In *Town and Country in Central and Eastern Africa*, David Parkin, ed., pp. 190–210. London: Oxford University Press.

———. 1988. *For Prayer and Profit: The Ritual, Economic, and Social Importance of Beer in Gwembe District, Zambia, 1950–1982*. Stanford, CA: Stanford University Press.

Connor, W. 1972. Nation-Building or Nation-Destroying. *World Politics* 24(3).

Cooper, F., and A. L. Stoler, eds. 1997. *Tensions of Empire: Colonial Cultures in a Bourgeois World*. Berkeley: University of California Press.

Council on International and Public Affairs. 2006. How Many Dollars at the Top? *Too Much: A Commentary on Excess and Inequality*. New York, April 24. http://www.toomuchonline.org/articlenew2006/April24a.html.

Crapo, R. H. 2006. *Anthropology of Religion: The Unity and Diversity of Religions.* Boston: McGraw-Hill.

Crate, S. A., and M. Nuttall 2008. *Anthropology and Climate Change: From Encounters to Actions.* Walnut Creek, CA: Left Coast Press.

Cresswell, T. 2006. *On the Move: Mobility in the Modern West.* New York: Routledge.

Crosby, A. W., Jr. 1986. *Ecological Imperialism: The Biological Expansion of Europe 900–1900.* Cambridge: Cambridge University Press.

———. 2003. *The Columbian Exchange: Biological and Cultural Consequences of 1492.* Westport, CT: Praeger.

Cultural Survival Quarterly. Quarterly Journal. Cambridge, MA: Cultural Survival, Inc.

———. 2009. A Closer Look: Sudan—The Peoples of Darfur. http://www.culturalsurvival.org/publications/cultural-survival-quarterly/sudan/closer-look-sudanbrthe-peoples-darfur.

Cunningham, G. 1999. *Religion and Magic: Approaches and Theories.* New York: New York University Press.

DaMatta, R. 1991. *Carnivals, Rogues, and Heroes: An Interpretation of the Brazilian Dilemma.* John Drury (trans.). Notre Dame, IN: University of Notre Dame Press.

D'Andrade, R. 1984. Cultural Meaning Systems. In *Culture Theory: Essays on Mind, Self, and Emotion,* R. A. Shweder and R. A. Levine, eds., pp. 88–119. Cambridge: Cambridge University Press.

Das, V., and D. Poole, eds. 2004. *Anthropology in the Margins of the State.* Santa Fe, NM: School of American Research Press.

Degler, C. 1970. *Neither Black nor White: Slavery and Race Relations in Brazil and the United States.* New York: Macmillan.

de la Peña, G. 2005. Social and Cultural Policies toward Indigenous Peoples: Perspectives from Latin America. *Annual Review of Anthropology* 34:717–739.

DeNavas-Walt, C., B. D. Proctor, and C. H. Lee. 2006. Income, Poverty, and Health Insurance Coverage in the United States: 2005, U.S. Census Bureau. Current Population Reports, Consumer Income. http://www.census.gov/rpod/2006pubs/p60–231.pdf.

Dentan, R. K. 1979. *The Semai: A Nonviolent People of Malaya,* Fieldwork ed. New York: Harcourt Brace.

De Vos, G. A., and H. Wagatsuma. 1966. *Japan's Invisible Race: Caste in Culture and Personality.* Berkeley: University of California Press.

De Vos, G. A., W. O. Wetherall, and K. Stearman. 1983. *Japan's Minorities: Burakumin, Koreans, Ainu and Okinawans.* Report no. 3. London: Minority Rights Group.

De Waal, F. B. M. 1997. *Bonobo: The Forgotten Ape.* Berkeley: University of California Press.

Di Leonardo, M., ed. 1991. *Toward a New Anthropology of Gender.* Berkeley: University of California Press.

Diamond, J. M. 1997. *Guns, Germs, and Steel: The Fates of Human Societies.* New York: Norton.

Dillon, S. 2006. In Schools Across U.S., the Melting Pot Overflows. *New York Times,* August 27. http://www.nytimes.com.

Divale, W. T., and M. Harris. 1976. Population, Warfare, and the Male Supremacist Complex. *American Anthropologist* 78: 521–538.

Douglass, W. A. 1969. *Death in Murelaga: Funerary Ritual in a Spanish Basque Village.* Seattle: University of Washington Press.

———. 1975. *Echalar and Murelaga: Opportunity and Rural Exodus in Two Spanish Basque Villages.* London: C. Hurst.

———. 1992. Basques. *Encyclopedia of World Cultures,* Vol. 4. Boston: G. K. Hall.

Draper, P. 1975. !Kung Women: Contrasts in Sexual Egalitarianism in Foraging and Sedentary Contexts. In *Toward an Anthropology of Women,* R. Reiter, ed., pp. 77–109. New York: Monthly Review Press.

Dressler, W. W., K. S. Oths, and C. C. Gravlee. 2005. Race and Ethnicity in Public Health Research. *Annual Review of Anthropology* 34:231–252.

Durkheim, E. 1951 (orig. 1897). *Suicide: A Study in Sociology.* Glencoe, IL: Free Press.

———. 1961 (orig. 1912). *The Elementary Forms of the Religious Life.* New York: Collier Books.

———. 2001 (orig. 1912). *The Elementary Forms of the Religious Life.* Carol Cosman (trans.). Abridged with an introduction and notes by Mark S. Cladis. New York: Oxford University Press.

Durrenberger, E. P., and T. D. King, eds. 2000. *State and Community in Fisheries Management: Power, Policy, and Practice.* Westport, CT: Bergin and Garvey.

Dwyer, K. 1982. *Moroccan Dialogues: Anthropology in Question.* Baltimore: Johns Hopkins University Press.

Earle, T. K. 1987. Chiefdoms in Archaeological and Ethnohistorical Perspective. *Annual Review of Anthropology* 16:279–308.

———. 1997. *How Chiefs Come to Power: The Political Economy in Prehistory.* Stanford, CA: Stanford University Press.

Eastman, C. M. 1975. *Aspects of Language and Culture.* San Francisco: Chandler and Sharp.

Echeverria, J. 1999. *Home Away from Home: A History of Basque Boardinghouses.* Reno: University of Nevada Press.

Eckert, P. 1989. *Jocks and Burnouts: Social Categories and Identity in the High School.* New York: Teachers College Press, Columbia University.

———. 2000. *Linguistic Variation as Social Practice: The Linguistic Construction of Identity in Belten High.* Malden, MA: Blackwell.

Eckert, P., and S. McConnell-Ginet. 2003. *Language and Gender.* New York: Cambridge University Press.

Edelman, M., and A. Haugerud. 2004. *The Anthropology of Development and Globalization: From Classical Political Economy to Contemporary Neoliberalism.* Malden, MA: Blackwell.

Escobar, A. 1991. Anthropology and the Development Encounter: The Making and Marketing of Development Anthropology. *American Ethnologist* 18:658–682.

———. 1994. Welcome to Cyberia: Notes on the Anthropology of Cyberculture. *Current Anthropology* 35(3):211–231.

———. 1995. *Encountering Development: The Making and Unmaking of the Third World.* Princeton, NJ: Princeton University Press.

Eskridge, W. N., Jr. 1996. *The Case for Same-Sex Marriage: From Sexual Liberty to Civilized Commitment.* New York: Free Press.

Evans-Pritchard, E. E. 1970. Sexual Inversion among the Azande. *American Anthropologist* 72:1428–1433.

Fagan, B. M. 1998. *World Prehistory: A Brief Introduction.* 4th ed. New York: Longman.

———. 2002. *World Prehistory: A Brief Introduction.* 5th ed. Upper Saddle River, NJ: Prentice Hall.

Farner, R. F., ed. 2004. *Nationalism, Ethnicity, and Identity: Cross-National and Comparative Perspectives.* New Brunswick, NJ: Transaction Publishers.

Farooq, M. 1966. Importance of Determining Transmission Sites in Planning Bilharziasis Control: Field Observations from the Egypt-49 Project Area. *American Journal of Epidemiology* 83:603–612.

Farr, D. M. L. 1980. British Empire. *Academic American Encyclopedia,* Vol. 3, pp. 495–496. Princeton, NJ: Arete.

Fasold, R. W. 1990. *The Sociolinguistics of Language.* Oxford: Blackwell.

Fearson, J. 2003. Ethnic Structure and Cultural Diversity around the World: A Cross-National Data Set on Ethnic Groups. *Stanford Education Working Papers.* http://stanford.edu/group/ethnic/workingpapers/egroups.pdf.

Ferguson, R. B. 1995. *Yanomami Warfare: A Political History.* Santa Fe, NM: School of American Research.

———. 2002. *The State, Identity, and Violence: Political Disintegration in the Post-Cold War Era.* New York: Routledge.

Ferraro, G. 2006. *The Cultural Dimension of International Business.* 5th ed. Upper Saddle River, NJ: Prentice Hall.

Fields, J. M. 2004. America's Families and Living Arrangements: 2003. U.S. Census Bureau. *Current Population Reports,* P20–553, November. http://www.census.gov.

Fields, J. M., and L. M. Casper. 2001. America's Families and Living Arrangements: Population Characteristics, 2000. U.S. Census

Bureau. *Current Population Reports,* P20–537, June. http://www
.census.gov/prod/2001pubs/p20–537.pdf.

Files, J. 2005. Report Describes Immigrants as Younger and More
Diverse. *New York Times,* National ed., June 10, p. A11.

Finkler, K. 1985. *Spiritualist Healers in Mexico: Successes and Failures of Alternative Therapeutics.* South Hadley, MA: Bergin and
Garvey.

Finnstrom, S. 1997. Postcoloniality and the Postcolony: Theories of the
Global and the Local. http://www.stg.brown.edu/projects/hypertext/
landow/post/poldiscourse/finnstrom/finnstrom1.html.

Fischer, Steven Roger. 2001. *A History of Writing.* London: Reaktion
Books.

Fiske, J. 1989. *Understanding Popular Culture.* Boston: Unwin
Hyman.

Fiske, J., and J. Hartley. 2003. *Reading Television.* New York:
Routledge.

Fleisher, M. L. 2000. *Kuria Cattle Raiders: Violence and Vigilantism
on the Tanzania/Kenya Frontier.* Ann Arbor: University of Michigan Press.

Food, Inc. promotional website. About the Issues. http://www
.foodincmovie.com/about-the-issues.php.

Ford, C. S., and F. A. Beach. 1951. *Patterns of Sexual Behavior.* New
York: Harper Torchbooks.

Fortes, M. 1950. Kinship and Marriage among the Ashanti. In *African
Systems of Kinship and Marriage,* A. R. Radcliffe-Brown and
D. Forde, eds., pp. 252–284. London: Oxford University Press.

Fortmann, Louise, Camille Antinori, and Nontokozo Nabane. 1997.
Fruits of Their Labors: Gender, Property Rights, and Tree Planting
in Two Zimbabwe Villages. *Rural Sociology* 62(3): 295–314.

Foster, G. M. 1965. Peasant Society and the Image of Limited Good.
American Anthropologist 67:293–315.

Foster, G. M., and B. G. Anderson. 1978. *Medical Anthropology.* New
York: McGraw-Hill.

Foucault, M. 1979. *Discipline and Punish: The Birth of the Prison.*
A. Sheridan (trans.). New York: Vintage Books.

———. 1990. *The History of Sexuality,* Vol. 2, *The Use of Pleasure.*
R. Hurley (trans.). New York: Vintage.

Fouts, R. S. 1997. *Next of Kin: What Chimpanzees Have Taught Me
about Who We Are.* New York: William Morrow.

Fouts, R. S., D. H. Fouts, and T. E. Van Cantfort. 1989. The Infant
Loulis Learns Signs from Cross-Fostered Chimpanzees. In *Teaching Sign Language to Chimpanzees,* R. A. Gardner, B. T. Gardner,
and T. E. Van Cantfort, eds., pp. 280–292. Albany: State University
of New York Press.

Frake, C. O. 1961. The Diagnosis of Disease among the Subanun of
Mindanao. *American Anthropologist* 63:113–132.

Franke, R. 1977. Miracle Seeds and Shattered Dreams in Java. In
Readings in Anthropology, pp. 197–201. Guilford, CT: Dushkin.

French, H. W. 2002. Whistling Past the Global Graveyard. *New
York Times,* July 14. http://www./nytimes.com/2002/01/14
.weekinreview/14FREN.html.

Fricke, T. 1994. *Himalayan Households: Tamang Demography and
Domestic Processes.* 2nd ed. New York: Columbia University Press.

Fried, M. H. 1960. On the Evolution of Social Stratification and the
State. In *Culture in History,* S. Diamond, ed., pp. 713–731. New
York: Columbia University Press.

———. 1967. *The Evolution of Political Society: An Essay in Political
Anthropology.* New York: McGraw-Hill.

Friedl, E. 1975. *Women and Men: An Anthropologist's View.* New York:
Holt, Rinehart & Winston.

Friedman, J., ed. 2003. *Globalization, the State, and Violence.* Walnut
Creek, CA: AltaMira.

Friedman, K. E., and J. Friedman. 2008. *The Anthropology of Global
Systems.* Lanham, MD: AltaMira.

Gal, S. 1989. Language and Political Economy. *Annual Review of
Anthropology* 18:345–367.

Gardner, R. A., B. T. Gardner, and T. E. Van Cantfort, eds. 1989. *Teaching Sign Language to Chimpanzees.* Albany: State University of
New York Press.

Geertz, C. 1973. *The Interpretation of Cultures.* New York: Basic
Books.

Geis, M. L. 1987. *The Language of Politics.* New York:
Springer-Verlag.

Gellner, E. 1997. *Nationalism.* New York: New York University Press.

Gezon, L. L. 2006. *Global Visions, Local Landscapes: A Political Ecology of Conservation, Conflict, and Control in Northern Madagascar.* Lanham, MD: AltaMira.

Giddens, A. 1973. *The Class Structure of the Advanced Societies.* New
York: Cambridge University Press.

———. 2000. *Runaway World: How Globalization Is Reshaping Our
Lives.* New York: Routledge.

Gilmore, D. D. 1987. *Aggression and Community: Paradoxes of Anda-
lusian Culture.* New Haven, CT: Yale University Press.

———. 1991. *Manhood in the Making: Cultural Concepts of Masculinity.* New Haven, CT: Yale University Press.

———. 2001. *Misogyny: The Male Malady.* Philadelphia: University
of Pennsylvania Press.

Gledhill, J. 2000. *Power and Its Disguises: Anthropological Perspectives on Politics.* Sterling, VA: Pluto Press.

Gmelch, G. 1978. Baseball Magic. *Human Nature* 1(8):32–40.

———. 2001. *Inside Pitch: Life in Professional Baseball.* Washington,
DC: Smithsonian Institution Press.

Gmelch, G., and W. Zenner, eds. 2002. *Urban Life: Readings in the
Anthropology of the City.* Prospect Heights, IL: Waveland.

Gogoi, Pallavi. 2005. Wal-Mart's China Card. *Bloomberg Business
Week,* July 26. http://www.businessweek.com.

Goldberg, D. T. 2002. *The Racial State.* Malden, MA: Blackwell.

Golden, T. 1997. Oakland Revamps Plan to Teach Black English. *New
York Times,* January 14. http://www.nytimes.com.

Goleman, D. 1992. Anthropology Goes Looking for Love in All the
Old Places. *New York Times,* November 24, 1992, p. B1.

Goode, Erich. 2008. Drugs in American Society. 7th ed. New York:
McGraw-Hill.

Gottdiener, M., ed. 2000. *New Forms of Consumption: Consumers, Culture, and Commodification.* Lanham, MD: Rowman & Littlefield.

Gough, E. K. 1959. The Nayars and the Definition of Marriage. *Journal of the Royal Anthropological Institute* 89:23–34.

Gramsci, A. 1971. *Selections from the Prison Notebooks.* Q. Hoare and
G. N. Smith, ed. and trans. London: Wishart.

Grasmuck, S., and P. Pessar. 1991. *Between Two Islands: Dominican
International Migration.* Berkeley: University of California Press.

Gray, J. 1986. With a Few Exceptions, Television in Africa Fails to
Educate and Enlighten. *Ann Arbor News,* December 8.

Greaves, T. C. 1995. Problems Facing Anthropologists: Cultural Rights
and Ethnography. *General Anthropology* 1(2):1, 3–6.

Green, E. C. 1992 (orig. 1987). The Integration of Modern and Tra-
ditional Health Sectors in Swaziland. In *Applying Anthropology,*
A. Podolefsky and P. J. Brown, eds., pp. 246–251. Mountain View,
CA: Mayfield.

Greenwood, D. J. 1976. *Unrewarding Wealth: The Commercialization
and Collapse of Agriculture in a Spanish Basque Town.* Cambridge:
Cambridge University Press.

Grekova, M. 2001. Postsocialist Societies. *International Encyclopedia
of the Social & Behavioral Sciences,* pp. 11877–11881. New York:
Elsevier.

Griffin, P. B., and A. Estioko-Griffin, eds. 1985. *The Agta of Northern
Luzon: Recent Studies.* Cebu City, Philippines: University of San
Carlos.

Gudeman, S., ed. 1999. *Economic Anthropology.* Northhampton, MA:
E. Elgar.

Gumperz, J. J., and S. C. Levinson, eds. 1996. *Rethinking Linguistic
Relativity.* New York: Cambridge University Press.

Gupta, A., and J. Ferguson. 1997a. Culture, Power, Place: Ethnography
at the End of an Era. In *Culture, Power, Place: Explorations in
Critical Anthropology,* A. Gupta and J. Ferguson, eds., pp. 1–29.
Durham, NC: Duke University Press.

———. 1997b. Beyond "Culture": Space, Identity, and the Politics
of Difference. In *Culture, Power, Place: Explorations in Critical*

Anthropology, A. Gupta and J. Ferguson, eds., pp. 33–51. Durham, NC: Duke University Press.

Gupta, A., and J. Ferguson, eds. 1997c. *Anthropological Locations: Boundaries and Grounds of a Field Science*. Berkeley: University of California Press.

———. 1997d. *Culture, Power, Place: Explorations in Critical Anthropology*. Durham, NC: Duke University Press.

Guyot, J., and C. Hughes. 2007. Researchers Find Earliest Evidence for Modern Human Behavior. *Arizona State University Research Magazine*. http://researchmag.asu.edu/2008/02researchers_find _earliest_evid.html.

Hall, Edward T. 1990 (orig. 1966). *The Hidden Dimension*. New York: Anchor.

Hallowell, A. I. 1955. *Culture and Experience*. Philadelphia: University of Pennsylvania Press.

Hansen, K. V. 2004. *Not-So-Nuclear Families: Class, Gender, and Networks of Care*. New Brunswick, NJ: Rutgers University Press.

Hansen, K. V., and A. I. Garey, eds. 1998. *Families in the U.S.: Kinship and Domestic Politics*. Philadelphia: Temple University Press.

Harding, S. 1975. Women and Words in a Spanish Village. In *Toward an Anthropology of Women*, R. Reiter, ed., pp. 283–308. New York: Monthly Review Press.

Harper, J. 2002. *Endangered Species: Health, Illness, and Death among Madagascar's People of the Forest*. Durham, NC: Carolina Academic Press.

Harris, M. 1964. *Patterns of Race in the Americas*. New York: Walker.

———. 1970. Referential Ambiguity in the Calculus of Brazilian Racial Identity. *Southwestern Journal of Anthropology* 26(1):1–14.

———. 1974. *Cows, Pigs, Wars, and Witches: The Riddles of Culture*. New York: Random House.

———. 1978. *Cannibals and Kings*. New York: Vintage Books.

———. 2001 (orig. 1968). *The Rise of Anthropological Theory*. Walnut Creek, CA: AltaMira.

Harris, M., and C. P. Kottak. 1963. The Structural Significance of Brazilian Racial Categories. *Sociologia* 25:203–209.

Harrison, G. G., W. L. Rathje, and W. W. Hughes. 1994. Food Waste Behavior in an Urban Population. In *Applying Anthropology: An Introductory Reader*, 3rd ed., A. Podolefsky and P. J. Brown, eds., pp. 107–112. Mountain View, CA: Mayfield.

Harrison, K. D. 2007. *When Languages Die: The Extinction of the World's Languages and the Erosion of Human Knowledge*. New York: Oxford University Press.

Hart, C. W. M., A. R. Pilling, and J. C. Goodale. 1988. *The Tiwi of North Australia*. 3rd ed. Fort Worth, TX: Harcourt Brace.

Harvey, D. J. 1980. French Empire. *Academic American Encyclopedia*, Vol. 8, pp. 309–310. Princeton, NJ: Arete.

Hastings, A. 1997. *The Construction of Nationhood: Ethnicity, Religion, and Nationalism*. New York: Cambridge University Press.

Hawkes, K., J. O'Connell, and K. Hill. 1982. Why Hunters Gather: Optimal Foraging and the Aché of Eastern Paraguay. *American Ethnologist* 9:379–398.

Hedges, C. 1992. Sudan Presses Its Campaign to Impose Islamic Law on Non-Muslims. *New York Times*, June 1, p. A7.

Helman, C. 2001. *Culture, Health, and Illness: An Introduction for Health Professionals*. 4th ed. Boston: Butterworth-Heinemann.

Henry, J. 1955. Docility, or Giving Teacher What She Wants. *Journal of Social Issues* 2:33–41.

Herdt, G. H. 1981. *Guardians of the Flutes*. New York: McGraw-Hill.

Herdt, G. H., ed. 1984. *Ritualized Homosexuality in Melanesia*. Berkeley: University of California Press.

Hill, J. H. 1978. Apes and Language. *Annual Review of Anthropology* 7:89–112.

Hill, K., H. Kaplan, K. Hawkes, and A. Hurtado. 1987. Foraging Decisions among Aché Hunter-gatherers: New Data and Implications for Optimal Foraging Models. *Ethology and Sociobiology* 8:1–36.

Hill-Burnett, J. 1978. Developing Anthropological Knowledge through Application. In *Applied Anthropology in America*, E. M. Eddy and W. L. Partridge, eds., pp. 112–128. New York: Columbia University Press.

Hobhouse, L. T. 1915. *Morals in Evolution*. Rev. ed. New York: Holt.

Hoebel, E. A. 1954. *The Law of Primitive Man*. Cambridge, MA: Harvard University Press.

———. 1968 (orig. 1954). The Eskimo: Rudimentary Law in a Primitive Anarchy. In *Studies in Social and Cultural Anthropology*, J. Middleton, ed., pp. 93–127. New York: Crowell.

Hoenisch, Steve. 2004. Identifying and Resolving Ambiguity. http://www.criticism.com/linguistics/types-of-ambiguity.php.

Hoge, W. 2001. Kautokeino Journal; Reindeer Herders, at Home on a (Very Cold) Range. *New York Times*, March 26, late ed.—final, sec. A, p. 4.

Holden, A. 2005. *Tourism Studies and the Social Sciences*. New York: Routledge.

Hopkins, T., and I. Wallerstein. 1982. Patterns of Development of the Modern World System. In *World System Analysis: Theory and Methodology*, by T. Hopkins, I. Wallerstein, R. Bach, C. Chase-Dunn, and R. Mukherjee, eds., pp. 121–141. Thousand Oaks, CA: Sage.

Hornborg, A., J. R. McNeill, and J. Martinez-Alier. 2007. *Rethinking Environmental History: World-System History and Global Environmental Change*. Lanham, MD: AltaMira.

Hornborg, A., and C. L. Crumley, eds. 2007. *The World System and the Earth System: Global Socioenvironmental Change and Sustainability since the Neolithic*. Walnut Creek, CA: Left Coast Press.

Hunt, R. C. 2007. *Beyond Relativism: Comparability in Cultural Anthropology*. Lanham, MD: AltaMira.

Hunter, M. L. 2005. *Race, Gender, and the Politics of Skin Tone*. New York: Routledge.

Hurtado, A. M., C. A. Lambourne, P. James, K. Hill, K. Cheman, and K. Baca. 2005. Human Rights, Biomedical Science, and Infectious Diseases among South American Indigenous Groups. *Annual Review of Anthropology* 34:639–665.

Inda, J. X., and R. Rosaldo, eds. 2008. *The Anthropology of Globalization: A Reader*. Malden, MA: Blackwell.

Ingraham, C. 2008. *White Weddings: Romancing Heterosexuality in Popular Culture*. 2nd ed. New York: Routledge.

Inhorn, M. C., and P. J. Brown. 1990. The Anthropology of Infectious Disease. *Annual Review of Anthropology* 19:89–117.

International Labor Rights Forum. 2009. About ILRF. http://www .laborrights.org/about-ilrf.

Iqbal, S. 2002. A New Light on Skin Color. *National Geographic Online Extra*. http://magma.nationalgeographic.com/ngm/0211/ feature2/online_extra.html.

Jablonski, N. G., and G. Chaplin. 2000. The Evolution of Human Skin Coloration. *Journal of Human Evolution* (39):57–106.

Jackson, J., and K. B. Warren. 2005. Indigenous Movements in Latin America, 1992–2004: Controversies, Ironies, New Directions. *Annual Review of Anthropology* 34:549–573.

Jayson, Sharon. 2009. Federally Funded Ad Campaign Holds Up Value of Marriage. *USA Today*, Feb. 17. http://www.usatoday.com.

Jenks, C. 2003. *Culture*. 2nd ed. New York: Routledge.

Johansen, B. E. 2003. *Indigenous Peoples and Environmental Issues: An Encyclopedia*. Westport, CT: Greenwood.

Johnson, A. W. 1978. *Quantification in Cultural Anthropology: An Introduction to Research Design*. Stanford, CA: Stanford University Press.

Johnson, A. W., and T. K. Earle. 2000. *The Evolution of Human Societies: From Foraging Group to Agrarian State*. 2nd ed. Stanford, CA: Stanford University Press.

Johnston, B. R. 2009. *Life and Death Matters: Human Rights, Environment, and Social Justice*. 2nd ed. Walnut Creek, CA: Left Coast Press.

Jones, D. 1999. Hot Asset in Corporate: Anthropology Degrees. *USA Today*, February 18, p. B1.

Joralemon, D. 2006. *Exploring Medical Anthropology*. 2nd ed. Boston: Pearson.

Jordan, A. 2003. *Business Anthropology*. Prospect Heights, IL: Waveland.

Kan, S. 1986. The 19th-Century Tlingit Potlatch: A New Perspective. *American Ethnologist* 13:191–212.

———. 1989. *Symbolic Immortality: The Tlingit Potlatch of the Nineteenth Century.* Washington, DC: Smithsonian Institution Press.

Kantor, P. 1996. Domestic Violence against Women: A Global Issue. http://metalab.unc.edu/ucis/pubs/Carolina_Papers/Abuse/figure1.html.

Kaufman, S. R., and L. M. Morgan. 2005. The Anthropology of the Beginnings and Ends of Life. *Annual Review of Anthropology* 34:317–341.

Kearney, M. 1996. *Reconceptualizing the Peasantry: Anthropology in Global Perspective.* Boulder, CO: Westview Press.

———. 2004. *Changing Fields of Anthropology: From Local to Global.* Lanham, MD: Rowman & Littlefield.

Kelly, R. C. 1976. Witchcraft and Sexual Relations: An Exploration in the Social and Semantic Implications of the Structure of Belief. In *Man and Woman in the New Guinea Highlands,* P. Brown and G. Buchbinder, eds., pp. 36–53. Special Publication no. 8. Washington, DC: American Anthropological Association.

Kelly, R. L. 1995. *The Foraging Spectrum: Diversity in Hunter-Gatherer Lifeways.* Washington, DC: Smithsonian Institution Press.

Kent, S. 1992. The Current Forager Controversy: Real versus Ideal Views of Hunter-gatherers. *Man* 27:45–70.

———. 1996. *Cultural Diversity among Twentieth-Century Foragers: An African Perspective.* New York: Cambridge University Press.

Kent, S., and H. Vierich. 1989. The Myth of Ecological Determinism: Anticipated Mobility and Site Organization of Space. In *Farmers as Hunters: The Implications of Sedentism,* S. Kent, ed., pp. 96–130. New York: Cambridge University Press.

Keppel, K. G., J. N. Pearch, and D. K. Wagener. 2002. Trends in Racial and Ethnic-Specific Rates for the Health Status Indicators: United States, 1990–98. *Healthy People Statistical Notes* No. 23. Hyattsville, MD: National Center for Health Statistics.

Kerbo, H. R. 2006. World Poverty: *Global Inequality and the Modern World System.* Boston: McGraw-Hill.

Keynes, J. M. 1927. *The End of Laissez-Faire.* London: L and Virginia Woolf.

———. 1936. *General Theory of Employment, Interest, and Money.* New York: Harcourt Brace.

Kimmel, M. S. 2007. *The Gendered Society.* 3rd ed. New York: Oxford University Press.

Kimmel, M. S., and M. A. Messner, eds. 2007. *Men's Lives.* 7th ed. Boston: Pearson.

Kimmel, M. S., and R. Plante. 2004. *Sexualities: Identities, Behaviors, and Society.* New York: Oxford University Press.

Kimmel, M. S., J. Hearn, and R. W. Connell. 2004. *Handbook of Studies on Men and Masculinities.* Thousand Oaks, CA: Sage.

Kinsey, A. C., W. B. Pomeroy, and C. E. Martin. 1948. *Sexual Behavior in the Human Male.* Philadelphia: W. B. Saunders.

Klass, M. 2003. *Mind over Mind: The Anthropology and Psychology of Spirit Possession.* Lanham, MA: Rowman & Littlefield.

Klein, R. G., with B. Edgar. 2002. *The Dawn of Human Culture.* New York: Wiley.

Kleinfeld, J. 1975. Positive Stereotyping: The Cultural Relativist in the Classroom. *Human Organization* 34:269–274.

Kluckhohn, C. 1944. *Mirror for Man: A Survey of Human Behavior and Social Attitudes.* Greenwich, CT: Fawcett.

Kottak, C. P. 1980. *The Past in the Present: History, Ecology, and Social Organization in Highland Madagascar.* Ann Arbor: University of Michigan Press.

———. 1990a. Culture and "Economic Development." *American Anthropologist* 93(3):723–731.

———. 1990b. *Prime-Time Society: An Anthropological Analysis of Television and Culture.* Belmont, CA: Wadsworth.

———. 1991. When People Don't Come First: Some Lessons from Completed Projects. In *Putting People First: Sociological Variables in Rural Development,* 2nd ed., M. Cernea, ed., pp. 429–464. New York: Oxford University Press.

———. 2004. An Anthropological Take on Sustainable Development: A Comparative Study of Change. *Human Organization* 63(4): 501–510.

———. 2006. *Assault on Paradise: The Globalization of a Little Community in Brazil.* 4th ed. New York: McGraw-Hill.

———. 2007. Return to Madagascar: A Forty Year Retrospective. *General Anthropology: Bulletin of the General Anthropology Division of the American Anthropological Association* 14(2):1–10.

Kottak, C. P., and K. A. Kozaitis. 2008. *On Being Different: Diversity and Multiculturalism in the North American Mainstream.* 3rd ed. Boston: McGraw-Hill.

Kottak, N. C. 2002. *Stealing the Neighbor's Chicken: Social Control in Northern Mozambique.* Ph.D. dissertation. Department of Anthropology, Emory University, Atlanta, GA.

Kreider, R. M., and J. M. Fields. 2002. Number, Timing and Duration of Marriages and Divorces: 1996. U.S. Census Bureau. *Current Population Reports,* P70–80, February. http://www.census.gov/prod/2002pubs/p70-80.pdf.

Kuhn, S. L., M. C. Stiner, and D. S. Reese. 2001. Ornaments of the Earliest Upper Paleolithic: New Insights from the Levant. *Proceedings of the National Academy of Sciences of the United States of America* 98(13):7641–7646.

Kulick, D. 1998. *Travesti: Sex, Gender, and Culture among Brazilian Transgendered Prostitutes.* Chicago: University of Chicago Press.

Kuper, L. 2006. *Race, Class, and Power: Ideology and Revolutionary Change in Plural Societies.* New Brunswick, NJ: Transaction Publishers.

Kurtz, D. V. 2001. *Political Anthropology: Power and Paradigms.* Boulder, CO: Westview Press.

Kutsche, P. 1998. *Field Ethnography: A Manual for Doing Cultural Anthropology.* Upper Saddle River, NJ: Prentice Hall.

Labov, W. 1972a. *Language in the Inner City: Studies in the Black English Vernacular.* Philadelphia: University of Pennsylvania Press.

———. 1972b. *Sociolinguistic Patterns.* Philadelphia: University of Pennsylvania Press.

La Fraugh, R. J. n.d. Euskara: The History, a True Mystery. The La Fraugh Name History. http://planetrjl.tripod.com/LaFraughName/id5.html.

Laguerre, M. 1984. *American Odyssey: Haitians in New York.* Ithaca, NY: Cornell University Press.

———. 1998. *Diasporic Citizenship: Haitian Americans in Transnational America.* New York: St. Martin's Press.

———. 1999. *The Global Ethnopolis: Chinatown, Japantown, and Manilatown in American Society.* New York: St. Martin's Press.

———. 2001. *Urban Multiculturalism and Globalization in New York City.* New York: Palgrave Macmillan.

Laird, S. A. 2002. *Biodiversity and Traditional Knowledge: Equitable Partnerships in Practice.* Sterling, VA: Earthscan.

Lakoff, R. T. 2000. *The Language War.* Berkeley: University of California Press.

———. 2004. *Language and Woman's Place.* Rev. ed. New York: Oxford University Press.

Lambek, M. 2008. *A Reader in the Anthropology of Religion.* Malden, MA: Blackwell.

Lancaster, R. N., and M. Di Leonardo, eds. 1997. *The Gender/Sexuality Reader: Culture, History, Political Economy.* New York: Routledge.

Lance, L. M., and E. E. Mckenna. 1975. Analysis of Cases Pertaining to the Impact of Western Technology on the Non-Western World. *Human Organization* 34:87–94.

Larson, A. 1989. Social Context of Human Immunodeficiency Virus Transmission in Africa: Historical and Cultural Bases of East and Central African Sexual Relations. *Review of Infectious Diseases* 11:716–731.

Lassiter, L. E. 1998. *The Power of Kiowa Song: A Collaborative Ethnography.* Tucson: University of Arizona Press.

Leach, E. R. 1955. Polyandry, Inheritance and the Definition of Marriage. *Man* 55:182–186.

———. 1961. *Rethinking Anthropology.* London: Athlone Press.

Lee, R. B. 1979. *The !Kung San: Men, Women, and Work in a Foraging Society.* New York: Cambridge University Press.

———. 1984. *The Dobe !Kung.* New York: Harcourt Brace.

———. 1993. *The Dobe Ju/'hoansi.* 2nd ed. Fort Worth, TX: Harcourt Brace.

———. 2003. *The Dobe Ju/'hoansi.* 3rd ed. Belmont, CA: Wadsworth.

Lee, R. B., and R. H. Daly. 1999. *The Cambridge Encyclopedia of Hunters and Gatherers.* New York: Cambridge University Press.

Lehmann, A. C., J. E. Meyers, and P. A. Moro, eds. 2005. *Magic, Witchcraft, and Religion: An Anthropological Study of the Supernatural.* 6th ed. Boston: McGraw-Hill.

Leman, J. 2001. *The Dynamics of Emerging Ethnicities: Immigrant and Indigenous Ethnogenesis in Confrontation.* New York: Peter Lang.

Lenski, G. 1966. *Power and Privilege: A Theory of Social Stratification.* New York: McGraw-Hill.

Levine, N. E. 2008. Alternative Kinship, Marriage, and Reproduction. *Annual Review of Anthropology* 37:17–35.

Lèvi-Strauss, C. 1963. *Totemism.* R. Needham (trans.). Boston: Beacon Press.

———. 1967. *Structural Anthropology.* New York: Doubleday.

Levy, J. E., with B. Pepper. 1992. *Orayvi Revisited: Social Stratification in an "Egalitarian" Society.* Santa Fe, NM: School of American Research Press, and Seattle: University of Washington Press.

Lewellen, T. C. 2003. *Political Anthropology: An Introduction.* 3rd ed. Westport, CT: Praeger.

Lewis, M. Paul, ed. 2009. *Ethnologue: Languages of the World.* 16th ed. Dallas: SIL International.

Lewis, P. 1992. U.N. Sees a Crisis in Overpopulation. *New York Times,* p. A6.

Lie, J. 2001. *Multiethnic Japan.* Cambridge, MA: Harvard University Press.

Lieban, R. W. 1977. The Field of Medical Anthropology. In *Culture, Disease, and Healing: Studies in Medical Anthropology,* D. Landy, ed., pp. 13–31. New York: Macmillan.

Lindenbaum, S. 1972. Sorcerers, Ghosts, and Polluting Women: An Analysis of Religious Belief and Population Control. *Ethnology* 11:241–253.

Linton, R. 1943. Nativistic Movements. *American Anthropologist* 45:230–240.

Little, K. 1965. *West African Urbanization: A Study of Voluntary Associations in Social Change.* Cambridge: Cambridge University Press.

———. 1971. *Some Aspects of African Urbanization South of the Sahara.* Reading, MA: Addison-Wesley, McCaleb Modules in Anthropology.

Lockwood, W. G. 1975. *European Moslems: Economy and Ethnicity in Western Bosnia.* New York: Academic Press.

Lohr, S. 2005. Cutting Here, but Hiring Over There. *New York Times,* June 24. http://www.nytimes.com.

Lowie, R. H. 1961 (orig. 1920). *Primitive Society.* New York: Harper & Brothers.

Lucentini, J. 2002. Bones Reveal Some Truth in "Noble Savage Myth." *Washington Post,* April 15, p. A09.

Lugaila, T. 1999. Married Adults Still in the Majority, Census Bureau Reports. http://www.census.gov/Press-Release/www/1999/cb99-03.html.

Madra, Y. M. 2004. Karl Polanyi: Freedom in a Complex Society. *Econ-Atrocity Bulletin: In the History of Thought.* http://www.fguide.org/Bulletin/polanyi.htm.

Malinowski, B. 1929. Practical Anthropology. *Africa* 2:23–38.

———. 1961 (orig. 1922). *Argonauts of the Western Pacific.* New York: Dutton.

———. 1978 (orig. 1931). The Role of Magic and Religion. In *Reader in Comparative Religion: An Anthropological Approach,* 4th ed., W. A. Lessa and E. Z. Vogt, eds., pp. 37–46. New York: Harper and Row.

Malkki, Liisa H. 1995. *Purity and Exile: Violence, Memory, and National Cosmology among Hutu Refugees in Tanzania.* Chicago: University of Chicago Press.

Maquet, J. 1964. Objectivity in Anthropology. *Current Anthropology* 5:47–55.

Mar, M. E. 1997. Secondary Colors: The Multiracial Option. *Harvard Magazine,* May–June, pp. 19–20.

Marcus, G. E., and D. Cushman. 1982. Ethnographies as Texts. *Annual Review of Anthropology* 11:25–69.

Marcus, G. E., and M. M. J. Fischer. 1986. *Anthropology as Cultural Critique: An Experimental Moment in the Human Sciences.* Chicago: University of Chicago Press.

———. 1999. *Anthropology as Cultural Critique: An Experimental Moment in the Human Sciences.* 2nd ed. Chicago: University of Chicago Press.

Marcus, G. E., and F. R. Myers, eds. 1995. *The Traffic in Culture: Refiguring Art and Anthropology.* Berkeley: University of California Press.

Margolis, M. L. 1984. *Mothers and Such: American Views of Women and How They Changed.* Berkeley: University of California Press.

———. 2000. *True to Her Nature: Changing Advice to American Women.* Prospect Heights, IL: Waveland.

———. 2003. The Relative Status of Men and Women. In *Encyclopedia of Sex and Gender: Men and Women in the World's Cultures,* C. Ember and M. Ember, eds., pp. 137–145. New York: Kluwer Academic/Plenum.

Martin, E. 1992. The End of the Body? *American Ethnologist* 19:121–140.

Martin, K., and B. Voorhies. 1975. *Female of the Species.* New York: Columbia University Press.

Martin, Steven P. 2005. Growing Evidence for a "Divorce Divide"? Education and Marital Dissolution Rates in the U.S. Since the 1970s. *Russell Sage Foundation Working Papers.*

Martinez, E., and A. Garcia. 2000. What Is "Neo-Liberalism"? A Brief Definition. http://www.globalexchange.org/campaigns/econ101/neoliberalDefined.html.pdf.

Marx, K., and F. Engels. 1976 (orig. 1948). *Communist Manifesto.* New York: Pantheon.

Mascia-Lees, F., and N. J. Black. 2000. *Gender and Anthropology.* Prospect Heights, IL: Waveland.

Mathews, G. 2000. *Global Culture/Individual Identity: Searching for Home in the Cultural Supermarket.* New York: Routledge.

Maugh, T. H., III. 2007. One Language Disappears Every 14 Days; about Half of the World's Distinct Tongues Could Vanish This Century, Researchers Say. *Los Angeles Times,* September 19.

Maybury-Lewis, D. 2002. *Indigenous Peoples, Ethnic Groups, and the State.* 2nd ed. Boston: Allyn & Bacon.

Mayell, H. 2004. Is Bead Find Proof Modern Thought Began in Africa? *National Geographic News,* March 31. http://news.nationalgeographic.com/news/2004/03/0331_040331_ostrichman.html.

McBrearty, S., and A. S. Brooks. 2000. The Revolution That Wasn't: A New Interpretation of the Origin of Modern Human Behavior. *Journal of Human Evolution* 39:453–563.

McElroy, A., and P. K. Townsend. 2003. *Medical Anthropology in Ecological Perspective.* 4th ed. Boulder, CO: Westview Press.

McKinnon, S. 2005. On Kinship and Marriage: A Critique of the Genetic and Gender Calculus of Evolutionary Psychology. In *Complexities: Beyond Nature and Nurture,* S. McKinnon and S. Silverman, eds., pp. 106–131. Chicago: The University of Chicago Press.

Meigs, A., and K. Barlow. 2002. Beyond the Taboo: Imagining Incest. *American Anthropologist* 104(1):38–49.

Merry, S. E. 2006. Anthropology and International Law. *Annual Review of Anthropology* 35:99–116.

Michaels, E. 1986. Aboriginal Content. Paper presented at the meeting of the Australian Screen Studies Association, December, Sydney.

Miles, H. L. 1983. Apes and Language: The Search for Communicative Competence. In *Language in Primates,* J. de Luce and H. T. Wilder, eds., pp. 43–62. New York: Springer Verlag.

Miller, B. D. 1997. *The Endangered Sex: Neglect of Female Children in Rural North India*. New York: Oxford University Press.

Miller, J. n.d. Alaskan Tlingit and Tsimtsian. Seattle: University of Washington Libraries, Digital Collections. http://content.lib .washington.edu/aipnw/miller1.html.

Miller, N., and R. C. Rockwell, eds. 1988. *AIDS in Africa: The Social and Policy Impact*. Lewiston, NY: Edwin Mellen.

Mintz, S. 1985. *Sweetness and Power: The Place of Sugar in Modern History*. New York: Viking Penguin.

Mitchell, J. C. 1966. Theoretical Orientations in African Urban Studies. In *The Social Anthropology of Complex Societies*, M. Banton, ed., pp. 37–68. London: Tavistock.

Moerman, M. 1965. Ethnic Identification in a Complex Civilization: Who Are the Lue? *American Anthropologist* 67(5, Part I):1215–1230.

Montagu, A., ed. 1997. *Man's Most Dangerous Myth: The Fallacy of Race*. Walnut Creek, CA: AltaMira.

Morgen, S., ed. 1989. *Gender and Anthropology: Critical Reviews for Research and Teaching*. Washington, DC: American Anthropological Association.

Motseta, S. 2006. Botswana Gives Bushmen Tough Conditions. *Tulsa World*, December 14.

Mukhopadhyay, C., and P. Higgins. 1988. Anthropological Studies of Women's Status Revisited: 1977–1987. *Annual Review of Anthropology* 17:461–495.

Mukhopadhyay, C., R. Henze, and Y. T. Moses. 2007. *How Real Is Race? A Sourcebook on Race, Culture, and Biology*. Lanham, MD: AltaMira.

Mullings, L., ed. 1987. *Cities of the United States: Studies in Urban Anthropology*. New York: Columbia University Press.

Murdock, G. P. 1934. *Our Primitive Contemporaries*. New York: Macmillan.

———. 1949. *Social Structure*. New York: Macmillan.

———. 1957. World Ethnographic Sample. *American Anthropologist* 59:664–687.

Murdock, G. P., and C. Provost. 1973. Factors in the Division of Labor by Sex: A Cross-Cultural Analysis. *Ethnology* XII(2):203–225.

Murphy, R. F., and L. Kasdan. 1959. The Structure of Parallel Cousin Marriage. *American Anthropologist* 61:17–29.

Murray, S. O., and W. Roscoe, eds. 1998. *Boy-wives and Female Husbands: Studies in African Homosexualities*. New York: St. Martin's Press.

Mydans, S. 1992a. Criticism Grows over Aliens Seized during Riots. *New York Times*, May 29, p. A8.

———. 1992b. Judge Dismisses Case in Shooting by Officer. *New York Times*, June 4, p. A8.

Nagel, J. 1996. *American Indian Ethnic Renewal: Red Power and the Resurgence of Identity and Culture*. New York: Oxford University Press.

Nanda, S. 2000. *Gender Diversity: Crosscultural Variations*. Prospect Heights, IL: Waveland.

National Academies. 2007. Understanding and Responding to Climate Change: Highlights of National Academies Reports. http://dels.nas .edu/basc/Climate-HIGH.pdf.

Naylor, L. L. 1996. *Culture and Change: An Introduction*. Westport, CT: Bergin and Garvey.

Nazarea, V. D. 2006. Local Knowledge and Memory in Biodiversity Conservation. *Annual Review of Anthropology* 35:317–335.

Newman, M. 1992. Riots Bring Attention to Growing Hispanic Presence in South-Central Area. *New York Times*, May 11, p. A10.

Nielsson, G. P. 1985. States and Nation-Groups: A Global Taxonomy. In *New Nationalisms of the Developed World*, E.A. Tiryakian and R. Rogowski, eds., pp. 27–56. Boston: Allen and Unwin.

Nolan, R. W. 2002. *Development Anthropology: Encounters in the Real World*. Boulder, CO: Westview Press.

———. 2003. *Anthropology in Practice*. Boulder, CO: Lynne Rienner.

Nordstrom, C. 2004. *Shadows of War: Violence, Power, and International Profiteering in the Twenty-First Century*. Berkeley: University of California Press.

Nugent, D., and J. Vincent, eds. 2004. *A Companion to the Anthropology of Politics*. Malden, MA: Blackwell.

Ohlemacher, S. 2006. 2006: The Year of the 300M Mark: Face of America Changes as Country Grows. *Charleston Post and Courier*, June 26, pp. 1A, 11A.

O'Leary, C. 2002. *Class Formation, Diet and Economic Transformation in Two Brazilian Fishing Communities*. Unpublished Ph.D. dissertation, University of Michigan, Ann Arbor.

Omohundro, J. T. 2001. *Careers in Anthropology*. 2nd ed. Boston: McGraw-Hill.

Ong, A. 1987. *Spirits of Resistance and Capitalist Discipline: Factory Women in Malaysia*. Albany: State University of New York Press.

———. 1989. Center, Periphery, and Hierarchy: Gender in Southeast Asia. In *Gender and Anthropology: Critical Reviews for Research and Teaching*, S. Morgen, ed., pp. 294–312. Washington, DC: American Anthropological Association.

Ong, A., and S. J. Collier, eds. 2005. *Global Assemblages: Technology, Politics, and Ethics as Anthropological Problems*. Malden, MA: Blackwell.

Ontario Consultants on Religious Tolerance. 1996. Religious Access Dispute Resolved. Internet Mailing List, April 12, http://www .religious tolerance.org/news_694.htm.

———. 2001. Religions of the World: Number of Adherents; Rates of Growth. http://www.religioustolerance.org/worldrel.htm.

Ortner, S. B. 1984. Theory in Anthropology Since the Sixties. *Comparative Studies in Society and History* 126(1):126–166.

Ott, S. 1981. *The Circle of Mountains: A Basque Shepherding Community*. Oxford: Clarendon Press.

Parkin, R., and L. Stone, eds. 2004. *Kinship and Family: An Anthropological Reader*. Malden, MA: Blackwell.

Patterson, F. 1978. Conversations with a Gorilla. *National Geographic*, October, pp. 438–465.

Paulson, T. E. 2005. Chimp, Human DNA Comparison Finds Vast Similarities, Key Differences. *Seattle Post-Intelligencer Reporter*, September 1. http:// seattlepi.nwsource.com/local/238852 _chimp01.html.

Peletz, M. 1988. *A Share of the Harvest: Kinship, Property, and Social History among the Malays of Rembau*. Berkeley: University of California Press.

Pelto, P. 1973. *The Snowmobile Revolution: Technology and Social Change in the Arctic*. Menlo Park, CA: Cummings.

Peplau, L. A., ed. 1999. *Gender, Culture, and Ethnicity: Current Research about Women and Men*. Mountain View, CA: Mayfield.

Peters, J. D. 1997. Seeing Bifocally: Media, Place, Culture. In *Culture, Power, Place: Explorations in Critical Anthropology*, A. Gupta and J. Ferguson, eds., pp. 75–92. Durham, NC: Duke University Press.

Peters-Golden, H. 2006. *Culture Sketches: Case Studies in Anthropology*. 4th ed. New York: McGraw-Hill.

Petraglia-Bahri, D. 1996. Introduction to Postcolonial Studies. http:// www.emory.edu/ENGLISH/Bahri/.

Piddington, R. 1960. Action Anthropology. *Journal of the Polynesian Society* 69:199–213.

Piddocke, S. 1969. The Potlatch System of the Southern Kwakiutl: A New Perspective. In *Environment and Cultural Behavior*, A. P. Vayda, ed., pp. 130–156. Garden City, NY: Natural History Press.

Plattner, S., ed. 1989. *Economic Anthropology*. Stanford, CA: Stanford University Press.

Podolefsky, A., and P. J. Brown, eds. 1992. *Applying Anthropology: An Introductory Reader*. 2nd ed. Mountain View, CA: Mayfield.

Polanyi, K. 1968. *Primitive, Archaic and Modern Economies: Essays of Karl Polanyi*, G. Dalton, ed., Garden City, NY: Anchor Books.

Pospisil, L. 1963. *The Kapauku Papuans of West New Guinea*. New York: Holt, Rinehart & Winston.

Potash, B., ed. 1986. *Widows in African Societies: Choices and Constraints*. Stanford, CA: Stanford University Press.

Price, R., ed. 1973. *Maroon Societies*. New York: Anchor Press/ Doubleday.

Race, Ethnicity, and Genetics Working Group. 2005. The Use of Racial, Ethnic, and Ancestral Categories in Human Genetics Research. *American Journal of Human Genetics* 77(4):519–532.

Radcliffe-Brown, A. R. 1965 (orig. 1962). *Structure and Function in Primitive Society.* New York: Free Press.

Ramirez, R. R., and G. P. de la Cruz. 2003. The Hispanic Population in the United States. U.S. Census Bureau. *Current Population Reports,* P20–545, March. http://www.census.gov/prod/2003pubs/p20–545.pdf.

Ranger, T. O. 1996. Postscript. In *Postcolonial Identities,* R. Werbner and T. O. Ranger, eds. London: Zed.

Rappaport, R. A. 1974. Obvious Aspects of Ritual. *Cambridge Anthropology* 2:2–60.

———. 1999. *Holiness and Humanity: Ritual in the Making of Religious Life.* New York: Cambridge University Press.

Rathje, W. L., and C. Murphy. 2001. *Rubbish!: The Archaeology of Garbage.* Tucson: University of Arizona Press.

Rathus, S. A., J. S. Nevid, and J. Fichner-Rathus. 2008. *Human Sexuality in a World of Diversity.* 7th ed. Boston: Allyn & Bacon.

Redfield, R. 1941. *The Folk Culture of Yucatan.* Chicago: University of Chicago Press.

Redfield, R., R. Linton, and M. Herskovits. 1936. Memorandum on the Study of Acculturation. *American Anthropologist* 38:149–152.

Reese, W. L. 1999. *Dictionary of Philosophy and Religion: Eastern and Western Thought.* Amherst, NY: Humanities Books.

Reiter, R. 1975. Men and Women in the South of France: Public and Private Domains. In *Toward an Anthropology of Women,* R. Reiter, ed., pp. 252–282. New York: Monthly Review Press.

Rickford, J. R. 1997. Suite for Ebony and Phonics, Discover, December. http://www.stanford.edu/~rickford/papers/SuiteForEbonyAndPhonics.html.

———. 1999. *African American Vernacular English: Features, Evolution, Educational Implications.* Malden, MA: Blackwell.

Rickford, J. R., and R. J. Rickford. 2000. *Spoken Soul: The Story of Black English.* New York: Wiley.

Roberts, S. 2010. More Men Marrying Wealthier Women. *New York Times,* January 18. http://www.nytimes.com.

Roberts, S., A. Sabar, B. Goodman, and M. Balleza. 2007. 51% of Women Are Now Living without Spouse. *New York Times,* January 16. http://www.nytimes.com.

Robertson, A. F. 1995. *The Big Catch: A Practical Introduction to Development.* Boulder, CO: Westview Press.

Robertson, J. 1992. *Koreans in Japan.* Paper presented at the University of Michigan Department of Anthropology, Martin Luther King Jr. Day Panel, January. Ann Arbor: University of Michigan Department of Anthropology (unpublished).

Rodseth, L., R. W. Wrangham, A. M. Harrigan, and B. Smuts. 1991. The Human Community as a Primate Society. *Current Anthropology* 32:221–254.

Rogers, S. More Criticism for Ethanol: Now it's Affecting Food Prices. *Earth First.* http://earthfirst.com.

Romaine, S. 1999. *Communicating Gender.* Mahwah, NJ: Erlbaum.

———. 2000. *Language in Society: An Introduction to Sociolinguistics.* 2nd ed. New York: Oxford University Press.

Root, D. 1996. *Cannibal Culture: Art, Appropriation, and the Commodification of Difference.* Boulder, CO: Westview Press.

Rosaldo, M. Z. 1980a. *Knowledge and Passion: Notions of Self and Social Life.* Stanford, CA: Stanford University Press.

———. 1980b. The Use and Abuse of Anthropology: Reflections on Feminism and Cross-Cultural Understanding. *Signs* 5(3):389–417.

Rouse, R. 1991. Mexican Migration and the Social Space of Postmodernism. *Diaspora* 1(1):8–23.

Royal Anthropological Institute. 1951. *Notes and Queries on Anthropology.* 6th ed. London: Routledge and Kegan Paul.

Ryan, Barbara E., Tom Colthurst, and Lance Segars. 2009. *College Alcohol Risk Assessment Guide: Environmental Approaches to Prevention.* A publication of the Higher Education Center for Alcohol and Other Drug Abuse and Violence Prevention Funded by the U.S. Department of Education. http://www.higheredcenter.org/files/product/cara.txt.

Ryan, S. 1990. *Ethnic Conflict and International Relations.* Brookfield, MA: Dartmouth.

Sahlins, M. D. 1968. *Tribesmen.* Englewood Cliffs, NJ: Prentice Hall.

———. 2004. *Stone Age Economics.* New York: Routledge.

Salzman, P. C. 1974. Political Organization among Nomadic Peoples. In *Man in Adaptation: The Cultural Present,* 2nd ed., Y. A. Cohen, ed., pp. 267–284. Chicago: Aldine.

———. 2004. *Pastoralists: Equality, Hierarchy, and the State.* Boulder, CO: Westview Press.

Salzmann, Z. 2007. *Language, Culture, and Society: An Introduction to Linguistic Anthropology.* 4th ed. Boulder, CO: Westview.

Sanday, P. R. 1974. Female Status in the Public Domain. In *Woman, Culture, and Society,* M. Z. Rosaldo and L. Lamphere, eds., pp. 189–206. Stanford, CA: Stanford University Press.

———. 2002. *Women at the Center: Life in a Modern Matriarchy.* Ithaca, NY: Cornell University Press.

Sapir, E. 1931. Conceptual Categories in Primitive Languages. *Science* 74:578–584.

Savage-Rumbaugh, E. Sue, Jeannine Murphy, Rose A. Sevcik, Karen E. Brakke, Shelly L. Williams, Duane M. Rumbaugh and Elizabeth Bates. 1993. Language Comprehension in Ape and Child. *Monographs of the Society for Research in Child Development* 58(3/4):i, iii, v–vi, 1–252.

Scheidel, W. 1997. Brother-Sister Marriage in Roman Egypt. *Journal of Biosocial Science* 29(3):361–371.

Scheinman, M. 1980. Imperialism. *Academic American Encyclopedia,* Vol. 11, pp. 61–62. Princeton, NJ: Arete.

Scheper-Hughes, Nancy. 1993. *Death Without Weeping: The Violence of Everyday Life in Brazil.* Berkeley: University of California Press.

Schneider, D. M. 1967. Kinship and Culture: Descent and Filiation as Cultural Constructs. *Southwestern Journal of Anthropology* 23:65–73.

Scholte, J. A. 2000. *Globalization: A Critical Introduction.* New York: St. Martin's Press.

Scott, J. C. 1985. *Weapons of the Weak.* New Haven, CT: Yale University Press.

———. 1990. *Domination and the Arts of Resistance.* New Haven, CT: Yale University Press.

Scudder, T., and E. Colson. 1980. *Secondary Education and the Formation of an Elite: The Impact of Education on Gwembe District, Zambia.* London: Academic Press.

Scupin, R. 2003. *Race and Ethnicity: An Anthropological Focus on the United States and the World.* Upper Saddle River, NJ: Prentice Hall.

Sebeok, T. A., and J. Umiker-Sebeok, eds. 1980. *Speaking of Apes: A Critical Anthropology of Two-Way Communication with Man.* New York: Plenum.

Service, E. R. 1962. *Primitive Social Organization: An Evolutionary Perspective.* New York: McGraw-Hill.

———. 1966. *The Hunters.* Englewood Cliffs, NJ: Prentice Hall.

Shanklin, E. 1995. *Anthropology and Race.* Belmont, CA: Wadsworth.

Shannon, T. R. 1996. *An Introduction to the World-System Perspective.* 2nd ed. Boulder, CO: Westview Press.

Sharma, A., and A. Gupta, eds. 2006. *The Anthropology of the State: A Reader.* Malden, MA: Blackwell.

Shivaram, C. 1996. Where Women Wore the Crown: Kerala's Dissolving Matriarchies Leave a Rich Legacy of Compassionate Family Culture. *Hinduism Today.* http://www.spiritweb.org/HinduismToday/96_02_Women_Wore_Crown.html.

Shostak, M. 1981. *Nisa: The Life and Words of a !Kung Woman.* Cambridge, MA: Harvard University Press.

Silberbauer, G. 1981. *Hunter and Habitat in the Central Kalahari Desert.* New York: Cambridge University Press.

Sillitoe, P., ed. 2007. *Local Science versus Global Science: Approaches to Indigenous Knowledge in International Development.* New York: Berghahn Books.

Bibliography

Singer, M., and H. Bauer. 2007. *Introducing Medical Anthropology: A Discipline in Action.* Lanham, MD: AltaMira.

Sinnott, M. J. 2004. *Toms and Dees: Transgender Identity and Female Same-Sex Relationships in Thailand.* Honolulu: University of Hawaii Press.

Slade, M. 1984. Displaying Affection in Public. *New York Times,* December 17.

Smart, A., and J. Smart. 2003. Urbanization and the Global Perspective. *Annual Review of Anthropology* 32:263–285.

Smith, A. T. 2003. *The Political Landscape: Constellations of Authority in Early Complex Polities.* Westport, CT: Praeger.

Smitherman, G. 1986 (orig. 1977). *Talkin and Testifyin: The Language of Black America.* Detroit: Wayne State University Press.

Sneath, Julie Z., Megehee, Carol M., and Deborah F. Spake. 2008. Social Identity in the American South: Mardi Gras Societies in Coastal Mississippi and Alabama. *International Journal of Culture, Tourism and Hospitality Research* 2(2):170–186.

Solway, J., and R. Lee. 1990. Foragers, Genuine and Spurious: Situating the Kalahari San in History (with CA treatment). *Current Anthropology* 31(2):109–146.

Spickard, P., ed. 2004. *Race and Nation: Ethnic Systems in the Modern World.* New York: Routledge.

Spindler, G. D. 2005. *New Horizons in the Anthropology of Education.* Mahwah, NJ: Erlbaum.

Spindler, G. D., ed. 2000. *Fifty Years of Anthropology and Education, 1950–2000: A Spindler Anthology.* Mahwah, NJ: Erlbaum.

Srivastava, J., N. J. H. Smith, and D. A. Forno. 1998. *Integrating Biodiversity in Agricultural Intensification: Toward Sound Practices.* Washington, DC: World Bank.

Stack, C. B. 1975. *All Our Kin: Strategies for Survival in a Black Community.* New York: Harper Torchbooks.

Statistical Abstract of the United States. 1991. 111th ed. Washington, DC: U.S. Bureau of the Census, U.S. Government Printing Office.

———. 1996. 116th ed. Washington, DC: U.S. Bureau of the Census, U.S. Government Printing Office.

———. 1999. 119th ed. Washington, DC: U.S. Bureau of the Census, U.S. Government Printing Office.

———. 2001. http://www.census.gov/prod/www/statistical-abstract-us .html.

———. 2002. http://www.census.gov/prod/www/statistical-abstract-us .html.

———. 2007. http://www.census.gov/prod/www/statistical-abstract .html.

———. 2008. http://www.census.gov/prod/www/statistical-abstract .html.

Statistics Canada. 2001. *1996 Census.* National Tables. http://www .statcan.ca/english/census96/nation.htm.

———. 2003. Religions in Canada. *2001 Census*—Release 8, May 13. http://www12.statcan.ca/english/census01/release/index.cfm.

Stein, R. L., and P. L. Stein. 2008. *The Anthropology of Religion, Magic, and Witchcraft.* Boston: Pearson.

Stevens, W. K. 1992. Humanity Confronts Its Handiwork: An Altered Planet. *New York Times,* May 5, pp. B5–B7.

Stevenson, D. 2003. *Cities and Urban Cultures.* Philadelphia: Open University Press.

Stoler, A. 1977. Class Structure and Female Autonomy in Rural Java. *Signs* 3:74–89.

Stone, L. S. 2004. Gay Marriage and Anthropology. *Anthropology News* 45(5). http://www.aaanet.org/press/an/0405if-comm4.htm.

Strathern, A., and P. J. Stewart. 1999. *Curing and Healing: Medical Anthropology in Global Perspective.* Durham, NC: Carolina Academic Press.

Sunderland, P. L., and R. M. Denny. 2007. *Doing Anthropology in Consumer Research.* Walnut Creek, CA: Left Coast Press.

Suttles, W. 1960. Affinal Ties, Subsistence, and Prestige among the Coast Salish. *American Anthropologist* 62:296–305.

Svoboda, E. 2005. UC Scientist Says Ethanol Uses More Energy Than It Makes / A Lot of Fossil Fuels Go into Producing the Gas Substitute. *San Francisco Chronicle,* June 27.

Swift, M. 1963. Men and Women in Malay Society. In *Women in the New Asia,* B. Ward, ed., pp. 268–286. Paris: UNESCO.

Tanaka, J. 1980. *The San Hunter-Gatherers of the Kalahari.* Tokyo: University of Tokyo Press.

Tannen, D. 1990. *You Just Don't Understand: Women and Men in Conversation.* New York: Ballantine Books.

Tannen, D., ed. 1993. *Gender and Conversational Interaction.* New York: Oxford University Press.

Taylor, C. 1987. Anthropologist-in-Residence. In *Applied Anthropology in America,* 2nd ed., E. M. Eddy and W. L. Partridge, eds. New York: Columbia University Press.

Terrace, H. S. 1979. *Nim.* New York: Knopf.

Thomas, L. 1999. *Language, Society and Power.* New York: Routledge.

Thomas, L., and S. Wareing, eds. 2004. *Language, Society, and Power: An Introduction.* New York: Routledge.

Thompson, W. 1983. Introduction: World System with and without the Hyphen. In *Contending Approaches to World System Analysis,* W. Thompson, ed., pp. 7–26. Thousand Oaks, CA: Sage.

Tice, K. 1997. Reflections on Teaching Anthropology for Use in the Public and Private Sector. In *The Teaching of Anthropology: Problems, Issues, and Decisions,* C. P. Kottak, J. J. White, R. H. Furlow, and P. C. Rice, eds., pp. 273–284. Mountain View, CA: Mayfield.

Tishkov, V. A. 2004. *Chechnya: Life in a War-Torn Society.* Berkeley: University of California Press.

Titiev, M. 1992. *Old Oraibi: A Study of the Hopi Indians of Third Mesa.* Albuquerque: University of New Mexico Press.

Toma, Catalina L., and Jeffrey T. Hancock. 2008. Separating Fact from Fiction: An Examination of Deceptive Self-Presentation in Online Dating Profiles. *Personality and Social Psychology Bulletin* 34(8):1023–1036.

Tomlinson, J. 1991. *Cultural Imperialism: A Critical Introduction.* Baltimore: Johns Hopkins University Press.

———. 1999. *Globalization and Culture.* Chicago: University of Chicago Press.

Toner, R. 1992. Los Angeles Riots Are a Warning, Americans Fear. *New York Times,* May 11, pp. A1, A11.

Trask, L. 1996. FAQs about Basque and the Basques. http://www.cogs .susx.ac.uk/users/larryt/basque.faqs.html.

Trevathan, W. R., Smith, E. O., and McKenna, J., eds. 2007. *Evolutionary Medicine and Health.* New York: Oxford University Press.

Trivedi, B. P. 2001. Scientists Identify a Language Gene. *National Geographic News,* October 4. http://news.nationalgeographic.com/ news/2001/10/1004_Tvlanguagegene.html.

Trudgill, P. 2000. *Sociolinguistics: An Introduction to Language and Society.* 4th ed. New York: Penguin Books.

Turnbull, C. 1965. *Wayward Servants: The Two Worlds of the African Pygmies.* Garden City, NY: Natural History Press.

Turner, V. W. 1974 (orig. 1967). *The Ritual Process.* Harmondsworth, England: Penguin Books.

———. 1995 (orig. 1969). *The Ritual Process.* Hawthorne, NY: Aldine de Gruyter.

Tylor, E. B. 1958 (orig. 1871). *Primitive Culture.* New York: Harper Torchbooks.

U.S. Census Bureau. 2000. http://www.census.gov.

———. 2004. *Statistical Abstract of the United States, 2003.* Table 688, p. 459. http://www.census.gov/prod/2004pubs/03statab/ income.pdf.

———. 2005. *Statistical Abstract of the United States, 2004.* http:// www.census.gov/prod/2004pubs/04statab/labor.pdf.

———. 2006. http://quickfacts.census.gov/qfd/index.html.

———. 2009. Trade with China: 2009. http://www.census.gov/foreign-trade/balance/c5700.html#2009.

Ulijaszek, S. J., and H. Lofink. 2006. Obesity in Biocultural Perspective. *Annual Review of Anthropology* 35:337–360.

Van Cantfort, T. E., and J. B. Rimpau. 1982. Sign Language Studies with Children and Chimpanzees. *Sign Language Studies* 34:15–72.

Van der Elst, D., and P. Bohannan. 2003. *Culture as Given, Culture as Choice.* 2nd ed. Prospect Heights, IL: Waveland.

Van Willigen, J. 2002. *Applied Anthropology: An Introduction.* 3rd ed. Westport, CT: Bergin and Garvey.

Vayda, A. P. 1968 (orig. 1961). Economic Systems in Ecological Perspective: The Case of the Northwest Coast. In *Readings in Anthropology,* 2nd ed., Vol. 2, M. H. Fried, ed., pp. 172–178. New York: Crowell.

Veblen, T. 1934. *The Theory of the Leisure Class: An Economic Study of Institutions.* New York: Modern Library.

Verdery, K. 2001. Socialist Societies: Anthropological Aspects. *International Encyclopedia of the Social & Behavioral Sciences,* pp. 14496–14500. New York: Elsevier.

Vidal, J. 2003. Every Third Person Will Be a Slum Dweller within 30 Years, UN Agency Warns: Biggest Study of World's Cities Finds 940 Million Already Living in Squalor. *The Guardian,* October 4. http://www.guardian.co.uk/international/story/0,3604,1055785,00.html.

Vigil, J. D. 2003. Urban Violence and Street Gangs. *Annual Review of Anthropology* 32: 225–242.

Viola, H. J., and C. Margolis. 1991. *Seeds of Change: Five Hundred Years since Columbus, a Quincentennial Commemoration.* Washington, DC: Smithsonian Institution Press.

Wade, N. 2005. For Gay Men, Different Scent of Attraction. *New York Times,* May 10, late ed.—final, p. A1.

Wade, P. 2002. *Race, Nature, and Culture: An Anthropological Perspective.* Sterling, VA: Pluto Press.

Wagley, C. W. 1968 (orig. 1959). The Concept of Social Race in the Americas. In *The Latin American Tradition,* C. Wagley, ed., pp. 155–174. New York: Columbia University Press.

Wallace, A. F. C. 1956. Revitalization Movements. *American Anthropologist* 58:264–281.

———. 1966. *Religion: An Anthropological View.* New York: McGraw-Hill.

———. 1969. *The Death and Rebirth of the Seneca.* New York: Knopf.

Wallerstein, I. M. 1982. The Rise and Future Demise of the World Capitalist System: Concepts for Comparative Analysis. In *Introduction to the Sociology of "Developing Societies,"* H. Alavi and T. Shanin, eds., pp. 29–53. New York: Monthly Review Press.

———. 2000. *The Essential Wallerstein.* New York: New Press, Norton.

———. 2004a. *The Decline of American Power: The U.S. in a Chaotic World.* New York: New Press.

———. 2004b. *World-Systems Analysis: An Introduction.* Durham, NC: Duke University Press.

Walmart Watch. 2009. Issues: Supplier Relathionships. http://walmartwatch.com/issues/supplier_relationships/.

Ward, M. C. 2003. *A World Full of Women.* 3rd ed. Needham Heights, MA: Allyn & Bacon.

Ward, M. C., and M. Edelstein. 2008. *A World Full of Women.* 5th ed. Needham Heights, MA: Allyn & Bacon.

Warms, R., J. Garber, and R. J. McGee, eds. 2009. *Sacred Realms: Readings in the Anthropology of Religion.* 2nd ed. New York: Oxford University Press.

Weber, M. 1958 (orig. 1904). *The Protestant Ethic and the Spirit of Capitalism.* New York: Scribner.

———. 1968 (orig. 1922). *Economy and Society.* E. Fischoff et al. (trans.). New York: Bedminster Press.

Webster's New World Encyclopedia. 1993. College Edition. Englewood Cliffs, NJ: Prentice Hall.

Wedel, J. 2002. *Blurring the Boundaries of the State-Private Divide: Implications for Corruption.* Paper presented at the European Association of Social Anthropologists (EASA) Conference in Copenhagen, August 14–17. http://www.anthrobase.com/Txt/W/Wedel_J_01.htm.

Weinberg, D. 1996. Press Briefing on 1995 Income, Poverty, and Health Insurance Estimates. Housing and Household Economic Statistics Division, U.S. Bureau of the Census. Washington, DC, September 26. http://www.census.gov/Press-Release/speech1.html.

Weise, E. 1999. Anthropologists Adapt Technology to World's Cultures. *USA Today,* May 26. http://www. usatoday.com/life/cyber/tech/ctf256.htm.

Weston, K. 1991. *Families We Choose: Lesbians, Gays, Kinship.* New York: Columbia University Press.

White, L. A. 1959. *The Evolution of Culture: The Development of Civilization to the Fall of Rome.* New York: McGraw-Hill.

Whorf, B. L. 1956. A Linguistic Consideration of Thinking in Primitive Communities. In *Language, Thought, and Reality: Selected Writings of Benjamin Lee Whorf,* J. B. Carroll, ed., pp. 65–86. Cambridge, MA: MIT Press.

Whyte, M. F. 1978. Cross-Cultural Codes Dealing with the Relative Status of Women. *Ethnology* XII(2):203–225.

Wilford, J. N. 2002. When Humans Became Human. *New York Times,* February 26, late ed.—final, sec. F, p. 1, col. 1. http://www.nytimes.com.

Wilk, R. R. 1996. *Economies and Cultures: An Introduction to Economic Anthropology.* Boulder, CO: Westview Press.

Williams, B. 1989. A Class Act: Anthropology and the Race to Nation across Ethnic Terrain. *Annual Review of Anthropology* 18:401–444.

Williams, L. M., and D. Finkelhor. 1995. Paternal Caregiving and Incest: Test of a Biosocial Model. *American Journal of Orthopsychiatry* 65(1):101–113.

Willie, C. V. 2003. *A New Look at Black Families.* Walnut Creek, CA: AltaMira.

Wilmsen, E. N. 1989. *Land Filled with Flies: A Political Economy of the Kalahari.* Chicago: University of Chicago Press.

Wilson, R., ed. 1996. *Human Rights: Culture and Context: Anthropological Perspectives.* Chicago: Pluto Press.

Winter, R. 2001. Religions of the World: Number of Adherents; Names of Houses of Worship; Names of Leaders; Rates of Growth. http://www.religioustolerance.org/worldrel.htm.

Winzeler, R. L. 2007. *Anthropology and Religion.* Lanham, MD: AltaMira.

Wittstock, L. W., and E. J. Salinas. 2010. *A Brief History of the American Indian Movement.* http://www.aimovement.org/ggc/history.html.

Wolcott, H. F. 2008. *Ethnography: A Way of Seeing.* 2nd ed. Lanham, MD: AltaMira.

Wolf, E. R. 1966. *Peasants.* Englewood Cliffs, NJ: Prentice Hall.

———. 1982. *Europe and the People without History.* Berkeley: University of California Press.

Wolf, E. R., with S. Silverman. 2001. *Pathways of Power: Building an Anthropology of the Modern World.* Berkeley: University of California Press.

Worsley, P. 1985 (orig. 1959). Cargo Cults. In *Readings in Anthropology* 85/86. Guilford, CT: Dushkin.

Yetman, N., ed. 1991. *Majority and Minority: The Dynamics of Race and Ethnicity in American Life.* 5th ed. Boston: Allyn & Bacon.

Yurchak, A. 2002. Entrepreneurial Governmentality in Postsocialist Russia. In *The New Entrepreneurs of Europe and Asia,* V. Bonnell and T. Gold, eds., p. 301. Armonk, NY: M. E. Sharpe.

———. 2005. *Everything Was Forever until It Was No More: The Last Soviet Generation.* Princeton, NJ: Princeton University Press.

Zimmer-Tamakoshi, L. 1997. The Last Big Man: Development and Men's Discontents in the Papua New Guinea Highlands. *Oceania* 68(2):107–122

Zou, Y., and E. T. Trueba. 2002. *Ethnography and Schools: Qualitative Approaches to the Study of Education.* Lanham, MD: Rowman & Littlefield.

Zulaika, J. 1988. *Basque Violence: Metaphor and Sacrament.* Reno: University of Nevada Press.

Chapter 1

p. xxxvi: Friedrich Stark/Alamy; p. 2B: Ron Gilling/Peter Arnold Inc.; p. 3: © Michael S. Yamashita/Corbis; p. 4L: © iStockphoto.com/Bartosz Hadyniak; p. 4R: BananaStock/Jupiterimages; p. 5T: David Samuel Robbins/Getty Images; p. 5B: Michael Dunning/Getty Images; p. 6: © National Anthropological Archives. Neg.#906-B; p. 7TL: © Hubert Stadler/Corbis; p. 7BL: © Nigel Pavitt/JAI/Corbis; p. 7TR: © Danita Delimont/Alamy; p. 7BR: © Ed George/National Geographic Image Collection; p. 8L: © Blickwinkel/Alamy; p. 8ML: dbimages/Alamy; p. 8MR: David Levenson/Alamy; p. 8R: © Ariadne Van Zandbergen/africanpictures.net/The Image Works; p. 11: SSPL/The Image Works; p. 12: © AP Images/Obama Presidential Campaign; p. 13TL: iStockphoto.com/ollo; p. 13TR: © iStockphoto.com/malerapaso; p. 13B: The Kobal Collection/Lucasfilm/Paramount Pictures; p. 14: © Randy Olson/Aurora Photos; p. 15TL: Digital Vision/Getty Images; p. 15TM: © Eric Martin/Iconotec.com; p. 15TR: © Photodisc/Gettty Images; p. 15B: Emma Wood/Alamy; p. 17T: © C Squared Studios/Getty Images; p. 17M: © Bruce Avera Hunter/National Geographic Image Collection; p. 17B: Glow Images/Getty Images

Chapter 2

p. 20: James L. Stanfield/National Geographic Stock; p. 22: © Ferdinando Scianna/Magnum Photos; p. 23: Royalty-Free/Corbis; p. 24TL: Jenny Matthews/Alamy; p. 24TR: © Neil Emmerson/Robert Harding World Imagery/Corbis; p. 24MR: © Mary Evans Picture Library/The Image Works; p. 24BR: Frederick M. Brown/Getty Images; p. 25T: Michael Loccisano/Getty Images; p. 25B: © Tim Pannell/Corbis; p. 26T © William Gottlieb/Corbis; p. 26B: © 2009 Jupiterimages Corporation; p. 27T: Siede Preis/Getty Images; p. 27B: © OSF/Clive Bromhall/Animals Animals; p. 28M: © iStockphoto.com/Eric Isselée; p. 28B: DAJ/Getty Images; p. 30T: © Stockbyte/PunchStock; p. 30L: © Hideo Haga/The Image Works; p. 30R: © Carl D. Walsh/Aurora Photos; p. 31L: Bob Rowan/Corbis; p. 31R: © Robert Holmes/Corbis; p. 32: © iStockphoto.com/Vasko Miokovic; p. 33T: © Frans Lemmens/Getty Images; p. 33B: © Mandel Ngan/AFP/Getty Images; p. 34: Monica Stevenson Photography/Getty Images; p. 35: Anders Ryman/Corbis; p. 36: © Bill Bachmann/Alamy; p. 37: © SuperStock

Chapter 3

p. 40: Melvin Konner/Anthro-Photo; p. 43T: © Peggy & Yoran Kahana/Peter Arnold/Photolibrary; p. 43B: Courtesy of Nancy Scheper-Hughes; p. 44: © AP Images; p. 45: Neil McAllister/Alamy; p. 46T: The McGraw-Hill Companies Inc./Ken Cavanagh Photographer; p. 46B: © Richard Lord/PhotoEdit; p. 47T: Asia Images/Getty Images; p. 48: © Historical Picture Archive/Corbis; p. 49T: © 20th Century Fox. All rights reserved/Courtesy Everett Collection; p. 49M: © Beawiharta/Reuters/Corbis; p. 49B: © Athar Hussain/Reuters/Corbis; p. 50: © Mary Evans Picture Library/The Image Works; p. 51: Courtesy of Conrad Kottak; p. 52: Courtesy of Lisa Gezon; p. 53: © Chris Fitzgerald/CandidatePhotos/The Image Works; p. 54L: Peggy & Yoran Kahana/Peter Arnold Inc.; p. 54R: © iStockphoto.com/Silvia Jansen; p. 55: © Bob Daemmrich/The Image Works

Chapter 4

p. 58: © Ian Berry/Magnum Photos; p. 60BL: © iStockphoto.com/JasonRWarren; p. 60BML: Getty Images/Photographer's Choice RF; p. 60BMR: Adam Gault/Getty Images; p. 60BR: Digital Vision/Getty Images; p. 62T: © Charles Harbutt/Actuality, Inc. ; p. 62B: © Mike Yamashita/Woodfin Camp & Associates; p. 63: Chris Maddaloni/Getty Images; p. 64: © J.L. Dugast/Lineair/Peter Arnold; p. 65T: Alexander Joe/AFP/Getty Images; p. 65B: © Betty Press/Woodfin Camp & Associates; p. 66: © Oleg Popov/Reuters/Cor-

bis; p. 67T: Gideon Mendel/ActionAid/Corbis; p. 67B: © Antonio Scorza/AFP/Getty Images; p. 68: The Kobal Collection/20th Century Fox Television; p. 69: © Photodisc/Getty Images; p. 71T: © Punchstock/Creatas; p. 71B: © UNEP/Peter Arnold/Photolibrary; p. 73: Corbis Super RF/Alamy; p. 74: © Najlah Feanny/Corbis; p. 75: Image Source/Getty Images

Chapter 5

p. 78: © Olivier Martel/Corbis; p. 80B: Donald Pye/Alamy; p. 81T: © Jason Lee/Reuters/Corbis; p. 81B: © Michael Nichols/National Geographic Image Collection; p. 82T: h.e.r./Getty Images; p. 83TL: Corbis; p. 83TR: © Digital Vision/Punchstock; p. 83B: © Sandro Vannini/Corbis; p. 84T: Per-Anders Pettersson/Getty Images; p. 84BL: The McGraw-Hill Companies, Inc./Andrew Resek, photographer; p. 84BR: Bloom Productions/Getty Images; p. 85T: Martin Thomas Photography/Alamy; p. 85B: Noel Hendrickson/Getty Images; p. 86: iStockphoto.com/Mark Strozier; p. 87T: © David Brabyn/Corbis; p. 87B: © Lonny Shavelson; p. 88T: Keijiro Komine/Getty Images; p. 88B: © Steven Kazlowski/Alaska Stock LLC/National Geographic Stock; p. 89T: Ryan McVay/Getty Images; p. 89B: Steve Smith/Getty Images; p. 90T: Bob Daemmrich/The Image Works; p. 90B: Blend Images/Hill Street Studios/Getty Images; p. 91T: © iStockphoto.com/Alexander Drack; p. 92T: Michael Siluk/The Image Works; p. 92B: © Lawrence Jackson, White House Photo; p. 93: Ben Rose/WireImage/Getty Images; p. 95B: © Brand X/JupiterImages/Getty Images; p. 95TL: Barbara Penoyar/Getty Images; p. 95TR: Barbara Penoyar/Getty Images; p. 95TML: Barbara Penoyar/Getty Images; p. 95TMR: Amos Morgan/Getty Images; p. 95TBL: Kevin Peterson/Getty Images; p. 95TBR: Barbara Penoyar/Getty Images; p. 95B: Brand X/JupiterImages/Getty Images

Chapter 6

p. 98: © Author's Image/PunchStock; p. 100B: Steve Raymer/Getty Images; p. 103T: Danita Delimont/Getty Images; p. 103B: © D. Halleux/BIOS/Peter Arnold/D. Halleux/BIOS/Photolibrary; p. 104: © Earl & Nazima Kowall/Corbis; p. 105B: Santokh Kochar/Getty Images; p. 107TL: MedioImages/Getty Images; p. 107TML: © iStockphoto.com/Morley Read; p. 107TM: Kent Knudson/PhotoLink/Getty Images; p. 107TMR: Getty Images; p. 107TR: Steve Allen/Brand X Pictures; p. 108T: © Carl D. Walsh/Aurora Photos; p. 109: © BananaStock/PunchStock; p. 110: Guang Niu/Getty Images; p. 111T: Steve Mason/Getty Images ; p. 111B: Jupiter Images; p. 112T: Burke/Triolo Productions/Getty Images; p. 113T: © Blend Images/Alamy; p. 113B: © John Eastcott/Yva Momatiuk/Woodfin Camp & Associates; p. 114: Frank Micelotta/Getty Images; p. 115T: Elbridge W. Merrill Collection Photograph Collection/Alaska State Library and Archives [P57–028]; p. 115B: Jesse Grant/WireImage/Getty Images

Chapter 7

p. 118: © Owen Franken/Corbis; p. 120B: © Alessandro Di Meo/epa/Corbis; p. 122T: Eduard Korniyenko/Reuters/Corbis; p. 122B © Joy Tessman/National Geographic Image Collection; p. 124: Photolibrary.com; p. 125: © Peer Grimm/epa/Corbis; p. 126: © Burt Glinn/Magnum Photos; p. 127T: Amos Morgan/Getty Images; p. 127BL: AKG Images/The Image Works; p. 127BR: The Kobal Collection/Marvel Enterprises; p. 129: © Douglas Kirkland; p. 131: © Peter Adams/Getty Images; p. 132: © Anders Ryman/Corbis; p. 134T: © Pawan Kumar/Reuters/Corbis; p. 134B: © Tim Mosenfelder/Getty Images; p. 135T: David W. Hamilton/Getty Images; p. 135TL: Library of Congress Prints and Photographs Division [LC-USZ62–13912]; p. 135TML: Brand X Pictures/PunchStock; p. 135TMR: © Bruno Morandi/Hemis/Corbis; p. 135TR: Royalty-Free/Corbis; p. 136: Hans Deryk/Reuters/Corbis; p. 137T: The Image Works; p. 137B: Ariel Skelley/Getty Images

Page references in **bold** refer to glossary definitions.

A

AAA (American Anthropological Association), 16–17, 42–44, 62
Aboriginal Australians, 94, 101, 256
academic anthropology, 61–62
acculturation, **35,** 35*f,* 253
Aché, 101
achieved status, 126–**127**
adaptation, **4**
    culture and, 26
    forms of, 3–5, 4*t,* 5*f*
adaptive strategies, 100–103, 107*t.*
    See also making a living
adat, 172
affection, expression of, 21
affinals, 155–156
African Americans
    Black English Vernacular, 92, 93*f*
    population of, 237
    Rodney King beating and, 239
    women, 175
age, social distinctions based on, 103
agency, 31
age sets, **128**–129, 129*f*
agnates, 152
agriculture, **104**
    animal domestication, 100–101, 104, 106
    compared with other strategies, 107*t*
    costs and benefits of, 105
    horticulture, 103–104, 103*f*
    independent invention of, 36
    indigenous models in, 66
    intensification of, 105–106
    irrigation, 63, 104–105
    pastoralism, 106
    sugarcane plantations, 205–206, 206*f*
    terracing, 104–105, 104*f*
Agta, 170
ahimsa, 193*f*
AIDS, 70–71
AIM (American Indian Movement), 259
Alaska Natives, vitamin D in, 10.
    See also Inuit
alienation, in industrial economies, 109–110

Al Jazeera, 257
alternative ends, 111
American Anthropological Association (AAA), 16–17, 42–44, 62
American anthropology, early, 6
American Indian Movement (AIM), 259
American Sign Language (ASL), 81–82
Anderson, Barbara, 71
Anderson, Benedict, 234–235
anencephaly, 11
animal domestication, 100–101, 104, 106
animism, **187**
Antankarana, 250
anthropology, **3**
    applied (*See* applied anthropology)
    archaeological, 5–6, 12–14, 17
    biological, 5–6, 14–15
    business and, 73–74, 73*f*
    careers in, 74–75
    cross-cultural perspective in, 2–3
    cultural, 5–6, 12, 13*t*
    cultural relativism and, 33–34
    early American, 6, 6*f*
    education and, 66–67, 66*f*
    ethics in, 42–44
    evolution of ethnography, 49–53, 50*f,* 51*f,* 52*f*
    human adaptability, 3–5
    linguistic (*See* linguistic anthropology)
    medical, 60, 70–73, 71*f*
    other academic fields and, 16
    race concept in, 6–12, 7*f,* 10*f,* 11*f,* 228–234
    urban, 67–69, 67*f*
anthropology and education, **66**–67, 66*f*
anxiety, 188, 190
apical ancestor, 149*f,* 150, 150*f*
Appiah, Kwame Anthony, 231
applied anthropology, **17,** 59–75
    academic anthropology *vs.,* 16–17, 61–62
    business and, 73–74, 73*f*
    careers in, 74–75
    current interests in, 62–63, 62*f*
    development anthropology, 63–64

early applications of, 61
in education, 63, 66–67, 66*f*
equity in, 63–64
indigenous models in, 66
innovation strategies, 64–66
medical anthropology, 60, 70–73, 71*f*
in subfields of anthropology, 60–61, 60*t*
urban anthropology, 67–69, 67*f*
archaeological anthropology, 5–6, 12–14, **13,** 17
archaic states, 130, 132, 133
Arembepe, Brazil
    C. Kottak in, 46, 47
    gender roles in, 167
    marriage in, 151
    phenotypical diversity in, 233–234
    team research in, 51–52
    traditional performances and tourism in, 255
Argonauts of the Western Pacific (Malinowski), 49
artifacts, 12
ascribed status, 126, **127**
asexuality, 178
ASL (American Sign Language), 81–82
assimilation, **235**–236, 240, 260
Atlantic slave trade, 134, 205–206
Australian Natives, 94, 101, 256
authoritarian systems, 216
authority, 120
autochthon, 260
autochthony, 260
Avatar (film), 49*f*
Aymarans, 7*f*
Azande, 179
Aztecs, 195

B

balanced reciprocity, 112–113
Balinese culture, 30*f*
bands, **102**
    foraging and, 102–103
    the Inuit as, 123–124, 123*f*
    political regulation of, 135*t*
    the San as, 122–123, 122*f*
    in Service's typology, 121
Barlow, Kathleen, 153
Barth, Fredrick, 236

Basarwa San, 101–102. *See also* San ("Bushmen")
baseball, magic in, 185
Basques, 240
Basseri, 106, 129–130, 130*f*
Beach, Frank A., 179
Bellah, Robert, 195–196
Benedict, Ruth, 6
berdaches, 155
Berry, Halle, 230*f*
Betsileo
    division of labor in, 108, 108*f*, 174
    gender roles in, 174
    key cultural consultants in, 48
    life-cycle events among, 30
    stipulated descent in, 150
    witchcraft accusations among, 194
BEV (Black English Vernacular), **92**, 93*f*
big man, **125**–127, 126*f*, 127*f*
bilharzia, 70
bilingual education, 67
biocultural perspective, 8
biological adaptation, 4–5, 4*t*, 5*f*
biological anthropology, 5–6, 14–15
biomedicine (Western medicine), 71, 72
bipedalism, 27
bisexuality, 178. *See also* sexual orientation
Black English Vernacular (BEV), **92**, 93*f*
blood feuds, 124, 136
BMOC (big man on campus), 119, 126*f*
Boas, Franz, 8, 12
Bodley, John, 215
body movements, communication by, 84–85, 85*f*
Bones, 68*f*
Bosnian Muslim families, 144, 240
Bourdieu, 92
bourgeoisie, **208**
Bourque, Susan, 165
brain size, 27
Braudel, Fernand, 204
Brazil. *See also* Arembepe, Brazil
    faith healers in, 193
    global needs and the Amazon, 251
    phenotype and fluidity in, 233–234, 233*f*
    sugarcane in, 205

telenovelas in, 257
traditional performances in, 255
in world system, 204–205
bridewealth, **156**–157
British colonialism, 211–212, 211*f*, 212*f*
British Sign Language (BSL), 81
Browne, Joy, 141
Buganda, 134, 159
Bumba Meu Boi festival, 255
burakumin, 232–233, 232*f*
Bushmen. *See* San
business, anthropology and, 73–74, 73*f*

C

call systems, **80**–81, 83*t*
campesinos, 259
Canada, minority population in, 231, 231*f*
candomblé, 47
capital, **204**
capitalism, 112, 208
capitalist world economy, **204**
Capoid racial classification, 8
carbon dioxide, 247, 248*f*, 249*f*
careers in anthropology, 74–75
cargo cults, **198**–199
Caribbean nations, sugarcane in, 205–206, 206*f*
Carnaval, 255
Carneiro, Robert, 130
caste system, **133**, 153–154
censuses, 134, 213*f*, 230–231, 230*f*, 234
ceremonial funds, 111
Chambers, Erve, 17
Chaplin, George, 10
Chegança, 255
Cherokee, 112
Chicanos, 227
chief, 132, 132*f*
chiefdoms, **121**
    archaic states and, 130–131
    emergence of stratification in, 132–133, 133*f*
    open- and closed-class systems in, 133–134
    political and economic systems in, 131, 131*f*
    political regulation of, 135*t*
    social status in, 132, 132*f*
children
    care of, 167–168, 168*f*

child labor, 204, 209*f*
    enculturation of, 3, 23
    multiracial, 230–231
    paternity of, 151
chimpanzees. *See also* primates
    call systems in, 80–81, 83*t*
    cultural features of, 27–29, 28*t*
    genetic speech deficit in, 83
    sign language in, 81–82
    tool use by, 27, 27*f*
cholera, 72
Chomsky, Noam, 86
Christianity, 195–196, 196*f*, 197, 253
Chukchee, 195
CIS (Commonwealth of Independent States), 240–241
Civilization and Capitalism, 15th–18th Century (Braudel), 204
civil unions, 155
clans, **150**–151
class consciousness, 208
class systems, 133–134, 208–210
climate change, 246–249, 246*f*, **247**, 248*f*, 249*f*
clitoridectomy, 33
Code of Ethics, 42–44, 62
Cohen, Yehudi, 100, 103
collateral households, 145
colonialism, **211**
    applied anthropology in, 61
    British, 211–212, 211*f*, 212*f*
    cultural imperialism, 254–255, 254*f*
    direct *vs.* indirect rule in, 213
    ethnic conflict and, 240
    French, 212–213, 213*f*
    identity and, 213–214
    imperialism *vs.*, 210
    origins of, 210–211
    postcolonial studies, 214
    settler *vs.* nonsettler countries, 214
color, skin. *See* skin color
color terms, 89
Colson, Elizabeth, 51
Common (music group), 93*f*
Commonwealth of Independent States (CIS), 240–241
communal religions, **195**
communication. *See also* language(s)
    globalization and, 37
    nonverbal, 84–85, 84*f*
    primate call systems, 80–81, 83*t*
    sign language, 81–83

social networking, 87f
Communism, 216–217, 216f
communism, 216
communitas, 186, 190f, **191**
complex societies, **54**–55
conflict resolution, **123,** 125
consumption, global culture of, 257–258, 257f
contagious magic, 188
Convention 169, 259
conversation, in field work, 46–47
cooperatives, 65
Copsa Mica, Romania, 220f
core nations, 204, **205,** 217, 217t
core values, **26**
correlations, **102**
corruption, 217
The Cosby Show, 145f
cremation, 30
creole languages, 87
crimes, 135
CRM (cultural resource management), **17,** 62
Cuban Americans, 227, 227f
cults, 191–192, 197–199, 198f
cultural adaptation, 4–5, 4t
cultural anthropology, 5–6, **12,** 13t
cultural change mechanisms, 34–36
cultural colonialism, **240**
cultural consultants, 48, **49**
cultural ecology, 115, 250. *See also* environmental anthropology
cultural imperialism, **254**–255, 254f
cultural learning, 23
cultural relativism, **33**–34
cultural resource management (CRM), **17,** 62
cultural rights, **34**
cultural sensitivity, 42–43
cultural transmission, **82**
culture(s), **3,** 21–37
   adaptive or maladaptive, 26
   agency and practice in, 31
   definitions of, 3, 22–23
   ethnocentrism and cultural relativism, 32–34
   evolutionary basis of, 26–29, 28t
   global culture of consumption, 257–258, 257f
   globalization and, 36–37
   ideal *vs.* real, 31
   indigenizing popular culture, 256
   influence on development, 1

interactions between, 12
language and thought in, 86–89, 87f, 88f, 89f
levels of, 31–32, 32t
mechanisms of change in, 34–36
nature and, 24–25
particularities in, 29, 30–31
qualities of, 22–26
symbols in, 23–24
transmission of, 3–4, 23
universals and generalities in, 29–30
curers, **71**–72, 71f

D

Dalits, 134f
Darfur, Sudan, 253–254, 254f
Darwin, Charles, 9, 15
daughter languages, **93**–94, 94f
Declaration of Indigenous Rights, 259
defecation, 25
deforestation, 252–253
demonstrated descent, 150
Descartes, Lara, 145f
descent, **229**–230
descent groups, **149**
   innovation and, 66
   patrilineal and matrilineal, 149–150, 149f, 150f
   status and, 132
   in tribal societies, 124
descriptive linguistics, **85**
development anthropology, **63**–64
dialects, 90, 92, 93
dialogic ethnography, 50
diaries, personal, 45
diasporas, **257**
Dickens, Charles, 208
differential access, **132**
diffusion, 30, **34**–35
diglossia, **90**
discrimination, **238**
disease, 49, **70**
displacement, linguistic, 82–**83**
Disraeli, Benjamin, 212
distribution and exchange
   coexistence of exchange principles, 114
   differential access and, 132
   market principle, 112
   potlatching, 114–115, 114f, 115f
   reciprocity, 112–113, 113f
   redistribution, 112, 131

diversity. *See also* ethnicity and race
   biological, 6–12, 7f, 10f, 11f
   human, 225
   multiculturalism, 236–238, 236f, 239
division of labor, 103, 107–109, 166–167, 166t, 167f
divorce, 147, 147f, 157–158, 158f
divorce divide, 158
domestic–public dichotomy, **168,** 175, 178
domestic violence shelters, 181f
dowry, **156**–157, 175
dowry murders, 175
drug use and abuse, 70, 72
Dunn, Janet, 52
Durkheim, Émile, 44, 186

E

Earle, Timothy, 132
ecological anthropology, 115, **250.** *See also* environmental anthropology
ecology, 13
economic production. *See* making a living
economic systems. *See also* making a living
   alienation and, 109–110, 110f
   distribution and exchange in, 112–115, 113f, 114f, 115f
   division of labor in, 103, 107–109, 166–167, 166t, 167f
   economizing and maximization in, 110–111
   means of production, 108–109
economy, **107**
ecosystems, 13
education
   applied anthropology in, 63, 66–67, 66f
   gender gap in, 178
Efe, 101
effervescence, religious, 186
egalitarian bands, 103
emic approach, **48**–49, 70
emotionalistic disease theories, 71
employment. *See* making a living
enculturation, 3, **23**
endogamy, **153**–154
Enduring Voices Project, 94
energy consumption, 218–219, 218f, 219f
enforcement systems, 136

environment
    adaptation to, 4–5, 4t, 5f
    biological anthropology and, 15
    industrial degradation, 219–221,
        220f
    intensive agriculture and, 105
    skull form and, 8
environmental anthropology
    in the 1950s–1970s, 249–250
    deforestation and, 252–253
    ecosystem management in, 250
    global assaults on local economy,
        251, 251f
equity, increased, **63**–64
Eskimos. *See* Inuit
essentialism, **260,** 261
estrus, 29
ethanol, 249
ethics
    AAA Code of Ethics, 42–44, 62
    in cultural resource management,
        62
    in development anthropology, 63
ethnic conflict
    after Rodney King beating, 239
    genocide, 214, 214f, 239–241,
        239f, 240f
    industrialism and, 219
    prejudice and discrimination, 238
    roots of, 238
    in Rwanda, 214, 214f
ethnic expulsion, 240
ethnic groups, 226–**227,** 228–229,
    234–235
ethnicity and race, 225–241, **227.**
    See also ethnic conflict
    assimilation, 235–236, 240, 260
    in Brazil, 233–234, 233f
    in the census, 230–231, 230f, 231f
    colonialism and, 240
    definition of ethnicity, 226–227
    essentialism in, 261
    ethnicity *vs.* race, 228–229, 228f,
        229f
    genocide, 214, 214f, 219, 239–
        241, 239f
    hypodescent, 229–230, 233–234
    indigenous peoples, 221, 259–
        261, 260f
    interethnic contact, 253–255, 254f
    in Japan, 231–233, 232f
    multiculturalism and ethnic iden-
        tity, 236–238, 236f, 261
    nationalities, 234–235
    pantribal movement, 259, 259f

plural society, 236
prejudice and discrimination, 238
race concept, 6–12, 7f, 10f, 227,
    228–229
status shifting, 227
in the United States, 226f, 230–
    231, 230f, 236–238, 236f
ethnic stereotypes, **238**
ethnocentrism, **32,** 62–63
ethnocide (genocide), 214, 214f,
    219, 239–241, 239f, **240**
ethnoecology, **250**
ethnographic present, 50
ethnographic realism, 49
ethnography, **2**
    defining, 2–3
    ethnology and, 12, 13t
    evolution of, 49–53, 50f, 51f, 52f
    problem-oriented, 51
    research methods in, 44–49
    salvage, 49
    survey research *vs.,* 54t
ethnology, **12,** 13t
ethnomusicology, 16
etic approach, **48**–49, 70
Etoro, 32–33, 178, 179–180
Evangelical Protestantism, 253
exogamy, 29, **152**–153, 152f
extended families, 143
extended family households,
    144–145
extradomestic labor, **173**

F

Facebook, 87f, 257
factories, 109–110, 110f, 206–207,
    209f
factors of production, **108**–109
faith healers, 192–193
families, 142–148, **143.** *See also*
    kinship
    changes in North American, 145–
        148, 146f, 147f, 148f, 149f
    extended, 143–144
    among foragers, 148
    industrialization and, 144–145
    nuclear, 29, 65, 143–144, 153
    parenting, 141
    polygynous, 142f, 159f
    single-parent, 147, 148f, 177,
        177f
    in states, 136
    working mothers and, 176–177,
        177f

family of orientation, **143**
family of procreation, **143**
Fantástico, 255
feasting, 115
female genital modification (FGM),
    33
The Feminine Mystique (Friedan),
    176
Ferguson, James, 52–53
field notes, 45
field work. *See* research methods
Finkelhor, David, 153
fiscal systems, 136–**137**
fisheries, 63–64
fishing, 100f
focal vocabulary, **88**–89, 88f
folate, 10–11
food origins, 206
food production, adaptation in, **4,** 5.
    See also agriculture
foraging/foragers
    compared with other strategies,
        107t
    conflict resolution in, 123–124
    correlates of, 102–103
    disease and, 70
    families and, 148
    gender and, 169–170, 170f
    historically known, 100–102,
        102f
    sharing by, 28–29
forced resettlement, 51
Ford, Clellan S., 179
forensic anthropologists, 60, 68f
Fortes, Meyer, 153
fossil fuels, climate change and, 247,
    248
Foster, George, 71
four-field approach, 5–6
FOXP2 gene, 83
fraternal polyandry, 151
French colonialism, 212–213, 213f
Fried, Morton, 120–121
Friedan, Betty, 176
funerals and burial practices, 30, 70

G

gangs, 69
garbology, 14, 60
Gardner, Beatrice, 81
Gardner, R. Allen, 81
Geertz, Clifford, 23, 50
gender, 163–181. *See also* women
    in agricultural societies, 173–174

childcare and, 167–168, 168f
in communication, 84, 84f, 95
definition of, 164–165
in division of labor, 103, 107–
    109, 166–167, 166t, 167f
double standards in sexual behav-
    ior, 168–169, 169f, 173
foraging and, 169–170, 170f
gender roles, 164–165
in horticultural societies, 170–
    173, 171f, 172f, 173f
in industrial societies, 175–177,
    176f, 177f
in matriarchies, 172
in matrilineal-matrilocal societies,
    171
nature and nurture in, 164–165
patriarchy and violence, 174–175,
    174f, 181f
in the patrilineal–patrilocal com-
    plex, 172–173
poverty and, 177
recurrent patterns in, 165–169,
    166t, 167f, 168f, 169f
reproductive strategies and, 168–
    169, 168f, 169f
sexual orientation, 32–33, 178–
    180, 178f
in speech, 90–91
stratification and, 124, 165, 171
U.S. labor force and, 176–177,
    177f
variability in, 178
gender roles, **164**–165
gender stereotypes, **164**–165
gender stratification, 124, **165**, 171
genealogical method, **47**–48
general anthropology, **4**–5. *See also*
    anthropology
generalities, **29**–30
generalized reciprocity, 112–113
genetics, 83, 164
genocide, 214, 214f, 219, 239–241,
    239f
German Roma, 144f
Gezon, Lisa, 2, 52f, 250
Glee, 229f
global climate change, 246–249,
    246f, **247**, 248f, 249f
globalization, **36**
    forces of, 36–37
    global assaults on local auton-
        omy, 251, 251f
    multiculturalism and, 237
    transnational migrations, 258–259

Globo TV, 257
Golden Rule, 194
Goodall, Jane, 27
Goode, Erich, 70
gorillas, language experiments with,
    82
greenhouse effect, **247**, 249f, 252
Guangzhou province, China, 7f
Gullah, 87
Gupta, Akhil, 52–53
Gwembe District, Zambia, 51
Gypsies, 144f

H

Haley, Shay, 93f
Hallowell, A. Irving, 153
Handsome Lake religion, 197–198,
    253
Harappa, 14f
Hard Times (Dickens), 208
Harrison, K. David, 94
health care systems, **71**–72
Henry, Jules, 66
herding, 100–101, 104, 106
Herdt, Gilbert, 180
heterosexuality, 178–179. *See also*
    sexual orientation
Hidatsa, 166, 167
high altitudes, adaptation to, 4–5, 5f
hijras, 178f
Hinduism, 193f, 196f
"Hispanics," 227, 227f, 228, 228f,
    237
historical linguistics, 16, **93**–95, 94f,
    95f
HIV/AIDS, 70–71
Hoebel, E. A., 123
holistic science, **3**
Holocaust, 219
holy water, 23–24
hominids, **26**
hominins, **26**
homonyms, 92
Homo sapiens, spoken language in,
    84
homosexuality, 32–33, 178–180,
    178f
Hopi, 87–88, 87f, 158
horses, 106, 128
horticulture, **103**
    compared with other strategies,
        107t
    gender roles and, 170–173, 171f,
        172f, 173f

overview of, 103–104, 103f
Hugo, Chad, 93f
human evolution, primate traits and,
    26–29, 28t
humanism, 16
humanistic science, 16
human rights, 33–**34**
hunter-gatherers. *See* foraging/
    foragers
hunting
    by early humans, 28, 100
    gender roles in, 166t, 167, 170,
        170f
    horses in, 106
    by primates, 28
Hutus, 213–214, 214f
hypodescent, **229**–230, 233–234

I

ideal types, 131
Ifugao, 104
Igbo, 156
illness, 49, **70**
Ilongots, 165
il-rah, 130
IMF (International Monetary Fund),
    215
imitative magic, 188
immigration, of labor to core coun-
    tries, 205
imperialism, 210, **211**. *See also*
    colonialism
incest, **152**–153, 152f
independent invention, **35**–36
Indiana Jones, 13f
indígena, 259
indigenized culture, **256**
indigenous models, 66
indigenous peoples, **221**, 259–261,
    260f
indigenous rights movement, 259–
    260, 260f
individualism, 21
industrial degradation, 219–221,
    220f
industrialism
    alienation and, 109–110
    compared with other strategies,
        107t
    family organization and,
        144–145
    gender and, 175–177, 176f, 177f
    industrial degradation, 219–221,
        220f

industrialism *(continued)*
    Industrial Revolution, 206–207, 207*f*
    perpetual expansion in, 210
    socioeconomic effects of, 207–210, 209*f*, 210*f*
Industrial Revolution, 206–**207**, 207*f*
infant care, 74
infertility, 157
informed consent, **43**, 46
innovation strategies, 64–66
intellectual property rights (IPR), **34**
Inter-American Development Bank, 215
interethnic contact, 253–255, 254*f*
Intergovernmental Panel on Climate Change (IPCC), 247
international culture, **31**–32, 32*t*
International Monetary Fund (IMF), 215
Internet, top 10 languages on, 95*f*
interpretive anthropology, 50
interracial classifications, 230–231, 230*f*
intervention philosophy, **215**
interviews, 47
interview schedule, **47**
intrinsic racism, 231
Inuit (Eskimos)
    band organization of, 123–124, 123*f*
    foraging by, 101, 169, 170*f*
    vitamin D in, 10
    words for snow, 88, 88*f*
IPCC (Intergovernmental Panel on Climate Change), 247
IPR (intellectual property rights), **34**
Iroquois, 197, 253
irrigation, 63, 104–105
Islam
    media portrayal of Muslims, 197*f*
    national change and, 197, 238
    number of adherents in, 196, 196*f*
    in the Sudan, 253–254, 254*f*

J

Jablonski, Nina, 10
Japan, burakumin in, 232–233, 232*f*
jati, 153
Al Jazeera, 257
Jenkins, Leigh, 87*f*
Jones, Doug, 52
judiciary systems, 135–136

Ju/'hoansi, 101, 170. *See also* San ("Bushmen")

K

Kalahari Desert, 101–102. *See also* San ("Bushmen")
Kanuri, 159
Kanzi (bonobo), 81
Kapauku Papuans, 125–127
Katrina, Hurricane, 247, 249*f*
Kelly, Raymond C., 179
Kent, Susan, 122
key cultural consultants, **48**
Keynes, John Maynard, 215
Keynesian economics, 215
khan, 130
Kibale National Park, Uganda, 28
Kiefer, Christie, 43*f*
kinesics, **84**–85
King, Rodney, 239
Kinsey report, 179
kinship, 141–160. *See also* descent groups; families; marriage
    changes in North American, 145–148, 146*f*, 147*f*, 148*f*, 149*f*
    endogamy and, 153–154
    genealogical method, 47–48
    in humans *vs.* primates, 29
    incest and exogamy, 152–153, 152*f*
    nuclear and extended families, 143–145
    patrilineage *vs.* matrilineage, 149–150, 149*f*, 150*f*
    residence rules, 150–151, 151*f*
    same-sex marriage and, 151, 154–156
    sororate and levirate, 157, 157*f*
    stratum endogamy and, 132
Kipling, Rudyard, 212
Kluckhohn, Clyde, 16
Koko (gorilla), 82–83
Korean Americans, 239
Kottak, Conrad
    on development projects, 64
    Media and Middle-Class Moms, 145
    on phenotypical diversity, 233–234, 233*f*
    photograph of, 51*f*
    research locations of, 2
    research methods of, 46, 47, 48, 52

    on stratification, 133
    on transnationalism, 203
Kottak, Isabel Wagley, 52
Kuikuru, 104
Kurds, 3*f*, 235
Kuria, 113
Kwakiutl, 114–115, 114*f*, 123*f*
Kyrgyzstan, 240*f*

L

labor
    alienation in, 109–110
    child, 204, 209*f*
    division of, 103, 109, 166–167, 166*t*, 167*f*
    in industrial societies, 175
    industrial stratification, 208–210, 208*f*, 209*f*, 210*f*
    labor movement, 208
    in nonindustrial societies, 109
Laguerre, Michel, 237
laissez-faire economics, 215
Lakher, 152
Lakoff, Robin, 90
land, as means of production, 108–109
language(s), 79–95. *See also* communication; linguistic anthropology; linguistics
    Black English Vernacular, 92, 93*f*
    call systems *vs.*, 83*t*
    creole, 87
    dialects, 90, 92, 93
    focal vocabulary, 88–89, 88*f*
    gender speech contrasts, 90–91, 95
    historical linguistics, 16, 93–95, 94*f*, 95*f*
    Hopi, 87–88, 87*f*
    on the Internet, 95*f*
    learning field languages, 46
    loss of, 94–95
    nonverbal communication, 84–85, 84*f*
    origin of, 83–84, 83*f*
    pidgin, 35, 35*f*, 86–87
    Sapir-Whorf hypothesis, 87–88, 87*f*
    sign language, 81–83
    sociolinguistics, 16, 89–92, 91*f*
    standardizing, 213
    stratification and, 91–92, 91*f*
    structure of, 85–86, 86*f*

thought and, 86–89, 87f, 88f, 89f
language subgroups, **93**, 94f
"Latinos," 227, 227f, 228, 228f
law, **123**, 135
law of supply and demand, 112
Leach, Edmund, 154
Leave It to Beaver, 145f
Lee, Richard, 101, 122
Lenski, Gerhard, 209
Less Developed Countries (LDCs), 68
leveling mechanisms, **194**
levirate, **157**, 157f
Levy, Jerome, 158
lexicons, **85**
life-cycle events, 30, 30f
life expectancy, 70
life histories, **48**
liminality, **190**–191, 191t
lineages, **150**–151
linguistic anthropology, **16**
    examples of, 60–61
    interests in, 79, 80
    as subfield of general anthropology, 5–6, 15–16
linguistics
    descriptive, 85
    displacement, 82–83
    historical, 16, 93–95, 94f, 95f
    sociolinguistics, 16, 89–92, 91f
liturgical orders, 189
livelihood. *See* making a living
Living Tongues Institute for Endangered Languages, 94
locally based demand, 59
longitudinal research, **51**
Loomis, W. F., 10
Lovedu, 156
Lucy (chimpanzee), 82

M

Madagascar, 251, 251f, 252
magic, 185, **188**, 189f
majority groups, **227**
making a living, 99–115. *See also* agriculture
    adaptive strategies in, 100–103, 107t
    alienation in, 109–110
    alternative ends, 111
    differential access and, 132
    distribution and exchange in, 112–115, 113f, 114f, 115f

division of labor, 103, 107–109, 166–167, 166t, 167f
economizing and maximization, 110–111
    foraging, 100–103, 102f, 107t
    horticulture, 103–104, 103f, 107t
    Industrial Revolution, 206–207, 207f
    means of production in, 108–109
    modes of production, 107
    peasants, 111
    subsistence activities, 166–167, 166f
maladaptive traits, 26
Malagasy, 66, 251, 252
Malays, 171
Malaysia, industrial alienation in, 109–110
male–female avoidance, 173
Malinowski, Bronislaw
    on diaries, 45
    focus on one site by, 52
    on magic, 185, 188, 190
    salvage ethnography of, 49–50, 50f
    on Westernization, 61
mana, **187**–188
Mardi Gras, 190
Margolis, Maxine, 175–176
market principle, **112**
Marrakesh, Morocco, 22f
marriage. *See also* families; kinship
    bridewealth and dowry, 156–157
    culture and, 25
    definition of, 151
    divorce, 147, 147f, 157–158, 158f
    endogamy, 153–154
    exogamy, 29, 152–153, 152f
    infertility and, 157
    Nayar, 144
    plural, 151, 157, 159–160, 168, 168f, 175
    ratio of divorce to, 147, 147f
    same-sex, 151, 154–156
    sororate and levirate, 157, 157f
    United States trends in, 158f
Martin, M. Kay, 170, 172, 173
Marx, Karl, 194, 208, 208f, 216
Masai, 128–129, 129f
mass hysteria, 110
mass media, 52–53, 256–257, 257f
masturbation, 179–180
matai system, 69
mating, in humans *vs.* primates, 29

matriarchy, **172**
matrilineal descent, **149**, 150f, 171
matrilocality, **150**–151, 158, 171
Mbuti, 101, 102, 113
McDonald's, 206
MDCs (More Developed Countries), 68, 72
Mead, Margaret, 41, 44, 44f
means of production, **108**–109
media, 52–53, 256–257, 257f
Media and Middle-Class Moms (Descartes and Kottak), 145f
mediators, 124
medical anthropology, 60, **70**–73, 71f
Meigs, Anna, 153
Melanesians, 187–188, 198–199, 198f
melanin, 9–11
men. *See* gender
Mende, 129
Merina, 159
mestizo, 259
Mexican Americans, 227, 227f
middle class, in the U.S., 209–210
migrations, 237, 258–259
militaries, 136
Miller, Barbara, 174
Minangkabau, 172, 172f
minority groups, **227**, 231f
mission civilisatrice, 213, 215
modern world system. *See* world system
modes of production, **107**
monocrop production, 205
monotheism, 187, **195**
Morales, Evo, **260**
More Developed Countries (MDCs), 68, 72
morphemes, 85
morphology, **85**
Motseta, Sello, 101–102
movimento, 68
Mozambique, 2f
multiculturalism, **236**–238, 236f, 239
multilocal living, 37

N

naming phase, 46
National Association for the Advancement of Colored People (NAACP), 230
National Council of La Raza, 230

national culture, **31**–32, 32*t*
nationalism, 235
nationalities, 234–**235**
National Organization of Women
    (NOW), 176
nation-state, **234**
Native Americans
    classification as, 230
    distribution and exchange, 112,
        113
    early anthropologists on, 6
    family in, 148
    foraging by, 101
    gender roles in, 166–168
    Handsome Lake religion, 197–
        198, 253
    horses and, 106, 128
    pan-Indian movements, 259
    pantribal sodalities in, 128
    potlatching by, 114–115, 114*f*,
        115*f*
    rites of passage among, 190
    same-sex marriages of, 155
Native Australians, 94, 101, 256
nativistic (revitalization) move-
    ments, 197–198
naturalistic disease theories, 71
natural selection, **9**–12, 10*f*, 11*f*
Navajo, 106
Nayar (Nair), 144
Ndembu, 190
negative reciprocity, 112–113
négritude, 235
neoliberalism, **215**–216
neolocality, **144**–145
neural tube defects (NTDs), 11
Nilotes, 8
nomadism, **106**, 129–130
nonverbal communication, 84–85,
    84*f*
norms, 123
NOW (National Organization of
    Women), 176
nuclear families, 29, 65, 143–144,
    153
Nuer, 88, 151, 155

O

Obama, Barack, 12*f*, 92*f*
observation, as field method, 45–46
office, **131**
O'Leary, Chris, 52

Olympian religions, **195**
Ong, Aihwa, 109–110, 165, 174
online dating, 151
open-class system, **133**
opposable thumbs, 26
osteology, 15
osteoporosis, 10
outcast groups, 154, 232, 232*f*
outsourcing, 205
overinnovation, **64**

P

Pacific Islanders, big man concept
    in, 125–126
paleoanthropology, 15
paleoecology, 13
paleontology, 15
pantheons, 195
pantribal sodalities, **128**
Papua New Guinea, 173, 173*f*, 198
Parker, Ely S. (Ha-sa-no-an-da), 6
participant observation, 44, **45**–46
particularities, **29**, 30–31
pastoralism, **106**, 107*t*
paternity, 151, 155
patriarchy, violence and, **174**–175,
    175*f*, 176*f*
patrilineal descent, **149**, 149*f*
patrilineal–patrilocal complex,
    172–**173**
patrilocality, **150**, 172–173
Pawnee, 166–167
peasants, **111**
periphery, **205**
personalistic disease theories, 71
personhood, 72
Peters, John Durham, 52
phenotype, 7–9, **233**
Phipps, Susie Guillory, 229
phonemes, **85**–86, 86*f*
phonemics, **86**
phonetics, **86**
phonology, **85**–86, 86*f*
pidgin, 35, 35*f*, 86–87
PIE (Proto-Indo-European), 93, 94*f*
plural marriages, **157**
    polyandry, 151, 157, 160, 168*f*
    polygyny, 142*f*, 157, 159–160,
        159*f*, 168*f*, 175
plural society, **236**
Polanyi, Karl, 112
political organization, 119–137

agricultural intensification and,
    105–106
bands, 102–103, 121, 122–124
chiefdoms, 121, 130–134, 131*f*,
    132*f*, 133*f*
definition of, 120–121
foraging and, 102–103
states, 130, 132–133, 134–137,
    135*t*
tribal societies, 124–130, 126*f*,
    127*f*
types and trends in, 121–122
political scientists, 12
polling, 54
polyandry, 151, **157**, 160, 168*f*
polygamy. *See* plural marriages
polygyny, **157**
    families in, 142*f*, 159*f*
    overview of, 157, 159–160
    polyandry and, 168, 168*f*
    protection for women in, 175
Polynesia
    chiefdoms in, 131
    racial classification and, 7
    religion in, 188
polytheism, 187, **195**
population control, 134–135
population growth, 207
Pospisil, Leopold, 125–126
postcolonial studies, **214**
postmodern, **259**
postmodernism, **259**
postmodernity, **258**, 259
postsocialist societies, 216–217
potlatch, **114**–115, 114*f*, 115*f*
poverty, 145, 177
power, 120, 127*f*, **133**
practical anthropology. *See* applied
    anthropology
practice theory, 31
pregnancy, folate deficiencies in,
    10–11
prejudice, **238**
prestige, **133**. *See also* status
    in chiefdoms and states, 132
    gender and, 124, 165
    in the Inuit, 124
    warfare and, 172–173
priesthoods, 195
primates, **15**. *See also* chimpanzees
    call systems in, 80–81, 83*t*
    humans compared with other,
        26–29, 28*t*
    incest in, 153

sign language in, 81–83
primatology, 15
private–public contrast, 169, 175, 178
problem-oriented ethnography, 51
productivity, **82**
profit motive, 110
progeny price, **156**–157
proletariat, **208**
Proto-Indo-European (PIE), 93, 94f
protolanguage, **93**–94, 94f
"psychic unity of humanity," 29
public archaeology, 17
Puerto Ricans, 227, 227f
"pygmies," 101, 113

Q

Qashqai, 106, 129–130, 130f
questionnaire procedures, 47

R

race concept, **227**. *See also* ethnicity and race
    biological diversity and, 6–12
    ethnicity and, 228–229
    "Hispanic" and, 227, 227f, 228, 228f
    hypodescent, 229–230, 230f
    in racial classification, 6–9
    social construction of, 229–234, 230f, 231f, 232f, 233f
racial classification, **6**–9
racial identity, 229–230
racism, **227**, 231–233
Rambo, 256
random sampling, **53**
Rathje, William, 14
reciprocity, **112**–113, 113f
reciprocity continuum, 112–**113**
Redfield, Robert, 68
redistribution, **112**, 131
reflexive ethnography, 50
refugees, **240**
religion, **186**. *See also individual religions*
    in chiefdoms, 131
    current world religions, 196, 196f
    definitions of, 186
    magic and, 185, 188, 189f
    Marx on, 194

powers and forces in, 187–188
proselytizing, 253–254
rites of passage, 190–192, 190f, 191t
rituals in, 189–190, 199
same-sex marriage and, 155
secular rituals and, 199, 199f
social change and, 197–199, 198f, 253
social control and, 192–194, 193f
solace and, 188–189, 189f
spiritual beings in, 187, 187f
totemism, 192
types of, 194–196, 195t
rent funds, 111
replacement funds, 111
reproductive strategies, 168–169, 168f, 169f
research methods, 44–55
    conversation and interviewing, 46–47
    culture, space, and scale in, 52–53
    in evolution of ethnography, 49–53, 50f
    genealogical method, 47–48
    interview schedule, 47
    key cultural consultants, 48
    life histories, 48
    local beliefs and perceptions, 48–49
    longitudinal research, 51
    observation and participant observation, 44, 45–46
    problem-oriented, 51
    survey research, 47, 53–55, 54t
    team research, 51–52
residence rules, 150–151, 151f
revitalization movements, **197**–199, 198f, 253
rice cultivation, 104f, 108, 108f
rickets, 10, 11f
rights, human *vs.* cultural, 34
rites of intensification, 192
rites of passage, **190**–192, 190f, 191t
rituals, **189**–190, 199, 199f
Robertson, Jennifer, 231
Roma, 144f
Roman Catholicism, 23–24
Romance languages, 93
Rosaldo, Michelle, 165
Roxo, Gui, 51f
rule of hypodescent, 229–230
rural-urban continuum, 68–69

Rwanda and Burundi, 213–214, 214f, 219

S

Salish, 114–115, 114f, 123f
salvage ethnography, 49
Samburu, 7f
same-sex marriages, 151, 154–156
Samis (Laplanders), 106
Samoans, 69, 132f
sample, **53**
San ("Bushmen")
    foraging by, 101–102
    gender and, 170
    land as means of production in, 109
    political organization of, 122–123, 122f
    racial classification and, 8
Sanday, Peggy, 168–169, 172
sanitary citizens, 72
Sapir, Edward, 87
Sapir-Whorf hypothesis, **87**–88, 87f
Scheper-Hughes, Nancy, 43
Schiavo, Terri, 72–73
schistosomiasis, 70
science, **16**
scientific medicine, **72**
Scudder, Thayer, 51
SE (Standard English), 86, 86f
Second World, 216–217, 216f
secret societies, 129
sectarian violence, 238
secular rituals, 199, 199f
Semai, 113
semantics, **89**
semiperiphery, 204–**205**
seniority of descent, 132
serial monogamy, 159
Service, Elman, 121
sexual behavior
    double standards in, 168–169, 169f, 173
    ethnocentrism and, 32–33
    incest, 152–153, 152f
    sexual orientation and, 32–33, 178–180, 178f
    variability in, 179–180
sexual dimorphism, **164**
sexually transmitted diseases (STDs), 71
sexual orientation, 32–33, **178**–180, 178f

Shaheen, Jack, 197*f*
shamans, 71, 124, **194**–195
shifting cultivation, 104
Shiites, 238
Shoshone, 148
sign language, 81–83
silent trade, 113
single-parent families, 147, 148*f*, 177, 177*f*
situational negotiation of social identity, 227
skin color
    difficulties of classification from, 7–9
    map of, 10*f*
    natural selection and, 9–12, 10*f*, 11*f*
slash-and-burn techniques, 103
slavery, **133**–134, 135, 205–206
Smart, Alan and Josephine, 67
Smith, Adam, 215
social funds, 111
social indicators, 55
social networking, 87*f*, 257
sociolinguistics, 16, **89**–92, 91*f*
sociopolitical typology, **121**–122
sodalities, 128
Soetoro, Stanley Ann Dunham, 12*f*
song battle, 124
sororate, **157,** 157*f*
South Ossetia, 240*f*
Soviet Union, 216–217, 216*f*, 240, 240*f*
species, definition of, 6
speech, 83, 85–86, 86*f*
spina bifida, 11–12
spirit possession, 110
sports, focal vocabulary in, 89, 89*f*
Standard (American) English (SE), 86, 86*f*
states (nation-states), **121**
    earliest, 130
    enforcement systems, 136
    fiscal systems, 136–137
    judiciary systems, 135–136
    political regulation of, 135*t*
    population control in, 134–135
    social status in, 132
    stratification in, 133
status, **127**. *See also* prestige; stratification
    ascribed *vs.* achieved, 126–127
    in chiefdoms and states, 132

language pronunciation and, 90, 91–92, 91*f*
STDs (sexually transmitted diseases), 71
stereotypes, **164**–165, **238**
stipulated descent, 150
Stoler, Ann, 165
Stonehenge, 131, 131*f*
stratification, **133**
    in chiefdoms, 132–133
    development and, 64, 64*f*
    gender, 124, 165, 171
    industrial, 208–210, 208*f*, 209*f*, 210*f*
    in Japan, 232
    open- and closed-class systems, 133–134
    sumptuary goods for the elites, 137
    symbolic domination and, 91–92, 91*f*
    Weber's dimensions of, 133, 133*f*
stratum endogamy, 132
style shifts, **90**
subcultures, **32**
subordinate stratum, **133**
subsistence funds, 111
subspecies, definition of, 6
Sudan, 253–254, 254*f*
sugarcane, 205–206, 206*f*
Sukuma, 213
sumptuary goods, 137
Sunnis, 238
superordinate stratum, **133**
survey research, 47, **53**–55, 54*t*
susto, 71
Suttles, Wayne, 115
swastikas, 24
symbiosis, 106
symbolic capital, 92
symbolic domination, 91–92, 91*f*
symbols, **23**–24
syntactic ambiguity, 85
syntax, **85**

T

taboos, **188**
Taliban Movement, 193–194, 193*f*
Tanala, 30*f*
Tannen, Deborah, 84, 91, 95
tarawads, 144
taxes, 137
team research, 51–52

technology, social impact of, 63–64
telenovelas, 257
television viewing, 256–257
Ten Commandments, 194
termiting, 27
Terrace, Herbert, 83
terracing, 104–105, 104*f*
theft, 124
Theory of the Leisure Class (Veblen), 114–115
time, language and, 87–88, 87*f*
Titiev, Mischa, 158
Tiwi, 159
Tlingit, 115*f*
Togo, 190*f*
tonowi, 126
tools, primates and, 27, 27*f*
top-down change, 59
totalitarian systems, 216
totemism, 192
totems, 150, 192
transhumance, **106**
transvestism, 179
tribal societies
    big man in, 125–127, 126*f*, 127*f*
    nomadic politics, 129–130
    pantribal sodalities and age grades, 127–129, 129*f*
    political regulation of, 135*t*
    village head in, 124–125, 125*f*
tribes, **121**
trickle-down economics, 216
Trobriand Islanders, 17*f*, 50*f*, 188, 189*f*
tropics, skin color and, 9–12, 10*f*, 11*f*
tulafale, 132*f*
Turkana, 106
Turner, Victor, 186, 191
Tutsis, 213–214, 214*f*
Twitter, 87*f*
Tylor, Edward Burnett, 22–23, 187

U

Uganda, 240
underdifferentiation, **65**–66, 65*f*
unilineal descent, **149**–150, 149*f*, 150*f*
United Nations, on human rights, 34
United States Census, 230–231, 230*f*
universal grammar, 86
universals, **29**–30
urban anthropology, 67–69, 67*f*, **68**

UV radiation, 9–12, 11*f*

V

van Vugt, Janine, 2*f*
variables, **54**
varna, 153
Vayda, Andrew, 115
Veblen, Thorstein, 114–115
vertical mobility, **133**
Vietnam War, 61, 62*f*
Vigil, James, 69
The Village Headmaster, 257
village heads, 124–**125,** 125*f*
violence
    domestic violence shelters, 181*f*
    by gangs, 69
    genocide, 214, 214*f,* 219
    patriarchy and, 174–175, 174*f,*
        175*f*
    sectarian, 238
vitamin D, 10–12, 11*f*
Voorhies, Barbara, 170, 172, 173

W

Wallace, Alfred Russel, 9, 194–195,
    195*t*
Wallace, Anthony F. C., 186
warfare
    gender and, 170
    in the patrilineal–patrilocal com-
        plex, 172–173
    tribal, 124
    women's work roles and, 175–
        176, 176*f*
Warren, Kay, 165
Washoe (chimpanzee), 81–82

wealth, **133**
wealth inequities, 209–210, 210*f*
The Wealth of Nations (Smith), 215
Weber, Max, 133, 133*f,* 208, 210,
    210*f*
Wedel, Janine, 217
weretigers, 110
Westernization, 61, **62,** 253
WGIP (Working Group on Indig-
    enous Populations), 259
When Languages Die (Harrison), 94
White, Leslie, 23
"white man's burden," 212, 213, 215
Whorf, Benjamin Lee, 87
Williams, Linda M., 153
Williams, Pharrell, 93*f*
Wilmsen, Edwin, 122
witchcraft accusations, 194
women. *See also* gender
    in agricultural societies, 173–174
    childcare by, 167–168, 168*f*
    poverty and, 177
    in U.S. labor force, 176–177, 177*f*
    violence against, 174–175, 174*f,*
        175*f,* 181*f*
work. *See* making a living
working class, **208**
Working Group on Indigenous Pop-
    ulations (WGIP), 259
World Bank, 215, 217
World Conference of Indigenous
    Peoples, 259, 259*f*
world system, 203–221
    ascent and decline of nations in,
        217–221, 217*t,* 218*f,* 219*f,*
        220*f*
    colonialism and, 61, 210–214,
        211*f,* 212*f,* 213*f*

communism in, 216–217, 216*f*
emergence of, 205–206
energy consumption in, 218–219,
    218*f,* 219*f*
indigenous peoples in, 221, 259–
    260, 260*f*
industrial degradation, 219–221,
    220*f*
Industrial Revolution and, 206–
    207, 207*f*
industrial stratification, 208–210,
    208*f,* 209*f,* 210*f*
postcolonial studies, 214
postsocialist transitions, 217
role of development in, 215–216
socioeconomic effects of, 207–
    210, 209*f,* 210*f*
transnationalism, 203
world-system theory, 204–205
world-system theory, 204–**205**
Worldwide Fund for Nature, 250
World Wildlife Fund, 250
wudu, 70

Y

Yanomami
    incest in, 153
    patrilineal–patrilocal complex in,
        172–173, 175
    specialization in, 109
    village head in, 124–125, 125*f*
Yeltsin, Boris, 217
Yurchak, Alexei, 217

Z

zadruga, 144

MAP ATLAS

CONTENTS

Map 1   Annual Percent of World Forest Loss, 1990–2000

Map 2   Major Primate Groups

Map 3   Evolution of the Primates

Map 4   Early Hominins (and Hominids): Origins and Diffusion

Map 5   The Emergence of Modern Humans

Map 6   Origins and Distribution of Modern Humans

Map 7   The Distribution of Human Skin Color (Before C.E. 1400)

Map 8   The Origin and Spread of Food Production

Map 9   Ancient Civilizations of the Old World

Map 10   Ethnographic Study Sites Prior to 1950

Map 11   Major Families of World Languages

Map 12   World Land Use, C.E. 1500

Map 13   Organized States and Chiefdoms, C.E. 1500

Map 14   Female/Male Inequality in Education and Employment

Map 15   World Religions

Map 16   Total Annual Energy Consumption by Country

Map 17   The Quality of Life: The Index of Human Development, 2007

Map 18   Global Warming

MAP 1

Annual Percent of World Forest Loss, 1990–2000

Deforestation is a major environmental problem. In the tropics, large corporations clear forests seeking hardwoods for the global market in furniture and fine woods. As well, the agriculturally driven clearing of the great rain forests of the Amazon Basin, west and central Africa, Middle America, and Southeast Asia has drawn public attention. Reduced forest cover means the world's vegetation system will absorb less carbon dioxide, resulting in global warming. Of concern, too, is the loss of biodiversity (large numbers of plants and animals), the destruction of soil systems, and disruptions in water supply that accompany clearing.

QUESTIONS

Look at Map 1, "Annual Percent of World Forest Loss, 1990–2000."

1. On what continents do you find stable or increased forest cover?

2. Are there areas of Africa with stable or increased forest cover? Where are they? What might the reasons be for this lack of deforestation?

3. How does deforestation in India compare with the area to its east, which includes mainland and insular Southeast Asia?

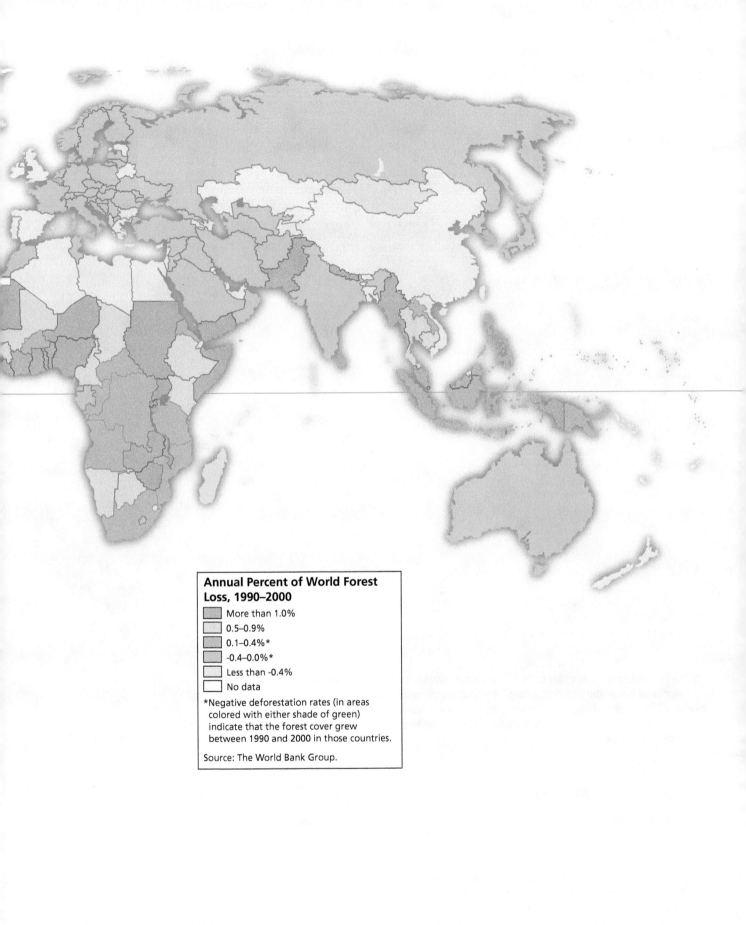

**Annual Percent of World Forest
Loss, 1990–2000**

More than 1.0%

0.5–0.9%

0.1–0.4%*

-0.4–0.0%*

Less than -0.4%

No data

*Negative deforestation rates (in areas
 colored with either shade of green)
 indicate that the forest cover grew
 between 1990 and 2000 in those countries.

Source: The World Bank Group.

MAP 2
Major Primate Groups

The primate zoological order includes prosimians (lemurs, lorises, and tarsiers), monkeys, apes, and humans. Except for humans, contemporary primates live mainly in the tropics. As the map shows, primates used to have a wider distribution. Fossils of ancient primates have been found outside the tropics, including North America and Europe.

QUESTIONS

Look at Map 2, "Major Primate Groups."

1. On what continents are there nonhuman primates today? How does this differ from the past? What primate thrives today in North America?

2. What nonhuman primates live on the island of Madagascar? Are they monkeys or what? Where do other members of their suborder live?

3. On what continents can you find apes in the wild today? What continent that used to have apes lacks them today (except, of course, in zoos).

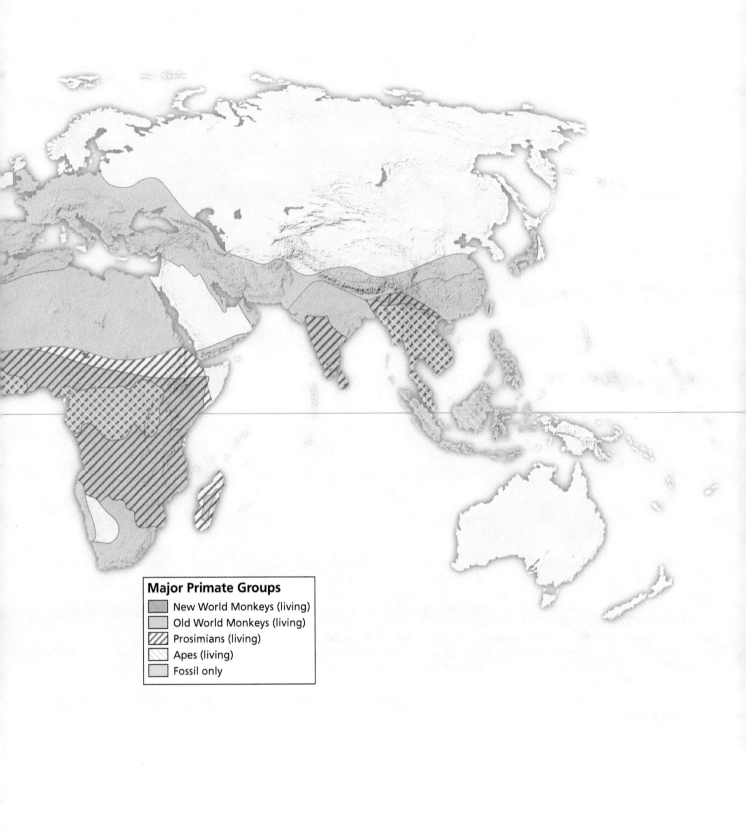

Major Primate Groups

- New World Monkeys (living)
- Old World Monkeys (living)
- Prosimians (living)
- Apes (living)
- Fossil only

MAP 3
Evolution of the Primates

Scientists trace modern primates, including humans, back to ancestral forms. Prosimians evolved earliest, perhaps by 60 million years ago. Their fossils have been found in North America, Europe, Asia, and Africa. Fossil sites with the ancestors of New World monkeys date back between 37 and 23 million years (to the Oligocene epoch). Old World monkeys and apes evolved at about the same time, but Old World monkeys spread into many parts of the Old World only in the last 5 million years. Apes lived in Africa, Europe, and Asia during the Miocene (23–5 million years ago).

QUESTIONS

Look at Map 3, "Evolution of the Primates."

1. What continent(s) had the first primates? What kinds of primates were those?

2. On what continent has the evolution of primates been most continuous? Does this have implications for human evolution?

3. Which continent with several of the earliest primates has the fewest non-human primates today?

Evolution of the Primates

Eocene: 57–37 million years ago

Oligocene: 37–23 million years ago

Miocene: 23–5 million years ago

OM Old World monkeys

NM New World monkeys

P Prosimians

A Apes

MAP 4
Early Hominins (and Hominids): Origins and Diffusion

The earliest hominins, including the ancestors of modern humans, evolved in Africa around 6 million years ago. Many sites date to the late Miocene (8–5 million years ago) when the lines leading to modern humans, chimps, and gorillas may have separated. Some sites dating to the end of the Pliocene epoch (5–1.8 million years ago) contain fossil remains of human ancestors, *Homo*. During the Pleistocene Era (1.8 million–11,000 years ago), humans spread all over the world. Scholars don't always agree on the evolutionary connections between the different fossils, as indicated in the question marks and broken lines on the time line.

QUESTIONS

Look at Map 4, "Early Hominins (and Hominids): Origins and Diffusion."

1. How many African countries have early hominin or hominid sites? Which countries contain sites of hominids that may not have been hominins? Name those two sites. How many African countries have sites from the Miocene? From the Pliocene? And from the Pleistocene?

2. Compare the African distribution of nonhuman primate fossils in Map 3 with the distribution of early hominins in Map 4. Which fossil record is better—the one for nonhuman primates or the one for hominins?

3. Compare the distribution of contemporary African apes, as shown in Map 2, with the distribution of early hominin sites in Map 4. Also look at the distribution of extinct African apes in Map 3. What patterns do you notice? Where did early hominins overlap with the African apes (extinct and contemporary)? Where were there apes but no known early hominins, and vice versa?

Pierolapithecus
catalaunicus

40°N

10°W

30°N

20°N

Bahr el
Ghazal

Toumai

CHAD

N'Djamena

10°N

Middle
Awash

Dikika

Hadar

W. Turkana

Omo

ETHIOPIA

Fejej

Lothagam

Koobi Fora

Black Skull

Kanapoi

Tugen Hills

Lukeino

Chesawanja

Kanam

Chemeron

0°

Peninj

KENYA

10°W

0°

10°E

ATLANTIC
OCEAN

TANZANIA

INDIAN
OCEAN

10°S

10°S

20°S

20°S

Gladysvale

Sterkfontein

Makapansgat

Swartkrans

Pretoria

Kromdraai

Johannesburg

**Early Hominins (and Hominids):
Origins and Diffusion**

◻ Late Miocene localities

◼ Pliocene localities

△ Early and Middle Pleistocene localities

Taung

Drimolen

Kimberley

30°S

30°S

SOUTH
AFRICA

Pinnacle Point

30°E

40°E

20°E

MAP 5

The Emergence of Modern Humans

Early forms of *Homo (H.) erectus,* sometimes called *H. ergaster,* have been found in East Africa and the former Soviet Georgia. By 1.7 million years ago, *H. erectus* had spread from Africa into Asia, including Indonesia, and eventually Europe. The *H. erectus* period may have lasted until 300,000 years ago. Other archaic forms of *Homo,* including fossils sometimes called *H. antecessor* and *H. heidelbergensis,* have been found in various parts of the Old World.

QUESTIONS

Look at Map 5, "The Emergence of Modern Humans."

1. Locate the site of Dmanisi (Georgia). Locate the site of Nariokotome (East Turkana, Kenya). These are sites where similarly dated early remains of *Homo erectus* (or *Homo ergaster*) have been found. Find two additional sites where hominins with similar dates (1.8–1.6 m.y.a.) have been found.

2. Considering Africa and Asia, name five sites (other than Dmanisi and Nariokotome) where *Homo erectus* fossils have been found.

3. Locate Heidelberg (Mauer) and Ceprano. What kinds of hominin fossils have been found there?

ATLANTIC OCEAN

Pinr

Okladnikov
Cave

ASIA

Dmanisi (1.7–1.8 m.y.a.)

CAUCASUS
MTS.

Black Sea

Caspian
Sea

Teshik Tash

Zhoukoudian, "Peking man"
(450,000 years ago)

Shanidar

Amud
Skhul
Tabun
Zuttiyen
ara Cave
Qafzeh

Lantian

Langtandong

Yunxian

Hominid
migration

Red Sea

Maba

Nazlet Khatir

Yuanmou
(Earliest evidence of
hominids in East Asia,
1.7 million years ago)

Tham Khuyen

Buia

RICA

Herto
Hadar

Bouri

Konso-Gardula

Omo
Nariokotome
Koobi Fora
Ileret
Lake Turkana,
"Nariokotome boy" (1.6 m.y.a.)

Olduvai Gorge

INDIAN OCEAN

Sangiran, Java (1.6–1.8 m.y.a.)

Kedungbrubus

Trinil, "Java man"
(700,000 years ago)

Flores

ARCHAEOLOGICAL SITE

- Homo habilis
- Homo erectus
- Archaic Homo sapiens
- Neandertals
- Homo sapiens
- Homo floresiensis

AUSTRALIA

e of Hearths
kfontein (2 m.y.a.)

Border Cave
Swartkrans (1.5 m.y.a.)

ver Mouth
me of the earliest
atomically modern
c. 100,000 years ago)

MAP 6

Origins and Distribution of Modern Humans

Anatomically modern humans (AMHs), appeared earliest in Africa (at Herto?) and migrated into the rest of the Old World, perhaps around 130,000 years ago. Whether these early modern humans interbred with archaic humans, such as Neandertals, outside of Africa is still debated. Sometime between 25,000 and 9,000 years ago, humans colonized the New World.

QUESTIONS

Look at Map 6, "Origins and Distribution of Modern Humans."

1. When and from where was Australia first settled?

2. When and from where was North America first settled? How many migrations are shown as figuring in the settlement of North America? How were these migrations related to the glacial ice cover? Did they all follow the same route?

3. Locate three sites providing early evidence of AMHs in Africa. How do their dates compare with those of AMHs in Europe?

LAURENTIDE ICE SHEET

St. Lawrence R.

NORTH AMERICA

Great Lakes

Corridor opened from 11,300 B.P.

BERINGIA (c. 80,000 to 7,000 B.P.)

ROCKY MTS.

Meadowcroft

GREAT PLAINS

APPALACHIAN MTS.

ATLANTIC OCEAN

Clovis

Rio Grande

Mississippi R.

West Indies

Orinoco R.

GUIANA HIGHLANDS

Nanchoc Valley

A N D E S

AMAZON BASIN

Pedra Furada

Monte Verde

PATAGONIA

ealand

Origins and Distribution of Modern Humans

↖ Possible settlement direction

▲ Archaic *Homo sapiens* (c. 650,000–28,000 B.P.)

△ Neandertals (c. 130,000–28,000? B.P.)

▪ Modern *Homo sapiens* (c. 130,000 B.P.–present)

☐ Areas covered by ice in late Pleistocene era (18,000 B.P.)

☐ Beringia

MAP 7

The Distribution of Human Skin Color (Before C.E. 1400)

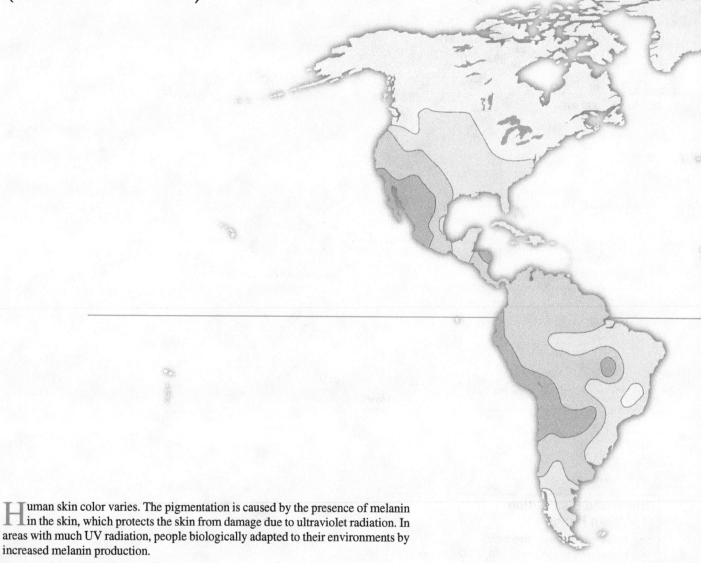

Human skin color varies. The pigmentation is caused by the presence of melanin in the skin, which protects the skin from damage due to ultraviolet radiation. In areas with much UV radiation, people biologically adapted to their environments by increased melanin production.

QUESTIONS

Look at Map 7, "The Distribution of Human Skin Color (Before C.E. 1400)."

1. Where are the Native Americans with the darkest skin color located? What factors help explain this distribution?

2. In both western and eastern hemispheres, is the lightest skin color found in the north or the south? Outside Asia, where do you find skin color closest to northern Asian skin color? Is this surprising given what you have read about migrations and settlement history?

3. Where are skin colors darkest? How might you explain this distribution?

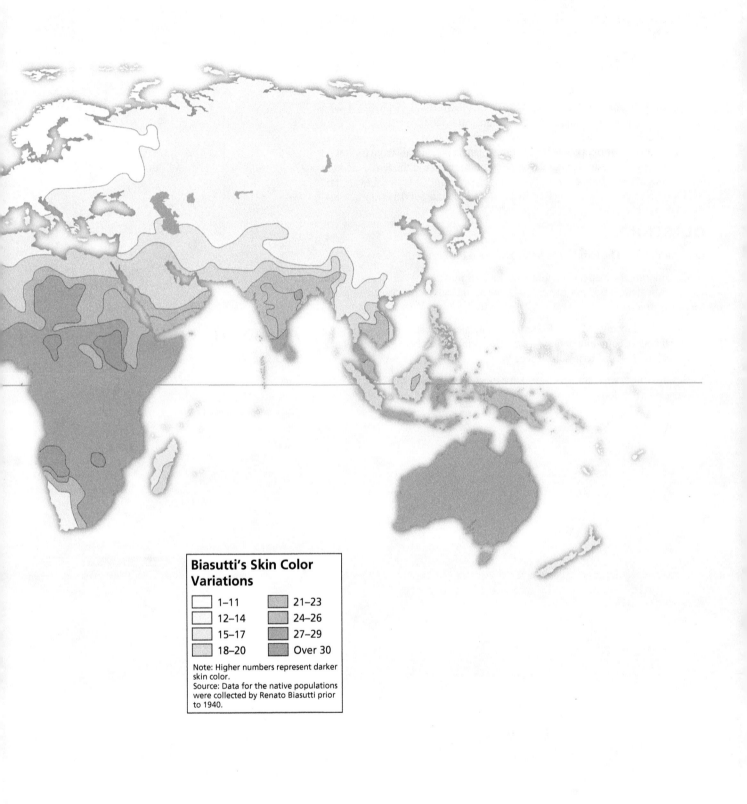

Biasutti's Skin Color Variations

- 1–11
- 12–14
- 15–17
- 18–20
- 21–23
- 24–26
- 27–29
- Over 30

Note: Higher numbers represent darker skin color.
Source: Data for the native populations were collected by Renato Biasutti prior to 1940.

MAP 8

The Origin and Spread of Food Production

The Neolithic, or New Stone Age, refers to the period of early farming settlements when people who had been foragers shifted to food production. This pattern of subsistence was based on the domestication of plants and animals. Through domestication, people transformed plants and animals from their wild state to a form more useful to humans. The Neolithic began in the fertile crescent area of the Middle East over 10,000 years ago. It spread to the Levant and Mediterranean, finally reaching Britain and Scandinavia around 5,000 years ago.

QUESTIONS

Look at Map 8, "The Origin and Spread of Food Production."

1. Considering the map and the timeline, name three regions where cattle were domesticated. Based on the timeline, what animals were domesticated in North America?

2. Did Ireland receive Middle Eastern domesticates? What is the origin of the "Irish potato," or white potato (see the timeline), which became, much later, the caloric basis of Irish subsistence?

3. Besides cattle, what animals were domesticated more than once? Where were those areas of domestication?

ATLANTIC OCEAN

Lake Ladoga

Lake Peipus

Baltic Sea

Elbe R.

Goose

Oder R.

Bug R.

Vistula R.

Danube R.

Dniester R.

Dnieper R.

Horse

Sea of Azov

Volga R.

Ural R.

Aral Sea

Caspian Sea

Early Neolithic Sites of the Middle East and Europe

- Settlement region and date
- Settlement sites
- Possible migration routes
- Areas of domestication

Po R.

Sava R.

7,500

7,700

7,700

7,800

Cattle

8,000

8,400

Adriatic Sea

Mediterranean Sea

7,800

9,000

9,000

8,900

Danube R.

7,800

9,600

9,800

Black Sea

Cattle

10,300

Pig

Sheep

Goat

Tigris R.

Euphrates R.

Goat

Persian Gulf

9,400?

10,300

Dromedary

Ass

Honey Bee

Cat

Mediterranean Domestication

Barley	Dates	Grapes
Cattle	Garlic	Lentils
Celery	Goat	Lettuce
		Olives

Yam, oil palm

Cat (Egypt)

Chickens (south-central Asia)

| 4000 | 3000 | 2000 | 1000 Years Ago |

Marsh elder
Sunflower
Squash

Lamb's quarters

Maize

North America

White potato

Southwest Asia Domestication

Barley	Duck	Melons
Beans	Fruits (seed	Oats
Beets	and stone)	Oil seeds
Camel (Bactrian)	Goat	Onions
Carrots	Grapes	Rye
Cattle	Hemp	Sheep
Dog	Horse	Wheat

MAP 9

Ancient Civilizations of the Old World

Archaic states developed in many parts of the Old World at different periods. The earliest civilizations, such as Mesopotamia, Egypt, and the Indus Valley, are generally placed at about 5500 B.P. States developed later in Asia, Africa, and the Americas (see Map 13).

QUESTIONS

Look at Map 9, "Ancient Civilizations of the Old World."

1. What contemporary nations would you have to visit if you wanted to see all the places where ancient civilizations developed in the Old World? Would some countries be off limits for political reasons? How do you think such limitations have affected the archaeological record?

2. Of the ancient states shown on Map 9, which developed latest? Why do you think the first states developed when and where they did?

3. In which of the ancient states shown on Map 9 were Middle Eastern domesticates basic to the economy? In which states shown on Map 9 were other domesticates basic to the economy?

Sea
of
Okhots

Lake
Baikal

n-Mycenaean
3050 B.P.
Çatal Hüyük

Caspian Sea

Harappa

Yellow River (Shang)
4000 B.P.–3027 B.P.

Sea
of
Japan

e a

Jericho

**Tigris-Euphrates
(Mesopotamia and
Babylonia)**
5500 B.P.–4000 B.P.

East
China
Sea

Mohenjo-daro

**Nile
(Ancient Egypt)**
4920 B.P.–3100 B.P.

Red Sea

Tell el-Ubaid

**Indus-Ganges
(Harappan and Vedic Civilizations)**
5000 B.P.–2150 B.P.

Nok Nok Tha

PACIFIC
OCEAN

Khmer
A.D. 802–1218

South
China
Sea

Arabian
Sea

Bay of Bengal

Funan
A.D. 100–546

eroe (Nubia)
2591 B.P.–
B.P. (A.D. 325)

Aksum/Axum
?2200 B.P.–1300 B.P. (A.D. 700)

Chenla
A.D. 611–802

INDIAN OCEAN

Zimbabwe
A.D. 1000–1450

**Ancient Civilizations of
the Old World**

Before 5500 B.P.
5500–3000 B.P.
4100–3000 B.P.
After 2600 B.P.

Funan

Meroe (Nubia)

Aksum/Axum

Chenla

Jenne-jeno

Ghana

Rome

Khmer

Zimbabwe

Mali

Songhay/Songhai

2500   2000   1500
(500 A.D)

1000
(1000 A.D)

500
(1500 A.D)

Years (B.P.)

MAP 10
Ethnographic Study Sites Prior to 1950

The development of anthropology as a scientific discipline can be traced to the middle to late part of the 19th century. In cultural anthropology, ethnographic field work became usual and common during the early 20th century. American ethnographers turned to the study of Native Americans, while European anthropologists often studied people living in world areas, such as Africa, which had been conquered and/or colonized by the anthropologist's nation of origin.

QUESTIONS

Look at Map 10, "Ethnographic Study Sites Prior to 1950."

1. Anthropology originated as the scientific study of nonwestern peoples and cultures. Yet Map 10 shows that many anthropological studies conducted prior to 1950 were done in North America. What societies were being studied in North America? Were they considered western or nonwestern? What does this tell us about the concept of "western"?

2. How would you describe the range of ethnographic sites prior to 1950? Were some world areas being neglected, such as the Middle East or mainland Asia? What might be the reasons for such omissions?

3. Think about how changes in transportation and communication have affected the way anthropologists do their research. How might a list of contemporary ethnographic sites contrast with the distribution shown in Map 10. How has longitudinal research been affected by changes in transportation and communication?

Ethnographic Study Sites Prior to 1950

North America
1. Eastern Eskimo
2. Central Eskimo
3. Naskapi
4. Iroquois
5. Delaware
6. Natchez
7. Shawnee
8. Kickapoo
9. Sioux
10. Crow
11. Nez Percé
12. Shoshone
13. Paviotso
14. Kwakiutl
15. Tsimshian
16. Haida
17. Tlingit
18. Navajo
19. Hopi
20. Zuñi
21. Aztec
22. Tzintzuntzan and Cuanajo
23. Maya
24. Cherokee
25. San Pedro

South America
Ecuador
26. Jívaro
Peru
27. Inca
28. Machiguenga
29. Achuara
30. Campa
Bolivia
31. Aymara
Chile
32. Yahgan
Venezuela
33. Yanomamö
Brazil
34. Tapirapé
35. Mundurucu
36. Mehinacu
37. Kuikuru
38. Caingang

Africa
Ghana
39. Ashanti
Nigeria
40. Kadar

Sudan
41. Fur
42. Dinka
43. Nuer
44. Azande
Uganda
45. Bunyoro
46. Ganda
Dem. Rep. of Congo
47. Mbuti
Rwanda
48. Watusi
Kenya
49. Masai
Tanzania
50. Nyakyusa
51. Lovedu
Zambia
52. Ndembu
53. Barotse
Mozambique
54. Bathonga
South Africa
55. !Kung Bushmen
56. Zulu

Asia
Sri Lanka
57. Vedda
58. Sinhalese
India
59. Andaman
60. Nayar
61. Tamil
62. Rajput
Siberia
63. Tungus
Japan
64. Ainu
China
65. Luts'un village
Taiwan
66. Taiwan Chinese
Vietnam
67. Mnong-Gar
Malaya
68. Semai

Pacific
Philippines
69. Tasaday
Indonesia Area
70. Dyaks
71. Alorese
72. Tetum
Australia
73. Tiwi
74. Arunta
75. Murngin
76. Saibai Islanders
New Guinea
77. Arapesh
78. Dani
79. Gururumba
80. Kai
81. Kapauku
82. Mae Enga
83. Kuma
84. Mundugumor
85. Tchambuli
86. Tsembaga Maring
87. Tavade
88. Foré
89. Etoro

Melanesian Islands
90. Manus Islanders
91. New Hanover Islanders
92. Trobriand Islanders
93. Dobuans
94. Rossel Islanders
95. Kaoka
96. Malaita Islanders
97. Espiritu Santo Islanders
98. Tana Islanders
99. Tikopia
100. Sivai

Polynesian Islands
101. Maori
102. Tongans
103. Samoans
104. Mangians
105. Tahitians
106. Hawailans

Micronesian Islands
107. Truk

MAP 11
Major Families
of World Languages

Language, like religion, is an important identifying and distinguishing characteristic of culture. Knowing the distribution of the major world languages and language families helps us understand some of the reasons behind important current events. In areas that have emerged from recent colonial rule, for example, the participants in conflicts over territory and power are often defined in terms of linguistic groups. Language distributions also help us understand our past by providing clues that enable us to chart the course of human migrations, as is suggested by the distribution of Indo-European, Austronesian, and Hamito-Semitic languages.

QUESTIONS

Look at Map 11, "Major Families of World Languages."

1. Name three language families or subfamilies that are spoken on more than one continent. How do you explain this distribution?

2. Where are the Austronesian languages spoken? How might one explain this distribution?

3. What language families are spoken on the African continent? Locate the Niger-Congo language family, of which the Bantu languages comprise a subfamily.

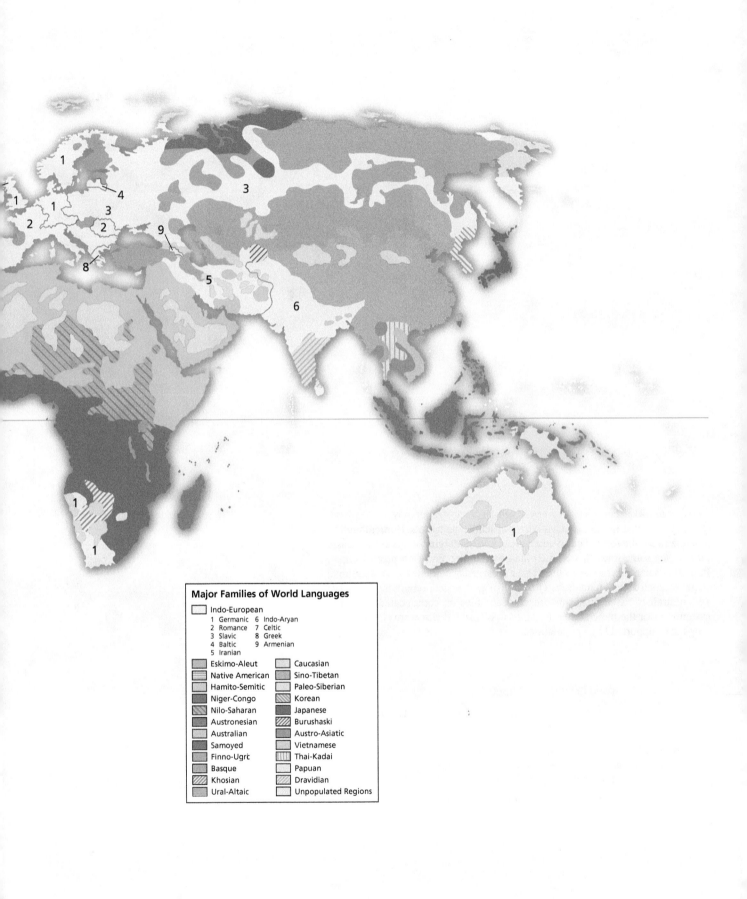

Major Families of World Languages

Indo-European
1 Germanic	6 Indo-Aryan
2 Romance	7 Celtic
3 Slavic	8 Greek
4 Baltic	9 Armenian
5 Iranian	

Eskimo-Aleut	Caucasian
Native American	Sino-Tibetan
Hamito-Semitic	Paleo-Siberian
Niger-Congo	Korean
Nilo-Saharan	Japanese
Austronesian	Burushaski
Australian	Austro-Asiatic
Samoyed	Vietnamese
Finno-Ugric	Thai-Kadai
Basque	Papuan
Khosian	Dravidian
Ural-Altaic	Unpopulated Regions

MAP 12
World Land Use,
C.E. 1500

In the late 1400s there were a variety of self-sustaining economies in the world. Foragers hunted and gathered wild forms of animals and plants. Horticulturalists practiced a simple form of cultivation, using hoes or digging sticks as their basic tools. They sometimes cleared their land by burning, and then planted crops. Pastoralists herded animals as their basic subsistence pattern. A few state-level societies, such as the Mongols, had pastoralism as their economic base. Intensive agriculturalists based their subsistence economies on complicated irrigation systems and/or the plow and draft animals. Wheat and rice were two kinds of crops that supported large populations

QUESTIONS

Look at Map 12, "World Land Use, C.E. 1500."

1. Name three continents with significant herding economies. On which continents was pastoralism absent?

2. How do the various types of agriculture vary among the continents? Which continent had the largest area under intensive cultivation? Which continent or continents had the least amount of intensive cultivation?

3. What were the main uses of land in Europe when the European age of discovery and conquest began?

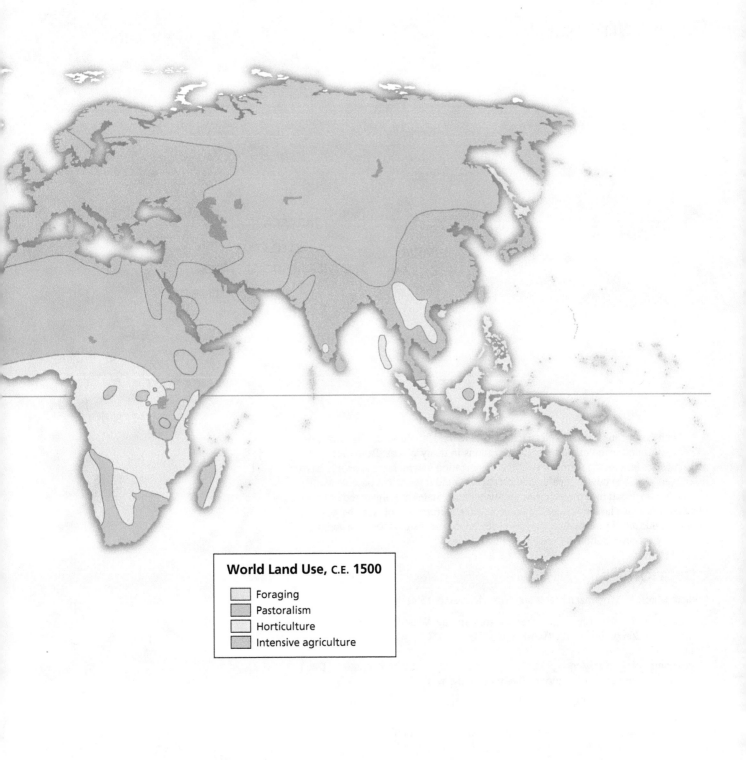

World Land Use, C.E. 1500

- Foraging
- Pastoralism
- Horticulture
- Intensive agriculture

MAP 13

Organized States and Chiefdoms, C.E. 1500

PACIFIC
OCEAN

ATLANT
OCEAN

TARASCA

AZTEC STATE

OTHER MEXICAN STATES

CHIBCHA

INCA STATE

When Europeans started exploring the world in the 15th through 17th centuries, they found complex political organizations in many places. Both chiefdoms and states are large-scale forms of political organization in which some people have privileged access to power, wealth, and prestige. Chiefdoms are kin-based societies in which redistribution is the major economic pattern. States are organized in terms of socioeconomic classes, headed by a centralized government that is led by an elite. States include a full-time bureaucracy and specialized subsystems for such activities as military action, taxation, and social control.

QUESTIONS

Look at Map 13, "Organized States and Chiefdoms, C.E. 1500."

1. Locate and name the states that existed in the Western Hemisphere in C.E. 1500. Compare Map 12, "World Land Use: C.E. 1500," with Map13. Looking at the Western Hemisphere, can you detect a correlation between land use (and economy) and the existence of states? What's the nature of that correlation? Does that correlation also characterize other parts of the world?

2. Locate three regions of the world where chiefdoms existed in C.E. 1500. Compare Map 12, "World Land Use: C.E. 1500," with Map 13. Can you detect a correlation between land use (and economy) and the existence of chiefdoms? What's the nature of that correlation?

3. Some parts of the world lacked either chiefdoms or states in C.E. 1500. What are some of those areas? What kinds of political systems did they probably have?

EUROPEAN STATES

SEMI NOMADIC STATES

ISLAMIC STATES

JAPAN

CHINA

PACIFIC OCEAN

INDIAN STATES

SONGHAI

KANEM-BORNU

ETHIOPIA

PHILIPPINES

HINDU/MUSLIM STATES

Ceylon
Strait of Malacca
Malaya
Moluccas
Sumatra

NEW GUINEA

OYO
BENIN

KONGO

LUBA

Zanzibar

Kilwa

THE EAST INDIES

Java

AUSTRALIA

INDIAN OCEAN

Sofala

MONOMATAPA

Organized States and Chiefdoms, C.E. **1500**

- No chiefdoms or states
- Chiefdoms
- States

MAP 14

Female/Male Inequality in Education and Employment

Women in developed countries have made significant advances in socioeconomic status in recent years. In most of the world, however, females suffer from significant inequality when compared with their male counterparts. Although women can vote in most countries, in over 90 percent of those countries that right was granted only during the last 50 years. In most regions, literacy rates for women still fall far short of those for men. In Africa and Asia, for example, only about half as many women are as literate as men. Inequalities in education and employment are perhaps the most telling indicators of the unequal status of women in most of the world. Even where women are employed in positions similar to those held by men, they tend to receive less compensation. The gap between rich and poor involves not only a clear geographic differentiation, but a clear gender differentiation as well.

QUESTIONS

Look at Map 14 "Female/Male Inequality in Education and Employment."

1. Locate and name three Third World countries with the same degree of gender-based inequality as the United States and Canada.

2. Two of the world's largest developing nations are coded as having "less inequality." What are they?

3. Most European countries are coded as having "least inequality." Which western European countries are exceptions?

Female/Male Inequality in Education and Employment

- Least inequality
- Less inequality
- Average inequality
- More inequality
- Most inequality
- No data

Wadaabe

Igbo

Azande

Mbuti 'pygmies'

Ju/'hoansi San

Betsileo

Bangalore (Bengaluru)

Ilongots

Agta

Negeri Sembilan

Minangkabau

Etoro, Kaluli, and Sambia

MAP 15
World Religions

Because religion is a fundamental characteristic of human culture, a depiction of the spatial distribution of religions comes close to a map of cultural patterns. More than just a set of behavior patterns having to do with worship and ceremony, religion influences the ways in which people deal with one another, with their institutions, and with their environments. An examination of this map in the context of conflict within and among nations also shows that the tension between countries and the internal stability of states are also functions of the spatial distribution of religion.

QUESTIONS

Look at Map 15, "World Religions."

1. Which continent has the most diversity with respect to the major religions?

2. Which continent is most Protestant? Why do you think that is the case?

3. Where in the world are "tribal" religions still practiced?

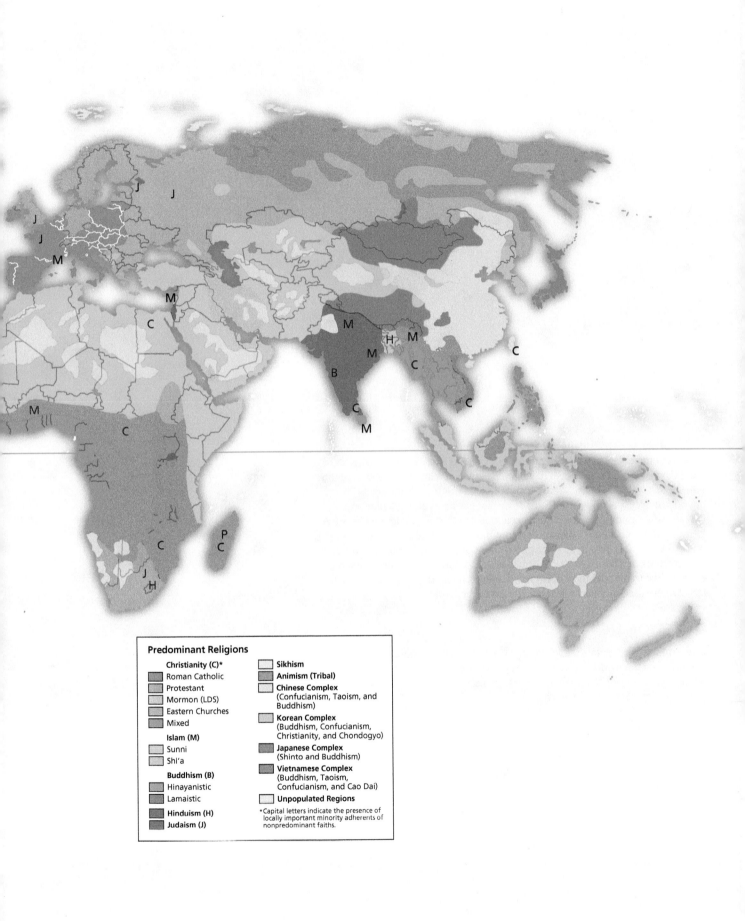

Predominant Religions

Christianity (C)*
- Roman Catholic
- Protestant
- Mormon (LDS)
- Eastern Churches
- Mixed

Islam (M)
- Sunni
- Shi'a

Buddhism (B)
- Hinayanistic
- Lamaistic

Hinduism (H)

Judaism (J)

- Sikhism
- **Animism (Tribal)**
- **Chinese Complex** (Confucianism, Taoism, and Buddhism)
- **Korean Complex** (Buddhism, Confucianism, Christianity, and Chondogyo)
- **Japanese Complex** (Shinto and Buddhism)
- **Vietnamese Complex** (Buddhism, Taoism, Confucianism, and Cao Dai)
- **Unpopulated Regions**

*Capital letters indicate the presence of locally important minority adherents of nonpredominant faiths.

MAP 16

Total Annual Energy Consumption by Country

All of the countries defined by the World Bank as having high incomes consume at least 100 gigajoules of commercial energy (the equivalent of more than 10 metric tons of coal) per person per year. With the exception of the oil-rich Persian Gulf states, where consumption figures include the costly "burning off" of excess energy in the form of natural gas flares at wellheads, most of the highest-consuming countries are concentrated in North America and Western Europe. At the other end of the scale are low-income countries, whose consumption rates are often less than 1 percent of those of the United States and other high consumers. These figures don't include the consumption of noncommercial energy—the traditional fuels of firewood, animal dung, and other organic matter—widely used in the less developed parts of the world.

QUESTIONS

Look at Map 16, "Total Annual Energy Consumption by Country." What five countries are the world's foremost energy consumers? Does this mean that the average person in each of these countries consumes more energy than the average European? Why or why not?

1. Compare energy consumption in Europe and North America. Do all European countries consume energy at the same rate as the United States and Canada?

2. What are some exceptions to the generalization that the highest rates of energy consumption are in core countries, with the lowest rates on the periphery?

3. How is energy consumption related to measures of the quality of life, as shown in Map 17?

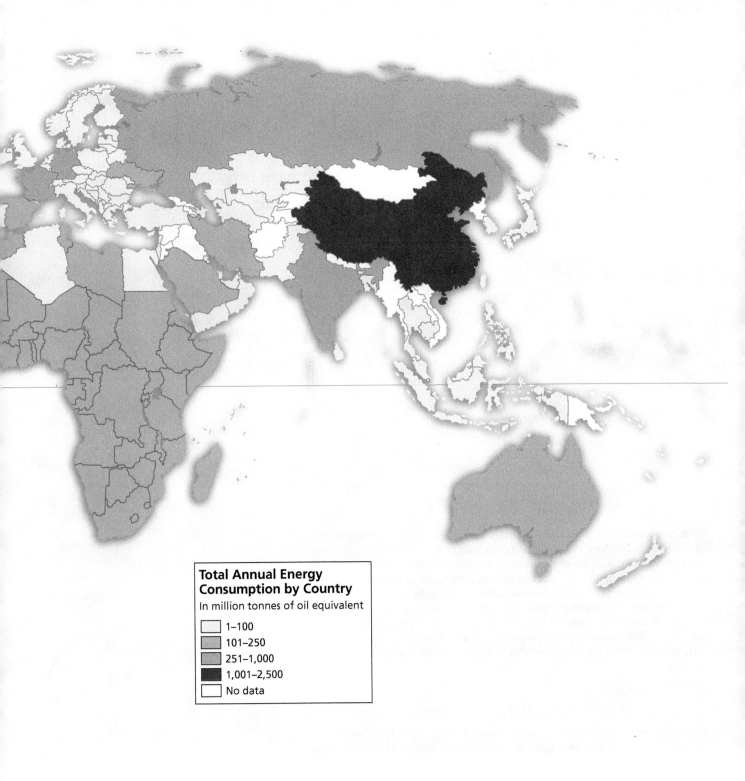

**Total Annual Energy
Consumption by Country**

In million tonnes of oil equivalent

- 1–100
- 101–250
- 251–1,000
- 1,001–2,500
- No data

MAP 17

The Quality of Life: The Index of Human Development, 2007

This map is based on a development index that considers a wide variety of demographic, health, and educational data, including population growth, per capita gross domestic income, longevity, literacy, and years of schooling. Compared with earlier years, there has been substantial improvement in the quality of life in Middle and South America. Africa and South Asia, however, face the challenge of providing basic access to health care, education, and jobs for rapidly increasing populations. This map illustrates an enduring difference in quality of life between those who inhabit the world's equatorial and tropical regions and those fortunate enough to live in the temperate zones, where the quality of life is significantly higher.

QUESTIONS

Look at Map 17, "The Quality of Life: The Index of Human Development, 2007."

1. What countries in central and South America have Human Development Index (HDI) scores comparable to those of some European nations? Does this surprise you?

2. Given that Brazil has one of the world's top 10 economies, does its HDI score surprise you? How do Brazil, Mexico, and Venezuela compare in terms of the HDI?

3. Do you notice a correlation between deforestation (Map 1) and quality of life? Does India fit this correlation?

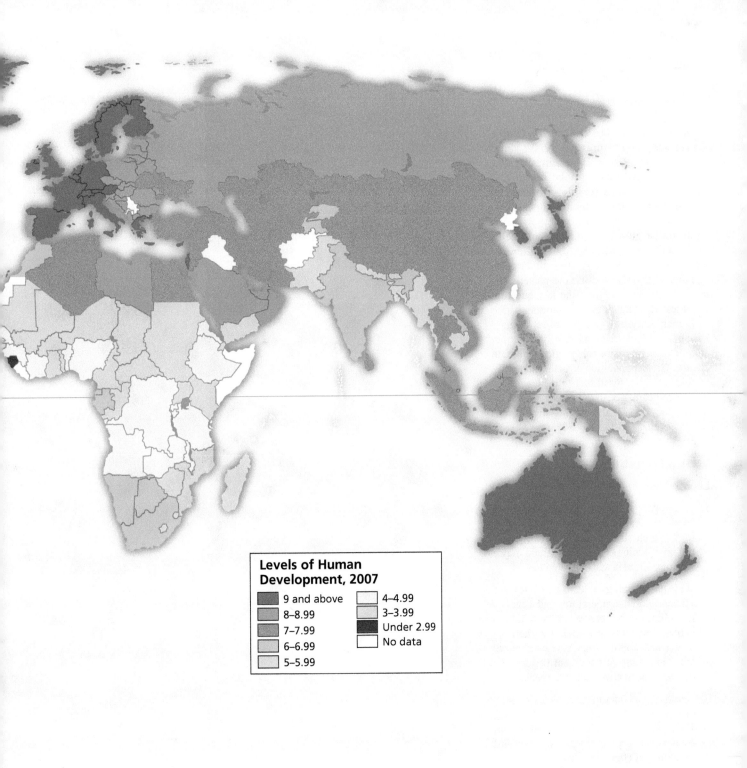

Levels of Human Development, 2007

- 9 and above
- 8–8.99
- 7–7.99
- 6–6.99
- 5–5.99
- 4–4.99
- 3–3.99
- Under 2.99
- No data

MAP 18
Global Warming

Since the early 20th century, the Earth's surface temperatures have risen about 1.4° F (0.7° C). Rising temperatures, shrinking glaciers, and melting polar ice provide additional evidence for global warming. Scientists prefer the term climate change to *global warming*. Scientific measurements confirm that global warming is not due to increased solar radiation, but rather are mainly *anthropogenic*—caused by humans and their activities. Because our planet's climate is always changing, the key question becomes: How much global warming is due to human activities versus natural climate variability. Most scientists agree that human activities play a major role in global climate change. Given population growth and rapidly increasing use of fossil fuels, the human factor is significant. The map represents the relative impact of global warming in different regions of the world.

QUESTIONS

Look at Map 18, "Global Warming."

1. Which geographical regions of the world show noticeable effects of global warming? Which show the least? What about the polar regions? Why are certain major sections of the oceans affected?

2. Widespread and long-term trends toward warmer global temperatures and a changing climate are referred to as "fingerprints." Researchers look for them to detect and confirm that climate change. What are some of the recent fingerprints that have been covered in the media?

3. "Harbingers" refer to such events as fires, exceptional droughts, and downpours. They can also include the spread of disease-bearing insects and widespread bleaching of coral reefs. Any and all may be directly or partly caused by a warmer climate. Have you noticed any recent harbingers in the U.S. in the past year? Have they been confined to any specific geographical regions?

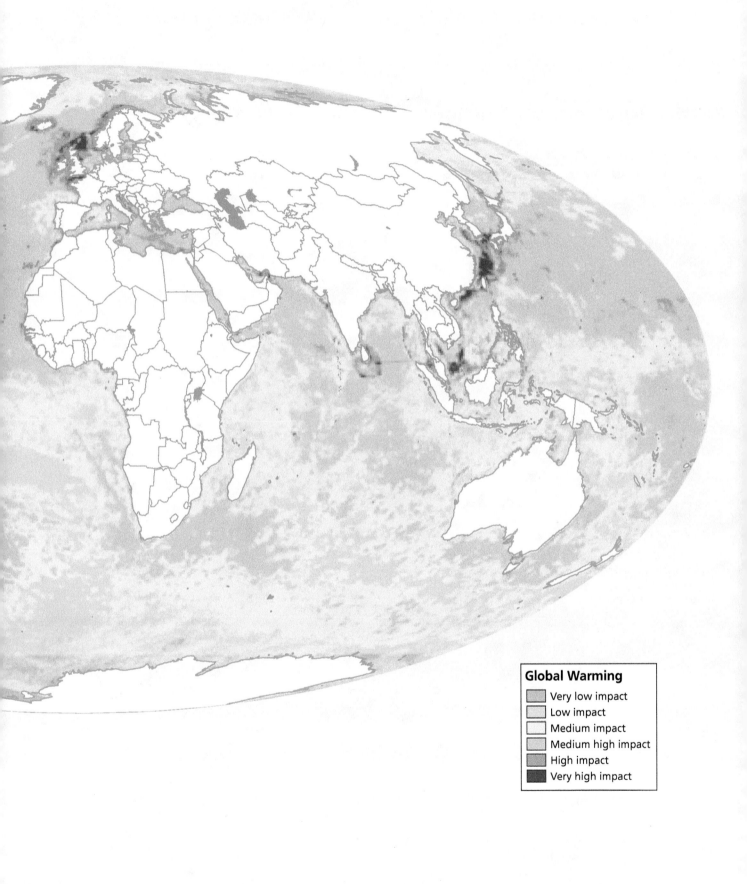

Global Warming

Very low impact
Low impact
Medium impact
Medium high impact
High impact
Very high impact

Editors/Academic Advisory Board

Members of the Academic Advisory Board are instrumental in the final selection of articles for each edition of ANNUAL EDITIONS. Their review of articles for content, level, and appropriateness provides critical direction to the editors and staff. We think that you will find their careful consideration well reflected in this volume.

ANNUAL EDITIONS: Anthropology 11/12
34th Edition

EDITOR

Elvio Angeloni
Pasadena City College

ACADEMIC ADVISORY BOARD MEMBERS

Preface

In publishing ANNUAL EDITIONS we recognize the enormous role played by the magazines, newspapers, and journals of the public press in providing current, first-rate educational information in a broad spectrum of interest areas. Many of these articles are appropriate for students, researchers, and professionals seeking accurate, current material to help bridge the gap between principles and theories and the real world. These articles, however, become more useful for study when those of lasting value are carefully collected, organized, indexed, and reproduced in a low-cost format, which provides easy and permanent access when the material is needed. That is the role played by ANNUAL EDITIONS.

This thirty-fourth edition of *Annual Editions: Anthropology* contains a variety of articles on contemporary issues in social and cultural anthropology. In contrast to the broad range of topics with minimum depth that is typical of standard textbooks, this anthology provides an opportunity to read firsthand accounts by anthropologists of their own research. In allowing scholars to speak for themselves about the issues in which they are experts, we are better able to understand the kind of questions anthropologists ask, the ways in which they ask them, and how they go about searching for answers. Indeed, where there is disagreement among anthropologists, this format allows the readers to draw their own conclusions. Given the very broad scope of anthropology—in time, space, and subject matter—the present collection of highly readable articles has been selected according to a certain criteria. The articles have been chosen from both professional and nonprofessional publications for the purpose of supplementing standard textbooks that are used in introductory courses. Some of the articles are considered classics in the field, while others have been selected for their timely relevance.

Included in this volume are a number of features that are designed to make it useful for students, researchers, and professionals in the field of anthropology. While the articles are arranged along the lines of broadly unifying themes, the *Topic Guide* can be used to establish specific reading assignments tailored to the needs of a particular course of study. Other useful features include the *Table of Contents* abstracts, which summarize each article and present key concepts in bold italics. In addition, each unit is preceded by an overview, which provides a background for informed reading of the articles, emphasizes critical issues, and presents *Learning Outcomes* in the form of questions. Finally, the *Internet References* section can be used to further explore the topics online.

Annual Editions: Anthropology 11/12 will continue to be updated annually. Those involved in producing the volume wish to make the next one as useful and effective as possible. Your criticism and advice are always welcome. Please fill out the postage-paid *Article Rating Form* on the last page of the book and let us know your opinions. Any anthology can be improved. This continues to be—annually.

Elvio Angeloni
Editor
evangeloni@gmail.com

Correlation Guide

The *Annual Editions* series provides students with convenient, inexpensive access to current, carefully selected articles from the public press. **Annual Editions: Anthropology 11/12** is an easy-to-use reader that presents articles on important topics such as *cultural diversity, language, social relationships,* and many more. For more information on *Annual Editions* and other *McGraw-Hill Contemporary Learning Series* titles, visit www.mhhe.com/cls.

This convenient guide matches the units in **Annual Editions: Anthropology 11/12** with the corresponding chapters in three of our best-selling McGraw-Hill Anthropology textbooks by Kottak and Lenkeit.

Annual Editions: Anthropology 11/12	Cultural Anthropology: Appreciating Cultural Diversity, 14/e by Kottak	Window on Humanity: A Concise Introduction to General Anthropology, 4/e by Kottak	Introducing Cultural Anthropology, 4/e by Lenkeit
Unit 1: Anthropological Perspectives	**Chapter 1:** What is Anthropology? **Chapter 2:** Culture **Chapter 3:** Method and Theory in Cultural Anthropology **Chapter 4:** Applying Anthropology	**Chapter 1:** What Is Anthropology? **Chapter 3:** Ethics and Methods **Chapter 18:** Applying Anthropology	**Chapter 1:** Anthropology **Chapter 3:** Fieldwork
Unit 2: Culture and Communication	**Chapter 2:** Culture **Chapter 5:** Language and Communication **Chapter 6:** Ethnicity and Race	**Chapter 2:** Culture **Chapter 10:** Language and Communication **Chapter 17:** Ethnicity and Race	**Chapter 2:** Culture **Chapter 4:** Language
Unit 3: The Organization of Society and Culture	**Chapter 10:** Families, Kinship, and Descent **Chapter 11:** Marriage **Chapter 13:** Arts, Media, and Sports	**Chapter 13:** Families, Kinship, and Marriage	**Chapter 5:** Subsistence Strategies and Resource Allocation I **Chapter 6:** Subsistence Strategies and Resource Allocation II **Chapter 10:** Political Order, Disorder, and Social Control
Unit 4: Other Families, Other Ways	**Chapter 10:** Families, Kinship, and Descent **Chapter 11:** Marriage	**Chapter 13:** Families, Kinship, and Marriage	**Chapter 7:** Marriage, Family, and Residence **Chapter 8:** Kinship and Descent
Unit 5: Gender and Status	**Chapter 9:** Gender	**Chapter 14:** Gender	**Chapter 9:** Gender and Sexuality
Unit 6: Religion, Belief and Ritual	**Chapter 8:** Political Systems **Chapter 12:** Religion **Chapter 15:** Global Issues Today	**Chapter 12:** Political Systems **Chapter 15:** Religion **Chapter 19:** Global Issues Today	**Chapter 11:** Belief Systems
Unit 7: Sociocultural Change	**Chapter 7:** Making a Living **Chapter 14:** The World System and Colonialism **Chapter 15:** Global Issues Today	**Chapter 11:** Making a Living **Chapter 16:** The World System and Colonialism **Chapter 19:** Global Issues Today	**Chapter 13:** Culture Change and Globalization **Chapter 14:** Applying Anthropology

Topic Guide

This topic guide suggests how the selections in this book relate to the subjects covered in your course. You may want to use the topics listed on these pages to search the Web more easily.

On the following pages a number of websites have been gathered specifically for this book. They are arranged to reflect the units of this Annual Editions reader. You can link to these sites by going to www.mhhe.com/cls

All the articles that relate to each topic are listed below the bold-faced term.

Acculturation
- 10. Macho Origin Myths
- 20. Who Needs Love!: In Japan, Many Couples Don't
- 26. Shamanisms: Past and Present
- 28. Understanding Islam
- 34. Yanomamo
- 35. The Arrow of Disease
- 36. The Americanization of Mental Illness
- 37. The Price of Progress
- 38. Seeing Conservation through the Global Lens
- 39. Der Indianer
- 40. What Native Peoples Deserve
- 41. Being Indigenous in the 21st Century

Aggression
- 2. Doing Fieldwork among the Yąnomamö
- 10. Macho Origin Myths
- 23. . . . but What If It's a Girl?
- 24. Missing Girls
- 25. Rising Number of Dowry Deaths in India
- 28. Understanding Islam
- 34. Yanomamo
- 35. The Arrow of Disease
- 40. What Native Peoples Deserve

Altruism
- 3. Eating Christmas in the Kalahari
- 10. Macho Origin Myths
- 15. Ties That Bind

Child care
- 1. A Dispute in Donggo: Fieldwork and Ethnography
- 13. Meet the Alloparents
- 16. Sick of Poverty
- 18. Death without Weeping
- 22. Where Fat Is a Mark of Beauty
- 23. . . . but What If It's a Girl?
- 24. Missing Girls

Children
- 13. Meet the Alloparents
- 16. Sick of Poverty
- 18. Death without Weeping
- 22. Where Fat Is a Mark of Beauty
- 23. . . . but What If It's a Girl?
- 24. Missing Girls

Communication
- 6. Whose Speech Is Better?
- 7. Do You Speak American?
- 8. Fighting for Our Lives
- 9. Shakespeare in the Bush
- 15. Ties That Bind
- 28. Understanding Islam

Cross-cultural experience
- 1. A Dispute in Donggo: Fieldwork and Ethnography
- 2. Doing Fieldwork among the Yąnomamö
- 3. Eating Christmas in the Kalahari
- 6. Whose Speech Is Better?
- 9. Shakespeare in the Bush
- 14. The Inuit Paradox
- 18. Death without Weeping
- 19. Arranging a Marriage in India
- 26. Shamanisms: Past and Present
- 28. Understanding Islam
- 34. Yanomamo
- 36. The Americanization of Mental Illness
- 39. Der Indianer
- 41. Being Indigenous in the 21st Century

Cultural change
- 7. Do You Speak American?
- 14. The Inuit Paradox
- 20. Who Needs Love!: In Japan, Many Couples Don't
- 23. . . . but What If It's a Girl?
- 24. Missing Girls
- 25. Rising Number of Dowry Deaths in India
- 26. Shamanisms: Past and Present
- 32. Why Can't People Feed Themselves?
- 33. The Tractor Invasion
- 34. Yanomamo
- 35. The Arrow of Disease
- 36. The Americanization of Mental Illness
- 37. The Price of Progress
- 38. Seeing Conservation through the Global Lens
- 39. Der Indianer
- 40. What Native Peoples Deserve
- 41. Being Indigenous in the 21st Century

Cultural diversity
- 6. Whose Speech Is Better?
- 7. Do You Speak American?
- 19. Arranging a Marriage in India
- 21. The Berdache Tradition
- 26. Shamanisms: Past and Present
- 28. Understanding Islam
- 36. The Americanization of Mental Illness
- 38. Seeing Conservation through the Global Lens
- 39. Der Indianer

Cultural identity
- 5. Can White Men Jump?: Ethnicity, Genes, Culture, and Success
- 6. Whose Speech Is Better?
- 14. The Inuit Paradox
- 22. Where Fat Is a Mark of Beauty
- 27. The Adaptive Value of Religious Ritual
- 28. Understanding Islam
- 39. Der Indianer
- 40. What Native Peoples Deserve
- 41. Being Indigenous in the 21st Century

Cultural relativity
- 3. Eating Christmas in the Kalahari
- 6. Whose Speech Is Better?
- 7. Do You Speak American?
- 14. The Inuit Paradox
- 19. Arranging a Marriage in India
- 28. Understanding Islam
- 36. The Americanization of Mental Illness

Ecology and society

14. The Inuit Paradox
17. When Brothers Share a Wife: Among Tibetans, the Good Life Relegates Many Women to Spinsterhood
32. Why Can't People Feed Themselves?
33. The Tractor Invasion
35. The Arrow of Disease
37. The Price of Progress
38. Seeing Conservation through the Global Lens

Economic systems

16. Sick of Poverty
17. When Brothers Share a Wife: Among Tibetans, the Good Life Relegates Many Women to Spinsterhood
18. Death without Weeping
23. . . . but What If It's a Girl?
24. Missing Girls
25. Rising Number of Dowry Deaths in India
32. Why Can't People Feed Themselves?
33. The Tractor Invasion
35. The Arrow of Disease
37. The Price of Progress
38. Seeing Conservation through the Global Lens

Ethnocentrism

3. Eating Christmas in the Kalahari
19. Arranging a Marriage in India
28. Understanding Islam
30. Body Ritual among the Nacirema
36. The Americanization of Mental Illness
39. Der Indianer

Ethnographic fieldwork

1. A Dispute in Donggo: Fieldwork and Ethnography
2. Doing Fieldwork among the Yąnomamö
3. Eating Christmas in the Kalahari
4. Tricking and Tripping: Fieldwork on Prostitution in the Era of AIDS
34. Yanomamo

Family systems

12. When Cousins Do More than Kiss
17. When Brothers Share a Wife: Among Tibetans, the Good Life Relegates Many Women to Spinsterhood
18. Death without Weeping
19. Arranging a Marriage in India
20. Who Needs Love!: In Japan, Many Couples Don't
22. Where Fat Is a Mark of Beauty
23. . . . but What If It's a Girl?
24. Missing Girls
25. Rising Number of Dowry Deaths in India

Gender

17. When Brothers Share a Wife: Among Tibetans, the Good Life Relegates Many Women to Spinsterhood
20. Who Needs Love!: In Japan, Many Couples Don't
21. The Berdache Tradition
23. . . . but What If It's a Girl?
24. Missing Girls
25. Rising Number of Dowry Deaths in India

Healing

26. Shamanisms: Past and Present
30. Body Ritual among the Nacirema
36. The Americanization of Mental Illness

Health

14. The Inuit Paradox
16. Sick of Poverty
18. Death without Weeping
22. Where Fat Is a Mark of Beauty

Hunter-gatherers

3. Eating Christmas in the Kalahari
10. Macho Origin Myths
11. How Cooking Frees Men
14. The Inuit Paradox

Industrial change

33. The Tractor Invasion
36. The Americanization of Mental Illness
40. What Native Peoples Deserve
41. Being Indigenous in the 21st Century

Kinship

12. When Cousins Do More than Kiss
13. Meet the Alloparents
17. When Brothers Share a Wife: Among Tibetans, the Good Life Relegates Many Women to Spinsterhood
18. Death without Weeping
20. Who Needs Love!: In Japan, Many Couples Don't
22. Where Fat Is a Mark of Beauty
25. Rising Number of Dowry Deaths in India

Language

6. Whose Speech Is Better?
7. Do You Speak American?
8. Fighting for Our Lives
9. Shakespeare in the Bush
28. Understanding Islam

Marriage systems

12. When Cousins Do More than Kiss
17. When Brothers Share a Wife: Among Tibetans, the Good Life Relegates Many Women to Spinsterhood
18. Death without Weeping
19. Arranging a Marriage in India
20. Who Needs Love!: In Japan, Many Couples Don't
22. Where Fat Is a Mark of Beauty
23. . . . but What If It's a Girl?
24. Missing Girls
25. Rising Number of Dowry Deaths in India

Medicine

16. Sick of Poverty
26. Shamanisms: Past and Present
30. Body Ritual among the Nacirema
36. The Americanization of Mental Illness

Participant observation

1. A Dispute in Donggo: Fieldwork and Ethnography
2. Doing Fieldwork among the Yąnomamö
3. Eating Christmas in the Kalahari
4. Tricking and Tripping: Fieldwork on Prostitution in the Era of AIDS
9. Shakespeare in the Bush

Patriarchy

20. Who Needs Love!: In Japan, Many Couples Don't

Political systems

16. Sick of Poverty
17. When Brothers Share a Wife: Among Tibetans, the Good Life Relegates Many Women to Spinsterhood
18. Death without Weeping

28. Understanding Islam
32. Why Can't People Feed Themselves?
35. The Arrow of Disease
37. The Price of Progress
38. Seeing Conservation through the Global Lens
40. What Native Peoples Deserve

Poverty

16. Sick of Poverty
18. Death without Weeping
32. Why Can't People Feed Themselves?
33. The Tractor Invasion
38. Seeing Conservation through the Global Lens
40. What Native Peoples Deserve

Rituals

22. Where Fat Is a Mark of Beauty
26. Shamanisms: Past and Present
27. The Adaptive Value of Religious Ritual
28. Understanding Islam
29. The Secrets of Haiti's Living Dead
30. Body Ritual among the Nacirema
31. Baseball Magic
39. Der Indianer

Sexuality

17. When Brothers Share a Wife: Among Tibetans, the Good Life Relegates Many Women to Spinsterhood
20. Who Needs Love!: In Japan, Many Couples Don't
21. The Berdache Tradition

Social change

7. Do You Speak American?
20. Who Needs Love!: In Japan, Many Couples Don't
23. . . . but What If It's a Girl?
24. Missing Girls
25. Rising Number of Dowry Deaths in India
28. Understanding Islam
32. Why Can't People Feed Themselves?
33. The Tractor Invasion
34. Yanomamo
35. The Arrow of Disease
36. The Americanization of Mental Illness
37. The Price of Progress

38. Seeing Conservation through the Global Lens
39. Der Indianer
40. What Native Peoples Deserve
41. Being Indigenous in the 21st Century

Social equality

11. How Cooking Frees Men
16. Sick of Poverty
20. Who Needs Love!: In Japan, Many Couples Don't
23. . . . but What If It's a Girl?
24. Missing Girls
25. Rising Number of Dowry Deaths in India
28. Understanding Islam
33. The Tractor Invasion
34. Yanomamo
37. The Price of Progress
38. Seeing Conservation through the Global Lens
40. What Native Peoples Deserve

Social relationships

3. Eating Christmas in the Kalahari
4. Tricking and Tripping: Fieldwork on Prostitution in the Era of AIDS
8. Fighting for Our Lives
11. How Cooking Frees Men
12. When Cousins Do More than Kiss
13. Meet the Alloparents
19. Arranging a Marriage in India
20. Who Needs Love!: In Japan, Many Couples Don't
23. . . . but What If It's a Girl?
24. Missing Girls
25. Rising Number of Dowry Deaths in India
27. The Adaptive Value of Religious Ritual
28. Understanding Islam
29. The Secrets of Haiti's Living Dead

Violence

2. Doing Fieldwork among the Yąnomamö
10. Macho Origin Myths
23. . . . but What If It's a Girl?
24. Missing Girls
25. Rising Number of Dowry Deaths in India
28. Understanding Islam
34. Yanomamo
40. What Native Peoples Deserve

Internet References

The following Internet sites have been selected to support the articles found in this reader. These sites were available at the time of publication. However, because websites often change their structure and content, the information listed may no longer be available. We invite you to visit www.mhhe.com/cls for easy access to these sites.

Annual Editions: Anthropology 11/12

General Sources

American Anthropologist Association
www.aaanet.org

Check out this site—the home page of the American Anthropology Association—for general information about the field of anthropology as well as access to a wide variety of articles.

Anthropology Links
http://anthropology.gmu.edu

George Mason University's Department of Anthropology website provides a number of interesting links.

Latin American Studies
www.library.arizona.edu/search/subjects

Click on Latin American Studies to access an extensive list of resources—links to encyclopedias, journals, indexes, almanacs, and handbooks, and to the Latin American Network Information Center and Internet Resources for Latin American Studies.

The Royal Anthropological Institute of Great Britain and Ireland (RAI)
www.therai.org.uk

The world's longest established scholarly association dedicated to the furtherance of anthropology in its broadest and most inclusive sense.

A Sociological Tour through Cyberspace
www.trinity.edu/~mkearl/anthro.html

This is an excellent starting point for anthropological resources, using links.

Web Resources for Visual Anthropology
www.usc.edu/dept/elab/urlist/index.html

This UR-List offers a mouse-click selection of web resources by cross-indexing 375 anthropological sites according to 22 subject categories.

UNIT 1: Anthropological Perspectives

Archaeology and Anthropology Computing and Study Skills
www.isca.ox.ac.uk/index.html

Consult this site of the Institute of Social and Cultural Anthropology to learn about ways to use the computer as an aid in conducting fieldwork, methodology, and analysis.

The Institute for Intercultural Studies
www.interculturalstudies.org/main.html

Established by Margaret Mead, the institute is directed by her daughter, Mary Catherine Bates. With links, it promotes accessibility to Mead's work as well as that of several of her associates, including Franz Boas, Ruth Benedict, and Gregory Bateson.

Introduction to Anthropological Fieldwork and Ethnography
http://web.mit.edu/dumit/www/syl-anth.html

This class outline can serve as an invaluable resource for conducting anthropological fieldwork. Addressing such topics as *The Interview and Power Relations in the Field,* the site identifies many important books and articles for further reading.

Theory in Anthropology
www.indiana.edu/~wanthro/theory.htm

These web pages cover sub-disciplines within anthropology, changes in perspectives over time, and prominent theorists, reflecting 30 years of dramatic changes in the field.

UNIT 2: Culture and Communication

Center for Nonverbal Studies
www.library.kent.edu/resource.php?id=2800

This site is from a private, non-profit research center with links to relevant news stories.

Exploratorium Magazine: "The Evolution of Languages"
www.exploratorium.edu/exploring/language

Where did languages come from and how did they evolve? This educational site explains the history and origin of language. You can also investigate words, word stems, and the similarities of different languages.

Hypertext and Ethnography
www.umanitoba.ca/anthropology

Presented by Brian Schwimmer of the University of Manitoba, this site will be of great value to people who are interested in culture and communication. Schwimmer addresses such topics as multi-vocality and complex symbolization.

International Communication Association
www.icahdq.org

The I.C.A. sponsors conferences and publishes books and journals having to do with cross-cultural communication.

Intute: Social Sciences
www.intute.ac.uk/socialsciences/cgi-bin/browse.pl?id=120052

This site provides links to linguistic associations, journals, and links to websites and data bases dedicated to the preservation and study of languages.

Language and Culture
http://anthro.palomar.edu/language/default.htm

This is a good introduction to the subject of linguistics and includes related websites.

Language Extinction
www.colorado.edu/iec

"An often overlooked fact in the ecological race against environmental extinction is that many of the world's languages

Internet References

are disappearing at an alarming rate." This article investigates language extinction and its possible consequences.

Nonverbal Behavior
www.usal.es/~nonverbal/researchcenters.htm

This site is the gateway to links to all other sites having to do with nonverbal behavior and communication. The site includes links to publications, research centers, experiments, and conferences.

Showcase Anthropology
www.anthropology.wisc.edu

Examples of documents that make innovative use of the web as a tool for "an anthropology of the future"—one consisting of multimedia representations in a nonlinear and interactive form—are provided on this website.

UNIT 3: The Organization of Society and Culture

Smithsonian Institution Website
www.si.edu

Looking through this site, which provides access to many of the enormous resources of the Smithsonian, will give a sense of the scope of anthropological inquiry today.

Sociology Guy's Anthropology Links
www.trinity.edu/~mkearl/anthro.html

This list of anthropology resources on the web is suggested by a sociology professor at Trinity University and includes cultures of Asia, Africa, the Middle East; Aztecan, Mayan, and aboriginal cultures; sections on Mythology, Folklore, Legends, and Archaeology; plus much more.

UNIT 4: Other Families, Other Ways

Kinship and Social Organization
www.umanitoba.ca/anthropology

Kinship, marriage systems, residence rules, incest taboos, and cousin marriages are explored in this kinship tutorial.

Sex and Marriage
http://anthro.palomar.edu/marriage/default.htm

This is a good cross-cultural survey of marriage customs, residence rules, and the treatment of homosexuality. Related websites are included.

Wedding Traditions and Customs
http://worldweddingtraditions.com

Marriage customs are summarized for every region of the world.

UNIT 5: Gender and Status

Reflections on Sinai Bedouin Women
www.sherryart.com/women/bedouin.html

Social anthropologist Ann Gardner tells something of her culture shock while first living with a Sinai Bedouin family as a teenager. She provides links to sites about organization of society and culture, particularly with regard to women.

Women Watch
www.un.org/womenwatch/about

As part of the United Nations, Women Watch serves as a conduit for information and resources on the promotion of gender equality and empowerment throughout the world.

UNIT 6: Religion, Belief, and Ritual

Anthropology Resources Page
www.usd.edu/anth

Many topics can be accessed from this University of South Dakota website. Repatriation and reburial are just two.

Apologetics Index
www.apologeticsindex.org/site/index-c

This site offers resources on religious cults, sects, religions, and doctrines.

Magic and Religion
http://anthro.palomar.edu/religion/default.htm

This site deals with the various aspects of folk religion and magic along with related Internet links.

Yahoo: Society and Culture: Death
http://dir.yahoo.com/Society_and_Culture/Death_and_Dying

This Yahoo site has an extensive index to diverse issues related to how different people approach death, such as beliefs about euthanasia, reincarnation, and burial.

UNIT 7: Sociocultural Change

Association for Political and Legal Anthropology
www.aaanet.org/apla/index.htm

As a branch of the American Anthropological Association, this organization supports workshops, lectures, and publications having to do with issues of contemporary importance in the fields of political and legal anthropology, such as nationalism, colonialism, and post-colonial public spheres, multiculturalism, and globalism.

Human Rights and Humanitarian Assistance
www.etown.edu/vl/humrts.html

Through this site you can conduct research into a number of human rights topics and issues affecting indigenous peoples in the modern era.

The Indigenous Rights Movement in the Pacific
www.inmotionmagazine.com/pacific.html

This article addresses issues that pertain to the problems of the Pacific Island peoples as a result of U.S. colonial expansion in the Pacific and Caribbean 100 years ago.

Murray Research Center
www.radcliffe.edu/murray_redirect/index.php

This site promotes the use of existing social science data to explore human development in the context of social change.

RomNews Network—Online
www.romnews.com/community/index.php

This is a website dedicated to news and information for and about the Roma (European Gypsies). Visit here to learn more about their culture and the discrimination they constantly face.

WWW Virtual Library: Indigenous Studies
http://cwis.org/wwwvl/indig-vl.html

This site presents resources collected by the Center for World Indigenous Studies (CWIS) in Africa, Asia, and the Middle East, Central and South America, Europe, and the Pacific.

World Map

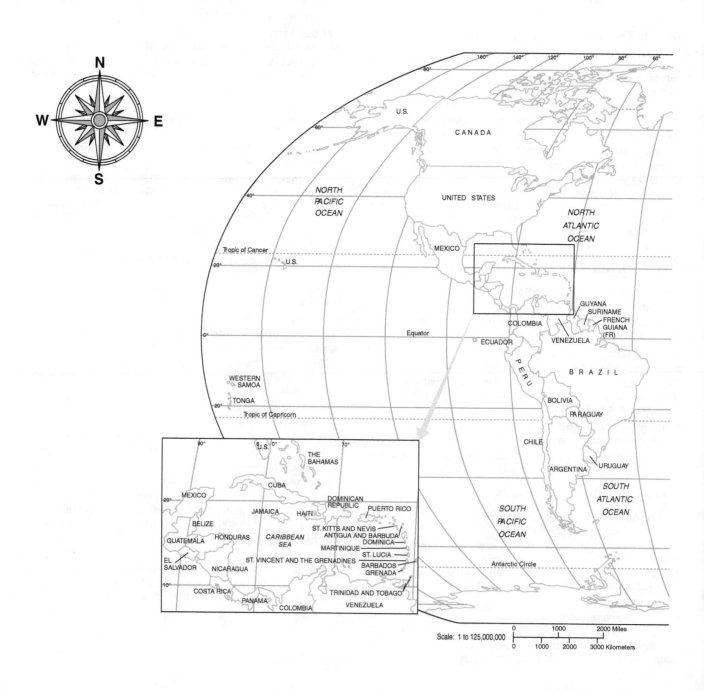

W E S

U.S.

CANADA

NORTH PACIFIC OCEAN

UNITED STATES

NORTH ATLANTIC OCEAN

Tropic of Cancer

U.S.

MEXICO

GUYANA
SURINAME
FRENCH GUIANA (FR)

COLOMBIA

Equator

VENEZUELA

ECUADOR

PERU

BRAZIL

WESTERN SAMOA

BOLIVIA

TONGA

PARAGUAY

Tropic of Capricorn

CHILE

URUGUAY

ARGENTINA

SOUTH ATLANTIC OCEAN

SOUTH PACIFIC OCEAN

Antarctic Circle

U.S.

THE BAHAMAS

CUBA

MEXICO

DOMINICAN REPUBLIC

JAMAICA   HAITI

PUERTO RICO

BELIZE

ST. KITTS AND NEVIS
ANTIGUA AND BARBUDA
DOMINICA

GUATEMALA   HONDURAS

CARIBBEAN SEA

MARTINIQUE
ST. LUCIA

EL SALVADOR   NICARAGUA

ST. VINCENT AND THE GRENADINES

BARBADOS
GRENADA

COSTA RICA

TRINIDAD AND TOBAGO

PANAMA

COLOMBIA

VENEZUELA

Scale: 1 to 125,000,000

0   1000   2000 Miles

0   1000   2000   3000 Kilometers

UNIT 1

Anthropological Perspectives

Unit Selections

1. **A Dispute in Donggo: Fieldwork and Ethnography,** John Monaghan and Peter Just
2. **Doing Fieldwork among the Yąnomamö,** Napoleon A. Chagnon
3. **Eating Christmas in the Kalahari,** Richard Borshay Lee
4. **Tricking and Tripping: Fieldwork on Prostitution in the Era of AIDS,** Claire E. Sterk
5. **Can White Men Jump?: Ethnicity, Genes, Culture, and Success,** David Shenk

Learning Outcomes

After reading this unit, you should be able to:

- Discuss how anthropology teaches us about whether humans are naturally cooperative or competitive.

- Describe some of the unique research strategies of anthropological fieldwork.

- Explain how anthropologists who become personally involved with a community through participant observation maintain their objectivity as scientists.

- Give examples of the kind of ethical obligations fieldworkers have toward their informants.

- Explain the ways in which the results of fieldwork depend on the kind of questions asked.

- Identify some of the lessons that can be learned about one's own culture by going to the field.

Student Website

www.mhhe.com/cls

Internet References

Archaeology and Anthropology Computing and Study Skills
www.isca.ox.ac.uk/index.html
The Institute for Intercultural Studies
www.interculturalstudies.org/main.html
Introduction to Anthropological Fieldwork and Ethnography
http://web.mit.edu/dumit/www/syl-anth.html
Theory in Anthropology
www.indiana.edu/~wanthro/theory.htm

For at least a century, the goals of anthropology have been to describe societies and cultures throughout the world and to compare and contrast the differences and similarities among them. Anthropologists study in a variety of settings and situations, ranging from small hamlets and villages to neighborhoods and corporate offices of major urban centers throughout the world. They study hunters and gatherers, peasants, farmers, labor leaders, politicians, and bureaucrats. They examine religious life in Latin America as well as revolutionary movements.

Wherever practicable, anthropologists take on the role of "participant observer." Through active involvement in the life ways of people, they hope to gain an insider's perspective without sacrificing the objectivity of the trained scientist. Sometimes the conditions for achieving such a goal seem to form an almost insurmountable barrier, but anthropologists call on persistence, adaptability, and imagination to overcome the odds against them. (See "A Dispute in Donggo: Fieldwork and Ethnography," by John Monaghan and Peter Just.)

The diversity of focus in anthropology means that it is earmarked less by its particular subject matter than by its perspective. Although the discipline relates to both the biological and social sciences, anthropologists know that the boundaries drawn between disciplines are highly artificial. For example, while in theory it is possible to examine only the social organization of a family unit or the organization of political power in a nation-state, in reality it is impossible to separate the biological from the social, from the economic, from the political. This explanatory perspective of anthropology is emphasized in "Can White Men Jump?" by David Shenk, in which we see how anthropologists as well as scientists in general now seek out interrelationships among all these factors.

Other articles in this unit illustrate varying kinds of research strategies employed by anthropologists as they take on the role of "participant observer." Napoleon Chagnon's essay, "Doing Fieldwork among the Yanomamö," shows the hardships imposed by certain physical conditions and the vast differences in values

© Royalty-Free/CORBIS

and attitudes to be bridged by the anthropologist just to get along.

Richard Borshay Lee, in "Eating Christmas in the Kalahari," came to realize that his behavior conveyed a certain attitude incompatible with the values of his hosts. In the process, he learned an important lesson about how these hunter-gatherers have been able to survive for so long under conditions that we would consider marginal at best. Then, there is "Tricking and Tripping: Fieldwork on Prostitution in the Era of AIDS," in which Claire E. Sterk describes the problems, both professional and personal, involved in trying to understand the precarious lives of prostitutes on the urban streets of America.

Much is at stake in these discussions as we attempt to achieve a more objective understanding of the diversity of peoples' ways. After all, the purpose of anthropology is not only to describe and explain, but also to develop a special vision of the world in which cultural alternatives (past, present, and future) can be measured against one another and used as guides for human action.

A Dispute in Donggo:
Fieldwork and Ethnography

JOHN MONAGHAN AND PETER JUST

As has often been said, if you want to understand what anthropology is, look at what anthropologists do. Above all else, what anthropologists do is *ethnography*. Ethnography is to the cultural or social anthropologist what lab research is to the biologist, what archival research is to the historian, or what survey research is to the sociologist. Often called—not altogether accurately—'participant observation', ethnography is based on the apparently simple idea that in order to understand what people are up to, it is best to observe them by interacting with them intimately and over an extended period. That is why anthropologists have tended traditionally to spend long periods–sometimes years at a stretch—living in the communities they study, sharing the lives of the people to as great an extent as they can. It is this approach that has defined our discipline and distinguished it from other social sciences. Now, we certainly do not dismiss the methods more characteristic of other disciplines, such as the use of questionnaires or the collection of quantitative behavioural data. But anthropologists have long felt that approaching the study of human beings in those ways is likely to produce an incomplete—even misleading—understanding of the people studied, especially when those people are members of foreign or unfamiliar societies.

It might also be said that fieldwork is what gives the enterprise of anthropology a good deal of its romance. It was certainly one of the things that attracted the two of us to the discipline. Today anthropologists conduct fieldwork in settings that are as unexotic as television stations in city centres, magistrate's courts in small towns, corporate boardrooms, and church congregations in middle-class suburbs. But in its infancy as a profession, anthropology was distinguished by its concentration on so-called 'primitive' societies: relatively small, non-Western communities in which social institutions appeared to be fairly limited and simple (not so, as it turned out!) and social interaction was conducted almost entirely face-to-face.

Such societies, it was felt, provided anthropologists with a simplified view of the 'elementary' workings of society, one that contrasted with the complexities of 'modern' (that is, Western) society. There was also a sense among anthropologists that the ways of life represented by these smaller societies were rapidly disappearing, and since many of them had no writing, it was an urgent task to preserve a record for posterity. This orientation of the discipline, and an early commitment to the first-hand collection of ethnographic data by means of participant observation, led anthropologists to some of the most remote and exotic places on earth. Most often working alone and in isolation from other Westerners, the ethnographer cut a bold figure indeed. Often this isolation created a sense of alienation and loneliness, especially in the early stages of fieldwork. But almost all anthropologists find themselves assimilating to the culture of their host communities to a greater or lesser degree—a few, it is said, even to the point of 'going native', completely adopting the lifestyle of their hosts and never returning home. All together, the process of immersing oneself in fieldwork can be a challenging and unique experience, one that continues to attract men and women to anthropology. It also so happens that participant observation seems to be the most effective way of understanding in depth the ways in which other people see the world and interact with it, and often provides a check on our own preconceptions and beliefs.

Let us begin with a story, a story that shows you not only how anthropologists work, but what is distinctive about anthropology as a discipline. This is a story about Peter's fieldwork with the Dou Donggo and how he came to be interested in the anthropology of law.

> One night I was sitting in the house of a friend in Doro Ntika, the village where I was conducting fieldwork. One of my friend's relatives burst into the room, shouting that his sister-in-law, a woman named ina Mone, had been assaulted by a young man, la Ninde.

We rushed over to ina Mone's house to see what had happened. Ina Mone sat on the floor of the room, one side of her face painted with a medicinal paste, where she said la Ninde had struck her.

She also showed us the shirt she had been wearing and that had been torn in the assault. Her male relatives were angry, and talked of 'taking down the spears and sharpening the bushknives', anxious to exact an immediate revenge on la Ninde. But everyone became calmer when ama Tife, one of the principal elders of the village, came by to assure us that he and the other elders of Doro Ntika would convene a court and exact justice according to tradition. The next morning they did just that. La Ninde was brought before a group of elders with most of the village looking on. Ina Mone showed her medicated face and torn shirt as evidence. La Ninde admitted to having shouted at her, but denied having laid hands upon her. A spirited and tumultuous drama ensued, as members of the court, led by ama Panci, berated la Ninde and finally extracted a confession. He was assessed a minor fine and was made to kneel before ina Mone begging forgiveness. She gave him a symbolic slap on the head, and he was let go.

Later that afternoon, I chatted with a friend. I said, 'Wasn't that terrible, what la Ninde did, assaulting ina Mone like that?' He answered, 'Yes, it was. But you know he never really hit her.' I was surprised. 'What about the torn shirt and her face?', I asked. 'Well', he said, 'anyone can tear a shirt, and who knows what's under the medicine.' I was deeply shocked. 'But that means la Ninde is innocent. Isn't this terribly unfair?' 'Not at all', he replied. 'What la Ninde was convicted of was more true than what really happened.' He then proceeded to fill me in on what everyone else in the village knew, indeed, what they had known all along. Ina Mone had seen la Ninde hanging around la Fia, a young woman who was betrothed to another young man, absent from Doro Ntika. Ina Mone had complained to la Ninde's mother, who in turn had admonished la Ninde. Furious at having been ratted out, la Ninde had gone to ina Mone's house and threatened her—a serious breach of etiquette—but had not in fact assaulted her.

This story is an account of a real event in the real world, as witnessed by an ethnographer. How would this event have been recorded and analysed by a historian or a sociologist? To begin with, to a historian who works primarily with archives or court records, the case of la Ninde's assault on ina Mone would be completely invisible. The Dou Donggo do not keep written records of disputes settled by village

elders, so this case and the great majority of cases would not appear in a form accessible to the historian working in an archive. Even a historian who adopts the ethnographic methods of an anthropologist and takes down oral histories might have difficulty in accessing this case, for among the Dou Donggo it is an accepted practice that one never discusses a dispute after it has been settled. Only because he was on the scene at the time the dispute erupted, was Peter able to record it and explore its meaning.

How would this case have appeared to a sociologist or a criminologist? Although some sociologists and criminologists are adept at using ethnographic methods, it is far more common for them to rely on surveys, questionnaires, and the analysis of official statistics. Again, to those relying on official statistics, this case would have been completely invisible. La Ninde's 'assault' might have appeared as a 'data point' in a survey of disputes in the community undertaken by a sociologist. But it seems unlikely that a survey would be so artfully constructed as to see beyond the superficial evidence of the case, or, more importantly, to uncover the notion that la Ninde's conviction of a crime he did not commit was 'more true than what really happened'. If the case had been recorded officially, researchers (including anthropologists) who rely on such data would probably assume the case of la Ninde was one of simple assault, leading to conclusions about Dou Donggo society that would be seriously incomplete, if not misleading.

Very well, then, what might the case described mean to an ethnographer? How might an anthropologist analyse this event to learn more about what the Dou Donggo believe and how they behave? First, after considerable questioning, it became clear to Peter that the case had little to do with assault and a very great deal to do with respect for the institution of marriage. Why had ina Mone complained to la Ninde's mother about his flirtations with la Fia? Because ina Mone had a real and vested interest in protecting the integrity of betrothals, particularly betrothals contracted by the family of ama Panci. Why? Because ina Mone's daughter was betrothed to ama Panci's son and another of ama Panci's sons was betrothed to la Fia!

One lesson, then, that Peter learned was that in disputes (at least among the Dou Donggo) things are often other than what they appear to be. A case of 'assault' may really be a case about 'alienation of affection'. What made this sort of realization possible? First of all, Peter was there to witness the event to begin with, something that would not have been possible had he not spent almost two years in this village. The ability to observe unusual, unique events is one of the principal advantages of the ethnographic method. It is important to recognize, as well, that Peter was able to observe the case in question from the outset not only because he lived in Doro Ntika for a long time, but because he lived there around the clock and as a member of the community. The case came to his attention not because he was seeking out information on disputes or even on betrothals, but because he just happened to be chatting with friends in a nearby house, long after a conventional 'working day' was over. It is this openness to the serendipitous discovery that gives the ethnographic method strength and flexibility not generally available to highly deductive social science methods, such as survey or statistical research. Indeed, anthropologists often find themselves doing significant research on unanticipated subjects. While there are those research topics we take with us to the field, there are also topics imposed upon us by the actual circumstances and events of people's everyday lives. Peter had not intended to study dispute settlement when he set off for Indonesia, but neither could he ignore the research opportunity he encountered that evening. The randomness of ethnographic serendipity is compensated for by the length of time a good ethnographer spends in the field; eventually, one hopes, one will accidentally encounter most social phenomena of significance.

Prolonged exposure to daily life in Doro Ntika also made Peter aware that it was necessary to look beyond the superficial events of the case, made him aware that issues like the fidelity of fiancés was a sensitive, even explosive, topic in this community. In other words, after more than a year living in this community, Peter had a rich and nuanced context into which the events of this case could be placed. The discrepancy between what a social event is apparently about and what it might 'really' be about is almost impossible to discern without the experiential context ethnographic fieldwork makes available. That is one of the advantages that anthropologists have traditionally relied upon for the insights they derive from their research and it is why traditional ethnographic fieldwork has placed a premium on long duration—often as much as two years for an initial study. Moreover, Peter was able to discover what the case was 'really about' because his long residence in the village had allowed him to build up relations of trust with people who were willing to confide in him and to explain events and motivations beyond superficial appearances. Having long-term cordial relations with people in the village—having friends, if you like—also enabled Peter to persist in his questions beyond the superficial and to evaluate the content of the answers he received.

What implications might an anthropologist see in the lessons of this case? Every ethnographic description at least implicitly participates in the cross-cultural comparisons that also engage anthropologists. Anthropology has long been engaged in relating the description of local beliefs and practices to categories of universal, pan-human significance. The case of la Ninde compelled Peter to bring into question his understanding of legal categories like 'evidence' and 'liability', to question the universality of the idea of 'justice' itself. What does it mean that virtually everyone in the village knew the physical evidence presented by ina Mone was false, yet was nonetheless accepted? What might it mean for our understanding of liability and responsibility if la Ninde could be convicted for what he *might have* done, rather than for what he actually did, without producing a sense among the villagers that he was a victim of trumpery or injustice? If evidence and liability could be handled in this way, what does that mean if we are to try to construct a sense of what justice means to human beings at large? It is this interplay between the specific and the general, between the local and the universal that gives anthropology much of its value as a social science. For not only are we engaged in recording the 'customs and manners' of people around the world, we are constantly bringing our appreciation of local knowledge to bear on a more general understanding of what it means to be a human being.

Fieldwork: Strategies and Practices

It should be obvious that a truly comprehensive description of any society's culture is far beyond the capacity of even a hundred researchers. An ethnographer goes to the field with the intention of studying some particular aspect of social life, which might range from ecological adaptation to indigenous theology, to relations between the genders, to grassroots political mobilization, and so on (see text box). The ethnographer does not enter into the enterprise unprepared. What ethnographers need to know is as diverse and varied as the studies they undertake. Most anthropologists begin their preparation with several years of study in the history and previous ethnographic literature of the region in which they propose to do fieldwork. Because anthropologists have felt it imperative that they conduct their fieldwork in the language of the people they study without using translators, an ethnographer may need to acquire at least passable fluency in several languages. In addition to such general preparation, ethnographers are usually trained in more specialized fields concerning the kind of problem they intend to investigate. A researcher who intends to study the medicinal use of plants among an Amazonian people, for example, needs to learn not only a good deal of conventional botany, but also needs to be familiar with how various of the world's peoples have categorized and used plants. Anthropologists are always anthropologists of something and somewhere: John is an anthropologist of religion and a Mesoamericanist; Peter is an anthropologist of law and a Southeast Asianist.

Half a Dozen Ethnographies

To give an idea of the range of people and places anthropologists study, here, in no particular order, are the titles of half a dozen ethnographies, each with a very brief description.

- *We Eat the Mines and the Mines Eat Us* June Nash's description of Bolivian tin miners and the ways in which transnational economic processes affect their lives (1979).
- *Beamtimes and Lifetimes* Sharon Traweek's account of the world of high-energy physicists (1988).
- *Tuhami. Portrait of a Moroccan* Vincent Crapanzano's ethnographic biography describes his encounter with 'an illiterate Moroccan tilemaker who believes himself married to a camel-footed she-demon' (1980).
- *In the Realm of the Diamond Queen* Anna Tsing's study of political and cultural marginality, linking a Borneo people to the Indonesian nation and the global politics of 'modernization' (1993).
- *The Channeling Zone: American Spirituality in an Anxious Age* Michael F. Brown presents a fascinating look at the lives and experiences of New Age 'channellers' and their place in contemporary American spiritual life (1997).
- *Medusa's Hair* Gananath Obeyesekere brings insights from psychoanalysis to bear on 'personal symbols and religious experience' among ecstatic priests and priestesses in Sri Lanka (1981).

Half a Dozen More Ethnographies

- *After Nature* Marilyn Strathern, whose work on gender and exchange in Papua New Guinea is much admired, turns to English kinship in the twentieth century (1992).
- *Corn Is Our Blood* Alan Sandstrom's examination of Nahua (Aztec) theology and its relation to ethnic identity (1991).
- *The Golden Yoke* Rebecca French, who is both a lawyer and an anthropologist, gives a masterful account of Buddhist cosmology and its relationship to the traditional legal system of Tibet (1995).
- *Geisha* Liza Dalby trained as a geisha in Kyoto and provides a fascinating look at the 'willow world' (1983).
- *Persuasions of the Witch's Craft* Tanya Luhrman delves into the world of witches and magicians in contemporary Britain exploring the implications of their beliefs in the context of modern society (1989).
- *Javanese Shadow Plays, Javanese Selves* Ward Keeler lived with a Javanese puppeteer for several years and wrote this fascinating account of an ancient art form, its practitioners, and its place in modern culture (1987).

An ethnographer's first task is to become established in the community. This is often a protracted and difficult process, during which more than a few projects have foundered. Once the ethnographer has found a source of funding for the project, it is often necessary to secure a variety of permits from various levels of government, local research institutions, and the host community. This can consume more than a year of the ethnographer's time, before he or she even sets foot in the field site. One colleague carrying out a research project at the headquarters of a major industrial concern needed to have his proposal reviewed by the company's lawyers before he could even enter the building to talk with anyone. Once they have arrived, ethnographers face many of the same problems anyone would encounter when moving into a new community, problems complicated by unfamiliarity with the language and the challenges of daily life in places lacking many of the amenities they may have been used to at home: electricity, indoor plumbing, or easy access to healthcare, news, or entertainment. Many anthropologists work in cities and suburbs in Europe and North America, where the challenges are of a different nature. Neither of us would be eager to trade places with colleagues we know who have worked with drug addicts in Spanish Harlem or the top executives of a multinational corporation in Philadelphia.

The ethnographer faces more subtle difficulties, too. Locally powerful individuals may try to use the ethnographer as a prize or a pawn in their rivalries. Members of the community may have an exaggerated idea of what the ethnographer can do for them, and make persistent demands that cannot be met. At the same time, the ethnographer often experiences the great joy of making new friends and the thrill of seeing and doing things he or she would never otherwise have been able to see or do. As a day-to-day experience, fieldwork can be filled with abruptly alternating emotional highs and lows. At its heart, the process of doing ethnography really is participant observation. By living among the people of the community as they themselves live, the ethnographer stands the best chance of becoming established.

Dialogue is the backbone of ethnography. While anthropologists make use of a variety of techniques to elicit and record data, the interview is by far the most important. Interviews can range in formality from highly structured question-and-answer sessions with indigenous specialists, to the recording of life histories, to informal conversations, or to a chance exchange during an unanticipated encounter. Ultimately, the key to ethnographic success is *being there,* available to observe, available to follow up, available to take advantage of the chance event. Beyond the apparently simple techniques of interview and dialogue, ethnographers also employ a variety of more specialized techniques. Audio recording of speech and music, photography, film, drawing, genealogy, mapping, census-taking, archival research, collecting material culture, collecting botanical or other natural samples, all have their ethnographic uses, depending on the ethnographer's specific research project.

Leaving the field can be almost as difficult as entering it: considering the effort required to establish oneself in a community, parting company with friends and now-familiar ways of life can be a wrenching experience. On an intellectual level, there are often nagging worries about whether one has really completed the research topic—a concern that is often justified. In a sense, no ethnographic research project is ever truly complete; it is always possible to learn more, to expand the temporal or spatial scope of one's understanding, or deepen the subtlety of that understanding. Epistemological misgivings, such as those discussed more fully in the next section, often bother the departing ethnographer. Nonetheless, a kind of closure is sometimes possible. Peter recalls relating his analysis of a particularly complex dispute to a friend who was one of the principal elders of Doro Ntika. His friend laughed, and slapping his thigh said, 'You really do understand the way things work around here! Looks like you weren't wasting the past two years after all!'

Critiques of Ethnographic Fieldwork

For all its virtues, we would not want to give the impression that ethnographic fieldwork is the best method for all kinds of social science research, nor that participant observation is the only method employed by anthropologists. Fieldwork brings with it a substantial set of methodological and epistemological problems. Fieldwork also carries with it a unique set of ethical dilemmas.

The very strengths of classical ethnographic research have sometimes also proved to be weaknesses. One problem with participant observation has been a temptation for the ethnographer to present the community in a kind of temporal and spatial isolation. Many ethnographers, particularly in the 'classic' accounts of the 1930s and 1940s, employed what came to be called the *ethnographic present* in which communities were presented as frozen in time, outside any historical context, and without reference to neighbouring societies or encapsulating states. For example, one of the most admired classics, Raymond Firth *We the Tikopia,* described the social organization and traditional religion of the Tikopia without reference to the fact that half the population had recently converted to Christianity. Indeed, anthropologists may sometimes be carried away by the romance of their own enterprise and value the 'unspoiled' traditions of a society far more than the people themselves do. A friend of ours visited Tikopia some twenty years after Firth had lived there, and was taken to a grotto by the sea where offerings to the gods of the old religion had been made. Seeing a single old offering, he asked his guide who had left it there, and was told 'Fossi left it there'. 'Fossi', of course, is the Tikopia pronunciation of Firth's name. Ethnographers are not always successful in guarding against a temptation to romanticize the 'otherness' of the people they study. Another criticism of the 'ethnographic present' has concerned the tendency of ethnographers to write in an omniscient third-person voice, as if they had not been actively involved in eliciting the information they present. For better or worse, the past ten years has seen the emergence of a genre of ethnography that seems as intent on conveying the ethnographer's personal experiences in collecting the data as in presenting the data themselves.

Participant observation—characterized by long-term intense interaction with relatively small groups of people—may allow the ethnographer to dig deeply into the complexities and subtleties of a community's social life. But how representative of larger social and cultural wholes can this be? Based on participant observation alone, it would be impossible for Peter to say to what extent the beliefs and values uncovered in the case of la Ninde are typical of the Dou Donggo in general, or of the regency of Bima, or of Indonesia, or of Southeast Asia. In approaching these problems we recall once again that ethnography is incomplete without the cross-cultural comparisons which allow the uniqueness of ethnographic description to find a comparative spatial and temporal context. Moreover, when it comes to matters of historicity and generalization, anthropologists often make use of the methods of allied disciplines such as history, psychology, and sociology.

There are also persistent questions about the 'objectivity' of the data collected by means of participant observation. When a chemist sets out to analyse a sample, she might use a spectroscope. Like any scientific instrument, a spectroscope can be *calibrated* so that the scientist can be reasonably sure that data collected with one spectroscope will be comparable to data collected with a spectroscope calibrated in another time or place. But what—or, more appropriately, who—is the instrument of data collection in anthropology? Obviously, it is the ethnographer, and calibrating a human being is a far more daunting prospect than calibrating a spectroscope. Each ethnographer is a unique individual, the product of a unique upbringing and education, replete with all the psychological predispositions—hidden as well as obvious—that constitute any human being. There have been notorious instances in which two anthropologists have studied the same community but come to very different conclusions about them. How, then, can we reconcile the inevitable subjectivity of participant observation with our desire for a calibrated uniformity of data collection? The short answer is that we can't, and it is this, more than anything else, that distinguishes social sciences such as anthropology from natural sciences such as chemistry, whatever their own problems of observer bias.

Can the problem of ethnographic subjectivity be overcome? The origins of participant observation as the hallmark method of anthropology began at the end of the last century as an attempt to compensate for the variable reliability of descriptions of non-Western peoples. Not content to rely on travellers' tales, missionary accounts, and official colonial reports of 'customs and manners', W. H. R. Rivers, Bronislaw Malinowski, Franz Boas, and others among the founders of modern professional anthropology insisted on the first-hand collection of ethnographic data by trained observers. It was their hope that training would suffice to compensate for the prejudices of the observer. In the 1951 edition of the Royal Anthropological Institute's *Notes and Queries on Anthropology* the uninitiated were told that 'amateurs untrained in anthropology . . . are apt to assume that they are free from bias. This, however, is far from the case; without a scientific training their observation will certainly be hampered by preconceived attitudes of mind.' Standardized categories for data collection, such as those presented in *Notes and Queries* and the Human Relations Area Files' *Outline of Cultural Materials,* had been created in an attempt to overcome observer bias and ensure the comparability of data collected by different ethnographers. In the 1930s some American anthropologists even went so far as to undergo psychoanalysis before fieldwork in an attempt to 'calibrate' the instrument of data collection, a practice quickly abandoned.

Other notable attempts to overcome these epistemological problems have included re-studies and studies undertaken by teams of ethnographers. One would think that a scientific approach to gathering ethnographic data would encourage anthropologists to re-study communities that had been studied before by other ethnographers as a check against subjectivity or bias. But this is far from common. To some extent this has been due to a sense of urgency among anthropologists to conduct *'salvage ethnography'*. Many have been concerned that most of the world's smaller societies and traditional ways of life are fast disappearing and that it is more important to record

those that have never been studied than to confirm results already collected. It must also be admitted that many anthropologists were first attracted to the field by the romantic image of the lone, intrepid explorer, and that an unspoken ethnographic 'machismo' has attached itself to those who have studied the previously unstudied. There has been, altogether, an understandable if misguided sense of proprietorship on the part of an ethnographer for 'his' or 'her people' which has made it very difficult for one ethnographer to 'poach' on the 'territory' of another. Finally, it has been rare for ethnographers working in communities that have been studied before to approach those communities interested in precisely the same theoretical or ethnographic issues as their predecessors. And because societies can change rapidly, separation in time of even a few years between an initial study and the next study also makes it difficult for re-studies to provide a check on ethnographic objectivity.

On occasion, anthropologists have engaged in the study of a particular community by a team of researchers, partly to provide greater comprehensiveness and partly to compensate for individual observer bias. The 'Modjokuto Project' engaged seven social scientists (mostly anthropologists) in the study of a small town in central Java in the early 1950s; while the Mexican town of Zinacantan was serially the focus of scores of ethnographic studies in the 1960s and 1970s under the general supervision of Evon Vogt. Problems of funding and logistics make such projects difficult to organize and so they have been rare. Nonetheless, in some countries, notably Mexico and Japan, ethnographers are institutionally inclined to engage in team efforts, usually consisting of a group of advanced graduate students led by their professor. For all of this, it is not clear that the data collected by teams of ethnographers are significantly less subjective than those collected by groups.

More recently, some anthropologists have argued that 'objectivity' is a false issue. Our bias—that is, our social and historical situation—is what gives us a point of view, and hence constitutes a resource we should openly draw upon in our interpretations. Others contend that any form of representation is an exercise in power and control. To these critics, the whole enterprise of ethnographic description is suspect so long as asymmetries of power persist between the observer and the observed. These critiques have occasioned new styles of ethnographic writing. In contrast to the language of omniscient objectivity that characterized earlier ethnography, some now favour the presentation of relatively unedited texts representing a variety of 'voices' other than the ethnographer's. Other ethnographers have adopted the inclusion of a more autobiographical style of presentation, in which the ethnographer's background and relations with his or her subjects become a central topic of the ethnography. In a way, we may have come full circle back to travellers' tales. Unfortunately, few ethnographers have proved to be as interesting as the people they study.

All the same, isn't it an act of extraordinary hubris for someone to propose to present a definitive account of another people, even when it is based on long-term 'participant observation'? And isn't it problematic that the vast majority of ethnographers are Westerners when the vast majority of their subjects have been non-Western? To some extent this is a self-correcting problem: more and more non-Western students are trained as anthropologists and more and more nations are developing their own traditions and styles of anthropological research. For example, most of the ethnography of Mexican communities is today written by Mexicans, in Spanish, which was not the case twenty years ago. The same can be said to be true of gender: women, who now constitute a majority of recent doctorates in American anthropology, are frequently engaged in the study of women, both at home and elsewhere. By the same token, a number of non-Western ethnographers have begun to turn their attention to the study of Western societies. The discipline as a whole can only benefit from additional perspectives. After all, Alexis de Toqueville's description of American society remains unsurpassed by any observation made by an American. In the same way, anthropologists have long regarded the 'outsider's perspective' they bring to their subjects as one of the principal advantages of ethnographic method. A person studying his or her own culture can be likened to a fish trying to describe water. While the insider is capable of noticing subtle local variations, the outsider is far more likely to notice the tacit understandings that local people take for granted as 'common sense' or 'natural' categories of thought. The outsider status of the ethnographer, then, can be regarded as a strength as well as a weakness, even as a strength crucial to the success of the enterprise.

The Ethics of Ethnography

The nature of ethnographic work is such that the researcher develops a unique set of relationships with the people he or she studies, with host institutions and governments, and with colleagues. As anthropology has matured, the moral issues raised by these relationships have become matters of concern. Various professional associations have debated the issues and framed codes of ethical conduct. For fieldworkers the first imperative is to ensure that one's research does not harm the people one studies. For example, John and a colleague wrote a history of a Maya town in Guatemala. In a book review, a geographer questioned their expertise and political commitment by noting that

the book failed to mention and criticize the establishment of an army garrison in the town in the 1980s. John and his colleague had certainly been aware of the army's presence (in 1979 a drunken soldier fired a machine gun into the house where John was sleeping). But John and his colleague declined to discuss the army in their book because, given the political situation in Guatemala at the time, and their close work with certain individuals and families in the town, critical mention of the army could have led to retaliation against their friends. Similarly, Peter's account of the case of la Ninde makes use of pseudonyms to protect the anonymity of the parties concerned—a fairly standard practice among anthropologists. Like other anthropologists, he also uses pseudonyms to refer to the places where he has worked.

A persistent source of ethical dilemma for ethnographers is to be found in the extent to which it is appropriate for ethnographers actively to influence the social, religious, or political life of the communities in which they work. In one celebrated case, for example, an ethnographer was presented with a situation in which members of her host community held the traditional belief that twins are inhuman and should be allowed to die of neglect. When twins were born to a village woman during her stay, she faced the dilemma of whether to intervene and if so, in what way. Should she try to persuade the mother not to abandon her newborn babies? Should she offer to adopt them herself? Should she inform village or government officials who disapproved of the traditional practice? Or, out of respect for the beliefs of her hosts, should she do nothing? For all our efforts to frame codes of professional behaviour, there is no consensus among anthropologists as to how such dilemmas are to be resolved. Admittedly, most of the dilemmas anthropologists face are not matters of life and death, but the degree to which the participant observer should really participate in the affairs of the community remains a persistent and vexing problem. In a similar vein, John has frequently been asked by Mixtecs to aid them in entering the United States without a visa. How should he respond? On the one hand he feels a deep sense of obligation to people who have been his friends and hosts in Mexico. On the other hand, helping them in this way violates the laws of his own country.

At the same time, ethnographers have often felt compelled to become advocates for the people they study. The peoples anthropologists study have often been among those most vulnerable to colonial and neocolonial oppression, genocide, displacement, poverty, and general powerlessness in the face of governments and other institutions. Anthropologists sometimes (although hardly always) have access to media and other means of publicizing the plight of the people they study and many have made use of this access. Advocacy has not been without risk to these anthropologists, who have suffered deportation, imprisonment, and even assassination in retaliation for their actions.

One ethical issue that has received increasing attention concerns intellectual property rights. Anthropologists have been criticized for 'profiting' from the 'expropriation' of indigenous cultural knowledge. Are indigenous peoples entitled to copyright knowledge that has traditionally been in the public domain? Should communities be able to exercise control over the publication of cultural knowledge? Should they be entitled to pass binding editorial judgement on the interpretations ethnographers make? Are ethnographers obliged to share what profits, if any, they make from the sale of ethnographic accounts with the subjects of their accounts?

Ultimately, we have to confront more general ethical issues. To whom does an ethnographer owe his or her greatest allegiance? Is it to the people studied, to the sovereign government of the country where research takes place, to the agency or foundation that funds the ethnographer's research, to the academic or research institution that employs the ethnographer, or to the community of scholars to which the ethnographer belongs? Should ethnographers be expected only to add to humanity's knowledge of itself or should they be expected to provide more tangible benefits to the people they study or to the world at large? Should ethnographers be held to a higher standard than the one applied to journalists, filmmakers, or photographers who also report on their fellow human beings? These, too, are unresolved questions, subject to lively debate.

What can we expect of ethnography and the ethnographer? For all of the claims made for and against the products of participant observation, anthropology has always relied on what amounts to a good-faith effort on the part of ethnographers to tell their stories as fully and honestly as possible. Similarly, we have relied on the common decency of ethnographers to act with due regard for the integrity of their profession. We all recognize that complete descriptive objectivity is impossible, that a comprehensive understanding of any society or culture is unattainable, and that ethical problems are more easily posed than resolved. That we continue to pose these questions is perhaps the best indication of the fundamental health of anthropology as both an academic discipline and a humanistic enterprise.

Assess Your Progress

1. In what respects does ethnographic fieldwork define the discipline of cultural anthropology and distinguish it from other disciplines?

2. Why is "participant observation" so important to the field?

3. How does the case of la Ninde and ina Mone illustrate the importance of the ethnographic experience in understanding a culture?

4. How does a cross-cultural comparison call into question the universality of "evidence," "liability," and "justice?"

5. In what ways must an anthropologist be prepared to work in the field?

6. In what ways can the very strengths of classical ethnographic research also prove to be its weaknesses?

7. In what ways have anthropologists attempted to overcome their own subjectivity? Can this ever truly be done?

8. What are some of the ethical dilemmas anthropologists face with respect to the people they are studying?

From *Social and Cultural Anthropology: A Very Short Introduction* by John Monaghan and Peter Just, (Oxford University Press, 2000). Copyright © 2000 by Oxford University Press, Ltd. Reprinted by permission.

Doing Fieldwork among the Yąnomamö[1]

Napoleon A. Chagnon

Vignette

The Yąnomamö are thinly scattered over a vast and verdant tropical forest, living in small villages that are separated by many miles of unoccupied land. They have no writing, but they have a rich and complex language. Their clothing is more decorative than protective. Well-dressed men sport nothing more than a few cotton strings around their wrists, ankles, and waists. They tie the foreskins of their penises to the waist string. Women dress about the same. Much of their daily life revolves around gardening, hunting, collecting wild foods, collecting firewood, fetching water, visiting with each other, gossiping, and making the few material possessions they own: baskets, hammocks, bows, arrows, and colorful pigments with which they paint their bodies. Life is relatively easy in the sense that they can 'earn a living' with about three hours' work per day. Most of what they eat they cultivate in their gardens, and most of that is plantains—a kind of cooking banana that is usually eaten green, either roasted on the coals or boiled in pots. Their meat comes from a large variety of game animals, hunted daily by the men. It is usually roasted on coals or smoked, and is always well done. Their villages are round and open—and very public. One can hear, see, and smell almost everything that goes on anywhere in the village. Privacy is rare, but sexual discreetness is possible in the garden or at night while others sleep. The villages can be as small as 40 to 50 people or as large as 300 people, but in all cases there are many more children and babies than there are adults. This is true of most primitive populations and of our own demographic past. Life expectancy is short.

The Yąnomamö fall into the category of Tropical Forest Indians called 'foot people.' They avoid large rivers and live in interfluvial plains of the major rivers. They have neighbors to the north, Carib-speaking Ye'kwana, who are true 'river people': They make elegant, large dugout canoes and travel extensively along the major waterways. For the Yąnomamö, a large stream is an obstacle and can be crossed only in the dry season. Thus, they have traditionally avoided larger rivers and, because of this, contact with outsiders who usually come by river.

They enjoy taking trips when the jungle abounds with seasonally ripe wild fruits and vegetables. Then, the large village—the *shabono*—is abandoned for a few weeks and everyone camps out for from one to several days away from the village and garden. On these trips, they make temporary huts from poles, vines, and leaves, each family making a separate hut.

Two major seasons dominate their annual cycle: the wet season, which inundates the low-lying jungle, making travel difficult, and the dry season—the time of visiting other villages to feast, trade, and politic with allies. The dry season is also the time when raiders can travel and strike silently at their unsuspecting enemies. The Yąnomamö are still conducting intervillage warfare, a phenomenon that affects all aspects of their social organization, settlement pattern, and daily routines. It is not simply 'ritualistic' war: At least one-fourth of all adult males die violently in the area I lived in.

Social life is organized around those same principles utilized by all tribesmen: kinship relationships, descent from ancestors, marriage exchanges between kinship/descent groups, and the transient charisma of distinguished headmen who attempt to keep order in the village and whose responsibility it is to determine the village's relationships with those in other villages. Their positions are largely the result of kinship and marriage patterns; they come from the largest kinship groups within the village. They can, by their personal wit, wisdom, and charisma, become autocrats, but most of them are largely 'greaters' among equals. They, too, must clear gardens, plant crops, collect wild foods, and hunt. They are simultaneously peacemakers and valiant warriors. Peacemaking often requires the threat or actual use of force, and most headmen have an acquired reputation for being *waiteri*: fierce.

The social dynamics within villages are involved with giving and receiving marriageable girls. Marriages are arranged by older kin, usually men, who are brothers, uncles, and the father. It is a political process, for girls are promised in marriage while they are young, and the men who do this attempt to create alliances with other men via marriage exchanges. There is a shortage of women due in part to a sex-ratio imbalance in the younger age categories, but also complicated by the fact that some men have multiple wives. Most fighting within the village stems from sexual affairs or failure to deliver a promised woman—or out-and-out seizure of a married woman by some other man. This can lead to internal fighting and conflict of such an intensity that villages split up and fission, each group then becoming a new village and, often, enemies to each other.

But their conflicts are not blind, uncontrolled violence. They have a series of graded forms of violence that ranges from chest-pounding and club-fighting duels to out-and-out shooting to kill. This gives them a good deal of flexibility in settling disputes without immediate resort to lethal violence. In addition, they have developed patterns of alliance and friendship that serve to limit violence—trading and feasting with others in order to become friends. These alliances can, and often do, result in intervillage exchanges of marriageable women, which leads to additional amity between villages. No good thing lasts forever, and most alliances crumble. Old friends become hostile and, occasionally, treacherous. Each village must therefore be keenly aware that its neighbors are fickle and must behave accordingly. The thin line between friendship and animosity must be traversed by the village leaders, whose political acumen and strategies are both admirable and complex.

Each village, then, is a replica of all others in a broad sense. But each village is part of a larger political, demographic, and ecological process, and it is difficult to attempt to understand the village without knowing something of the larger forces that affect it and its particular history with all its neighbors.

Collecting the Data in the Field

I have now spent over 60 months with Yąnomamö, during which time I gradually learned their language and, up to a point, submerged myself in their culture and way of life.[2] As my research progressed, the thing that impressed me most was the importance that aggression played in shaping their culture. I had the opportunity to witness a good many incidents that expressed individual vindictiveness on the one hand and collective bellicosity on the other hand. These ranged in seriousness from the ordinary incidents of wife beating and chest pounding to dueling and organized raids by parties that set out with the intention of ambushing and killing men from enemy villages. One of the villages was raided approximately twenty-five times during my first 15 months of fieldwork—six times by the group among whom I was living. And, the history of every village I investigated, from 1964 to 1991, was intimately bound up in patterns of warfare with neighbors that shaped its politics and determined where it was found at any point in time and how it dealt with its current neighbors.

The fact that the Yąnomamö have lived in a chronic state of warfare is reflected in their mythology, ceremonies, settlement pattern, political behavior, and marriage practices. Accordingly, I have organized this case study in such a way that students can appreciate the effects of warfare on Yąnomamö culture in general and on their social organization and political relationships in particular.

I collected the data under somewhat trying circumstances, some of which I will describe to give a rough idea of what is generally meant when anthropologists speak of 'culture shock' and 'fieldwork.' It should be borne in mind, however, that each field situation is in many respects unique, so that the problems I encountered do not necessarily exhaust the range of possible problems other anthropologists have confronted in other areas. There are a few problems, however, that seem to be nearly universal among anthropological fieldworkers, particularly those having to do with eating, bathing, sleeping, lack of privacy, loneliness, or discovering that the people you are living with have a lower opinion of you than you have of them or you yourself are not as culturally or emotionally 'flexible' as you assumed.

The Yąnomamö can be difficult people to live with at times, but I have spoken to colleagues who have had difficulties living in the communities they studied. These things vary from society to society, and probably from one anthropologist to the next. I have also done limited fieldwork among the Yąnomamö's northern neighbors, the Carib-speaking Ye'kwana Indians. By contrast to many experiences I had among the Yąnomamö, the Ye'kwana were very pleasant and charming, all of them anxious to help me and honor bound to show any visitor the numerous courtesies of their system of etiquette. In short, they approached the image of 'primitive man' that I had conjured up in my mind before doing fieldwork, a kind of 'Rousseauian' view, and it was sheer pleasure to work with them. Other anthropologists have also noted sharp contrasts in the people they study from one field situation to another. One of the most startling examples of this is in the work of Colin Turnbull, who first studied the Ituri Pygmies (1965, 1983) and found them delightful to live with, but then studied the Ik (1972) of the desolate outcroppings of the Kenya/Uganda/Sudan border region, a people he had difficulty coping with intellectually, emotionally, and physically. While it is possible that the anthropologist's reactions to a particular people are personal and idiosyncratic, it nevertheless remains true that there are enormous differences between whole peoples, differences that affect the anthropologist in often dramatic ways.

Hence, what I say about some of my experiences is probably equally true of the experiences of many other fieldworkers. I describe some of them here for the benefit of future anthropologists—because I think I could have profited by reading about the pitfalls and field problems of my own teachers. At the very least I might have been able to avoid some of my more stupid errors. In this regard there is a growing body of excellent descriptive work on field research. Students who plan to make a career in anthropology should consult these works, which cover a wide range of field situations in the ethnographic present.[3]

The Longest Day: The First One

My first day in the field illustrated to me what my teachers meant when they spoke of 'culture shock.' I had traveled in a small, aluminum rowboat propelled by a large outboard motor for two and a half days. This took me from the territorial capital, a small town on the Orinoco River, deep into Yąnomamö country. On the morning of the third day we reached a small mission settlement, the field 'headquarters' of a group of Americans who were working in two Yąnomamö villages. The missionaries had come out of these villages to hold their annual conference on the progress of their mission work and were conducting their meetings when I arrived. We picked up a passenger at the mission station, James P. Barker, the first non-Yąnomamö to make a sustained, permanent contact with the tribe (in 1950). He had just returned from a year's furlough in the United States, where I had earlier visited him before leaving for Venezuela. He agreed to accompany me to the village I had selected for my base of operations to introduce me to the Indians. This village was also his own home base, but he had not been there for over a year and did not plan to join me for another three months. Mr. Barker had been living with this particular group about five years.

We arrived at the village, Bisaasi-teri, about 2:00 P.M. and docked the boat along the muddy bank at the terminus of the path used by Yąnomamö to fetch their drinking water. It was hot and muggy, and my clothing was soaked with perspiration. It clung uncomfortably to my body, as it did thereafter for the remainder of the work. The small biting gnats, *bareto,* were out in astronomical numbers, for it was the beginning of the dry season. My face and hands were swollen from the venom of their numerous stings. In just a few moments I was to meet my first Yąnomamö, my first primitive man. What would he be like? I had visions of entering the village and seeing 125 social facts running about altruistically calling each other kinship terms and sharing food, each waiting and anxious to have me collect his genealogy. I would wear them out in turn. Would they like me? This was important to me; I wanted them to be so fond of me that they would adopt me into their kinship system and way of life. I had heard that successful anthropologists always get adopted by their people. I had learned during my seven years of anthropological training at the University of Michigan that kinship was equivalent to society in primitive tribes and that it was a moral way of life, 'moral' being something 'good' and 'desirable.' I was determined to work my way into their moral system of kinship and become a member of their society—to be 'accepted' by them.

How Did They Accept You?

My heart began to pound as we approached the village and heard the buzz of activity within the circular compound. Mr. Barker commented that he was anxious to see if any changes had taken place while he was away and wondered how many of them had died during his absence. I nervously felt my back pocket to make sure that my notebook was still there and felt personally more secure when I touched it.

The entrance to the village was covered over with brush and dry palm leaves. We pushed them aside to expose the low opening to the village. The excitement of meeting my first Yanomamö was almost unbearable as I duck-waddled through the low passage into the village clearing.

I looked up and gasped when I saw a dozen burly, naked, sweaty, hideous men staring at us down the shafts of their drawn arrows! Immense wads of green tobacco were stuck between their lower teeth and lips making them look even more hideous, and strands of dark-green slime dripped or hung from their nostrils—strands so long that they clung to their pectoral muscles or drizzled down their chins. We arrived at the village while the men were blowing a hallucinogenic drug up their noses. One of the side effects of the drug is a runny nose. The mucus is always saturated with the green powder and they usually let it run freely from their nostrils. My next discovery was that there were a dozen or so vicious, underfed dogs snapping at my legs, circling me as if I were to be their next meal. I just stood there holding my notebook, helpless and pathetic. Then the stench of the decaying vegetation and

filth hit me and I almost got sick. I was horrified. What kind of welcome was this for the person who came here to live with you and learn your way of life, to become friends with you? They put their weapons down when they recognized Barker and returned to their chanting, keeping a nervous eye on the village entrances.

We had arrived just after a serious fight. Seven women had been abducted the day before by a neighboring group, and the local men and their guests had just that morning recovered five of them in a brutal club fight that nearly ended in a shooting war. The abductors, angry because they had lost five of their seven new captives, vowed to raid the Bisaasi-teri. When we arrived and entered the village unexpectedly, the Indians feared that we were the raiders. On several occasions during the next two hours the men in the village jumped to their feet, armed themselves, nocked their arrows and waited nervously for the noise outside the village to be identified. My enthusiasm for collecting ethnographic facts diminished in proportion to the number of times such an alarm was raised. In fact, I was relieved when Barker suggested that we sleep across the river for the evening. It would be safer over there.

As we walked down the path to the boat, I pondered the wisdom of having decided to spend a year and a half with these people before I had even seen what they were like. I am not ashamed to admit that had there been a diplomatic way out, I would have ended my fieldwork then and there. I did not look forward to the next day—and months—when I would be left alone with the Yąnomamö; I did not speak a word of their language, and they were decidedly different from what I had imagined them to be. The whole situation was depressing, and I wondered why I ever decided to switch from physics and engineering in the first place. I had not eaten all day, I was soaking wet from perspiration, the *bareto* were biting me, and I was covered with red pigment, the result of a dozen or so complete examinations I had been given by as many very pushy Yąnomamö men. These examinations capped an otherwise grim day. The men would blow their noses into their hands, flick as much of the mucus off that would separate in a snap of the wrist, wipe the residue into their hair, and then carefully examine my face, arms, legs, hair, and the contents of my pockets. I asked Barker how to say, 'Your hands are dirty'; my comments were met by the Yąnomamö in the following way: They would 'clean' their hands by spitting a quantity of slimy tobacco juice into them, rub them together, grin, and then proceed with the examination.

Mr. Barker and I crossed the river and slung our hammocks. When he pulled his hammock out of a rubber bag, a heavy disagreeable odor of mildewed cotton and stale wood smoke came with it. 'Even the missionaries are filthy,' I thought to myself. Within two weeks, everything I owned smelled the same way, and I lived with that odor for the remainder of the fieldwork. My own habits of personal cleanliness declined to such levels that I didn't even mind being examined by the Yąnomamö, as I was not much cleaner than they were after I had adjusted to the circumstances. It is difficult to blow your nose gracefully when you are stark naked and the invention of handkerchiefs is millenia away.

Life in the Jungle: Oatmeal, Peanut Butter, and Bugs

It isn't easy to plop down in the Amazon Basin for a year and get immediately into the anthropological swing of things. You have been told about horrible diseases, snakes, jaguars, electric eels, little spiny fish that will swim up your urine into your penis, quicksand, and getting lost. Some of the dangers are real, but your imagination makes them more real and threatening than many of them really are. What my teachers never bothered to advise me about, however, was the mundane, nonexciting, and trivial stuff—like eating, defecating, sleeping, or keeping clean. These turned out to be the bane of my existence during the first several months of field research. I set up my household in Barker's abandoned mud hut, a few yards from the village of Bisaasi-teri, and immediately set to work building my own mud/thatch hut with the help of the Yąnomamö. Meanwhile, I had to eat and try to do my 'field research.' I soon discovered that it was an enormously time-consuming task to maintain my own body in the manner to which it had grown accustomed in the relatively antiseptic environment of the northern United States. Either I could be relatively well fed and relatively comfortable in a fresh change of clothes and do very little fieldwork, or I could do considerably more fieldwork and be less well fed and less comfortable.

It is appalling how complicated it can be to make oatmeal in the jungle. First, I had to make two trips to the river to haul the water. Next, I had to prime my kerosene stove with alcohol to get it burning, a tricky procedure when you are trying to mix powdered milk and fill a coffee pot at the same time. The alcohol prime always burned out before I could turn the kerosene on, and I would have to start all over. Or, I would turn the kerosene on, optimistically hoping that the Coleman element was still hot enough to vaporize the fuel, and start a small fire in my palm-thatched hut as the liquid kerosene squirted all over the table and walls and then ignited. Many amused Yąnomamö onlookers quickly learned the English phrase 'Oh, Shit!' and, once they discovered that the phrase offended and irritated the missionaries, they used it as often as they could in their presence. I usually had to start over with the alcohol. Then I had to boil the oatmeal and pick the bugs out of it. All my supplies, of course, were carefully stored in rat-proof, moisture-proof, and insect-proof containers, not one of which ever served its purpose adequately. Just taking things out of the multiplicity of containers and repacking them afterward was a minor project in itself. By the time I had hauled the water to cook with, unpacked my food, prepared the oatmeal, milk, and coffee, heated water for dishes, washed and dried the dishes, repacked the food in the containers, stored the containers in locked trunks, and cleaned up my mess, the ceremony of preparing breakfast had brought me almost up to lunch time!

Eating three meals a day was simply out of the question. I solved the problem by eating a single meal that could be prepared in a single container, or, at most, in two containers, washed my dishes only when there were no clean ones left, using cold river water, and wore each change of clothing at least a week to cut down on my laundry problem—a courageous

undertaking in the tropics. I reeked like a jockstrap that had been left to mildew in the bottom of some dark gym locker. I also became less concerned about sharing my provisions with the rats, insects, Yąnomamö, and the elements, thereby eliminating the need for my complicated storage process. I was able to last most of the day on *café con leche*, heavily sugared espresso coffee diluted about five to one with hot milk. I would prepare this in the evening and store it in a large thermos. Frequently, my single meal was no more complicated than a can of sardines and a package of soggy crackers. But at least two or three times a week I would do something 'special' and sophisticated, like make a batch of oatmeal or boil rice and add a can of tuna fish or tomato paste to it. I even saved time by devising a water system that obviated the trips to the river. I had a few sheets of tin roofing brought in and made a rain water trap; I caught the water on the tin surface, funneled it into an empty gasoline drum, and then ran a plastic hose from the drum to my hut. When the drum was exhausted in the dry season, I would get a few Yąnomamö boys to fill it with buckets of water from the river, 'paying' them with crackers, of which they grew all too fond all too soon.

I ate much less when I traveled with the Yąnomamö to visit other villages. Most of the time my travel diet consisted of roasted or boiled green plantains (cooking bananas) that I obtained from the Yąnomamö, but I always carried a few cans of sardines with me in case I got lost or stayed away longer than I had planned. I found peanut butter and crackers a very nourishing 'trail' meal, and a simple one to prepare. It was nutritious and portable, and only one tool was required to make the meal: a hunting knife that could be cleaned by wiping the blade on a convenient leaf. More importantly, it was one of the few foods the Yąnomamö would let me eat in relative peace. It looked suspiciously like animal feces to them, an impression I encouraged. I referred to the peanut butter as the feces of babies or 'cattle.' They found this disgusting and repugnant. They did not know what 'cattle' were, but were increasingly aware that I ate several canned products of such an animal. Tin cans were thought of as containers made of 'machete skins,' but how the cows got inside was always a mystery to them. I went out of my way to describe my foods in such a way as to make them sound unpalatable to them, for it gave me some peace of mind while I ate: They wouldn't beg for a share of something that was too horrible to contemplate. Fieldworkers develop strange defense mechanisms and strategies, and this was one of my own forms of adaptation to the fieldwork. On another occasion I was eating a can of frankfurters and growing very weary of the demands from one of the onlookers for a share in my meal. When he finally asked what I was eating, I replied: 'Beef.' He then asked: 'Shaki![4] What part of the animal are you eating?' To which I replied, 'Guess.' He muttered a contemptuous epithet, but stopped asking for a share. He got back at me later, as we shall see.

Meals were a problem in a way that had nothing to do with the inconvenience of preparing them. Food sharing is important to the Yąnomamö in the context of displaying friendship. 'I am hungry!' is almost a form of greeting with them. I could not possibly have brought enough food with me to feed the

13

entire village, yet they seemed to overlook this logistic fact as they begged for my food. What became fixed in their minds was the fact that I did not share my food with whomsoever was present—usually a small crowd—at each and every meal. Nor could I easily enter their system of reciprocity with respect to food. Every time one of them 'gave' me something 'freely,' he would dog me for months to 'pay him back,' not necessarily with food but with knives, fishhooks, axes, and so on. Thus, if I accepted a plantain from someone in a different village while I was on a visit, he would most likely visit me in the future and demand a machete as payment for the time that he 'fed' me. I usually reacted to these kinds of demands by giving a banana, the customary reciprocity in their culture—food for food—but this would be a disappointment for the individual who had nursed visions of that single plantain growing into a machete over time. Many years after beginning my fieldwork, I was approached by one of the prominent men who demanded a machete for a piece of meat he claimed he had given me five or six years earlier.

Despite the fact that most of them knew I would not share my food with them at their request, some of them always showed up at my hut during mealtime. I gradually resigned myself to this and learned to ignore their persistent demands while I ate. Some of them would get angry because I failed to give in, but most of them accepted it as just a peculiarity of the subhuman foreigner who had come to live among them. If or when I did accede to a request for a share of my food, my hut quickly filled with Yąnomamö, each demanding their share of the food that I had just given to one of them. Their begging for food was not provoked by hunger, but by a desire to try something new and to attempt to establish a coercive relationship in which I would accede to a demand. If one received something, all others would immediately have to test the system to see if they, too, could coerce me.

A few of them went out of their way to make my meals downright unpleasant—to spite me for not sharing, especially if it was a food that they had tried before and liked, or a food that was part of their own cuisine. For example, I was eating a cracker with peanut butter and honey one day. The Yąnomamö will do almost anything for honey, one of the most prized delicacies in their own diet. One of my cynical onlookers—the fellow who had earlier watched me eating frankfurters—immediately recognized the honey and knew that I would not share the tiny precious bottle. It would be futile to even ask. Instead, he glared at me and queried icily, 'Shaki! What kind of animal semen are you pouring onto your food and eating?' His question had the desired effect and my meal ended.

Finally, there was the problem of being lonely and separated from your own kind, especially your family. I tried to overcome this by seeking personal friendships among the Yąnomamö. This usually complicated the matter because all my 'friends' simply used my confidence to gain privileged access to my hut and my cache of steel tools and trade goods—and looted me when I wasn't looking. I would be bitterly disappointed that my erstwhile friend thought no more of me than to finesse our personal relationship exclusively with the intention of getting at my locked up possessions, and my depression

would hit new lows every time I discovered this. The loss of the possessions bothered me much less than the shock that I was, as far as most of them were concerned, nothing more than a source of desirable items. No holds were barred in relieving me of these, since I was considered something subhuman, a non-Yąnomamö.

The hardest thing to learn to live with was the incessant, passioned, and often aggressive demands they would make. It would become so unbearable at times that I would have to lock myself in my hut periodically just to escape from it. Privacy is one of our culture's most satisfying achievements, one you never think about until you suddenly have none. It is like not appreciating how good your left thumb feels until someone hits it with a hammer. But I did not want privacy for its own sake; rather, I simply had to get away from the begging. Day and night for almost the entire time I lived with the Yąnomamö, I was plagued by such demands as: 'Give me a knife, I am poor!'; 'If you don't take me with you on your next trip to Widokai-yateri, I'll chop a hole in your canoe!'; 'Take us hunting up the Mavaca River with your shotgun or we won't help you!'; 'Give me some matches so I can trade with the Reyaboböwei-teri, and be quick about it or I'll hit you!'; 'Share your food with me, or I'll burn your hut!'; 'Give me a flashlight so I can hunt at night!'; 'Give me all your medicine, I itch all over!'; 'Give me an ax or I'll break into your hut when you are away and steal all of them!' And so I was bombarded by such demands day after day, month after month, until I could not bear to see a Yanomamö at times.

It was not as difficult to become calloused to the incessant begging as it was to ignore the sense of urgency, the impassioned tone of voice and whining, or the intimidation and aggression with which many of the demands were made. It was likewise difficult to adjust to the fact that the Yąnomamö refused to accept 'No' for an answer until or unless it seethed with passion and intimidation—which it did after a few months. So persistent and characteristic is the begging that the early 'semi-official' maps made by the Venezuelan Malaria Control Service (Malarialogía) designated the site of their first permanent field station, next to the village of Bisaasi-teri, as *Yaba-buhii:* 'Gimme.' I had to become like the Yąnomamö to be able to get along with them on their terms: somewhat sly, aggressive, intimidating, and pushy.

It became indelibly clear to me shortly after I arrived there that had I failed to adjust in this fashion I would have lost six months of supplies to them in a single day or would have spent most of my time ferrying them around in my canoe or taking them on long hunting trips. As it was, I did spend a considerable amount of time doing these things and did succumb often to their outrageous demands for axes and machetes, at least at first, for things changed as I became more fluent in their language and learned how to defend myself socially as well as verbally. More importantly, had I failed to demonstrate that I could not be pushed around beyond a certain point, I would have been the subject of far more ridicule, theft, and practical jokes than was the actual case. In short, I had to acquire a certain proficiency in their style of interpersonal politics and to learn how to imply subtly that certain potentially undesirable, but unspecified, consequences might follow if they did such and such to me. They do this to each other incessantly in order to establish precisely the point at which they cannot goad or intimidate an individual any further without precipitating some kind of retaliation. As soon as I realized this and gradually acquired the self-confidence to adopt this strategy, it became clear that much of the intimidation was calculated to determine my flash point or my 'last ditch' position—and I got along much better with them. Indeed, I even regained some lost ground. It was sort of like a political, interpersonal game that everyone had to play, but one in which each individual sooner or later had to give evidence that his bluffs and implied threats could be backed up with a sanction. I suspect that the frequency of wife beating is a component in this syndrome, since men can display their *waiteri* (ferocity) and 'show' others that they are capable of great violence. Beating a wife with a club is one way of displaying ferocity, one that does not expose the man to much danger—unless the wife has concerned, aggressive brothers in the village who will come to her aid. Apparently an important thing in wife beating is that the man has displayed his presumed potential for violence and the intended message is that other men ought to treat him with circumspection, caution, and even deference.

After six months, the level of Yąnomamö demand was tolerable in Bisaasi-teri, the village I used for my base of operations. We had adjusted somewhat to each other and knew what to expect with regard to demands for food, trade goods, and favors. Had I elected to remain in just one Yąnomamö village for the entire duration of my first 15 months of fieldwork, the experience would have been far more enjoyable than it actually was. However, as I began to understand the social and political dynamics of this village, it became patently obvious that I would have to travel to many other villages to determine the demographic bases and political histories that lay behind what I could understand in the village of Bisaasi-teri. I began making regular trips to some dozen neighboring Yąnomamö villages as my language fluency improved. I collected local genealogies there, or rechecked and cross-checked those I had collected elsewhere. Hence, the intensity of begging was relatively constant and relatively high for the duration of my fieldwork, for I had to establish my personal position in each village I visited and revisited.

For the most part, my own 'fierceness' took the form of shouting back at the Yąnomamö as loudly and as passionately as they shouted at me, especially at first, when I did not know much of the language. As I became more fluent and learned more about their political tactics, I became more sophisticated in the art of bluffing and brinksmanship. For example, I paid one young man a machete (then worth about $2.50) to cut a palm tree and help me make boards from the wood. I used these to fashion a flooring in the bottom of my dugout canoe to keep my possessions out of the water that always seeped into the canoe and sloshed around. That afternoon I was working with one of my informants in the village. The long-awaited mission supply boat arrived and most of the Yąnomamö ran out of the village to see the supplies and try to beg items from the crew. I continued to work in the village for another hour or

so and then went down to the river to visit with the men on the supply boat. When I reached the river I noticed, with anger and frustration, that the Yąnomamö had chopped up all my new floor boards to use as crude paddles to get their own canoes across the river to the supply boat.[5] I knew that if I ignored this abuse I would have invited the Yąnomamö to take even greater liberties with my possessions in the future. I got into my canoe, crossed the river, and docked amidst their flimsy, leaky craft. I shouted loudly to them, attracting their attention. They were somewhat sheepish, but all had mischievous grins on their impish faces. A few of them came down to the canoe, where I proceeded with a spirited lecture that revealed my anger at their audacity and license. I explained that I had just that morning paid one of them a machete for bringing me the palmwood, how hard I had worked to shape each board and place it in the canoe, how carefully and painstakingly I had tied each one in with vines, how much I had perspired, how many *bareto* bites I had suffered, and so on. Then, with exaggerated drama and finality, I withdrew my hunting knife as their grins disappeared and cut each one of their canoes loose and set it into the strong current of the Orinoco River where it was immediately swept up and carried downstream. I left without looking back and huffed over to the other side of the river to resume my work.

They managed to borrow another canoe and, after some effort, recovered their dugouts. Later, the headman of the village told me, with an approving chuckle, that I had done the correct thing. Everyone in the village, except, of course, the culprits, supported and defended my actions—and my status increased as a consequence.

Whenever I defended myself in such ways I got along much better with the Yąnomamö and gradually acquired the respect of many of them. A good deal of their demeanor toward me was directed with the forethought of establishing the point at which I would draw the line and react defensively. Many of them, years later, reminisced about the early days of my fieldwork when I was timid and *mohode* ("stupid") and a little afraid of them, those golden days when it was easy to bully me into giving my goods away for almost nothing.

Theft was the most persistent situation that required some sort of defensive action. I simply could not keep everything I owned locked in trunks, and the Yąnomamö came into my hut and left at will. I eventually developed a very effective strategy for recovering almost all the stolen items: I would simply ask a child who took the item and then I would confiscate that person's hammock when he was not around, giving a spirited lecture to all who could hear on the antisociality of thievery as I stalked off in a faked rage with the thief's hammock slung over my shoulder. Nobody ever attempted to stop me from doing this, and almost all of them told me that my technique for recovering my possessions was ingenious. By nightfall the thief would appear at my hut with the stolen item or send it over with someone else to make an exchange to recover his hammock. He would be heckled by his covillagers for having got caught and for being embarrassed into returning my item for his hammock. The explanation was usually, 'I just borrowed your ax! I wouldn't think of stealing it!'

Collecting Yąnomamö Genealogies and Reproductive Histories

My purpose for living among Yąnomamö was to systematically collect certain kinds of information on genealogy, reproduction, marriage practices, kinship, settlement patterns, migrations, and politics. Much of the fundamental data was genealogical—who was the parent of whom, tracing these connections as far back in time as Yąnomamö knowledge and memory permitted. Since 'primitive' society is organized largely by kinship relationships, figuring out the social organization of the Yąnomamö essentially meant collecting extensive data on genealogies, marriage, and reproduction. This turned out to be a staggering and very frustrating problem. I could not have deliberately picked a more difficult people to work with in this regard. They have very stringent name taboos and eschew mentioning the names of prominent living people as well as all deceased friends and relatives. They attempt to name people in such a way that when the person dies and they can no longer use his or her name, the loss of the word in their language is not inconvenient. Hence, they name people for specific and minute parts of things, such as 'toenail of sloth,' 'whisker of howler monkey,' and so on, thereby being able to retain the words 'toenail' or 'whisker' but somewhat handicapped in referring to these anatomical parts of sloths and monkeys respectively. The taboo is maintained even for the living, for one mark of prestige is the courtesy others show you by not using your name publicly. This is particularly true for men, who are much more competitive for status than women in this culture, and it is fascinating to watch boys grow into young men, demanding to be called either by a kinship term in public, or by a teknonymous reference such as 'brother of Himotoma.' The more effective they are at getting others to avoid using their names, the more public acknowledgment there is that they are of high esteem and social standing. Helena Valero, a Brazilian woman who was captured as a child by a Yąnomamö raiding party, was married for many years to a Yąnomamö headman before she discovered what his name was (Biocca, 1970; Valero, 1984). The sanctions behind the taboo are more complex than just this, for they involve a combination of fear, respect, admiration, political deference, and honor.

At first I tried to use kinship terms alone to collect genealogies, but Yąnomamö kinship terms, like the kinship terms in all systems, are ambiguous at some point because they include so many possible relatives (as the term 'uncle' does in our own kinship system). Again, their system of kin classification merges many relatives that we 'separate' by using different terms: They call both their actual father and their father's brother by a single term, whereas we call one 'father' and the other 'uncle.' I was forced, therefore, to resort to personal names to collect unambiguous genealogies or 'pedigrees.' They quickly grasped what I was up to and that I was determined to learn everyone's 'true name,' which amounted to an invasion of their system of prestige and etiquette, if not a flagrant violation of it. They reacted to this in a brilliant but devastating manner: They invented false names for everybody in the village and systematically learned them, freely revealing to me the 'true' identities of everyone. I smugly thought I had cracked the system

and enthusiastically constructed elaborate genealogies over a period of some five months. They enjoyed watching me learn their names and kinship relationships. I naively assumed that I would get the 'truth' to each question and the best information by working in public. This set the stage for converting my serious project into an amusing hoax of the grandest proportions. Each 'informant' would try to outdo his peers by inventing a name even more preposterous or ridiculous than what I had been given by someone earlier, the explanations for discrepancies being 'Well, he has two names and this is the other one.' They even fabricated devilishly improbable genealogical relationships, such as someone being married to his grandmother, or worse yet, to his mother-in-law, a grotesque and horrifying prospect to the Yąnomamö. I would collect the desired names and relationships by having my informant whisper the name of the person softly into my ear, noting that he or she was the parent of such and such or the child of such and such, and so on. Everyone who was observing my work would then insist that I repeat the name aloud, roaring in hysterical laughter as I clumsily pronounced the name, sometimes laughing until tears streamed down their faces. The 'named' person would usually react with annoyance and hiss some untranslatable epithet at me, which served to reassure me that I had the 'true' name. I conscientiously checked and re-checked the names and relationships with multiple informants, pleased to see the inconsistencies disappear as my genealogy sheets filled with those desirable little triangles and circles, thousands of them.

My anthropological bubble was burst when I visited a village about 10 hours' walk to the southwest of Bisaasi-teri some five months after I had begun collecting genealogies on the Bisaasi-teri. I was chatting with the local headman of this village and happened to casually drop the name of the wife of the Bisaasi-teri headman. A stunned silence followed, and then a village-wide roar of uncontrollable laughter, choking, gasping, and howling followed. It seems that I thought the Bisaasi-teri headman was married to a woman named "hairy cunt." It also seems that the Bisaasi-teri headman was called 'long dong' and his brother 'eagle shit.' The Bisaasi-teri headman had a son called "asshole" and a daughter called 'fart breath.' And so on. Blood welled up my temples as I realized that I had nothing but nonsense to show for my five months' of dedicated genealogical effort, and I had to throw away almost all the information I had collected on this the most basic set of data I had come there to get. I understood at that point why the Bisaasi-teri laughed so hard when they made me repeat the names of their covillagers, and why the 'named' person would react with anger and annoyance as I pronounced his 'name' aloud.

I was forced to change research strategy—to make an understatement to describe this serious situation. The first thing I did was to begin working in private with my informants to eliminate the horseplay and distraction that attended public sessions. Once I did this, my informants, who did not know what others were telling me, began to agree with each other and I managed to begin learning the 'real' names, starting first with children and gradually moving to adult women and then, cautiously, adult men, a sequence that reflected the relative degree of intransigence at revealing names of people. As I built up a core of accurate genealogies and relationships—a core that all independent informants had verified repetitiously—I could 'test' any new informant by soliciting his or her opinion and knowledge about these 'core' people whose names and relationships I was confident were accurate. I was, in this fashion, able to immediately weed out the mischievous informants who persisted in trying to deceive me. Still, I had great difficulty getting the names of dead kinsmen, the only accurate way to extend genealogies back in time. Even my best informants continued to falsify names of the deceased, especially closely related deceased. The falsifications at this point were not serious and turned out to be readily corrected as my interviewing methods improved (see below). Most of the deceptions were of the sort where the informant would give me the name of a living man as the father of some child whose actual father was dead, a response that enabled the informant to avoid using the name of a deceased kinsman or friend.

The quality of a genealogy depends in part on the number of generations it embraces, and the name taboo prevented me from making any substantial progress in learning about the deceased ancestors of the present population. Without this information, I could not, for example, document marriage patterns and interfamilial alliances through time. I had to rely on older informants for this information, but these were the most reluctant informants of all for this data. As I became more proficient in the language and more skilled at detecting fabrications, any informants became better at deception. One old man was particularly cunning and persuasive, following a sort of Mark Twain policy that the most effective lie is a sincere lie. He specialized in making a ceremony out of false names for dead ancestors. He would look around nervously to make sure nobody was listening outside my hut, enjoin me never to mention the name again, become very anxious and spooky, and grab me by the head to whisper a secret name into my ear. I was always elated after a session with him, because I managed to add several generations of ancestors for particular members of the village. Others steadfastly refused to give me such information. To show my gratitude, I paid him quadruple the rate that I had been paying the others. When word got around that I had increased the pay for genealogical and demographic information, volunteers began pouring into my hut to 'work' for me, assuring me of their changed ways and keen desire to divest themselves of the 'truth.'

Enter Rerebawä: Inmarried Tough Guy

I discovered that the old man was lying quite by accident. A club fight broke out in the village one day, the result of a dispute over the possession of a woman. She had been promised to a young man in the village, a man named Rerebawä, who was particularly aggressive. He had married into Bisaasi-teri and was doing his 'bride service'—a period of several years during which he had to provide game for his wife's father and mother, provide them with wild foods he might collect, and help them in certain gardening and other tasks. Rerebawä had already been given one of the daughters in marriage and was promised her younger sister as his second wife. He was enraged when the younger sister, then about 16 years old, began having

an affair with another young man in the village, Bäkotawä, making no attempt to conceal it. Rerebawä challenged Bäkotawä to a club fight. He swaggered boisterously out to the duel with his 10-foot-long club, a roof-pole he had cut from the house on the spur of the moment, as is the usual procedure. He hurled insult after insult at both Bäkotawä and his father, trying to goad them into a fight. His insults were bitter and nasty. They tolerated them for a few moments, but Rerebawä's biting insults provoked them to rage. Finally, they stormed angrily out of their hammocks and ripped out roof-poles, now returning the insults verbally, and rushed to the village clearing. Rerebawä continued to insult them, goading them into striking him on the head with their equally long clubs. Had either of them struck his head—which he held out conspicuously for them to swing at—he would then have the right to take his turn on their heads with his club. His opponents were intimidated by his fury, and simply backed down, refusing to strike him, and the argument ended. He had intimidated them into submission. All three retired pompously to their respective hammocks, exchanging nasty insults as they departed. But Rerebawä had won the showdown and thereafter swaggered around the village, insulting the two men behind their backs at every opportunity. He was genuinely angry with them, to the point of calling the older man by the name of his long-deceased father. I quickly seized on this incident as an opportunity to collect an accurate genealogy and confidentially asked Rerebawä about his adversary's ancestors. Rerebawä had been particularly 'pushy' with me up to this point, but we soon became warm friends and staunch allies: We were both 'outsiders' in Bisaasi-teri and, although he was a Yąnomamö, he nevertheless had to put up with some considerable amount of pointed teasing and scorn from the locals, as all inmarried 'sons-in-law' must. He gave me the information I requested of his adversary's deceased ancestors, almost with devilish glee. I asked about dead ancestors of other people in the village and got prompt, unequivocal answers: He was angry with everyone in the village. When I compared his answers to those of the old man, it was obvious that one of them was lying. I then challenged his answers. He explained, in a sort of 'you damned fool, don't you know better?' tone of voice that everyone in the village knew the old man was lying to me and gloating over it when I was out of earshot. The names the old man had given to me were names of dead ancestors of the members of a village so far away that he thought I would never have occasion to check them out authoritatively. As it turned out, Rerebawä knew most of the people in that distant village and recognized the names given by the old man.

I then went over all my Bisaasi-teri genealogies with Rerebawä, genealogies I had presumed to be close to their final form. I had to revise them all because of the numerous lies and falsifications they contained, much of it provided by the sly old man. Once again, after months of work, I had to recheck everything with Rerebawä's aid. Only the living members of the nuclear families turned out to be accurate; the deceased ancestors were mostly fabrications.

Discouraging as it was to have to recheck everything all over again, it was a major turning point in my fieldwork. Thereafter, I began taking advantage of local arguments and animosities in selecting my informants, and used more extensively informants who had married into the village in the recent past. I also began traveling more regularly to other villages at this time to check on genealogies, seeking out villages whose members were on strained terms with the people about whom I wanted information. I would then return to my base in the village of Bisaasi-teri and check with local informants the accuracy of the new information. I had to be careful in this work and scrupulously select my local informants in such a way that I would not be inquiring about *their* closely related kin. Thus, for each of my local informants, I had to make lists of names of certain deceased people that I dared not mention in their presence. But despite this precaution, I would occasionally hit a new name that would put some informants into a rage, or into a surly mood, such as that of a dead 'brother' or 'sister'[6] whose existence had not been indicated to me by other informants. This usually terminated my day's work with that informant, for he or she would be too touchy or upset to continue any further, and I would be reluctant to take a chance on accidentally discovering another dead close kinsman soon after discovering the first.

These were unpleasant experiences, and occasionally dangerous as well, depending on the temperament of my informant. On one occasion I was planning to visit a village that had been raided recently by one of their enemies. A woman, whose name I had on my census list for that village, had been killed by the raiders. Killing women is considered to be bad form in Yąnomamö warfare, but this woman was deliberately killed for revenge. The raiders were unable to bushwhack some man who stepped out of the village at dawn to urinate, so they shot a volley of arrows over the roof into the village and beat a hasty retreat. Unfortunately, one of the arrows struck and killed a woman, an accident. For that reason, her village's raiders *deliberately* sought out and killed a woman in retaliation—whose name was on my list. My reason for going to the village was to update my census data on a name-by-name basis and estimate the ages of all the residents. I knew I had the name of the dead woman in my list, but nobody would dare to utter her name so I could remove it. I knew that I would be in very serious trouble if I got to the village and said her name aloud, and I desperately wanted to remove it from my list. I called on one of my regular and usually cooperative informants and asked him to tell me the woman's name. He refused adamantly, explaining that she was a close relative—and was angry that I even raised the topic with him. I then asked him if he would let me whisper the names of *all* the women of that village in his ear, and he would simply have to nod when I hit the right name. We had been 'friends' for some time, and I thought I was able to predict his reaction, and thought that our friendship was good enough to use this procedure. He agreed to the procedure, and I began whispering the names of the women, one by one. We were alone in my hut so that nobody would know what we were doing and nobody could hear us. I read the names softly, continuing to the next when his response was a negative. When I ultimately hit the dead woman's name, he flew out of his chair, enraged and trembling violently, his arm raised to strike me: 'You son-of-a-bitch!' he screamed. 'If you say her name in my presence again, I'll kill you in an instant!' I sat there, bewildered,

shocked, and confused. And frightened, as much because of his reaction, but also because I could imagine what might happen to me should I unknowingly visit a village to check genealogy accuracy without knowing that someone had just died there or had been shot by raiders since my last visit. I reflected on the several articles I had read as a graduate student that explained the 'genealogical method,' but could not recall anything about its being a potentially lethal undertaking. My furious informant left my hut, never again to be invited back to be an informant. I had other similar experiences in different villages, but I was always fortunate in that the dead person had been dead for some time, or was not very closely related to the individual into whose ear I whispered the forbidden name. I was usually cautioned by one of the men to desist from saying any more names lest I get people 'angry.'[7]

Kaobawä: The Bisaasi-teri Headman Volunteers to Help Me

I had been working on the genealogies for nearly a year when another individual came to my aid. It was Kaobawä, the headman of Upper Bisaasi-teri. The village of Bisaasi-teri was split into two components, each with its own garden and own circular house. Both were in sight of each other. However, the intensity and frequency of internal bickering and argumentation was so high that they decided to split into two separate groups but remain close to each other for protection in case they were raided. One group was downstream from the other; I refer to that group as the 'Lower' Bisaasi-teri and call Kaobawä's group 'Upper' (upstream) Bisaasi-teri, a convenience they themselves adopted after separating from each other. I spent most of my time with the members of Kaobawä's group, some 200 people when I first arrived there. I did not have much contact with Kaobawä during the early months of my work. He was a somewhat retiring, quiet man, and among the Yąnomamö, the outsider has little time to notice the rare quiet ones when most everyone else is in the front row, pushing and demanding attention. He showed up at my hut one day after all the others had left. He had come to volunteer to help me with the genealogies. He was 'poor,' he explained, and needed a machete. He would work only on the condition that I did not ask him about his own parents and other very close kinsmen who had died. He also added that he would not lie to me as the others had done in the past.

This was perhaps the single most important event in my first 15 months of field research, for out of this fortuitous circumstance evolved a very warm friendship, and among the many things following from it was a wealth of accurate information on the political history of Kaobawä's village and related villages, highly detailed genealogical information, sincere and useful advice to me, and hundreds of valuable insights into the Yąnomamö way of life. Kaobawä's familiarity with his group's history and his candidness were remarkable. His knowledge of details was almost encyclopedic, his memory almost photographic. More than that, he was enthusiastic about making sure I learned the truth, and he encouraged me, indeed, *demanded* *that* I learn all details I might otherwise have ignored. If there were subtle details he could not recite on the spot, he would advise me to wait until he could check things out with someone else in the village. He would often do this clandestinely, giving me a report the next day, telling me who revealed the new information and whether or not he thought they were in a position to know it. With the information provided by Kaobawä and Rerebawä, I made enormous gains in understanding village interrelationships based on common ancestors and political histories and became lifelong friends with both. And both men knew that I had to learn about his recently deceased kin from the other one. It was one of those quiet understandings we all had but none of us could mention.

Once again I went over the genealogies with Kaobawä to recheck them, a considerable task by this time. They included about two thousand names, representing several generations of individuals from four different villages. Rerebawä's information was very accurate, and Kaobawä's contribution enabled me to trace the genealogies further back in time. Thus, after nearly a year of intensive effort on genealogies, Yąnomamö demographic patterns and social organization began to make a good deal of sense to me. Only at this point did the patterns through time begin to emerge in the data, and I could begin to understand how kinship groups took form, exchanged women in marriage over several generations, and only then did the fissioning of larger villages into smaller ones emerge as a chronic and important feature of Yąnomamö social, political, demographic, economic, and ecological adaptation. At this point I was able to begin formulating more sophisticated questions, for there was now a pattern to work from and one to flesh out. Without the help of Rerebawä and Kaobawä it would have taken much longer to make sense of the plethora of details I had collected from not only them, but dozens of other informants as well.

I spent a good deal of time with these two men and their families, and got to know them much better than I knew most Yąnomamö. They frequently gave their information in a way which related themselves to the topic under discussion. We became warm friends as time passed, and the formal 'informant/anthropologist' relationship faded into the background. Eventually, we simply stopped 'keeping track' of work and pay. They would both spend hours talking with me, leaving without asking for anything. When they wanted something, they would ask for it no matter what the relative balance of reciprocity between us might have been at that point. . . .

For many of the customary things that anthropologists try to communicate about another culture, these two men and their families might be considered to be 'exemplary' or 'typical.' For other things, they are exceptional in many regards, but the reader will, even knowing some of the exceptions, understand Yąnomamö culture more intimately by being familiar with a few examples.

Kaobawä was about 40 years old when I first came to his village in 1964. I say "about 40" because the Yąnomamö numeration system has only three numbers: one, two, and more-than-two. It is hard to give accurate ages or dates for events when the informants have no means in their language to reveal such detail. Kaobawä is the headman of his village,

meaning that he has somewhat more responsibility in political dealings with other Yąnomamö groups, and very little control over those who live in his group except when the village is being raided by enemies. We will learn more about political leadership and warfare in a later chapter, but most of the time men like Kaobawä are like the North American Indian 'chief' whose authority was characterized in the following fashion: "One word from the chief, and each man does as he pleases." There are different 'styles' of political leadership among the Yąnomamö. Some leaders are mild, quiet, inconspicuous most of the time, but intensely competent. They act parsimoniously, but when they do, people listen and conform. Other men are more tyrannical, despotic, pushy, flamboyant, and unpleasant to all around them. They shout orders frequently, are prone to beat their wives, or pick on weaker men. Some are very violent. I have met headmen who run the entire spectrum between these polar types, for I have visited some 60 Yąnomamö villages. Kaobawä stands at the mild, quietly competent end of the spectrum. He has had six wives thus far—and temporary affairs with as many more, at least one of which resulted in a child that is publicly acknowledged as his child. When I first met him he had just two wives: Bahimi and Koamashima. Bahimi had two living children when I first met her; many others had died. She was the older and enduring wife, as much a friend to him as a mate. Their relationship was as close to what we think of as 'love' in our culture as I have seen among the Yąnomamö. His second wife was a girl of about 20 years, Koamashima. She had a new baby boy when I first met her, her first child. There was speculation that Kaobawä was planning to give Koamashima to one of his younger brothers who had no wife; he occasionally allows his younger brother to have sex with Koamashima, but only if he asks in advance. Kaobawä gave another wife to one of his other brothers because she was *beshi* ("horny"). In fact, this earlier wife had been married to two other men, both of whom discarded her because of her infidelity. Kaobawä had one daughter by her. However, the girl is being raised by Kaobawä's brother, though acknowledged to be Kaobawä's child.

Bahimi, his oldest wife, is about five years younger than he. She is his cross-cousin—his mother's brother's daughter. Ideally, all Yąnomamö men should marry a cross-cousin. . . . Bahimi was pregnant when I began my field work, but she destroyed the infant when it was born—a boy in this case—explaining tearfully that she had no choice. The new baby would have competed for milk with Ariwari, her youngest child, who was still nursing. Rather than expose Ariwari to the dangers and uncertainty of an early weaning, she chose to terminate the newborn instead. By Yąnomamö standards, this has been a very warm, enduring marriage. Kaobawä claims he beats Bahimi only 'once in a while, and only lightly' and she, for her part, never has affairs with other men.

Kaobawä is a quiet, intense, wise, and unobtrusive man. It came as something of a surprise to me when I learned that he was the headman of his village, for he stayed at the sidelines while others would surround me and press their demands on me. He leads more by example than by coercion. He can afford to be this way at his age, for he established his reputation for being forthright and as fierce as the situation required when he was younger, and the other men respect him. He also has five mature brothers or half-brothers in his village, men he can count on for support. He also has several other mature 'brothers' (parallel cousins, whom he must refer to as 'brothers' in his kinship system) in the village who frequently come to his aid, but not as often as his 'real' brothers do. Kaobawä has also given a number of his sisters to other men in the village and has promised his young (8-year-old) daughter in marriage to a young man who, for that reason, is obliged to help him. In short, his 'natural' or 'kinship' following is large, and partially because of this support, he does not have to display his aggressiveness to remind his peers of his position.

Rerebawä is a very different kind of person. He is much younger—perhaps in his early twenties. He has just one wife, but they have already had three children. He is from a village called Karohi-teri, located about five hours' walk up the Orinoco, slightly inland off to the east of the river itself. Kaobawä's village enjoys amicable relationships with Rerebawä's, and it is for this reason that marriage alliances of the kind represented by Rerebawä's marriage into Kaobawä's village occur between the two groups. Rerebawä told me that he came to Bisaasi-teri because there were no eligible women from him to marry in his own village, a fact that I later was able to document when I did a census of his village and a preliminary analysis of its social organization. Rerebawä is perhaps more typical than Kaobawä in the sense that he is chronically concerned about his personal reputation for aggressiveness and goes out of his way to be noticed, even if he has to act tough. He gave me a hard time during my early months of fieldwork, intimidating, teasing, and insulting me frequently. He is, however, much braver than the other men his age and is quite prepared to back up his threats with immediate action—as in the club fight incident just described above. Moreover, he is fascinated with political relationships and knows the details of intervillage relationships over a large area of the tribe. In this respect he shows all the attributes of being a headman, although he has too many competent brothers in his own village to expect to move easily into the leadership position there.

He does not intend to stay in Kaobawä's group and refuses to make his own garden—a commitment that would reveal something of an intended long-term residence. He feels that he has adequately discharged his obligations to his wife's parents by providing them with fresh game, which he has done for several years. They should let him take his wife and return to his own village with her, but they refuse and try to entice him to remain permanently in Bisaasi-teri to continue to provide them with game when they are old. It is for this reason that they promised to give him their second daughter, their only other child, in marriage. Unfortunately, the girl was opposed to the marriage and ultimately married another man, a rare instance where the woman in the marriage had this much influence on the choice of her husband.

Although Rerebawä has displayed his ferocity in many ways, one incident in particular illustrates what his character can be like. Before he left his own village to take his new wife in Bisaasi-teri, he had an affair with the wife of an older brother. When it was discovered, his brother attacked him with a club.

Rerebawä responded furiously: He grabbed an ax and drove his brother out of the village after soundly beating him with the blunt side of the single-bit ax. His brother was so intimidated by the thrashing and promise of more to come that he did not return to the village for several days. I visited this village with Kaobawä shortly after this event had taken place; Rerebawä was with me as my guide. He made it a point to introduce me to this man. He approached his hammock, grabbed him by the wrist, and dragged him out on the ground: 'This is the brother whose wife I screwed when he wasn't around!' A deadly insult, onc that would usually provoke a bloody club fight among more valiant Yąnomamö. The man did nothing. He slunk sheepishly back into his hammock, shamed, but relieved to have Rerebawä release his grip.

Even though Rerebawä is fierce and capable of considerable nastiness, he has a charming, witty side as well. He has a biting sense of humor and can entertain the group for hours with jokes and clever manipulations of language. And, he is one of few Yąnomamö that I feel I can trust. I recall indelibly my return to Bisaasi-teri after being away a year—the occasion of my second field trip to the Yąnomamö. When I reached Bisaasi-teri, Rerebawä was in his own village visiting his kinsmen. Word reached him that I had returned, and he paddled downstream immediately to see me. He greeted me with an immense bear hug and exclaimed, with tears welling up in his eyes, 'Shaki! Why did you stay away so long? Did you not know that my will was so cold while you were gone that I could not at times eat for want of seeing you again?' I, too, felt the same way about him—then, and now.

Of all the Yąnomamö I know, he is the most genuine and the most devoted to his culture's ways and values. I admire him for that, although I cannot say that I subscribe to or endorse some of these values. By contrast, Kaobawä is older and wiser, a polished diplomat. He sees his own culture in a slightly different light and seems even to question aspects of it. Thus, while many of his peers enthusiastically accept the 'explanations' of things given in myths, he occasionally reflects on them—even laughing at some of the most preposterous of them. . . . Probably more of the Yąnomamö are like Rerebawä than like Kaobawä , or at least try to be. . . .

Notes

1. The word Yąnomamö is nasalized through its entire length, indicated by the diacritical mark ','. When this mark appears on any Yąnomamö word, the whole word is nasalized. The vowel 'ö' represents a sound that does not occur in the English language. It is similar to the umlaut 'ö' in the German language or the 'oe' equivalent, as in the poet Goethe's name. Unfortunately, many presses and typesetters simply eliminate diacritical marks, and this has led to multiple spellings of the word Yąnomamiö—and multiple mispronunciations. Some anthropologists have chosen to introduce a slightly different spelling of the word Yąnomamö since I began writing about them, such as Yąnomami, leading to additional misspellings as their diacriticals are characteristically eliminated by presses, and to the *incorrect* pronunciation 'Yąnomameee.' Vowels indicated as 'ä' are pronounced as the 'uh' sound in the word 'duck'. Thus, the name Kaobawä would be pronounced 'cowba-wuh,' but entirely nasalized.

2. I spent a total of 60 months among the Yąnomamö between 1964 and 1991. The first edition of this case study was based on the first 15 months I spent among them in Venezuela. I have, at the time of this writing, made 20 field trips to the Yąnomamö and this edition reflects the new information and understandings I have acquired over the years. I plan to return regularly to continue what has now turned into a lifelong study.

3. See Spindler (1970) for a general discussion of field research by anthropologists who have worked in other cultures. Nancy Howell has recently written a very useful book (1990) on some of the medical, personal, and environmental hazards of doing field research, which includes a selected bibliography on other fieldwork programs.

4. They could not pronounce "Chagnon." It sounded to them like their name for a pesky bee, shaki, and that is what they called me: pesky, noisome bee.

5. The Yąnomamö in this region acquired canoes very recently. The missionaries would purchase them from the Ye'kwana Indians to the north for money, and then trade them to the Yąnomamö in exchange for labor, produce, or 'informant' work in translating. It should be emphasized that those Yąnomamö who lived on navigable portions of the Upper Orinoco River moved there recently from the deep forest in order to have contact with the missionaries and acquire the trade goods the missionaries (and their supply system) brought.

6. Rarely were there actual brothers or sisters. In Yąnomamö kinship classifications, certain kinds of cousins are classified as siblings.

7. Over time, as I became more and more 'accepted' by the Yąnomamö, they became less and less concerned about my genealogical inquiries and now provide me with this information quite willingly because I have been very discrete with it. Now, when I revisit familiar villages I am called aside by someone who whispers to me things like, "Don't ask about so-and-so's father."

Assess Your Progress

1. Describe the Yąnomamö culture in general, according to Chagnon.

2. How extensive is Yąnomamö warfare?

3. Describe the "headmen" in Yąnomamö society.

4. What is the importance of marriage and how are marriage practices and violence interrelated?

5. Describe and explain the graded series of violence.

6. In what respects is aggression an important part of their lives?

7. In general, what were the trying circumstances of working among the Yąnomamö?

8. In what ways did Chagnon experience "culture shock" on his very first day with the Yąnomamö?

9. In what ways did Chagnon have to change his ways in order to do fieldwork? In particular, how did he deal with the Yąnomamö custom of reciprocity? How was his need for friendship exploited by them?

10. Why did Chagnon seek privacy? What would happen if he gave in to their demands? How did he cope with this problem? How does wife-beating fit into their type of behavior? Why did the problem of aggressive demands remain fairly constant?

11. What was the most persistent situation requiring action and how did Chagnon cope with it?

12. Why was data collection a special problem? In what ways was this solved?

13. From the two personal profiles, what can you say about how a Yąnomamö attains leadership status in his society?

Eating Christmas in the Kalahari

RICHARD BORSHAY LEE

The !Kung Bushmen's knowledge of Christmas is third-hand. The London Missionary Society brought the holiday to the southern Tswana tribes in the early nineteenth century. Later, native catechists spread the idea far and wide among the Bantu-speaking pastoralists, even in the remotest corners of the Kalahari Desert. The Bushmen's idea of the Christmas story, stripped to its essentials, is "praise the birth of white man's god-chief"; what keeps their interest in the holiday high is the Tswana-Herero custom of slaughtering an ox for his Bushmen neighbors as an annual goodwill gesture. Since the 1930s, part of the Bushmen's annual round of activities has included a December congregation at the cattle posts for trading, marriage brokering, and several days of trance-dance feasting at which the local Tswana headman is host.

As a social anthropologist working with !Kung Bushmen, I found that the Christmas ox custom suited my purposes. I had come to the Kalahari to study the hunting and gathering subsistence economy of the !Kung, and to accomplish this it was essential not to provide them with food, share my own food, or interfere in any way with their food-gathering activities. While liberal handouts of tobacco and medical supplies were appreciated, they were scarcely adequate to erase the glaring disparity in wealth between the anthropologist, who maintained a two-month inventory of canned goods, and the Bushmen, who rarely had a day's supply of food on hand. My approach, while paying off in terms of data, left me open to frequent accusations of stinginess and hard-heartedness. By their lights, I was a miser.

The Christmas ox was to be my way of saying thank you for the cooperation of the past year; and since it was to be our last Christmas in the field, I determined to slaughter the largest, meatiest ox that money could buy, insuring that the feast and trance-dance would be a success.

Through December I kept my eyes open at the wells as the cattle were brought down for watering. Several animals were offered, but none had quite the grossness that I had in mind. Then, ten days before the holiday, a Herero friend led an ox of astonishing size and mass up to our camp. It was solid black, stood five feet high at the shoulder, had a five-foot span of horns, and must have weighed 1,200 pounds on the hoof. Food consumption calculations are my specialty, and I quickly figured that bones and viscera aside, there was enough meat—at least four pounds—for every man, woman, and child of the 150 Bushmen in the vicinity of /ai/ai who were expected at the feast.

Having found the right animal at last, I paid the Herero £20 ($56) and asked him to keep the beast with his herd until Christmas day. The next morning word spread among the people that the big solid black one was the ox chosen by /ontah (my Bushman name; it means, roughly, "whitey") for the Christmas feast. That afternoon I received the first delegation. Ben!a, an outspoken sixty-year-old mother of five, came to the point slowly.

"Where were you planning to eat Christmas?"

"Right here at /ai/ai," I replied.

"Alone or with others?"

"I expect to invite all the people to eat Christmas with me."

"Eat what?"

"I have purchased Yehave's black ox, and I am going to slaughter and cook it."

"That's what we were told at the well but refused to believe it until we heard it from yourself."

"Well, it's the black one," I replied expansively, although wondering what she was driving at.

"Oh, no!" Ben!a groaned, turning to her group. "They were right." Turning back to me she asked, "Do you expect us to eat that bag of bones?"

"Bag of bones! It's the biggest ox at /ai/ai."

"Big, yes, but old. And thin. Everybody knows there's no meat on that old ox. What did you expect us to eat off it, the horns?"

Everybody chuckled at Ben!a's one-liner as they walked away, but all I could manage was a weak grin.

That evening it was the turn of the young men. They came to sit at our evening fire. /gaugo, about my age, spoke to me man-to-man.

"/ontah, you have always been square with us," he lied. "What has happened to change your heart? That sack of guts and bones of Yehave's will hardly feed one camp, let alone all the Bushmen around ai/ai." And he proceeded to enumerate the seven camps in the /ai/ai vicinity, family by family. "Perhaps you have forgotten that we are not few, but many. Or are you too blind to tell the difference between a proper cow and an old wreck? That ox is thin to the point of death."

"Look, you guys," I retorted, "that is a beautiful animal, and I'm sure you will eat it with pleasure at Christmas."

"Of course we will eat it; it's food. But it won't fill us up to the point where we will have enough strength to dance. We will eat and go home to bed with stomachs rumbling."

That night as we turned in, I asked my wife, Nancy: "What did you think of the black ox?"

"It looked enormous to me. Why?"

"Well, about eight different people have told me I got gypped; that the ox is nothing but bones."

"What's the angle?" Nancy asked. "Did they have a better one to sell?"

"No, they just said that it was going to be a grim Christmas because there won't be enough meat to go around. Maybe I'll get an independent judge to look at the beast in the morning."

Bright and early, Halingisi, a Tswana cattle owner, appeared at our camp. But before I could ask him to give me his opinion on Yehave's black ox, he gave me the eye signal that indicated a confidential chat. We left the camp and sat down.

"/ontah, I'm surprised at you: you've lived here for three years and still haven't learned anything about cattle."

"But what else can a person do but choose the biggest, strongest animal one can find?" I retorted.

"Look, just because an animal is big doesn't mean that it has plenty of meat on it. The black one was a beauty when it was younger, but now it is thin to the point of death."

"Well I've already bought it. What can I do at this stage?"

"Bought it already? I thought you were just considering it. Well, you'll have to kill it and serve it, I suppose. But don't expect much of a dance to follow."

My spirits dropped rapidly. I could believe that Ben!a and /gaugo just might be putting me on about the black ox, but Halingisi seemed to be an impartial critic. I went around that day feeling as though I had bought a lemon of a used car.

In the afternoon it was Tomazo's turn. Tomazo is a fine hunter, a top trance performer . . . and one of my most reliable informants. He approached the subject of the Christmas cow as part of my continuing Bushman education.

"My friend, the way it is with us Bushmen," he began, "is that we love meat. And even more than that, we love fat. When we hunt we always search for the fat ones, the ones dripping with layers of white fat: fat that turns into a clear, thick oil in the cooking pot, fat that slides down your gullet, fills your stomach and gives you a roaring diarrhea," he rhapsodized.

"So, feeling as we do," he continued, "it gives us pain to be served such a scrawny thing as Yehave's black ox. It is big, yes, and no doubt its giant bones are good for soup, but fat is what we really crave and so we will eat Christmas this year with a heavy heart."

The prospect of a gloomy Christmas now had me worried, so I asked Tomazo what I could do about it.

"Look for a fat one, a young one . . . smaller, but fat. Fat enough to make us //gom ('evacuate the bowels'), then we will be happy."

My suspicions were aroused when Tomazo said that he happened to know of a young, fat, barren cow that the owner was willing to part with. Was Tomazo working on commission, I wondered? But I dispelled this unworthy thought when we approached the Herero owner of the cow in question and found that he had decided not to sell.

The scrawny wreck of a Christmas ox now became the talk of the /ai/ai water hole and was the first news told to the outlying groups as they began to come in from the bush for the feast. What finally convinced me that real trouble might be brewing was the visit from u!au, an old conservative with a reputation for fierceness. His nickname meant spear and referred to an incident thirty years ago in which he had speared a man to death. He had an intense manner; fixing me with his eyes, he said in clipped tones:

"I have only just heard about the black ox today, or else I would have come here earlier. /ontah, do you honestly think you can serve meat like that to people and avoid a fight?" He paused, letting the implications sink in. "I don't mean fight you, /ontah; you are a white man. I mean a fight between Bushmen. There are many fierce ones here, and with such a small quantity of meat to distribute, how can you give everybody a fair share? Someone is sure to accuse another of taking too much or hogging all the choice pieces. Then you will see what happens when some go hungry while others eat."

The possibility of at least a serious argument struck me as all too real. I had witnessed the tension that surrounds the distribution of meat from a kudu or gemsbok kill, and had documented many arguments that sprang up from a real or imagined slight in meat distribution. The owners of a kill may spend up to two hours arranging and rearranging the piles of meat under the gaze of a circle of recipients before handing them out. And I also knew that the Christmas feast at /ai/ai would be bringing together groups that had feuded in the past.

Convinced now of the gravity of the situation, I went in earnest to search for a second cow; but all my inquiries failed to turn one up.

The Christmas feast was evidently going to be a disaster, and the incessant complaints about the meagerness of the ox had already taken the fun out of it for me. Moreover, I was getting bored with the wisecracks, and after losing my temper a few times, I resolved to serve the beast anyway. If the meat fell short, the hell with it. In the Bushmen idiom, I announced to all who would listen:

"I am a poor man and blind. If I have chosen one that is too old and too thin, we will eat it anyway and see if there is enough meat there to quiet the rumbling of our stomachs."

On hearing this speech, Ben!a offered me a rare word of comfort. "It's thin," she said philosophically, "but the bones will make a good soup."

At dawn Christmas morning, instinct told me to turn over the butchering and cooking to a friend and take off with Nancy to spend Christmas alone in the bush. But curiosity kept me from retreating. I wanted to see what such a scrawny ox looked like on butchering and if there *was* going to be a fight, I wanted to catch every word of it. Anthropologists are incurable that way.

The great beast was driven up to our dancing ground, and a shot in the forehead dropped it in its tracks. Then, freshly cut branches were heaped around the fallen carcass to receive the meat. Ten men volunteered to help with the cutting. I asked /gaugo to make the breast bone cut. This cut, which begins the butchering process for most large game, offers easy access for removal of the viscera. But it also allows the hunter to spot-check the amount of fat on the animal. A fat game animal carries a white layer up to an inch thick on the chest, while in a thin one, the knife will quickly cut to bone. All eyes fixed on his hand as /gaugo, dwarfed by the great carcass, knelt to the breast. The first cut opened a pool of solid white in the black skin. The second and third cut widened and deepened the creamy white. Still no bone. It was pure fat; it must have been two inches thick.

"Hey /gau," I burst out, "that ox is loaded with fat. What's this about the ox being too thin to bother eating? Are you out of your mind?"

"Fat?" /gau shot back, "You call that fat? This wreck is thin, sick, dead!" And he broke out laughing. So did everyone else. They rolled on the ground, paralyzed with laughter. Everybody laughed except me; I was thinking.

I ran back to the tent and burst in just as Nancy was getting up. "Hey, the black ox. It's fat as hell! They were kidding about it being too thin to eat. It was a joke or something. A put-on. Everyone is really delighted with it!"

"Some joke," my wife replied. "It was so funny that you were ready to pack up and leave /ai/ai."

If it had indeed been a joke, it had been an extraordinarily convincing one, and tinged, I thought, with more than a touch of malice as many jokes are. Nevertheless, that it was a joke lifted my spirits considerably, and I returned to the butchering site where the shape of the ox was rapidly disappearing under the axes and knives of the butchers. The atmosphere had become festive. Grinning broadly, their arms covered with blood well past the elbow, men packed chunks of meat into the big cast-iron cooking pots, fifty pounds to the load, and muttered and chuckled all the while about the thinness and worthlessness of the animal and /ontah's poor judgment.

We danced and ate that ox two days and two nights; we cooked and distributed fourteen potfuls of meat and no one went home hungry and no fights broke out.

But the "joke" stayed in my mind. I had a growing feeling that something important had happened in my relationship with the Bushmen and that the clue lay in the meaning of the joke. Several days later, when most of the people had dispersed back to the bush camps, I raised the question with Hakekgose, a Tswana man who had grown up among the !Kung, married a !Kung girl, and who probably knew their culture better than any other non-Bushman.

"With us whites," I began, "Christmas is supposed to be the day of friendship and brotherly love. What I can't figure out is why the Bushmen went to such lengths to criticize and belittle the ox I had bought for the feast. The animal was perfectly good and their jokes and wisecracks practically ruined the holiday for me."

"So it really did bother you," said Hakekgose. "Well, that's the way they always talk. When I take my rifle and go hunting with them, if I miss, they laugh at me for the rest of the day. But even if I hit and bring one down, it's no better. To them, the kill is always too small or too old or too thin; and as we sit down on the kill site to cook and eat the liver, they keep grumbling, even

with their mouths full of meat. They say things like, 'Oh this is awful! What a worthless animal! Whatever made me think that this Tswana rascal could hunt!'"

"Is this the way outsiders are treated?" I asked.

"No, it is their custom; they talk that way to each other too. Go and ask them."

/gaugo had been one of the most enthusiastic in making me feel bad about the merit of the Christmas ox. I sought him out first.

"Why did you tell me the black ox was worthless, when you could see that it was loaded with fat and meat?"

"It is our way," he said smiling. "We always like to fool people about that. Say there is a Bushman who has been hunting. He must not come home and announce like a braggard, 'I have killed a big one in the bush!' He must first sit down in silence until I or someone else comes up to his fire and asks, 'What did you see today?' He replies quietly, 'Ah, I'm no good for hunting. I saw nothing at all [pause] just a little tiny one.' Then I smile to myself," /gaugo continued, "because I know he has killed something big."

"In the morning we make up a party of four or five people to cut up and carry the meat back to the camp. When we arrive at the kill we examine it and cry out, 'You mean to say you have dragged us all the way out here in order to make us cart home your pile of bones? Oh, if I had known it was this thin I wouldn't have come.' Another one pipes up, 'People, to think I gave up a nice day in the shade for this. At home we may be hungry but at least we have nice cool water to drink.' If the horns are big, someone says, 'Did you think that somehow you were going to boil down the horns for soup?'"

"To all this you must respond in kind. 'I agree,' you say, 'this one is not worth the effort; let's just cook the liver for strength and leave the rest for the hyenas. It is not too late to hunt today and even a duiker or a steenbok would be better than this mess.'"

"Then you set to work nevertheless; butcher the animal, carry the meat back to the camp and everyone eats," /gaugo concluded.

Things were beginning to make sense. Next, I went to Tomazo. He corroborated /gaugo's story of the obligatory insults over a kill and added a few details of his own.

"But," I asked, "why insult a man after he has gone to all that trouble to track and kill an animal and when he is going to share the meat with you so that your children will have something to eat?"

"Arrogance," was his cryptic answer.

"Arrogance?"

"Yes, when a young man kills much meat he comes to think of himself as a chief or a big man, and he thinks of the rest of us as his servants or inferiors. We can't accept this. We refuse one who boasts, for someday his pride will make him kill somebody. So we always speak of his meat as worthless. This way we cool his heart and make him gentle."

"But why didn't you tell me this before?" I asked Tomazo with some heat.

"Because you never asked me," said Tomazo, echoing the refrain that has come to haunt every field ethnographer.

The pieces now fell into place. I had known for a long time that in situations of social conflict with Bushmen I held all the cards. I was the only source of tobacco in a thousand square miles, and I was not incapable of cutting an individual off for non-cooperation. Though my boycott never lasted longer than a few days, it was an indication of my strength. People resented my presence at the water hole, yet simultaneously dreaded my leaving. In short I was a perfect target for the charge of arrogance and for the Bushmen tactic of enforcing humility.

I had been taught an object lesson by the Bushmen; it had come from an unexpected corner and had hurt me in a vulnerable area. For the big black ox was to be the one totally generous, unstinting act of my year at /ai/ai, and I was quite unprepared for the reaction I received.

As I read it, their message was this: There are no totally generous acts. All "acts" have an element of calculation. One black ox slaughtered at Christmas does not wipe out a year of careful manipulation of gifts given to serve your own ends. After all, to kill an animal and share the meat with people is really no more than Bushmen do for each other every day and with far less fanfare.

In the end, I had to admire how the Bushmen had played out the farce—collectively straight-faced to the end. Curiously, the episode reminded me of the *Good Soldier Schweik* and his marvelous encounters with authority. Like Schweik, the Bushmen had retained a thorough-going skepticism of good intentions. Was it this independence of spirit, I wondered, that had kept them culturally viable in the face of generations of contact with more powerful societies, both black and white? The thought that the Bushmen were alive and well in the Kalahari was strangely comforting. Perhaps, armed with that independence and with their superb knowledge of their environment, they might yet survive the future.

Assess Your Progress

1. To what extent do the Bushmen typically celebrate Christmas?
2. Why did Lee wish to slaughter an ox for the Bushmen?
3. What was it about the Bushman ways of life and Lee's role as an anthropologist that led to their reactions to his generosity?
4. Why was the Bushman reaction "strangely comforting" to Lee in the final analysis?

RICHARD BORSHAY LEE is a full professor of anthropology at the University of Toronto. He has done extensive fieldwork in southern Africa, is coeditor of *Man the Hunter* (1968) and *Kalahari Hunter-Gatherers* (1976), and author of *The !Kung San: Men, Women, and Work in a Foraging Society.*

From *Natural History,* December 1969, pp. 14–22, 60–64. Copyright © 1969 by Natural History Magazine. Reprinted by permission.

Tricking and Tripping
Fieldwork on Prostitution in the Era of AIDS

CLAIRE E. STERK

S tudents often think of anthropological fieldwork as requiring travel to exotic tropical locations, but that is not necessarily the case. This reading is based on fieldwork in the United States—on the streets in New York City as well as Atlanta. Claire Sterk is an anthropologist who works in a school of public health and is primarily interested in issues of women's health, particularly as it relates to sexual behavior. In this selection, an introduction to a recent book by the same title, she describes the basic fieldwork methods she used to study these women and their communities. Like most cultural anthropologists, Sterk's primary goal was to describe "the life" of prostitution from the women's own point of view. To do this, she had to be patient, brave, sympathetic, trustworthy, curious, and nonjudgmental. You will notice these characteristics in this selection; for example, Sterk begins her book with a poem written by one of her informants. Fieldwork is a slow process, because it takes time to win people's confidence and to learn their language and way of seeing the world. In this regard, there are probably few differences between the work of a qualitative sociologist and that of a cultural anthropologist (although anthropologists would not use the term "deviant" to describe another society or a segment of their own society).

Throughout the world, HIV/AIDS is fast becoming a disease found particularly in poor women. Sex workers or prostitutes have often been blamed for AIDS, and they have been further stigmatized because of their profession. In reality, however, entry into prostitution is not a career choice; rather, these women and girls are themselves most often victims of circumstances such as violence and poverty. Public health officials want to know why sex workers do not always protect their health by making men wear condoms. To answer such questions, we must know more about the daily life of these women. The way to do that, the cultural anthropologist would say, is to ask and to listen.

As you read this selection, ask yourself the following questions:

- What happens when Sterk says, "I'm sorry for you" to one of her informants? Why?
- Why do you think fieldwork might be a difficult job?
- Do you think that the fact that Sterk grew up in Amsterdam, where prostitution is legal, affected her research?
- Which of the six themes of this work, described at the end of the article, do you think is most important?

O ne night in March of 1987 business was slow. I was hanging out on a stroll with a group of street prostitutes. After a few hours in a nearby diner/coffee shop, we were kicked out. The waitress felt bad, but she needed our table for some new customers. Four of us decided to sit in my car until the rain stopped. While three of us chatted about life, Piper wrote this poem. As soon as she read it to us, the conversation shifted to more serious topics—pimps, customers, cops, the many hassles of being a prostitute, to name a few. We decided that if I ever finished a book about prostitution, the book would start with her poem.

This book is about the women who work in the lower echelons of the prostitution world. They worked in the streets and other public settings as well as crack houses. Some of these women viewed themselves primarily as prostitutes, and a number of them used drugs to cope with the pressures of the life. Others identified themselves more as drug users, and their main reason for having sex for money or other goods was to support their own drug use and often the habit of their male partner. A small group of women interviewed for this book had left prostitution, and most of them were still struggling to integrate their past experiences as prostitutes in their current lives.

The stories told by the women who participated in this project revealed how pimps, customers, and others such as police officers and social and health service providers treated them as "fallen" women. However, their accounts also showed their strengths and the many strategies they developed to challenge these others. Circumstances, including their drug use, often forced them to sell sex, but they all resisted the notion that they might be selling themselves. Because they engaged in an illegal profession, these women had little status: their working conditions were poor, and their work was physically and mentally exhausting. Nevertheless, many women described the ways in which they gained a sense of control over their lives. For instance, they learned how to manipulate pimps, how to control the types of services and length of time bought by their customers, and how to select customers. While none of these schemes explicitly enhanced their working conditions, they did make the women feel stronger and better about themselves.

In this book, I present prostitution from the point of view of the women themselves. To understand their current lives, it was necessary to learn how they got started in the life, the various processes involved in their continued prostitution careers, the link between prostitution and drug use, the women's interactions with their pimps and customers, and the impact of the AIDS epidemic and increasing violence on their experiences. I also examined the implications for women. Although my goal was to present the women's thoughts, feelings, and actions in their own words, the final text is a sociological monograph compiled by me as the researcher. Some women are quoted more than others because I developed a closer relationship with them, because they were more able to verbalize and capture their circumstances, or simply because they were more outspoken.

The Sample

The data for this book are qualitative. The research was conducted during the last ten years in the New York City and Atlanta metropolitan areas. One main data source was participant observation on streets, in hotels and other settings known for prostitution activity, and in drug-use settings, especially those that allowed sex-for-drug exchanges. Another data source was in-depth, life-history interviews with 180 women ranging in age from 18 to 59 years, with an average age of 34. One in two women was African-American and one in three white; the remaining women were Latina. Three in four had completed high school, and among them almost two-thirds had one or more years of additional educational training. Thirty women had graduated from college.

Forty women worked as street prostitutes and did not use drugs. On average, they had been prostitutes for 11 years. Forty women began using drugs an average of three years after they began working as prostitutes, and the average time they had worked as prostitutes was nine years. Forty women used drugs an average of five years before they became prostitutes, and on the average they had worked as prostitutes for eight years. Another forty women began smoking crack and exchanging sex for crack almost simultaneously, with an average of four years in the life. Twenty women who were interviewed were ex-prostitutes.

Comments on Methodology

When I tell people about my research, the most frequent question I am asked is how I gained access to the women rather than what I learned from the research. For many, prostitution is an unusual topic of conversation, and many people have expressed surprise that I, as a woman, conducted the research. During my research some customers indeed thought I was a working woman, a fact that almost always amuses those who hear about my work. However, few people want to hear stories about the women's struggles and sadness. Sometimes they ask questions about the reasons why women become prostitutes. Most of the time, they are surprised when I tell them that the prostitutes as well as their customers represent all layers of society. Before presenting the findings, it seems important to discuss the research process, including gaining access to the women, developing relationships, interviewing, and then leaving the field.[1]

Locating Prostitutes and Gaining Entree

One of the first challenges I faced was to identify locations where street prostitution took place. Many of these women worked on strolls, streets where prostitution activity is concentrated, or in hotels known for prostitution activity. Others, such as the crack prostitutes, worked in less public settings such as a crack house that might be someone's apartment.

I often learned of well-known public places from professional experts, such as law enforcement officials and health care providers at emergency rooms and sexually transmitted disease clinics. I gained other insights from lay experts, including taxi drivers, bartenders, and community representatives such as members of neighborhood associations. The contacts universally mentioned some strolls as the places where many women worked, where the local police focused attention, or where residents had organized protests against prostitution in their neighborhoods.

As I began visiting various locales, I continued to learn about new settings. In one sense, I was developing ethnographic maps of street prostitution. After several visits to a specific area, I also was able to expand these maps by adding information about the general atmosphere on the stroll, general characteristics of the various people present, the ways in which the women and customers connected, and the overall flow of action. In addition, my visits allowed the regular actors to notice me.

I soon learned that being an unknown woman in an area known for prostitution may cause many people to notice you, even stare at you, but it fails to yield many verbal interactions. Most of the time when I tried to make eye contact with one of the women, she quickly averted her eyes. Pimps, on the other hand, would stare at me straight on and I ended up being the one to look away. Customers would stop, blow their horn, or wave me over, frequently yelling obscenities when I ignored them. I realized that gaining entree into the prostitution world was not going to be as easy as I imagined it. Although I lacked such training in any of my qualitative methods classes, I decided to move slowly and not force any interaction. The most I said during the initial weeks in a new area was limited to "how are you" or "hi." This strategy paid off during my first visits to one of the strolls in Brooklyn, New York. After several appearances, one of the women walked up to me and sarcastically asked if I was looking for something. She caught me off guard, and all the answers I had practiced did not seem to make sense. I mumbled something about just wanting to walk around. She did not like my answer, but she did like my accent. We ended up talking about the latter and she was especially excited when I told her I came from Amsterdam. One of her friends had gone to Europe with her boyfriend, who was in the military. She understood from her that prostitution and drugs were legal in the Netherlands. While explaining to her that some of her friend's impressions were incorrect, I was able to show off some of my knowledge about prostitution. I mentioned that I was interested in prostitution and wanted to write a book about it.

Despite the fascination with my background and intentions, the prostitute immediately put me through a Streetwalker 101 test, and apparently I passed. She told me to make sure to come back. By the time I left, I not only had my first conversation but also my first connection to the scene. Variations of this entry process occurred on the other strolls. The main lesson I learned in these early efforts was the importance of having some knowledge of the lives of the people I wanted to study, while at the same time refraining from presenting myself as an expert.

Qualitative researchers often refer to their initial connections as gatekeepers and key respondents. Throughout my fieldwork I learned that some key respondents are important in providing initial access, but they become less central as the research evolves. For example, one of the women who introduced me to her lover, who was also her pimp, was arrested and disappeared for months. Another entered drug treatment soon after she facilitated my access. Other key respondents provided access to only a segment of the players on a scene. For example, if a woman worked for a pimp, [she] was unlikely . . . to introduce me to women working for another pimp. On one stroll my initial contact was with a pimp whom nobody liked. By associating with him, I almost lost the opportunity to meet other pimps. Some key respondents were less connected than promised—for example, some of the women who worked the street to support their drug habit. Often their connections were more frequently with drug users and less so with prostitutes.

Key respondents tend to be individuals central to the local scene, such as, in this case, pimps and the more senior prostitutes. Their function as gatekeepers often is to protect the scene and to screen outsiders. Many times I had to prove that I was not an undercover police officer or a woman with ambitions to become a streetwalker. While I thought I had gained entree, I quickly learned that many insiders subsequently wondered about my motives and approached me with suspicion and distrust.

Another lesson involved the need to proceed cautiously with self-nominated key respondents. For example, one of the women presented herself as knowing everyone on the stroll. While she did know everyone, she was not a central figure. On the contrary, the other prostitutes viewed her as a failed streetwalker whose drug use caused her to act unprofessionally. By associating with me, she hoped to regain some of her status. For me, however, it meant limited access to the other women because I affiliated myself with a woman who was marginal to the scene. On another occasion, my main key respondent was a man who claimed to own three crack houses in the neighborhood. However, he had a negative reputation, and people accused him of cheating on others. My initial alliance with him delayed, and almost blocked, my access to others in the neighborhood. He intentionally tried to keep me from others on the scene, not because he would gain something from that transaction but because it made him feel powerful. When I told him I was going to hang out with some of the other people, he threatened me until one of the other dealers stepped in and told him to stay away. The two of them argued back and forth, and finally

I was free to go. Fortunately, the dealer who had spoken up for me was much more central and positively associated with the local scene. Finally, I am unsure if I would have had success in gaining entrance to the scene had I not been a woman.

Developing Relationships and Trust

The processes involved in developing relationships in research situations amplify those involved in developing relationships in general. Both parties need to get to know each other, become aware and accepting of each other's roles, and engage in a reciprocal relationship. Being supportive and providing practical assistance were the most visible and direct ways for me as the researcher to develop a relationship. Throughout the years, I have given countless rides, provided child care on numerous occasions, bought groceries, and listened for hours to stories that were unrelated to my initial research questions. Gradually, my role allowed me to become part of these women's lives and to build rapport with many of them.

Over time, many women also realized that I was uninterested in being a prostitute and that I genuinely was interested in learning as much as possible about their lives. Many felt flattered that someone wanted to learn from them and that they had knowledge to offer. Allowing women to tell their stories and engaging in a dialogue with them probably were the single most important techniques that allowed me to develop relationships with them. Had I only wanted to focus on the questions I had in mind, developing such relationships might have been more difficult.

At times, I was able to get to know a woman only after her pimp endorsed our contact. One of my scariest experiences occurred before I knew to work through the pimps, and one such man had some of his friends follow me on my way home one night. I will never know what plans they had in mind for me because I fortunately was able to escape with only a few bruises. Over a year later, the woman acknowledged that her pimp had gotten upset and told her he was going to teach me a lesson.

On other occasions, I first needed to be screened by owners and managers of crack houses before the research could continue. Interestingly, screenings always were done by a man even if the person who vouched for me was a man himself. While the women also were cautious, the ways in which they checked me out tended to be much more subtle. For example, one of them would tell me a story, indicating that it was a secret about another person on the stroll. Although I failed to realize this at the time, my field notes revealed that frequently after such a conversation, others would ask me questions about related topics. One woman later acknowledged that putting out such stories was a test to see if I would keep information confidential.

Learning more about the women and gaining a better understanding of their lives also raised many ethical questions. No textbook told me how to handle situations in which a pimp abused a woman, a customer forced a woman to engage in unwanted sex acts, a customer requested unprotected sex from a woman who knew she was HIV infected, or a boyfriend had realistic expectations regarding a woman's earnings to support his drug habit. I failed to know the proper response when asked to engage in illegal activities such as holding drugs or money a woman had stolen from a customer. In general, my response was to explain that I was there as a researcher. During those occasions when pressures became too severe, I decided to leave a scene. For example, I never returned to certain crack houses because pimps there continued to ask me to consider working for them.

Over time, I was fortunate to develop relationships with people who "watched my back." One pimp in particular intervened if he perceived other pimps, customers, or passersby harassing me. He also was the one who gave me my street name: Whitie (indicating my racial background) or Ms. Whitie for those who disrespected me. While this was my first street name, I subsequently had others. Being given a street name was a symbolic gesture of acceptance. Gradually, I developed an identity that allowed me to be both an insider and an outsider. While hanging out on the strolls and other gathering places, including crack houses, I had to deal with some of the same uncomfortable conditions as the prostitutes, such as cold or warm weather, lack of access to a rest room, refusals from owners for me to patronize a restaurant, and of course, harassment by customers and the police.

I participated in many informal conversations. Unless pushed to do so, I seldom divulged my opinions. I was more open with my feelings about situations and showed empathy. I learned quickly that providing an opinion can backfire. I agreed that one of the women was struggling a lot and stated that I felt sorry for her. While I meant to indicate my "genuine concern for her, she heard that I felt sorry for her because she was a failure. When she finally, after several weeks, talked with me again, I was able to explain to her that I was not judging her, but rather felt concerned for her. She remained cynical and many times asked me for favors to make up for my mistake. It took me months before I felt comfortable telling her that I felt I had done enough and that it was time to let go. However, if she was not ready, she needed to know that I would no longer go along. This was one of many occasions when I learned that although I wanted to facilitate my work as a researcher, that I wanted people to like and trust me, I also needed to set boundaries.

Rainy and slow nights often provided good opportunities for me to participate in conversations with groups of women. Popular topics included how to work safely, what to do about condom use, how to make more money. I often served as a health educator and a supplier of condoms, gels, vaginal douches, and other feminine products. Many women were very worried about the AIDS epidemic. However, they also were worried about how to use a condom when a customer refused to do so. They worried particularly about condom use when they needed money badly and, consequently, did not want to propose that the customer use one for fear of rejection. While some women became experts at "making" their customers use a condom—for example, "by hiding it in their mouth prior to beginning oral sex—others would carry condoms to please me but never pull one out. If a woman was HIV positive and I knew she failed to use a condom, I faced the ethical dilemma of challenging her or staying out of it.

Developing trusting relationships with crack prostitutes was more difficult. Crack houses were not the right environment for informal conversations. Typically, the atmosphere was tense and everyone was suspicious of each other. The best times to talk with these women were when we bought groceries together, when I helped them clean their homes, or when we shared a meal. Often the women were very different when they were not high than they were when they were high or craving crack. In my conversations with them, I learned that while I might have observed their actions the night before, they themselves might not remember them. Once I realized this, I would be very careful to omit any detail unless I knew that the woman herself did remember the event.

In-Depth Interviews

All interviews were conducted in a private setting, including women's residences, my car or my office, a restaurant of the women's choice, or any other setting the women selected. I did not begin conducting official interviews until I developed relationships with the women. Acquiring written informed consent prior to the interview was problematic. It made me feel awkward. Here I was asking the women to sign a form after they had begun to trust me. However, often I felt more upset about this technicality than the women themselves. As soon as they realized that the form was something the university required, they seemed to understand. Often they laughed about the official statements, and some asked if I was sure the form was to protect them and not the school.[2] None of the women refused to sign the consent form, although some refused to sign it right away and asked to be interviewed later.

In some instances the consent procedures caused the women to expect a formal interview. Some of them were disappointed when they saw I only had a few structured questions about demographic characteristics, followed by a long list of open-ended questions. When this disappointment occurred, I reminded the women that I wanted to learn from them and that the best way to do so was by engaging in a dialogue rather than interrogating them. Only by letting the women identify their salient issues and the topics they wanted to address was I able to gain an insider's perspective. By being a careful listener and probing for additional information and explanation, I as the interviewer, together with the women, was able to uncover the complexities of their lives. In addition, the nature of the interview allowed me to ask questions about contradictions in a woman's story. For example, sometimes a woman would say that she always used a condom. However, later on in the conversation she would indicate that if she needed drugs she would never use one. By asking her to elaborate on this, I was able to begin developing insights into condom use by type of partner, type of sex acts, and social context.

The interviewer becomes much more a part of the interview when the conversations are in-depth than when a structured questionnaire is used. Because I was so integral to the process, the way the women viewed me may have biased their answers. On the one hand, this bias might be reduced because of the extent to which both parties already knew each other; on the other, a woman might fail to give her true opinion and reveal her actions if she knew that these went against the interviewer's opinion. I suspected that some women played down the ways in which their pimps manipulated them once they knew that I was not too fond of these men. However, some might have taken more time to explain the relationship with their pimp in order to "correct" my image.

My background, so different from that of these women, most likely affected the nature of the interviews. I occupied a higher socioeconomic status. I had a place to live and a job. In contrast to the nonwhite women, I came from a different racial background. While I don't know to what extent these differences played a role, I acknowledge that they must have had some effect on this research.

Leaving the Field

Leaving the field was not something that occurred after completion of the fieldwork, but an event that took place daily. Although I sometimes stayed on the strolls all night or hung out for several days, I always had a home to return to. I had a house with electricity, a warm shower, a comfortable bed, and a kitchen. My house sat on a street where I had no fear of being shot on my way there and where I did not find condoms or syringes on my doorstep.

During several stages of the study, I had access to a car, which I used to give the women rides or to run errands together. However, I will never forget the cold night when everyone on the street was freezing, and I left to go home. I turned up the heat in my car, and tears streamed down my cheeks. I appreciated the heat, but I felt more guilty about that luxury than ever before. I truly felt like an outsider, or maybe even more appropriate, a betrayer.

Throughout the years of fieldwork, there were a number of times when I left the scene temporarily. For example, when so many people were dying from AIDS, I was unable to ignore the devastating impact of this disease. I needed an emotional break.

Physically removing myself from the scene was common when I experienced difficulty remaining objective. Once I became too involved in a woman's life and almost adopted her and her family. Another time I felt a true hatred for a crack house owner and was unable to adhere to the rules of courteous interactions. Still another time, I got angry with a woman whose steady partner was HIV positive when she failed to ask him to use a condom when they had sex.

I also took temporary breaks from a particular scene by shifting settings and neighborhoods. For example, I would invest most of my time in women from a particular crack house for several weeks. Then I would shift to spending more time on one of the strolls, while making shorter and less frequent visits to the crack house. By shifting scenes, I was able to tell people why I was leaving and to remind all of us of my researcher role.

While I focused on leaving the field, I became interested in women who had left the life. It seemed important to have an understanding of their past and current circumstances. I knew some of them from the days when they were working, but identifying others was a challenge. There was no gathering place for ex-prostitutes. Informal networking, advertisements in local newspapers, and local clinics and community settings allowed me to reach twenty of these women. Conducting interviews with them later in the data collection process prepared me to ask specific questions. I realized that I had learned enough about the life to know what to ask. Interviewing ex-prostitutes also prepared me for moving from the fieldwork to writing.

It is hard to determine exactly when I left the field. It seems like a process that never ends. Although I was more physically removed from the scene, I continued to be involved while analyzing the data and writing this book. I also created opportunities to go back, for example, by asking women to give me feedback on parts of the manuscript or at times when I experienced writer's block and my car seemed to automatically steer itself to one of the strolls. I also have developed other research projects in some of the same communities. For example, both a project on intergenerational drug use and a gender-specific intervention project to help women remain HIV negative have brought me back to the same population. Some of the women have become key respondents in these new projects, while others now are members of a research team. For example, Beth, one of the women who has left prostitution, works as an outreach worker on another project.

Six Themes in the Ethnography of Prostitution

The main intention of my work is to provide the reader with a perspective on street prostitution from the point of view of the women themselves. There are six fundamental aspects of the women's lives as prostitutes that must be considered. The first concerns the women's own explanations for their involvement in prostitution and their descriptions of the various circumstances that led them to become prostitutes. Their stories include justifications such as traumatic past experiences, especially sexual abuse, the lack of love they experienced as children, pressures by friends and pimps, the need for drugs, and most prominently, the economic forces that pushed them into the life. A number of women describe these justifications as excuses, as reflective explanations they have developed after becoming a prostitute.

The women describe the nature of their initial experiences, which often involved alienation from those outside the life. They also show the differences in the processes between women who work as prostitutes and use drugs and women who do not use drugs.

Although all these women work either on the street or in drug-use settings, their lives do differ. My second theme is a typology that captures these differences, looking at the women's prostitution versus drug-use identities. The typology distinguishes among (a) streetwalkers, women who work strolls and who do not use drugs; (b) hooked prostitutes, women who identify themselves mainly as prostitutes but who upon their entrance into the life also began using drugs; (c) prostituting addicts, women who view themselves mainly as drug users and who became prostitutes to support their drug habit; and (d) crack prostitutes, women who trade sex for crack.

This typology explains the differences in the women's strategies for soliciting customers, their screening of customers, pricing of sex acts, and bargaining for services. For example, the streetwalkers have the most bargaining power, while such power appears to be lacking among the crack prostitutes.

Few prostitutes work in a vacuum. The third theme is the role of pimps, a label that most women dislike and for which they prefer to substitute "old man" or "boyfriend." Among the pimps, one finds entrepreneur lovers, men who mainly employ streetwalkers and hooked prostitutes and sometimes prostituting addicts. Entrepreneur lovers engage in the life for business reasons. They treat the women as their employees or their property and view them primarily as an economic commodity. The more successful a woman is in earning them money, the more difficult it is for that woman to leave her entrepreneur pimp.

Most prostituting addicts and some hooked prostitutes work for a lover pimp, a man who is their steady partner but who also lives off their earnings. Typically, such pimps employ only one woman. The dynamics in the relationship between a prostitute and her lover pimp become more complex when both partners use drugs. Drugs often become the glue of the relationship.

For many crack prostitutes, their crack addiction serves as a pimp. Few plan to exchange sex for crack when they first begin using; often several weeks or months pass before a woman who barters sex for crack realizes that she is a prostitute.

Historically, society has blamed prostitutes for introducing sexually transmitted diseases into the general population. Similarly, it makes them scapegoats for the spread of HIV/AIDS. Yet their pimps and customers are not held accountable. The fourth theme in the anthropological study of prostitution is the impact of the AIDS epidemic on the women's lives. Although most are knowledgeable about HIV risk behaviors and the ways to reduce their risk, many misconceptions exist. The women describe the complexities of condom use, especially with steady partners but also with paying customers. Many women have mixed feelings about HIV testing, wondering how to cope with a positive test result while no cure is available. A few of the women already knew their HIV-infected status, and the discussion touches on their dilemmas as well.

The fifth theme is the violence and abuse that make common appearances in the women's lives. An ethnography of prostitution must allow the women to describe violence in their neighborhoods as well as violence in prostitution and drug-use settings. The most common violence they encounter is from customers. These men often assume that because they pay for sex they buy a woman. Apparently, casual customers pose more of a danger than those who are regulars. The types of abuse the women encounter are emotional, physical, and sexual. In addition to customers, pimps and boyfriends abuse the women. Finally, the women discuss harassment by law enforcement officers.

When I talked with the women, it often seemed that there were no opportunities to escape from the life. Yet the sixth and final theme must be the escape from prostitution. Women who have left prostitution can describe the process of their exit from prostitution. As ex-prostitutes they struggle with the stigma of their past, the challenges of developing a new identity, and the impact of their past on current intimate relationships. Those who were also drug users often view themselves as ex-prostitutes and recovering addicts, a perspective that seems to create a role conflict. Overall, most ex-prostitutes find that their past follows them like a bad hangover.

Notes

1. For more information about qualitative research methods, see, for example, Patricia Adler and Peter Adler, *Membership Roles in Field Research* (Newbury Park: Sage, 1987); Michael Agar, *The Professional Stranger* (New York: Academic Press, 1980) and *Speaking of Ethnography* (Beverly Hills: Sage, 1986); Howard Becker and Blanche Geer, "Participant Observation and Interviewing: A Comparison," *Human Organization* 16 (1957): 28–32; Norman Denzin, *Sociological Methods: A Sourcebook* (Chicago: Aldine, 1970); Barney Glaser and Anselm Strauss, *The Discovery of Grounded Theory: Strategies for Qualitative Research* (Chicago: Aldine, 1967); Y. Lincoln and E. Guba, *Naturalistic Inquiry* (Beverly Hills: Sage, 1985); John Lofland, "Analytic Ethnography: Features, Failings, and Futures," *Journal of Contemporary Ethnography* 24 (1996): 30–67; and James Spradley, *The Ethnographic Interview* (New York: Holt, Rinehart and Winston, 1979) and *Participant Observation* (New York: Holt, Rinehart and Winston, 1980).

2. For a more extensive discussion of informed consent procedures and related ethical issues, see Bruce L. Berg, *Qualitative Research Methods for the Social Sciences,* 3rd edition, Chapter 3: "Ethical Issues" (Boston: Allyn and Bacon, 1998).

Assess Your Progress

1. How do prostitutes gain a sense of control over their lives?

2. How does the author describe the women in her study?

3. How does the author describe people's reactions when she tells them what her research is about?

4. How and where did she find places of prostitution?

5. What was the main lesson she learned in her early efforts?

6. How does she describe "key respondents?"

7. How did she manage to develop relationships with prostitutes? What was the single most important technique?

8. How did the author handle situations involving ethical questions?

9. Describe the author's interview techniques and the rationale behind them.

10. How did the author feel about being able to "leave the field" daily?

11. Under what circumstances would she leave a scene temporarily?

12. What explanations do the women themselves give for their involvement in prostitution?

13. What is the author's typology regarding prostitutes? What kinds of strategies are thereby explained? Which has the most bargaining power? Which has the least?

14. How does the author describe the different kinds of pimps?

15. Who is historically held responsible for the spread of HIV/AIDS? Who is not held responsible?

16. How does the author describe the violence and abuse suffered by prostitutes and who is likely to inflict it?

17. With what do ex-prostitutes come to struggle?

Can White Men Jump?

Ethnicity, Genes, Culture, and Success

Clusters of ethnic and geographical athletic success prompt suspicions of hidden genetic advantages. The real advantages are far more nuanced—and less hidden.

DAVID SHENK

At the 2008 Summer Olympics in Beijing, the world watched in astonishment as the tiny island of Jamaica captured six gold medals in track and field and eleven overall. Usain Bolt won (and set world records in) both the men's 100-meter and the men's 200-meter races. Jamaican women took the top three spots in the 100-meter and won the 200-meter as well. "They brought their A game. I don't know where we left ours," lamented American relay runner Lauryn Williams.

A poor, underdeveloped nation of 2.8 million people—one-hundredth the size of the United States—had somehow managed to produce the fastest humans alive.

How?

Within hours, geneticists and science journalists rushed in with reports of a "secret weapon": biologically, it turned out that almost all Jamaicans are flush with alpha-actinin-3, a protein that drives forceful, speedy muscle contractions. The powerful protein is produced by a special gene variant called *ACTN3*, at least one copy of which can be found in 98 percent of Jamaicans—far higher than in many other ethnic populations.

An impressive fact, but no one stopped to do the math. Eighty percent of Americans also have at least one copy of *ACTN3*—that amounts to 240 million people. Eighty-two percent of Europeans have it as well—that tacks on another 597 million potential sprinters. "There's simply no clear relationship between the frequency of this variant in a population and its capacity to produce sprinting superstars," concluded geneticist Daniel MacArthur.

What, then, is the Jamaicans' secret sauce?

This is the same question people asked about champion long-distance runners from Finland in the 1920s and about great Jewish basketball players from the ghettos of Philadelphia and New York in the 1930s. Today, we wonder how tiny South Korea turns out as many great female golfers as the United States—and how the Dominican Republic has become a factory for male baseball players.

The list goes on and on. It turns out that sports excellence commonly emerges in geographic clusters—so commonly, in fact, that a small academic discipline called "sports geography" has developed over the years to help understand it. What they've discovered is that there's never a single cause for a sports cluster. Rather, the success comes from many contributions of climate, media, demographics, nutrition, politics, training, spirituality, education, economics, and folklore. In short, athletic clusters are not genetic, but systemic.

Unsatisfied with this multifaceted explanation, some sports geographers have also transformed themselves into sports geneticists. In his book *Taboo: Why Black Athletes Dominate Sports and Why We're Afraid to Talk About It,* journalist Jon Entine insists that today's phenomenal black athletes—Jamaican sprinters, Kenyan marathoners, African American basketball players, etc.—are propelled by "high performance genes" inherited from their West and East African ancestors. Caucasians and Asians don't do as well, he says, because they don't share these advantages. "White athletes appear to have a physique between central West Africans and East Africans," Entine writes. "They have more endurance but less explosive running and jumping ability than West Africans; they tend to be quicker than East Africans but have less endurance."

In the finer print, Entine acknowledges that these are all grosser-than-gross generalizations. He understands that there are extraordinary Asian and Caucasian athletes in basketball, running, swimming, jumping, and cycling. (In fact, blacks do not even dominate the latter three of these sports as of 2008.) In his own book, Entine quotes geneticist Claude Bouchard: "They key point is that these biological characteristics *are not unique* to either West or East African blacks. These characteristics are seen in all populations, including whites." (Italics mine.) (Entine also acknowledges that we haven't in fact found the actual genes he's alluding to. "These genes will likely be identified early in the [twenty-first century]," he predicts.)

Actual proof for his argument is startlingly thin. But Entine's message of superior genes seems irresistible to a world steeped in gene-giftedness—and where other influences and dynamics are nearly invisible.

Take the running Kenyans. Relatively new to international competition, Kenyans have in recent years become overwhelmingly dominant in middle- and long-distance races. "It's pointless for me to run on the pro circuit," complained American 10,000-meter champion Mike Mykytok to the *New York Times* in 1998. "With all the Kenyans, I could set a personal best time, still only place 12th and win $200."

Ninety percent of the top-performing Kenyans come from the Kalenjin tribe in the Great Rift Valley region of western Kenya, where they have a centuries-old tradition of long-distance running. Where did this tradition come from? Kenyan-born journalist John Manners suggests it came from cattle raiding. Further, he proposes how a few basic economic incentives became a powerful evolutionary force. "The better a young man was at raiding [cattle]—in large part a function of his speed and endurance—the more cattle he accumulated," Manners says. "And since cattle were what a prospective husband needed to pay for a bride, the more a young man had, the more wives he could buy, and the more children he was likely to father. It is not hard to imagine that such a reproductive advantage might cause a significant shift in a group's genetic makeup over the course of a few centuries."

Whatever the precise origin, it is true that the Kalenjin have long had a fierce dedication to running. But it wasn't until the 1968 Olympics that they became internationally renowned for their prowess, thanks to the extraordinary runner Kipchoge Keino.

The son of a farmer and ambitious long-distance runner, Keino caught the running bug early in life. He wasn't the most precocious or "natural" athlete among his peers, but running was simply woven into the fabric of his life: along with his schoolmates, Keino ran many miles per day as a part of his routine. "I used to run from the farm to school and back," he recalled. "We didn't have a water tap in the house, so you run to the river, take your shower, run home, change, [run] to school . . . Everything is running." Slowly, Keino emerged as a serious competitor. He built himself a running track on the farm where his family worked and by his late teens was showing signs of international-level performance. After some success in the early 1960s, he competed admirably in the 1964 Olympics and became the leader of the Kenyan running team for the 1968 games in Mexico City. It was Kenya's fourth Olympics.

In Mexico City, things did not begin well for Keino. After nearly collapsing in pain during his first race, the 10,000 meters, he was diagnosed with gallstones and ordered by doctors not to continue. At the last minute, though, he stubbornly decided to race the 1,500 meters and hopped in a cab to Mexico City's Aztec Stadium. Caught in terrible traffic, Keino did the only thing he could do, the thing he'd been training his whole life for: he jumped out of the cab and ran the last mile to the event, arriving on the track only moments before the start of the race, winded and very sick. Still, when the gun sounded, Keino was off, and his performance that day shattered the world record and left his rival, American Jim Ryun, in the dust.

The dramatic victory made Keino one of the most celebrated men in all Africa and helped catalyze a new interest in world-class competition. Athletic halls and other venues all over Kenya were named after him. World-class coaches like Fred Hardy and Colm O'Connell were recruited to nurture other Kenyan aspirants. In the decades that followed, the long-standing but profitless Kalenjin running tradition became a well-oiled economic-athletic engine. Sports geographers point to many crucial ingredients in Kenya's competitive surge but no single overriding factor. High-altitude training and mild year-round climate are critical, but equally important is a deeply ingrained culture of asceticism—the postponement of gratification—and an overriding preference for individual over team sports. (Soccer, the overwhelming Kenyan favorite, is all but ignored among the Kalenjin; running is all.) In testing, psychologists discovered a particularly strong cultural "achievement orientation," defined as the inclination to seek new challenges, attain competence, and strive to outdo others. And then there was the built-in necessity as virtue: as Keino mentioned, Kalenjin kids tend to run long distances as a practical matter, an average of eight to twelve kilometers per day from age seven.

Joke among elite athletes: How can the rest of the world defuse Kenyan running superiority? Answer: Buy them school buses.

With the prospect of international prize money, running in Kenya has also become a rare economic opportunity to catapult oneself into Western-level education and wealth. Five thousand dollars in prize money is a very nice perk for an American; for a Kenyan, it is instant life-changing wealth. Over time, a strong culture of success has also bred even more success. The high-performance benchmark has stoked higher and higher levels of achievement—a positive feedback loop analogous to technological innovation in Silicon Valley, combat skills among Navy SEALs, and talents in other highly successful microcultures. In any competitive arena, the single best way to inspire better performance is to be surrounded by the fiercest possible competitors and a culture of extreme excellence. Success begets success.

There is also an apparent sacrificial quality particular to Kenyan training, wherein coaches can afford to push their athletes to extreme limits in a way that coaches in other parts of the world cannot. *Sports Illustrated*'s Alexander Wolff writes that with a million Kenyan schoolboys running so enthusiastically, "coaches in Kenya can train their athletes to the outer limits of endurance—up to 150 miles a week—without worrying that their pool of talent will be meaningfully depleted. Even if four out of every five runners break down, the fifth will convert that training into performance."

And what of genetics? Are Kenyans the possessors of rare endurance genes, as some insist? No one can yet know for sure, but the new understanding of GxE and some emergent truths in genetic testing strongly suggest otherwise, in two important ways:

1. Despite Appearances to the Contrary, Racial and Ethnic Groups Are *Not* Genetically Discrete

Skin color is a great deceiver; actual genetic differences between ethnic and geographic groups are very, very limited. All human beings are descended from the same African ancestors, and it is well established among geneticists that there is roughly ten times more genetic variation within large populations than there is between populations. "While ancestry is a useful way to classify species (because species are isolated gene pools, most of the time)," explains University of Queensland philosopher of biology John Wilkins, "it is rarely a good way to classify populations within species . . . [and definitely not] in humans. We move about too much."

By no stretch of the imagination, then, does any ethnicity or region have an exclusive lock on a particular body type or secret high-performance gene. Body shapes, muscle fiber types, etc., are actually quite varied and scattered, and true athletic potential is widespread and plentiful.

2. Genes Don't Directly Cause Traits; They Only Influence the System

Consistent with other lessons of GxE, the surprising finding of the $3 billion Human Genome Project is that only in rare instances do specific gene variants directly cause specific traits or diseases. Far more commonly, they merely increase or decrease the likelihood of those traits/diseases. In the words of King's College developmental psychopathologist Michael Rutter, genes are "probabilistic rather than deterministic."

As the search for athletic genes continues, therefore, the overwhelming evidence suggests that researchers will instead locate genes prone to certain types of interactions: gene variant A in combination with gene variant B, provoked into expression by X amount of training + Y altitude + Z will to win + a hundred other life variables (coaching, injury rate, etc.), will produce some specific result R. What this means, of course, is that we need to dispense rhetorically with the thick firewall between biology (nature) and training (nurture). The reality of GxE assures that each person's genes interact with his climate, altitude, culture, meals, language, customs, and spirituality—everything—to produce unique life trajectories. Genes play a critical role, but as dynamic instruments, not a fixed blueprint. A seven- or fourteen- or twenty-eight-year-old outfitted with a certain height, shape, muscle-fiber proportion, and so on is not that way merely because of genetic instruction.

• • •

As for John Manners's depiction of cattle-raiding Kenyans becoming genetically selected to be better and better runners over the generations, it's an entertaining theory that fits well with the popular gene-centric view of natural selection. But developmental biologists would point out that you could take exactly the same story line and flip the conclusion on its head: the fastest man earns the most wives and has the most kids—but rather than passing on quickness genes, he passes on crucial external ingredients, such as the knowledge and means to attain maximal nutrition, inspiring stories, the most propitious attitude and habits, access to the best trainers, the most leisure time to pursue training, and so on. This nongenetic aspect of inheritance is often overlooked by genetic determinists: culture, knowledge, attitudes, and environments are also passed on in many different ways.

The case for the hidden performance gene is even further diminished in the matter of Jamaican sprinters, who turn out to be a quite heterogeneous genetic group—nothing like the genetic "island" that some might imagine. On average, Jamaican genetic heritage is about the same as African American heritage, with roughly the same mix of West African, European, and native American ancestry. That's on average; individually, the percentage of West African origin varies widely, from 46.8 to 97.0 percent. Jamaicans are therefore *less* genetically African and *more* European and native American than their neighboring Barbadians and Virgin Islanders. "Jamaica . . . may represent a 'crossroads' within the Caribbean," conclude the authors of one DNA study. Jamaica was used as a "transit point by colonists between Central and South America and Europe [which] may have served to make Jamaica more cosmopolitan and thus provided more opportunities for [genetic] admixture to occur. *The large variance in both the global and individual admixture estimates in Jamaica attests to the cosmopolitan nature of the island.*"

In other words, Jamaica would be one of the very last places in the region expected to excel, according to a gene-gift paradigm.

Meanwhile, specific cultural explanations abound for the island's sprinting success—and for its recent competitive surge. In Jamaica, track events are beloved. The annual high school Boys' and Girls' Athletic Championships is as important to Jamaicans as the Super Bowl is to Americans. "Think Notre Dame football," write *Sports Illustrated*'s Tim Layden and David Epstein. "Names like Donald Quarrie and Merlene Ottey are holy on the island. In the United States, track and field is a marginal, niche sport that pops its head out of the sand every four years and occasionally produces a superstar. In Jamaica . . . it's a major sport. When *Sports Illustrated* [recently] visited the island . . . dozens of small children showed up for a Saturday morning youth track practice. That was impressive. That they were all wearing spikes was stunning."

With that level of intensity baked right into the culture, it's no surprise that Jamaicans have for many decades produced a wealth of aggressive, ambitious young sprinters. Their problem, though, was that for a long time they didn't have adequate college-level training resources for these promising teenagers. Routinely, the very best athletes would leave the country for Britain (Linford Christie) or Canada (Ben Johnson) and often never return.

Then, in the 1970s, former champion sprinter Dennis Johnson did come back to Jamaica to create a college athletic program based on what he'd experienced in the United States.

That program, now at the University of Technology in Kingston, became the new core of Jamaican elite training. After a critical number of ramp-up years, the medals started to pour in. It was the final piece in the systemic machinery driven by national pride and an ingrained sprinting culture.

Psychology was obviously a critical part of the mix. "We genuinely believe that we'll conquer," says Jamaican coach Fitz Coleman. "It's a mindset. We're small and we're poor, but we believe in ourselves." On its own, it might seem laughable that self-confidence can turn a tiny island into a breeding ground for champion sprinters. But taken in context of the developmental dynamic, psychology and motivation become vital. Science has demonstrated unequivocally that a person's mind-set has the power to dramatically affect both short-term capabilities and the long-term dynamic of achievement. In Jamaica, sprinting is a part of the national identity. Kids who sprint well are admired and praised; their heroes are sprinters; sprinting well provides economic benefits and ego gratification and is even considered a form of public service.

All things considered, it seems obvious that the mind is the most athletic part of any Jamaican athlete's body.

The nvotion that the mind is of such paramount importance to athletic success is something that we all have to accept and embrace if we're going to advance the culture of success in human society. Within mere weeks of British runner Roger Bannister becoming the first human being to crack the four-minute mile, several other runners also broke through. Bannister himself later remarked that while biology sets ultimate limits to performance, it is the mind that plainly determines how close individuals come to those absolute limits.

And we keep coming closer and closer to them. "The past century has witnessed a progressive, indeed remorseless improvement in human athletic performance," writes South African sports scientist Timothy David Noakes. The record speed for the mile, for example, was cut from 4:36 in 1865 to 3:43 in 1999. The one-hour cycling distance record increased from 26 kilometers in 1876 to 49 kilometers in 2005. The 200-meter freestyle swimming record decreased from 2:31 in 1908 to 1:43 in 2007. Technology and aerodynamics are a part of the story, but the rest of it has to do with training intensity, training methods, and sheer competitiveness and desire. It used to be that 67 kilometers per week was considered an aggressive level of training. Today's serious Kenyan runners, Noakes points out, will cover 230 kilometers per week (at 6,000 feet in altitude).

These are not superhumans with rare super-genes. They are participants in a culture of the extreme, willing to devote more, to ache more, and to risk more in order to do better. Most of us will understandably want nothing to do with that culture of the extreme. But that is our choice.

Assess Your Progress

1. How does the author describe the evidence for sports excellence with respect to "geographic clusters" and "high performance genes?"

2. Why do people of the Kalenjin tribe in Kenya excel at long-distance running?

3. How does the author describe the actual genetic differences between people? Why does he say that genes are not "a fixed blueprint?"

4. What is the author's response to the notion of the "hidden performance gene?" What cultural explanations abound for the Jamaicans' performance in track events?

5. In what sense does the "culture of the extreme" explain the continued breaking of athletic records?

Academic Editor's Note: GxEs refers to genes *interacting* with the environment rather than simply genes *plus* environment.

From *The Genius in All of Us* by David Shenk (Doubleday, 2010). Copyright © 2010 by David Shenk. Reprinted by permission of Doubleday, a division of Bantam Doubleday Dell.

UNIT 2

Culture and Communication

Unit Selections

6. **Whose Speech Is Better?,** Donna Jo Napoli
7. **Do You Speak American?,** Robert MacNeil
8. **Fighting for Our Lives,** Deborah Tannen
9. **Shakespeare in the Bush,** Laura Bohannan

Learning Outcomes

After reading this unit, you should be able to:

- Discuss the ways in which all languages are "equal."

- Explain how language can restrict our thought processes.

- Decide whether the monitors of the English language (such as teachers and dictionaries) should be prescriptive or descriptive.

- Describe the relationship between a people's language, culture, and interaction with their environment.

- Explain how the "argument culture" has affected the way we conduct ourselves vis-à-vis others.

- Give examples of the ways in which communication is difficult in a cross-cultural situation.

- Explain how this section has enhanced your ability to communicate more effectively.

Student Website

www.mhhe.com/cls

Internet References

Center for Nonverbal Studies
www.library.kent.edu/resource.php?id=2800
Exploratorium Magazine: "The Evolution of Languages"
www.exploratorium.edu/exploring/language
Hypertext and Ethnography
www.umanitoba.ca/anthropology
International Communication Association
www.icahdq.org
Intute: Social Sciences
www.intute.ac.uk
Language and Culture
http://anthro.palomar.edu/language/default.htm
Language Extinction
www.colorado.edu/iec
Nonverbal Behavior
www.usal.es/~nonverbal/researchcenters.htm
Showcase Anthropology
www.anthropology.wisc.edu

Anthropologists are interested in all aspects of human behavior and how they interrelate. Language is a form of such behavior (albeit, primarily verbal behavior) and, therefore, worthy of study. Although it changes over time, language is patterned and passed down from one generation to the next through learning, not instinct. In keeping with the idea that language is integral to human social interactions, it has long been recognized that human communication through language is, by its nature, different from the communication found among other animals. Central to this difference is the fact that humans communicate abstractly, with symbols that have meaning independent of the immediate sensory experiences of either the sender or the receiver of the message. Thus, for instance, humans are able to refer to the future and the past and not just the present.

Recent experiments have shown that anthropoid apes can be taught a small portion of Ameslan or American Sign Language. It must be remembered, however, that their very rudimentary ability has to be tapped by painstaking human effort, and that the degree of difference between apes and humans serves only to emphasize the peculiar need of humans for, and development of, language.

Just as the abstract quality of symbols lifts our thoughts beyond immediate sense perception, it also inhibits our ability to think about and convey the full meaning of our personal experience. No categorical term can do justice to its referents—the variety of forms to which the term refers. The degree to which this is an obstacle to clarity of thought and communication relates to the degree of abstraction involved in the symbols. The word "chair," for instance, would not present much difficulty, since it has objective referents. However, consider the trouble we have in thinking and communicating with words whose referents are not tied to immediate sense perception—words such as "freedom," "democracy," and "justice." Deborah Tannen's discussion of the "argument culture" (in "Fighting for Our Lives") is a prime example of this. At best, the likely result is symbolic confusion: an inability to think or communicate in objectively definable symbols. At worst, language may be used to purposefully obfuscate.

A related issue has to do with the fact that languages differ as to what is relatively easy to express within the restrictions of their particular vocabularies and grammatical structure. Thus, although a given language may not have enough words to cope

with a new situation or a new field of activity, the typical solution is to invent words or to borrow them. In this way, it has been claimed that any language can be used to say anything. This point is challenged, however, by Laura Bohannan's attempt to convey the "true" meaning of Shakespeare's *Hamlet* to the West African Tiv (see "Shakespeare in the Bush"). Much of her task was devoted to finding the most appropriate words in the Tiv language to convey her Western thoughts. At least part of her failure was due to the fact that some of the words just don't exist in the native language, and her inventions were unacceptable to the Tiv.

In a somewhat different manner, Donna Jo Napoli in "Whose Speech Is Better?" points out that there are subtleties to language that cannot be found in a dictionary and whose meaning can only be interpreted in the context of the social situation. In fact, Robert MacNeil shows in "Do You Speak American?" that linguistic diversity within the United States is alive and well and, in spite of the homogenizing effects of the mass media, is actually on the increase.

In summary, the articles in this unit show how symbolic confusion may occur between individuals or groups; they illustrate the beauty and wonder inherent in this uniquely human form of communication we call "language," and they demonstrate the tremendous potential of recent research to enhance effective communication among all of us.

Whose Speech Is Better?

Donna Jo Napoli

Not all speakers of a given language speak the same way. You've noticed speech variations on television. Maybe you've seen the movie *My Fair Lady,* in which Henry Higgins believes that the Queen's English is the superior language of England (and, perhaps, of the world). So the question arises, whose speech is better? And this question is subsumed under the larger question of whether any language is intrinsically superior to another.

Before facing this issue, though, we need to face another matter. Consider these utterances:

Would you mind if I borrowed that cushion for a few moments?

Could I have that pillow for a sec?

Give me that, would you?

All of these utterances could be used to request a pillow.

Which one(s) would you use in addressing a stranger? If you use the first one, perhaps you sense that the stranger is quite different from you (such as a much older person or a person with more stature or authority). Perhaps you're trying to show that you're polite or refined or not a threat. Pay attention to the use of the word "cushion" instead of "pillow." Pillows often belong behind our heads, typically in bed. If you wanted to avoid any hint of intimacy, you might choose to use the word "cushion" for what is clearly a pillow.

Consider the third sentence. It's harder for some people to imagine using this one with a stranger. When I help to renovate urban housing for the poor with a group called Chester Community Improvement Project and I am pounding in nails next to some guy and sweat is dripping off both our brows, I have no hesitation in using this style sentence. With the informality of such a sentence, I'm implying, or perhaps trying to bring about, a sense of comradery.

Of course, it's easy to imagine a scene in which you could use the second sentence with a stranger.

Which one(s) would you use in addressing someone you know well? Again, it could be all three. But now if you use the first one, you might be insulting the addressee. It's not hard to think of a scenario in which this sentence carries a nasty tone rather than a polite one. And you can describe scenarios for the second and third sentences easily.

The point is that we command different registers of language. We can use talk that is fancy or ordinary or extremely informal, and we can choose which register to use in which situations to get the desired effect. So we have lots of variation in our own speech in the ways we phrase things (syntax) and the words we use (lexicon vocabulary).

Other variation in an individual's speech involves sound rules (phonology). Say the third sentence aloud several times, playing with different ways of saying it. Contrast "give me" to "gimme" and "would you" to "wudja." When we say words in a sequence, sometimes we contract them, but even a single word can be said in multiple ways. Say the word "interesting" in several sentences, imagining scenarios that differ in formality. Probably your normal (or least marked) pronunciation has three syllables: "in-tres-ting." But maybe it has four, and if it does, they are probably "in-er-es-ting."

The pronunciation that is closest to the spelling ("in-ter-es-ting") is more formal and, as a result, is sometimes used for humor (as in "very in-ter-es-ting," with a noticeably foreign flair to the pronunciation of "very" or with a drawn-out "e" in "very").

So you have plenty of variation in your own speech, no matter who you are, and the more different speech communities you belong to, the more variation you will have. With my mother's relatives, I will say, for example, "I hate lobsters anymore," whereas with other people I'm more likely to say, "I hate lobsters these days." This particular use of "anymore" is common to people from certain geographical areas (the North and South Midland, meaning the area from Philadelphia westward through southern Pennsylvania, northern West Virginia, Ohio, Indiana, and Illinois to the Mississippi River) but not to people from other places, who may not even understand what I mean. With my sister, I used to say, "Ain't nobody gonna tell me what to do," but I'd never say that to my mother or to other people unless I was trying to make a sociolinguistic point. This kind of talk signaled for us a comradery outside of the socioeconomic group my mother aspired to. In a speech to a convention of librarians recently, I said, "That had to change, for I, like you, do not lead a charmed life," but I'd probably never say that in conversation to anyone—it's speech talk. Also, think about the language you use in e-mail and contrast it to your job-related writings, for example.

Although we cannot explicitly state the rules of our language, we do choose to use different rules in different contexts. We happily exploit variation, which we encounter in a wide range, from simple differences in pronunciation and vocabulary to more marked differences that involve phrasing and sentence structure. When the differences are greater and more numerous, we tend to talk of dialects rather than just variations. Thus the languages of upper class and lower class Bostonians would probably be called variations of American English, whereas the languages of upper class and lower class Londoners (Queen's English versus Cockney) would probably be called dialects of British English. When the dialects are so different as to be mutually incomprehensible and/or when they gain a cultural or political status, we tend to talk of separate languages (such as French versus Spanish).

There's one more point I want to make before we return to our original question. I often ask classes to play the game of telephone in the following way. We line up twenty-one chairs, and volunteers sit on them. Then I whisper in the middle person's ear, perhaps something very simple, such as "Come with me to the store." The middle person then whispers the phrase into the ears of people on both sides, and the whisper chain goes on to each end of the line. Finally, the first and twenty-first persons say aloud what they heard.

Next we do the same experiment but this time with a sentence that's a little more tricky, perhaps something such as "Why choose white shoes for winter sports?" Then we do the experiment with a sentence in a language that the first whisperer (who is often not me at this point) speaks reasonably well and might be familiar to some of the twenty-one people in the chairs—perhaps something such as *La lune, c'est magnifique* (which in French means "the moon is wonderful"). Finally, we do the experiment with a sentence whispered initially by a native speaker of a language that none of the twenty-one people speak.

Typically, the first and twenty-first persons do not come up with the same results. Furthermore, the distance between them seems greater with each successive experiment.

Part of the problem is in the listening. We don't all hear things the same way. When we haven't heard something clearly, we ask people to repeat what they said. But sometimes we don't realize we haven't heard something clearly, until our inappropriate response is corrected. At times the other person doesn't correct us and the miscommunication remains, leading to various other difficulties.

Part of the problem in the experiment is in the repeating. You may say, "My economics class is a bore," and you begin the second word with the syllable "eek." I might repeat the sentence but use my pronunciation of the second word, which would begin with "ek." If you speak French well, you might say "magnifique" quite differently from me. In high school or college language classes, the teacher drilled the pronunciation of certain words over and over—but some people never mimicked to her satisfaction. A linguist told me a story about a little girl who introduced herself as "Litha." The man she was introducing herself to said, "Litha?" The child said, "No, Litha." The man said, "Litha?" The child said, "No, no. Litha. Li-tha." The man said, "Lisa?" The child smiled and said, "Right." Repetitions are not exact and lead to change.

Imperfections in hearing and repeating are two of the reasons that language must change over time. When the Romans marched into Gaul and into the Iberian peninsula and northeastward into what is now Romania, they brought large populations who stayed and spoke a form of street Latin. But over time, the street Latin in Gaul developed into French; that in the Iberian Peninsula developed into Portuguese along the west and Spanish along the east and central portions; that in Romania developed into Romanian. Moreover, the street Latin spoken in the original community on the Italian peninsula changed as well, developing into Italian.

Other factors (besides our imperfections in hearing and in repeating sounds) can influence the speed with which language changes and the ways in which it changes—but the fact is that living languages necessarily change. They always have and they always will.

Many political groups have tried to control language change. During the French Revolution, a controlling faction decided that a standard language would pave the way for unity. Parish priests, who were ordered to survey spoken language, found that many dialects were spoken in different geographic areas, and many of them were quite distinct from the dialect of Paris. Primary schools in every region of France were established with teachers proficient in the Parisian dialect. The effect of this educational reform was not significant until 1881, when state education became free and mandatory, and the standard dialect (that is, Parisian) took hold more firmly. Still, the geographic dialects continued, though weakened, and most important, the standard kept changing. Standard French today is different from the Parisian dialect of 1790. In addition, new varieties of French have formed, as new subcultures have appeared. Social dialects persist and/or arise even when geographic dialects are squelched. Change is the rule in language, so variation will always be with us.

Now we can ask whose speech is better. This is a serious question because our attitudes about language affect how we treat speakers in personal, as well as in business and professional, situations. In what follows I will use the term "standard American English" (a term riddled with problems, which will become more and more apparent as you read)—the variety that we hear in news reports on television and radio. It doesn't seem to be strongly associated with any particular area of the country, although those who aren't from the Midwest often call it midwestern. This variety is also more frequently associated with the middle class than with the lower class, and it is more frequently associated with whites than with other races.

A few years ago a white student from Atlanta, Georgia, recorded herself reading a passage of James Joyce both in standard American English pronunciation and in her Atlanta pronunciation. She then asked strangers (adults of varying ages who lived in the town of Swarthmore, Pennsylvania) to listen to the two readings and answer a set of questions she had prepared. She did not tell the strangers that the recordings were made by a single person (nor that they were made by her). Without exception, the strangers judged the person who read the passage with standard English pronunciation as smarter and better educated, and most of them judged the person who read the passage with Atlanta pronunciation as nicer and more laid-back. This was just a small, informal study, but its findings are consistent with those of larger studies.

Studies have shown that prejudice against certain varieties of speech can lead to discriminatory practices. For example, Professor John Baugh of Stanford University directed a study of housing in which he used different English pronunciations when telephoning people who had advertised apartments for rent. In one call he would use standard American pronunciation; in another, African-American; in another, Latino. (He is African American, but he grew up in the middle class in Los Angeles with many Latino friends. He can sound white, African American, or Latino, at will.) He said exactly the same words in every call, and he controlled for the order in which he made the calls (i.e., sometimes the Latino pronunciation would be used first, sometimes the African-American, and sometimes the standard). He asked if the apartments were still available. More were available when he used the standard pronunciation. Thus it is essential that we examine carefully the question of "better" with regard to language variety.

When I knock on a door and my friend inside says, "Who's there?" I'm likely to answer, "It's me," but I don't say, "It's I" (or, even more unlikely for me, "It is I"). Do you? If you do, do you say that naturally, that is, not self-consciously? Or do you say it because you've been taught that that's the correct thing to say? If you do it naturally, your speech contains an archaism—a little fossil from the past. We all have little fossils. I say, "I'm different from you." Most people today would say, "I'm different than you." My use of "from" after "different" was typical in earlier generations, but it's not typical today. Some of us hold onto archaisms longer than others, and even the most linguistically innovative of us probably have some. So don't be embarrassed by your fossils: They're a fact of language.

But if you say "It's I" self-consciously because you've been taught that that's correct, what does "correct" mean in this situation? If that's what most people used to say but is not what most people say today, you're saying it's correct either because you revere the past (which many of us do) or because you believe that there's a rule of language that's being obeyed by "It's I" and being broken by "It's me."

I'm going to push the analysis of just this one contrast—"It's I" versus "It's me"—quite a distance because I believe that many relevant issues about how people view language will come out of the discussion. Consider the former reason for preferring "It's I," that of revering the past. Many people have this reason for using archaic speech patterns and for preferring that others use them. For some reason, language is treated in a unique way here. We certainly don't hold up the past as superior in other areas, for example, mathematics or physics. So why do some of us feel that changes in language are evidence of decay?

If it were true that the older way of saying something were better simply because it's older, your grandparents spoke better than your parents and your great-grandparents spoke better than your grandparents and so on. Did Chaucer speak a form of English superior to that spoken by Shakespeare? Shall we go further back than Chaucer for our model? There is no natural stopping point. We can go all the way to prehistoric times if we use "older" as the only standard for "better."

The latter reason—believing that "It's I" obeys a rule that "It's me" breaks—is more defensible, if it is indeed true. Defenders of the "It's I" school of speech point out that with the verb "be" the elements on both sides of it are grammatically equivalent—so they should naturally have the same case.

I've used a linguistic term here: "case." To understand it (or review it), look at these Hungarian sentences:

Megnézhetem a szobát?

Van rádió a szobában?

Hol a szoba?

May I see the room?

Is there a radio in the room?

Where's the room?

I have translated the sentences in a natural way rather than word by word. Can you pick out the word in each sentence that means "room"? I hope you chose *szobát*, *szobában*, and *szoba*. These three forms can be thought of as variants of the same word. The difference in form is called case marking. Textbooks on Hungarian typically claim that a form like *szoba* is used when the word is the subject of the sentence, a form like *szobát* when the word is the direct object, and a form like *szobában* when the word conveys a certain kind of location (comparable to the object of the preposition "in" in English). So a word can have various forms—various cases—based on how it is used in the sentence.

English does not have different case forms for nouns (with the exception of genitive nouns, such as "boy's" in "the boy's book"). So in the English translations of the Hungarian sentences above, the word "room" was invariable. However, English does have different case forms for pronouns:

I like tennis.

That tennis racket is mine.

Everyone likes me.

These three forms indicate the first-person singular: "I," "mine," and "me." They distinguish subjects ("I") from genitives ("mine") from everything else ("me").

Now let's return to "It's I." Must elements on either side of "be" be equivalent? In the following three sentences, different syntactic categories are on either side of "be" (here "NP" stands for "noun phrase"):

Bill is tall.

Bill is off his rocker.

Bill is to die for.

NP "be" AP

NP "be" PP

NP "be" VP

"Tall" is an adjective (here, an adjective phrase, AP). "Off" is a preposition, and it's part of the prepositional phrase (PP) "off his rocker." "To die for" is a verb phrase (VP). Thus the two elements that flank "be" do not have to be equivalent in category.

Still, in the sentence "It's I," the elements that flank "be" are both pronouns ("It" and "I"), so maybe these elements are equivalent in this sentence. Let's test that claim by looking at agreement. Verbs agree with their subject in English, whether that subject precedes or follows them:

John's nice.

Is John nice?

But "be" in our focus sentence agrees with the NP to its left, not to its right:

It's I.

*It am I.

No one would say "It am I." Therefore, the NP to the right of "be" is not the subject of the sentence, which means that the NPs flanking "be" are not equivalent—"It" is the subject, but "I" is not.

Perhaps you think that the equivalency that matters here has to do with meaning, not with syntax. Let's pursue that: Do "It" and "I" have equivalent meaning in "It's I"? Notice that you can also say:

"It's you."

In fact, the slot after "It's" can be filled by several different pronouns. "It" in these sentences is not meaningful; it is simply a place holder, just as in sentences about time and weather:

It's four o'clock.

It's hailing.

But "I" is meaningful because it refers to a person (the speaker). Therefore, "It" and "I" are not equivalent in meaning in the sentence "It's I."

In sum, it's not clear that the elements on either side of "be" in the sentence "It's I" are equivalent in any linguistic way. We can conclude something even stronger. We noted that "It" in these sentences is the subject and that the pronoun following a form of "be" is not the subject. But the pronoun following "be" is also not a genitive. Given the pronoun case system of English discussed above, we expect the pronoun to take the third form (the "elsewhere" form), which is "me," not "I." In other words, our case system would lead us to claim that "It's me" is the grammatical sentence.

I am not saying "It's I" is ungrammatical. I want to show that the issue may not be as clean-cut as you might have thought. Indeed, the conclusion I come to is that more than one case system is at play here. Those who say "It's me" are employing regular case rules. But those who say "It's I" have a special case rule for certain sentences that contain "be." The important point is that both sets of speakers have rules that determine what they say. Their speech is systematic; they are not speaking randomly.

That is the key issue of this whole chapter. When we consider variation in language, we must give up the idea of errors and accept the idea of patterns. Some people produce one pattern because they are following one set of rules; other people produce a different pattern because they are following a different set of rules. (For several different types of language variations in English, visit the websites of the West Virginia Dialect Project: www.as.wvu.edu/dialect.) From a linguistic perspective, asking whose speech is better would amount to asking whose system is better. But what standards do we have for evaluating systems? What standards do you, as a speaker of the language, employ when you judge between varieties of speech? To answer that question, consider variation in your own speech. Do you consider some varieties better than others? And which ones? If you're like most people, you consider formal or polite speech to be better. But that standard concerns behavior in society—behavior that may reveal or perhaps even determine one's position. We tend to think that the speech of those who hold cultural, economic, or other social power is better, but this has little to do with linguistic structure. Now ask yourself what standards you are using to judge the speech of others.

Such questions often boil down to your politics (who do you esteem?) or to your experience (what are you familiar with?) but not to your grammatical rules. Consider the common claim that some varieties of speech are lazy. Try to find a recording of English speech that you consider lazy. Now mimic it. Some people are good at mimicking the speech of others, but accurately mimicking the speech of anyone else (anyone at all) takes a good ear, good control over the parts of your body that produce speech, and mostly a grasp of the sound rules that are being used. So the speech you thought was lazy wasn't lazy at all. Rather, different rules are being employed in different varieties of speech. What makes each variety distinct from others is its inventory of rules.

Consider learning a foreign language. People who feel confident about their ability to speak and to understand a foreign language in a classroom often visit a place where that language is spoken, only to find that no one is speaking the classroom variety. One of the big differences is usually speed: Ordinary speech can be quite rapid. Again, some claim that fast speech is sloppy, but fast speech is notoriously hard to mimic. It is typically packed with sound rules, so it takes more experience with the language to master all the rules and to be able to produce fast speech.

Among American speakers a common misconception is that British speech is superior to American speech. Part of this belief follows from reverence of the past, already discussed. Part of it follows from the misperception that American upper class speech is closer to British speech—so British speech is associated with high society and with politeness. In fact, the speech of the British changed over time, just as the speech of the American colonialists changed over time. Therefore, modern British speech is not, in general, closer to older forms of English than American speech is. Pockets of conservative varieties of English occur both in the British Isles and in the United States, but most varieties on either side of the Atlantic Ocean have changed considerably. Also, British society is stratified, just as American society is, and not all British speech is either upper class or polite.

Linguists claim that all varieties of a language—all dialects and all languages, for that matter—are equal linguistic citizens. Linguists have recognized that all languages are systematic, obeying certain universal principles regarding the organization and interaction of sounds, the ways we build words and phrases and sentences, and how we code meaning. However, this doesn't mean that all language is esthetically equal. I can recognize a beautiful line in a poem or a story, as I'm sure you can (though we might not agree). But that beautiful line might be in archaic English, formal contemporary English, ordinary contemporary English, very informal contemporary English, African-American Atlanta English, Italian-American Yonkers English, Philadelphia gay English, Chinese-American Seattle English, or so many others. Within our different varieties of speech, we can speak in ways that affect people's hearts or resonate in their minds, or we can speak in ways that are unremarkable. These are personal (esthetic or political) choices.

Some possible effects of the goal of the English only movement (EOM) of minimizing certain language variations in the United States [exist]. But even if English were declared the official language of the United States, variation would not be wiped out. What would be threatened is the richness of the range of variation most speakers are exposed to. Once that exposure is lost, Americans might start thinking that English is a superior language simply because they would no longer hear other languages being spoken by people they know personally and respect. They might become severely provincial in their linguistic attitudes, and given the necessity of global respect these days, such provincialism could be dangerous.

The fact that variation in language is both unavoidable and sometimes the result of esthetic and political choices does not mean that educational institutions should not insist that children master whatever variety of language has been deemed the standard—just for purely practical reasons. There's little doubt that linguistic prejudice is a reality. The adult who cannot speak and write the standard variety may encounter a range of difficulties, from finding suitable employment to achieving social advancement.

At the same time, all of us—and educational institutions, in particular—should respect all varieties of language and show that respect in relevant ways. Look at one notorious controversy: In 1996 the school board in Oakland, California, declared Ebonics to be the official language of the district's African-American students. Given funding regulations for bilingual education in that time and place, this decision had the effect of allowing the school district to use funds set aside for bilingual education to teach their African-American children in Ebonics, as well as in the standard language.

The debate was particularly hot, I believe, because of the sociological issues involved. Many people thought that Ebonics should be kept out of the classroom purely because the dialect was associated with race. Some of these people were African Americans who did not want their children to be disadvantaged by linguistic prejudice; they were afraid that teaching in Ebonics would exaggerate racial linguistic prejudice rather than redress it. Many good books written about the Ebonics controversy for the general public look at the issue from a variety of perspectives (see the suggested readings). But from a linguistic perspective, the issue is more a question of bilingual (or bidialectal) education than anything else.

In sum, variation in language is something we all participate in, and, as a linguist and a writer, I believe it's something we should revel in. Language is not a monolith, nor can it be, nor should it be, given the complexity of culture and the fact that language is the fabric of culture. Some of us are more eloquent than others, and all of us have moments of greater or lesser eloquence. But that range in eloquence is found in every language, every dialect, and every variety of speech.

Further Readings on Variation

Andersson, L. G., and P. Trudgill. 1990. *Bad language.* Cambridge: Blackwell.

Baron, D. 1994. *Guide to home language repair.* Champaign, Ill.: National Council of Teachers of English.

Baugh, J. 1999. *Out of the mouths of slaves.* Austin: University of Texas Press.

Biber, D., and E. Finegan. 1997. *Sociolinguistic perspectives on register.* Oxford: Oxford University Press.

Cameron, D. 1995. *Verbal hygiene.* London: Routledge.

Carver, C. 1989. *American regional dialects: A word geography.* Ann Arbor: University of Michigan Press.

Coulmas, F. 1998. *Handbook of sociolinguistics.* Cambridge: Blackwell.

Fasold, R. 1984. *The sociolinguistics of society.* New York: Blackwell.

Finegan, E. 1980. *Attitudes toward language usage.* New York: Teachers College Press.

Fishman, J. 1968. *Readings in the sociology of language.* Paris: Mouton.

Herman, L. H., and M. S. Herman. 1947. *Manual of American dialects for radio, stage, screen, and television.* New York: Ziff Davis.

Hock, H., and B. Joseph. 1996. *An introduction to historical and comparative linguistics.* Berlin: Mouton de Gruyter.

Labov, W. 1972. *The logic of nonstandard English in language and social context: Selected readings.* Compiled by Pier Paolo Giglioli. Baltimore Md.: Penguin.

Labov, W. 1972. *Sociolinguistic patterns.* Philadelphia: University of Pennsylvania Press.

LeClerc, F., Schmitt, B. H., and Dube, L. 1994, May. Foreign branding and its effects on product perceptions and attitudes. *Journal of Marketing Research,* 31: 263–270.

Lippi-Green, R. 1997. *English with an accent.* New York: Routledge.

McCrum, R., W. Cran, and R. MacNeil. 1986. *The story of English.* New York: Viking Penguin.

Millward, C. M. 1989. *A biography of the English language.* Orlando, Fla.: Holt, Rinehart and Winston.

Milroy, J., and L. Milroy. 1991. *Authority in language,* 2nd ed. London: Routledge.

Moss, B., and K. Walters. 1993. Rethinking diversity: Axes of difference in the writing classroom. In L. Odell, ed., *Theory and practice in the teaching of writing: Rethinking the discipline.* Carbondale: Southern Illinois University Press.

Peyton, J., S. McGinnis, and D. Ranard, eds. 2001. *Heritage languages in America: Preserving a national resource* (from Delta Systems, phone 800-323-8270), Arlington, Va.

Romaine, S. 1994. *Language in society: An introduction to sociolinguistics.* Oxford: Oxford University Press.

Scherer, K., and H. Giles, eds. 1979. *Social markers in speech.* New York: Cambridge University Press.

Seligman, C. R., G. R. Tucker, and W. Lambert. 1972. The effects of speech style and other attributes on teachers' attitudes toward pupils. *Language and Society,* 1: 131–42.

Trask, R. L. 1994. *Language change.* London: Routledge.

Weinreich, U. [1953] 1968. *Languages in contact.* The Hague: Mouton.

Wolfram, W. 1991. *Dialects and American English.* Englewood Cliffs, N.J.: Prentice Hall.

Wolfram, W., and N. Schilling-Estes. 1998. *American English—dialects and variation.* Oxford: Blackwell.

Further Readings on Ebonics

Adger, C. 1994. Enhancing the delivery of services to black special education students from non-standard English backgrounds. Final Report. University of Maryland, Institute for the Study of Exceptional Children and Youth. (Available through ERIC Document Reproduction Service. Document No. ED 370 377.)

Adger, C., D. Christian, and O. Taylor. 1999. *Making the connection: Language and academic achievement among African American students.* Washington, D.C. and McHenry, Ill.: Center for Applied Linguistics and Delta Systems.

Adger, C., W. Wolfram, and J. Detwyler. 1993. Language differences: A new approach for special educators. *Teaching Exceptional Children,* 26, no. (1): 44–47.

Adger, C., W. Wolfram, J. Detwyler, and B. Harry. 1993. Confronting dialect minority issues in special education: Reactive and proactive perspectives. In *Proceedings of the Third National Research Symposium on Limited English Proficient Student Issues: Focus on Middle and High School Issues,* 2: 737–62. U.S. Department of Education, Office of Bilingual Education and Minority Languages Affairs. (Available through ERIC Document Reproduction Service. Document No. ED 356 673.)

Baratz, J. C., and R. W. Shuy, eds. 1969. Teaching black children to read. Available as reprints from the University of Michigan, Ann Arbor (313-761-4700).

Baugh, J. 2000. *Beyond Ebonics.* New York: Oxford University Press.

Christian, D. 1997. Vernacular dialects and standard American English in the classroom. ERIC Minibib. Washington, D.C.: ERIC Clearinghouse on Languages and Linguistics. (This minibibliography cites seven journal articles and eight documents related to dialect usage in the classroom. The documents can be accessed on microfiche at any institution with the ERIC collection, or they can be ordered directly from EDRS.)

Dillard, J. L. 1972. *Black English: Its history and use in the U.S.* New York: Random House.

Fasold, R. W. 1972. Tense marking in black English: A linguistic and social analysis. Available as reprints from the University of Michigan, Ann Arbor (313-761-4700).

Fasold, R. W., and R. W. Shuy, eds. 1970. *Teaching standard English in the inner city.* Washington, D.C.: Center for Applied Linguistics.

Wiley, T. G. 1996. The case of African American language. In *Literacy and language diversity in the United States,* pp. 125–32. Washington, D. C.: Center for Applied Linguistics and Delta Systems.

Wolfram, W. 1969. A sociolinguistic description of Detroit Negro speech. Available as reprints from the University of Michigan, Ann Arbor (313-761-4700).

Wolfram, W. 1990, February. Incorporating dialect study into the language arts class. *ERIC Digest.* Available from the ERIC Clearinghouse on Languages and Linguistics, Center for Applied Linguistics, 4646 40th Street NW, Washington, D.C. 20016-1859, (202-362-0700).

Wolfram, W. 1994. Bidialectal literacy in the United States. In D. Spencer, ed., *Adult biliteracy in the United States,* pp. 71–88. Washington, D.C.: Center for Applied Linguistics and Delta Systems.

Wolfram, W., and C. Adger. 1993. *Handbook on language differences and speech and language pathology: Baltimore City public schools.* Washington, D.C.: Center for Applied Linguistics.

Wolfram, W., C. Adger, and D. Christian. 1999. Dialects in schools and communities. Mahwah, N.J.: Erlbaum.

Wolfram, W., and N. Clarke, eds. 1971. *Black-white speech relationships.* Washington, D.C.: Center for Applied Linguistics.

Assess Your Progress

1. What are some of the factors that account for variations in speech?

2. What evidence is there that people discriminate on the basis of speech patterns?

3. When considering variations in language, why must we "give up the idea of errors and accept the idea of patterns?"

4. Why is there no such thing as "lazy speech?"

5. Are all varieties of language equal? Explain. Are they all esthetically equal? Explain.

6. What would be threatened if language variation were to be wiped out?

Do You Speak American?

**"Well, butter my butt and call me a biscuit"; a documentary
on the English language, as spoken in the U.S., is airing on PBS.**

Robert MacNeil

On Columbus Avenue in New York, a young waitress approaches our table and asks, "How are you guys doin'?" My wife and I are old enough to be her grandparents, but we are "you guys" to her. Today, in American English, guys can be guys, girls, or grandmothers. Girls call themselves guys, even dudes. For a while, young women scorned the word girls, but that is cool again, probably because African-American women use it and it can be real cool—even empowering—to whites to borrow black talk, like the word cool. It is empowering to gay men to call themselves queer, once a hated homophobic term, but now used to satirize the whole shifting scene of gender attitudes in the TV reality show, "Queer Eye for the Straight Guy." As society changes, so does language, and American society has changed enormously in recent decades. Moreover, when new norms are resented or feared, language often is the target of that fear or resentment.

How we use the English language became a hot topic during the 1960s, and it remains so today—a charged ingredient in the culture wars, as intensely studied and disputed as any other part of our society. That is appropriate because nothing is more central to our identity and sense of who we are and where we belong. "Aside from a person's physical appearance, the first thing someone will be judged by is how he or she talks," maintains linguist Dennis Baron.

Many feel that the growing informality of American life, the retreat from fixed standards, ("the march of casualization," *The New York Times* recently called it)—in clothing, manners, sexual mores—is reflected in our language and is corrupting it. They see schools lax about teaching grammar and hear nonstandard forms accepted in broadcasting, newspapers, politics, and advertising. They believe the slogan "Winston tastes good like a cigarette should" is so embedded in the national psyche that few Americans would now balk at the use of "like" (instead of "as") because that usage is fast becoming the new standard. They hate such changes in the language and they despair for our culture.

Others, however, believe language is thriving—as inventive and vigorous as English was in the time of the Elizabethans—and they see American English as the engine driving what is now a global language.

This deep disagreement is one of the issues explored in a survey producer William Cran and I recently completed and a three-hour documentary, "Do You Speak American?"

We address the controversies, issues, anxieties, and assumptions swirling around language today—some highly emotional and political. Why are black and white Americans speaking less and less like each other? We explain. Does Hispanic immigration threaten the English language? We do not think so. Is our exposure to national media wiping out regional differences and causing us all to speak the same? We think not. Is the language really in serious decline? Well, we have quite a debate about that.

The people who believe so are known as prescriptivists: those who want us to obey prescribed rules of grammar. They do not mind being called curmudgeons and they alternate between pleasure and despair—pleasure in correcting their fellow citizens: despair that they cannot stop the language from going to hell in our generation.

The Prince of Prescriptivists

One of the leading curmudgeons of our time—he has been called the Prince of Prescriptivists—is John Simon, theater critic for *New York Magazine,* and he comes to do battle in "Do You Speak American?" Simon sees the language today as "unhealthy, poor, sad, depressing, and probably fairly hopeless." In the foreword to a new book, *The Dictionary of Disagreeable English,* he writes: "No damsel was ever in such distress, no drayhorse more flogged, no defenseless child more drunkenly abused than the English language today."

The enemies for Simon are the descriptivists, those content to describe language as it actually is used. They include the editors of great dictionaries who, Simon charges, have grown dangerously permissive, abandoning advice on what is correct and what is not. He calls descriptivist linguists "a curse on their race."

One such individual is Jesse Sheidlower, American editor of the august *Oxford English Dictionary.* Does he believe the language is being ruined by the great informality of American life? "No, it is not being ruined at all," he replies. Sheidlower believes that Simon and other language conservatives actually are complaining that linguists and dictionary writers no longer are focused on the language of the elite. They look at the old days and say, "Well, everything used to be very proper, and now we have all these bad words and people are being careless, and so forth." In fact, he insists people always have spoken that way. "It's just that you didn't hear them because the media would only report on the language of the educated upper middle class," Sheidlower points out. "Nowadays . . . we see the language of other groups, of other social groups, of other income levels, in a way that we never used to.

"Language change happens and there's nothing you can do about it." To which Simon replies, "Maybe change is inevitable—maybe. Maybe dying from cancer is also inevitable, but I don't think we should help it along."

Helping it along, to Simon, would mean surrendering to the word "hopefully," one of his pet peeves. "To say, 'Hopefully it won't rain tomorrow'—who, or what, is filled with hope? Nothing. So you have to say, 'I hope it won't rain tomorrow.' But you can say, 'I enter a room hopefully,' because you are the vessel for that hopefulness."

Sheidlower replies that modern computer databases make it possible to check texts back over the centuries: "We see that 'hopefully' is not in fact very new. . . . It goes back hundreds of years, and it has been very common even in highly educated speech for much of the time."

This battle—the stuff of angry skirmishes in books, magazines, and seminars—is only one part of what makes our language news today. Other findings may surprise many people because they challenge widely held popular conceptions, or misconceptions, about the language.

Our study took the form of a journey starting in the Northeast, down to the mid-Atlantic states, west to the Great Lakes, Midwest, Appalachia, then toward the South, through Louisiana, Texas, and California into the Pacific Northwest. In linguistic terms, we traveled through the main dialect areas of the nation. Professional linguists, students of the science of language, were the key to our understanding of the forces changing the language as rapidly as the society has changed in the past 50 years.

While computers, information technology, globalization, digital communications, and satellites have revolutionized how we work, equally potent revolutions have occurred concerning the home, family structure and marriage, sexual mores, the role of women, race relations, and the rise of teenagers as a major consumer and marketing force. With this has come alterations in our public manners, eating habits, clothing, and tolerance of different lifestyles—all of which have been swept by a tide of informality.

Linguists Spring into Action

Observing how these rapid social changes have altered our language have been the linguists, whose new branch of the social sciences really came into its own in the 1960s, followed more recently by sociolinguistics, the study of how language and society interact. They have produced a body of fascinating research that usually is couched in technical language difficult for non-linguists to understand. Dozens of linguists have lent their skills to help us translate their findings, and marry their scholarship to our sampling of the actual speech of ordinary Americans in all its variety, vitality, and humor, drawn from the widest social spectrum. They include waitresses, cowboys, hip-hop artists, Marine drill sergeants, Border Patrol agents, Mexican immigrants, Cajun musicians, African-American and Hispanic broadcasters, and Silicon Valley techies (who try to make computers talk like real people), as well as writers and editors, teachers and teenagers, surfers and snowboarders, actors and screenwriters, and presidents and politicians.

Did they all sound the same? One of the most common assumptions is that our total immersion in the same mass media is making

us all speak in a similar manner. Not true, claim the linguists. We are not talking more alike, but less.

One of the enduring themes in American life is the pull of national against regional interests and regret for local distinctiveness erased in the relentless march of uniformity. It surfaced in the song "Little Boxes" by Pete Seeger, about people put into little boxes of identical houses made of "ticky tacky" and who all come out the same. Today, with more and more national franchising of basic elements—food, mobile homes, clothing, hotels, recreation—the U.S. can seem like one giant theme park endlessly reduplicated, the triumph of the cookie cutter culture and its distinctive art form, the national TV commercial.

Paradoxically, however, language is one fundamental aspect of our cultural identity in which growing homogenization is a myth. While some national trends are apparent, regional speech differences not only thrive, in some places they are becoming more distinctive. Local differences, pride, and identity with place are asserting themselves strongly, perhaps as instinctive resistance to the homogenizing forces of globalization. One remarkable example is the speech of urban African-Americans, which is diverging from standard mainstream English. After decades of progress in civil rights, and the growth of a large and successful black middle class, African-American speech in our big cities dramatically is going its own way.

Two linguists, Guy Bailey, provost of the University of Texas at San Antonio, and Patricia Cukor-Avila of the University of North Texas at Denton have documented this. For 18 years, they have studied a small community in East Central Texas they named "Springville," which appears to live in a time warp from a century ago, when it was the center for local cotton sharecroppers, black and white. Little remains now but the original general store. During the late 1930s, the Works Progress Administration recorded the voices of elderly blacks, some former slaves, some the children of slaves.

One of them, Laura Smalley, was born to a slave mother. She was nine at the time of Emancipation in 1863. She told how the slave owner kept them ignorant of Lincoln's Proclamation for six months. "An' I thought ol' master was dead, but he wasn'. . . . He'd been off to the war an' come back. All the niggers gathered aroun' to see ol' master again. You know, an' ol' master didn' tell, you know, they was free. . . . They worked there, I think now they say they worked them six months after that, six months. And turn them loose on the 19th of June. That's why, you know, they celebrate that day. Colored folks celebrates that day."

Black and White Dialects

Reviewing the speech of Smalley and others, the linguists were taken by how similar it was to the speech of rural whites of that time and place, but now dissimilar to the speech of blacks today. Features characteristic of modern black speech, what linguists call African-American vernacular English—such as the invariant "be," as in "they 'be' working," or the deleted copular, leaving out the auxiliary verb in "they working"—were absent.

Here are samples of modern speech of African-Americans in large cities:

"When the baby be sleep, and the othe' kids be at school, and my husband be at work, then . . . I might can finally sit down."

"She told David they Mama had went to Chicago to see her sister and her sister's new baby."

45

These examples show the invariant "be," and the construction "had went." Bailey and Cukor-Avila say that these features did not exist in black speech before World War II. They conclude that, after the great migration to the North from World War I to the 1970s, blacks were segregated in urban ghettoes, had less contact with whites than they had in places like Springville, and their speech began to develop new features, as all human speech does when people are separated culturally and have little communication.

This has serious consequences in efforts to reduce the school dropout rate among blacks. Not only white teachers, but many African-American instructors, despise the "street talk" or "slang" as they call it, and often treat the children as if they were stupid or uneducable. In 1979, a Federal judge in Detroit ruled that an Ann Arbor, Mich., school, ironically named after Martin Luther King, Jr., was discriminating against black kids because of their language and ordered the school to remedy it. Yet, the prejudice lives on elsewhere. In 1997, Oakland schools tried to get black speech recognized not as a dialect of English but a separate language, Ebonics, to qualify for Federal money to teach English as a second language. That backfired amid furious protests nationally from black and white educators.

What is shocking to linguists is the manner in which many newspaper columnists excoriate black English, using terms such as "gibberish." In the linguistic community, black English is recognized as having its own internal consistency and grammatical forms. It certainly is not gibberish (which means something unintelligible) because it works effectively for communication within the urban community.

One of the first to give black English this measure of respect was William Labov of the University of Pennsylvania, who testified at a Senate hearing during the Ebonics furor in 1997: "This African-American vernacular English . . . is not a set of slang words, or a random set of grammatical mistakes, but a well-formed set of rules of grammar and pronunciation that is capable of conveying complex logic and reasoning."

To linguists, the fault lies not in a particular dialect, but in what attitudes others bring to it. Steve Harvey, an African-American who hosts the most popular morning radio show in Los Angeles, told us: "I speak good enough American. You know, I think there's variations of speaking American. I don't think there's any one set way, because America's so diverse." He added, "You do have to be bilingual in this country, which means you can be very adept at slang, but you also have to be adept at getting through the job interview."

Now, without fanfare, some Los Angeles schools have been trying a more sympathetic approach to help minority students become bilingual—by teaching them the differences between African-American Language, as they call it, and Mainstream American English. We visited PS 100 in Watts to watch fifth-graders play a "Jeopardy"-like game in which they won points for "translating" such sentences as "Last night we bake cookies."

Teacher: "What language is it in?"

Student: "AAL."

Teacher: "It is in African-American Language. What linguistic feature is in AAL?"

Student: "Past-tense marker-ed."

Teacher: "Past-tense marker-ed. That's cool! And how do you code-switch it to Mainstream American English?"

Student: "Last night we baked cookies."

Teacher: "You got five hundred more points." Big cheers from the kids.

So, four decades after the passage of landmark legislation outlawing racial discrimination, the news is that it blatantly survives in language. Columnists would not dream of describing other attributes of being African-American with epithets like "gibberish." They could, however, get away with it in writing about black language, which remains a significant barrier to success in school and ultimately in the job market and housing—pathways to the American dream.

Ironically, as much as it is despised, black English is embraced and borrowed by whites, especially young whites in thrall to the appeal of hip hop music. There are divergences just as dramatic within the English of white Americans. Around the Great Lakes, people are making what Labov believes are "revolutionary changes in the pronunciation of short vowels that have remained relatively stable in the language for a thousand years."

Labov is director of an effort to determine the boundaries of different dialects within American speech. Traditionally, that was achieved by comparing distinctive local or regional words people used for every day things. One surviving example is the different terms for the long sandwich that contains cold cuts, cheese, and lettuce—a grinder in some parts of New England; a wedge in Rhode Island; a spuky in Boston; a hero in New York; a hoagie in Philadelphia; a submarine in Ohio and farther west. By drawing lines around places where each term is used, linguists can form maps of dialect areas. Many such regional terms are dying out because old craft skills are replaced by products marketed nationally. Labov leads a new method in which the different ways people pronounce words are recorded with colored dots on a map of the U.S. Connecting the dots produces the Atlas of North American English.

Labov and his colleagues found startling pronunciation changes in cities such as Chicago, Cleveland, and Detroit and New York State's Rochester and Syracuse. On a computer in his office in Philadelphia, we heard a woman say the word "black," then the complete phrase: "Old senior citizens living on one 'black,'" and it was apparent that she was pronouncing "block" like "black." Similarly, another woman mentions what sounds like "bosses." The full sentence reveals she means "buses:" "I can vaguely remember when we had 'bosses' with the antennas on top."

When one vowel changes, so do the neighboring ones: "caught" shifts toward "cot," "cot" toward "cat," "cat" toward "kit" or "keeyat." Labov thinks these changes are quite important. "From our point of view as linguists, we want to understand why people should become more different from each other. We're all watching the same radio and television; we live side by side. And it's important to recognize that people don't always want to behave in the same way."

Labov has a theory that, behind changes like these, are women, the primary transmitters of language. Traditionally enjoying less economic power than men, women rely on the symbolic power offered by words. Labov believes women are more apt than men to adopt "prestige forms" of language and symbols of nonconformism—new or "stigmatized forms" that can acquire a kind of "covert prestige." Labov writes that women are quicker and more forceful in employing the new social symbolism, whatever it may be. Working on his landmark study, "The Principles of Linguistic Change," he identifies a particular type of woman—working class, well-established in her community—who takes pleasure in being nonconformist and is strong enough to influence others. He sees parallels between leadership in fashion and language change. Most young women are alert to novelty in fashion; some have the confidence to embrace it and the natural authority to induce others to follow.

These are mysterious forces working on our language from underneath, as it were, and producing startling changes that, far from homogenizing our speech, actually create more diversity. Despite all the forces of global and national uniformity in products and trends, Americans clearly still want to do their own thing linguistically. An example is Pittsburgh, where the local dialect, or Pittsburghese, is celebrated, constantly talked about, and made a commodity. They know themselves as "Yinzers," from "yinz," the plural of "you," or "you ones." They use "slippy" for "slippery"; "red up" means to "tidy up"; and "anymore" as in "'Anymore,' there's so many new buildings you can't tell which is which." In downtown Pittsburgh—pronounced "dahntahn"—the question, "Did you eat yet?" sounds like "Jeet jet?" If you haven't, the response is, "No, 'jew?'"

Barbara Johnstone, a linguist from Pittsburgh, thinks the pride in their local speech is a way for Pittsburghers to talk about who they are and what it means to live there. People treasure their local accents, because where they come from, or where they feel they belong, still does matter. In the words of California linguist, Carmen Fought, "People want to talk like the people they want to be like." This contradicts the common assumption that media exposure is making everyone sound the same.

Local Accents Prevail

Yet, amusingly, people often are quite unaware of how their own speech sounds to others. Linguists we met were full of stories about people in Texas or coastal North Carolina with strong local accents who were convinced they sounded like Walter Cronkite. It happened to me. I grew up in the Canadian province of Nova Scotia, so fascinated with words that I called a memoir of my childhood *Wordstruck*. Even in my own family, I often heard the same words said differently. My grandfather, from Nova Scotia's south shore, said "garridge" while his daughter, my mother, said "gar-aghe."

Until I first came to the U.S. in 1952, I was unaware how different my speech was even from that of neighboring New England. I was 21 and (briefly, thank God!) an aspiring actor, thrilled to be working in a summer theater in Massachusetts. The first time I stepped on to the stage and opened my mouth, the director said, "You can't talk like that." I was stunned, not knowing until that moment that I was pronouncing "out" to rhyme with "oat," and "about" with "aboat"—still the common Nova Scotian pronunciation. Anxious not to close any career doors, I immediately began trying to modify the "oat" sound, but 50 years later, when I am tired or back with my brothers in Canada, I still slip into the pronunciations I grew up with.

What appears to be the determining force in whether regional dialects survive or disappear is not media influence, but rather the movements of people. We talked to John Coffin, a lobsterman in South Freeport, Me. Once a quiet fishing and ship-building harbor

but now a bustling outlet shopping center, the town has attracted so many new visitors and residents that Coffin fears the Maine way of speaking—with its characteristic "ayeh" for "yes"—is disappearing: "I think in this area it's going to be a lost thing," and that makes him sad. "I'd like to think my children and grandchildren talk that way, whether people laugh at you, wherever we go—whatever." Do people laugh at his Maine accent? "Oh, yes, lots of times. When I was in the military, they made fun of me wicked."

"Wicked" is a typical Maine word, meaning "very," as in "wicked' good."

This homogenizing trend is obvious on some of the islands, like Ocrakoke, off the coast of North Carolina, home of the Hoi Toiders, people who pronounce "high tide" as "hoi toid." These islands have become meccas for individuals from elsewhere building vacation homes, displacing locals and their dialect.

Still, the national media are having some effect: Labov notes two sound changes that have spread nationally, probably from California. One is the vowel in "do," which increasingly sounds like "dew." Labov calls it "oo-fronting"; the sound is produced more to the front of the mouth. You also hear it in the word "so," which sounds like "so-ew." Another trend, more noticeable among young women, but also some men, is a rising inflection at the ends of sentences, making statements such as "The bus station is around *the corner*" sound like a query. One of the regions where "oo-fronting" is common is the South, where there are changes just as dramatic as those in the North. Southern ghosts do not say "boo," but "bew."

The most prevalent shift is that Southerners increasingly are pronouncing the "r" at the ends of words such as father. In part, this is due to the large migration of Northerners to Southern cities. Partly it is the historic decline in influence of the coastal Southern areas that once boasted the great slave-holding plantation culture, and the kind of r-less pronunciation we associated with languid belles posing in hoop skirts on the porches of antebellum houses. This advancing "r" marks the growing prestige of what linguists call Inland Southern, the speech deriving from Appalachia. That pattern goes back to the earliest days of British settlement, when people from parts of England who did not pronounce "r" settled the coastal areas, while the Scots-Irish, settlers from Northern Ireland who spoke with a strong "r," moved into the hills of Appalachia because the easily-cultivated coastal land already was taken.

Their speech has been given a huge boost by the rise of country music, no longer a regional craze, but a national phenomenon. Those who "sing country," wherever they come from, "talk country" and "talkin' country" has become a kind of default way of speaking informal American. It is considered easygoing and friendly. Pres. George W. Bush has made it his trademark, with no disadvantage politically because, like him, a great many Americans say, "Howya doin'? Doin' fine!" and they are not more particular than he is about making subject agree with verb in sentences such as, "There's no negotiations with North Korea."

The economic rise of the South has had another startling result. So many Americans have moved into the South and Southwest and happily adopted Southernisms—such as "y'all" and "fixin' to" and pronouncing "I" as "all," not the Northern "eye-ee"—that more Americans now speak some variety of Southern than any other dialect. That is the conclusion of linguist John Fought, who believes that, as the population shift to the Sun Belt continues, "In time, we should expect 'r-full' southern to become accepted as standard American speech."

That news will come as a shock to Northerners conditioned over generations to despise Southern talk, considering it evidence of stupidity and backwardness. In the film "Sweet Home Alabama," the good ol' boy played by Josh Lucas says to his Northernized wife, Reese Witherspoon, "Just because I talk slow, doesn't mean I'm stupid." The context leads the audience to believe him.

The comedian Jeff Foxworthy still fills huge theaters North and South with his hilarious routine ridiculing Southern speech and Northern attitudes towards it. He kills them with his list of Southern "words:'"

"May-o-naise. Man, a's a lotta people here tonight,"

"Urinal. I told my brother, 'You're in a lotta trouble when Daddy gets home.'"

"Wichadidja. Hey, you didn't bring your track with you, did you?"

Northern attitudes to Southerners may be ameliorating slightly, possibly because it no longer is uncool in Northern cities to like country music and the culture that goes with it. Yet, an ingrained sense of the prestige of some dialects and scorn for others is very much alive. Linguist Dennis Preston of Michigan State University has spent years studying the prejudices Americans have concerning speech different from their own. He joined us on a train west from Philadelphia, demonstrating his regular technique. Establishing quick rapport with other passengers, he got them to mark on a map of the U.S. where they thought people spoke differently. Almost without exception, they circled the South and New York to locate the worst English. Referring to New York, a Pennsylvania woman told Preston contemptuously, "They say waader!" Preston asked, "What do you say?" "Water!" she declared proudly.

A Distinct New York Voice

Preston, though, detects another emotion creeping in beneath the scorn, and that is pleasure. People may think Southern or New York speech is not good, but they find them charming, and that must be partly an effect of media exposure, for instance, to the sympathetic New York characters in the TV series "Law and Order." Linguists believe that broadcasting and the movies help all Americans understand different dialects, perhaps appreciating the diversity in our culture. Moreover, no matter how they themselves speak, Americans learn to understand the language of network broadcasters, which is the closest thing to an overall American standard. That standard coincides with the speech that Preston's subjects inevitably identify as the best American speech—that of the Midwest—because it has the fewest regional features.

That Midwest standard is relevant to the cutting edge of computer research in Silicon Valley. There is heavy investment in efforts to make computers speak like us and understand us. The researchers believe they will achieve that in 10 to 15 years but it is an incredible challenge.

What these efforts demonstrate is how infinitely complex our language and understanding of it is, how meaning turns on the subtlest changes in intonation, how vast any computer data base must be to catch all the nuances we take for granted. How do you program a computer to avoid those charming errors in context which foreigners make in perfectly grammatical sentences? For instance, a sign in an Egyptian hotel states: "Patrons need have no anxiety about the water. It has all been passed by the management." Or, this in a Swiss hotel: "Due to the impropriety of entertaining guests of the opposite sex in the bedrooms, it is suggested that the lobby be used for this purpose."

The effort to make computers understand speech raises other questions about the future of language. Will the technology, and the business imperatives behind it, create an irresistible drive toward more standard speech? If so, which accents or varieties of American speech will that leave out? Whom will it disenfranchise because of their dialect—African-Americans, Hispanics, Cajuns in Louisiana? A couple of years ago, the police chief of Shreveport, La., complained that the computer voice-recognition system used to route nonemergency calls did not understand the local accent. Researchers point out, however, that if you speak like someone from the Midwest, computers will understand you.

The emerging technology is irresistible for business. When United Airlines introduced a computerized voice-recognition system for flight information—replacing live bodies—it saved a reported $25,000,000. As these systems become more sophisticated, a lot of companies will want them to replace expensive warm bodies. Inevitably, more and more of our lives will involve talking to and being understood by computers. Being understood will be increasingly important. Will the technology work to reinforce existing linguistic stereotypes—about your race, ethnicity, gender, or where you live—or help to break them down? Will we have to talk as computers would like us to in order for them to obey us?

During the California portion of filming "Do You Speak American?" I drove a car equipped with an elaborate voice-recognition system. I speak a version of standard broadcast American English, and I tried to enunciate clearly. Occasionally, it worked, but often it did not and the car kept saying, "Pardon me? Pardon me?" and I gave it up.

Everything in the American experience, each new frontier encountered—geographical, spiritual, technological—has altered our language. What kind of a frontier are we crossing by teaching computers our most fundamental human skill, that of the spoken word?

Assess Your Progress

1. How do the "prescriptivists" and the "descriptivists" differ with respect to how the English language is changing?

2. Why does the author say that the "growing homogenization" of the English language is a myth?

3. How and why has African American speech diverged from that of rural whites? In what sense does discrimination still exist in the area of language?

4. Why does Labov think that women have been a force for linguistic change?

5. How is the movement of people a determining force in whether regional dialects survive?

6. What role will the media and emerging technology play in linguistic change?

ROBERT MACNEIL, former co-anchor of PBS's Emmy Award-winning "MacNeil/Lehrer NewsHour," is a member of the Television Academy Hall of Fame and the author of several books.

From *USA Today Magazine*, January 2005, pp. 18–22. Copyright © 2005 by Society for the Advancement of Education, Inc. Reprinted by permission.

Fighting for Our Lives

Deborah Tannen, PhD

This is not another book about civility. "Civility" suggests a superficial, pinky-in-the-air veneer of politeness spread thin over human relations like a layer of marmalade over toast. This book is about a pervasive war-like atmosphere that makes us approach public dialogue, and just about anything we need to accomplish, as if it were a fight. It is a tendency in Western culture in general, and in the United States in particular, that has a long history and a deep, thick, and far-ranging root system. It has served us well in many ways but in recent years has become so exaggerated that it is getting in the way of solving our problems. Our spirits are corroded by living in an atmosphere of unrelenting contention—an argument culture.

The argument culture urges us to approach the world—and the people in it—in an adversarial frame of mind. It rests on the assumption that opposition is the best way to get anything done: The best way to discuss an idea is to set up a debate; the best way to cover news is to find spokespeople who express the most extreme, polarized views and present them as "both sides"; the best way to settle disputes is litigation that pits one party against the other; the best way to begin an essay is to attack someone; and the best way to show you're really thinking is to criticize.

Our public interactions have become more and more like having an argument with a spouse. Conflict can't be avoided in our public lives any more than we can avoid conflict with people we love. One of the great strengths of our society is that we can express these conflicts openly. But just as spouses have to learn ways of settling their differences without inflicting real damage on each other, so we, as a society, have to find constructive ways of resolving disputes and differences. Public discourse requires *making* an argument for a point of view, not *having* an argument—as in having a fight.

The war on drugs, the war on cancer, the battle of the sexes, politicians' turf battles—in the argument culture, war metaphors pervade our talk and shape our thinking. Nearly everything is framed as a battle or game in which winning or losing is the main concern. These all have their uses and their place, but they are not the only way—and often not the best way—to understand and approach our world. Conflict and opposition are as necessary as cooperation and agreement, but the scale is off balance, with conflict and opposition

overweighted. In this book, I show how deeply entrenched the argument culture is, the forms it takes, and how it affects us every day—sometimes in useful ways, but often creating more problems than it solves, causing rather than avoiding damage. As a sociolinguist, a social scientist, I am trained to observe and explain language and its role in human relations, and that is my biggest job here. But I will also point toward other ways for us to talk to each other and get things done in our public lives.

The Battle of the Sexes

My interest in the topic of opposition in public discourse intensified in the years following the publication of *You Just Don't Understand,* my book about communication between women and men. In the first year I appeared on many television and radio shows and was interviewed for many print articles in newspapers and magazines. For the most part, that coverage was extremely fair, and I was—and remain—indebted to the many journalists who found my ideas interesting enough to make them known to viewers, listeners, and readers. But from time to time—more often than I expected—I encountered producers who insisted on setting up a television show as a fight (either between the host and me or between another guest and me) and print journalists who made multiple phone calls to my colleagues, trying to find someone who would criticize my work. This got me thinking about what kind of information comes across on shows and in articles that take this approach, compared to those that approach topics in other ways.

At the same time, my experience of the academic world that had long been my intellectual home began to change. For the most part, other scholars, like most journalists, were welcoming and respectful in their responses to my work, even if they disagreed on specific points or had alternative views to suggest. But about a year after *You Just Don't Understand* became a best-seller—the wheels of academia grind more slowly than those of the popular press—I began reading attacks on my work that completely misrepresented it. I had been in academia for over fifteen years by then, and had valued my interaction with other researchers as one of the greatest rewards of academic life. Why, I wondered, would someone represent me as having said things I had never said or as having failed to say things I had said?

The answer crystallized when I put the question to a writer who I felt had misrepresented my work: "Why do you need to make others wrong for you to be right?" Her response: "It's an argument!" Aha, I thought, that explains it. When you're having an argument with someone, your goal is not to listen and understand. Instead, you use every tactic you can think of—including distorting what your opponent just said—in order to win the argument.

Not only the level of attention *You Just Don't Understand* received but, even more, the subject of women and men, triggered the tendency to polarize. This tendency to stage a fight on television or in print was posited on the conviction that opposition leads to truth. Sometimes it does. But the trouble is, sometimes it doesn't. I was asked at the start of more than one talk show or print interview, "What is the most controversial thing about your book?" Opposition does not lead to truth when the most controversial thing is not the most important.

The conviction that opposition leads to truth can tempt not only members of the press but just about anyone seeking to attract an audience to frame discussions as a fight between irreconcilable opposites. Even the Smithsonian Institution, to celebrate its 150th anniversary, sponsored a series of talks billed as debates. They invited me to take part in one titled "The Battle of the Sexes." The organizer preempted my objection: "I know you won't be happy with this title, but we want to get people interested." This is one of many assumptions I question in this book: Is it necessary to frame an interchange as a battle to get people interested? And even if doing so succeeds in capturing attention, does it risk dampening interest in the long run, as audiences weary of the din and begin to hunger for more substance?

Thought-Provoking or Just Provocative?

In the spring of 1995, Horizons Theatre in Arlington, Virginia, produced two one-act plays I had written about family relationships. The director, wanting to contribute to the reconciliation between Blacks and Jews, mounted my plays in repertory with two one-act plays by an African American playwright, Caleen Sinnette Jennings. We had both written plays about three sisters that explored the ethnic identities of our families (Jewish for me, African-American for her) and the relationship between those identities and the American context in which we grew up. To stir interest in the plays and to explore the parallels between her work and mine, the theater planned a public dialogue between Jennings and me, to be held before the plays opened.

As production got under way, I attended the audition of actors for my plays. After the auditions ended, just before everyone headed home, the theater's public relations volunteer distributed copies of the flyer announcing the public

dialogue that she had readied for distribution. I was horrified. The flyer announced that Caleen and I would discuss "how past traumas create understanding and conflict between Blacks and Jews today." The flyer was trying to grab by the throat the issue that we wished to address indirectly. Yes, we were concerned with conflicts between Blacks and Jews, but neither of us is an authority on that conflict, and we had no intention of expounding on it. We hoped to do our part to ameliorate the conflict by focusing on commonalities. Our plays had many resonances between them. We wanted to talk about our work and let the resonances speak for themselves.

Fortunately, we were able to stop the flyers before they were distributed and devise new ones that promised something we could deliver: "a discussion of heritage, identity, and complex family relationships in African-American and Jewish-American culture as represented in their plays." Jennings noticed that the original flyer said the evening would be "provocative" and changed it to "thought-provoking." What a world of difference is implied in that small change: how much better to make people think, rather than simply to "provoke" them—as often as not, to anger.

It is easy to understand why conflict is so often highlighted: Writers of headlines or promotional copy want to catch attention and attract an audience. They are usually under time pressure, which lures them to established, conventionalized ways of expressing ideas in the absence of leisure to think up entirely new ones. The promise of controversy seems an easy and natural way to rouse interest. But serious consequences are often unintended: Stirring up animosities to get a rise out of people, though easy and "provocative," can open old wounds or create new ones that are hard to heal. This is one of many dangers inherent in the argument culture.

For the Sake of Argument

In the argument culture, criticism, attack, or opposition are the predominant if not the only ways of responding to people or ideas. I use the phrase "culture of critique" to capture this aspect. "Critique" in this sense is not a general term for analysis or interpretation but rather a synonym for criticism.

It is the *automatic* nature of this response that I am calling attention to—and calling into question. Sometimes passionate opposition, strong verbal attack, are appropriate and called for. No one knows this better than those who have lived under repressive regimes that forbid public opposition. The Yugoslavian-born poet Charles Simic is one. "There are moments in life," he writes, "when true invective is called for, when it becomes an absolute necessity, out of a deep sense of justice, to denounce, mock, vituperate, lash out, in the strongest possible language." I applaud and endorse this view. There are times when it is necessary and right to fight—to defend your country or yourself, to argue for right against wrong or against offensive or dangerous ideas or actions.

What I question is the ubiquity, the knee-jerk nature, of approaching almost any issue, problem, or public person in an adversarial way. One of the dangers of the habitual use of adversarial rhetoric is a kind of verbal inflation—a rhetorical boy who cried wolf: The legitimate, necessary denunciation is muted, even lost, in the general cacophony of oppositional shouting. What I question is using opposition to accomplish *every* goal, even those that do not require fighting but might also (or better) be accomplished by other means, such as exploring, expanding, discussing, investigating, and the exchanging of ideas suggested by the word "dialogue." I am questioning the assumption that *everything* is a matter of polarized opposites, the proverbial "two sides to every question" that we think embodies open-mindedness and expansive thinking.

In a word, the type of opposition I am questioning is what I call "agonism." I use this term, which derives from the Greek word for "contest," *agonia*, to mean an automatic warlike stance—not the literal opposition of fighting against an attacker or the unavoidable opposition that arises organically in response to conflicting ideas or actions. An agonistic response, to me, is a kind of programmed contentiousness—a prepatterned, unthinking use of fighting to accomplish goals that do not necessarily require it.

How Useful Are Fights?

Noticing that public discourse so often takes the form of heated arguments—of having a fight—made me ask how useful it is in our personal lives to settle differences by arguing. Given what I know about having arguments in private life, I had to conclude that it is, in many cases, not very useful.

In close relationships it is possible to find ways of arguing that result in better understanding and solving problems. But with most arguments, little is resolved, worked out, or achieved when two people get angrier and less rational by the minute. When you're having an argument with someone, you're usually not trying to understand what the other person is saying, or what in their experience leads them to say it. Instead, you're readying your response: listening for weaknesses in logic to leap on, points you can distort to make the other person look bad and yourself look good. Sometimes you know, on some back burner of your mind, that you're doing this—that there's a kernel of truth in what your adversary is saying and a bit of unfair twisting in what you're saying. Sometimes you do this because you're angry, but sometimes it's just the temptation to take aim at a point made along the way because it's an easy target.

Here's an example of how this happened in an argument between a couple who had been married for over fifty years. The husband wanted to join an HMO by signing over their Medicare benefits to save money. The wife objected because it would mean she could no longer see the doctor she knew and trusted. In arguing her point of view, she said, "I like Dr. B. He knows me, he's interested in me. He calls me by my first name." The husband parried the last point: "I don't

like that. He's much younger than we are. He shouldn't be calling us by first name." But the form of address Dr. B. uses was irrelevant. The wife was trying to communicate that she felt comfortable with the doctor she knew, that she had a relationship with him. His calling her by first name was just one of a list of details she was marshaling to explain her comfort with him. Picking on this one detail did not change her view—and did not address her concern. It was just a way to win the argument.

We all are guilty, at times, of seizing on irrelevant details, distorting someone else's position the better to oppose it, when we're arguing with those we're closest to. But we are rarely dependent on these fights as sources of information. The same tactics are common when public discourse is carried out on the model of personal fights. And the results are dangerous when listeners are looking to these interchanges to get needed information or practical results.

Fights have winners and losers. If you're fighting to win, the temptation is great to deny facts that support your opponent's views and to filter what you know, saying only what supports your side. In the extreme form, it encourages people to misrepresent or even to lie. We accept this risk because we believe we can tell when someone is lying. The problem is, we can't.

Paul Ekman, a psychologist at the University of California, San Francisco, studies lying. He set up experiments in which individuals were videotaped talking about their emotions, actions, or beliefs—some truthfully, some not. He has shown these videotapes to thousands of people, asking them to identify the liars and also to say how sure they were about their judgments. His findings are chilling: Most people performed not much better than chance, and those who did the worst had just as much confidence in their judgments as the few who were really able to detect lies. Intrigued by the implications of this research in various walks of life, Dr. Ekman repeated this experiment with groups of people whose jobs require them to sniff out lies: judges, lawyers, police, psychotherapists, and employees of the CIA, FBI, and ATF (Bureau of Alcohol, Tobacco, and Firearms). They were no better at detecting who was telling the truth than the rest of us. The only group that did significantly better were members of the U.S. Secret Service. This finding gives some comfort when it comes to the Secret Service but not much when it comes to every other facet of public life.

Two Sides to Every Question

Our determination to pursue truth by setting up a fight between two sides leads us to believe that every issue has two sides—no more, no less: If both sides are given a forum to confront each other, all the relevant information will emerge, and the best case will be made for each side. But opposition does not lead to truth when an issue is not composed of two opposing sides but is a crystal of many sides. Often the truth is in the complex middle, not the oversimplified extremes.

We love using the word "debate" as a way of representing issues: the abortion debate, the health care debate, the affirmative action debate—even "the great backpacking vs. car camping debate." The ubiquity of this word in itself shows our tendency to conceptualize issues in a way that predisposes public discussion to be polarized, framed as two opposing sides that give each other no ground. There are many problems with this approach. If you begin with the assumption that there *must* be an "other side," you may end up scouring the margins of science or the fringes of lunacy to find it. As a result, proven facts, such as what we know about how the earth and its inhabitants evolved, are set on a par with claims that are known to have no basis in fact, such as creationism.

The conviction that there are two sides to every story can prompt writers or producers to dig up an "other side," so kooks who state outright falsehoods are given a platform in public discourse. This accounts, in part, for the bizarre phenomenon of Holocaust denial. Deniers, as Emory University professor Deborah Lipstadt shows, have been successful in gaining television airtime and campus newspaper coverage by masquerading as "the other side" in a "debate."

Appearance in print or on television has a way of lending legitimacy, so baseless claims take on a mantle of possibility. Lipstadt shows how Holocaust deniers dispute established facts of history, and then reasonable spokespersons use their having been disputed as a basis for questioning known facts. The actor Robert Mitchum, for example, interviewed in *Esquire,* expressed doubt about the Holocaust. When the interviewer asked about the slaughter of six million Jews, Mitchum replied, "I don't know. People dispute that." Continual reference to "the other side" results in a pervasive conviction that everything has another side—with the result that people begin to doubt the existence of any facts at all.

The Expense of Time and Spirit

Lipstadt's book meticulously exposes the methods used by deniers to falsify the overwhelming historic evidence that the Holocaust occurred. That a scholar had to invest years of her professional life writing a book unraveling efforts to deny something that was about as well known and well documented as any historical fact has ever been—while those who personally experienced and witnessed it are still alive—is testament to another way that the argument culture limits our knowledge rather than expanding it. Talent and effort were wasted when individuals who have been unfairly attacked must spend years of their creative lives defending themselves rather than advancing their work. The entire society loses their creative efforts. This is what happened with scientist Robert Gallo.

Dr. Gallo is the American virologist who codiscovered the AIDS virus. He is also the one who developed the technique for studying T-cells, which made that discovery possible. And Gallo's work was seminal in developing the test to detect the AIDS virus in blood, the first and for a long time the only means known of stemming the tide of death from AIDS. But in 1989, Gallo became the object of a four-year investigation into allegations that he had stolen the AIDS virus from Luc Montagnier of the Pasteur Institute in Paris, who had independently identified the AIDS virus. Simultaneous investigations by the National Institutes of Health, the office of Michigan Congressman John Dingell, and the National Academy of Sciences barreled ahead long after Gallo and Montagnier settled the dispute to their mutual satisfaction. In 1993 the investigations concluded that Gallo had done nothing wrong. Nothing. But this exoneration cannot be considered a happy ending. Never mind the personal suffering of Gallo, who was reviled when he should have been heralded as a hero. Never mind that, in his words, "These were the most painful years and horrible years of my life." The dreadful, unconscionable result of the fruitless investigations is that Gallo had to spend four years fighting the accusations instead of fighting AIDS.

The investigations, according to journalist Nicholas Wade, were sparked by an article about Gallo written in the currently popular spirit of demonography: not to praise the person it features but to bury him—to show his weaknesses, his villainous side. The implication that Gallo has stolen the AIDS virus was created to fill a requirement of the discourse: In demonography, writers must find negative sides of their subjects to display for readers who enjoy seeing heroes transformed into villains. The suspicion led to investigations, and the investigations became a juggernaut that acquired a life of its own, fed by the enthusiasm for attack on public figures that is the culture of critique.

Metaphors: We Are What We Speak

Perhaps one reason suspicions of Robert Gallo were so zealously investigated is that the scenario of an ambitious scientist ready to do anything to defeat a rival appeals to our sense of story; it is the kind of narrative we are ready to believe. Culture, in a sense, is an environment of narratives that we hear repeatedly until they seem to make self-evident sense in explaining human behavior. Thinking of human interactions as battles is a metaphorical frame through which we learn to regard the world and the people in it.

All language uses metaphors to express ideas; some metaphoric words and expressions are novel, made up for the occasion, but more are calcified in the language. They are simply the way we think it is natural to express ideas. We don't think of them as metaphors. Someone who says, "Be careful: You aren't a cat, you don't have nine lives," is explicitly comparing you to a cat, because the cat is named in words. But what if someone says, "Don't pussyfoot around; get to the point"? There is no explicit comparison to a cat, but the comparison is there nonetheless, implied in the word "pussyfoot." This expression probably developed as a reference to the movement of a cat cautiously circling a suspicious object. I doubt that individuals using the word "pussyfoot" think consciously of cats. More often than not, we use expressions without thinking about their metaphoric implications. But that doesn't mean those implications are not influencing us.

At a meeting, a general discussion became so animated that a participant who wanted to comment prefaced his remark by saying, "I'd like to leap into the fray." Another participant called out, "Or share your thoughts." Everyone laughed. By suggesting a different phrasing, she called attention to what would probably have otherwise gone unnoticed: "Leap into the fray" characterized the lively discussion as a metaphorical battle.

Americans talk about almost everything as if it were a war. A book about the history of linguistics is called *The Linguistics Wars*. A magazine article about claims that science is not completely objective is titled "The Science Wars." One about breast cancer detection is "The Mammogram War"; about competition among caterers, "Party Wars"—and on and on in a potentially endless list. Politics, of course, is a prime candidate. One of innumerable possible examples, the headline of a story reporting that the Democratic National Convention nominated Bill Clinton to run for a second term declares, "DEMOCRATS SEND CLINTON INTO BATTLE FOR A 2ND TERM." But medicine is as frequent a candidate, as we talk about battling and conquering disease.

Headlines are intentionally devised to attract attention, but we all use military or attack imagery in everyday expressions without thinking about it: "Take a shot at it," "I don't want to be shot down," "He went off half cocked," "That's half the battle." Why does it matter that our public discourse is filled with military metaphors? Aren't they just words? Why not talk about something that matters—like actions?

Because words matter. When we think we are using language, language is using us. As linguist Dwight Bolinger put it (employing a military metaphor), language is like a loaded gun: It can be fired intentionally, but it can wound or kill just as surely when fired accidentally. The terms in which we talk about something shape the way we think about it—and even what we see.

The power of words to shape perception has been proven by researchers in controlled experiments. Psychologist Elizabeth Loftus and John Palmer, for example, found that the terms in which people are asked to recall something affect what they recall. The researchers showed subjects a film of two cars colliding, then asked how fast the cars were going; one week later, they asked whether there had been any broken glass. Some subjects were asked, "About how fast were the cars going when they smashed into each other?" Those who read the question with the verb "smashed" estimated that the cars were going faster. They were also more likely to "remember" having seen broken glass. (There wasn't any.)

This is how language works. It invisibly molds our way of thinking about people, actions, and the world around us. Military metaphors train us to think about—and see—everything in terms of fighting, conflict, and war. This perspective then limits our imaginations when we consider what we can do about situations we would like to understand or change.

Even in science, common metaphors that are taken for granted influence how researchers think about natural phenomena. Evelyn Fox Keller describes a case in which acceptance of a metaphor led scientists to see something that was not there. A mathematical biologist, Keller outlines the fascinating behavior of cellular slime mold. This unique mold can take two completely different forms: It can exist as single-cell organisms, or the separate cells can come together to form multicellular aggregates. The puzzle facing scientists was: What triggers aggregation? In other words, what makes the single cells join together? Scientists focused their investigations by asking what entity issued the order to start aggregating. They first called this bosslike entity a "founder cell," and later a "pacemaker cell," even though no one had seen any evidence for the existence of such a cell. Proceeding nonetheless from the assumption that such a cell must exist, they ignored evidence to the contrary: For example, when the center of the aggregate is removed, other centers form.

Scientists studying slime mold did not examine the interrelationship between the cells and their environment, nor the interrelationship between the functional systems within each cell, because they were busy looking for the pacemaker cell, which, as eventually became evident, did not exist. Instead, under conditions of nutritional deprivation, each individual cell begins to feel the urge to merge with others to form the conglomerate. It is a reaction of the cells to their environment, not to the orders of a boss. Keller recounts this tale to illustrate her insight that we tend to view nature through our understanding of human relations as hierarchical. In her words, "We risk imposing on nature the very stories we like to hear." In other words, the conceptual metaphor of hierarchical governance made scientists "see" something—a pacemaker cell—that wasn't there.

Among the stories many Americans most like to hear are war stories. According to historian Michael Sherry, the American war movie developed during World War II and has been with us ever since. He shows that movies not explicitly about war were also war movies at heart, such as westerns with their good guy–bad guy battles settled with guns. *High Noon*, for example, which became a model for later westerns, was an allegory of the Second World War: The happy ending hinges on the pacifist taking up arms. We can also see this story line in contemporary adventure films: Think of *Star Wars*, with its stirring finale in which Han Solo, having professed no interest in or taste for battle, returns at the last moment to destroy the enemy and save the day. And precisely the same theme is found in a contemporary low-budget independent film, *Sling Blade*, in which a peace-loving retarded man becomes a hero at the end by murdering the man who has been tormenting the family he has come to love.

Put up Your Dukes

If war provides the metaphors through which we view the world and each other, we come to view others—and ourselves—as warriors in battle. Almost any human encounter can be framed as a fight between two opponents. Looking at it this way brings particular aspects of the event into focus and obscures others.

Framing interactions as fights affects not only the participants but also the viewers. At a performance, the audience, as well as the performers, can be transformed. This effect was noted by a reviewer in *The New York Times,* commenting on a musical event:

> **Showdown at Lincoln Center.** Jazz's ideological war of the last several years led to a pitched battle in August between John Lincoln Collier, the writer, and Wynton Marsalis, the trumpeter, in a debate at Lincoln Center. Mr. Marsalis demolished Mr. Collier, point after point after point, but what made the debate unpleasant was the crowd's blood lust; humiliation, not elucidation, was the desired end.

Military imagery pervades this account: the difference of opinions between Collier and Marsalis was an "ideological war," and the "debate" was a "pitched battle" in which Marsalis "demolished" Collier (not his arguments, but him). What the commentator regrets, however, is that the audience got swept up in the mood instigated by the way the debate was carried out: "the crowd's blood lust" for Collier's defeat.

This is one of the most dangerous aspects of regarding intellectual interchange as a fight. It contributes to an atmosphere of animosity that spreads like a fever. In a society that includes people who express their anger by shooting, the result of demonizing those with whom we disagree can be truly tragic.

But do audiences necessarily harbor within themselves a "blood lust," or is it stirred in them by the performances they are offered? Another arts event was set up as a debate between a playwright and a theater director. In this case, the metaphor through which the debate was viewed was not war but boxing—a sport that is in itself, like a debate, a metaphorical battle that pitches one side against the other in an all-out effort to win. A headline describing the event set the frame: "AND IN THIS CORNER . . . ," followed by the subhead "A Black Playwright and White Critic Duke It Out." The story then reports:

> the face-off between August Wilson, the most successful black playwright in the American theater, and Robert Brustein, longtime drama critic for *The New Republic* and artistic director of the American Repertory Theatre in Cambridge, Mass. These two heavyweights had been battling in print since last June. . . .
>
> Entering from opposite sides of the stage, the two men shook hands and came out fighting—or at least sparring.

Wilson, the article explains, had given a speech in which he opposed Black performers taking "white" roles in color-blind casting; Brustein had written a column disagreeing; and both followed up with further responses to each other.

According to the article, "The drama of the Wilson-Brustein confrontation lies in their mutual intransigence." No one would question that audiences crave drama. But is intransigence the most appealing source of drama? I happened to hear this debate broadcast on the radio. The line that triggered the loudest cheers from the audience was the final question put to the two men by the moderator, Anna Deavere Smith: "What did you each learn from the other in this debate?" The loud applause was evidence that the audience did not crave intransigence. They wanted to see another kind of drama: the drama of change—change that comes from genuinely listening to someone with a different point of view, not the transitory drama of two intransigent positions in stalemate.

To encourage the staging of more dramas of change and fewer of intransigence, we need new metaphors to supplement and complement the pervasive war and boxing match metaphors through which we take it for granted issues and events are best talked about and viewed.

Mud Splatters

Our fondness for the fight scenario leads us to frame many complex human interactions as a battle between two sides. This then shapes the way we understand what happened and how we regard the participants. One unfortunate result is that fights make a mess in which everyone is muddied. The person attacked is often deemed just as guilty as the attacker.

The injustice of this is clear if you think back to childhood. Many of us still harbor anger as we recall a time (or many times) a sibling or playmate started a fight—but both of us got blamed. Actions occur in a stream, each a response to what came before. Where you punctuate them can change their meaning just as you can change the meaning of a sentence by punctuating it in one place or another.

Like a parent despairing of trying to sort out which child started a fight, people often respond to those involved in a public dispute as if both were equally guilty. When champion figure skater Nancy Kerrigan was struck on the knee shortly before the 1994 Olympics in Norway and the then-husband of another champion skater, Tonya Harding, implicated his wife in planning the attack, the event was characterized as a fight between two skaters that obscured their differing roles. As both skaters headed for the Olympic competition, their potential meeting was described as a "long-anticipated figure-skating shootout." Two years later, the event was referred to not as "the attack on Nancy Kerrigan" but as "the rivalry surrounding Tonya Harding and Nancy Kerrigan."

By a similar process, the Senate Judiciary Committee hearings to consider the nomination of Clarence Thomas for Supreme Court justice at which Anita Hill was called to testify are regularly referred to as the "Hill-Thomas hearings," obscuring the very different roles played by Hill and Thomas. Although testimony by Anita Hill was the occasion for reopening the hearings, they were still the Clarence Thomas confirmation hearings: Their purpose was to evaluate Thomas's candidacy. Framing these hearings as a two-sides dispute between Hill and Thomas allowed the senators to focus their investigation on cross-examining Hill rather than seeking other sorts of evidence, for example by consulting experts on sexual harassment to ascertain whether Hill's account seemed plausible.

Slash-and-Burn Thinking

Approaching situations like warriors in battle leads to the assumption that intellectual inquiry, too, is a game of attack, counterattack, and self-defense. In this spirit, critical thinking is synonymous with criticizing. In many classrooms, students are encouraged to read someone's life work, then rip it to shreds. Though criticism is one form of critical thinking—and an essential one—so are integrating ideas from disparate fields and examining the context out of which ideas grew. Opposition does not lead to the whole truth when we ask only "What's wrong with this?" and never "What can we use from this in building a new theory, a new understanding?"

There are many ways that unrelenting criticism is destructive in itself. In innumerable small dramas mirroring what happened to Robert Gallo (but on a much more modest scale), our most creative thinkers can waste time and effort responding to critics motivated less by a genuine concern about weaknesses in their work than by a desire to find something to attack. All of society loses when creative people are discouraged from their pursuits by unfair criticism. (This is particularly likely to happen since, as Kay Redfield Jamison shows in her book *Touched with Fire,* many of those who are unusually creative are also unusually sensitive; their sensitivity often drives their creativity.)

If the criticism is unwarranted, many will say, you are free to argue against it, to defend yourself. But there are problems with this, too. Not only does self-defense take time and draw off energy that would better be spent on new creative work, but any move to defend yourself makes you appear, well, defensive. For example, when an author wrote a letter to the editor protesting a review he considered unfair, the reviewer (who is typically given the last word) turned the very fact that the author defended himself into a weapon with which to attack again. The reviewer's response began, "I haven't much time to waste on the kind of writer who squanders his talent drafting angry letters to reviewers."

The argument culture limits the information we get rather than broadening it in another way. When a certain kind of interaction is the norm, those who feel comfortable with that type of interaction are drawn to participate, and those who do not feel comfortable with it recoil and go elsewhere. If public discourse included a broad range of types, we would be making room for individuals with different temperaments to take part and contribute their perspectives and insights. But when debate, opposition, and fights overwhelmingly predominate, those who enjoy verbal sparring are likely to take part—by calling in to talk shows, writing letters to the editor or articles, becoming journalists—and those who cannot comfortably take part in oppositional discourse, or do not wish to, are likely to opt out.

This winnowing process is easy to see in apprenticeship programs such as acting school, law school, and graduate school. A woman who was identified in her university drama program as showing exceptional promise was encouraged to go to New York to study acting. Full of enthusiasm, she was accepted by a famous acting school where the teaching method entailed the teacher screaming at students, goading and insulting them as a way to bring out the best in them. This worked well with many of the students but not with her. Rather than rising to the occasion when attacked, she cringed, becoming less able to draw on her talent, not more. After a year, she dropped out. It could be that she simply didn't have what it took—but this will never be known, because the adversarial style of teaching did not allow her to show what talent she had.

Polarizing Complexity: Nature or Nurture?

Few issues come with two neat, and neatly opposed, sides. Again, I have seen this in the domain of gender. One common polarization is an opposition between two sources of differences between women and men: "culture," or "nurture," on one hand and "biology," or "nature," on the other.

Shortly after the publication of *You Just Don't Understand,* I was asked by a journalist what question I most often encountered about women's and men's conversational styles. I told her, "Whether the differences I describe are biological or cultural." The journalist laughed. Puzzled, I asked why this made her laugh. She explained that she had always been so certain that any significant differences are cultural rather than biological in origin that the question struck her as absurd. So I should not have been surprised when I read, in the article she wrote, that the two questions I am most frequently asked are "Why do women nag?" and "Why won't men ask for directions?" Her ideological certainty that the question I am most frequently asked was absurd led her to ignore my answer and get a fact wrong in her report of my experience.

Some people are convinced that any significant differences between men and women are entirely or overwhelmingly due to cultural influences—the way we treat girls and boys, and men's dominance of women in society. Others are convinced that any significant differences are entirely or overwhelmingly due to biology: the physical facts of female and male bodies, hormones, and reproductive functions. Many problems are caused by framing the question as a dichotomy: Are behaviors that pattern by sex biological or cultural? This polarization encourages those on one side to demonize those who take the other view, which leads in turn to misrepresenting the work of those who are assigned to the opposing camp. Finally, and most devastatingly, it prevents us from exploring the interaction of biological and cultural factors—factors that must, and can only, be understood together. By posing the question as either/or, we reinforce a false assumption that biological and cultural factors are separable and preclude the investigations that would help us understand their interrelationship. When a problem is posed in a way that polarizes, the solution is often obscured before the search is under way.

Who's Up? Who's Down?

Related to polarization is another aspect of the argument culture: our obsession with ratings and rankings. Magazines offer the 10, 50, or 100 best of everything: restaurants, mutual funds, hospitals, even judges. Newsmagazines tell us Who's up, Who's down, as in *Newsweek*'s "Conventional Wisdom Watch" and *Time*'s "Winners and Losers." Rankings and ratings pit restaurants, products, schools, and people against each other on a single scale, obscuring the myriad differences among them. Maybe a small Thai restaurant in one neighborhood can't really be compared to a pricey French one in another, any more than judges with a vast range of abilities and beliefs can be compared on a single scale. And timing can skew results: Ohio State University protested to *Time* magazine when its football team was ranked at the bottom of a scale because only 29 percent of the team graduated. The year before it would have ranked among the top six with 72 percent.

After a political debate, analysts comment not on what the candidates said but on the question "Who won?" After the president delivers an important speech, such as the State of the Union Address, expert commentators are asked to give it a grade. Like ranking, grading establishes a competition. The biggest problem with asking what grade the president's speech deserves, or who won and who lost a campaign debate, is what is not asked and is therefore not answered: What was said, and what is the significance of this for the country?

An Ethic of Aggression

In an argument culture aggressive tactics are valued for their own sake. For example, a woman called in to a talk show on which I was a guest to say, "When I'm in a place where a man is smoking, and there's a no-smoking sign, instead of saying to him 'You aren't allowed to smoke in here. Put that out,' I say, 'I'm awfully sorry, but I have asthma, so your smoking makes it hard for me to breathe. Would you mind terribly not smoking?' Whenever I say this, the man is extremely polite and solicitous, and he puts his cigarette out, and I say, 'Oh,

thank you, thank you!' as if he's done a wonderful thing for me. Why do I do that?"

I think this woman expected me to say that she needs assertiveness training to learn to confront smokers in a more aggressive manner. Instead, I told her that there was nothing wrong with her style of getting the man to stop smoking. She gave him a face-saving way of doing what she asked, one that allowed him to feel chivalrous rather than chastised. This is kind to him, but it is also kind to herself, since it is more likely to lead to the result she desires. If she tried to alter his behavior by reminding him of the rules, he might well rebel: "Who made you the enforcer? Mind your own business!" Indeed, who gives any of us the authority to set others straight when we think they're breaking rules?

Another caller disagreed with me, saying the first caller's style was "self-abasing" and there was no reason for her to use it. But I persisted: There is nothing necessarily destructive about conventional self-effacement. Human relations depend on the agreement to use such verbal conventions. I believe the mistake this caller was making—a mistake many of us make—was to confuse *ritual* self-effacement with the literal kind. All human relations require us to find ways to get what we want from others without seeming to dominate them. Allowing others to feel they are doing what you want for a reason less humiliating to them fulfills this need.

Thinking of yourself as the wronged party who is victimized by a lawbreaking boor makes it harder to see the value of this method. But suppose you are the person addicted to smoking who lights up (knowingly or not) in a no-smoking zone. Would you like strangers to yell at you to stop smoking, or would you rather be allowed to save face by being asked politely to stop in order to help them out? Or imagine yourself having broken a rule inadvertently (which is not to imply rules are broken only by mistake; it is only to say that sometimes they are). Would you like some stranger to swoop down on you and begin berating you, or would you rather be asked politely to comply?

As this example shows, conflicts can sometimes be resolved without confrontational tactics, but current conventional wisdom often devalues less confrontational tactics even if they work well, favoring more aggressive strategies even if they get less favorable results. It's as if we value a fight for its own sake, not for its effectiveness in resolving disputes.

This ethic shows up in many contexts. In a review of a contentious book, for example, a reviewer wrote, "Always provocative, sometimes infuriating, this collection reminds us that the purpose of art is not to confirm and coddle but to provoke and confront." This false dichotomy encapsulates the belief that if you are not provoking and confronting, then you are conforming and coddling—as if there weren't myriad other ways to question and learn. What about exploring, exposing, delving, analyzing, understanding, moving, connecting, integrating, illuminating . . . or any of innumerable verbs that capture other aspects of what art can do?

The Broader Picture

The increasingly adversarial spirit of our contemporary lives is fundamentally related to a phenomenon that has been much remarked upon in recent years: the breakdown of a sense of community. In this spirit, distinguished journalist and author Orville Schell points out that in his day journalists routinely based their writing on a sense of connection to their subjects—and that this sense of connection is missing from much that is written by journalists today. Quite the contrary, a spirit of demonography often prevails that has just the opposite effect: Far from encouraging us to feel connected to the subjects, it encourages us to feel critical, superior—and, as a result, distanced. The cumulative effect is that citizens feel more and more cut off from the people in public life they read about.

The argument culture dovetails with a general disconnection and breakdown of community in another way as well. Community norms and pressures exercise a restraint on the expression of hostility and destruction. Many cultures have rituals to channel and contain aggressive impulses, especially those of adolescent males. In just this spirit, at the 1996 Republican National Convention, both Colin Powell and Bob Dole talked about growing up in small communities where everyone knew who they were. This meant that many people would look out for them, but also that if they did something wrong, it would get back to their parents. Many Americans grew up in ethnic neighborhoods that worked the same way. If a young man stole something, committed vandalism, or broke a rule or law, it would be reported to his relatives, who would punish him or tell him how his actions were shaming the family. American culture today often lacks these brakes.

Community is a blend of connections and authority, and we are losing both. As Robert Bly shows in his book by that title, we now have a *Sibling Society:* Citizens are like squabbling siblings with no authority figures who can command enough respect to contain and channel their aggressive impulses. It is as if every day is a day with a substitute teacher who cannot control the class and maintain order.

The argument culture is both a product of and a contributor to this alienation, separating people, disconnecting them from each other and from those who are or might have been their leaders.

What Other Way Is There?

Philosopher John Dewey said, on his ninetieth birthday, "Democracy begins in conversation." I fear that it gets derailed in polarized debate.

In conversation we form the interpersonal ties that bind individuals together in personal relationships; in public discourse, we form similar ties on a larger scale, binding individuals into a community. In conversation, we exchange the many types of information we need to live our lives as members of a community. In public discourse, we exchange the information that citizens in a democracy need in order to decide how to vote. If public discourse provides entertainment first and foremost—and if entertainment is first and foremost watching fights—then citizens do not get the information they need to make meaningful use of their right to vote.

Of course it is the responsibility of intellectuals to explore potential weaknesses in others' arguments, and of journalists to represent serious opposition when it exists. But when opposition becomes the overwhelming avenue of inquiry—a formula that *requires* another side to be found or a criticism to be voiced; when the lust for opposition privileges extreme views and obscures complexity; when our eagerness to find weaknesses blinds us to strengths; when the atmosphere of animosity precludes respect and poisons our relations with one another; then the argument culture is doing more damage than good.

I offer this book not as a formal assault in the argument culture. That would be in the spirit of attack that I am questioning. It is an attempt to examine the argument culture—our use of attack, opposition, and debate in public discourse—to ask, What are its limits as well as its strengths? How has it served us well, but also how has it failed us? How is it related to culture and gender? What other options do we have?

I do not believe we should put aside the argument model of public discourse entirely, but we need to rethink whether this is the *only* way, or *always* the best way, to carry out our affairs. A step toward broadening our repertoires would be to pioneer reform by experimenting with metaphors other than sports and war, and with formats other than debate for framing the exchange of ideas. The change might be as simple as introducing a plural form. Instead of asking "What's the other side?" we might ask instead, "What are the other sides?" Instead of insisting on hearing "both sides," we might insist on hearing "all sides."

Another option is to expand our notion of "debate" to include more dialogue. This does not mean there can be no negativity, criticism, or disagreement. It simply means we can be more creative in our ways of managing all of these, which are inevitable and useful. In dialogue, each statement that one person makes is qualified by a statement made by someone else, until the series of statements and qualifications moves everyone closer to a fuller truth. Dialogue does not preclude negativity. Even saying "I agree" makes sense only against the background assumption that you might disagree. In dialogue, there is opposition, yes, but no head-on collision. Smashing heads does not open minds.

There are times when we need to disagree, criticize, oppose, and attack—to hold debates and view issues as polarized battles. Even cooperation, after all, is not the absence of conflict but a means of managing conflict. My goal is not a make-nice false veneer of agreement or a dangerous ignoring of true opposition. I'm questioning the *automatic* use of adversarial formats—the assumption that it's *always* best to address problems and issues by fighting over them. I'm hoping for a broader repertoire of ways to talk to each other and address issues vital to us.

Notes

Note: Sources referred to by short form are cited in full in the References.

[Numbers indicate page numbers of original document. Ed]

7. *"culture of critique"*: I first introduced this term in an op-ed essay, "The Triumph of the Yell," *The New York Times,* Jan. 14, 1994, p. A29.

7. *"There are moments"*: Charles Simic, "In Praise of Invective," *Harper's,* Aug. 1997, pp. 24, 26–27; the quote is from p. 26. The article is excerpted from *Orphan Factory* (Ann Arbor: University of Michigan Press, 1997). I am grateful to Amitai Etizioni for calling this article to my attention.

8. Both the term "agonism" and the phrase "programmed contentiousness" come from Walter Ong, *Fighting for Life.*

10. *"the great backpacking vs. car camping debate"*: Steven Hendrix, "Hatchback vs. Backpack," *The Washington Post Weekend,* Mar. 1, 1996, p. 6.

11. *creationism:* See, for example, Jessica Mathews, "Creationism Makes a Comeback," *The Washington Post,* Apr. 8, 1996, p. A21.

11. *"People dispute that"*: Lipstadt, *Denying the Holocaust,* p. 15. Lipstadt cites *Esquire,* Feb. 1983, for the interview with Mitchum.

12. *Gallo had to spend:* See Nicholas Wade, "Method and Madness: The Vindication of Robert Gallo," *The New York Times Magazine,* Dec. 26, 1993, p. 12, and Elaine Richman, "The Once and Future King," *The Sciences,* Nov.–Dec. 1996, pp. 12–15. The investigations of Gallo were among a series of overly zealous investigations of suspected scientific misconduct—all of which ended in the exoneration of the accused, but not before they had caused immense personal anguish and professional setbacks. Others similarly victimized were Gallo's colleague Mike Popovic, immunologist Thereza Imanishi-Kari, and her coauthor (not accused of wrongdoing but harmed as a result of his defense of her), Nobel Prize winner David Baltimore. On Popovic, see Malcolm Gladwell, "Science Friction," *The Washington Post Magazine,* Dec. 6, 1992, pp. 18–21, 49–51. On Imanishi-Kari and Baltimore, see *The New Yorker,* May 27, 1996, pp. 94–98ff.

14. *potentially endless list:* Randy Allen Harris, *The Linguistics Wars* (New York: Oxford University Press, 1993); "The Science Wars," *Newsweek,* Apr. 21, 1997, p. 54; "The Mammogram War," *Newsweek,* Feb. 24, 1997, p. 54; "Party Wars," *New York,* June 2, 1997, cover. The subhead of the latter reads, "In the battle to feed New York's elite, the top caterers are taking off their white gloves and sharpening their knives."

14. "DEMOCRATS SEND CLINTON": *The New York Times,* Aug. 29, 1996, p. A1.

15. *"We risk imposing"*: Keller, *Reflections on Gender and Science,* p. 157. Another such case is explained by paleontologist Stephen Jay Gould in his book *Wonderful Life* about the Burgess shale—a spectacular deposit of 530-million-year-old fossils. In 1909, the first scientist to study these fossils missed the significance of the find, because he "shoehorned every last Burgess animal into a modern group, viewing the fauna collectively as a set of primitive or ancestral versions of later, improved forms" (p. 24). Years later, observers looked at the Burgess shale fossils with a fresh eye and saw a very different reality: a panoply of life forms, far more diverse and numerous than what exists today. The early scientists missed what was right before their eyes because, Gould shows, they proceeded from a metaphoric understanding of evolution as a linear march of progress from the ancient and primitive to the modern and complex, with humans the inevitable, most complex apex. Accepting the metaphor of "the cone of increasing diversity" prevented the early scientists from seeing what was really there.

16. *"Showdown at Lincoln Center"*: Peter Watrous, "The Year in the Arts: Pop & Jazz/1994," *The New York Times,* Dec. 25, 1994, sec. 2, p. 36.

17. *"the face-off between"*: Jack Kroll, "And in This Corner . . . ," *Newsweek,* Feb. 10, 1997, p. 65.

18. *a fight between two skaters:* Though Harding was demonized somewhat more as an unfeminine, boorish "Wicked Witch of the West" (George Vecsey, "Let's Begin the Legal Olympics," *The New York Times,* Feb. 13, 1994, sec. 8, p. 1.), Kerrigan was also demonized as cold and aloof, an "ice princess."

18. *"long-anticipated figure-skating shootout"*: Jere Longman, "Kerrigan Glides Through Compulsory Interviews," *The New York Times,* Feb. 13, 1994, sec. 8, p. 9.

18. *"the rivalry surrounding"*: Paul Farhi, "For NBC, Games Not Just for Guys; Network Tailors Its Coverage to Entice Women to Watch," *The Washington Post,* July 26, 1996, p. A1.

20. *"I haven't time"*: *The Washington Post Book World,* June 16, 1996, p. 14.

21. *even judges: Washingtonian,* June 1996, ranked judges.

22. *Ohio State University protested:* Letter to the editor by Malcolm S. Baroway, Executive Director, University Communications, *Time,* Oct. 3, 1994, p. 14.

22. Overlaid on the talk show example is the gender issue: The woman who called wished she had the courage to stand up to a man and saw her habitual way of speaking as evidence of her insecurity. This interpretation is suggested by our assumptions about women and men. Many people, researchers included, start from the assumption that women are insecure, so ways they speak are scrutinized for evidence of insecurity. The result is often a failure to understand or appreciate women's styles on their own terms, so women are misinterpreted as defective men.

23. *"Always provocative, sometimes infuriating"*: Jill Nelson, "Fighting Words," review of Ishmael Reed, *Airing Dirty Laundry, The New York Times Book Review,* Feb. 13, 1994, p. 28.

24. *In this spirit:* John Krich, "To Teach Is Glorious: A Conversation with the New Dean of Cal's Journalism School," Orville Schell, *Express,* Aug. 23, 1996, pp. 1, 14–16, 18, 20–22. The remark is from p. 15.

24. *Many cultures have rituals:* See Schlegel and Barry, *Adolescence.*

25. *"Democracy begins in conversation"*: *Dialogue on John Dewey,* Corliss Lamont, ed. (New York: Horizon Press, 1959), p. 88. Thanks to Pete Becker for this reference.

26. *In dialogue, there is:* This insight comes from Walter Ong, who writes, "There is opposition here but no head-on collision, which stops dialogue. (Of course, sometimes dialogue has to be stopped, but that is another story.)" (*Fighting for Life,* p. 32).

References

Gould, Stephen Jay. *Wonderful Life: The Burgess Shale and the Nature of History* (New York: W. W. Norton, 1989).

Keller, Evelyn Fox. *Reflections on Gender and Science* (New Haven: Yale University Press, 1985).

Krich, John. "To Teach Is Glorious: A Conversation with the New Dean of Cal's Journalism School, Orville Schell." *Express,* Aug. 23, 1996, pp. 1, 14–16, 18, 20–22.

Lipstadt, Deborah. *Denying the Holocaust: The Growing Assault on Truth and Memory* (New York: Free Press, 1993).

Ong, Walter J. *Fighting for Life: Contest, Sexuality, and Consciousness* (Ithaca, N.Y.: Cornell University Press, 1981).

Schlegel, Alice, and Herbert Barry III. *Adolescence: An Anthropological Inquiry* (New York: Free Press, 1991).

Assess Your Progress

1. What is "the argument culture?" What should public discourse be, and not be?

2. How is the argument culture expressed in metaphors? How does the author see this as a problem?

3. How does the author describe "an argument?"

4. What conviction is behind the tendency to stage a fight? What is the problem with this idea? What assumption does the author challenge?

5. Why is conflict so often highlighted? Why is this dangerous?

6. What is the "culture of critique?" Are there times when passionate opposition is called for? What does the author question and why? What is "agonism" or an "agonistic response?"

7. Describe what happens when people have "an argument."

8. What did Paul Ekman's experiments show about the ability to detect lies?

9. What is the problem with the idea that "every issue has two sides?"

10. Describe the problem with assuming that there *must* be an "other side" and list the examples cited.

11. How can talent and effort be wasted by the argument culture?

12. How is people's thinking influenced by metaphors, especially the metaphor of war? Why is this a problem? How is the experiment by Loftus and Palmer relevant? In what ways are our imaginations limited by metaphors?

13. What is one of the "most dangerous aspects" of regarding intellectual interchange as a fight?

14. Be generally aware of how the argument culture:
    (a) limits the information we get rather than broadening it;
    (b) polarizes issues;
    (c) leads to an obsession with ratings and rankings;
    (d) encourages aggressive tactics for their own sake.

15. In what ways is the argument culture related to a general disconnection and breakdown of community?

16. What alternatives to the argument culture does the author propose? What is her goal?

DEBORAH TANNEN is best known as the author of *You Just Don't Understand: Women and Men in Conversation,* which was on *The New York Times* bestseller list for nearly four years, including eight months as number one, and has been translated into twenty-four languages. Her book, *Talking from 9 to 5: Women and Men in the Workplace: Language, Sex, and Power,* was a *New York Times* Business bestseller. She has written for and been featured in *The New York Times, Newsweek, Time, USA Today, People,* and *The Washington Post.* Her many national television and radio appearances include *20/20, 48 Hours,* CBS *News,* ABC *World News Tonight,* and *Good Morning America.* She is one of only three University Professors at Georgetown University in Washington, D.C., where she is on the Linguistics Department faculty. *The Argument Culture* is her sixteenth book.

Deborah Tannen has also published short stories, essays, and poems. Her first play, *An Act of Devotion,* is included in *Best Short Plays 1993–1994.* It was produced, together with her play *Sisters,* by Horizons Theatre in Arlington, VA.

Shakespeare in the Bush

Laura Bohannan

Just before I left Oxford for the Tiv in West Africa, conversation turned to the season at Stratford. "You Americans," said a friend, "often have difficulty with Shakespeare. He was, after all, a very English poet, and one can easily misinterpret the universal by misunderstanding the particular."

I protested that human nature is pretty much the same the whole world over; at least the general plot and motivation of the greater tragedies would always be clear—everywhere—although some details of custom might have to be explained and difficulties of translation might produce other slight changes. To end an argument we could not conclude, my friend gave me a copy of *Hamlet* to study in the African bush: it would, he hoped, lift my mind above its primitive surroundings, and possibly I might, by prolonged meditation, achieve the grace of correct interpretation.

It was my second field trip to that African tribe, and I thought myself ready to live in one of its remote sections—an area difficult to cross even on foot. I eventually settled on the hillock of a very knowledgeable old man, the head of a homestead of some hundred and forty people, all of whom were either his close relatives or their wives and children. Like the other elders of the vicinity, the old man spent most of his time performing ceremonies seldom seen these days in the more accessible parts of the tribe. I was delighted. Soon there would be three months of enforced isolation and leisure, between the harvest that takes place just before the rising of the swamps and the clearing of new farms when the water goes down. Then, I thought, they would have even more time to perform ceremonies and explain them to me.

I was quite mistaken. Most of the ceremonies demanded the presence of elders from several homesteads. As the swamps rose, the old men found it too difficult to walk from one homestead to the next, and the ceremonies gradually ceased. As the swamps rose even higher, all activities but one came to an end. The women brewed beer from maize and millet. Men, women, and children sat on their hillocks and drank it.

People began to drink at dawn. By midmorning the whole homestead was singing, dancing, and drumming. When it rained, people had to sit inside their huts: there they drank and sang or they drank and told stories. In any case, by noon or before, I either had to join the party or retire to my own hut and my books. "One does not discuss serious matters when there is beer. Come, drink with us." Since I lacked their capacity for the thick native beer, I spent more and more time with *Hamlet*. Before the end of the second month, grace descended on me. I was quite sure that *Hamlet* had only one possible interpretation, and that one universally obvious.

Early every morning, in the hope of having some serious talk before the beer party, I used to call on the old man at his reception hut—a circle of posts supporting a thatched roof above a low mud wall to keep out wind and rain. One day I crawled through the low doorway and found most of the men of the homestead sitting huddled in their ragged cloths on stools, low plank beds, and reclining chairs, warming themselves against the chill of the rain around a smoky fire. In the center were three pots of beer. The party had started.

The old man greeted me cordially. "Sit down and drink." I accepted a large calabash full of beer, poured some into a small drinking gourd, and tossed it down. Then I poured some more into the same gourd for the man second in seniority to my host before I handed my calabash over to a young man for further distribution. Important people shouldn't ladle beer themselves.

"It is better like this," the old man said, looking at me approvingly and plucking at the thatch that had caught in my hair. "You should sit and drink with us more often. Your servants tell me that when you are not with us, you sit inside your hut looking at a paper."

The old man was acquainted with four kinds of "papers": tax receipts, bride price receipts, court fee receipts, and letters. The messenger who brought him letters from the chief used them mainly as a badge of office, for he always knew what was in them and told the old man. Personal letters for the few who had relatives in the government or mission stations were kept until someone went to a large market where there was a letter writer and reader. Since my arrival, letters were brought to me to be read. A few men also brought me bride price receipts, privately, with requests to change the figures to a higher sum. I found moral arguments were of no avail, since in-laws are fair game, and the technical hazards of forgery difficult to explain to an illiterate people. I did not wish them to think me silly enough to look at any such papers for days on end, and I hastily explained that my "paper" was one of the "things of long ago" of my country.

"Ah," said the old man. "Tell us."

I protested that I was not a storyteller. Story telling is a skilled art among them; their standards are high, and the audiences critical—and vocal in their criticism. I protested in vain. This morning they wanted to hear a story while they drank. They threatened to tell me no more stories until I told them one of mine. Finally, the old man promised that no one would criticize my style "for we know you are struggling with our language." "But," put in one of the elders, "you must explain what we do not understand, as we do when we tell you our stories." Realizing that here was my chance to prove *Hamlet* universally intelligible, I agreed.

The old man handed me some more beer to help me on with my storytelling. Men filled their long wooden pipes and knocked coals from the fire to place in the pipe bowls; then, puffing contentedly, they sat back to listen. I began in the proper style, "Not yesterday, not yesterday, but long ago, a thing occurred. One night three men were keeping watch outside the homestead of the great chief, when suddenly they saw the former chief approach them."

"Why was he no longer their chief?"

"He was dead," I explained. "That is why they were troubled and afraid when they saw him."

"Impossible," began one of the elders, handing his pipe on to his neighbor, who interrupted, "Of course it wasn't the dead chief. It was an omen sent by a witch. Go on."

Slightly shaken, I continued. "One of these three was a man who knew things"—the closest translation for scholar, but unfortunately it also meant witch. The second elder looked triumphantly at the first. "So he spoke to the dead chief saying, 'Tell us what we must do so you may rest in your grave,' but the dead chief did not answer. He vanished, and they could see him no more. Then the man who knew things—his name was Horatio—said this event was the affair of the dead chief's son, Hamlet."

There was a general shaking of heads round the circle. "Had the dead chief no living brothers? Or was this son the chief?"

"No," I replied. "That is, he had one living brother who became the chief when the elder brother died."

The old men muttered: such omens were matters for chiefs and elders, not for youngsters; no good could come of going behind a chief's back; clearly Horatio was not a man who knew things.

"Yes, he was," I insisted, shooing a chicken away from my beer. "In our country the son is next to the father. The dead chief's younger brother had become the great chief. He had also married his elder brother's widow only about a month after the funeral."

"He did well," the old man beamed and announced to the others, "I told you that if we knew more about Europeans, we would find they really were very like us. In our country also," he added to me, "the younger brother marries the elder brother's widow and becomes the father of his children. Now, if your uncle, who married your widowed mother, is your father's full brother, then he will be a real father to you. Did Hamlet's father and uncle have one mother?"

His question barely penetrated my mind; I was too upset and thrown too far off balance by having one of the most important elements of *Hamlet* knocked straight out of the picture. Rather uncertainly I said that I thought they had the same mother, but I wasn't sure—the story didn't say. The old man told me severely that these genealogical details made all the difference and that when I got home I must ask the elders about it. He shouted out the door to one of his younger wives to bring his goatskin bag.

Determined to save what I could of the mother motif, I took a deep breath and began again. "The son, Hamlet, was very sad because his mother had married again so quickly. There was no need for her to do so, and it is our custom for a widow not to go to her next husband until she has mourned for two years."

"Two years is too long," objected the wife, who had appeared with the old man's battered goatskin bag. "Who will hoe your farms for you while you have no husband?"

"Hamlet," I retorted without thinking, "was old enough to hoe his mother's farms himself. There was no need for her to remarry." No one looked convinced. I gave up. "His mother and the great chief told Hamlet not to be sad, for the great chief himself would be

a father to Hamlet. Furthermore, Hamlet would be the next chief: therefore he must stay to learn the things of a chief. Hamlet agreed to remain, and all the rest went off to drink beer."

While I paused, perplexed at how to render Hamlet's disgusted soliloquy to an audience convinced that Claudius and Gertrude had behaved in the best possible manner, one of the younger men asked me who had married the other wives of the dead chief.

"He had no other wives," I told him.

"But a chief must have many wives! How else can he brew beer and prepare food for all his guests?"

I said firmly that in our country even chiefs had only one wife, that they had servants to do their work, and that they paid them from tax money.

It was better, they returned, for a chief to have many wives and sons who would help him hoe his farms and feed his people; then everyone loved the chief who gave much and took nothing—taxes were a bad thing.

I agreed with the last comment, but for the rest fell back on their favorite way of fobbing off my questions: "That is the way it is done, so that is how we do it."

I decided to skip the soliloquy. Even if Claudius was here thought quite right to marry his brother's widow, there remained the poison motif, and I knew they would disapprove of fratricide. More hopefully I resumed, "That night Hamlet kept watch with the three who had seen his dead father. The dead chief again appeared, and although the others were afraid, Hamlet followed his dead father off to one side. When they were alone, Hamlet's dead father spoke."

"Omens can't talk!" The old man was emphatic.

"Hamlet's dead father wasn't an omen. Seeing him might have been an omen, but he was not." My audience looked as confused as I sounded. "It *was* Hamlet's dead father. It was a thing we call a 'ghost.'" I had to use the English word, for unlike many of the neighboring tribes, these people didn't believe in the survival after death of any individuating part of the personality.

"What is a 'ghost?' An omen?"

"No, a 'ghost' is someone who is dead but who walks around and can talk, and people can hear him and see him but not touch him."

They objected. "One can touch zombis."

"No, no! It was not a dead body the witches had animated to sacrifice and eat. No one else made Hamlet's dead father walk. He did it himself."

"Dead men can't walk," protested my audience as one man.

I was quite willing to compromise. "A 'ghost' is the dead man's shadow."

But again they objected. "Dead men cast no shadows."

"They do in my country," I snapped.

The old man quelled the babble of disbelief that arose immediately and told me with that insincere, but courteous, agreement one extends to the fancies of the young, ignorant, and superstitious, "No doubt in your country the dead can also walk without being zombis." From the depths of his bag he produced a withered fragment of kola nut, bit off one end to show it wasn't poisoned, and handed me the rest as a peace offering.

"Anyhow," I resumed, "Hamlet's dead father said that his own brother, the one who became chief, had poisoned him. He wanted Hamlet to avenge him. Hamlet believed this in his heart, for he did not like his father's brother." I took another swallow of beer. "In the country of the great chief, living in the same homestead, for it was a very large one, was an important elder who was often with the chief to advise and help him. His name was Polonius. Hamlet was courting his daughter, but her father and her brother . . . [I cast hastily about for some tribal analogy] warned her not to let Hamlet visit her when she was alone on her farm, for he would be a great chief and so could not marry her."

"Why not?" asked the wife, who had settled down on the edge of the old man's chair. He frowned at her for asking stupid questions and growled, "They lived in the same homestead."

"That was not the reason," I informed them. "Polonius was a stranger who lived in the homestead because he helped the chief, not because he was a relative."

"Then why couldn't Hamlet marry her?"

"He could have," I explained, "but Polonius didn't think he would. After all, Hamlet was a man of great importance who ought to marry a chief's daughter, for in his country a man could have only one wife. Polonius was afraid that if Hamlet made love to his daughter, then no one else would give a high price for her."

"That might be true," remarked one of the shrewder elders, "but a chief's son would give his mistress's father enough presents and patronage to more than make up the difference. Polonius sounds like a fool to me."

"Many people think he was," I agreed. "Meanwhile Polonius sent his son Laertes off to Paris to learn the things of that country, for it was the homestead of a very great chief indeed. Because he was afraid that Laertes might waste a lot of money on beer and women and gambling, or get into trouble by fighting, he sent one of his servants to Paris secretly, to spy out what Laertes was doing. One day Hamlet came upon Polonius's daughter Ophelia. He behaved so oddly he frightened her. Indeed"—I was fumbling for words to express the dubious quality of Hamlet's madness—"the chief and many others had also noticed that when Hamlet talked one could understand the words but not what they meant. Many people thought that he had become mad." My audience suddenly became much more attentive. "The great chief wanted to know what was wrong with Hamlet, so he sent for two of Hamlet's age mates [school friends would have taken long explanation] to talk to Hamlet and find out what troubled his heart. Hamlet, seeing that they had been bribed by the chief to betray him, told them nothing. Polonius, however, insisted that Hamlet was mad because he had been forbidden to see Ophelia, whom he loved."

"Why," inquired a bewildered voice, "should anyone bewitch Hamlet on that account?"

"Bewitch him?"

"Yes, only witchcraft can make anyone mad, unless, of course, one sees the beings that lurk in the forest."

I stopped being a storyteller, took out my notebook and demanded to be told more about these two causes of madness. Even while they spoke and I jotted notes, I tried to calculate the effect of this new factor on the plot. Hamlet had not been exposed to the beings that lurk in the forests. Only his relatives in the male line could bewitch him. Barring relatives not mentioned by Shakespeare, it had to be Claudius who was attempting to harm him. And, of course, it was.

For the moment I staved off questions by saying that the great chief also refused to believe that Hamlet was mad for the love of Ophelia and nothing else. "He was sure that something much more important was troubling Hamlet's heart."

"Now Hamlet's age mates," I continued, "had brought with them a famous storyteller. Hamlet decided to have this man tell the chief and all his homestead a story about a man who had poisoned his brother because he desired his brother's wife and wished to be chief himself. Hamlet was sure the great chief could not hear the story without making a sign if he was indeed guilty, and then he would discover whether his dead father had told him the truth."

The old man interrupted, with deep cunning, "Why should a father lie to his son?" he asked.

I hedged: "Hamlet wasn't sure that it really was his dead father." It was impossible to say anything, in that language, about devil-inspired visions.

"You mean," he said, "it actually was an omen, and he knew witches sometimes send false ones. Hamlet was a fool not to go to one skilled in reading omens and divining the truth in the first place. A man-who-sees-the-truth could have told him how his father died, if he really had been poisoned, and if there was witchcraft in it; then Hamlet could have called the elders to settle the matter."

The shrewd elder ventured to disagree. "Because his father's brother was a great chief, one-who-sees-the-truth might therefore have been afraid to tell it. I think it was for that reason that a friend of Hamlet's father—a witch and an elder—sent an omen so his friend's son would know. Was the omen true?"

"Yes," I said, abandoning ghosts and the devil; a witch-sent omen it would have to be. "It was true, for when the storyteller was telling his tale before all the homestead, the great chief rose in fear. Afraid that Hamlet knew his secret he planned to have him killed."

The stage set of the next bit presented some difficulties of translation. I began cautiously. "The great chief told Hamlet's mother to find out from her son what he knew. But because a woman's children are always first in her heart, he had the important elder Polonius hide behind a cloth that hung against the wall of Hamlet's mother's sleeping hut. Hamlet started to scold his mother for what she had done."

There was a shocked murmur from everyone. A man should never scold his mother.

"She called out in fear, and Polonius moved behind the cloth. Shouting, 'A rat!' Hamlet took his machete and slashed through the cloth." I paused for dramatic effect. "He had killed Polonius!"

The old men looked at each other in supreme disgust. "That Polonius truly was a fool and a man who knew nothing! What child would not know enough to shout, 'It's me!'" With a pang, I remembered that these people are ardent hunters, always armed with bow, arrow, and machete; at the first rustle in the grass an arrow is aimed and ready, and the hunter shouts "Game!" If no human voice answers immediately, the arrow speeds on its way. Like a good hunter Hamlet had shouted, "A rat!"

I rushed in to save Polonius's reputation. "Polonius did speak. Hamlet heard him. But he thought it was the chief and wished to kill him earlier that evening. . . ." I broke down, unable to describe to these pagans, who had no belief in individual afterlife, the difference between dying at one's prayers and dying "unhousell'd, disappointed, unaneled."

This time I had shocked my audience seriously. "For a man to raise his hand against his father's brother and the one who has become his father—that is a terrible thing. The elders ought to let such a man be bewitched."

I nibbled at my kola nut in some perplexity, then pointed out that after all the man had killed Hamlet's father.

"No," pronounced the old man, speaking less to me than to the young men sitting behind the elders. "If your father's brother has killed your father, you must appeal to your father's age mates; *they* may avenge him. No man may use violence against his senior relatives." Another thought struck him. "But if his father's brother had indeed been wicked enough to bewitch Hamlet and make him mad that would be a good story indeed, for it would be his fault that Hamlet, being mad, no longer had any sense and thus was ready to kill his father's brother."

There was a murmur of applause. *Hamlet* was again a good story to them, but it no longer seemed quite the same story to me. As I thought over the coming complications of plot and motive, I lost courage and decided to skim over dangerous ground quickly.

"The great chief," I went on, "was not sorry that Hamlet had killed Polonius. It gave him a reason to send Hamlet away, with his two treacherous mates, with letters to a chief of a far country, saying that Hamlet should be killed. But Hamlet changed the writing on their papers, so that the chief killed his age mates instead." I encountered a reproachful glare from one of the men whom I had told undetectable forgery was not merely immoral but beyond human skill. I looked the other way.

"Before Hamlet could return, Laertes came back for his father's funeral. The great chief told him Hamlet had killed Polonius. Laertes swore to kill Hamlet because of this, and because his sister Ophelia, hearing her father had been killed by the man she loved, went mad and drowned in the river."

"Have you already forgotten what we told you?" The old man was reproachful. "One cannot take vengeance on a madman; Hamlet killed Polonius in his madness. As for the girl, she not only went mad, she was drowned. Only witches can make people drown. Water itself can't hurt anything. It is merely something one drinks and bathes in."

I began to get cross. "If you don't like the story, I'll stop."

The old man made soothing noises and himself poured me some more beer. "You tell the story well, and we are listening. But it is clear that the elders of your country have never told you what the story really means. No, don't interrupt! We believe you when you say your marriage customs are different, or your clothes and weapons are different, but people are the same everywhere; therefore, there are always witches and it is we, the elders, who know how witches work. We told you it was the great chief who wished to kill Hamlet, and now your own words have proved us right. Who were Ophelia's male relatives?"

"There were only her father and her brother." *Hamlet* was clearly out of my hands.

"There must have been many more; this also you must ask of your elders when you get back to your country. From what you tell us, since Polonius was dead, it must have been Laertes who killed Ophelia, although I do not see the reason for it."

We had emptied one pot of beer, and the old men argued the point with slightly tipsy interest. Finally one of them demanded of me, "What did the servant of Polonius say on his return?"

With difficulty I recollected Reynaldo and his mission. "I don't think he did return before Polonius was killed."

"Listen," said the elder, "and I will tell you how it was and how your story will go, then you may tell me if I am right. Polonius knew his son would get into trouble, and so he did. He had many fines to pay for fighting, and debts from gambling. But he had only two ways of getting money quickly. One was to marry off his sister at once, but it is difficult to find a man who will marry a woman desired by the son of a chief. For if the chief's heir commits adultery with your wife, what can you do? Only a fool calls a case against a man who will someday be his judge. Therefore Laertes had to take the second way: he killed his sister by witchcraft, drowning her so he could secretly sell her body to the witches."

I raised an objection. "They found her body and buried it. Indeed Laertes jumped into the grave to see his sister once more—so, you see, the body was truly there. Hamlet, who had just come back, jumped in after him."

"What did I tell you?" The elder appealed to the others. "Laertes was up to no good with his sister's body. Hamlet prevented him, because the chief's heir, like a chief, does not wish any other man to grow rich and powerful. Laertes would be angry, because he would have killed his sister without benefit to himself. In our country he would try to kill Hamlet for that reason. Is this not what happened?"

"More or less," I admitted. "When the great chief found Hamlet was still alive, he encouraged Laertes to try to kill Hamlet and arranged a fight with machetes between them. In the fight both the young men were wounded to death. Hamlet's mother drank the poisoned beer that the chief meant for Hamlet in case he won the fight. When he saw his mother die of poison, Hamlet, dying, managed to kill his father's brother with his machete."

"You see, I was right!" exclaimed the elder.

"That was a very good story," added the old man, "and you told it with very few mistakes. There was just one more error, at the very end. The poison Hamlet's mother drank was obviously meant for the survivor of the fight, whichever it was. If Laertes had won, the great chief would have poisoned him, for no one would know that he arranged Hamlet's death. Then, too, he need not fear Laertes' witchcraft; it takes a strong heart to kill one's only sister by witchcraft.

"Sometime," concluded the old man, gathering his ragged toga about him, "you must tell us some more stories of your country. We, who are elders, will instruct you in their true meaning, so that when you return to your own land your elders will see that you have not been sitting in the bush, but among those who know things and who have taught you wisdom."

Assess Your Progress

1. What attitude did Laura Bohannan have about cross-cultural translation of Shakespeare before visiting the Tiv?

2. What differences in custom and belief hampered her telling of "Hamlet" and how?

3. Was there a difference between Laura Bohannan and the Tiv in terms of what they got out of this experience? Explain.

LAURA BOHANNAN is a former professor of anthropology at the University of Illinois, at Chicago.

UNIT 3

The Organization of Society and Culture

Unit Selections

10. **Macho Origin Myths,** Franz de Waal
11. **How Cooking Frees Men,** Richard Wrangham
12. **When Cousins Do More than Kiss,** Anthony Layng
13, **Meet the Alloparents,** Sarah Blaffer Hrdy
14. **The Inuit Paradox,** Patricia Gadsby
15. **Ties That Bind,** Peter M. Whiteley
16. **Sick of Poverty,** Robert Sapolsky

Learning Outcomes

After reading this unit, you should be able to:

- Describe the impact of cooking on human social evolution.

- Explain why marriage between cousins has been so common in the human past.

- Discuss the importance of "alloparenting" with regard to the success of the human species.

- Identify the traditional Inuit (Eskimo) practices that are important for their survival in the circumstances they live in and contrast them with the values professed by the society you live in.

- Discuss what contemporary hunter-collector societies teach us about the quality of life in the prehistoric past.

- Define the "Inuit paradox" and explain what we can learn from it with regard to modern-day eating practices.

- Explain the significance of "the gift" in traditional Hopi society.

- Determine how much of the relationship between poverty and health is a function of the relative disparities of socioeconomic status rather than simply the material circumstances of being poor.

Student Website
www.mhhe.com/cls

Internet References

Smithsonian Institution Website
   www.si.edu
Sociology Guy's Anthropology Links
   www.trinity.edu/~mkearl/anthro.html

Human beings do not interact with one another or think about their world in random fashion. They engage in structured and recurrent physical and mental activities. In this section, such patterns of behavior and thought—referred to here as the organization of society and culture—may be seen in a number of different contexts, from the mating preferences of hunter-gatherer bands (see "When Cousins Do More than Kiss") to the value the Hopi place on the gift as a symbol of social relations built on kinship and altruism (as discussed in "Ties That Bind").

Of special importance are the ways in which people make a living—in other words, the production, distribution, and consumption of goods and services. It is only by knowing the basic subsistence systems that we can hope to gain insight into other levels of social and cultural phenomena, for they are all inextricably bound together. (See "Macho Origin Myths" by Franz de Waal.) Noting the various aspects of a sociocultural system in harmonious balance, however, does not imply an anthropological seal of approval. To understand infanticide (killing of the newborn) in the manner that it is practiced among some peoples is neither to condone nor condemn it. The adaptive patterns that have been in existence for a great length of time, such as many of the patterns of hunters and gatherers, probably owe their existence to their contributions to long-term human survival (see "How Cooking Frees Men," "Meet the Alloparents," and "The Inuit Paradox").

Anthropologists, however, are not content with the data derived from individual experience. On the contrary, personal descriptions must become the basis for sound anthropological theory. Otherwise, they remain meaningless, isolated relics of culture in the manner of museum pieces. Thus, in "Sick of Poverty," Robert Sapolsky tells us that the subjective state of *feeling* poor may be just as important in predicting ill health as is the objective case of *being* poor.

In other words, while the articles in this unit are to some extent descriptive, they also serve to challenge both the academic and commonsense notions about why people behave and think the way they do. They remind us that assumptions are never really safe. As long as anthropologists are kept on their toes, the field as a whole will be better.

© PhotoLink/Getty Images

Macho Origin Myths

Franz de Waal

It was a typical primate conflict over dinner in a fancy Italian restaurant: one human male challenging another—me—in front of his girlfriend. Knowing my writings, what better target than humanity's place in nature? "Name one area in which it's hard to tell humans apart from animals," he said, looking for a test case. Before I knew it, between two bites of delicious pasta, I replied, "The sex act."

Perhaps reminded of something unmentionable, I could see that this took him aback a little, but only momentarily. He launched into a great defense of passion as peculiarly human, stressing the recent origin of romantic love, the wonderful poems and serenades that come with it, while pooh-poohing my emphasis on the mechanics of *l'amore,* which are essentially the same for humans, hamsters, and guppies (male guppies are equipped with a penislike modified fin). He pulled a deeply disgusted face at these mundane anatomical details.

Alas for him, his girlfriend was a colleague of mine, who with great enthusiasm jumped in with more examples of animal sex, so we had the sort of dinner conversation that primatologists love but that embarrasses almost everyone else. A stunned silence fell at neighboring tables when the girlfriend exclaimed that "he had *such* an erection!" It was unclear if the reaction concerned what she had just said, or that she had indicated what she meant holding thumb and index finger only slightly apart. She was talking about a small South American monkey.

Our argument was never resolved, but by the time desserts arrived it fortunately had lost steam. Such discussions are a staple of my existence: I believe that we are animals, whereas others believe we are something else entirely. Human uniqueness may be hard to maintain when it comes to sex, but the situation changes if one considers airplanes, parliaments, or skyscrapers. Humans have a truly impressive capacity for culture and technology. Even though many animals do show some elements of culture, if you meet a chimp in the jungle with a camera, you can be pretty sure he didn't produce it himself.

But what about humans who have missed out on the cultural growth spurt that much of the world underwent over the last few thousand years? Hidden in far-flung corners, these people do possess all the hallmarks of our species, such as language, art, and fire. We can study how they survive without being distracted by the technological advances of today. Does their way of life fit widely held assumptions about humanity's "state of nature"—a concept with a rich history in the West? Given the

way this concept figured in the French Revolution, the U.S. Constitution, and other historical steps toward modern democracy, it's no trivial matter to establish how humans may have lived in their original state.

A good example are the "Bushmen" of southwest Africa, who used to live in such simplicity that their lifestyle was lampooned in the 1980 movie *The Gods Must Be Crazy.* As a teenager, anthropologist Elizabeth Marshall Thomas went with her parents, also anthropologists, to the Kalahari Desert to live among them. Bushmen, also known as the San, are a small, lithe people who have carved out a very modest niche in a grassy, open ecosystem that for half of the year is so low on water that the few reliable water-holes seriously restrict human movement. They have lived this way for thousands and thousands of years, which is why Marshall Thomas titled her book on them *The Old Way.*

The old way includes minimal clothing made out of antelope hides, a modest grass shelter, a sharpened digging stick, and an ostrich eggshell to transport water on day trips. Shelters are built and rebuilt all the time by putting a few sticks into the ground, interwining the top, and covering the frame with grass. It reminded Marshall Thomas of the way apes build one-night nests in the trees by quickly weaving a few branches together into a platform before they go to sleep. This way, they stay off the ground, where danger lurks.

When Bushmen travel, they walk in single file, with a man in the lead who watches out for fresh predator tracks, snakes, and other dangers. Women and children occupy safer positions. This, too, is reminiscent of chimpanzees, who at dangerous moments—such as when they cross a human dirt road—have adult males in the lead and rear, with females and juveniles in between. Sometimes the alpha male stands guard at the road until everyone has crossed it.

Our ancestors may have been higher on the food chain than most primates, but they definitely were not at the apex. They had to watch their backs. This brings me to the first false myth about our state of nature, which is that our ancestors ruled the savanna. How could this be true for bipedal apes that stood only four feet tall? They must have lived in terror of the bear-sized hyenas of those days, and the saber-toothed cats that were twice the size of our lions. As a result, they had to content themselves with second-rate hunting time. Darkness is the best cover, but like the Bushmen today, early human hunters likely opted for the heat of the day, when their prey could see them coming from miles away, because they had to leave the night to the "professional" hunters.

Lions are the supreme rulers of the savanna, as reflected in our "lion king" stories and the Bushmen's high regard for lions. Significantly, Bushmen never use their deadly poison arrows on these animals, knowing that this may start a battle they can't win. The lions leave them alone most of the time, but when for some reason the lions in some places become man-eaters, people have had no choice but to leave. Danger is so much on the Bushmen's mind that at night, while the others sleep, they keep their fire going, which means getting up to stoke it. If the glow-in-the-dark eyes of nightly predators are spotted, appropriate action will be taken, such as picking up a burning branch from the fire and waving it over one's head (making one look larger-than-life) while urging the predator in a calm but steady voice to go find something better to do. Bushmen do have courage, but pleading with predators hardly fits the idea of humans as the dominant species.

The old way must have been quite successful, though, for even in the modern world we still show the same tendency to come together for safety. At times of danger, we forget what divides us. This was visible, for example, after the 9/11 attack on the World Trade Center in New York, an unbelievably traumatic experience for those who lived through it. Nine months afterward, when asked how they saw relations between the races, New Yorkers of all races called those relations mostly good, whereas in foregoing years, they had called them mostly bad. The postattack feeling of "we're in this together" had fostered unity in the city.

These reflexes go back to the deepest, most ancient layers of our brain, layers that we share with many animals, not just mammals. Look at how fish, such as herring, swim in schools that tighten instantly when a shark or porpoise approaches. Or how schools turn abruptly in one silvery flash, making it impossible for the predator to target any single fish. Schooling fish keep very precise individual distances, seek out companions of the same size, and perfectly match their speed and direction, often in a fraction of a second. Thousands of individuals thus act almost like a single organism. Or look at how birds, such as starlings, swarm in dense flocks that in an instant evade an approaching hawk. Biologists speak of "selfish herds," in which each individual hides among a mass of others for its own security. The presence of other prey dilutes the risk for each one among them, not unlike the old joke about two men being chased by a bear: There's no need to run faster than the bear so long as you outrun your pal.

Even bitter rivals seek companionship at times of danger. Birds that in the breeding season fight one another to death over territory may end up in the same flock during migration. I know this tendency first-hand from my fish, each time I redo one of my large tropical aquariums. Many fish, such as cichlids, are quite territorial, displaying with spread fins and chasing one another to keep their corner free of intruders. I clean my tanks out every couple of years, during which time I keep the fish in a barrel. After a few days they are released back into the tank, which by then looks quite different from before. I am always amused at how they suddenly seek out the company of their own kind. Like best buddies, the biggest fighters now swim side by side, exploring their new environment together. Until, of course, they start to feel confident again, and claim a piece of real estate.

Security is the first and foremost reason for social life. This brings me to the second false origin myth: that human society is the voluntary creation of autonomous men. The illusion here is that our ancestors had no need for anybody else. They led uncommitted lives. Their only problem was that they were so competitive that the cost of strife became unbearable. Being intelligent animals, they decided to give up a few liberties in return for community life. This origin story, proposed by French philosopher Jean-Jacques Rousseau as the *social contract,* inspired America's founding fathers to create the "land of the free." It is a myth that remains immensely popular in political science departments and law schools, since it presents society as a negotiated compromise rather than something that came naturally to us.

Granted, it can be instructive to look at human relations *as if* they resulted from an agreement among equal parties. It helps us think about how we treat, or ought to treat, one another. It's good to realize, though, that this way of framing the issue is a leftover from pre-Darwinian days, based on a totally erroneous image of our species. As is true for many mammals, every human life cycle includes stages at which we either depend on others (when we are young, old, or sick) or others depend on us (when we care for the young, old, or sick). We very much rely on one another for survival. It is this reality that ought to be taken as a starting point for any discussion about human society, not the reveries of centuries past, which depicted our ancestors as being as free as birds and lacking any social obligations.

We descend from a long line of group-living primates with a high degree of interdependence. How the need for security shapes social life became clear when primatologists counted long-tailed macaques on different islands in the Indonesian archipelago. Some islands have cats (such as tigers and clouded leopards), whereas others don't. The same monkeys were found traveling in large groups on islands with cats, but in small groups on islands without. Predation thus forces individuals together. Generally, the more vulnerable a species is, the larger its aggregations. Ground-dwelling monkeys, like baboons, travel in larger groups than tree dwellers, which enjoy better escape opportunities. And chimpanzees, which because of their size have little to fear in the daytime, typically forage alone or in small groups.

Few animals lack a herd instinct. When former U.S. Senate majority leader Trent Lott titled his memoir *Herding Cats,* he was referring to the impossibility of reaching consensus. This may be frustrating when it comes to politicians, but for cats it's entirely logical. Domestic cats are solitary hunters, so don't need to pay much attention to one another. But all animals that either rely on one another for the hunt, such as members of the dog family, or are prey themselves, such as wildebeests, have a need to coordinate movements. They tend to follow leaders and conform to the majority. When our ancestors left the forest and entered an open, dangerous environment, they became prey and evolved a herd instinct that beats that of many animals.

We excel at bodily synchrony and actually derive pleasure from it. Walking next to someone, for example, we automatically fall into the same stride. We coordinate chants and "waves" during sporting events, oscillate together during pop concerts, and take aerobics classes where we all jump up and down to the same beat. As an exercise, try to clap after a lecture when no one else is clapping, or try *not* to clap when everyone else is. We are group animals to a terrifying degree. Since political leaders are masters at crowd psychology, history is replete with people following them en masse into insane adventures. All that a leader has to do is create an outside threat, whip up fear, and voilà: The human herd instinct takes over.

Here we arrive at the third false origin myth, which is that our species has been waging war for as long as it has been around. In the 1960s, following the devastations of World War II, humans were routinely depicted as "killer apes"—as opposed to real apes, which were considered pacifists. Aggression was seen as the hallmark of humanity. While it's far from my intention to claim humans are angels of peace, we do need to draw a line between homicide and warfare. Warfare rests on a tight hierarchical structure of many parties, not all of which are driven by aggression. In fact, most are just following orders. Napoleon's soldiers didn't march into freezing Russia in an aggressive mood, nor did American soldiers fly to Iraq because they wanted to kill somebody. The decision to go to war is typically made by older men in the capital. When I look at a marching army, I don't necessarily see aggression in action. I see the herd instinct: thousands of men in lockstep, willing to obey superiors.

In recent history, we have seen so much war-related death that we imagine that it must always have been like this, and that warfare is written into our DNA. In the words of Winston Churchill, "The story of the human race is War. Except for brief and precarious interludes, there has never been peace in the world; and before history began, murderous strife was universal and unending." But is Churchill's war-mongering state of nature any more plausible than Rousseau's noble savage? Although archeological signs of individual murder go back hundreds of thousands of years, we lack similar evidence for warfare (such as graveyards with weapons embedded in a large number of skeletons) from before the agricultural revolution. Even the walls of Jericho, considered one of the first pieces of evidence of warfare and famous for having come tumbling down in the Old Testament, may have served mainly as protection against mudflows.

Long before this, our ancestors lived on a thinly populated planet, with altogether only a couple of million people. Their density may have resembled that of the Bushmen, who live on ten square miles per capita. There are even suggestions that before this, about seventy thousand years ago, our lineage was at the edge of extinction, living in scattered small bands with a global population of just a couple of thousand. These are hardly the sort of conditions that promote continuous warfare. Furthermore, our ancestors probably had little worth fighting over, again like the Bushmen, for whom the only such exceptions are water and women. But Bushmen share water with thirsty visitors, and regularly marry off their children to neighboring groups. The latter practice ties groups together and means that the men in one group are often related to those in the other. In the long run, killing one's kin is not a successful trait.

Marshall Thomas witnessed no warfare among Bushmen and takes the absence of shields as evidence that they rarely fight with strangers. Shields, which are easily made out of strong hides, offer effective protection against arrows. Their nonexistence suggests that Bushmen are not too worried about intergroup hostilities. This is not to say that war is totally absent in preliterate societies: We know many tribes that engage in it occasionally, and some that do so regularly. My guess is that for our ancestors war was always a possibility, but that they followed the pattern of present-day hunter-gatherers, who do exactly the opposite of what Churchill surmised: They alternate long stretches of peace and harmony with brief interludes of violent confrontation.

Comparisons with apes hardly resolve this issue. Since it has been found that chimpanzees sometimes raid their neighbors and brutally take their enemies' lives, these apes have edged closer to the warrior image that we have of ourselves. Like us, chimps wage violent battles over territory. Genetically speaking, however, our species is exactly equally close to another ape, the bonobo, which does nothing of the kind. Bonobos can be unfriendly to their neighbors, but soon after a confrontation has begun, females often rush to the other side to have sex with both males and other females. Since it is hard to have sex and wage war at the same time, the scene rapidly turns into a sort of picnic. It ends with adults from different groups grooming each other while their children play. Thus far, lethal aggression among bonobos is unheard of.

The only certainty is that our species has a *potential* for warfare, which under certain circumstances will rear its ugly head. Skirmishes do sometimes get out of control and result in death, and young men everywhere have a tendency to show off their physical prowess by battling outsiders with little regard for the consequences. But at the same time, our species is unique in that we maintain ties with kin long after they have dispersed. As a result there exist entire networks between groups, which promote economic exchange and make warfare counterproductive. Ties with outsiders provide survival insurance in unpredictable environments, allowing the risk of food or water shortages to be spread across groups.

Polly Wiessner, an American anthropologist, studied "risk pooling" among the Bushmen and offers the following description of the delicate negotiations to obtain access to resources outside their territory. The reason these negotiations are done so carefully and indirectly is that competition is never absent from human relations:

> In the 1970s, the average Bushman spent over three months a year away from home. Visitors and hosts engaged in a greeting ritual to show respect and seek permission to stay. The visiting party sat down under a shade tree at the periphery of the camp. After a few hours, the hosts would come to greet them. The visitors would tell about people and conditions at home in a rhythmic form of speech. The hosts would confirm each statement by repeating the last words followed by "eh he." The host typically complained

of food shortage, but the visitors could read how serious this was. If it was serious, they would say that they only had come for a few days. If the host did not stress shortages or problems, they knew they could stay longer. After the exchange, visitors were invited into camp where they often brought gifts, though they'd give them very subtly with great modesty so as not to arouse jealousy.

Because of interdependencies between groups with scarce resources, our ancestors probably never waged war on a grand scale until they settled down and began to accumulate wealth by means of agriculture. This made attacks on other groups more profitable. Instead of being the product of an aggressive drive, it seems that war is more about power and profit. This also implies, of course, that it's hardly inevitable.

So much for Western origin stories, which depict our forebears as ferocious, fearless, and free. Unbound by social commitments and merciless toward their enemies, they seem to have stepped straight out of your typical action movie. Present-day political thought keeps clinging to these macho myths, such as the belief that we can treat the planet any way we want, that humanity will be waging war forever, and that individual freedom takes precedence over community.

None of this is in keeping with the old way, which is one of reliance on one another, of connection, of suppressing both internal and external disputes, because the hold on subsistence is so tenuous that food and safety are the top priorities. The women gather fruits and roots, the men hunt, and together they raise small families that survive only because of their embeddedness in a larger social fabric. The community is there for them and they are there for the community. Bushmen devote much time and attention to the exchange of small gifts in networks that cover many miles and multiple generations. They work hard to reach decisions by consensus, and fear ostracism and isolation more than death itself. Tellingly, one woman confided, "It is bad to die, because when you die you are alone."

We can't return to this preindustrial way of life. We live in societies of a mind-boggling scale and complexity that demand quite a different organization than humans ever enjoyed in their state of nature. Yet, even though we live in cities and are surrounded by cars and computers, we remain essentially the same animals with the same psychological wants and needs.

Assess Your Progress

1. What are three myths about the human "state of nature" and how does the author answer them?

2. Why does the author claim that our ancestors probably never waged war on a grand scale? Why did warfare begin with agriculture?

3. Why was such conflict not compatible with the "old way of life?"

How Cooking Frees Men

RICHARD WRANGHAM

"Voracious animals . . . both feed continually and as incessantly eliminate, leading a life truly inimical to philosophy and music, as Plato has said, whereas nobler and more perfect animals neither eat nor eliminate continually."

—GALEN, *Galen on the Usefulness
of the Parts of the Body*

Diet has long been considered a key to understanding social behavior across species. The food quest is fundamental to evolutionary success, and social strategies affect how well individuals eat. Group size in chimpanzees rapidly adjusts to monthly changes in the density and distribution of fruiting trees. Chimpanzee society differs markedly from gorilla society, thanks to the gorillas' reliance on herbs. Humans are no exception to such relationships. The Man-the-Hunter hypothesis has inspired such potent explanations of bonding between males and females that it has seemed to some researchers that no other explanation is necessary. In 1968 physical anthropologists Sherwood Washburn and Chet Lancaster wrote, "Our intellect, interests, emotions and basic social life, all are evolutionary products of the hunting adaptation." Such ideas have been highly influential, but they have rarely looked beyond meat. The adoption of cooking must have radically changed the way our ancestors ate, in ways that would have changed our social behavior too.

Take softness. Foods soften when they are cooked, and as a result, cooked food can be eaten more quickly than raw food. Reliance on cooked food has therefore allowed our species to thoroughly restructure the working day. Instead of chewing for half of their time, as great apes tend to do, women in subsistence societies tend to spend the active part of their days collecting and preparing food. Men, liberated from the simple biological demands of a long day's commitment to chewing raw food, engage in productive or unproductive labor as they wish. In fact, I believe that cooking has made possible one of the most distinctive features of human society: the modern form of the sexual division of labor.

The sexual division of labor refers to women and men making different and complementary contributions to the household economy. Though the specific activities of each sex vary by culture, the gendered division of labor is a human universal. It is therefore assumed to have appeared well before modern humans started spreading across the globe sixty thousand to seventy thousand years ago. So discussion of the evolution of the sexual division of labor centers on hunter-gatherers. The 750-strong Hadza tribe are one such group. They live in northern Tanzania, scattered among a series of small camps in dry bush country around a shallow lake.

The Hadza are modern-day people. Neighboring farmers and pastoralists trade with them and marry some of their daughters. Government officials, tourists, and researchers visit them. The Hadza use metal knives and money, wear cotton clothes, hunt with dogs, and occasionally trade for agricultural foods. Much has changed since the time, perhaps two thousand years ago, when they last lived in an exclusive world of hunter-gatherers. Nevertheless, they are one of the few remaining peoples who obtain the majority of their food by foraging in an African woodland of a type that was once occupied by ancient humans.

Dawn sees people emerging from their sleeping huts to eat scraps of food from the previous night's meal. As consensus quietly develops about the day's activity; most of the women in camp—six or more, perhaps—take up their digging sticks and go toward a familiar *ekwa* patch a couple of kilometers (more than a mile) away. Some take their babies in slings, and one or more carries a smoldering log with which to start a fire if needed. Older children walk alongside. Meanwhile, in ones and twos, various men and their dogs also walk off with bows and arrows in hand. Some men are going hunting, others to visit neighbors. A scattering of people remain in camp—a couple of old women, perhaps, looking after toddlers whose mothers have gone for food, and a young man resting after a long hunt the previous day.

The women walk slowly, in pace with the younger children. They stop occasionally to pick small fruits that they eat on the spot. After less than an hour they break into smaller parties as each forager finds her own choice site in calling distance of her companions. The digging is hard and uncomfortable but it does not take long. A couple of hours later the women's karosses—cloaks made of animal skins—are covered in piles of thick, brown, foot-long roots. These *ekwa* tubers are a year-round staple for the Hadza, always easily found. As the karosses fill, someone starts a fire, and shortly afterward the foragers gather for a well-deserved snack. They bake their *ekwa* by leaning the tubers against the coals. In barely twenty minutes, the smaller ones are ready. After the simple meal, some women chat while others dig up a few more *ekwa* to make sure they have enough for the rest of the day. Most have found other foods as well—a few bulbs, perhaps. They tie up their karosses and start homeward. Each woman totes at least 15 kilograms (33 pounds). They are back in camp by early afternoon, tired from the hard work.

Anthropologists sometimes debate whether hunting and gathering is a relaxed way of life. Lorna Marshall worked alongside Nyae Nyae !Kung women gathering in the Kalahari in the 1950s. "They did not have pleasurable satisfaction," she said, "in remembering their hot, monotonous, arduous days of digging and picking and trudging home with their heavy loads." But times and cultures vary. Anthropologist Phyllis Kaberry, who worked with aborigines in the Kimberley region of northwestern Australia, said the women enjoyed one another's company and their foraging routine.

Back in the Hadza camp, each woman empties her kaross in her own hut. By early evening she has a fire, and a pile of *ekwa* lies baked and ready. She hopes the men will bring some meat to complete the meal. During the evening hours several men return. Some have honey, a few have nothing, and one arrives with the carcass of a warthog. After he singes the animal's hair off in a fire, men and women gather to divide it. Following the typical practice of hunter-gatherers, many men in the camp get a share, but the successful hunter makes sure his friends, family, and relatives get the most. Soon each household fire is cooking meat. The delicious smells enrich the night air. The meat and the roasted *ekwa* are quickly consumed. As the camp settles into sleep, enough *ekwa* remains for breakfast the following day.

The Hadza illustrate two major features of the sexual division of labor among hunter-gatherers that differentiate humans sharply from nonhuman primates. Women and men spend their days seeking different kinds of foods, and the foods they obtain are eaten by both sexes. Why our species forages in such an unusual way (compared to primates and all other animals, whose adults do not share food with one another) has never been fully resolved. There are many variations in the particular foods obtained. Tierra del Fuego's bitter climate provided few plant foods, so while men hunted sea mammals, women would dive for shellfish in the frigid shallows. In the tropical islands of northern Australia, there was so much plant food that women brought enough to feed all the family and still found time to hunt occasional small animals. Men there did little hunting, mostly playing politics instead.

Although the specific food types varied from place to place, women always tended to provide the staples, whether roots, seeds, or shellfish. These foods normally needed processing, which could involve a lot of time and laborious work. Many Australian tribes prepared a kind of bread called damper from small seeds, such as from grasses. Women gathered the plants and heaped them so their seeds would drop and collect in a pile. They threshed the seeds by trampling, pounding, or rubbing them in their hands, winnowed them in long bark dishes, and ground them into a paste. The result was occasionally eaten raw but was more often cooked on hot ashes. The whole process could take more than a day. Women worked hard at such tasks because their children and husbands relied on the staples women prepared.

Men, by contrast, tended to search for foods that were especially appreciated but could not be found easily or predictably. They hoped for such prizes as meat and honey, which tended to come in large amounts and tasted delicious. Their arrival in camp made the difference between happiness and sadness. Phyllis Kaberry's description of an aborigine camp in western Australia is typical: "The Aborigines continually craved for meat, and any man was apt to declare, 'me hungry alonga bingy,' though he had had a good meal of yams and damper a few minutes before. The camp on such occasions became glum, lethargic, and unenthusiastic about dancing." Hunting large game was a predominantly masculine activity in 99.3 percent of recent societies.

Hints of comparable sex differences in food procurement have been detected in primates. Female lemurs tend to eat more of the preferred foods than males. In various monkeys such as macaques, guenons, and mangabeys, females eat more insects and males eat more fruit. Among chimpanzees, females eat more termites and ants, and males eat more meat. But such differences are minor because in every nonhuman primate the overwhelming majority of the foods collected and eaten by females and males are the same types.

Even more distinctive of humans is that each sex eats not only from the food items they have collected themselves, but also from their partner's finds. Not even a hint of this complementarity is found among nonhuman primates. Plenty of primates, such as gibbons and gorillas, have family groups. Females and males in those species spend all day together, are nice to each other, and bring up their offspring together, but, unlike people, the adults never give each other food. Human couples, by contrast, are expected to do so.

In foraging societies a woman always shares her food with her husband and children, and she gives little to anyone other than close kin. Men likewise share with their wives, whether they have received meat from other men or have brought it to camp themselves and shared part of it with other men. The exchanges between wife and husband permeate families in every society. The contributions might involve women digging roots and men hunting meat in one culture, or women shopping and men earning a salary in another. No matter the specific items each partner contributes, human families are unique compared to the social arrangements of other species because each household is a little economy.

Attempts to understand how the sexual division of labor arose in our evolutionary history have been strongly affected by whether women or men are thought to have provided more of the food. It used to be thought that women typically produced most of the calories, as occurs among the Hadza. Worldwide across foraging groups, however, men probably supplied the bulk of the food calories more often than women did. This is particularly true in the high, colder latitudes where there are few edible plants, and hunting is the main way to get food. In an analysis of nine well-studied groups, the proportion of calories that came from foods collected by women ranged from a maximum of 57 percent, in the desert-living Gwi Bushmen of Namibia, down to a low of 16 percent in the Aché

Indians of Paraguay. Women provided one-third of the calories in these societies, and men two-thirds. But such averages do not give an accurate sense of the value of items each sex contributes. At different times of year, the relative importance of foods obtained by women and men can change, and overall each sex's foods can be just as critical as the other's in maintaining health and survival. Furthermore, each sex makes vital contributions to the overall household economy regardless of any difference in the proportion of food calories contributed.

The division of labor by sex affects both household subsistence and society as a whole. Sociologist Emile Durkheim thought that its most important result was to promote moral standards, by creating a bond within the family. Specialization of labor also increases productivity by allowing women and men to become more skilled at their particular tasks, which promotes efficient use of time and resources. It is even thought to be associated with the evolution of some emotional and intellectual skills, because our reliance on sharing requires a cooperative temperament and exceptional intelligence. For such reasons anthropologists Jane and Chet Lancaster described the sexual division of labor as the "fundamental platform of behavior for the genus *Homo*," and the "true watershed for differentiating ape from human lifeways." Whether they were right in thinking the division began with the genus *Homo* is debated. Though I agree with the Lancasters, many think the division of labor by sex started much later. But there is no doubt of its importance in making us who we are.

The classic explanation in physical anthropology for this social structure is essentially what Jean Anthelme Brillat-Savarin proposed: when meat became an important part of the human diet, it was harder for females than males to obtain. Males with a surplus would have offered some to females, who would have appreciated the gift and returned the favor by gathering plant foods to share with males. The result was an incipient household. Physical anthropologist Sherwood Washburn put it this way:

> When males hunt and females gather, the results are shared and given to the young, and the habitual sharing between a male, a female, and their offspring becomes the basis for the human family. According to this view, the human family is the result of the reciprocity of hunting, the addition of a male to the mother-plus-young social group of the monkeys and apes.

Washburn's statement captures a core feature of conventional wisdom, which is that the way to explain the evolution of the sexual division of labor is to imagine that, together, meat eating and plant eating allowed a household. An unstated assumption was that the food was raw. But if food was raw, the sexual division of labor is unworkable. Nowadays a man who has spent most of the day hunting can satisfy his hunger easily when he returns to camp, because his evening meal is cooked. But if the food waiting for him in camp had all been raw, he would have had a major problem.

The difficulty lies in the large amount of time it takes to eat raw food. Great apes allow us to estimate it. Simply because they are big—30 kilograms (66 pounds) and more—they need

a lot of food and a lot of time to chew. Chimpanzees in Gombe National Park, Tanzania, spend more than six hours a day chewing. Six hours may seem high considering that most of their food is ripe fruit: Bananas or grapefruit would slip down their throats easily, and for this reason, chimpanzees readily raid the plantations of people living near their territories. But wild fruits are not nearly as rewarding as those domesticated fruits. The edible pulp of a forest fruit is often physically hard, and it may be protected by a skin, coat, or hairs that have to be removed. Most fruits have to be chewed for a long time before the pulp can be fully detached from the pieces of skin or seeds, and before the solid pieces are mashed enough to give up their valuable nutrients. Leaves, the next most important food for chimpanzees, are also tough and likewise take a long time to chew into pieces small enough for efficient digestion. The other great apes (bonobos, gorillas, and orangutans) commit similarly long hours to chewing their food. Because the amount of time spent chewing is related to body size among primates, we can estimate how long humans would be obliged to spend chewing if we lived on the same kind of raw food that great apes do. Conservatively, it would be 42 percent of the day, or just over five hours of chewing in a twelve-hour day.

People spend much less than five hours per day chewing their foods. Brillat-Savarin claimed to have seen the vicar of Bregnier eat the following within forty-five minutes: a bowl of soup, two dishes of boiled beef, a leg of mutton, a handsome capon, a generous salad, a ninety-degree wedge from a good-sized white cheese, a bottle of wine, and a carafe of water. If Brillat-Savarin was not exaggerating, the amount of food eaten by the vicar in less than an hour would have provided enough calories for a day or more. It is hard to imagine a wild chimpanzee achieving such a feat.

A few careful studies using direct observation confirm how relatively quickly humans eat their food. In the United States, children from nine to twelve years of age spend a mere 10 percent of their time eating, or just over an hour per twelve-hour day. This is close to the daily chewing time for children recorded by anthropologists in twelve subsistence societies around the world, from the Ye'kwana of Venezuela to the Kipsigi of Kenya and the Samoans of the South Pacific. Girls ages six to fifteen chewed for an average of 8 percent of the day, with a range of 4 percent to 13 percent. Results for boys were almost identical: they chewed for an average of 7 percent of the day, again ranging from 4 percent to 13 percent.

The children's data show little difference between the industrialized United States and subsistence societies. In the twelve measured cultures, adults chewed for even less time than the children. Women and men each spent an average of 5 percent of their time chewing. One might object that the people in the subsistence societies were observed only from dawn to dusk. Since people often have a big meal after dark, the total time eating per day might be more than indicated by the 5 percent figure, which translates to only thirty-six minutes in a twelve-hour day. But even if people chewed their evening meals for an hour after dark, which is an improbably long time, the total time spent eating would still be less than 12 percent of a fourteen-hour day, allowing two hours for the evening meal. However we look at the data, humans devote between a fifth and a tenth as much time to chewing as do the great apes.

This reduction in chewing time clearly results from cooked food being softer. Processed plant foods experience similar physical changes to those of meat. As the food canning industry knows all too well, it is hard to retain a crisp, fresh texture in heated vegetables or fruits. Plant cells are normally glued together by pectic polysaccharides. These chemicals degrade when heated, causing the cells to separate and permitting teeth to divide the tissue more easily. Hot cells also lose rigidity, a result of both their walls swelling and their membranes being disrupted by denaturation of proteins. The consequences are predictable. By measuring the amount of force needed to initiate a crack in food, researchers have shown that softness (or hardness) closely predicts the number of times someone chews before swallowing. The effect works for animals too. Wild monkeys spend almost twice as long chewing per day if their food is low-quality. Observers have recorded the amount of time spent chewing by wild primates that obtain human foods (such as garbage stolen from hotels). As the proportion of human foods rises in the diet, the primates spend less time chewing, down to less than 10 percent when all of the food comes from humans.

Six hours of chewing per day for a chimpanzee mother who consumes 1,800 calories per day means that she ingests food at a rate of around 300 calories per hour of chewing. Humans comparatively bolt their food. If adults eat 2,000 to 2,500 calories a day, as many people do, the fact that they chew for only about one hour per day means that the average intake rate will average 2,000 to 2,500 calories an hour or higher, or more than six times the rate for a chimpanzee. The rate is doubtless much more when people eat high-calorie foods, such as hamburgers, candy bars, and holiday feasts. Humans have clearly had a long history of much more intense calorie consumption than primates are used to. Thanks to cooking, we save ourselves around four hours of chewing time per day.

Before our ancestors cooked, then, they had much less free time. Their options for subsistence activities would therefore have been severely constrained. Males could not afford to spend all day hunting, because if they failed to get any prey, they would have had to fill their bellies on plant foods instead, which would take a long time just to chew. Consider chimpanzees, who hunt little and whose raw-food diet can be safely assumed to be similar to the diet of australo-pithecines. At Ngogo, Uganda, chimpanzees hunt intensely compared to other chimpanzee populations, yet males still average less than three minutes per day hunting. Human hunters have lots of time and walk for hours in the search for prey. A recent review of eight hunter-gatherer societies found that men hunted for between 1.8 and 8.2 hours daily. Hadza men were close to the average, spending more than 4 hours a day hunting—about eighty times as long as an Ngogo chimpanzee.

Almost all hunts by chimpanzees follow a chance encounter during such routine activities as patrolling their territorial boundaries, suggesting that chimpanzees are unwilling to risk spending time on a hopeful search. When chimpanzees hunt

their favorite prey—red colobus monkeys—the colobus rarely move out of the tree where they are attacked. The monkeys appear to feel safer staying in one place, rather than jumping to adjacent trees where chimpanzees might ambush them. The monkeys' immobility allows chimpanzees to alternate between sitting under the prey and making repeated rushes at them. In theory, the chimpanzees could spend hours pursuing this prey. But at Ngogo the longest hunt observed was just over one hour, and the average length of hunts is only eighteen minutes. At Gombe I found that the average interval between plant-feeding bouts was twenty minutes, almost the same as the length of a hunt. The similarity between the average hunt duration and the average interval between plant-feeding bouts suggests that chimpanzees can afford a break of twenty minutes from eating fruits or leaves to hunt, but if they take much longer they risk losing valuable plant-feeding time.

The time budget for an ape eating raw food is also constrained by the rhythm of digestion, because apes have to pause between meals. Judging from data on humans, the bigger the meal, the longer it takes for the stomach to empty. It probably takes one to two hours for a chimpanzee's full stomach to empty enough to warrant feeding again. Therefore, a five-hour chewing requirement becomes an eight- or nine-hour commitment to feeding. Eat, rest, eat, rest, eat. An ancestor species that did not cook would presumably have experienced a similar rhythm.

These time constraints are inescapable for a large ape or habiline eating raw unprocessed food. Males who did not cook would not have been able to rely on hunting to feed themselves. Like chimpanzees, they could hunt in opportunistic spurts. But if they devoted many hours to hunting, the risk of failure to obtain prey could not be compensated rapidly enough. Eating their daily required calories in the form of their staple plant foods would have taken too long.

Washburn and other anthropologists have proposed that the human division of labor by sex was based on hunting. They suggest that on days when a male failed to find meat, honey, or other prizes, a female could provide food to him. As we now see, this would not have been sufficient, because a returning male who had not eaten during the day would not have had enough time left in the evening to chew his plant-food calories. The same time constraints apply whether our precooking ancestor obtained his staple plant diet by his own labor or received it from a female. A division of labor into hunting and gathering would not have afforded consumption of sufficient calories, as long as the food was consumed raw.

Suppose that a hunter living on raw food has a mate who is willing to feed him, that his mate could collect enough raw foods for him (while satisfying her own needs) and would bring them back to a central place, to be met by her grateful mate. Then suppose the male has had an unsuccessful day of hunting. Even modern hunter-gatherers armed with efficient weapons often fail. Among the Hadza there are stretches of a week or more several times per year when hunters bring no big-game meat to camp. The hungry hunter needs to consume, say, two thousand calories, but he cannot eat after dark. To do so would be too dangerous, scrabbling in the predator-filled night to feel for the nuts, leaves, or roots his gatherer friend brought him. If the hunter slept on the ground, he would be exposed to predators and large ungulates as he fumbled for his food. If he were in a tree, he would find it hard to have his raw foods with him because they do not come in tidy packages.

So to eat his fill he would have to do most of his eating before dusk, which falls between about 6 and 7 P.M. in equatorial regions. If he had eaten nothing while on the hunt, he would need to be back in camp before midday, and there he would find his mate's gathered foods (assuming she had been able to complete her food gathering so early in the day). He would then have to spend the rest of the day eating, resting, eating, resting, and eating. In short, the long hours of chewing necessitated by a raw diet would have sharply reduced hunting time. It is questionable whether the sexual division of labor would have been possible at all.

The use of fire solved the problem. It freed hunters from previous time constraints by reducing the time spent chewing. It also allowed eating after dark. The first of our ancestral line to cook their food would have gained several hours of daytime. Instead of being an opportunistic activity, hunting could have become a more dedicated pursuit with a higher potential for success. Nowadays men can hunt until nightfall and still eat a large meal in camp. After cooking began, therefore, hunting could contribute to the full development of the family household, reliant as it is on a predictable economic exchange between women and men.

Assess Your Progress

1. What is the Man-the-Hunter hypothesis?
2. How did the cooking of food allow our ancestors to restructure the working day?
3. What is the sexual division of labor and why does its evolution center on hunter-gatherers?
4. Describe the Hadza way of life with respect to traditional hunting and gathering.
5. What are two major features of the sexual division of labor represented by the Hadza?
6. In what sense is there complementarity in food sharing among humans that is not found among primates?
7. How has the division of labor by sex been thought to have affected society as a whole?
8. How has the introduction of meat eating itself been thought to generate the sexual division of labor?
9. Why does the author believe that cooking food was an essential factor in allowing for the sexual division of labor?

When Cousins Do More than Kiss

Anthony Layng

Now that same-sex marriage increasingly is becoming acceptable in the U.S., might not incestuous marriage be next? Both have been condemned by legal sanctions and religious beliefs. However, since these are subject to change, what is to prevent first cousin marriage from gaining popularity?

While visiting recently with a group of my Catholic in-laws, the subject of incest came up. Actually, no one used the term "incest" but when my brother-in-law mentioned that he once dated his first cousin, others in the room clearly were shocked. After all, it says in the Bible that sex with close relatives, even some in-laws, is abhorrent to God. This reaction encouraged me to play anthropologist by pointing out that in some societies, the most preferred marriages are between first cousins. Predictably, someone asked, "What about inbreeding?" Since most Americans probably would ask the same question, here is my professorial answer

Incest taboos in practically all societies prohibit copulation between parent and child and, with a few rare exceptions, sex between siblings is not allowed. Beyond these relationships, there is very little international agreement concerning the extent to which incest taboos should apply to relatives outside one's nuclear family and, where marriage between certain cousins is the ideal, other cousins strictly may be off-limits. For instance, among the Trobriand Islanders of the South Pacific, a man is forbidden to have sex with the daughter of his mother's sister, and yet he is encouraged to marry a daughter of his mother's brother. Both are, of course, first cousins and equally close genetic relatives.

The scope of incest taboos varies widely from one society to another. Where descent is traced strictly through males, as among the Lakher of Southeast Asia, one cannot marry anyone within his or her clan or lineage, including many distant cousins. Likewise, many mairi lineal societies, like the inhabitants of Chuuk (Truk) in the central Pacific, frequently extend incest taboos to all matrilineal relatives. That means that a man cannot even marry his mother's mother's mother's sister's daughter's daughter's daughter's daughter—a third cousin once removed. In China, traditionally, people with the same surname are discouraged from marrying even when there was no indication of common kinship. In some states in the U.S., it used to be illegal for in-laws to marry, especially for a man to marry his stepdaughter. Clearly, this did not represent any concern about inbreeding.

Another interesting variable regarding incest taboos has to do with the fact that some societies permit certain exceptions. Historically, royal siblings in Egypt, Hawaii, and Peru were expected to marry each other to produce an heir, thus preventing dilution of royal blood. The Tonga of East Africa sometimes encouraged an esteemed hunter to have sexual intercourse with his daughter prior to stalking lions.

Given the fact that many tribal societies have westernized their incest taboos as a result of Christian missionary influence, illustrating how flexible they can be, we must ask: If incest taboos are instinctual as so many believe, why do they vary so from one society to another, and why are they so subject to change over time? Yet, first we have to ask: How did incest taboos get started? The Australian Tiwi of Bathurst Island are a particularly interesting case. To them, a child was considered unrelated to his or her mother's husband. Daddy was seen as playing only a mechanical role in inducing pregnancy, making it possible for some family ancestor to complete spiritual conception. A man's children, strictly speaking, were not considered to be his offspring. Nevertheless, the mother's husband was not allowed to have sex with her daughters. If this prohibition is not based on genetic considerations, how do we explain it?

In most societies, violations of incest taboos do occur, as in our own country. For every case of father-daughter or brother-sister incest that is brought to the attention of authorities, there must be many that go unreported. After all, shame and guilt can be strong motives to remain silent. Believing that you either have been a perpetrator of sin or a victim of a sinful act, especially when the participants are immediate family members, makes most of us disinclined to go public.

Given the variability of the range of these taboos and the fact that exceptions are made in some places, the numerous illegal cases of incest involving parents, siblings, and cousins, and those societies where conception was considered to be caused by dead ancestors, it seems unlikely that humans have some sort of instinct regarding inbreeding. Also, it is not probable that genetic closeness is the major concern here. After all, the children of your father's brother and the children of your mother's brother share the same amount of common genes with you but in tribal societies, seldom are considered equally close relatives.

We all have heard the stories of European royal cousins who perpetuated a high incidence of hemophilia in their offspring. Yet, just as unfortunate genetic propensities can show up more readily when people marry close relatives, desirable propensities can be encouraged in the same way. Understandably, given the emotionally charged nature of this subject we have had little opportunity to learn much about the biological consequences of incest. It is interesting to note that among chimpanzees, our closest living nonhuman relatives, mother-son copulation has been observed, although the mothers usually protest.

In this country, we are encouraged to focus on assumed deleterious genetic abnormalities, believing that it is this concern that initially gave rise to incest taboos and the laws enacted to prohibit inbreeding. However, it seems quite possible that American incest taboos essentially are a case of retaining ancient tribal beliefs.

Let us consider a nonbiological explanation for how incest taboos got started. Unlike what it says in the Bible about our earliest ancestors being farmers, they actually lived in small, vulnerable hunter-gatherer bands that needed to form alliances with others to ensure their survival. To the extent that marriage between siblings and some close cousins was discouraged, many of the young men would have to seek mates from outside their band. Incest taboos would have served them well in this regard, encouraging kinship ties among bands. This greatly facilitated cooperation and exchanges of food and information regarding where and how to hunt and gather. In regions where food scarcity was severe from time to time, bands that maintained incest taboos had an advantage because of the cooperation fostered by kinship affiliation with other bands. Members could call on kin in other bands who were likely to share whatever food they had.

Where incest was not prohibited, there were fewer kin ties among bands, so assistance and practical knowledge from others would be less available. Survival was more hazardous under these circumstances because starvation was more likely. Such bands produced fewer children who reached adulthood and reproduced, giving rise, over thousands of years, to incest taboos becoming a cultural universal.

In this age of computers and a global economy, what utility do moral restrictions on sex with close relatives have now? Perhaps we hold on to incest taboos today not merely because of Bible lore or the fact that we favor some degree of eugenics, but because they still benefit us socially. After all, in spite of the prevalence of in-law jokes, having an extensive network of relatives continues to be quite useful when we need a favor, such as help in acquiring a job or a stock tip. Given the importance of such benefits, it is not unsuitable that we continue to act as if incest is harmful biologically to our society. If the only reason we had in mind for avoiding sex with first cousins and siblings was sociological, it is unlikely that most of us would consider that such avoidance was absolutely imperative. At the very least, we would be more inclined to question such restrictions, and copulation and even marriage of close relatives would be far more common than it is now, resulting in less extensive kinship networks. On the other hand, the assumed genetic role played by incest perpetuates the belief that incest is forbidden by God and, therefore, sinful. Such thinking is very helpful in ensuring that we keep the benefits of having in-laws that can expand the number of persons we can look to for assistance.

Since incest taboos are so ancient and continue today very much as they did in the past having near unanimity regarding their moral necessity, it seems safe to assume that they still serve some practical need. As in our tribal past, incest taboos may have far more to do with maintaining a pragmatic and orderly society than with presumed deleterious effects on our genes.

Assess Your Progress

1. What evidence is there that the incest taboos vary widely from one society to another?

2. What examples are there that some societies even provide exceptions to their own incest taboos?

3. Why does it seem unlikely that humans have an instinct regarding inbreeding? Why does genetic closeness not seem to be a concern?

4. What social benefits derive from the incest taboo?

5. Why is it still important that humans think that there would be dangerous biological consequences of incest?

ANTHONY LAYNG is professor emeritus of anthropology at Elmira (N. Y.) College.

Meet the Alloparents

Sarah Blaffer Hrdy

We cram our bodies into the plane's narrow seats, elbow-to-elbow, making eye contact with nods and resigned smiles as we yield to latecomers pushing past. Most ignore the crying baby, or pretend to. A few of us even signal the mother with a sideways nod and a wry smile. We want her to know that we know how she feels, and that the disturbance she thinks her baby is causing is not nearly as annoying as she imagines—even though we can tell (as can she) that the young man beside her, eyes determinedly glued to the screen of his laptop, does indeed mind every bit as much as she fears.

Thus does every frequent flier employ our species' peculiarly empathetic aptitude for intuiting the mental states and intentions of other people. Cognitive scientists and philosophers have long called this awareness of others' inner life "theory of mind," but many psychologists now refer to it as "intersubjectivity," a broader concept that roots our sophisticated skill at mind reading in the capacity to share in the emotional states and experiences of others. Whatever we call it, this ability to divine and care about the mental experiences of others makes humans more adept at cooperating than other apes are.

Imagine what would happen if one were traveling with a plane load of chimpanzees. We would be lucky to disembark with all our fingers, testicles, and toes attached, and with the baby still breathing and unmaimed. But human passengers fill some 2 billion airline seats every year and submit to being compressed and manhandled, with no dismemberments reported yet! Along with our 1,350-cubic-centimeter brains and capacity for language, such unusually well-developed impulses to cooperate have helped propel our success as a species. But why did humans become such "other-regarding" apes?

Although the genus Homo arose before the beginning of the Pleistocene epoch (1.8 million to 12,000 years ago), H. sapiens—anatomically modern humans with upright bodies and big brains—evolved only within the last 200,000 years. And behaviorally modern humans, capable of symbolic thought and language, emerged more recently still, within the last 80,000 years. Most evolutionists have assumed that our unusually sophisticated capacities for attributing mental states and feelings to others coincided with those late-Pleistocene behavioral transformations, and corresponded with the need for members of one group to get along so as to outcompete and defend themselves against other groups.

But there are difficulties with that scenario. There is abundant archaeological evidence for early warfare, but none dates back much before 12,000 years ago, when people began to settle down and live in more complex societies with property to protect. Moreover, genetic evidence suggests that our foraging ancestors in the Pleistocene lived at low densities. Although individuals no doubt fought and sometimes killed one another, there is no evidence that whole groups fought. More to the point, if the drive to outcompete members of opposing groups was the source of our hypersocial tendencies, why didn't selection favor even greater and more Machiavellian intelligence, better mind reading, and better capacities to cooperate against hostile neighbors among the ancestors of today's chimpanzees? Chimpanzees are competitive, dominance-oriented, aggressive, and reflexively xenophobic: wouldn't they have benefited just as much, or more, from being able to cooperate to wipe out competing groups?

Consider, however, an alternative explanation, the possibility that our empathetic impulses grew out of the peculiar way that children in the genus Homo were reared. I believe that at an early stage in human evolution, our bipedal ape ancestors were increasingly cared for and provisioned not just by parents but also by other group members, known as alloparents.

In my view, cooperative breeding (as sociobiologists term the reproductive strategy in which alloparents help both care for and provision young) came before big brains. I believe it first emerged among upright apes that were only beginning to look like us, and further evolved during the Pleistocene in African H. erectus (also called H. ergaster)—creatures that did not think or use language to communicate the way we do. Alloparental care and provisioning set the stage for children to grow up slowly and remain dependent on others for many years, paving the way for the evolution of anatomically modern people with even bigger brains. It was not the other way around: bigger brains required care more than caring required big brains.

Comparisons across cooperatively breeding species show how nonessential a sapient mentality is for shared care, and provide our best hope for understanding what selection pressures induce individuals to help rear someone else's young. Insights from such comparisons help explain why mothers among highly social apes living in Africa about 1.8 million years ago might have begun to abandon mother-only care, setting our ancestors on the road to emotional modernity.

Although at first caring for and provisioning someone else's offspring seems to defy evolutionary logic, cooperative breeding has evolved many times in a taxonomically diverse array of arthropod, avian, and mammalian species. It occurs in 9 percent of the 10,000 living species of birds and in perhaps 3 percent of mammals. The advantages for parents are well documented, with significant demographic consequences.

Mothers able to confidently entrust helpless offspring to groupmates' care conserve energy, stay better nourished, and remain safer from predators and other hazards, leading longer lives with greater reproductive success. Because mammal mothers that have aid also wean babies sooner, many reproduce again sooner, and so give birth to a greater number of young over their lifetimes. More important, the extra help ensures the young have a better chance of survival. Certain species therefore spread successfully thanks to cooperative breeding and, with it, a faster pace of reproduction and the flexibility permitting young to survive in a wide range of habitats.

But how could natural selection ever favor caring for someone else's young? Why would young magpie jays in Costa Rica, ones that have never reproduced, bring back beakful after beakful of food to begging fledglings? Those allomothers often provide more food than the chicks' own parents do. Ornithologists J. David Ligon of the University of New Mexico and D. Brent Burt of Stephen F. Austin State University in Texas propose a two-step process for such development. Start with a species with particularly helpless, slow-maturing young, in which selection will favor high sensitivity to the cues emitted by needy babies as a parental trait. Then add some special benefit that encourages maturing individuals to linger in their natal place, such as defensible and heritable resources. As a result, group members will be exposed to sensory cues from chicks (or pups) and will be primed to respond. This "misplaced parental care" hypothesis helps explain why cooperative breeding is three times more likely to evolve in taxa that produce altricial (helpless) young rather than precocial young (those that are soon able to survive on their own).

Not all such caretaking is as self-sacrificing as it may appear. Often, alloparents only babysit when no more self-serving option is available. They may proffer food only when they do not actually need it themselves. They may volunteer only when they have energy to spare, or when they are still too young or lack the opportunity to reproduce themselves. Or if two cohabiting mothers are reproducing, as occurs among lions, ruffed lemurs, bush babies, and some mice, they may take turns as alloparents. One mother may suckle the other's offspring while the other mother is "at work" foraging. And where practice is critical for learning how to parent, as is the case for many primates, babysitters derive valuable experience by first caring for another's young.

In other cases, however, helping is more of a one-way street—and by no means entirely voluntary. Subordinate meerkat, wild dog, and wolf females that have never conceived (and may never do so) sometimes undergo a "pseudopregnancy," developing a swollen belly and mammary glands. Then, once the alpha female's pups are born, the nonmothers secrete milk for the alpha's pups. By becoming a wet-nurse, a subordinate may increase her chances of being tolerated in the group. Had she given birth herself, her young might have been killed by the alpha female.

Of course, it makes good evolutionary sense for individuals to enhance the reproductive success of relatives with whom they share genes. But helpers are not always kin, and even kin can be less than kind: some meerkat and marmoset alphas eliminate their own daughters' offspring—the grandmothers from hell.

In roughly half the 300-odd species of living primates, including all four great apes and many of the best-known species of Old World monkeys, such as rhesus macaques and savanna baboons, mothers alone care for their infants. A chimpanzee, gorilla, or orangutan mother will be literally "in touch" with her infant for almost every moment during its first six months of life, and the orangutan nurses her baby for up to seven years. Such continuous maternal care cannot be attributed to lack of interest from would-be babysitters, however. In all primates, babies are a source of attraction, most often to subadult females. The mother's possessiveness is the determining factor. A wild ape mother is adamant that others will not hold or carry her baby.

Elsewhere in the primate order, mothers are more tolerant of allomaternal overtures. Shared care with at least minimal provisioning (often no more than one female allowing another female's infant to briefly nurse) is found in some 20 percent of primate genera. But only among marmosets and tamarins, members of the family Callitrichidae, do we find shared infant care combined with extensive alloparental provisioning, such as we also see in humans. In that respect, those tiny-brained South American monkeys, which last shared a common ancestor with humans more than 35 million years ago, may provide more insights into the early evolution of human family life than do more closely related species such as chimpanzees.

Marmoset and tamarin mothers tend to produce twins (together weighing up to 20 percent of the mother's body weight) as often as twice a year. But the social arrangements lighten the load. Usually, only the group's most dominant female breeds, although groups with two breeding females sometimes occur. Fathers and alloparents of both sexes are unusually eager to help mothers rear their young. Babies are carried throughout most of the day by one or more adult males, which expend so much energy doing so that they actually lose weight. Other helpers, typically but not exclusively kin, voluntarily deliver even prized animal prey to youngsters.

Group members are also unusually tolerant of one another during foraging. Observing moustached tamarins in the wild, University of Illinois primatologist Paul A. Garber recorded only one aggressive act for every fifty-two cooperative ones he saw, such as collaborating to gnaw open hard fruits. When tested in the lab, cotton-top tamarins studied by psychologist Marc D. Hauser's team at Harvard, and marmosets studied by evolutionary anthropologists Judith M. Burkart and Carel P. van Schaik at the University of Zurich, turn out to be unusually attentive to the needs of others. They are far more willing to deliver food to individuals (including nonrelatives) in an adjacent cage than are chimpanzees in comparable experiments. Marmosets go out of their way to provide food to others, and tamarins even keep track of and reciprocate generosity. Burkart argues that the combined mutual tolerance and spontaneous generosity of cooperative breeders are conducive to social learning, in particular to the ability of youngsters to glean information from and about their caretakers.

In every human hunting-and-gathering society about which we have information, mothers allow others to hold newborns. But how could selfish apes ever make the transition from mother-only care to such cooperative breeding? At some point in the emergence of the genus Homo, mothers must have become more relaxed about handing even quite young infants over to others to temporarily hold and carry. No infant is more costly than a human one, and a growing body of evidence from traditional societies makes clear that wherever rates of child mortality were high, children with alloparental provisioning were more likely to survive. I believe that was the case among our ancestors in the Pleistocene.

Among ethnographically recorded hunter-gatherers, provisioning by allomothers starts early and goes on for years, beginning with "kiss-feeding" of un-weaned infants with saliva sweetened by honey or with premasticated mouthfuls of other food. That encourages infants to pay attention to others, including their own mothers, with whom they are eager to maintain visual and vocal contact. An infant temporarily out of its mother's arms will spend more time monitoring her whereabouts and looking at her face. Youngsters also have a big incentive to learn who else might be available and willing to care, and children with several trusted attachment figures learn to integrate multiple perspectives. In the words of pioneering child psychologists Ted Ruffman of the University of Otago and Josef Perner of the University of Salzberg, "theory of mind is contagious"—you catch it from older siblings and other caretakers.

Among our Pleistocene ancestors, infants with multiple caretakers would have been challenged in ways that no ape had ever been before. The needy youngster would have had to decipher not only its mother's commitment but also the moods and intentions of others who might be seduced into helping. How best to attract care in varied circumstances? Through crying? With smiles, funny faces, gurgling, or babbling? The youngster best at mind reading would be best cared for and best fed. Such novel (for an ape) selection pressures favored a very different type of ape—one that we might call emotionally modern.

Almost all primates live in social groups, and it is generally advantageous for a mother to be in a group that includes close kin. Their help is especially critical when an inexperienced young female first gives birth. In most social mammals, and in the majority of monkeys, females remain with the group where they are born, and maturing males strike out to make their fortunes. But among our nearest living relatives, the great apes, only a tiny minority of new mother apes ever have matrilineal kin nearby. Evolutionary biologists have taken for granted that, like other apes, our female ancestors must have left their natal groups to breed in another community. There they would have encountered unrelated females, possibly competing mothers, who might be not only unsupportive but actually infanticidal.

Until recently, in fact, evolutionary biologists assumed hunter-gatherers followed a similar pattern of female dispersal. But in 2004, in an exhaustive review of ethnographic studies, University of Utah anthropologist Helen Alvarez concluded that mothers living in hunting-and-gathering groups were likely to have their mothers and other kin nearby when they gave birth.

For example, Stanford University anthropologists Brooke A. Scelza and Rebecca Bliege Bird found that among the traditionally polygamous Mardu hunter-gatherers of Australia's Western Desert, older mothers would relocate to be near daughters of childbearing age, especially if the daughter lacked an older cowife to advise and help her. Mothers were also eager to join a daughter if she was married to the same man as her sister. In consequence, half of married Mardu women between the ages of fourteen and forty had a mother in the same group, while many had sisters or cousins as well, often as cowives. On average, female group members had an 11 percent chance of sharing a gene by common descent—just as do females of some of the nonhuman primate species that practice infant-sharing.

Something happened in the line leading to H. sapiens that encouraged female relatives to stick together. The impetus, I believe, had to do with food.

By 1.8 million years ago H. erectus had new ways of finding, processing, and digesting food needed to support both larger bodies and energetically more expensive, larger brains. The most plausible scenario, set forth by anthropologists James F. O'Connell and Kristen Hawkes of the University of Utah, is that long-term trends toward a cooler, drier climate leading up to the Pleistocene pressured the precursors of H. erectus to supplement a diet that had consisted mostly of fruit and occasionally meat. Game was increasingly important, but its availability unpredictable. A division of labor emerged between male hunters and female gatherers, and social bonds ensuring that men and women shared became increasingly essential.

O'Connell and others suggest that when other foods were scarce, our ancestors relied on the large underground tubers that plants in dry areas use to stockpile carbohydrates. Those storage organs occur throughout the savanna, but are protected by a deep layer of sunbaked earth. Savanna-dwelling baboons dig up rhizomes and undergound stems called corms, both found nearer the surface, and at least one unusual population of savanna-dwelling chimpanzees is known to use sticks to dig out the shallower tubers, suggesting that early bipedal apes may have done so as well. But it takes special knowledge and equipment to dig out the deeply situated larger tubers.

Tubers are not only hard to extract, they are fibrous and difficult to digest, hardly ideal food for children. Like nuts, they need skilled processing. To eat them, weaned juveniles would have to depend on capable providers. Nevertheless, evidence is increasing that starchy tubers were an important fallback food for African hunter-gatherers. A 2007 report in *Nature Genetics* revealed that people like the Hadza of Tanzania, who rely on roots and tubers, have accumulated extra copies of a gene that makes an enzyme useful in the digestion of starch, salivary amylase. While we can't test the saliva or sequence the genes of African H. erectus, isotopic analysis of their tooth enamel yields results consistent with a diet substantially reliant on underground roots. Once H. erectus developed the use of fire, perhaps as early as 800,000 years ago, roasting tough, fibrous tubers would have rendered them more digestible, and more useful still.

Even before cooking, the addition of tubers to nuts and other plant foods gathered and processed by women would have provided new incentives for food sharing between hunters and gatherers, as well as new opportunities for postreproductive women motivated to share. In their "grandmother hypothesis," Hawkes and O'Connell propose that Darwinian selection would have favored experienced, hardworking women who live on for decades after menopause, not just for a few more years, as in other primates. Such women could help provision younger kin, without the distraction of infants of their own.

Across traditional societies, where it is not unusual for 40 percent or more of individuals to die prior to maturity, mortality rates depend a lot on family composition. Not surprisingly, presence of the mother matters' most. The father's impact varies from being vitally important to having no detectable impact, depending on local conditions and who else is around to help. When it comes to alloparents, older siblings and grandmothers, especially maternal grandmothers, have the most reliably beneficial impact. Under some circumstances, their presence cuts the chance of dying during childhood in half.

In purely practical terms, we can envision a sequence that begins with hunters and gatherers sharing the fruits (and tubers) of foraging and then moving toward cooperative breeding. That would have allowed our Pleistocene ancestors to produce young that depended on many caretakers, for a long time. No ape produces such big babies that mature so slowly, yet not only did our ancestors manage to survive, but our species eventually expanded beyond Africa and around the globe.

In terms of cognition and emotions, the transformations wrought by shared care and provisioning were even more profound. Our bipedal ape ancestors were surely as clever and manipulative as are living chimpanzees, able to manufacture and use tools; they must have been at least as empathetic in some circumstances, and endowed with a rudimentary theory of mind. But when they adopted what was, for an ape, a novel mode of rearing young, one that produced individuals more mutually tolerant and other-regarding than other apes, they laid the foundations for ever higher levels of empathy and cooperation. In such modest beginnings we can identify the groundwork for spectacular later developments.

Assess Your Progress

1. What is it that makes humans more adept at cooperating than apes are?
2. What difficulties does the author see with the notion that our ancestors cooperated so as to out-compete and defend themselves against other groups?
3. What alternative explanation does the author provide for our empathic impulses?
4. What is the relationship between caring for children and big brains?
5. What are some of the advantages of cooperative breeding?
6. In what context does "misplaced parental care" occur?
7. Are alloparents always self-sacrificing? Explain.
8. What happened in the human line of evolution that encouraged female relatives to stick together?

SARAH BLAFFER HRDY, an anthropologist and mother, is a professor emerita at the University of California, Davis. Her book *The Woman That Never Evolved* (1981) was selected by the *New York Times* as one of the Notable Books of that year, and *Mother Nature* was chosen by both *Publishers Weekly* and *Library Journal* as one of the best books of 1999. Hrdy is a frequent contributor to *Natural History;* "Meet the Alloparents" is her ninth article for the magazine.

The Inuit Paradox

How can people who gorge on fat and rarely see a vegetable be healthier than we are?

Patricia Gadsby

Patricia Cochran, an Inupiat from Northwestern Alaska, is talking about the native foods of her childhood: "We pretty much had a subsistence way of life. Our food supply was right outside our front door. We did our hunting and foraging on the Seward Peninsula and along the Bering Sea."

"Our meat was seal and walrus, marine mammals that live in cold water and have lots of fat. We used seal oil for our cooking and as a dipping sauce for food. We had moose, caribou, and reindeer. We hunted ducks, geese, and little land birds like quail, called ptarmigan. We caught crab and lots of fish—salmon, whitefish, tomcod, pike, and char. Our fish were cooked, dried, smoked, or frozen. We ate frozen raw whitefish, sliced thin. The elders liked stinkfish, fish buried in seal bags or cans in the tundra and left to ferment. And fermented seal flipper, they liked that too."

Cochran's family also received shipments of whale meat from kin living farther north, near Barrow. Beluga was one she liked; raw muktuk, which is whale skin with its underlying blubber, she definitely did not. "To me it has a chew-on-a-tire consistency," she says, "but to many people it's a mainstay." In the short subarctic summers, the family searched for roots and greens and, best of all from a child's point of view, wild blueberries, crowberries, or salmonberries, which her aunts would mix with whipped fat to make a special treat called *akutuq*—in colloquial English, Eskimo ice cream.

Now Cochran directs the Alaska Native Science Commission, which promotes research on native cultures and the health and environmental issues that affect them. She sits at her keyboard in Anchorage, a bustling city offering fare from Taco Bell to French cuisine. But at home Cochran keeps a freezer filled with fish, seal, walrus, reindeer, and whale meat, sent by her family up north, and she and her husband fish and go berry picking—"sometimes a challenge in Anchorage," she adds, laughing. "I eat fifty-fifty," she explains, half traditional, half regular American.

No one, not even residents of the northernmost villages on Earth, eats an entirely traditional northern diet anymore. Even the groups we came to know as Eskimo—which include the Inupiat and the Yupiks of Alaska, the Canadian Inuit and Inuvialuit, Inuit Greenlanders, and the Siberian Yupiks—have probably seen more changes in their diet in a lifetime than their ancestors did over thousands of years. The closer people live to towns and the more access they have to stores and cash-paying jobs, the more likely they are to have westernized their eating. And with westernization, at least on the North American continent, comes processed foods and cheap carbohydrates—Crisco, Tang, soda, cookies, chips, pizza, fries. "The young and urbanized," says Harriet Kuhnlein, director of the Centre for Indigenous Peoples' Nutrition and Environment at McGill University in Montreal, "are increasingly into fast food." So much so that type 2 diabetes, obesity, and other diseases of Western civilization are becoming causes for concern there too.

Today, when diet books top the best-seller list and nobody seems sure of what to eat to stay healthy, it's surprising to learn how well the Eskimo did on a high-protein, high-fat diet. Shaped by glacial temperatures, stark landscapes, and protracted winters, the traditional Eskimo diet had little in the way of plant food, no agricultural or dairy products, and was unusually low in carbohydrates. Mostly people subsisted on what they hunted and fished. Inland dwellers took advantage of caribou feeding on tundra mosses, lichens, and plants too tough for humans to stomach (though predigested vegetation in the animals' paunches became dinner as well). Coastal people exploited the sea. The main nutritional challenge was avoiding starvation in late winter if primary meat sources became too scarce or lean.

These foods hardly make up the "balanced" diet most of us grew up with, and they look nothing like the mix of grains, fruits, vegetables, meat, eggs, and dairy we're accustomed to seeing in conventional food pyramid diagrams. How could such a diet possibly be adequate? How did people get along on little else but fat and animal protein?

The diet of the Far North shows that there are no essential foods—only essential nutrients.

What the diet of the Far North illustrates, says Harold Draper, a biochemist and expert in Eskimo nutrition, is that there are no essential foods—only essential nutrients. And humans can get those nutrients from diverse and eye-opening sources.

One might, for instance, imagine gross vitamin deficiencies arising from a diet with scarcely any fruits and vegetables. What furnishes vitamin A, vital for eyes and bones? We derive much of ours from colorful plant foods, constructing it from pigmented plant precursors called carotenoids (as in carrots). But vitamin A, which is oil soluble, is also plentiful in the oils of cold-water fishes and sea mammals, as well as in the animals' livers, where fat is processed. These dietary staples also provide vitamin D, another oil-soluble vitamin needed for bones. Those of us living in temperate and tropical climates, on the other hand, usually make vitamin D indirectly by exposing skin to strong sun—hardly an option in the Arctic winter—and by consuming fortified cow's milk, to which the indigenous northern groups had little access until recent decades and often don't tolerate all that well.

As for vitamin C, the source in the Eskimo diet was long a mystery. Most animals can synthesize their own vitamin C, or ascorbic acid, in their livers, but humans are among the exceptions, along with other primates and oddballs like guinea pigs and bats. If we don't ingest enough of it, we fall apart from scurvy, a gruesome connective-tissue disease. In the United States today we can get ample supplies from orange juice, citrus fruits, and fresh vegetables. But vitamin C oxidizes with time; getting enough from a ship's provisions was tricky for early 18th- and 19th-century voyagers to the polar regions. Scurvy—joint pain, rotting gums, leaky blood vessels, physical and mental degeneration—plagued European and U.S. expeditions even in the 20th century. However, Arctic peoples living on fresh fish and meat were free of the disease.

Impressed, the explorer Vilhjalmur Stefansson adopted an Eskimo-style diet for five years during the two Arctic expeditions he led between 1908 and 1918. "The thing to do is to find your antiscorbutics where you are," he wrote. "Pick them up as you go." In 1928, to convince skeptics, he and a young colleague spent a year on an Americanized version of the diet under medical supervision at Bellevue Hospital in New York City. The pair ate steaks, chops, organ meats like brain and liver, poultry, fish, and fat with gusto. "If you have some fresh meat in your diet every day and don't overcook it," Stefansson declared triumphantly, "there will be enough C from that source alone to prevent scurvy."

In fact, all it takes to ward off scurvy is a daily dose of 10 milligrams, says Karen Fediuk, a consulting dietitian and former graduate student of Harriet Kuhnlein's who did her master's thesis on vitamin C. (That's far less than the U.S. recommended daily allowance of 75 to 90 milligrams—75 for women, 90 for men.) Native foods easily supply those 10 milligrams of scurvy prevention, especially when organ meats—preferably raw—are on the menu. For a study published with Kuhnlein in 2002, Fediuk compared the vitamin C content of 100-gram (3.55-ounce) samples of foods eaten by Inuit women living in the Canadian Arctic: Raw caribou liver supplied almost 24 milligrams, seal brain close to 15 milligrams, and raw kelp more than 28 milligrams. Still higher levels were found in whale skin and muktuk.

As you might guess from its antiscorbutic role, vitamin C is crucial for the synthesis of connective tissue, including the matrix of skin. "Wherever collagen's made, you can expect vitamin C," says Kuhnlein. Thick skinned, chewy, and collagen rich, raw muktuk can serve up an impressive 36 milligrams in a 100-gram piece, according to Fediuk's analyses. "Weight for weight, it's as good as orange juice," she says. Traditional Inuit practices like freezing meat and fish and frequently eating them raw, she notes, conserve vitamin C, which is easily cooked off and lost in food processing.

Hunter-gatherer diets like those eaten by these northern groups and other traditional diets based on nomadic herding or subsistence farming are among the older approaches to human eating. Some of these eating plans might seem strange to us—diets centered around milk, meat, and blood among the East African pastoralists, enthusiastic tuber eating by the Quechua living in the High Andes, the staple use of the mongongo nut in the southern African !Kung—but all proved resourceful adaptations to particular eco-niches. No people, though, may have been forced to push the nutritional envelope further than those living at Earth's frozen extremes. The unusual makeup of the far-northern diet led Loren Cordain, a professor of evolutionary nutrition at Colorado State University at Fort Collins, to make an intriguing observation.

Four years ago, Cordain reviewed the macronutrient content (protein, carbohydrates, fat) in the diets of 229 hunter-gatherer groups listed in a series of journal articles collectively known as the Ethnographic Atlas. These are some of the oldest surviving human diets. In general, hunter-gatherers tend to eat more animal protein than we do in our standard Western diet, with its reliance on agriculture and carbohydrates derived from grains and starchy plants. Lowest of all in carbohydrate, and highest in combined fat and protein, are the diets of peoples living in the Far North, where they make up for fewer plant foods with extra fish. What's equally striking, though, says Cordain, is that these meat-and-fish diets also exhibit a natural "protein ceiling." Protein accounts for no more than 35 to 40 percent of their total calories, which suggests to him that's all the protein humans can comfortably handle.

Wild-animal fats are different from other fats. Farm animals typically have lots of highly saturated fat.

This ceiling, Cordain thinks, could be imposed by the way we process protein for energy. The simplest, fastest way to make energy is to convert carbohydrates into glucose, our body's primary fuel. But if the body is out of carbs, it can burn fat, or if necessary, break down protein. The name given to the convoluted business of making glucose from protein is gluconeogenesis. It takes place in the liver, uses a dizzying slew of enzymes, and creates nitrogen waste that has to be converted into urea and disposed of through the kidneys. On a truly traditional diet, says Draper, recalling his studies in the 1970s, Arctic people had plenty of protein but little carbohydrate, so they often relied on gluconeogenesis. Not only did they have bigger livers to handle the additional work but their urine volumes were also typically larger to get rid of the extra urea. Nonetheless, there appears to be a limit on how much protein the human liver can safely cope with: Too much overwhelms the liver's waste-disposal system, leading to protein poisoning—nausea, diarrhea, wasting, and death.

Whatever the metabolic reason for this syndrome, says John Speth, an archaeologist at the University of Michigan's Museum of Anthropology, plenty of evidence shows that hunters through the ages avoided protein excesses, discarding fat-depleted animals even when food was scarce. Early pioneers and trappers in North America encountered what looks like a similar affliction, sometimes referred to as rabbit starvation because rabbit meat is notoriously lean. Forced to subsist on fat-deficient meat, the men would gorge themselves, yet wither away. Protein can't be the sole source of energy for humans, concludes Cordain. Anyone eating a meaty diet that is low in carbohydrates must have fat as well.

Stefansson had arrived at this conclusion, too, while living among the Copper Eskimo. He recalled how he and his Eskimo companions had become quite ill after weeks of eating "caribou so skinny that there was no appreciable fat behind the eyes or in the marrow." Later he agreed to repeat the miserable experience at Bellevue Hospital, for science's sake, and for a while ate nothing but defatted meat. "The symptoms brought on at Bellevue by an incomplete meat diet [lean without fat] were exactly the same as in the Arctic . . . diarrhea and a feeling of general baffling discomfort," he wrote. He was restored with a fat fix but "had lost considerable weight." For the remainder of his year on meat, Stefansson tucked into his rations of chops and steaks with fat intact. "A normal meat diet is not a high-protein diet," he pronounced. "We were really getting three-quarters of our calories from fat." (Fat is more than twice as calorie dense as protein or carbohydrate, but even so, that's a lot of lard. A typical U.S diet provides about 35 percent of its calories from fat.)

Stefansson dropped 10 pounds on his meat-and-fat regimen and remarked on its "slenderizing" aspect, so perhaps it's no surprise he's been co-opted as a posthumous poster boy for Atkins-type diets. No discussion about diet these days can avoid Atkins. Even some researchers interviewed for this article couldn't resist referring to the Inuit way of eating as the "original Atkins." "Superficially, at a macronutrient level, the two diets certainly look similar," allows Samuel Klein, a nutrition researcher at Washington University in St. Louis, who's attempting to study how Atkins stacks up against conventional weight-loss diets. Like the Inuit diet, Atkins is low in carbohydrates and very high in fat. But numerous researchers, including Klein, point out that there are profound differences between the two diets, beginning with the type of meat and fat eaten.

Fats have been demonized in the United States, says Eric Dewailly, a professor of preventive medicine at Laval University in Quebec. But all fats are not created equal. This lies at the heart of a paradox—the Inuit paradox, if you

will. In the Nunavik villages in northern Quebec, adults over 40 get almost half their calories from native foods, says Dewailly, and they don't die of heart attacks at nearly the same rates as other Canadians or Americans. Their cardiac death rate is about half of ours, he says. As someone who looks for links between diet and cardiovascular health, he's intrigued by that reduced risk. Because the traditional Inuit diet is "so restricted," he says, it's easier to study than the famously heart-healthy Mediterranean diet, with its cornucopia of vegetables, fruits, grains, herbs, spices, olive oil, and red wine.

A key difference in the typical Nunavik Inuit's diet is that more than 50 percent of the calories in Inuit native foods come from fats. Much more important, the fats come from wild animals.

Wild-animal fats are different from both farm-animal fats and processed fats, says Dewailly. Farm animals, cooped up and stuffed with agricultural grains (carbohydrates) typically have lots of solid, highly saturated fat. Much of our processed food is also riddled with solid fats, or so-called trans fats, such as the reengineered vegetable oils and shortenings cached in baked goods and snacks. "A lot of the packaged food on supermarket shelves contains them. So do commercial french fries," Dewailly adds.

Trans fats are polyunsaturated vegetable oils tricked up to make them more solid at room temperature. Manufacturers do this by hydrogenating the oils—adding extra hydrogen atoms to their molecular structures—which "twists" their shapes. Dewailly makes twisting sound less like a chemical transformation than a perversion, an act of public-health sabotage: "These man-made fats are dangerous, even worse for the heart than saturated fats." They not only lower high-density lipoprotein cholesterol (HDL, the "good" cholesterol) but they also raise low-density lipoprotein cholesterol (LDL, the "bad" cholesterol) and triglycerides, he says. In the process, trans fats set the stage for heart attacks because they lead to the increase of fatty buildup in artery walls.

Wild animals that range freely and eat what nature intended, says Dewailly, have fat that is far more healthful. Less of their fat is saturated, and more of it is in the monounsaturated form (like olive oil). What's more, cold-water fishes and sea mammals are particularly rich in polyunsaturated fats called n-3 fatty acids or omega-3 fatty acids. These fats appear to benefit the heart and vascular system. But the polyunsaturated fats in most Americans' diets are the omega-6 fatty acids supplied by vegetable oils. By contrast, whale blubber consists of 70 percent monounsaturated fat and close to 30 percent omega-3s, says Dewailly.

Dieting is the price we pay for too little exercise and too much mass-produced food.

Omega-3s evidently help raise HDL cholesterol, lower triglycerides, and are known for anticlotting effects. (Ethnographers have remarked on an Eskimo propensity for nosebleeds.) These fatty acids are believed to protect the heart from life-threatening arrhythmias that can lead to sudden cardiac death. And like a "natural aspirin," adds Dewailly, omega-3 polyunsaturated fats help put a damper on runaway inflammatory processes, which play a part in atherosclerosis, arthritis, diabetes, and other so-called diseases of civilization.

You can be sure, however, that Atkins devotees aren't routinely eating seal and whale blubber. Besides the acquired taste problem, their commerce is extremely restricted in the United States by the Marine Mammal Protection Act, says Bruce Holub, a nutritional biochemist in the department of human biology and nutritional sciences at the University of Guelph in Ontario.

"In heartland America it's probable they're not eating in an Eskimo-like way," says Gary Foster, clinical director of the Weight and Eating Disorders Program at the Pennsylvania School of Medicine. Foster, who describes himself as open-minded about Atkins, says he'd nonetheless worry if people saw the diet as a green light to eat all the butter and bacon—saturated fats—they want. Just before rumors surfaced that Robert Atkins had heart and weight problems when he died, Atkins officials themselves were stressing saturated fat should account for no more than 20 percent of dieters' calories. This seems to be a clear retreat from the diet's original don't-count-the-calories approach to bacon and butter and its happy exhortations to "plow into those prime ribs." Furthermore, 20 percent of calories from saturated fats is *double* what most nutritionists advise. Before plowing into those prime ribs, readers of a recent edition of the *Dr. Atkins' New Diet Revolution* are urged to take omega-3 pills to help protect their hearts. "If you watch carefully," says Holub wryly, "you'll see many popular U.S. diets have quietly added omega-3 pills, in the form of fish oil or flaxseed capsules, as supplements."

Needless to say, the subsistence diets of the Far North are not "dieting." Dieting is the price we pay for too little exercise and too much mass-produced food. Northern diets were a way of life in places too cold for agriculture, where food, whether hunted, fished, or foraged, could not be taken for granted. They were about keeping weight on.

This is not to say that people in the Far North were fat: Subsistence living requires exercise—hard physical work. Indeed, among the good reasons for native people to maintain their old way of eating, as far as it's possible today, is that it provides a hedge against obesity, type 2 diabetes, and heart disease. Unfortunately, no place on Earth is immune to the spreading taint of growth and development. The very well-being of the northern food chain is coming under threat from global warming, land development, and industrial pollutants in the marine environment. "I'm a pragmatist," says Cochran, whose organization is involved in pollution monitoring and disseminating food-safety information to native villages. "Global warming we don't have control over. But we can, for example, do cleanups of military sites in Alaska or of communication cables leaching lead into fish-spawning areas. We can help communities make informed food choices. A young woman of childbearing age may choose not to eat certain organ meats that concentrate contaminants. As individuals, we do have options. And eating our salmon and our seal is still a heck of a better option than pulling something processed that's full of additives off a store shelf."

Not often in our industrial society do we hear someone speak so familiarly about "our" food animals. We don't talk of "our pig" and "our beef." We've lost that creature feeling, that sense of kinship with food sources. "You're taught to think in boxes," says Cochran. "In our culture the connectivity between humans, animals, plants, the land they live on, and the air they share is ingrained in us from birth.

"You truthfully can't separate the way we get our food from the way we live," she says. "How we get our food is intrinsic to our culture. It's how we pass on our values and knowledge to the young. When you go out with your aunts and uncles to hunt or to gather, you learn to smell the air, watch the wind, understand the way the ice moves, know the land. You get to know where to pick which plant and what animal to take."

"It's part, too, of your development as a person. You share food with your community. You show respect to your elders by offering them the first catch. You give thanks to the animal that gave up its life for your sustenance. So you get all the physical activity of harvesting your own food, all the social activity of sharing and preparing it, and all the spiritual aspects as well," says Cochran. "You certainly don't get all that, do you, when you buy prepackaged food from a store."

"That's why some of us here in Anchorage are working to protect what's ours, so that others can continue to live back home in the villages," she adds. "Because if we don't take care of our food, it won't be there for us in the future. And if we lose our foods, we lose who we are." The word Inupiat means "the real people." "That's who we are," says Cochran.

Assess Your Progress

1. What kinds of diseases are on the increase among the Inuit and why?

2. How does their traditional high-protein, high-fat diet compare with the "balanced diet" most of us grew up with? What does this mean, according to Harold Draper?

3. What are the contrasting sources of vitamins A, D, and C between our diet and the diet of the Inuit? What is the advantage of eating meat and fish raw?

4. What is a "protein ceiling?" How did hunter-gatherers cope with this problem?

5. Where do the more healthful fats (monounsaturated and omega-3 fatty acids) come from? What are their benefits?

6. Why is it that Atkins-dieters are not really eating in an "Eskimo-like way?"

7. What are the differences between the subsistence diets of the Far North and "dieting?"

8. Were people of the Far North fat? Why not? In what ways did the old way of eating protect them?

9. How is the northern food chain threatened?

10. In what sense is there a kinship with food sources in the Far North that our industrial societies do not have? Why is it also a part of one's development as a person?

From *Discover*, October 2004, pp. 48, 50, 52, 54. Copyright © 2004 by Patricia Gadsby. Reprinted by permission of the author.

Ties That Bind

Hopi gift culture and its first encounter with the United States.

PETER M. WHITELEY

In 1852, shortly after the United States had nominally annexed Hopi country, in northern Arizona, the Hopi people arranged for a diplomatic packet to reach President Millard Fillmore at the White House. Part message and part magical gift, the packet was delivered by a delegation of five prominent men from another Pueblo tribe, the Tewas of Tesuque Pueblo in New Mexico, who wanted to gain legal protection from Anglo and Hispanic settlers who were encroaching on their lands. The delegation traveled for nearly three months, on horseback, steamboat, and train, from Santa Fe to Washington, D.C., more than 2,600 miles away. The five men spoke fluent Spanish, the dominant European language of the region at the time—which made them ideally suited to convey the gift packet and its message to the president.

At the time, no U.S. government official had visited the Hopi (and few would do so before the 1890s). Their "unique diplomatic pacquet," in the words of the nineteenth-century ethnologist Henry Rowe Schoolcraft, offered "friendship and intercommunication . . . opening, symbolically, a road from the Moqui [Hopi] country to Washington." The packet was in two parts. The first part comprised two *pahos,* or prayer-sticks, at either end of a long cotton cord, dyed for part of its length. Separating the dyed from the undyed part of the cord were six varicolored feathers, knotted into a bunch. The *pahos* "represent the Moqui [Hopi] people and the President [respectively]," Schoolcraft wrote; "the cord is the road which separates them; the [bunch of feathers] tied to the cord is the meeting point."

As well as encoding a message, the *pahos* were an offering of a kind that Hopi deities such as Taawa, the Sun god, traditionally like to receive. By giving the president *pahos* worthy of the Sun, the Hopi signaled their expectation that he would reciprocate. Just as the Sun, on receiving the appropriate offerings, would send rain clouds for sustaining life and growth, so, too, the president would send protection for Hopi lives and lands—in this instance, protection from assaults by neighboring tribes such as the Navajo.

The second part of the packet comprised a cornstalk cigarette filled with tobacco ("to be smoked by the president") and a small cornhusk package that enclosed honey-soaked cornmeal. According to the Tesuque delegation, the honey-meal package was "a charm to call down rain from heaven." When the president smoked the cigarette, he would exhale clouds of smoke, which would sympathetically attract the clouds of the sky. Then, when he chewed the cornmeal and spat the wild honey on ground that needed rain, the Tesuque statement concluded, "the Moquis assure him that it [the rain] will come."

In sum, the packet was three things at once: message, offering, and gift of magical power. In conveying those elements, the Hopi sought to open diplomatic relations with the U.S.

But their intent appears to have been lost on their recipient. As so often happens when two cultures make contact, deep misunderstandings can arise: What does a gift mean? What, if anything, does the gift giver expect in return? Do the giver and the recipient both assign the same value to the gift? In twenty-five years of ethnographic fieldwork with the Hopi, it has been my goal to learn something of their history and culture. Recently I turned my attention to certain important events, such as the Millard Fillmore episode, that might shed light on how Hopi society changed as the U.S. developed. In that context Hopi gift giving and the ways it functions as a pillar of Hopi social organization have been central to my studies. One lesson of my work shines through: When nations exchange gifts, all the parties would do best to keep in mind the old adage, "It's the thought that counts."

Given the differences between Hopi and Western traditions and culture, perhaps it is not surprising that the Hopi idea of "gift" is only loosely equivalent to the Western one. In 1852 the Hopi people were still little affected by outside populations, and Hopi land use spread across much of northern Arizona and even into southern Utah. At that time, the Hopi lifestyle was traditional, based on farming, foraging, and some pastoralism. Even today, important elements of the subsistence economy persist, though wage labor and small business provide supplemental income.

The Hopi typically divide their work according to gender. Work done by men (such as farming and harvesting of crops) is perceived as a gift to the women; work done by women (such as gardening, gathering of piñon nuts, grasses, wild fruits, berries, and the like) is perceived as a gift to the men. Women also own and manage the distribution of their household's goods and crops. In fact, Hopi women control most of the material economic life, whereas Hopi men largely control the ritual and spiritual aspects.

The Hopi take part in an elaborate cycle of religious ceremonies, to which a range of specialized offices and privileges is attached. But individuals gain those distinctive social positions not through material wealth but rather through gender and kinship relations, which are ordered in a matrilineal manner. In fact, clan heads and chiefs of religious societies are typically worse off materially than the average member of the clan. Hopi leaders are supposed to be materially poor, and a wealthy individual is often criticized as *qahopi,* un-Hopi, for failing to share. Wealth and status among the Hopi is thus phrased in ritual terms: a poor person is one without ceremonial prerogatives, not one without money. So averse are the Hopi to material accumulation that in May 2004, for the second time, they voted against casino gambling, despite substantial poverty on the reservation.

Does such a primacy of value placed on ceremonial roles explain the evanescent nature of the gift given to President Fillmore? In what world of meaning did the packet represent great value? Indeed, what's in a gift?

Anthropologists have been making hay of that last question ever since 1925, when the French anthropologist Marcel Mauss published his groundbreaking *Essai sur le Don* (translated into English as "The Gift"). Mauss convincingly argued that in small-scale societies (10,000 or fewer persons) gifts are "total social facts." What he meant is that, in gift- or barter-based social systems, divisions of social life into discrete domains—such as economy, politics, law, or religion—are meaningless; each sphere interpenetrates and overlaps the others.

As in strict barter, an exchange in Hopi culture that begins by making a gift to someone does not involve money, but it does require reciprocity. Thus goods, services, or knowledge "given" to an individual or a group are answered with something of equivalent value. "Gifts" develop an interconnectedness between Hopi individuals in a way that outright purchases cannot. Furthermore, the Hopi offer gifts in a much broader range of circumstances than people in Western cultures do, and the value of those gifts extends to the religious realm, tying individuals and groups to each other and to the realm of the spirits.

Probably the key to understanding a gift-based system such as that of the Hopi is to recognize that such systems are built on kinship. "Kinship"—the godzilla that has driven multitudes of college students screaming from anthropology 101—is, in this regard at least, straightforward. It means simply that the great majority of human social activity is framed in terms of reciprocal family ties. Where all personal relationships are cast within the "kinship idiom" there are no members of the society who are not kin to me, nor I to them.

Kinship terms encode behavioral expectations as well as familial role. As anthropologists never tire of saying, such terms are primarily social, not biological: obviously if I call fifteen women "mother," as the average Hopi can do, I do not assume that each woman physically gave birth to me. But my "mothers" all have rights and duties in relation to me. And, reciprocally, I have duties and rights with respect to them: in fact, their duties are my rights, and my duties are their rights in the relationship. That is what reciprocity is all about. You give me food, I plant your cornfield, to give a crude example. But, in a kinship society, such a basic structure of mutual expectations forms the foundation for an entire apparatus of courtesy and manners, deference and respect, familiarity or distance. Those expectations are concretely expressed by gifts—spontaneous and planned, routine and special, trivial and grand. Gifts are thus communications in a language of social belonging.

So averse are the Hopi to material accumulation that in May 2004 they voted against casino gambling.

So-called gift economies entail a certain kind of sociality, or sense of what it means to belong to a community. In such an economy, one gives a gift to mark social relations built on kinship and altruism, but without the expectation of direct repayment. According to some arguments, gifts are also given to foster a sense of community, as well as sustainable interrelations with the local environment. In fact, in some respects the giver still "owns" some part of the gift, and it is the intangible connection between the two parties, mediated by the gift, that forms the basis of interpersonal relationships.

In contrast, in exchange economies, commodities dominate social interchange. Competitive markets, governed by the profit motive, connect buyer and seller, and social relations are characterized by individualism. A gift, once given, belongs entirely to the recipient; only when the item given has sentimental value does it keep the bond between giver and recipient alive.

That is not to say the Hopi did not engage in the more impersonal, "Western" forms of material exchange. In the Hopi language, as in English, several words describe how an item is transferred from one person to another: *maqa* ("to give"); *hùuya* ("to barter or trade"); and *tu'i* ("to buy"). Those words all antedate the arrival of Europeans—and anthropological classifications. Barter and purchase, as well as gifts, have all long been present in Hopi life. Furthermore, gift exchange in the West can also function as it does among the Hopi, as part of kinship obligations or ordinary social life.

What is distinctive about Hopi custom is the fact that the gift economy is responsible for the great majority of exchanges. Furthermore, there is no such thing as a free gift. The strong interpersonal bonds created by a gift make giving almost de rigueur at ceremonial events. Gifts, particularly gifts of food or utensils, are transmitted during ceremonies of personal milestones (at a birth or a marriage), as well as at public gatherings.

For example, at the annual so-called basket dances, girls and women distribute a variety of objects they have collected for the occasion. The dances illustrate the Hopi lack of acquisitiveness. The women form a semicircle and dance and sing; after each song two girls fling gifts into the crowd of men assembled outside the circle. Among the gifts are valuable baskets and buckskins, though inexpensive utensils and manufactured items are also popular. Each man zealously grabs for the flying objects, and if two men happen to catch the same item, both wrestle with the object, often until it has been totally destroyed.

Although gift giving has been a pillar of Hopi society, trade has also flourished in Hopi towns since prehistory, with a network that extended from the Great Plains to the Pacific Coast, and from the Great Basin, centered on present-day Nevada and Utah, to the Valley of Mexico. Manufactured goods, raw materials, and gems drove the trade, supplemented by exotic items such as parrots. The Hopis were producers as well, manufacturing large quantities of cotton cloth and ceramics for the trade. To this day, interhousehold trade and barter, especially for items of traditional manufacture for ceremonial use (such as basketry, bows, cloth, moccasins, pottery, and rattles), remain vigorous.

For hundreds of years, at least, the Hopi traded with the Rio Grande Pueblos to acquire turquoise, *heishi* (shell necklaces), and buckskins; one long string of *heishi,* for instance, was worth two Hopi woven cotton mantas. Similarly, songs, dances, and other ritual elements were often exchanged for an agreed-upon equivalent.

The high value the Hopi placed on the items they acquired by trade correlate, in many respects, with the value Europeans placed on them. Silver, for instance, had high value among both Westerners and Native Americans as money and as jewelry. *Siiva,* the Hopi word both for "money" and for "silver jewelry" was borrowed directly from the English word "silver." Paper money itself was often treated the way traditional resources were: older Hopi men bundled it and stored it in trunks, stacked by denomination.

It was not until the 1890s, however, that silver jewelry began to be produced by the Hopi. A man named Sikyatala learned silversmithing from a Zuni man, and his craftsmanship quickly made silver jewelry into treasured adornments. Those among the Hopi who cared for it too much, though, were criticized for vanity; one nickname, Siisiva ("[wearing] a lot of silver"), characterized a fop.

Some jewels, such as turquoise, traditionally had a sacred value, beyond adornment. Even today, flakes of turquoise are occasionally offered to the spirits in religious ceremonies. Turquoise and shell necklaces appear in many ritual settings, frequently adorning the costumes of *katsinas* (ceremonial figures) and performers in the social dances.

How much the Hopi value turquoise becomes apparent toward the close of a ritual enactment known as the Clown Ceremony. The "clowns"—more than mere entertainers—represent unbridled human impulses. Warrior *katsinas* arrive to punish the clowns for licentious behavior and teach them good Hopi behavior: modest and quiet in conduct, careful and decorous in speech, abstemious and sharing about food, and unselfish about other things. The clowns fail miserably (and hilariously) at their lessons. Eventually the warrior chief presents an ultimatum: stop flaunting chaos or die. The clown chief then offers him a turquoise necklace as a "mortgage" on the clowns' lives. The warrior chief accepts, the clowns receive a lesser punishment, and community life goes on—not with perfection, but with a human mixture of the virtuous and the flawed.

In Hopi tradition, the first clan among the Hopi, and the one that supplied the *kikmongwi,* or village chief, was Bear. When other clans arrived, their leaders approached the *kikmongwi* to request entry into the village. He asked what they had to contribute, such as a beneficial ceremony. So challenged, each clan performed its ceremony, and if successful, say, in producing rain, its members were invited to live in the village, assigned an area for housing, and granted agricultural lands to work in the valley below. In return, the clan agreed to perform its ceremony, as part of a cycle of ceremonies throughout the year, and to intermarry with the other clans of the community, a practice called exogamous marriage. In that way, the Snake clan brought the Snake Dance, the Badger clan introduced principal katsina ceremonies, and the Fire clan brought the Warriors' society to the Hopi village. The villages thus came to be made up of mutually interdependent clans.

One of the essential principles expressed here, and the very cornerstone of Hopi society and sociality, is the exchange of mutually beneficial gifts—ceremonies for land, people in exogamous marriage—and the relationships reconfigured by those exchanges. And the same model is extended to the supernatural world: the gods must be propitiated with offerings of ritual gifts, and thus reminded of their dependence upon and obligations to mortal people.

The items sent to President Fillmore conform to the archetypal Hopi offering. Seeking to incorporate the president into the Hopi world, the appropriate strategy was to give him valuable presents that sought something in return, and to make sure he understood what that meant. Addressing him with prayer-sticks the way they might address the Sun father, the delegation sought to engage him within the gifting and kinship idiom. The instructions delivered with the packet—even across a succession of translations—spoke clearly of the Hopi intent. As with the turquoise mortgage of the *katsina* clowns, the idea of reciprocity is central. If the president wants more of, say, rain-magic, he must give back: he must receive the gift and its political proposal, and provide something in return.

Alas, the magico-religious sensibility of the Hopi worldview and the offer of serial reciprocity clashed with Manifest Destiny and the assimilationist ideology of Fillmore's presidency. Historical records make it clear that he did not smoke the cigarette, nor chew nor spit the honey-meal, and, so far as we know, he sent no formal reply. None of the objects has survived.

What the five men of the Tesuque delegation received no doubt perplexed them as much as the packet they delivered perplexed the president: Each man was given a Millard Fillmore peace medal, a Western-style business suit, and a daguerreotype portrait (all now lost, as well). They also got a tour of standard destinations in Washington, including the Patent Office and the Smithsonian Institution, where they were introduced to the "wonders of electricity," according to a contemporary newspaper account in the *Daily National Intelligencer.* In their meeting with Fillmore they heard the president say he "hoped the Great Spirit would bless and sustain them till they again returned to the bosom of their families."

Certainly Fillmore expressed the goodwill of the U.S. toward the Pueblos in general and to the Tesuque party in particular—who, in all probability, conveyed that sentiment to the Hopi. But the dissonance between gift and exchange economies helps explain why the Hopis did not achieve their goals. (The U.S. did not protect the Hopi from intrusions by the Navajo or by anyone else.)

The Hopi sought to embrace the president in their own sphere of sociality and mutuality—to extend kinship to him. But in a social system like the president's, where gifts are not total social facts, the political belongs in a separate domain from the religious or the economic, and kinship is secondary. The gift of a jeweled sword, for instance, might have impressed Fillmore more, but for the Hopi, its strictly symbolic value—as an item for display, but with no political, religious, or social value—would not have ensured a return, a social connection built on mutual exchange. More, by Hopi standards, presenting such a gift might have seemed inhospitable and materialistic, indeed, undiplomatic and even selfish. Thus does understanding fail between nations.

Assess Your Progress

1. What was the intent of the diplomatic packet sent to President Millard Fillmore by the Hopi?

2. Describe Hopi lifestyle and attitudes toward material wealth.

3. What is the significance of a "gift" in Hopi culture?

4. In what sense is Hopi kinship social, not biological?

5. What is the difference between a gift economy and an exchange economy? How does the "gift" differ in these two contexts?

6. What are the distinctive qualities of gifts in Hopi culture?

7. Although the Hopi do trade, what indications are there that exchanges are primarily ceremonial and are conducted as gifts?

8. Why did the Hopi not achieve their goal of reciprocity with President Fillmore?

Sick of Poverty

New studies suggest that the stress of being poor has a staggeringly harmful influence on health.

ROBERT SAPOLSKY

Rudolph Virchow, the 19th-century German neuroscientist, physician and political activist, came of age with two dramatic events—a typhoid outbreak in 1847 and the failed revolutions of 1848. Out of those experiences came two insights for him: first, that the spread of disease has much to do with appalling living conditions, and second, that those in power have enormous means to subjugate the powerless. As Virchow summarized in his famous epigram, "Physicians are the natural attorneys of the poor."

Physicians (and biomedical scientists) are advocates of the underprivileged because poverty and poor health tend to go hand in hand. Poverty means bad or insufficient food, unhealthy living conditions and endless other factors that lead to illness. Yet it is not merely that poor people tend to be unhealthy while everyone else is well. When you examine socioeconomic status (SES), a composite measure that includes income, occupation, education and housing conditions, it becomes clear that, starting with the wealthiest stratum of society, every step downward in SES correlates with poorer health.

This "SES gradient" has been documented throughout Westernized societies for problems that include respiratory and cardiovascular diseases, ulcers, rheumatoid disorders, psychiatric diseases and a number of cancers. It is not a subtle statistical phenomenon. When you compare the highest versus the lowest rungs of the SES ladder, the risk of some diseases varies 10-fold. Some countries exhibit a five- to 10-year difference in life expectancy across the SES spectrum. Of the Western nations, the U.S. has the steepest gradient; for example, one study showed that the poorest white males in America die about a decade earlier than the richest.

So what causes this correlation between SES and health? Lower SES may give rise to poorer health, but conversely, poorer health could also give rise to lower SES. After all, chronic illness can compromise one's education and work productivity, in addition to generating enormous expenses.

Nevertheless, the bulk of the facts suggests that the arrow goes from economic status to health—that SES at some point in life predicts health measures later on. Among the many demonstrations of this point is a remarkable study of elderly American nuns. All had taken their vows as young adults and had spent many years thereafter sharing diet, health care and housing, thereby controlling for those lifestyle factors. Yet in their old age, patterns of disease, incidence of dementia and longevity were still significantly predicted by their SES status from when they became nuns, at least half a century before.

Inadequate Explanations

So, to use a marvelous phrase common to this field, how does SES get "under the skin" and influence health? The answers that seem most obvious, it turns out, do not hold much water. One such explanation, for instance, posits that for the poor, health care may be less easily accessible and of lower quality. This possibility is plausible when one considers that for many of the poor in America, the family physician does not exist, and medical care consists solely of trips to the emergency room.

But that explanation soon falls by the wayside, for reasons made clearest in the famed Whitehall studies by Michael G. Marmot of University College London over the past three decades. Marmot and his colleagues have documented an array of dramatic SES gradients in a conveniently stratified population, namely, the members of the British civil service (ranging from blue-collar workers to high-powered executives). Office messengers and porters, for example, have far higher mortality rates from chronic heart disease than administrators and professionals do. Lack of access to medical attention cannot explain the phenomenon, because the U.K., unlike the U.S., has universal health care. Similar SES gradients also occur in other countries with socialized medicine, including the health care Edens of Scandinavia, and the differences remain significant even after researchers factor in how much the subjects actually use the medical services.

Another telling finding is that SES gradients exist for diseases for which health care access is irrelevant. No amount of medical check-ups, blood tests and scans will change the likelihood of someone getting type 1 (juvenile-onset) diabetes or rheumatoid arthritis, yet both conditions are more common among the poor.

The next "obvious" explanation centers on unhealthy lifestyles. As you descend the SES ladder in Westernized societies, people are more likely to smoke, to drink excessively, to be obese, and to live in a violent or polluted or densely populated neighborhood. Poor people are also less likely to have access to clean water, healthy food and health clubs, not to mention adequate heat in the winter and air-conditioning in the summer. Thus, it seems self-evident that lower SES gets under the skin by increasing risks and decreasing protective factors. As mordantly stated by Robert G. Evans of the University of British Columbia, "Drinking sewage is probably unwise, even for Bill Gates."

What is surprising, though, is how little of the SES gradient these risk and protective factors explain. In the Whitehall studies, controlling for factors such as smoking and level of exercise accounted for only about a third of the gradient. This same point is made by studies comparing health and wealth among, rather than within, nations. It is reasonable to assume that the wealthier a country, the more financial resources its citizens have to buy protection and avoid risk. If so, health should improve incrementally as one moves up the wealth gradient among nations, as well as among the citizens within individual nations. But it does not. Instead, among the wealthiest quarter of countries on earth, there is no relation between a country's wealth and the health of its people.

Thus, health care access, health care utilization, and exposure to risk and protective factors explain the SES/health gradient far less well than one might have guessed. One must therefore consider whether most of the gradient arises from a different set of considerations: the psychosocial consequences of SES.

Psychosocial Stress

Ideally, the body is in homeostatic balance, a state in which the vital measures of human function—heart rate, blood pressure, blood sugar levels and so on—are in their optimal ranges. A stressor is anything that threatens to disrupt homeostasis. For most organisms, a stressor is an acute physical challenge—for example, the need for an injured gazelle to sprint for its life or for a hungry predator to chase down a meal. The body is superbly adapted to dealing with short-term physical challenges to homeostasis. Stores of energy, including the sugar glucose, are released, and cardiovascular tone increases to facilitate the delivery of fuel to exercising muscle throughout the body. Digestion, growth, tissue repair, reproduction and other physiological processes not needed to survive the crisis are suppressed. The immune system steps up to thwart opportunistic pathogens. Memory and the senses transiently sharpen.

But cognitively and socially sophisticated species, such as we primates, routinely inhabit a different realm of stress. For us, most stressors concern interactions with our own species, and few physically disrupt homeostasis. Instead these psychosocial stressors involve the anticipation (accurate or otherwise) of an impending challenge. And the striking characteristic of such psychological and social stress is its chronicity. For most mammals, a stressor lasts only a few minutes. In contrast, we humans can worry chronically over a 30-year mortgage.

Unfortunately, our body's response, though adaptive for an acute physical stressor, is pathogenic for prolonged psychosocial stress. Chronic increase in cardiovascular tone brings stress-induced hypertension. The constant mobilization of energy increases the risk or severity of diseases such as type 2 (adult-onset) diabetes. The prolonged inhibition of digestion, growth, tissue repair and reproduction increases the risks of various gastrointestinal disorders, impaired growth in children, failure to ovulate in females and erectile dysfunction in males. A too-extended immune stress response ultimately suppresses immunity and impairs disease defenses. And chronic activation of the stress response impairs cognition, as well as the health, functioning and even survival of some types of neurons.

An extensive biomedical literature has established that individuals are more likely to activate a stress response and are more at risk for a stress-sensitive disease if they (a) feel as if they have minimal control over stressors, (b) feel as if they have no predictive information about the duration and intensity of the stressor, (c) have few outlets for the frustration caused by the stressor, (d) interpret the stressor as evidence of circumstances worsening, and (e) lack social support—for the duress caused by the stressors.

Psychosocial stressors are not evenly distributed across society. Just as the poor have a disproportionate share of physical stressors (hunger, manual labor, chronic sleep deprivation with a second job, the bad mattress that can't be replaced), they have a disproportionate share of psychosocial ones. Numbing assembly-line work and an occupational lifetime spent taking orders erode workers' sense of control. Unreliable cars that may not start in the morning and paychecks that may not last the month inflict unpredictability. Poverty rarely allows stress-relieving options such as health club memberships, costly but relaxing hobbies, or sabbaticals for rethinking one's priorities. And despite the heartwarming stereotype of the "poor but loving community," the working poor typically have less social support than the middle and upper classes, thanks to the extra jobs, the long commutes on public transit, and other burdens. Marmot has shown that regardless of SES, the less autonomy one has at work, the worse one's cardiovascular health. Furthermore, low control in the workplace accounts for about half the SES gradient in cardiovascular disease in his Whitehall population.

Feeling Poor

Three lines of research provide more support for the influence of psychological stress on SES-related health gradients. Over the past decade Nancy E. Adler of the University of California, San Francisco, has explored the difference between objective and subjective SES and the relation of each to health. Test subjects were shown a simple diagram of a ladder with 10 rungs and then asked, "In society, where on this ladder would you rank yourself in terms of how well you're doing?" The very openness of the question allowed the person to define the comparison group that felt most emotionally salient.

As Adler has shown, a person's subjective assessment of his or her SES takes into account the usual objective measures (education, income, occupation and residence) as well as measures of life satisfaction and of anxiety about the future. Adler's provocative finding is that subjective SES is at least as good as objective SES at predicting patterns of cardiovascular function, measures of metabolism, incidences of obesity and levels of stress hormones—suggesting that the subjective feelings may help explain the objective results.

This same point emerges from comparisons of the SES/health gradient among nations. A relatively poor person in the U.S. may objectively have more financial resources to purchase health care and protective factors than a relatively wealthy person in a less developed country yet, on average, will still have a shorter life expectancy. For example, as Stephen Bezruchka of the University of Washington emphasizes, people in Greece on average earn half the income of Americans yet have a longer life expectancy. Once the minimal resources are available to sustain a basic level of health through adequate food and housing, absolute levels of income are of remarkably little importance to health. Although Adler's work suggests that the objective state of being poor adversely affects health, at the core of that result is the subjective state of feeling poor.

Being Made to Feel Poor

Another body of research arguing that psychosocial factors mediate most of the SES/health gradient comes from Richard Wilkinson of the University of Nottingham in England. Over the past 15 years he and his colleagues have reported that the extent of income inequality in a community is even more predictive than SES for an array of health measures. In other words, absolute levels of income aside, greater disparities in income between the poorest and the wealthiest in a community predict worse average health. (David H. Abbott of the Wisconsin National Primate Research Center and I, along with our colleagues, found a roughly equivalent phenomenon in animals: among many nonhuman primate species, less egalitarian social structures correlate with higher resting levels of a key stress hormone—an index for worse health—among socially subordinate animals.)

Wilkinson's subtle and critical finding has generated considerable controversy. One dispute concerns its generality. His original work suggested that income inequality was relevant to health in many European and North American countries and communities. It has become clear, however, that this relation holds only in the developed country with the greatest of income inequalities, namely, the U.S.

Whether considered at the level of cities or states, income inequality predicts mortality rates across nearly all ages in the U.S. Why, though, is this relation not observed in, say, Canada or Denmark? One possibility is that these countries have too little income variability to tease out the correlation.

Some critics have questioned whether the linkage between income inequality and worse health is merely a mathematical quirk. The relation between SES and health follows an asymptotic curve: dropping from the uppermost rung of society's ladder to the next-to-top step reduces life expectancy and other measures much less drastically than plunging from the next-to-bottom rung to the lowest level. Because a community with high levels of income inequality will have a relatively high number of individuals at the very bottom, where health prospects are so dismal, the community's average life expectancy will inevitably be lower than that of an egalitarian community, for reasons that have nothing to do with psychosocial factors. Wilkinson has shown, however, that decreased income inequality predicts better health for both the poor and the wealthy. This result strongly indicates that the association between illness and inequality is more than just a mathematical artifact.

Wilkinson and others in the field have long argued that the more unequal income in a community is, the more psychosocial stress there will be for the poor. Higher income inequality intensifies a community's hierarchy and makes social support less available: truly symmetrical, reciprocal, affiliative support exists only among equals. Moreover, having your nose rubbed in your poverty is likely to lessen your sense of control in life, to aggravate the frustrations of poverty and to intensify the sense of life worsening.

If Adler's work demonstrates the adverse health effects of feeling poor, Wilkinson's income inequality work suggests that the surest way to feel poor is to be made to feel poor—to be endlessly made aware of the haves when you are a have-not. And in our global village, we are constantly made aware of the moguls and celebrities whose resources dwarf ours.

John W. Lynch and George A. Kaplan of the University of Michigan at Ann Arbor have recently proposed another way that people are made to feel poor. Their "neomaterialist" interpretation of the income inequality phenomenon—which is subtle reasonable and, ultimately, deeply depressing—runs as follows: Spending money on public goods (better public transit, universal health care and so on) is a way to improve the quality of life for the average person. But by definition, the bigger the income inequality in a society, the greater the financial distance between the average and the wealthy. The bigger this distance, the less the wealthy have to gain from expenditures on the public good. Instead they would benefit more from keeping their tax money to spend on their private good—a better chauffeur, a gated community, bottled water, private schools, private health insurance. So the more unequal the income is in a community, the more incentive the wealthy will have to oppose public expenditures benefiting the health of the community. And within the U.S., the more income inequality there is, the more power will be disproportionately in the hands of the wealthy to oppose such public expenditures. According to health economist Evans, this scenario ultimately leads to "private affluence and public squalor."

This "secession of the wealthy" can worsen the SES/health gradient in two ways: by aggravating the conditions in low-income communities (which account for at least part of the increased health risks for the poor) and by adding to the psychosocial stressors. If social and psychological stressors are entwined with feeling poor, and even more so with feeling poor while being confronted with the wealthy, they will be even more stressful when the wealthy are striving to decrease the goods and services available to the poor.

Social Capital

A third branch of support for psychosocial explanations for the relation between income inequality and health comes from the work of Ichiro Kawachi of Harvard University, based on the concept of "social capital." Although it is still being refined as a measure, social capital refers to the broad levels of trust and efficacy in a community. Do people generally trust one another and help one another out? Do people feel an incentive to take care of commonly held resources (for example, to clean up graffiti in public parks)? And do people feel that their organizations—such as unions or tenant associations—actually have an impact? Most studies of social capital employ two simple measures, namely, how many organizations people belong to and how people answer a question such as, "Do you think most people would try to take advantage of you if they got a chance?"

What Kawachi and others have shown is that at the levels of states, provinces, cities and neighborhoods, low social capital predicts bad health, bad self-reported health and high mortality rates. Using a complex statistical technique called path analysis, Kawachi has demonstrated that (once one controls for the effects of absolute income) the strongest route from income inequality to poor health is through the social capital measures—to wit, high degrees of income inequality come with low levels of trust and support, which increases stress and harms health.

None of this is surprising. As a culture, America has neglected its social safety nets while making it easier for the most successful to sit atop the pyramids of inequality. Moreover, we have chosen to forgo the social capital that comes from small, stable communities in exchange for unprecedented opportunities for mobility and anonymity. As a result, all measures of social epidemiology are worsening in the U.S. Of Westernized nations, America has the greatest income inequality (40 percent of the wealth is controlled by 1 percent of the population) and the greatest discrepancy between expenditures on health care (number one in the world) and life expectancy (as of 2003, number 29).

The importance of psychosocial factors in explaining the SES/health gradient generates a critical conclusion: when it comes to health, there is far more to poverty than simply not having enough money. (As Evans once stated, "Most graduate students have had the experience of having very little money, but not of poverty. They are very different things.") The psychosocial school has occasionally been accused of promulgating an anti-progressive message: don't bother with universal health care, affordable medicines and other salutary measures because there will still be a robust SES/health gradient after all the reforms. But the lesson of this research is not to abandon such societal change. It is that so much more is needed.

Overview/Status and Health

- Researchers have long known that people with low socioeconomic status [SES] have dramatically higher disease risks and shorter life spans than do people in the wealthier strata of society. The conventional explanations—that the poor have less access to health care and a greater incidence of harmful lifestyles such as smoking and obesity—cannot account for the huge discrepancy in health outcomes.
- New studies indicate that the psychosocial stresses associated with poverty may increase the risks of many illnesses. The chronic stress induced by living in a poor, violent neighborhood, for example, could increase one's susceptibility to cardiovascular disease, depression and diabetes.
- Other studies have shown a correlation between income inequality and poor health in the U.S. Some researchers believe that the poor feel poorer, and hence suffer greater stress, in communities with wide gaps between the highest and lowest incomes.

The Good and Bad Effects of Stress

The human body is superb at responding to the acute stress of a physical challenge, such as chasing down prey or escaping a predator. The circulatory, nervous and immune systems are mobilized while the digestive and reproductive processes are suppressed. If the stress becomes chronic, though, the continual repetition of these responses can cause major damage.

Effects of Acute Stress

Brain Increased alertness and less perception of pain

Thymus Gland and Other Immune Tissues Immune system readied for possible injury

Circulatory System Heart beats faster, and blood vessels constrict to bring more oxygen to muscles

Adrenal Glands Secrete hormones that mobilize energy supplies

Reproductive Organs Reproductive functions are temporarily suppressed

Effects of Chronic Stress

Brain Impaired memory and increased risk of depression

Thymus Gland and Other Immune Tissues Deteriorated immune response

Circulatory System Elevated blood pressure and higher risk of cardiovascular disease

Adrenal Glands High hormone levels slow recovery from acute stress

Reproductive Organs Higher risks of infertility and miscarriage

More to Explore

Mind the Gap: Hierarchies, Health and Human Evolution. Richard Wilkinson. Weidenfeld and Nicolson, 2000.

The Health of Nations: Why Inequality Is Harmful to Your Health. Ichiro Kawachi and Bruce P. Kennedy. New Press, 2002.

The Status Syndrome. Michael Marmot. Henry Holt and Company, 2004.

Why Zebras Don't Get Ulcers: A Guide to Stress, Stress-Related Diseases and Coping. Robert Sapolsky. Third edition. Henry Holt and Company, 2004.

Assess Your Progress

1. How does health correlate with socioeconomic status? In which direction does the arrow of causation go? How did the study of elderly American nuns confirm this?

2. Why are some of the most obvious explanations for poor health inadequate, according to the author?

3. How does human stress differ from that of animal stress?

4. Under what circumstances are individuals more likely to activate a stress response?

5. How does the author support his claim that psychosocial stressors are not evenly distributed across society?

6. What evidence is there that a person's subjective assessment of socioeconomic status is just as important for health as one's objective socioeconomic status?

7. What evidence is there that income inequality in a society is an important factor in people's health?

8. How does "low social capital" predict poor health?

ROBERT SAPOLSKY is professor of biological sciences, neurology and neurological sciences at Stanford University and a research associate at the National Museums of Kenya. In his laboratory work, he focuses on how stress can damage the brain and on gene therapy for the nervous system. In addition, he studies populations of wild baboons in East Africa, trying to determine the relation between the social rank of a baboon and its health. His latest book is *Monkeyluv and Other Essays on Our Lives as Animals* [Scribner, 2005].

UNIT 4

Other Families, Other Ways

Unit Selections

17. **When Brothers Share a Wife: Among Tibetans, the Good Life Relegates Many Women to Spinsterhood,** Melvyn C. Goldstein
18. **Death without Weeping,** Nancy Scheper-Hughes
19. **Arranging a Marriage in India,** Serena Nanda
20. **Who Needs Love! In Japan, Many Couples Don't,** Nicholas D. Kristof

Learning Outcomes

After reading this unit, you should be able to:

- Discuss why "fraternal polyandry" is socially acceptable in Tibet but not in our society.

- Describe how dietary changes have affected birth rates and women's health.

- List the pros and cons of arranged marriages versus love marriages.

- Determine whether the stability of Japanese marriages implies compatibility and contentment.

Student Website

www.mhhe.com/cls

Internet References

Kinship and Social Organization
    www.umanitoba.ca/anthropology
Sex and Marriage
    http://anthro.palomar.edu/marriage/default.htm
Wedding Traditions and Customs
    http://worldweddingtraditions.com/

Because most people in small-scale societies of the past spent their whole lives within a local area, it is understandable that their primary interactions—economic, religious, and otherwise—were with their relatives. It also makes sense that, through marriage customs, they strengthened those kinship relationships that clearly defined their mutual rights and obligations. Indeed, the resulting family structure may be surprisingly flexible and adaptive, as witnessed in the essays "When Brothers Share a Wife: Among Tibetans, the Good Life Relegates Many Women to Spinsterhood" by Melvyn Goldstein, and "Arranging a Marriage in India" by Serena Nanda.

For these reasons, anthropologists have looked upon family and kinship as the key mechanisms for transmitting culture from one generation to the next. Social changes may have been slow to take place throughout the world, but as social horizons have widened, family relationships and community alliances are increasingly based upon new principles. Even as birth rates have increased, kinship networks have diminished in size and strength. As people have increasingly become involved with others as co-workers in a market economy, our associations depend more and more upon factors such as personal aptitudes, educational backgrounds, and job opportunities. Yet the family still exists. Except for some rather unusual exceptions, the family is small, but still functions in its age-old nurturing and protective role, even under conditions where there is little affection (see "Who Needs Love! In Japan, Many Couples Don't" by Nicholas Kristof) or under conditions of extreme poverty and a high infant mortality rate (see "Death without Weeping" by Nancy Scheper-Hughes). Beyond the immediate family, the situation is in a state of flux. Certain ethnic groups, especially those in poverty, still have a need for the broader network and in some ways seem to be reformulating those ties.

We do not know where the changes described in this section will lead us and which ones will ultimately prevail. One thing is certain: anthropologists will be there to document the trends, for the discipline of anthropology has had to change as well. One important feature of the essays in this section is the growing interest of anthropologists in the study of complex societies where old theoretical perspectives are inadequate.

The current trends, however, do not necessarily depict the decline of the kinship unit. The large family network is still the best guarantee of individual survival and well-being in an urban setting.

© Santokh Kochar/Getty Images

When Brothers Share a Wife

Among Tibetans, the Good Life Relegates Many Women to Spinsterhood

Melvyn C. Goldstein

Eager to reach home, Dorje drives his yaks hard over the 17,000-foot mountain pass, stopping only once to rest. He and his two older brothers, Pema and Sonam, are jointly marrying a woman from the next village in a few weeks, and he has to help with the preparations.

Dorje, Pema, and Sonam are Tibetans living in Limi, a 200-square-mile area in the northwest corner of Nepal, across the border from Tibet. The form of marriage they are about to enter—fraternal polyandry in anthropological parlance—is one of the world's rarest forms of marriage but is not uncommon in Tibetan society, where it has been practiced from time immemorial. For many Tibetan social strata, it traditionally represented the ideal form of marriage and family.

The mechanics of fraternal polyandry are simple. Two, three, four, or more brothers jointly take a wife, who leaves her home to come and live with them. Traditionally, marriage was arranged by parents, with children, particularly females, having little or no say. This is changing somewhat nowadays, but it is still unusual for children to marry without their parents' consent. Marriage ceremonies vary by income and region and range from all the brothers sitting together as grooms to only the eldest one formally doing so. The age of the brothers plays an important role in determining this: very young brothers almost never participate in actual marriage ceremonies, although they typically join the marriage when they reach their mid-teens.

The eldest brother is normally dominant in terms of authority, that is, in managing the household, but all the brothers share the work and participate as sexual partners. Tibetan males and females do not find the sexual aspect of sharing a spouse the least bit unusual, repulsive, or scandalous, and the norm is for the wife to treat all the brothers the same.

Offspring are treated similarly. There is no attempt to link children biologically to particular brothers, and a brother shows no favoritism toward his child even if he knows he is the real father because, for example, his other brothers were away at the time the wife became pregnant. The children, in turn, consider all of the brothers as their fathers and treat them equally, even if they also know who is their real father. In some regions children use the term "father" for the eldest brother and "father's brother" for the others, while in other areas they call all the brothers by one term, modifying this by the use of "elder" and "younger."

Unlike our own society, where monogamy is the only form of marriage permitted, Tibetan society allows a variety of marriage types, including monogamy, fraternal polyandry, and polygyny. Fraternal polyandry and monogamy are the most common forms of marriage, while polygyny typically occurs in cases where the first wife is barren. The widespread practice of fraternal polyandry, therefore, is not the outcome of a law requiring brothers to marry jointly. There is choice, and in fact, divorce traditionally was relatively simple in Tibetan society. If a brother in a polyandrous marriage became dissatisfied and wanted to separate, he simply left the main house and set up his own household. In such cases, all the children stayed in the main household with the remaining brother(s), even if the departing brother was known to be the real father of one or more of the children.

The Tibetans' own explanation for choosing fraternal polyandry is materialistic. For example, when I asked Dorje why he decided to marry with his two brothers rather than take his own wife, he thought for a moment, then said it prevented the division of his family's farm (and animals) and thus facilitated all of them achieving a higher standard of living. And when I later asked Dorje's bride whether it wasn't difficult for her to cope with three brothers as husbands, she laughed and echoed the rationale of avoiding fragmentation of the family and land, adding that she expected to be better off economically, since she would have three husbands working for her and her children.

Exotic as it may seem to Westerners, Tibetan fraternal polyandry is thus in many ways analogous to the way primogeniture functioned in nineteenth-century England. Primogeniture dictated that the eldest son inherited the family estate, while younger sons had to leave home and seek their own employment—for example, in the military or the clergy. Primogeniture maintained family estates intact over generations by permitting only one heir per generation. Fraternal polyandry also accomplishes this but does so by keeping all the brothers together with just one wife so that there is only one *set* of heirs per generation.

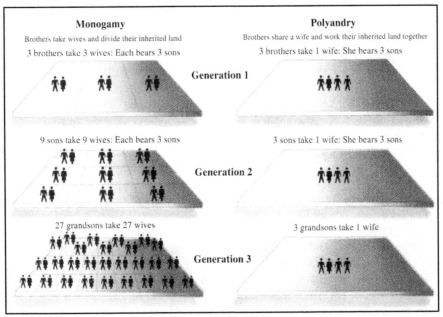

Monogamy

Brothers take wives and divide their inherited land

3 brothers take 3 wives: Each bears 3 sons

Generation 1

9 sons take 9 wives: Each bears 3 sons

Generation 2

27 grandsons take 27 wives

Generation 3

Polyandry

Brothers share a wife and work their inherited land together

3 brothers take 1 wife: She bears 3 sons

3 sons take 1 wife: She bears 3 sons

3 grandsons take 1 wife

Joe LeMonnier

Family Planning in Tibet   An economic rationale for fraternal polyandry is outlined in the diagram, which emphasizes only the male offspring in each generation. If every wife is assumed to bear three sons, a family splitting up into monogamous households would rapidly multiply and fragment the family land. In this case, a rule of inheritance, such as primogeniture, could retain the family land intact, but only at the cost of creating many landless male offspring. In contrast, the family practicing fraternal polyandry maintains a steady ratio of persons to land.

While Tibetans believe that in this way fraternal polyandry reduces the risk of family fission, monogamous marriages among brothers need not necessarily precipitate the division of the family estate: brothers could continue to live together, and the family land could continue to be worked jointly. When I asked Tibetans about this, however, they invariably responded that such joint families are unstable because each wife is primarily oriented to her own children and interested in their success and well-being over that of the children of the other wives. For example, if the youngest brother's wife had three sons while the eldest brother's wife had only one daughter, the wife of the youngest brother might begin to demand more resources for her children since, as males, they represent the future of the family. Thus, the children from different wives in the same generation are competing sets of heirs, and this makes such families inherently unstable. Tibetans perceive that conflict will spread from the wives to their husbands and consider this likely to cause family fission. Consequently, it is almost never done.

Although Tibetans see an economic advantage to fraternal polyandry, they do not value the sharing of a wife as an end in itself. On the contrary, they articulate a number of problems inherent in the practice. For example, because authority is customarily exercised by the eldest brother, his younger male siblings have to subordinate themselves with little hope of changing their status within the family. When these younger brothers are aggressive and individualistic, tensions and difficulties often occur despite there being only one set of heirs.

In addition, tension and conflict may arise in polyandrous families because of sexual favoritism. The bride normally sleeps with the eldest brother, and the two have the responsibility to see to it that the other males have opportunities for sexual access. Since the Tibetan subsistence economy requires males to travel a lot, the temporary absence of one or more brothers facilitates this, but there are also other rotation practices. The cultural ideal unambiguously calls for the wife to show equal affection and sexuality to each of the brothers (and vice versa), but deviations from this ideal occur, especially when there is a sizable difference in age between the partners in the marriage.

Dorje's family represents just such a potential situation. He is fifteen years old and his two older brothers are twenty-five and twenty-two years old. The new bride is twenty-three years old, eight years Dorje's senior. Sometimes such a bride finds the youngest husband immature and adolescent and does not treat him with equal affection; alternatively, she may find his youth attractive and lavish special attention on him. Apart from that consideration, when a younger male like Dorje grows up, he may consider his wife "ancient" and prefer the company of a woman his own age or younger. Consequently, although men and women do not find the idea of sharing a bride or bridegroom repulsive, individual likes and dislikes can cause familial discord.

Two reasons have commonly been offered for the perpetuation of fraternal polyandry in Tibet: that Tibetans practice female infanticide and therefore have to marry polyandrously, owing to a shortage of females; and that Tibet, lying at extremely high altitudes, is so barren and bleak that Tibetans would starve without resort to this mechanism. A Jesuit who lived in Tibet during the eighteenth century articulated this second view: "One reason for this most odious custom is the sterility of the soil, and the small amount of land that can be cultivated owing to the lack of water. The crops may suffice if the brothers all live together, but if they form separate families they would be reduced to beggary."

Both explanations are wrong, however. Not only has there never been institutionalized female infanticide in Tibet, but Tibetan society gives females considerable rights, including inheriting the family estate in the absence of brothers. In such cases, the woman takes a bridegroom who comes to live in her family and adopts her family's name and identity. Moreover, there is no demographic evidence of a shortage of females. In Limi, for example, there were (in 1974) sixty females and fifty-three males in the fifteen- to thirty-five-year age category, and many adult females were unmarried.

The second reason is also incorrect. The climate in Tibet is extremely harsh, and ecological factors do play a major role perpetuating polyandry, but polyandry is not a means of preventing starvation. It is characteristic, not of the poorest segments of the society, but rather of the peasant landowning families.

In the old society, the landless poor could not realistically aspire to prosperity, but they did not fear starvation. There was a persistent labor shortage throughout Tibet, and very poor families with little or no land and few animals could subsist through agricultural labor, tenant farming, craft occupations such as carpentry, or by working as servants. Although the per person family income could increase somewhat if brothers married polyandrously and pooled their wages, in the absence of inheritable land, the advantage of fraternal polyandry was not generally sufficient to prevent them from setting up their own households. A more skilled or energetic younger brother could do as well or better alone, since he would completely control his income and would not have to share it with his siblings. Consequently, while there was and is some polyandry among the poor, it is much less frequent and more prone to result in divorce and family fission.

An alternative reason for the persistence of fraternal polyandry is that it reduces population growth (and thereby reduces the pressure on resources) by relegating some females to lifetime spinsterhood. Fraternal polyandrous marriages in Limi (in 1974) averaged 2.35 men per woman, and not surprisingly, 31 percent of the females of child-bearing age (twenty to forty-nine) were unmarried. These spinsters either continued to live at home, set up their own households, or worked as servants for other families. They could also become Buddhist nuns. Being unmarried is not synonymous with exclusion from the reproductive pool. Discreet extramarital relationships are tolerated, and actually half of the adult unmarried women in Limi had one or more children. They raised these children as single mothers, working for wages or weaving cloth and blankets for sale. As a group, however, the unmarried woman had far fewer off-spring than the married women, averaging only 0.7 children per woman, compared with 3.3 for married women, whether polyandrous, monogamous, or polygynous. While polyandry helps regulate population, this function of polyandry is not consciously perceived by Tibetans and is not the reason they consistently choose it.

If neither a shortage of females nor the fear of starvation perpetuates fraternal polyandry, what motivates brothers, particularly younger brothers, to opt for this system of marriage? From the perspective of the younger brother in a land-holding family, the main incentive is the attainment or maintenance of the good life. With polyandry, he can expect a more secure and higher standard of living, with access not only to this family's land and animals but also to its inherited collection of clothes, jewelry, rugs, saddles, and horses. In addition, he will experience less work pressure and much greater security because all responsibility does not fall on one "father." For Tibetan brothers, the question is whether to trade off the greater personal freedom inherent in monogamy for the real or potential economic security, affluence, and social prestige associated with life in a larger, labor-rich polyandrous family.

A brother thinking of separating from his polyandrous marriage and taking his own wife would face various disadvantages. Although in the majority of Tibetan regions all brothers theoretically have rights to their family's estate, in reality Tibetans are reluctant to divide their land into small fragments. Generally, a younger brother who insists on leaving the family will receive only a small plot of land, if that. Because of its power and wealth, the rest of the family usually can block any attempt of the younger brother to increase his share of land through litigation. Moreover, a younger brother may not even get a house and cannot expect to receive much above the minimum in terms of movable possessions, such as furniture, pots, and pans. Thus, a brother contemplating going it on his own must plan on achieving economic security and the good life not through inheritance but through his own work.

The obvious solution for younger brothers—creating new fields from virgin land—is generally not a feasible option. Most Tibetan populations live at high altitudes (above 12,000 feet), where arable land is extremely scarce. For example, in Dorje's village, agriculture ranges only from about 12,900 feet, the lowest point in the area, to 13,300 feet. Above that altitude, early frost and snow destroy the staple barley crop. Furthermore, because of the low rainfall caused by the Himalayan rain shadow, many areas in Tibet and northern Nepal that are within the appropriate altitude range for agriculture have no reliable sources of irrigation. In the end, although there is plenty of unused land in such areas, most of it is either too high or too arid.

Even where unused land capable of being farmed exists, clearing the land and building the substantial terraces necessary for irrigation constitute a great undertaking. Each plot has to be completely dug out to a depth of two to two and half feet so that the large rocks and boulders can be removed. At best, a man might be able to bring a few new fields under cultivation in the first years after separating from his brothers, but he could not expect to acquire substantial amounts of arable land this way.

In addition, because of the limited farmland, the Tibetan subsistence economy characteristically includes a strong emphasis on animal husbandry. Tibetan farmers regularly maintain cattle, yaks, goats, and sheep, grazing them in the areas too high for agriculture. These herds produce wool, milk, cheese, butter, meat, and skins. To obtain these resources, however, shepherds must accompany the animals on a daily basis. When first setting up a monogamous household, a younger brother like Dorje would find it difficult to both farm and manage animals.

In traditional Tibetan society, there was an even more critical factor that operated to perpetuate fraternal polyandry—a form of hereditary servitude somewhat analogous to serfdom in

Europe. Peasants were tied to large estates held by aristocrats, monasteries, and the Lhasa government. They were allowed the use of some farmland to produce their own subsistence but were required to provide taxes in kind and corvée (free labor) to their lords. The corvée was a substantial hardship, since a peasant household was in many cases required to furnish the lord with one laborer daily for most of the year and more on specific occasions such as the harvest. This enforced labor, along with the lack of new land and ecological pressure to pursue both agriculture and animal husbandry, made polyandrous families particularly beneficial. The polyandrous family allowed an internal division of adult labor, maximizing economic advantage. For example, while the wife worked the family fields, one brother could perform the lord's corvée, another could look after the animals, and a third could engage in trade.

Although social scientists often discount other people's explanations of why they do things, in the case of Tibetan fraternal polyandry, such explanations are very close to the truth. The custom, however, is very sensitive to changes in its political and economic milieu and, not surprisingly, is in decline in most Tibetan areas. Made less important by the elimination of the traditional serf-based economy, it is disparaged by the dominant non-Tibetan leaders of India, China, and Nepal. New opportunities for economic and social mobility in these countries, such as the tourist trade and government employment, are also eroding the rationale for polyandry, and so it may vanish within the next generation.

Assess Your Progress

1. What is "fraternal polyandry?" How is it arranged?
2. How do marriage ceremonies vary? When do younger brothers typically join the marriage?
3. How are authority, work, and sex dealt with?
4. Describe the relationship between fathers and children. How is family structure reflected in kinship terminology?
5. What types of marriage are allowed in Tibetan society? Which are the most common? When does polygyny typically occur? Is fraternal polyandry a matter of law or choice? What happens if a brother is dissatisfied? What about his children?
6. How do the Tibetans explain fraternal polyandry? How is this analogous to primogeniture in 19th century England?
7. Why does it seem that monogamous marriages among brothers in the same household would not work?
8. What kinds of problems occur with fraternal polyandry that make it less than ideal?
9. What two reasons have been commonly offered for the perpetuation of fraternal polyandry in Tibet and how does the author refute these?
10. What percentage of women remain unmarried in Tibetan society? What happens to them? To what extent does polyandry thereby limit population growth? Are the Tibetans aware of this effect?
11. Why would a younger brother accept such a marriage form?
12. How is the polyandrous family more adaptive to the system of hereditary servitude in traditional Tibet?
13. Why is the custom of fraternal polyandry in decline?

MELVYN C. GOLDSTEIN, now a professor of anthropology at Case Western Reserve University in Cleveland, has been interested in the Tibetan practice of fraternal polyandry (several brothers marrying one wife) since he was a graduate student in the 1960s.

Death without Weeping

Has poverty ravaged mother love in the shantytowns of Brazil?

NANCY SCHEPER-HUGHES

I have seen death without weeping,
The destiny of the Northeast is death,
Cattle they kill,
To the people they do something worse
　　　　　—Anonymous Brazilian singer (1965)

"Why do the church bells ring so often?" I asked Nailza de Arruda soon after I moved into a corner of her tiny mud-walled hut near the top of the shantytown called the Alto do Cruzeiro (Crucifix Hill). I was then a Peace Corps volunteer and community development/ health worker. It was the dry and blazing hot summer of 1965, the months following the military coup in Brazil, and save for the rusty, clanging bells of N. S. das Dores Church, an eerie quiet had settled over the market town that I call Bom Jesus da Mata. Beneath the quiet, however, there was chaos and panic. "It's nothing," replied Nailza, "just another little angel gone to heaven."

Nailza had sent more than her share of little angels to heaven, and sometimes at night I could hear her engaged in a muffled but passionate discourse with one of them, two-year-old Joana. Joana's photograph, taken as she lay propped up in her tiny cardboard coffin, her eyes open, hung on a wall next to one of Nailza and Ze Antonio taken on the day they eloped.

Nailza could barely remember the other infants and babies who came and went in close succession. Most had died unnamed and were hastily baptized in their coffins. Few lived more than a month or two. Only Joana, properly baptized in church at the close of her first year and placed under the protection of a powerful saint, Joan of Arc, had been expected to live. And Nailza had dangerously allowed herself to love the little girl.

In addressing the dead child, Nailza's voice would range from tearful imploring to angry recrimination: "Why did you leave me? Was your patron saint so greedy that she could not allow me one child on this earth?" Ze Antonio advised me to ignore Nailza's odd behavior, which he understood as a kind of madness that, like the birth and death of children, came and went. Indeed, the premature birth of a stillborn son some months later "cured" Nailza of her "inappropriate" grief, and the day came when she removed Joana's photo and carefully packed it away.

More than fifteen years elapsed before I returned to the Alto do Cruzeiro, and it was anthropology that provided the vehicle of my return. Since 1982 I have returned several times in order to pursue a problem that first attracted my attention in the 1960s. My involvement with the people of the Alto do Cruzeiro now spans a quarter of a century and three generations of parenting in a community where mothers and daughters are often simultaneously pregnant.

The Alto do Cruzeiro is one of three shantytowns surrounding the large market town of Bom Jesus in the sugar plantation zone of Pernambuco in Northeast Brazil, one of the many zones of neglect that have emerged in the shadow of the now tarnished economic miracle of Brazil. For the women and children of the Alto do Cruzeiro the only miracle is that some of them have managed to stay alive at all.

The Northeast is a region of vast proportions (approximately twice the size of Texas) and of equally vast social and developmental problems. The nine states that make up the region are the poorest in the country and are representative of the Third World within a dynamic and rapidly industrializing nation. Despite waves of migrations from the interior to the teeming shantytowns of coastal cities, the majority still live in rural areas on farms and ranches, sugar plantations and mills.

Life expectancy in the Northeast is only forty years, largely because of the appallingly high rate of infant and child mortality. Approximately one million children in Brazil under the age of five die each year. The children of the Northeast, especially those born in shantytowns on the periphery of urban life, are at a very high risk of death. In these areas, children are born without the traditional protection of breast-feeding, subsistence gardens, stable marriages, and multiple adult caretakers that exists in the interior. In the hillside shantytowns that spring up around cities or, in this case, interior market towns, marriages are brittle, single parenting is the norm, and women are frequently forced into the shadow economy of domestic work in the homes of the rich or into unprotected and oftentimes "scab" wage labor on the surrounding sugar plantations, where they clear land for planting and weed for a pittance, sometimes less than a dollar a day. The women of the Alto may not bring their babies with them into the homes of the wealthy, where the often-sick infants are considered sources of contamination, and they cannot carry the little ones to the riverbanks where they wash clothes because the river is heavily infested with schistosomes and other deadly parasites. Nor can they carry their young children to the plantations, which are often several miles away. At wages of a dollar a day, the women of the Alto cannot hire baby sitters. Older children who are not in school will sometimes serve as somewhat indifferent caretakers. But any child not in school is also expected to find wage work. In most cases, babies are simply left at home alone, the door securely fastened. And so many also die alone and unattended.

Bom Jesus da Mata, centrally located in the plantation zone of Pernambuco, is within commuting distance of several sugar plantations and mills. Consequently, Bom Jesus has been a magnet for rural workers forced off their small subsistence plots by large landowners wanting to use every available piece of land for sugar cultivation. Initially, the rural migrants to Bom Jesus were squatters who were given tacit approval by the mayor to put up temporary straw huts on each of the three hills overlooking the town. The Alto do Cruzeiro is the oldest, the largest, and the poorest of the shantytowns. Over the past three decades many of the original migrants have become permanent residents, and the primitive and temporary straw huts have been replaced by small homes (usually of two rooms) made of wattle and daub, sometimes covered with plaster. The more affluent residents use bricks and tiles. In most Alto homes, dangerous kerosene lamps have been replaced by light bulbs. The once tattered rural garb, often fashioned from used sugar sacking, has likewise been replaced by store-bought clothes, often castoffs from a wealthy *patrão* (boss). The trappings are modern, but the hunger, sickness, and death that they conceal are traditional, deeply rooted in a history of feudalism, exploitation, and institutionalized dependency.

My research agenda never wavered. The questions I addressed first crystalized during a veritable "die-off" of Alto babies during a severe drought in 1965. The food and water shortages and the political and economic chaos occasioned by the military coup were reflected in the handwritten entries of births and deaths in the dusty, yellowed pages of the ledger books kept at the public registry office in Bom Jesus. More than 350 babies died in the Alto during 1965 alone—this from a shantytown population of little more than 5,000. But that wasn't what surprised me. There were reasons enough for the deaths in the miserable conditions of shantytown life. What puzzled me was the seeming indifference of Alto women to the death of their infants, and their willingness to attribute to their own tiny offspring an aversion to life that made their death seem wholly natural, indeed all but anticipated.

Although I found that it was possible, and hardly difficult, to rescue infants and toddlers from death by diarrhea and dehydration with a simple sugar, salt, and water solution (even bottled Coca-Cola worked fine), it was more difficult to enlist a mother herself in the rescue of a child she perceived as ill-fated for life or better off dead, or to convince her to take back into her threatened and besieged home a baby she had already come to think of as an angel rather than as a son or daughter.

I learned that the high expectancy of death, and the ability to face child death with stoicism and equanimity, produced patterns of nurturing that differentiated between those infants thought of as thrivers and survivors and those thought of as born already "wanting to die." The survivors were nurtured, while stigmatized, doomed infants were left to die, as mothers say, *a mingua*, "of neglect." Mothers stepped back and allowed nature to take its course. This pattern, which I call mortal selective neglect, is called passive infanticide by anthropologist Marvin Harris. The Alto situation, although culturally specific in the form that it takes, is not unique to Third World shantytown communities and may have its correlates in our own impoverished urban communities in some cases of "failure to thrive" infants.

I use as an example the story of Zezinho, the thirteen-month-old toddler of one of my neighbors, Lourdes. I became involved with Zezinho when I was called in to help Lourdes in the delivery of another child, this one a fair and robust little tyke with a lusty cry. I noted that while Lourdes showed great interest in the newborn, she totally ignored Zezinho who, wasted and severely malnourished, was curled up in a fetal position on a piece of urine- and feces-soaked cardboard placed under his mother's hammock. Eyes open and vacant, mouth slack, the little boy seemed doomed.

When I carried Zezinho up to the community day-care center at the top of the hill, the Alto women who took turns caring for one another's children (in order to free themselves for part-time work in the cane fields or washing clothes) laughed at my efforts to save Ze, agreeing with Lourdes that here was a baby without a ghost of a chance. Leave him alone, they cautioned. It makes no sense to fight with death. But I did do battle with Ze, and after several weeks of force-feeding (malnourished babies lose their interest in food), Ze began to succumb to my ministrations. He acquired some flesh across his taut chest bones, learned to sit up, and even tried to smile. When he seemed well enough, I returned him to Lourdes in her miserable scrap-material lean-to, but not without guilt about what I had done. I wondered whether returning Ze was at all fair to Lourdes and to his little brother. But I was busy and washed my hands of the matter. And Lourdes did seem more interested in Ze now that he was looking more human.

When I returned in 1982, there was Lourdes among the women who formed my sample of Alto mothers—still struggling to put together some semblance of life for a now grown Ze and her five other surviving children. Much was made of my reunion with Ze in 1982, and everyone enjoyed retelling the story of Ze's rescue and of how his mother had given him up for dead. Ze would laugh the loudest when told how I had had to force-feed him like a fiesta turkey. There was no hint of guilt on the part of Lourdes and no resentment on the part of Ze. In fact, when questioned in private as to who was the best friend he ever had in life, Ze took a long drag on his cigarette and answered without a trace of irony, "Why my mother, of course." "But of course," I replied.

Part of learning how to mother in the Alto do Cruzeiro is learning when to let go of a child who shows that it "wants" to die or that it has no "knack" or no "taste" for life. Another part is learning when it is safe to let oneself love a child. Frequent child death remains a powerful shaper of maternal thinking and practice. In the absence of firm expectation that a child will survive, mother love as we conceptualize it (whether in popular terms or in the psychobiological notion of maternal bonding) is attenuated and delayed with consequences for infant survival. In an environment already precarious to young life, the emotional detachment of mothers toward some of their babies contributes even further to the spiral of high mortality—high fertility in a kind of macabre lock-step dance of death.

The average woman of the Alto experiences 9.5 pregnancies, 3.5 child deaths, and 1.5 stillbirths. Seventy percent of all child deaths in the Alto occur in the first six months of life, and 82 percent by the end of the first year. Of all deaths in the community each year, about 45 percent are of children under the age of five.

Women of the Alto distinguish between child deaths understood as natural (caused by diarrhea and communicable diseases) and those resulting from sorcery, the evil eye, or other magical or supernatural afflictions. They also recognize a large category of infant deaths seen as fated and inevitable. These hopeless cases are classified by mothers under the folk terminology "child sickness" or "child attack." Women say that there are at least fourteen different types of hopeless child sickness, but most can be subsumed under two categories—chronic and acute. The chronic cases refer to infants who are born small and wasted. They are deathly pale, mothers say, as well as weak and passive. They demonstrate no vital force, no liveliness. They do not suck vigorously; they hardly cry. Such babies can be this way at birth or they can be born sound but soon show no resistance, no "fight" against the common crises of infancy: diarrhea, respiratory infections, tropical fevers.

The acute cases are those doomed infants who die suddenly and violently. They are taken by stealth overnight, often following convulsions that bring on head banging, shaking, grimacing, and shrieking. Women say it is horrible to look at such a baby. If the infant begins to foam at the mouth or gnash its teeth or go rigid with its eyes turned back inside its head, there is absolutely no hope. The infant is "put aside"—left alone—often on the floor in a back room, and allowed to die. These symptoms (which accompany high fevers, dehydration, third-stage malnutrition, and encephalitis) are equated by Alto women with madness, epilepsy, and worst of all, rabies, which is greatly feared and highly stigmatized.

Most of the infants presented to me as suffering from chronic child sickness were tiny, wasted famine victims, while those labeled as victims of acute child attack seemed to be infants suffering from the deliriums of high fever or the convulsions that can accompany electrolyte imbalance in dehydrated babies.

Local midwives and traditional healers, praying women, as they are called, advise Alto women on when to allow a baby to die. One midwife explained: "If I can see that a baby was born unfortuitously, I tell the mother that she need not wash the infant or give it a cleansing tea. I tell her just to dust the infant with baby powder and wait for it to die." Allowing nature to take its course is not seen as sinful by these often very devout Catholic women. Rather, it is understood as cooperating with God's plan.

Often I have been asked how consciously women of the Alto behave in this regard. I would have to say that consciousness is always shifting between allowed and disallowed levels of awareness. For example, I was awakened early one morning in 1987 by two neighborhood children who had been sent to fetch me to a hastily organized wake for a two-month-old infant whose mother I had unsuccessfully urged to breast-feed. The infant was being sustained on sugar water, which the mother referred to as *soro* (serum), using a medical term for the infant's starvation regime in light of his chronic diarrhea. I had cautioned the mother that an infant could not live on *soro* forever.

The two girls urged me to console the young mother by telling her that it was "too bad" that her infant was so weak that Jesus had to take him. They were coaching me in proper Alto etiquette. I agreed, of course, but asked, "And what do *you* think?" Xoxa, the eleven-year-old, looked down at her dusty flip-flops and blurted out, "Oh, Dona Nanci, that baby never got enough to eat, but you must never say that!" And so the death of hungry babies remains one of the best kept secrets of life in Bom Jesus da Mata.

Most victims are waked quickly and with a minimum of ceremony. No tears are shed, and the neighborhood children form a tiny procession, carrying the baby to the town graveyard where it will join a multitude of others. Although a few fresh flowers may be scattered over the tiny grave, no stone or wooden cross will mark the place, and the same spot will be reused within a few months' time. The mother will never visit the grave, which soon becomes an anonymous one.

What, then, can be said of these women? What emotions, what sentiments motivate them? How are they able to do what, in fact, must be done? What does mother love mean in this inhospitable context? Are grief, mourning, and melancholia present, although deeply repressed? If so, where shall we look for them? And if not, how are we to understand the moral visions and moral sensibilities that guide their actions?

I have been criticized more than once for presenting an unflattering portrait of poor Brazilian women, women who are, after all, themselves the victims of severe social and institutional neglect. I have described these women as allowing some of their children to die, as if this were an unnatural and inhuman act rather than, as I would assert, the way any one of us might act, reasonably and rationally, under similarly desperate conditions. Perhaps I have not emphasized enough the real pathogens in this environment of high risk: poverty, deprivation, sexism, chronic hunger, and economic exploitation. If mother love is, as many psychologists and some feminists believe, a seemingly natural and universal maternal script, what does it mean to women for whom scarcity, loss, sickness, and deprivation have made that love frantic and robbed them of their grief, seeming to turn their hearts to stone?

Throughout much of human history—as in a great deal of the impoverished Third World today—women have had to give birth and to nurture children under ecological conditions and social arrangements hostile to child survival, as well as to their own well-being. Under circumstances of high childhood mortality, patterns of selective neglect and passive infanticide may be seen as active survival strategies.

100

They also seem to be fairly common practices historically and across cultures. In societies characterized by high childhood mortality and by a correspondingly high (replacement) fertility, cultural practices of infant and child care tend to be organized primarily around survival goals. But what this means is a pragmatic recognition that not all of one's children can be expected to live. The nervousness about child survival in areas of northeast Brazil, northern India, or Bangladesh, where a 30 percent or 40 percent mortality rate in the first years of life is common, can lead to forms of delayed attachment and a casual or benign neglect that serves to weed out the worst bets so as to enhance the life chances of healthier siblings, including those yet to be born. Practices similar to those that I am describing have been recorded for parts of Africa, India, and Central America.

Life in the Alto do Cruzeiro resembles nothing so much as a battlefield or an emergency room in an overcrowded inner-city public hospital. Consequently, mortality is guided by a kind of "life-boat ethics," the morality of triage. The seemingly studied indifference toward the suffering of some of their infants, conveyed in such sayings as "little critters have no feelings," is understandable in light of these women's obligation to carry on with their reproductive and nurturing lives.

In their slowness to anthropomorphize and personalize their infants, everything is mobilized so as to prevent maternal over-attachment and, therefore, grief at death. The bereaved mother is told not to cry, that her tears will dampen the wings of her little angel so that she cannot fly up to her heavenly home. Grief at the death of an angel is not only inappropriate, it is a symptom of madness and of a profound lack of faith.

Infant death becomes routine in an environment in which death is anticipated and bets are hedged. While the routinization of death in the context of shantytown life is not hard to understand, and quite possible to empathize with, its routinization in the formal institutions of public life in Bom Jesus is not as easy to accept uncritically. Here the social production of indifference takes on a different, even a malevolent, cast.

In a society where triplicates of every form are required for the most banal events (registering a car, for example), the registration of infant and child death is informal, incomplete, and rapid. It requires no documentation, takes less than five minutes, and demands no witnesses other than office clerks. No questions are asked concerning the circumstances of the death, and the cause of death is left blank, unquestioned and unexamined. A neighbor, grandmother, older sibling, or common-law husband may register the death. Since most infants die at home, there is no question of a medical record.

From the registry office, the parent proceeds to the town hall, where the mayor will give him or her a voucher for a free baby coffin. The full-time municipal coffinmaker cannot tell you exactly how many baby coffins are dispatched each week. It varies, he says, with the seasons. There are more needed during the drought months and during the big festivals of Carnaval and Christmas and São Joao's Day because people are too busy, he supposes, to take their babies to the clinic. Record keeping is sloppy.

Similarly, there is a failure on the part of city-employed doctors working at two free clinics to recognize the malnutrition

of babies who are weighed, measured, and immunized without comment and as if they were not, in fact, anemic, stunted, fussy, and irritated starvation babies. At best the mothers are told to pick up free vitamins or a health "tonic" at the municipal chambers. At worst, clinic personnel will give tranquilizers and sleeping pills to quiet the hungry cries of "sick-to-death" Alto babies.

The church, too, contributes to the routinization of, and indifference toward, child death. Traditionally, the local Catholic church taught patience and resignation to domestic tragedies that were said to reveal the imponderable workings of God's will. If an infant died suddenly, it was because a particular saint had claimed the child. The infant would be an angel in the service of his or her heavenly patron. It would be wrong, a sign of a lack of faith, to weep for a child with such good fortune. The infant funeral was, in the past, an event celebrated with joy. Today, however, under the new regime of "liberation theology," the bells of N. S. das Dores parish church no longer peal for the death of Alto babies, and no priest accompanies the procession of angels to the cemetery where their bodies are disposed of casually and without ceremony. Children bury children in Bom Jesus da Mata. In this most Catholic of communities, the coffin is handed to the disabled and irritable municipal gravedigger, who often chides the children for one reason or another. It may be that the coffin is larger than expected and the gravedigger can find no appropriate space. The children do not wait for the gravedigger to complete his task. No prayers are recited and no sign of the cross made as the tiny coffin goes into its shallow grave.

When I asked the local priest, Padre Marcos, about the lack of church ceremony surrounding infant and childhood death today in Bom Jesus, he replied; "In the old days, child death was richly celebrated. But those were the baroque customs of a conservative church that wallowed in death and misery. The new church is a church of hope and joy. We no longer celebrate the death of child angels. We try to tell mothers that Jesus doesn't want all the dead babies they send him." Similarly, the new church has changed its baptismal customs, now often refusing to baptize dying babies brought to the back door of a church or rectory. The mothers are scolded by the church attendants and told to go home and take care of their sick babies. Baptism, they are told, is for the living; it is not to be confused with the sacrament of extreme unction, which is the anointing of the dying. And so it appears to the women of the Alto that even the church has turned away from them, denying the traditional comfort of folk Catholicism.

The contemporary Catholic church is caught in the clutches of a double bind. The new theology of liberation imagines a kingdom of God on earth based on justice and equality, a world without hunger, sickness, or childhood mortality. At the same time, the church has not changed its official position on sexuality and reproduction, including its sanctions against birth control, abortion, and sterilization. The padre of Bom Jesus da Mata recognizes this contradiction intuitively, although he shies away from discussions on the topic, saying that he prefers to leave questions of family planning to the discretion and the "good consciences" of his impoverished parishioners. But this, of course, sidesteps the extent to which those good consciences have been shaped by traditional church teachings in Bom Jesus, especially by his recent predecessors. Hence, we can begin to see that the seeming indifference of Alto mothers toward the death of some of their infants is but a pale reflection of the official indifference of church and state to the plight of poor women and children.

Nonetheless, the women of Bom Jesus are survivors. One woman, Biu, told me her life history, returning again and again to the themes of child death, her first husband's suicide, abandonment by her father and later by her second husband, and all the other losses and disappointments she had suffered in her long forty-five years. She concluded with great force, reflecting on the days of Carnaval '88 that were fast approaching:

> No, Dona Nanci, I won't cry, and I won't waste my life thinking about it from morning to night. . . . Can I argue with God for the state that I'm in? No! And so I'll dance and I'll jump and I'll play Carnaval! And yes, I'll laugh and people will wonder at a *pobre* like me who can have such a good time.

And no one did blame Biu for dancing in the streets during the four days of Carnaval—not even on Ash Wednesday, the day following Carnaval '88 when we all assembled hurriedly to assist in the burial of Mercea, Biu's beloved *casula,* her last-born daughter who had died at home of pneumonia during the festivities. The rest of the family barely had time to change out of their costumes. Severino, the child's uncle and godfather, sprinkled holy water over the little angel while he prayed: "Mercea, I don't know whether you were called, taken, or thrown out of this world. But look down at us from your heavenly home with tenderness, with pity, and with mercy." So be it.

Assess Your Progress

1. How is the poverty of the Brazilian Northeast reflected in its life expectancy and infant and child mortality?
2. What traditional protections are absent for the children?
3. How does the author characterize marriage and the lives of women and their children?
4. Under what circumstances have people come to Bom Jesus?
5. What puzzled the author about the death of infants? How was it possible to rescue their children and yet difficult to enlist the mothers' help?
6. Describe "mortal selective neglect" (or "passive infanticide").
7. Describe the case of "Ze" as it illustrates the author's later points.
8. What must one learn to be a mother?
9. Why is "allowing nature to take its course" not seen as sinful?
10. What is "one of the best kept secrets of life?"
11. How does the author explain the mothers' "delayed attachment" and "benign neglect?"
12. How is infant death "routinized" with respect to official records and medical care? How has the church contributed to this indifference? What changes have occurred under "liberation theology?"
13. How is the church caught in a "double bind?"

NANCY SCHEPER-HUGHES is a professor in the Department of Anthropology at the University of California, Berkeley. She has written *Death Without Weeping: Violence of Everyday Life in Brazil* (1992).

Arranging a Marriage in India

SERENA NANDA

Sister and doctor brother-in-law invite correspondence from North Indian professionals only, for a beautiful, talented, sophisticated, intelligent sister, 5'3", slim, M.A. in textile design, father a senior civil officer. Would prefer immigrant doctors, between 26–29 years. Reply with full details and returnable photo. A well-settled uncle invites matrimonial correspondence from slim, fair, educated South Indian girl, for his nephew, 25 years, smart, M.B.A., green card holder, 5'6". Full particulars with returnable photo appreciated.

—*Matrimonial Advertisements,*
India Abroad

In India, almost all marriages are arranged. Even among the educated middle classes in modern, urban India, marriage is as much a concern of the families as it is of the individuals. So customary is the practice of arranged marriage that there is a special name for a marriage which is not arranged: It is called a "love match."

On my first field trip to India, I met many young men and women whose parents were in the process of "getting them married." In many cases, the bride and groom would not meet each other before the marriage. At most they might meet for a brief conversation, and this meeting would take place only after their parents had decided that the match was suitable. Parents do not compel their children to marry a person who either marriage partner finds objectionable. But only after one match is refused will another be sought.

As a young American woman in India for the first time, I found this custom of arranged marriage oppressive. How could any intelligent young person agree to such a marriage without great reluctance? It was contrary to everything I believed about the importance of romantic love as the only basis of a happy marriage. It also clashed with my strongly held notions that the choice of such an intimate and permanent relationship could be made only by the individuals involved. Had anyone tried to arrange my marriage, I would have been defiant and rebellious!

At the first opportunity, I began, with more curiosity than tact, to question the young people I met on how they felt about this practice. Sita, one of my young informants, was a college graduate with a degree in political science. She had been waiting for over a year while her parents were arranging a match for her. I found it difficult to accept the docile manner in which this well-educated young woman awaited the outcome of a process that would result in her spending the rest of her life with a man she hardly knew, a virtual stranger, picked out by her parents.

"How can you go along with this?" I asked her, in frustration and distress. "Don't you care who you marry?"

"Of course I care," she answered. "This is why I must let my parents choose a boy for me. My marriage is too important to be arranged by such an inexperienced person as myself. In such matters, it is better to have my parents' guidance."

I had learned that young men and women in India do not date and have very little social life involving members of the opposite sex. Although I could not disagree with Sita's reasoning, I continued to pursue the subject.

Young men and women do not date and have very little social life involving members of the opposite sex.

"But how can you marry the first man you have ever met? Not only have you missed the fun of meeting a lot of different people, but you have not given yourself the chance to know who is the right man for you."

"Meeting with a lot of different people doesn't sound like any fun at all," Sita answered. "One hears that in America the girls are spending all their time worrying about whether they will meet a man and get married. Here we have the chance to enjoy our life and let our parents do this work and worrying for us."

She had me there. The high anxiety of the competition to "be popular" with the opposite sex certainly was the most prominent feature of life as an American teenager in the late fifties. The endless worrying about the rules that governed our behavior and about our popularity ratings sapped both our self-esteem and our enjoyment of adolescence. I reflected that absence of this competition in India most certainly may have contributed to the self-confidence and natural charm of so many of the young women I met.

And yet, the idea of marrying a perfect stranger, whom one did not know and did not "love," so offended my American ideas of individualism and romanticism, that I persisted with my objections.

"I still can't imagine it," I said. "How can you agree to marry a man you hardly know?"

"But of course he will be known. My parents would never arrange a marriage for me without knowing all about the boy's family background. Naturally we will not rely only on what the family tells us. We will check the particulars out ourselves. No one will want their daughter to marry into a family that is not good. All these things we will know beforehand."

Impatiently, I responded, "Sita, I don't mean know the family, I mean, know the man. How can you marry someone you don't know personally and don't love? How can you think of spending your life with someone you may not even like?"

"If he is a good man, why should I not like him?" she said. "With you people, you know the boy so well before you marry, where will be the fun to get married? There will be no mystery and no romance. Here we have the whole of our married life to get to know and love our husband. This way is better, is it not?"

Her response made further sense, and I began to have second thoughts on the matter. Indeed, during months of meeting many intelligent young Indian people, both male and female, who had the same ideas as Sita, I saw arranged marriages in a different light. I also saw the importance of the family in Indian life and realized that a couple who took their marriage into their own hands was taking a big risk, particularly if their families were irreconcilably opposed to the match. In a country where every important resource in life—a job, a house, a social circle—is gained through family connections, it seemed foolhardy to cut oneself off from a supportive social network and depend solely on one person for happiness and success.

Six years later I returned to India to again do fieldwork, this time among the middle class in Bombay, a modern, sophisticated city. From the experience of my earlier visit, I decided to include a study of arranged marriages in my project. By this time I had met many Indian couples whose marriages had been arranged and who seemed very happy. Particularly in contrast to the fate of many of my married friends in the United States who were already in the process of divorce, the positive aspects of arranged marriages appeared to me to outweigh the negatives. In fact, I thought I might even participate in arranging a marriage myself. I had been fairly successful in the United States in "fixing up" many of my friends, and I was confident that my matchmaking skills could be easily applied to this new situation, once I learned the basic rules. "After all," I thought, "how complicated can it be? People want pretty much the same things in a marriage whether it is in India or America."

An opportunity presented itself almost immediately. A friend from my previous Indian trip was in the process of arranging for the marriage of her eldest son. In India there is a perceived shortage of "good boys," and since my friend's family was eminently respectable and the boy himself personable, well educated, and nice looking, I was sure that by the end of my year's fieldwork, we would have found a match.

The basic rule seems to be that a family's reputation is most important. It is understood that matches would be arranged only within the same caste and general social class, although some crossing of subcastes is permissible if the class positions of the bride's and groom's families are similar. Although dowry is now prohibited by law in India, extensive gift exchanges took place with every marriage. Even when the boy's family do not "make demands," every girl's family nevertheless feels the obligation to give the traditional gifts, to the girl, to the boy, and to the boy's family. Particularly when the couple would be living in the joint family—that is, with the boy's parents and his married brothers and their families, as well as with unmarried siblings—which is still very common even among the urban, upper-middle class in India, the girls' parents are anxious to establish smooth relations between their family and that of the boy. Offering the proper gifts, even when not called "dowry," is often an important factor in influencing the relationship between the bride's and groom's families and perhaps, also, the treatment of the bride in her new home.

In a society where divorce is still a scandal and where, in fact, the divorce rate is exceedingly low, an arranged marriage is the beginning of a lifetime relationship not just between the bride and groom but between their families as well.

In a society where divorce is still a scandal and where, in fact, the divorce rate is exceedingly low, an arranged marriage is the beginning of a lifetime relationship not just between the bride and groom but between their families as well. Thus, while a girl's looks are important, her character is even more so, for she is being judged as a prospective daughter-in-law as much as a prospective bride. Where she would be living in a joint family, as was the case with my friend, the girls's ability to get along harmoniously in a family is perhaps the single most important quality in assessing her suitability.

My friend is a highly esteemed wife, mother, and daughter-in-law. She is religious, soft-spoken, modest, and deferential. She rarely gossips and never quarrels, two qualities highly desirable in a woman. A family that has the reputation for gossip and conflict among its womenfolk will not find it easy to get good wives for their sons. Parents will not want to send their daughter to a house in which there is conflict.

My friend's family were originally from North India. They had lived in Bombay, where her husband owned a business, for forty years. The family had delayed in seeking a match for their eldest son because he had been an Air Force pilot for several years, stationed in such remote places that it had seemed fruitless to try to find a girl who would be willing to accompany him. In their social class, a military career, despite its economic security, has little prestige and is considered a drawback in finding a suitable bride. Many families would not allow their daughters

Even today, almost all marriages in India are arranged. It is believed that parents are much more effective at deciding whom their daughters should marry.

to marry a man in an occupation so potentially dangerous and which requires so much moving around.

The son had recently left the military and joined his father's business. Since he was a college graduate, modern, and well traveled, from such a good family, and, I thought, quite handsome, it seemed to me that he, or rather his family, was in a position to pick and choose. I said as much to my friend.

While she agreed that there were many advantages on their side, she also said, "We must keep in mind that my son is both short and dark; these are drawbacks in finding the right match." While the boy's height had not escaped my notice, "dark" seemed to me inaccurate; I would have called him "wheat" colored perhaps, and in any case, I did not realize that color would be a consideration. I discovered, however, that while a boy's skin color is a less important consideration than a girl's, it is still a factor.

An important source of contacts in trying to arrange her son's marriage was my friend's social club in Bombay. Many of the women had daughters of the right age, and some had already expressed an interest in my friend's son. I was most enthusiastic about the possibilities of one particular family who had five daughters, all of whom were pretty, demure, and well educated. Their mother had told my friend, "You can have your pick for your son, whichever one of my daughters appeals to you most."

I saw a match in sight. "Surely," I said to my friend, "we will find one there. Let's go visit and make our choice." But my friend held back; she did not seem to share my enthusiasm, for reasons I could not then fathom.

When I kept pressing for an explanation of her reluctance, she admitted, "See, Serena, here is the problem. The family has so many daughters, how will they be able to provide nicely for any of them? We are not making any demands, but still, with so many daughters to marry off, one wonders whether she will even be able to make a proper wedding. Since this is our eldest son, it's best if we marry him to a girl who is the only daughter, then the wedding will truly be a gala affair." I argued that surely the quality of the girls themselves made up for any deficiency in the elaborateness of the wedding. My friend admitted this point but still seemed reluctant to proceed.

"Is there something else," I asked her, "some factor I have missed?" "Well," she finally said, "there is one other thing. They have one daughter already married and living in Bombay. The mother is always complaining to me that the girl's in-laws don't let her visit her own family often enough. So it makes me wonder, will she be that kind of mother who always wants her daughter at her own home? This will prevent the girl from adjusting to our house. It is not a good thing." And so, this family of five daughters was dropped as a possibility.

Somewhat disappointed, I nevertheless respected my friend's reasoning and geared up for the next prospect. This was also the daughter of a woman in my friend's social club. There was clear interest in this family and I could see why. The family's reputation was excellent; in fact, they came from a subcaste slightly higher than my friend's own. The girl, who was an only daughter, was pretty and well educated and had a brother studying in the United States. Yet, after expressing an interest to me in this family, all talk of them suddenly died down and the search began elsewhere.

"What happened to that girl as a prospect?" I asked one day. "You never mention her any more. She is so pretty and so educated, what did you find wrong?"

"She is too educated. We've decided against it. My husband's father saw the girl on the bus the other day and thought her forward. A girl who 'roams about' the city by herself is not the girl for our family." My disappointment this time was even greater, as I thought the son would have liked the girl very much. But then I thought, my friend is right, a girl who is going to live in a joint family cannot be too independent or she will make life miserable for everyone. I also learned that if the family of the girl has even a slightly higher social status than the family of the boy, the bride may think herself too good for them, and this too will cause problems. Later my friend admitted to me that this had been an important factor in her decision not to pursue the match.

The next candidate was the daughter of a client of my friend's husband. When the client learned that the family was looking for a match for their son, he said, "Look no further, we have a daughter." This man then invited my friends to dinner to see the girl. He had already seen their son at the office and decided that "he liked the boy." We all went together for tea, rather than dinner—it was less of a commitment—and while we were there, the girl's mother showed us around the house. The girl was studying for her exams and was briefly introduced to us.

After we left, I was anxious to hear my friend's opinion. While her husband liked the family very much and was impressed with his client's business accomplishments and reputation, the wife didn't like the girl's looks. "She is short, no doubt, which is an important plus point, but she is also fat and wears glasses." My friend obviously thought she could do better for her son and asked her husband to make his excuses to his client by saying that they had decided to postpone the boy's marriage indefinitely.

By this time almost six months had passed and I was becoming impatient. What I had thought would be an easy matter to arrange was turning out to be quite complicated. I began to believe that between my friend's desire for a girl who was modest enough to fit into her joint family, yet attractive and educated enough to be an acceptable partner for her son, she would not find anyone suitable. My friend laughed at my impatience: "Don't be so much in a hurry," she said. "You Americans want everything done so quickly. You get married quickly and then just as quickly get divorced. Here we take marriage more seriously. We must take all the factors into account. It is not enough for us to learn by our mistakes. This is too serious a business. If a mistake is made we have not only ruined the life of our son or daughter, but we have spoiled the reputation of our family as

well. And that will make it much harder for their brothers and sisters to get married. So we must be very careful."

If a mistake is made we have not only ruined the life of our son or daughter, but we have spoiled the reputation of our family as well.

What she said was true and I promised myself to be more patient, though it was not easy. I had really hoped and expected that the match would be made before my year in India was up. But it was not to be. When I left India my friend seemed no further along in finding a suitable match for her son than when I had arrived.

Two years later, I returned to India and still my friend had not found a girl for her son. By this time, he was close to thirty, and I think she was a little worried. Since she knew I had friends all over India, and I was going to be there for a year, she asked me to "help her in this work" and keep an eye out for someone suitable. I was flattered that my judgment was respected, but knowing now how complicated the process was, I had lost my earlier confidence as a matchmaker. Nevertheless, I promised that I would try.

It was almost at the end of my year's stay in India that I met a family with a marriageable daughter whom I felt might be a good possibility for my friend's son. The girl's father was related to a good friend of mine and by coincidence came from the same village as my friend's husband. This new family had a successful business in a medium-sized city in central India and were from the same sub-caste as my friend. The daughter was pretty and chic; in fact, she had studied fashion design in college. Her parents would not allow her to go off by herself to any of the major cities in India where she could make a career, but they had compromised with her wish to work by allowing her to run a small dress-making boutique from their home. In spite of her desire to have a career, the daughter was both modest and home-loving and had had a traditional, sheltered upbringing. She had only one other sister, already married, and a brother who was in his father's business.

I mentioned the possibility of a match with my friend's son. The girl's parents were most interested. Although their daughter was not eager to marry just yet, the idea of living in Bombay—a sophisticated, extremely fashion-conscious city where she could continue her education in clothing design—was a great inducement. I gave the girl's father my friend's address and suggested that when they went to Bombay on some business or whatever, they look up the boy's family.

Returning to Bombay on my way to New York, I told my friend of this newly discovered possibility. She seemed to feel there was potential but, in spite of my urging, would not make any moves herself. She rather preferred to wait for the girl's family to call upon them. I hoped something would come of this introduction, though by now I had learned to rein in my optimism.

A year later I received a letter from my friend. The family had indeed come to visit Bombay, and their daughter and my

Appendix
Further Reflections on Arranged Marriage . . .

This essay was written from the point of view of a family seeking a daughter-in-law. Arranged marriage looks somewhat different from the point of view of the bride and her family. Arranged marriage continues to be preferred, even among the more educated, Westernized sections of the Indian population. Many young women from these families still go along, more or less willingly, with the practice, and also with the specific choices of their families. Young women do get excited about the prospects of their marriage, but there is also ambivalence and increasing uncertainty, as the bride contemplates leaving the comfort and familiarity of her own home, where as a "temporary guest" she had often been indulged, to live among strangers. Even in the best situation she will now come under the close scrutiny of her husband's family. How she dresses, how she behaves, how she gets along with others, where she goes, how she spends her time, her domestic abilities—all of this and much more—will be observed and commented on by a whole new set of relations. Her interaction with her family of birth will be monitored and curtailed considerably. Not only will she leave their home, but with increasing geographic mobility, she may also live very far from them, perhaps even on another continent. Too much expression of her fondness for her own family, or her desire to visit them, may be interpreted as an inability to adjust to her new family, and may become a source of conflict. In an arranged marriage the burden of adjustment is clearly heavier for a woman than for a man. And that is in the best of situations.

In less happy circumstances, the bride may be a target of resentment and hostility from her husband's family, particularly her mother-in-law or her husband's unmarried sisters, for whom she is now a source of competition for the affection, loyalty, and economic resources of their son or brother. If she is psychologically, or even physically abused, her options are limited, as returning to her parents' home, or divorce, are still very stigmatized. For most Indians, marriage and motherhood are still considered the only suitable roles for a woman, even for those who have careers, and few women can comfortably contemplate remaining unmarried. Most families still consider "marrying off" their daughters as a compelling religious duty and social necessity. This increases a bride's sense of obligation to make the marriage a success, at whatever cost to her own personal happiness.

The vulnerability of a new bride may also be intensified by the issue of dowry, which although illegal, has become a more pressing issue in the consumer conscious society of contemporary urban India. In many cases, where a groom's family is not satisfied with the amount of dowry a bride brings to her marriage, the young bride will be constantly harassed to get her parents to give more. In extreme cases, the bride may even be murdered, and the murder disguised as an accident or suicide. This also offers the husband's family an opportunity to arrange another match for him, thus bringing in another dowry. This phenomena, called dowry death, calls attention not just to the "evils of dowry" but also to larger issues of the powerlessness of women as well.

Serena Nanda
March 1998

---

friend's daughter, who were near in age, had become very good friends. During that year, the two girls had frequently visited each other. I thought things looked promising.

Last week I received an invitation to a wedding: My friend's son and the girl were getting married. Since I had found the match, my presence was particularly requested at the wedding. I was thrilled. Success at last! As I prepared to leave for India, I began thinking, "Now, my friend's younger son, who do I know who has a nice girl for him . . .?"

Assess Your Progress

1. To what extent are marriages arranged in India? How do middle class families in modern urban India feel about marriage? What is a "love match?"

2. How does the author describe the process of the parents' "getting them married" (with regard to young men and women)? Why did the author find this "oppressive?"

3. Describe the arguments and counter-arguments regarding arranged marriages as revealed in the verbal exchanges between the author and Sita.

4. In what sense did the author see arranged marriage as successful in contrast to marriage in the United States?

5. Why was the author so sure that a match could be made quickly for her friend's son?

6. What factors must be taken into account in arranging a marriage?

7. Why was the friend's son originally not considered a good match? What happened that would change his prospects? What drawbacks remained?

8. Describe the "problems" that arose with regard to the various "prospects" as well as the positive factors involved in the final match.

Edited by Philip R. DeVita.

Who Needs Love!

In Japan, Many Couples Don't

Nicholas D. Kristof

Yuri Uemura sat on the straw tatami mat of her living room and chatted cheerfully about her 40-year marriage to a man whom, she mused, she never particularly liked.

"There was never any love between me and my husband," she said blithely, recalling how he used to beat her. "But, well, we survived."

A 72-year-old midwife, her face as weathered as an old baseball and etched with a thousand seams, Mrs. Uemura said that her husband had never told her that he liked her, never complimented her on a meal, never told her "thank you," never held her hand, never given her a present, never shown her affection in any way. He never calls her by her name, but summons her with the equivalent of a grunt or a "Hey, you."

"Even with animals, the males cooperate to bring the females some food," Mrs. Uemura said sadly, noting the contrast to her own marriage. "When I see that, it brings tears to my eyes."

In short, the Uemuras have a marriage that is as durable as it is unhappy, one couple's tribute to the Japanese sanctity of family.

The divorce rate in Japan is at a record high but still less than half that of the United States, and Japan arguably has one of the strongest family structures in the industrialized world. As the United States and Europe fret about the disintegration of the traditional family, most Japanese families remain as solid as the small red table on which Mrs. Uemura rested her tea.

It does not seem that Japanese families survive because husbands and wives love each other more than American couples, but rather because they perhaps love each other less.

A study published last year by the Population Council, an international nonprofit group based in New York, suggested that the traditional two-parent household is on the wane not only in America but throughout most of the world. There was one prominent exception: Japan.

In Japan, for example, only 1.1 percent of births are to unwed mothers—virtually unchanged from 25 years ago. In the United States, the figure is 30.1 percent and rising rapidly.

Yet if one comes to a little Japanese town like Omiya to learn the secrets of the Japanese family, the people are not as happy as the statistics.

"I haven't lived for myself," Mrs. Uemura said, with a touch of melancholy, "but for my kids, and for my family, and for society."

Mrs. Uemura's marriage does not seem exceptional in Japan, whether in the big cities or here in Omiya. The people of Omiya, a community of 5,700 nestled in the rain-drenched hills of the Kii Peninsula in Mie Prefecture, nearly 200 miles southwest of Tokyo, have spoken periodically to a reporter about various aspects of their daily lives. On this visit they talked about their families.

Survival Secrets, Often the Couples Expect Little

Osamums Torida furrowed his brow and looked perplexed when he was asked if he loved his wife of 33 years.

"Yeah, so-so, I guess," said Mr. Torida, a cattle farmer. "She's like air or water. You couldn't live without it, but most of the time, you're not conscious of its existence."

The secret to the survival of the marriage, Mr. Torida acknowledged, was not mutual passion.

"Sure, we had fights about our work," he explained as he stood beside his barn. "But we were preoccupied by work and our debts, so we had no time to fool around."

That is a common theme in Omiya. It does not seem that Japanese families survive because husbands and wives love each other more than American couples, but rather because they perhaps love each other less.

"I think love marriages are more fragile than arranged marriages," said Tomika Kusukawa, 49, who married her high-school sweetheart and now runs a car repair shop with him. "In love marriages, when something happens or if the couple falls out of love, they split up."

If there is a secret to the strength of the Japanese family it consists of three ingredients: low expectations, patience, and shame.

GETTING ALONG

Matchmaker, Matchmaker

How countries compare on an index of compatibility of spouses, based on answers to questions about politics, sex, social issues, religion and ethics, from a survey by the Dentsu Research Institute and Leisure Development Center in Japan. A score of 500 would indicate perfect compatibility.

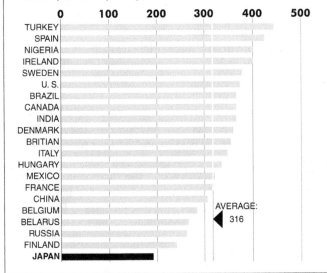

New York Times

The advantage of marriages based on low expectations is that they have built in shock absorbers. If the couple discover that they have nothing in common, that they do not even like each other, then that is not so much a reason for divorce as it is par for the course.

Even the discovery that one's spouse is having an affair is often not as traumatic in a Japanese marriage as it is in the West. A little sexual infidelity on the part of a man (though not on the part of his wife) was traditionally tolerated, so long as he did not become so besotted as to pay his mistress more than he could afford.

Tsuzuya Fukuyama, who runs a convenience store and will mark her 50th wedding anniversary this year, toasted her hands on an electric heater in the front of the store and declared that a woman would be wrong to get angry if her husband had an affair.

The durability of the Japanese family is particularly wondrous because couples are, by international standards, exceptionally incompatible.

"It's never just one side that's at fault," Mrs. Fukuyama said sternly. "Maybe the husband had an affair because his wife wasn't so hot herself. So she should look at her own faults."

Mrs. Fukuyama's daughter came to her a few years ago, suspecting that her husband was having an affair and asking what to do.

"I told her, 'Once you left this house, you can only come back if you divorce; if you're not prepared to get a divorce, then you'd better be patient,'" Mrs. Fukuyama recalled. "And so she was patient. And then she got pregnant and had a kid, and now they're close again."

The word that Mrs. Fukuyama used for patience is "gaman," a term that comes up whenever marriage is discussed in Japan. It means toughing it out, enduring hardship, and many Japanese regard gaman with pride as a national trait.

Many people complain that younger folks divorce because they do not have enough gaman, and the frequency with which the term is used suggests a rather bleak understanding of marriage.

"I didn't know my husband very well when we married, and afterward we used to get into bitter fights," said Yoshiko Hirowaki, 56, a store owner. "But then we had children, and I got very busy with the kids and with this shop. Time passed."

Now Mrs. Hirowaki has been married 34 years, and she complains about young people who do not stick to their vows.

"In the old days, wives had more gaman," she said. "Now kids just don't have enough gaman."

The durability of the Japanese family is particularly wondrous because couples are, by international standards, exceptionally incompatible.

One survey asked married men and their wives in 37 countries how they felt about politics, sex, religion, ethics and social issues. Japanese couples ranked dead last in compatibility of views, by a huge margin. Indeed, another survey found that if they were doing it over again, only about one-third of Japanese would marry the same person.

A national survey found that 30 percent of fathers spend less than 15 minutes a day on weekends talking with or playing with their children.

Incompatibility might not matter so much, however, because Japanese husbands and wives spend very little time talking to each other.

"I kind of feel there's nothing new to say to her," said Masayuki Ogita, an egg farmer, explaining his reticence.

In a small town like Omiya, couples usually have dinner together, but in Japanese cities there are many "7-11 husbands," so called because they leave at 7 A.M. and return after 11 P.M.

Masahiko Kondo now lives in Omiya, working in the chamber of commerce, but he used to be a salesman in several big cities. He would leave for work each morning at 7, and about four nights a week would go out for after-work drinking or mah-jongg sessions with buddies.

"I only saw my baby on Saturdays or Sundays," said Mr. Kondo, a lanky good-natured man of 37. "But in fact, I really enjoyed that life. It didn't bother me that I never spent time with my kid on weekdays."

Mr. Kondo's wife, Keiko, had her own life, spent with her child and the wives of other workaholic husbands.

"We had birthday parties, but they were with the kids and the mothers," she remembers. "No fathers ever came."

A national survey found that 30 percent of fathers spend less than 15 minutes a day on weekdays talking with or playing with their children. Among eighth graders, 51 percent reported that they never spoke with their fathers on weekdays.

Traditionally, many companies were reluctant to promote employees who had divorced or who had major problems at home.

As a result, the figures in Japan for single-parent households can be deceptive. The father is often more a theoretical presence than a homework-helping reality.

Still, younger people sometimes want to see the spouses in daylight, and a result is a gradual change in focus of lives from work to family. Two decades ago, nearly half of young people said in surveys that they wanted their fathers to put priority on work rather than family. Now only one-quarter say that.

Social Pressures
Shame Is Keeping Bonds in Place

For those who find themselves desperately unhappy, one source of pressure to keep plugging is shame.

"If you divorce, you lose face in society," said Tatsumi Kinoshita, a tea farmer. "People say, 'His wife escaped.' So folks remain married because they hate to be gossiped about."

Shame is a powerful social sanction in Japan, and it is not just a matter of gossip. Traditionally, many companies were reluctant to promote employees who had divorced or who had major problems at home.

"If you divorce, it weakens your position at work," said Akihiko Kanda, 27, who works in a local government office. "Your bosses won't give you such good ratings, and it'll always be a negative factor."

The idea, Mr. Kanda noted, is that if an employee cannot manage his own life properly, he should not be entrusted with important corporate matters.

Financial sanctions are also a major disincentive for divorce. The mother gets the children in three-quarters of divorces, but most mothers in Japan do not have careers and have few financial resources. Fathers pay child support in only 15 percent of all divorces with children, partly because women often hesitate to go to court to demand payments and partly because men often fail to pay even when the court orders it.

"The main reason for lack of divorce is that women can't support themselves," said Mizuko Kanda, a 51-year-old housewife. "My friends complain about their husbands and say that they'd divorce if they could, but they can't afford to."

The result of these social and economic pressures is clear.

Even in Japan, there are about 24 divorces for every 100 marriages, but that compares with 32 in France, and 42 in England, and 55 in the United States.

The Outlook
Change Creeps in, Imperiling Family

But society is changing in Japan, and it is an open question whether these changes will undermine the traditional family as they have elsewhere around the globe.

The nuclear family has already largely replaced the extended family in Japan, and shame is eroding as a sanction. Haruko Okumura, for example, runs a kindergarten and speaks openly about her divorce.

"My Mom was uneasy about it, but I never had an inferiority complex about being divorced," said Mrs. Okumura, as dozens of children played in the next room. "And people accepted me easily."

Mrs. Okumura sees evidence of the changes in family patterns every day: fathers are playing more of a role in the kindergarten. At Christmas parties and sports contests, fathers have started to show up along with mothers. And Mrs. Okumura believes that divorce is on the upswing.

"If there's a weakening of the economic and social pressures to stay married," she said, "surely divorce rates will soar."

Already divorce rates are rising, approximately doubling over the last 25 years. But couples are very reluctant to divorce when they have children, and so single-parent households account for exactly the same proportion today as in 1965.

Shinsuke Kawaguchi, a young tea farmer, is one of the men for whom life is changing. Americans are not likely to be impressed by Mr. Kawaguchi's open-mindedness, but he is.

"I take good care of my wife," he said. "I may not say 'I love you,' but I do hold her hand. And I might say, after she makes dinner, 'This tastes good.'"

"Of course," Mr. Kawaguchi quickly added, "I wouldn't say that unless I'd just done something really bad."

Even Mrs. Uemura, the elderly woman whose husband used to beat her, said that her husband was treating her better.

"The other day, he tried to pour me a cup of tea," Mrs. Uemura recalled excitedly. "It was a big change. I told all my friends."

Assess Your Progress

1. How does the author describe the marriage of Yuri Uemura?

2. How does the current Japanese divorce rate compare with the past and with that of the United States?

3. What are the statistics regarding unwed mothers?

4. In what sense are love marriages more fragile than arranged marriages?

5. What three ingredients add to the strength of Japanese marriages?

6. How do low expectations strengthen Japanese marriages?

7. Why is an affair "not as traumatic?"

8. What is "gaman" and how important is it to the Japanese?

9. To what extent are Japanese couples incompatible? What is the measure of this? Why does it not seem to matter much?

10. How much time do Japanese fathers spend with their children? What trend does the author see in this regard?

11. What are the social pressures working against divorce?

12. What changes does the author see with regard to the nuclear family versus the extended family and with regard to shame as a social sanction?

13. What changes are occurring with regard to the role of the father?

14. Are divorce rates rising? Under what specific circumstances?

From *The New York Times*, February 11, 1996, pp. 1, 12. Copyright © 1996 by The New York Times Company. Reprinted by permission via PARS International.

UNIT 5

Gender and Status

Unit Selections

21. **The Berdache Tradition,** Walter L. Williams
22. **Where Fat Is a Mark of Beauty,** Ann M. Simmons
23. **. . . but What If It's a Girl?,** Carla Power
24. **Missing Girls,** Michelle Goldberg
25. **Rising Number of Dowry Deaths in India,** Amanda Hitchcock

Learning Outcomes

After reading this unit, you should be able to:

• Define "berdache" and explain how it highlights the ways in which different societies accommodate atypical individuals.

• Explain how and why perceptions of feminine beauty vary from culture to culture.

• Describe the social forces that have contributed to the increasing death rate of females in Asia.

• Explain why there is a rising number of dowry deaths in India.

Student Website

www.mhhe.com/cls

Internet References

Reflections on Sinai Bedouin Women
   www.sherryart.com/women/bedouin.html
Women Watch
   www.un.org/womenwatch/about/

The feminist movement in the United States has had a significant impact upon the development of anthropology. Feminists have rightly charged that anthropologists have tended to gloss over the lives of women in studies of society and culture. In part this is because, until recent times, most anthropologists have been men. The result has been an undue emphasis on male activities as well as male perspectives in descriptions of particular societies.

These charges, however, have proven to be a firm corrective. In the last few years, anthropologists have begun to study women and, more particularly, the division of labor based on gender and its relation to biology, as well as to social and political status. In addition, these changes in emphasis have been accompanied by an increase in the number of women in the field.

Feminist anthropologists have begun to attack critically many of the established anthropological beliefs. They have shown, for example, that field studies of nonhuman primates, which were often used to demonstrate the evolutionary basis of male dominance, distorted the actual evolutionary record by focusing primarily on baboons. (Male baboons are especially dominant and aggressive.) Other, less-quoted primate studies show how dominance and aggression are highly situational phenomena, sensitive to ecological variation. Feminist anthropologists have also shown that the subsistence contribution of women has likewise been ignored by anthropologists. A classic case is that of the !Kung, a hunting and gathering group in southern Africa, where women provide the bulk of the foodstuffs, including most of the available protein, and who, not coincidentally, enjoy a more egalitarian relationship than usual with men. Thus, since political control is a matter of cultural variation, male authority is not biologically predetermined. In fact, there are many cultures in which some men may play a more feminine or, at least, asexual role, as described in "The Berdache Tradition" and, as we see in "Where Fat Is a Mark of Beauty," gender relationships are deeply embedded in social experience.

Lest we think that gender issues are primarily academic, we need only consider the articles, ". . . but What If It's a Girl?" by Carla Power "Missing Girls" by Michelle Goldberg and "Rising Number of Dowry Deaths in India" by Amanda Hitchcock to realize that gender equality in this world is still a distant dream.

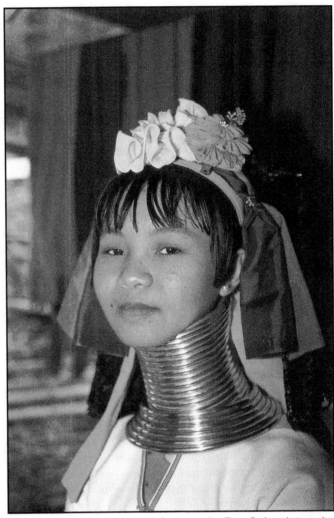

The Berdache Tradition

WALTER L. WILLIAMS

Because it is such a powerful force in the world today, the Western Judeo-Christian tradition is often accepted as the arbiter of "natural" behavior of humans. If Europeans and their descendant nations of North America accept something as normal, then anything different is seen as abnormal. Such a view ignores the great diversity of human existence.

This is the case of the study of gender. How many genders are there? To a modern Anglo-American, nothing might seem more definite than the answer that there are two: men and women. But not all societies around the world agree with Western culture's view that all humans are either women or men. The commonly accepted notion of "the opposite sex," based on anatomy, is itself an artifact of our society's rigid sex roles.

Among many cultures, there have existed different alternatives to "man" or "woman." An alternative role in many American Indian societies is referred to by anthropologists as *berdache*. . . . The role varied from one Native American culture to another, which is a reflection of the vast diversity of aboriginal New World societies. Small bands of hunter-gatherers existed in some areas, with advanced civilizations of farming peoples in other areas. With hundreds of different languages, economies, religions, and social patterns existing in North America alone, every generalization about a cultural tradition must acknowledge many exceptions.

This diversity is true for the berdache tradition as well, and must be kept in mind. My statements should be read as being specific to a particular culture, with generalizations being treated as loose patterns that might not apply to peoples even in nearby areas.

Briefly, a berdache can be defined as a morphological male who does not fill a society's standard man's role, who has a nonmasculine character. This type of person is often stereotyped as effeminate, but a more accurate characterization is androgyny. Such a person has a clearly recognized and accepted social status, often based on a secure place in the tribal mythology. Berdaches have special ceremonial roles in many Native American religions, and important economic roles in their families. They will do at least some women's work, and mix together much of the behavior, dress, and social roles of women and men. Berdaches gain social prestige by their spiritual, intellectual, or craftwork/artistic contributions, and by their reputation for hard work and generosity. They serve a mediating function between women and men, precisely because their character is seen as distinct from either sex. They are not seen as men, yet they are not seen as women either. They occupy an alternative gender role that is a mixture of diverse elements.

In their erotic behavior berdaches also generally (but not always) take a nonmasculine role, either being asexual or becoming the passive partner in sex with men. In some cultures the berdache might become a wife to a man. This male-male sexual behavior became the focus of an attack on berdaches as "sodomites" by the Europeans who, early on, came into contact with them. From the first Spanish conquistadors to the Western frontiersmen and the Christian missionaries and government officials, Western culture has had a considerable impact on the berdache tradition. In the last two decades, the most recent impact on the tradition is the adaptation of a modern Western gay identity.

To Western eyes berdachism is a complex and puzzling phenomenon, mixing and redefining the very concepts of what is considered male and female. In a culture with only two recognized genders, such individuals are gender nonconformist, abnormal, deviant. But to American Indians, the institution of another gender role means that berdaches are not deviant—indeed, they do conform to the requirements of a custom in which their culture tells them they fit. Berdachism is a way for society to recognize and assimilate some atypical individuals without imposing a change on them or stigmatizing them as deviant. This cultural institution confirms their legitimacy for what they are.

Societies often bestow power upon that which does not neatly fit into the usual. Since no cultural system can explain everything, a common way that many cultures deal with these inconsistencies is to imbue them with negative power, as taboo, pollution, witchcraft, or sin. That which is not understood is seen as a threat. But an alternative method of dealing with such things, or people, is to take them out of the realm of threat and to sanctify them.[1] The berdaches' role as mediator is thus not just between women and men, but also between the physical and the spiritual. American Indian cultures have taken what Western culture calls negative, and made it a positive; they have successfully utilized the different skills and insights of a class of people that Western culture has stigmatized and whose spiritual powers have been wasted.

Many Native Americans also understood that gender roles have to do with more than just biological sex. The standard

Western view that one's sex is always a certainty, and that one's gender identity and sex role always conform to one's morphological sex is a view that dies hard. Western thought is typified by such dichotomies of groups perceived to be mutually exclusive: male and female, black and white, right and wrong, good and evil. Clearly, the world is not so simple; such clear divisions are not always realistic. Most American Indian worldviews generally are much more accepting of the ambiguities of life. Acceptance of gender variation in the berdache tradition is typical of many native cultures' approach to life in general.

Overall, these are generalizations based on those Native American societies that had an accepted role for berdaches. Not all cultures recognized such a respected status. Berdachism in aboriginal North America was most established among tribes in four areas: first, the Prairie and western Great Lakes, the northern and central Great Plains, and the lower Mississippi Valley; second, Florida and the Caribbean; third, the Southwest, the Great Basin, and California; and fourth, scattered areas of the Northwest, western Canada, and Alaska. For some reason it is not noticeable in eastern North America, with the exception of its southern rim. . . .

American Indian Religions

Native American religions offered an explanation for human diversity by their creation stories. In some tribal religions, the Great Spiritual Being is conceived as neither male nor female but as a combination of both. Among the Kamia of the Southwest, for example, the bearer of plant seeds and the introducer of Kamia culture was a man-woman spirit named Warharmi.[2] A key episode of the Zuni creation story involves a battle between the kachina spirits of the agricultural Zunis and the enemy hunter spirits. Every four years an elaborate ceremony commemorates this myth. In the story a kachina spirit called *ko'lhamana* was captured by the enemy spirits and transformed in the process. This transformed spirit became a mediator between the two sides, using his peacemaking skills to merge the differing lifestyles of hunters and farmers. In the ceremony, a dramatic reenactment of the myth, the part of the transformed *ko'lhamana* spirit, is performed by a berdache.[3] The Zuni word for berdache is *lhamana,* denoting its closeness to the spiritual mediator who brought hunting and farming together.[4] The moral of this story is that the berdache was created by the deities for a special purpose, and that this creation led to the improvement of society. The continual reenactment of this story provides a justification for the Zuni berdache in each generation.

In contrast to this, the lack of spiritual justification in a creation myth could denote a lack of tolerance for gender variation. The Pimas, unlike most of their Southwestern neighbors, did not respect a berdache status. *Wi-kovat,* their derogatory word, means "like a girl," but it does not signify a recognized social role. Pima mythology reflects this lack of acceptance, in a folk tale that explains male androgyny as due to Papago witchcraft. Knowing that the Papagos respected berdaches, the Pimas blamed such an occurrence on an alien influence.[5] While the Pimas' condemnatory attitude is unusual, it does point out the importance of spiritual explanations for the acceptance of gender variance in a culture.

Other Native American creation stories stand in sharp contrast to the Pima explanation. A good example is the account of the Navajos, which presents women and men as equals. The Navajo origin tale is told as a story of five worlds. The first people were First Man and First Woman, who were created equally and at the same time. The first two worlds that they lived in were bleak and unhappy, so they escaped to the third world. In the third world lived two twins, Turquoise Boy and White Shell Girl, who were the first berdaches. In the Navajo language the world for berdache is *nadle,* which means "changing one" or "one who is transformed." It is applied to hermaphrodites—those who are born with the genitals of both male and female—and also to "those who pretend to be *nadle,*" who take on a social role that is distinct from either men or women.[6]

In the third world, First Man and First Woman began farming, with the help of the changing twins. One of the twins noticed some clay and, holding it in the palm of his/her hand, shaped it into the first pottery bowl. Then he/she formed a plate, a water dipper, and a pipe. The second twin observed some reeds and began to weave them, making the first basket. Together they shaped axes and grinding stones from rocks, and hoes from bone. All these new inventions made the people very happy.[7]

The message of this story is that humans are dependent for many good things on the inventiveness of *nadle.* Such individuals were present from the earliest eras of human existence, and their presence was never questioned. They were part of the natural order of the universe, with a special contribution to make.

Later on in the Navajo creation story, White Shell Girl entered the moon and became the Moon Bearer. Turquoise Boy, however, remained with the people. When First Man realized that Turquoise Boy could do all manner of women's work as well as women, all the men left the women and crossed a big river. The men hunted and planted crops. Turquoise Boy ground the corn, cooked the food, and weaved cloth for the men. Four years passed with the women and men separated, and the men were happy with the *nadle.* Later, however the women wanted to learn how to grind corn from the *nadle,* and both the men and women had decided that it was not good to continue living separately. So the women crossed the river and the people were reunited.[8]

They continued living happily in the third world, until one day a great flood began. The people ran to the highest mountaintop, but the water kept rising and they all feared they would be drowned. But just in time, the ever-inventive Turquoise Boy found a large reed. They climbed upward inside the tall hollow reed, and came out at the top into the fourth world. From there, White Shell Girl brought another reed, and they climbed again to the fifth world, which is the present world of the Navajos.[9]

These stories suggest that the very survival of humanity is dependent on the inventiveness of berdaches. With such a mythological belief system, it is no wonder that the Navajos held *nadle* in high regard. The concept of the *nadle* is well formulated in the creation story. As children were educated by these stories, and all Navajos believed in them, the high status accorded to gender variation was passed down from generation to generation. Such stories also provided instruction for *nadle* themselves to live by. A spiritual explanation guaranteed a special place for a person who was considered different but not deviant.

For American Indians, the important explanations of the world are spiritual ones. In their view, there is a deeper reality than the here-and-now. The real essence or wisdom occurs when one finally gives up trying to explain events in terms of "logic" and "reality." Many confusing aspects of existence can better be explained by actions of a multiplicity of spirits. Instead of a concept of a single god, there is an awareness of "that which we do not understand." In Lakota religion, for example, the term *Wakan Tanka* is often translated as "god." But a more proper translation, according to the medicine people who taught me, is "The Great Mystery."[10]

While rationality can explain much, there are limits to human capabilities of understanding. The English language is structured to account for cause and effect. For example, English speakers say, "It is raining," with the implication that there is a cause "it" that leads to rain. Many Indian languages, on the other hand, merely note what is most accurately translated as "raining" as an observable fact. Such an approach brings a freedom to stop worrying about causes of things, and merely to relax and accept that our human insights can go only so far. By not taking ourselves too seriously, or overinflating human importance, we can get beyond the logical world.

The emphasis of American Indian religions, then, is on the spiritual nature of all things. To understand the physical world, one must appreciate the underlying spiritual essence. Then one can begin to see that the physical is only a faint shadow, a partial reflection, of a supernatural and extrarational world. By the Indian view, everything that exists is spiritual. Every object—plants, rocks, water, air, the moon, animals, humans, the earth itself—has a spirit. The spirit of one thing (including a human) is not superior to the spirit of any other. Such a view promotes a sophisticated ecological awareness of the place that humans have in the larger environment. The function of religion is not to try to condemn or to change what exists, but to accept the realities of the world and to appreciate their contributions to life. Everything that exists has a purpose.[11]

One of the basic tenets of American Indian religion is the notion that everything in the universe is related. Nevertheless, things that exist are often seen as having a counterpart: sky and earth, plant and animal, water and fire. In all of these polarities, there exist mediators. The role of the mediator is to hold the polarities together, to keep the world from disintegrating. Polarities exist within human society also. The most important category within Indian society is gender. The notions of Woman and Man underlie much of social interaction and are comparable to the other major polarities. Women, with their nurtural qualities, are associated with the earth, while men are associated with the sky. Women gatherers and farmers deal with plants (of the earth), while men hunters deal with animals.

The mediator between the polarities of woman and man, in the American Indian religious explanation, is a being that combines the elements of both genders. This might be a combination in a physical sense, as in the case of hermaphrodites.

Many Native American religions accept this phenomenon in the same way that they accept other variations from the norm. But more important is their acceptance of the idea that gender can be combined in ways other than physical hermaphroditism. The physical aspects of a thing or a person, after all, are not nearly as important as its spirit. American Indians use the concept of a person's *spirit* in the way that other Americans use the concept of a person's *character*. Consequently, physical hermaphroditism is not necessary for the idea of gender mixing. A person's character, their spiritual essence, is the crucial thing.

The Berdache's Spirit

Individuals who are physically normal might have the spirit of the other sex, might range somewhere between the two sexes, or might have a spirit that is distinct from either women or men. Whatever category they fall into, they are seen as being different from men. They are accepted spiritually as "Not Man." Whichever option is chosen, Indian religions offer spiritual explanations. Among the Arapahos of the Plains, berdaches are called *haxu'xan* and are seen to be that way as a result of a supernatural gift from birds or animals. Arapaho mythology recounts the story of Nih'a'ca, the first *haxu'xan*. He pretended to be a woman and married the mountain lion, a symbol for masculinity. The myth, as recorded by ethnographer Alfred Kroeber about 1900, recounted that "These people had the natural desire to become women, and as they grew up gradually became women. They gave up the desires of men. They were married to men. They had miraculous power and could do supernatural things. For instance, it was one of them that first made an intoxicant from rainwater."[12] Besides the theme of inventiveness, similar to the Navajo creation story, the berdache role is seen as a product of a "natural desire." Berdaches "gradually became women," which underscores the notion of woman as a social category rather than as a fixed biological entity. Physical biological sex is less important in gender classification than a person's desire—one's spirit.

They myths contain no prescriptions for trying to change berdaches who are acting out their desires of the heart. Like many other cultures' myths, the Zuni origin myths simply sanction the idea that gender can be transformed independently of biological sex.[13] Indeed, myths warn of dire consequences when interference with such a transformation is attempted. Prince Alexander Maximilian of the German state of Wied, traveling in the northern Plains in the 1830s, heard a myth about a warrior who once tried to force a berdache to avoid women's clothing. The berdache resisted, and the warrior shot him with an arrow. Immediately the berdache disappeared, and the warrior saw only a pile of stones with his arrow in them. Since then, the story concluded, no intelligent person would try to coerce a berdache.[14] Making the point even more directly, a Mandan myth told of an Indian who tried to force *mihdake* (berdaches) to give up their distinctive dress and status, which led the spirits to punish many people with death. After that, no Mandans interfered with berdaches.[15]

With this kind of attitude, reinforced by myth and history, the aboriginal view accepts human diversity. The creation story of the Mohave of the Colorado River Valley speaks of a time when people were not sexually differentiated. From this perspective, it is easy to accept that certain individuals might combine elements of masculinity and femininity.[16] A respected Mohave elder, speaking in the 1930s, stated this viewpoint simply: "From the very beginning of the world it was meant that there should be [berdaches], just as it was instituted that there should be shamans. They were intended for that purpose."[17]

This elder also explained that a child's tendencies to become a berdache are apparent early, by about age nine to twelve, before the child reaches puberty: "That is the time when young persons become initiated into the functions of their sex. . . . None but young people will become berdaches as a rule."[18] Many tribes have a public ceremony that acknowledges the acceptance of berdache status. A Mohave shaman related the ceremony for his tribe: "When the child was about ten years old his relatives would begin discussing his strange ways. Some of them disliked it, but the more intelligent began envisaging an initiation ceremony." The relatives prepare for the ceremony without letting the boy know of it. It is meant to take him by surprise, to be both an initiation and a test of his true inclinations. People from various settlements are invited to attend. The family wants the community to see it and become accustomed to accepting the boy as an *alyha*.

On the day of the ceremony, the shaman explained, the boy is led into a circle: "If the boy showed a willingness to remain standing in the circle, exposed to the public eye, it was almost certain that he would go through with the ceremony. The singer, hidden behind the crowd, began singing the songs. As soon as the sound reached the boy he began to dance as women do." If the boy is unwilling to assume *alyha* status, he would refuse to dance. But if his character—his spirit—is *alyha*, "the song goes right to his heart and he will dance with much intensity. He cannot help it. After the fourth song he is proclaimed." After the ceremony, the boy is carefully bathed and receives a woman's skirt. He is then led back to the dance ground, dressed as an *alyha*, and announces his new feminine name to the crowd. After that he would resent being called by his old male name.[19]

Among the Yuman tribes of the Southwest, the transformation is marked by a social gathering, in which the berdache prepares a meal for the friends of the family.[20] Ethnographer Ruth Underhill, doing fieldwork among the Papago Indians in the early 1930s, wrote that berdaches were common among the Papago Indians, and were usually publicly acknowledged in childhood. She recounted that a boy's parents would test him if they noticed that he preferred female pursuits. The regular pattern, mentioned by many of Underhill's Papago informants, was to build a small brush enclosure. Inside the enclosure they placed a man's bow and arrows, and also a woman's basket. At the appointed time the boy was brought to the enclosure as the adults watched from outside. The boy was told to go inside the circle of brush. Once he was inside, the adults "set fire to the enclosure. They watched what he took with him as he ran out and if it was the basketry materials, they reconciled themselves to his being a berdache."[21]

What is important to recognize in all of these practices is that the assumption of a berdache role was not forced on the boy by others. While adults might have their suspicions, it was only when the child made the proper move that he was considered a berdache. By doing woman's dancing, preparing a meal, or taking the woman's basket he was making an important symbolic gesture. Indian children were not stupid, and they knew the implications of these ceremonies beforehand. A boy in the enclosure could have left without taking anything, or could have taken both the man's and the woman's tools. With the community standing by watching, he was well aware that his choice would mark his assumption of berdache status. Rather than being seen as an involuntary test of his reflexes, this ceremony may be interpreted as a definite statement by the child to take on the berdache role.

Indians do not see the assumption of berdache status, however, as a free will choice on the part of the boy. People felt that the boy was acting out his basic character. The Lakota shaman Lame Deer explained:

> They were not like other men, but the Great Spirit made them *winktes* and we accepted them as such. . . . We think that if a woman has two little ones growing inside her, if she is going to have twins, sometimes instead of giving birth to two babies they have formed up in her womb into just one, into a half-man/half-woman kind of being. . . . To us a man is what nature, or his dreams, make him. We accept him for what he wants to be. That's up to him.[22]

While most of the sources indicate that once a person becomes a berdache it is a lifelong status, directions from the spirits determine everything. In at least one documented case, concerning a nineteenth-century Klamath berdache named Lele'ks, he later had a supernatural experience that led him to leave the berdache role. At that time Lele'ks began dressing and acting like a man, then married women, and eventually became one of the most famous Klamath chiefs.[23] What is important is that both in assuming berdache status and in leaving it, supernatural dictate is the determining factor.

Dreams and Visions

Many tribes see the berdache role as signifying an individual's proclivities as a dreamer and a visionary. . . .

Among the northern Plains and related Great Lakes tribes, the idea of supernatural dictate through dreaming—the vision quest—had its highest development. The goal of the vision quest is to try to get beyond the rational world by sensory deprivation and fasting. By depriving one's body of nourishment, the brain could escape from logical thought and connect with the higher reality of the supernatural. The person doing the quest simply sits and waits for a vision. But a vision might not come easily; the person might have to wait for days.

The best way that I can describe the process is to refer to my own vision quest, which I experienced when I was living on a Lakota reservation in 1982. After a long series of prayers and blessings, the shaman who had prepared me for the ceremony took me out to an isolated area where a sweat lodge had been set up for my quest. As I walked to the spot, I worried that I might not be able to stand it. Would I be overcome by hunger?

Could I tolerate the thirst? What would I do if I had to go to the toilet? The shaman told me not to worry, that a whole group of holy people would be praying and singing for me while I was on my quest.

He had me remove my clothes, symbolizing my disconnection from the material would, and crawl into the sweat lodge. Before he left me I asked him, "What do I think about?" He said, "Do not think. Just pray for spiritual guidance." After a prayer he closed the flap tightly and I was left in total darkness. I still do not understand what happened to me during my vision quest, but during the day and a half that I was out there, I never once felt hungry or thirsty or the need to go to the toilet. What happened was an intensely personal experience that I cannot and do not wish to explain, a process of being that cannot be described in rational terms.

When the shaman came to get me at the end of my time, I actually resented having to end it. He did not need to ask if my vision quest was successful. He knew that it was even before seeing me, he explained, because he saw an eagle circling over me while I underwent the quest. He helped interpret the signs I had seen, then after more prayers and singing he led me back to the others. I felt relieved, cleansed, joyful, and serene. I had been through an experience that will be a part of my memories always.

If a vision quest could have such an effect on a person not even raised in Indian society, imagine its impact on a boy who from his earliest years had been waiting for the day when he could seek his vision. Gaining his spiritual power from his first vision, it would tell him what role to take in adult life. The vision might instruct him that he is going to be a great hunter, a craftsman, a warrior, or a shaman. Or it might tell him that he will be a berdache. Among the Lakotas, or Sioux, there are several symbols for various types of visions. A person becomes *wakan* (a sacred person) if she or he dreams of a bear, a wolf, thunder, a buffalo, a white buffalo calf, or Double Woman. Each dream results in a different gift, whether it is the power to cure illness or wounds, a promise of good hunting, or the exalted role of a *heyoka* (doing things backward).

A white buffalo calf is believed to be a berdache. If a person has a dream of the sacred Double Woman, this means that she or he will have the power to seduce men. Males who have a vision of Double Woman are presented with female tools. Taking such tools means that the male will become a berdache. The Lakota word *winkte* is composed of *win*, "woman," and *kte*, "would become."[24] A contemporary Lakota berdache explains, "To become a *winkte,* you have a medicine man put you up on the hill, to search for your vision. "You can become a *winkte* if you truly are by nature. You see a vision of the White Buffalo Calf Pipe. Sometimes it varies. A vision is like a scene in a movie."[25] Another way to become a *winkte* is to have a vision given by a *winkte* from the past.[26] . . .

By interpreting the result of the vision as being the work of a spirit, the vision quest frees the person from feeling responsible for his transformation. The person might even claim that the change was done against his will and without his control. Such a claim does not suggest a negative attitude about berdache status, because it is common for people to claim reluctance to fulfill their spiritual duty no matter what vision appears to them. Becoming any kind of sacred person involves taking on various social responsibilities and burdens.[27] . . .

A story was told among the Lakotas in the 1880s of a boy who tried to resist following his vision from Double Woman. But according to Lakota informants "few men succeed in this effort after having taken the strap in the dream." Having rebelled against the instructions given him by the Moon Being, he committed suicide.[28] The moral of that story is that one should not resist spiritual guidance, because it will lead only to grief. In another case, an Omaha young man told of being addressed by a spirit as "daughter," whereupon he discovered that he was unconsciously using feminine styles of speech. He tried to use male speech patterns, but could not. As a result of this vision, when he returned to his people he resolved himself to dress as a woman.[29] Such stories function to justify personal peculiarities as due to a fate over which the individual has no control.

Despite the usual pattern in Indian societies of using ridicule to enforce conformity, receiving instructions from a vision inhibits others from trying to change the berdache. Ritual explanation provides a way out. It also excuses the community from worrying about the cause of that person's difference, or the feeling that it is society's duty to try to change him.[30] Native American religions, above all else, encourage a basic respect for nature. If nature makes a person different, many Indians conclude, a mere human should not undertake to counter this spiritual dictate. Someone who is "unusual" can be accommodated without being stigmatized as "abnormal." Berdachism is thus not alien or threatening; it is a reflection of spirituality.

Notes

1. Mary Douglas, *Purity and Danger* (Baltimore: Penguin, 1966), p. 52. I am grateful to Theda Perdue for convincing me that Douglas's ideas apply to berdachism. For an application of Douglas's thesis to berdaches, see James Thayer, "The Berdache of the Northern Plains: A Socioreligious Perspective," *Journal of Anthropological Research 36* (1980): 292–93.

2. E. W. Gifford, "The Kamia of Imperial Valley," *Bureau of American Ethnology Bulletin 97* (1931): 12.

3. By using present tense verbs in this text, I am not implying that such activities are necessarily continuing today. I sometimes use the present tense in the "ethnographic present," unless I use the past tense when I am referring to something that has not continued. Past tense implies that all such practices have disappeared. In the absence of fieldwork to prove such disappearance, I am not prepared to make that assumption, on the historic changes in the berdache tradition.

4. Elsie Clews Parsons, "The Zuni La' Mana," *American Anthropologist 18* (1916): 521; Matilda Coxe Stevenson, "Zuni Indians," *Bureau of American Ethnology Annual Report 23* (1903): 37; Franklin Cushing, "Zuni Creation Myths," *Bureau of American Ethnology Annual Report 13* (1894): 401–3. Will Roscoe clarified this origin story for me.

5. W. W. Hill, "Note on the Pima Berdache," *American Anthropologist 40* (1938): 339.

6. Aileen O'Bryan, "The Dine': Origin Myths of the Navaho Indians," *Bureau of American Ethnology Bulletin 163* (1956): 5;

W. W. Hill, "The Status of the Hermaphrodite and Transvestite in Navaho Culture,"*American Anthropologist 37* (1935): 273.

7. Martha S. Link, *The Pollen Path: A Collection of Navajo Myths* (Stanford: Stanford University Press, 1956).

8 O'Bryan, "Dine'," pp. 5, 7, 9–10.

9. Ibid.

10. Lakota informants, July 1982. See also William Powers, *Oglala Religion* (Lincoln: University of Nebraska Press, 1977).

11. For this admittedly generalized overview of American Indian religious values, I am indebted to traditionalist informants of many tribes, but especially those of the Lakotas. For a discussion of native religions see Dennis Tedlock, *Finding the Center* (New York: Dial Press, 1972); Ruth Underhill, *Red Man's Religion* (Chicago: University of Chicago Press, 1965); and Elsi Clews Parsons, *Pueblo Indian Religion* (Chicago: University of Chicago Press, 1939).

12. Alfred Kroeber, "The Arapaho," *Bulletin of the American Museum of Natural History 18* (1902–7): 19.

13. Parsons, "Zuni La' Mana," p. 525.

14. Alexander Maximilian, *Travels in the interior of North America, 1832–1834,* vol. 22 of *Early Western Travels,* ed. Reuben Gold Thwaites, 32 vols. (Cleveland: A. H. Clark, 1906), pp. 283–84, 354. Maximilian was quoted in German in the early homosexual rights book by Ferdinand Karsch-Haack, *Das Gleichgeschlechtliche Leben der Naturvölker* (The same-sex life of nature peoples) (Munich: Verlag von Ernst Reinhardt, 1911; reprinted New York: Arno Press, 1975), pp. 314, 564.

15. Oscar Koch, *Der Indianishe Eros* (Berlin: Verlag Continent, 1925), p. 61.

16. George Devereux, "Institutionalized Homosexuality of the Mohave Indians," *Human Biology 9* (1937): 509.

17. Ibid., p. 501

18. Ibid.

19. Ibid., pp. 508–9.

20. C. Daryll Forde, "Ethnography of the Yuma Indians," *University of California Publications in American Archaeology and Ethnology 28* (1931): 157.

21. Ruth Underhill, *Social Organization of the Papago Indians* (New York: Columbia University Press, 1938), p. 186. This story is also mentioned in Ruth Underhill, ed., *The Autobiography of a Papago Woman* (Menasha, Wisc.: American Anthropological Association, 1936), p. 39.

22. John Fire and Richard Erdoes, *Lame Deer, Seeker of Visions* (New York: Simon and Schuster, 1972), pp. 117, 149.

23. Theodore Stern, *The Klamath Tribe: A People and Their Reservation* (Seattle: University of Washington Press, 1965), pp. 20, 24; Theodore Stern, "Some Sources of Variability in Klamath Mythology,"*Journal of American Folklore 69* (1956): 242ff; Leshe Spier, *Klamath Ethnography* (Berkeley: University of California Press, 1930), p. 52.

24. Clark Wissler, "Societies and Ceremonial Associations in the Oglala Division of the Teton Dakota," *Anthoropological Papers of the American Museum of Natural History 11,* pt. 1 (1916): 92; Powers, *Oglala Religion,* pp. 57–59.

25. Ronnie Loud Hawk, Lakota informant 4, July 1982.

26. Terry Calling Eagle, Lakota informant 5, July 1982.

27. James S. Thayer, "The Berdache of the Northern Plains: A Socioreligious Perspective," *Journal of Anthropological Research 36* (1980): 289.

28. Fletcher, "Elk Mystery," p. 281.

29. Alice Fletcher and Francis La Flesche, "The Omaha Tribe," *Bureau of American Ethnology Annual Report 27* (1905–6): 132.

30. Harriet Whitehead offers a valuable discussion of this element of the vision quest in "The Bow and the Burden Strap: A New Look at Institutionalized Homosexuality in Native North America," in *Sexual Meanings,* ed. Sherry Ortner and Harriet Whitehead (Cambridge: Cambridge University Press, 1981), pp. 99–102. See also Erikson, "Childhood," p. 329.

Assess Your Progress

1. What is a berdache? What special roles have berdaches played in Native American societies?

2. What kinds of erotic behavior have they exhibited?

3. How have Europeans and American Indians differed in their treatment of the berdaches? How does the author explain these two different approaches?

4. How does the author contrast Western thought with Native American views regarding gender?

5. Why do Native Americans explain things in spiritual terms rather than "logic" and "reality"?

6. What is the emphasis of American Indian religions? What is the function of such religion?

7. What is one of the most basic tenets of American Indian religion? What kinds of polarities exist? Why are mediators necessary?

8. What is the most important category within Indian society? How do men and women differ?

9. Describe some of the Native American beliefs regarding the berdache.

Where Fat Is a Mark of Beauty

In a rite of passage, some Nigerian girls spend months gaining weight and learning customs in a special room. "To be called a 'slim princess' is an abuse," says a defender of the practice.

ANN M. SIMMONS

Margaret Bassey Ene currently has one mission in life: gaining weight.

The Nigerian teenager has spent every day since early June in a "fattening room" specially set aside in her father's mud-and-thatch house. Most of her waking hours are spent eating bowl after bowl of rice, yams, plantains, beans and *gari,* a porridge-like mixture of dried cassava and water.

After three more months of starchy diet and forced inactivity, Margaret will be ready to reenter society bearing the traditional mark of female beauty among her Efik people: fat.

In contrast to many Western cultures where thin is in, many culture-conscious people in the Efik and other communities in Nigeria's southeastern Cross River state hail a woman's rotundity as a sign of good health, prosperity and allure.

The fattening room is at the center of a centuries-old rite of passage from maidenhood to womanhood. The months spent in pursuit of poundage are supplemented by daily visits from elderly matrons who impart tips on how to be a successful wife and mother. Nowadays, though, girls who are not yet marriage-bound do a tour in the rooms purely as a coming-of-age ceremony. And sometimes, nursing mothers return to the rooms to put on more weight.

"The fattening room is like a kind of school where the girl is taught about motherhood," said Sylvester Odey, director of the Cultural Center Board in Calabar, capital of Cross River state. "Your daily routine is to sleep, eat and grow fat."

Like many traditional African customs, the fattening room is facing relentless pressure from Western influences. Health campaigns linking excess fat to heart disease and other illnesses are changing the eating habits of many Nigerians, and urban dwellers are opting out of the time-consuming process.

Effiong Okon Etim, an Efik village chief in the district of Akpabuyo, said some families cannot afford to constantly feed a daughter for more than a few months. That compares with a stay of up to two years, as was common earlier this century, he said.

But the practice continues partly because "people might laugh at you because you didn't have money to allow your child to pass through the rite of passage," Etim said. What's more, many believe an unfattened girl will be sickly or unable to bear children.

Etim, 65, put his two daughters in a fattening room together when they were 12 and 15 years old, but some girls undergo the process as early as age 7, after undergoing the controversial practice of genital excision.

Bigger Is Better, According to Custom

As for how fat is fat enough, there is no set standard. But the unwritten rule is the bigger the better, said Mkoyo Edet, Etim's sister.

"Beauty is in the weight," said Edet, a woman in her 50s who spent three months in a fattening room when she was 7. "To be called a 'slim princess' is an abuse. The girl is fed constantly whether she likes it or not."

In Margaret's family, there was never any question that she would enter the fattening room.

"We inherited it from our forefathers; it is one of the heritages we must continue," said Edet Essien Okon, 25, Margaret's stepfather and a language and linguistics graduate of the University of Calabar. "It's a good thing to do; it's an initiation rite."

His wife, Nkoyo Effiong, 27, agreed: "As a woman, I feel it is proper for me to put my daughter in there, so she can be educated."

Effiong, a mother of five, spent four months in a fattening room at the age of 10.

Margaret, an attractive girl with a cheerful smile and hair plaited in fluffy bumps, needs only six months in the fattening room because she was already naturally plump, her stepfather said.

During the process, she is treated as a goddess, but the days are monotonous. To amuse herself, Margaret has only an instrument made out of a soda bottle with a hole in it, which she taps on her hand to play traditional tunes.

Still, the 16-year-old says she is enjoying the highly ritualized fattening practice.

"I'm very happy about this," she said, her belly already distended over the waist of her loincloth. "I enjoy the food, except for *gari.*"

Day in, day out, Margaret must sit cross-legged on a special stool inside the secluded fattening room. When it is time to eat, she sits on the floor on a large, dried plantain leaf, which also serves as her bed. She washes down the mounds of food with huge pots of water and takes traditional medicine made from leaves and herbs to ensure proper digestion.

As part of the rite, Margaret's face is decorated with a white, claylike chalk.

"You have to prepare the child so that if a man sees her, she will be attractive," Chief Etim said.

Tufts of palm leaf fiber, braided and dyed red, are hung around Margaret's neck and tied like bangles around her wrists and ankles. They are adjusted as she grows.

Typically, Margaret would receive body massages using the white chalk powder mixed with heavy red palm oil. But the teen said her parents believe the skin-softening, blood-stimulating massages might cause her to expand further than necessary.

Margaret is barred from doing her usual chores or any other strenuous physical activities. And she is forbidden to receive visitors, save for the half a dozen matrons who school Margaret in the etiquette of the Efik clan.

They teach her such basics as how to sit, walk and talk in front of her husband. And they impart wisdom about cleaning, sewing, child care and cooking—Efik women are known throughout Nigeria for their chicken pepper soup, pounded yams and other culinary creations.

"They advise me to keep calm and quiet, to eat the *gari,* and not to have many boyfriends so that I avoid unwanted pregnancy," Margaret said of her matron teachers. "They say that unless you have passed through this, you will not be a full-grown woman."

What little exercise Margaret gets comes in dance lessons. The matrons teach her the traditional *ekombi,* which she will be expected to perform before an audience on the day she emerges from seclusion—usually on the girl's wedding day, Etim said.

But Okon said his aim is to prepare his stepdaughter for the future, not to marry her off immediately. Efik girls receive more education than girls in most parts of Nigeria, and Okon hopes Margaret will return to school and embark on a career as a seamstress before getting married.

Weddings Also Steeped in Tradition

Once she does wed, Margaret will probably honor southeastern Nigeria's rich marriage tradition. It begins with a letter from the family of the groom to the family of the bride, explaining that "our son has seen a flower, a jewel, or something beautiful in your family, that we are interested in," said Josephine Effah-Chukwuma, program officer for women and children at the Constitutional Rights Project, a law-oriented nongovernmental organization based in the Nigerian commercial capital of Lagos.

If the girl and her family consent, a meeting is arranged. The groom and his relatives arrive with alcoholic beverages, soft drinks and native brews, and the bride's parents provide the food. The would-be bride's name is never uttered, and the couple are not allowed to speak, but if all goes well, a date is set for handing over the dowry. On that occasion, the bride's parents receive about $30 as a token of appreciation for their care of the young woman. "If you make the groom pay too much, it is like selling your daughter," Effah-Chukwuma said. Then, more drinks are served, and the engagement is official.

On the day of the wedding, the bride sits on a specially built wooden throne, covered by an extravagantly decorated canopy. Maidens surround her as relatives bestow gifts such as pots, pans, brooms, plates, glasses, table covers—everything she will need to start her new home. During the festivities, the bride changes clothes three times.

The high point is the performance of the *ekombi,* in which the bride twists and twirls, shielded by maidens and resisting the advances of her husband. It is his task to break through the ring and claim his bride.

Traditionalists are glad that some wedding customs are thriving despite the onslaught of modernity.

Traditional weddings are much more prevalent in southeastern Nigeria than so-called white weddings, introduced by colonialists and conducted in a church or registry office.

"In order to be considered married, you have to be married in the traditional way," said Maureen Okon, a woman of the Qua ethnic group who wed seven years ago but skipped the fattening room because she did not want to sacrifice the time. "Tradition identifies a people. It is important to keep up a culture. There is quite a bit of beauty in Efik and Qua marriages."

Assess Your Progress

1. How do the Efik contrast with many Western cultures with respect to a woman's "rotundity?"

2. What was the traditional role of the fattening room? What purpose does it serve today?

3. What kind of pressure does the fattening room face today? Why does the practice continue today?

4. What is the unwritten rule about "how fat?"

5. How does the author describe the fattening room experience? What exercise does Margaret get and why?

... but What If It's a Girl?

Modern technology is helping parents in Asia indulge in a hideous practice—killing off their girl children. It's never been easier to identify a female foetus and abort it.

CARLA POWER

Grey hair pulled into a tidy bun, blood-orange sari crisp, Sangam Satyavathi marches into the hospital, her team scurrying after her. She is on a raid. As district health officer for Hyderabad, Dr. Satyavathi is on a "sting operation"—a surprise visit to a maternity hospital to check its ultrasound records. A nervous knot of doctors and nurses forms around her, under a portrait of the baby Krishna and an advertisement for a General Electric ultrasound machine. This features a pregnant belly and the slogan "We bring good things to life". Satyavathi and her team frown over ledgers and a pile of Form Fs, required whenever a pregnant woman has an ultrasound scan. Like all the other hospitals in Hyderabad District, this one has been ordered, as part of a local campaign against female foeticide, to present detailed records of any such procedures.

"No reports," says Satyavathi, frowning. "And no consent forms."

"Consent form we are not taking, madam," ventures a doctor.

More poring over ledgers. "You haven't submitted your forms on time."

"Next time, madam."

"Next time?" she asks. "Now we are going to seize the machine."

Dr. Satyavathi's men go to work. They shroud the ultrasound machine in a sheet, then wrap it in lashings of surgical gauze. They drip red molten wax on the knots. Satyavathi whips out a five-rupee coin and presses it to the wax, sealing the suspect machine with the design of the three-headed lion, symbol of the Indian government.

"You see," she says grimly. "The act is so powerful."

The Prenatal Diagnostic Techniques Act is powerful indeed, but rarely enforced. Passed after India realised that modern medical techniques such as ultrasound scans and amniocentesis were frequently being used to identify female foetuses—which are then aborted—the PNDT Act requires the registration of all ultrasound machines, and bans doctors from revealing the sex of the foetus to expectant parents. The 1994 law was an attempt to reverse India's rampant use of sex-selective abortion, and

the lopsided sex ratio this has produced. India's 2001 census showed that there were 927 girls to every 1,000 boys, down from 945:1,000 in 1991 and 962:1,000 in 1981. Until recently, no doctors had been put in prison under the PNDT Act. But late last month a doctor was jailed for three years after telling an undercover investigator that her foetus was female, and hinting that she could abort it. Arvind Kumar, Hyderabad district collector and Satyavathi's boss, sees the law as the only practical tool for tackling India's female foeticide epidemic. Doctors who practise sex-selective abortion, he says, "like any other criminals, should be treated like criminals".

It is uncertain how many such crimes have been committed. A January study in the *Lancet* estimated that ten million female foeticides had occurred in India over the past two decades. Both the Indian Medical Association and anti-sex-selection activists disputed the findings, saying the numbers were too high. While the numbers may be a matter of debate, the general trend is not: the ratio of girls to boys in India has been dwindling over the past two decades. In 1991, not a single district in India had a child sex ratio of less than 800:1,000. By 2001, there were 14. "What we're dealing with," says Sabu George, India's leading activist, "is a genocide."

The prospects are even bleaker elsewhere in Asia. In South Korea and China, official numbers suggest that there are 855 girls for every 1,000 boys. In the case of China, independent experts put it even lower, at 826:1,000. Whichever is correct, the Chinese demographic picture is more unbalanced than back in 1990, when the statistics showed 901 girls for every 1,000 boys. Today, in parts of Hainan and Guangdong Provinces, the ratio is 769:1,000. The Chinese scenario has already produced a glut of bachelors, which experts say will only get worse. A 2002 article in *International Security* magazine estimated that by 2020 there will be up to 33 million guang guan ("bare branches"), as these young, unmarried men are known. Some demographers have put the figure even higher, at 40 million.

The unwanted girl has a long history in Asia. The first written record of female infanticide dates back to Japan's Tokugawa period, between 1600 and 1868, when there were nine times as many boys born as girls. A British colonial official in India recorded cases of female infanticide as long ago as the 1780s. In rural India today, there are dais, traditional birth attendants, who still know how to get rid of unwanted baby girls. Classic methods include feeding the newborn rice or salt, or smothering the baby with a pillow.

In recent decades, female infanticide has been eclipsed by modern methods of sex determination, including amniocentesis or ultrasound scan, followed by abortion. Activists say female foeticide is merely the first assault on Indian women, and cannot be seen as separate from the whole life cycle of anti-girl practices in India: girl-child neglect, early marriage, the dowry system, domestic violence and honour killings. "Being a girl," says Sabu George, "is considered a congenital defect."

It is tempting to dismiss Asia's female foeticide problem as a product of the sexism of "backward" societies. To be sure, the problem stems from traditional belief systems favouring boys, but the prevalence of sex selection is an unexpected side effect of modernity. Female foeticide has been boosted by precisely the trends that make China and India the great success stories of the Noughties: economic liberalisation, growing affluence, increased access to technology, and controlled population explosions.

Asia's dearth of girls, say researchers, is partly a function of official reproductive health policies. In the late 20th century, both China and India embarked on population-control programmes. In China, from the 1950s to the 1970s, when the government needed female workers, female infanticide dropped to the lowest levels the country had ever known, a 2004 study in the *Journal of Population Research* reported. After 1979, however, when the infamous one-child policy was introduced, female infanticide and foeticide became more common. In India, the muscular public health campaigns of the 1970s and 1980s drummed home the official line: happy families were small ones. Abortion, legalised in 1970, "was pursued with an almost patriotic zeal", recalls Dr. Puneet Bedi, a Delhi obstetrician and anti-sex-selection activist. Tellingly, the Indian states that did particularly well in curbing population growth—the Punjab, Delhi and Haryana among them—are today those with the most skewed sex ratios. "A large part of the small-family ideal is achieved by eliminating girls," says George. Pressured by the government to keep their families small, and by society to produce boys, Indian women turned to modern technology to ensure that they got their treasured sons.

India's new open markets have made it easier. Economic liberalisation in the early 1990s brought not just foreign cars and the outsourcing boom, but the rise of what Bedi calls "medical entrepreneurship". Easy credit and aggressive marketing by foreign companies made it possible for thousands of clinics to buy ultrasound machines. "The ultrasound machine was marketed like Coca-Cola," Bedi says. Between 1988 and 2003, there was a 33-fold increase in the annual manufacture of ultrasound equipment in India. Doctors advertised their possibilities widely. "Boy or girl?" asked adverts, before the PNDT Act outlawed them. A 2005 report by the Geneva Centre for the Democratic Control of Armed Forces noted that sex selection had become "a booming business" not only in India, but also in China and South Korea.

In India, the recent *Lancet* study found sex-selective abortion was far more prevalent among the urban middle classes than the illiterate poor: the more educated the mother, the less likely she was to give birth to a second child who was a girl. Though the practice has recently begun to spread to remote areas and to the south, it has been most widely practised in cities, particularly in the north. It is rare among Dalits and remote tribes and common among Sikhs and Jains, historically wealthy business communities. In Delhi, the leafiest suburbs have the worst sex ratios. Shailaja Chandra, a top-tier civil servant, says that preference for boys is common among the capital's elites.

"They want to keep property in the family," she says. "Because boys traditionally inherit the wealth, people want boys."

For many activists, India's female foeticide problem is entwined with the consumer society the country has become over the past 15 years. If one can order a BMW, goes the mindset, one can order a boy. Mira Shiva, a member of both the National Commission for Women and the National Commission on Population, sees the issue of female foeticide as just one example of the rise in violent crime against women, created by India's quicksilver modernisation. "We're going through a time of increasing consumerism and materialism, where our values are changing," she says. "Marketwise, things that are deemed not of value are expendable."

Other traditions have helped make girls seem expendable in Asia. Usually boys, not girls, carry on the family name. In Hinduism, it is the son who lights the funeral pyre when his parents die. In China and South Korea, ancestor-worship rituals are performed by sons and grandsons. In both China and India, boys are viewed as pension schemes, supporting their parents in old age.

If boys are a boon, girls are a liability. In India, the birth of a girl eventually entails a dowry, an increasingly expensive proposition. Where the grandmothers of today recall going to their husbands' homes with a pot or two and a few rupees, a modern dowry can cost hundreds of thousands of rupees. Girls are viewed as both an economic drain and a hassle. The protection of their virginity—central to family honour—creates further stress for parents. Boy-preference is so ingrained in the Indian family system that many women don't feel they have done their wifely duty until they produce a son. "They want to bend their heads, like sheep being slaughtered," observes Dr. Soubhagya Bhat, an obstetrician-gynaecologist in Belgaum, Karnataka. "The only way they feel their life is fulfilled is if they produce a son."

Governments are trying to change the conventional mindset. In 2003, India's national government launched a policy of paying homeless women money to help with their newborn babies: girls get double the rupees boys do. In Delhi, the Directorate of Family Welfare has recently come out with a clutch of "Respect the Girls" advertisements, with slogans such as: "If you kill daughters, you will keep searching for mothers, daughters and wives" and "Indira Gandhi and Mother Teresa: your daughter can be one of them!" They haven't worked. The latest statistics suggest that Delhi's sex ratio stands at roughly 814 girls to 1,000 boys. This is down from 845:1,000 in 2003.

If such trends continue, the future could be nightmarish. In their 2004 book *Bare Branches: The security implications of*

Asia's surplus male population, the political scientists Andrea den Boer and Valerie Hudson argue that the existence of all these millions of frustrated Asian bachelors will boost crime and lawlessness. They speculate that, to find an outlet for the continent's sex-starved males, Asian governments might even need to resort to fomenting wars. Indian activists also fear that the girl shortage will create a hyper-macho society.

Spiralling numbers of rapes and rates of violence will lead to the increasing sequestration of women. Men with money will be able to afford wives, who will quickly become a status symbol. "Powerful men would maintain zanankhanas [harems] to demonstrate their power and influence," writes the activist R. P. Ravindra. Poorer men, "finding no companions, might resort to any means to force a woman into a sexual/marital relationship".

In pockets of India, this has already begun. In Haryana and the Punjab, home to India's most unbalanced sex ratios, trafficking in women has skyrocketed. Men from these wealthy areas are purchasing wives from impoverished eastern states such as East Bengal and Bihar. This trend of "killing girls in the womb in western states is hurting girls in eastern states who have survived in the womb", argues Kamal Kumar Pandey, a lawyer with the Shakti Vahini network, an anti-trafficking NGO.

Rishi Kant, the network's founder, brandishes a recent snapshot showing a bloody, decapitated corpse: a 12-year-old bride wearing a yellow dress. The girl was murdered by the man who bought her for 25,000 rupees, says Kant, because she had refused to sleep with his brother. Tales of violence against bought women, and of brothers sharing wives, are increasingly common in parts of northern India.

The spectre of millions of lawless bachelors seems a far cry from the bureaucratic world-view of Arvind Kumar in Hyderabad. If India's officials could just implement the PNDT Act, he believes, the demographic tide could be reversed. He is just

18 months into the campaign, and so he sounds cautious, but the latest figures suggest that Hyderabad's sex ratio might be tilting back into balance. He tells of a letter he received recently from a 13-year-old girl who was being belittled by her family for not being a son. Just hearing of his work, she had written, had given her strength enough not to be ashamed of being a girl.

Assess Your Progress

1. Describe the problems that the Prenatal Diagnostic Techniques Act is intended to deal with and how.

2. In what sense is the situation even bleaker in China?

3. What evidence is there that the "unwanted girl has a long history in Asia?

4. What are the modern methods being employed for sex determination?

5. Describe the "whole life cycle of anti-girl practices in India."

6. In what respects is sex selection an unexpected side effect of modernity? Of official reproductive health policies in China and India? How has economic liberalization made it even easier?

7. In what segments of Indian society is sex-selective abortion more common and why?

8. What are some other Asian traditions helping to make girls seem expendable?

9. Why are girls seen as a liability?

10. In what ways are governments trying to change the conventional mindset?

11. How would the future become "nightmarish" if present trends continue? In what sense has this already begun in pockets of India?

Missing Girls

MICHELLE GOLDBERG

Fatehgarh Sahib, a district in the northern India state of Punjab, is rich in rupees and poor in girls. Called the breadbasket of India, Punjab's wealth is built on agriculture; flat fields of ripe, gold wheat stretch out from straight, smooth highways, plowed by giant tractors driven by turbaned Sikh farmers. Unlike in southern India, women have little role in agriculture here, which is one of several reasons that so many in Punjab see them as a useless investment, one better avoided altogether.

India, like other Asian countries, has long had a pronounced son preference, which has translated into a population with more males than females. Punjab is one of several Indian states with a history of female infanticide that shocked the British colonialists, who found entire villages without a single girl.[1] The British banned female infanticide in 1870—almost a hundred years after they discovered the practice—yet more subtle forms of discrimination and neglect continued to cull India's population of girls, who were, and still are, fed less than boys and given less medical care.

"The actual murder of little girls has in a great measure ceased, but it has been replaced in some tribes by a degree of carelessness hardly less criminal," one observer wrote toward the end of the 1800s. "It is found in some districts that, when fever is prevalent, girls' deaths, especially in the first three years of life, so largely exceed those of males that it is impossible not to believe that but small attempts are made to save the girls, and in many places deaths caused by disease of the lungs or malnutrition suggest the same conclusion."[2]

The care deficit has never been eliminated, but it seemed to have been improving throughout the twentieth century, and in India in the 1950s and 1960s there were almost as many female children as male.[3] Even Punjab saw a sustained increase in girls relative to boys. That's why the publication of India's 2001 census came as such a painful shock. Girls and women were living longer thanks to increased medical care, but the sex ratio had nonetheless gone seriously askew.* In seventy districts, the ratio of girls to boys had declined by more than 50 points in the previous decade.[4] With 798 female children for every thousand males, Punjab had the worst sex ratio in India, and Fatehgarh Sahib, with a sex ratio of 766, was the worst district in Punjab.

The decline was overwhelmingly due to the epidemic spread of sex-selective abortion, which most people in India refer to as "female feticide." Sex determination tests first appeared in India in the 1970s through the use of amniocentesis and chorionic villus sampling, both relatively invasive procedures that had to be done by a doctor. It wasn't until ultrasound, which spread throughout the country in the 1990s, that sex determination became easy and accessible. According to a 2006 study by *The Lancet,* a conservative estimate is that there are half a million sex-selective abortions in India each year.[5]

"Ultrasound really came as a WMD," said Puneet Bedi, a Delhi gynecologist who is one of the country's most vocal activists against sex selection. "Parts of India where there is no drinking water or flush toilets, you can find ultrasound. They have no electricity—they carry their own car batteries." Ultrasound can only detect sex at around four months, meaning sex-selective abortions are usually late-term abortions, a more complicated, dangerous procedure than early abortions. It doesn't matter: Some women go through them over and over again, sacrificing their bodies for a boy.

General Electric, which dominates India's ultrasound market in concert with the Indian company Wipro, provided cheap credit to help practitioners buy the machines. "The present marketing strategy of GE-WIPRO to target smaller towns is a matter of concern," wrote Sabu George, a leading anti–sex selection activist.

> Once a private practitioner in a small town buys a machine then there is great pressure on other doctors to buy. Multiple machines where there is little demand for legitimate prenatal care increases competition, reduces scan rates and motivates abuses like fetal sex determination so that clinics can recover their investment. . . . At the global level, it is imperative that those concerned with human rights expose the transnational corporations involved in marketing ultrasound machines for these purposes.[6]

But the bitter problem of the missing girls cannot simply be laid at the door of even the most callous corporate behemoth. The sins of capitalism may exacerbate it, but behind it

---

*Sex ratio can be defined in several different ways. Internationally, most use the number of boys per 100 or 1,000 girls, which means that discrimination results in high sex ratios. But Indians tend to use the number of girls per 1,000 boys, so that areas of discrimination against girls are said to have low sex ratios.

are fantastically complex hierarchies of the world's most multifarious country, where feudalism and technocapitalism, extreme superstition and hypermodernity, purdah and professional women all coexist. Even as it highlights the desperate need for women's empowerment, sex-selective abortion sometimes looks, in a bizarre way, like a symptom of it. For reproductive rights advocates the whole issue has a looking-glass quality to it. It is a moral labyrinth that leads everyone but absolutists to sometimes uncomfortable and contradictory positions.

"You're going to get multiple opinions on everything on this," said Ena Singh, UNFPA's assistant representative in India and a particularly impassioned combatant against sex-selective abortion. (The day I met her a major Punjabi pop star, Rabbi Shergill, surprised her in her office; she had convinced him to make sex selection the theme of a new music video, which was about to debut on Indian TV.)

You're going to get multiple opinions on terminology; you're going to get multiple opinions on policy; you're going to get multiple opinions about rights, choice, gender, the way the law should be framed, the way it should be implemented, who should be implementing it. Because this issue is so fundamental, it's so deep, it impacts everything. It's about men and women—about every aspect of that relationship. It's about existence; it's about marriage; it's about love; it's about sex; it's about children; it's about globalization; it's about economics; it's about rights; it's about norms; it's about the media; it's about crime; it's about medicine; it's about medical ethics; it's about dowry; it's about property; and a hundred other things. Tell me what this is not about!

According to Amarjit Singh, a thirty-one-year-old family planning fieldworker from Fatehgarh Sahib, ultrasound exploded throughout his area in 1994. "Even remote villages knew about it," he said. Infamous advertisements went up across the region: "Spend 500 Rupees today and save 500,000 Rupees later." The numbers were a reference to the sometimes crushing cost of dowry, the main reason Indians give for the misery that commonly greets the birth of girls. Amarjit* remembers salesmen traveling to Punjabi villages touting the wonders of the new innovations. The same year India passed a law banning sex-determination tests for the purpose of sex-selective abortion, but it was widely ignored. "Everything was practiced very openly," said Amarjit.

A tall man with an easy smile and a shadow of a beard, Amarjit donates some of his time to the Voluntary Health Association of Punjab, the primary NGO addressing sex-selective abortion in that state. Like most of the district's residents he's a Sikh, though he long ago cut his hair and stopped wearing a turban except on special occasions. Sikhs have the worst sex ratio of all the groups in India, and the worst among the Sikhs are the Jat Sikhs, the land-owning caste that Amarjit belongs to.

He recalled an old chant he heard from relatives. Decades before he was born, when infanticide was committed openly, it was sung by those killing girl babies.

Eat the jaggery

Spin the cotton

You should not come

Send your brother

Today Amarjit is as active an opponent of sex selection as one is likely to find in Fatehgarh Sahib. He has allied himself with Manmohan Sharma, the founder of the Voluntary Health Association of Punjab, a frail, ardently committed social scientist who has dedicated the last fifteen years to combating his state's inequities, particularly those arising from sex discrimination. Amarjit insists that the mind-set that values men over women must be wiped out. And yet, less than twenty minutes after we first met, he explained to me why, in certain cases, he supports "female feticide."

"Supposing somebody has three, four, five girl children. In that case I think it's right that they plan a female feticide," he said. "You cannot change the idea of that woman who has three daughters. She keeps producing children in hopes of producing a son. So I think in such a situation it is acceptable. Sometimes in hopes of a son they produce too many girl children. They have no proper nutrition, education, or security. In that situation, it is very painful. Girls will be maltreated. They will not get good husbands."

The problem of sex-selective abortion is not, of course, limited to India. Across Asia it is reshaping the population in unprecedented ways. In most populations around 105 boys are born for every 100 girls. Male infants are weaker and more susceptible to illness, leading ratios to even out over time. The arrival of sex-selection technology has profoundly disrupted this equilibrium. According to the UNFPA, in 2005 six Asian countries reported imbalances of more than 108 male children for every 100 females: India, South Korea, Georgia, Azerbaijan, China, and Armenia. In China and India the situation has clearly deteriorated since the 1980s. "The fact that the child sex ratio has unexpectedly increased is going to influence the entire population over the coming decades: the entire population will gradually grow increasingly more masculine in their make-up, as the new generations born after the 1980s grow older," demographer Christophe Z. Guilmoto wrote of Asia.[7]

Immigration, meanwhile, has brought sex selection to the United States, Britain, and Canada, where advertisements for sex determination have appeared in newspapers aimed at the Indian diaspora.[8] A 2008 article in the *Proceedings of the National Academy of Sciences* documented skewed sex ratios among the children of Chinese, Korean, and Indian parents in the United States. "Using the 2000 U.S. Census, we find that the sex ratio of the oldest child to be normal, but that of subsequent

---

*Because so many Sikh men have the last name "Singh," and Sikh women the last name "Kaur," when dealing with groups, I'm going to refer to people by their first names to avoid confusion.

children to be heavily male if there was no previous son," it said.[9]

But the problem of the missing girls has been especially confounding in India, one of the two countries in the world where it is most prevalent. In the other, China, widespread sex selection is happening in the context of government compulsion. That makes the solution easy enough to see: End the one-child policy. India's situation is more complicated. It would be comforting to think that sex-selective abortion there is the product of poverty-driven desperation, of a kind of backwardness that could be remedied by development and education. Comforting, but wrong. In fact, while sex-selective abortion is sometimes motivated by economic need, other times it's the product of a twisted kind of consumerism.

It is widely practiced by India's emerging middle class, those with enough money and education to skirt the law and take advantage of technology. They fully embrace the two-child ideal that India's government—with outside help—pushed for decades, but only on the condition that they have at least one son. In a modernizing but still rigidly patriarchal society, boys hold out the prospect of a lifetime of economic security for their parents, while girls, who will join the household of their in-laws, are widely seen as simply a drain on expenses.

Female education is a remedy for almost every form of discrimination against girls—except this one. Indeed, in much of India higher rates of female literacy are correlated with higher rates of sex-selective abortion. This contrasts with China, where urbanites and those with higher education have the most normal sex ratios—despite the fact that the one-child policy is enforced more strictly in the cities.[10]

The posh, leafy suburbs of South Delhi, full of gracious homes occupied by professional couples with multiple servants, have sex ratios well under 900 girls for every 1,000 boys.[11] Bedi, a specialist in fetal medicine—and the father of two girls—has his practice there, in an elite neighborhood called Haus Kauz. He is a bearish man with a gray mustache, a Sikh from a caste, ironically, famous for female infanticide. A copy of the Dalai Lama's poem "A Precious Human Life" hangs on the wall of his office. On his desktop is one of his anti-sex selection PowerPoint presentations, which begins with a quote from Malcolm X: "It isn't that time is running out—time has run out!"

"This whole myth of somehow the poor women being forced to undergo sex determination and abortion is the biggest bullshit," said Bedi. "Seventy percent of the women who come to me [asking for sex determination], their husbands or their families don't even know that they're coming. The first demand for female feticide comes from the mother herself."

Bedi's patients, of course, are hardly representative of Indian women. They represent the richest sliver of Indian society: As he himself says, no one else can afford him. If the problem of sex-selective abortion were confined to people like them, it would barely show up in censuses. Still, the fact that even such privileged women seek out sex selection says much about how entrenched the preference for sons is throughout Indian society.

Given that Bedi is a high-profile crusader against sex selection, it seems strange that any of his patients would ask him for help in finding out the sex of their fetuses. That they do is evidence of how much cynicism and corruption surrounds efforts to ban the practice. According to Bedi, most doctors who declaim against sex selection in public profit from it in private, a view I heard echoed by doctors in Punjab as well. He speaks about sex-selective abortion in the shrillest possible terms, calling it a genocide, a holocaust. Still, some women assume that he must not really mean it, that for the right price he'll help them avoid the burden of girls.

Bedi exudes a poignant mix of urgency and fatalism; he believes that everything possible must be done to stop sex-selective abortion, and that none of his activism is having any impact at all. In the last fifteen years, he said, he has talked two women out of aborting female fetuses, one of whom was pregnant after a long period of infertility. Both of them come to see him every year or two to castigate him for ruining their lives. They come, he said, to "remind me what a mistake they made because they listened to me, while everybody in their peer group has sons, [women] who were also my patients but had gone to better doctors later and got sons and abortions, while they had not."

These women are not cowering victims, he insisted. They "are women like you, like my wife and my sister. Empowered, with big cars, big houses, and the best possible college degrees."

T here are several reasons for the counterintuitive connection between prosperity, education, and sex discrimination. Wealthier communities in India's northwest—precisely those who can most afford decent schools for their children—have always been the most averse to the birth of daughters. Members of the urban middle class want smaller families than poor people in the countryside, leaving less room for girls. Those with at least some education are better able to navigate the medical system, especially now that sex-determination tests have become illegal.

Most of all, though, more prosperous families are rejecting daughters because of the toxic, exponential growth of dowries. Dowry has been illegal in India since 1961, but that law is hardly enforced. In theory, dowry is a gift parents give to a daughter to ensure her future security; because she won't inherit any of her parents' property, it represents her share of their wealth. As it's practiced, though, dowry is a kind of tribute paid to the family of the groom. In much of northern India it's not a one-time gift, either: A girl's parents are expected to offer a continuous flow of presents to her husband's family, and to be somewhat abject before them. "In the power relations between the bride's and groom's families, the former always have to give in and put up with any humiliation, indignity, and oblique or direct insults on the part of the latter," wrote Indian sociologist Tulsi Patel.[12]

In recent years, with India suddenly awash in consumerist bounty, dowry demands have exploded, turning the whole thing into a materialistic free-for-all. In the high-caste communities where dowry had long been established, demands became inflated. At the same time, the custom took hold in places where it had never existed before as the upwardly mobile tried to imitate those further up the caste and class hierarchy.[13]

Historically, female infanticide was practiced mostly by the upper castes in India's highly conservative, Pakistan-bordering northern and northwestern plains, which stretch from Gujarat to Punjab, and that is where the problem of sex-selective abortion is most acute. Dowry is out of control in the region. "We have a developing society, and so much consumerism," said Nirupama Dutt, editor of the Punjabi edition of the *Sunday Indian,* a national newsmagazine. "It's so important to have the modern gadgets, ostentatious weddings." Her cousin, she said, from "a slightly backward rural area," considers the minimum acceptable dowry to include a television, a motorcycle, a refrigerator, and a washing machine, as well as quantities of gold. "This is the done thing," said Dutt. "Newspapers advertise package deals. And among the landlords, the Jats, a car is a must."

Exorbitant demands have been spreading from the north to the rest of the country, and as they have, sex-selective abortion has made inroads in parts of India where female infanticide had been unknown. A slight female deficit even appeared among children in the southernmost state of Kerala, where matriarchal traditions and leftist government combined to create a relative idyll of gender equality, with a female literacy rate of almost 90 percent, compared to less than 50 percent in India as a whole.

When dowry demands continue after marriage, a woman can become a kind of hostage in her in-laws' home, tormented, beaten, and even killed if enough money isn't forthcoming. In a not atypical story from May 2008, the *Times of India* reported that twenty-four-year-old Astha Jain was found hanging in her South Delhi home on her one-year wedding anniversary, her suicide note saying she could no longer bear her husband's family's dowry harassment. The in-laws owned a steel factory; her parents owned a paper business. According to her parents, they had already spent a crore—10 million rupees, or a quarter million dollars—during her wedding, and had given a Mercedes to the groom, Amit Jain, and gold rings to every member of the wedding party. In order to placate Amit's parents, they had handed over another 35 lakh, or $86,500, a few months before Astha's death. Their "greed could not be satisfied," said one of her relatives.[14]

On a searingly hot spring day in 2008, Amarjit Singh took me to one of the Fatehgarh Sahib villages where he worked. The people who live there are far from the rarefied realm of the Jains or of Bedi's patients, but the upper-caste Sikhs' section of the village has nearly as many modern conveniences as an American suburb. The houses are two stories high, with satellite dishes and designer water tanks shaped like birds or soccer balls perched on top. Behind the gates are courtyards big enough to park cars and John Deere tractors. Here, said Amarjit, there aren't more than 400 girls for every 1,000 boys. "The numbers look better because of Muslims and migrants," he said, both groups that have higher birthrates and more females.

Harpreet Singh, a lean, attractive man in white kurta pajamas and an orange turban, shared his late father's house with his brother, Narpreet. Each of them had one son. Harpreet, whose boy was six years old, planned to stop while he was ahead.

"The money that I earn is not enough to raise a girl child," he said. "I have already got one son, so I don't want any second child at all." Another boy would create his own problems, forcing Harpreet to split his share of his father's land in two. If dowries keep growing as they have been, meanwhile, he estimated he'd have to spend at least 15 lakh—1.5 million rupees, or $37,000—by the time any daughter of his would marry. With one boy he feels assured that his family line will continue and his wealth won't be dispersed.

"I know my district is famous for having the least number of girl children," he said. He worries, sometimes, about where his son will find a bride. But no one wanted to spend their own fortune providing wives for Punjab's boys: As the famous Punjabi saying goes, "Raising a daughter is like watering your neighbor's garden." If anything, Harpreet thought that increasing competition for women made it all the more imperative that he invest everything in his only boy. With so few girls, he said, "the time will come when the girls will be choosers in marriage. So in most cases the girls will choose the richer families to be married into. So those who are financially weaker, they will not get brides. That will be a very big crisis in our society."

Faced with such economic fears, he found official attempts to change attitudes wholly unconvincing. Like elsewhere in India, when people in the village have sons, they decorate their houses and hand out sweets. Usually, there is no celebration for a girl. Lately, people connected to the government and NGOs had been distributing sweets for daughters as well, which Harpreet saw as insincere "showing off." Deep down, he insisted, they're as desperate for boys as everyone else.

A short walk down a brick lane led us to the home of Balwant Singh, a milk seller and practitioner of ayurvedic medicine, and his wife, Gurjit Kaur. They had two daughters, twenty and twenty-two, and a five-year-old son. "I am very happy that I have two girls," Balwant insisted. "Clinton has only one daughter, but I have two daughters." Both girls were studying: The eldest, Ranbir, was working on a master's degree in commerce, and the younger, Satvir, was getting a BA in ayurvedic medicine, like her father.

In the curio case in the small sitting room, though, along with the birds made of seashells, the stuffed dog, and the yellow fabric flowers, there were no photos of Ranbir or Satvir. There were only pictures of little Inderbir, a boisterous boy who ran around the room soaking up attention as his sisters sat decorously to the side or went back and forth to the kitchen with drinks.

"Those people who have only girls in a family, the neighbors think that family is useless," said Gurjit, forty-four. "I'm thankful to God that I have a son."

Balwant's sister, Charanjit, and her husband, Harpreet, a young policeman in a light blue turban, were visiting that day with their only son. They were silent as their relatives and I talked about sex selection until, suddenly, Harpreet's indignation boiled over. He burst out, speaking Punjabi, "Take a look at Muslim families in other states—they have got nine children, twelve children. Take a look at the girls in this family. One is studying ayurveda, one is preparing for her MBA. These are smaller families, and we are planning them rather well, we think. Whatever is being practiced here, take a look at how we have controlled the population growth."

Harpreet continued in a rapid soliloquy: "I am a Jat Sikh. I feel bad that people are always blaming us for killing our girl children. We love all our children—we love our boy children, and also we love our girl children. But through this thing, we have controlled our population in such a way that—take a look at our families—we don't have the kind of poverty that exists in other parts of the country, where they have five children, six children, seven children. They cannot even feed their children, forget about their education." His son, he said, is studying in the top school in the area. "If I had five children, I couldn't afford to keep him in the best school."

Harpreet's wife was sterilized, and as a government employee, he was rewarded for her operation. Policemen like him who have two children or fewer, and foreclose the possibility of having any more, get an extra five hundred rupees, or twelve dollars, every month. Thus, Harpreet was incensed that his community's highly successful mode of population control is now under attack.

"The government took such big trouble during Sanjay Gandhi's time to do all these things," Harpreet continued, exasperated. "But we are naturally doing it! We are not being coerced, we are not being forced. So what's the problem?"

For all his passion Harpreet spoke elliptically, avoiding any actual mention of sex-selective abortion, instead calling it "this thing." Only once, during a particularly heated moment, did he use the phrase *kudi maar*, which means girl killer.

I ndia's government has spent the last half century trying to persuade, cajole, and sometimes coerce its population into having smaller families, and they have largely succeeded. In 2005 the country's total fertility rate averaged 2.9 children per woman, down more than 17 percent in just the last decade. Women in India's cities average only 2.1 children each. The decline has been felt even among poor people in remote areas. In rural Rajasthan, for example, the total fertility rate dropped from 4.7 in the mid 1990s to 4.0 ten years later.[15]

Son preference, though, has remained unchanged. "Since the desired family size has come down to two or three—two in many cases—they still want *at least* one if not more sons," said Saroj Pachauri, Asia region director of the Population Council. "That's where the distortions are occurring."

Population control, divorced from an appreciable increase in women's status, replaced one demographic problem with another. "Some things are so ironic when you look back," Pachauri said sadly, recalling her long history in India's population movement. "We did this with such good intentions, and it backfired on us."

A grandmotherly woman with a gentle face, bobbed hair, and a fashionably understated *salwar kameez*, Pachauri has been involved in the movement since the early 1970s; in many ways, its history is her own. She worked at the Ford Foundation's India office when Adrienne Germain was representing Ford in Bangladesh; like Germain she struggled to make population

programs more responsive to women's rights. "I am absolutely convinced that unless you address the underlying gender problem, you will get nowhere," she said.

Yet India's population programs never did this before Cairo, when the focus was on reducing fertility at all costs. While the central government has become much more sensitive since then, some state governments continue to employ punitive targets and quotas, barring people with more than two children from local political office and denying them maternity benefits. Among India's elite there continues to be near unanimity about the necessity of population control. (As recently as 2003, India's Supreme Court characterized "the torrential increase in the population" as "more dangerous than a hydrogen bomb.")

It's impossible to say how much of India's fertility decline is due to state policy and how much to increasing wealth, urbanization, and decreasing agricultural plot sizes in the countryside. But the government has almost certainly played a partial role, suggesting that a colossal official mobilization can over time help change social norms. Had the campaign, with all its resources, focused on women's rights from the start, India's success in addressing overpopulation may not have come so much at girls' expense.

Despite the small recent decline in its child sex ratio, Kerala remains a model of what's possible. Until 1971, Kerala had the highest population growth rate in India, with an average of 4.1 children per woman. By 1992, enormous investments in women's education, freely available family planning, and comprehensive health care had led to India's lowest infant mortality rate, all helping to push fertility down to 1.8 children per woman without coercion or, at the time, a decrease in the proportion of girls to boys.[16] Kerala's women still both outlive and outnumber its men, although unless current trends are halted, their demographic superiority may not last.[17]

A s early as the 1970s some predicted—approvingly—that sex selection could be a tool for limiting population. In May 1975, when amniocentesis was first being used for prenatal diagnoses in India, a group of Indian doctors published a report in the journal *Indian Pediatrics* that mentioned the potential of the new method for population control. "In India, cultural and economical factors make the parents desire a son, and in many instances the couple keeps on reproducing just to have a son," they wrote. "Prenatal determination of sex would put an end to this unnecessary fecundity. There is of course the tendency to abort the fetus if it is female. This may not be acceptable to persons in the West, but in our patients this plan of action was followed in seven of eight patients who had the test carried out primarily for the determination of sex of the fetus."[18]

After protests from women's groups, the government of India banned sex tests in public hospitals in 1976. Within a few years, though, private clinics offering sex determination appeared. In the mid 1980s a study commissioned by anti-sex-selection activists found that 84 percent of gynecologists in Bombay were performing amniocentesis for sex determination. "A majority of the doctors thought the sex-determination tests were a humane service for women who did not want any more daughters, and some even felt that they could be an important family planning device for our country," the activists wrote.[19] At one city hospital, of 8,000 abortions following amniocentesis, 7,999 were of female fetuses.[20]

Through the efforts of feminist organizers, the state of Maharashtra, where Bombay is located, outlawed sex-determination tests in 1988, and the central government followed suit in 1994. But sex-selective abortion was too popular to control. Most people are willing to leave their first child up to chance, but after one or two daughters they take matters into their own hands. "[I]t is with regards to later pregnancies among sonless couples that SRB [sex-ratio at birth] values tend to surge," wrote Guilmoto. "Parents want to avoid the 'worst-case' scenario—i.e., a family without a son."[21] Following the 2001 census the government made the anti-sex-selection law more stringent, and as a result prices went up, but other than that there was little evidence that people were being deterred.

Although feminists have taken a leading role in India's anti-sex-selection campaign, it's a supremely tricky issue for those who care deeply about abortion rights. Women's rights activists with experience in Western countries worry that the language of the campaign is shading into the idiom of the Western antiabortion movement. "Murder in the Womb" was the title of a six-part exposé aired on the national news channel *Sahara Samay*. Educational posters, produced by the government and by local NGOs, show swords and daggers pointed at fetuses. The almost universal use of the term "female feticide" or, in Hindi, *kanya bhronn hatya*, which literally means "the killing of young girls," begs the question of why feticide in general is OK.

Abortion up to twenty weeks was legalized in India in 1971 as part of the country's attempt to control population growth. It was never about women's rights. The Medical Termination of Pregnancy Act allows abortion for a wide range of reasons, including failure of contraception, but it is the doctor, not the woman, who has the right to decide whether an abortion is warranted. Unlike the legalization of abortion in the United States, the MTP Act wasn't associated with any sort of social upheaval or disruption in gender roles—premarital sex remained as taboo as ever, and notions of wifely obedience as deeply engrained. That's likely why it passed without controversy, and why India has never had a serious antiabortion movement.

Yet while abortion is legal, unsafe abortion remains a major problem; in many places safe services either aren't available or aren't known, leading millions of women to seek abortions from traditional midwives and unqualified quacks. Research in the mid-1990s showed botched abortions were responsible for 13 percent of India's staggeringly high maternal mortality rate.[22]

Most abortions in India are for unwanted pregnancies, not sex selection.[23] Still, with the campaign against sex-selective abortion injecting the idea of fetal rights into the public conversation as never before, there was reason to fear that efforts to expand access to safe abortion would be hurt. "The biggest danger, which is the one we're dealing with right now, is that

the anti-sex-selection campaigns not turn into antiabortion campaigns," said Gita Sen, the longtime women's rights activist and Cairo lobby veteran.

Dr. Sharad Iyengar and his wife, Dr. Kirti Iyengar, run an NGO called Action Research and Training for Health in the poor desert state of Rajasthan. They provide child immunizations, family planning, and prenatal care and safe delivery, running two friendly and basic but clean clinics that are open twenty-four hours a day for people in the surrounding villages. Thanks to a scheme meant to reduce India's maternal mortality, women are paid cash to have their babies in government hospitals, but some of the poor women ARTH serves would rather forgo that money and instead pay a nominal fee to ARTH to deliver at their centers, where they're treated with care and dignity.

Safe abortion is an important part of ARTH's work; health volunteers in the villages steer women away from the quacks, who are known as "Bengali doctors," and rotating gynecologists perform both manual vacuum aspiration and medical abortions at its clinics. These services are crucial. On a scorching April day in 2008 I visited a village where ARTH works, in a hilly, marble-mining area in Rajasthan's south. A small group of illiterate women, dressed brightly and wearing big, beaded nose rings and tarnished silver ankle bracelets, sat on the dusty ground around an ARTH employee using a specially designed picture book to teach them about reproductive and child health. One woman quickly volunteered that before ARTH local women used to seek abortions from a nearby practitioner "who gave some tablets and used some instruments." There was a lot of pain and bleeding, but they wouldn't tell anyone or go to the hospital. A young woman in a green sari—a teenager, or a little older—added that her mother died after taking some abortifacient plants given by a local *dai*, or midwife.

According to Sharad Iyengar, the campaign against sex-selective abortion has had a chilling effect on legitimate abortion providers in Rajasthan. "There is stigmatization of abortion. A lot of providers have become averse to providing abortion services," he said. "Some gynecologists are now against abortions. Those who do it, do it quietly—they're not ready to talk about it. The public health dimensions of unsafe abortion never were on the agenda."

Elsewhere in India enterprising local officials tackled the problem of sex selection by targeting women who had had abortions. Krishan Kumar, deputy commissioner of the Nawanshahr district of Punjab, made national news for his success in combating sex-selective abortion. Partly, he did it through an impressive crackdown on illegal ultrasound operations and unscrupulous doctors. One gynecologist arrested during his reign, back at work after Kumar was transferred, told me with obvious self-pity that Kumar had been a "dictator." The gynecologist remained unapologetic: Anyone with a daughter should be allowed sex determination for her next pregnancy, he insisted, adding, "In no situation should there be a third child."

But Kumar also humiliated many women, organizing groups of volunteers to stage loud, public mourning ceremonies outside the homes of women thought to have had sex-selective abortions. "Two days ago when news came that an unborn girl had been murdered in her mother Manjit Kaur's womb, hundreds of villagers wearing white assembled outside Manjit Kaur's house and took out a 'funeral procession,'" reported the *Times of India,* noting that "sadness was writ large in the eyes of Manjit, who is already a mother of a three-year-old daughter."[24]

Feminists have been understandably alarmed. They've struggled against the phrase "female feticide," but it is used so widely that even the UNFPA sometimes employs it, prioritizing effective grassroots communication over global abortion politics. Worse, in local efforts, "female" is sometimes dropped. Official campaigns against "feticide" are especially problematic, given that many rural Indians are already unaware that abortion is legal.[25]

Some campaigners dismiss anxieties about abortion rights as a Western projection, noting that India has never had a real antiabortion movement. "Please understand, in this country there was no pro-life, pro-choice debate," said Bedi. "Nobody has ever fought for fetal rights. The medical profession has not. The ethicists have not. The temples and the gurudawaras have not. So to say that any voice against [sex-selective abortion] will give vent to the prolifers and hence restrict the reproductive choice of a woman is ridiculous."

Perhaps. But India *does* have pronatalist Hindu rightists, who have urged women to have more sons for the sake of communal demographic strength. The secretary of the Vishwa Hindu Parishad, a hard-line Hindu nationalist group, encouraged every Hindu woman to become an *Ashtaputra,* or mother of eight sons. The leader of the Rashtriya Swayamsevak Sangh, the VHP's parent organization, called on Hindu women to produce at least three sons each to ensure that Hindus do not become outnumbered by Muslims.[26]

With increasing efforts afoot to enlist religious figures in the fight against sex selection, some fear that they'll start attacking abortion rather than the preference for sons. "One of India's biggest pluses in being able to hold up women's reproductive rights around abortion has always been that the religious dimension has never been very strong," said Sen. "That doesn't mean that with the Hindu fundamentalists running riot all over the country, some crackpot doesn't pick that up."

Sex selection poses an additional challenge to women's rights activists, one that's philosophical rather than tactical. To confront the issue of sex-selective abortion as a feminist is to see the world in much the same way pro-lifers do, at least for a moment. It's to look in horror at a culture where potential life is tossed away in the quest for economic advancement and status, debasing all involved. It's to see some choices as illegitimate.

The American antiabortion movement has relished pointing out the contradiction. "It is perhaps obvious why sex-selective abortion is an embarrassment to feminism: while the preference for sons is deeply rooted in history, the other factors, such as reduced family size and cultural acceptance of abortion, are central pillars of feminist thought," wrote Douglas A. Sylva of the Catholic Family and Human Rights Institute in the *Weekly Standard.* "Since at least the 1995 Beijing Women's Conference, feminist champions have argued that international 'gender justice' could only be established if women possessed

the reproductive rights necessary to reduce their family sizes, thereby liberating them for higher education and successful careers." It is never pleasant, he continued, "to admit that one's revolutionaries have begun to devour their own."[27]

There is indeed an inconsistency between believing in absolute reproductive choice and in wanting to outlaw abortions performed for the "wrong" reason. That's why American feminists tend to see domestic attempts to ban sex selection as threats to *Roe v. Wade.* Indian feminists, though, have never prioritized the concept of choice the way Westerners do, in part because whatever choices Indian women face are so constrained. Women's rights activists in India fight against the "choice" of families to pay dowry to marry their daughters off, and to both practice and glorify *sati,* in which living widows burn with their husbands on their funeral pyres.

"My own view is that the question of reproductive rights is much bigger than the question of just reproductive choice," said Sen. "The language of choice, while it's very useful in holding up individual rights, often misses that behind the way in which people make choices are a lot of social pressures, forces, relationships, and so on." A woman's choice to have a sex-selective abortion, said Sen, "may reflect the fact that she has very few rights."

This approach doesn't jibe with the debate about abortion in the United States, where rights and choice are seen as synonymous, and where feminists are constantly defending the right of women to make reproductive decisions unencumbered by others' beliefs about what is best for them or for society. But it is not, obviously, the job of Indian feminists to map their politics onto the ideological topography of the West. There may be no overarching philosophy that can reconcile the two stances, except perhaps for solidarity between groups of women working in vastly different contexts.

Distorted sex ratios pose a concrete threat to Indian women that goes beyond the disturbing demonstration of how little they are esteemed. Some have suggested, based on crude economic logic, that the deficit in women would raise their value. On the ground, this has not been the case. Already in northern India shortages of women have led to increases in sexual violence and trafficking for both marriage and prostitution. Though dowry has persisted unabated, men who can't find wives have begun importing poor women from the country's south and east, who then find themselves isolated in an alien culture where they don't even speak the language and may be treated as little more than chattel.

Parts of Haryana, which borders Punjab and has India's second-worst sex ratio, have witnessed a return of polyandry, in which one woman is shared among several brothers. In February 2006, Tripala Kurmari, an eighteen-year-old girl from one of India's minority tribes, was murdered there. "The tribal girl was brought to Haryana by an agent who promised to get her a job," wrote Gita Aravamudan, author of the book *Disappearing Daughters: The Tragedy of Female Foeticide.* "She was 'married' to Ajmer Singh who desperately wanted a male heir. However, soon after her marriage she found she was expected to sleep with all his brothers. When she refused, he killed her. The murder of Tripala Kumari gave a gruesome face to a form of sexual exploitation which has become increasingly popular in the women-starved states of Punjab and Haryana."[28] And this was before the hardest-hit generation in those states reached adulthood.

Sexual violence, meanwhile, reinforced some families' motives for rejecting daughters in the first place. The investment of family honor in girls' sexual purity, and the terror of losing it, long played a role in northern India's tradition of infanticide. As Amarjit Singh explained, "The Afghan plunderers on horseback used to come to Punjab to plunder and rob this area. They picked up beautiful women." People thought it was "better to kill the girls before they are picked up, raped, and taken away." In the twenty-first century there are no more invading hordes from the north and west, but the constant vigilance required to keep girls safe from violation is one reason people say they don't want them in the first place.

Declining sex ratios curtail female freedom in additional ways as well. Guilmoto speculated that the increased demand for women to serve as wives and mothers will cut off other opportunities. "The reduced number of women in these areas would have an interesting corollary, in that women's roles as wife, daughter-in-law or mother would become more essential to society," he wrote. "The enhancement of this traditional family role will, however, come at the expense of other life trajectories, such as remaining single or a career-oriented strategy. Indeed, if new incentives towards early marriage and childbearing are offered to women, this could lead to their temporary or permanent withdrawal from the workforce."[29] Evidence from societies with highly uneven sex ratios bear him out; in such places women have lower levels of literacy and labor force participation, and higher rates of suicide, than in countries where the numbers of men and women are more even.[30]

It's not just women whose futures are imperiled. Countries with millions of alienated, unmarriageable men are likely to be both more internally insecure and externally belligerent. In their book *Bare Branches: The Security Implications of Asia's Surplus Male Population,* political scientists Valerie M. Hudson and Andrea M. den Boer show how historically, in areas where men have outnumbered women due to widespread female infanticide, superfluous single men have played a violently destabilizing role. To channel their aggression governments have sometimes embarked on campaigns of expansion, threatening nearby countries.

"The evidence suggests that high-sex-ratio societies, especially those with unequal resource distribution and generalized resource scarcity, breed chronic violence and persistent social disorder and corruption," they concluded. "Indeed, bare branches in high-sex-ratio societies contribute to this disruption on a larger scale than might be possible in societies with lower sex ratios."[31]

Hudson and den Boer adopt the term "bare branches" from nineteenth-century China, where surplus bachelors formed criminal gangs that eventually coalesced into rebel militias. Like India, China has a long history of female infanticide, practiced for many of the same reasons. Women's status, thought to be relatively high during the Shang and Zhou dynasties (1766–1122 B.C. and 1122–221 B.C.) fell during the Qin and Han eras (221–206 B.C. and 206 B.C.–A.D. 220) as arranged marriages, female seclusion, and the cult of chastity became institutionalized.[32] As in India, dowries portended financial ruin for parents of daughters, and a mania for virginity made the killing of girls seem less shameful than the threat of premarital sex. Hudson and den Boer quote a scholar from the time of the Song dynasty (960–1279) who claimed, "[T]o starve to death is a very minor matter, but to lose one's chastity is a major matter."[33]

In the first half of the nineteenth century, Hudson and den Boer write, the Huai-pei region of northeast China had a series of natural disasters. The resulting poverty led to an increase in female infanticide and a sex ratio of around 129 men for every 100 women. Polygamy and concubinage, they write, further decreased the supply of wives. Thus, many poor men were unable to settle down and achieve the status of respectable adults; instead, they built a kind of antisocial subculture based on crime and martial arts. Eventually, the small bands of bandits started to organize on a larger scale to try to overthrow the Qing dynasty in the Nien Rebellion.

"The Nien Rebellion," write Hudson and den Boer, "is an example of how exaggerated offspring sex selection can threaten the stability of entire regions, and even great empires."[34]

Beyond questions of demographics and geopolitics, India's epidemic of sex-selective abortion—and, more generally, its pathological mania for sons—victimizes individual women. It is way too simple to claim that all women who abort female fetuses are forced into it, but despite the experiences of Puneet Bedi and his elite patients, for some coercion is very real.

"In Gujarat, women do not decide whether they will have male children or female children," said Ila Pathak, secretary of the Ahmedabad Women's Action Group, a feminist organization based in Gajarat's largest city. "To be frank, she is never consulted whether she will go to bed with the man. So there is no freedom of decision."

Prosperous Gujarat, birthplace of Jawaharlal Nehru and cradle of India's independence struggle, is famous in more recent years for right-wing Hindu programs against Muslims. While Punjab has agriculture, Gujarat has trade and industry; the Gujarati businessman is a national stereotype. Like elsewhere in India, its wealth is inverse to its tolerance for girls. The state's sex ratio is 883 girls for every 1,000 boys. In Ahmedabad, it is 836. Pathak, a white-haired, soft-spoken, retired English professor, has studied violence against women in Gujarat extensively, spending several years combing through police records to produce a systematic analysis of domestic violence cases and of the circumstances surrounding women's deaths. "In Gujarat, so many women die or commit suicide because they give birth to daughters," she said. "Husbands torturing wives because of the birth of a daughter is not unique."

At around 8:00 P.M. one evening in May 2007, two confused, terrified women, Sunita Rajput and her cowife, Kajal, appeared with their daughters at the Kasturba Gandhi Memorial Trust, a shelter for abused women on the outskirts of Ahmedabad. They could barely walk and had to be helped from the gate. Both were covered with welts from beatings with a belt. Sunita needed a blood transfusion. They had just escaped from their husband, Rajesh Rajput, seller of ayurvedic remedies, a sadist who had forced the women to have eight abortions between them because they hadn't produced a boy.

When I met Sunita a year later she was in her late twenties. Her huge obsidian eyes, perfect almonds fringed by thick lashes, were still shadowed and often blank, and she often broke into tears as she spoke. She found it too painful to recount much of her past in detail, so Pratima Pandya, the shelter's director, told her story instead.

Sunita, who has a seventh-grade education, had married Rajesh ten years earlier, and after a year her first daughter, Anjali, was born. A year and a half later there was another girl, Kashish. It is the sperm that determines whether a baby will be male or female, but Rajesh blamed his wife, and, furious at his failure to have a son, he would beat Sunita terribly. His mother blamed Sunita as well, and after the first two daughters, she and Rajesh arranged for ultrasound tests followed by abortions for each of Sunita's next four pregnancies.

Each time she went, Sunita recalled with an angry little laugh, there was a sign outside announcing, as per the law, that the clinics did not perform sex-determination tests. "They should be stopped, they should not exist," she said. It should have been obvious to the doctors, she said, that she was there under duress: "Of course no mother wants to kill her baby. Of course Rajesh took me there forcibly."

The next two times Sunita was pregnant, Rajesh, assuming she was incapable of having sons, didn't even take her for ultrasound—he just brought her for abortions. Meanwhile, flouting Hindu law, he married another woman, Kajal, hoping that she could give him a son. At first he installed Kajal in his brother's house, not bringing her home until she was seven months pregnant. He treated her decently until she too gave birth to a girl. Rajesh didn't go to the hospital to see the newborn, and when Kajal brought her home, he held her up by one leg and started hitting her. Together, the two women rushed at him, fighting to save the girl's life. From then on he would torture the two of them together—beating them daily, driving nails into their fingers and ears, even forcing them to drink his urine. They weren't allowed any contact with the outside world. Kajal would eventually have two abortions as well. As Rajesh's persecution increased, Sunita stopped eating. They started to go mad.

The torments Sunita and Kajal faced, said Pandya, exceed anything she's seen in her many years at the shelter. It is not unusual, though, for abuse to escalate following the birth of a girl. "Almost for twenty years I have been working in this field," she said. "If a boy is born, [a woman's] position in the family becomes consolidated. If a girl is born, she has to face the usual torture."

Finally, when Sunita was pregnant for the ninth time, the two women made their escape together. Neither had any idea where to go—Kajal was an orphan and Sunita's family was too poor to help her. Fleeing their village, they got in a rickshaw and asked to go to the nearest town. They were sobbing, and the rickshaw driver asked what was wrong. They told him their story. Fortunately, he'd heard of the Kasturba Gandhi Trust, and he brought them there.

In addition to medical treatment, Pandya called the police and got the women legal representation. Rajesh was arrested and jailed, and two clinics where Sunita had undergone ultrasounds had their registrations suspended. Meanwhile, the story hit the local media. A young woman named Usha, who had been raped and branded with hot metal by cousins of the mentally retarded man she'd been married to, read about it in *Chitralekha*, a popular magazine. It inspired her to run away, too; today she shares a room with Sunita and her children at the shelter. At least one other woman also fled to Kasturba Gandhi after seeing Sunita's story.

Usha may have been moved by Sunita's strength, but Sunita feels anything but powerful. Several months after arriving at the shelter she gave birth, in a cosmic irony, to a boy, whom she named Dharmik. In jail Rajesh read about Dharmik in the paper and began sending letters to the shelter, demanding that Sunita and his son be returned to him and promising that he would no longer torture her now that she's succeeded in producing a male heir.

To Sunita's horror, Rajesh was released from jail pending the outcome of the trial, which, given India's glacial legal system, could take years. Hoping to pressure her, he beat up her father and brother. "Bring back Sunita to me," he told them. "I want my son back." As long as he's free she lives in terror that he will try to take Dharmik. Compounding her shock, Kajal, restless at the shelter, returned to Rajesh, assuming the more legitimate role of his only wife. (According to Pandya, a momentarily solicitous Rajesh, hoping to stop Kajal from testifying against him, promised to put the house, now partly in Sunita's name, in Kajal's instead.) "They are in that home," said Sunita, "and I am in an orphanage."

Sunita never leaves Kasturba Gandhi except for medical and legal appointments. She's learning handicrafts—embroidery and beading—but can't imagine how she'll ever support herself independently. The day we met she was sitting in one of the shelter's airy cement common rooms, which is half open to the leafy compound outside. Other residents were sifting wheat for chapatis. Eyes downcast, she rocked Dharmik in a rustic cradle; her lovely daughters, saucer-eyed and solemn, were perched protectively beside her.

She had only one wish: She wanted Rajesh back in jail. Please, she implored, wasn't there something I could do? "I don't want anything but that Rajesh should be punished." She started crying. "I don't have an identity!" she said, repeating it over and over, "I don't have an identity!" Her only hope was in the sleeping six-month-old. "When Dharmik grows up," she said, "I will have someone to cling to."

In the end, as long as women lack an identity without a husband or a son, sex-selective abortion will continue to deform India's—and Asia's—demographics. That's why what is happening in India is more complicated than modernization gone awry. Rather, social modernization has proven unable to catch up with technological progress. Indian society is reforming, slowly and incrementally. The very fact that Sunita escaped her hellish home, said Pandya, is evidence of a small shift. Twenty years ago, "she would have committed suicide," Pandya said. "That Sunita came here, it is a sign of seeking freedom." Gradually, she insisted, women are moving beyond utter dependence on men. Due to increased education, she said, "twenty, twenty-five percent of women who have faced such torture are trying their best to get out, the way Sunita or Usha did."

If you look hard you can see such faintly hopeful signs everywhere. Dutt, the editor of the *Sunday Indian,* comes from a family with an infanticidal history. Of her grandfather's sisters just one survived; an elderly female member of her great-grandfather's family put the others to sleep with overdoses of opium. Just two generations later she chose to remain single and to adopt a baby girl.

Some believe only a boy can light his parents' funeral pyres; indeed, that's said to be one of the many reasons Hindus are so desperate for sons. "Now girls are doing it," said Dutt. "I lit my mother's funeral pyre." Dutt, a large woman with a sweet smile, was wearing a royal blue *salwar kameez;* as she spoke, her teenage daughter, wearing jeans, did homework at the kitchen table. They seem more a remarkable exception than the edge of an emerging trend, but they are there nonetheless, in one of the most hostile parts of the country. There has been "slow change," said Dutt. "There has been a lot of change from the late nineteenth century until now. When I was born my mother distributed sweets. She was bored of having sons—I had six brothers. I opted to adopt a girl child. So there are exceptions like that, and slow change, but it is very, very rare."

The coming of sex-selection technology overtook this sluggish process, amplifying all the country's atavisms. Skewed gender ratios are the terrible result of one kind of progress. The ultimate solution will have to be progress of another kind. "Culture and tradition is not a monolith," said Bedi. "It is not permanent. It changes. For example, twenty years ago it was ridiculous to see a girl from a small town from [the state of] Utter Pradesh to come to Delhi, live on her own, and earn money, because the money she earned was a pittance. Now she works in a call center and earns ten times more than her father, and it is acceptable. Social acceptability follows economic compulsions." He is fulsomely cynical about the "awareness campaigns" and street plays put on by many NGOs. But, he said, "if people realize after two hundred years that those who have two daughters have a better quality of life than those who have two sons, then it will obviously change."

South Korea, the first Asian country to begin to reverse the trend of sex selection, offers a hopeful example that such change needn't take two hundred years. To be sure, South Koreans continue to have more boys than girls, but the ratio of male to female births has been declining since the 1990s. Interestingly, it has been falling in tandem with the total fertility rate, the opposite of the usual pattern, in which the desire for fewer children leaves less space for daughters.[35]

"Until a few years ago, South Korea appeared to epitomize the pattern of rising sex ratios despite rapid development—with dramatic increases in levels of education, industrialization, and urbanization, as well as in women's education and participation in the formal labor force," researchers Woojin Chung and Monica Das Gupta wrote in a 2007 World Bank paper. "By the mid-1990s, South Korea was officially included as a member of the developed countries' club, the [Organization for Economic Co-operation and Development]. Yet sex ratios at birth rose steeply during this period."[36]

It was the same paradox now seen in India. As Chung and Das Gupta point out, "This flew in the face of over a century of social science theory," which had always posited that modernization lessened the pull of tradition and made status dependent on individual achievement rather than immutable identity. It also seemed to challenge the idea that increased education and female employment reduce gender inequalities within households.[37]

The operative word is "seemed." Chung and Das Gupta make an important distinction "between the *intensity* of son preference felt by people, and its actual *manifestation* on the ground in sex ratios," and they show that the two can actually move in opposite directions. When new technology makes sex selection accessible, sex ratios can get worse even as attitudes are getting more progressive. "Moreover," they write, "since educated women are typically better able to access and implement these new technologies, studies can even appear to suggest that gender outcomes for children are worsened by development, and even by improvements in the position of women."

This is a distortion, though, caused by a lag between social change and technological advancement. In fact, the number of South Korean women who said they "must have a son" fell slowly between 1985 and 1991, and then precipitously after that. Son preference, Chung and Das Gupta found, "declines with increasing socio-economic status, lower parental control, younger birth cohort, and older age at marriage." Less intense desire for boys is significantly correlated with living in cities, especially big ones.[38] It took a few years for behavior to catch up with beliefs, but eventually the new values snowballed through the population.

Interestingly, these changes took place despite the fact that until very recently South Korean government policy purposely worked to prop up patriarchy. (Abortion, in fact, is highly restricted in South Korea, though safe illgal terminations, performed by doctors, are widely available.) Thus, Chung and Das Gupta speculate that change could come to China and India even before they reach Korea's level of modernization. "It is notable that in China and India, public policies have sought to lead changes in social norms, whereas in South Korea public policies sought to *prevent* changes in social norms," they write. "Without these countervailing public policies, son preference may have declined in South Korea before it reached such high levels of development. This offers hope that in China and India, public policies will accelerate the process of change such that son preference may decline before they reach South Korea's levels of development."[39]

Despite such cause for optimism, though, to experts and activists in India the crisis is too acute to wait for an evolution in gender norms. Besides, as Sen pointed out, the Indian case is complicated by dowry. Had outsize dowry demands not proliferated across southern India, perhaps that region, more socially progressive than the north, might have seen something akin to the South Korean phenomenon, she said. As it is, though, sex selection can't be effectively tackled without taking on the system that turns women into financial liabilities—an epochal challenge, one that will require something close to a revolution in deeply rooted ideas about marriage and family. Dowry, said Sen, was a major issue for the women's movement in the 1980s, but it proved so implacable that dispiritedness set in. But no matter the difficulty, such efforts have to be revived, both for their own sake and for there to be any hope of righting the country's gender balance. "I think this is a nexus that has to be dealt with together," she said.

With masculinization out of control, almost everyone sees the need for more immediate intervention. "I think it's a struggle over the long haul, but some sort of tough and salutary short-term punishments for doctors who provide the service wouldn't hurt," said Sen. Some in the government clearly agree. In April 2008 the Health minister, responding to "shockingly low" conviction rates, called for tough new measures against sex determination practitioners, including longer jail terms, higher fines, and special public prosecutors to handle cases. "Launching the country's biggest ever campaign against the 'inhuman and uncivilised practise' of female feticide, Prime Minister Manmohan Singh . . . said no nation, society or community could hold its head high and claim to be part of a civilised world if it condoned the practice of discriminating against women," reported the *Times of India*.[40]

It remains to be seen whether this time the law will be enforced with more zeal than in the past. While most experts welcome such a move, few believe it will be nearly enough. Already technology is one step ahead. Though illegal, in vitro fertilization clinics offer sex selection without abortion to those who can afford it. Meanwhile, some Western companies are marketing at-home tests with names like Pink or Blue over the Internet for a few hundred dollars. Women using them send a drop of blood to the companies' laboratories, which claim they can tell the sex of the fetus a mere six or seven weeks after conception by analyzing fetal DNA in the mother's bloodstream. The Indian government has talked about blocking access to the companies' Web sites, an idea that only underscores how powerless it is to stem the adoption of new innovations by a free people hungry for them.[41]

There will be no easy answer. Once again India is faced with the specter of demographic catastrophe, and once again the only sustainable solution lies in making a massive commitment to women's rights. Doing what needs to be done would be controversial, socially disruptive, and extraordinarily difficult politically. As disparate as India's cultures are, most of them are bound up with female submission. Any threat to that order would arouse the rage of those who see the self-abnegation of women as the essence of virtue and the guarantee of group identity. Like any democracy, India will probably find it easier to slouch toward disaster than to infuriate the defenders of patriarchy. Ultimately, though, unless the country finds a way to break through the encrustations of centuries of misogyny, its democracy itself could be in danger from an unmanageable excess of men.

Notes

1. Barbara D. Miller, *The Endangered Sex* (Ithaca, NY: Cornell University Press, 1981), pp. 50–51.

2. Ibid., p. 58.

3. Christophe Z. Guilmoto, "Characteristics of Sex-Ratio Imbalance in India, and Future Scenarios," United Nations Population Fund. Presented at the Fourth Asia Pacific Conference on Reproductive and Sexual Health and Rights. Hyderabad, India, October 29–31, 2007.

4. United Nations Population Fund, *Missing: Mapping the Adverse Child Sex Ratio in India,* November 2003.

5. Prabhat Jha, Rajesh Kumar, Priya Vasa, Neeraj Dhingra, Deva Thiruchelvam, and Rahim Moineddin, "Low Male-to-Female Sex Ratio of Children Born in India: National Survey of 1.1 Million Households," *The Lancet,* vol. 367, iss. 9506 (January 21, 2006), pp. 211–18.

6. Sabu George, "Sex Selection/Determination in India: Contemporary Developments," *Reproductive Health Matters,* vol. 10, no. 19, *Abortion: Women Decide* (special issue, May 2002), pp. 190–92.

7. Christophe Z. Guilmoto, "Sex-ratio Imbalance in Asia: Trends, Consequences and Policy Responses," United Nations Population Fund. Available at the UNFPA website, www.unfpa.org

8. "Vernacular Dailies Pulling NRIs Back Home for Sex Tests," *Times of India,* August 19, 2007.

9. Douglas Almond and Lena Edlund, "Son-Biased Sex Ratios in the 2000 United States Census," Proceedings of the National Academy of Science, March 31, 2008.

10. Valerie M. Hudson and Andrea M. den Boer, *Bare Branches: The Security Implications of Asia's Surplus Male Population* (Cambridge, MA: MIT Press, 2004), pp. 164–67.

11. *Missing: Mapping the Adverse Child Sex Ratio in India.*

12. Tulsi Patel, "The Mindset Behind Eliminating the Female Foetus," in *Sex-Selective Abortion in India: Gender Society and New Reproductive Technology,* Tulsi Patel, ed. (New Delhi: Sage Publications, 2007), p. 170.

13. Ibid., pp. 161–62, 170–71.

14. "Dowry 'Kills' Her on 1st Anniversary," *Times of India.* May 1, 2008.

15. "Sample Registration System Statistic Report 2005," Office of the Registrar General, India.

16. Data available on the Kerala government website, www.kerala.org

17. Ibid.

18. Ishwar C. Verma, Rose Joseph, Kusum Verma, Kamal Buckshee, and O. P. Ghai, "Prenatal Diagnosis of Genetic Disorders," *Indian Pediatrics* (May 1975).

19. Forum Against Sex Determination and Sex Pre-selection, "Using Technology, Choosing Sex, the Campaign Against

Sex Determination and the Question of Choice," *Development Dialogue,* vol. 1, no. 2 (1992), pp. 91–102.

20. John Ward Anderson and Molly Moore, "Born Oppressed: Women in the Developing World Face Cradle-to-Grave Discrimination, Poverty," *Washington Post,* February 14, 1993.

21. Guilmoto, "Characteristics of Sex-Ratio Imbalance in India."

22. Ravi Duggal and Vimala Ramachandran, "The Abortion Assessment Project—India: Key Findings and Recommendations," *Reproductive Health Matters,* vol. 12, no. 24, Supplement: Abortion Law, Policy, and Practice in Transition (November 2004), pp. 122–29.

23. Ibid.

24. "Punjab Village Cries for Unborn Girls," *Times of India,* January 19, 2006.

25. According to the World Health Organization, a survey in the state of Madhya Pradesh showed that 49 percent of women thought abortion was illegal, and 36 percent did not know its legal status. *Unsafe Abortion: Global and Regional Estimates of the Incidence of Unsafe Abortion and Associated Mortality in 2003,* World Health Organization, 2007. Available at the WHO website, www.who.int

26. Manisha Gupte, "Declining Sex Ratio. The Two Child Norm, and Women's Status," in *Coercion Versus Empowerment: Perspectives from the Peoples Tribunal on India's Coercive Population Policies and Two-Child Norm,* Shruti Pandey, Abhijit Das, Shravanti Reddy, and Binamrata Rani, eds. (New Delhi: Human Rights Law Network, 2006), p. 55. See also, "Defeat Because Hindutva Agenda Abandoned: VHP," *Times of India,* October 17, 2004.

27. Douglas A. Sylva, "The Lost Girls," *Weekly Standard,* March 21, 2007.

28. Gita Aravamudan, "Who Killed the Girls?" *Deccan Herald,* August 5, 2007.

29. Guilmoto, "Sex-Ratio Imbalance in Asia."

30. Scott J. South and Katherine Trent, "Sex Ratios and Women's Roles: A Cross-National Analysis," *American Journal of Sociology,* vol. 93, no. 5 (March 1988).

31. Hudson and den Boer, *Bare Branches,* p. 261.

32. Ibid., pp. 134–36.

33. Ibid., p. 140.

34. Ibid., pp. 208–11.

35. Woojin Chung and Monica Das Gupta, "Why Is Son Preference Declining in South Korea? The Role of Development and Public Policy, and the Implications for China and India," Policy Research Working Paper, the World Bank Development Research Group, Human Development and Public Services Team (October 2007).

36. Ibid.

37. Ibid.

38. Ibid.

39. Ibid.

40. *Times of India,* "Save the Girl Child, Says Manmohan Singh," April 29, 2008.

41. Maria Cheng, "Next Test Tells Fetus Sex After 6 Weeks," Associated Press, May 15, 2007; "Easy Availability of Gender ID Kits on Net a Threat: Minister," Indo-Asian News Service, March 15, 2008.

Assess Your Progress

1. Why were there historically fewer females in the Indian state of Punjab? Why, after decades of improvement, was there another decline in females shown in the 2001 census?

2. What is the relationship between prosperity, education and sex discrimination in India?

3. Why is the dowry becoming more characteristic of the upwardly mobile, whereas traditionally it was practiced by the upper castes?

4. Why has India never had an anti-abortion movement? What is the dilemma faced by women's rights activitst with regard to abortion in India?

5. How have distorted sex ratios posed a threat to Indian women beyond the disturbing demonstration of how little they are esteemed? How might this exacerbate the problems for society as a whole?

6. How are women being victimized as individuals?

7. What does the author mean by pointing out that social modernization has proven unable to catch up with technological progress?

8. How does South Korea serve as a hopeful sign that the changes need does not have to take two hundred years?

9. Why does the author claim that a sustainable solution to the problems of women in India requires a massive commitment to women's rights?

Rising Number of Dowry Deaths in India

Amanda Hitchcock

May 27: Young Housewife Burnt Alive for Dowry

Lucknow: For nineteen-year-old Rinki the dream of a happily married life was never to be. Barely a month after her marriage, she was allegedly tortured and then set ablaze by her in-laws for dowry in Indiranagar in the small hours of Saturday. Daughter of late Gyan Chand, a fish contractor who expired a year ago, Rinki was married to Anil on April 19 . . . However, soon after the marriage, Balakram [Anil's father] demanded a colour television instead of a black and white one and a motorcycle as well. When Rinki's mother failed to meet their demands, the teenage housewife was subjected to severe physical torture, allegedly by her husband and mother-in-law . . . On Saturday morning she [her mother] was informed that Rinki was charred to death when a kerosene lamp accidentally fell on her and her clothes caught fire. However, prima-facie it appeared that the victim was first attacked as her teeth were found broken. Injuries were also apparent on her wrist and chest.

June 7: Woman Ends Life Due to Dowry Harassment

Haveri: Dowry harassment claimed yet another life here recently. Jyoti, daughter of Chandrashekhar Byadagi, married to Ajjappa Siddappa Kaginelle in Guttal village (Haveri taluk) had taken her life after being allegedly harassed by her husband Ajjappa, mother-in-law Kotravva, sister-in-law Nagavva and father-in-law Siddappa for more dowry, the police said. Police said that the harassment compelled her to consume poison. . . . The Guttal police have arrested her husband and father-in-law.

June 7: Body Found Floating

Haveri: The police said that a woman's body was found floating in a well at Tilawalli (Hanagal taluk) near here. . . . The deceased has been identified as Akhilabanu Yadawad (26). The police said that Akhilabanu was married to Abdul Razaksab Yadawad five years ago. In spite of dowry being given, her husband and his family tortured her to bring some more dowry. Her father, Abdulrope Pyati in his complaint, alleged that she was killed by them. Her husband and his two brothers have been arrested, the police added.

These three chilling reports from *The Times of India* are typical of the many accounts of dowry-related deaths that take place in the country every year. One cannot help but be struck by the offhand way in which a young woman's life and death is summed up, matter of factly, without any undue cause for alarm or probing of the causes. It is much as one would report a traffic accident or the death of a cancer patient—tragic certainly, but such things are to be expected.

The character of the articles points to the fact that the harassment, beating and in some cases murder of women over dowry is both common and commonly ignored or even tacitly condoned in official circles—by the police, the courts, politicians and media. These crimes are not isolated to particular groups, social strata, geographical regions or even religions. Moreover, they appear to be on the rise.

According to an article in *Time* magazine, deaths in India related to dowry demands have increase 15-fold since the mid-1980s from 400 a year to around 5,800 a year by the middle of the 1990s. Some commentators claim that the rising number simply indicates that more cases are being reported as a result of increased activity of women's organisations. Others, however, insist that the incidence of dowry-related deaths has increased.

An accurate picture is difficult to obtain, as statistics are varied and contradictory. In 1995, the National Crime Bureau of the Government of India reported about 6,000 dowry deaths every year. A more recent police report stated that dowry deaths had risen by 170 percent in the decade to 1997. All of these official figures are considered to be gross understatements of the real situation. Unofficial estimates cited in a 1999 article by Himendra Thakur "Are our sisters and daughters for sale?" put the number of deaths at 25,000 women a year, with many more left maimed and scarred as a result of attempts on their lives.

Some of the reasons for the under-reporting are obvious. As in other countries, women are reluctant to report threats and abuse to the police for fear of retaliation against themselves and their families. But in India there is an added disincentive. Any attempt to seek police involvement in disputes over dowry transactions may result in members of the woman's own family being subject to criminal proceedings and potentially imprisoned. Moreover, police action is unlikely to stop the demands for dowry payments.

The anti-dowry laws in India were enacted in 1961 but both parties to the dowry—the families of the husband and wife—are criminalised. The laws themselves have done nothing to halt dowry transactions and the violence that is often associated with them. Police and the courts are notorious for turning a blind eye to cases of violence against women and dowry associated deaths. It was not until 1983 that domestic violence became punishable by law.

Many of the victims are burnt to death—they are doused in kerosene and set light to. Routinely the in-laws claim that what happened was simply an accident. The kerosene stoves used in many poorer households are dangerous. When evidence of foul play is too obvious to ignore, the story changes to suicide—the wife, it is said, could not adjust to new family life and subsequently killed herself.

Research done in the late 1990s by Vimochana, a women's group in the southern city of Bangalore, revealed that many deaths are quickly written off by police. The police record of interview with the dying woman—often taken with her husband and relatives present—is often the sole consideration in determining whether an investigation should proceed or not. As Vimochana was able to demonstrate, what a victim will say in a state of shock and under threat from her husband's relatives will often change markedly in later interviews.

Of the 1,133 cases of "unnatural deaths" of women in Bangalore in 1997, only 157 were treated as murder while 546 were categorised as "suicides" and 430 as "accidents". But as Vimochana activist V. Gowramma explained: "We found that of 550 cases reported between January and September 1997, 71 percent were closed as 'kitchen/cooking accidents' and 'stove-bursts' after investigations under section 174 of the Code of Criminal Procedures." The fact that a large proportion of the victims were daughters-in-law was either ignored or treated as a coincidence by police.

Figures cited in *Frontline* indicate what can be expected in court, even in cases where murder charges are laid. In August 1998, there were 1,600 cases pending in the only special court in Bangalore dealing with allegations of violence against women. In the same year three new courts were set up to deal with the large backlog but cases were still expected to take six to seven years to complete. Prosecution rates are low. *Frontline* reported the results of one court: "Of the 730 cases pending in his court at the end of 1998, 58 resulted in acquittals and only 11 in convictions. At the end of June 1999, out of 381 cases pending, 51 resulted in acquittals and only eight in convictions."

Marriage as a Financial Transaction

Young married women are particularly vulnerable. By custom they go to live in the house of their husband's family following the wedding. The marriage is frequently arranged, often in response to advertisements in newspapers. Issues of status, caste and religion may come into the decision, but money is nevertheless central to the transactions between the families of the bride and groom.

The wife is often seen as a servant, or if she works, a source of income, but has no special relationship with the members of her new household and therefore no base of support. Some 40 percent of women are married before the legal age of 18. Illiteracy among women is high, in some rural areas up to 63 percent. As a result they are isolated and often in no position to assert themselves.

Demands for dowry can go on for years. Religious ceremonies and the birth of children often become the occasions for further requests for money or goods. The inability of the bride's family to comply with these demands often leads to the daughter-in-law being treated as a pariah and subject to abuse. In the worst cases, wives are simply killed to make way for a new financial transaction—that is, another marriage.

A recent survey of 10,000 Indian women conducted by India's Health Ministry found that more than half of those interviewed considered violence to be a normal part of married life—the most common cause being the failure to perform domestic duties up to the expectations of their husband's family.

The underlying causes for violence connected to dowry are undoubtedly complex. While the dowry has roots in traditional Indian society, the reasons for prevalence of dowry-associated deaths have comparatively recent origins.

Traditionally a dowry entitled a woman to be a full member of the husband's family and allowed her to enter the marital home with her own wealth. It was seen as a substitute for inheritance, offering some security to the wife. But under the pressures of cash economy introduced under British colonial rule, the dowry like many of the structures of pre-capitalist India was profoundly transformed.

Historian Veena Oldenburg in an essay entitled "Dowry Murders in India: A Preliminary Examination of the Historical Evidence" commented that the old customs of dowry had been perverted "from a strongly spun safety net twist into a deadly noose". Under the burden of heavy land taxes, peasant families were inevitably compelled to find cash where they could or lose their land. As a result the dowry increasingly came to be seen as a vital source of income for the husband's family.

Oldenburg explains: "The will to obtain large dowries from the family of daughters-in-law, to demand more in cash, gold and other liquid assets, becomes vivid after leafing through pages of official reports that dutifully record the effects of indebtedness, foreclosures, barren plots and cattle dying for lack of fodder. The voluntary aspects of dowry, its meaning as a mark of love for the daughter, gradually evaporates. Dowry becomes dreaded payments on demand that accompany and follow the marriage of a daughter."

What Oldenburg explains about the impact of money relations on dowry is underscored by the fact that dowry did not wither away in India in the 20th century but took on new forms. Dowry and dowry-related violence is not confined to rural areas or to the poor, or even just to adherents of the Hindu religion. Under the impact of capitalism, the old custom has been transformed into a vital source of income for families desperate to meet pressing social needs.

A number of studies have shown that the lower ranks of the middle class are particularly prone. According to the Institute of Development and Communication, "The quantum of dowry exchange may still be greater among the middle classes, but 85 percent of dowry death and 80 percent of dowry harassment occurs in the middle and lower stratas." Statistics produced by Vimochana in Bangalore show that 90 percent of the cases of dowry violence involve women from poorer families, who are unable to meet dowry demands.

There is a definite market in India for brides and grooms. Newspapers are filled with pages of women seeking husbands and men advertising their eligibility and social prowess, usually using their caste as a bargaining chip. A "good" marriage is often seen by the wife's family as a means to advance up the social ladder. But the catch is that there is a price to be paid in the form of a dowry. If for any reason that dowry arrangements cannot be met then it is the young woman who suffers.

One critic, Annuppa Caleekal, commented on the rising levels of dowry, particularly during the last decade. "The price of the Indian groom astronomically increased and was based on his qualifications, profession and income. Doctors, charted accountants and engineers even prior to graduation develop the divine right to expect a 'fat' dowry as they become the most sought after cream of the graduating and educated dowry league."

The other side of the dowry equation is that daughters are inevitably regarded as an unwelcome burden, compounding the already oppressed position of women in Indian society. There is a high incidence of gender-based abortions—almost two million female babies a year. One article noted the particularly crass billboard advertisements in Bombay encouraging pregnant women to spend 500 rupees on a gender test to "save" a potential 50,000 rupees on dowry in the future. According to the UN Population Fund report for the year 2000, female infanticide has also increased dramatically over the past decade and infant mortality rates are 40 percent higher for girl babies than boys.

Critics of the dowry system point to the fact that the situation has worsened in the 1990s. As the Indian economy has been opened up for international investment, the gulf between rich and poor widened and so did the economic uncertainty facing the majority of people including the relatively well-off. It was a recipe for sharp tensions that have led to the worsening of a number of social problems.

One commentator Zenia Wadhwani noted: "At a time when India is enjoying unprecedented economic advances and boasts the world's fastest growing middle class, the country is also experiencing a dramatic escalation in reported dowry deaths and bride burnings. Hindu tradition has been transformed as a means to escaping poverty, augmenting one's wealth or acquiring the modern conveniences that are now advertised daily on television."

Domestic violence against women is certainly not isolated to India. The official rate of domestic violence is significantly lower than in the US, for example, where, according to UN statistics, a woman is battered somewhere in the country on average once every 15 seconds. In all countries this violence is bound up with a mixture of cultural backwardness that relegates women to an inferior status combined with the tensions produced by the pressures of growing economic uncertainty and want.

In India, however, where capitalism has fashioned out of the traditions of dowry a particularly naked nexus between marriage and money, and where the stresses of everyday life are being heightened by widening social polarisation, the violence takes correspondingly brutal and grotesque forms.

Assess Your Progress

1. What is implied by the character of the three articles cited, according to the author?

2. Why are the number of dowry deaths in India under-reported?

3. What are the typical explanations for why a woman might be burned to death?

4. Why are so many such deaths quickly written off by the police?

5. Why are young married women in such a vulnerable situation?

6. Why does the dowry system lead to their abuse?

7. How did the dowry function traditionally? How and why has it been transformed? In what segment of society are women most vulnerable?

8. What have been the consequences with respect to gender-based abortion and female infant mortality rates?

UNIT 6

Religion, Belief, and Ritual

Unit Selections

26. **Shamanisms: Past and Present,** David Kozak
27. **The Adaptive Value of Religious Ritual,** Richard Sosis
28. **Understanding Islam,** Kenneth Jost
29. **The Secrets of Haiti's Living Dead,** Gino Del Guercio
30. **Body Ritual among the Nacirema,** Horace Miner
31. **Baseball Magic,** George Gmelch

Learning Outcomes

After reading this unit, you should be able to:

- Determine how we can best identify shamans and shamanic traditions apart from our own assumptions, stereotypes, desires, and expectations about them.

- Explain how beliefs about the supernatural contribute to a sense of personal security, individual responsibility, and social harmony.

- Describe the basic tenets of Islam and explain whether or not they really clash with Western values.

- Discuss how voodoo has become an important form of social control in rural Haiti.

- Explain the ways in which magic rituals are practical and rational.

- Describe how rituals and taboos were established in the first place.

- Discuss the role of rituals and taboos in our modern industrial society.

Student Website

www.mhhe.com/cls

Internet References

Anthropology Resources Page
www.usd.edu/anth
Apologetics Index
www.apologeticsindex.org/site/index-c
Magic and Religion
http://anthro.palomar.edu/religion/default.htm
Yahoo: Society and Culture: Death
http://dir.yahoo.com/Society_and_Culture/Death_and_Dying

The anthropological interest in religion, belief, and ritual is not concerned with the scientific validity of such phenomena but rather with the way in which people relate various concepts of the supernatural to their everyday lives. From this practical perspective, some anthropologists have found that some traditional spiritual healing is just as helpful in the treatment of illness, as is modern medicine; that voodoo is a form of social control (as in "The Secrets of Haiti's Living Dead"); and that the ritual and spiritual preparation for playing the game of baseball can be just as important as spring training (see "Baseball Magic"). The placing of belief systems in these types of social contexts thus helps to not only counter popular stereotypes, but also serves to promote a greater understanding of and appreciation for other viewpoints (see "Understanding Islam").

Every society is composed of feeling, thinking, and acting human beings who, at one time or another, are either conforming to or altering the social order into which they were born. As described in "The Adaptive Value of Religious Ritual," religion is an ideological framework that gives special legitimacy and validity to human experience within any given socio-cultural system. In this way, monogamy as a marriage form, or monarchy as a political form, ceases to be simply one of many alternative ways in which a society can be organized, but becomes, for the believer, the only legitimate way. Religion considers certain human values and activities as sacred and inviolable. It is this mythic function that helps explain the strong ideological attachments that some people have, regardless of the scientific merits of their points of view.

While, under some conditions, religion may in fact be "the opiate of the masses," under other conditions such a belief system may be a rallying point for social and economic protest. A contemporary example of the former might be the "Moonies" (members of the Unification Church founded by Sun Myung Moon), while a good example of the latter is the role of the Black Church in the American Civil Rights movement, along with the

© Royalty-Free/CORBIS

prominence of religious figures such as Martin Luther King Jr. and Jesse Jackson. A word of caution must be set forth concerning attempts to understand belief systems of other cultures. At times, the prevailing attitude seems to be, "What I believe in is religion, and what you believe in is superstition." While anthropologists generally do not subscribe to this view, some tend to explain such behavior as incomprehensible and impractical without considering its full meaning and function within its cultural context. The articles in this unit should serve as a strong warning concerning the pitfalls of that approach.

Finally, it should be pointed out that mystical beliefs and rituals are not absent from the modern world. "Body Ritual among the Nacirema" reveals that even our daily routines have mystic overtones.

In summary, the writings in this unit show religion, belief, and ritual in relationship to practical human affairs.

Shamanisms
Past and Present

DAVID KOZAK

For centuries, the exotic and romantic image and story line of the shaman as a religious virtuoso who takes magical, hallucinatory flights into the supernatural world, learning from or skirmishing with animal spirits and human ghosts, capturing and returning lost souls, and dwelling in a nether world of trance and ecstacy, has dominated both the scholarly and popular imaginations. The shaman has been perceived and represented as the prototypic, primordial religious practitioner who has direct contact with the supernatural, nonordinary realm of the phantasmic, a perception that has led to the widespread assumption that this is the central defining characteristic of this specialist. Along these lines, the shaman is viewed by some—in the past and in the present—as representative of a person who pursues an "authentic" religious experience and who consider shamanism as an "authentic" religious system when compared to various "inauthentic" institutionalized world religions. This often exotic and romantic image of shamans and shamanisms misrepresents or at least it misunderstands them. And importantly, if not ironically, to understand shamans and shamanisms we must look to ourselves and the stories we have told and continue to tell about them.

The study of shamans and shamanisms has been plagued with a number of conceptual problems. At root is the ethnographic-based difficulty in creating a satisfactory standardized definition. This is because, on the one hand, shamanisms are highly diverse, culturally and historically relative phenomena, encompassing a vast array of social behaviors and beliefs. On the other hand, it is possible to identify shared or perhaps core shamanic phenomena. Yet, to pin a tidy label and definition on what shamanism is, is to risk the social scientific sin of overly particularizing or generalizing a constellation of behaviors and beliefs. Another problem relates to how the shaman's psychological and phenomenological status has taken precedence in the literature. Central to this precedence is the interest in what is today called Altered States of Consciousness (ASC), the affective, inspirational, emotional, and ecstatic states experienced by many shamans. This emphasis is problematic because it largely ignores the very real problems of social history that place each shamanism in context and the individual culture history that drives the transformations that all individual shamanisms experience. While ASC is certainly important, it is debatable that it should be taken as an unproblematic feature of shamanisms. Finally, and related to the emphasis on ASC and shaman phenomenology, is that it has contributed to a line of self-help, self-actualization "New Age," neo-shamanism literature that often bears surprisingly little resemblance to what the ethnographic record tells us of indigenous forms of shamanism.

In this essay I propose to work backwards in that I will begin with a general discussion of the difficulties with the conflation of scholarly and popular writings and perceptions of shamanisms in the present. I then move toward providing a rough working definition and general description of shamanism. How anthropologists and other scholars explain shamanism is outlined prior to my offering three ethnographic (particularistic) case studies. I trust that the case-study approach that focuses on cultural particulars will demonstrate the difficulties inherent in defining the generalities of this subject matter. Moreover, my selection of case studies is intended to juxtapose the so-called "classical" Siberian shamanism with how colonialism, global capitalization, and Christian missionization have differentially affected Tohono O'odham and Putumayo shamanisms. This essay is not intended to be comprehensive—a perhaps impossible task. However, refer to Jane M. Atkinson and Joan B. Townsend for excellent literature reviews and discussions of the relevant issues.[1] Here I offer a more modest goal: to provide the reader a basis for exploring and learning more about this most important religious phenomenon.

The Stories We Tell

Shamans and shamanic traditions continue to captivate both the scholarly and popular consciousness. This captivation has run and continues to run the gamut of admiration to condemnation, acceptance to persecution, emulation to fear. While it may sound strange, shamans and shamanisms as we know them are in part the rhetorical inventions of the Western intellectual and popular cultural imaginations. Oftentimes the stories that outsiders to shamanic traditions tell about them are based less in empirical reality than in the storyteller's own assumptions, stereotypes, desires and expectations about what they themselves want from the exotic "other." The inaccuracies in these stories have less to do with cultural secrecy or of shamans intentionally misleading anthropologists than with the author's failure to appropriately document the phenomena. Perhaps such ill-informed storytelling is innocuous enough, but it is frequently the case that such storytelling serves political, cultural, social, "racial," even personal ends, from the usurping of sacred cultural traditions for personal needs at one end of a continuum to outright state-level political repression, domination, and oppression at the other end. Moreover, shamanism has served as a multivocal symbol for social, political, and religious purposes of the West. For instance, in the past, animistic religions were viewed by late nineteenth-century social evolutionists (e.g., E.B. Tylor, Sir James Frazer) as occupying an inferior or impoverished level of religious evolution and achievement, far behind the assumed superiority of monotheism found in the "civilized" West. Juxtaposed to this unfavorable view, shamanism is today frequently adopted by people who are unhappy with institutionalized and patriarchal Christianity. In the United States, the "New Age," neo-shamanism, and self-actualization movements make much use of shamanic (tribal) symbolism and ideas, taken largely out of context, in order to cobble together a personal religious belief system and ritual practice that satisfies the individual's needs. Whether historically or contemporarily, shamanism is often uncritically evoked as either impoverished as a pagan and archaic religious expression or exalted as the solution to contemporary human ecological, existential, and personal crises.

Anthropologists early recognized the importance of shamanism in human religious history and cultures and have formulated various explanations and interpretations. The explanatory and interpretive stories that anthropologists tell include evolutionary, functional, structural, psychological, Marxist, cultural, and political-economic strategies. And while the emphasis of shamanistic research has been on the shaman as healer, as bridge between this and other worlds, as individual, as an evolutionary type, a more recent trend has emerged with an emphasis on the role of the shaman and shamanisms as parts of larger political, historical, and economic contexts in the burgeoning global political economy. Various anthropologists have rightly criticized the emphasis that had been placed on such things as the distinctions made between the so-called "classical" shamans of Siberia and all others, the affective and hallucinatory states that shamans experience, the abnormal personality traits supposedly exhibited by individual shamans, and so on. The emphasis has also been on the universal characteristics shared by shamans and shamanistic systems. In response to the bulk of the literature, some anthropologists have gone so far as to say that "shamanism" is an invented and contentious category of disparate items, ripped out of context, artificially if artfully associated and all of it dreamed up in the West with little basis in reality.[2]

As indicated, anthropologists are not the only ones who find shamanisms of interest. In fact, the scholarly and the popular images merge with shamanism. Today there is a burgeoning popular, nonacademic and practitioner-based interest in shamans, and particularly in their altered states of consciousness, and ultimately in self-help and self-actualization as grounded frequently in Jungian psychology. And while the self-actualization approach is largely denigrated by anthropologists as opportunistic, superficial, and self-serving in its treatment of shamanism, it was originally anthropologists who promoted, if indirectly, the current popularity. It is reasonable to say that the current popular and self-help interest of the neo-shamanism, New Age, and self-actualization movements stem from the publications of anthropologists Carlos Casteñada, Ake Hultkrantz, and Michael Harner, and the religious historian Mircea Eliade.[3] There is a distinct romanticizing and exoticizing of shamanism in their publications which appeals to a consumer group who feels that their lives as members of Western industrial societies are vacuous and that institutional forms of religion are inauthentic. In this literature, whether stated implicitly or not, shamanism offers what is believed to be an authentic method for establishing a relation between the individual and the natural and supernatural worlds.

The overarching rhetorical strategy used by the aforementioned authors is what I call the "shaman-as-hero" archetype, as the striving, seeking, brave, self-assured individual (the image is usually male). With not a little irony, this shaman-as-hero is transformed by such speculations and interpretations into the quintessential laissez faire "self-made man," the rugged individualist-equivalent of the non-Western, "primitive" world. In other words, the shaman becomes imbued with the idealistic Western characteristics of hyper-individualism in order to better correspond to the lives of people who wish to use shamanism for their own psychic and spiritual needs, rather than for understanding the shaman on his or her own cultural terms. The shaman-as-hero archetype and hero rhetoric, as rugged individualist, thus become acceptable and appropriable. But in this process, the shaman becomes yet another commodity for consumer culture. Herein lies the crux of the storytelling quandary.

The shaman has been used to tell stories distinctly not of the shaman's making. Rather, the stories often tell as much if not more about the tellers of scholarly or popular culture stories. All such characterizations are deeply flawed as they neglect to account for the social context in which all shamans are a part. Shamanism is nothing, after all, if not a community-centered activity. What lacks in much of the literature on shamanisms is an appreciation for the social, political, historical, gendered, and economic contexts that shamans participate in. The struggles of shamans with other shamans, with other villagers, and with outside forces have significantly modified their cultures and religious practices. And the danger of representing the shaman as the rugged individual hero and archetype is that shamanism is trivialized, reduced to a caricature, and is literally eviscerated of its social meaning and context. This trivilization, of course, serves an important storytelling purpose: It affords outsiders easy access to the complex traditions of shamanism without forcing them to understand the intricacies of context or to become part of a community where shamanism is only a fraction of a much larger social and cultural whole. Importantly, it allows the storyteller's imagination to conjure and speculate freely; shamanism as aesthetics rather than science. But this is ideally not what the anthropological study of shamans and shamanisms is about. Rather, anthropologists wish to understand and perhaps partly explain some of the phenomena associated with this compelling and important social role and religious practice. Anthropological understanding is gained up close, through fieldwork observation and participation, through learning the language of the shaman's community, and distinctly not from a "safe" distance where insight derives from one's own imaginative flights of fancy or creative speculation.

Defining Shamanisms

Defining shamans and shamanisms is not an easy task. In fact, shamanism is truly many things to many people. For myself, I would prefer to avoid making categorical or definitional statements altogether. Yet it is reasonably possible to make a few general statements about shamans and shamanisms. Realize, however, that generalizations on this subject are tentative and any claim must be viewed and evaluated in the context of ethnographic data.

Let us begin by saying that a shaman is a ritualist who is able to divine, predict, and effect future outcomes, provide medical care, who is believed to have direct access to the supernatural, phantasmic realm, and who gains his or her powers and abilities by being tutored by spirits including deceased ancestors. Shamans are frequently skilled orators or singers. The social role of the shaman is often the only or one of only a few distinct social roles available in the culture. This general definition of the shaman shares characteristics with other ritualists known variously as medicine man, medium, spirit or faith healer, priest, oracle, witch doctor, among others.

Origins of shamanism. For many anthropologists today the origins of shamanism is a moot question because it must remain largely conjectural reconstruction and is ultimately unprovable. Despite this, hypothesizing and research continue. Siberian and Arctic shamanism is considered by some to be the original source and prototypic form of shamanism in the world. The word "shaman" was originally derived from the Tungus (a central Siberian tribe) word *saman,* with the English word shaman

being derived from the German noun *der schaman.* Others argue that Tungus shamanism was itself influenced by Buddhism. For this latter suggestion a linguistic affiliation has been explored with the Sanskrit word *sramana,* which translates as "one who practices austerities." Siberian origin also relates to the Bering Straights land bridge hypothesis which explains the peopling of the New World. This hypothesis is widely accepted by archaeologists and argues that the ancestors of today's Native Americans migrated from Northern Asia to North America, bringing their religious and shamanic practices with them. This diaspora hypothesis is based on linguistic and physiological data and partly on the similar, cross culturally shared shamanic practices which indicate a common heritage.[4]

Ancient rock art has produced some of the more intriguing sources of data and interpretation regarding the origins question. Several researchers suggest that some rock art styles are actually the renderings of the shaman's altered states of consciousness and of the shamanic cosmos dating to as long ago as 8,000 to 25,000 years. Rock art data suggesting paleolithic origins derive from Lascaux cave paintings in France, southern Africa, and the British Isles and are based on neurologically based entoptic phenomenon. Entoptic phenomena are those visual phenomena that people see while experiencing various altered states of consciousness, visual phenomena that are argued to follow distinctive pan-human patterns and forms. It is claimed that these visual forms and patterns were then chiseled or painted on stone and were used as sacred mnemonic and didactic devices. Moreover, it is argued that shamanistic power came to reside in the shaman's ability to control such altered states and visions and the creation of sacred images.[5]

While it is not possible to know the absolute origins of shamanism, interesting research and hypothesizing continue to be accomplished. The assumption that Siberian shamanism is prototypical and diffused outward, as with all origin theories, must be viewed with a healthy skepticism. The fact that cultures change, adapting and culling beliefs and practices, in myriad patterns, it becomes impossible to pinpoint the genesis of the shamanic science and art.

Where shamanisms are found. Shamans and shamanisms are found throughout North and South America, Siberia, parts of Asia, Polynesia, and Africa, virtually throughout the entire world. The ethnographic record reveals that shamanisms are related to a variety of levels of social structure. Gatherer-hunter, egalitarian populations like the San of southern Africa are the most likely to possess a shamanistic system. Yet, pastoralists like the Tungus of Siberia or the Somali of northeastern Africa and agriculturalists like the Pima of southern Arizona also have shamanic traditions. Recent studies of highly stratified, state-level systems of governing, as in Korea, have also documented the presence of shamanistic systems. Therefore, much of where we find shamanisms depends on how shamans are defined. Gatherer-hunter populations are largely egalitarian with minor status differentiation who subsist on a diet characterized by feast-and-famine food availability which radically fluctuates throughout the yearly cycle. The shaman's role in an often tenuous subsistence setting, for example, is that of mediator between his or her village and the environment where they live and the spirit forces that control food and water availability. The shaman divines to locate game animals and to diagnose and cure spirit sicknesses, soul loss, and sorcery malevolence. Spirit-caused sicknesses are frequently the result of human inattention to or disrespect for the spirit and natural worlds.

Shamanic cosmos. The cosmos is frequently, though not always, divided into a series of horizontally stacked layers, three or more. Humans occupy a middle earth level that is loosely demarcated by permeable boundaries by upper and lower spirit worlds. The upper and lower worlds are nonphysical in character and accessible only through spiritual means. The various levels are linked and readily accessible to shamans. The spirit worlds are sources of power for human benefit. A version of "balance" between these worlds is the desired state and it is the shaman whose job it is to maintain this balance. Imbalances are manifested in humans as illnesses, or in the lack of game animals, or in natural disasters. As in the human world, so too in the spirit world, there is an emphasis on reciprocity with the spirits who inhabit the supernatural realm. A shaman's job is to keep the spirits happy or at least mollified and fellow villagers healthy. The afterlife locality is conceived of as either an improved version of the human community or an ill-defined place. It is usually not a location of punishment or reward for a person's actions in life. The concept of sin seems to be absent. Spirits, including human ghosts or ancestors, may be malevolent, benevolent, both, or benign. In any case, spirits have a significant impact on the human community.

A shaman's training. Direct contact with spirits is a universal feature of the shaman's practice. A shaman's contact with spirits makes the power from the other nonearthly cosmos layers accessible to a larger community of people in the middle earth level. A shaman is taught this power by a spirit(s) and the teaching consists of learning songs, chants, speeches, ritual techniques, and in the construction and use of shaman's tools such as a drum or other musical instruments, clothing, smoke, feathers, rattles, and crystals. A shaman ideally uses this supernatural knowledge and power to aid his or her community members' health and well-being, although shamans are also able to use this power to harm other humans. Frequently, a shaman has the ability for soul flight, or at the very least the shaman is capable of making nocturnal journeys as guided by spirit tutelaries.

A shaman may inherit his or her abilities or be selected by spirits to accept this important social responsibility. A person may be approached by spirits as a child or at any time in one's life for that matter. Often, the selection occurs during an acute or trying period in a person's life such as psychological stress, physical illness, accident, or a "near death" experience. A person often has the choice of accepting or rejecting a spirit's advances, and the shaman role. If a person accepts a spirit's advances, the spirit(s) will tutor their pupil in the shamanic sciences during nocturnal dreams or in hallucinatory or trance-induced states. A shaman's training is a lifelong process and a shaman's abilities and effectiveness may wax and wane over a lifetime.

States of consciousness. The literature is crowded with discussions of the shaman's altered state of consciousness, Shamanic State of Consciousness (SSC), magic flight, trance, hallucinatory, inspirational, and ecstatic abilities. Made famous by Mircea Eliade, the shaman's ecstacy has come largely to define—as discussed above—much of what we think of as quintessentially shamanic. Altered states of consciousness are either induced with hallucinogenic plants, including fungi, or with nonhallucinogenic alcoholic drinks, tobacco smoke, hyperventilation, meditation, and rhythmic drumming. It is not the altered state per se that is important but rather the communication that the altered state facilitates between spirit-animal and shaman or shaman and the lost soul that he or she searches for. As mentioned above, the altered state is also a time when the shaman is tutored by spirits.

Sacramental actions. Blowing, sucking, singing, massaging, spitting, smudging, painting, chanting, touching, fanning, seeing, and sprinkling water, ashes, and corn meal are all sacramental actions used by shamans as taught to them by spirit tutelaries. By sacramental I mean how a shaman uses his soul, augmented by the soul(s) of his spirit helpers or tutelaries and tools (i.e., feathers, water, smoke, peyote, or other hallucinogens) to positively affect the soul of a patient and/or of an entire community. The sacramental act of blowing, for instance, may come in the form of singing songs to patients, reciting chants to spirits, or even of blowing cigarette smoke over a patient to illuminate embedded sickness or discover the location of sorcery objects. A sacrament's performative intent is to improve the living condition of a person or of a community through sacredly endowed actions: blessings made physically manifest for all to see. A shaman's sacramental actions are always for good; in comparison, sorcery could be classified as an antisacramental act.

Shamanic discourses. The verbalizations of shamans provide a rich avenue for understanding shamanism. Songs, chants, narratives, and verbal explanations given by shamans are ways to examine the internal and cultural dimensions and perceptions held by practitioners themselves. This area of research is perhaps the most challenging for an anthropologist as it demands the researcher to possess a firm grasp of the shaman's own language.[6] Text transcription and translation become central in this work and interpretations and explanations of a single or a few key words may be the foundation for an entire study. A rich corpus of song and chant texts has revealed the art of various shamanisms, but also the meaning and centrality of shamanic discourses in the work of healing or divining.

Empirical observations. Since the social evolutionist E.B. Tylor's time (late 1800s), some anthropologists have argued that religious beliefs and practices are ultimately based in people's systematic observations of the sentient world around them. Empirical observations of the physical world serve as a template for their ultimate conceptions of the soul, human body, the sacred, and the role of religious belief in human affairs. Furthermore, people are also astute observers of human-animal and human-plant interactions. As such, the empirical observations and experiments that people conduct in their natural world serve as the basis for their public and private religious lives.

Explaining Shamanisms

Anthropologists use various theoretical orientations to understand and explain the shamanism phenomenon. I will briefly discuss two general orientations: the psychological-physiological and the political-economic. This brief discussion lumps together general tendencies and the two theoretical categories could be divided in other ways.

Psychology and physiology. The belief that shamans are mentally ill, who suffer from neuroses, psychoses, or schizophrenia, has roots in the eighteenth century. During that time shamanic practices competed, if indirectly, with the ascendancy of rationalist principles being developed with the scientific revolution. At the time, inspirationally or mythically based ways of knowing were being systematically discredited as irrational and as nonsense. The shaman as crazy person penetrated well into the twentieth century with anthropologists such as A.L. Kroeber, Ralph Linton, and A.F.C. Wallace. These anthropologists, using one or another psychoanalytic theory, concluded that the shaman and potential shamans suffer from a number of severe mental or physical complaints. Kroeber went so far as to say that so-called primitive cultures not only condoned but exalted psychotic behavior, that the shaman's claim to see and deal with spirits was nothing other than a delusional psychopathology. The mental illness theory of the shaman persisted until the 1960s when counter-arguments mounted against this unfortunate interpretation. By the late 1960s shaman's behaviors were considered psychologically normal. And as Jane M. Atkinson has pointed out, the change of attitude that occurred in the 1960s toward shamanic psychology and behavior was affected by changing notions of consciousness in general spurred on by hallucinogenic-modified consciousness in particular and the effectiveness of shamanism as psychotherapy in general.[7]

The continued interest in the psychic states of shamans, anthropologists, and other behavioralist researchers, wishing to ground their work on a scientific footing, developed their research around the concept of altered states of consciousness or shamanic states of consciousness. The emphasis of this research is on the phenomenological experience of the practitioner, the cross-culturally shared trance-state characteristics, and more recently an interest in the neurophysiological bases of ASC. Of note in this regard are studies related to the role of endorphins and other chemicals released in the brain during rituals. More recently is an interest in what Michael Winkelman calls "neurognostic structures" of the psyche. He argues that shamanism is a biologically based transpersonal mode of consciousness.[8] It is suggested that the capacity for shamanic behavior—that is, trance and vision flights—is a biologically based memory device of sorts, a shamanistic

equivalent of a Chomskyan "deep structure" of linguistic ability or a Jungian "archetype" of collective consciousness, whereby shamanic behavior is a hard-wired and universal human characteristic and is evidenced in the similarities shared by shamans in vastly different cultures.

Politics, economics, and history. Complementing the biological- and psychological-based explanations for shamanism is a recent interest in the political, historical, and economic factors related to shamans, cultures with shamanic systems, and how these relate to state-level and global capitalist structures of power and institutionalized religions. This interest area reflects a general trend in anthropology that emphasizes historical and political economic factors.

Foremost in this approach is an appreciation for how shamanisms have been affected by various state, economic, and institutionalized religious structures. Due to the impacts of colonialism and neo-colonialism, the historical and political economic approach takes for granted that much of what we know of as shamanism today is the result of contact and change initiated by institutions stemming from the West. The implication is that to understand shamanism we must also understand how the structures of power have been manifested at the local level. Thus, much of the published work stemming from this general orientation takes change as inevitable, that shamanic-oriented cultures have been victimized, and that the search for pristine and "authentic" versions of shamanisms is fallacious and naïve. In response to the psychological-physiological approaches, to understand shaman psychology, ASC, and ritual actions, the researcher must be rigorous in defining the social, political, and economic context(s) in which individual shamanisms are expressed. Thus, this general approach emphasizes the social rather than the individual, the historical rather than the immediate, the cultural rather than the psychological, and the relations of power rather than altered states.[9]

The primary drawback to this general political economy orientation is that it may sacrifice the richness of local-level interpretations and individualistic articulations for its emphasis on structure, history, and power relations. Real people are often lost in a maze of political and economic and historic factors that seemingly override the agency of individual actors.

In sum, the theories that anthropologists use to explain or interpret shamanisms are of necessity incomplete. This is because human experience is far more complex and rich than our abstractions of it. Thus, our theories are ways to assist our comprehension of a culturally rich realm of humanness and each theory tends to privilege partial elements of that richness.

Three Case Studies

Ethnographic description, the product of intensive fieldwork conducted by an anthropologist who lives for an extended time with the people being studied, is crucial to the work of sociocultural anthropologists. The ethnographic method is perhaps the superior way for understanding shamanisms and it also offers the potential for a critical appraisal and reevaluation of past storytelling inaccuracies and excesses regarding the study of shamanisms around the world. Because the fieldwork experience demands that the anthropologist live among and participate in the subject's community life and have a familiarity with the host culture's language, the anthropological perspective holds out promise for a nuanced understanding and documentation to be found in this religious-medicinal practice. It is also a valuable source for critiquing the frequently problematic categories, analyses, and assumptions made by outside observers of shamanic phenomena. To illustrate this point and present a fragment of the diversity of shamanisms found in the world today, and to demonstrate its range of applicability, I here offer three case studies of shamanism in Northern Asia, North America, and South America. The case studies reveal that shamanisms are a complex interweaving of cultural practices, gifted individual practitioners, political economic issues, and ASC. They reveal how shamanisms change, how they are influenced by the institutionalized religions like Christianity, and by global capitalism and social change. Each case study demonstrates in its own way how the category of a generalized shamanism is a theoretical oversimplification at best and that shamanisms undergo change and modification to fit the needs of a people.

Siberian Shamanisms

Siberian shamanism is often referred to as the "classical" form that used to exist. Mircea Eliade made Siberian shamanism famous and identified it by their exotic and mystical rituals and costumes, hallucinations, trances, the mastering of spirits, and cosmic travels. Since Eliade's work, many shamanisms have been evaluated and compared with it. As Caroline Humphrey[10] has pointed out, Eliade's characterization is seriously flawed as it lacks social and historical context. Moreover, she criticizes Eliade's representations for effectively crystallizing the current belief in the context-free view of shamanism as a mysterious and purely inspirational phenomenon. In order to offer a context to Siberian shamanism I draw extensively from the research of Roberte Hamayon.[11]

According to Hamayon there are two primary types of Siberian shamanism: hunting and pastoral. Each corresponds to distinct social organizational forms, economic, and political characteristics. Siberian "hunting shamanism" is present in tribal, noncentralized, forest-dwelling societies like the Chugchee. Hunting shamanism is characteristic of the form Eliade spoke of in his writings. "Pastoral shamanism" as found among the Tungus is characterized by people who are patrilineal and patrilocal, who domesticate livestock, and live in regions that border the forest and steppe regions. A potential third type, what Hamayon calls "peripheral shamanism," is only marginally identifiable as shamanism as it is related to state formation and how the traditional shaman's

role and power were usurped by Lamaist Buddhist lamas and through the decentralization and feminization of the shaman's role in Siberian shamanic societies. With state formation, institutional religion gains power and pushes traditional inspirational religious practices and beliefs to the margins of society where women may become shamans as men become Buddhist lamas. In many ways state or institutionalized religion delegitimizes shamanism.

The fundamental element of "hunting shamanism" is that spirits of animal species are contacted directly by a shaman who makes compacts with them in order to supply humans with good luck at hunting. The divinely inspired and experienced shaman-spirit compacts assure food availability for human consumption. This compact is not conceived as one-sided in that while animal spirits supply humans with food through hunting successes, the other half of the compact is that humans will eventually supply the spirits with human flesh and blood. Such is the source and cause of much human sickness and death. The task, however, is for the shaman to limit the amount of human sickness and death while maximizing the amount of animal flesh available for human consumption. A shaman's success at this depends on another kind of compact: that of his ritual marriage to the daughter of the game spirit (an elk or reindeer spirit).

The exchanges and compacts established between spirit-animals and humans make them trading partners in an ongoing economic and social relationship. The relationship is a form of generalized reciprocity where the exchanges are never equally balanced and immediate in return. Rather, delayed and nonequivalent exchanges keep the relationship alive and in need of continual tinkering by the shaman and spirit(s). To balance out their reciprocity would mean an end to their relationship. Thus, a shaman's power resides in his ability to maintain this reciprocity. His authority in the human community, therefore, stems from his usefulness to his peers, in the shaman's ability to secure a plentiful supply of game animals while minimizing sickness and death.

The human-animal compacts—of food and marriage—serve as the model of social organization. The dualistic spirit-human relationship is replicated in human-animal relations and in the human kinship system of moieties or clan subdivisions. Here, too, in the human world of marriage alliances, society is predicated on compacts between moieties just as the shaman makes compacts with the animal-spirit world.

Reliance on the domestication of animals (pastoralism) presents a second type of Siberian shamanism and is related to alterations in inheritance patterns which are linked to changes in social organization which is in turn linked to a transformation in conceptions of the supernatural. With "pastoral shamanism," no longer does food flow directly from compacts made in the supernatural world but it instead derives from various locations in the observable environment where grazing and herding occur. For the Tungus, pasturage is associated with patrilineal descent groups (in this case, clan segments), and nearby mountains become the locations where ancestors reside after death. Patrilocal residence becomes important and land or pasture inheritance follows the male line. Sickness is no longer caused by animal spirits but is associated with transgressions of patrilineal kinship rules and by one's ancestral spirits. Pastoral shamans do not make compacts with spirit animals, nor do they ritually marry the daughter of the game spirit as food comes from other sources. Here the shaman's role changes in that it is entrusted with ensuring the fertility of both the domesticated animals and human villagers. Pastoralist shamans are related to tribal mythology where the shaman is synonymous with the tribal founder.

Here we see that even the classic Siberian shamanism takes several forms. Importantly, the forms are related to the mode of subsistence, social organization, residence patterns, and whether the shaman has intimate contact with animal spirits or deceased ancestor spirits who participate with the shaman in ongoing reciprocal exchanges.

Tohono O'odham Christian-Shamanism

The Tohono O'odham (formerly known as Papago) of southern Arizona and northern Sonora, Mexico, were gatherer-hunters and horticulturalists until the early part of the twentieth century.[12] This form of shamanism is comparable to the hunting shamanism of Siberia. Their subsistence strategy made the best of an existence in the heart of the Sonoran Desert where scarce and unpredictable rainfall made growing corn, beans, and squash very tenuous. Despite this, O'odham subsistence practices emphasized the importance of rain and crop production. In fact, O'odham ritual life— both individual and public—centered around moisture. The public ritual of the annual rain ceremony focused the community's religious sentiments on securing adequate moisture for plant, animal, and human consumption.

Village well-being was symbolized by sufficient rainfall, and the village shaman was in part responsible for securing it. Shamans worked together to sing for, divine, and encourage the rains to fall. They directed the annual rain festivities by overseeing the production of a mildly intoxicating wine brewed from the syrup of saguaro cactus fruits. During the rain dance ceremony, shamans from various villages gave speeches and sang songs to attract the rain clouds from the "rain houses" positioned at the cardinal directions. The proper execution of the ceremony secured the ultimate fertility of the natural and human worlds.

The other central role of O'odham shamans was to diagnose a series of sicknesses unique to the O'odham people. Until the middle of the twentieth century it was thought in O'odham cosmology and medical theory that there were approximately 50 "staying sicknesses" (only O'odham contract them) that were caused by the spirit protectors of various animal-persons (e.g., deer, badger, coyote), insect-persons (e.g., fly, butterfly), natural phenomena-persons (e.g., wind, lightning), humans (e.g., ghosts, prostitutes),

plant-persons (e.g., peyote, jimson weed), reptile-persons (e.g., rattle snake, chuckwalla), and bird-persons (e.g., eagle, owl, swallow) species. Being sickened is the result of a human's impropriety or disrespect toward or transgression on the integrity of the spirit species. The person does not know the moment that sickness is contracted, but once symptoms emerge, the person consults a shaman for diagnosis. Once diagnosed, which can take a quick or a protracted form, the person is instructed to have the appropriate curing songs sung for them.

A shaman's ability to diagnose, and to cure, derives from spirit helpers who tutor the shaman during nighttime dreams. Thus spirits both cause sicknesses and provide the means for their cure. This tutoring takes the form of learning songs that are authored and sung by the spirit species to the shaman who memorizes them verbatim. The songs are densely meaningful, haiku-like poems that tell brief stories of experiences that the shaman has had with the spirit, present images of a landscape, or are statements about the quirkiness of the spirit itself.

This version of O'odham shamanism has been modified during the past three hundred years of contact with Spanish, then Mexican, and finally with American colonizers and Catholic missionaries. Catholicism has made significant inroads in O'odham religious culture since their early contact with the Jesuit priest Eusebio Kino in the late 1690s. Catholicism continues to be a strong element of O'odham identity. Another significant source of change came with the introduction of cattle into the U.S. Southwest regional economy. The external influences of Catholicism and cattle capitalism prompted changes in O'odham shamanism in several ways. First, shamans gained power from Christian deities as spirit tutelaries, primarily the saints, but Jesus and God also, just as they did from the traditional spirit-beings. As the O'odham adopted Catholic public rituals and theological beliefs, and as they began to adopt saints for village patrons and for individuals, people began to be sickened by these Christian spirits in a manner similar to that described above. Saint sickness became an illness diagnosed and treated by shamans.

Second, the O'odham also began, by the late 1880s, to be sickened by the instruments of frontier capitalism—cattle and horses (known collectively as devil sickness). O'odham readily adopted a cowboy lifestyle and are still cattle ranchers to this day. Here too O'odham shamans became charged with the responsibility of contending with the new contagions. Today, devil sickness is thought by some O'odham to be the most commonly diagnosed staying sickness.

Saint and devil sicknesses in the O'odham theory of sickness and cure represent what I call Christian-shamanism. Not only do shamans continue to use the traditional tools of tobacco smoke, eagle and owl feathers, and crystals to augment their power in diagnostic sessions, but many shamans also use saints' images, a Christian cross, and holy water. Perhaps more telling is the fact that the Christian deities (spirits) also come to shamans in the same manner as the traditional spirits—in dreams, singing and tutoring their human pupils in the diagnostic healing art and science.

Christian-shamanism can be understood as a manifestation of significant political, religious, and economic changes that affected this culture. For the O'odham, shamanism has been effectively used to attend to and ameliorate the changes conceived in the three-hundred-year plus period of colonization and missionization. Some might conclude that the O'odham shamanic system as described has been "corrupted" or "polluted" by the Christian influence. I do not think so, nor do I think that most O'odham think so either. In many ways, the O'odham are merely using all that is available to them to make their lives better and healthier.

Shamanism, Terror, and the Putumayo of Colombia

By the turn of the twentieth century, in the industrializing West, the demand for rubber expanded quickly. Far from the crowded cities of London, Los Angeles, Chicago, and Paris, the Putumayo Indians of the sparsely populated lowland Amazonian jungles of southern Colombia were being forcibly incorporated into the Industrial Revolution as rubber tree tappers. This incorporation was often violent and terrifying. To coerce work out of this recalcitrant labor force, the Putumayo Indians were subjected to systematic torture, murder, and sexual abuses. This troubling period in Putumayo and Colombian social history continues to haunt and permeate the present in the form of *mal aire* (evil wind)[13] and in the shamanistic beliefs and practices that heal it. Current shamanic practice can be partly understood as an attempt to ameliorate the unquiet souls of the violently tortured and murdered Putumayo Indians of the southern Amazon jungle.[14]

Michael Taussig argues in his provocative book *Shamanism, Colonialism, and the Wild Man* that contemporary *yagé* (a hallucinogenic drink) shamanism in southern Colombia is an effort to heal the tortured memories of the violently killed Putumayo Indians. Sorcery and evil air are the two sicknesses that shamans currently treat. It is the latter that stems directly from rubber tapping and Christianization. Currently, both Indians and non-Indians of the region view the ancient ones, called the Huitoto (ancestral Putumayo), as sorcerers, demonic, and evil. Huitoto means "the people from below"— below the ground and below in the jungles. They were the people conquered during the Spanish conquest, people who were labeled and viewed by Europeans as evil, devil worshipping idolaters since Spanish times. The ideology of the Spanish was that they were violent, sorcerers, cannibals, and thus fearsome. This ideologically charged characterization persisted until the time of rubber exploration and production. The image of the savage other and of the wild, primordial jungles struck fear in the hearts of the rubber plantation managers. The managers saw Indian conspiracies and treachery everywhere. In their zeal to extract rubber and labor, company managers hired and trained gangs to carry out retribution stemming from their fears of the "savage" Putumayo. Rumors of the atrocities committed by the rubber companies led to an investigation and the eventual publication of Sir Roger Casement's revealing report in 1912 which substantiated the rumors' veracity.

The violent memories created in the colonial, and later the capitalist, contexts revisioned the shamanism of the region. Sickness was now thought to be caused by the evil airs emanating from below in the jungles, from the rotting evil ancestors (savages) buried beneath the ground. This miasmatic theory is perpetuated by locals, native and nonnative alike.

In this context, according to Taussig, Putumayo shamanism is above all else a healing of history, a healing of the excesses of Christian ideology and capitalist extraction. It is as if the former set the stage for the latter. Hence, for the Putumayo, shamanism is the method through which people attend to the horrific memories embedded in the history of the region. It is as if it is history-as-sorcery that today's Putumayo shamans strive to cure.

The three examples come nowhere near exhausting the possible ethnographic variation that continues to exist in the world today. Research into questions of history, global economy, and exploitation add to an already rich anthropological literature on the shaman's ASC, personality, and phenomenological characteristics. It is through a continued documentation of local expressions of shamanism, juxtaposed to macrolevel processes, that our understanding will be improved in this most dynamic arena of human spirituality.

Conclusion

The interest and study of shamanism has a long and often checkered history. Shamanism storytellings are varied and continue to be tightly bound to the defining culture's attitude toward indigenous peoples and their cultural practices. In the 1990s shamanisms have not only been tolerated but they have also been exulted as the true, authentic religious expression worthy of emulation. As discussed, this admiration has not always been the preferred story. Yet, this admiration, while meant with the best of intentions, must also be seen as potentially problematic, as it is yet another way people use shamanism in other than their intended contexts. And whether shamanisms are exalted or denigrated, both are equally stereotypic responses. It is my suspicion that shamans and shamanisms will continue to serve the rhetorical needs of members of Western or other dominant societies. It appears that the need for people to tell stories about other people remains strong. It also appears to matter not that the stories are only loosely, at best, based in empirical reality. And as I began this essay, it is important to remember that the stories we tell about others may say more about ourselves than about those of whom we supposedly tell the stories.

Notes

1. The combined reviews of Jane Monnig Atkinson, "Shamanisms Today," *Annual Review of Anthropology* 21:307–330, 1992, and Joan B. Townsend, "Shamanism," in Stephan Glazier, ed., *Anthropology of Religion: A Handbook* (Westport, CT: Greenwood Press, 1997), offer a wide-ranging and thorough overview of the subjects. One book by religious studies scholar Margaret Stutley, *Shamanism: An Introduction* (London: Routledge, 2003) provides general descriptive materials of shamanism throughout the world.

2. Perhaps most strident in this regard is Michael Taussig, who argues in "The Nervous System: Homesickness and Dada," *Stanford Humanities Review* 1(1):44–81, 1989, that shamanism is a "made-up," "artful reification of disparate practices" that are the creations of academic programs such as religious studies and anthropology. Much earlier, Clifford Geertz in "Religion as a Cultural System," in Michael Banton, ed., *Anthropological Approaches to the Study of Religion* (London: Tavistock, 1966), came to the same conclusion as Taussig. What Taussig and Geertz criticize are the overly large generalizations and characterizations that anthropologists and others have made of shamanisms, and, particularly for Taussig, how such characterizations reflect Western notions of religiosity. More recently, anthropologist Alice Kehoe takes up this critical stance in *Shamans and Religion: An Anthropological Exploration in Critical Thinking* (Prospect Heights, IL: Waveland Press, 2000).

3. Among the most influential of both anthropology and popular interest in shamanism are Eliade's *Shamanism: Archaic Techniques of Ecstacy* (Princeton, NJ: Princeton University Press, 1964); Casteñada's *The Teachings of Don Juan: A Yaqui Way of Knowledge* (New York: Ballantine Books, 1968); Harner's *Hallucinogens and Shamanism* (Oxford: Oxford University Press, 1973); and Hultkrantz's various articles on the subject: "An Ecological Approach to Religion," *Ethos* 31:131–150, 1966; "Spirit Lodge: A North American Shamanistic Seance," in Carl-Martin Edsman, ed., *Studies in Shamanism* (Stockholm: Almqvist and Wiksell, 1967); and "A Definition of Shamanism," *Temenos* 9:25–37, 1973. Of these works, it is perhaps the first two that have had the longest and most profound impact on shamanic studies in general and popular consciousness in particular.

4. Alice Kehoe in "Primal Gaia," in J. Clifton, ed., *The Invented Indian* (Somerset, NJ: Transaction Press, 1990); Michael Winkelman in "Shamans and Other 'Magico-Religious' Healers," *Ethos* 18(3):308–352, 1990; Ake Hultkrantz in "Ecological and Phenomenological Aspects of Shamanism, in L. Backman and A. Hultkrantz, eds. *Studies in Lapp Shamanism* (Stockholm: Almquivst and Wiksell, 1978); J.D. Lewis-Williams and T. Dowson in "The Signs of All Times," *Current Anthropology* 29(2):201–245, 1988; and Peter Furst in "The Roots and Continuities of Shamanism," in A. Brodzky, R. Daneswich, and N. Johnson, eds., *Stones, Bones, and Skin* (Toronto: Society for Art Publications, 1977), offer various perspectives of the paleolithic origins question. In general, origins are traced to the Siberian and Arctic shamanisms and are considered the "classic" form. Yet others such as Sergei Shirokogoroff in *Psychomental Complex of the Tungus* (London: Kegan Paul, Trench, Trubner and Company, 1935) and Mircea Eliade in *Shamanism: Archaic Techniques of Ecstacy* (Princeton, NJ: Princeton University Press, 1964), postulate that Buddhist Lamaism drastically modified Tungus shamanism. Thus, one version of origins suggests that shamanisms have a Tibetan source.

5. J.D. Lewis-Williams's name is synonymous with the work on entoptic phenomena. His works *Believing and Seeing* (New York: Academic Press, 1981) and "Cognitive and Optical Illusions in San Rock Art," *Current Anthropology* 27:171–178,

1986 are exemplary in this regard. See also his collaboration with T.A. Dowson, "The Signs of All Times," 1988, and "On Vision and Power in the Neolithic," *Current Anthropology* 34:55–65, 1993.

6. *Piman Shamanism and Staying Sickness* by Donald Bahr, Juan Gregorio, David Lopez, and Albert Alvarez (Tucson: University of Arizona Press, 1974) stands out as one of the first and is still one of the finest discussions between a shaman, Gregorio, an anthropologist, Donald Bahr, and two native speaker-translators, Lopez and Alvarez. Bahr has also written on shamanic song texts in "A Grey and Fervent Shamanism," *Journal of the Society of the Americas,* 67:7–26, 1991. Other collaborative and innovative work has been completed by Larry Evers and Felipe Molina in *Yaqui Deer Songs* (Tucson: University of Arizona Press, 1987), Jane Monnig Atkinson's *Wana Shamanship* (Berkeley: University of California Press, 1989), Anna Siikala's "Two Types of Shamanizing and Categories of Shamanistic Songs," in L. Honko and V. Voigt, eds., *Akademiai Kiado* (Budapest, 1980), and in B. Walraven's *Muga: The Songs of Korean Shamanism* (Dordredt: ICG Printing, 1985). A general beautifully illustrated guide to Native American Indian shamanism is Norman Bancroft Hunt, *Shamanism in North America* (Buffalo, NY: Firefly Books, 2003).

7. For arguments against the mentally ill shaman stereotype, see Alfred Kroeber, *The Nature of Culture* (Chicago: University of Chicago Press, 1952); L.B. Boyer, "Shamans: To Set the Record Straight," *American Anthropologist* 71(2):307–309, 1969; D. Handelman, "Shamanizing on an Empty Stomach," *American Anthropologist* 70(2):353–356, 1968; and George Murdock, "Tenino Shamanism," *Ethnology* 4:165–171, 1965, among others.

8. The desire to empirically ground the study of shamanic consciousness has led to this interesting version of a biopsychological approach. For a general discussion of this hypothesis, see C. Laughlin, J. McManus, and E. d'Aquili, *Brain, Symbol and Experience: Toward a Neurophenomenology of Consciousness* (New York: Columbia University Press, 1992) and Michael Winkelman, "Trance States: A Theoretical Model and Cross-Cultural Analysis," *Ethos* 14(2):174–203, 1986, and "Altered States of Consciousness and Religious Behavior," in S. Glazier, ed., *Anthropology of Religion* (Westport, CT: Greenwood Press, 1997).

9. A few recent examples of this work include Michael Taussig's *Shamanism, Colonialism, and the Wild Man* (Chicago: University of Chicago Press, 1987); N. Thomas and C. Humphrey's edited volume *Shamanism, History, and the State* (Ann Arbor: University of Michigan Press, 1994); and Atkinson's book cited in Endnote 6.

10. Refer to C. Humphrey's "Shamanic Practices and the State in Northern Asia," in Nicholas Thomas and Carolyn Humphrey, eds., *Shamanism, History and the State* (Ann Arbor: University of Michigan Press, 1994).

11. This section on Siberian shamanism draws heavily from the two works of R. Hamayon: *La Chasse à l'âme: Esquisse d'une Theorie du Chamanisme Siberien* (Société d'ethnologie Nanterre, 1990) and "Shamanism in Siberia," in N. Thomas and C. Humphrey, eds., *Shamanism, History, and the State* (Ann Arbor: University of Michigan Press, 1994). Her research and writing are exemplary for placing shamanism into a nuanced format rather than reifying much of what is assumed to be true about Siberian shamanism. See also Caroline Humphrey's, "Shamanic Practices and the State in Northern Asia," in N. Thomas and C. Humphrey, eds., *Shamanism, History, and the State* (Ann Arbor: University of Michigan Press, 1994).

12. This section on Tohono O'odham shamanism is based on my own research in various communities on the Sells Reservation

and on several published monographs. See Ruth Underhill's classic, *Papago Indian Religion* (New York: Columbia University Press, 1946) and the collaborative work *Piman Shamanism and Staying Sickness* by Donald Bahr, Juan Gregorio, David Lopez, and Albert Alvarez (Tucson: University of Arizona Press, 1974). For a detailed treatment of a single staying sickness, see my *Devil Sickness and Devil Songs: Tohono O'odham Poetics* (Washington, DC: Smithsonian Institution Press, 1999).

13. Mal aire is a widespread "folk" illness found throughout parts of North and South America as well as in parts of Europe. Evil air sickness in the New World is thought by most observers to be an import from the Old World.

14. This case study relies on the intriguing and ingenious work of M. Taussig, "History as Sorcery," *Representations* 7:87–109, 1984, and *Shamanism, Colonialism, and the Wild Man* (Chicago: University of Chicago Press, 1987).

Assess Your Progress

1. What are the conceptual problems that have plagued the study of shamans and shamanism?

2. To what ends has the inaccurate "storytelling" about shamanism been used in the past?

3. In what sense have the scholarly and the popular images of shamanism merged?

4. How does the author explain the "shaman-as-hero" archetype?

5. In what sense are all such characterizations "deeply flawed?" Explain.

6. What is the danger of such trivialization? How does this contradict what the anthropological study of shamanism is all about?

7. How does the author define shamanism?

8. What have been the most prominent hypotheses about the origins of shamanism? Why must this remain speculative?

9. Where are shamanisms found?

10. Describe the "shamanic cosmos."

11. How do shamans typically acquire their ability to contact the spirit world?

12. How does the author characterize the sacramental actions of the shaman?

13. Why were shamans characterized as mentally ill until recently? How and why did this view change?

14. How does the author describe and explain the differences between "hunting shamanism" and "pastoral shamanism" in Siberia?

15. What was the role of shamans among the gatherer-hunters and horticulturalist Tohono O'odham people? What is "Christians-hamanism?"

16. In what sense does Putumayo shamanism represent a "healing of history?"

17. Why is it that "the stories we tell about others may say more about ourselves?"

The Adaptive Value of Religious Ritual

Rituals promote group cohesion by requiring members to engage in behavior that is too costly to fake.

RICHARD SOSIS

I was 15 years old the first time I went to Jerusalem's Old City and visited the 2,000-year-old remains of the Second Temple, known as the Western Wall. It may have foreshadowed my future life as an anthropologist, but on my first glimpse of the ancient stones I was more taken by the people standing at the foot of the structure than by the wall itself. Women stood in the open sun, facing the Wall in solemn worship, wearing long-sleeved shirts, head coverings and heavy skirts that scraped the ground. Men in their thick beards, long black coats and fur hats also seemed oblivious to the summer heat as they swayed fervently and sang praises to God. I turned to a friend, "Why would anyone in their right mind dress for a New England winter only to spend the afternoon praying in the desert heat?" At the time I thought there was no rational explanation and decided that my fellow religious brethren might well be mad.

Of course, "strange" behavior is not unique to ultraorthodox Jews. Many religious acts appear peculiar to the outsider. Pious adherents the world over physically differentiate themselves from others: Moonies shave their heads, Jain monks of India wear contraptions on their heads and feet to avoid killing insects, and clergy almost everywhere dress in outfits that distinguish them from the rest of society. Many peoples also engage in some form of surgical alteration. Australian aborigines perform a ritual operation on adolescent boys in which a bone or a stone is inserted into the penis through an incision in the urethra. Jews and Muslims submit their sons to circumcision, and in some Muslim societies daughters are also subject to circumcision or other forms of genital mutilation. Groups as diverse as the Nuer of Sudan and the Iatmul of New Guinea force their adolescents to undergo ritual scarification. Initiation ceremonies, otherwise known as rites of passage, are often brutal. Among Native Americans, Apache boys were forced to bathe in icy water, Luiseno initiates were required to lie motionless while being bitten by hordes of ants, and Tukuna girls had their hair plucked out.

How can we begin to understand such behavior? If human beings are rational creatures, then why do we spend so much time, energy and resources on acts that can be so painful or, at the very least, uncomfortable? Archaeologists tell us that our species has engaged in ritual behavior for at least 100,000 years, and every known culture practices some form of religion. It even survives covertly in those cultures where governments have attempted to eliminate spiritual practices. And, despite the unparalleled triumph of scientific rationalism in the 20th century, religion continued to flourish. In the United States a steady 40 percent of the population attended church regularly throughout the century. A belief in God (about 96 percent), the afterlife (about 72 percent), heaven (about 72 percent) and hell (about 58 percent) remained substantial and remarkably constant. Why do religious beliefs, practices and institutions continue to be an essential component of human social life?

Such questions have intrigued me for years. Initially my training in anthropology did not provide an answer. Indeed, my studies only increased my bewilderment. I received my training in a subfield known as human behavioral ecology, which studies the adaptive design of behavior with attention to its ecological setting. Behavioral ecologists assume that natural selection has shaped the human nervous system to respond successfully to varying ecological circumstances. All organisms must balance trade-offs: Time spent doing one thing prevents them from pursuing other activities that can enhance their survival or reproductive success. Animals that maximize the rate at which they acquire resources, such as food and mates, can maximize the number of descendants, which is exactly what the game of natural selection is all about.

Behavioral ecologists assume that natural selection has designed our decision-making mechanisms to optimize the rate at which human beings accrue resources under diverse ecological conditions—a basic prediction of *optimal foraging theory.* Optimality models offer predictions of the "perfectly adapted" behavioral response, given a set of environmental constraints. Of course, a perfect fit with the environment is almost never achieved because organisms rarely have perfect information and because environments are always changing. Nevertheless, this assumption has provided a powerful framework to analyze a variety of decisions, and most research (largely conducted among foraging populations) has shown that our species broadly conforms to these expectations.

If our species is designed to optimize the rate at which we extract energy from the environment, why would we engage in religious behavior that seems so counterproductive? Indeed, some religious practices, such as ritual sacrifices, are a conspicuous display of wasted resources. Anthropologists can explain why foragers regularly share their food with others in the group, but why would anyone share their food with a dead ancestor by burning it to ashes on an altar? A common response to this question is that people believe in the efficacy of the rituals and the tenets of the faith that give meaning to the ceremonies. But this response merely begs the question. We must really ask why natural selection has favored a psychology that believes in the supernatural and engages in the costly manifestations of those beliefs.

Ritual Sacrifice

Behavioral ecologists have only recently begun to consider the curiosities of religious activities, so at first I had to search other disciplines to understand these practices. The scholarly literature suggested that I wasn't the only one who believed that intense religious behavior was a sign of madness. Some of the greatest minds of the past two centuries, such as Marx and Freud, supported my thesis. And the early anthropological theorists also held that spiritual beliefs were indicative of a primitive and simple mind. In the 19th century, Edward B. Tylor, often noted as one of the founding fathers of anthropology, maintained that religion arose out of a misunderstanding among "primitives" that dreams are real. He argued that dreams about deceased ancestors might have led the primitives to believe that spirits can survive death.

Eventually the discipline of anthropology matured, and its practitioners moved beyond the equation that "primitive equals irrational." Instead, they began to seek functional explanations of religion. Most prominent among these early 20th-century theorists was the Polish-born anthropologist Bronislaw Malinowski. He argued that religion arose out of "the real tragedies of human life, out of the conflict between human plans and realities." Although religion may serve to allay our fears of death, and provide comfort from our incessant search for answers, Malinowski's thesis did not seem to explain the origin of rituals. Standing in the midday desert sun in several layers of black clothing seems more like a recipe for increasing anxiety than treating it. The classical anthropologists didn't have the right answers to my questions. I needed to look elsewhere.

Fortunately, a new generation of anthropologists has begun to provide some explanations. It turns out that the strangeness of religious practices and their inherent costs are actually the critical features that contribute to the success of religion as a universal cultural strategy and why natural selection has favored such behavior in the human lineage. To understand this unexpected benefit we need to recognize the adaptive problem that ritual behavior solves. William Irons, a behavioral ecologist at Northwestern University, has suggested that the universal dilemma is the promotion of cooperation within a community. Irons argues that the primary adaptive benefit of religion is its ability to facilitate cooperation within a group—while hunting, sharing food, defending against attacks and waging war—all critical activities in our evolutionary history. But, as Irons points out, although everyone is better off if everybody cooperates, this ideal is often very difficult to coordinate and achieve. The problem is that an individual is even better off if everyone else does the cooperating, while he or she remains at home enjoying an afternoon siesta. Cooperation requires social mechanisms that prevent individuals from free riding on the efforts of others. Irons argues that religion is such a mechanism.

The key is that religious rituals are a form of communication, which anthropologists have long maintained. They borrowed this insight from ethologists who observed that many species engage in patterned behavior, which they referred to as "ritual." Ethologists recognized that ritualistic behaviors served as a form of communication between members of the same species, and often between members of different species. For example, the males of many avian species engage in courtship rituals—such as bowing, head wagging, wing waving and hopping (among many other gestures)—to signal their amorous intents before a prospective mate. And, of course, the vibration of a rattlesnake's tail is a powerful threat display to other species that enter its personal space.

Irons's insight is that religious activities signal commitment to other members of the group. By engaging in the ritual, the member effectively says, "I identify with the group and I believe in what the group stands for." Through its ability to signal commitment, religious behavior can overcome the problem of free riders and promote cooperation within the group. It does so because trust lies at the heart of the problem: A member must assure everyone that he or she will participate in acquiring food or in defending the group. Of course, hunters and warriors may make promises—"you have my word, I'll show up tomorrow"—but unless the trust is already established such statements are not believable.

It turns out that there is a robust way to secure trust. Israeli biologist Amotz Zahavi observes that it is often in the best interest of an animal to send a dishonest signal—perhaps to fake its size, speed, strength, health or beauty. The only signal that can be believed is one that is too costly to fake, which he referred to as a "handicap." Zahavi argues that natural selection has favored the evolution of handicaps. For example, when a springbok antelope spots a predator it often *stots*—it jumps up and down. This extraordinary behavior puzzled biologists for years: Why would an antelope waste precious energy that could be used to escape the predator? And why would the animal make itself more visible to something that wants to eat it? The reason is that the springbok is displaying its quality to the predator—its ability to escape, effectively saying, "Don't bother chasing me. Look how strong my legs are, you won't be able to catch me." The only reason a predator believes the springbok is because the signal is too costly to fake. An antelope that is not quick enough to escape cannot imitate the signal because it is not strong enough to repeatedly jump to a certain height. Thus, a display can provide honest information if the signals are so costly to perform that lower quality organisms cannot benefit by imitating the signal.

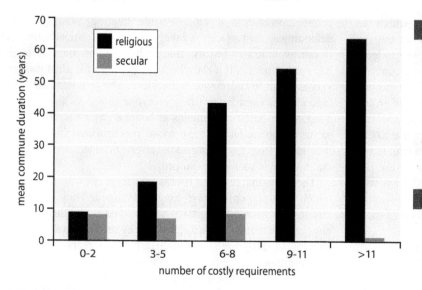

behaviors that are constrained

consumption of:
coffee, alcohol, tobacco, meat, other foods or
beverages

use and ownership of:
photographs, jewelry, certain technology, other
material items

activities:
monogamous marriage, gambling, communication
with the outside, living as a nuclear family,
maintaining rights to biological children

behaviors that are required

trial period for membership, surrender of material
belongings, learn a body of knowledge, endure
public sessions of criticism, certain clothing styles,
certain hairstyles, fasting

In much the same way, religious behavior is also a costly signal. By donning several layers of clothing and standing out in the midday sun, ultraorthodox Jewish men are signaling to others: "Hey! Look, I'm a *haredi* Jew. If you are also a member of this group you can trust me because why else would I be dressed like this? No one would do this *unless* they believed in the teachings of ultraorthodox Judaism and were fully committed to its ideals and goals." The quality that these men are signaling is their level of commitment to a specific religious group.

Adherence to a set of religious beliefs entails a host of ritual obligations and expected behaviors. Although there may be physical or psychological benefits associated with some ritual practices, the significant time, energy and financial costs involved serve as effective deterrents for anyone who does not believe in the teachings of a particular religion. There is no incentive for nonbelievers to join or remain in a religious group, because the costs of maintaining membership—such as praying three times a day, eating only kosher food, donating a certain part of your income to charity and so on—are simply too high.

Those who engage in the suite of ritual requirements imposed by a religious group can be trusted to believe sincerely in the doctrines of their respective religious communities. As a result of increased levels of trust and commitment among group members, religious groups minimize costly monitoring mechanisms that are otherwise necessary to overcome free-rider problems that typically plague communal pursuits. Hence, the adaptive benefit of ritual behavior is its ability to promote and maintain cooperation, a challenge that our ancestors presumably faced throughout our evolutionary history.

Benefits of Membership

One prediction of the "costly signaling theory of ritual" is that groups that impose the greatest demands on their members will elicit the highest levels of devotion and commitment. Only committed members will be willing to dress and behave in ways that differ from the rest of society. Groups that maintain more-committed members can also offer more because it's easier for them to attain their collective goals than groups whose members

are less committed. This may explain a paradox in the religious marketplace: Churches that require the most of their adherents are experiencing rapid rates of growth. For example, the Church of Jesus Christ of Latter-day Saints (Mormons), Seventh-day Adventists and Jehovah's Witnesses, who respectively abstain from caffeine, meat and blood transfusions (among other things), have been growing at exceptional rates. In contrast, liberal Protestant denominations such as the Episcopalians, Methodists and Presbyterians have been steadily losing members.

Economist Lawrence Iannaccone, of George Mason University, has also noted that the most demanding groups also have the greatest number of committed members. He found that the more distinct a religious group was—how much the group's lifestyle differed from mainstream America—the higher its attendance rates at services. Sociologists Roger Finke and Rodney Stark, of Penn State and the University of Washington, respectively, have argued that when the Second Vatican Council in 1962 repealed many of the Catholic Church's prohibitions and reduced the level of strictness in the church, it initiated a decline in church attendance among American Catholics and reduced the enrollments in seminaries. Indeed, in the late 1950s almost 75 percent of American Catholics were attending Mass weekly, but since the Vatican's actions there has been a steady decline to the current rate of about 45 percent.

The costly signaling theory of ritual also predicts that greater commitment will translate into greater cooperation within groups. My colleague Eric Bressler, a graduate student at McMaster University, and I addressed this question by looking at data from the records of 19th-century communes. All communes face an inherent problem of promoting and sustaining cooperation because individuals can free ride on the efforts of others. Because cooperation is key to a commune's survival, we employed commune longevity as a measure of cooperation. Compared to their secular counterparts, the religious communes did indeed demand more of their members, including such behavior as celibacy, the surrender of all material possessions and vegetarianism. Communes that demanded more of their members survived longer, overcoming the fundamental challenges of cooperation. By placing greater demands on their

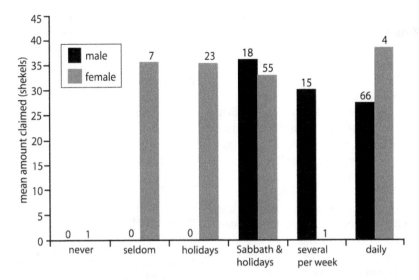

members, they were presumably able to elicit greater belief in and commitment toward the community's common ideology and goals.

I also wanted to evaluate the costly signaling theory of ritual within modern communal societies. The kibbutzim I had visited in Israel as a teenager provided an ideal opportunity to examine these hypotheses. For most of their 100-year history, these communal societies have lived by the dictum, "From each according to his abilities, to each according to his needs." The majority of the more than 270 kibbutzim are secular (and often ideologically antireligious); fewer than 20 are religiously oriented. Because of a massive economic failure—a collective debt of more than $4 billion—the kibbutzim are now moving in the direction of increased privatization and reduced communality. When news of the extraordinary debt surfaced in the late 1980s, it went largely unnoticed that the religious kibbutzim were financially stable. In the words of the Religious Kibbutz Movement Federation, "the economic position of the religious kibbutzim is sound, and they remain uninvolved in the economic crisis."

The success of the religious kibbutzim is especially remarkable given that many of their rituals inhibit economic productivity. For example, Jewish law does not permit Jews to milk cows on the Sabbath. Although rabbinic rulings now permit milking by kibbutz members to prevent the cows from suffering, in the early years none of this milk was used commercially. There are also significant constraints imposed by Jewish law on agricultural productivity. Fruits are not allowed to be eaten for the first few years of the tree's life, agricultural fields must lie fallow every seven years, and the corners of fields can never be harvested—they must be left for society's poor. Although these constraints appear detrimental to productivity, the costly signaling theory of ritual suggests that they may actually be the key to the economic success of the religious kibbutzim.

I decided to study this issue with economist Bradley Ruffle of Israel's Ben Gurion University. We developed a game to determine whether there were differences in how the members of secular and religious kibbutzim cooperated with each other. The game involves two members from the same kibbutz who remain anonymous to each other. Each member is told there are 100 shekels in an envelope to which both members have access. Each participant decides how many shekels to withdraw and keep. If the sum of both requests exceeds 100 shekels, both members receive no money and the game is over. However, if the requests are less than or equal to 100 shekels, the money remaining in the envelope is increased by 50 percent and divided evenly among the participants. Each member also keeps the original amount he or she requested. The game is an example of a common-pool resource dilemma in which publicly accessible goods are no longer available once they are consumed. Since the goods are available to more than one person, the maintenance of the resources requires individual self-restraint; in other words, cooperation.

After we controlled for a number of variables, including the age and size of the kibbutz and the amount of privatization, we found not only that religious kibbutzniks were more cooperative with each other than secular kibbutzniks, but that male religious kibbutz members were also significantly more cooperative than female members. Among secular kibbutzniks we found no sex differences at all. This result is understandable if we appreciate the types of rituals and demands imposed on religious Jews. Although there are a variety of requirements that are imposed equally on males and females, such as keeping kosher and refraining from work on the Sabbath, male rituals are largely performed in public, whereas female rituals are generally pursued privately. Indeed, none of the three major requirements imposed exclusively on women—attending a ritual bath, separating a portion of dough when baking bread and lighting Shabbat and holiday candles—are publicly performed. They are not rituals that signal commitment to a wider group; instead they appear to signal commitment to the family. Men, however, engage in highly visible rituals, most notably public prayer, which they are expected to perform three times a day. Among male religious kibbutz members, synagogue attendance is positively correlated with cooperative behavior. There is no similar correlation among females. This is not surprising given that women are not required to attend services, and so their presence does not signal commitment to the group. Here the costly signaling theory of ritual provides a unique explanation of these findings. We expect that further work will provide even more insight into the ability of ritual to promote trust, commitment and cooperation.

We know that many other species engage in ritual behaviors that appear to enhance trust and cooperation. For example, anthropologists John Watanabe of Dartmouth University and Barbara Smuts at the University of Michigan have shown that greetings between male olive baboons serve to signal trust and commitment between former rivals. So why are human rituals often cloaked in mystery and the supernatural? Cognitive anthropologists Scott Atran of the University of Michigan and Pascal Boyer at Washington University in St. Louis have pointed out that the counterintuitive nature of supernatural concepts are more easily remembered than mundane ideas, which facilitates their cultural transmission. Belief in supernatural agents such as gods, spirits and ghosts also appears to be critical to religion's ability to promote long-term cooperation. In our study of 19th-century communes, Eric Bressler and I found that the strong positive relationship between the number of costly requirements imposed on members and commune longevity only held for religious communes, not secular ones. We were surprised by this result because secular groups such as militaries and fraternities appear to successfully employ costly rituals to maintain cooperation. Cultural ecologist Roy Rappaport explained, however, that although religious and secular rituals can both promote cooperation, religious rituals ironically generate greater belief and commitment because they sanctify unfalsifiable statements that are beyond the possibility of examination. Since statements containing supernatural elements, such as "Jesus is the son of God," cannot be proved or disproved, believers verify them "emotionally." In contrast to religious propositions, the kibbutz's guiding dictum, taken from Karl Marx, is not beyond question; it can be evaluated by living according to its directives by distributing labor and resources appropriately. Indeed, as the economic situation on the kibbutzim has worsened, this fundamental proposition of kibbutz life has been challenged and is now disregarded by many who are pushing their communities to accept differential pay scales. The ability of religious rituals to evoke emotional experiences that can be associated with enduring supernatural concepts and symbols differentiates them from both animal and secular rituals and lies at the heart of their efficiency in promoting and maintaining long-term group cooperation and commitment.

Evolutionary research on religious behavior is in its infancy, and many questions remain to be addressed. The costly signaling theory of ritual appears to provide some answers, and, of course, it has given me a better understanding of the questions I asked as a teenager. The real value of the costly signaling theory of ritual will be determined by its ability to explain religious phenomena across societies. Most of us, including ultraorthodox Jews, are not living in communes. Nevertheless, contemporary religious congregations that demand much of their members are able to achieve a close-knit social community—an impressive accomplishment in today's individualistic world.

Religion has probably always served to enhance the union of its practitioners; unfortunately, there is also a dark side to this unity. If the intragroup solidarity that religion promotes is one of its significant adaptive benefits, then from its beginning religion has probably always played a role in intergroup conflicts. In other words, one of the benefits for individuals of intragroup solidarity is the ability of unified groups to defend and compete against other groups. This seems to be as true today as it ever was, and is nowhere more apparent than the region I visited as a 15-year-old boy—which is where I am as I write these words. As I conduct my fieldwork in the center of this war zone, I hope that by appreciating the depth of the religious need in the human psyche, and by understanding this powerful adaptation, we can learn how to promote cooperation rather than conflict.

References

Atran, S. 2002. *In Gods We Trust.* New York: Oxford University Press.

Iannaccone, L. 1992. Sacrifice and stigma: Reducing free-riding in cults, communes, and other collectives. *Journal of Political Economy* 100:271–291.

Iannaccone, L. 1994. Why strict churches are strong. *American Journal of Sociology* 99:1180–1211.

Irons, W. 2001. Religion as a hard-to-fake sign of commitment. In *Evolution and the Capacity for Commitment,* ed. R. Nesse, pp. 292–309. New York: Russell Sage Foundation.

Rappaport, R. 1999. *Ritual and Religion in the Making of Humanity.* Cambridge: Cambridge University Press.

Sosis, R. 2003. Why aren't we all Hutterites? Costly signaling theory and religious behavior. *Human Nature* 14:91–127.

Sosis, R., and C. Alcorta. 2003. Signaling, solidarity, and the sacred: The evolution of religious behavior. *Evolutionary Anthropology* 12:264–274.

Sosis, R., and E. Bressler. 2003. Cooperation and commune longevity: A test of the costly signaling theory of religion. *Cross-Cultural Research* 37:211–239.

Sosis, R., and B. Ruffle. 2003. Religious ritual and cooperation: Testing for a relationship on Israeli religious and secular kibbutzim. *Current Anthropology* 44:713–722.

Zahavi, A., and A. Zahavi. 1997. *The Handicap Principle.* New York: Oxford University Press.

Assess Your Progress

1. What is the universal dilemma with regard to cooperation in a community, according to William Irons?

2. In what sense is religious ritual a form of communication?

3. What is the only kind of signal that can be believed? How does the example of the springbok antelope illustrate the point?

4. Why is there no incentive for nonbelievers to join or remain in a religious group? Are there costly monitoring mechanisms? Explain.

5. What is the relationship between demands upon members and levels of devotion and commitment? What paradox does this explain?

6. What groups have the most committed members?

7. What was observed among American Catholics once the Vatican Council reduced the level of strictness in the church?

8. Which 19th century communes survived long and why?

9. Which kibbutzim survived better and why? What constraints existed among the religious kibbutzim and what effect did they have?

10. Describe the overall results of the game experiment with regard to religious versus secular kibbutzim and men versus women.

11. Why are religious rituals more successful at promoting belief than are secular rituals?

12. What is the "dark side" to the unity provided by religious intragroup solidarity?

RICHARD SOSIS is an assistant professor of anthropology at the University of Connecticut. His research interests include the evolution of cooperation, utopian societies and the behavioral ecology of religion. Address: Department of Anthropology, U-2176, University of Connecticut, Storrs, CT 06269–2176. Internet: richard.sosis@uconn.edu

From *American Scientist*, March/April 2004, pp. 166–172. Copyright © 2004 by American Scientist, magazine of Sigma Xi, The Scientific Research Society. Reprinted by permission.

Understanding Islam

KENNETH JOST

Is Islam Compatible with Western Values?

With more than 1 billion adherents, Islam is the world's second-largest religion after Christianity. Within its mainstream traditions, Islam teaches piety, virtue and tolerance. Ever since the Sept. 11, 2001, terrorist attacks in the United States, however, many Americans have associated Islam with the fundamentalist groups that preach violence against the West and regard "moderate" Muslims as heretics. Mainstream Muslims and religious scholars say Islam is wrongly blamed for the violence and intolerance of a few. But some critics say Muslims have not done enough to oppose terrorism and violence. They also contend that Islam's emphasis on a strong relationship between religion and the state is at odds with Western views of secularism and pluralism. Some Muslims are calling for a more progressive form of Islam. But radical Islamist views are attracting a growing number of young Muslims in the Islamic world and in Europe.

Overview

Aishah Azmi was dressed all in black, her face veiled by a *niqab* that revealed only her brown eyes through a narrow slit.

"Muslim women who wear the veil are not aliens," the 24-year-old suspended bilingual teaching assistant told reporters in Leeds, England, on Oct. 19. "Integration [of Muslims into British society] requires people like me to be in the workplace so that people can see that we are not to be feared or mistrusted."

But school officials defended their decision to suspend Azmi for refusing to remove her veil in class with a male teacher, saying it interfered with her ability to communicate with her students—most of them Muslims and, like Azmi, British Asians.

"The school and the local authority had to balance the rights of the children to receive the best quality education possible and Mrs. Azmi's desire to express her cultural beliefs," said local Education Minister Jim Dodds.

Although an employment tribunal rejected Azmi's discrimination and harassment claims, it said the school council had handled her complaint poorly and awarded her 1,100 British pounds—about $2,300.

Azmi's widely discussed case has become part of a wrenching debate in predominantly Christian England over relations with the country's growing Muslim population.

In September, a little more than a year after subway and bus bombings in London claimed 55 lives, a government minister called on Muslim parents to do more to steer their children away from violence and terrorism. Then, in October, a leaked report being prepared by the interfaith adviser of the Church of England complained that what he called the government's policy of "privileged attention" toward Muslims had backfired and was creating increased "disaffection and separation."

The simmering controversy grew even hotter after Jack Straw, leader of the House of Commons and former foreign secretary under Prime Minister Tony Blair, called full-face veils "a visible statement of separation and difference" that promotes separatism between Muslims and non-Muslims. Straw, whose constituency in northwestern England includes an estimated 25 percent Muslim population aired the comments in a local newspaper column.

Hamid Qureshi, chairman of the Lancashire Council of Mosques, called Straw's remarks "blatant Muslim-bashing."

"Muslims feel they are on center stage, and everybody is Muslim-bashing," says Anjum Anwar, the council's director of education. "They feel very sensitive."

Britain's estimated 1.5 million Muslims—comprising mostly Pakistani or Indian immigrants and their British-born children—are only a tiny fraction of Islam's estimated 1.2 billion adherents worldwide. But the tensions surfacing in the face-veil debate exemplify the increasingly strained relations between the predominantly Christian West and the Muslim world.

The world's two largest religions—Christianity has some 2 billion adherents—have had a difficult relationship at least since the time of the European Crusades against Muslim rulers, or caliphs, almost 1,000 years ago. Mutual suspicion and hostility have intensified since recent terrorist attacks around the world by militant Islamic groups and President George W. Bush proclaimed a worldwide "war on terror" in response to the Sept. 11, 2001, attacks in the United States.

Bush, who stumbled early on by referring to a "crusade" against terrorism, has tried many times since then to dispel perceptions of any official hostility toward Islam or Muslims generally. In Britain, Blair's government has carried on a 40-year-old policy of "multiculturalism" aimed at promoting cohesion among the country's various communities, Muslims in particular.

Despite those efforts, widespread distrust of Islam and Muslims prevails on both sides of the Atlantic. In a recent poll in the United States, 45 percent of those surveyed said they had an unfavorable view of Islam—a higher percentage than registered in a similar poll four years earlier.

British Muslim leaders also say they feel increasingly hostile anti-Muslim sentiments from the general public and government officials. "Muslims are very fearful, frustrated, upset, angry," says Asghar Bukhari, a spokesman for the Muslim Public Affairs Committee in London. "It's been almost like a mental assault on the Muslim psyche here."

As the face-veil debate illustrates, the distrust stems in part from an array of differences between today's Christianity and Islam as variously practiced in the so-called Muslim world, including the growing Muslim diaspora in Europe and North America.

In broad terms, Islam generally regards religion as a more pervasive presence in daily life and a more important source for civil law than contemporary Christianity, according to the British author Paul Grieve, who wrote a comprehensive guide to Islam after studying Islamic history and thought for more than three years. "Islam is a system of rules for all aspects of life," Grieve writes, while Western liberalism limits regulation of personal behavior. In contrast to the secular nation-states of the West, he explains, Islam views the ideal Muslim society as a universal community—such as the *ummah* established by the Prophet Muhammed in the seventh century.

Those theological and cultural differences are reflected, Grieve says, in Westerners' widespread view of Muslims as narrow-minded and extremist. Many Muslims correspondingly view Westerners as decadent and immoral.

The differences also can be seen in the debates over the role Islam plays in motivating terrorist violence by Islamic extremist groups such as al Qaeda and the objections raised by Muslims to what they consider unflattering and unfair descriptions of Islam in the West.

Muslim leaders generally deny responsibility for the violence committed by Islamic terrorists, including the 9/11 terrorist attacks in the United States and subsequent attacks in Indonesia, Spain and England. "Muslim organizations have done more than ever before in trying to advance community cohesion," Anwar says. They also deny any intention to deny freedom of expression, even though Muslims worldwide denounced a Danish cartoonist's satirical portrayal of Muhammad and Pope Benedict XVI's citation of a medieval Christian emperor's description of Islam as a violent religion.

For many Westerners, however, Islam is associated with radical Muslims—known as Islamists—who either advocate or appear to condone violence and who take to the streets to protest unfavorable depictions of Islam. "A lot of traditional or moderate Islam is inert," says Paul Marshall, a senior fellow at Freedom House's Center for Religious Freedom in Washington. "Many of the people who disagree with radicals don't have a developed position. They keep their heads down."

Meanwhile, many Muslims and non-Muslims alike despair at Islam's sometimes fratricidal intrafaith disputes. Islam split within the first decades of its founding in the seventh century

into the Sunni and Shiite (Shia) branches. The Sunni-Shiite conflict helps drive the escalating insurgency in Iraq three years after the U.S.-led invasion ousted Saddam Hussein, a Sunni who pursued generally secularist policies. "A real geopolitical fracturing has taken place in the Muslim world since the end of the colonial era," says Reza Aslan, an Iranian-born Shiite Muslim now a U.S. citizen and author of the book *No god but God*.

The tensions between Islam and the West are on the rise as Islam is surging around the world, growing at an annual rate of about 7 percent. John Voll associate director of the Prince Alwaleed bin Talal Centre for Christian-Muslim Understanding at Georgetown University, notes that the growth is due largely to conversions, not the high birth rates that are driving Hinduism's faster growth.

Moreover, Voll says, Muslims are growing more assertive. "There has been an increase in intensity and an increase in strength in the way Muslims view their place in the world and their place in society," he says.

Teaching assistant Azmi's insistence on wearing the *niqab* exemplifies the new face of Islam in parts of the West. But her choice is not shared by all, or even, most of her fellow Muslim women. "I don't see why she needs to wear it," says Anwar. "She's teaching young children under 11." (Azmi says she wears it because she works with a male classroom teacher.)

Muslim experts generally agree the Koran does not require veils, only modest dress. Observant Muslim women generally comply with the admonition with a head scarf and loose-fitting attire. In particularly conservative cultures, such as Afghanistan under Taliban rule, women cover their entire bodies, including their eyes.

Still, despite the varying practices, many Muslim groups see a disconnect between the West's self-proclaimed tolerance and its pressure on Muslims to conform. "It's a Muslim woman's right to dress as she feels appropriate, given her religious views," says Ibrahim Hooper, director of communications for the Council on American-Islamic Relations in Washington. "But then when somebody actually makes a choice, they're asked not to do that."

Indeed, in Hamtramck, Mich., a judge recently came under fire for throwing out a small-claims case because the Muslim plaintiff refused to remove her full-face veil.

As the debates continue, here are some of the questions being considered:

Is Islam a Religion That Promotes Violence?

Within hours of the London subway and bus bombings on July 7, 2005, the head of the Muslim World League condemned the attacks as un-Islamic. "The heavenly religions, notably Islam, advocate peace and security," said Abdallah al-Turki, secretary-general of the Saudi-funded organization based in Mecca.

The league's statement echoed any number of similar denunciations of Islamist-motivated terrorist attacks issued since 9/11 by Muslims in the United States and around the world. Yet many non-Muslim public officials, commentators, experts and others say Muslims have not done enough to speak out against terrorism committed in the name of their religion.

"Mainstream Muslims have not stepped up to the plate, by and large," says Angel Rabasa, a senior fellow at the Rand Corp., a California think tank, and lead author of a U.S. Air Force-sponsored study, *The Muslim World after 9/11*.

Muslim organizations voice indignant frustration in disputing the accusation. "We can always do more," says Hooper. "The problem is that it never seems to be enough. But that doesn't keep us from trying."

Many Americans, in fact, believe Islam actually encourages violence among its adherents. A CBS poll in April 2006 found that 46 percent of those surveyed believe Islam encourages violence more than other religions. A comparable poll four years earlier registered a lower figure: 32 percent.

Those perceptions are sometimes inflamed by U.S. evangelical leaders. Harsh comments about Islam have come from religious leaders like Franklin Graham, Jerry Falwell, Pat Robertson and Jerry Vines, the former president of the Southern Baptist Convention. Graham called Islam "a very evil and wicked religion," and Vines called Muhammad, Islam's founder and prophet, a "demon-possessed pedophile." Falwell, on the CBS news magazine "60 Minutes" in October 2002, declared, "I think Muhammad was a terrorist."

Mainstream Muslims insist Islam is a peaceful religion and that terrorist organizations distort its tenets and teachings in justifying attacks against the West or other Muslims. But Islamic doctrine and history sometimes seem to justify the use of violence in propagating or defending the faith. The dispute revolves around the meaning of *jihad,* an Arabic word used in the Koran and derived from a root meaning "to strive" or "to make an effort for." Muslim scholars can point to verses in the Koran that depict *jihad* merely as a personal, spiritual struggle and to others that describe *jihad* as encompassing either self-defense or conquest against non-believers.

Georgetown historian Voll notes that, in contrast to Christianity, Islam achieved military success during Muhammad's life and expanded into a major world empire within decades afterward. That history "reinforces the idea that militancy and violence can, in fact, be part of the theologically legitimate plan of the Muslim believer," says Voll.

"Islam, like all religions, has its historical share of violence," acknowledges Stephen Schwartz, an adult convert to Islam and executive director of the Center for Islamic Pluralism in Washington. "But there's no reason to single out Islam."

Modern-day jihadists pack their public manifestos with Koranic citations and writings of Islamic theologians to portray themselves as warriors for Allah and defenders of true Islam. But Voll and others stress that the vast majority of Muslims do not subscribe to their views. "You have a highly visible minority that represents a theologically extreme position in the Muslim world," Voll says.

In particular, writes Seyyed Hossein Nasr, a professor of Islamic studies at George Washington University, Islamic law prohibits the use of force against women, children or civilians—even during war. "Inflicting injuries outside of this context," he writes, "is completely forbidden by Islamic law."

Rabasa says, however, that Muslims who disapprove of terrorism have not said enough or done enough to mobilize opposition to terrorist attacks. "Muslims see themselves as part of a community and are reluctant to criticize radical Muslims," he says.

In addition, many Muslims are simply intimidated from speaking out, he explains. "Radicals are not reluctant to use violence and the threat of violence," he says. Liberal and moderate Muslims are known to receive death threats on their cell phones, even in relatively peaceful Muslim countries such as Indonesia.

Voll also notes that Islamic radicals have simply outorganized the moderates. "There is no moderate organization that even begins to resemble some of the radical organizations that have developed," he says.

In Britain, Bukhari of the Muslim Public Affairs Committee criticizes Muslim leaders themselves for failing to channel young people opposed to Britain's pro-U.S. foreign policy into non-violent political action. "Children who could have been peaceful react to that foreign policy in a way that they themselves become criminals," he says.

The Council on American-Islamic Relations' Hooper details several anti-terrorism pronouncements and drives issued following the London bombings by various Muslim groups and leaders in Britain and in the United States, including *fatwas,* or legal opinions, rejecting terrorism and extremism.

For his part, Omid Safi, an associate professor of Islamic studies at the University of North Carolina in Chapel Hill, points out that virtually every Muslim organization in the United States issued condemnations of violence almost immediately after the 9/11 terrorist attacks.

"How long must we keep answering this question?" Safi asks in exasperation. But he concedes a few moments later that the issue is more than perception. "Muslims must come to terms with our demons," he says, "and one of those demons is violence."

Is Islam Compatible with Secular, Pluralistic Societies?

In 2003, Germany's famed Deutsche Oper staged an avant-garde remake of Mozart's opera "Idomeneo," which dramatizes the composer's criticism of organized religion, with a scene depicting the severed heads of Muhammad, Jesus, Buddha and Poseidon. That production was mounted without incident, but the company dropped plans to restage it in November 2006 after police warned of a possible violent backlash from Muslim fundamentalists.

The cancellation prompted protests from German officials and artistic-freedom advocates in Europe and in the United States, who saw the move as appeasement toward terrorists. Wolfgang Bornsen, a spokesman for conservative Chancellor Angela Merkel, said the cancellation was "a signal" to other artistic companies to avoid any works critical of Islam.

The debate continued even after plans were discussed to mount the production after all—with enhanced security and the blessing of German Muslim leaders. "We live in Europe, where democracy was based on criticizing religion," remarked Philippe Val, editor of the French satirical magazine *Charlie Hebdo.* "If we lose the right to criticize or attack religions in our free countries . . . we are doomed."

As with the issue of violence, Islam's doctrines and history can be viewed as pointing both ways on questions of pluralism and tolerance. "There are a great many passages [in the Koran] that support a pluralistic interpretation of Islam," says the Rand Corp.'s Rabasa. "But you also find a great many that would support an intolerant interpretation."

"Intellectual pluralism is traditional Islam," says Schwartz at the Center for Islamic Pluralism. An oft-quoted verse from the Koran specifically prohibits compulsion in religion, he says. Voll and other historians agree that Muslim countries generally tolerated Christians and Jews, though they were often subject to special taxes or other restrictions.

"Islam is the only major religious system that has built-in protections for minorities," says Hooper at the Council on American-Islamic Relations. "You don't see the kind of persecutions of minorities that we often saw in Europe for hundreds of years. Many members of the Jewish community fled to find safety within the Muslim world."

Even so, Islam's view of religion and politics as inseparable creates difficult issues. Outside the Arab world, most Muslims live in practicing democracies with fair to good human-rights records. But some Muslim countries—Arab and non-Arab—have either adopted or been urged to adopt provisions of Islamic law—*sharia*—that are antithetical to modern ideas of human rights, such as limiting women's rights and prescribing stoning or amputations as criminal penalties.

Muslims participating in a society as a minority population face different issues, according to author Grieve. "Islam is difficult to accommodate in a determinedly secular Western society where almost all views are equally respected, and none is seen as either right or wrong," he writes.

The tensions played out in a number of controversies in recent years were provoked by unflattering depictions of Islam in Europe. A Danish cartoonist's satirical view of Muhammad provoked worldwide protests from Muslim leaders and groups after they were publicized in early 2006. Scattered violence resulted in property damage and more than 30 deaths.

Somewhat similarly, Pope Benedict XVI drew sharp criticism after a Sept. 12, 2006, lecture quoting a medieval Christian emperor's description of Islam as "evil and inhuman." Along with verbal denunciations, protesters in Basra, Iraq, burned an effigy of the pope. Within a week, he disclaimed the remarks and apologized.

Freedom House's Marshall says such controversies, as well as the cancellation of the opera in Berlin, strengthens radical Muslim elements. "Bending to more radical demands marginalizes the voices of moderate Muslims and hands over leadership to the radicals," he says.

Many Muslims in European countries, however, view the controversies—including the current debate over the veil in England—as evidence of pervasive hostility from the non-Muslim majorities. "There is a growing hatred of Muslims in Britain, and anybody who bashes Muslims can only get brownie points," says Bukhari of the Muslim Public Affairs Committee.

"These are not friendly times for Western Muslims," says Safi, at the University of North Carolina. "Whenever people

---

Basic Tenets of Islam

Islam is the youngest of the world's three major monotheistic religions. Like the other two, Judaism and Christianity, Islam (the word means both "peace" and "submission") holds there is but one God (Allah). Muslims believe God sent a number of prophets to teach mankind how to live according to His law. Muslims consider Jesus, Moses and Abraham as prophets of God and hold the Prophet Muhammad as his final and most sacred messenger. Many accounts found in Islam's sacred book, the Koran (Qur'an), are also found in sacred writings of Jews and Christians.

There are five basic pillars of Islam:

- Creed—Belief in God and Muhammad as his Prophet.
- Almsgiving—Giving money to charity is considered a sacred duty.
- Fasting—From dawn to dusk during the month of Ramadan.
- Prayer—Five daily prayers must be given facing Mecca, Islam's holiest city.
- Pilgrimage—All Muslims must make a baff to Mecca at least once during their lifetime, if they are physically able.

---

find themselves under assault, opening their arms and opening their hearts is difficult."

Does Islam Need a "Reformation"?

If Pakistan's Punjab University expected a chorus of approval when it decided to launch a master's program in musicology in fall 2006, it was in for a surprise. At the Lahore campus, the conservative Islamic Assembly of Students, known as I.J.T., rose up in protest.

Handbills accused school authorities of forsaking Islamic ideological teachings in favor of "the so-called enlightened moderation" dictated by "foreign masters." Undeterred, administrators opened the program for enrollment in September. When fewer students applied than expected, they blamed the poor response in part on the I.J.T. campaign.

The episode reflects how Islam today is evolving differently in the West and in some parts of the Muslim world. Many Muslim writers and scholars in the United States and Europe are calling for Islam to adapt to modern times by, for example, embracing pluralism and gender equality. Introducing a collection of essays by "progressive" Muslims, the University of North Carolina's Safi says the movement seeks to "start swimming through the rising waters of Islam and modernity, to strive for justice in the midst of society."

In much of the Muslim world, however, Islam is growing—in numbers and intensity—on the strength of literal interpretations of the Koran and exclusivist attitudes toward the non-Muslim world. "In the Muslim world in general, more extreme or reactionary forms of Islam are getting stronger—in Africa, Asia and the Middle East," says Freedom House's Marshall, who has previously worked on issues pertaining to persecution of Christians around the world.

Islamist groups such as I.J.T. talk about "reforming" or "purifying" Islam and adopting Islamic law as the primary or exclusive source of civil law. In fact, one version of reformed Islam—Wahhabism[1] or the currently preferred term Salafism—espouses a literalistic reading of the Koran and a puritanical stance toward such modern practices as listening to music or watching television. It has been instituted in Saudi Arabia and has advanced worldwide because of financial backing from the oil-rich kingdom and its appeal to new generations of Muslims.

"The Salafi movement is a fringe," says the Rand Corp.'s Rabasa. "But it's growing because it's dynamic and revolutionary, whereas traditional Islam tends to be conservative. It has this appeal to young people looking for identity."

But the Center for Islamic Pluralism's Schwartz, an outspoken critic of Salafism, says many Muslims are rejecting it because of its tendency to view other branches of Islam as apostasy. "People are getting sick of this," he says. "They're tired of the social conflict and upheaval."

Voll at the Center for Christian-Muslim Understanding also says some Muslim legal scholars are disputing literalistic readings of *sharia* by contending that the Islamic law cited as divinely ordained is actually "a human construct subject to revision."

Some Western commentators refer to a "reformation" in calling for a more liberal form of Islam. Nicholas D. Kristof, a *New York Times* columnist who focuses on global human-rights issues, sees "hopeful rumblings . . . of steps toward a Muslim Reformation," especially on issues of gender equality. He notes that feminist Muslim scholars are reinterpreting passages in the Koran that other Muslims cite in justifying restrictions on women, such as the Saudi ban on women driving.

Safi says he avoids the term reformation because it has been adopted by Salafists and also because it suggests a need to break from traditional Islam. He says "progressive" Muslims return to the Prophet's vision of the common humanity of all human beings and seek "to hold Muslim societies accountable for justice and pluralism."

Rabasa also says reformation is historically inappropriate as a goal for liberal or progressive Muslims. "What is needed is not an Islamic reformation but an Islamic enlightenment," says Rabasa. The West's liberal tradition, he notes, was produced not by the Reformation but by the Enlightenment—the 18th-century movement that used reason to search for objective truth.

Whatever terms are used, the clash between different visions of Islam will be less susceptible to resolution than analogous disputes within most branches of Christianity because Islam lacks any recognized hierarchical structure. Islam has no pope or governing council. Instead, each believer is regarded as having a direct relationship with God, or Allah, with no ecclesiastical intermediary.

"In the face of contemporary Islam, there is absolutely the sense of an authority vacuum," says Safi. Islam's future, he adds, "is a question that can only be answered by Muslims."

Note

1. Wahhabism originated in the Arabian peninsula in the late 1700s from the teachings of Arabian theologian Muhammand ibn Abd al Wahhab (1703–1792).

Assess Your Progress

1. What are the main points of contention regarding the strained relationship between the Christian West and Muslim world?

2. Does Islam encourage violence? Explain.

3. Is Islam compatible with secular, pluralistic societies? Explain.

4. Does Islam need a "Reformation?" Explain.

The Secrets of Haiti's Living Dead

A Harvard botanist investigates mystic potions, voodoo rites, and the making of zombies.

GINO DEL GUERCIO

Five years ago, a man walked into l'Estère, a village in central Haiti, approached a peasant woman named Angelina Narcisse, and identified himself as her brother Clairvius. If he had not introduced himself using a boyhood nickname and mentioned facts only intimate family members knew, she would not have believed him. Because, eighteen years earlier, Angelina had stood in a small cemetery north of her village and watched as her brother Clairvius was buried.

The man told Angelina he remembered that night well. He knew when he was lowered into his grave, because he was fully conscious, although he could not speak or move. As the earth was thrown over his coffin, he felt as if he were floating over the grave. The scar on his right cheek, he said, was caused by a nail driven through his casket.

The night he was buried, he told Angelina, a voodoo priest raised him from the grave. He was beaten with a sisal whip and carried off to a sugar plantation in northern Haiti where, with other zombies, he was forced to work as a slave. Only with the death of the zombie master were they able to escape, and Narcisse eventually returned home.

Legend has it that zombies are the living dead, raised from their graves and animated by malevolent voodoo sorcerers, usually for some evil purpose. Most Haitians believe in zombies, and Narcisse's claim is not unique. At about the time he reappeared, in 1980, two women turned up in other villages saying they were zombies. In the same year, in northern Haiti, the local peasants claimed to have found a group of zombies wandering aimlessly in the fields.

But Narcisse's case was different in one crucial respect; it was documented. His death had been recorded by doctors at the American-directed Schweitzer Hospital in Deschapelles. On April 30, 1962, hospital records show, Narcisse walked into the hospital's emergency room spitting up blood. He was feverish and full of aches. His doctors could not diagnose his illness, and his symptoms grew steadily worse. Three days after he entered the hospital, according to the records, he died. The attending physicians, an American among them, signed his death certificate. His body was placed in cold storage for twenty hours, and then he was buried. He said he remembered hearing his doctors pronounce him dead while his sister wept at his bedside.

At the Centre de Psychiatrie et Neurologie in Port-au-Prince, Dr. Lamarque Douyon, a Haitian-born, Canadian-trained psychiatrist, has been systematically investigating all reports of zombies since 1961. Though convinced zombies were real, he had been unable to find a scientific explanation for the phenomenon. He did not believe zombies were people raised from the dead, but that did not make them any less interesting. He speculated that victims were only made to *look* dead, probably by means of a drug that dramatically slowed metabolism. The victim was buried, dug up within a few hours, and somehow reawakened.

The Narcisse case provided Douyon with evidence strong enough to warrant a request for assistance from colleagues in New York. Douyon wanted to find an ethnobotanist, a traditional-medicines expert, who could track down the zombie potion he was sure existed. Aware of the medical potential of a drug that could dramatically lower metabolism, a group organized by the late Dr. Nathan Kline—a New York psychiatrist and pioneer in the field of psychopharmacology—raised the funds necessary to send someone to investigate.

The search for that someone led to the Harvard Botanical Museum, one of the world's foremost institutes of ethnobiology. Its director, Richard Evans Schultes, Jeffrey professor of biology, had spent thirteen years in the tropics studying native medicines. Some of his best-known work is the investigation of curare, the substance used by the nomadic people of the Amazon to poison their darts. Refined into a powerful muscle relaxant called D-tubocurarine, it is now an essential component of the anesthesia used during almost all surgery.

Schultes would have been a natural for the Haitian investigation, but he was too busy. He recommended another Harvard ethnobotanist for the assignment, Wade Davis, a 28-year-old Canadian pursuing a doctorate in biology.

Davis grew up in the tall pine forests of British Columbia and entered Harvard in 1971, influenced by a *Life* magazine story on the student strike of 1969. Before Harvard, the only Americans he had known were draft dodgers, who seemed very exotic. "I used to fight forest fires with them," Davis says. "Like everybody else, I thought America was where it was at. And I wanted to go to Harvard because of that *Life* article. When I got there, I realized it wasn't quite what I had in mind."

Davis took a course from Schultes, and when he decided to go to South America to study plants, he approached his professor for guidance. "He was an extraordinary figure," Davis remembers. "He was a man who had done it all. He had lived alone for years in the Amazon." Schultes sent Davis to the rain forest with two letters of introduction and two pieces of advice: wear a pith helmet and try ayahuasca, a powerful hallucinogenic vine. During that expedition and others, Davis proved himself an "outstanding field man," says his mentor. Now, in early 1982, Schultes called him into his office and asked if he had plans for spring break.

"I always took to Schultes's assignments like a plant takes to water," says Davis, tall and blond, with inquisitive blue eyes. "Whatever Schultes told me to do, I did. His letters of introduction opened up a whole world." This time the world was Haiti.

Davis knew nothing about the Caribbean island—and nothing about African traditions, which serve as Haiti's cultural basis. He certainly did not believe in zombies. "I thought it was a lark," he says now.

Davis landed in Haiti a week after his conversation with Schultes, armed with a hypothesis about how the zombie drug—if it existed—might be made. Setting out to explore, he discovered a country materially impoverished, but rich in culture and mystery. He was impressed by the cohesion of Haitian society; he found none of the crime, social disorder, and rampant drug and alcohol abuse so common in many of the other Caribbean islands. The cultural wealth and cohesion, he believes, spring from the country's turbulent history.

During the French occupation of the late eighteenth century, 370,000 African-born slaves were imported to Haiti between 1780 and 1790. In 1791, the black population launched one of the few successful slave revolts in history, forming secret societies and overcoming first the French plantation owners and then a detachment of troops from Napoleon's army, sent to quell the revolt. For the next hundred years Haiti was the only independent black republic in the Caribbean, populated by people who did not forget their African heritage. "You can almost argue that Haiti is more African than Africa," Davis says. "When the west coast of Africa was being disrupted by colonialism and the slave trade, Haiti was essentially left alone. The amalgam of beliefs in Haiti is unique, but it's very, very African."

Davis discovered that the vast majority of Haitian peasants practice voodoo, a sophisticated religion with African roots. Says Davis, "It was immediately obvious that the stereotypes of voodoo weren't true. Going around the countryside, I found clues to a whole complex social world." Vodounists believe they communicate directly with, indeed are often possessed by, the many spirits who populate the everyday world. Vodoun society is a system of education, law, and medicine; it embodies a code of ethics that regulates social behavior. In rural areas, secret vodoun societies, much like those found on the west coast of Africa, are as much or more in control of everyday life as the Haitian government.

Although most outsiders dismissed the zombie phenomenon as folklore, some early investigators, convinced of its reality, tried to find a scientific explanation. The few who sought a zombie drug failed. Nathan Kline, who helped finance Davis's expedition, had searched unsuccessfully, as had Lamarque Douyon, the Haitian psychiatrist. Zora Neale Hurston, an American black woman, may have come closest. An anthropological pioneer, she went to Haiti in the thirties, studied vodoun society, and wrote a book on the subject, *Tell My Horse,* first published in 1938. She knew about the secret societies and was convinced zombies were real, but if a power existed, she too failed to obtain it.

Davis obtained a sample in a few weeks.

He arrived in Haiti with the names of several contacts. A BBC reporter familiar with the Narcisse case had suggested he talk with Marcel Pierre. Pierre owned the Eagle Bar, a bordello in the city of Saint Marc. He was also a voodoo sorcerer and had supplied the BBC with a physiologically active powder of unknown ingredients. Davis found him willing to negotiate. He told Pierre he was a representative of "powerful but anonymous interests in New York," willing to pay generously for the priest's services, provided no questions were asked. Pierre agreed to be helpful for what Davis will only say was a "sizable sum." Davis spent a day watching Pierre gather the ingredients—including human bones—and grind them together with mortar and pestle. However, from his knowledge of poison, Davis knew immediately that nothing in the formula could produce the powerful effects of zombification.

Three weeks later, Davis went back to the Eagle Bar, where he found Pierre sitting with three associates. Davis challenged him. He called him a charlatan. Enraged, the priest gave him a second vial, claiming that this was the real poison. Davis pretended to pour the powder into his palm and rub it into his skin. "You're a dead man," Pierre told him, and he might have been, because this powder proved to be genuine. But, as the substance had not actually touched him, Davis was able to maintain his bravado, and Pierre was impressed. He agreed to make the poison and show Davis how it was done.

The powder, which Davis keeps in a small vial, looks like dry black dirt. It contains parts of toads, sea worms, lizards, tarantulas, and human bones. (To obtain the last ingredient, he and Pierre unearthed a child's grave on a nocturnal trip to the cemetery.) The poison is rubbed into the victim's skin. Within hours he begins to feel nauseated and has difficulty breathing. A pins-and-needles sensation afflicts his arms and legs, then progresses to the whole body. The subject becomes paralyzed; his lips turn blue for lack of oxygen. Quickly—sometimes within six hours—his metabolism is lowered to a level almost indistinguishable from death.

As Davis discovered, making the poison is an inexact science. Ingredients varied in the five samples he eventually acquired, although the active agents were always the same. And the poison came with no guarantee. Davis speculates that sometimes instead of merely paralyzing the victim, the compound kills him. Sometimes the victim suffocates in the coffin before he can be resurrected. But clearly the potion works well enough often enough to make zombies more than a figment of Haitian imagination.

Analysis of the powder produced another surprise. "When I went down to Haiti originally," says Davis, "my hypothesis was that the formula would contain *concombre zombi,* the 'zombie's cucumber,' which is a *Datura* plant. I thought somehow *Datura*

Richard Schultes

His students continue his tradition of pursuing botanical research in the likeliest of unlikely places.

Richard Evans Schultes, Jeffrey professor of biology emeritus, has two homes, and they could not be more different. The first is Cambridge, where he served as director of the Harvard Botanical Museum from 1970 until last year, when he became director emeritus. During his tenure he interested generations of students in the exotic botany of the Amazon rain forest. His impact on the field through his own research is worldwide. The scholarly ethnobotanist with steel-rimmed glasses, bald head, and white lab coat is as much a part of the Botanical Museum as the thousands of plant specimens and botanical texts on the museum shelves.

In his austere office is a picture of a crew-cut, younger man stripped to the waist, his arms decorated with tribal paint. This is Schultes's other persona. Starting in 1941, he spent thirteen years in the rain forests of South America, living with the Indians and studying the plants they use for medicinal and spiritual purposes.

Schultes is concerned that many of the people he has studied are giving up traditional ways. "The people of so-called primitive societies are becoming civilized and losing all their forefathers' knowledge of plant lore," he says. "We'll be losing the tremendous amounts of knowledge they've gained over thousands of years. We're interested in the practical aspects with the hope that new medicines and other things can be developed for our own civilization."

Schultes's exploits are legendary in the biology department. Once, while gathering South American plant specimens hundreds of miles from civilization, he contracted beri-beri. For forty days he fought creeping paralysis and overwhelming fatigue as he paddled back to a doctor. "It was an extraordinary feat of endurance," says disciple Wade Davis. "He is really one of the last nineteenth-century naturalists."

Hallucinogenic plants are one of Schultes's primary interests. As a Harvard undergraduate in the thirties, he lived with Oklahoma's Kiowa Indians to observe their use of plants. He participated in their peyote ceremonies and wrote his thesis on the hallucinogenic cactus. He has also studied other hallucinogens, such as morning glory seeds, sacred mushrooms, and ayahuasca, a South American vision vine. Schultes's work has led to the development of anesthetics made from curare and alternative sources of natural rubber.

Schultes's main concern these days is the scientific potential of plants in the rapidly disappearing Amazon jungle. "If chemists are going to get material on 80,000 species and then analyze them, they'll never finish the job before the jungle is gone," he says. "The short cut is to find out what the [native] people have learned about the plant properties during many years of living in the very rich flora."

—G.D.G.

---

was used in putting people down." *Datura* is a powerful psychoactive plant, found in West Africa as well as other tropical areas and used there in ritual as well as criminal activities. Davis had found *Datura* growing in Haiti. Its popular name suggested the plant was used in creating zombies.

But, says Davis, "there were a lot of problems with the *Datura* hypothesis. Partly it was a question of how the drug was administered. *Datura* would create a stupor in huge doses, but it just wouldn't produce the kind of immobility that was key. These people had to appear dead, and there aren't many drugs that will do that."

One of the ingredients Pierre included in the second formula was a dried fish, a species of puffer or blowfish, common to most parts of the world. It gets its name from its ability to fill itself with water and swell to several times its normal size when threatened by predators. Many of these fish contain a powerful poison known as tetrodotoxin. One of the most powerful nonprotein poisons known to man, tetrodotoxin turned up in every sample of zombie powder that Davis acquired.

Numerous well-documented accounts of puffer fish poisoning exist, but the most famous accounts come from the Orient, where *fugu* fish, a species of puffer, is considered a delicacy. In Japan, special chefs are licensed to prepare *fugu*. The chef removes enough poison to make the fish nonlethal, yet enough remains to create exhilarating physiological effects—tingles up and down the spine, mild prickling of the tongue and lips,

euphoria. Several dozen Japanese die each year, having bitten off more than they should have.

"When I got hold of the formula and saw it was the *fugu* fish, that suddenly threw open the whole Japanese literature," says Davis. Case histories of *fugu* poisoning read like accounts of zombification. Victims remain conscious but unable to speak or move. A man who had "died" after eating *fugu* recovered seven days later in the morgue. Several summers ago, another Japanese poisoned by *fugu* revived after he was nailed into his coffin. "Almost all of Narcisse's symptoms correlated. Even strange things such as the fact that he said he was conscious and could hear himself pronounced dead. Stuff that I thought had to be magic, that seemed crazy. But, in fact, that is what people who get *fugu*-fish poisoning experience."

Davis was certain he had solved the mystery. But far from being the end of his investigation, identifying the poison was, in fact, its starting point. "The drug alone didn't make zombies," he explains. "Japanese victims of puffer-fish poisoning don't become zombies, they become poison victims. All the drug could do was set someone up for a whole series of psychological pressures that would be rooted in the culture. I wanted to know why zombification was going on," he says.

He sought a cultural answer, an explanation rooted in the structure and beliefs of Haitian society. Was zombification simply a random criminal activity? He thought not. He had discovered that Clairvius Narcisse and "Ti Femme," a second victim he interviewed, were village pariahs. Ti Femme was regarded as a thief. Narcisse had abandoned his children and deprived his brother of land that was rightfully his. Equally suggestive, Narcisse claimed that his aggrieved brother had sold him to a *bokor,* a voodoo priest who dealt in black magic; he made cryptic reference to having been tried and found guilty by the "masters of the land."

Gathering poisons from various parts of the country, Davis had come into direct contact with the vodoun secret societies. Returning to the anthropological literature on Haiti and pursuing his contacts with informants, Davis came to understand the social matrix within which zombies were created.

Davis's investigations uncovered the importance of the secret societies. These groups trace their origins to the bands of escaped slaves that organized the revolt against the French in the late eighteenth century. Open to both men and women, the societies control specific territories of the country. Their meetings take place at night, and in many rural parts of Haiti the drums and wild celebrations that characterize the gatherings can be heard for miles.

Davis believes the secret societies are responsible for policing their communities, and the threat of zombification is one way they maintain order. Says Davis, "Zombification has a material basis, but it also has a societal logic." To the uninitiated, the practice may appear a random criminal activity, but in rural vodoun society, it is exactly the opposite—a sanction imposed by recognized authorities, a form of capital punishment. For rural Haitians, zombification is an even more severe punishment than death, because it deprives the subject of his most valued possessions: his free will and independence.

The vodounists believe that when a person dies, his spirit splits into several different parts. If a priest is powerful enough, the spiritual aspect that controls a person's character and individuality, known as *ti bon ange,* the "good little angel," can be captured and the corporeal aspect, deprived of its will, held as a slave.

From studying the medical literature on tetrodotoxin poisoning, Davis discovered that if a victim survives the first few hours of the poisoning, he is likely to recover fully from the ordeal. The subject simply revives spontaneously. But zombies remain without will, in a trance-like state, a condition vodounists attribute to the power of the priest. Davis thinks it possible that the psychological trauma of zombification may be augmented by *Datura* or some other drug; he thinks zombies may be fed a *Datura* paste that accentuates their disorientation. Still, he puts the material basis of zombification in perspective: "Tetrodotoxin and *Datura* are only templates on which cultural forces and beliefs may be amplified a thousand times."

Davis has not been able to discover how prevalent zombification is in Haiti. "How many zombies there are is not the question," he says. He compares it to capital punishment in the United States: "It doesn't really matter how many people are electrocuted, as long as it's a possibility." As a sanction in Haiti, the fear is not of zombies, it's of becoming one.

Davis attributes his success in solving the zombie mystery to his approach. He went to Haiti with an open mind and immersed himself in the culture. "My intuition unhindered by biases served me well," he says. "I didn't make any judgments." He combined this attitude with what he had learned earlier from his experiences in the Amazon. "Schultes's lesson is to go and live with the Indians as an Indian." Davis was able to participate in the vodoun society to a surprising degree, eventually even penetrating one of the Bizango societies and dancing in their nocturnal rituals. His appreciation of Haitian culture is apparent. "Everybody asks me how did a white person get this information? To ask the question means you don't understand Haitians—they don't judge you by the color of your skin."

As a result of the exotic nature of his discoveries, Davis has gained a certain notoriety. He plans to complete his dissertation soon, but he has already finished writing a popular account of his adventures. To be published in January by Simon and Schuster, it is called *The Serpent and the Rainbow,* after the serpent that vodounists believe created the earth and the rainbow spirit it married. Film rights have already been optioned; in October Davis went back to Haiti with a screenwriter. But Davis takes the notoriety in stride. "All this attention is funny," he says. "For years, not just me, but all Schultes's students have had extraordinary adventures in the line of work. The adventure is not the end point, it's just along the way of getting the data. At the Botanical Museum, Schultes created a world unto itself. We didn't think we were doing anything above the ordinary. I still don't think we do. And you know," he adds, "the Haiti episode does not begin to compare to what others have accomplished—particularly Schultes himself."

Assess Your Progress

1. What were the circumstances of Clairvius Narcisse's disappearance for eighteen years and what makes this case of "zombification" unique?

2. Describe and explain the cohesion of Haitian society.

3. Describe voodoo and its place in Haitian society.

4. How is the poison used and what are its effects on the victim? Why does it come with no guarantee?

5. What is the one ingredient which turns up in all of the formulas and where does it come from? How and why is this poison used in Japan? What effects have been observed there?

6. What is the "cultural answer" to the zombie mystery? Describe the secret societies and their importance in maintaining order.

7. Why is zombification seen as a punishment more severe than death?

8. How do the priests continue their control over the individual after the effects of tetrodotoxin have worn off, according to Davis?

9. Is it important that there be a lot of zombies in Haiti for social control to be achieved?

GINO DEL GUERCIO is a national science writer for United Press International.

From *Harvard Magazine,* January/February 1986, pp. 31–37. Copyright © 1986 by Gino Del Guercio. Reprinted by permission of the author.

Body Ritual among the Nacirema

HORACE MINER

The anthropologist has become so familiar with the diversity of ways in which different peoples behave in similar situations that he is not apt to be surprised by even the most exotic customs. In fact, if all of the logically possible combinations of behavior have not been found somewhere in the world, he is apt to suspect that they must be present in some yet undescribed tribe. This point has, in fact, been expressed with respect to clan organization by Murdock (1949: 71). In this light, the magical beliefs and practices of the Nacirema present such unusual aspects that it seems desirable to describe them as an example of the extremes to which human behavior can go.

Professor Linton first brought the ritual of the Nacirema to the attention of anthropologists twenty years ago (1936: 326), but the culture of this people is still very poorly understood. They are a North American group living in the territory between the Canadian Cree, the Yaqui and Tarahumare of Mexico, and the Carib and Arawak of the Antilles. Little is known of their origin, though tradition states that they came from the east. According to Nacirema mythology, their nation was originated by a culture hero, Notgnishaw, who is otherwise known for two great feats of strength—the throwing of a piece of wampum across the river Pa-To-Mac and the chopping down of a cherry tree in which the Spirit of Truth resided.

Nacirema culture is characterized by a highly developed market economy which has evolved in a rich natural habitat. While much of the people's time is devoted to economic pursuits, a large part of the fruits of these labors and a considerable portion of the day are spent in ritual activity. The focus of this activity is the human body, the appearance and health of which loom as a dominant concern in the ethos of the people. While such a concern is certainly not unusual, its ceremonial aspects and associated philosophy are unique.

The fundamental belief underlying the whole system appears to be that the human body is ugly and that its natural tendency is to debility and disease. Incarcerated in such a body, man's only hope is to avert these characteristics through the use of the powerful influences of ritual and ceremony. Every household has one or more shrines devoted to this purpose. The more powerful individuals in the society have several shrines in their houses and, in fact, the opulence of a house is often referred to in terms of the number of such ritual centers it possesses. Most houses are of wattle and daub construction, but the shrine rooms of the more wealthy are walled with stone. Poorer families imitate the rich by applying pottery plaques to their shrine walls.

While each family has at least one such shrine, the rituals associated with it are not family ceremonies but are private and secret. The rites are normally only discussed with children, and then only during the period when they are being initiated into these mysteries. I was able, however, to establish sufficient rapport with the natives to examine these shrines and to have the rituals described to me.

The focal point of the shrine is a box or chest which is built into the wall. In this chest are kept the many charms and magical potions without which no native believes he could live. These preparations are secured from a variety of specialized practitioners. The most powerful of these are the medicine men, whose assistance must be rewarded with substantial gifts. However, the medicine men do not provide the curative potions for their clients, but decide what the ingredients should be and then write them down in an ancient and secret language. This writing is understood only by the medicine men and by the herbalists who, for another gift, provide the required charm.

The charm is not disposed of after it has served its purpose, but is placed in the charm-box of the household shrine. As these magical materials are specific for certain ills, and the real or imagined maladies of the people are many, the charm-box is usually full to overflowing. The magical packets are so numerous that people forget what their purposes were and fear to use them again. While the natives are very vague on this point, we can only assume that the idea in retaining all the old magical materials is that their presence in the charm-box, before which the body rituals are conducted, will in some way protect the worshipper.

Beneath the charm-box is a small font. Each day every member of the family, in succession, enters the shrine room, bows his head before the charm-box, mingles different sorts of holy water in the font, and proceeds with a brief rite of ablution. The holy waters are secured from the Water Temple of the community, where the priests conduct elaborate ceremonies to make the liquid ritually pure.

In the hierarchy of magical practitioners, and below the medicine men in prestige, are specialists whose designation is best translated "holy-mouth-men." The Nacirema have an almost pathological horror and fascination with the mouth, the condition of which is believed to have a supernatural influence on all social relationships. Were it not for the rituals of the mouth, they believe that their teeth would fall out, their gums bleed, their jaws shrink, their friends desert them, and their lovers reject them. (They also believe that a strong relationship exists between oral and moral characteristics. For example, there is a ritual ablution of the mouth for children which is supposed to improve their moral fiber.)

The daily body ritual performed by everyone includes a mouth-rite. Despite the fact that these people are so punctilious about care of the mouth, this rite involves a practice which strikes the uninitiated stranger as revolting. It was reported to me that the ritual consists of inserting a small bundle of hog hairs into the mouth, along with certain magical powders, and then moving the bundle in a highly formalized series of gestures.

In addition to the private mouth-rite, the people seek out a holy-mouth-man once or twice a year. These practitioners have an impressive set of paraphernalia, consisting of a variety of augers, awls, probes, and prods. The use of these objects in the exorcism of the evils of the mouth involves almost unbelievable ritual torture of the client. The holy-mouth-man opens the client's mouth and, using the above mentioned tools, enlarges any holes which decay may have created in the teeth. Magical materials are put into these holes. If there are no naturally occurring holes in the teeth, large sections of one or more teeth are gouged out so that the supernatural substance can be applied. In the client's view, the purpose of these ministrations is to arrest decay and to draw friends. The extremely sacred and traditional character of the rite is evident in the fact that the natives return to the holy-mouth-men year after year, despite the fact that their teeth continue to decay.

It is to be hoped that, when a thorough study of the Nacirema is made, there will be a careful inquiry into the personality structure of these people. One has but to watch the gleam in the eye of a holy-mouth-man, as he jabs an awl into an exposed nerve, to suspect that a certain amount of sadism is involved. If this can be established, a very interesting pattern emerges, for most of the population shows definite masochistic tendencies. It was to these that Professor Linton referred in discussing a distinctive part of the daily body ritual which is performed only by men. This part of the rite involves scraping and lacerating the surface of the face with a sharp instrument. Special women's rites are performed only four times during each lunar month, but what they lack in frequency is made up in barbarity. As part of this ceremony, women bake their heads in small ovens for about an hour. The theoretically interesting point is that what seems to be a preponderantly masochistic people have developed sadistic specialists.

The medicine men have an imposing temple, or *latipso,* in every community of any size. The more elaborate ceremonies required to treat very sick patients can only be performed at this temple. These ceremonies involve not only the thaumaturge but a permanent group of vestal maidens who move sedately about the temple chambers in distinctive costume and headdress.

The *latipso* ceremonies are so harsh that it is phenomenal that a fair proportion of the really sick natives who enter the temple ever recover. Small children whose indoctrination is still incomplete have been known to resist attempts to take them to the temple because "that is where you go to die." Despite this fact, sick adults are not only willing but eager to undergo the protracted ritual purification, if they can afford to do so. No matter how ill the supplicant or how grave the emergency, the guardians of many temples will not admit a client if he cannot give a rich gift to the custodian. Even after one has gained admission and survived the ceremonies, the guardians will not permit the neophyte to leave until he makes still another gift.

The supplicant entering the temple is first stripped of all his or her clothes. In every-day life the Nacirema avoids exposure of his body and its natural functions. Bathing and excretory acts are performed only in the secrecy of the household shrine, where they are ritualized as part of the body-rites. Psychological shock results from the fact that body secrecy is suddenly lost upon entry into the *latipso.* A man, whose own wife has never seen him in an excretory act, suddenly finds himself naked and assisted by a vestal maiden while he performs his natural functions into a sacred vessel. This sort of ceremonial treatment is necessitated by the fact that the excreta are used by a diviner to ascertain the course and nature of the client's sickness. Female clients, on the other hand, find their naked bodies are subjected to the scrutiny, manipulation, and prodding of the medicine men.

Few supplicants in the temple are well enough to do anything but lie on their hard beds. The daily ceremonies, like the rites of the holy-mouth-men, involve discomfort and torture. With ritual precision, the vestals awaken their miserable charges each dawn and roll them about on their beds of pain while performing ablutions, in the formal movements of which the maidens are highly trained. At other times they insert magic wands in the supplicant's mouth or force him to eat substances which are supposed to be healing. From time to time the medicine men come to their clients and jab magically treated needles into their flesh. The fact that these temple ceremonies may not cure, and may even kill the neophyte, in no way decreases the people's faith in the medicine men.

There remains one other kind of practitioner, known as a "listener." This witch-doctor has the power to exorcise the devils that lodge in the heads of people who have been bewitched. The Nacirema believe that parents bewitch their own children. Mothers are particularly suspected of putting a curse on children while teaching them the secret body rituals. The counter-magic of the witch-doctor is unusual in its lack of ritual. The patient simply tells the "listener" all his troubles and fears, beginning with the earliest difficulties he can remember. The memory displayed by the Nacirema in these exorcism sessions is truly remarkable. It is not uncommon for the patient to bemoan the rejection he felt upon being weaned as a babe, and a few individuals even see their troubles going back to the traumatic effects of their own birth.

In conclusion, mention must be made of certain practices which have their base in native esthetics but which depend upon the pervasive aversion to the natural body and its functions. There are ritual fasts to make fat people thin and ceremonial feasts to make thin people fat. Still other rites are used to make women's breasts large if they are small, and smaller if they are large. General dissatisfaction with breast shape is symbolized in the fact that the ideal form is virtually outside the range of human variation. A few women afflicted with almost inhuman hypermammary development are so idolized that they make a handsome living by simply going from village to village and permitting the natives to stare at them for a fee.

Reference has already been made to the fact that excretory functions are ritualized, routinized, and relegated to secrecy. Natural reproductive functions are similarly distorted. Intercourse is taboo as a topic and scheduled as an act. Efforts are made to avoid pregnancy by the use of magical materials or by limiting intercourse to certain phases of the moon. Conception is actually very infrequent. When pregnant, women dress so as to hide their condition. Parturition takes place in secret, without friends or relatives to assist, and the majority of women do not nurse their infants.

Our review of the ritual life of the Nacirema has certainly shown them to be a magic-ridden people. It is hard to understand how they have managed to exist so long under the burdens which they have imposed upon themselves. But even such exotic customs as these take on real meaning when they are viewed with the insight provided by Malinowski when he wrote (1948:70):

> Looking from far and above, from our high places of safety in the developed civilization, it is easy to see all the crudity and irrelevance of magic. But without its power

and guidance early man could not have mastered his practical difficulties as he has done, nor could man have advanced to the higher stages of civilization.

References

Linton, Ralph. 1936. *The Study of Man.* New York, D. Appleton-Century Co.

Malinowski, Bronislaw. 1948. *Magic, Science, and Religion.* Glencoe, The Free Press.

Murdock, George P. 1949. *Social Structure.* New York, The Macmillan Co.

Assess Your Progress

1. What is "Nacirema" spelled backwards? Where are they actually located on a map? Who are they, really?

2. Why do the customs of the Nacirema seem so bizarre when they are written about in anthropological style?

3. Having read the article, do you view American culture any differently than you did before? If so, how?

4. Has this article helped you to view other cultures differently? If so, how?

5. If this article has distorted the picture of American culture, how difficult is it for all of us, anthropologists included, to render objective descriptions of other cultures?

From *American Anthropologist*, by Horace Miner, June 1956, pp. 503–507.

Baseball Magic

GEORGE GMELCH

On each pitching day for the first three months of a winning season, Dennis Grossini, a pitcher on a Detroit Tiger farm team, arose from bed at exactly 10:00 A.M. At 1:00 P.M. he went to the nearest restaurant for two glasses of iced tea and a tuna fish sandwich. When he got to the ballpark at 3:00 P.M., he put on the sweatshirt and jock he wore during his last winning game; one hour before the game he chewed a wad of Beech-Nut chewing tobacco. After each pitch during the game he touched the letters on his uniform and straightened his cap after each ball. Before the start of each inning he replaced the pitcher's rosin bag next to the spot where it was the inning before. And after every inning in which he gave up a run, he washed his hands.

When I asked which part of his ritual was most important, he said, "You can't really tell what's most important so it all becomes important. I'd be afraid to change anything. As long as I'm winning, I do everything the same."

Trobriand Islanders, according to anthropologist Bronislaw Malinowski, felt the same way about their fishing magic. Trobrianders fished in two different settings: in the *inner lagoon* where fish were plentiful and there was little danger, and on the *open sea* where fishing was dangerous and yields varied widely. Malinowski found that magic was not used in lagoon fishing, where men could rely solely on their knowledge and skill. But when fishing on the open sea, Trobrianders used a great deal of magical ritual to ensure safety and increase their catch.

Baseball, America's national pastime, is an arena in which players behave remarkably like Malinowski's Trobriand fishermen. To professional ballplayers, baseball is more than just a game, it is an occupation. Since their livelihoods depend on how well they perform, many use magic in an attempt to control the chance that is built into baseball. There are three essential activities of the game—pitching, hitting, and fielding. In the first two, chance can play a surprisingly important role. The pitcher is the player least able to control the outcome of his efforts. He may feel great and have good stuff warming up in the bullpen and then get in the game and get clobbered. He may make a bad pitch and see the batter miss it for a strike or see it hit hard but right into the hands of a fielder for an out. Conversely, his best pitch may be blooped for a base hit. He may limit the opposing team to just a few hits yet lose the game, and he may give up many hits and win. And the good and bad luck don't always average out over the course of a season. For instance, this past season (2007) Matt Cain gave up fewer runs per game than his teammate Noah Lowry but only won 7 games while losing 16 while Lowry won 14 games and only lost 8. Both pitched for the same team—the San Francisco Giants—which meant they had the same fielders behind them. By chance, when Cain pitched the Giants scored few runs while his teammate Lowry enjoyed considerable run support. Regardless of how well a pitcher performs, the outcome of the game also depends upon the proficiency of his teammates, the ineptitude of the opposition, and luck.

Hitting, which many observers call the single most difficult task in the world of sports, is also full of uncertainty. Unless it's a home run, no matter how hard the batter hits the ball, fate determines whether it will go into a waiting glove or find a gap between the fielders. The uncertainty is compounded by the low success rate of hitting: the average hitter gets only one hit in every four trips to the plate, while the very best hitters average only one hit in every three trips. Fielding, which we will return to later, is the one part of baseball where chance does not play much of a role.

How does the risk and uncertainty in pitching and hitting affect players? How do they try to control the outcomes of their performance? These are questions that I first became interested in many years ago both as a ballplayer and as an anthropology student. I had devoted much of my youth to baseball, and played professionally as a first baseman in the Detroit Tiger organization in the 1960s. It was shortly after the end of one baseball season that I took an anthropology course called "Magic, Religion, and Witchcraft." As I listened to my professor describe the magical rituals of the Trobriand Islanders, it occurred to me that what these so-called "primitive" people did wasn't all that different from what my teammates and I did for luck and confidence at the ballpark.

Routines and Rituals

The most common way players attempt to reduce chance and their feelings of uncertainty is to develop a routine—a course of action which is regularly followed. Talking about the routines of ballplayers, Pittsburgh Pirates coach Rich Donnelly said:

> They're like trained animals. They come out here [ball-park] and everything has to be the same, they don't like anything that knocks them off their routine. Just look at the dugout and you'll see every guy sitting in the same spot every night. It's amazing, everybody in the same spot. And don't you dare take someone's seat. If a guy comes up from the minors and sits here, they'll say, 'Hey, Jim sits here, find another seat.' You watch the pitcher warm up and he'll do the same thing every time. . . You got a routine and you adhere to it and you don't want anybody knocking you off it.

Routines are comforting, they bring order into a world in which players have little control. The varied elements in routines can produce the tangible benefit of helping the player concentrate. All ballplayers know that it is difficult to think and hit at the same time, and that following a routine can keep them from thinking too much. But often what players do goes beyond mere routine. These actions become what anthropologists define as *ritual*—prescribed behaviors in which there is no empirical connection between the means (e.g., tapping home plate three times) and the desired end (e.g., getting a base hit). Because there is no real connection between the two, rituals are not rational. Sometimes they are quite irrational. Similar to rituals are the nonrational beliefs that form the basis of taboos and fetishes, which players also use to bring luck to their side. But first let's take a close look at rituals.

Baseball rituals are infinitely varied. Most are personal, and are performed by individuals rather than by a team or group. Most are done in a private and unemotional manner, in much the same way players apply pine tar and rosin to their bats to improve the grip. A ballplayer may ritualize any activity that he considers important or somehow linked to good performance. Recall the variety of things that Dennis Grossini does, from specific times for waking and eating to foods and dress. Many pitchers listen to the same song on their I-pods on the day they are scheduled to start. Pitcher Al Holland always played with two dollar bills in his back pocket. The Oriole's Glenn Davis used to chew the same gum every day during hitting streaks, saving it under his cap. Astros infielder Julio Gotay always played with a cheese sandwich in his back pocket (he had a big appetite, so there might also have been a measure of practicality here). Red Sox Wade Boggs ate chicken before every game during his career, and that was just one of many elements in his pre- and post game routine, which also included leaving his house for the ballpark at precisely the same time each day (1:47 for a night game), running wind sprints at 7:17 for a 7:35 start, and drawing a chai—the Hebrew symbol for life—upon entering the batter's box.

Many hitters go through a series of preparatory rituals before stepping into the batter's box. These include tugging on their caps, touching their uniform letters or medallions, crossing themselves, and swinging, tapping, or bouncing the bat on the plate a prescribed number of times. Consider the Dodger's Nomar Garciaparra. After each pitch he steps out of the batters box, kicks the dirt with each toe, adjusts his right batting glove, adjusts his left batting glove, and touches his helmet before getting back into the box. He insists that it is a routine, not superstition. "I'm just doing it to get everything tight. I like everything tight, that's all it is, really." Mike Hargrove, former Cleveland Indian first baseman, had so many time-consuming elements in his batting ritual that he was nicknamed "the human rain delay." Both players believe their batting rituals helped them regain their concentration after each pitch. But others wondered if the two had become prisoners of their elaborate superstitions.

Players who have too many or particularly bizarre rituals risk being labeled as flakes, and not just by teammates but by fans and the media as well. For example, ex-Mets pitcher Turk Wendell's eccentric rituals, which include chewing black licorice while pitching, only to spit it out, brush his teeth and reload the candy between innings, and wearing a necklace of teeth from animals he has killed, made him a cover story subject in the *New York Times Sunday Magazine.*

Baseball fans observe a lot of this ritual behavior, such as pitchers smoothing the dirt on the mound before each new batter and position players tagging a base when leaving and returning to the dugout between innings, never realizing its importance to the player. The one ritual many fans do recognize, largely because it's a favorite of TV cameramen, is the "rally cap"—players in the dugout folding their caps and wearing them bill up in hopes of sparking a rally.

Rituals grow out of exceptionally good performances. When a player does well, he seldom attributes his success to skill alone; he knows that his skills don't change much from day to day. So, then, what was different about today which can explain his three hits? He makes a correlation. That is, he attributes his success, in part, to an object, a food he ate, not having shaved, a new shirt he bought that day, or just about any behavior out of the ordinary. By repeating those behaviors, the player seeks to gain control over his performance, to bring more good luck. Outfielder John White explained how one of his rituals started:

> I was jogging out to centerfield after the national anthem when I picked up a scrap of paper. I got some good hits that night and I guess I decided that the paper had something to do with it. The next night I picked up a gum wrapper and had another good night at the plate . . . I've been picking up paper every night since.

When outfielder Ron Wright played for the Calgary Cannons he shaved his arms once a week. It all began two years before when after an injury he shaved his arm so it could be taped, and then hit three homers. Now he not only has one of the smoothest swings in the minor leagues, but two of the smoothest forearms. Wade Boggs' routine of eating chicken before every game began when he was a rookie in 1982 and noticed a correlation between multiple-hit games and poultry plates (his wife has 40 chicken recipes). One of Montreal Expo farmhand Mike Saccocio's rituals also concerned food: "I got three hits one night after eating at Long John Silver's. After that when we'd pull into town, my first question would be, "Do you have a Long John Silver's?" Unlike Boggs, Saccocio abandoned his ritual and looked for a new one when he stopped hitting well.

During one game New York Yankee manager Joe Torre stood on the dugout steps instead of sitting on the bench when his team was batting. The Yankees scored a few runs, so he decided to keep on doing it. As the Yankees won nine games in a row, Torre kept standing. Torre explained, "I have a little routine going now . . . As long as we score, I'll be doing the same thing."

When in a slump, most players make a deliberate effort to change their routines and rituals in an attempt to shake off their bad luck. One player tried taking different routes to the ballpark, another tried sitting in a different place in the dugout, another shaved his head, and several reported changing what they ate before the game. I had one manager who would rattle the bat bin when the team was not hitting well, as if the bats were in a stupor and could be aroused by a good shaking. Some of my teammates rubbed their hands along the handles of the bats protruding from the bat bin in hopes of picking up some luck from the bats of others. Diamondbacks left fielder Luis Gonzalez sometimes places his bats in the room where Baseball Chapel – a Sunday church service—is about to get underway. Gonzalez hopes his bats will get some benefit, though he doesn't usually attend the service himself.

Taboo

Taboos (the word comes from a Polynesian term meaning prohibition) are the opposite of rituals. These are things you shouldn't do. Breaking a taboo, players believe, leads to undesirable consequences or bad luck. Most players observe at least a few taboos, such as never stepping on the chalk foul lines. A few, like Nomar Garciaparra, leap over the entire base path. One teammate of mine would never watch a movie on a game day, despite our playing virtually every day from April to September. Another teammate refused to read anything before a game because he believed it weakened his batting eye.

Many taboos take place off the field, out of public view. On the day a pitcher is scheduled to start, he is likely to avoid activities he believes will sap his strength and detract from his effectiveness. On the day they are to start, some pitchers avoid shaving, eating certain foods and even having sex (this nostrum is probably based on an 18th century belief about preserving vital body fluids, but experts now agree there is no ill effect and there may actually be a small benefit).

Taboos usually grow out of exceptionally poor performances, which players attribute to a particular behavior. During my first season of pro ball I ate pancakes before a game in which I struck out three times. A few weeks later I had another terrible game, again after eating pancakes. The result was a pancake taboo: I never again ate pancakes during the season. (Conversely, Orioles pitcher Jim Palmer, after some success, insisted on eating pancakes before each of his starts).

While most taboos are idiosyncratic, there are a few that all ballplayers hold and that do not develop out of individual experience or misfortune. These form part of the culture of baseball, and are sometimes learned as early as Little League. Mentioning a no-hitter while one is in progress is a well-known example. The origins of such shared beliefs are lost in time, though some scholars have proposed theories. For example, the taboo against stepping on the chalk foul lines when running onto or off the field between innings, suggests National Baseball Hall of Fame research director Tim Wiles, may be rooted in the children's superstition, "step on a crack, break your mother's back."

Fetishes

Fetishes are charms, material objects believed to embody supernatural power that can aid or protect the owner. Good-luck charms are standard equipment for some ballplayers. These include a wide assortment of objects from coins, chains, and crucifixes to a favorite baseball hat. The fetishized object may be a new possession or something a player found that coincided with the start of a streak and which he holds responsible for his good fortune. While playing in the Pacific Coast League, Alan Foster forgot his baseball shoes on a road trip and borrowed a pair from a teammate. That night he pitched a no-hitter, which he attributed to the shoes. Afterwards he bought them from his teammate and they became a fetish. Expo farmhand Mark LaRosa's rock has a different origin and use:

I found it on the field in Elmira after I had gotten bombed. It's unusual, perfectly round, and it caught my attention. I keep it to remind me of how important it is to concentrate. When I am going well I look at the rock and remember to keep my focus. The rock reminds me of what can happen when I lose my concentration.

For one season Marge Schott, former owner of the Cincinnati Reds, insisted that her field manager rub her St. Bernard "Schotzie" for good luck before each game. When the Reds were on the road, Schott would sometimes send a bag of the dog's hair to the field manager's hotel room. Religious medallions, which many Latino players wear around their necks and sometimes touch before going to the plate or mound, are also fetishes, though tied to their Roman Catholicism. Also relating to their religion, some players some make the sign of the cross or bless themselves before every at bat (a few like Pudge Rodriguez do so before every pitch), and a few point or blow a kiss to the heavens after hitting a home run.

Some players regard certain uniform numbers as lucky. When Ricky Henderson came to the Blue Jays in 1993, he paid teammate Turner Ward $25,000 for the right to wear number 24. Don Sutton got off cheaper. When he joined the Dodgers he convinced teammate Bruce Boche to give up number 20 in exchange for a new set of golf clubs. Oddly enough, there is no consensus about the effect of wearing number 13. Some players shun it, while a few request it. When Jason Giambi arrived with the Oakland A's his favorite number 7 was already taken, so he settled for 16 (the two numbers add up to 7). When he signed with the Yankees, number 7 (Mickey Mantle's old number) was retired and 16 was taken, so he settled for 25 (again, the numbers add up to 7).

Number preferences emerge in different ways. A young player may request the number of a former star, sometimes hoping that it will bring him the same success. Or he may request a number he associates with good luck. Colorado Rockies' Larry Walker's fixation with the number 3 has become well known to baseball fans. Besides wearing 33, he takes three practice swings before stepping into the box, he showers from the third nozzle, sets his alarm for three minutes past the hour and he was wed on November 3 at 3:33 P.M.[1] Fans in ballparks all across America rise from their seats for the seventh-inning stretch before the home club comes to bat because the number 7 is lucky, although the specific origin of this tradition has been lost.[2]

Clothing, both the choice and the order in which it is put on, combine elements of both ritual and fetish. Some players put on the part of their uniform in a particular order. Expos farmhand Jim Austin always puts on his left sleeve, left pants leg, and left shoe before the right. Most players, however, single out one or two lucky articles or quirks of dress for ritual elaboration. After hitting two home runs in a game, for example, ex-Giant infielder Jim Davenport discovered that he had missed a buttonhole while dressing for the game. For the remainder of his career he left the same button undone. Phillies' Len Dykstra would discard his batting gloves if he failed to get a hit in a single at-bat. In a hitless game, he might go through four pair of gloves. For outfielder Brian Hunter the focus is shoes: "I have a pair of high tops and a pair of low tops. Whichever shoes don't get a hit that game, I switch to the other pair." At the time of our interview, he was struggling at the plate and switching shoes almost every day. For Birmingham Baron pitcher Bo Kennedy the arrangement of the different pairs of baseball shoes in his locker is critical:

> I tell the clubbies [clubhouse boys] when you hang stuff in my locker don't touch my shoes. If you bump them move them back. I want the Ponys in front, the turfs to the right, and I want them nice and neat with each pair touching each other . . . Everyone on the team knows not to mess with my shoes when I pitch.

During hitting or winning streaks players may wear the same clothes day after day. Once I changed sweatshirts midway through the game for seven consecutive nights to keep a hitting streak going. Clothing rituals, however, can become impractical. Catcher Matt Allen was wearing a long sleeve turtle neck shirt on a cool evening in the New York-Penn League when he had a three-hit game. "I kept wearing the shirt and had a good week," he explained. "Then the weather got hot as hell, 85 degrees and muggy, but I would not take that shirt off. I wore it for another ten days—catching—and people thought I was crazy." Former Phillies, Expos, Twins, and perhaps taking a ritual to the extreme, Leo Durocher, managing the Brooklyn Dodgers to a pennant in 1941, spent three and a half weeks in the same gray slacks, blue coat, and knitted blue tie. Losing streaks often produce the opposite effect, such as the Oakland A's players who went out and bought new street clothes after losing 14 in a row.

Former Oakland A's manager Art Howe often wouldn't wash his socks after the A's were victorious; and he would also write the line up card with the same pen, and tape the pregame radio show in the same place on the field. In the words of one veteran, "It all comes down to the philosophy of not messing with success—or deliberately messing with failure."

Baseball's superstitions, like most everything else, change over time. Many of the rituals and beliefs of early baseball are no longer observed. In the 1920s-30s sportswriters reported that a player who tripped en route to the field would often retrace his steps and carefully walk over the stumbling block for "insurance." A century ago players spent time on and off the field intently looking for items that would bring them luck. To find a hairpin on the street, for example, assured a batter of hitting safely in that day's game. A few managers were known to strategically place a hairpin on the ground where a slumping player would be sure to find it. Today few women wear hairpins—a good reason the belief has died out. In the same era, Philadelphia Athletics manager Connie Mack hoped to ward off bad luck by employing a hunchback as a mascot. Hall of Famer Ty Cobb took on a young black boy as a good luck charm, even taking him on the road during the 1908 season. It was a not uncommon then for players to rub the head of a black child for good luck.

To catch sight of a white horse or a wagon-load of barrels were also good omens. In 1904 the manager of the New

York Giants, John McGraw, hired a driver with a team of white horses to drive past the Polo Grounds around the time his players were arriving at the ballpark. He knew that if his players saw white horses, they would have more confidence and that could only help them during the game. Belief in the power of white horses survived in a few backwaters until the 1960s. A gray-haired manager of a team I played for in Drummondville, Quebec, would drive around the countryside before important games and during the playoffs looking for a white horse. When he was successful, he would announce it to everyone in the clubhouse.

One belief that appears to have died out recently is a taboo about crossed bats. Several of my Latino teammates in the 1960s took it seriously. I can still recall one Dominican player becoming agitated when another player tossed a bat from the batting cage and it landed on top of his bat. He believed that the top bat might steal hits from the lower one. In his view, bats contained a finite number of hits. It was once commonly believed that when the hits in a bat were used up no amount of good hitting would produce any more. Hall of Famer Honus Wagner believed each bat contained only 100 hits. Regardless of the quality of the bat, he would discard it after its 100th hit. This belief would have little relevance today, in the era of light bats with thin handles—so thin that the typical modern bat is lucky to survive a dozen hits without being broken. Other superstitions about bats do survive, however. Position players on the Class A Asheville Tourists would not let pitchers touch or swing their bats, not even to warm up. Poor-hitting players, as most pitchers are, were said to pollute or weaken the bats.

While the elements in many rituals have changed over time, the reliance of players on them has not. Moreover, that reliance seems fairly impervious to advances in education. Way back in the 1890s, in an article I found in the archives of the National Baseball Hall of Fame, one observer predicted that the current influx of better educated players into the game and the "gradual weeding out of bummers and thugs" would raise the intellectual standard of the game and reduce baseball's rampant superstitions. It didn't. I first researched baseball magic in the late 1960s; when I returned 30 years later to study the culture of baseball, I expected to find less superstition. After all, I reasoned, unlike in my playing days most of today's players have had some college. I did find that today's players are less willing to admit to having superstitions, but when I asked instead about their "routines" they described rituals and fetishes little different from my teammates in the 60s.

Uncertainty and Magic

The best evidence that players turn to rituals, taboos, and fetishes to control chance and uncertainty is found in their uneven application. They are associated mainly with pitching and hitting—the activities with the highest degree of chance—and not fielding. I met only one player who had any ritual in connection with fielding, and he was an error-prone shortstop. Unlike hitting and pitching, a fielder has almost complete control over the outcome of his performance. Once a ball has been hit in his direction, no one can intervene and ruin his chances of catching it for an out (except in the unlikely event of two fielders colliding). Compared with the pitcher or the hitter, the fielder has little to worry about. He knows that in better than 9.7 times out of 10 he will execute his task flawlessly. With odds like that there is little need for ritual.

Clearly, the rituals of American ballplayers are not unlike those of the Trobriand Islanders studied by Malinowski many years ago.[3] In professional baseball, fielding is the equivalent of the inner lagoon while hitting and pitching are like the open sea.

While Malinowski helps us understand how ballplayers respond to chance and uncertainty, behavioral psychologist B. F. Skinner sheds light on why personal rituals get established in the first place.[4] With a few grains of seed Skinner could get pigeons to do anything he wanted. He merely waited for the desired behavior (e.g. pecking) and then rewarded it with some food. Skinner then decided to see what would happen if pigeons were rewarded with food pellets regularly, every fifteen seconds, regardless of what they did. He found that the birds associate the arrival of the food with a particular action, such as tucking their head under a wing or walking in clockwise circles. About ten seconds after the arrival of the last pellet, a bird would begin doing whatever it associated with getting the food and keep doing it until the next pellet arrived. In short, the pigeons behaved as if their actions made the food appear. They learned to associate particular behaviors with the reward of being given seed.

Ballplayers also associate a reward—successful performance—with prior behavior. If a player touches his crucifix and then gets a hit, he may decide the gesture was responsible for his good fortune and touch his crucifix the next time he comes to the plate. Unlike pigeons, however, most ballplayers are quicker to change their rituals once they no longer seem to work. Skinner found that once a pigeon associated one of its actions with the arrival of food or water, only sporadic rewards were necessary to keep the ritual going. One pigeon, believing that hopping from side to side brought pellets into its feeding cup, hopped ten thousand times without a pellet before finally giving up. But, then, Wade Boggs ate chicken before every game, through slumps and good times, for seventeen years.

Obviously the rituals and superstitions of baseball do not make a pitch travel faster or a batted ball find the gaps between the fielders, nor do the Trobriand rituals calm the seas or bring fish. What both do, however, is give their practitioners a sense of control, and with that added confidence. And we all know how important that is. If you really believe eating chicken or hopping over the foul lines will make you a better hitter, it probably will.

References

Gmelch, G. *Inside Pitch: Life in Professional Baseball* (Smithsonian Institution Press, 2001).

Malinowski, B. *Magic, Science and Religion and Other Essays* (Glencoe, Ill., 1948).

Skinner, B.F. *Behavior of Organisms: An Experimental Analysis* (D. Appleton-Century Co., 1938).

Skinner, B.F. *Science and Human Behavior* (New York: Macmillan, 1953).

Torrez, D. *High Inside: Memoirs of a Baseball Wife* (New York: G.P. Putnam's Sons, 1983.)

Notes

1. *Sports Illustrated . . .* , 48
2. Allen, *The Superstitions of Baseball Players,* 104.
3. Malinowski, B., *Magic, Science and Religion and Other Essays*
4. Skinner, B.F., *Behavior of Organisms: An Experimental Analysis*

Assess Your Progress

1. Describe the two forms of fishing among the Trobriand Islanders and explain why magic is associated with one and not the other.

2. How does the author describe the importance of baseball to baseball players and the use of magic in baseball?

3. When do people resort to the use of magic? Are rituals of magic common in technologically advanced societies as well as in simple societies? What is the purpose of magic? In what sense is it irrational? In what sense is it rational?

4. What are the three essential activities in baseball? With which are magic and ritual associated and why?

5. Which player is least able to control the outcome of the game and why?

6. Why is hitting full of risk and uncertainty? Why do batters suffer from the fear of being hit by a pitch?

7. How does the author describe and explain the certainty of fielding? Is there magic associated with it?

8. What is the most common form of magic in professional baseball? How is it performed? Why is such ritual "infinitely varied?"

9. Out of what do rituals usually grow? Why wouldn't a player attribute success to skills alone?

10. What is meant by "taboo?" Out of what do taboos grow?

11. What are fetishes and charms? How do ordinary objects acquire power? What parallel does the author see during World War II?

12. Why do pitchers perform rituals less frequently? Are the rituals just as important? Why are such rituals more complex?

13. Can uniform numbers have significance? Is there a consensus about the number thirteen? What is "imitative magic" and how is it relevant?

14. When taboos are not personal, how are they learned? Describe the "no-hitter" example.

15. Describe B.F. Skinner's research on how specific rituals and taboos get established and how this is related to baseball magic.

16. Are magical practices a waste of time? Explain.

UNIT 7

Sociocultural Change

Unit Selections

32. **Why Can't People Feed Themselves?,** Frances Moore Lappé and Joseph Collins
33. **The Tractor Invasion,** Laura Graham
34. **Yanomamo,** Leslie E. Sponsel
35. **The Arrow of Disease,** Jared Diamond
36. **The Americanization of Mental Illness,** Ethan Watters
37. **The Price of Progress,** John Bodley
38. **Seeing Conservation through the Global Lens,** Jim Igoe
39. **Der Indianer,** Noemi Lopinto
40. **What Native Peoples Deserve,** Roger Sandall
41. **Being Indigenous in the 21st Century,** Wilma Mankiller

Learning Outcomes

After reading this unit you should be able to:

- Define a subsistence system and discuss the effects of colonialism on former subsistence-oriented socioeconomic systems.

- Explain how the production of cash crops inevitably leads to class distinctions and poverty.

- Determine what ethical obligations industrial societies have toward human rights and the cultural diversity of traditional communities.

- Explain how globalization is undermining local conceptions of self and modes of healing.

- Explain why so many indigenous people look upon conservation with disdain.

- Decide whether the German "hobbyist" movement honors Native Americans by paying homage to them or whether it is demeaning them.

- Determine if wealth and power is distributed fairly across the world.

- Describe what your nation's policy should be toward genocidal practices in other countries.

- Show how exploitation of indigenous people has persisted in Africa even after political independence.

- Discuss if it is possible for the world's indigenous people to make their way into the modern world without losing sight of who they are.

Student Website

www.mhhe.com/cls

Internet References

Association for Political and Legal Anthropology
www.aaanet.org/apla/index.htm

Human Rights and Humanitarian Assistance
www.etown.edu/vl/humrts.html

The Indigenous Rights Movement in the Pacific
www.inmotionmagazine.com/pacific.html

Murray Research Center
www.radcliffe.edu/murray_redirect/index.php

RomNews Network—Online
www.romnews.com/community/index.php

WWW Virtual Library: Indigenous Studies
www.cwis.org/wwwvl/indig-vl.html

The origins of academic anthropology lie in the colonial and imperial ventures of the past five hundred years. During this period, many people of the world were brought into a relationship with Europe and the United States that was usually exploitative and often socially and culturally disruptive. For over a century, anthropologists have witnessed this process, and the transformations that have taken place in those social and cultural systems brought under the umbrella of a world economic order. Early anthropological studies—even those widely regarded as pure research—directly or indirectly served colonial interests. Many anthropologists certainly believed that they were extending the benefits of Western technology and society, while preserving the cultural rights of those people whom they studied. But representatives of poor nations challenge this view, and are far less generous in describing the past role of the anthropologist. Most contemporary anthropologists, however, have a deep moral commitment to defending the legal, political, and economic rights of the people with whom they work.

When anthropologists discuss social change, they usually mean the change brought about in pre-industrial societies through longstanding interaction with the nation-states of the industrialized world. In early anthropology, contact between the West and the remainder of the world was characterized by the terms "acculturation" and "culture contact." These terms were used to describe the diffusion of cultural traits between the developed and the less-developed countries. Often this was analyzed as a one-way process, in which cultures of the less developed world were seen, for better or worse, as receptacles for Western cultural traits. Nowadays, many anthropologists believe that the diffusion of cultural traits across social, political, and economic boundaries was emphasized at the expense of the real issues of dominance, subordination, and dependence that characterized the colonial experience. Just as important, many anthropologists recognize that the present-day forms of cultural, economic, and political interaction between the developed and the so-called underdeveloped world are best characterized as neocolonial. Most of the authors represented in this unit take the perspective that anthropology should be critical as well as descriptive. They raise questions about cultural contact and subsequent economic and social disruption.

In keeping with the notion that the negative impact of the West on traditional cultures began with colonial domination, this unit opens with "Why Can't People Feed Themselves?," "The Tractor Invasion," and "Yanomamo." Continuing with "The Arrow of Disease," "The Americanization of Mental Illness," and "The Price of Progress," we see that "progress" for the West has often meant poverty, hunger, disease, and death for traditional peoples.

None of this is to say that indigenous peoples can or even should be left entirely alone to live in isolation from the rest of the world. A much more sensible, as well as more practical, approach

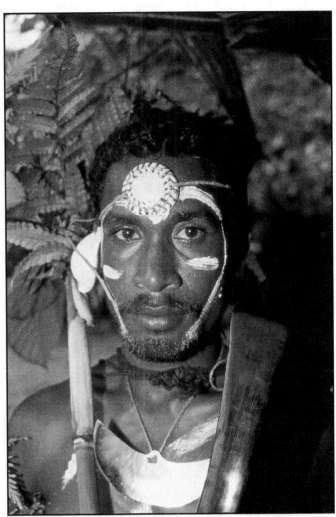

© The McGraw-Hill Companies, Inc./Barry Barker, photographer

would involve some degree of self determination (as discussed in "What Native Peoples Deserve" and "Being Indigenous in the 21st Century") and considerably more respect for their cultures (see "Der Indianer").

Of course, traditional peoples are not the only losers in the process of cultural destruction. In "Seeing Conservation through the Global Lens," we learn that the more we deprive the traditional stewards (the Indigenous peoples) of their land, the greater the loss in overall biodiversity. All of humanity stands to suffer, as a vast store of human knowledge—embodied in tribal subsistence practices, language, medicine, and folklore—is obliterated, in a manner not unlike the burning of the library of Alexandria 1,600 years ago. We can only hope that it is not too late to save what is left.

Why Can't People Feed Themselves?

FRANCES MOORE LAPPÉ AND JOSEPH COLLINS

Question: You have said that the hunger problem is not the result of overpopulation. But you have not yet answered the most basic and simple question of all: Why can't people feed themselves? As Senator Daniel P. Moynihan put it bluntly, when addressing himself to the Third World, "Food growing is the first thing you do when you come down out of the trees. The question is, how come the United States can grow food and you can't?"

Our Response: In the very first speech I, Frances, ever gave after writing *Diet for a Small Planet,* I tried to take my audience along the path that I had taken in attempting to understand why so many are hungry in this world. Here is the gist of that talk that was, in truth, a turning point in my life:

When I started I saw a world divided into two parts: a *minority* of nations that had "taken off" through their agricultural and industrial revolutions to reach a level of unparalleled material abundance and a *majority* that remained behind in a primitive, traditional, undeveloped state. This lagging behind of the majority of the world's peoples must be due, I thought, to some internal deficiency or even to several of them. It seemed obvious that the underdeveloped countries must be deficient in natural resources—particularly good land and climate—and in cultural development, including modern attitudes conducive to work and progress.

But when looking for the historical roots of the predicament, I learned that my picture of these two separate worlds was quite false. My two separate worlds were really just different sides of the same coin. One side was on top largely because the other side was on the bottom. Could this be true? How were these separate worlds related?

Colonialism appeared to me to be the link. Colonialism destroyed the cultural patterns of production and exchange by which traditional societies in "underdeveloped" countries previously had met the needs of the people. Many precolonial social structures, while dominated by exploitative elites, had evolved a system of mutual obligations among the classes that helped to ensure at least a minimal diet for all. A friend of mine once said: "Precolonial village existence in subsistence agriculture was a limited life indeed, but it's certainly not Calcutta." The

misery of starvation in the streets of Calcutta can only be understood as the end-point of a long historical process—one that has destroyed a traditional social system.

"Underdeveloped," instead of being an adjective that evokes the picture of a static society, became for me a verb (to "underdevelop") meaning the *process* by which the minority of the world has transformed—indeed often robbed and degraded—the majority.

That was in 1972. I clearly recall my thoughts on my return home. I had stated publicly for the first time a world view that had taken me years of study to grasp. The sense of relief was tremendous. For me the breakthrough lay in realizing that today's "hunger crisis" could not be described in static, descriptive terms. Hunger and underdevelopment must always be thought of as a *process.*

To answer the question "why hunger?" it is counterproductive to simply *describe* the conditions in an underdeveloped country today. For these conditions, whether they be the degree of malnutrition, the levels of agricultural production, or even the country's ecological endowment, are not static factors—they are not "givens." They are rather the *results* of an ongoing historical process. As we dug ever deeper into that historical process for the preparation of this book, we began to discover the existence of scarcity-creating mechanisms that we had only vaguely intuited before.

We have gotten great satisfaction from probing into the past since we recognized it is the only way to approach a solution to hunger today. We have come to see that it is the *force* creating the condition, not the condition itself, that must be the target of change. Otherwise we might change the condition today, only to find tomorrow that it has been recreated—with a vengeance.

Asking the question "Why can't people feed themselves?" carries a sense of bewilderment that there are so many people in the world not able to feed themselves adequately. What astonished us, however, is that there are not *more* people in the world who are hungry—considering the weight of the centuries of effort by the few to undermine the capacity of the majority to feed themselves. No, we are not crying "conspiracy!" If these forces were entirely conspiratorial, they would be easier to detect and many more people would by now have risen up to resist. We are talking about something more subtle and insidious; a heritage of a colonial order in which people with the advantage of considerable power sought their own self-interest, often arrogantly believing they were acting in the interest of the people whose lives they were destroying.

The Colonial Mind

The colonizer viewed agriculture in the subjugated lands as primitive and backward. Yet such a view contrasts sharply with documents from the colonial period now coming to light. For example, A. J. Voelker, a British agricultural scientist assigned to India during the 1890s wrote:

> Nowhere would one find better instances of keeping land scrupulously clean from weeds, of ingenuity in device of water-raising appliances, of knowledge of soils and their capabilities, as well as of the exact time to sow and reap, as one would find in Indian agriculture. It is wonderful too, how much is known of rotation, the system of "mixed crops" and of fallowing. . . . I, at least, have never seen a more perfect picture of cultivation.[1]

None the less, viewing the agriculture of the vanquished as primitive and backward reinforced the colonizer's rationale for destroying it. To the colonizers of Africa, Asia, and Latin America, agriculture became merely a means to extract wealth—much as gold from a mine—on behalf of the colonizing power. Agriculture was no longer seen as a source of food for the local population, nor even as their livelihood. Indeed the English economist John Stuart Mill reasoned that colonies should not be thought of as civilizations or countries at all but as "agricultural establishments" whose sole purpose was to supply the "larger community to which they belong." The colonized society's agriculture was only a subdivision of the agricultural system of the metropolitan country. As Mill acknowledged, "Our West India colonies, for example, cannot be regarded as countries. . . . The West Indies are the place where England *finds it convenient* to carry on the production of sugar, coffee and a few other tropical commodities."[2]

Prior to European intervention, Africans practiced a diversified agriculture that included the introduction of new food plants of Asian or American origin. But colonial rule simplified this diversified production to single cash crops—often to the exclusion of staple foods—and in the process sowed the seeds of famine.[3] Rice farming once had been common in Gambia. But with colonial rule so much of the best land was taken over by peanuts (grown for the European market) that rice had to be imported to counter the mounting prospect of famine. Northern Ghana, once famous for its yams and other foodstuffs, was forced to concentrate solely on cocoa. Most of the Gold Coast thus became dependent on cocoa. Liberia was turned into a virtual plantation subsidiary of Firestone Tire and Rubber. Food production in Dahomey and southeast Nigeria was all but abandoned in favor of palm oil; Tanganyika (now Tanzania) was forced to focus on sisal and Uganda on cotton.

The same happened in Indochina. About the time of the American Civil War the French decided that the Mekong Delta in Vietnam would be ideal for producing rice for export. Through a production system based on enriching the large landowners,

Vietnam became the world's third largest exporter of rice by the 1930s; yet many landless Vietnamese went hungry.[4]

Rather than helping the peasants, colonialism's public works programs only reinforced export crop production. British irrigation works built in nineteenth-century India did help increase production, but the expansion was for spring export crops at the expense of millets and legumes grown in the fall as the basic local food crops.

Because people living on the land do not easily go against their natural and adaptive drive to grow food for themselves, colonial powers had to force the production of cash crops. The first strategy was to use physical or economic force to get the local population to grow cash crops instead of food on their own plots and then turn them over to the colonizer for export. The second strategy was the direct takeover of the land by large-scale plantations growing crops for export.

Forced Peasant Production

As Walter Rodney recounts in *How Europe Underdeveloped Africa,* cash crops were often grown literally under threat of guns and whips.[5] One visitor to the Sahel commented in 1928: "Cotton is an artificial crop and one the value of which is not entirely clear to the natives . . . " He wryly noted the "enforced enthusiasm with which the natives . . . have thrown themselves into . . . planting cotton."[6] The forced cultivation of cotton was a major grievance leading to the Maji Maji wars in Tanzania (then Tanganyika) and behind the nationalist revolt in Angola as late as 1960.[7]

Although raw force was used, taxation was the preferred colonial technique to force Africans to grow cash crops. The colonial administrations simply levied taxes on cattle, land, houses, and even the people themselves. Since the tax had to be paid in the coin of the realm, the peasants had either to grow crops to sell or to work on the plantations or in the mines of the Europeans.[8] Taxation was both an effective tool to "stimulate" cash cropping and a source of revenue that the colonial bureaucracy needed to enforce the system. To expand their production of export crops to pay the mounting taxes, peasant producers were forced to neglect the farming of food crops. In 1830, the Dutch administration in Java made the peasants an offer they could not refuse; if they would grow government-owned export crops on one fifth of their land, the Dutch would remit their land taxes.[9] If they refused and thus could not pay the taxes, they lost their land.

Marketing boards emerged in Africa in the 1930s as another technique for getting the profit from cash crop production by native producers into the hands of the colonial government and international firms. Purchases by the marketing boards were well below the world market price. Peanuts bought by the boards from peasant cultivators in West Africa were sold in Britain for more than *seven times* what the peasants received.[10]

The marketing board concept was born with the "cocoa hold-up" in the Gold Coast in 1937. Small cocoa farmers refused to sell to the large cocoa concerns like United Africa Company (a subsidiary of the Anglo-Dutch firm, Unilever—which we know as Lever Brothers) and Cadbury until they got a higher price. When the British government stepped in and agreed to buy the cocoa directly in place of the big business concerns, the smallholders must have thought they had scored at least a minor victory. But had they really? The following year the British formally set up the West African Cocoa Control Board. Theoretically, its purpose was to pay the peasants a reasonable price for their crops. In practice, however, the board, as sole purchaser, was able to hold down the prices paid the peasants for their crops when the world prices were rising. Rodney sums up the real "victory":

> None of the benefits went to Africans, but rather to the British government itself and to the private companies. . . . Big companies like the United African Company and John Holt were given . . . quotas to fulfill on behalf of the boards. As agents of the government, they were no longer exposed to direct attack, and their profits were secure.[11]

These marketing boards, set up for most export crops, were actually controlled by the companies. The chairman of the Cocoa Board was none other than John Cadbury of Cadbury Brothers (ever had a Cadbury chocolate bar?) who was part of a buying pool exploiting West African cocoa farmers.

The marketing boards funneled part of the profits from the exploitation of peasant producers indirectly into the royal treasury. While the Cocoa Board sold to the British Food Ministry at low prices, the ministry upped the price for British manufacturers, thus netting a profit as high as 11 million pounds in some years.[12]

These marketing boards of Africa were only the institutionalized rendition of what is the essence of colonialism—the extraction of wealth. While profits continued to accrue to foreign interests and local elites, prices received by those actually growing the commodities remained low.

Plantations

A second approach was direct takeover of the land either by the colonizing government or by private foreign interests. Previously self-provisioning farmers were forced to cultivate the plantation fields through either enslavement or economic coercion.

After the conquest of the Kandyan Kingdom (in present day Sri Lanka), in 1815, the British designated all the vast central part of the island as crown land. When it was determined that coffee, a profitable export crop, could be grown there, the Kandyan lands were sold off to British investors and planters at a mere five shillings per acre, the government even defraying the cost of surveying and road building.[13]

Java is also a prime example of a colonial government seizing territory and then putting it into private foreign hands. In 1870, the Dutch declared all uncultivated land—called waste land—property of the state for lease to Dutch plantation enterprises. In addition, the Agrarian Land Law of 1870 authorized foreign companies to lease village-owned land. The peasants, in chronic need of ready cash for taxes and foreign consumer goods, were only too willing to lease their land to the foreign companies for very modest sums and under terms dictated by the firms. Where land was still held communally, the village

headman was tempted by high cash commissions offered by plantation companies. He would lease the village land even more cheaply than would the individual peasant or, as was frequently the case, sell out the entire village to the company.[14]

The introduction of the plantation meant the divorce of agriculture from nourishment, as the notion of food value was lost to the overriding claim of "market value" in international trade. Crops such as sugar, tobacco, and coffee were selected, not on the basis of how well they feed people, but for their high price value relative to their weight and bulk so that profit margins could be maintained even after the costs of shipping to Europe.

Suppressing Peasant Farming

The stagnation and impoverishment of the peasant food-producing sector was not the mere by-product of benign neglect, that is, the unintended consequence of an overemphasis on export production. Plantations—just like modern "agro-industrial complexes"—needed an abundant and readily available supply of low-wage agricultural workers. Colonial administrations thus devised a variety of tactics, all to undercut self-provisioning agriculture and thus make rural populations dependent on plantation wages. Government services and even the most minimal infrastructure (access to water, roads, seeds, credit, pest and disease control information, and so on) were systematically denied. Plantations usurped most of the good land, either making much of the rural population landless or pushing them onto marginal soils. (Yet the plantations have often held much of their land idle simply to prevent the peasants from using it—even to this day. Del Monte owns 57,000 acres of Guatemala but plants only 9000. The rest lies idle except for a few thousand head of grazing cattle.)[15]

In some cases a colonial administration would go even further to guarantee itself a labor supply. In at least twelve countries in the eastern and southern parts of Africa the exploitation of mineral wealth (gold, diamonds, and copper) and the establishment of cash-crop plantations demanded a continuous supply of low-cost labor. To assure this labor supply, colonial administrations simply expropriated the land of the African communities by violence and drove the people into small reserves.[16] With neither adequate land for their traditional slash-and-burn methods nor access to the means—tools, water, and fertilizer—to make continuous farming of such limited areas viable, the indigenous population could scarcely meet subsistence needs, much less produce surplus to sell in order to cover the colonial taxes. Hundreds of thousands of Africans were forced to become the cheap labor source so "needed" by the colonial plantations. Only by laboring on plantations and in the mines could they hope to pay the colonial taxes.

The tax scheme to produce reserves of cheap plantation and mining labor was particularly effective when the Great Depression hit and the bottom dropped out of cash crop economies. In 1929 the cotton market collapsed, leaving peasant cotton producers, such as those in Upper Volta, unable to pay their colonial taxes. More and more young people, in some years as many as 80,000, were thus forced to migrate to the Gold Coast to compete with each other for low-wage jobs on cocoa plantations.[17]

The forced migration of Africa's most able-bodied workers—stripping village food farming of needed hands—was a recurring feature of colonialism. As late as 1973 the Portuguese "exported" 400,000 Mozambican peasants to work in South Africa in exchange for gold deposited in the Lisbon treasury.

The many techniques of colonialism to undercut self-provisioning agriculture in order to ensure a cheap labor supply are no better illustrated than by the story of how, in the mid-nineteenth century, sugar plantation owners in British Guiana coped with the double blow of the emancipation of slaves and the crash in the world sugar market. The story is graphically recounted by Alan Adamson in *Sugar Without Slaves.*[18]

Would the ex-slaves be allowed to take over the plantation land and grow the food they needed? The planters, many ruined by the sugar slump, were determined they would not. The planter-dominated government devised several schemes for thwarting food self-sufficiency. The price of crown land was kept artificially high, and the purchase of land in parcels smaller than 100 acres was outlawed—two measures guaranteeing that newly organized ex-slave cooperatives could not hope to gain access to much land. The government also prohibited cultivation on as much as 400,000 acres—on the grounds of "uncertain property titles." Moreover, although many planters held part of their land out of sugar production due to the depressed world price, they would not allow any alternative production on them. They feared that once the ex-slaves started growing food it would be difficult to return them to sugar production when world market prices began to recover. In addition, the government taxed peasant production, then turned around and used the funds to subsidize the immigration of laborers from India and Malaysia to replace the freed slaves, thereby making sugar production again profitable for the planters. Finally, the government neglected the infrastructure for subsistence agriculture and denied credit for small farmers.

Perhaps the most insidious tactic to "lure" the peasant away from food production—and the one with profound historical consequences—was a policy of keeping the price of imported food low through the removal of tariffs and subsidies. The policy was double-edged: first, peasants were told they need not grow food because they could always buy it cheaply with their plantation wages; second, cheap food imports destroyed the market for domestic food and thereby impoverished local food producers.

Adamson relates how both the Governor of British Guiana and the Secretary for the Colonies Earl Grey favored low duties on imports in order to erode local food production and thereby release labor for the plantations. In 1851 the governor rushed through a reduction of the duty on cereals in order to "divert" labor to the sugar estates. As Adamson comments, "Without realizing it, he [the governor] had put his finger on the most mordant feature of monoculture: . . . its convulsive need to destroy any other sector of the economy which might compete for 'its' labor."[19]

Many colonial governments succeeded in establishing dependence on imported foodstuffs. In 1647 an observer in the West Indies wrote to Governor Winthrop of Massachusetts: "Men are so intent upon planting sugar that they had rather buy food at very dear rates than produce it by labour, so infinite is the profitt of sugar workes. . . ."[20] By 1770, the West Indies were importing most of the continental colonies' exports of dried fish, grain, beans, and vegetables. A dependence on imported food made the West Indian colonies vulnerable to any disruption in supply. This dependence on imported food stuffs spelled disaster when the thirteen continental colonies gained independence and food exports from the continent to the West Indies were interrupted. With no diversified food system to fall back on, 15,000 plantation workers died of famine between 1780 and 1787 in Jamaica alone.[21] The dependence of the West Indies on imported food persists to this day.

Suppressing Peasant Competition

We have talked about the techniques by which indigenous populations were forced to cultivate cash crops. In some countries with large plantations, however, colonial governments found it necessary to *prevent* peasants from independently growing cash crops not out of concern for their welfare, but so that they would not compete with colonial interests growing the same crop. For peasant farmers, given a modicum of opportunity, proved themselves capable of outproducing the large plantations not only in terms of output per unit of land but, more important, in terms of capital cost per unit produced.

In the Dutch East Indies (Indonesia and Dutch New Guinea) colonial policy in the middle of the nineteenth century forbade the sugar refineries to buy sugar cane from indigenous growers and imposed a discriminatory tax on rubber produced by native smallholders.[22] A recent unpublished United Nations study of agricultural development in Africa concluded that large-scale agricultural operations owned and controlled by foreign commercial interests (such as the rubber plantations of Liberia, the sisal estates of Tanganyika [Tanzania], and the coffee estates of Angola) only survived the competition of peasant producers because "the authorities actively supported them by suppressing indigenous rural development."[23]

The suppression of indigenous agricultural development served the interests of the colonizing powers in two ways. Not only did it prevent direct competition from more efficient native producers of the same crops, but it also guaranteed a labor force to work on the foreign-owned estates. Planters and foreign investors were not unaware that peasants who could survive economically by their own production would be under less pressure to sell their labor cheaply to the large estates.

The answer to the question, then, "Why can't people feed themselves?" must begin with an understanding of how colonialism actively prevented people from doing just that.

Colonialism

- forced peasants to replace food crops with cash crops that were then expropriated at very low rates;
- took over the best agricultural land for export crop plantations and then forced the most able-bodied workers to leave the village fields to work as slaves or for very low wages on plantations;

- encouraged a dependence on imported food;
- blocked native peasant cash crop production from competing with cash crops produced by settlers or foreign firms.

These are concrete examples of the development of underdevelopment that we should have perceived as such even as we read our history schoolbooks. Why didn't we? Somehow our schoolbooks always seemed to make the flow of history appear to have its own logic—as if it could not have been any other way. I, Frances, recall, in particular, a grade-school, social studies pamphlet on the idyllic life of Pedro, a nine-year-old boy on a coffee plantation in South America. The drawings of lush vegetation and "exotic" huts made his life seem romantic indeed. Wasn't it natural and proper that South America should have plantations to supply my mother and father with coffee? Isn't that the way it was *meant* to be?

Notes

1. Radha Sinha, *Food and Poverty* (New York: Holmes and Meier, 1976), p. 26.
2. John Stuart Mill, *Political Economy,* Book 3, Chapter 25 (emphasis added).
3. Peter Feldman and David Lawrence, "Social and Economic Implications of the Large-Scale Introduction of New Varieties of Foodgrains," Africa Report, preliminary draft (Geneva: UNRISD, 1975), pp. 107–108.
4. Edgar Owens, *The Right Side of History,* unpublished manuscript, 1976.
5. Walter Rodney, *How Europe Underdeveloped Africa* (London: Bogle-L'Ouverture Publications, 1972), pp. 171–172.
6. Ferdinand Ossendowski, *Slaves of the Sun* (New York: Dutton, 1928), p. 276.
7. Rodney, *How Europe Underdeveloped Africa,* pp. 171–172.
8. Ibid., p. 181.
9. Clifford Geertz, *Agricultural Involution* (Berkeley and Los Angeles: University of California Press, 1963), pp. 52–53.
10. Rodney, *How Europe Underdeveloped Africa,* p. 185.
11. Ibid., p. 184.
12. Ibid., p. 186.
13. George L. Beckford, *Persistent Poverty: Underdevelopment in Plantation Economies of the Third World* (New York: Oxford University Press, 1972), p. 99.
14. Ibid., p. 99, quoting from Erich Jacoby, *Agrarian Unrest in Southeast Asia* (New York: Asia Publishing House, 1961), p. 66.
15. Pat Flynn and Roger Burbach, North American Congress on Latin America, Berkely, California, recent investigation.
16. Feldman and Lawrence, "Social and Economic Implications," p. 103.
17. Special Sahelian Office Report, Food and Agriculture Organization, March 28, 1974, pp. 88–89.
18. Alan Adamson, *Sugar Without Slaves: The Political Economy of British Guiana, 1838–1904* (New Haven and London: Yale University Press, 1972).
19. Ibid., p. 41.
20. Eric Williams, *Capitalism and Slavery* (New York: Putnam, 1966), p. 110.
21. Ibid., p. 121.
22. Gunnar Myrdal, *Asian Drama,* vol. 1 (New York: Pantheon, 1966), pp. 448–449.
23. Feldman and Lawrence, "Social and Economic Implications," p. 189.

Assess Your Progress

1. In relation to hunger, what do the authors mean when they say that "it is the force creating the condition, not the condition itself that must be the target of change?"

2. How did colonizers view agriculture in the subjugated lands? How did they view their own agriculture?

3. What kind of agriculture was practiced prior to colonization? after colonization?

4. What were the two basic strategies to force cash crop production?

5. What were the functions of taxes? Marketing boards?

6. How does Java represent a prime example of how a colonial government seizes land and then puts it into foreign hands? What did the introduction of the plantation mean regarding nourishment?

7. What techniques have been used to actively force peasants off their land?

8. How did British Guiana cope with the "double blow of the emancipation of slaves and the crash in the world sugar market?"

9. Why do some countries prevent peasants from independently growing cash crops?

Frances Moore Lappé and **Dr. Joseph Collins** are founders and directors of the Institute for Food and Development Policy, located in San Francisco and New York.

The Tractor Invasion

For the Indigenous Peoples of the Cerrado, plowshares might as well be swords, as agribusiness increasingly turns their homelands into farmlands.

LAURA GRAHAM

It was evening in the Xavante community of Etéñhiritipa in central Brazil as the moon rose over the Serra do Roncador. We had just finished a refreshing bath in the river and were seated against the wall of a house facing the cleared red-earth plaza in the community's center (clearing the swath of vegetation around the houses and in the central plaza means there are no snakes to deal with near people's homes). Twilight settled over the thatched houses as the adolescent novitiates sang and danced a dreamed song around the semicircular ring of houses and the adult men gathered in the central plaza for their nightly men's council.

The rhythm of daily life felt almost the same as it did more than 25 years ago when, as a graduate student, I began my ethnographic studies of Xavante peoples among this group. The dramatic changes that are taking place in the central Brazilian plateau seemed far away, almost undetectable at a first glance inside the community. But changes there are, and they especially threaten the land rights of the Xavante people. I was in Etéñhiritipa with Cultural Survival Executive Director Ellen Lutz, who came to learn the challenges Xavante now face and to explore ways that Cultural Survival could support their efforts.

The Xavante live in the vast Brazilian savanna called the Cerrado, an area the size of the American Great Plains. A Ge-speaking people, they retreated from contact with national society in the mid-1800s and earned a reputation for fierceness and determined isolationism. Xavante groups did not begin to establish peaceful relationships with representatives of national society until 1946. Even then, some groups refused contact until the mid-1960s.

Fifty years after colonization, the Xavante continue many of their traditional cultural practices, and their spiritual and ceremonial lives are rich. They also face tremendous challenges. Their homeland is now just a 12-hour drive from Brasilia and lies in the heart of Brazil's new agricultural and economic engine. The nine small reserves that the government began carving out for the Xavante in the late 1970s today seem like islands in a sea of soy. And agribusiness has its sights set on even these small reserves where, in indigenous areas such as these, the rich and unique Cerrado ecosystem is still intact.

While large-scale agriculturalists and related corporations are reaping enormous profits from Mato Grosso's burgeoning soy industry and making plans for multimillion-dollar development projects, many Xavante don't have enough to eat, and those who live in the smallest of the Xavante areas can't find sufficient game or even palm fronds to construct their thatched homes. The health situation in Xavante areas is abysmal: infant mortality is high, well above the regional and national averages and close to that of Northeastern Brazil, the nation's poorest region. Xavante mortality rates are high because they are exposed to many infectious diseases and have poor health care; an epidemic of hypertension and diabetes is imminent.

The Xavante are one of many central Brazilian groups whose homelands and livelihoods have been severely affected over the last two decades by the proliferation of colossal agroindustry. In some areas it is soy; in others, sugarcane for biofuels; and in still others, fast-growing eucalyptus for firewood to process soy oil in factories.

"The Cerrado is a source of life to the Indigenous community," says Elcio, from the Terena village of Cachoeirinha. "It is very important to us, and we worry about the devastation of the Cerrado, especially in our region, where the farmers are cutting the forests down. The Cerrado has enormous biodiversity, and it sustains our lives, because our foods come from the Cerrado: it is where we hunt and fish, collect fruits and honey. Burning down the forests is also threatening the biodiversity of the Cerrado. The burnings are destroying the guavira, a delicious fruit that we eat and can also sell."

The Xavante are more fortunate than some because they live in legally protected reserves—even if those protections are frequently disregarded and the areas are small. Many other groups live on lands that have yet not been legally demarcated. For many, their claims have been languishing for decades in the drawers and filing cabinets of the government agency responsible for granting Indigenous Peoples legal title to their lands.

Ellen and I, along with our companions, Hiparidi Top'tiro, a Xavante leader from the Sangradouro Reserve, and activist Daniela Lima, made the trip from Brasilia to the Xavante areas in less than a day. Paved roads carried us to within about

40 miles of the Pimentel Barbosa reserve. This was a journey that in 1982 had taken me a minimum of three days (usually more), traveling in a sturdy four-wheel-drive truck over rough dirt roads and unstable bridges, often no more than two planks precariously set over logs. In the rainy season, when torrential downpours hammer the Cerrado, the road was frequently impassable, and washed-out bridges were common. On this trip, we made rapid time. Our small sedan wove in and out between heavily laden trucks that were barreling down the highway at speeds that made me nervous. These immense truck caravans were transporting agricultural produce, particularly soybeans, out of Mato Grosso, Brazil's largest soy-producing state, to ports and commercial centers where most of these crops would be exported, mainly to markets in Europe, China, and Japan.

Our journey took us past miles and miles of deforested Cerrado fields, much of it owned by large and powerful farming and ranching corporations. We passed huge grain elevators, silos, and storage facilities and billboards with transnational names: Cargill, Bunge, ADM, Maggi, Monsanto. Towns that I previously knew as small hamlets had mushroomed into sizeable cities; municipalities in this region are some of the fastest-growing cities in the nation.

The galloping, massive growth in the agroindustry is putting enormous pressure on the Xavante and other Indigenous groups. The prevailing attitude in the region is pro-development, pro-agribusiness. Anyone who takes an alternative position meets strong resentment and antagonism. This is especially true for Indigenous Peoples who, in defending their constitutionally granted rights to territory, clean environment, and the ability to live according to their traditional ways, are perceived as presenting obstacles to progress.

The Brazilian Cerrado extends across the vast central Brazilian Plateau, stretching over approximately 800,000 square miles, almost one third of the nation's land mass and spanning 12 states. Its total area is equivalent to the combined area of Spain, France, Germany, Italy, and England (or, if you prefer, three times the size of Texas). It is one of the world's most biologically diverse tropical savanna regions and the nation's second major biome, after the Amazon rainforest. Conservation International identifies it as a "Conservation Hotspot," one of "the richest and most threatened reservoirs of plant and animal life on Earth." The Cerrado houses the watersheds for three of South America's major river basins: the Amazon, Sao Francisco, and Paraná/Paraguai. As Xavante leader Cipassé Xavante says, "The fight to save the Cerrado isn't just for us, it is for all humanity." What happens in the Cerrado has broad human and planetary effects.

Soy agribusiness began to aggressively expand into Brazil's central western Cerrado in the late 1980s, when soy varieties that could tolerate the tropical climate became commercially available. This accelerating agricultural boom, together with huge related infrastructure development projects (road construction, hydroelectric dams, colossal hydroengineering projects to transform rivers into water highways), as well as illegal mining and timber extraction in Indigenous areas, is destroying the fragile Cerrado environment and having devastating effects on the region's Indigenous inhabitants.

Socially and culturally diverse Indigenous Peoples have lived in the Cerrado for centuries, but reliable demographic information on the current Indigenous populations does not exist. Brazil's central-west region alone (the states of Mato Grosso, Mato Grosso do Sul, Goiais, Tocantins) is home to some 53,000 Indigenous people who belong to 42 distinct ethnic groups. All of these groups are confronting serious challenges, and some are responding by building alliances with members of other Indigenous groups and other traditional peoples, and also with national and international organizations like Cultural Survival. In the face of formidable focs and challenges, they are asserting themselves to take control over processes that are influencing their lives.

The Rise of Colonization

During the 1960s and into the 1980s, the Brazilian government used large-scale colonization schemes and generous fiscal incentives to attract settlers and commercial cattle ranching from the south into remote Cerrado regions. As the frontier moved westward, there were increasing conflicts between settlers and Indigenous Peoples, and communities were devastated by new diseases, like measles, against which they had no immunity. In a pattern repeated over and over, government agents or missionaries used those problems to attract distressed Indigenous groups to specific locales—government posts or missions—where they received sanctuary and medical treatment. With a region's original inhabitants corralled into defined areas, the state then sold their lands, with titles certifying the land as "free of Indians."

One of the most egregious examples of purging Indigenous Peoples from their lands occurred in the Xavante area known as Maräwaitsede, located in the region of the Suya-Missú River near what is now the Xingu National Park. (The park is Brazil's "postcard" Indigenous Territory, an area of 108,000 square miles that is home to approximately 4,700 people Indigenous Peoples belonging to 14 distinct groups.) After a Säo Paulo-based rancher fraudulently purchased lands inhabited by Xavante, he flew an airplane over the area everyday and dropped food in a specific location. Eventually the Xavante relocated to the site to receive rations. The rancher then moved the group multiple times and finally settled it close to ranch headquarters, where he forced the Xavante to work for food, and subjected them to continuous harassment by the ranch's non-Indigenous employees. Conditions for Xavante deteriorated so severely that, in 1966, the owners—at that point the powerful Italian-based Olmetto group, whose corporate land holdings reached 6,000 square miles—in collaboration with Salesian missionaries, the government Indian agency, and the Brazilian Air Force, solved their "Indian problem" by airlifting the remaining Xavante some 250 miles away to the Salesian mission at Säo Marcos. Within two weeks after their arrival, more than 100 Xavante died of a measles epidemic.

In 1994, Xavante from this area finally won a long battle to recoup some of this land when the state demarcated the Maräwäitsede Indigenous Territory. But despite the ruling, ranchers who had moved onto the land refused to leave or allow the Xavante to move back to their territory. They even encouraged settlers to take their place and deforest large tracts. When, in 2004, a determined Xavante group attempted to enter their lands, they were prevented by armed gunmen. The refugees set up camp on the opposite side of the dirt highway (BR-158) and lived for 11 months in improvised shelters. Three babies died of pneumonia exacerbated by the incessant dust from camping alongside the road. When a team carrying out a study for the UN High Commissioner for Human Rights attempted to reach the area by road, ranchers burned bridges in an attempt to stop them. The team hired planes and reached the area by air. This area is still plagued by conflict, and powerful ranchers continue to challenge the Xavante's rights to this land in the courts.

Cattle ranchers continue to deforest huge areas of Cerrado lands for pasture around Indigenous areas as well as within them. Deforestation and the aggressive, intrusive grasses that ranchers plant for cattle severely disrupt the Cerrado flora and fauna, reducing game populations that are important sources of protein in Native peoples' diets. And because hunting is central to many important ceremonials, lack of game has forced many groups, such as the Parecí of western Mato Grosso, to abandon traditional activities that are fundamental to their social organization and culture.

Prior to Brazil's new constitution of 1988, state policy was directed toward assimilating Indigenous Peoples into the nation's social fabric and economy. In the Cerrado area, the government attempted to transform Indigenous Peoples into capitalist ranchers and commercial agriculturalists. For example, in the 1970s, when many Cerrado ranchers were turning to commercial rice cultivation for domestic markets, the National Indian Foundation (FUNAI) implemented colossal mechanized rice cultivation projects in Xavante areas. The state used these projects to justify the creation of their reserves. Instead of "wasting" this land on Indigenous Peoples, these areas (along with Indigenous labor) would contribute to the region's GNP just like other commercial ranches in the region. Many large-scale ranchers and agriculturalists oppose the creation or amplification of Indigenous reserves because, they argue, it removes potentially productive lands from development.

For Xavante, the rice projects were immensely destructive: they created massive technological dependency, exacerbated tensions within and across communities, and, since Xavante substituted rice for nutritious traditional foods, dramatically altered their diet. Malnutrition is now a serious problem, and new diseases are endemic, especially hypertension and diabetes, which are associated with excessive reliance on refined foods and the new sedentary lifestyle. The projects also provided opportunities for corrupt Indian agents to siphon monies in every type of financial transaction, from equipment repair to the sale of crops harvested from Xavante lands. Although these projects were eventually abandoned in the late 1980s, many of the problems they created persist.

1990s—The Soy Boom

Commercial agriculture in the central Brazilian Cerrado began with rice and some soy in the 1970s and exploded into a massive export-oriented agroindustry during the late 1980s and 1990s. Soybean cultivation is highly mechanized, capital intensive, and uses large amounts of chemical fertilizers, herbicides, and pesticides. Its explosion in the Cerrado coincided with increased global demand in the wake of the mad-cow scare, when Europeans turned to soy for high protein animal feed, and with the expansion of world markets for soy oil, especially in China and Japan. In 2000, Mato Grosso became the country's leading soy-producing state, and in 2004, Brazil displaced the United States as the world's leading soy-exporting nation. In Mato Grosso, the area dedicated to soy cultivation increased 81 percent in just three years, between 1991–1994. This area nearly doubled again by 2003, and estimates indicate that the state has the potential to plant 10 times that amount—an area almost the size of California.

The environmental and social consequences of this immense and rapid agricultural explosion are staggering, especially for the region's vulnerable Indigenous inhabitants, particularly those who do not have legal title to their land. Although Brazil's constitution guarantees Indigenous Peoples the right to permanently occupy lands they traditionally inhabited, the government has been lamentably slack in carrying out its obligation to identify and legally demarcate those lands. In many cases, large landholders and corporations tie up the land claims in lawsuits that can drag on for years and, in some cases, such as Serra Raposa do Sol in Roraima, for decades.

And, of course, while the cases are being decided (or not decided), the landholders and corporations can continue developing and profiting from Indigenous land. They build roads, fences, silos, warehouses, buildings, and sometimes even cities in areas that Indigenous Peoples claim. These "improvements" reduce the likelihood that the government will have sufficient political will or the ability to compensate developers for the cost of their investments, and this increases the likelihood that the state will concede to the more powerful party.

There are many cases, like the Xavante in Marãwaitsede who ended up camped on the roadside, in which farmers and ranchers refuse to leave Indigenous lands, even after they have received compensation. One notable case happened on the Ilha do Bananal, an island the size of New Jersey in the middle of the Araguaia River that is home to Karajá, Javaé, and Ava Canoeiro. Despite the ranchers being compensated for having to move, their cattle remain on the island degrading the environment and polluting the waters.

Indigenous groups that challenge powerful landholders are subjected to tremendous pressure. Sometimes they even become martyrs to their cause. In 2007 and 2008, three Xacriabá leaders were assassinated over land disputes. In Mato Grosso do Sul, where Guarani Kaiowa, Nândeva, and other Native communities are squeezed into tiny areas, 80 Indigenous people are imprisoned. Indigenous Peoples in this region suffer extreme social disorganization, and the incidence of suicide is disturbingly high. Eliso da Lopes is one such leader who, because of persecution from ranchers, has not seen his family in over a year. "We want our land returned so that we can plant and produce," he says. "Even though this is our land we are living on the edge of an interstate highway. This is a sad situation, but we are not going to pull back. If the ranchers kill one Indigenous leader, 1,000 leaders will arise."

Some ranchers have taken a more insidious approach to the issue. Among the Parecí of Mato Grosso, for example, neighboring farmers convinced some leaders to become "agricultural partners," even though commercial agriculture within Indigenous areas is illegal. Instead of standing up for Indigenous rights, the state governor, Blairo Maggi, a millionaire farmer whose Maggi Group is the world's largest soy producer, condoned and officially recognized these arrangements. In 1995 the Parecí agreed to allow 130 acres to be planted, an area that has expanded each year. Despite using the term "partners" to describe the Parecí, the farmers take 98 percent of the profits, leaving only 2 percent for the Parecí from the soy grown on their lands with their labor.

Governor Maggi is known in Brazil as O Rei da Soja, "the King of Soy," but environmentalists call him "the King of Deforestation." Mato Grosso leads Brazilian states in the number of agricultural burnings and the rate of deforestation. One hundred and fifteen thousand square miles of forest and savanna (an area the size of Arizona) have been replaced with plantations in the last twenty years, according to the World Wildlife Fund.

Deforestation, especially around the headwaters of rivers and streams, causes severe erosion and increases pollution. During the rainy season heavy rains wash toxic chemicals used in soy agriculture—like the Monsanto herbicide Roundup—directly into rivers where Indigenous Peoples drink, bathe, and catch fish. Because Cerrado soils are acidic and nutrient poor, they demand large amounts of lime and chemical fertilizers to be productive. These, as well as pesticides used in intensive monocropping, seep into water supplies and contaminate groundwater, making even well water dangerous. In the Guarani Aquifer, the world's largest, contaminants have reached 80 percent of the level acceptable for human consumption.

Chemicals are also dropped or carried by wind onto Indigenous lands. This happened during the last planting season in the Xavante territory of Sangradouro, and Paulo Supretaprâ, leader of Etéñhiritipa, reports that this also happens in the Pimentel Barbosa Indigenous Territory. Also, since Brazil's president, Luiz Inácio da Silva, lifted the ban on genetically modified organisms in August 2003, soy farmers plant modified varieties immediately next to, and sometimes inside Indigenous areas, even though their environmental and human impacts are unknown. As Paulo Cipassé says, Xavante are concerned that game animals they hunt and eat may be ingesting toxic substances outside of Indigenous areas. With plans to expand sugarcane planting and installation of factories for converting this crop into biofuels, pressure on Indigenous territories is likely to increase in the future.

Reshaping the Cerrado

With soybean production booming, at more than 4.5 million tons per year in Mato Grosso alone and predictions that production will continue to rise, Brazil has plans for huge infrastructural projects—part of a state plan known as Avança Brasil ("Forward Brazil")—to make the region more accessible and transport the huge harvests to ports and commercial centers. The Tocantins-Araguaia Hidrovia, also known as the Central-Northern Multimodal Transport Corridor, is a multimillion dollar project that would transform the most extensive river basin of central Brazil and the eastern Amazon into a commercial waterway to support barge convoys mostly for transporting soy, but also carrying agricultural toxins, which makes Indigenous Peoples very nervous. In total, the project would alter 1,700 miles of the Tocantins-Araguaia-Rio das Mortes river system. It includes large-scale engineering works including hydroelectric facilities, locks, and dams and the construction of new ports. Two of the planned "small" hydroelectric projects will be constructed in or next to the Xavante areas of São Marcos and Sangradouro, and the project will directly affect the Xavante territories of Areões and Pimentel Barbosa, where Ellen Lutz and I spent the last night of our Xavante trip. A recently constructed dam next to the Parabubure reserve, one of many planned on headwaters to the Xingu River, is already operating.

In addition, the project will affect at least six other Indigenous groups: the Apinajé, Javaé, Karajá, Krahó, Krikati and Tapirapé. In all, the Hidrovia would directly affect the lives of more than 10,000 Indigenous people who depend on the river's flora and fauna for their livelihoods. But the Indigenous Peoples are fighting the project, and a lawsuit filed by the Xavante of Pimentel Barbosa in collaboration with the Brazilian organization, Instituto Socioambiental, has delayed the work. It is not clear, though, whether they will be able to stop it.

Although Ellen and I only visited a few of the 200 Xavante communities that exist today, we were heartened to learn about many positive projects that Xavante are undertaking to improve conditions in their reserves. Cipassé, the leader of the Wederä community in Pimentel Barbosa, gave us a tour of a recently inaugurated school in his community that had been built with government funds, with state-of-the-art kitchen equipment and a room ready for computers. He also told us of the community's project to manage, and hopefully increase, the population of white-lipped peccary in the reserve. Wederä and many other Xavante communities are also undertaking projects, often in collaboration with NGOs, that validate traditional knowledge of Cerrado plants, many of which have medicinal properties. They want to revitalize collecting and processing practices that have been abandoned and encourage the eating of nutritious Cerrado foods. Small projects like these, which can make a tremendous difference in Indigenous Peoples' lives, are underway in many Indigenous communities throughout the Cerrado. The Krahó, for example, are helping to enrich the environment by participating in a Cerrado fruit project and earning some income at the same time.

We were glad that our trip provided opportunities for our companions, Hiparidi Top'tiro and Daniela Lima, to spend time with Xavante leaders and community members. Among other things, they discussed a project known as Maräna Bödödi, or Forest Path, which would unite the disparate Xavante and Bororo Indigenous territories that lie along the Rio das Mortes into a single contiguous protected area.

As part of our effort to understand ways that Cultural Survival may best support Xavante, we met with staff from the National Indian Foundation's department of territorial affairs and the office of the Attorney General that deals with Indigenous affairs. It was very encouraging to find that the officials we met were very supportive of this and other Indigenous efforts to protect their lands.

Brazil's constitution is a strong weapon for Indigenous Peoples, but putting their rights into practice takes dedication and very long, hard work. The Xavante Warä Association and an expanding network called the Mobilization of Indigenous Peoples of the Cerrado are taking action to advance the struggle of Indigenous Peoples of the Cerrado. Kuiusi Kisêdjê, leader of the Ngojwere community in the Xingu, spoke for many when he said, "We fight to recoup this land because it is sacred to us; our ancestors are buried here. A lot of people think that we only care about money, but what we want is our land."

Assess Your Progress

1. What is the contrast between the expansion and prosperity of the large-scale agriculturalists and the conditions of the Xavante? How are the Xavante "more fortunate than some?"

2. What evidence is there of massive growth in the agroindustry? What is the prevailing attitude in the region regarding this?

3. What are the other developments destroying the fragile Cerrado?

4. How has the government's policy of colonization affected the indigenous people?

5. How have cattle ranchers changed the land and the ability of the Xavante to hunt?

6. Prior to 1988, what was state policy regarding assimilation and land use?

7. How were the rice projects destructive? What have been the health consequences?

8. How has the legal process failed the Indigenous Peoples?

9. What happens to those who challenge the powerful landholders?

10. What have been the consequences of deforestation and the use of chemicals?

11. How will the water projects affect the people of the area?

12. What are some positive projects being undertaken by the Xavante?

Yanomamo

LESLIE E. SPONSEL

As one of the most famous of all cultures in anthropology and beyond, the Yanomami are ethnographic celebrities. They are a large population of indigenous people living in a vast area of some 192,000 square kilometers in the Amazon rain forest. The heart of their homeland is the Sierra Parima, part of the Guyana Highlands, the mountainous divide between the watersheds of the two most famous rivers of the Amazon region, the Orinoco and the Amazon itself. Their territory overlaps the border between northwestern Brazil and southeastern Venezuela. Some 21,000 Yanomami reside in 363 scattered communities that range in size from 30 to 90 individuals with a few reaching more than 200 in size. Although very little archaeological research has been conducted in the area, two other independent lines of evidence, linguistics and blood group genetics, indicate that the Yanomami have been a separate population for 2,000 years. Their language remains classified as independent, unrelated to any others on the continent of South America.

Surely among the reasons for their survival for millennia is one of the most outstanding attributes that distinguishes this unique culture, reciprocity. It is a pivotal social principle applied in almost every aspect of their daily life, and most commonly through kindness, sharing, cooperation, and camaraderie. However, this principle is also applied in resolving disputes, occasionally even through violence between individuals, groups, or villages. In various ways reciprocity extends beyond ordinary life to their relationships with the spiritual component of their world as well. For example, every Yanomami hunter has a counterpart in the form of an animal spirit in the forest that he cannot kill without seriously endangering himself. The unity, interconnectedness, and interdependence of all life is a fundamental tenet of the religion and philosophy of the Yanomami, another expression of reciprocity.

The Yanomami world is intensely intimate, socially and ecologically. Traditionally people dwell together in a big, palm leaf thatched, communal, round house with a large open central plaza. Their egalitarian society is structured primarily along lines of kinship. In this communal shelter, the hammocks of each nuclear or extended family are arranged around a hearth along the back perimeter. Each village is relatively autonomous politically with a charismatic headman who can lead only by persuasion in developing a consensus. There is no chief or other authority uniting more than one community, let alone Yanomami society as a whole, although alliances with several other villages are common for economic, social, and political purposes. In Yanomami society the units of residence, kinship, and politics are not isomorphic, but overlap in diverse, complex, and fluid ways. This dynamic is mirrored by the subsistence economy that entails almost daily forays into the surrounding forest for gardening, hunting, fishing, and gathering. Accordingly, individuals accumulate an extensive detailed knowledge of the ecology of their habitat from such regular intimate experience.

Yanomami society successfully adapted to the diverse *terra firme* (interfluvial) forest ecosystems within its territory for two millennia. They developed an ecologically sustainable society in terms of their low population density; limited interest in material culture; high mobility; rotational subsistence economy; environmental knowledge; and worldview, values, and attitudes. They practice a rotational system of land and resource use not only in their shifting or swidden farming, but also in their hunting, fishing, and gathering. The last three activities emphasize extensive trekking several times a year when they may camp in the forest for a week to a month or so at a time. Their environmental knowledge includes well over a hundred species of wild plants that they use for food, medicinal, and other purposes. Furthermore, their worldview, values, and attitudes usually help promote respect for nature. For instance, they have a system of extensive prohibitions on consuming certain animal species, some of which apply to everyone in the community whereas others are specific to individual circumstances. These food taboos reduce pressure on prey species. Thus, after millennia of use the forest and its wildlife remain intact. The sustainability of traditional Yanomami society is no romantic illusion.

The ancestral homeland of the Yanomami is a region of high biological diversity in several respects: tropical rain forest ecosystems; altitudinal zonation and other variations in climate, soils, and biota from lowlands to highlands; *tepuis;* and *refugia.* *Tepuis,* or *inselbergs,* are isolated tabletop mountains that are like islands of biological evolution with relatively high species endemicity. *Refugia* are areas of relict forest surviving from periods of wet and dry climatic oscillations during the Pleistocene. For environmentalists and others concerned with Amazonian ecosystems and biological diversity, the optimum route for conservation would be the continued survival and welfare of the Yanomami and other indigenous societies.

Until recently, Yanomami territory was also a refuge in two other respects, political and cultural. The Yanomami may have retreated to the core of their territory in the Sierra Parima to escape slave raids from adjacent Carib neighbors during the colonial period. They are one of the unique indigenous cultures remaining in the Amazon, part of the cultural diversity of this region that is increasingly endangered through serious violations of the human rights of the indigenous peoples by some colonists, miners, ranchers, government agents, military, missionaries, anthropologists, tourists, and other foreigners.

Although not generally recognized, the Yanomami in Brazil and Venezuela have been influenced in varying ways and degrees for centuries at least indirectly by Western "civilization," and sometimes even by direct contact on the margins of their territory. However, only since the 1970s have they progressively become an endangered people, first as the result of the construction of the Northern Perimeter highway that penetrated 225 kilometers into the southern portion of their traditional territory, and since the mid-1980s by the invasion of tens of thousands of illegal gold miners, initially in Brazil, and then more recently also hundreds infiltrating into Venezuela. This cannot be labeled with euphemisms such as cultural contact, acculturation, cultural change, or even catastrophic cultural change—rather clearly in effect it amounts to ecocide, ethnocide, and genocide.

One of the most serious threats of all to the Yanomami in the past two decades has been placer mining, although mainly in Brazil. It is conducted on the land surface by washing away alluvial sediments along river and stream banks with high-pressure hoses and through dredging the bottom of rivers. This causes deforestation, game depletion and displacement, biodiversity reduction, mercury and other pollution, river and stream bank destruction and siltation, and fishery degradation. Subsistence and sport hunting by gold miners, and noise from airplanes and gold mining machinery all combine to degrade the habitat of game and fish as well as deplete and displace their populations. Obviously this has deleterious effects on the animal protein resources, nutrition, health, and disease resistance of local Yanomami communities. Some Yanomami go hungry and even beg for food from the miners, something unknown in their traditional society. For the first time, Yanomami are experiencing poverty and inequality. Other detrimental new practices are introduced such as alcohol abuse and prostitution. Consequently, every aspect of Yanomami society, culture, and ecology is in effect attacked at all levels.

Introduced disease is certainly the most serious immediate threat to all Yanomami. In Brazil, at least 15% of the Yanomami population has already died, mostly as a result of epidemic diseases introduced by the gold miners: tuberculosis, venereal diseases, and even AIDS. The incidence of previously existing diseases, such as malaria and onchocerciasis (African river blindness), has markedly increased as well. Although this medical emergency has long been recognized, and was even predicted in advance of the earlier road construction, the Brazilian and Venezuelan governments have consistently failed to provide adequate medical assistance for the Yanomami. However, the efforts of the Pro-Yanomami Commission in Brazil together with the French organization called Doctors Without Borders have brought more medical assistance to some Yanomami communities. Unfortunately, there are no comparable efforts in Venezuela, although the situation appears to be less dire.

There have been homicides and even mass murders of Yanomami by gold miners that were subsequently investigated and documented. For instance, the Hashimu massacre involved a series of events from June through August of 1993. The 12 victims included women, children, and elderly. Several of the bodies were mutilated and some even decapitated.

The miners have brought prostitution that spreads diseases. They have also introduced trade goods that can trigger competition and aggression among Yanomami. They have even given Yanomami shotguns, perhaps to win over friends in areas where they mine. The negative effects on the Yanomami of venereal disease, competition for trade goods, and shotguns may sometimes be inadvertent, or sometimes even intentional.

Although the number of miners in Yanomami territory has declined substantially in recent years from a high of around 40,000 in 1987, there are still regular invasions each dry season. Moreover, changes in the national and regional economies, increases in the price of gold, or discoveries of new kinds of minerals could easily and quickly lead to catastrophic explosions of the mining population at any time in the future with grave consequences for the Yanomami.

Since the 1980s, the territory of the Yanomami nation in the country of Brazil has been turned, in effect, into killing fields because of the illegal invasion of many thousands of gold miners with a multitude of negative health, social, and environmental consequences. However, this disturbing human tragedy is not simply an inadvertent result of the activity of the miners and those who support and profit from their activity. It is also clearly the direct result of the failure of the state and provincial governments of Brazil and Venezuela to adequately protect and promote the human rights of the Yanomami, even though both countries have joined in numerous international agreements on human rights and also have significant protections specified in their own constitutions and laws. After decades of a mixture of governmental apathy, incompetence, corruption, and even complicity, all of which is well documented in numerous sources, the Yanomami are an endangered society. They will continue to be threatened, unless the international community marshals a much more concerted, systematic, forceful, and sustained initiative on their behalf.

Anthropologists are part of the international community, and some, such as those who are members of the American Anthropological Association, are supposed to follow a formal code of professional ethics that assigns first priority to the welfare of the host community in research. Furthermore, anthropologists have knowledge of some 500 years of recurrent historical trends in situations in which Western "civilization" made war against indigenous societies. From a diversity of sources the profession also has access to substantial specific knowledge about Yanomami culture and ecology as well as the continuing crisis they suffer. Anthropology in the United States and other countries has its own organizations and contacts with relevant governmental and nongovernmental organizations. In short, anthropologists already possess sufficient knowledge to act on behalf of social and environmental justice for the Yanomami. Yet, with few outstanding exceptions, anthropologists individually and collectively have been grossly negligent in this regard.

By now more than three-dozen anthropologists have worked with the Yanomami in various areas and ways for widely different lengths of time. For instance, the eminent Yanomami ethnographer, Jacques Lizot, actually lived with them for more than a quarter of a century. By now more than 60 books have been published about the Yanomami, albeit with diverse approaches, coverage, quality, and accuracy. With so many different anthropologists publishing this much on the Yanomami for more than a century, it is feasible to compare accounts to identify points of agreement, presumably indicative of ethnographic reality, and other points of disagreement, reflecting the individual ethnographer's interpretation, idiosyncrasies, biases, and other phenomena. For example, only a couple of these dozens of authors are obsessed with the violence in Yanomami society to the extent of exaggeration and distortion as well as to the neglect of the violence committed by outsiders against the Yanomami: Ettore Biocca and Napoleon Chagnon. Another important consideration that has yet to receive much systematic research attention is the fact that there is tremendous variation in the geography, ecology, economy, culture, and history among the some 363 Yanomami villages scattered over the enormous area of 192,000 square kilometers. Communities are located from the Orinoco lowlands into the Guyana Highlands within an altitudinal range of 250 to 1,200 meters above sea level.

It is also feasible to identify historical trends in Yanomami studies (Yanomamalogy). The orientation of anthropological research among the Yanomami has evolved to emphasize more humanitarian, applied, and advocacy work in recent decades. Starting in the late 18th century, various explorers and naturalists like Alexander von Humboldt published anecdotal accounts of brief encounters with the Yanomami. Much later this stage was followed, during the 1960s and 1970s, by salvage ethnography, an attempt to systematically describe as much about Yanomami culture and life as possible. This was guided by the assumption that, as a supposedly "primitive" people surviving from a previous stage of cultural evolution, the Yanomami were destined for extinction in the face of civilization and "progress," or at least for profound cultural change through acculturation and assimilation. The first comprehensive ethnography on the Yanomami was published by Louis Cocco in 1971 after he had lived with them as a Salesian missionary for 15 years. Already at this time there was enough research on the Yanomami by various investigators to allow Cocco to include a whole section on the history of Yanomami studies.

During the 1980s, research on the Yanomami in Venezuela became more problem-oriented, much of it focusing on the causes of their so-called warfare and related issues. Actually the most intense form of Yanomami inter-village aggression is more akin to the famous blood feud between the Hatfield and McCoy families in the Appalachian Mountains between Kentucky and Virginia from 1882 to 1890. In any case, the extended debate about the causes of aggression in Yanomami society was over competing sociobiological and ecological explanations proposed mainly by Napoleon Chagnon and Marvin Harris, respectively. Until Brian Ferguson's subsequent meticulous ethno-historical research, the Yanomami were falsely treated as some kind of a pristine isolate. In addition, the consequences on aggression and other aspects of their society of the movement of some villages to the lowlands in pursuit of trade goods and other Western resources were mostly ignored. Furthermore, there is no scientific or other justification in affording internal aggression in Yanomami society so much attention while largely, if not entirely, ignoring aggressive external forces that clearly threaten their survival, welfare, and rights as fellow human beings.

Simultaneously in Brazil, however, with the dire consequences of road construction and then mining in the southern territory of the Yanomami, research in that country shifted in emphasis from basic to applied and advocacy work as exemplified by the heroic efforts of anthropologists like Bruce Albert, Gale Goodwin Gomez, Alcida Ramos, and Kenneth Taylor, among others. In Venezuela, where the situation was not as grave and urgent, basic research persisted. However, the controversy over the allegations of serious violations of professional ethics and of the human rights of the Yanomami on the part of Napoleon Chagnon and associates made in Patrick Tierney's controversial book in late 2000 have aroused increased concern with social responsibility and relevance in anthropological research in both Venezuela and Brazil. Accordingly, many no longer consider it justifiable to collect scientific data merely to feed careerism and the vague promise of contributing to human knowledge. Such egocentric work not only dehumanizes the host communities in which the research is conducted, but the researcher as well. The Yanomami and the profession deserve far better.

Fortunately, the Yanomami themselves are increasingly working to sustain their self-determination and other human rights, territorial integrity, and ethnic identity, as well as to meet their own medical, educational, political, and other needs. For instance, one of their leaders, Davi Kopenawa Yanomami, has traveled internationally to publicize their situation and needs. He has addressed organizations such as the British House of Commons and the United Nations. Some schools in Yanomami communities in Brazil are teaching computer literacy with equipment provided by donations raised by Cultural Survival, Inc. It may well be just a matter of time before there are even Yanomami trained as anthropologists documenting their own culture and critically assessing what others have published about their society. Thus, although Yanomami face many serious threats because of the failures of the state and provincial governments of Brazil and Venezuela in protecting and advancing their human rights, they are not merely passive victims of cultural contact and change, but increasingly active agents in struggling to determine their own future. The only anachronism is those racist and ethnocentric outsiders who continue to view them as primitive, worthy only as a source of scientific data and not of voicing their own opinions—including opinions about anthropologists. The Yanomami are neither noble nor ignoble savages, but rather they are fellow human beings with a distinctive culture. Indeed, the word *Yanomami* simply means human being.

References

Borofsky, R. (2005). *Yanomami: The fierce controversy and what we can learn from it.* Berkeley, CA: University of California Press.

Chagnon, N. A. (1997). *Yanomamo.* New York: Harcourt Brace College.

Cooco, L. (1972). *Iyewei-Teri: Quince años entre los Yanomamos* [Fifteen years among the Yanomamos]. Caracas, Venezuela: Libreria Editorial Salesiana.

Ferguson, R. B. (1995). *Yanomami warfare: A political history.* Santa Fe, NM: School of American Research Press.

Lizot, J. (1985). *Tales of the Yanomami: Daily life in the Venezuelan forest.* New York: Cambridge University Press.

Ramos, A. R. (1995). *Sanuma memories: Yanomami ethnography in times of crisis.* Madison, WI: University of Wisconsin Press.

Rocha, J. (1999). *Murder in the rain forest: The Yanomami, the gold miners, and the Amazon.* London, UK: Latin American Bureau.

Smole, W. J. (1976). *The Yanomama Indians: A cultural geography.* Austin, TX: University of Texas Press.

Tierney, P. (2001). *Darkness in El Dorado: How scientists and journalists devastated the Amazon.* New York: W. W. Norton & Co.

Assess Your Progress

1. How important is the principle of reciprocity to the Yanomami?

2. In what ways is the Yanomami world "intensely intimate?"

3. In what ways have the Yanomami become an endangered people?

4. Why are anthropologists uniquely positioned to act on behalf of the Yanomami?

5. Why does the author complain that external sources of aggression in Yanomami society have not been given enough attention?

6. Why does he express concern regarding social responsibility and relevance in anthropological research?

The Arrow of Disease

When Columbus and his successors invaded the Americas, the most potent weapon they carried was their germs. But why didn't deadly disease flow in the other direction, from the New World to the Old?

JARED DIAMOND

The three people talking in the hospital room were already stressed out from having to cope with a mysterious illness, and it didn't help at all that they were having trouble communicating. One of them was the patient, a small, timid man, sick with pneumonia caused by an unidentified microbe and with only a limited command of the English language. The second, acting as translator, was his wife, worried about her husband's condition and frightened by the hospital environment. The third person in the trio was an inexperienced young doctor, trying to figure out what might have brought on the strange illness. Under the stress, the doctor was forgetting everything he had been taught about patient confidentiality. He committed the awful blunder of requesting the woman to ask her husband whether he'd had any sexual experiences that might have caused the infection.

As the young doctor watched, the husband turned red, pulled himself together so that he seemed even smaller, tried to disappear under his bed sheets, and stammered in a barely audible voice. His wife suddenly screamed in rage and drew herself up to tower over him. Before the doctor could stop her, she grabbed a heavy metal bottle, slammed it onto her husband's head, and stormed out of the room. It took a while for the doctor to elicit, through the man's broken English, what he had said to so enrage his wife. The answer slowly emerged: he had admitted to repeated intercourse with sheep on a recent visit to the family farm; perhaps that was how he had contracted the mysterious microbe.

This episode, related to me by a physician friend involved in the case, sounds so bizarrely one of a kind as to be of no possible broader significance. But in fact it illustrates a subject of great importance: human diseases of animal origins. Very few of us may love sheep in the carnal sense. But most of us platonically love our pet animals, like our dogs and cats; and as a society, we certainly appear to have an inordinate fondness for sheep and other livestock, to judge from the vast numbers of them that we keep.

Some of us—most often our children—pick up infectious diseases from our pets. Usually these illnesses remain no more than a nuisance, but a few have evolved into far more. The major killers of humanity throughout our recent history—smallpox, flu, tuberculosis, malaria, plague, measles, and cholera—are all infectious diseases that arose from diseases of animals. Until World War II more victims of war died of microbes than of gunshot or sword wounds. All those military histories glorifying Alexander the Great and Napoleon ignore the ego-deflating truth: the winners of past wars were not necessarily those armies with the best generals and weapons, but those bearing the worst germs with which to smite their enemies.

The grimmest example of the role of germs in history is much on our minds this month, as we recall the European conquest of the Americas that began with Columbus's voyage of 1492. Numerous as the Indian victims of the murderous Spanish conquistadores were, they were dwarfed in number by the victims of murderous Spanish microbes. These formidable conquerors killed an estimated 95 percent of the New World's pre-Columbian Indian population.

Why was the exchange of nasty germs between the Americas and Europe so unequal? Why didn't the reverse happen instead, with Indian diseases decimating the Spanish invaders, spreading back across the Atlantic, and causing a 95 percent decline in *Europe's* human population?

Similar questions arise regarding the decimation of many other native peoples by European germs, and regarding the decimation of would-be European conquistadores in the tropics of Africa and Asia.

Naturally, we're disposed to think about diseases from our own point of view: What can we do to save ourselves and to kill the microbes? Let's stamp out the scoundrels, and never mind what *their* motives are!

In life, though, one has to understand the enemy to beat him. So for a moment, let's consider disease from the microbes' point of view. Let's look beyond our anger at their making us sick in bizarre ways, like giving us genital sores or diarrhea, and ask why it is that they do such things. After all, microbes are as much a product of natural selection as we are, and so their actions must have come about because they confer some evolutionary benefit.

Basically, of course, evolution selects those individuals that are most effective at producing babies and at helping those babies find suitable places to live. Microbes are marvels at this latter requirement. They have evolved diverse ways of spreading from one person to another, and from animals to people. Many of our symptoms of disease actually represent ways in which some clever bug modifies our bodies or our behavior such that we become enlisted to spread bugs.

The most effortless way a bug can spread is by just waiting to be transmitted passively to the next victim. That's the strategy practiced by microbes that wait for one host to be eaten by the next—salmonella bacteria, for example, which we contract by eating already-infected eggs or meat; or the worm responsible for trichinosis, which waits for us to kill a pig and eat it without properly cooking it.

As a slight modification of this strategy; some microbes don't wait for the old host to die but instead hitchhike in the saliva of an insect that bites the old host and then flies to a new one. The free ride may be provided by mosquitoes, fleas, lice, or tsetse flies, which spread malaria, plague, typhus, and sleeping sickness, respectively. The dirtiest of all passive-carriage tricks is perpetrated by microbes that pass from a woman to her fetus—microbes such as the ones responsible for syphilis, rubella (German measles), and AIDS. By their cunning these microbes can already be infecting an infant before the moment of its birth.

Other bugs take matters into their own hands, figuratively speaking. They actively modify the anatomy or habits of their host to accelerate their transmission. From our perspective, the open genital sores caused by venereal diseases such as syphilis are a vile indignity. From the microbes' point of view, however, they're just a useful device to enlist a host's help in inoculating the body cavity of another host with microbes. The skin lesions caused by smallpox similarly spread microbes by direct or indirect body contact (occasionally very indirect, as when U.S. and Australian whites bent on wiping out "belligerent" native peoples sent them gifts of blankets previously used by smallpox patients).

More vigorous yet is the strategy practiced by the influenza, common cold, and pertussis (whooping cough) microbes, which induce the victim to cough or sneeze, thereby broadcasting the bugs toward prospective new hosts. Similarly the cholera bacterium induces a massive diarrhea that spreads bacteria into the water supplies of potential new victims. For modification of a host's behavior, though, nothing matches the rabies virus, which not only gets into the saliva of an infected dog but drives the dog into a frenzy of biting and thereby infects many new victims.

Thus, from our viewpoint, genital sores, diarrhea, and coughing are "symptoms" of disease. From a bug's viewpoint, they're clever evolutionary strategies to broadcast the bug. That's why it's in the bug's interests to make us "sick." But what does it gain by killing us? That seems self-defeating, since a microbe that kills its host kills itself.

Though you may well think it's of little consolation, our death is really just an unintended by-product of host symptoms that promote the efficient transmission of microbes. Yes, an untreated cholera patient may eventually die from producing diarrheal fluid at a rate of several gallons a day. While the patient lasts, though, the cholera bacterium profits from being massively disseminated into the water supplies of its next victims. As long as each victim thereby infects, on average, more than one new victim, the bacteria will spread, even though the first host happens to die.

So much for the dispassionate examination of the bug's interests. Now let's get back to considering our own selfish interests: to stay alive and healthy, best done by killing the damned bugs. One common response to infection is to develop a fever. Again, we consider fever a "symptom" of disease, as if it developed inevitably without serving any function. But regulation of body temperature is under our genetic control, and a fever doesn't just happen by accident. Because some microbes are more sensitive to heat than our own bodies are, by raising our body temperature we in effect try to bake the bugs to death before we get baked ourselves.

We and our pathogens are now locked in an escalating evolutionary contest, with the death of one contestant the price of defeat, and with natural selection playing the role of umpire.

Another common response is to mobilize our immune system. White blood cells and other cells actively seek out and kill foreign microbes. The specific antibodies we gradually build up against a particular microbe make us less likely to get reinfected once we are cured. As we all know there are some illnesses, such as flu and the common cold, to which our resistance is only temporary; we can eventually contract the illness again. Against other illnesses, though—including measles, mumps, rubella, pertussis, and the now-defeated menace of smallpox—antibodies stimulated by one infection confer lifelong immunity. That's the principle behind vaccination—to stimulate our antibody production without our having to go through the actual experience of the disease.

Alas, some clever bugs don't just cave in to our immune defenses. Some have learned to trick us by changing their antigens, those molecular pieces of the microbe that our antibodies recognize. The constant evolution or recycling of new strains of flu, with differing antigens, explains why the flu you got two years ago didn't protect you against the different strain that arrived this year. Sleeping sickness is an even more slippery customer in its ability to change its antigens rapidly.

Among the slipperiest of all is the virus that causes AIDS, which evolves new antigens even as it sits within an individual patient, until it eventually overwhelms the immune system.

Our slowest defensive response is through natural selection, which changes the relative frequency with which a gene appears from generation to generation. For almost any disease some people prove to be genetically more resistant than others. In an epidemic, those people with genes for resistance to that particular microbe are more likely to survive than are people lacking such genes. As a result, over the course of history human populations repeatedly exposed to a particular pathogen tend to be made up of individuals with genes that resist the appropriate microbe just because unfortunate individuals without those genes were less likely to survive to pass their genes on to their children.

Fat consolation, you may be thinking. This evolutionary response is not one that does the genetically susceptible dying individual any good. It does mean, though, that a human population as a whole becomes better protected.

In short, many bugs have had to evolve tricks to let them spread among potential victims. We've evolved counter-tricks, to which the bugs have responded by evolving counter-counter-tricks. We and our pathogens are now locked in an escalating evolutionary contest, with the death of one contestant the price of defeat, and with natural selection playing the role of umpire.

The form that this deadly contest takes varies with the pathogens: for some it is like a guerrilla war, while for others it is a blitzkrieg. With certain diseases, like malaria or hookworm, there's a more or less steady trickle of new cases in an affected area, and they will appear in any month of any year. Epidemic diseases, though, are different: they produce no cases for a long time, then a whole wave of cases, then no more cases again for a while.

Among such epidemic diseases, influenza is the most familiar to Americans, this year having been a particularly bad one for us (but a great year for the influenza virus). Cholera epidemics come at longer intervals, the 1991 Peruvian epidemic being the first one to reach the New World during the twentieth century. Frightening as today's influenza and cholera epidemics are, though, they pale beside the far more terrifying epidemics of the past, before the rise of modern medicine. The greatest single epidemic in human history was the influenza wave that killed 21 million people at the end of the First World War. The black death, or bubonic plague, killed one-quarter of Europe's population between 1346 and 1352, with death tolls up to 70 percent in some cities.

The infectious diseases that visit us as epidemics share several characteristics. First, they spread quickly and efficiently from an infected person to nearby healthy people, with the result that the whole population gets exposed within a short time. Second, they're "acute" illnesses: within a short time, you either die or recover completely. Third, the fortunate ones of us who do recover develop antibodies that leave us immune against a recurrence of the disease for a long time, possibly our entire lives. Finally, these diseases tend to be restricted to humans; the bugs causing them tend not to live in the soil or in other animals. All four of these characteristics apply to what Americans think of as the once more-familiar acute epidemic diseases of childhood, including measles, rubella, mumps, pertussis, and smallpox.

It is easy to understand why the combination of those four characteristics tends to make a disease run in epidemics. The rapid spread of microbes and the rapid course of symptoms mean that everybody in a local human population is soon infected, and thereafter either dead or else recovered and immune. No one is left alive who could still be infected. But since the microbe can't survive except in the bodies of living people, the disease dies out until a new crop of babies reaches the susceptible age—and until an infectious person arrives from the outside to start a new epidemic.

A classic illustration of the process is given by the history of measles on the isolated Faeroe Islands in the North Atlantic. A severe epidemic of the disease reached the Faeroes in 1781, then died out, leaving the islands measles-free until an infected carpenter arrived on a ship from Denmark in 1846. Within three months almost the whole Faeroes population—7,782 people—had gotten measles and then either died or recovered, leaving the measles virus to disappear once again until the next epidemic. Studies show that measles is likely to die out in any human population numbering less than half a million people. Only in larger populations can measles shift from one local area to another, thereby persisting until enough babies have been born in the originally infected area to permit the disease's return.

Rubella in Australia provides a similar example, on a much larger scale. As of 1917 Australia's population was still only 5 million, with most people living in scattered rural areas. The sea voyage to Britain took two months, and land transport within Australia itself was slow. In effect, Australia didn't even consist of a population of 5 million, but of hundreds of much smaller populations. As a result, rubella hit Australia only as occasional epidemics, when an infected person happened to arrive from overseas and stayed in a densely populated area. By 1938, though, the city of Sydney alone had a population of over one million, and people moved frequently and quickly by air between London, Sydney, and other Australian cities. Around then, rubella for the first time was able to establish itself permanently in Australia.

What's true for rubella in Australia is true for most familiar acute infectious diseases throughout the world. To sustain themselves, they need a human population that is sufficiently numerous and densely packed that a new crop of susceptible children is available for infection by the time the disease would otherwise be waning. Hence the measles and other such diseases are also known as "crowd diseases."

Crowd diseases could not sustain themselves in small bands of hunter-gatherers and slash-and-burn farmers. As tragic recent experience with Amazonian Indians and Pacific Islanders confirms, almost an entire tribelet may be wiped out by an epidemic brought by an outside visitor, because no one in the tribelet has any antibodies against the microbe. In addition, measles and some other "childhood" diseases are more likely to kill infected adults than children, and all adults in the tribelet are susceptible. Having killed most of the tribelet, the epidemic then disappears. The small population size explains why tribelets can't sustain epidemics introduced from the outside; at the same time it explains why they could never evolve epidemic diseases of their own to give back to the visitors.

That's not to say that small human populations are free from all infectious diseases. Some of their infections are caused by microbes capable of maintaining themselves in animals or in soil, so the disease remains constantly available to infect people. For example, the yellow fever virus is carried by African wild monkeys and is constantly available to infect rural human populations of Africa. It was also available to be carried to New World monkeys and people by the transAtlantic slave trade.

Other infections of small human populations are chronic diseases, such as leprosy and yaws, that may take a very long time to kill a victim. The victim thus remains alive as a reservoir of microbes to infect other members of the tribelet. Finally, small human populations are susceptible to nonfatal infections against which we don't develop immunity, with the result that the same person can become reinfected after recovering. That's the case with hookworm and many other parasites.

All these types of diseases, characteristic of small, isolated populations, must be the oldest diseases of humanity. They were the ones that we could evolve and sustain through the early millions of years of our evolutionary history, when the total human population was tiny and fragmented. They are also shared with, or are similar to the diseases of, our closest wild relatives, the African great apes. In contrast, the evolution of our crowd diseases could only have occurred with the buildup of large, dense human populations, first made possible by the rise of agriculture about 10,000 years ago, then by the rise of cities several thousand years ago. Indeed, the first attested dates for many familiar infectious diseases are surprisingly recent: around 1600 B.C. for smallpox (as deduced from pockmarks on an Egyptian mummy), 400 B.C. for mumps, 1840 for polio, and 1959 for AIDS.

Agriculture sustains much higher human population densities than do hunting and gathering—on average, 10 to 100 times higher. In addition, hunter-gatherers frequently shift camp, leaving behind their piles of feces with their accumulated microbes and worm larvae. But farmers are sedentary and live amid their own sewage, providing microbes with a quick path from one person's body into another person's drinking water. Farmers also become surrounded by disease-transmitting rodents attracted by stored food.

The explosive increase in world travel by Americans, and in immigration to the United States, is turning us into another melting pot— this time of microbes that we'd dismissed as causing disease in far-off countries.

Some human populations make it even easier for their own bacteria and worms to infect new victims, by intentionally gathering their feces and urine and spreading it as fertilizer on the fields where people work. Irrigation agriculture and fish farming provide ideal living conditions for the snails carrying schistosomes, and for other flukes that burrow through our skin as we wade through the feces-laden water.

If the rise of farming was a boon for our microbes, the rise of cities was a veritable bonanza, as still more densely packed human populations festered under even worse sanitation conditions. (Not until the beginning of the twentieth century did urban populations finally become self-sustaining; until then, constant immigration of healthy peasants from the countryside was necessary to make good the constant deaths of city dwellers from crowd diseases.) Another bonanza was the development of world trade routes, which by late Roman times effectively joined the populations of Europe, Asia, and North Africa into one giant breeding ground for microbes. That's when smallpox finally reached Rome as the "plague of Antonius," which killed millions of Roman citizens between A.D. 165 and 180.

Similarly, bubonic plague first appeared in Europe as the plague of Justinian (A.D. 542–543). But plague didn't begin to hit Europe with full force, as the black death epidemics, until 1346, when new overland trading with China provided rapid transit for flea-infested furs from plague-ridden areas of Central Asia. Today our jet planes have made even the longest intercontinental flights briefer than the duration of any human infectious disease. That's how an Aerolíneas Argentinas airplane, stopping in Lima, Peru, earlier this year, managed to deliver dozens of cholera-infected people the same day to my city of Los Angeles, over 3,000 miles away. The explosive increase in world travel by Americans, and in immigration to the United States, is turning us into another melting pot—this time of microbes that we previously dismissed as just causing exotic diseases in far-off countries.

When the human population became sufficiently large and concentrated, we reached the stage in our history when we could at last sustain crowd diseases confined to our species. But that presents a paradox: such diseases could

never have existed before. Instead they had to evolve as new diseases. Where did those new diseases come from?

Evidence emerges from studies of the disease-causing microbes themselves. In many cases molecular biologists have identified the microbe's closest relative. Those relatives also prove to be agents of infectious crowd diseases—but ones confined to various species of domestic animals and pets! Among animals too, epidemic diseases require dense populations, and they're mainly confined to social animals that provide the necessary large populations. Hence when we domesticated social animals such as cows and pigs, they were already afflicted by epidemic diseases just waiting to be transferred to us.

For example, the measles virus is most closely related to the virus causing rinderpest, a nasty epidemic disease of cattle and many wild cud-chewing mammals. Rinderpest doesn't affect humans. Measles, in turn, doesn't affect cattle. The close similarity of the measles and rinderpest viruses suggests that the rinderpest virus transferred from cattle to humans, then became the measles virus by changing its properties to adapt to us. That transfer isn't surprising, considering how closely many peasant farmers live and sleep next to cows and their accompanying feces, urine, breath, sores, and blood. Our intimacy with cattle has been going on for 8,000 years since we domesticated them—ample time for the rinderpest virus to discover us nearby. Other familiar infectious diseases can similarly be traced back to diseases of our animal friends.

Given our proximity to the animals we love, we must constantly be getting bombarded by animal microbes. Those invaders get winnowed by natural selection, and only a few succeed in establishing themselves as human diseases. A quick survey of current diseases lets us trace four stages in the evolution of a specialized human disease from an animal precursor.

In the first stage, we pick up animal-borne microbes that are still at an early stage in their evolution into specialized human pathogens. They don't get transmitted directly from one person to another, and even their transfer from animals to us remains uncommon. There are dozens of diseases like this that we get directly from pets and domestic animals. They include cat scratch fever from cats, leptospirosis from dogs, psittacosis from chickens and parrots, and brucellosis from cattle. We're similarly susceptible to picking up diseases from wild animals, such as the tularemia that hunters occasionally get from skinning wild rabbits.

In the second stage, a former animal pathogen evolves to the point where it does get transmitted directly between people and causes epidemics. However, the epidemic dies out for several reasons—being cured by modern medicine, stopping when everybody has been infected and died, or stopping when everybody has been infected and become immune. For example, a previously unknown disease termed *o'nyong-nyong* fever appeared in East Africa in 1959 and infected several million Africans. It probably arose from a virus of monkeys and was transmitted to humans by mosquitoes. The fact that patients recovered quickly and became immune to further attack helped cause the new disease to die out quickly.

The annals of medicine are full of diseases that sound like no known disease today but that once caused terrifying epidemics before disappearing as mysteriously as they had come. Who alive today remembers the "English sweating sickness" that swept and terrified Europe between 1485 and 1578, or the "Picardy sweats" of eighteenth- and nineteenth-century France?

A third stage in the evolution of our major diseases is represented by former animal pathogens that establish themselves in humans and that do not die out; until they do, the question of whether they will become major killers of humanity remains up for grabs. The future is still very uncertain for Lassa fever, first observed in 1969 in Nigeria and caused by a virus probably derived from rodents. Better established is Lyme disease, caused by a spirochete that we get from the bite of a tick. Although the first known human cases in the United States appeared only as recently as 1962, Lyme disease is already reaching epidemic proportions in the Northeast, on the West Coast, and in the upper Midwest. The future of AIDS, derived from monkey viruses, is even more secure, from the virus's perspective.

The final stage of this evolution is represented by the major, long-established epidemic diseases confined to humans. These diseases must have been the evolutionary survivors of far more pathogens that tried to make the jump to us from animals—and mostly failed.

Diseases represent evolution in progress, as microbes adapt by natural selection to new hosts. Compared with cows' bodies, though, our bodies offer different immune defenses and different chemistry. In that new environment, a microbe must evolve new ways to live and propagate itself.

The best-studied example of microbes evolving these new ways involves myxomatosis, which hit Australian rabbits in 1950. The myxoma virus, native to a wild species of Brazilian rabbit, was known to cause a lethal epidemic in European domestic rabbits, which are a different species. The virus was intentionally introduced to Australia in the hopes of ridding the continent of its plague of European rabbits, foolishly introduced in the nineteenth century. In the first year, myxoma produced a gratifying (to Australian farmers) 99.8 percent mortality in infected rabbits. Fortunately for the rabbits and unfortunately for the farmers, the death rate then dropped in the second year to 90 percent and eventually to 25 percent, frustrating hopes of eradicating rabbits completely from Australia. The problem was that the myxoma virus evolved to serve its own interest, which differed from the farmers' interests and those of the rabbits. The virus changed to kill fewer rabbits and to permit lethally infected ones to live longer before dying. The result was bad for Australian farmers but good for the virus: a less lethal myxoma virus spreads baby viruses to more rabbits than did the original, highly virulent myxoma.

For a similar example in humans, consider the surprising evolution of syphilis. Today we associate syphilis with genital sores and a very slowly developing disease, leading to the death of untreated victims only after many years. However, when syphilis was first definitely recorded in Europe in 1495, its pustules often covered the body from the head to the knees, caused flesh to fall off people's faces, and led to death within a few months. By 1546 syphilis had evolved into the disease with the symptoms known to us today. Apparently, just as with myxomatosis, those syphilis spirochetes evolved to keep their victims alive longer in order to transmit their spirochete offspring into more victims.

How, then, does all this explain the outcome of 1492—that Europeans conquered and depopulated the New World, instead of Native Americans conquering and depopulating Europe?

In the century or two following Columbus's arrival in the New World, the Indian population declined by about 95 percent. The main killers were European germs, to which the Indians had never been exposed.

Part of the answer, of course, goes back to the invaders' technological advantages. European guns and steel swords were more effective weapons than Native American stone axes and wooden clubs. Only Europeans had ships capable of crossing the ocean and horses that could provide a decisive advantage in battle. But that's not the whole answer. Far more Native Americans died in bed than on the battlefield—the victims of germs, not of guns and swords. Those germs undermined Indian resistance by killing most Indians and their leaders and by demoralizing the survivors.

The role of disease in the Spanish conquests of the Aztec and Inca empires is especially well documented. In 1519 Cortés landed on the coast of Mexico with 600 Spaniards to conquer the fiercely militaristic Aztec Empire, which at the time had a population of many millions. That Cortés reached the Aztec capital of Tenochtitlán, escaped with the loss of "only" two-thirds of his force, and managed to fight his way back to the coast demonstrates both Spanish military advantages and the initial naïveté of the Aztecs. But when Cortés's next onslaught came, in 1521, the Aztecs were no longer naïve; they fought street by street with the utmost tenacity.

What gave the Spaniards a decisive advantage this time was smallpox, which reached Mexico in 1520 with the arrival of one infected slave from Spanish Cuba. The resulting epidemic proceeded to kill nearly half the Aztecs. The survivors were demoralized by the mysterious illness that killed Indians and spared Spaniards, as if advertising the Spaniards' invincibility. By 1618 Mexico's initial population of 20 million had plummeted to about 1.6 million.

Pizarro had similarly grim luck when he landed on the coast of Peru in 1531 with about 200 men to conquer the Inca Empire. Fortunately for Pizarro, and unfortunately for the Incas, smallpox had arrived overland around 1524, killing much of the Inca population, including both Emperor Huayna Capac and his son and designated successor, Ninan Cuyoche. Because of the vacant throne, two other sons of Huayna Capac, Atahuallpa and Huáscar, became embroiled in a civil war that Pizarro exploited to conquer the divided Incas.

When we in the United States think of the most populous New World societies existing in 1492, only the Aztecs and Incas come to mind. We forget that North America also supported populous Indian societies in the Mississippi Valley. Sadly, these societies too would disappear. But in this case conquistadores contributed nothing directly to the societies' destruction; the conquistadores' germs, spreading in advance, did everything. When De Soto marched through the Southeast in 1540, he came across Indian towns abandoned two years previously because nearly all the inhabitants had died in epidemics. However, he was still able to see some of the densely populated towns lining the lower Mississippi. By a century and a half later, though, when French settlers returned to the lower Mississippi, almost all those towns had vanished. Their relics are the great mound sites of the Mississippi Valley. Only recently have we come to realize that the mound-building societies were still largely intact when Columbus arrived, and that they collapsed between 1492 and the systematic European exploration of the Mississippi.

When I was a child in school, we were taught that North America had originally been occupied by about one million Indians. That low number helped justify the white conquest of what could then be viewed as an almost empty continent. However, archeological excavations and descriptions left by the first European explorers on our coasts now suggest an initial number of around 20 million. In the century or two following Columbus's arrival in the New World, the Indian population is estimated to have declined by about 95 percent.

The main killers were European germs, to which the Indians had never been exposed and against which they therefore had neither immunologic nor genetic resistance. Smallpox, measles, influenza, and typhus competed for top rank among the killers. As if those were not enough, pertussis, plague, tuberculosis, diphtheria, mumps, malaria, and yellow fever came close behind. In countless cases Europeans were actually there to witness the decimation that occurred when the germs arrived. For example, in 1837 the Mandan Indian tribe, with one of the most elaborate cultures in the Great Plains, contracted smallpox thanks to a steamboat traveling up the Missouri River from St. Louis. The population of one Mandan village crashed from 2,000 to less than 40 within a few weeks.

The one-sided exchange of lethal germs between the Old and New Worlds is among the most striking and consequence-laden facts of recent history. Whereas over a dozen major infectious diseases of Old World origins became established in the New World, not a single major killer reached Europe from the Americas. The sole possible exception is syphilis, whose area of origin still remains controversial.

That one-sidedness is more striking with the knowledge that large, dense human populations are a prerequisite for the evolution of crowd diseases. If recent reappraisals of the pre-Columbian New World population are correct, that population was not far below the contemporaneous population of Eurasia. Some New World cities, like Tenochtitlán, were among the world's most populous cities at the time. Yet Tenochtitlán didn't have awful germs waiting in store for the Spaniards. Why not?

One possible factor is the rise of dense human populations began somewhat later in the New World than in the Old. Another is that the three most populous American centers—the Andes, Mexico, and the Mississippi Valley—were never connected by regular fast trade into one gigantic breeding ground for microbes, in the way that Europe, North Africa, India, and China became connected in late Roman times.

The main reason becomes clear, however, if we ask a simple question: From what microbes could any crowd diseases of the Americas have evolved? We've seen that Eurasian crowd diseases evolved from diseases of domesticated herd animals. Significantly, there were many such animals in Eurasia. But there were only five animals that became domesticated in the Americas: the turkey in Mexico and parts of North America, the guinea pig and llama/alpaca (probably derived from the same original wild species) in the Andes, and Muscovy duck in tropical South America, and the dog throughout the Americas.

That extreme paucity of New World domestic animals reflects the paucity of wild starting material. About 80 percent of the big wild mammals of the Americas became extinct at the end of the last ice age, around 11,000 years ago, at approximately the same time that the first well-attested wave of Indian hunters spread over the Americas. Among the species that disappeared were ones that would have yielded useful domesticates, such as American horses and camels. Debate still rages as to whether those extinctions were due to climate changes or to the impact of Indian hunters on prey that had never seen humans. Whatever the reason, the extinctions removed most of the basis for Native American animal domestication—and for crowd diseases.

The few domesticates that remained were not likely sources of such diseases. Muscovy ducks and turkeys don't live in enormous flocks, and they're not naturally endearing species (like young lambs) with which we have much physical contact. Guinea pigs may have contributed a trypanosome infection like Chagas' disease or leishmaniasis to our catalog of woes, but that's uncertain.

Initially the most surprising absence is of any human disease derived from llamas (or alpacas), which are tempting to consider as the Andean equivalent of Eurasian livestock. However, llamas had three strikes against them as a source of human pathogens: their wild relatives don't occur in big herds as do wild sheep, goats, and pigs; their total numbers were never remotely as large as the Eurasian populations of domestic livestock, since llamas never spread beyond the Andes; and llamas aren't as cuddly as piglets and lambs and aren't kept in such close association with people. (You may not think of piglets as cuddly, but human mothers in the New Guinea highlands often nurse them, and they frequently live right in the huts of peasant farmers.)

The importance of animal-derived diseases for human history extends far beyond the Americas. Eurasian germs played a key role in decimating native peoples in many other parts of the world as well, including the Pacific islands, Australia, and southern Africa. Racist Europeans used to attribute those conquests to their supposedly better brains. But no evidence for such better brains has been forthcoming. Instead, the conquests were made possible by Europeans' nastier germs, and by the technological advances and denser populations that Europeans ultimately acquired by means of their domesticated plants and animals.

So on this 500th anniversary of Columbus's discovery, let's try to regain our sense of perspective about his hotly debated achievements. There's no doubt that Columbus was a great visionary, seaman, and leader. There's also no doubt that he and his successors often behaved as bestial murderers. But those facts alone don't fully explain why it took so few European immigrants to initially conquer and ultimately supplant so much of the native population of the Americas. Without the germs Europeans brought with them—germs that were derived from their animals—such conquests might have been impossible.

Assess Your Progress

1. What are the major killers of humanity and where do they come from? How did most victims of war die before World War II? What determined the winners of past wars? What percentage of the pre-Columbian Indian population was killed by Spanish microbes?

2. How might a bug such as salmonella be passively transmitted to its next victim? What examples does the author provide of microbes getting a "free ride" to its next victim? How might they modify the anatomy or habits of their host in order to accelerate their transmission?

3. How does the author, therefore, describe such "symptoms" of disease? Why is it in the bug's interest to make us "sick?"

Is it in the bug's interest to kill us? How does the author explain death? How do bacteria survive even though the hosts die?

4. What "common responses" do we use to stay alive?

5. Explain the principle of vaccination. How do the bugs "trick us?" Why is the AIDS virus one of the "slipperiest of all?"

6. What is our slowest defense mechanism? How does the author describe the "escalating evolutionary context?"

7. Explain the difference between pathogens that fight a "guerrilla war," creating a steady trickle of new cases, versus those that conduct a "blitzkrieg" and cause epidemics.

8. What characteristics are shared by infectious diseases that visit us as epidemics?

9. Why does measles die out in populations of less than half a million people but persists in larger population?

10. Why can't such "crowd diseases" sustain themselves in small bands of hunter-gatherers and slash-and burn farmers?

11. Does this mean that small human populations are free from all infectious diseases? Explain. Why does the author believe these to be the oldest diseases of humanity?

12. When did crowd diseases first develop and what are the various reasons for their increased frequency?

13. What is the paradox regarding these diseases? Where did they come from? Why does the author say we must be constantly bombarded by them?

14. Describe the four stages in the evolution of a specialized human disease from an animal precursor.

15. In what sense do diseases represent evolution in progress? How do the mixoma virus and the Australian rabbits provide an example?

16. How were Europeans technologically superior to Native Americans? What gave Cortez the decisive advantage over the Aztecs? Why were the surviving Aztecs demoralized? What was Pizarro's similar "grim luck?" What happened to the Mound Builders of the Mississippi Valley?

17. What was the author taught in school that originally justified conquest? What do we know now?

18. Why was there "one-sidedness" to the disease transmission in spite of the large Native American populations? Explain the author's reasoning.

JARED DIAMOND is a contributing editor of *Discover,* a professor of physiology at the UCLA School of Medicine, a recipient of a MacArthur genius award, and a research associate in ornithology at the American Museum of Natural History. Expanded versions of many of his *Discover* articles appear in his book *The Third Chimpanzee: The Evolution and Future of the Human Animal,* which won Britain's 1992 COPUS prize for best science book. Not least among his many accomplishments was his rediscovery in 1981 of the long-lost bowerbird of New Guinea. Diamond wrote about pseudo-hermaphrodites for *Discover's* special June issue on the science of sex.

From *Discover*, October 1992, pp. 64, 66–68, 70–73. Copyright © 1992 by Jared Diamond. Reprinted by permission of the author.

The Americanization of Mental Illness

ETHAN WATTERS

Americans, particularly if they are of a certain leftward-leaning, college-educated type, worry about our country's blunders into other cultures. In some circles, it is easy to make friends with a rousing rant about the McDonald's near Tiananmen Square, the Nike factory in Malaysia or the latest blowback from our political or military interventions abroad. For all our self-recrimination, however, we may have yet to face one of the most remarkable effects of American-led globalization. We have for many years been busily engaged in a grand project of Americanizing the world's understanding of mental health and illness. We may indeed be far along in homogenizing the way the world goes mad.

This unnerving possibility springs from recent research by a loose group of anthropologists and cross-cultural psychiatrists. Swimming against the biomedical currents of the time, they have argued that mental illnesses are not discrete entities like the polio virus with their own natural histories. These researchers have amassed an impressive body of evidence suggesting that mental illnesses have never been the same the world over (either in prevalence or in form) but are inevitably sparked and shaped by the ethos of particular times and places. In some Southeast Asian cultures, men have been known to experience what is called amok, an episode of murderous rage followed by amnesia; men in the region also suffer from koro, which is characterized by the debilitating certainty that their genitals are retracting into their bodies. Across the fertile crescent of the Middle East there is zar, a condition related to spirit-possession beliefs that brings forth dissociative episodes of laughing, shouting and singing.

The diversity that can be found across cultures can be seen across time as well. In his book "Mad Travelers," the philosopher Ian Hacking documents the fleeting appearance in the 1890s of a fugue state in which European men would walk in a trance for hundreds of miles with no knowledge of their identities. The hysterical-leg paralysis that afflicted thousands of middle-class women in the late 19th century not only gives us a visceral understanding of the restrictions set on women's social roles at the time but can also be seen from this distance as a social role itself—the troubled unconscious minds of a certain class of women speaking the idiom of distress of their time.

"We might think of the culture as possessing a 'symptom repertoire'—a range of physical symptoms available to the unconscious mind for the physical expression of psychological conflict," Edward Shorter, a medical historian at the University of Toronto, wrote in his book "Paralysis: The Rise and Fall of a 'Hysterical' Symptom." "In some epochs, convulsions, the sudden inability to speak or terrible leg pain may loom prominently in the repertoire. In other epochs patients may draw chiefly upon such symptoms as abdominal pain, false estimates of body weight and enervating weakness as metaphors for conveying psychic stress."

In any given era, those who minister to the mentally ill—doctors or shamans or priests—inadvertently help to select which symptoms will be recognized as legitimate. Because the troubled mind has been influenced by healers of diverse religious and scientific persuasions, the forms of madness from one place and time often look remarkably different from the forms of madness in another.

That is until recently.

For more than a generation now, we in the West have aggressively spread our modern knowledge of mental illness around the world. We have done this in the name of science, believing that our approaches reveal the biological basis of psychic suffering and dispel prescientific myths and harmful stigma. There is now good evidence to suggest that in the process of teaching the rest of the world to think like us, we've been exporting our Western "symptom repertoire" as well. That is, we've been changing not only the treatments but also the expression of mental illness in other cultures. Indeed, a handful of mental-health disorders—depression, post-traumatic stress disorder and anorexia among them—now appear to be spreading across cultures with the speed of contagious diseases. These symptom clusters are becoming the lingua franca of human suffering, replacing indigenous forms of mental illness.

Dr. Sing Lee, a psychiatrist and researcher at the Chinese University of Hong Kong, watched the Westernization of a mental illness firsthand. In the late 1980s and early 1990s, he was busy documenting a rare and culturally specific form of anorexia nervosa in Hong Kong.

Unlike American anorexics, most of his patients did not intentionally diet nor did they express a fear of becoming fat. The complaints of Lee's patients were typically somatic—they complained most frequently of having bloated stomachs. Lee was trying to understand this indigenous form of anorexia and, at the same time, figure out why the disease remained so rare.

As he was in the midst of publishing his finding that food refusal had a particular expression and meaning in Hong Kong, the public's understanding of anorexia suddenly shifted. On Nov. 24, 1994, a teenage anorexic girl named Charlene Hsu Chi-Ying collapsed and died on a busy downtown street in Hong Kong. The death caught the attention of the media and was featured prominently in local papers. "Anorexia Made Her All Skin and Bones: Schoolgirl Falls on Ground Dead," read one headline in a Chinese-language newspaper. "Thinner Than a Yellow Flower, Weight-Loss Book Found in School Bag, Schoolgirl Falls Dead on Street," reported another Chinese-language paper.

In trying to explain what happened to Charlene, local reporters often simply copied out of American diagnostic manuals. The mental-health experts quoted in the Hong Kong papers and magazines confidently reported that anorexia in Hong Kong was the same disorder that appeared in the United States and Europe. In the wake of Charlene's death, the transfer of knowledge about the nature of anorexia (including how and why it was manifested and who was at risk) went only one way: from West to East.

Western ideas did not simply obscure the understanding of anorexia in Hong Kong; they also may have changed the expression of the illness itself. As the general public and the region's mental-health professionals came to understand the American diagnosis of anorexia, the presentation of the illness in Lee's patient population appeared to transform into the more virulent American standard. Lee once saw two or three anorexic patients a year; by the end of the 1990s he was seeing that many new cases each month. That increase sparked another series of media reports. "Children as Young as 10 Starving Themselves as Eating Ailments Rise," announced a headline in one daily newspaper. By the late 1990s, Lee's studies reported that between 3 and 10 percent of young women in Hong Kong showed disordered eating behavior. In contrast to Lee's earlier patients, these women most often cited fat phobia as the single most important reason for their self-starvation. By 2007 about 90 percent of the anorexics Lee treated reported fat phobia. New patients appeared to be increasingly conforming their experience of anorexia to the Western version of the disease.

What is being missed, Lee and others have suggested, is a deep understanding of how the expectations and beliefs of the sufferer shape their suffering. "Culture shapes the way general psychopathology is going to be translated partially or completely into specific psychopathology," Lee says. "When there is a cultural atmosphere in which professionals, the media, schools, doctors, psychologists all recognize and

endorse and talk about and publicize eating disorders, then people can be triggered to consciously or unconsciously pick eating-disorder pathology as a way to express that conflict."

The problem becomes especially worrisome in a time of globalization, when symptom repertoires can cross borders with ease. Having been trained in England and the United States, Lee knows better than most the locomotive force behind Western ideas about mental health and illness. Mental-health professionals in the West, and in the United States in particular, create official categories of mental diseases and promote them in a diagnostic manual that has become the worldwide standard. American researchers and institutions run most of the premier scholarly journals and host top conferences in the fields of psychology and psychiatry. Western drug companies dole out large sums for research and spend billions marketing medications for mental illnesses. In addition, Western-trained traumatologists often rush in where war or natural disasters strike to deliver "psychological first aid," bringing with them their assumptions about how the mind becomes broken by horrible events and how it is best healed. Taken together this is a juggernaut that Lee sees little chance of stopping. "As Western categories for diseases have gained dominance, microcultures that shape the illness experiences of individual patients are being discarded," Lee says. "The current has become too strong."

Would anorexia have so quickly become part of Hong Kong's symptom repertoire without the importation of the Western template for the disease? It seems unlikely. Beginning with scattered European cases in the early 19th century, it took more than 50 years for Western mental-health professionals to name, codify and popularize anorexia as a manifestation of hysteria. By contrast, after Charlene fell onto the sidewalk on Wan Chai Road on that late November day in 1994, it was just a matter of hours before the Hong Kong population learned the name of the disease, who was at risk and what it meant.

The idea that our Western conception of mental health and illness might be shaping the expression of illnesses in other cultures is rarely discussed in the professional literature. Many modern mental-health practitioners and researchers believe that the scientific standing of our drugs, our illness categories and our theories of the mind have put the field beyond the influence of endlessly shifting cultural trends and beliefs. After all, we now have machines that can literally watch the mind at work. We can change the chemistry of the brain in a variety of interesting ways and we can examine DNA sequences for abnormalities. The assumption is that these remarkable scientific advances have allowed modern-day practitioners to avoid the blind spots and cultural biases of their predecessors.

Modern-day mental-health practitioners often look back at previous generations of psychiatrists and psychologists with a thinly veiled pity, wondering how they could have been so swept away by the cultural currents of their time. The confident pronouncements of Victorian-era doctors regarding the epidemic of hysterical women are now dismissed as cultural artifacts. Similarly, illnesses found only in other cultures are often treated like carnival sideshows. Koro, amok and the like can be found far back in the American diagnostic manual (DSM-IV, Pages 845–849) under the heading "culture-bound syndromes." Given the attention they get, they might as well be labeled "Psychiatric Exotica: Two Bits a Gander."

Western mental-health practitioners often prefer to believe that the 844 pages of the DSM-IV prior to the inclusion of culture-bound syndromes describe real disorders of the mind, illnesses with symptomatology and outcomes relatively unaffected by shifting cultural beliefs. And, it logically follows, if these disorders are unaffected by culture, then they are surely universal to humans everywhere. In this view, the DSM is a field guide to the world's psyche, and applying it around the world represents simply the brave march of scientific knowledge.

Of course, we can become psychologically unhinged for many reasons that are common to all, like personal traumas, social upheavals or biochemical imbalances in our brains. Modern science has begun to reveal these causes. Whatever the trigger, however, the ill individual and those around him invariably rely on cultural beliefs and stories to understand what is happening. Those stories, whether they tell of spirit possession, semen loss or serotonin depletion, predict and shape the course of the illness in dramatic and often counterintuitive ways. In the end, what cross-cultural psychiatrists and anthropologists have to tell us is that all mental illnesses, including depression, P.T.S.D. and even schizophrenia, can be every bit as influenced by cultural beliefs and expectations today as hysterical-leg paralysis or the vapors or zar or any other mental illness ever experienced in the history of human madness. This does not mean that these illnesses and the pain associated with them are not real, or that sufferers deliberately shape their symptoms to fit a certain cultural niche. It means that a mental illness is an illness of the mind and cannot be understood without understanding the ideas, habits and predispositions—the idiosyncratic cultural trappings—of the mind that is its host.

Even when the underlying science is sound and the intentions altruistic, the export of Western biomedical ideas can have frustrating and unexpected consequences. For the last 50-odd years, Western mental-health professionals have been pushing what they call "mental-health literacy" on the rest of the world. Cultures became more "literate" as they adopted Western biomedical conceptions of diseases like depression and schizophrenia. One study published in The International Journal of Mental Health, for instance, portrayed those who endorsed the statement that "mental illness is an illness like any other" as having a "knowledgeable, benevolent, supportive orientation toward the mentally ill."

Mental illnesses, it was suggested, should be treated like "brain diseases" over which the patient has little choice or responsibility. This was promoted both as a scientific fact and as a social narrative that would reap great benefits. The logic seemed unassailable: Once people believed that the onset of mental illnesses did not spring from supernatural forces, character flaws, semen loss or some other prescientific notion, the sufferer would be protected from blame and stigma. This idea has been promoted by mental-health providers, drug companies and patient-advocacy groups like the National Alliance on Mental Illness in the United States and SANE in Britain. In a sometimes fractious field, everyone seemed to agree that this modern way of thinking about mental illness would reduce the social isolation and stigma often experienced by those with mental illness. Trampling on indigenous prescientific superstitions about the cause of mental illness seemed a small price to pay to relieve some of the social suffering of the mentally ill.

But does the "brain disease" belief actually reduce stigma?

In 1997, Prof. Sheila Mehta from Auburn University Montgomery in Alabama decided to find out if the "brain disease" narrative had the intended effect. She suspected that the biomedical explanation for mental illness might be influencing our attitudes toward the mentally ill in ways we weren't conscious of, so she thought up a clever experiment.

In her study, test subjects were led to believe that they were participating in a simple learning task with a partner who was, unbeknownst to them, a confederate in the study. Before the experiment started, the partners exchanged some biographical data, and the confederate informed the test subject that he suffered from a mental illness.

The confederate then stated either that the illness occurred because of "the kind of things that happened to me when I was a kid" or that he had "a disease just like any other, which affected my biochemistry." (These were termed the "psychosocial" explanation and the "disease" explanation respectively.) The experiment then called for the test subject to teach the confederate a pattern of button presses. When the confederate pushed the wrong button, the only feedback the test subject could give was a "barely discernible" to "somewhat painful" electrical shock.

Analyzing the data, Mehta found a difference between the group of subjects given the psychosocial explanation for their partner's mental-illness history and those given the brain-disease explanation. Those who believed that their partner suffered a biochemical "disease like any other" increased the severity of the shocks at a faster rate than those who believed they were paired with someone who had a mental disorder caused by an event in the past.

"The results of the current study suggest that we may actually treat people more harshly when their problem is described in disease terms," Mehta wrote. "We say we are being kind, but our actions suggest otherwise." The problem, it appears, is that the biomedical narrative about an illness like schizophrenia carries with it the subtle assumption that a brain made ill through biomedical or genetic abnormalities is more thoroughly broken and permanently abnormal than one made ill though life events. "Viewing those with mental disorders as diseased sets them apart and may lead to our perceiving them as physically distinct. Biochemical aberrations make them almost a different species."

In other words, the belief that was assumed to decrease stigma actually increased it. Was the same true outside the lab in the real world?

The question is important because the Western push for "mental-health literacy" has gained ground. Studies show that much of the world has steadily adopted this medical model of mental illness. Although these changes are most extensive in the United States and Europe, similar shifts have been documented elsewhere. When asked to name the sources of mental illness, people from a variety of cultures are increasingly likely to mention "chemical imbalance" or "brain disease" or "genetic/inherited" factors.

Unfortunately, at the same time that Western mental-health professionals have been convincing the world to think and talk about mental illnesses in biomedical terms, we have been simultaneously losing the war against stigma at home and abroad. Studies of attitudes in the United States from 1950 to 1996 have shown that the perception of dangerousness surrounding people with schizophrenia has steadily increased over this time. Similarly, a study in Germany found that the public's desire to maintain distance from those with a diagnosis of schizophrenia increased from 1990 to 2001.

Researchers hoping to learn what was causing this rise in stigma found the same surprising connection that Mehta discovered in her lab. It turns out that those who adopted biomedical/genetic beliefs about mental disorders were the same people who wanted less contact with the mentally ill and thought of them as more dangerous and unpredictable. This unfortunate relationship has popped up in numerous studies around the world. In a study conducted in Turkey, for example, those who labeled schizophrenic behavior as akil hastaligi (illness of the brain or reasoning abilities) were more inclined to assert that schizophrenics were aggressive and should not live freely in the community than those who saw the disorder as ruhsal hastagi (a disorder of the spiritual or inner self). Another study, which looked at populations in Germany, Russia and Mongolia, found that "irrespective of place . . . endorsing biological factors as the cause of schizophrenia was associated with a greater desire for social distance."

Even as we have congratulated ourselves for becoming more "benevolent and supportive" of the mentally ill, we have steadily backed away from the sufferers themselves. It appears, in short, that the impact of our worldwide anti-stigma campaign may have been the exact opposite of what we intended.

Nowhere are the limitations of Western ideas and treatments more evident than in the case of schizophrenia. Researchers have long sought to understand what may be the most perplexing finding in the cross-cultural study of mental illness: people with schizophrenia in developing countries appear to fare better over time than those living in industrialized nations.

This was the startling result of three large international studies carried out by the World Health Organization over the course of 30 years, starting in the early 1970s. The research showed that patients outside the United States and Europe had significantly lower relapse rates—as much as two-thirds lower in one follow-up study. These findings have been widely discussed and debated in part because of their obvious incongruity: the regions of the world with the most resources to devote to the illness—the best technology, the cutting-edge medicines and the best-financed academic and private-research institutions—had the most troubled and socially marginalized patients.

Trying to unravel this mystery, the anthropologist Juli McGruder from the University of Puget Sound spent years in Zanzibar studying families of schizophrenics. Though the population is predominantly Muslim, Swahili spirit-possession beliefs are still prevalent in the archipelago and commonly evoked to explain the actions of anyone violating social norms—from a sister lashing out at her brother to someone beset by psychotic delusions.

McGruder found that far from being stigmatizing, these beliefs served certain useful functions. The beliefs prescribed a variety of socially accepted interventions and ministrations that kept the ill person bound to the family and kinship group. "Muslim and Swahili spirits are not exorcised in the Christian sense of casting out demons," McGruder determined. "Rather they are coaxed with food and goods, feted with song and dance. They are placated, settled, reduced in malfeasance." McGruder saw this approach in many small acts of kindness. She watched family members use saffron paste to write phrases from the Koran on the rims of drinking bowls so the ill person could literally imbibe the holy words. The spirit-possession beliefs had other unexpected benefits. Critically, the story allowed the person with schizophrenia a cleaner bill of health when the illness went into remission. An ill individual enjoying a time of relative mental health could, at least temporarily, retake his or her responsibilities in the kinship group. Since the illness was seen as the work of outside forces, it was understood as an affliction for the sufferer but not as an identity.

For McGruder, the point was not that these practices or beliefs were effective in curing schizophrenia. Rather, she said she believed that they indirectly helped control the course of the illness. Besides keeping the sick individual in the social group, the religious beliefs in Zanzibar also allowed for a type of calmness and acquiescence in the face of the illness that she had rarely witnessed in the West.

The course of a metastasizing cancer is unlikely to be changed by how we talk about it. With schizophrenia, however, symptoms are inevitably entangled in a person's complex interactions with those around him or her. In fact, researchers have long documented how certain emotional reactions from family members correlate with higher relapse rates for people who have a diagnosis of schizophrenia. Collectively referred to as "high expressed emotion," these reactions include criticism, hostility and emotional overinvolvement (like overprotectiveness or constant intrusiveness in the patient's life). In one study, 67 percent of white American families with a schizophrenic family member were rated as "high EE." (Among British families, 48 percent were high EE; among Mexican families the figure was 41 percent and for Indian families 23 percent.)

Does this high level of "expressed emotion" in the United States mean that we lack sympathy or the desire to care for our mentally ill? Quite the opposite. Relatives who were "high EE" were simply expressing a particularly American view of the self. They tended to believe that individuals are the captains of their own destiny and should be able to overcome their problems by force of personal will. Their critical comments to the mentally ill person didn't mean that these family members were cruel or uncaring; they were simply applying the same assumptions about human nature that they applied to themselves. They were reflecting an "approach to the world that is active, resourceful and that emphasizes personal accountability," Prof. Jill M. Hooley of Harvard University concluded. "Far from high criticism reflecting something negative about the family members of patients with schizophrenia, high criticism (and hence high EE) was associated with a characteristic that is widely regarded as positive."

Widely regarded as positive, that is, in the United States. Many traditional cultures regard the self in different terms—as inseparable from your role in your kinship group, intertwined with the story of your ancestry and permeable to the spirit world. What McGruder found in Zanzibar was that families often drew strength from this more connected and less isolating idea of human nature. Their ability to maintain a low level of expressed emotion relied on these beliefs. And that level of expressed emotion in turn may be key to improving the fortunes of the schizophrenia sufferer.

Of course, to the extent that our modern psychopharmacological drugs can relieve suffering, they should not be denied to the rest of the world. The problem is that our biomedical advances are hard to separate from our particular cultural beliefs. It is difficult to distinguish, for example, the biomedical conception of schizophrenia—the idea that the disease exists within the biochemistry of the brain—from the more inchoate Western assumption that the self resides there as well. "Mental illness is feared and has such a stigma because it represents a reversal of what Western humans . . . have come to value as the essence of human nature," McGruder concludes. "Because our culture so highly values . . . an illusion of self-control and control of circumstance, we become abject when contemplating mentation that seems more changeable, less restrained and less controllable, more open to outside influence, than we imagine our own to be."

Cross-cultural psychiatrists have pointed out that the mental-health ideas we export to the world are rarely unadulterated scientific facts and never culturally neutral. "Western mental-health discourse introduces core components of Western culture, including a theory of human nature, a definition of personhood, a sense of time and memory and a source of moral authority. None of this is universal," Derek Summerfield of the Institute of Psychiatry in London observes. He has also written: "The problem is the overall thrust that comes from being at the heart of the one globalizing culture. It is as if one version of human nature is being presented as definitive, and one set of ideas about pain and suffering. . . . There is no one definitive psychology."

Behind the promotion of Western ideas of mental health and healing lie a variety of cultural assumptions about human nature. Westerners share, for instance, evolving beliefs about what type of life event is likely to make one psychologically traumatized, and we agree that venting emotions by talking is more healthy than stoic silence. We've come to agree that the human mind is rather fragile and that it is best to consider many emotional experiences and mental states as illnesses that require professional intervention. (The National Institute of Mental Health reports that a quarter of Americans have diagnosable mental illnesses each year.) The ideas we export often have at their heart a particularly American brand of hyperintrospection—a penchant for "psychologizing" daily existence. These ideas remain deeply influenced by the Cartesian split between the mind and the body, the Freudian duality between the conscious and unconscious, as well as the many self-help philosophies and schools of therapy that have encouraged Americans to separate the health of the individual from the health of the group. These Western ideas of the mind are proving as seductive to the rest of the world as fast food and rap music, and we are spreading them with speed and vigor.

No one would suggest that we withhold our medical advances from other countries, but it's perhaps past time to admit that even our most remarkable scientific leaps in understanding the brain haven't yet created the sorts of cultural stories from which humans take comfort and meaning. When these scientific advances are translated into popular belief and cultural stories, they are often stripped of the complexity of the science and become comically insubstantial narratives. Take for instance this website text advertising the antidepressant Paxil: "Just as a cake recipe requires you to use flour, sugar and baking powder in the right amounts, your brain needs a fine chemical balance in order to perform at its best." The Western mind, endlessly analyzed by generations of theorists and researchers, has now been reduced to a batter of chemicals we carry around in the mixing bowl of our skulls.

All cultures struggle with intractable mental illnesses with varying degrees of compassion and cruelty, equanimity and fear. Looking at ourselves through the eyes of those living in places where madness and psychological trauma are still embedded in complex religious and cultural narratives, however, we get a glimpse of ourselves as an increasingly insecure and fearful people. Some philosophers and psychiatrists have suggested that we are investing our great wealth in researching and treating mental illness—medicalizing ever larger swaths of human experience—because we have rather suddenly lost older belief systems that once gave meaning and context to mental suffering.

If our rising need for mental-health services does indeed spring from a breakdown of meaning, our insistence that the rest of the world think like us may be all the more problematic. Offering the latest Western mental-health theories, treatments and categories in an attempt to ameliorate the psychological stress sparked by modernization and globalization is not a solution; it may be part of the problem. When we undermine local conceptions of the self and modes of healing, we may be speeding along the disorienting changes that are at the very heart of much of the world's mental distress.

Assess Your Progress

1. What evidence is there that mental illness has never been the same the world over?

2. What is meant by the "symptom repertoire" of a culture? How has this been aided by those who minister to the mentally ill?

3. Describe the process by which we in the West have spread our modern knowledge of mental illness along with our "symptom repertoire."

4. How was Dr. Sing Lee able to observe a unique form of anorexia in Hong Kong evolve into a Westernized version of the disease?

5. How has globalization enabled Western symptom repertoires to spread across borders with ease?

6. Why do Western health professionals believe their concepts of mental illness are free of cultural bias? How does the author respond?

7. What is the logic behind seeing mental illness as a "brain disease?" Why does it increase the stigma rather than decrease it?

8. How does the belief that spiritual possession causes schizophrenia illustrate the limitations of Western ideas regarding treatment of the disease? How does this relate to differing concepts of self?

9. How is that "offering the latest Western mental-health theories, treatments and categories in an attempt to ameliorate the psychological stress sparked by modernization and globalization is not a solution; it may be part of the problem?"

ETHAN WATTERS lives in San Francisco. This essay is adapted from his book *Crazy Like Us: The Globalization of the American Psyche.*

The Price of Progress

JOHN BODLEY

In aiming at progress . . . you must let no one suffer by too drastic a measure, nor pay too high a price in upheaval and devastation, for your innovation.

Maunier, 1949: 725

Until recently, government planners have always considered economic development and progress beneficial goals that all societies should want to strive toward. The social advantage of progress—as defined in terms of increased incomes, higher standards of living, greater security, and better health—are thought to be positive, *universal* goods, to be obtained at any price. Although one may argue that tribal peoples must sacrifice their traditional cultures to obtain these benefits, government planners generally feel that this is a small price to pay for such obvious advantages.

In earlier chapters [in *Victims of Progress,* 3rd ed.], evidence was presented to demonstrate that autonomous tribal peoples have not *chosen* progress to enjoy its advantages, but that governments have *pushed* progress upon them to obtain tribal resources, not primarily to share with the tribal peoples the benefits of progress. It has also been shown that the price of forcing progress on unwilling recipients has involved the deaths of millions of tribal people, as well as their loss of land, political sovereignty, and the right to follow their own life style. This chapter does not attempt to further summarize that aspect of the cost of progress, but instead analyzes the specific effects of the participation of tribal peoples in the world-market economy. In direct opposition to the usual interpretation, it is argued here that the benefits of progress are often both illusory and detrimental to tribal peoples when they have not been allowed to control their own resources and define their relationship to the market economy.

Progress and the Quality of Life

One of the primary difficulties in assessing the benefits of progress and economic development for any culture is that of establishing a meaningful measure of both benefit and detriment. It is widely recognized that *standard of living,* which is the most frequently used measure of progress, is an intrinsically ethnocentric concept relying heavily upon indicators that lack universal cultural relevance. Such factors as GNP, per capita income, capital formation, employment rates, literacy, formal education, consumption of manufactured goods, number of doctors and hospital beds per thousand persons, and the amount of money spent on government welfare and health programs may be irrelevant measures of actual *quality* of life for autonomous or even semiautonomous tribal cultures. In its 1954 report, the Trust Territory government indicated that since the Micronesian population was still largely satisfying its own needs within a cashless subsistence economy, "Money income is not a significant measure of living standards, production, or well-being in this area" (TTR, 1953: 44). Unfortunately, within a short time the government began to rely on an enumeration of certain imported consumer goods as indicators of a higher standard of living in the islands, even though many tradition-oriented islanders felt that these new goods symbolized a lowering of the quality of life.

A more useful measure of the benefits of progress might be based on a formula for evaluating cultures devised by Goldschmidt (1952: 135). According to these less ethnocentric criteria, the important question to ask is: Does progress or economic development increase or decrease a given culture's ability to satisfy the physical and psychological needs of its population, or its stability? This question is a far more direct measure of quality of life than are the standard economic correlates of development, and it is universally relevant. Specific indication of this *standard* of living could be found for any society in the nutritional status and general physical and mental health of its population, the incidence of crime and delinquency, the demographic structure, family stability, and the society's relationship to its natural resource base. A society with high rates of malnutrition and crime, and one degrading its natural environment to the extent of threatening its continued existence, might be described as at a lower standard of living than is another society where these problems did not exist.

Careful examination of the data, which compare, on these specific points, the former condition of self-sufficient tribal peoples with their condition following their incorporation into the world-market economy, leads to the conclusion that their standard of living is *lowered,* not raised, by economic progress—and often to a dramatic degree. This is perhaps the most outstanding and inescapable fact to emerge from the years of research that anthropologists have devoted to the study of culture change and modernization. Despite the best intentions of those who have promoted change and improvement, all too often the results have been poverty, longer working hours, and much greater physical exertion, poor health, social disorder, discontent, discrimination, overpopulation, and environmental deterioration—combined with the destruction of the traditional culture.

Diseases of Development

Perhaps it would be useful for public health specialists to start talking about a new category of diseases. . . . Such diseases could be called the "diseases of development" and would consist of those pathological conditions which are based on the usually unanticipated consequences of the implementation of developmental schemes.

Hughes & Hunter, 1972: 93

Economic development increases the disease rate of affected peoples in at least three ways. First, to the extent that development is successful, it makes developed populations suddenly become vulnerable to all of the diseases suffered almost exclusively by "advanced" peoples. Among these are diabetes, obesity, hypertension, and a variety of circulatory problems. Second, development disturbs traditional environmental balances and may dramatically increase certain bacterial and parasite diseases. Finally, when development goals prove unattainable, an assortment of poverty diseases may appear in association with the crowded conditions of urban slums and the general breakdown in traditional socioeconomic systems.

Outstanding examples of the first situation can be seen in the Pacific, where some of the most successfully developed native peoples are found. In Micronesia, where development has progressed more rapidly than perhaps anywhere else, between 1958 and 1972 the population doubled, but the number of patients treated for heart disease in the local hospitals nearly tripled, mental disorder increased eightfold, and by 1972 hypertension and nutritional deficiencies began to make significant appearances for the first time (TTR, 1959, 1973, statistical tables).

Although some critics argue that the Micronesian figures simply represent better health monitoring due to economic progress, rigorously controlled data from Polynesia show a similar trend. The progressive acquisition of modern degenerative diseases was documented by an eight-member team of New Zealand medical specialists, anthropologists, and nutritionists, whose research was funded by the Medical Research Council of New Zealand and the World Health Organization. These researchers investigated the health status of a genetically related population at various points along a continuum of increasing cash income, modernizing diet, and urbanization. The extremes on this acculturation continuum were represented by the relatively traditional Pukapukans of the Cook Islands and the essentially Europeanized New Zealand Maori, while the busily developing Rarotongans, also of the Cook Islands, occupied the intermediate position. In 1971, after eight years of work, the

team's preliminary findings were summarized by Dr. Ian Prior, cardiologist and leader of the research, as follows:

We are beginning to observe that the more an islander takes on the ways of the West, the more prone he is to succumb to our degenerative diseases. In fact, it does not seem too much to say our evidence now shows that the farther the Pacific natives move from the quiet, carefree life of their ancestors, the closer they come to gout, diabetes, atherosclerosis, obesity, and hypertension.

Prior, 1971: 2

In Pukapuka, where progress was limited by the island's small size and its isolated location some 480 kilometers from the nearest port, the annual per capita income was only about thirty-six dollars and the economy remained essentially at a subsistence level. Resources were limited and the area was visited by trading ships only three or four times a year; thus, there was little opportunity for intensive economic development. Predictably, the population of Pukapuka was characterized by relatively low levels of imported sugar and salt intake, and a presumably related low level of heart disease, high blood pressure, and diabetes. In Rarotonga, where economic success was introducing town life, imported food, and motorcycles, sugar and salt intakes nearly tripled, high blood pressure increased approximately ninefold, diabetes two- to threefold, and heart disease doubled for men and more than quadrupled for women, while the number of grossly obese women increased more than tenfold. Among the New Zealand Maori, sugar intake was nearly eight times that of the Pukapukans, gout in men was nearly double its rate on Pukapuka, and diabetes in men was more than fivefold higher, while heart disease in women had increased more than sixfold. The Maori were, in fact, dying of "European" diseases at a greater rate than was the average New Zealand European.

Government development policies designed to bring about changes in local hydrology, vegetation, and settlement patterns and to increase population mobility, and even programs aimed at reducing certain diseases, have frequently led to dramatic increases in disease rates because of the unforeseen effects of disturbing the preexisting order. Hughes and Hunter (1972) published an excellent survey of cases in which development led directly to increased disease rates in Africa. They concluded that hasty development intervention in relatively balanced local cultures and environments resulted in "a drastic deterioration in the social and economic conditions of life."

Traditional populations in general have presumably learned to live with the endemic pathogens of their environments, and in some cases they have evolved genetic adaptations to specific diseases, such as the sickle-cell trait, which provided an immunity to malaria. Unfortunately, however, outside intervention has entirely changed this picture. In the late 1960s, sleeping sickness suddenly increased in many areas of Africa and even spread to areas where it did not formerly occur, due to the building of new roads and migratory labor, both of which caused increased population movement. Large-scale relocation schemes, such as the Zande Scheme, had disastrous results when natives were moved from their traditional disease-free refuges into infected areas. Dams and irrigation developments inadvertently created ideal conditions for the rapid proliferation of snails carrying schistosomiasis (a liver fluke disease), and major epidemics suddenly occurred in areas where this disease had never before been a problem. DDT spraying programs have been temporarily successful in controlling malaria, but there is often a rebound effect that increases the problem when spraying is discontinued, and the malarial mosquitoes are continually evolving resistant strains.

Urbanization is one of the prime measures of development, but it is a mixed blessing for most former tribal peoples. Urban health standards are abysmally poor and generally worse than in rural areas for the detribalized individuals who have crowded into the towns and cities throughout Africa, Asia, and Latin America seeking wage employment out of new economic necessity. Infectious diseases related to crowding and poor sanitation are rampant in urban centers, while greatly increased stress and poor nutrition aggravate a variety of other health problems. Malnutrition and other diet-related conditions are, in fact, one of the characteristic hazards of progress faced by tribal peoples and are discussed in the following sections.

The Hazards of Dietary Change

The traditional diets of tribal peoples are admirably adapted to their nutritional needs and available food resources. Even though these diets may seem bizarre, absurd, and unpalatable to outsiders, they are unlikely to be improved by drastic modifications. Given the delicate balances and complexities involved in any subsistence system, change always involves risks, but for tribal people the effects of dietary change have been catastrophic.

Under normal conditions, food habits are remarkably resistant to change, and indeed people are unlikely to abandon their traditional diets voluntarily in favor of dependence on difficult-to-obtain exotic imports. In some cases it is true that imported foods may be identified with powerful outsiders and are therefore sought as symbols of greater prestige. This may lead to such absurdities as Amazonian Indians choosing to consume imported canned tunafish when abundant high-quality fish is available in their own rivers. Another example of this situation occurs in tribes where mothers prefer to feed their infants expensive nutritionally inadequate canned milk from unsanitary, but *high status,* baby bottles. The high status of these items is often promoted by clever traders and clever advertising campaigns.

Aside from these apparently voluntary changes, it appears that more often dietary changes are forced upon unwilling tribal peoples by circumstances beyond their control. In some areas, new food crops have been introduced by government decree, or as a consequence of forced relocation or other policies designed to end hunting, pastoralism, or shifting cultivation. Food habits have also been modified by massive disruption of the natural environment by outsiders—as when sheepherders transformed the Australian Aborigines' foraging territory or when European invaders destroyed the bison herds that were the primary element in the Plains Indians' subsistence patterns. Perhaps the most frequent cause of diet change occurs when formerly self-sufficient peoples find that wage labor, cash cropping, and other economic development activities that feed tribal resources into the world-market economy must inevitably divert time and energy away from the production of subsistence foods. Many developing peoples suddenly discover that, like it or not, they are unable to secure traditional foods and must spend their newly acquired cash on costly, and often nutritionally inferior, manufactured foods.

Overall, the available data seem to indicate that the dietary changes that are linked to involvement in the world-market economy have tended to *lower* rather than raise the nutritional levels of the affected tribal peoples. Specifically, the vitamin, mineral, and protein components of their diets are often drastically reduced and replaced by enormous increases in starch and carbohydrates, often in the form of white flour and refined sugar.

Any deterioration in the quality of a given population's diet is almost certain to be reflected in an increase in deficiency diseases and a general decline in health status. Indeed, as tribal peoples have shifted to a diet based on imported manufactured or processed foods, there has been a dramatic rise in malnutrition, a massive increase in dental problems, and a variety of other nutritional-related disorders. Nutritional physiology is so complex that even well-meaning dietary changes have had tragic consequences. In many areas of Southeast Asia, government-sponsored protein supplementation programs supplying milk to protein-deficient populations caused unexpected health problems and increased mortality. Officials failed to anticipate that in cultures where adults do not normally drink milk, the enzymes needed to digest it are no longer produced and milk *intolerance* results (Davis & Bolin, 1972). In Brazil, a similar milk distribution program caused an epidemic of permanent blindness by aggravating a preexisting vitamin A deficiency (Bunce, 1972).

Teeth and Progress

There is nothing new in the observation that savages, or peoples living under primitive conditions, have, in general, excellent teeth. . . . Nor is it news that most civilized populations possess wretched teeth which begin to decay almost before they have erupted completely, and that dental caries is likely to be accompanied by periodontal disease with further reaching complications.

Hooton, 1945: xviii

Anthropologists have long recognized that undisturbed tribal peoples are often in excellent physical condition. And it has often been noted specifically that dental caries and the other dental abnormalities that plague industrialized societies are absent or rare among tribal peoples who have retained their traditional diets. The fact that tribal food habits may contribute to the development of sound teeth, whereas modernized diets may do just the opposite, was illustrated as long ago as 1894 in an article in the *Journal of the Royal Anthropological Institute* that described the results of a comparison between the teeth of ten Sioux Indians who were examined when they came to London as members of Buffalo Bill's Wild West Show and were found to be completely free of caries and in possession of all their teeth, even though half of the group were over thirty-nine years of age. Londoners' teeth were conspicuous for both their caries and their steady reduction in number with advancing age. The difference was attributed primarily to the wear and polishing caused by the traditional Indian diet of coarse food and the fact that they chewed their food longer, encouraged by the absence of tableware.

One of the most remarkable studies of the dental conditions of tribal peoples and the impact of dietary change was conducted in the 1930s by Weston Price (1945), an American dentist who was interested in determining what caused normal, healthy teeth. Between 1931 and 1936, Price systematically explored tribal areas throughout the world to locate and examine the most isolated peoples who were still living on traditional foods. His fieldwork covered Alaska, the Canadian Yukon, Hudson Bay, Vancouver Island, Florida, the Andes, the Amazon, Samoa, Tahiti, New Zealand, Australia, New Caledonia, Fiji, the Torres Strait, East Africa, and the Nile. The study demonstrated both the superior quality of aboriginal dentition and the devastation that occurs as modern diets are adopted. In nearly every area where traditional foods were still being eaten, Price found perfect teeth with normal dental arches and virtually no decay, whereas caries and abnormalities increased steadily as new diets were adopted. In many cases the change was sudden and striking. Among Eskimo groups subsisting entirely on traditional food he found caries totally absent, whereas in groups eating a considerable quantity of store-bought food approximately 20 percent of their teeth were decayed. This figure rose to more than 30 percent with Eskimo groups subsisting almost exclusively on purchased or government-supplied food, and reached an incredible 48 percent among the Vancouver Island Indians. Unfortunately for many of these people, modern dental treatment did not accompany the new food, and their suffering was appalling. The loss of teeth was, of course, bad enough in itself, and it certainly undermined the population's resistance to many new diseases, including tuberculosis. But new foods were also accompanied by crowded, misplaced teeth, gum diseases, distortion of the face, and pinching of the nasal cavity. Abnormalities in the dental arch appeared in the new generation following the change in diet, while caries appeared almost immediately even in adults.

Price reported that in many areas the affected peoples were conscious of their own physical deterioration. At a mission school in Africa, the principal asked him to explain to the native schoolchildren why they were not physically as strong as children who had had no contact with schools. On an island in the Torres Strait the natives knew exactly what was causing their problems and resisted—almost to the point of bloodshed—government efforts to establish a store that would make imported food available. The government prevailed, however, and Price was able to establish a relationship between the length of time the government store had been established and the increasing incidence of caries among a population that showed an almost 100 percent immunity to them before the store had been opened.

In New Zealand, the Maori, who in their aboriginal state are often considered to have been among the healthiest, most perfectly developed of people, were found to have "advanced" the furthest. According to Price:

Their modernization was demonstrated not only by the high incidence of dental caries but also by the fact that 90 percent of the adults and 100 percent of the children had abnormalities of the dental arches.

Price, 1945: 206

Malnutrition

Malnutrition, particularly in the form of protein deficiency, has become a critical problem for tribal peoples who must adopt new economic patterns. Population pressures, cash cropping, and government programs all have tended to encourage the replacement of traditional crops and other food sources that were rich in protein with substitutes, high in calories but low in protein. In Africa, for example, protein-rich staples such as millet and sorghum are being replaced systematically by high-yielding manioc and plantains, which have insignificant amounts of protein. The problem is increased for cash croppers and wage laborers whose earnings are too low and unpredictable to allow purchase of adequate amounts of protein. In some rural areas, agricultural laborers have been forced systematically to deprive nonproductive members (principally children) of their households of their minimal nutritional requirements to satisfy the need of the productive members. This process has been documented in northeastern Brazil following the introduction of large-scale sisal plantations (Gross & Underwood, 1971). In urban centers the difficulties of obtaining nutritionally adequate diets are even more serious for tribal immigrants, because costs are higher and poor quality foods are more tempting.

One of the most tragic, and largely overlooked, aspects of chronic malnutrition is that it can lead to abnormally undersized brain development and apparently irreversible brain damage; it has been associated with various forms of mental impairment or retardation. Malnutrition has been linked clinically with mental retardation in both Africa and Latin America (see, for example, Mönckeberg, 1968), and this appears to be a worldwide phenomenon with serious implications (Montagu, 1972).

Optimistic supporters of progress will surely say that all of these new health problems are being overstressed and that the introduction of hospitals, clinics, and the other modern health institutions will overcome or at least compensate for all of these difficulties. However, it appears that uncontrolled population growth and economic impoverishment probably will keep most of these benefits out of reach for many tribal peoples, and the intervention of modern medicine has at least partly contributed to the problem in the first place.

The generalization that civilization frequently has a broad negative impact on tribal health has found broad empirical support (see especially Kroeger & Barbira-Freedman [1982] on Amazonia; Reinhard [1976] on the Arctic; and Wirsing

[1985] globally), but these conclusions have not gone unchallenged. Some critics argue that tribal health was often poor before modernization, and they point specifically to tribals' low life expectancy and high infant mortality rates. Demographic statistics on tribal populations are often problematic because precise data are scarce, but they do show a less favorable profile than that enjoyed by many industrial societies. However, it should be remembered that our present life expectancy is a recent phenomenon that has been very costly in terms of medical research and technological advances. Furthermore, the benefits of our health system are not enjoyed equally by all members of our society. High infant mortality could be viewed as a relatively inexpensive and egalitarian tribal public health program that offered the reasonable expectation of a healthy and productive life for those surviving to age fifteen.

Some critics also suggest that certain tribal populations, such as the New Guinea highlanders, were "stunted" by nutritional deficiencies created by tribal culture and are "improved" by "acculturation" and cash cropping (Dennett & Connell, 1988). Although this argument does suggest that the health question requires careful evaluation, it does not invalidate the empirical generalizations already established. Nutritional deficiencies undoubtedly occurred in densely populated zones in the central New Guinea highlands. However, the specific case cited above may not be widely representative of other tribal groups even in New Guinea, and it does not address the facts of outside intrusion or the inequities inherent in the contemporary development process.

Ecocide

"How is it," asked a herdsman . . . "how is it that these hills can no longer give pasture to my cattle? In my father's day they were green and cattle thrived there; today there is no grass and my cattle starve." As one looked one saw that what had once been a green hill had become a raw red rock.

Jones, 1934

Progress not only brings new threats to the health of tribal peoples, but it also imposes new strains on the ecosystems upon which they must depend for their ultimate survival. The introduction of new technology, increased consumption, lowered mortality, and the eradication of all traditional controls have combined to replace what for most tribal peoples was a relatively stable balance between population and natural resources, with a new system that is imbalanced. Economic development is forcing *ecocide* on peoples who were once careful stewards of their resources. There is already a trend toward widespread environmental deterioration in tribal areas, involving resource depletion, erosion, plant and animal extinction, and a disturbing series of other previously unforeseen changes.

After the initial depopulation suffered by most tribal peoples during their engulfment by frontiers of national expansion, most tribal populations began to experience rapid growth. Authorities generally attribute this growth to the introduction of modern medicine and new health measures and the termination of intertribal warfare, which lowered morality rates, as well as to new technology, which increased food production. Certainly all of these factors played a part, but merely lowering mortality rates would not have produced the rapid population growth that most tribal areas have experienced if traditional birth-spacing mechanisms had not been eliminated at the same time. Regardless of which factors were most important, it is clear that all of the natural and cultural checks on population growth have suddenly been pushed aside by culture change, while tribal lands have been steadily reduced and consumption levels have risen. In many tribal areas, environmental deterioration due to overuse of resources has set in, and in other areas such deterioration is imminent as resources continue to dwindle relative to the expanding population and increased use. Of course, population expansion by tribal peoples may have positive political consequences, because where tribals can retain or regain their status as local majorities they may be in a more favorable position to defend their resources against intruders.

Swidden systems and pastoralism, both highly successful economic systems under traditional conditions, have proved particularly vulnerable to increased population pressures and outside efforts to raise productivity beyond its natural limits. Research in Amazonia demonstrates that population pressures and related resource depletion can be created indirectly by official policies that restrict swidden peoples to smaller territories. Resource depletion itself can then become a powerful means of forcing tribal people into participating in the world-market economy—thus leading to further resource depletion. For example, Bodley and Benson (1979) showed how the Shipibo Indians in Peru were forced to further deplete their forest resources by cash cropping in the forest area to replace the resources that had been destroyed earlier by the intensive cash cropping necessitated by the narrow confines of their reserve. In this case, certain species of palm trees that had provided critical housing materials were destroyed by forest clearing and had to be replaced by costly purchased materials. Research by Gross (1979) and others showed similar processes at work among four tribal groups in central Brazil and demonstrated that the degree of market involvement increases directly with increases in resource depletion.

The settling of nomadic herders and the removal of prior controls on herd size have often led to serious overgrazing and erosion problems where these had not previously occurred. There are indications that the desertification problem in the Sahel region of Africa was aggravated by programs designed to settle nomads. The first sign of imbalance in a swidden system appears when the planting cycles are shortened to the point that garden plots are reused before sufficient forest regrowth can occur. If reclearing and planting continue in the same area, the natural patterns of forest succession may be disturbed irreversibly and the soil can be impaired permanently. An extensive tract of tropical rainforest in the lower Amazon of Brazil was reduced to a semiarid desert in just fifty years through such a process (Ackermann, 1964). The soils in the Azande area are also now seriously threatened with laterization and other problems as a result of the government-promoted cotton development scheme (McNeil, 1972).

209

The dangers of overdevelopment and the vulnerability of local resource systems have long been recognized by both anthropologists and tribal peoples themselves. But the pressures for change have been overwhelming. In 1948 the Maya villagers of Chan Kom complained to Redfield (1962) about the shortening of their swidden cycles, which they correctly attributed to increasing population pressures. Redfield told them, however, that they had no choice but to go "forward with technology" (Redfield, 1962: 178). In Assam, swidden cycles were shortened from an average of twelve years to only two or three within just twenty years, and anthropologists warned that the limits of swiddening would soon be reached (Burling, 1963: 311–312). In the Pacific, anthropologists warned of population pressures on limited resources as early as the 1930s (Keesing, 1941: 64–65). These warnings seemed fully justified, considering the fact that the crowded Tikopians were prompted by population pressures on their tiny island to suggest that infanticide be legalized. The warnings have been dramatically reinforced since then by the doubling of Micronesia's population in just the fourteen years between 1958 and 1972, from 70,600 to 114,645, while consumption levels have soared. By 1985 Micronesia's population had reached 162,321.

The environmental hazards of economic development and rapid population growth have become generally recognized only since worldwide concerns over environmental issues began in the early 1970s. Unfortunately, there is as yet little indication that the leaders of the new developing nations are sufficiently concerned with environmental limitations. On the contrary, governments are forcing tribal peoples into a self-reinforcing spiral of population growth and intensified resource exploitation, which may be stopped only by environmental disaster or the total impoverishment of the tribals.

The reality of ecocide certainly focuses attention on the fundamental contrasts between tribal and industrial systems in their use of natural resources, who controls them, and how they are managed. Tribal peoples are victimized because they control resources that outsiders demand. The resources exist because tribals managed them conservatively. However, as with the issue of the health consequences of detribalization, some anthropologists minimize the adaptive achievements of tribal groups and seem unwilling to concede that ecocide might be a consequence of cultural change. Critics attack an exaggerated "noble savage" image of tribals living in perfect harmony with nature and having no visible impact on their surroundings. They then show that tribals do in fact modify the environment, and they conclude that there is no significant difference between how tribals and industrial societies treat their environments. For example, Charles Wagley declared that Brazilian Indians such as the Tapirape

are not "natural men." They have human vices just as we do.... They do not live "in tune" with nature any more than I do; in fact, they can often be as destructive of their environment, within their limitations, as some civilized men. The Tapirape are not innocent or childlike in any way.

Wagley, 1977: 302

Anthropologist Terry Rambo demonstrated that the Semang of the Malaysian rain forests have a measurable impact on their environment. In his monograph *Primitive Polluters,* Rambo (1985) reported that the Semang live in smoke-filled houses. They sneeze and spread germs, breathe, and thus emit carbon dioxide. They clear small gardens, contributing "particulate matter" to the air and disturbing the local climate because cleared areas proved measurably warmer and drier than the shady forest. Rambo concluded that his research "demonstrates the essential functional similarity of the environmental interactions of primitive and civilized societies" (1985: 78) in contrast to a "noble savage" view (Bodley, 1983) which, according to Rambo (1985: 2), mistakenly "claims that traditional peoples almost always live in essential harmony with their environment."

This is surely a false issue. To stress, as I do, that tribals tend to manage their resources for sustained yield within relatively self-sufficient subsistence economies is not to make them either innocent children or natural men. Nor is it to deny that tribals "disrupt" their environment and may never be in absolute "balance" with nature.

The ecocide issue is perhaps most dramatically illustrated by two sets of satellite photos taken over the Brazilian rain forests of Rôndonia (Allard & McIntyre, 1988: 780–781). Photos taken in 1973, when Rôndonia was still a tribal domain, show virtually unbroken rain forest. The 1987 satellite photos, taken after just fifteen years of highway construction and "development" by outsiders, show more than 20 percent of the forest destroyed. The surviving Indians were being concentrated by FUNAI (Brazil's national Indian foundation) into what would soon become mere islands of forest in a ravaged landscape. It is irrelevant to quibble about whether tribals are noble, childlike, or innocent, or about the precise meaning of balance with nature, carrying capacity, or adaptation, to recognize that for the past 200 years rapid environmental deterioration on an unprecedented global scale has followed the wresting of control of vast areas of the world from tribal groups by resource-hungry industrial societies.

Deprivation and Discrimination

Contact with European culture has given them a knowledge of great wealth, opportunity and privilege, but only very limited avenues by which to acquire these things.

Crocombe, 1968

Unwittingly, tribal peoples have had the burden of perpetual relative deprivation thrust upon them by acceptance—either by themselves or by the governments administering them—of the standards of socioeconomic progress set for them by industrial civilizations. By comparison with the material wealth of industrial societies, tribal societies become, by definition, impoverished. They are then forced to transform their cultures and work to achieve what many economists now acknowledge to be unattainable goals. Even though in many cases the modest GNP goals set by development planners for the developing nations during the "development decade" of the 1960s were often met, the results were hardly noticeable for most of the tribal people involved. Population growth, environmental limitations, inequitable distribution of wealth, and the continued rapid growth of the industrialized nations have all meant that both the absolute and the relative gap between the rich and poor in the world is steadily widening. The prospect that tribal peoples will actually be able to attain the levels of resource consumption to which they are being encouraged to aspire is remote indeed except for those few groups who have retained effective control over strategic mineral resources.

Tribal peoples feel deprivation not only when the economic goals they have been encouraged to seek fail to materialize, but also when they discover that they are powerless, second-class citizens who are discriminated against and exploited by the dominant society. At the same time, they are denied the satisfactions of their traditional cultures, because these have been sacrificed in the process of modernization. Under the impact of major economic change family life is disrupted, traditional social controls are often lost, and many indicators of social anomie such as alcoholism, crime, delinquency, suicide, emotional disorders, and despair may increase. The inevitable frustration resulting from this continual deprivation finds expression in the cargo cults, revitalization movements, and a variety of other political and religious movements that have been widespread among tribal peoples following their disruption by industrial civilization.

References

Ackermann, F. L. 1964. *Geologia e Fisiografia da Região Bragantina, Estado do Pará*. Manaus, Brazil: Conselho Nacional de Pesquisas, Instituto Nacional de Pesquisas da Amazonia.

Allard, William Albert, and Loren McIntyre. 1988. Rondônia's settlers invade Brazil's imperiled rain forest. *National Geographic* 174(6):772–799.

Bodley, John H. 1970. *Campa Socio-Economic Adaptation*. Ann Arbor: University Microfilms.

_____. 1983. *Der Weg der Zerstörung: Stammesvölker und die industrielle Zivilization*. Munich: Trickster-Verlag. (Translation of *Victims of Progress*.)

Bodley, John H., and Foley C. Benson. 1979. Cultural ecology of Amazonian palms. *Reports of Investigations,* no. 56. Pullman: Laboratory of Anthropology, Washington State University.

Bunce, George E. 1972. Aggravation of vitamin A deficiency following distribution of non-fortified skim milk: An example of nutrient interaction. In *The Careless Technology: Ecology and International Development,* ed. M. T. Farvar and John P. Milton, pp. 53–60. Garden City, N.Y.: Natural History Press.

Burling, Robbins. 1963. *Rengsanggri: Family and Kinship in a Garo Village*. Philadelphia: University of Pennsylvania Press.

Davis, A. E., and T. D. Bolin. 1972. Lactose intolerance in Southeast Asia. In *The Careless Technology: Ecology and International Development,* ed. M. T. Farvar and John P. Milton, pp. 61–68. Garden City, N.Y.: Natural History Press.

Dennett, Glenn, and John Connell. 1988. Acculturation and health in the highlands of Papua New Guinea. *Current Anthropology* 29(2):273–299.

Goldschmidt, Walter R. 1972. The interrelations between cultural factors and the acquisition of new technical skills. In *The Progress of Underdeveloped Areas,* ed. Bert F. Hoselitz, pp. 135–151. Chicago: University of Chicago Press.

Gross, Daniel R., et al. 1979. Ecology and acculturation among native peoples of Central Brazil. *Science* 206(4422): 1043–1050.

Hughes, Charles C., and John M. Hunter. 1972. The role of technological development in promoting disease in Africa. In *The Careless Technology: Ecology and International Development,* ed. M. T. Farvar and John P. Milton, pp. 69–101. Garden City, N.Y.: Natural History Press.

Keesing, Felix M. 1941. *The South Seas in the Modern World*. Institute of Pacific Relations International Research Series. New York: John Day.

Kroeger, Axel, and François Barbira-Freedman. 1982. *Culture Change and Health: The Case of South American Rainforest Indians*. Frankfurt am Main: Verlag Peter Lang. (Reprinted in Bodley, 1988a:221–236.)

McNeil, Mary. 1972. Lateritic soils in distinct tropical environments: Southern Sudan and Brazil. In *The Careless Technology: Ecology and International Development,* ed. M. T. Farvar and John P. Milton, pp. 591–608. Garden City, N.Y.: Natural History Press.

Mönckeberg, F. 1968. Mental retardation from malnutrition. *Journal of the American Medical Association* 206:30–31.

Montagu, Ashley. 1972. Sociogenic brain damage. *American Anthropologist* 74(5):1045–1061.

Rambo, A. Terry. 1985. *Primitive Polluters: Semang Impact on the Malaysian Tropical Rain Forest Ecosystem*. Anthropological Papers no. 76, Museum of Anthropology, University of Michigan.

Redfield, Robert. 1953. *The Primitive World and Its Transformations*. Ithaca, N.Y.: Cornell University Press.

_____. 1962. *A Village That Chose Progress: Chan Kom Revisited*. Chicago: University of Chicago Press, Phoenix Books.

Smith, Wilberforce. 1894. The teeth of ten Sioux Indians. *Journal of the Royal Anthropological Institute* 24:109–116.

TTR: *See under* United States.

United States, Department of the Interior, Office of Territories. 1953. *Report on the Administration of the Trust Territory of the Pacific Islands* (by the United States to the United Nations) for the Period July 1, 1951, to June 30, 1952.

_____. 1954. *Annual Report, High Commissioner of the Trust Territory of the Pacific Islands to the Secretary of the Interior* (for 1953).

United States, Department of State. 1955. *Seventh Annual Report to the United Nations on the Administration of the Trust Territory of the Pacific Islands* (July 1, 1953, to June 30, 1954).

_____. 1959. *Eleventh Annual Report to the United Nations on the Administration of the Trust Territory of the Pacific Islands* (July 1, 1957, to June 30, 1958).

_____. 1964. *Sixteenth Annual Report to the United Nations on the Administration of the Trust Territory of the Pacific Islands* (July 1, 1962 to June 30, 1963).

_____. 1973. *Twenty-Fifth Annual Report to the United Nations on the Administration of the Trust Territory of the Pacific Islands* (July 1, 1971, to June 30, 1972).

Assess Your Progress

1. Why is "standard of living" an intrinsically ethnocentric concept as a measure of progress? What is a more useful measure and why? What does a careful examination based upon the specific points show?

2. In what ways does economic development increase the disease rate of affected peoples?

3. How does the author answer critics who argue that such figures simply represent better health monitoring? List the examples cited.

4. Explain the effects of government policy on peoples' adaptations to local environmental conditions.

5. Describe the circumstances under which peoples' dietary habits have been changed as a result of outside influences. What has happened to nutritional levels and why?

6. To what was attributed the differences in dental health between the Sioux Indians of Buffalo Bill's Wild West Show and Londoners?

7. What did Weston Price find in his studies?

8. Describe the chain of events that goes from the adoption of new economic patterns to changes in the kinds of crops grown to low wages to nutritional deprivation (principally of children).

9. What is one of the most tragic, and largely overlooked, aspects of chronic malnutrition?

10. What are the prospects that modern health institutions will overcome these problems?

11. How does the author respond to critics who charge that tribal peoples have always had low life expectancies, high infant mortality rates and nutritional deficiencies?

12. What factors have contributed to population growth?

13. What are the consequences for each of the following:
   - Official policy restricting swidden people to smaller territories?
   - Resource depletion forcing people to participate in the world-market economy?
   - The settling of nomadic herders and the removal of prior controls on herd size?
   - Shortening the planting cycles?

14. How does the reality of ecocide focus attention on the fundamental contrasts between tribal and industrial systems in their use of natural resources? Who controls such resources and how are they managed?

15. What do the critics of the "noble savage" image claim? How does the author respond?

16. In what respects do tribal peoples feel deprivation as a result of "modernization?"

From *Victims of Progress* by John Bodley, (Mayfield Publishing, 1998). Copyright © 1998 by The McGraw-Hill Companies. Reprinted by permission.

Seeing Conservation through the Global Lens

Jim Igoe

Popular Notions and Painful Realities about Conservation and Globalization

You probably have some idea of what both conservation and globalization are about. A person would have to have been living in a cave not to have heard of conservation. Indeed, conservation now enjoys an unquestioned place in American popular culture: Earth Day, the Earth Summit, Al Gore's book *Earth in the Balance*, Sting's rainforest benefits, Green Peace, and the Green Party. McDonald's has habitat conservation areas on the median separating their drive through windows from their parking lots. Even George W. Bush, not exactly a noted conservationist, pays lip service to the environment, while proposing to drill for oil in the Alaskan Wilderness Preserve. Although Americans might not all agree about what form conservation should take, most are aware that it is important.

The idea of globalization is less well known, but still has a tremendous impact on how people think about the world. The image that defines globalization is the photograph of Earth taken by astronauts in the 1960s. The importance of this image to "one world" thinking is evidenced by the fact that it is often used in appeals that "we are all in this together." Most Americans are familiar with slogans like "space-ship earth," "a green and peaceful planet," and "the global village." They are also broadly aware that the world is becoming a smaller place, not physically smaller, but easier to communicate around and travel over. There's really no place on earth that a person can't reach in a couple of days, assuming he or she has the money to pay for the ticket. Americans are also aware that localized environmental destruction threatens the entire planet. This is why the Amazon Rainforest is now referred to as "the lungs" of the planet. Clearly, therefore, notions of conservation and globalization are interlinked.

Globalization as a Homogenizing Process

Another important aspect of globalization is the fact that it is a homogenizing process. Americans might "celebrate diversity," but the implicit assumption of globalization is that it will transform other people in the world to become more like the West. So fundamental are these transformations that many Americans do not recognize that they are happening at all. Being a consumer, for instance, is something that Westerners take for granted. However, it is not a "natural" way of being for many peoples. Being a consumer means having money and accumulating things. It also assumes that people are naturally self-interested and acquisitive. As it turns out, however, this ideology is frequently incompatible with the ways in which many people live their lives. A large part of the world's people grow their own food, build their houses from materials that they find in their environment, and require little in the way of consumer goods (a situation that is rapidly changing of course). In many of these societies acquisitiveness and competition are frowned on. People share and cooperate. Those who do not are viewed with suspicion. Such cultural proclivities are often seen as a barrier to globalization and progress; people who hold them are said to have the wrong "mind-set."

Many other categories that Americans take for granted imply transformation for others in the process of globalization. A short list might include categories of citizen, entrepreneur, and wage laborer. These categories are part and parcel of globalization, but they are also widely resisted by people around the world. Even Americans sometimes need to be reminded that they are citizens and consumers. In the wake of the 9/11 attacks, the Bush administration reminded Americans constantly that the most patriotic thing they could do was to go shopping. It also discouraged them from thinking about themselves as African Americans, Native Americans, Irish Americans, or what have you, reminding them that they were U.S. citizens first and foremost. The upshot is that globalization requires people to conform to certain categories, categories that even Americans need to be actively reminded of from time to time. For people who lack a traditional category of citizen-consumer, this can be an extremely painful process.

Globalization and Indigenous People

. . . The most common definition of indigenous people is the original inhabitants of a particular place. However, this definition is being broadened to include those who have maintained their traditional ways of life in spite of the modernization and social change. Such definitions are necessary for places like Africa, where Europeans and other outsiders make up a small percentage of the population (the exception being South Africa), and so, practically speaking, everyone is indigenous. And yet, in a movie such as *The Gods Must Be Crazy*, the viewer can definitely tell the difference between the bushman who wears a loin cloth and coexists with elephants, and the African who gets up when his alarm clock goes off and stands in a busy intersection directing traffic in a pressed white uniform. The bushman, who remains indigenous, has not been globalized. The man directing traffic has.

Few people, if any, still live the idyllic indigenous lifestyle of the people in *The Gods Must Be Crazy*. The idea shown in the movie that people living in the Kalahari have never seen a bottle of Coca-Cola is simply preposterous. Coca-Cola is so widely available in Africa that it is easier to get than clean drinking water in many places. A more accurate portrayal of the Bushmen (or !Kung as they call themselves) can be seen in the anthropological documentary *N!ai: Portrait of a !Kung Woman* (the explanation point stands for the clicking sound so common in the !Kung language). This film shows the making of *The Gods Must Be Crazy*, and the confusion of the !Kung actors about the ways in which the director wanted to portray their culture. Far from living an idyllic existence in the Kalahari, these actors have been forced to live on a reservation, where they rely on government handouts and tourist money, rather than on hunting antelope as portrayed in the movie. If you haven't seen *N!ai* or *The Gods Must Be Crazy*, I strongly urge you to do so.

Such conditions are typical of indigenous communities around the world: pushed off their land by commercial enterprises and national parks, relegated to government-designated reservations, living in poverty because they have not been fully integrated into the modern economy, and yet no longer able to pursue their traditional economic activities. Through all of this, indigenous communities strive to maintain their traditions after some fashion. I would argue that this effort to maintain tradition in the face of globalization is the foundation of a global indigenous identity. That is to say that until recently groups like the !Kung, the Maasai, the Sherpa, the Kayapo, the Anangu, and the Inuit were first and foremost !Kung or Maasai or what have you. They did not identify strongly with people in similar straits in other parts of the world or even necessarily know of their existence. With globalization, however, came improved communication and a growing recognition of a common problem. Networking by indigenous activists eventually led to the recognition of a global indigenous community by the United Nations (UN) and other transnational institutions. A global indigenous identity began to emerge.

Introducing the Maasai

. . . Like other indigenous peoples, the Maasai are economically, culturally, and politically marginalized. Their traditional culture is distinct from the dominant cultures of Kenya and Tanzania, the two countries in which most Maasai live. Unlike most other Kenyans and Tanzanians, who speak English and/or Swahili, most Maasai speak their own language. In more remote Maasai communities, it is sometimes difficult to find anyone who speaks Swahili, the national language of Tanzania, let alone English, which is spoken primarily by educated people in urban areas.

The Maasai have also struggled to maintain their traditional herding economy, which revolves around the ability to keep large herds of cattle, sheep, and goats. . . .it also requires a certain amount of mobility because the Maasai have traditionally moved their herds in search of pasture and water. This movement was informed by traditional environmental knowledge and seasonal cycles. Traditional Maasai resource management systems were complex.

My liberal use of the past tense has probably cued you to the fact that the Maasai (at least the majority of them) no longer pursue their traditional herding economy.

Increasingly they rely on subsistence farming, even though most of the areas in which they live are too arid to ensure a successful crop. Most Maasai can no longer be mobile because they have lost their traditional grazing lands to global processes. This change began with colonialism, when British settlers took over high-quality Maasai pasture for farms and cattle ranches. More recently the Maasai have lost land to African and foreign investors who have claimed large areas for bean farms, commercial hunting safaris, and wildlife viewing. These investors came into East Africa in recent years in response to policies designed to transform the economies of Kenya and Tanzania so that they could become more fully integrated into the world economy. The expectation, of course, was that Africans would also be transformed into wage-earning consumers instead of subsistence-oriented peasants. For the most part, however, this hasn't happened. The Maasai (in fact most rural Africans) have wound up left out of the process altogether. They have lost their land and their subsistence economy, but they haven't been able to benefit from the integration of their countries into the world economy.

Many of the elders I interviewed lamented that these processes were leading to the demise of their traditional values. In Maasai society, cattle are everything, in about the same way that money is everything in the United States. That is, although it may be a bit of an exaggeration to say that "it's everything," people certainly do spend a lot of time thinking about it and trying to accumulate it. The fact that Americans need to remind themselves that "money isn't everything" reflects the fact that they often behave as though it is. However, Americans don't have money in their creation myth: the Maasai creation myth holds that when God created the earth He gave cattle to the Maasai and proclaimed that they were the only people on earth with the right to own it. Throughout their history the Maasai have used this myth as a justification to raid neighboring ethnic groups and take away their cattle by force. If God proclaimed cattle to be the sole property of the Maasai, then other people must have obtained their cattle by less than honorable means. It may have been generations ago, but that is not important. It is the right, nay the duty, of the Maasai to reclaim their God-given cattle whenever possible.

The ability of the Maasai to control large herds of cattle, as well as to take other people's cattle when they took a fancy to it, was based on their superior military organization. In fact when the British arrived in East Africa at the turn of the 20th century, they saw the Maasai as the single biggest threat to their colonial project. Their initial approach, therefore, was to seek alliances with the Maasai, rather than to try and dominate them by military force. In this respect, the British did not appear terribly different to the Maasai than the numerous African groups who had sought similar alliances with them over the years. Because they controlled so many cattle and such a large territory, the Maasai were seen as desirable allies and trading partners for ethnic groups throughout East Africa. While God may have decreed that all cattle belonged to the Maasai, almost everyone wanted them, meaning that "being Maasai" was one of the most prestigious things that someone could achieve in pre-colonial East Africa (Spear and Waller 1993).

The central importance of livestock to the Maasai economy is reflected in its traditional (but diminishing) use as a medium of exchange in Maasai society. Gifts of livestock are presented to boys as they are initiated into warriorhood. Friendships, called stock associations by anthropologists, are cemented by periodic gifts of livestock. Wealthy men frequently lend animals to poorer men in an effort to build a loyal following of clients. Perhaps most important, livestock in Maasai society is used as a medium of marriage exchange. When a young man wishes to marry, he presents the parents of his potential bride with gifts of livestock. If the gift is acceptable, then he will periodically add new gifts of livestock to this original gift until the marriage is made official through a series of rituals, also involving livestock exchange. Even once the marriage is complete the husband will continue to present his in-laws with livestock for the rest of their lives. These gifts, which were the intended subject of my original research project, cement relationships between two social groups: the bride givers and the bride takers. If the marriage is dissolved then the livestock must be returned. As you can imagine, this creates huge pressures against divorce in Maasai society. One of the unfortunate effects of this tradition is that it makes it exceedingly difficult for Maasai women to escape abusive marriages.

The social exchange of livestock also serves ecological and group survival functions. One of the defining characteristics of Maasai country is its unpredictable weather patterns and periodic lack of rain. Rain may come for seven years to one area, and then not at all for another seven. By giving and loaning livestock to friends and clients, Maasai herders effectively scatter their herds all over the place. When the area in which a herder lives is dry and several of his animals die, the area of his stock associates may receive abundant rains. Traditionally this means that this man's stock associates will present him with livestock, or if he is wealthy, his clients may return some of the animals he lent to them, allowing his herd to recover from the drought. The social networks created by these livestock exchanges are also useful in that such networks make it possible for herders to relocate their entire herd to the country of their stock associates, a greater benefit than all but the most generous gifts of stock.

While herders have always tried to spread their livestock over large areas, certain places have been traditionally recognized as better than others. Some had permanent sources of water; others were at higher elevations and so received more rain. Other areas have ancient wells, which were dug by and belong to specific Maasai clans. My research area, Simanjiro, was once considered an especially great place to keep livestock. Elders who came to Simanjiro from other places told stories about its reputation. During the 1940s and 1950s many herders relocated to Simanjiro because of its abundant pasture and water. Elders who came to Simanjiro during this period describe how they prospered as their herds doubled, tripled, and even quadrupled. One man in particular, who was my host for much of my time in Tanzania, is rumored to have over 10,000 head of cattle. He claims to have been able to build this herd because of Simanjiro's favorable climate.

Since the 1950s, however, the reputation of Simanjiro as a great place to keep livestock has declined immensely. Most of the pasture and water that were the foundation of Simanjiro's booming herding economy have been lost to other concerns. Because of the central importance of cattle to the Maasai of Simanjiro, the decline of this herding economy has had devastating effects on their culture. The ability to live the "pure pastoralist life style," which has been a central cultural value, is now enjoyed by only a handful of wealthy herders. As the herding economy declined, so did the number of livestock available for social exchange. Local people believe that social relationships within their society have suffered accordingly. Most important, for most Maasai, the tradition of wealthy herders sharing their animals with poorer ones has been steadily disappearing. The result has been increased wealth discrepancies within Maasai society as a few wealthy men, who are now able to hire laborers for cash, accumulate large numbers of animals, while many others decline into poverty. The resentment that these poorer herders felt towards their former patrons was evident in many of my interviews.

What about Conservation?

One of the central processes that have contributed to the displacement of Maasai herders in Simanjiro is conservation. Specifically, the creation of Tarangire National Park has enclosed pasture and water resources essential to the herding economy, a process that has also contributed to ecological deterioration. Many of my informants described conservation as indistinguishable from any of the other global processes they confronted in their daily lives. Its bottom line was the alienation of traditional grazing lands for the benefit and enjoyment of other people, the majority of whom, from their perspective, were white and not even from Tanzania. As far as they were concerned, this was essentially unfair.

Of course this perspective is different from how most Americans imagine conservation. A student in my "Culture and the Environment" class once told me that for him the class had been as much about unlearning as it had been about learning. He had to unlearn things that he previously believed about conservation before he could begin to explore concepts addressed in the class. This process of unlearning is essential, because many people (myself included) hold preconceived ideas about conservation. Too often, these ideas are formed by popular notions that conceal the painful reality of how conservation affects indigenous communities around the world. . . .

Conservation and Globalization: Some Issues of Definition
Conservation

It is difficult to see what objections anyone could have to conservation. Defining this term broadly, it simply means using natural resources in ways that ensure they will be available to future generations. Conservation is also what we mean when we talk about sustainable development: cutting down a tree means planting a new one, finding alternative power sources instead of exhausting fossil fuels, and recycling or reusing the packaging of consumer goods. While these types of conservation and sustainable practice would certainly benefit the planet, they don't represent the kind of conservation that I am concerned about.

Most Western conservationists seeking to do conservation in indigenous communities also aren't talking about this kind of conservation. Almost all indigenous peoples have traditional ways of using natural resources in ways that will ensure their continued availability to future generations. In other words, they engage in sustainable resource management practices. This doesn't mean that their resource management systems are perfect, and I want to avoid popular notions of indigenous peoples living in harmony with their environment. For the most part, however, people who have used natural resources in the same area for many generations have gotten pretty good at it. If they haven't destroyed their resource base and perished as a result (and this has certainly happened to indigenous communities), they have learned from their mistakes. Through this process, they have developed resource management practices that are suited to the particular environment in which they live.

Most of people living in Western consumer culture do not face the same kinds of immediate environmental constraints as indigenous communities. The global capitalist system can destroy resources in one area and simply move to exploit the same resources in a completely different part of the world. As long as they don't use up all of a particular resource in the world, business can continue as usual. This system, and the high standards of living it provides for some, has wreaked environmental havoc from the Great Lakes to the Amazon Rainforest. It is somewhat ironic, therefore, that most Western conservationists working with indigenous peoples operate under the assumption that indigenous conservation models (if they acknowledge that such a thing exists at all) are inherently inferior to the ones of their own society. This situation is now changing somewhat, but it is changing very slowly and still has a long way to go. . . .

As a distinctly Western conservation model, parks are usually incompatible with indigenous conservation models, which aren't usually premised on the total exclusion of community members over large territories. This is the type of conservation that is usually funded by Western conservation organizations. It is also the type of conservation with which indigenous peoples are most directly familiar. It should come as no surprise, therefore, that I have heard Native Americans and indigenous Africans speak of conservation(ists) with disdain on many occasions. While the concept is too big to define comprehensively, certain aspects of globalization are especially relevant to this study and more generally to cultural anthropology. Globalization revolves around a network of institutions that have now reached almost every part of the world. These institutions include governments and markets, as well as transnational bodies such as the UN, the World Bank, and the International Monetary Fund (IMF). They also include transnational conservation organizations such as the World Wildlife Fund (WWF) and the International Union for the Conservation of Nature and Natural Resources (IUCN), as well as transnational human rights organizations such as OXFAM, Amnesty International, and Africa Watch. Among these global institutions, I also include national parks, which link to governments and transnational bodies such as the UN and the WWF.

This global institutional network forms a system of money and ideas. Money moves through the network, but it is also attached to certain types of ideas. Those who are able to articulate the right ideas are more likely to be able to gain access to this global network and the money it controls. For instance, the IMF operates on the idea that free markets should exist in every part of the world. Third world governments that agree to promote free markets can obtain economic assistance from the IMF; others cannot. Likewise, third world governments that promote Western conservation models can expect to get a lot of economic support from groups like the IUCN, as well as from Western governments. The problem is that the ideas attached to the money are almost always those of powerful people who run the institutions in this global network. The ideas of marginalized people are almost never considered or implemented, although there are important exceptions to this rule.

Since the fall of the Soviet Union, this global network has been transformed, making it more accessible to indigenous communities, or at least certain community members. The end of European communism also meant the end of state-centered development. Development policies began to revolve around the idea that governments should do less. This idea was another one to which large sums of money were attached. The institutions that replaced governments in a variety of functions have come to be known simply as NGOs (non-governmental organizations). NGOs have existed for a long time—they were called charities. Since the fall of the Soviet Union, however, the number of NGOs around the world has exploded. So many of these organizations came into existence in the early 1990s that some observers called it a "global associational revolution."

The Maasai, along with many other indigenous groups around the world, have taken full advantage of this "global associational revolution." By the late 1980s, most development aid to African countries came with the stipulation that their governments would promote the emergence of a vibrant NGO sector. Tanzania, where I did my dissertation research, was no exception. In the early 1980s, only 17 registered NGOs were working in this country. By the end of the 1990s, there were nearly 1,000 NGOs. Because development money became tied to the idea that NGOs were better than African governments at delivering services and promoting democracy, Tanzania experienced its own "associational revolution." . . .

As with other global institutions, the money Western conservation organizations offered to Maasai NGOs has been attached to certain ideas. In this case, these ideas revolve around Western conservation models. Specifically, Western conservation organizations hold that it would be a good thing if indigenous groups like the Maasai would embrace Western conservation models and help promote them. On an abstract level, however, these ideas draw from certain Western fantasies about Africa in general, and the Maasai in particular. It is important to explore these fantasies, because they are the very kind of popular notions that so often mask the painful realities of indigenous communities.

While Western conservation organizations often evoke these popular notions in their fund raising appeals, they rarely address their implications for what they are trying to achieve. These fantasies, therefore, are also tied to money circulating in the global institutional network. Because their money gives Western conservation organizations power over Maasai NGOs, it is important to understand who they are, where they come from, and what their objectives are. In the following section, I address these fantasies by way of introduction to conservation in East Africa.

East Africa as an Ecocultural Theme Park
Western Media Fantasies about Wildlife and the Maasai

Although you may not be able to find Tanzania quickly on a globe (see Figure 1), you are probably familiar with conservation in Africa. Perhaps you have watched the *Discovery Channel* and saw a pride of lions take down zebra on the Serengeti Plain. Or you may have seen video footage of the annual wildebeest migrations along the Great Rift Valley in Tanzania and Kenya. Tens of thousands of these animals plunge into flooded rivers, apparently oblivious to the racing current and the waiting crocodiles. Some drown and some are eaten, but most survive to complete the journey. Or possibly you are familiar with images of machine-gunned elephants, with gaping holes in their faces where poachers have crudely extracted their tusks. These images were indispensable to several highly successful fund-raising campaigns by American conservation organizations in the 1980s (cf. Bonner 1993). Through these popular media images, most Americans "know" that conservation in Africa is about animals. More specifically, it is about the preservation of endangered species, most notably rhino and elephants. While I suspect that few Americans actually sit around and worry about African rhinos in their spare time, most associate Africa with wild animals.

Maasai are nearly as familiar to Westerners as the lions of the Serengeti. Whether you know it or not, you probably have an idea of what they look like. Maasai warriors, with their flowing red togas and spears in hand have become a quintessential symbol for

Figure 1 This map shows the relative size and location of the country of Tanzania on the continent of Africa.

vanishing Africa. They have appeared on the *Discovery Channel*, leaping into the air in exuberant dances and (in their calmer moments) leaning on their spears gazing out over a vast African landscape of waving savanna grasses. In the movie *Out of Africa* they appear racing across the arid savanna on a mysterious mission. A lighter movie, *The Air Up There*, presents an unlikely story of a college basketball coach who goes to Kenya to recruit a Maasai warrior for his school's team. The movie climaxes with a game between the "traditional" Maasai and some "nontraditional" urban Africans. (I won't spoil the ending by telling you who wins.) A recent commercial from Nissan features a group of Maasai warriors congratulating each other on the purchase of a brand new Altima. Standing in a row outside of their mud houses, they marvel at the latest in midsize family sedans while an elephant lazily wanders by in the distant background.

This bizarre scenario captures the essence of Western fantasies about Africa, which are frequently used to market something. Both African people and African wildlife are portrayed as exotic and inhabiting an unspoiled world that no longer exists in the West. Just as important, the two are portrayed as separate from one another. People exist in one realm, and animals in another. Viewers may see lions on the *Discovery Channel*, and viewers may see Maasai on the *Discovery Channel*. It is unlikely, however, that they will ever see lions and Maasai on the *Discovery Channel* at the same time. For most Westerners this seems like a "natural" arrangement: African wildlife exists in wilderness or nature, a place untouched by the ravaging effects of human activities. This imaginary vision is difficult to resolve with the reality of a traffic jam of zebra-striped safari vans converging on a rhino that happens to be wearing a collar that allows authorities to monitor his movements with a high-tech satellite tracking

217

system. Nevertheless, it is an idea that many hold dear: national parks equal nature and nature does not include humans. If you are fortunate enough to visit this nature, you should "take nothing but pictures and leave nothing but footprints." Westerners expect other cultures to conform to this imperative.

These expectations raise important questions for the other half of the equation: the Maasai. If they don't live in nature along with wild animals, where exactly do they live? In one respect the answer to this question is a simple: somewhere else. If you examine Western stereotypes of the Maasai closely, however, this answer doesn't make much sense. As I have already explained, the Maasai are commonly portrayed as living in a vast steppe, with nothing to see from horizon to horizon but tall savanna grasses. The reality of the situation is drastically different. A glimpse at a map of East Africa reveals that much of their rangeland has been encroached on by national parks and urban sprawl. Nairobi, a city of nearly 5 million people, sits squarely in the middle of traditional Maasai territory. I have seen Maasai herders grazing their livestock in the median of a major highway and by airport runways. In the rural areas, mechanized farms and commercial ranches have taken over much of the best grazing land outside of national parks. In short, the idea that the Maasai herd their cattle in wide-open spaces is largely inaccurate.

Disneyfication and Ecocultural Tourism in East Africa

Obviously there are some serious discrepancies between Western media fantasies about wildlife and the Maasai and the "on-the-ground" realities of life in East Africa. As long as images of African people and animals are experienced at a distance, these discrepancies are not terribly significant. As most Americans are well aware, mediums like TV, movies, and the Internet can construct "virtual realities" that are convincing to the consumer but have absolutely no relationship to the real world. But what about fantasies that are experienced as "actual reality"? Is it possible for Western fantasies about people and the environment to be imposed on the "real world" and in effect become a reality? As bizarre as this proposition may initially appear, it is something with which Americans are intimately familiar, through institutions such as subdivisions, shopping malls, and especially theme parks.

So pervasive are the effects of theme parks on the ways that Westerners look at the world that some social scientists refer to the process by which artificial realities are constructed as "Disneyfication." In his book, *The Culture of Nature* (1992), Alexander Wilson describes how the fantasy realities of Disney theme parks are created through a process known as *illusioneering* in industry-speak. He quotes one Disney *illusioneer*, who explains:

> The environments we create are more utopian, more romanticized and more like the guest imagined they would be. The negative elements are discreetly eliminated, while positive aspects are in some cases embellished to tell the story more clearly. (pp. 161–162)

Thus, riders on Disney's Jungle Cruise see pygmy villages, wild animals, and a jungle temple. They don't see lumber companies clearing the forest with bulldozers, cattle grazing the deforested areas to dust, local people being displaced by hydroelectric dams, nor any signs of poverty or malnutrition. Of even more relevance to this book is Disney World's African Safari Ride, which simulates the African safari experience, to the extent of importing animals and people from Africa. Riders board a four-wheel drive vehicle that takes them through rutted dirt roads and swollen rivers before they finally encounter herds of animals listlessly grazing on an artificial savanna. An African man then runs up to the vehicle yelling, *"Bwana! Bwana!* The poachers are stealing the baby elephant!" The ride then becomes a high-speed chase, ending with the rescue of the baby elephant, which is a mechanical elephant's trunk sticking out of a wooden crate. The animals that the visitors encounter are not native; they were raised in captivity and descended from animals that were captured somewhere in Africa like the mechanical baby elephant who is "saved" from such a fate over and over again by the thousands of visitors who go on the ride every day.

In an article aptly entitled "The Maasai and the Lion King", anthropologist Edward Bruner (2001) describes how the types of fantasies produced by the "Disney dream machine" make their way back to Africa where they are repackaged and sold to Western tourists. Westerners usually go to East Africa on safari to see two things: animals and "traditional" Africans. To see animals they go to national parks. To see "traditional" Africans they don't even have to leave the comfort of their luxury hotels. Most resorts feature Maasai dancers at least a couple nights a week. What most tourists don't realize, however, is that many of these dancers are not actually Maasai. Tourists will pay to see "the Maasai." In a society with rampant unemployment, it only makes sense that young men should take advantage of this opportunity by dressing up like Maasai and learning "traditional" Maasai dances. More adventurous tourists might also visit "cultural villages," where they can see how the Maasai "really live" and pay to take some pictures for the folks back home. Unlike real Maasai villages, however, cultural villages lack cows, their manure, and the swarms of flies they inevitably attract.

Maasai "cultural villages" are exactly the type of controlled experience that Western tourists pay for when they purchase a luxury safari. Like the rides at Disney World, luxury safaris highlight the utopian and the romantic, presenting tourists with a world that is more like they imagined it would be. They are met at the airport by an English-speaking guide in a safari suit who whisks them away to the Nairobi Hilton. They traverse the short distance from the van to the lobby with the assistance of porters dressed in brass-buttoned suits. The hotel shopping arcade offers everything from *The New York Times* to a pith helmet, without ever stepping outside. The same vehicle that brought them from the airport will transport them to a luxury lodge inside of one of Kenya's world-famous parks. From there they will be driven about, taking pictures of elephants, lions, and zebra. Then it's back to the Hilton, back to the airport, and back to the Western city from whence they came. With luck, the only Africans they will have encountered are servants and the "traditional" people who danced for their entertainment. Dangerous animals will have been viewed from the comfort and safety of their safari vehicle.

Also like the riders on Jungle Cruise and the African Safari Ride, these tourists will be spared the unpleasant realities of the real world that their "Disneyfied" experiences are modeled after. If they were only to step outside the Nairobi Hilton, less than a block away they would encounter 6-year-old boys sniffing glue on garbage heaps, shrouded lepers begging for money, and teenage girls forced into prostitution by poverty and despair. If they were only to stop outside the national parks that they came to visit, they would encounter whole communities of people who have been displaced and impoverished by those very parks. Because these people and their poverty are discreetly eliminated from the safari experience, very few tourists will make the connection between the luxury hotels, where they are spared from these unpleasant sights, and the vast wealth discrepancies that exist in countries like Tanzania and Kenya. It is one of the central contentions of this book, however, that the negative impacts of conservation and economic development in East Africa are intertwined with the Western fantasies played out in African wildlife safaris.

Do Western Fantasies about the Maasai and the Environment Actually Affect Communities?

The relationship between Western fantasies about Africa and the poverty concealed by the luxury safari experience is by no means simple. For one thing the illusion is never complete. Tourists do see poverty, even if only in fleeting glimpses. The received wisdom, however, is that tourism generates revenues that will help alleviate poverty, and that it also helps pay for the protection of valuable endangered species. These two "articles of faith" make up the creed of ecotourism. That ecotourism frequently has the exact opposite effect is a proposition that does not mesh well with these popularly held ideals.

Another important question is whether changing peoples' perceptions would actually have meaningful impacts on poverty and environmental degradation in East Africa. This type of question has been hotly debated within cultural anthropology and other social sciences. In overly simplistic terms such debates pit anthropologists influenced by the ideas of Karl Marx (who believed that ideas are nothing more than a superfluous by-product of material processes), and those influenced by Michel Foucault (who believed that ideas are a powerful force that actually shape peoples' realities). Traditional Marxists would argue that it matters little how tourists imagine Africa. Poverty is the result of material processes, whereby Africans were dispossessed of their land and other forms of natural wealth by colonialism and international capitalism. If there was money to be made by building luxury lodges in national parks, then ideas about conservation and wildlife protection were nothing more than post hoc justifications for the dispossession that building these lodges entailed. Foucauldians, on the other hand, would argue that ideas and discourses have everything to do with what happened in East Africa. Powerful ideas about wilderness and the value of wildlife, shrouded in the scientific veneer of ecology, were a driving force in the creation of national parks in this part of the world.

Most anthropologists, myself included, fall somewhere in between. The enclosure of Maasai grazing lands by national parks and commercial farms is a material process with observable social and ecological impacts. It would be wrong to argue, however, that the ideas that accompanied this process were merely ideological byproducts. Notions of wilderness, wildlife, and "natural man" run deep in the Western psyche. They not only shape what Western tourists want to see when they go to East Africa, they also inform policy, science, and the formation of government agencies and NGOs. In this respect they have a much deeper impact on life in East Africa than you might initially suspect. Anthropologists' understanding of conservation in East Africa must encompass these types of ideas, as well as the historical processes of dispossession that they accompanied. For some readers this ambitious goal may seem to push the limits of cultural anthropology. Many people are attracted to this discipline for its emphasis on isolated non-Western people living in harmony with nature—an existence that seems to have been lost in the West. Ironically, these are the same ideas that inform the types of problems this book seeks to address.

The Ethnography of Conservation and Globalization
Shedding My Fantasies about Africa, or Yet Another Ethnographer's Dramatic Entrance Tale

The depth of Western fantasies about traditional Africans and pristine wildernesses are reflected in my own experience of becoming an anthropologist. I will be the first to admit that I entered the field because it offered adventure. As a child my worldview was influenced by *Dr. Doolittle* (Rex Harrison not Eddy Murphy), *Mutual of Omaha's Wild Kingdom*, a short-lived series called *Daktari* (about an American doctor living in Kenya), and a set of National Geographic books called *Peoples of the Earth*. Going to high school in suburban Detroit nearly burned this sense of adventure out of my soul, but then I went away to college and took "Introduction to Cultural Anthropology." One of the books we read in this class was *The Forest People* by Colin Turnbull. His experiences among the Mbuti of Central Africa, living in a mud house and participating in the daily life of his host community intrigued me. At the time, I was a dishwasher and selling plasma twice a week to make ends meet. Anthropological fieldwork appeared as an exciting alternative to my lifestyle of financial and intellectual impoverishment. I decided to become a cultural anthropologist. I never considered who would pay me to live among exotic people and write a book about it; I just decided it was the job for me.

As it turned out, I did get to live in a mud house. However, my experiences in the field were far more confusing and complex than those described by Turnbull. The Maasai warriors where I lived rode motorcycles, listened to reggae, and watched Jackie Chan movies on a portable video monitor. People were engaged in struggles with commercial farms and national parks that were encroaching on their land, and organizing their own NGOs. Through these NGOs, Maasai leaders were becoming active at the national and international levels. There was a great deal going on, not all of it was local, and none of it was easy to understand. Since I have left the field, Maasai warriors who have made it big as gemstone miners have begun coordinating their herding activities with cell phones (Amy Cooke, personal communication, November 2002). Tanzania also boasts a Maasai warrior rap star named Mr. Ebbo who sings about the wonders of privatization. The reality of the situation was exceedingly different from my romantic expectations of fieldwork.

In retrospect, my expectations seem rather misplaced. I didn't read *The Forest People* and rush off to Africa the next day. I went to Tanzania as a doctoral student with several years of theoretical training. Yet my ideas of social change among the Maasai were naïve. I believed that I could find communities that were essentially unaffected by modernization. I was interested in cattle markets, since many development projects for the Maasai were premised on the idea that they refused to market their livestock. It didn't take long to discover that the Maasai had been selling their animals for a long time (since probably before European contact), that some even made a living from this business, and that many considered it an important strategy for managing their herds. I also discovered that poverty was forcing many Maasai to sell off the last of their animals and out of the herding business altogether. It soon became clear that most Maasai men knew a great deal about markets and marketing, and that my assumptions about recent transformations to the Maasai herding economy were largely unfounded. Many Maasai frankly stated that my study, which was looking at the impact of cattle marketing on traditional marriage payments, wasn't very interesting.

My views of African nature and wildlife were also essentially unexamined. I knew that my intended field communities were on the borders of a national park. This concerned me, because I imagined that a lion would probably eat me. Otherwise, I didn't give the matter much thought. I was there to study social and economic change among the Maasai. What could wildlife or national parks have to do with that? The animals were inside the park, where they belonged (except for the lions that might wander out and eat me). The people, and the processes of social change that I was interested in recording, were outside the park. This seemed reasonable to me. Of course, I now realize that it doesn't make sense. Even then I had begun to acknowledge that the whole arrangement seemed kind of funny. I suspected that at some point in time the Maasai must have lived in the area that was now the park. However, these niggling doubts were overridden by my uncritical assumption that parks were nature. I didn't consider conservation as part of the economic and social transformation that I wanted to study, until people in my study area complained so loudly and frequently about it that I couldn't ignore the issue any longer.

Chance Encounters and a New Way of Looking at Things

A Change in research direction. So how did I get from this original state of mystification and ignorance to my current analysis of conservation in East Africa? In a word: gradually. When I first went to Tanzania 1992 I had no funding for my project. I hoped to get funding, but I couldn't convince myself that it was terribly important. To make matters worse, I didn't feel right about bothering people with lots of seemingly irrelevant questions. My lack of confidence was exacerbated by my fear of lions, the fact that so many Maasai held my project in low-esteem, and that the local authorities seemed bent on making my life as difficult as possible. I also discovered that I didn't like smoke-filled houses, sleeping on cowhide beds, and having goats slaughtered in my honor. My temptation was to stay in the city of Arusha. Here I could go to the movies, eat Indian food, and hang out by the Novotel swimming pool. Because of the exchange rates that existed at the time, I could do this all for a few dollars a day. It would have been a perfect setup, except that I couldn't relax and enjoy it. My career appeared to be going down the drain before it even got started. Besides, what would I tell my advisor? The matter was clear, I was going to have to stay out of Arusha for a long time. The next day I boarded an overfilled dump truck, which was listing worrisomely to the left, and embarked on an extended survey of the southern Maasai markets.

This survey resulted in a contact that was crucial to my research. Traveling from market to market required that I spend the night in different villages. Occasionally this put me in the position of having to seek the hospitality of strangers. On one such occasion I was directed to a house that turned out to be the headquarters of a newly registered political party (Tanzania was a one-party state until the year I started my research). The local organizer of this party was a man named Saruni Ndelelya[1]. . . . Saruni was a man in his thirties who had been trained as a school teacher in the 1970s, and who had insisted on returning to his home village of Orkesumet to educate another generation of Maasai. As an educated member of his community he was a natural leader, and people constantly came to him when confronted with problems that they could not solve on their own. Saruni was also one of the founders of an NGO called Pastoralists of the Highlands (*Ilaramatak Lorkornerie*). This NGO was one of the first Maasai NGOs, and it received a great deal of attention from international donors in the mid-1990s.

Saruni taught me more in two days than I learned in the entire month of my market survey. He explained that both the NGO and the political party were products of a local social movement protesting land grabbing by European and Tanzanian investors. Local people felt that the government had discriminated against the Maasai for long enough, especially now that land grabbing was happening at an unprecedented rate. . . . they hoped that the new NGO would promote local control of land and natural resources and become a platform from which to advocate for rights of cultural autonomy. This was far more exciting than anything I had previously imagined. . . .

The 1993 NGO Workshop
Maasai NGO Leaders

. . . Based on my background and training, Maasai NGOs seemed like the ultimate solution to the problem of pastoralist development. No longer would misinformed outsiders be designing socially and ecologically inappropriate development programs. New programs could be designed by the Maasai for the Maasai. What could be a better arrangement? I now know that I had merely adopted a slightly more sophisticated version of my romantic (but still largely uninformed) notion of the Maasai. At the time, however, this newfound enthusiasm was just what I needed. I finally had a reason to be excited about my fieldwork. I would make NGOs the new focus of my dissertation research! Unfortunately, I was almost completely out of money. I returned to the United States to write another round of funding proposals. Apparently my enthusiasm for Maasai NGOs was convincing, because in December 1994 I returned to Tanzania with a funded project. Aside from almost dying of malaria the following year and almost cutting my arm off the year after that, my research continued without a hitch. Well, that's not exactly true, but I did manage to get enough data to write my dissertation, not to mention this book.

Conservation and Conflict in My Research Area

Coming back to the field with something important to work on helped me to overcome my apathy for research. However, my reluctance to bother people with my prying questions still hindered me. I was especially averse to bothering NGO leaders, who were always exceedingly busy. With all of the environmental and social problems that they had to deal with, what possible interest could they have in a dissertation project? To make matters worse, Saruni was in Ireland on a development studies course. I had to make my contacts all over again. I managed to do this and began tagging along to community meetings. One community meeting in particular became a turning point in my field project. Organized by leaders of the Pastoralists of the Highlands, it allowed local people to address representatives of several British charities, as well as a BBC reporter. Local people had lost a lot of land to a Dutch seed company called Royal Sluis. Local people explained how the seed farm had disrupted their economy as well as the local ecosystem. I realized that a study of Maasai NGOs would need to address the issue of land grabbing in Maasai communities. Furthermore, any data that I produced on this issue would also be useful to NGOs themselves.

My research assistant, Edward Oloure, and I created an extensive land-use survey, designed to reveal the connections between land grabbing and changes in Maasai resource management practices. We spent several months conducting this survey in five villages. We also spent time with Maasai elders, who told us about the history of resource management in the area. These oral histories were indispensable, because they allowed us to see differences in past resource management practices during a time when more land and water were available to herders and practices that have emerged in the context of large-scale land loss. We also spent time "truth-testing" through independent cross-checks with Maasai elders in other villages. After we had published our findings (Igoe & Brockington 1999), I learned from another researcher that they were consistent with satellite data that she was analyzing for her dissertation project. While these outcomes do not unequivocally prove my data, they support the possibility that local knowledge of the environment is frequently accurate. The Maasai men and women whom I interviewed in this

Figure 2 Map showing the relative size and location of Simanjiro District and Tarangire National Park in Tanzania.

survey presented a coherent picture of the social and environmental changes taking place in their communities. . . .

People living on the borders of Tarangire National Park complained that natural resources now inside the park were essential to the traditional economy of Simanjiro. With the enclosure of the park in 1971, followed by the arrival of commercial farms in the 1980s, herd mobility became increasingly restricted. Herders could no longer move their animals in search of pasture and water as they had done in the past. Without fallow periods in which it could recover, pasture in the area began to decline. This situation became especially tenuous during periods of drought, which happen periodically throughout East Africa. During recent drought, many herders in my research area lost all or most of their animals. Some moved away altogether; many others turned to farming in an effort to feed themselves and their families. For the most part, however, their semi-arid rangelands proved unsuitable for cultivation. The exception to this rule was the higher, wetter areas taken over by commercial farms. Herders described themselves as squeezed between the park and the commercial farms with no place left to go.

In addition to the ecological and economic stresses herders attributed to Tarangire, relationships between communities and park authorities have been consistently antagonistic. Local women expressed fear over collecting firewood in the vicinity of the park because of the danger of sexual harassment by park rangers. Men reported having their livestock confiscated, being tied up, beat up, threatened with guns, and being arrested. Fines for being arrested and retrieving confiscated livestock run into several hundreds or thousands of dollars. Local people do not view the park as a public resource, nor do they believe that those who deny them access are interested in conservation. Many were of the opinion that tourism benefited wealthy Europeans and Tanzanian elites, while bringing few benefits to the people who are forced to pay with the loss of their traditional natural resource base. This view is not entirely inaccurate; luxury lodges inside the park are highly lucrative ventures. Some lodges have already had negative environmental impacts, such as taxing local water tables (Bonner 1993).

Local concerns about Tarangire National Park came to a head in the middle 1980s, when a group of conservationists floated a proposal to extend its boundaries. Communities near the park would be incorporated into a conservation area, where agriculture would be forbidden and herding practices highly restricted. Some people would be forcefully relocated away from the park. The proposal was leaked to community leaders by a sympathetic conservationist. Alarmed by the proposal, these leaders organized the Committee to Stop Conservation in Simanjiro (translated from Swahili by the author) or the Anti-Conservation Committee for short. In fact, the proposed conservation area would probably never have materialized anyway. Nevertheless, the campaign to stop it has had a profound effect on local people's perceptions of anything called conservation. The very idea of an Anti-Conservation Committee unequivocally presents conservation as a wholly negative thing. Even when people knew little about the specific aims of Western conservation, most felt that they knew enough. To local Maasai, people who promoted conservation were outsiders who thought animals were more important than people, and who wanted to take away Maasai rangeland in order to accommodate wildlife at the Maasai's expense.

This was the prevailing view of conservation expressed by respondents to my land-use survey in 1996. During this same year a new type of conservation initiative was taking place in my research area. The European Union sponsored a group of researchers to conduct an extensive research project on the interaction of people and wildlife to the east of Tarangire National Park. One of the team members, an American economist, was conducting a community mapping project using GIS technology.[2] Towards this end, she elicited the help of local herders in identifying key resources within their communities, such as pasture, farms, water, and forests. Once completed the maps would become a resource for future resource management projects. Not surprisingly, people were suspicious. An armed park ranger accompanied the researcher, and local children had seen the project airplane flying up and down the park border. Rumors began to circulate that this was simply a more sophisticated way to expand park boundaries. By this time Saruni was back from Ireland. He and other leaders in the Pastoralists of the Highlands were instrumental in blocking the mapping project.

A New Type of Conservation?

The mapping project was part of a resource management paradigm called community-based conservation, which takes its model from Zimbabwe's Communal Areas Management Program for Indigenous Resources (CAMPFIRE) program. CAMPFIRE premised that giving local people a stake in wildlife would increase their incentive to conserve it. Wildlife would thereby become an important engine of local economic development (Kiss 1990; Murphree 1996). In other words, community-based conservation seeks to create a synthesis of conservation and development. Several local observers pointed out that this would be a bad deal. Conservation denied people access to

natural resources in favor of preserving wild animals. Development, during the socialist period (1967 to 1980), entailed the forced resettlement of Maasai communities. Lately it appeared to revolve around the transfer of community resources to strangers and outsiders. What would local people gain from programs that combined these two projects? Assertions that this was a new kind of conservation were met with public skepticism. As one elder put it, "A warthog's tusks can be as dangerous as an elephant's."

Conversations between conservationists and local people took place in community meetings, sponsored by Tanzania National Parks. The meetings were part of a pilot project called Good Neighborliness (*Ujirani Mwema*). They were designed to enroll people in the community-mapping project, and to introduce them to the concept of community-based conservation. It was immediately clear that conservationists and local people (mostly male elders) were working at cross-purposes. Conservationists (both Western and Tanzanian) extolled the potential values of wildlife for local communities, and encouraged people to stop farming in wildlife migration corridors. Local people, on the other hand, demanded access to land and other natural resources inside of Tarangire National Park. This was a concession that conservationists were unable (and that most were unwilling) to make. At one meeting a Tanzanian official invoked the ritual pageantry of Maasai celebrations saying, "When you go to a feast or a party, you wear your best clothes. On most days, however, you wear your regular clothes." He concluded that land inside the parks was like ritual clothing and land outside the parks was like regular clothes. This prompted a question from a young Maasai: Why weren't the people of Simanjiro invited to the feast?

All of the community-based conservation meetings that I attended during my time in the field revolved around this impasse. Promoters of community-based conservation spoke of using tourist revenues to fund local development projects (ranging from tented safari camps to ostrich farms), which implicitly assumed local economic transformations. Not all local people were opposed to economic transformation, and some were even interested in the potential revenue of these projects. However, most were primarily concerned about the land and natural resources on which the survival of their herds depended. Revenue sharing and income-generating projects could not begin to compensate for the resources enclosed by the national park (cf. Brockington 2002). Many pointed out the irony of a program of good neighborliness premised on excluding people from high-quality pasture. Good-neighborliness in Maasai culture is closely related to a system of mutual access to land and natural resources. A Maasai elder highlighted this discrepancy at another community-based conservation meeting:

> Tanzania National Parks can't teach us about good neighborliness. We had good neighborliness before Tanzania National Parks ever came here. If it doesn't rain here, I know that I can take my cattle to Naberera [a neighboring village]. The people at Naberera won't turn me away. They will let me stay so that my cattle will not die. They will help me, because they may need my help another year. This is good neighborliness. Tanzania National

Parks does not understand this. Their livestock [wildlife] come to graze in our villages, and we do not bother them. If it rains in the park we can't go there, even if our cattle are dying. If we do, we are beaten up and our cattle are taken away. This is not good neighborliness. I know all about Tanzania National Parks Good Neighborliness. I've seen it with my own eyes, and we don't need it here. We would all be better off if Tanzania National Parks took their Good Neighborliness and went away. . . .

Connecting the Dots: Multisited Ethnography and Globalization

This brief overview outlines a complex state of affairs. Studies of this nature have become increasingly common in cultural anthropology, as anthropologists struggle to describe the connections between specific communities and the rest of the world. Local conflicts over land are also conflicts over meaning taking place at multiple levels. Is it traditional rangeland, a world heritage site, or a resource to be harnessed for national development? The rise of the Maasai NGOs brings a new set of questions to these debates. Suddenly questions over meanings of land are intertwined with questions of what it means to be Maasai and especially whether the Maasai have special rights as indigenous people.

The cast of players in this scene is also dauntingly complex, including local people, Maasai NGO leaders, government officials (categories that often overlap), Western conservationists, human rights advocates, missionaries, entrepreneurs, and tourists. In talking about what's going on, these people mix and match an equally confusing array of ideas: Western stereotypes about the Maasai, conservation, free trade, national sovereignty, indigenous rights, to name a few. To complicate matters further, this scene is connected to institutions like the Tanzanian government, Western governments, NGOs, and the World Bank.

In a situation like this an anthropologist struggles to understand the complexity of the local situation and the various interests and perspectives that he or she may encounter there. She or he must then try and understand the connections of this complex local situation to other institutions and places. To do this she or he will probably have to engage in what is known in anthropology as multisited ethnography. My own study, for example, began in specific Maasai communities. From what I learned at this particular ethnographic site I found it necessary to pursue additional research at meetings in workshops in the cities of Arusha and Dar-es-Salaam. I also gathered data from human rights organizations in the United Kingdom. I expect that future research along these lines might take me to Canada, Washington D.C., and maybe even Australia. Research of this nature can also take place at virtual sites on the Internet and television. I learned a great deal from visiting human rights and conservation Web sites connected to the Maasai. These virtual sites taught me a great deal about how Maasai and Western NGO leaders were representing the types of problems that I was trying to understand. As I have already mentioned, these types of representations often invoke images and stereotypes of Africa and the Maasai that have their roots in the colonial period. . . .

Notes

1. The use of first and last names in this text follows Tanzanian usage and may appear inconsistent to the Western reader—the idea of people having first and last names was brought by Europeans.

2. Geographic Information Technology (GIS) is a form of satellite technology used to make maps. Conservation biologists use it to map such things as wildebeest migration routes. Anthropologists can use it to map resource conflicts.

Assess Your Progress

1. In what respects are conservation and globalization linked?

2. How is globalization a "homogenizing process?"

3. How does the author describe the conditions of indigenous people today?

4. How have the Maasai been marginalized? What changes have been taking place?

5. Describe the importance of livestock to Maasai culture, ecology and survival.

6. How have social relationships suffered with the decline of the herding economy?

7. How has conservation hurt the Maasai?

8. What kind of conservation is practiced by indigenous communities? How does this differ from what we usually think of as conservation?

9. Why is the western model of the park usually incompatible with the indigenous conservation model?

10. Why do third world governments promote free markets and Western models of conservation?

11. What is the "global associational revolution?"

12. Describe the process of Disneyfication and ecocultural tourism in East Africa.

13. What is the "received wisdom" regarding tourism? Does changing people's perceptions have a meaningful impact on poverty and environmental degradation? Explain.

14. In what respects were the author's expectations about the Maasai, the national park and the wildlife misplaced?

15. Describe the ways in which the Maasai have been negatively affected by the creation of Tarangire National Park.

16. How did the proposal to expand park boundaries present conservation as a negative thing to the Maasai?

17. Why do local people resist the idea of using tourist revenues for local economic transformation? How do conservationists and Maasai see "good-neighborliness" differently?

Der Indianer

Some 40,000 Germans spend their weekends dressed as North American aboriginals. Why?

Noemi Lopinto

The first thing John Blackbird learned when he was growing up on the Canadian prairies was that his people were no good. Indians were history's losers: dethroned, displaced, rounded up and ghettoized on the reserves. Raised by a white family from the age of nine, Blackbird heard from friends and classmates that natives were unreliable, lazy and unemployable. Even in childhood games, nobody wanted to be the Indian. They all wanted to play the gallant cowboy or the stalwart RCMP officer. But, like it or not, he was an Indian. He was taunted by the meaner white kids at school—and Blackbird responded the only way he could: with his fists.

Today, in Germany, John Blackbird is a star, a celebrity even. He's seen as a descendant of the wild and free people of the plains, an embodiment of environmental respect and cooperation, a defender of the land the white man has despoiled. The 37-year-old Cree filmmaker and writer is routinely trailed on the streets by fans; he even signs autographs. He tours the country's military installations, universities and elementary schools and is an honoured guest in people's homes. He is consulted for his opinion on everything from the environment, to politics, spirituality and Native studies; he frequently holds workshops on these subjects. From the moment he got off the plane in Frankfurt in the mid-1990s, he was celebrated, feted and spoiled.

"They were so excited to [meet] me because Indians were admired in their storybooks," says Blackbird. "I was amazed. When I was a kid, Indians definitely weren't seen as heroes."

Born in Saskatchewan and educated in Alberta, Blackbird was introduced to the German propensity for Indian hero-worship after meeting and marrying a German citizen in Meadow Lake, Sask., where he worked at the local television station. They had a child, and at his wife's urging they relocated to Oldenburg in northwestern Germany. Within a few weeks, Blackbird was confronted with what is called the "hobbyist" movement. Its 40,000 members grew up fascinated with Native North American culture, thanks in no small part to the bestselling German author of all time, Karl May. May wrote four books and many short stories about an Apache warrior named Winnetou and his sidekick and German blood-brother, Old Shatterhand. First penned in 1892, the books' characters roam the North American plains, using their nearly superhuman powers to fight off the land-hungry government and thuggish, violent pioneers. Fans of the stories included Adolf Hitler and Albert Einstein.

May was imprisoned for fraud several times and wrote under many pen names, including his wife's. Contrary to his public declarations, he never visited North America. He made factual mistakes throughout his fiction; for example, he assumed the US southwest resembled the Sahara desert and described the Apache as living in pueblos and travelling in birch canoes in what is now Texas. But Winnetou was a great success and the author attracted worshipful crowds wherever he went. His books even made their way into communist countries, where they were handed from person to person in secrecy. In the 1960s, Winnetou and Old Shatterhand were immortalized in five films starring the French actor Pierre Brice and the American Lex Barker. Soon hobbyist (or "woodcraft" movements as they were called in communist countries), began forming across Europe. There are now over 400 hobbyist clubs in Germany alone.

Hobbyists take their proclivities very seriously. They spend their weekends trying to live exactly as Indians of the plains did over two centuries ago. They recreate teepee encampments in forests, public parks or on private farms, dress in animal skins and furs as "true" Sioux or Lakota did before the advent of modernity, and forgo modern tools, using moss, sticks and stone to make fire and handmade bone knives to cut and prepare food. They address each other by adopted Indian-sounding names such as "White Wolf." Their materials,

> **Hobbyists take their proclivities very seriously. They spend their weekends trying to live exactly as Indians of the plains did over two centuries ago. They address each other by adopted Indian-sounding names such as "White Wolf."**

including blankets, drums and rattles, smudge and tomahawks, can be purchased from websites such as that of Indianershop Seven Arrows, based in Offstein. Some meticulously craft their own objects, using only the materials and technologies of the 17th and 18th centuries. Many feel an intense spiritual link to native myths and spirituality. They talk about "feeling" native on the inside.

"The hobbyists' hearts are in the right place," says Blackbird. "But it is strange to see so many white people taking photographs of themselves dressed in powwow regalia, facing each other like two warriors and looking as mean as they can. If I didn't grow up with Mr. Dressup, I might have issues with it."

Some aboriginals do take issue. When David Redbird Baker first went to Germany over a decade ago and saw adult Germans playing "Cowboys and Indians," he thought it was cute. But he was offended when the hobbyists began staging sacred ceremonies like ghost and sun dances, naming ceremonies and sweat lodges. Baker lives in Mönchengladbach between Düsseldorf and the Dutch border, with his German wife and their son. An Ojibwa, Baker used to dance at German powwows and sell native crafts and beadwork through his website. When I spoke to him, he was in the process of closing up shop.

"They take the social and religious ceremonies and change them beyond recognition," says Baker. "I feel bad because I used to encourage sharing. It would have been better to have kept my mouth shut."

He says hobbyists have begun to develop a sense of ownership over aboriginal culture and claim the right to improvise on the most sacred rituals. They've held pipe and naming ceremonies, held dances where anyone in modern dress is barred from attending—even visiting aboriginals. They buy sacred items like eagle feathers on the Internet (even though some eagle species are endangered) and add them to their regalia. They've allowed women to dance during their "moon time," which is, according to Baker, the equivalent of a cardinal sin. He compares it to an Indian walking into a Catholic church dressed in a priest's vestments on a Sunday, drinking holy water out of a coffee cup and making a sandwich out of the host.

Baker says the most common story he hears from hobbyists is that they're the illegitimate children of a missing or mysterious Native American soldier. Only one hobbyist he ever met was able to prove some link to native ancestry, and it turned out he was actually half-Mexican. "He was wandering around calling himself an Apache, a descendant of Geronimo," he says.

Despite his frustration, Baker says he stays in Europe for his family's sake. He suffered a stroke in 2003 and the family enjoys European medical and social benefits. But he insists he is never going to dance in Germany again.

"I'll go back home to dance," Baker says. "I won't get myself involved with these people anymore. Everything encourages them. In Germany they'll believe anything they see on paper and not believe the truth when it's standing there talking to them. But if it were written in a book, it would be great. I've thought about getting some friends to make me up as a dancer in lederhosen, a short hat with a feather, wooden shoes and coming out during one of their grand entries slapping my hands. Maybe I should."

Over 420,000 German tourists visit Canada each year. The Alberta government, in their international marketing strategy, notes German tourists are a "priority" market—and actively cultivates their interest in aboriginal culture. For many Germans, the Calgary Stampede, Head-Smashed-In Buffalo Jump and Blackfoot Crossing are "must-sees." Hobbyists go even further, hiring local aboriginals to take them on hunting trips or renting land to set up their teepees so they can sleep under an authentic prairie sky.

But there is traffic in both directions, and always has been, even dating back a few hundred years. Toward the end of the 19th century, many famous chiefs escaped poor living conditions by going to Europe, usually as part of a variety show dedicated to the glorification of the US froniter. When the Apache warrior Geronimo was in his dotage (and technically a prisoner of war), he travelled to Europe with Buffalo Bill's Wild West Show in the late 1890s with other famous warriors: Sitting Bull of the Lakota, Chief Joseph of the Nez Perce, Sioux Chief Rains-in-the-Face, and Black Elk, an Oglala Sioux. They were extremely popular. Some stayed in Europe after the tour was over.

According to Carmen Kwasny of the Native American Association of Germany, in a country of some 82 million people, North American aboriginals number no more than a few hundred. Unless they apply for citizenship, their comings and goings are likely to remain invisible. Established in the 1980s by a couple of native soldiers in Heidelberg, the NAAOG began as a kind of a social club. They sponsored a few mini-powwows with other native dancers serving in the US armed forces. When they were shipped back home, a Hopi Native-American kept up the organization. He was a singer who had a small drum group and would use non-native dancers, mainly German women, to help raise money for the group. When he left, the NAAOG's remaining members were all Germans.

As the new chairwoman, Kwasny still stages powwows, but she insists she is not like the hobbyists. "Some of them are really good people," she says. "They put hard work into it. It's amazing how much time they spend doing these arts. They can set up teepees in a really short time, skin an animal or make an arrowhead out of stone. But the problems come up when they try to be what they can't be. They say, 'My heart is like [a] Native American heart. I feel like a Native American,' and then they think they would like to have their spiritual feelings. So many are looking for something they will probably never find.

"They mainly get their knowledge out of books," she continues. "But then they mix it up, and [their] little group develops something new that doesn't really exist, that never did, but they think it was like that. They say, 'We want to be authentic,' and I say, 'How can you be authentic? You're German.'"

Ever since she learned to read, the 43-year-old Kwasny has been interested in aboriginal culture. She read May's books and more: books about Wounded Knee, Custer's last stand and the ongoing struggle for land rights. She has been a regular at German powwows since 1989. Born in Bavaria in an industrial area surrounded by towers and factories, there were few green areas where she grew up—mostly bushes and the odd tree. She remembers longing for an intimate connection to nature and freedom of movement. She is convinced that Germans' fascination with *der Indianer* comes from a lack of interaction with the natural environment in increasingly crowded, industrial cities.

Add the demise of the church, and you have a people also looking for a new way to connect with God. "After all these years, I found the freedom inside myself," Kwasny says. "I don't have to go outside. I can do this work because I can see them just as people, beyond the colour of their skin. People in Germany are trying to look for some closeness, a new religion, new way of thinking. The conflict is they have to find out that Native Americans are just people."

They have to get past Karl May, in other words. His fiction, of course, makes no mention of the realities of colonization, oppression and discrimination that aboriginal people still face in Canada today. And local tour guides, in shuttling all those everyday Germans and hobbyists alike around Alberta, don't typically schedule a visit to any of the homes of the 156,000 descendants of the First Nations, Métis and Inuit and who still live in the province.

That's because the May fans and hobbyists are "fantasists," says visual anthropologist Marta Carlson, a member of California's Yurok tribe and a native studies teacher at the University of Massachusetts. If they knew the conditions in which a lot of natives live today, Germans would have no interest in recreating them authentically. "No one wants to be living below the poverty level on a [North American] reservation," says Carlson. "It lacks a certain romance."

Carlson is also troubled by the idea of North American aboriginals turning themselves into "cultural entrepreneurs" for Europeans' benefit. "It feeds into and helps maintain the stereotype of Native Americans as living in the late 1800s," she says. "It keeps aboriginal people in cultural stasis. And who has control over that image? The hobbyists."

In her visits to hobbyist camps in Germany, Carlson has noticed two divides in the movement: east from west, and men from women. East Germans, she says, are more communal, less acquisitive of native products and tend to be more aware of and involved in aboriginal political causes. West hobbyist camps tend to be more materialistic, the regalia more magnificent and the participants more obsessed with authenticity. Carlson once attended a camp where you had to emulate the style of a certain tribe in a certain year: you had to park your car kilometres away, drag your stuff in on foot and you couldn't wear glasses, contact lenses, socks or underwear. She describes hobbyism as very much a man's game: the women are usually hidden away inside the teepees socializing while the men whoop it up outside. It was usually western German hobbyists who would tell her she didn't know her own culture.

"German hobbyists consider culture a product, a kind of capital that they're trying to acquire," she says. "The effects of them doing our spiritual ceremonies… [they] have no idea what damage they could be doing. They could be unknowingly upsetting the balance of energy in our world."

Carlson says that since first contact with Europeans, everything has been taken from North American aboriginals—their land, their freedom of movement, languages, their way of life. "Why can't they leave us with our spirituality?" she asks. "I know people who have no problem sharing it, but it has to be done correctly. It can't just be appropriated. It's ours, and if you get upset with that, there is something wrong with you."

Powwows are among the least contentious of hobbyist activities because they're not religious or spiritual ceremonies. A powwow is a dance competition, a social event which may incorporate spiritual elements but whose purpose is akin to a county fair. A sweat lodge, on the other hand, is a sacred ritual akin to a church service where adherents go to find emotional and spiritual healing.

A Blackfoot creation legend says the sweat lodge was given to aboriginal people in trust, as a sacred gift. As the story goes, the Sun wanted to help a young warrior named Scarface. He led the young man into the first of four sweat lodges and showed him how to rub the smoke over his body on the right and left sides, purifying his body and wiping away his disfiguring scar. He also gave Scarface smudge, the sacred pipe, ochre, a forked stick for lifting hot embers and a braid of sweetgrass to make incense. Sun dances, ghost dances and pipe and naming ceremonies are also sacred rituals, usually hosted by a community or spiritual leader.

Casey Eagle Speaker, a Blackfoot elder from southern Alberta, believes German interest in aboriginal spiritual practice is the beginning of realization of a Blackfoot prophecy that says that four races of man, represented by the colours red, white, black and yellow, will one day come together in complete harmony. He points out that aboriginal people are involved in western religions, too.

Casey Eagle Speaker believes German interest in aboriginal spiritual practice is the beginning of realization of a Blackfoot prophecy that says that the four races of man . . . will one day come together in complete harmony.

"There has to be equality at some level to call upon the Creator for help, whether it's at a church, sweat lodge or any other ceremonies," he says. "Is there any wrong way to pray? No. These are spiritual practices, and every person is their own spiritual authority. As long as it is done with respect, there should be no boundary, no discrimination based on the shell you carry."

As for German hobbyists, Eagle Speaker says it's part of human nature to be interested in other people's spiritual practices. "The Great Spirit exists in all people no matter what their colour or gender," he says. "No person should be denied if they choose to be a part of a ceremony."

When he lived in Canada, John Blackbird was alienated from his Indian family growing up, and as an adult felt too shy to participate in powwows. But since moving to Europe he has been forced to educate himself on Cree customs in order to sell his main product: himself.

He often feels frustrated with his role as a "dime-store Indian," never being seen as a full person. But then he comes home to the prairies and sees the small "redskin" dolls with their chubby brick-red faces and fake buckskin breechcloths in the airport gift shop; the sweatshirts and mugs stamped with the faces of chiefs who were ignored, persecuted and imprisoned during their lifetimes.

He knows that if he looks for a job and an apartment, he will face a wall of racism. Canadian aboriginals' wages are at the lowest rung of the economic ladder, lower even than what is made by other visible minorities. Even though they make up less than 3 per cent of the population in most provinces, aboriginals account for 18.5 percent of the federal prison population, and their overall incarceration rate is almost nine times higher. On the whole, Blackbird's two daughters could expect to have poorer health, lower levels of education and higher rates of unemployment as adults on their own land.

So he stays in Deutschland and dances for the NAAOG. He also writes for a local website and promotes the documentary film he finished in 2005. Entitled *Powwow,* it follows several male and female dancers as they perform a variety of dances from across a broad spectrum of aboriginal traditions. The film's protagonists talk about the complexities of modern times, about residential schools, the church's influence, the broken treaties, loss of land rights and the need to move forward.

"It's hard being an Indian, but I love my Indian ways," says a powwow announcer at the end of the film. Blackbird says he is trying to show Germans that aboriginal dances are thriving and evolving art forms, not the ancient rituals of an extinct people.

Once, as part of his promotion efforts, he described his documentary in an e-mail to a hobbyist organization as being about "Indian life." He received a quick response informing him that the proper term was "First Nations," that he would do well not to use outdated, racist terminology and that First Nations in North America never used the term.

"I am an Indian!" Blackbird shot back. "My friends are Indians, my family are Indians. We have always called ourselves Indians. I have a status card from the Canadian government that tells me I am an Indian. You have no right to tell me what I am."

Assess Your Progress

1. What did John Blackbird learn about being Indian when he was growing up? Why is he seen as a star in Germany today?

2. Describe the "hobbyist" movement. Why are some aboriginals offended by it?

3. In what respects are May fans and hobbyists "fantasists?" Why would they not have an interest in recreating native life if they knew the truth?

4. What is the problem with North American aboriginals being "cultural entrepreneurs?"

5. What are the differences between East German and West German hobbyists, according to anthropologist Marta Carlson? Why does she say that hobbyism is a "man's game" and that hobbyism is a kind of "product?"

6. Do you think hobbyists should pursue the spiritual aspects of aboriginal culture? Discuss.

7. In what ways is John Blackbird uncomfortable in Canada?

8. What does his film try to show to Germans?

9. What was Blackbird's response to the German who advised him not to refer to himself as an "Indian?"

Originally from Montreal, **NOEMI LOPINTO** came west to become the managing editor of a small-town newspaper in northern Saskatchewan, where she first encountered the hobbyist movement. She now lives in Edmonton.

What Native Peoples Deserve

ROGER SANDALL

The Roosevelt Indian Reservation in the Amazon rain forest is not a happy place. Last year, the Cinta Larga Indians slaughtered 29 miners there, and in October the Brazilian who was trying to mediate the conflict was murdered at a cash machine. Neither of these events represented anything new. The reserve, located 2,100 miles northwest of Rio de Janeiro, and named for Theodore Roosevelt when he visited Brazil in 1913, is also where a notorious massacre of Cinta Larga by rubber tappers took place in 1963; only one child in the village survived.

The immediate cause of the recent violence is not rubber but diamonds. The Roosevelt Indian Reservation may be sitting on one of the world's largest deposits, and no one wants to leave it in the ground—neither the Indians, nor the itinerant diggers (*garimpeiros*), nor the government. But, under present Brazilian law, no one is free to begin digging, either. And this brings us to the deeper cause of murder and mayhem in the region.

Under Brazil's constitution, the country's Indians are not full citizens. Instead, they are legal minors, with the status of a protected species. This has one singular benefit for the Indians: the twelve Cinta Larga responsible for last year's killing of 29 wildcat prospectors may enjoy immunity from prosecution and never face jail. But there is also a downside. As wards of the state, the Indians are denied the right to mine their own land.

As for outsiders, they must apply for permits to dig, and face endless bureaucratic delays that more often than not lead nowhere. The outcome is predictable: frustrated in their own wishes, and hard-pressed by the impatient diggers, Indians make private deals, which then go sour—and the shooting starts.

At issue here is not just the law; the law is itself the product of an idea, or a set of ideas, concerning certain underlying questions. What should be done about endangered enclave societies in the midst of a modern nation? Can they, or their land, or their minerals be cut off and preserved, frozen in time, pristine and inviolate, forever? Should they be?

The massacre of the Cinta Larga in 1963 gave rise to a Brazilian state inquiry that became known as the Figueiredo Report (after the official in charge of the investigation). The inquiry was meant to find out about the shockingly grave deficiencies and abuses that were then being tolerated by the Indian Protection Service, including the use of individual Indians as slaves. Once it was completed, the old agency was closed down, and a new one created to replace it.

There the matter might have rested had not the London *Sunday Times* caught a whiff of scandal. The paper dispatched the travel writer Norman Lewis to Brazil; though he did not meet any Indians, he found all he needed in the Figueiredo Report. "By the descriptions of all who had seen them," Lewis reported, "there were no more inoffensive and charming human beings on the planet than the forest Indians of Brazil."

Having established a scene of primal innocence, Lewis proceeded to tell of the atrocities against the Cinta Larga, warning that they were being pushed to the brink of extinction and that there might not be a single Indian left by 1980. He concluded: "What a tragedy, what a reproach it will be for the human race if this is allowed to happen!" Reprinted all over the globe, his sensational article had profound and lasting effects.

The first of these effects was to enshrine a form of extreme protectionism, not only as a temporary means to an end—the human and cultural survival of the indigenous peoples of Brazil—but as an end in itself. Soon, all those working for Indian interests were of a single opinion: the only way to protect these tribal peoples was to create inviolable sanctuaries where they would "live their own lives preserving their own culture on their own land."

The second effect was to galvanize a number of English explorers, writers, and anthropologists into setting up a permanent international lobby. The name of this flourishing body is Survival, self-described as "the world's leading organization supporting tribal peoples." Two men who have been associated with it from the outset are John Hemming and Robin Hanbury-Tenison.

Hemming, who served for two decades as the director of the Royal Geographical Society, has written a number of books about South America, among them an indispensable three volume history of the impact of civilization on Brazil's indigenous peoples—*Red Gold, Amazon Frontier,* and *Die If You Must,* the last of which appeared in 2003.[*] Hanbury-Tenison, Hemming's long-time friend, was also a founder of Survival and is today its president. Less well-known but also important is the documentary filmmaker Adrian Cowell, who has spoken up on behalf of the Amazonian Indians for nearly 50 years.

According to a recent article by Hemming in the British monthly *Prospect,* the campaign to ensure the survival of the Amazonian peoples appears to have succeeded. This is also the gist of the final chapter of *Die If You Must,* where he wrote:

> The Indians will survive physically. Their populations have grown steadily since a nadir of near-extinction in the mid-20th century. Having fallen to little more than 100,000 in the 1950's, they have more than tripled to some 350,000 and are generally rising fast.

---

[*]Macmillan, 887 pp., $28.50 (paper)

The health of the Indians is basically good, Hemming reported in *Die If You Must*. The killers of yesteryear—measles, TB, pneumonia, cholera, and smallpox—are rare. Their land is also secure: "a remarkable 11 percent of the land-mass of Brazil is now reserved for Indians. The 587 indigenous areas total almost 260 million acres—an area greater than France, Germany, and Benelux combined." Environmentalist ideals and indigenous interests have been reconciled: "From the air, [one reservation] now stands out as an immense rectangle of verdant vegetation framed by the dismal brown of arid ranch-lands."

It was in the 1950's and 60's that Hemming, Hanbury-Tenison, and Cowell, three young men from Oxford and Cambridge, launched themselves on the world. They were talented and energetic, they had good connections, and above all they shared a boyish taste for adventure. At Eton they probably read about Lawrence of Arabia; at Oxford, where Hemming and Hanbury-Tenison roomed together, they already knew that "exploring" was what they wanted to do most. They regarded the rain forests of Brazil as a natural field for their endeavors, and in no time they were paddling up the Amazon in canoes.

Adrian Cowell was a Cambridge man, and his precocity as an explorer makes an impressive tale in itself. As a student in 1954 he joined a university Trans-Africa Expedition. The following year he was in Asia. Then, as he relates in *The Heart of the Forest* (1961), "the Oxford and Cambridge Expedition to South America . . . brought me to the Amazon forest." Thereafter he joined the Brazilian Centro Expedition, an enterprise associated with the creation of the new national capital of Brasilia. Its purpose was "to canoe down the Xingu River and burn an airstrip at the exact geographical center of Brazil."

It was all tremendous fun and very romantic—a word that occurs spontaneously in the books of Hanbury-Tenison, who has written voluminously about his explorations and today runs a booking agency for exotic locations. Here, from his website, is a typical passage about an early adventure in Afghanistan:

> A sound like distant thunder made me look up at the rich blue cloudless sky before I turned to see twenty wild horsemen in turbans and flowing robes bearing down on me. They carried long-barreled rifles and had daggers in their belts. Beside their spirited horses loped large, hairy hounds. With their Genghis Khan moustaches and fine, aquiline noses they were almost caricatures of the bandits we had been warned about. I should have been frightened, but all I could think was that if I had to go I could not have found a more romantic end.

This tells us quite a bit about the attitude of all three men toward indigenous peoples. In light of that attitude, Hanbury-Tenison must have been taken aback when, in 1971, he called on the anthropologist Margaret Mead at the Museum of Natural History in New York to tell her about Survival International (as Survival was then called), and she gave him a piece of her mind. Mead at the age of seventy was a very different person from the idealistic young woman who had visited Samoa in 1926. By 1971, she was fiercely *un*romantic, and the spectacle of yet another young Oxford "explorer" embarking on yet another expedition up the Amazon must have set her teeth on edge. With sturdy good sense she tried to talk him out of his fantasies.

In his 1973 book, *A Question of Survival*, Hanbury-Tenison describes this "small, beady-eyed dumpling of a lady who sailed into the attack as I came through the door":

> The main point that annoyed [Mead] was the concept, unstated by me, that primitive peoples were any better off as they were. She said she was "maddened by antibiotic-ridden idealists who

wouldn't stand three weeks in the jungle" . . . and the whole "noble savage" concept almost made her foam at the mouth. "All primitive peoples," she said, "lead miserable, unhappy, cruel lives, most of which are spent trying to kill each other." The reason they lived in the unpleasant places they did, like the middle of the Brazilian jungle, was that nobody else would.

There was much talk in those days about the pharmaceutical benefits of rain forests, and Hanbury-Tenison and his friends were sure that the Amazon was about to make a huge contribution to the world's health. (This was a little before the discovery of the supposed wonders of jojoba oil.) But Mead was having none of it:

> She said that to protect [the Indians] on the grounds that they could be useful to us or contribute anything was nonsense. "No primitive person has *ever* contributed *anything*, or ever will," she said. She had no time for suggestions of medical knowledge or the value of jungle lore.

The only grounds on which Mead relented were broadly humanitarian. For one thing, the Indians' "art, culture, dancing, music, etc. was pleasant and attractive and their grandchildren might thank us for trying to preserve or at best record it now that we have the proper technical means [i.e., tape and film] for doing so." For another thing, "it was bad for the world to let these people die, and the effort to prevent their extermination was good for mankind even if it failed."

For the rest, however, Mead vehemently denied that the Indians had any special reasons for being protected, as she denied any advantage of one race over another. She also claimed emphatically that they all wanted one thing only, and that was to have as many material possessions and comforts as possible. Those still running away in the jungle were the ones who had encountered the most unpleasant savagery from Europeans, and even though they might be having no contact now, if they could possibly get hold of any aluminum pots they would use them.

Although faithfully recorded by Hanbury-Tenison, Mead's argument was as lost on him in 1971 as it is lost today on legions of like-minded people who teach or mouth the slogans of multiculturalism. What Mead herself failed to grasp was that, naive though he may have sounded, Hanbury-Tenison and his friends had been radicalized, and they were never going to accept her bleak view of the tribal world. It was not that they had been reading Marx; instead, they had been reading Norman Lewis's digest of the worst parts of the Figueiredo Report, including Figueiredo's judgment that "the Indians [had] suffered tortures similar to those of Treblinka and Dachau."

Torture, indeed, was too tame a word for what had taken place. In 1963, there had been massacres of the Cinta Larga tribe in Rondonia. One gunman's taped testimony describes how an employee of a rubber company named Chico Luis

> gave the chief a burst with his tommy gun to make sure, and after that he let the rest of them have it. . . . [A]ll the other guys had to do was finish off anyone still showing signs of life. . . . [T]here was a young Indian girl they didn't shoot, with a kid of about five in one hand, yelling his head off. . . . Chico shot the kid through the head with his .45 and then grabbed hold of the woman—who by the way was very pretty. "Be reasonable," I said, "why do you have to kill her?" In my view it was a waste. "What's wrong with giving her to the boys? They haven't set eyes on a woman for six weeks. Or we could give her as a present to [their boss] de Brito."

But Chico would not listen:

> He tied the Indian girl up and hung her head downward from a tree, legs apart, and chopped her in half right down the middle with his machete. Almost with a single chop I'd say. The village was like a slaughterhouse. He calmed down after he'd cut the woman up, and told us to burn down all the huts and throw the bodies into the river.

This is unbearable: but it is not essentially different from what had happened to many Indians in Latin America after 1492. The lawless frontier was for centuries a refuge for loners, criminals, and violent psychopaths who had nothing to lose and could act with impunity. Those who went searching for El Dorado in the 1540's behaved like packs of marauding wolves, seizing food from the same Indian villagers whom they then enslaved as porters, and who were tortured or killed when they failed to cooperate. As one learns from Hemming's three-volume work, this sort of thing has had a very long history indeed.

Colonial nations fashion their heroes from the timber at hand, much of which is twisted and full of knots. Australia, for example, invites its citizens to admire an unappealing Irish bandit named Ned Kelly. But the Kellys smell sweet alongside Brazil's much romanticized *bandeirantes.* What are often referred to as expeditions of "pathfinders" from São Paulo into the interior in the first half of the 17th century were mostly slave raids aimed at catching, chaining, and marching back to the coast as many Indians as a group of well-armed and ruthless men could seize.

To be sure, there was sometimes a genuinely exploratory aspect to such forays. In *Red Gold,* Hemming offers a balanced account of this phase of Brazilian expansion inland, and fairly describes the ordeals of the *bandeirantes* themselves. Since slave-raiding was a central feature of traditional Indian culture, too, the journeys engaged whites, Indians, and those of mixed ancestry (*mamelucos*) in a common enterprise:

> The Indians contributed their forest skills and geographical knowledge. They soon grasped the purpose of the mission and became expert enslavers of other natives. Although brutalized and worked hard by the captains of the *bandeiras,* the Indians probably enjoyed service on them. It was quite normal for Tupi warriors to make long marches through the forests to attack enemy tribes.

In the course of his own periodic visits to Brazil, Adrian Cowell appears to have come rather closer to the realities of Amazonian Indian life than either Hanbury-Tenison or Hemming. As a result, although aware of the horrors long endured by Indians at the hands of slavers, settlers, and frontier psychopaths, he was also more prepared to face up to the grimmer aspects of the native cultures themselves, and of the horrors Indians had long inflicted on each other.

In *The Heart of the Forest* (1961), Cowell writes in idyllic prose of the partnership he formed with an Indian hunter, carrying his friend's gun and studying his craft, teaching himself to decoy wildfowl by imitating their calls. But he also reports how, in 1958 on the Xingu River, there were continual killings of itinerant Brazilian rubber tappers (*seringueiros*) by Indians, and of Indians by *seringueiros.* A Juruna Indian told him how

> first we lived lower down the Xingu and worked for the *seringueiros,* but they killed many [Indians] with rifles. So we came up here past the great rapids and lived till the *seringueiros*

say they are friends and gave us rifles. So we went downriver again and worked for the *seringueiros* till they killed more Juruna. Then we killed many *seringueiros* and came back here and killed Trumai and Kamayura Indians. Then the Txukahamae tribe came and killed almost all of us so that we are only twelve now.

That is the way things were and always had been. And this, too, was a seemingly ineradicable aspect of the culture that Cowell thought worthy of being saved. Back in 1967, he had joined the brothers Claudio and Orlando Villas-Boas in an attempt to contact and "pacify" the elusive Kreen-Akrore. But violence in the camp was making it hard to manage a community where different tribal groups had been brought together for their own safety. The captions on a page of photographs in Cowell's 1973 book, *The Tribe that Hides from Man,* read like the list of casualties on some exotic war memorial: "*Above:* Javaritu, a Trumai killed by Tapiokap. *Above:* Pionim, a Kayabi, killed Tapiokap to avenge his brother-in-law." And so on.

Much has been written about the endeavor of the Villas-Boas brothers to establish the Xingu Indian refuge and entice the tribal remnants of the Kayabi or Txikao or Suya to join it. A passage from *The Tribe that Hides from Man* offers a glimpse into the thought processes of Claudio, a "Marxist philosopher" in the Latin American manner:

> Look around this camp and you will see Indians are more loving than we are. But the expression of their love is confined to the limits of this society. They cut a hole in the wilderness to contain their family, but outside this camp is the jungle where they kill meat for food, bamboo for arrows, leaves for their beds. Killing is the essence of forest existence, and if you stopped it, the forest and the Indian would die. Within the Indian mind there is a complete division between the duties within the group and the absence of duty in the land of killing outside.

At one time, Claudio suggested that Indians should feel free to kill white *seringueiros* or any other uninvited marauders who came into the Xingu Park. While warning them of the inevitable costs of this practice as a permanent way of life, he understood that, according to the tribal code, revenge killing was natural, habitual, and inevitable. Nor was this the only aspect of Amazonian Indian culture that was hard to reconcile with modern life. Strict rules of seclusion were found among all the upper-Xingu tribes. Women were subjected to draconian punishments for violations of taboo. In a British television documentary from the 1970's, a young Mehinacu woman was asked what would happen if she were to glimpse, even accidentally, the sacred flutes played by the men. She would be gang-raped, she replied, smiling sadly as if in recognition that in the genteel world of her white interviewer, such sexual punishments—culturally authorized, approved, indeed mandatory—were unthinkable.

Hemming's account of Amazonian life is hard on the efforts of Christian missionaries, and especially hard on Jesuits ("fanatical missionaries intent on replacing native society and beliefs with their own Christian model"). One line of grudging appreciation will be followed by the word "but" and ten lines of disparagement. As his impressive study proceeds from volume to volume, he is consistently severe, his language becomes more tendentious, and an austere secularism dictates his judgment of religious matters. In his recent article in *Prospect,* he seems to approve wholeheartedly only of the politically radical priests who began to appear in the 1960's— "trained anthropologists who did not try to undermine indigenous beliefs and ceased to be aggressive proselytizers." Before that point, his view of Catholic missionary activity is mainly negative.

But what exactly were the religious authorities to do when they first arrived from Portugal and had to deal, for example, with the Tupinamba? Did they not have a clear obligation both to undermine and to prohibit certain indigenous beliefs? In modern times, we have seen the rise of whole political cultures gripped by pathology, with hideous consequences; so, too, sick ethnic cultures evolved historically in the tribal world. Few quite so sick as the Tupinamba have been recorded before or since.

They loved human flesh. Prestige and power centered on the ritual slaughtering of prisoners. In an account prepared by Alfred Métraux for the Smithsonian's *Handbook of South American Indians* (1948), we read that the killing and eating of these prisoners (who were fattened for the purpose) "were joyful events which provided these Indians with the opportunity for merrymaking, aesthetic displays, and other emotional outlets." Métraux then describes what took place at a cannibal feast after the victim's skull was shattered:

Old women rushed to drink the warm blood, and children were invited to dip their hands in it. Mothers would smear their nipples with blood so that even babies could have a taste of it. The body, cut into quarters, was roasted on a barbecue, and the old women, who were the most eager for human flesh, licked the grease running along the sticks. Some portions, reputed to be delicacies or sacred, such as the fingers or the grease around the liver or heart, were allotted to distinguished guests.

That Portuguese settlers in the 16th century did not cope very well with this aspect of the Indian tribal world is probably true. That the missionaries who came after them did not handle the situation as they might have done is also likely. But if they had been around at the time, would John Hemming, or Robin Hanbury-Tenison, or Adrian Cowell, or the entire staff of Survival have done much better? Would any of us?

"All primitive peoples," Margaret Mead had said to her young Oxford visitor, "lead miserable, unhappy, cruel lives, most of which are spent trying to kill each other." She was overdoing it, but she had a point—a point largely lost sight of in today's systematic sentimentalizing of the Stone Age.

Of course, as we have seen, Mead also acknowledged that certain aspects of Indian culture—"their art, culture, dancing, music, etc."—deserved to survive, for the enjoyment of the people themselves and for the admiration of humanity as a whole. That, indeed, is more or less what has happened today in the Xingu Park and places like it elsewhere. On display in such places is a pacified, deranged, and somewhat feminized version of Amazonian culture, of the kind that middle-class travelers from the West like to see: a theatrical world where dressing-up in feathered regalia, ritual ceremonies, and communal dancing never stop.

Hemming, who welcomes the prospect of self-determination, claims that "modern indigenous policy seeks to empower tribes to manage their own affairs." Yet both self-determination and empowerment imply literacy and modern education; and here the picture is less clear. Officially, the children are learning to read and write, and in the last chapter of *Die If You Must*—a chapter with the title "Present and Future" Hemming makes three rather perfunctory references to schooling. But at the same time, he strongly implies that in his vision of the future it does not matter whether the children learn to read and write or not, because others will be there to do things for them.

Who are these others? According to Hemming, the external political affairs of the Indians on the Xingu reserve are "supported by a remarkable contingent of 33 non-government organizations, a fireless band of missionaries, anthropologists, well-wishers, journalists, doctors, and lawyers, both in Brazil and abroad." As for their internal welfare, that is served by a "resident tribe of whites, composed of social scientists, doctors, teachers, nurses, biologists, and agronomists from all parts of Brazil." With friends like these, who needs self-determination?

What Hemming is describing is the fruit of the inviolable-sanctuary approach to cultural survival. This rests on what might be called fortress theory, and has two cardinal principles: that "culture" and "people" and "land" should be seen as indivisible, and that they can be kept this way forever in a suitably constructed territorial redoubt. Whatever is happening in the world around them, ethnic cultures should, insofar as possible, be preserved unchanged. With the help of an army of administrative personnel, custodially responsible for seeing to it that they go on wanting only the same things they have always wanted, their heritage will be kept alive. Social change—at least as it affects these picturesque tribal peoples—is bad, and should be stopped.

Among the Xingu Park Indians, it is in fact safe to say that the older generation remains strongly attached to its remote lands, and intends to go on living there, hunting animals and gathering fruits. But what do younger Indians want to do with their lives? If there is one thing we have learned from modern history, it is that individuals often outgrow their ethnic cultures, find life in a fortress claustrophobic, and choose to move on. In contrast to museum exhibits, real human beings have a way of developing ideas and ambitions and desires—including for aluminum pots—beyond the ken of conservators. Fortress theory, multicultural "essentialism," and the enduring cult of the noble savage are the enemies of those ambitions and human desires.

In the final paragraph of *Die If You Must*, Hemming wonders uneasily whether the pessimists might have the last laugh after all—whether the Amazon's "beautiful, ancient, and intricate cultures will be maintained only artificially as curiosities for tourists, researchers, or politically correct enthusiasts." That is quite possible. But it is hardly the only undesirable possibility. Preserving ancient cultural patterns is laudable, but it is not enough. No society in history has ever stood still, and however beautiful, and ancient, and intricate traditional cultures may be, it is wrong to lock people up inside them and throw away the key. Uprooting the dishonest and patronizing Western cult of the noble savage will be the work of generations; but as far as today's Amazonian Indians are concerned, the main priority must surely be to ensure that those among them who do not want to play the obliging role of historical curiosities, endlessly dressing up for visitors whose expectations they feel bound to fulfill, are able to find something else to do in the modern world—on the reservation or off it. In that quest we can only wish them well.

Assess Your Progress

1. What was the immediate cause of the violence in Cinta Larga?

2. What is the status of Brazil's Indians under the constitution and what are its implications? Why was the Indian Protection Service closed down?

3. What did the Figueiredo Report reveal, and what happened as a result of it?

4. What were the two effects of the Norman Lewis article?

5. How does John Hemming describe the situation today?

6. Explain Margaret Mead's take on "primitive peoples."

7. In what respects is "torture" too tame a word for the treatment of Indians?

8. For whom was the lawless frontier a refuge? Why does the author characterize these people as "marauding wolves?"

9. What were the "pathfinders" of Brazil doing?

10. Who were the slave-raiders?

11. What is "on display" in the Xingu Park today?

12. How does Hemming describe "modern indigenous policy?"

13. What do "self-determination and empowerment" imply?

14. Upon what two principles does "fortress theory" depend?

15. How does the author contrast the older generation with the younger in terms of what they want? What are the "enemies of those ambitions and desires?"

16. Given the two alterative possibilities for their future, what does the author think should be the main priority?

ROGER SANDALL taught anthropology for many years at the University of Sydney in Australia and is the author most recently of *The Culture Cult*. His essay, "Can Sudan Be Saved?," appeared in the December 2004 Commentary.

Being Indigenous in the 21st Century

With a shared sense of history and a growing set of tools, the world's Indigenous Peoples are moving into a future of their own making without losing sight of who they are and where they come from.

Wilma Mankiller

There are more than 300 million indigenous people, in virtually every region of the world, including the Sámi peoples of Scandinavia, the Maya of Guatemala, numerous tribal groups in the Amazonian rainforest, the Dalits in the mountains of Southern India, the San and Kwei of Southern Africa, Aboriginal people in Australia, and, of course the hundreds of Indigenous Peoples in Mexico, Central and South America, as well as here in what is now known as North America.

There is enormous diversity among communities of Indigenous Peoples, each of which has its own distinct culture, language, history, and unique way of life. Despite these differences, Indigenous Peoples across the globe share some common values derived in part from an understanding that their lives are part of and inseparable from the natural world.

Onondaga Faith Keeper Oren Lyons once said, "Our knowledge is profound and comes from living in one place for untold generations. It comes from watching the sun rise in the east and set in the west from the same place over great sections of time. We are as familiar with the lands, rivers, and great seas that surround us as we are with the faces of our mothers. Indeed, we call the earth Etenoha, our mother from whence all life springs."

Indigenous people are not the only people who understand the interconnectedness of all living things. There are many thousands of people from different ethnic groups who care deeply about the environment and fight every day to protect the earth. The difference is that indigenous people have the benefit of being regularly reminded of their responsibilities to the land by stories and ceremonies. They remain close to the land, not only in the way they live, but in their hearts and in the way they view the world. Protecting the environment is not an intellectual exercise; it is a sacred duty. When women like Pauline Whitesinger, an elder at Big Mountain, and Carrie Dann, a Western Shoshone land rights activist, speak of preserving the land for future generations, they are not just talking about future generations of humans. They are talking about future generations of plants, animals, water, and all living things. Pauline and Carrie understand the relative insignificance of human beings in the totality of the planet.

Aside from a different view of their relationship to the natural world, many of the world's Indigenous Peoples also share a fragmented but still-present sense of responsibility for one another. Cooperation always has been necessary for the survival of tribal people, and even today cooperation takes precedence over competition in more traditional communities. It is really quite miraculous that a sense of sharing and reciprocity continues into the 21st century given the staggering amount of adversity Indigenous Peoples have faced. In many communities, the most respected people are not those who have amassed great material wealth or achieved great personal success. The greatest respect is reserved for those who help other people, those who understand that their lives play themselves out within a set of reciprocal relationships.

There is evidence of this sense of reciprocity in Cherokee communities. My husband, Charlie Soap, leads a widespread self-help movement among the Cherokee in which low-income volunteers work together to build walking trails, community centers, sports complexes, water lines, and houses. The self-help movement taps into the traditional Cherokee value of cooperation for the sake of the common good. The projects also build a sense of self-efficacy among the people.

Besides values, the world's Indigenous Peoples are also bound by the common experience of being "discovered" and subjected to colonial expansion into their territories that has led to the loss of an incalculable number of lives and millions and millions of acres of land and resources. The most basic rights of Indigenous Peoples were disregarded, and they were subjected to a series of policies that were designed to dispossess them of their land and resources and assimilate them into colonial society and culture. Too often the policies resulted in poverty, high infant mortality, rampant unemployment, and substance abuse, with all its attendant problems.

The stories are shockingly similar all over the world. When I read Chinua Achebe's *Things Fall Apart*, which chronicled the systematic destruction of an African tribe's social, cultural, and economic structure, it sounded all too familiar: take the land, discredit the leaders, ridicule the traditional healers, and send the children off to distant boarding schools.

And I was sickened by the Stolen Generation report about Aboriginal children in Australia who were forcibly removed from their families and placed in boarding schools far away from their families and communities. My own father and my Aunt Sally were taken from my grandfather by the U.S. government and placed in a government boarding school when they were very young. There is a connection between us. Indigenous Peoples everywhere are connected both by our values and by our oppression.

When contemplating the contemporary challenges and problems faced by Indigenous Peoples worldwide, it is important to remember that the roots of many social, economic, and political problems can be found in colonial policies. And these policies continue today across the globe.

Several years ago Charlie and I visited an indigenous community along the Rio Negro in the Brazilian rainforest. Some of the leaders expressed concern that some environmentalists, who should be natural allies, focus almost exclusively on the land and appear not to see or hear the people at all. One leader pointed out that a few years ago it was popular for famous musicians to wear T-shirts emblazoned with the slogan "Save the Rainforests," but no one ever wore a T-shirt with the slogan "Save the People of the Rainforest," though the people of the forest possess the best knowledge about how to live with and sustain the forests.

With so little accurate information about Indigenous Peoples available in educational institutions, in literature, films, or popular culture, it is not surprising that many people are not even conscious of Indigenous Peoples.

The battle to protect the human and land rights of Indigenous Peoples is made immeasurably more difficult by the fact that so few people know much about either the history or contemporary lives of our people. And without any kind of history or cultural context, it is almost impossible for outsiders to understand the issues and challenges faced by Indigenous Peoples.

This lack of accurate information leaves a void that is often filled with nonsensical stereotypes, which either vilify Indigenous Peoples as troubled descendants of savage peoples, or romanticize them as innocent children of nature, spiritual but incapable of higher thought.

Public perceptions will change in the future as indigenous leaders more fully understand that there is a direct link between public perception and public policies. Indigenous Peoples must frame their own issues, because if they don't frame the issues for themselves, their opponents most certainly will. In the future, as more indigenous people become filmmakers, writers, historians, museum curators, and journalists, they will be able to use a dazzling array of technological tools to tell their own stories, in their own voice, in their own way.

Once, a journalist asked me whether people in the United States had trouble accepting the government of the Cherokee Nation during my tenure as principal chief. I was a little surprised by the question. The government of the Cherokee Nation predated the government of the United States and had treaties with other countries before it executed a treaty with one of the first U.S. colonies.

Cherokee and other tribal leaders sent delegations to meet with the English, Spanish, and French in an effort to protect their lands and people. Traveling to foreign lands with a trusted interpreter, tribal ambassadors took maps that had been painstakingly drawn by hand to show their lands to heads of other governments. They also took along gifts, letters, and proclamations. Though tribal leaders thought they were being dealt with as heads of state and as equals, historical records indicate they were often objects of curiosity, and that there was a great deal of disdain and ridicule of these earnest delegates.

Tribal governments in the United States today exercise a range of sovereign rights. Many tribal governments have their own judicial systems, operate their own police force, run their own schools, administer their own clinics and hospitals, and operate a wide range of business enterprises. There are now more than two dozen tribally controlled community colleges. All these advancements benefit everyone in the community, not just tribal people. The history, contemporary lives, and future of tribal governments is intertwined with that of their neighbors.

One of the most common misperceptions about Indigenous Peoples is that they are all the same. There is not only great diversity among Indigenous Peoples, there is great diversity within each tribal community, just as there is in the larger society. Members of the Cherokee Nation are socially, economically, and culturally stratified. Several thousand Cherokee continue to speak the Cherokee language and live in Cherokee communities in rural northeastern Oklahoma. At the other end of the spectrum, there are enrolled tribal members who have never been to even visit the Cherokee Nation. Intermarriage has created an enrolled Cherokee membership that includes people with Hispanic, Asian, Caucasian, and African American heritage.

So what does the future hold for Indigenous Peoples across the globe? What challenges will they face moving further into the 21st century?

To see the future, one needs only to look at the past. If, as peoples, we have been able to survive a staggering loss of land, of rights, of resources, of lives, and we are still standing in the early 21st century, how can I not be optimistic that we will survive whatever challenges lie ahead, that 100 or 500 years from now we will still have viable indigenous communities? Without question, the combined efforts of government and various religious groups to eradicate traditional knowledge systems has had a profoundly negative impact on the culture as well as the social and economic systems of Indigenous Peoples. But if we have been able to hold onto our sense of community, our languages, culture, and ceremonies, despite everything, how can I not be optimistic about the future?

And though some of our original languages, medicines, and ceremonies have been irretrievably lost, the ceremonial fires of many Indigenous Peoples across the globe have survived all the upheaval. Sometimes indigenous communities have almost had to reinvent themselves as a people but they have never given up their sense of responsibility to one another and to the land. It is this sense of interdependence that has sustained tribal people thus far and I believe it will help sustain them well into the future.

Indigenous Peoples know about change and have proven time and time again they can adapt to change. No matter where they go in the world, they hold onto a strong sense of tribal identity while fully interacting with and participating in the larger society around them. In my state of Oklahoma alone, we have produced an indigenous astronaut, two United States congressmen, a Pulitzer Prize-winning novelist, and countless others who have made great contributions to their people, the state, and the world.

One of the great challenges for Indigenous Peoples in the 21st century will be to develop practical models to capture, maintain, and pass on traditional knowledge systems and values to future generations. Nothing can replace the sense of continuity that a genuine understanding of traditional tribal knowledge brings. Many communities are working on discrete aspects of culture, such as language or medicine, but it is the entire system of knowledge that needs to be maintained, not just for Indigenous Peoples but for the world at large.

Regrettably, in the future the battle for human and land rights will continue. But the future does look somewhat better for tribal people. Last year, after 30 years of advocacy by Indigenous Peoples, the United Nations finally passed a declaration supporting their distinct human rights. The challenge will be to make sure the provisions of the declaration are honored and that the rights of Indigenous Peoples all over the world are protected.

Indigenous Peoples simply do better when they have control of their own lives. In the case of my own people, after we were forcibly removed by the United States military from the southeastern part of the United States to Indian Territory, now Oklahoma, we picked ourselves up and rebuilt our nation, despite the fact that approximately 4,000 Cherokee lives were lost during the forced removal. We started some of the first schools west of the Mississippi, Indian or non-Indian, and built schools for the higher education of women. We printed our own newspapers in Cherokee and English and were more literate than our neighbors in adjoining states. Then, in the early 20th century, the federal government almost abolished the Cherokee Nation, and within two decades, our educational attainment levels dropped dramatically and many of our people were living without the most basic amenities. But our people never gave up the dream of rebuilding

the Cherokee Nation. In my grandfather's time, Cherokee men rode horses from house to house to collect dimes in a mason jar so they could send representatives to Washington to remind the government to honor its treaties with the Cherokee people.

Over the past 35 years, we have revitalized the Cherokee Nation and once again run our own school, and we have an extensive array of successful education programs. The youth at our Sequoyah High School recently won the state trigonometry contest, and several are Gates Millennium Scholars. We simply do better when we have control over our own destiny.

Assess Your Progress

1. What do the 300 million indigenous people of the world have in common? Where does such knowledge come from?

2. In what ways do indigenous people differ from others who care about the environment?

3. In what respects is there a "shared sense of responsibility for one another" among indigenous people?

4. Describe the Indigenous People's common experience of "being discovered" and "being subjected to colonial expansion."

5. Why is it important to not just "save the rainforests," but also to "save the people?"

6. How is the battle to protect the human and land rights of Indigenous Peoples made immeasurably more difficult? How does the author suggest that such public perceptions be changed?

7. In what respects were tribal groups, such as the Cherokee, independent entities at one time?

8. In what respects do tribal governments in the United States still exercise a range of sovereign rights?

9. Why is the author optimistic about the future survival of indigenous communities?

10. What challenges lie ahead for Indigenous Peoples and how does the author suggest that they are meeting these challenges?

11. How have the Cherokee shown that "Indigenous Peoples simply do better when they have control over their own lives?"

Test-Your-Knowledge Form

We encourage you to photocopy and use this page as a tool to assess how the articles in *Annual Editions* expand on the information in your textbook. By reflecting on the articles you will gain enhanced text information. You can also access this useful form on a product's book support website at www.mhhe.com/cls

NAME: DATE:

_____

TITLE AND NUMBER OF ARTICLE:

_____

BRIEFLY STATE THE MAIN IDEA OF THIS ARTICLE:

_____

LIST THREE IMPORTANT FACTS THAT THE AUTHOR USES TO SUPPORT THE MAIN IDEA:

_____

WHAT INFORMATION OR IDEAS DISCUSSED IN THIS ARTICLE ARE ALSO DISCUSSED IN YOUR TEXTBOOK OR OTHER READINGS THAT YOU HAVE DONE? LIST THE TEXTBOOK CHAPTERS AND PAGE NUMBERS:

_____

LIST ANY EXAMPLES OF BIAS OR FAULTY REASONING THAT YOU FOUND IN THE ARTICLE:

_____

LIST ANY NEW TERMS/CONCEPTS THAT WERE DISCUSSED IN THE ARTICLE, AND WRITE A SHORT DEFINITION:

We Want Your Advice

ANNUAL EDITIONS revisions depend on two major opinion sources: one is our Advisory Board, listed in the front of this volume, which works with us in scanning the thousands of articles published in the public press each year; the other is you—the person actually using the book. Please help us and the users of the next edition by completing the prepaid article rating form on this page and returning it to us. Thank you for your help!

ANNUAL EDITIONS: Anthropology 11/12

ARTICLE RATING FORM

Here is an opportunity for you to have direct input into the next revision of this volume.
We would like you to rate each of the articles listed below, using the following scale:

1. **Excellent: should definitely be retained**
2. **Above average: should probably be retained**
3. **Below average: should probably be deleted**
4. **Poor: should definitely be deleted**

Your ratings will play a vital part in the next revision.
Please mail this prepaid form to us as soon as possible.
Thanks for your help!

RATING	ARTICLE	RATING	ARTICLE
	1. A Dispute in Donggo: Fieldwork and Ethnography		20. Who Needs Love! In Japan, Many Couples Don't
	2. Doing Fieldwork among the Yąnomamö		21. The Berdache Tradition
	3. Eating Christmas in the Kalahari		22. Where Fat Is a Mark of Beauty
	4. Tricking and Tripping: Fieldwork on Prostitution in the Era of AIDS		23. . . . but What If It's a Girl?
	5. Can White Men Jump?: Ethnicity, Genes, Culture and Success		24. Missing Girls
			25. Rising Number of Dowry Deaths in India
	6. Whose Speech Is Better?		26. Shamanisms: Past and Present
	7. Do You Speak American?		27. The Adaptive Value of Religious Ritual
	8. Fighting for Our Lives		28. Understanding Islam
	9. Shakespeare in the Bush		29. The Secrets of Haiti's Living Dead
	10. Macho Origin Myths		30. Body Ritual among the Nacirema
	11. How Cooking Frees Men		31. Baseball Magic
	12. When Cousins Do More than Kiss		32. Why Can't People Feed Themselves?
	13. Meet the Alloparents		33. The Tractor Invasion
	14. The Inuit Paradox		34. Yanomamo
	15. Ties That Bind		35. The Arrow of Disease
	16. Sick of Poverty		36. The Americanization of Mental Illness
	17. When Brothers Share a Wife: Among Tibetans, the Good Life Relegates Many Women to Spinsterhood		37. The Price of Progress
			38. Seeing Conservation through the Global Lens
	18. Death without Weeping		39. Der Indianer
	19. Arranging a Marriage in India		40. What Native Peoples Deserve
			41. Being Indigenous in the 21st Century

BUSINESS REPLY MAIL
FIRST CLASS MAIL PERMIT NO. 551 DUBUQUE IA

POSTAGE WILL BE PAID BY ADDRESSEE

McGraw-Hill Contemporary Learning Series
501 BELL STREET
DUBUQUE, IA 52001

ABOUT YOU

Name

Date

_____

Are you a teacher? ❏ A student? ❏
Your school's name

_____

Department

_____

Address   City   State   Zip

_____

School telephone #

_____

YOUR COMMENTS ARE IMPORTANT TO US!

Please fill in the following information:
For which course did you use this book?

_____

Did you use a text with this ANNUAL EDITION? ❏ yes ❏ no
What was the title of the text?

_____

What are your general reactions to the Annual Editions concept?

_____

Have you read any pertinent articles recently that you think should be included in the next edition? Explain.

_____

Are there any articles that you feel should be replaced in the next edition? Why?

_____

Are there any World Wide Websites that you feel should be included in the next edition? Please annotate.

_____

May we contact you for editorial input? ❏ yes ❏ no
May we quote your comments? ❏ yes ❏ no